THE NAKED TRUTH

ABOUT

THE NAKED TRUTH

ABOUT GOD

The Quest to Find Evidence for Whether God Exists
Reveals an Epic Discovery that has
Eluded Religion and Science

As a fellow Toastmaster, you were present since the initial spark in the year 2011... it would be seven years later that the final form of this book emerged! Thank you for your enduring friendship, most especially during the many painful and lonely lows. I hope this book will challenge your beliefs and infuse your life with knowledge that has been hidden for eons. — Fond Thoughts Always

BRIAN GOEDKEN

Arkenstone Media

11 July 2018

Arkenstone Media

RADIATING KNOWLEDGE™

Chandler, Arizona

RIGHTS, COPYRIGHT NOTICE, FAIR USE, AND COPYRIGHT PERMISSION GUIDANCE

Copyright Acknowledgments For Biblical Scripture Quotations

CONTACT

To Jennifer

We are mere *blips* of light amidst the

fathomless shadows of space

and the irrepressible clockwork of time.

To my companion *blip* Jennifer

whose aura has luminesced my brief cosmic journey.

To all those past and present

who have been misguided or suffered injustice

by a warped interpretation of God.

CONTENTS

PART I ◊ FOUNDATIONAL CONCEPTS FOR THE ZETETIC PATH

Introduction – *Mankind's Big Questions* 1

1 *Mankind's Search for God* 7

2 *Defining God* 63

PART II ◊ TRADITIONAL AND FRONTIER RELIGION

3 *The Disappearing Gods: A Detective Story* 83

4 *The Revealing Truth of Biblical Antiquities* 113

5 *Rediscovering the Origins of Christianity* 143

6 *The Historicity of the Resurrection... Did Jesus Rise from the Dead?* 183

7 *Testing the Truth of the Resurrection* 269

8 *Jesus' Divinity and Position in the Godhead.* 283

9 *The Probability for God's Existence & Is God Still Alive?* 307

10 *Pluralism & the New Sciences of Religion* 349

PART III ◊ SCIENCE ON GOD

11 *Teleology and Emergence –*
   Evidence of God's Hand Strokes at Work in the Universe? 371

12 *The Cognitive Science of Religion* 409

13 *The Scientific Theories of Creation –*
   Viewing God from the Cosmic Keyhole. 451

14 *Time, Infinity, and the Cosmological Argument* 505

PART IV ◊ THE SIX TOWERS OF GOD

15 *The Six Towers of God.* 535

16 *Chiseling the Stone of History* 579

CONTENTS CONTINUED

Appendix - Copyright Permissions and Fair Use Provisions. 593

Glossary 597

Works Cited. 627

Photo and Illustration Credits 683

Index 689

Acknowledgments 741

About the Author 743

LIST OF FIGURES

Figure 1-1. Do you believe in God? (a census of opinion in the United States) 29

Figure 1-2. Religious Conversions for the Abrahamic Traditions across 40 Countries . 31

Figure 2-1. Member Count of Major Religious Traditions (U.S. 2014). 68

Figure 2-2. Results from 35-Question Religious Knowledge Survey (U.S. 2010). 73

Figure 2-3. Aggregated Belief (U.S.) 75

Figure 2-4. Dogma Righteousness and Path to Eternal Life (U.S. 2008). 75

Figure 3-1. The Dingir – the Sumerian cuneiform IDEOGRAM for the word "Deity" 84

Figure 3-2. Empires of Ancient Near East. 89

Figure 3-3. Pithoi (Storage Jars) from Kuntillet 'Ajrud – Bes or Yahweh? 98

Figure 3-4. Statuettes of deities Bes and Beset. 101

Figure 3-5. The deity El and the goddess Asherah 103

Figure 3-6. Development Timeline for Abrahamic Religions 106

Figure 3-7. The Christian Shield of the Trinity. 108

Figure 5-1. The Rylands Papyrus P⁵² ($\mathfrak{P}^{52}$) 149

Figure 5-2. The Two Oldest Bibles 150

Figure 5-3. Ordering of the New Testament Books 177

Figure 6-1. Codex Sinaiticus – The Blank Column at the end of Mark 16 Verse 8 219

Figure 6-2. Attributes of Jesus' Life Compared to Other Legendary & Mythical Heroes .242

Figure 8-1. Major Schisms of Christianity. 301

Figure 10-1. Summary of Worldwide Affiliation. 350

Figure 10-2. Worldwide Affiliation by Major Groups 351

Figure 10-3. Affiliation by Adults (United States) 351

Figure 11-1. The Autocatalytic Process 378

Figure 12-1. Microtubules inside Neuron 442

Figure 13-1. Chronology of the Universe (Hot Inflationary Big Bang Model). 454

Figure 13-2. A Conical Singularity 459

Figure 13-3. Big Bang with and without Cosmic Inflation 463

LIST OF FIGURES CONTINUED

Figure 13-4. Hot Inflationary Big Bang Universe Model vs. the Cosmon Field Model . .485

Figure 13-5. Evolution of cosmon field strength 487

Figure 13-6. Source of Cosmological Redshift 493

Figure 14-1. William Lane Craig's—"Craigian"—Worldview 508

Figure 14-2. Subjunctive Possibility 512

Figure 14-3. Concepts of Different Types of Time Intervals 516

Figure 15-1. Ontological Propositions for a Transcendent God 550

Figure 15-2. Ontological Propositions for an Immanent God 551

Figure 15-3. The Six Towers of God Worldview and the Perimeter of God (Zeteticism). .565

Figure 15-4. Level of Plausibility for God's Existence Among the Six Towers 569

LIST OF TABLES

Table 1-1. Eight Criteria that Constitute the Truth of Reality 50

Table 3-1. Excerpts: The Code of Hammurabi. 84

Table 3-2. Types of Theism 87

Table 4-1. The Talpiot "Tomb A" (Garden Tomb) Ossuaries and the James Ossuary . . .133

Table 5-1. Foundational Truth Claims of Christianity. 149

Table 6-1. Historicity Tests 186

Table 6-2. Christian Evidence for the Resurrection. 195

Table 6-3. Biblical Post-death Jesus Appearances 212

Table 6-4. Was Jesus a Mythic/Legendary Hero? 241

Table 6-5. Swinburne's Symbology and Probability Estimate for the Resurrection . . .258

Table 7-1. Resurrection Hypothesis vs. Mortal Jesus Hypothesis 277

Table 9-1. Belief / Knowledge of Iran's Militarized Nuclear Ambitions 330

Table 9-2. Catholic Doctrine - Apophatic & Cataphatic Mysticism 337

Table 15-1. God's Nature: Categories for The Six Towers of God Paradigm. 556

Table 16-1. Religious and Scientific Institutional Change 585

LIST OF BOXES

Box 1 – An Estimate for the Existence of Technologically Advanced Exo-Civilizations in the Universe 35

Box 2 – Common Misconception of Christianity's Origin 157

Box 3 – Clement of Alexandria. 169

Box 4 – The Jesus Papers: Exposing the Greatest Cover-Up in History. 173

Box 5 – Arianism 292

Box 6 – A Brief Refresher of Theisms .382

PART I
FOUNDATIONAL CONCEPTS
FOR THE ZETETIC PATH

INTRODUCTION

Mankind's Big Questions

WELL BEFORE THE DAWN OF civilized man, our ancestors used their intellectual wares to call out into the forbidding darkness to beckon the favor of unseen spirits. Most ancient cultures—Egyptian, Mesopotamian, Indian, and Hellenistic—believed that a plurality of gods held dominion over the world-universe. In present-day times, most of us would regard our forbears' primeval knowledge of God as acutely unenlightened. In fact, we no longer refer to them as religions, but have demoted them to mythologies because we are certain they cannot be true conceptions for God. Better than half of the denizens of the world now believe in a singular almighty God and unlike the ancestral gods of lost societies, this God, according to adherents, has revealed his existence via scriptural revelation, epiphanies, and in the case of Christianity, **THEOPHANIC**[1] visitation. Many who hold a belief in God hold that our majestic universe is evidence unto itself that it was crafted by an Intelligent Designer due to the inconceivably exact parameters that govern the cosmos. Our 'just-so' universe generated conditions conducive to the evolution of self-reflective life-forms and furthermore that we and it are moving toward some purposive divine end (the so-called **ANTHROPIC COSMOLOGICAL PRINCIPLE**). Of course, the greatest motivation to invoke the existence of God is that the universe came into being. How else could the universe been realized?

God is commonly envisioned as an all-powerful singular Being who is interested in the destiny of mankind. He is the sovereign authority of all that is. Some say the wicked or the nonbeliever will forsake a privileged existence in the afterlife whereas the benevolent God will protect his faithful. Others hold that we can personally commune with this deity. This circumscription may be an oversimplification, but it strikes close enough to center. Nevertheless, what is the correct way to probe our faith to develop a systematic (i.e., comprehensively justified) belief in God?

This book guides you on a bold quest of self-discovery to tackle the many questions we all wonder about, sometimes with great frequency, but we seldom, if ever, come to any solid conclusions. **Can we hope to even fractionally prove God's existence and attributes?**

---

1. Words that are in **BOLDFACE-SMALL CAPS** have Glossary entries.

Is the Bible, or religious Scripture generally, a reliable testament of God? Is it irrational to believe in an unseen God? Can we compute the statistical probability that God exits? What is consciousness? What is reality? Is the property of natural time real? What is the meaning of life? Do we have a soul? Is the universe singular or are we but one among an uncountable multitude? Was the universe created or is it eternally existent? What are the odds that we are the only intelligent life in the universe? Is there a practical course to unify or otherwise harmonize the many divisions between world religions? How can we neutralize violent religious radicalism? These questions form the thread for which you will sew together a comprehensive and cohesive framework to understand how to approach answering these Big Questions. It is probably not well understood by most, but many of these questions are highly-interrelated and we cannot effectively answer one without answering the others.

For ages, mankind's greatest thinkers have opined many clues to elucidate answers to the intractable Big Questions. All too often, however, a critical oversight hampers the outcome. They employ a reductionist mentality to levy answers that rely on a subset of relevant knowledge sources. A theologian or philosopher may produce an answer using a preferred direction of philosophical mentation, a weighty sum of assumptions, and a dusting of science to give their conclusion more umpf. A scientist, on the other hand, will overlook salient philosophical constraints, elevate a favored set of physical theories, and dazzle with powerful mathematical manipulations. I asked myself, "How can we arrive at the best answers to these Big Questions if we continue to neglect the existence of many other silos of knowledge that should be brought to bear?" I will tender an answer to this question toward the end of this Introduction.

The Age of Science has succeeded in whittling away some of God's former territory. Many once-miraculous phenomena have been explained away as being the unextraordinary consequences of physics. But by no means has science expunged God from reality. The Science-Religion dialogue has been going in uncertain circles ever since Aristotle and classical antiquity. The ERUDITION of this long-running debate has become far too arcane for the Common Man to decipher or assimilate whatever wisdom might be had. **The Common Man prefers a simple wisdom by which to live out his or her own life. We want a liberty of conscience, not one that is weighed down with entangling and overbearing detail.** What we find is that if we do not ask penetrating questions, then it easier to find a comfortable, uncomplicated philosophy. But an unenlightened philosophy is all too often ignorance masquerading as truth. If we want to encircle the hard truth, we have to successively ask—and answer—a host of deeply challenging questions. To perform that task with any chance of success, we have to navigate around, and at times dismantle and rebuild, our prevailing beliefs. We also have to be tirelessly curious to push our way through many thorny passages which invariably will scrawl trails into our skin.

I grew up in a Midwestern city where 79% of the population was Christian, 82% of whom were Catholic.[1] There were only trace populations for other religious traditions and one-in-five were unaffiliated. For most of my adult life, I lived with an uncomplicated but sometimes tormented belief in the God of Catholicism. My collegiate studies instilled in me something that, if I am to be honest, has followed me so closely it is principally responsible for compelling me to write this book. It is this—whenever one tackles a problem, one must ALWAYS QUESTION THE ASSUMPTIONS THROUGHOUT THE ENTIRE PROBLEM SOLVING PROCESS. A corollary axiom is: THE FEWER THE ASSUMPTIONS NECESSARY, THE BETTER. When we are conscientiously and continuously engaged in this fashion, we will better understand the extent of the reliability and legitimacy of our logic.

I was also animated by another force. Ever since the Persian Gulf War, I became increasingly unnerved to hear time and again of beastly religious zealots perpetrating acts of unspeakable barbarism and subjugation of the indigenous populace. The current surge of religious extremism in the form of ISIL hasn't only affected those murdered, but has created a spillover refugee crisis of many millions of people fleeing their homes across Syria and neighboring countries needing humanitarian aid. While I was free to practice or not practice my religion here in the United States, this choice is stolen from many who live in far off lands. I felt powerless to prevent this perversion of God, even if I was equivocating upon my own Catholic worldview. The agitation swelled as I reflected more seriously on Christianity's and Judaism's shared heritage of violence even if this had occurred in centuries or millennia past or in light of the Bible's portrayal of righteous action. While it is not my place to atone for the repugnant acts of others dead and gone, it did weigh on my conscious. Indeed, there is no shortage of examples of civil strife past or present that bear the mark of a warped image of God. I steadily realized that the only way to peacefully counter further repetition of new acrimonies was to intellectualize this thing we call *faith in God*.

Now, to fulfill my earlier promise, how we are to solve the *Big Questions*? The only promising method I see as fit enough to accomplish the awesome task ahead is what I refer to as an integrative meta-synthesis of knowledge. We have to scour a broad range of disciplines under the headings of science, philosophy, and theology—both ancient and contemporary. More specifically, we will venture into the cavernous scholastic domains of: Abrahamic theology, Process Theology (i.e., God dynamically-acting to continually sustain the course of the universe), philosophy of religion, philosophy of mind, scriptural hermeneutics (i.e., biblical interpretation), biblical archaeology, evolutionary biology, neuroscience, neurotheology, quantum mechanics/quantum biology, cosmology, cosmogony—the study of the origins of the universe—mathematics, and statistics. My goal is to sieve the **PEDAGOGUERY** to be more digestible to those unfamiliar with the mind-numbing intricacies. Beyond the incessant hours of research, this was the most difficult goal to achieve for the simple fact that scholastic writing is able to discuss complex topics in a condensed language set. Writing this book with a presumption that the reader is only tangentially aware of a small subset of ideas for any given topic placed a sizable onus on me to explicate things in plain speak. The result, unfortunately, is a very thick book! It would have been my wish to write a much shorter book or a multi-volume set. The first option was impossible and the second option would have unacceptably broken the chain of reasoning that tracks throughout this book.

If you see your pilgrimage to the end, remain open to challenging your own beliefs, you will be rewarded with what we all seek—a coherent, deeply rational, well-informed, and simple philosophy. More curtly, we would call this a *systematic philosophy*. And in due course, you will have gained great insights on the aforementioned *Big Questions*.

SOME FINAL COMMENTS TO AID YOUR JOURNEY

The book is written with a continuity that entreats you to read each chapter successively in the presented order. If you were to jump ahead, you will greatly impair the chain of reasoning that is incrementally constructed. Content from previous chapters is frequently referenced. If you skip ahead to the final chapters, the conclusions will lose their full resonance. In most instances, I have provided summaries at the end of each chapter to enhance your comprehension of the chapter's subject matter. Some of the material introduced will be challenging to absorb. I wish some things could have been made easier to grapple with, but there was a constant trade-off between reaching the required depth and breadth in the many complex topics brought forward. In an attempt to make it a little easier, I have provided a rich glossary of terminology. A glossary entry is displayed in **BOLDFACE SMALL-CAP LETTERING** the first time it is used or where I deem it necessary to provide a definition of the term(s).

To challenge the verity of one's own beliefs is to be courageous. To separate the truth from falsity is to be wise. To take action against the headwinds of the status quo is to be a pioneer. The **TROIKA** of courage, wisdom, and a pioneering spirit is all that you need to embark on this odyssey. Steady yourself and venture forth.

CHAPTER 1

Mankind's Search for God

As for the search for truth, I know from my own painful searching, with its many blind alleys, how hard it is to take a reliable step, be it ever so small, towards the understanding of that which is truly significant.[1]

– Albert Einstein
A letter from Einstein to an intellectual admirer, February 13th, 1934

Academic chairs are many, but wise and noble teachers are few; lecture-rooms are numerous and large, but the number of young people who genuinely thirst after truth and justice is small. Nature scatters her common wares with a lavish hand, but the choice sort she produces but seldom. We all know that, so why complain? Was it not ever thus and will it not ever thus remain? Certainly, and one must take what Nature gives as one finds it. But there is also such a thing as a spirit of the times, an attitude of mind characteristic of a particular generation, which is passed on from individual to individual and gives a society its particular tone. Each of us has to do his little bit towards transforming this spirit of the times.[2]

– From The World As I See It by Albert Einstein

Truth always lags last, limping along on the arm of Time.[3]

– Baltasar Gracián y Morales
Spanish Jesuit and philosopher, 1647

Truth is seldom the sweet nectar we would have it be. It is more often the bitter taste of steel as the once nocked arrow strikes the palate of our conscious. It is no wonder why the sullied truth is the more delectable of the two.

– Present Author

It is a capital mistake to theorise before you have all the evidence. It biases the judgment.[61]

– Sir Arthur Conan Doyle
Fictional character Detective Sherlock Holmes speaking to his friend and assistant, Dr. Watson.

SET ATOP THIS TINY CRUSTAL rock we call Earth, we are but an impermanent ripple in the cosmic sea—insatiably transfixed by our origins, purpose, destiny, and the quandary concerning God. The progeny of eons of both cataclysmic and innocuous events alike have, for reasons to be explored, brought humankind to this **DAMOCLESIAN** moment in human history. In this very instant, we are deciding our future and our legacy. Whether by the snap of God's fingers or by the solitary yawn of the cosmic Big Bang, we as sentient beings have been given a singular opportunity to imprint our story—a most privileged narrative—on this otherwise unexceptional, almost quiescent corner of the universe.

THE GRAND OBSERVER AND THE SCHOLARLY DRAGONS

Before we heed this call to etch the cold and oft forgotten stone of history, envisage if you will a celestial *Grand Observer*[1] positioned in a remote sector of space far, far from our own. From his **ARCHIMEDEAN** vantage point, this spectator of the cosmos surveils our planet as a silent witness, studying it with an air of indifference. He exists in a quasi-temporal/timeless state. This otherworldly Being has at its command a network of telescopes of unfathomable capability dispatched throughout the cosmos. They are linked by a **QUANTUM COUPLING-QUANTUM ENTANGLEMENT** computer that permits instantaneous intra-communication in spite of the millions of **LIGHT-YEARS** of separation between each device. The telescopes offer simultaneous panoramic recording and the ability to freely magnify objects to sub-microscopic resolutions. With mere thought projection traversing an otherwise silent observatory, the Grand Observer tinkers with the telescope's controls to target the appartus on planet Earth. The view-field erupts with a myriad of blinking images depicting events taking place across the globe, and by some impossible act, in 360-degree, three-dimensional, ultra-high definition. In one image, the Grand Observer spies a nomadic herder on the Serengeti Plain, and in another, a team of scientists are drilling for 15 million year-old extremophile *Anthrobacter* bacteria locked away in a light-free subglacial Antarctic ice shelf. Soon, thousands of real-time movies flood the viewport and eerily self-sort into a comprehensible layout. Every cosmic event that ever was is chronicled on the telescope's information recording system, a veritable catalog of the unfiltered true history of all things. The Grand Observer leans back into a pensive posture as the frantic ant-like energy moving about the planet's surface is juxtaposed by an otherwise serene pale blue dot[2] careening around its central star heeding its vow of silence.

After a time, the Grand Observer commands the complex of telescope barrels to simultaneously pan across one quadrant then another to train onto the frontiers of **SPACETIME**. This incomprehensibly vast no man's land is positioned well beyond Earth's **LIGHT HORIZON**,

---

1. The Grand Observer is not to be confused with the "Ultimate Observer" conjectured by physicists John Barrow and Frank Tipler (*The Anthropic Cosmological Principle*, 1986, pp. 468 – 471, Oxford University Press)

2. The reference "pale blue dot" is an honorific reference to the eponymously named book by Carl Sagan, *Pale Blue Dot: A Vision of the Human Future in Space*, 1994, Random House.

to a time and place no human shall ever see no matter how advanced a civilization we may become. The Grand Observer dispassionately surveys the most ancient phenomena of the universe as the edges of **SPACETIME** furiously unfurl into the unknown void. The Being makes another gesture and his observatory looks back in Earth's direction. The alien telescope array gathers every photon emission to display the synchronal panchromatic[3] vista in unparalleled purity of detail. A switch is telekinetically-toggled by Observer's mind and the intergalactic scaffolding of **DARK MATTER** comes into view against the backdrop of the newly-discovered-to-humans Higgs field[4] visualized as a smooth, all-encompassing sea of scintillating colors.

The solemn figure gestures with his hand, tracing an arc from left to right, and the universal recorder jumps into action rewinding all matter-energy transactions throughout cosmic history ... spacetime curls back contracting the size of the universe ... **QUASARS** power down as **BLACK HOLES** belch-out billions upon billions of once-swallowed stars, shrinking ever more until their host supernovae unexplode ... Earth is serially de-populated, tectonic plates shift, oceans dry-up, mountains flatten, and the atmosphere toxifies. Soon, Earth atomizes into stellar dust ... galaxies disband ... the universe dies as all animate life blinks out of existence. The celestial chronometer obediently peels backward 13.8 billion years[5] as the universes' uncountable stars[6] progressively disintegrate into their founding nebulae nurseries which then disperse into a homogeneous field of relic radiation sprawling from one cosmic horizon to the other. The shrunken universe is now soley comprised of an ocean of uncondensed particulate matter.

Atoms begin to fly apart, forming a foam-like structure of **IONIZED PLASMA** making the universe dimmer and dimmer until the universe is blanketed in an absolute cosmic darkening some 380,000 years after the universe was first created. At this time the universe

---

3. *Synchronal panchromatic* means to see all the frequencies of light at the same time from long wavelength radio waves to short gamma waves. Photons are elementary particles of light (i.e., electromagnetic) energy.

4. The Higgs field is an energy field that permeates the universe that is responsible for mass being imparted (but not generated or created) to all elementary particles that possess mass. There are two confirmed types of massless particles which do not interact with the Higgs field. The most prominently known of the two are photons (e.g., particles which mediate the electromagnetic interaction; more simply, a component of which is visible light). The other is the gluon particle. Otherwise, the Higgs field affects all other matter.

5. The most current estimate for the age of our universe is 13.799 ± 0.038 billion years based on analysis of Planck space observatory data in 2013. (Planck Collaboration: R. Adam, *et al.*, 2015, arXiv:1502.01582v2, p. 27, Table 9)

6. It is not possible to accurately determine the number of stars in the *observable* universe, but astronomers have generally estimated the number in the range 2×10^{22} (20 billion-trillion) to 3×10^{23} (300 sextillion) based on the more estimable number of galaxies in the universe which is 100 billion (10^{11}) to 350 billion galaxies. However, as presented later in this chapter (see Box 1), a recent discovery indicates the number of stars and galaxies far exceed these estimates.

was opaque to human eyes due to the intensity of radiation being outside of the visible range. With each advancing frame of the Grand Observer's recorder the universe gets smaller and smaller. The 93 billion light-year universe is now crunched to less than one light-year in every direction. The fizzling plasma becomes increasingly agitated, stewed to a mad furor. Twenty minutes before the Big Bang event, atomic nuclei begin to rip apart. A mere 17 minutes pass and the first of all atoms is uncreated. With only three minutes on the countdown clock, a surge of electrons and positron antimatter burst into existence as the two un-annihilate their counterpart. Fleeting moments elapse as the recorder crosses the threshold of the very first second of the universe. Temperatures hurtle past a trillion degrees and in the next few fractions of a second every single proton and neutron bursts into their constituent **QUARKS**—fragmenting into a rapidly shrinking micro-verse. Temperatures scream past ten quadrillion (1×10^{16}) degrees as quarkian matter and antimatter un-annihilate like their electron-positron cousins did three minutes prior. More physical interactions take place in this tiny instant than all subsequent interactions that ever occurred in the universe combined.

Abruptly, the universe deflates exponentially in size through a reversal of **COSMIC INFLATION**. In a matter of a billionth of a trillionth, of a trillionth of a second ($\sim 10^{-33} - 10^{-32}$ seconds) all existent matter and energy is exponentially crushed so tightly that the four Fundamental Forces[7] unite into a single 'superforce'. In a handful of Planck times[8] the unitary superforce disappears altogether and the universe becomes a lawless, infinitesimally compact, inconceivably hot,[9] boundless state of roiling pure energy. Belgian Catholic priest, Fr. Lemaître, the proposer of the Big Bang theory, famously termed this initial state the "primeval atom."[4] Then, as the very first Planck time is uncreated, we arrive at the terminus of this regression ... *initio temporis* ... the impenetrable barrier to all human discernment and natural existents, and to some, the doorstep to God's domain.[10] If the Grand Observer were to rewind the telescope's recorder just a stitch further, would we witness the thunderclap of God detonate the Big Bang **CREATIO EX NIHILO** (i.e., creation from nothing) or would we

---

7. The four fundamental forces are *gravity, electromagnetism,* and the *strong* and *weak nuclear* forces. The strong force is responsible for binding protons and neutrons together and the weak force is involved in radioactivity and acts as the initiator of the nuclear fusion process that powers our Sun and all stars.

8. A unit of Planck time has the value of 5.39×10^{-44} second. This is commonly numerically rounded as 10^{-43} second.

9. The temperature at the first Planck time is on the order of 2.55 quadrillion-quadrillion (2.55×10^{32}) degrees Fahrenheit, and is called the Planck temperature.

10. The sequence of events is based loosely from data collected from the web page: *Timeline of the Big Bang* (http://www.physicsoftheuniverse.com/topics_bigbang_timeline.html). Last accessed 24 Nov 2015. Not all events are depicted in the outline are described by the present author.

suddenly find ourselves in a timeless,[11] dimensionless, and godless nothingness? Perhaps, as some cosmologists speculate, we might gaze upon an infinite number of godless universes—the so-called multiverse.[12]

What would the Grand Observer's recordings of our *true history* reveal about the 'godliness' of men and how we have honored our gift of sentient life? With all of our achievements throughout history, have we genuinely gained in a moral sense if only some nations have improved while others remain transfixed in human strife? Or, will we be bound to **Sisyphus'** tragedy to ceaselessly advance only to lose the same ground time and again? Or worse, will the Damoclesian sword be brought down upon our heads by our own negligence?

In the last few minutes you spent reading about the Grand Observer's observatory and the reversal of our universe's time history in the relative tranquility of your surrounds, the Earth sped some 2,500 to 3,500 miles along its orbital path around the Sun at 90 times faster than a typical rifle bullet. Simultaneously, the solar system whirled about our galactic center at a speed 7.35 times faster than Earth's solar journey.[13] In spite of such tremendous speeds, if we are lucky enough to live an average lifespan, we only make it a paltry 0.000032 percent of a complete galactic orbit. Since the dawn of humanity, we have made anemic progress achieving less than one percent (0.89 percent) of a single revolution. The incomprehensible scale and grandeur of our cosmos are the source of humanity's wonderment and it stirs our mind to ask ... and ... answer ... the greatest of all questions. What is the meaning of (human) life? What is reality? Is there an afterlife? And perhaps the ultimate **DYADIC** question of all—*Does God exist? And if so, does religion hold the truth about God?* I would propound that we can better frame the question "Does God exist?" by stating it as, ***How can we know whether or not God is real*? An intelligent response not only embeds the answer to God's existence *but also requires that we justify the answer*.** A question asked less frequently is, *What are we to do if God doesn't exist or if he does exist and is* **APATHETIC** *to us human beings?* The answers to these questions have been the **DESIDERATA** of every generation.

---

11. Timelessness is a condition where the property of natural time is non-existent. In some special circumstances, timelessness might also be equated with undifferentiated time whereby successive intervals of time may have different durations.

12. The multiverse is a predicted outcome from 'M-Theory' which itself evolved out of the *Many-Worlds Interpretation of Quantum Mechanics* (late 1950's), *Big Bang Inflation Theory* (1980's), and not too long after, *String Theory* which was itself corrected by *Superstring Theory*.

13. The Earth's speed around the Sun varies, but on average is 18.9 miles per second. The solar system's orbital speed around the Milky Way's galactic core is on the order of 138.9 miles per second.

Few ideas are freighted with higher ambiguity than this final triad of questions which inspire the underlying theme of this book. The God-debate animates our thoughts in an intellectual land where much falsehood masquerades as fact. If any are familiar with these ramblings one is struck with the utter chaos that has emerged which defy the ability for the Common Man to acquire a contemporary and rational justification for God. The Common Man is my parlance for the everyday person who is neither an academic nor an **ECCLESIASTICAL** authority but who retains a high measure of intellectual curiosity toward the **TRANSCENDENT**. Some say it is pure folly to think we shall ever come to any conclusion, much less a consensus, on these existential questions. Others have chosen to be indifferent to the answer (or even the question), while others still have become settled enough in one position or another based on some accumulation of knowledge they have garnered. Of special importance is that there is a tremendous variance on the relative set of knowledge any given person brings to bear to inform their beliefs.

While the prehistoric worship of deities and spirits existed long before, it was not until knowledge-seeking took root in the form of Indian **VEDIC** philosophy (c. 1500 – 1100 **BCE**) and Greek philosophy in Asia Minor (c. 600 BCE) when humans applied a measure of rationality to this **METAPHYSICAL** enigma. As our intellectualism expanded, philosophy and theology evolved to formalize and critique intellectual claims. Whereas philosophy is grounded more so in applying analytical rigor in the form of reason and logic, theology additionally introduces supernatural claims emanating from myth, revelation, religious knowledge (e.g., Scripture, sacred writings), and human experience. While astronomical knowledge existed in preliterate society (c. 9,000 BCE), it was in the Hindu *Rgveda* (c. 1500 – 1200 BCE) that the Vedic Indians rationally contemplated how it was that the universe came into being from non-existence, the organization of the cosmos, and the spherical shape of the Earth. The *Rgveda* also depicts a 12-month/360-day calendaring system much as we know it today.[5] Somewhat later, the Vedic *Mukhya Upanishads*, often referred to as the Principal Upanishads, were written to convey, in part, that to understand the spiritual, we must engage the universe through our sensorial experience and cognitive capacities, even though the product of such efforts is necessarily limited.

> You cannot see the seer of seeing; you cannot hear the hearer of hearing; you cannot think of the thinker of thinking; you cannot know the knower of knowing. This is your self that is within all; everything else but this is perishable.[6]
>
> Brihadaranyaka Upanishad (III.iv.2)

This pre-Buddhist reflection was written c. 700 BCE plus or minus a century. It advances a powerful statement from ancient philosophers who believed that human consciousness cannot fully comprehend reality because consciousness cannot discern itself. It is not a 'thing' or an object, rather it is integral to reality, as in a reality-consciousness, and thus it cannot be distinct from it. Because human consciousness cannot understand itself, it is powerless to know the absolute intelligence which is the ultimate self-knowing cosmic consciousness. It took millennia until discovery and innovation aided scientists and engineers to probe knowledge claims via hypothesis testing wherein empirical data could be objectively and independently confirmed by repetition. Century after century our cosmic environment grew more familiar against the backdrop of religious belief that was, by then, well embedded within society. The world-universe became impossibly larger while also becoming more reachable.

Religion **METASTASIZES** both generationally and geographically and we are therefore more often than not the inheritors of our closest ancestor's religion. Like generations for millennia, we were taught our religious or nonreligious worldview at a very young age during a time when we were not suitably equipped with mental tools to critique the influx of knowledge. With the many burdens of survival, we adapt the best we can and our worldview solidifies into a workable framework that we might roughly characterize as 'good enough'. Life keeps us very busy and it falls outside the realm of what is possible to objectively deconstruct our entire worldview to question what we first learned. It becomes, then, a radical and uncomfortable act for us to re-contemplate our fundamental beliefs.

It is probably not far from the truth to say that most people—the Common Man or otherwise—are not all too sure how to properly rationalize God. This idea of a 'proper rationalization' is highlighted in the next section. Because we lack the tools that would guide us in contemplating God, we tend to think rather superficially of how God could be manifested in reality and by what mechanisms he applies his various capacities. When we forego developing robust rationale for things concerning God, it becomes rather easy to believe this or that about God. Should we decide to put our beliefs in God under a microscope so to speak, major fault lines in our thinking invariably become evident.

Ultimately, in the course of your life you have a basic decision to make. Are you more interested in acquiring a philosophy that brings you peace and comfort, knowing full-well that some number of your beliefs are entirely irrational or are poorly conceived? Or, do you want to develop a philosophy that is congruent with actual reality as best we *collectively* understand it? The choice will yield two different prescriptions and outcomes. The first type of philosophy aims to minimize cognitive effort by looking for a relatively simplified belief system. Sometimes one's mental framework is more unduly influenced by the thoughts of others because the individual has not the desire or capacity to think independently. Once it has developed enough to weather the hum-drum of life, there is a strong tendency to shield oneself from altering it to any appreciable extent. We might call this eventual culmination a closed-minded philosophy. The second philosophy represents an enduring pursuit to challenge one's own beliefs and core values throughout life. Relatively speaking, it is a more rigorous and continual concern to seek out new knowledge and to more consciously adapt one's prevailing philosophy. This does not mean it is less complete than what is produced from the choosing the former approach, rather, it tends to produce a more robust modality of thinking that propels one to thrive as opposed to survive life's drama. Those choosing the latter philosophical approach possess a more wide-eyed, exploratory mindset and tend to be more understanding of other people's differences. While this produces a richer more fulfilling life experience, there is a significant cost in terms of time and energy that must be exacted to follow this course. Too many people for reasons just and otherwise live their lives in a sort of self-imposed cognitive slumber.

Relative to the pursuit of God, theologians and philosophers far and wide have pursued the development of what is called a **SYSTEMATIC THEOLOGY** which is the discipline to categorically explicate the phenomena of God's existence and nature. That is, they have performed the heavy-lifting to develop a complete framework or worldview concerning the considerable number of questions that arise when we start intelligizing God. A systematic theology would fully explain things such as, (1) how it is that we know God exists, (2) how we are to ascertain the number of deities and their interrelationship, (3) how God is physically or non-physically manifested, (4) what capabilities God possesses, (5) how God operates within or upon the universe (e.g, via revelation), (6) God's relationship to natural time, (7) why humanity is of any concern to God, (8) do humans have souls, (9) how can we redeem ourselves before God, (10) did God create the universe and when will the universe end, and so on. If, as an individual or as a religious order, one cannot offer suitably justified reasoning for questions of this ilk, then this is an indicator that the belief system may not comport with the truth of reality. When we are short on answers, often the next step is to call forth something we call '*faith*' to connect the gap between what we think we know and what we are uncertain of. However, to erect this 'faith bridge', there is a rarely acknowledged philosophical and societal cost that has to be paid to support the bridge itself. And because this penalty has gone unacknowledged and ignored, we find ourselves paying a significant price but not really understanding why sectors of society have become dysfunctional. Let us delve deeper into this thing we call 'faith' to understand what this societal cost is.

Toward a Revised Understanding of Faith and its Implications

A *belief* is sometimes an intellectualized opinion or judgment in which a person is fully persuaded but does not necessarily reflect reality. Religious faith for some is the dynamism captured by the famous words of Christian philosopher St. Anselm of Canterbury's *Fides Quaerens Intellectum* (Latin for 'Faith Seeking Understanding'). For Anselm, faith is an active love for God and it is through this love that one's knowledge of him grows. Faith then is dynamic and evolving and requires one to constantly query their knowledge of God. For our purposes, faith is to be taken as a set of beliefs retained by an individual that are inherently uncertain. The uncertainty arises because the belief framework depends on informational details that are difficult to partially or fully validate as being true of reality. Understanding faith is one of the motivating forces behind this venture because it plays such a central role in the ability to engage in a useful COLLOQUY on the question of God's existence. I will conjecture that faith is multi-spectral in character and this nature serves to confuse matters extraordinarily so. If one who believes in God is conversationally asked if and why they would believe in God, the most frequent retort is the rounded response "While I can't prove it, we must take it on faith that God exists." To which is often added or inferred is, "What else could explain the life-giving universe, the many miraculous actions that take place even today, or be responsible for human consciousness?"

When it comes to God, use of the word 'proof' is a loaded term because it immediately begs the question what constitutes *proof*. It can be well agreed from the start that proving God's existence has vexed our intellect and abilities for thousands of years and in spite of heroic efforts to do so, there has been no absolute definitive proof ever elucidated, either for or against. And, should we find an absence of quality evidence, it is inappropriate to state that God does not exist, for in such a situation there will be a non-zero probability that God might exist. That is, the absence of evidence is not evidence of absence. Fortunately, there are prospective evidences available that need to be deliberately considered in the form of physical objects consisting of historical documents (e.g., scrolls, papyri, inscriptions, books, and illustrations) and artifacts (e.g., a burial shroud, a rusty nail in a male heel bone, jewelry, paintings, and various forms of statuettes and sculptures). NOETICALLY, at our disposal are philosophic rationale (deduction, induction, ABDUCTION, and reduction), other forms of logic, scientific inquiry, and the mathematical sciences (e.g., proofs, axioms, and statistics). We also have abundant examples of sentient and intelligent life on our planet and a vast cosmos to explicate. And, lest we forget, some might also propound that we have oral narratives passed-down generationally, personal sensorial and revelatory experiences, and miracles to serve as authoritative testaments to the existence of a deity.

Beyond these notions of proof and evidence, it obliges us to ask whether the basic concept of faith is rational. That is, by itself, is it coherent and sensible to believe as true of reality something beyond our ability to verify its existence? It is here we need to draw clear lines to classify faith into three groups, namely, Fideistic, Complementary, and Co-Essential. **FIDEISTIC FAITH** is an orientation of belief that adheres to the precept that one does not have to forward any justification in the form of evidence or reasoning. When individual beliefs within a fideistic worldview are in agreement with naturalistic data educed from evidentiary sources or from cognitive analysis, then this may simply be coincidental. Nevertheless, it would be feasible to categorize the applicable subset of beliefs into one of the other two types of faith yet to be discussed. However, when **FIDEISM** is wholly or partially in conflict with natural data, fideistic faith becomes an irrational belief which is to say that it is discordant with reason or logic. Whereas fideism is the defiant or absolutist position that faith needn't be evidenced in any way, **BLIND FAITH** is a parallel ideology that more passively accepts that the unknown can remain wholly unexamined or believed on a basis of poorly qualified information.

Fideism is principally *non-rational* and blind faith is a position of professed *ignorance* that is also commonly affiliated with a disinterest to question or deliberate truths concerning God. Both positions are apt to be both epically incomplete and tragically irrational when it comes to characterizing the existence and nature of what we call God (feel free to choose your **THEONYM**). Are these two approaches to faith in God guilty of a crime of omission? Technically, No. Practically, Yes. How many times in history have fanatical religious zealots extolled their God as the one true God and that his will is not to be questioned? They become convinced, indeed divinely compelled, to eradicate or convert non-believers. This by no means impeaches peacefully acting faith dwellers. But we begin to see that when people are left free to radicalize theistic ideas, even if they numerically represent the fringe, it can have awful effects on broad swaths of society.

The process can appear rather benign at first but can steadily escalate in scale and seriousness. When religious adherents take the position that God is so great a Being that his existence, capabilities, will, motivations, words, or actions are not to be questioned by mankind, he is only to be obeyed, it generates a number of implications for the individual believer and potentially for those with whom the individual may come into contact with. If one blindly (unquestioningly) accepts that God expects mankind to believe or act in a particular way or else he will become displeased, this arrangement immediately creates internal and social tension. When one is further guided by a belief that a displeased God will bring suffering to humans here on Earth or jeopardize a much-prized idyllic afterlife, the tension increases. Frictions further intensify if the fideistic/blind faith believer takes to heart a duty to evangelize God's mission and to increase the membership of his or her in-group. When cultural values and political policies are perceived to be at odds with 'God's ways', the individual and group may react with counteractions. By separating God in this way, putting him on an untouchable pedestal if you will, the believer effectively disconnects all cognitive critiquing processes. If convictions are strong enough, God's mission becomes a rallying point for the in-group. If sacred Scriptures or God's intentions are interpreted in such a way that God expects his followers to act zealously, even violently if necessary, to enact God's vision, then all else becomes secondary, including moral concerns for the out-group. We have the alchemy necessary to generate what these religious adherents consider justified violent religious radicalism. We come upon a rather morose dichotomy that the religious extremist who unquestioningly (i.e., unjustifiably) believes in this sort of schema for God somehow feels well-justified in their abhorrent actions.

In attempting to understand the sociological and individual roots of religiously-motivated terrorism and the associated will to kill others, Anthropologist Scott Atran *et al.* have conducted field interviews of would-be and convicted religious terrorists. What he and his colleagues identified were three essential components. The first ingredient is a zealous and inviolable personal belief in sacred values that are also shared with his or her affiliated ingroup. These values are so sacrosanct that the individual holds them higher than his concerns for others, including his family and/or clan members. The third factor is that the group perceives themselves as being spiritually formidable towards its adversaries meaning that they are more willing to commit to personal and in-group sacrifice to defend or advance its values.[63] Many militants are additionaly spawned because of family or friends who wish to exact revenge for the fallen terrorist will take-up the cause. So when one is killed, the group size is maintained or becomes enlarged.

There is yet another component to consider when rejecting the need to question our belief or faith in God. ***If one is to adopt any position on God that is based wholly or largely on faith, then the individual is axiomatically compelled to grant others the same right to make propositions of their own.*** Fair enough you say, but what price does one need to pay to maintain their fideistic or weakly justified faith?[14] It is a rather simple and even off-putting tradeoff most easily explained by example. If, for instance, you were to hold a fideistic faith

---

14. A weakly justified faith may be characterized by a belief system that is, in part or whole, logically incoherent and/or has simplistic, too few, or overly vague would-be evidences. The framework may also be incomplete (i.e., not systematic) in that one's belief system may only answer a subset of core issues that arise in attempting to describe God. Generally, analytic philosophy, science, and mathematics are needed to help adjudicate what constitutes inadequately justified faith.

in the Abrahamic God,[15] then any other person is to be granted the license to envision God as any or all of the Hindu deities, *or* as a ten-armed, five-headed, twenty-eyed, purple giant living inside the core of our Sun, *or* as a physical Being with a throneship situated distantly in our galaxy, *or* as a formless diffuse essence distributed throughout the universe, perhaps entirely outside of it, or both. We could conjecture a breathtaking array of powers such as the ability to create matter and energy out of nothing, the ability to generate antigravity or defy it altogether, or to stop the passage of time with but a single thought. One could also envision that "X" number of deities exist, where "X" could be any integer value (e.g., 34 gods or 99 gods). Whether singular or plural, God could even be conceived as a supremely evil Being or one that is totally apathetic toward humans.

The crux of the matter is that **ALL** of these conceptions are on **EQUAL** footing because there is no requirement for any of the belief holders to provide a credible rational justification. I refer to this as the **Many-Faced God Conundrum**. **If you believe in a substantially faith-based God and you refuse to accept alternative definitions of God because you find them to be too nutty, delusional, or objectionable, then** *your own* **thinking would be irrational.** "Fine.", you say. "Call me irrational if you like and let the crackpots think what they may." However, most people do more than simply think about the most magnificent thing in all of reality, the holder of higher truth and morality beyond that of mortal men. Many *act* upon their religious belief which invariably affects others. If you are caught in the trappings of the Many-Faced God Conundrum, then you ought not have any compunction or distress when other people evangelize their version of God over yours, or worse, commit or condone unspeakable barbarism in the name of their God. **They are only responding to their own conception of God** _which is compatible with your own ideas in the context of people freely associating with unjustified supreme Beings_. With respect to religious theological beliefs, if you demand moral, civilized, and sympathetic action from others, _then you have little other choice than to defend your faith by credibly intellectualizing God_ (thereby rejecting fideism and blind faith).

We intellectualize God by seeking out natural data in a variety of formats to support the underlying belief. Often, those who maintain that they have adopted a blind faith in actuality have, perhaps unconsciously, integrated into their framework naturalistic data through inherited belief from friends, family, and religious teachers, knowledge of Scripture, or a sense of wonderment at the scale of the universe and an importance/relevance of our

---

15. The Abrahamic God is the contemporary view that the God of Judaism, Christianity, and Islam is by and large the same God.

position as human beings. Almost universally, people **ANTHROPOMORPHIZE** God by ascribing him with representational human-like traits.

An especially salient issue is the special case that arises as to whether or not it is properly warranted to apply **intuitive faculties** as a means for justifying God's **ONTOLOGY**. The theistically inclined would like to summarily invoke the right to wield intuitive powers as a conduit to the transcendent; however, there is good reason to be unyielding in ruling out its usage. This matter falls into the discipline of the Philosophy of Mind and there is no unanimity on what intuition precisely is. What can be said with certainty is that it is a phenomenon of the mind that seeks to acquire knowledge without the utilization of inference, logic, or reason (that is, no use of our deductive, inductive, or abductive capacities). However, there is an implied access to a limited level of cognition in the form of dull sensory inputs. Dull in this context means that the mind has registered incoming data at a low level but the information has not been well-processed or integrated into the rest of the greater cognitive schema.

Intuition is an *A PRIORI* position that yields an interpretive expression based on poorly comprehended and/or incomplete strata of information where one has a sense that such and such is true, but cannot put a finger on it. Intuition, then, is what I call the **PARAINTELLECT** because of its limited semi-reliance on our cognitive assets. It should also be clarified that intuition is *not* the situation in which someone takes several pieces of knowledge and 'intuits' (i.e., guesses) some relationship or idea about some other mentation. This set of circumstances is considered an inference which employs higher-order cognition. A follow-on point is that my use of the words "low level" and "higher-order" is not to be taken as a defense of the idea that the brain has physical or mental stratification. Rather, all that is meant is that the relative amount, areas of the brain, and types cognitive processes utilized will yield different results. The organization of the brain will be discussed in Chapter 12.

By way of example, our intuition tells us that it should be right and proper for elementary particles (e.g., photons, quarks, and **NEUTRINOS**) to consistently behave just like ordinary matter (e.g., air molecules, billiard balls, and stones). That is, reality should function the same at any scale large or small. If a billiard ball were to be placed onto a pool table, it should stay put in its original position unless something in the environment changes sufficiently to alter its location to somewhere else. Also, we have good reason to believe that the ball could never be in two or more locations simultaneously. This, one would conclude, applies to elementary particles of which the billiard ball is made from. However, the scientific theory of **QUANTUM MECHANICS** tells us with extreme certainty that free particles can suddenly disappear, teleport, and suddenly reappear at some other location. They can also be in two different locations at exactly the same time. And, this process is continually reoccurring many, many times over and again as you read this. This phenomenon defies our intuitive sense that such things could ever happen in our reality. Nevertheless, our intuition is very wrong. In a second example, ancient philosophers (generally regarded as highly intelligent and wise individuals) intuited that the Earth was positioned at the center of the universe. We know now that this is certainly not the case. These two examples are not put forward to negate the possibility that our paraintellect can be correct on occasion—it very well can be—but it is to say that in general it is a very unreliable human faculty.

We also have to be particularly wary of imaginative thought processes for we can very easily create things and ideas in our minds that are outright impossible or highly improbable to be manifested in the world-universe which we then deceive ourselves into thinking that they are either certain or probable likelihoods. We often take several different pieces of information or instilled beliefs and loosely wed them together to bestow some greater meaning which falsely represents reality.

Examples of this are so many and varied it is impossible to encapsulate this succinctly. Nevertheless, let us consider the domain of ufology (the study of unidentified flying objects) and the existence of extraterrestrial aliens—always a popular debate topic. People have conceived all manner of appearance and capability of aliens and their host spacecraft supported by what is believed to be a litany of evidence. Even so, hard (scientifically valid) evidence is scant. Putting aside the controversy as to whether or not extraterrestrials do exist and are visiting Earth, certainly not all of these imaginings can be real. The vast majority of claims are solidly discredited with only a small subset qualifying as being unexplainable for a range of reasons. Many like to believe that these aliens freely traverse the vast distances of space via worm holes—tunnels that connect disparate parts of the universe that permit physics-defeating rapid transport from one place to another. Some postulate that aliens have been observing mankind and our planet from an unknown (even undetectable) outpost in space for huge sums of time. These are easily imagined possibilities but there is a burden to be shouldered to demonstrate that they are factual (i.e., strongly validated theory). In most instances, there is a chasm between these two states of mentation. Ultimately, given the awesome imaginative power of the human mind, we must resolve ourselves to the fact that to gain a useful comprehension of belief, faith, and truth it is paramount that we proceed with a disciplined, objective, and systematic approach.

It is also instructive to understand that human beings are mentally programmed to be irrational. Research psychologist Peter Ditto outlines that "Irrational thinking stems from cognitive biases [...] 'People don't think like scientists; they think like lawyers. They hold the belief they want to believe and then they recruit anything they can to support it.' Motivated reasoning—our tendency to filter facts to support our preexisting belief systems—is the standard way we process information. [...] As much as we'd like to think otherwise, most human judgments aren't based on reason, but on emotion."[2] And furthermore, because "We don't have time to evaluate every piece of evidence on every issue, [...] we look to people we trust in our in-groups to help us make judgments."[2] While Ditto's comments are used in the context of how irrationality applies to the acceptance or rejection of scientific ideas, the principles involved equally parlay into the transmission of religious beliefs from one to another, especially generationally. It is also important to clarify Ditto's comment that, while cognitive biases are apt to influence one's thinking, it doesn't mean that there are not defenses available to combat such biases. People are simply ignorant or lazy in many cases to confront them. He points to scientists because their discipline demands that all information is supposed to be critically evaluated to address relevant biases either by removing such distortions or by acknowledging their actual or potential effect regarding the work being performed.

Human beings by and large act in accordance with their retained (and very often biased) beliefs regardless of whether the beliefs coincide with the true nature of ultimate reality. All too seldom are cognitive biases consciously deliberated. Thus, **religious faith is considered irrational when beliefs are not undergirded by a reasoned framework. When faith lacks reason, faith is better described as imaginative thought which is not burdened with a need to be rational. For faith to be considered a rational belief there must be solid grounding provided by well-constructed reasoning and external-to-the-individual evidences so that another individual could be afforded the opportunity to evaluate those claims as being sound judgment. A *justified rational faith* goes further by thoroughly validating the reasoning and evidences as being a valid characterization of ultimate reality. Since we do not possess a total lock on what ultimate reality is, the individual claiming to possess a justified rational belief must not only defend why their views conform to reality, but *also* provide their definition for ultimate reality. Only when someone puts forth a complete systematic belief system can it be judged on its full merits whether it can be considered justified rational faith.**

We can summarize our personal beliefs in a relatively simple conceptual mathematical framework. Our personal beliefs (P_B) can be equated to a combination of three factors: (1) fideistic belief ($B_{fideistic}$), (2) evidence that is given mental consideration ($E_{considered}$) to which it is affirmed, denied, or left uncertain in the mind of the individual, and lastly, (3) information or evidence that has been given little to no consideration because it is unknown or otherwise inaccessible to the individual. This relatively simple relationship captures the underlying essence that beliefs are founded on well-processed information, poorly-processed information, and information that is not processed whatsoever. The reason why this third component is included is that a person's belief might change in the future if previously unknown information or evidence is brought to the attention of the individual. This is identified in the equation as the term 'E_{future}'. The sigma symbol, '$\sum$', is the univeral mathematical symbol meaning that we need to add together all the currently considered and future evidences. In the first summation term, $\sum_0^m E_{considered}$, this is a compact way to express the summation of currently considered evidences: $E_{c_1} + E_{c_2} + E_{c_3} + \ldots + E_{c_m}$. This is similarly the case for $\sum_0^z E_{future}$.

$$\text{Personal Belief} = P_B = \overbrace{B_{fideistic}}^{\text{No Evidence}} + \overbrace{\sum_0^m E_{considered} + \sum_0^z E_{future}}^{\text{All Evidence}}$$

For individual pieces of evidence we can decide to affirm it or disconfirm it. We can also decide that the evidence offers information that makes it too difficult to discern one way or the other and therefore we mark this as being uncertain. These choices are represented as shown below.

$$B_{fideistic} = \begin{cases} \text{Affirm} \\ \text{Deny} \end{cases}; \quad E_{considered} = \begin{matrix} \text{past or present} \\ \text{evidence} \end{matrix} \begin{cases} \text{Affirm} \\ \text{Deny} \\ \text{Uncertain} \end{cases}; \quad E_{future} = \begin{matrix} \text{future} \\ \text{evidence} \end{matrix} \begin{cases} \text{Affirm} \\ \text{Deny} \\ \text{Uncertain} \end{cases}$$

We cannot assign numeric values to evidentiary sources or beliefs. The central point is that sometimes we willfully refuse to consider the necessity to be informed ($B_{fideistic}$) and more often we have weighed only a subset of the relevant information available. What is being brought to the fore is that **an individual's beliefs regarding God are fundamentally limited by his or her knowledge of the evidence and possibly other factors such as the cognitive capacities of our evolutionarily-supplied brains**. This is not to suggest that people possessing the exact same evidences for God would automatically hold the same beliefs about God. The formation and evolution of belief is affected in complex ways by emotional states, ancillary knowledge, other existent beliefs of the individual, and influences from other people.

To move closer to the truth, we have to interrogate the evidences with applicable faculties to carefully weigh evidence. The more deliberate and curious we are to seek the truth, the more likely we are to detect and correct any errors. In the words of American revolutionist, abolitionist, biblical critic, and philosopher Thomas Paine,[16] "It is error only, and not the truth, that shrinks from inquiry."[8]

---

16. Thomas Paine was a Deist, believing in a Creator-God but was not affiliated with any doctrinal religion.

The second type of faith is *Complementary Faith* which attempts to harmonize reason, evidence, and science by extending it where rationality leaves off. Pivotally, this is where **THEISTIC MYSTICISM** and **METAPHYSICS** comes into play. The former will be discussed in Chapter 2 and again in Chapter 9 whereas metaphysics is entertained throughout the entire discourse. In this way, *natural religion*, as in religion justified by *natural evidences as opposed to supernatural postulations*, is complemented by more vague and uncertain inquiry. The third type of faith is *Co-Essential Faith* which is the view that faith and reason are indispensable to each other, with one informing the other. Co-Essential Faith adds to Complementary Faith the concept of God's **PREVENIENT GRACE** and sacred mysteries (i.e., sacraments). Co-Essential Faith is chiefly affiliated with the **DOCTRINE** of Roman Catholicism. It will be examined how well these two types of faith stack-up against the Many-Faced God Conundrum.

In his **ENCYCLICAL** entitled *Fides et Ratio* (Faith and Reason), Pope John Paul II argues that faith without reason leads to superstition and reason without faith to **NIHILISM** and **RELATIVISM**.[2] John Paul II is referring principally to **EXISTENTIAL** and **MORAL NIHILISMS**. In short, he declares that fideistic/blind faith is insufficient to understand God. We require reason, evidence, and science to comprehend God — a highly important proclamation by the religious leader of billions to acknowledge that science poses questions of existential significance and furthermore can provide insights as to the answers. St. Thomas Aquinas, the most important doctor of the Catholic Church, in his **MAGNUM OPUS**, the *Summa Theologica* (1265 – 1274 **CE**), essentially provides that faith is given to us by God and is witnessed by God's word and his miraculous deeds.[17]

> Faith is a kind of knowledge, inasmuch as the intellect is determined by faith to some knowable object. But this determination to one object does not proceed from the vision of the believer, but from the vision of Him who is believed. Thus as far as faith falls short of vision, it falls short of the knowledge which belongs to science, for science determines the intellect to one object by the vision and understanding of first principles.[10] Faith has not that research of natural reason which demonstrates what is believed, but a research into those things whereby a man is induced to believe, for instance that such things have been uttered by God and confirmed by miracles.[11]
>
> St. Thomas Aquinas, Summa Theologica I.12.13

As a point of order, throughout this book, I will only use **THEONYMS** where necessary, however, more generally I shall refer to this entity as God or *"God-by-whatever-name"*— a neutral, yet respectful, catch-all phrase coined by religion scholar William Grassie.[12]

---

17. Throughout, there is no intention to ascribe a gender to God other than specific references to Jesus Christ or any of his affiliated names. Otherwise, the male pronoun is used solely due to custom.

This God-by-whatever-name and his role in the creation and evolution of the universe have beleaguered the greatest and the commonest of minds. If God were merely an academic concept with no particular ramifications, we might come to peace with the fact that we may never know if he was in fact the cosmic progenitor of man and universe. But, we propose, and many believe, that this *Being* we call by many names is a potent force in our world. Lacking indisputable proof one way or another, all that may be left are evidentiary sources and interpretations therein. We painstakingly excavate ancient bedrock, parse arcane texts, scan the heavens, formulate exotic theories of physics, discover mathematical absolutes, split atomic nucleons in city-sized particle colliders, dissect our DNA, and conduct philosophic inquests of conscience—all to probe the natural world to AUGUR the truth of God-by-whatever-name.

After centuries of divination and discernment there has been no consensus among the assembly of erudite and often PEDANTIC scholars—academic philosophers, theologians, historians, scientists, secularists, and religious headmasters—on an array of questions about God. If anything, these indefatigable Dragons spark fire and fork lightening in a battle royale to claim higher enlightenment. It is for all intents and purposes an academic *Glass Bead Game*[18] where polarizations and exaggerations abound just as much as they do in politics. While the dragonish scholars radiate knowledge, their views and arguments are often forsaken to become the property of the educationally privileged as we commoners bide our time while the HIEROPHANTS sit enthroned in their professor's chair fail time after time to reach any accord. For the views that are able to escape and become popularized, they are often biased and narrow in scope, and some are simply the product of flamboyant imaginings that are allowed in everyday university life. Very often, they become lost in the esotericism of their own making so much so that their SOPHISTRIES are very difficult to unwind. It would be mistaken to cast all highbrow scholastic God-science debate as incendiary POLEMICS. Most encounters carry-on with a sense of decorum—a polite swashbuckling of insightful ripostes and even-tempered platitudes. Nevertheless, the venues for such interchanges are private club-like forums that seldom engage the outside world to any substantive extent. The pattern of dialogue is a spiral toward indefiniteness. As the melee plays out decade after decade, century after century, the Common Man is betwixt and left with a confused imagery for God-by-whatever-name. ***All the Common Man wants is a digestible wisdom that can be***

---

18. The Glass Bead Game paraphrases Hermann Hesse' *The Glass Bead Game* (Jonathan Cape, 1970) which is fundamentally about the struggle to identify the purpose and meaning in one's life. More directly here, it refers to a game that was once played with glass beads to mark the progress of the game which has now been transformed to a form of pure mental art. The mind and realm of scholarly debate, then, is a playground for savants and intellectuals where the scholar endeavors to impress his or her colleagues to achieve higher status in the academic hierarchy.

conveyed in relatively simple terms. Riding shotgun is a trail of massive social injustice by those who leverage God's name to advance nefarious agendas. Disoriented, society scuffles 'forward' in a grim perpetual cycle.

The metaphorical reference to dragons in the PERDURING pursuit for God may seem a quizzical choice of words and its LOCUTION is in order. As we shall see in Chapter 3, the Mesopotamian culture of the Sumerians, the first recognized civilization, will be one of our first stops on our journey to find evidences of God's existence. Clay tablets tell the well-worn story of the EPIC OF GILGAMESH (c. 2100 BCE). The prologue depicts a Mesopotamian beast named *Kur* who was present before Creation and co-existed with the gods. It would not be until the Greek's morphed the story to fit into the Greek's pantheon of supernatural beings when these beasts were bestowed with the name *drákōn*. While we know them today to be mythical creatures, at the time, dragons were considered a part of human reality, even though they were never seen. Like the gods, they played out their role in the heavens. Dragons existed in many forms and lore has it that they were wildly intelligent, some were good-natured, and others were duplicitous, weaving guile and wisdom into the same sentence. They knew the gods well and dispensed parcels of this knowledge in riddle form to deserving mortals. To this end, philosophy, religion, science, and their scholarly disciples are the modern-day equivalent of the mythical dragons. Their wisdom is likewise strewn with bias and cryptic parlance making comprehension of the sacred and the scientific opaque to the Common Man.

Since well before the Age of Enlightenment (c. 1685 – 1815 CE), there was a HERMETIC boundary between religion and science. In the last several decades, scientific discovery has forced open the hand of religion. To the Vatican's credit as it were, its posture toward the scientific community has progressed from prosecutorial to a tepid, even enthusiastic, embrace. In 1967, then-Cardinal Ratzinger, Prefect of the Congregation for the Doctrine of the Faith, in support of Vatican II reforms, removed the mandate for all clergy and nuns to take the *Oath Against Modernism.*[19] And in a letter to the Director of the Vatican Observatory, Pope John Paul II wrote "Christians will inevitably assimilate the prevailing ideas about the world, and today these are deeply shaped by science. The only question is whether they will do this critically or unreflectively, with depth and nuance or with a shallowness that

---

19. On December 8, 1864, Pope Pius IX issued the *Syllabus of Errors* which condemned pantheism, naturalism, absolute rationalism, and most notably modernism (Source 1). Modernism was an intellectual movement largely influenced by Protestant theologians but included Rationalism, Secularism, modern philosophical traditions (e.g., Immanuel Kant), and other Enlightenment ideals (Source 2). The oath can be viewed in English at http://www.papalencyclicals.net/Pius10/p10moath.htm.

Source 1: https://en.wikipedia.org/wiki/Syllabus_of_Errors

Source 2: https://en.wikipedia.org/wiki/Modernism_in_the_Catholic_Church

debases the Gospel and leaves us ashamed before history."[13] Recognizing the revelations that science was making, Pope John Paul II later prompted the conception and development of the STOQ Project (Science, Theology and the **ONTOLOGICAL** Quest) which is currently in operation working toward identifying compatibility and developing dialogue and debate between Catholicism, philosophy, theology, and science.

There has been recognition that religion and science are not necessarily **ANTIPODES** and we should no longer refer to the practitioners as '*The God Makers*' and '*The God Takers*'. There is a new reality that, in some respects, the two may actually be of benefit to the other. Even so, a chasm remains between a useful reconciliation of mutual prejudices. And as we go forward, let us be ever mindful that religion and science are both the principle causators and the prospective cures of our predicament. To take a "reliable step"[20] on a hero's journey, we shall place upon our nose the spectacles of a scholar—sans adulterating biases—to study the Great Dilemma of God-by-whatever-name as we vivisect the seamy underbelly of these Dragons one-by-one.

CAPTIOUS intellectual debates and winged lizards aside, the consequences of having god(s) in the midst of man have had **BROBDINGNAGIAN** effects on our record of godliness. Religion teaches that to attain salvation or a state of perfection (depending on the ideology); by and large we must follow the codification of that particular religious order. Such codifications, even if divinely inspired by Scripture or revelation, are subject to human interpretation. Some come to the conclusion, wrongly, that it is a right or moral duty to infringe on the liberties of others who resist the righteous path or otherwise challenge the truth of the code. As the Grand Observer's report will clearly show, the **ABRAHAMIC RELIGIONS**—the faith of billions—are disarranged with zealots who expunge those marked as heretics and apostates, sometimes in vile and reprehensible ways. Many have been sacrificed on the altar of religion. Here we call to mind ancient polytheistic practices of human sacrifice to worship the gods, the Sanhedrin Jews who sent Jesus Christ to his death, Christianity's many Inquisitions, the military Crusades by both Christians and Muslims, the Colonial conquest of the Native American Indians, the African slave trade, the conflict in Northern Ireland, and the most recent fanatical jihadist movement by violent religious extremists affiliated with al-Qaeda, Boko Haram, and the Islamic State of Iraq and the Levant (ISIL).[21] Acting under the armor and spear tip of God, incalculable injustice has been committed.

---

20. Refer to the first of Einstein's quotations at the commencement of this chapter.

21. ISIL, also known as ISIS, officially shortened its name to "Islamic State" in English. Here I preference the use of ISIL so as to avoid confusion with 'Isis' the Egyptian goddess of health, marriage, and love.

As the eminent American mythologist Joseph Campbell (b. 1904 – d. 1987) articulated so cogently in his brilliantly unique style of prose:

> Totem, tribal, racial, and aggressively missionizing cults represent only partial solutions of the psychological problem of subduing hate by love; they only partially initiate. Ego is not annihilated in them; rather, it is enlarged; instead of thinking only of himself, the individual becomes dedicated to the whole of *his* society. [emphasis by Campbell] The rest of the world meanwhile (that is to say, by far the greater portion of mankind) is left outside the sphere of his sympathy and protection because [they are] outside the sphere of protection of his god. And there takes place, then, that dramatic divorce of the two principles of love and hate which the pages of history so bountifully illustrate. Instead of clearing his own heart the zealot tries to clear the world. The laws of the City of God are applied only to his in-group (tribe, church, nation, class, or what not) while the fire of a perpetual holy war is hurled (with good conscience, and indeed a sense of pious service) against whatever uncircumcised, barbarian, heathen, "native," or alien people happens to occupy the position of neighbor.[14]

While we have established the *International Bill of Human Rights* and various Conventions that expand the former to protect the propriety of life, liberty and self-determination for all, the aspirations of this social contract are far — very far — from being realized. All too often, life can be snatched with little or no provocation, and unchecked human wickedness takes place with our full knowledge and it may be years or decades until several ounces of moral justice is meted out. There can be no true justice for those whose life is unwillingly snuffed-out in the name of God. It was acknowledged by the 2005 *United Nations World Summit* that more safeguards were necessary to prevent genocides and other forms of capital crimes against humanity by stipulating that the sovereignty of individual nation states can be superseded if they are not looking after the welfare of its people.[22] But, renegade organizations such as ISIL, al-Qaeda's Syrian affiliate Jabat al-Nusra, and Nigerian-based Boko Haram, and others of their ilk continue to engage in savagery.

So, we see that installation of civic magna cartas, as necessary as they are, is no guarantee to change the recurrence of misdeeds. This is not to suggest that notwithstanding the veracity of doctrinal assertions that religion is bereft of certain social utility — far from it. It just reaffirms that religious codes are easily bent to justify the needs of the self-serving. And while corruption and violence by no means requires an invocation of God, I see it as a

---

22. Refer to A/RES/60/1, paragraph 138-140, http://tinyurl.com/hjg46ys. Last accessed 29 Sep 2016.

moral imperative to coalesce the evidence for God, assess the veracity of theological tenets, and to seek the counsel of the sciences to enable us to change the narrative of mankind.

As inferred earlier, many great minds have prepared radiant works propositioning the definition, defense, and invalidation of God-by-whatever-name. What remains to be said is to bring the Common Man up to speed with a contemporary understanding of applicable philosophy, theology, religion, history, and the many disciplines of scientific inquiry. However, I contend that before we can consult science, we *first* have to deal with religious beliefs upfront to deconstruct the built-up theological framework *on their own terms* to appreciate the relative coherency or lack thereof. Whenever we ask a defender of religion or a defender of science to understand the perspective of the other, without stripping things down in the manner I suggest, it is akin to asking someone, "What color is the object in my hand?" as they peer through colored lenses. Using this metaphor, we have to remove the spectacles and appreciate the object for what it truly is.

Ultimately, regardless of what can be said about God-by-whatever-name, throughout history, religion has been decidedly disobedient to its moral obligation of universal civility throughout its ranks. I do not believe it is a legitimate argument to carte blanche release 'peaceful religions' from responsibility when religiously radicalized militants commit violence based on contorted interpretations of the underlying tenants of these same religions. People will always interpret religion in their own way. When zealots come to believe that those external to, in opposition of, or simply are non-believing must be converted or be vanquished this becomes a *dual problem* of religious ideology and a demented amoral psyche that can no longer differentiate right from wrong. In some cases, differentiation suffers because of a religious belief where God's will as interpreted from religious texts trump inferior human conceptions of morality. In other cases, morality may be lost, subjugated, or co-mingled with ideologies trained on gaining power and influence. If the related materials for a given religion did not exist in the first place, there would be no launch pad for its adulteration. Hence, the violent religious fanaticism would be otherwise disempowered. This is why it becomes incumbent for the leaders of organized religion and individual adherents alike to fully justify and articulate their tenants in unambiguous and unequivocal terminology which are presumptively evocative of peaceful intentions toward all.

FAITH IN FLUX AND SECULARIZATION TODAY

A vast mall of religious and spiritual options exists. It is conjectured that approximately 10,000 religions exist worldwide.[23, 15] According to United States census data, more than six in ten are completely certain that a deity of some sort exists (refer to Figure 1-1[16]).

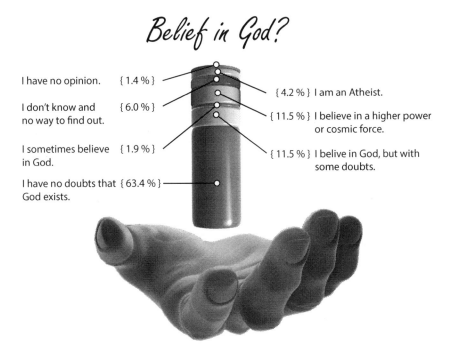

Belief in God?

I have no opinion. { 1.4 % }

I don't know and { 6.0 % }
no way to find out.

I sometimes believe { 1.9 % }
in God.

I have no doubts that { 63.4 % }
God exists.

{ 4.2 % } I am an Atheist.

{ 11.5 % } I believe in a higher power
or cosmic force.

{ 11.5 % } I belive in God, but with
some doubts.

Figure 1-1. Do you believe in God? (a census of opinion in the United States)

Based on the number of adherents, there are between seven to ten *major* religions—though this divisional outlook hardly matters. With so much diversity in belief systems, it is not all too surprising that people are apt to change their faith, sometimes several times, in their lifetime. According to a 2009 Pew Research Center study, 44 percent of people in the United States change their faith from that which they were raised.[17] In close agreement with this, parental influence is responsible for the religious transmission of their faith for six out of every ten children.[18] Among Catholics who have left the Church to become "unaffiliated,"[24] 75 percent

---

23. For comparison purposes, the *Encyclopedia of World Religions* (Foreign Media Group, 2006) lists 4,500 entries.

24. All of the numerical figures presented for Catholics are also comparable for Protestants who have become unaffiliated. Unaffiliation (or disaffiliation) generally means such individuals may still be religious and in some state of transition to some other faith. Only a small percentage elects to adopt an indifference or rejection to religion.

agree that many religions are partially true.[19] A slightly fewer number (66 percent) think that ecclesiastical leadership is more centrally focused on increasing their influence, positions, and financial gain rather than the pursuit of spiritual concerns.[19] The advances of scientific knowledge have also eroded the belief in many of these professed unaffiliated individuals whereby 32 percent of former Catholics now believe that religion is nothing more than superstition.[19]

The Rise of the Religiously Unaffiliated

According to a Pew Research Center study, the vast majority of adult Americans (79%) identify themselves as being religiously affiliated, though this has declined about 3% in the timeframe of 2007 – 2012. In this same timeframe, those who are religiously unaffiliated has risen about 4.3% to account for 19.6% of our population.[20] The unaffiliated population, sometimes referred to as the "Nones," is subdivided into ATHEISTS, AGNOSTICS, and those who have no particular belief. Among adults, atheists number about 5.6 million people (2.4% of population) and agnostics number 7.7 million (3.3% of population) which totals nearly 13.4 million people.[20] Those who have no particular belief represent about one-in-five Americans (13.9%)[20] and constitute 71% of all the "Nones" (unaffiliated).[21] Interestingly, of the Nones as a whole, only ten percent of these individuals are seeking a new religion to join so it would seem that they are largely settled in their state of disaffiliation from religion.[22] From 2007 – 2014, there has been a noticeable drop in the share of Christians overall, down 7.8% to 70.6% due to a decrease in Protestants and Catholics by 4.8% and 3.1%, respectively.[23] From 2012 – 2014, the unaffiliated increased from 19.6% to 22.8% which is an amazingly swift change.[20, 23] On a percentage-basis, the unaffiliated as a group now outnumber Catholics (22.8% vs. 20.8%, respectively).[23]

Religious Conversions

A fascinating even if not all too surprising statistic is that those who change religions seldom cross engrained boundaries between major faith traditions. As Figure 1-2[24] illustrates, those who originally believed in one of the Abrahamic religions — Christianity, Judaism, or Islam — overwhelmingly converted to become unaffiliated rather than making a wholesale change to one of the other two religions. The percentage of people that switch from one to another Abrahamic religion is a rare event in the overall scheme of conversions. The choice seems to be to either believe in nothing in particular (though remain loosely spiritual) or to disengage entirely from religion and become agnostic/atheistic.

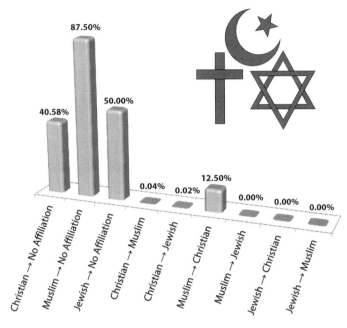

Religious Conversion From One Belief to Another

Worldwide Religious Transitions for People Aged 30 and Over
(40 countries surveyed, Year 2001)

Figure 1-2. Religious Conversions for the Abrahamic Traditions across 40 Countries

The largest majority of cross-boundary transitions occur from Islam-to-Christianity which is all the more remarkable considering the fact that some Muslim cultures where **SHARIA LAW** is practiced, punishments can be quite cruel. Often, the individual who has renounced Islam is required to convert back under extreme pressure by family members and/or their Imam or else face the penalty of death. Stories abound of so-called 'honor killings' whereby the family seeks to regain the good graces of their religious community by killing the family member who converted

SECULARISM TODAY

Worldwide, it is estimated that 11.8 percent are nonreligious with 9.8 percent claiming to be agnostic and just 2.0 percent identify as atheists.[25] Interestingly, data suggests that just 1.4 percent of U.S. and Canadian college students reared in a religious family later disaffiliated their institutional religion *in toto* (i.e., to commit **APOSTASY**),[26, 27] embracing tacitly or directly agnosticism or atheism. The realm of the unchurched is actually rather complex, far from being monochromatic. Influential sociologist Peter Berger frames secularization as the process whereby religious institutions and their associated beliefs and symbols become subordinated or extricated from sectors of society and culture.[28] Secularization might be considered an extension of the late 17th- and 18th-century Age of Enlightenment movement that challenged tradition and faith in favor of advancing knowledge through the scientific method. <u>What we find is that individuals are spiritually divorcing formalized orthodoxies in favor of more individualized perspectives.</u>[29, 30] As sociologist Phil Gorski postulates, Christianity is not so much declining as a share of the population but rather is returning to a state of **POLYSEMISM**[25] in which the beliefs practiced by Christians are no longer following orthodox theism.[31] <u>What is happening in the West is that people are developing their own personal theology which is often a **SYNCRETIC** combination of religious ideas from multiple faiths.</u> This is also just as true in Europe. Belgian Catholic theologian Lieven Boeve, a former chairman of the *European Society of Catholic Theology*, remarks that "The processes of detraditionalisation have not led to the disappearance of religion in Europe, but to its transformation. The continuing institutional and mental dechristianisation of Europe have not led to a secular culture and society, but to a new kind of vague religiosity. [...] This vague religiosity can be analysed as both the symptom of and the solution to the crisis of the modern subject, who has become conscious of the fact that he/she is no longer the master of him/herself. In a search for identity, meaning, harmony, stability, security, the human subject engages in a movement of self-transcendence toward something divine, which both reveal the limits of the subject as well as enables it to cope with these limits."[32, 33]

PRESCINDING the pedagogy of these last remarks, it is clear that the considerable majority of people profess belief in some representation of God and that religion is a near universal human phenomenon, and such has been the case for many millennia. Is it enough that billions of people believe in the existence of a supernatural Being for it to be true?[26] We certainly understand that this type of assertion is not a defensible position. If we resign ourselves to the inevitable fact that there is no undeniable proof that an external God exists and that God is not self-evident, what then should we base our belief in a higher power? And by use of the phrase

---

25. Gorski uses the words "return to polysemism" as he suggests that today's world is not unlike pre-Christian Rome when there were many types of gurus, preachers, sorcerers, mystagogues, and their ilk purveying a wide number of belief systems. Pre-Christianity will be explored in depth in Chapter 5.

26. Some individuals are uncomfortable with use of the word 'supernatural' in connection with God because by some definitions God is natural in the sense that he is a part of or pervades the universe. I will not quibble on such distinctions. If one is so inclined, one may exchange the word 'supernatural' for 'deific agency'.

'external God', what I mean to say is that God is a reality that exists outside of ourselves and is not a noetic internal fabrication of our mind-brain.

THE SEARCH FOR PURPOSE

Whether religious, spiritual, unaffiliated, or nonreligious, we all must find our way in the laboratory of our own existence. The vast majority of people's consciousness' regularly ponders how they fit into the grand scheme of things and what their purpose is in life. In America, 67% of the general public is frequently reflecting on the meaning to life, with only 10% rarely giving it much thought. While religiously affiliated people tend to mirror the general public in these regards, among the religiously unaffiliated, only 45% frequently think about the meaning of life with a relatively higher number seldom thinking on such things (17%).[34] In any case, this equates to a great deal of brain power devoted to understanding our place in our universe and the deity(ies) that may have created it. It is this enduring fascination that has motivated me to write this book and why, I think, many will share my passion and interest to join in the quest to find the most probable truths about what we can know about God-by-whatever-name.

QUESTIONING FAITH AND KNOWLEDGE

Let us consider a scenario whereby you and I have a chance encounter at a local coffee shop and we engage in a conversation. After a time, you reveal that you you have a congenital brain disorder and that it requires an invasive transcranial surgical procedure. I indicate that I happen to have developed a new machine to perform brain surgeries and that I can take care of this for you. Would you take it on faith that I could use this machine and correct your brain disorder?! The likelihood is that you would not. You would initially be very skeptical regarding my abilities or the machine to execute this complex operation. You would want some evidence as to my credentials to perform this type of medical procedure. You might also inquire how the machine works and has it been certified in any way. You would probably like to see some performance data on positive outcomes. Maybe you would ask your primary care doctor or ask to talk to other patients. And you would look for other more mundane clues such as my clothes, mannerisms, and whether I spoke intelligibly on this issue.

If you wouldn't take it on faith that I could perform this mortally critical surgery successfully, why would you unquestioningly entrust your way of life in a religion that was conceived (some may say divinely revealed) thousands of years ago by NEOLITHIC fishermen, farmers, and sheepherding folk or their ancient descendants about whom you know virtually nothing about, whose cultural placement in history was steeped in mythology, knew nothing of science, and that you can't directly question? One would suppose an equal or greater scrutiny would go into the decision toward belief in an existential God and the associated investment in lifelong efforts and sacrifices required of religious homage. Alas, the vast majority of people grow up with their religion and never question its *real* foundations. We will explore what I mean by "real" in the next several chapters. Many, perhaps most, religionists/ spiritualists, are unknowing or very uncertain how to go about critically evaluating their faith.

Neophytes (which I was most certainly one for far too long) were told by religious **PEDAGOGUES** that one should question and explore their personal faith. But the hidden subtext is that divine **AGENCY** must be presupposed and that you still ought to believe in the religion-by-whatever-name. The only tools to ask questions were to consult one's conscious and to earnestly read Scripture to enhance his or her understanding of faith. This may help one to gain knowledge of a religion but it seeks to do so by looking for spiritual verities from the inside-out. It is akin to sitting at the edge of an inward spiraling vortex where one constantly reaffirms the same information with different perspectives. What we study, we then become. We do not objectively question the truth of God per se; rather we **INCULCATE** ourselves in a **Pavlovian** ritual to institutionalize the initial belief. This type of introspective study is not a critical evaluation; rather it plays right into the hands of our fault-prone mind-brains. If we are told enough times, we begin to believe such and such is true.

Should we accept so easily that God in his awesome power created this incomprehensively vast universe, who then decided to populate this one planet with humans to pay him tribute? As of November 8, 2017, the *Kepler* Mission has confirmed the existence of 2,515 exoplanets which brings the total exoplanet discoveries to 3,550.[27] Among the 290 or so habitable planets, the closest are *Proxima b*, *Ross 128 b*, and *Wolf 1061c* located 4.22, 11, and 14 light-years from Earth, respectively.[28, 35, 36] But this does not even scratch the surface because scientists have recently estimated that **40 *billion*** roughly Earth-sized planets may exist in our own Milky Way Galaxy.[37-39] When we extend this out to the observable universe in its entirety, there may be many trillions of life-bearing planets! (refer to Box 1) Some religionists go further to claim that God made us in his own physical and/or mental image and delivered to us his only Son. As a person of faith, why would you so readily want to devote your entire life to any number

---

27. The *Kepler* Mission is a space satellite survey to observe portions of the Milky Way galaxy for planetary bodies. The 2,515 figure include 2,337 planets confirmed by the original Kepler Mission and 178 planets by the follow-on K2 Mission. (Source: NASA Exoplanet Archive, http://exoplanetarchive.ipac.caltech.edu/index.html)

28. An interactive database of confirmed planet discoveries is archived at: http://exoplanetarchive.ipac.caltech.edu/

of religious tenets such as abstaining from sexual intercourse (premarital sex, priestly celibacy, or otherwise), prejudicing against or even self-suppressing homosexuality, invest countless hours of religious worship, abstain from eating particular foods, risk being trampled to death on a Hajj pilgrimage to Mecca, wear special garb that signifies your piety, strap on a suicide vest, or any number of other things you might consider honorific to your religion? Even though the marshals in the Age of Enlightenment made a valiant attempt to break minds free from millennia of myths, hearsay, and blind acceptance of truth claims by religious monarchies, it is clear that a greater force for illumination is required to avoid further regrets of our past, or as Joseph Campbell puts it, "regrets are illuminations come too late."[40]

BOX 1 – AN ESTIMATE FOR THE EXISTENCE OF TECHNOLOGICALLY ADVANCED EXO-CIVILIZATIONS IN THE UNIVERSE

Until the latter part of 2016, astronomical estimates provided for the existence of some 100 – 200 billion galaxies in the universe. However, a recent study using data from NASA's Hubble Space Telescope has revealed that more than 90 percent of galaxies are not visible from Earth. That is, there are 10 times the number of galaxies than previously thought, concluding that our universe contains some two trillion galaxies (2×10^{12}).[62] In the last few years, it has been determined that approximately 22 percent of all stars in the Milky Way galaxy have an Earth-like planet positioned in a circumstellar habitable zone.[38]

If we were to assume that this arrangement held as an average for all other galaxies, we can make an appraisal for how many life-bearing planets might exist in the cosmos. Using an astronomical relationship called the *initial mass function* which describes the probability distribution of main sequence stars (such as our Sun), we can estimate the number of sun-like stars. Prior to the aforementioned Hubble Telescope study, we would have posited that there are on the order of 400 billion-billion (4×10^{20}) stars like our Sun (± 30 percent of one solar mass) in the observable universe. This would yield a conclusion that there may be 8.8 $\times 10^{19}$ or approximately 90 billion-billion Earth-like planets currently existent throughout the known universe. This agrees closely with a different estimate from U.S. astronomers Peter Behroozi and Molly Peeples (2015) who predicted the number to be ~10^{20} Earth-like planets. However, with the inferred discovery of so many more galaxies, we have to multiply these figures ten-fold. Thus, there may be as many as four sextillion (4×10^{21}) sun-like stars that are hosts to some 880 billion-billion (8.8×10^{20})—or equivalently, 0.88 sextillion—Earth-like planets! Behroozi's and Peoples' research also indicates that, while Earth formed after 80 percent of these habitable planets formed, only 8 percent of the free gas in the universe has been used toward star formation. *This means that roughly 92 percent of all Earth-like planets have yet to form in the universe.*[41] The universe will eventually birth an **additional** 10.1 sextillion (10.1 x 10^{21}) Earth-like planets! This is truly a dumbfounding thought to consider.

We can rationalize that many star systems with Earth-like planets still encounter major problems for the conception and sustainment of life. For example, the majority of star systems are binary—that is, planets will be affected gravitationally and otherwise by two stars. Some stars are not stable, and may, for example sporadically belch-out ultra-intense radiation blasts that would affect planetary life or may even 'go supernova' and annihilate its encircling planetary system. By some estimates, there are 30 supernovae every second in the universe.[42] This also needs to be increased to around 300 now that our universe plays host to two trillion galaxies. In our own galaxy, there is one supernova event about every 50 years.

Some planets may have everything going for it, but are stationed too close to an asteroid field whereby the planet's surface is under constant bombardment which interrupts biological processes. We have nary an understanding how biologic life arises from inanimate substances which means it is chiefly guess-work to postulate whether life will begin even when the conditions are 'just so'. And just because the top-level key factors are in place, it does not mean favorable conditions are sufficiently persistent or whether there are second-tier nullifying conditions that would prevent life from establishing itself. Scientists postulate the existence of the *Bottleneck Effect* which is a process of restriction or outright elimination of previously existent populations (e.g., mass extinctions from ecosystem collapse). It is recognition that there appear to be sustainability constraints that invoke time limits for exponential growth patterns to operate. With periodic collpases almost a certainty, it helps to explain why the sustainability of living things is so fragile in the long term.

There are currently between 7.4 – 10 million animal species on Earth.[43] Mass extinction events on Earth indicate that the vast majority of species have gone extinct signaling how difficult it is to successfully achieve human-like intelligence. This is a baseline to suggest that there is about a one-in-ten million chance—

an order of magnitude lower—that microbial life evolves to human-like maybe or better intelligence. With only one point of reference it is impossibleto know how well our situation fits in the broader context of the presently existing 880 billion-billion (8.8 x 10^{20}) Earth-like planets. to know how well our situation fits in the broader context of the presently existing 880 billion-billion (8.8 x 10^{20}) Earth-like planets. *Being presumptuous that this scaling applies universally, it would put the number of intelligent, technologically advanced exo-civilizations that have existed thus far anywhere between a mind-bending 8.8 trillion (8.8 x 10^{12}) to 88 trillion (8.8 x 10^{13})!*

However, we also have to take into account the lifespan of technologically advanced aliens and the longevity of their civilization. Human civilization has been around for some 10,000 years give or take. Some alien civilizations may be of a similar age whereas it is conceivable that others could have existed for ten or even 100 times longer, old enough and advanced enough to document significant evolution of their own species. The universe has been stable enough to support the development of solar systems for 13 billion years. *Given the relatively short life-cycle of any given intelligent civilization, it means that the considerable majority—potentially trillions—of exo-civilizations have already come and gone!* However, future planet formation activities would yield ~10^{14} – ~10^{15} more intelligent civilizations (i.e., between *0.1 quadrillion* to *one quadrillion* civilizations).

If we were to assume that of the 40 billion Earth-like planets in the Milky Way that *one-in-ten million* to *one-in-one hundred million* harbored intelligent life—rather scant odds—*that would mean that our galaxy will eventually be host to 400 – 4,000 technologically advanced alien civilizations*. Statistically, however, only a few handfuls would be our contemporaries and by contemporary I mean living within several million years past or present. *The number of exo-civilizations that exist right at this instant might be countable on two hands.* Our galaxy will eventually merge with the Andromeda galaxy, which according to Behroozi and Peeples, will shift Earth's position in the timeline of galactic planet formation. Whereas, before the galactic merger, Earth originated after 80 percent of other Earth-like planets formed, after the combination with Andromeda, this will be altered such that the Earth will become among the first 39 percent of all planets to be formed.[44] While astronomers at the present time are not able to gauge with any substantial certainty how many Earth-like extragalactic exoplanets may exist in Andromeda, we can grossly extrapolate a doubling or tripling of the total number of intelligent civilizations to 800 – 12,000 given that M31 contains approximately three times as many stars which also happen to be younger on-average.

In considering interstellar or intergalactic travel, there are formidable barriers to consider, especially for the transport of organic life. A major concern is the environmental hostilities of deep space owing to the persistent conditions of cosmic radiation and temperature extremes. We already know that physical shielding based on the use of lead, water-based barriers, or hydrogen-infused materials would not meet all the requirements necessary for long term journeys. The most likely technology to offer the requisite protection from cosmic rays would be to mimic Earth's protective magnetosphere by enveloping a spaceship in an artificial plasma or electromagnetic deflector shield to repel or redirect harmful particles. While such a system works in theory, constructing a viable system is still very uncertain. We also need to consider food supply and the typical lifespans of living things, the operational lifespan of equipment, along with the practical consideration of sustained civility among the alien travelers onboard a cramped spaceship galleon.

Finally, there are fundamental limits to the maximum speed one can obtain from a spaceship propulsion system. Future technology in the form of fusion or fission/fusion rockets is believed to be constrained to less than 10 percent of the speed of light. At such speeds, travel from the nearest star to Earth would take somewhere between one-half to a full century (basically, a human lifetime). Antimatter rocket concepts, of which there are several conceived methods, are limited to about five times the speed of fission rockets; however, the means to create and contain antimatter present many intractable problems. The propulsion system offering the fastest travel is by an Alcubierre warp drive. Such a system generates a spherical bubble or ring-like structure of flat space (i.e., a warp bubble) around a spacecraft. Then, space is compressed in front of the bubble while simultaneously expanding space behind the bubble thereby creating a 'space-wave' which can theoretically push the spacecraft up to near-light speeds and potentially faster. Nevertheless, every technologically-tantalizing concept brings with it a host of engineering problems that make any given ultra-advanced propulsion system rather improbable for mankind or any advanced species to fabricate.

Even if one considered the notion of serial colonization—'island hopping'—of intermediate solar systems to make spaceship repairs or for resupply, the odds are not much improved for alien life to have ever reached Earth. The greatest likelihood is that the overwhelming number of species is locked to their planet of origin or at best to its nearest stellar neighbors. It would be more feasible for an alien civilization to send lightweight emissaries in the form of robotic-like probes that might also be autonomous. These probes would need to travel at some decent fraction of the speed of light. But even then, they would have to know what direction to send them. The oldest (and now virtually undetectable) radio transmissions from Earth only go out 100 light-years in any direction so it is highly unlikely they would know of our existence considering how distant they are likely to be (the Milky Way is about 100,000 light-years across).

Ultimately, it appears that mathematical probability presents us with a powerful dichotomy that stymies the conscious. On one hand, biologic life is likely to be common throughout the universe. On the other, time and distance scales along with biological longevity significantly alter the calculus that our civilization could be in the same room with an intelligent exo-civilization so to speak. The best we can hope for in the near future is to infer possible locations of exolife based on spectrographic signatures. Maybe in the next few centuries we will launch hundreds of probes ourselves and wait centuries for feedback. Or, if we are lucky (maybe unlucky), we may be visited by an alien probe because they saw promise in the Earth's orbital parameters and spectrographic signature. It is feasible that such a probe could belong to a now extinct civilization whose citizens sent tens of thousands or millions of years ago.

Religion makes hefty claims that any rational person should place a great deal of *initial* skepticism until credible evidences are presented *and validated*. We must initiate with the fact that religion is festooned with immense historical power so much so that many believers have neglected to question the origin and evolution of belief systems and have not properly consulted the body scientific to appreciate a contemporary view of the data. We leave it to scholars to sort these things out who disseminate the bread crumbs in a 'here and over there' fashion. Frustratingly, while the scholars are busy debating among themselves, Common Men are simply expected by our religious leaders to trust in the "mystery of God" and that he is in our midst, responding to our prayers, allowing a semblance of free will and yet in some queer sense nudging us along Omega's cord of destiny in some divine pretext.

Pope Francis stated six months after his papal inauguration in his characteristically plain language:

> "When intelligence tries to explain a mystery, it always -- always -- becomes crazy," [...] The mystery of salvation "can only be understood on one's knees, in contemplation." [...] To enter into a mystery one needs "intelligence, heart, knees praying -- all together."[45]

Pope Francis, 2013

His expression is quite correct that the allegorical dragons—especially the manyfold religions—make one "crazy" when attempting to discern the true nature of God. Christian theology asserts that there is a *knowability of God*,[46] suggesting that we cannot know God in all respects, but we can know meaningful things about God because of revelatory actions in the form of Scripture, bodily visitation on Earth, and by psychic personal communication. Furthermore, God will continue to reveal more of himself as time goes on. I will grant that an encyclopedic understanding of the full dimensionality of God is outside of our grasp, I do think, however, it is equally unjustifiable that we just throw up our arms and wait for our mortality to wrest our last breath to find out what we cannot, can, do, and might come to know about this enigmatic God.

Beyond personal ruminations and scriptural reflections, religious headmasters point to human role models to substantiate and perpetuate God's abiding presence in our lives. We are presented with any number of miraculous examples of God's benevolence. Between 22[47] to 27[48] percent of American sports fans believe that God influences the outcome of sports contests[29] and half of American fans (48[47] to 53[48] percent) believe that athletes profit from a divine source with gifts of health and success. We bear witness to God's purported work when U.S. Presidents seek to inspire a nation with the invocation of biblical passages in a passionate national speech or we hear how someone overcame drug addiction by the intervention of God, or by a loved one miraculously escaping certain death or grave infirmity. Then we have the soul-wrenching stories of the marginalized who are uplifted. These serve to exemplify the power and effect of religion in society. While we will investigate the concept of human belief in detail, none of these would-be anecdotal stories qualifies as convincing evidence that a supernatural God is actually responsible for **SALVIFIC** acts. At best, it amounts to circumstantial evidence which offers an exceptionally loose causal connection between one thing and another. That is, there could be a host of other plausible natural causes

---

29. Break down by religious affiliation for those that believe God intervenes in sport contests: 40% Minority Christians, 38% White Evangelical Protestants, 29% Catholics, 19% White Mainline Protestants, 12% Religiously Unaffiliated

that have similar or greater explanatory power. More likely, we are apt to identify a long chain of indistinct *natural* causes that have brought about such circumstances. Here, I eschew the use of the concept of *miracles* because it imports theological assumptions. Let us put aside all discussion of miracle-claims until we come to a point where there is nothing else natural can be offered.

Zeteo Alétheia – The Systematic Search for God

Religious belief is a very personal and typically communal phenomenon. Therefore, questioning religion and theistic belief is often tagged with great emotion and is apt to trigger a defensive posture. Without performing a deep inquiry into what can be said about deific agency, we do ourselves as individuals and as a society a disservice by making avowals of faith under gaping ambiguities (or "mysteries" as Pope Francis puts it). By disservice I mean to say that without such an **INTERLOCUTION**, it greatly affects the ability to evolve humankind to become a better society than it is today. How certain are you that religious scriptures are the inspired oracles for God-by-whatever-name? Have you examined the origins and precursors of religion (yours and others) in a deep, independent, critical, and conscientiously objective manner? More generally, how certain are you that religion can offer an accurate depiction of and provide solid evidence for God-by-whatever-name?

Should we start our quest to find God with the explicit assumption and defense that some form of deity or deities exist in conjunction with a particular religious view therein, we immediately pollute the ability to have an objective discussion. We will have jumped squirrely-foot onto a playground merry-go-round with little hope of forward advancement or otherwise. To arrive at the best answers to the existential questions posed earlier on, we need to *initially* adopt the null hypothesis (that is, God does not exist) and then employ evidence-based thinking and study the global dimensions of far flung disciplines to fully engage the nexus of information accumulated over history. In this way, we work toward a justification in terms of the most well-wrought rationale whether or not God exists.

In searching for answers, Andrew Newberg, a prominent neuroscientist and psychiatrist suggests a new field of study, namely *neurotheology*—a combination of neuroscience and theology. In acknowledging that the human brain may not be able to definitively determine truths about reality, he suggests that "perhaps the only way around this would be to utilize a constellation of approaches. Thus combining sciences, theology, philosophy, and mathematics might yield a better, more complete answer regarding the nature of reality than any of those approaches individually."[42] His insights could not be more on point as this is the very course we shall follow. We shall employ methodological pluralism to traverse the vast terrain of our accumulated knowledge sources to parse philosophy, theology, and science vis-à-vis scriptural hermeneutics (biblical interpretation), historical and biblical archaeological analysis, evolutionary biology, neuroscience, evolutionary psychology, cosmogony (the scientific study for the origins of the universe), mathematics, statistics, and the nascent fields of neurotheology and quantum biology (biology at the fundamentally smallest scales of reality) to appreciate what each of these can tell us about God-by-whatever-name both by themselves and when looking at them holistically. These bodies of knowledge are attributed with their common moniker because human knowledge is forever afflicted with a level of uncertainty and because there is much that is unknown, only some of which may be discovered in centuries to come. In due course we can assemble and weigh the motivating evidences, then construct a synthetic framework to form the most intelligible outlook for God—more or less exactly what Newberg prescribes. *We can subsequently render a considered* EPISTEMIC *judgment based on the preponderance of evidence. Ultimately, this is a meta-synthesis of how religion has attempted to define God and to what degree our abilities and available evidences are able to more appropriately circumscribe the potentiality of an otherworldly ultra-Being.* It amounts to assembling one of the greatest jigsaw puzzles of all time. The road forward is therefore narrow, long, and often bumpy and we must position ourselves into uncomfortable spaces as it will become clear that no *single* worldview may be wholly or even partially true (i.e., a religious, scientific, philosophical, historical, or psychological view).

Herein I have opted to dispense with the DIALECTICAL SOCRATIC METHOD; as such the synthetic framework will not be formed from a balanced point–counterpoint engagement, at least not in any strict sense. As witnessed by the racks upon racks of scholarly APOLOGETIC literature, religion has already exhaustively staked-out and defended its position. The conversation herein is focused on skeptically dissecting key aspects of the theological and philosophical framework to bring the concepts at work into sharper focus. Also, I will re-highlight that the line of questioning is to critique theistic claims on the terms provided by the respective religion. Meaning, there is no implicit intention to malign a particular claim in some unfair fashion. Instead, it will be studied for what it is and as impartially as possible. Ultimately, if we are to illumine anything about religion's God-by-whatever-name we should initiate from a sterile origin (the null state). To my mind this means that we shrug-off all the intractable attachments to religion, and along with it, as much subjectivity and emotion as possible. By DENUDING ourselves from all prior interpretations of God and committed bias, we may then build a cognitive approach rooted in a ZETETIC process of DEDUCTIVE, INDUCTIVE, ABDUCTIVE, and finally REDUCTIVE methods of discernment.

The term *zetetic* is derived from the Greek verb *Zeteo*; which means *to seek out to find.*[30] Another salient Greek word is that for 'truth'—*Alétheia*—as in the factuality of reality. This leads us to the central thesis of this book which is to seek out the truth about God by critical inquiry, the essence of this effort being captured by these two ancient words— **Zeteo Alétheia**.[31] Zetetics is to be distinguished from the normative connotation of skepticism which is to say that skeptics sit back with their hands clasped, questioning and even scoffing at everything. Rather, Zetetics calls the inquirer, the believer, and the skeptic to stand on the same platform and to engage as intellectually honest participants in sourcing the truth to the question, "How can we know whether or not God is real?"

The zetetic journey necessarily initiates with the *a priori* position that there is no causal priority between the existence of God and the existence of the known universe (what I referred to earlier as the null state). The relationship between the potential existence of God and the universe will be entertained through a rigorous process of reflection. Given the dependence on, and the general unreliability of human cognition, a cautious advance is warranted. What we will find on our zetetic odyssey is that, to open the corridor to the most truthful nature of God, we will necessarily close certain theological doors.

Furthermore, we shall subtract from our point of origin any cogitation on the caused or uncaused existence of any deity(ies) with causal powers. This, by definition, excludes a reliance on miracles to describe any of our knowledge, experiences, and evidences. A related concern is Christianity's firm belief in a personally accessible living God which shall be given an extensive turn at the table in later chapters. In the next section, we will discuss the concept of truth. Suffice it to say that if 'Person A' believes as true that the Christian God is accessible to all individuals, this by itself does not make it necessarily true for 'Person B'. No more so than if Person B believes as true that 'God' is a species of generally unseen, conniving, and powerful aliens that manipulate our environment to see how humans respond to a complex set of stimuli (that is, we are the rats in the experiment box). These two beliefs/faiths are incompatible but, by themselves, are logical equals. 'Person C' may think both Persons A and B got it all wrong and that *their* personal judgment tells them something entirely different about what God is. Therefore, **it is encumbent upon us to establish a basis for what qualifies as a truth**, which is what we will do before the close of this chapter.

---

30. I wish to clarify that the usage of the words 'Zetetic, Zeteticism, Zeteticist' herein are completely distinct from the same terminology being used by the Universal Zetetic Society, the purveyors of the Flat Earth Hypothesis—the view that the Earth is shaped like a disk.

31. The formal pronunciation for the Greek words *Zeteo Alétheia* is *Dzay-teh'-o Aleeth-ee-a.*

Importantly, the initial adoption of the null state does **not** rule out God by FIAT, nor is it to be considered Empiricism,[32] Rationalism,[33] Religious Naturalism, or Traditional Naturalism.[34] It is also not at the outset grounding ourselves in ATHEISM or AGNOSTICISM which are effectively position statements on Modern DEISM and THEISM. If we are to apply a definition, it may be said that the approach to be taken herein shares aspects of the revisionary character of Ramified Natural Theology (RNT). This phrase was coined by analytic philosopher Richard Swinburne and is an extension (hence the meaning of the word 'ramified') of the age-old construct of traditional natural theology which seeks to establish the rational feasibility of theism. Natural theology proceeds by employing our natural endowments of sensory perceptions (experience) and reason (rationality) to comprehend the existence of a generic God, that is, not a God defined with the specific attributes as extolled by Judaism, Christianity, Islam, etc. Often, natural theology attempts to deduce the existence of an almighty deity from the apparent deliberate design of the physical universe. Furthermore, natural theology is by definition prohibited from making any appeals to the authority of divine revelation, supernaturalism, or miracle-making.

Ramified (extended) Natural Theology goes further than Traditional Naturalism to attempt to characterize God in a particular format (e.g., the Jewish God or the Christian God) using *natural evidences*, eschewing reliance on supernatural claims. While RNT could be used by any of the Abrahamic religions, it has become predominantly affiliated with and recognized as the most effective contemporary defense of the Christian interpretation of God. While the zetetic approach parallels this theology in light of our investigation of natural evidences, we diverge thereafter as will be explained further on. We will review key aspects of RNT in much more depth in Chapters 6, 7, and 9.

The zetetic approach shares some kinship with eminent philosopher Immanuel Kant's (b. 1724 – d. 1804) worldview who believed that we gain all knowledge from our mind's perceptions and subjective experiences to interpret the world and that these must be examined under the light of reason. By use of the word *interpret*, it is meant that we analyze,

---

32. Empiricism is a theory which states that knowledge is predominantly acquired from sensory experience and evidence.

33. Rationalism is a theory that all knowledge is sourced and tested by human reason. The criterion of the truth is not sensory but intellectual and deductive. It is a rival theory to Empiricism.

34. Religious Naturalism is non-theistic view that portends a belief that nature is itself sacred and highly interrelated. Furthermore, there is no justification necessary for nature's existence and sourcing deeper meaning for nature's reality is to appreciate its simplicity and complexity from many perspectives with no appeal to the divine. The religious aspects are characterized in terms of generating enhanced awareness of the sacredness of nature. It possesses an orientation toward Empiricism.

deconstruct, reduce, and synthesize all sources of information, namely empirical data, mathematics, physical laws, and the ways in which our brains process the internal cognitive, emotional, and subjective experiences and phenomena therein. Therefore, where our senses perceive reality, it is the brain and its limitations therein that makes sense of these perceptions. Kant also argued for a 'two-worlds' interpretation of reality, the *phenomenal* world accessible to our senses and the *noumenal* world which is inaccessible by any direct means. It is unclear if Kant meant that these two-worlds are ontologically (that is, physically) existent as separate domains or just that there is just one reality and we can only sense part of that single reality.

In either case, in at least one sense, Kant was right because there is much in the universe we cannot directly sense, but we can infer its existence indirectly. For example, the human body or mind cannot directly sense the radio waves that are bouncing all around us. Yet we know that until they are converted by electrical equipment (i.e., radios), radio waves exist beyond our sensory modalities of sight, sound, smell, touch, and taste. Another example is the confirmed existence of the invisible Higgs field present everywhere throughout the universe.[35] Relative to God, Kant is largely regarded as an agnostic so if God were to exist, Kant would regard him as residing outside of our senses. In the end, the zetetic approach goes so far as to say that there is a larger reality outside of our collective senses but that aspects (but not all) of this larger reality are *indirectly* accessible to us. Furthermore, the zetetic program remains open to the idea that there are both direct and indirect aspects of reality we can never know as a result of the limitations of our cognitive and physical abilities. For example, we may never be able to characterize with any useful certainty what happens deep within a cosmic black hole. We also know that no matter how powerful of an instrument or how fast a spaceship we can construct, we will never be able to experience in any way whatsoever the furthest reaches of the unobservable universe. Likewise, if multiple universes happen to exist; we can learn nothing definitive about them. The zetetic process specifically does not presume at the outset the existence of some other realm (e.g., the spirit world, heaven, firmament, paradise, fifth dimension, or higher level of reality) or even that there is such a thing as 'beyond the universe'.

Some might contend that the treatment contained herein is antithetical toward traditional religions. I would clarify this by saying that the approach is neither polemical nor antithetical toward *religion* per se, as the target herein is strictly about *theological claims*.

---

35. Experimental discovery of the Higgs boson (and by inference, the Higgs field) was preliminarily announced at the annual *Rencontres de Moriond* conference in Italy on July 4, 2012 with a 99 percent confidence level in the data. Later, on March 13, 2013, after additional data collection, it was announced that this level reached the highest bar of scientific statistical certainty of 5-sigma, or 99.9 percent.

Theology is to religion as a foundation is to a house. The foundation supports the full weight of the house, but it does not constitute the house in its entirety. Additionally, the statement is correct in the sense that we *initiate* with a sterile nontheistic position that does not accept or deny the *possibility* of God, whereas traditional religions start out of the gate with a great many theological assumptions about how to perceive and interact with God-by-whatever-name. The differences will become rather stark when we study the genesis and development of some of the dominant religious traditions as well as several of the more recently created religions. Traditional religions begin their story with rather mysterious origins, rely upon the CREDULITY of individuals, and an adoption of faith. While we lack the Grand Observer's extraordinary network of otherworldly telescopes and transcendent intelligence to assist the zetetic process, we will do our level best to unwind history to the beginning of religion as we understand it. From there we will endeavor to accumulate successive information in the context of the time that the sources of the information were conceived as well as how it can be viewed in contemporary terms.

In the end, after we have exhausted our power of reason and evidence and we have circumscribed God to the maximal extent warranted, then we will have positioned ourselves at the edge of a new boundary. Some may elect to step across this boundary in what some may say is a *justified* leap of faith. That is, the aforementioned Persons A, B, and C will have been provided the most contemporary perspectives about what we can know about God. With such knowledge, one can be more confident and comforted in their decision about their belief (or nonblief) in the existence of God-by-whatever-name.

What Constitutes 'The Truth'?

Epistemology is the investigation of what distinguishes *justified belief* from opinion. The word is derived from the Greek words *episteme* (knowledge) and *logos* (study of). As a philosophy it is the set of theories of knowledge that aim to understand the nature of knowledge by its methods of capture, its validity, and its scope of application. Intimately associated are the concepts of truth, belief, and justification. In discussing the idea of God's existence, use of epistemology is inescapably endemic to the process.

A *belief* is simply defined as accepting as true any given cognitive content and a *belief system* is a set of beliefs. For example, a Roman Catholic, as an action to affirm their faith, might declare their belief by saying, "I believe in all the tenants of the Nicene Creed" (mock quote). A Muslim might offer words to the effect, "According to our Holy Scriptures, Jesus was a mortal prophet" (mock quote). *Truth*, on the other hand, has proven to be impervious to the achievement of a unified definition. Linguist and philosopher Michael Glanzberg has written extensively on the topic of Truth Theory. He cogently circumscribes the situation by contending that, even though the concept of truth is an especially salient ingredient to a constellation of philosophical issues, having garnered a vast amount of philosophical discourse, there remains a deep controversy on which constraints on truth or falsity should be accepted and whether any theory of truth is correct.[50]

Initially, truth was the preserve of philosophy and theology. As science grabbed hold of the reins, empirical truth thoroughly tested the ancient and postmodern theories of truth. In applying the scientific method to feed our experiential knowledge-base, empirically-derived information yields a confidence that reality works a certain way and therefore provides an ability to separate truths from falsities. The hegemony of the sciences grew (and continues to do so) at an unbridled rate, far out-pacing philosophic developments which have appeared to stand still by comparison. Unwilling to surrender their province, contemporary philosophers and theologians argue by force that science is out of its depth. They intone that the demagoguery of scientific introspection is inherently confined, limiting the ability of the rationalistic enterprise to speak only narrowly, if at all, of absolute truths. Physical theories, for all their virtues, are built upon a scaffold of fundamental premises that cannot themselves be independently validated which is the essence of the 20th-century Duhem–Quine thesis. Many questions naturally arise from these discussions. Does reality exist independent of our mind or only within our mind? Does *justified belief* unequivocally constitute *truth*? What is knowledge? What is consciousness? There are many, difficult to understand, theories for all of these questions. Ultimately, these questions are left as unsolved by philosophy if one is to judge a solution as one where there is unanimity of opinion. Human beings are to be forever relegated to 'argue from within' as we can never hope to gain purchase of a utopic Archimedean perspective. And around and around we go.

Generally speaking, philosophy has one hand bound behind its back because it can only ply the lone hand of reason to manipulate these intricate and formidable problems. Theology, in this regard, has both hands free to apply reason on one hand and revelation/deific agency on the other. Unfortunately, this second appendage is a magician's hand that has ready access to a fog-making machine that obscures and confuses rather than clarifies matters in a convincing way. When theology makes claims that go beyond our capacity to rationalize, it not only confounds others but it also defeats the theologian because when we cross the line, what we will call the 'beyond reason line', then we have all entered a land of 'anything goes'. Anyone can claim anything because it is beyond reproach. And so, therein we come upon the ever impossible act of interlacing our fingers from the land of naturalism to the ethereal outpost of the metaphysical.

The Philosophical Tests of Truth

There are many criteria to analyze the accuracy of whether or not something is true of reality, though, as we will see, some criteria are more valid than others. We can, for instance, *appeal to the authority* of highly qualified individuals (e.g., scholars, specialists, experts).[51] However, as this book testifies, there is often a lack of agreement between scholars. And, while I have relied heavily on scholarly opinions, the views are balanced by other truth tests.

We can also judge truth claims by the *consensus view* and/or a *majority rule*. This approach carries with it a number of inherent problems and as such these criteria are used sparingly. Another test proposed by some is whether the claims have stood the test of time. Here again there are a number of shortcomings.[51] By way of example, if we used this criterion to judge religious truth, it would require us to believe the oldest truth presented. And there are many examples where we believed something was true at one time and then later determined that the initial assessment was incorrect.

Of special importance to our task, some would want to include *intuition* and *revelation* as tests for truth. These ideas initiate with a presumptive state of truthfulness and are independent of a rational examination of the relevant facts. Also, if we used these criteria, any conclusion that would be drawn would be considered highly constestable due to the associated inherent uncertainty. This is akin to one group of people intuiting that, given the rapid advances in science, in 1,000 years we will have a spaceship capable of transporting astronauts that can travel at the 75-percent the speed of light. However, a second group would intuit that this will not be possible in even 10,000 years. We achieve no meaningful insights.

The concept of *correspondence* is to characterize truth statements as true or false based solely on how they relate to and how effectively it describes our world.[52] If we were to make a claim that human physical traits are defined by DNA molecules, this would be considered true because it corresponds to objective data that such molecules do indeed exist in our world and by all evidences appear responsible for the compositional characteristics and appearances of people. However, for as many examples that we might point to that 'most people' would agree that our collective thoughts are capable of accurately depicting reality of some set of circumstances, there could be a large contingent of people who disagree. Thus, truth becomes relative to the observer and we are disabled to discern the true reality for we lack a 'God's eye' vantage point. So while the correspondence principle helps us to define what truth is, additional benchmarks are required to more precisely pinpoint what is real versus what is not.[53]

A final criterion to be considered is that of *coherency of truth* (there is also a distinctly different but related idea referred to as *coherency of belief*). Coherency refers to the requirement for all the facts and beliefs of the individual to be arranged in a consistent and cohesive manner. Consistency is the quality that the claims and supporting information must not be contradictory to itself (i.e., it must be internally consistent) or with the other information within the set of claims.[54] Arguments have been wagered against the validity of coherency because it can lead to circular and implausible 'truths'. The *Alice's Adventures in Wonderland* story provides a good example of circularity.

Alice speaks to Cheshire Cat:

[Alice]	'What sort of people live about here?'
[Cheshire Cat]	'In that direction,' the Cat said, waving its right paw round, 'lives a Hatter: and in that direction,' waving the other paw, 'lives a March Hare. Visit either you like: they're both mad.'
[Alice]	'But I don't want to go among mad people,' Alice remarked.
[Cheshire Cat]	'Oh, you can't help that,' said the Cat: 'we're all mad here. I'm mad. You're mad.'
[Alice]	'How do you know I'm mad?' said Alice.
[Cheshire Cat]	'You must be,' said the Cat, 'or you wouldn't have come here.'
[Alice]	Alice didn't think that proved it at all ... [55]

Additionally, by referring only to the individual's belief system, this theory of truth cuts off access to the external world (the so-called *isolation objection*). Yet another problem, the plurality objection, is the situation whether two or more equally coherent belief systems could also be incompatible. Additional concerns are raised by others which we will not review here.[56]

What we come to is that fact that philosophers, scientists, mathematicians—no one for that matter—knows how to define what is a truth in the universe. It simply remains an unsolved dilemma. Therefore, we have to invoke a degree of pragmatism to produce a working definition if we are to make any appreciable advance.

THE CRUCIBLE OF TRUTH

The Common Man is not going to bother with the esotericism of all these theories, especially if none can be adequately be shown to be accurate or accessible. To equalize the pressure in this vacuum most people make-do by simply equating their belief system as the truth. Before we take a worrisome leap like this, let us move forward with the establishment of a framework of Truth Criteria (TC).

Table 1-1. Eight Criteria that Constitute the Truth of Reality

[TC-1] **Accessibility Limits of Reality**. In our zetetic search for God, we shall accept that reality, knowledge, and consciousness exist and that our individual consciousness's comprise a part of, but do not wholly constitute, all of reality. That is, there are aspects of reality that are beyond any human being's current comprehension (e.g., we have no intelligible idea of what happens inside of a black hole or what exists beyond the visible universe).

[TC-2] **Dimensionality of Reality**. Reality is of spatiotemporal construction and plays out in the four known dimensions — three spatial and one temporal. If someone wishes to pose additional hidden, higher, or additional dimensions then that shall require a special rigor to understand this in context.

[TC-3] **Temporality of Reality**. Time is a fundamental property of reality which is a continuum defined by ordered intervals that permit one to refer to the past, present, and future. However, time can be quickened or slowed. This alteration of time is dictated by fundamental laws (relations) of the physical universe which will be elaborated on in later chapters. Time is also considered progressive in the context that past moments are locked away from access by both present and future time. Chapter 14 provides more in-depth remarks concerning the ontology and **TOPOLOGY** of time.

[TC-4] **Jurisprudence of Reality**. This spatiotemporal reality we call the universe operates in accordance to physical laws (known or unknown) and apply to all materiality. Immaterial abstract things also exist. Mathematical and statistical axioms define fundamental and absolute truths (we might say attributes) of the entire universe, however large it may be. Anything that might exist externally to the full universe is the province of speculation of the highest order.

[TC-5] **Complexity of Reality**. While there is a complexity of organization and structure to the universe which emerges over time, we will not presuppose a divine purpose for the establishment of biological life. We will also accept that individuals can and do experience reality in largely similar ways though there are many unique experiences as well. For example, someone with a physical disease, mental illness, is under the influence of medicinal substances, or those that live in very different cultures from our own, or are of different age or gender, may well perceive the very same reality, differently.

[TC-6] **Objectivity of Reality**. We will furthermore agree that absolute objective truth exists. By absolute truth we will take this to mean that there exist unalterable facts about reality (e.g., abstract objects such as numbers and sets exist, analytic truths such as there are no planar circular triangles or planar triangular circles) and that such truths are of logical necessity. We may even go so far as to say that many natural laws (e.g., universal mathematical principles and physical laws) are unalterable. The objective truths are facts that are stripped free of human prejudice and bias. Some absolute objective truths may be beyond our current or future ability to access them, that is, they are unknowable. We also must recognize and accept that applying objectivity is dependent on how large an individual's vessel of knowledge is (that is, their relative access to evidences) and the attendant ability of the individual to interpret and process that knowledge without bias. Subjective relative truth is associated chiefly with matters of personal experience, emotion, preconceived mentation, and primitive and/or inherited behavior that act as a matrix of filters to process reality.

[TC-7] **Temporal Relativity of Reality**. While it makes things a little fuzzier, truth can take on a transitory and contextual character as well. For example, we might all concede that in the year 1,000 BCE, the fastest means of transport was by horseback. Back then, it was probably believed that the maximum transport speed humans could ever attain could be equated to a speed less than 200 mph. However, with the advent of jet aircraft, rockets, and spacecraft, the maximum speed is now much faster. We might call such circumstances an *underdetermination of the truth* which is to say that at any given time, we may have insufficient information in which to establish a particular belief as the truth. We have to be very careful in applying this sort of truth condition because it can lead us to mistakenly regard something as being irrational when in fact it may be true. The point here is that taking truth positions for future events or being over-confident of current ones is to be taken on warily.

[TC-8] Coherency of Reality. One of the most important criterion of truth we will apply is that truth claims must be coherent in that they are not contradictory and cohere to our collective understanding of reality (that is, not just our *own* truths as in the case of the coherency of truth theory above). Truth comports with cause-and-effect processes and our ability to empirically evaluate natural events. This enforces that all constituent components are *self-consistent* and *logically constructed*. The following statements exemplify these ideas.

Self-Consistent:

1. Martin has heterogametic sex chromosomes (i.e., XY chromosomes) and is therefore a human male.

Logical Coherence:

2. Veronica needed to be at an appointment located in Dallas, Texas by 5:00pm today. It is now 8:00am. Veronica lives in a city in the same time zone as Dallas.

3. An airline has a 2-hour long flight leaving at 11:00am.

4. Veronica can take this flight to arrive in Dallas on time for her appointment.

Not Self-Consistent:

5. John is a human male that became pregnant with a child.

Logical Incoherence:

6. Jessica is a virginal human female that subsequently became pregnant with a child.

7. Jessica, currently of child-bearing age, was born on an island. No male human has ever set foot on the island and she has no access to male reproductive biological material.

In the fifth statement, it is inconsistent to believe that human males can become pregnant with a child in such a manner. In the final set of claims, each statement is completely rational and self-consistent, but when taken together, they run counter to the process of human conception and are therefore incoherent to reality.

I would tender that the terms TC-1 – TC-8 would be fully or generally agreeable to the considerable majority of people. With this presumption, we can proceed to apply these truth criteria in conjunction with analytical techniques applicable to the respective knowledge disciplines of interest. If it is not demonstrated otherwise, then it must necessarily fall outside the crucible of truth into the melting pot of imaginative thought, irrational thought, or false reality. The key takeaway is that we have to be aware of our all too ready tendency toward biased and irrational thinking and to judge things based on their internal consistency and logical coherency. If we are able to do that, we will move closer to the truth.

An Author's Perspective – A Full Disclosure

On the personal side of things, overcoming inherited or otherwise adopted religious commitments is extraordinarily difficult and placing oneself in this sterilized zetetic position is no small request. Most adult minds have found a level of comfort in the way they have chosen to lead their lives and even if the proverbial applecart shudders under an abrupt blow intended for the betterment of the individual, it is still perceived as an unwelcome assault. There is to be no doubt that many would prefer to remain ignorant in the face of a dissonant world order than to be dashed upon the jagged rocks of truth. At such times, calling to mind Thomas Gray's idiom "Ignorance is Bliss"[36] is apropos. Let me be clear that this is not a campaign to drop napalm onto religion or, more importantly, to disrespect individual choices. This treatise is more akin to removing obfuscation by the peeling away the uncountable layers of a several thousand-year old onion whose growth cycle never ceased. The core layers are encrusted and breaching them requires considerable effort. Can we in fact find truthful evidence for God-by-whatever name? In our efforts to suss out the truth, we will come to appreciate the **INIMICAL** stewardship both ancient and established religion has had on this devilishly difficult task.

It is only human for us to see the world from our own vantage point built by decade upon decade of life experiences. This is known as the *inside-out* perspective. This book attempts to negotiate past **EPISTEMOLOGICAL** barriers with the adoption of a multidimensional viewpoint. We will not only view our evidences from the inside-out, but we will plumb for significance from the *outside-in, top-down, bottom-up,* and most importantly *holistically.* The outside-in

---

36. In 1742, Thomas Gray authored the poem *Ode on A Distant Prospect of Eton College* in which the full context of the quote is presented as: *"Thought would destroy their paradise. No more. Where ignorance is bliss, 'tis folly to be wise."*

vantage point considers all the informational sources outside the set of knowledge and beliefs of a given philosophy/theology. Some of that information may be coincidentally shared by the 'inside-philosophy' but not the other way around. The bottom-up approach, noted earlier, is to start from a sterile position and to build a new framework 'from scratch'; in the same vein as humanity did hundreds of millennia ago but with the special advantage of today's body of knowledge. The bottom-up metaphor also refers to the use of inductive logic where premises will be suggestive (but never certain) of the truth. In contrast, the top-down approach leans on the use of deductive reasoning linking premises to offer a certain conclusion. It also relies on the use of reductive techniques whereby the whole is split into simpler, easier to understand components or 'chunks'. Finally, the holistic viewpoint will be aided extensively by the use of abductive reasoning to navigate the crowded underbrush of various theories to arrive at inferences to the best explanation.

We all take different paths on our intellectual pilgrimage through life. To be fair to you the reader, like so many, I keep my own existential doubts. I have lived the majority of my life in an equal mix of wonderment and bemusement of the Catholic Christian God and how he may be manifesting himself in my life. The more I study religious and scientific ecosystems, the more profound and complex it becomes, to the point that it becomes as meaningless as a jumble of rocks in a sack—ponderous, unfeeling, and forever discordant. Due to the geometric if not exponential expansion of knowledge, science has become a sprawling expanse of sub-specializations so numerous it stymies the conscious. We are on the verge if not past it already where generalizations are too difficult to prescribe because the knowledge found within these 'nano-domains' makes it impossibly difficult to extrapolate with any workable certainty. Contributions amount to adding a grain of sand to an amorphous beach head, adding no detail whatsoever.

In the time of Plato and Socrates or even during the Renaissance, one could be proficient across multiple domains. One might be a mix of philosopher, physician, mathematician, scientist, and musician as the circumscribed knowledge of each was relatively small. Nowadays, an astronomer may be engaged in astrochemistry and another in astrometry (the measurement and motion of celestial objects) and those in the respective fields could for all intents and purposes be incompetent to perform the work of their colleague's discipline. This siloing of knowledge can be mitigated by working in interdisciplinary teams, though this does not happen but for well-funded projects. And yet, by the relentless toil and perseverance of laborers far and wide, there are times when the world's conscious is punctuated by some great discovery that align the sand crystals into something both discernible and incredible (e.g., the prediction and subsequent confirmatory discovery of the Higgs field and the related

Higgs boson particle). More often than not, however, theories are more hype than anything else, and the revelation is often invalidated by some new theory if one waits long enough. It nevertheless is heaped onto the pile of 'knowledge' further entangling the list of hypothetical garbage. The net result is a creeping spasmodic 'progression' toward the understanding of truth and reality.

As to my Catholicism, on countless occasions I bade the Almighty to work toward my self-serving ends. Certainly not in the manner of zealots who desire to harm their fellow man. Rather I am aware that with so few years on planet Earth I must act quickly and decisively and having an omnipotent agent in my corner would be extremely useful. For as long as I can remember, I have been a seeker of knowledge, both physical and metaphysical. I have inherited it would seem from our forefathers a deep longing for a sense of unification amidst a minefield of divided sectarian perspectives. I was born and churched in the ways of the soulful American Catholic where God and Jesus were my constant yet perpetually mysterious companions. I kept my religion close well into my adulthood.

My young mind was hewn by the ideas fathered by the giants of science and engineering—from the peerless Isaac Newton, the inimitable Albert Einstein, and Gottfried Wilhelm Leibniz—Newton's contemporary—who famously asked about the existence of the universe, "Why is there anything at all rather than nothing whatsoever?" From the protection of their long shadows, I was carried further by a legion of modern-day erudite professors and collegiate fellows who instilled within me a servile obedience to good moral character, impartiality, a spirit of independence and creative thought, and most of all a methodical rigor in solving challenging problems. In this respect, I am much the student of the scientific method.

In some ways, for a time, I was embroiled in a theater of mental conflict, fortifying both the religious and scientific factions in equal measure so that none would prevail. Initially, religious incoherencies were nothing more than dormant specters that only caused me to wonder on occasion. These phantoms permeated the INTERSTITIAL spaces of my mind. As my appreciation and knowledge of religion and science steadily grew, the light beams crawled through the inner recesses disturbing the hidden spirits. I became all the more implacable to unlearn what I must if it were to unveil a greater truth. It began to ring hollow as my religious headmasters impressed upon me a Co-Essential Faith that could only describe God as a 'mystery'. **How can we consider ourselves to be rational and proclaim that God is INEFFABLE—beyond our frail human abilities to comprehend him—and in the same stroke of the pen develop a list of ORTHODOXICAL beliefs of what God is and is not!?** If *anything* is to be nonsensical, then this is it! What bothered me most is that in all the Church masses or religious-oriented education in general, never once did we engage in a rigorous examination of the fundamental assumption of God's existence. He was simply presumed to exist and the Catholic Bible and our personal relationship with God were to be our proof. I could not 'keep the faith', lest not in the same way I had been doing it for decades. I wondered, if I were born on an isolated island where no one passed on their religion, but had access to other worldly knowledge, would I come to the same conclusions held by Christianity? After much contemplation, it was decided. I needed to shadowbox God. Placing the gloves of science on one hand and philosophy on the other, I sought to outwit deific parries with well-placed thrusts and jabs until he was worked into a corner, perhaps not **INDUBITABLY** so, but with a far greater degree of conviction.

With scientific theories and religious theologies being of a provisional character, the only certainty we have is the continual grabbing of our own tail. With an open mind and a good measure of effort, we can erase a considerable amount of the ambiguity clouding our conscious' to attain, with reasonable probability, a heretofore clarity concerning the metaphysical, the ultimate meaning, and ultimate value of human kind. It is with this mindset I changed my fortunes from being tormented by the faith-science conflict with the adoption of the adventurer's mind. If we commit to being a mindful explorer, we will make the trek to find God a far more fruitful and intellectually stimulating journey. And in the process, we may come to find that simple wisdom that we yearn for.

My **TELOS** therefore is three-fold. The first of these is to ascertain zetetic wisdom as it relates to theological concepts and the idea of God-by-whatever-name circumscribed by objectively reasoned (as opposed to blind faith) beliefs. This will be counter-balanced with the scientific perspective which will also be skeptically cross-examined. The second obligation is to reduce the utter complexity of this to something more digestible to you the reader. And the third, dependent wholly on the success of the former, is to appeal to the universal brotherhood to change our convictions and our course to one that is bereft of the many inhumanities that have beset our kind in favor of a viral toehold toward liberty, self-determinism, and shared compassion in all quarters. To put a fine point on it, I harbor an enmity for the vile cretins that murder or subjugate others in the name of religion and the only way I know how to personally take action to mitigate further atrocity is to foster the education of society. It is a delicate and formidable task because there are many complex forces at work. Religion has been a polarizing double-edged weapon, exercised in the name of moral justice and mighty injustice alike. Given this awesome or awful affect (depending on your view) it has had on our world, we are obliged to understand its origins, its evolution, and how it must be reshaped to end the song of bitter and somber notes that have sounded too often. Religion *and* science must be seen for what they are so that we can better chart what they must become.

THE ZETETIC JOURNEY

The book's content is organized by covering the specifics of the Great Religions in anticipation of addressing the more general question of God's existence. This may seem counterintuitive as the question immediately arises; why not tackle the fundamental question of God's existence right out of the gate? In response to this I reflected on the fact that the majority of people in the United States are religious and come to this study with a wide range of embedded preconceptions of God-by-whatever-name. Similarly, there are many who count themselves among the nonreligious who may possess an imprecise or otherwise inadequate understanding of religious doctrine both ancient and contemporary. If we were to initiate the journey from the general point of view, the reader would be continually examining their specific beliefs against the greater context and more than likely fail to make the necessary connections. Rather, by proceeding to critique the theological doctrine of specific religions at the outset, we systematically address the many core beliefs so that those that are ill-fitting of a rational explanation of God-by-whatever-name can fall to the floor, unburdening the journey as we move forward. It is what I later refer to as the separation of the philosophical and theological chaff from the wheat. And, as we will see, there is a temporal evolution linking faith traditions for which we can better surgically examine how these have originated and evolved and to what degree they carry any weight in modern-day times. As we exit the specific critiques, we can enter into the wider discussion of God's ontological and metaphysical status with considerably less mental baggage.

With this in mind, we will begin with the historical development of Judaism and its unitary deity, Yahweh. This will be followed by an extensive dissection of Christianity and its conception of the Trinity—Father, Son, and Holy Spirit. The third branch of the Abrahamic religions, Islam, is treated more referentially in the context of the theological construction of the other two religions due to their shared claim on their lineage to Abraham, the Old Testament patriarch who is thought to have been born c. 2000 BCE. All three religions affirm that a single God had created the universe and has intervened in our worldly matters. In some ways he has revealed himself indirectly (e.g., a thunderous voice, a burning bush, a bright light, visions), through angelic messengers, prophetic oracles, and inspired Scriptures. They also believe in 'end times' whereby all of humanity will be judged for possible entry into the perpetual bliss of heaven or damned for all eternity.

We shall also examine religious pluralism which seeks to find religious truth in the larger body of world religions as well as the panentheistic mentation on God-by-whatever-name which focuses more on the dynamic actions of a cosmically-active agent. This book arcs from theological/philosophical perspectives toward an integrative discussion on biological, psychological, and neuroscientific perspectives on God. From there, we move forward to include contemporary cosmological perspectives to **ADJUDICATE** whether there are theistic inspirations that can be solicited from these scientific domains. It will be in the latter chapters that we will examine the primary question of God's existence in a more generic sense.

Your odyssey into the border realms of the scholarly Dragon-horde is near. Our first trek will be a relatively modest exposition of dominant religions, past and present. Religion has been with us in written form for over five thousand years and the voluminous body of work demands that we seek out and give our attention to the more precious evidences. By itself, the Vatican Secret Archives contains 85 kilometers (53 miles) of shelving.[57] The Vatican's main library has over 1.6 million printed books and 180,000 manuscripts.[58] This is an astounding amount of predominantly religious and historical literature in which a great many clues are ostensibly buried. This can be multiplied many times when one considers Christian literature in general and that of the other Abrahamic religions. When one gives this a moment of consideration, it becomes evident that it is beyond our human abilities to adequately synopsize religion let alone the scientific disciplines that might be able to comment on religion.

When questioning religion then, it becomes a fool's errand to think that every possible angle of introspection can be covered. After all, we are talking about disseminating the most salient ideas from a compilation of information amassed over thousands of years! It may be **PRESCIENT** to assert that any slicing of the loaf will invite a rabble of tempestuous critics to the table alleging bias, selective debunking of arguments, misrepresentation, and the annoying and often ignorant complaint of 'cherry-picking of the data'. The task of great enormity herein is to source and elucidate the most important evidences from the overwhelming collection of pertinent knowledge. Selecting the best epistemological kernels of knowledge is akin to surgically excising a specific cell from among the many billions deep within the living brain. So, yes, in a sense, there is what some may claim is a cherry-picking of the evidences. But if I may be **PROLEPTIC**, I have made my best attempt to be objective given my stated approach of starting from a clean slate as it were and to take religious claims and dissect them using the scalpel of balanced rationalism. On this point, I grant that the reader has had no input on such decisions.

The next step is to translate the scholarly codifications that invariably surround the **VERIDICALITY** of religious knowledge. Toward this end, by and large, I have sourced the opinions of eminent scholars both ancient and contemporary. Here again, I have had to sample a handful from the legion of scholars that I felt best represented the strongest theories (which notably may or may not be the prevailing theory of our time). In interpreting what this selection of combined set of knowledge has to say about religious truth claims and how they relate to the evidence for God-by-whatever-name, my third job is to translate this to the Common Man so that many more can appreciate contemporary musings on God-by-whatever-name. In writing this book, I have accepted, perhaps with great naiveté, the daunting challenge of walking barefoot on the proverbial razor's edge. The coverage needs to adequately span the yawning breadth and depth of many domains of knowledge. At the same time, it must delicately balance the delivery of specifics versus generality in such a way as to neither devolve into a burdensome slog, nor to become vague and ineffectual.

The next great slice off the 'loaf of knowledge' will be to limit primary attention to the **ABRAHAMIC** traditions, with a particular emphasis on the Judaic and Christian **MILIEU**. It is non-debatable that Christianity has been subjected to the most vigorous and ongoing **DIALECTICAL** exchange by an almost countless number of commentators. This is to say that the theological underpinnings have been under continual examination and re-examination like no other. The journey will shy away from a comparative analysis of religions as many such treatises can be accessed elsewhere. This examination will conclude with elucidation of promising thoughts from newer religious movements—Religious Pluralism, Ramified Natural Theology, the New Sciences of Religion, and Modern Christian Panentheism.

After we have scoured the aforementioned venerable and upstart religions for clues, we will tack our ship toward the headwinds of the great scientific frontier. The expedition will become both more difficult and more fascinating as we harvest, unify, and deploy insights from a constellation of scientific disciplines such as neurotheology, psychology of religion, evolutionary biology, physics, mathematics, statistics, and **COSMOGONY**. While science has been the secularist's hulking juggernaut—cleaving away in relentless fashion the supernatural limbs of religious **POLEMICS**—it has suffered under the weight of its own success and inherent limitations. As we shall see, the increased hegemony of science and knowledge in general is yoked with an ever growing complexity creating hyper-domain specialization. So too, the high burden of proof to ascertain truth claims is manifest making it inexorably problematic to take those "reliable steps" that Albert Einstein alluded to.

With these remarks in mind, this book is principally written to (1) those who inherited their (organized) religion from their parents or up-bringers and who have not deeply interrogated their faith, (2) to individuals who consider themselves unaffiliated or disengaged, perhaps because religions formerly tried did not offer a system of transcendental thought that they felt was convincing enough or would like more factual knowledge about the validity of religions, and (3) to those who are of an epistemic leaning wherein gathering comprehension and perspective of the natural realm and that which lies beyond constitutes a large percentage of their mindshare.

One final word before we embark on this intrepid journey. As you survey the horizon and then steady your gaze into the darkness that is the Dragon's chamber of secrets, I encourage you to remove your armor and lay down your sword, as it shall only encumber you as we squeeze through uncomfortable passages. Each reader comes to this book with an **ENDOGENOUS** narrative; an overarching story of oneself and a set of convictions and perhaps faith. Beliefs are what we as individuals take to be the truth, an amalgamation of what has been parceled together under a great many influences. Truth and belief are very often not congruent with one another. **What I argue for herein is for you to intellectualize your belief and to engage with me in an honest inquiry. I also ask that you suspend your faith and beliefs—that is what you think you know to be true—as well as your emotional defenses for the duration of this book. This is a unique opportunity to be naked in your search for the understanding of God-by-whatever-name. If you enter with your prejudices, you will have robbed yourself of this opportunity to engage in a unique, carefully reasoned inquest of the real and the metaphysical.**

For those willing to trouble settled convictions and to be intellectually honest with themselves, such individuals will exit as a well-informed, if not entirely changed person. If you are strongly religious, you may find that you become a more fervent foot solider of your faith. You might also become a conscientious objector of said faith. If you consider yourself to be religious but not practicing because you feel disenfranchised or spiritually shipwrecked, then you will most certainly gain clarity. And, if a skeptic, you will readily identify with the proposed methodical approach, but you may develop a fortification of your position or cause yourself to re-think what you thought to be certain knowledge. When you have completed the book, it is then I ask you to reflect on your former position and ask the same fundamental questions we set out to inform and answer.

The God debate can be likened to looking down the barrel of a crystalline prism. The light bedazzles and bewilders the eye and we struggle mightily to generate recognizable patterns—that is to see only what we want to see. When we are unable to identify a recognizable pattern, we become confused or frustrated. In the end, my abundant hope is to **DISABUSE** the Common Man from the vagaries and enchantments of the scholarly Dragons to instill a more refined understanding of religion, theology, philosophy, and science and to then write a more respectable story upon the stone of history. It is, I hope, a story of mankind's redemption from depravity, social injustice, and intellectual dormancy to become a race of peoples unified toward our most noble objectives of the time in which we live.

With deep reflection on the grandeur of our consciousness, the sameness of our humanity, and our collective smallness in this stunningly profound universe we will raise awareness of our mutual condition. I want nothing less than for the Grand Observer to witness the reshaping of our human frontier as we ply our wit and grit to recast our imprint in our tiny sector of the cosmos. To accomplish this feat we must unlock ourselves from the things that dreadfully hinder us by grasping onto a simple, but well-reasoned, philosophy that ennobles the truth as best we can understand it.

With the mind so prepared, let your hero's journey begin ...

The Hero's Journey

A hero ventures forth from the world of common day into a region of supernatural wonder: fabulous forces are there encountered and a decisive victory is won: The hero comes back from this mysterious adventure with the power to bestow boons on his fellow man.[59]

> Joseph Campbell (b. 1904 – d. 1987)
> American Mythologist
> from *The Hero with a Thousand Faces*

Greater Than We Seem

We are not brought into existence by chance nor thrown up into earth-life like wreckage cast along the shore, but are here for infinitely noble purposes.[60]

> Katherine Tingley (b. 1847 – d. 1929)
> Leader of the American Group of the Theosophical Society
> from *Greater Than We Seem*

The Theosophical Society is a philosophical system and religious movement that seeks to explore the mysteries of the world at large and to develop a unified explication of humanity and divinity in the context of the cosmos.

CHAPTER 2

Defining God

I am a deeply religious man. I cannot conceive of a God who rewards and punishes his creatures, or has a will of the type of which we are conscious in ourselves. An individual who should survive his physical death is also beyond my comprehension, nor do I wish it otherwise; such notions are for the fears or absurd egoism of feeble souls. Enough for me the mystery of the eternity of life, and the inkling of the marvellous structure of reality, together with the single-hearted endeavor to comprehend a portion, be it never so tiny, of the reason that manifests itself in nature.[1]

– Albert Einstein
The World As I See It, an Essay

Violence destroys what it claims to defend: the dignity, the life, the freedom of human beings.[2]

– Pope John Paul II
Homily at Drogheda, Ireland, 1979

The mind once enlightened cannot again become dark.

– Thomas Paine
A Letter Addressed to the Abbe Raynal of the Affairs of North America, 1792

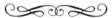

THE IMPETUS TO FIND GOD

A **CENTRAL QUANDARYF OF OUR TIME** is the immiscibility between the creed of religion and the hegemony of scientific advancement. The bifurcations that exist between these behemoths spawn division and animosity between nation, state, and neighbor and there does not appear to be any fast-acting catalyst to alter the chemistry of this dichotomy. Violent religious extremism has risen from the fold to coopt the international conscience. This bloody fundamentalism is based on foundational principles of **RELIGIOUS EXCLUSIVISM**, a perverse and fanatical interpretation of scriptural references, purist dogmatism, and decayed morality. Emblematic of such nefarious ideologies are al-Qaeda and the barbarous ISIL, an aggrieved religious sect of orthodox Sunni Islam. As of the year 2000, 50 percent of the 14 ongoing civil wars were religious in nature revealing a steady increase from the 1940s wherein only 19 percent of civil wars were religiously oriented.[3] While religious deviance is the 'now problem', it really is a modern story with ancient echoes.

For thousands of years, the perversion of religion has been a steady prescription to commandeer the physical, mental, spiritual, and financial resources of the populace, and it would be remiss not to mention the extermination, murder, enslavement, extreme torture, rape, false imprisonment, and prolonged starvation committed in the name of religion. That isn't to say that all people viewed such subjugation negatively as some people saw it as a necessary deed to 'keep the house in order'. With so much at stake, it is EXIGENT that we take action to comprehend the ongoing role of religiosity in our culture if we are to cull these abhorrent practices.

To this end, an examination of the arguments for and against God—whether evocative of reverence or revulsion—is an imperative. It could be averred that enlightenment, if not absolute answers, to the *Big Question* of God's existence could offer great benefit to society in the long run. We are not likely to achieve a state of total unification or undisputed wisdom as there will always be detractors, but we must seek a broadening of comprehension. If, on the basis of religious, philosophic, and scientific introspection we come to the conclusion that God does or is likely to exist, then we are sure to arrive at a new crossroads to decide on how we can recalibrate individual and societal actions to achieve (rather than aspire to) a universal and inviolable sanctification for the equality of life, liberty, and self-determination. If we find summary evidence to the contrary, that God does not or is not likely to exist, this would be even more profound. I hasten to say that if religion is determined to be incorrect about the existence of God-by-whatever-name, it does not necessarily parlay into a need for the elimination of religion. Firstly, even if God's existence were to be determinant in some measure, as we have seen in other worldly endeavors, educating a global populace is an agonizingly difficult millstone to turn. And, secondly, aspects of religion do provide a range of societal benefits. Notwithstanding these terms, if amity between people and nations as well as an enhanced purity of truth about God is the sole output, then the impetus is well justified.

Some such as evolutionary biologist Richard Dawkins and other so-called New Atheists go headlong into invective rants against religion which can be tempting when one is so sure of oneself. However, my thinking is that any exposition on God must be engaged with an abiding humility for the simple fact that we *Homo sapiens sapiens*[1] (Latin for 'wise man')—the most recent in a long line of social primates—are equipped with a set of fallible (yes biologic) senses, mixed motivations, and a bounded intellect to interpret our local environment and the universe at large. We should also be wary of professing absolutes, as Lord Alfred Tennyson's

---

1. *Homo sapiens sapiens* refers to Modern Humans of today and the earliest modern humans, the Cro-Magnon. *Homo sapiens* include earlier species (e.g., Neanderthals).

maxim reminds us "the vow that binds too strictly snaps itself."[4] While humans can posit breathtakingly **ABSTRUSE** mathematical treatises, after 100 years since publication of Einstein's theory of general relativity[2]—a theory of gravity—and in spite of its exceptional precision and its resilience to being deposed by thousands of experiments, there remains much contention as to whether or not it is fundamentally accurate in defining reality or is a mere approximation thereof. As for our fallibility, one only need recall the prestidigitation in a magic coin trick to realize how easily the senses can be misled.

Before diving deeply into specific evidences justifying or negating the existence of God, we ought to develop a coherency in our conversation by reviewing the intentional meaning of the word 'God' both connotatively and contextually in our culture. At the outset, this task may seem unnecessary because everyone knows that God is purported to be the all-powerful Being that created the universe. However, the lack of agreement on where God resides in the universe (location or time), whether he is more than one Being, what are his specific properties and/or capabilities, or whether God is a super-advanced alien species visiting us from interstellar space beckons at least a brief review.

THE LANGUAGE OF GOD

What then are we to look for as we pursue the identity of a cosmic animating force? We might start by ascribing some meaning as to *what* God is. However, no sooner than we plant our first footstep, we are immediately confronted by a lack of unanimity. Because of the **PROFUSION** of religion, God is **VARIEGATED** in form and meaning. And we also find that God is contextualized within our culture which as the sands in the desert, shifts over time. Language, therefore, takes on a special role. Bernard Spilka, a religion psychologist, and his co-authors summarize the situation thusly—"Bernstein (1964) tells us that 'Language marks out what is relevant, affectively, cognitively, and socially, and experiences transform what is made relevant' [...] Such relevance is well demonstrated by studies showing that religious persons possess a religious language and use it to describe their experience. There is a reason to believe that the presence of such a language designates an experience as religious instead of aesthetic or some other possibility [...]. Meaning to the experiencing individual appears in part to be a function of language and vocabulary available to the person, and this clearly relates to the individual's background and interests. There is much in the idea that thought is a slave of language, and the thoughts that breed attributions are clearly influenced by the language the attributer is set to use [...]."[5] In psychological terms, people who are religious exhibit a proclivity toward **COGNITIVE BIAS** (perceptual distortions) by

---

2. Einstein's field equations were published November 25, 1915

<u>defining a human experience in religious terms rather than critically assessing alternative explanations</u>. As a testament to this, people tend to feel the presence of God or affix divine interpretations to experiences during major struggles of life (e.g., death, illness, job loss) and during gatherings of a religious nature as opposed to times when they may be engaged in more mundane tasks of life.

We know the state is dire when we find ourselves paralyzed to make a distinction between two of the most commonly used words—'*religion*' and '*spirituality*'. Spilka *et al.* dedicate no fewer than seven pages of their tome reviewing historic attempts to unsuccessfully differentiate the meaning of these two words! We will take religion to mean an *institutional* framework designed to formulate, encode, organize, protect, transmit, and cyclically perpetuate information in the form of beliefs, values, worship practices, rituals, symbols, culture, language, and truth claims that accede to the primacy and allegiance to a sacred or transcendent Being(s).[3] In contrast, spirituality is a *personal* framework that values material and/or immaterial (metaphysical) nature which may or may not include subscription to an ascendant deity. So, one can be spiritual but not religious, but religious experience intrinsically involves expression of some component of spirituality and as such religion gives more shape to spirituality.

Another definition is in order. Whereas religion entails a variety of large categories—belief, culture, language, rituals, world views, and truth claims—theology is the systematic and rational study of concepts of God regarding his existence and the nature of his existence and associated truth claims therein. It is therefore unfortunate that the unwavering battle of ideology has been historically cast as the 'religion-science controversy'. It would be more precise to call it the 'science-theology' discourse because the core issues for scientists are much more to do about the veracity of theologically-oriented truth claims (doctrinal choices) and not the extracurricular religious customs, rituals, dress, language, culture or the peaceful practice therein. Where the tension resides is in religious people asserting truth claims that may not be substantiated as rationally true (to the satisfaction of skeptical minds) into the fabric of society. Also frustrating scientists is what they see as an indulgence in the procreation and reinforcement of irrational thinking. In past centuries, freedom of religious expression was much less free than it is today, though even today, this freedom is all too often geographically bound. It is therefore a central focus on this book to engage in the *science-theology discourse* and to appreciate the ramifications it has for the future denizens of Earth. And, specifically to always respect an individual's choice to *peacefully* contemplate,

---

3. Aspects of this definition are borrowed from John Bowker (see Bowker, *The Sense of God: Sociological, Anthropological and Psychological Approaches to the Origin of the Sense of God*, 1995, Oneworld Publications, p. x)

even if irrationally-so, how humanity and the cosmos came into being so long as they do not infringe on the life, liberty, or freedoms of any other person. But, given that we do not live in a utopia at the moment, the way forward is to invest in an education and outreach to seek out the most rationally justified truth about God-by-whatever-name and to restrict all activities to the nonviolent pursuit therein.

Earlier, religion and theology were analogized as being a house and its foundation. Another **HOMOLOGY** can be considered whereby religion can be likened to an automobile and theology to its engine. Without a theology, religion is like a car without motive force to make a car, a car. It just becomes a motionless shell. The foremost challenge about theology is that it is often highly abstract with its own complex language set. **The overwhelming majority of people shy away from abstraction and the investment of time necessary to grapple with complexity.** Drawing again on the car analogy, most people are aware that cars have an engine (gasoline, electric, or hybrid), but only a subset of people understand how the engine works mechanistically, electrically, or chemically. The vast majority of people simply appreciate the car for its styling, ride handling experience, speed, and utility to get from one place to another. Even if the belts are screaming or smoke is billowing out of the exhaust pipe, they would rather not be bothered to understand why the engine isn't functioning properly. Instead, they drive it to the mechanic's shop to let others figure out the problem. **Theology then, is the poorly understood engine and religion is the surrounding structure. People can become very comfortable with their religion even though they are acutely unaware of its inner-workings.**

Going back to the language issue, my focus is largely limited to Abrahamic religions and more so to the Judeo-Christian view therein. While Indian (e.g., Buddhism, Hinduism, Sikhism) and Eastern (e.g., Taoism, Shintoism, Confucianism) religious and spiritual traditions are worthy of discussion, the nuances of Abrahamic terminology is difficult enough to contend with in our context. Non-Abrahamic faiths will be broadly considered under the umbrella discussion of Religious Pluralism (Chapter 9). Consistent with the comments on secularism in Chapter 1, we find that Americans commonly engage in multiple faiths by mixing elements of religious traditions. Christians incorporate the beliefs of New Age spiritualism or Eastern philosophy creating for themselves a brand of unorthodox Christianity. For instance, 22% of Christians believe in reincarnation and just as many (23%) believe in astrology and/or the spiritual energy contained with inanimate things (e.g., 'energy crystals', Stonehenge, pyramids, mountains, trees).[6] There is also a significant number of Christians who believe in the casting of curses (17%). Additionally, other **SYNCRETISTIC** Christian practitioners believe that we can commune with the dead (29%) or that we can see ghosts (17%).[7] All of these statistics very closely mirror that of the general public which is not all too surprising since Christianity comprises about 70% of the U.S. population. As Figure 2-1 illustrates, confining discussion to the Abrahamic religions captures the overwhelming number of theistic adherents in the United States.[4, 5] In any case, limiting the discussion to religions practiced more widely in the United States is justified as science has no *a priori* reason to privilege one religion over another.

Member Count of U.S. Major Religious Studies (2014)

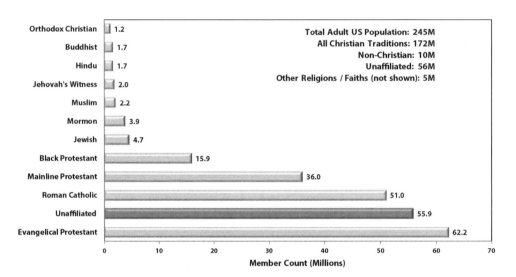

Figure 2-1. Member Count of Major Religious Traditions (U.S. 2014)

(The Unaffiliated include atheists, agnostics, and those with no particular religion) [8]

GOD AND THE FUZZY LOGIC OF MYSTICISM

Defining God is akin to finding sure footing on a wetted brook stone weathered smooth by racing waters. Is it better to define what *God is* or by what he *is not*? In either case, it is not an easy task if one is looking for a defensible line of evidence. We find that theologians and those

---

4. Atheists and Agnostics represent about 7.1% of the US adult population. It is divided as follows: Agnostics (9.8 million, 4%) and Atheists (7.6M, 3%). Source: *America's Changing Religious Landscape*, Pew Research Center, 12 May 2015.

5. For reference, worldwide, there are 2.2 billion Christians (31.4% of world population), 1.6 billion Muslims (23.2%), 1.1 billion religiously unaffiliated (16%), 1.0 billion Hindus (15.0%), 487.8 million Buddhists (7.1%). Source: *The Future of World Religions: Population Growth Projections, 2010-2050*; Pew Research Center, 2 April 2015.

fearful of opening a flank for criticism eagerly avail themselves to **MYSTICISM**. By employing mysticism the characterization of God is affirmed as fuzzy, mysterious, and enigmatic. An ill-defined metaphysical problem is the nectar of philosophers and theologians alike whose very discipline is to generate erudite theses and dispense tortured wisdoms. And so, there have been numerous nuanced conceptions of what God is. While this approach has greatly favored the perpetuation of religion for millennia, the advent and hegemony of science has blown off some of the fog. In the past it was adequate to maintain that God was angry with its people and he punished his minions with pestilence and adversity. In contemporary times we understand the origins of disease, meteorological patterns, and natural causation to a far greater degree which has defogged the mystery somewhat. This has led to an invigorated Philosophy of Religion to refine concepts that no longer hold up to rational inquiry.

A case in point is our medieval Christian ancestors who rolled-out the mystical theological constructs of **CATAPHATIC MYSTICISM**[6] and **APOPHATIC MYSTICISM** to formulate a basis on which to study the nature of God. These are very much in use today and apart from Christianity one finds the use of mysticism in most religious traditions. Cataphasis is often referred to as *positive theology* (*via postiva*) and apophasis as *negative theology* (*via negativa*). While both cataphatic and apophatic theology were integrally used in formulating early Christian doctrine (e.g., by Clement of Alexandria, b. c. 150 – d. c. 215 CE), the concepts at this time were not well developed. In fact, the concepts have evolved over time so much so that their original use as compared to contemporary use is quite different. Why? Not only were documents written in many languages (Greek, Latin, Coptic, Aramaic, Syriac), but there is an underlying challenge of describing God in terms that, when taken collectively, are suitably logical. It has required constant tinkering by theologians. These challenges will be extensively explored throughout this book. Suffice it to say for now, that even after two thousand years, the comprehensibility of these ideas has actually *lessened* because there have been so many attempts that have been unable to crisply defend the implications of the definitions affixed to these two words.

Cataphatic mysticism characterizes God based on divine revelation (as in Scripture) and what can be learned by natural reason. Cataphatic interpretations emphatically state that God exists and possesses certain, often human-like, attributes and these are knowable in some measure. This is highly evident when God speaks to Moses in the form a burning bush (Old Testament, Exodus 3:1–5) and by theophanic visitation when God became flesh and blood in the form of Jesus of Nazareth (New Testament). Positive theology maintains that

---

6. Sometimes spelled "kataphatic". The word is of Greek origin where "kata" is an intensifier to the word "phanai", which means to speak. Together it means to "affirmatively speak". In like manner, "apo" in Greek means "other than", so apophasis is translated as "negatively speak", where negative means "the denial or negation of" speaking.

we are able to capture the essence of God's nature by his omnipotence (infinite power) and omniscience (infinite knowledge) among other **HYPERBOLIC** parlance. It also conjectures that the Almighty is a personal God, someone with whom we can have a relationship with. Western Christianity goes further to say that God is **TRIUNE**, that is to say, comprised of three Persons. Comparatively, apophasis is the argument from learned ignorance or silence, often referred to as the unknowingness of God. He is neither an object nor a Being. He was uncreated, not self-generated or generated from another; furthermore he transcends time and space and is neither existent nor nonexistent in the physical realm and thereby is not within the realm of human perception. God is beyond human language and all past, present, or future ability to comprehend him and to to put it in single word, God is **INEFFABLE**. The only point at which God will be understood is in the afterlife where all human souls will be in the company of God.

These two modes of quasi-intellectualism have fundamentally divided Christianity for nearly two thousand years. Western (Latin) Christianity has long adhered to positive theology whereas Orthodox Christians (Eastern Catholic Orthodox Church and Oriental Orthodox Church) affiliate with negative theology.[7] These two theologies exhibit a creative tension that in more recent times, some say, work harmoniously to describe God.[9-11] By way of approximation these attempts try to justify the idea that while God is wholly unknowable and has no existence (even nonexistence) that we would understand, he is inexplicably able to exert his divine will across time, space, materiality, and immateriality. He furthermore performs miracles that defy what we believe to be inviolable rules for physical matter and processes and the underlying spatiotemporal fabric on which all such things are tied to. The explanations become esoteric and contorted products of the imagination that utterly fail the tests of truth and logic.

Christian mysticism has an identity crisis. The cornerstone of positive theology is the inherent presumption that there is truth in the Scriptures and that human reason is capable of formalizing truths about God. Additionally, it professes that God exhibits human-like attributes and allows access to his goodwill. As we will see in later chapters, the validity of Christian truth claims has been under sustained and heavy attack over the centuries. There has been a litany of claims that their sacred Scriptures contain undeniable errancies. So too science has been dispelling certain myths and other particularities (e.g., **GEOCENTRISM**).

---

7. Western and Eastern Orthodox churches believe that Jesus is one Person of two undivided natures–human and divine–making him forever fully human and fully divine. The Oriental Orthodox Church holds that Jesus is of singular nature which is undivided union of a divine component and a human component. Jesus is therefore neither all human nor all divine.

So too there have been many intellectualizations on the nature of Jesus and whether he was (1) merely a man chosen by God, (2) was one nature, part human and part divine, (3) of two natures, fully human and fully divine, or (4) was purely divine with an appearance of a man. Beyond that, there are more questions how Jesus is affiliated with God. This variegated view of God and Jesus as a divine pair makes Christian mysticism even more confused. It is a result of studying the contrasting evidences that negative theology has made a comeback of sorts in the Western traditions because it has become a more defensible position because they can explain away inexplicable things under the umbrella of 'God is a mystery'.[11] Christianity finds itself on the horns of a dilemma. **If the core of negative theology maintains that God cannot exist in our realm, theologian's DIALECTICAL attempts have denuded themselves of a rational cataphatic claim that Christian's can have a personal relationship with God since he cannot be accessed. There will always be incompatibility between the two ideas that prevent their full reconciliation. This is logically problematic**. We will take up these two concepts in Chapter 9 after we have studied the depths of Christianity to better appreciate these nuanced descriptions of the Christian God and whether either are proper ways to appreciate what we can or cannot know about God.

In an effort to take our first reliable step forward and begin to fashion our first bit of cohesion, we shall have to overlook this special conflict with Christian doctrine. For now, it may be agreed that a quality of God is that he can possess either a *communicable* or *incommunicable* characteristic.[12] The former are attributes that humans can also be endowed with, to a degree, whereas for the latter, can only be affiliated with God. For instance, both God and man can experience the communicable attributes of love, justice, and forgiveness. However, the incommunicable aspects of God speak to his ineffability and transcendence. Religions espouse hyperbolically that he is one or more of the following: OMNISCIENT, OMNIPRESENT, OMNIPOTENT, OMNIBENEVOLENT, OMNITEMPORAL, ATEMPORAL, beginningless, ETERNAL, EVERLASTING, TIMELESS,[8] TRANSCATEGORICAL, IMMORTAL, incorruptible, sovereign, self-existent (or equivalently uncaused or having ASEITY), IMPASSIBLE, spaceless,

---

8. Atemporal is defined as being free from the limitations of time. Timeless and timelessness is a condition whereby the natural property of time is nonexistent and expressly is a state outside of the domain of time. Thus, a timeless state is a hypothetical state. Eternal is defined as the absolute lack of a beginning (beginningless), end (endless), or sequence. In some contexts, some speak of a division of eternity as past-eternal or future-eternal relative to the present time. Everlastingness is nearly equivalent to Eternal, however, it is suggestive of a successive temporality (a sense of sequence) but that there is no beginning or end. Omnitemporal means to exist temporally for all past, present, and future time. The concept of an atemporal God works best for a completely transcendent God. For a God that acts in the universe's temporal realm, use of the term omnitemporal or everlasting would be appropriate.

IMMUTABLE,[9] **CHANGELESS**, the perpetual sustainer of the universe, and **NECESSARY**. Usually these words are prefaced with the words 'infinite' or 'perfect'. When philosophers or theologians employ a reference to *Perfect Being Theology*, it generally means a God that is the perfection of all the following: omniscient, omnipresent, omnipotent, omnibenevolent, and impassible, though there are variations to this list. I will refer to the full list simply as God's '*omni-perfections*'. Some religions (e.g., Mormonism, **PANTHEISM**) suggest that God is **IMMANENT**, that is, present in all materials of Creation. Immanence and omnipresence are similar constructs, but there are key differences. Whereas omnipresence means that God's will is extended everywhere at all times, immanence can mean the same thing, but it additionally indicates that God is physically manifested in and through all things. More broadly, other religions use the term 'immanence' to convey that God is able to exist or act within the domain of our universe. As we progress, the permanence of the defining characteristics shall be put to the test for any departure from these absolutes may provide us with certain evidences. **The omni-perfection terminology describing God's prospective attributes will be referred to extensively throughout the balance of this book. It is therefore strongly suggested to re-read this paragraph and the associated footnotes and Glossary terms to become familiar with these ideas before proceeding.**

While this captures God's prospective innateness, there exists divergence on whether the Supreme Being is accessible to us in our daily lives. An estimated 60%[13] to 67.5%[14] of adults in the United States maintain that the Creator is a relational entity that subscribes to 'personal relationships' with his minions and that he shares with us human-like emotions (i.e., love, happiness, anger, grief). One-quarter of people feel that God is a dispassionate Master not prone to human intercession. Interestingly, almost as many Catholics (29%) as Agnostics (36%) believe the latter; which for Catholics is in opposition of what the Catechism[15] teaches.[10] There are salient differences, too, between how one is able to access this personal relationship. Christianity, for example, teaches that God has unconditional love for all people. That is, there is no precondition or partiality from God on whether God loves an individual. In contrast, the Qur'an teaches that there is a wage for a personal relationship with God. The individual must believe and worship God in return for his love. For some who wish to divide Christianity from Islam, this difference is a central argument that the God encountered in the Qur'an cannot possibly be omnibenevolent.

---

9. Note, '*immutable*' is different from '*unchanging*'. Immutable means that nothing in the natural world can change God. God, however, is changing as witnessed by the biblical references when God changes his mind and/or his emotional state. This is more clearly seen in accounts of Jesus' frustration with his disciple Thomas or the theocrats and Greco-Roman rulers of his day. However, this change does not alter God's essence.

10. Other study results – *Belief that God is an Impersonal Force*: Protestant (19%), Mormon (6%), Jewish (50%)

WHAT PEOPLE KNOW ABOUT RELIGION

While language tells us how people communicate about and attribute their experiences to God, it is also important to benchmark our general knowledge of religion. In writing this book, I walk a difficult line to appease educated critics of the soundness of what is presented while also working to convey this knowledge in a manner that others less knowing of the intricacies could find it to be accessible. In 2010, the Pew Research Center surveyed United States participants by asking 32 interfaith questions, varying in difficulty (refer to Figure 2-2).[16] Rather than provide sample questions, the reader is encouraged to take the quick-to-complete on-line survey to compare their own knowledge of religion.[11] The study authors acknowledge that the survey questions do not necessarily reflect the most essential facts to know about religion, but are a representative sampling of the body of important knowledge. The general majority did no better than answering 50% of the questions correctly reflecting the fact that people possess, at best, a rudimentary comprehension of salient aspects of religion. Of course, the study focused on presenting interfaith questions and the knowledge of one's own religion would presumably be at least as great. *Some may be surprised that Atheists and Agnostics alike have a greater knowledge about religion on average than religious adherents.* It is conjectured that a greater number of adherents are more or less satisfied with their chosen faith tradition and unless otherwise stimulated to do so, see a limited need to learn about other religious perspectives. Relative to one another, religious groups have historically tended toward insular attitudes.

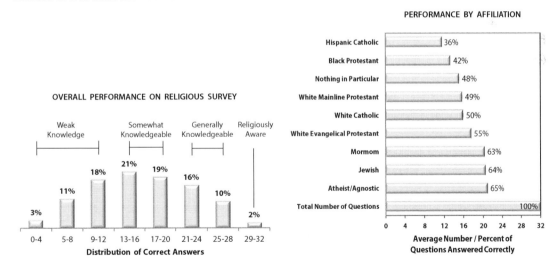

11. The PEW *Religion Knowledge Survey*, in addition to other surveys, can be accessed at author's website: http://www.zeteticpath.com/

Figure 2-2. Results from 35-Question Religious Knowledge Survey (U.S. 2010)

Another factor affecting people's ability to digest knowledge, religious or otherwise, is general information overload created by the fast-paced, Internet society we live in along with people tending to be overworked and overstressed leaving less time to devote to practicing their own faith let alone accumulating anything more than incidental knowledge of other religions.

In Chapter 1, the wisdom of the scholarly 'Dragons' was lambasted for their raw intractability to communicate their wisdoms to the Common Man. The concepts and arguments are deeply complex and an entire language set has been erected to characterize the knowledge therein. However, as much as the scholars are to blame, we see that most people only have a superficial grasp of the basics of religion and the same can be said of science and mathematics. The effective knowledge of the majority is akin to the amount of water drawn from a pail of water with the single dip of a thimble. This chasm of factual knowledge between the intellectual and the uninformed is highly problematic. **Many of us, wishing to be spared of the industry required to understand all the details, gladly accept what tradition teaches us. We are not talking about unimportant acquaintance of trivia, rather it points to awareness that we are unlearned about constructs of the so-called Great Religions and that we have a tenuous understanding of our fellow man when it comes to spiritual belief.** We also find that when faced with complexity or lack key information, individuals often employ psychological heuristics to simplify and short-cut the decision process (we'll talk more about heuristics in Chapter 12). This has a range of positive and negative impacts on the outcomes of the decisions we make as will be illuminated further on.

Institutional Precepts versus Actual Enactment of Belief

If one thing can be said about Americans, we are an independent thinking bunch. Even though institutionalized religion has perpetually echoed its positions on a range of religious topics, when it comes to what an individual actually subscribes to—or enacts—in one's life, people are not so dogmatic. Figure 2-3 illustrates the aggregated beliefs for a number of Christian doctrinal concerns.[17] Roughly three-quarters of U.S. Christians believe in miracles, Heaven, Hell, the Devil, an afterlife and less than one-half believe in the divinity of the Bible.[12] One will find that the numbers vary considerably for individual denominations and even more so when looking at the results for other countries. It is very much a case that the average is not a very useful statistic other than to say that there is a sizable divergence between

---

12. Similar data for the belief in miracles, angels, and demons can be found in *U.S. Religious Landscape Survey*, Pew Forum on Religion & Public Life, pp. 26-35, 2008.

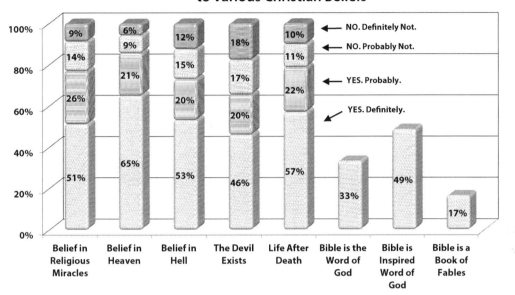

Figure 2-3. Aggregated Belief (U.S.)

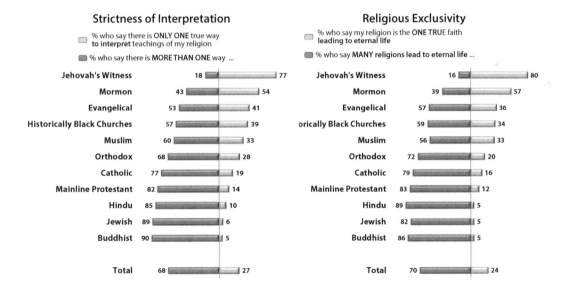

Figure 2-4. Dogma Righteousness and Path to Eternal Life (U.S. 2008)

what theological headmasters say *is* the truth about spiritual matters versus what any given adherent elects to believe.

On an aggregate level, we again find that roughly 70 percent of religious people (not speaking of institutions) accept that there is more than one correct interpretation of their religion and that there is more than one way to achieve eternal life (refer to Figure 2-4[18]). However, a sizable populace for certain traditions see themselves as more strict and righteous than others. Such believers subscribe to the fact that God has designed a unique to path to eternal salvation of the soul. More generally, those religions, namely Christianity and Islam, that purport a requirement to accept or otherwise be converted to the faith are said to be Exclusivists. Judaism was also once considered to be an exclusivist religion because Judaism proclaimed that they alone were God's 'Chosen People'. However, to avoid the full stigma of superiority associated with exclusivism, there has been an attitude of *triumphalism*, which is not necessarily doctrinally articulated, but is an acknowledgment that a degree of inclusion would be warranted if certain key aspects of the faith are accepted.

Our First Evidence Concerning God's Nature

The aforementioned statistical sampling of the U.S. population quantifies the multitudinous character of religious opinions that exist and furthermore why it is that so many denominations, cults, and sects abound. The summary point is that when dialoging about religion, there is a fuzzy fidelity such that any volley sent its way is returned with a shotgun pattern confounding the ability to achieve useful *quid pro quo*. By chasing every BB that erupts from the casing, religion greatly benefits because it either forces interrogation of many dozens of facets or forces a generalized response that can be criticized for a lack of specificity. Did God intend for such division to rule our world?

While we forewarned ourselves about making any absolute statements, we can say with absolute conviction that different religions make contradictory claims for the fundamental fact that they are logically inconsistent. We find this to be true when entertaining doctrinal questions that have binary answers. In his book entitled *The Evidence for God: Religious Knowledge Rexamined* religion philosopher Paul Moser reminds us of how major religions logically exclude one another. He points to a stark case wherein Judaism claims a single god and Hinduism holds that many gods exist.[19] Furthermore, Christianity and Mormonism claim that Jesus is divine. Judaism and Islam deny this. There can be no logical reconciliation in cases such as these.

It would seem reasonable at this point to put forward the idea that not every religion in existence can represent what God is in reality—in whole or part—unless, that is, we are willing to accept that he is literally all things to all people. Such a statement strikes one as counterfactual as it attempts to land square on a steeply angled slope as it would inherently require that we include Satanists or any deviant cult for that matter that claims existence of 'deity-like' Being(s). Not only that, but it would also mean that all the 'good' and 'bad' in the physical world, no matter how indecent or immoral, would be implicitly, even if unequally, acceptable to God. Here we hit upon the topic of **THEODICY** which seeks to define why God permits the manifestation of evil (which could be absolute or relative). While I am compelled to sidestep a detailed exposition of theodicy theory for the sake of brevity, it bears saying that its **PROVENANCE** was that of the ancient skeptics. The oldest extant reference to the Problem of Evil is provided by the Greek physician and philosopher Sextus Empiricus in his manual of skepticism (*Outlines of Scepticism*, c. 200 CE), though it is possible that the idea originated by Greek scholar Carneades (b. 214 – d. 129 BCE).[20] With two thousand years of additional thought under our belts, in spite of generating dozens of interesting perspectives and philosophical expositions thereof, all have failed by a considerable margin to provide a consensual or impenetrable solution to the Problem of Evil and why an all-loving deity allows vile immorality to persist.

What I will put forward are some notions for you to ponder. If God exists and is intentional whereby he maintains a set of ordained plans for humanity, evil deeds must be an innate component of his plan to come to fruition, even though this evil presumably emanates from demonic sources and not from God himself. It could also be that God is less inclined to impose a script on humanity and in an act of indifference permits us to act upon his gift of free will to forge any path, **SALVIFIC** or otherwise. As in the former case, even though he is not the author of evil, God implicitly sanctions the presence of evil by allowing it to be a part of our reality. The Abrahamic religions actually believe in a mixture of these two ideas. They profess an illogical construct that God affords us 'free will' to act benevolently or immorally most of the time but God intervenes of his own accord to ensure that his master plan (a directedness of nature) is realized. Most of the time God works in mysterious ways while at other times his presence is more recognizable as in the case of miracle-making. All the while, evil interpenetrates in grand scale 24 hours a day, day in and day out. There is of course the idea that 'good' and 'evil' do not exist at all and are simply human constructs that are defined by human-developed concepts of civility, morality, and ethics (i.e., moral relativism).[13]

---

13. Values are qualities that signify what is important and serves as the basis of moral codes. Morals are individual and societal codes of conduct that govern behavior that are an expression of values and are contingent on and help define a culture. Ethics is a systematic and rational framework that uses moral values for decision-making on a case-by-case basis.

I would have you consider another scenario. Physicists and astronomers have both theorized and experimentally confirmed the existence of so-called black holes. These magnificent, prolific, and enigmatic wanderers of the universe possess a gravitational field so inconceivably mighty that nothing in the cosmos can escape its clutches should it perforate its **EVENT HORIZON**. If tomorrow the Earth were to be succumbed by a black hole, would the Earth's destruction be considered evil or just random chance? Why would God allow such a thing to happen to his *entire* populace? Some might consider this thought experiment as being beyond the realm of possibility. In fact, there is chance, albeit small, such circumstances could come about. As it happens, in about 4 billion years, our galaxy, the Milky Way (also called 'G' in the **ARGOT** of astronomy) will inexorably collide with the Andromeda galaxy (known as M31) and the Triangulum galaxy (M33).[14] While it is predicted that the Earth is not likely to be destroyed in the galactic collision itself (that is by a star or planet striking the Earth), no one can say whether a black hole will show up in our solar system's neighborhood between now and then or whether one is hurled toward us as part of the collision process. With (roughly) one of every one thousand stars becoming a progenitor of a stellar black hole upon its death; our galaxy harbors something on the order of one hundred million black holes with a comparative number existing in M31. Many of these are so-called *stealthy black holes* because they are not actively consuming enough material to detect their presence.

In the end, logical analysis dictates that only some religions can potentially offer a true nature of God, should he exist at all. That is, there is a contingent of the religions in circulation that cannot be true. We have at last circumscribed our first evidence by pruning the Tree of Religion. We cannot say at this juncture what the shape of tree is (that is, what religions have been cleaved and what others remain) and we certainly have not cut it down. In Einstein's parlance it is an "ever so small"[21] a step, but a step nonetheless.[15]

SUMMARY

Many religious concepts were synopsized in this chapter. It is to be recognized that language plays a critical role in defining religion and more to the point who and what God is or is not. One does not have to wade deeply into theological or philosophical literature to appreciate that their writings are rarefied esotericism and all but impossible to comprehend without a considerable working knowledge of these disciplines.

---

14. It isn't clear if M33 will collide with our galaxy first or after the great M31 – G collision. To view a simulation of the event, I refer you to the following website which offers video footage in multiple formats. http://hubblesite.org/newscenter/archive/releases/2012/20/video/a/. Last accessed 01 October 2016.

15. Refer to the first of Einstein's quote at the beginning of Chapter 1

In spite of the challenges, a sufficiently clear definition for religion, spirituality, belief and faith were advanced. Also exposed is that the majority of people retain some level of affiliation with theism. Importantly, the theological constructs of cataphasis (positive theology) and apophasis (negative theology) were briefly explored toward their application in Christianity. Here we find that Christianity has put itself into an intractable position of characterizing the nature of God. If Christians wish to extol that God is indescribable (ineffable) then they must subscribe to an impersonal deity for how can we communicate with a God beyond our language? If God is personal, then we can apply our faculties and discover facts and evidences to clarify God's nature. Ultimately, mysticism presents a fuzzy, ill-defined concept of God. As will be seen in later chapters, it also leads to irrational beliefs.

I opted to overlook this flawed theologically-inspired 'logic' for the time being to enable continuance of our search for the perimeter of God's existence. It was stated that God has been characterized with some or all of the following ascriptions: omniscient, omnipresent, omnipotent, omnibenevolent, omnitemporal, atemporal, beginningless, eternal, everlasting, timeless, transcategorical, immortal, incorruptible, self-existent (aseity), impassible, and immutable (changeless), immanent, and necessary (refer to the Glossary for definitions of this terminology). I proceeded to quantify in more concrete terms the extent of people's knowledge of religion as well as what individuals in the United States believe about God, Heaven, Hell, the afterlife, and the Bible.

It becomes evident that the application of basic logic dictates that some religions are erroneous in their interpretation of God. We broached the intractable Problem of Evil to appreciate the fact that the concept of good and evil paralyzes, if not imperils, our ability to conceive of a God consistent with perfect goodwill toward humanity. Also discussed is the illogic that exists if adherents are to maintain that we have genuine free will if we also suggest that God also requires that some events are predestined by divine will.

I conclude this chapter with the first evidence in our attempt to circumscribe God to the effect that not every religion can legitimately claim to represent the true nature of God, though, without defining which religions might be cleaved from the fold. It is conceded that this is not a prophetic or all too significant of a step forward. But, it is best to establish an initial perimeter, even if its path and extent is fuzzily defined. We take this knowledge forward to examine the faiths that retain the greatest number of believers to understand what side of the perimeter they reside on.

PART II

TRADITIONAL AND
FRONTIER RELIGION

CHAPTER 3

The Disappearing Gods:
A Detective Story

Even if the open windows of science at first make us shiver after the cosy indoor warmth of traditional humanizing myths, in the end the fresh air brings vigour, and the great spaces have a splendour of their own.[1]

– Bertrand Russell, 1925
Nobel Laureate in Literature, mathematician,
and a founder of analytic philosophy

Seeking what is true is not seeking what is desirable.[2]

– Albert Camus, 1955
Nobel Laureate in Literature, philosopher

THE ORIGINS AND MYTHIC EVOLUTION OF RELIGION

WITH THE DISCOVERY OF OUR first modest trinket in hand, namely that not all religions can correctly interpret God's nature, we reset our landscape and lengthen our historical perspective. In this chapter we begin to familiarize ourselves with our rather vague knowledge of how the worship of gods originated and evolved as part of the rise of 'civilized' societies. The main focus is to gain an appreciation how **POLYTHEISM** gave way to the introduction of **MONOTHEISM**. I believe it is safe to venture the thought that the overwhelming majority of people, including many religious thinkers and purveyors, think that monotheism simply started at some fairly distinct point in time in history. The data suggests an altogether different view in that monotheism transitioned unevenly from polytheism over many centuries.

We move our quest to the time of antiquity and the land of Sumer (*soo-mer*), what is now modern-day southern Iraq. Settled permanently in the mid-Stone Age era (c. 4500 – 4000 BCE), it is alleged that no society has contributed more to culture than the Sumerians. Here we find that our penchant for religiously motivated aggression extends back centuries before the Sumerians invented the wheel and pictographic writing in 3200 BCE (this form of writing is called cuneiform script, refer to Figure 3-1). In spite of Sumer's eponymous namesake as the *Land of Civilized Kings*, war, ritualistic, and lawless killing among Mesopotamian tribes was a continual fact of everyday life. Circa 1780 BCE, in a rueful attempt to stem anarchy, the Sumerians adopted a primitive constitution called the 'Code'. More commonly referred to today as the *Code of Hammurabi*, it was instituted by Hammurabi, the sixth king of Babylon who had ruled for 43 years. It also happens to be the longest surviving text from the Old Babylonian period. The code sought to implement a system of law and order using the principle of reciprocity. Among the 282 laws, it established what the Bible (refer to Exodus and Leviticus), Torah, and Qur'an later termed the *lex talionis*, Latin for 'eye for an eye' system of retaliatory justice (refer to Law #196 – Table 3-1) [4].

Figure 3-1. The Dingir – the Sumerian cuneiform IDEOGRAM for the word "Deity"

It is also referential to the supreme Sumerian-Akkadian god called 'An'–the sky-god [3]

Table 3-1. Excerpts: The Code of Hammurabi

Law #2	If any one bring an accusation against a man, and the accused go to the river and leap into the river, if he sink in the river his accuser shall take possession of his house. But if the river prove that the accused is not guilty, and he escape unhurt, then he who had brought the accusation shall be put to death, while he who leaped into the river shall take possession of the house that had belonged to his accuser.
Law #195	If a son strike his father, his hands shall be hewn off.
Law #196	If a man put out the eye of another man, his eye shall be put out.
Law #209	If a man strike a free-born woman so that she lose her unborn child, he shall pay ten shekels for her loss.
Law #210	If the woman die, his daughter shall be put to death.

Sumer was organized into independent city-states each governed by a Priest King in a near complete THEOCRACY with the primacy of action directed toward appeasement of the gods at any cost. Routinely, people were ritually sacrificed to mollify the gods and to honor the death of royalty. Archaeological excavations at the city-state of Ur (southern Iraq), the once coastal city at the mouth of the Euphrates River and the Persian Gulf, establish that royal tombs for the elite also contained the sacrificed remains of their servant retainers. Outside of the chambers of those who were in the upper echelons of power were many dozens, in some cases over a hundred people who were dispatched and buried to form layers over the royal burial chamber. Initially, C. Leonard Woolley, the English archaeologist who directed the investigations at the Royal Cemetery of Ur concluded that the people were self-sacrificed by the ingestion of poison. However, subsequent forensic examination in 2009 concluded that they were killed with a pike driven into their heads. This may have been with a slight degree of willingness from the victims because it was an acknowledged custom for family members, servants, and royals to be sacrificed upon the death of their Priest King and they may have believed that they would follow their king into the afterlife.

Sumerians like other Mesopotamian tribal nations of the time were a polytheistic society having belief in major deities, lesser deities, primordial Beings (often dragons), demigods, heroes, spirits, demons, beasts, and **PARAHUMANS**. **THERIOMORPHISM** (gods depicted in animal form) was commonplace. Given the persistent state of conflict, it comes as no surprise that Sumerian mythos revered multiple gods of war. Even though the generally accepted demarcation for the start of religion is coincident with the invention of writing, the Sumerians did not invent religion. Protohumans have existed for some two million years but our best efforts tenuously trace human religion back to the dawn of our Neanderthalic evolutionary cousins some 225,000 year ago—the end of the Early Stone Age[1]—when deliberate disposal of deceased individuals in funerary caches marked the emergence of pseudo-religion with ceremonial burial rites.[5] Though, some archaeological data relating to the fact that the burial holes were small and that the skeletal remains were contorted into fetal positions suggests that the mortuary practice had more to do with mitigating the scavenging of the remains by wild animals.[6-8]

While prior research present us with a sketchy understanding of when Homo sapiens or Neanderthals may have buried their deceased for spiritual reasons, a revelatory discovery was made in 2013, reported in 2015, that a new relative of the human species had been unearthed.[9, 10] In the South African *Rising Star Cave*, some 1,500 bones from the skeletal remains of at least 15 *Homo naledi* were found some 80 meters deep into the cave and 30 meters beneath the surface in what is called the Dinaledi Chamber. In a second section of the cave called the Lesedi Chamber, 133 fossils from three individuals have been found. There are likely to be more fossils that are yet to be excavated.[50]

---

1. The Early Stone Age is also referred to as the *Lower Paleolithic Period* which lasted between 2.5 million – 200,000 years ago.

The skeletons included infant, teen, adult, and elderly individuals. The dating of the bones has proven to be a complicated affair and it was originally thought that the bones were over one million years old and perhaps more than twice that. This would place these creatures in the timeframe of early Neanderthals. However, it has since been determined that the bones are quite younger, dating to between 335,000 and 236,000 years old.[51] These smaller-brained species would have shared the African plains with the first early modern humans. In any case, the archaeological find confirms that purposeful burial customs were practiced by multiple human species at least a quarter-million years ago.

Prior to 3200 BCE, because no written documentation explaining their belief systems now exists, there is limited understanding of prehistoric religious beliefs of any species of protohumans. We only have glimpses obtained from archaeological relics and **PETROGLYPHS**. Behavioral modernity occurred roughly 50,000 years ago in the Upper Paleolithic period with the emergence of symbolic culture, language, and specialized **LITHIC TECHNOLOGY** adorning their sanctuaries, tools, and weapons.[11] Fulfilling the **QUOTIDIAN** demands during those times was arduous indeed where seeking protection from the elements and wildlife, obtaining adequate nourishment, and avoidance of injury was a full time endeavor. While humans at this time had controlled use of fire, it served as a small comfort in the cold, predator filled nights. Neanderthalic societies may have practiced **TOTEMISM**[2] wherein mystical associations were conferred upon plants and animals. Additionally, tribal leaders may have been revered in a god-like fashion as *Spirit Guides* (somewhat analogous to **SHAMANS**) who had access to direct revelations from the spirit world. Over many thousands of years, these belief systems evolved into what we understand as polytheism. Polytheism was the most widespread form of religion during the Bronze Age and Iron Age (c. 3000 – 587 BCE)[3] all the way up to the Axial Age (c. 800 – 200 BCE) and the beginnings of philosophy. To put things into overall perspective, leading up to the time of Jesus Christ, this represents 99 percent of all human history.

Up until the inception of the Common Era, societies were relatively geographically constrained by a lack of rapid transport. So, for a time, there was no large-scale migration of religious ideas between lower Europe, Africa, Scandinavia, Asia, and the Far East. It is of little surprise then that the conception of God-by-whatever-name evolved differently by geographical and cultural region. At this junction, it is useful to briefly review various categories of theistic belief in order to prepare our path forward in the zetetic process. Those marked with an asterisk will be covered in some detail and it will therefore be an important aid to recall the sometimes subtle differences between each category.

---

2. Totemism is probably better referred to as Animism, though some consider the former a subcategory of the latter.

3. The start and ending of the Iron Age is highly varied based on geographical location as technological progress was uneven.

Table 3-2. Types of Theism

Type of Theism	General Beliefs About God	Affiliated Religion
Polytheism*	The belief that multiple distinct deities exist.	• Ancient Judaism (c. 2000 BCE – late 9th-century BCE) • Ancient Egyptian, Greek, and Roman Mythology
Classical Theism* (Thomism)	The belief in a single deity existent as a single, distinct, separate Being that is absolutely and maximally ultimate and perfect possessing five attributes—transcendence, omnipotence, omniscience, omnipresence, and omnibenevolence. Aquinas maintains that God is ontologically (that is, existent as) simple, immutable, timeless (atemporal), impassible, and sovereign (God ordains all to occur). Additionally, some contend that God is also perpetually immanent and omnipresent in our physical realm though this position creates philosophical dilemmas as to how he exists as an undetectable cosmic Being, why evil is prevalent, and to what degree God is controlling events of the universe.	Largely affiliated with Medieval Christianity and the writings of Thomas Aquinas
Monotheism*	The belief in a single deity existent as a single, distinct, separate Entity, Being, or Essence outside (i.e., transcendent) of the four dimensions of the physical universe.	• Modern Judaism (6th-century BCE to present-day) • Modern Christianity • Islam • Sikhism
Deism*	The belief in a single deity, God, who created the universe but transcends the natural realm and does not intervene. Deists have no belief in miracles, prophets, special revelation, or Scriptures and regard God as incomprehensible, impersonal, and abstract. Deists base their belief on reason, experience, and nature. Deistic views have varied over time, so this is only a generalization.	World Union of Deists
Monolatrism*	The belief that more than one god may exist, but others are not worthy of worship. A subtype of Henotheism (refer to next page).	• Early Judaism (c. late 9th-century BCE – early 6th-century BCE). • Mormonism

* Explicitly discussed in this book

TABLE 3-2. TYPES OF THEISM (CONTINUED)

Type of Theism	General Beliefs About God	Affiliated Religion
Henotheism	The belief and worship of a single god. Accept actual or possible existence of other gods that may be worthy of worship. Less exclusive than Monolatrism.	Hinduism
Kathenoism	The belief that more than one god exists and worthy of worship. The difference with Henotheism is that gods are worshiped in a succession, one at a time.	Hinduism
Transtheism	Worship no god. It is neither theistic nor atheistic.	• Buddhism* • Jainism • Bahkti
Pantheism	The belief that 'Everything is God' or God is identically the world-universe. God exists not as a single Being / distinct Entity, but persists as a pervasive indwelling Essence in and of the universe, often referred to as an immanent God. Importantly, God does not transcend the universe. Pantheists can believe in one or more gods.	• Hinduism • Taoism
Panentheism*	The belief that 'Everything is *in* God' whereby he is both transcendent *and* immanent. Unlike pantheism (above) whereby God is diffused throughout all the cosmos, panentheism understands God as interpenetrating nature's four dimensions but is a distinct, separate Entity from the universe. Panentheists can believe in one or more gods. Some forms of panentheism are Christian-oriented and such versions are commonly referred to under the heading of Process Theology.	• Pagan Panentheism • Christian Panentheism

* Explicitly discussed in this book

THE GREAT SECRET OF ANCIENT & EARLY JUDAISM

What very few people seem to be aware of is that the long trek from polytheism to the now predominant monotheism was bridged in some ancient cultures by a **LIMINAL** period of **MONOLATRISM** whereby many gods were recognized as existent, but only one deity consistently worshiped (refer to Table 3-2, p. 87). Judaism, the oldest of the Abrahamic religions, evolved in three somewhat overlapping time periods: Ancient, Early, and Modern. Ancient Judaism emerged in southwestern Mesopotamia circa 2000 – 1800 BCE. At the turn of the second millennium BCE, centered in northern Mesopotamia was the settlements of the Hurrians (southern Turkey/northern Syria)—refer to Figure 3-2[12]. To the west of the Hurrians were the Hittites (southern Turkey) and just south of the Hittites were the closely affiliated Ugarit people (southern Turkey/northwestern Syria). To the east of the Hurrians were the Assyrians (northern Syria/northern Iraq/northwest Iran). On the southern border of the Hurrian kingdom were the Semitic-speaking Syrian Amorites who ventured further southward to capture large swaths of Mesopotamia, usurping the Sumerian, Ammon, and Akkadian empires. It was in the 18th-century BCE that Amorite King Hammurabi grew the town of Babylon into a great city and who had developed the Code of Hammurabi. This newly captured land would come to be the land of the Jewish Israelites and the pagan Canaanites and what we now know today as the Levant consisting of present-day Israel, Palestine, Lebanon, Cyprus, Jordan, Syria and sometimes Iraq and southern Turkey.

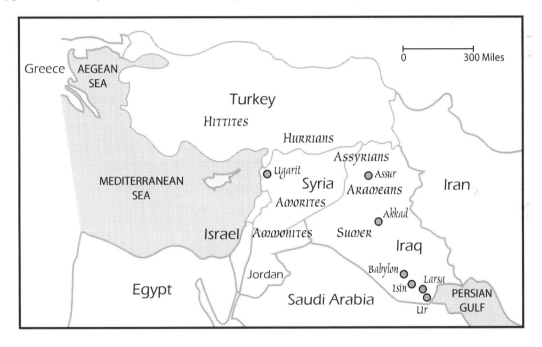

Figure 3-2. Empires of Ancient Near East

Mesopotamian kingdoms and the lands under their keep changed frequently.[4]

---

4. The purpose of this map is solely to provide a general idea regarding the kingdoms and prominent cities that once existed in the approximate timeframe of 3000 – 1500 BCE. Mesopotamian kingdoms and their positions on the map are only intended to be approximate. The boundaries of the kingdoms changed-over many times and not all kingdoms that existed are shown. The country names are the approximate geo-political boundaries in the present-day. Some countries are not shown (e.g., Palestine, Lebanon, and Cyprus).

Widely accepted today by the general populace and even by many Jewish scholars is that Judaism is *and always was* a monotheistic religion. However, there are evidences that strongly lead to the conclusion that Judaism followed a spectrum of beliefs originating in Judaic polytheistic cultism (Ancient Judaism) subsequently maturing into monolatrism over many centuries (Early Judaism), which in turn rather slowly and unevenly transitioned to full monotheism (Modern Judaism). We have a relatively sparse amount of literary, archaeological, or ICONOGRAPHIC information relating to the mid to late Bronze Age (2100 – 1200 BCE) to develop a well-connected, detailed, and inarguable history of the many societies present in the cradle of civilization. It would not be until we exit prehistoric times (what some call the proto-historic phase) and enter into Iron Age I (1200 – 1050 BCE) when alphabetic characters are invented to enhance written language. This new form of human expression enabled the development of what we now call literature. The Ugaritic realm develops into one of the literary centers of the age. As we get to the time of the Jewish monarchy (the reign of the Kings Saul, David, and Solomon, c. 1050 - 920 BCE) we still face a relative paucity of historically-solid literature. It would not be until the middle to the end of Iron Age II (1050 – 550 BCE) that we are on firmer ground relative to our sources of historical knowledge.

What we do know is that during the Bronze and Iron Ages, is that, like their southern Phoenician counterparts in Egypt, the northern Mesopotamians far and wide practiced polytheism. It was during the transitional period of the late Bronze-early Iron Ages that the epochal event called the *Catastrophe* seized the Aegean region (Greece, Crete, Western Turkey), Anatolia (Turkey), the eastern Mediterranean (Syria, Lebanon, Israel) and inland Mesopotamia, as well as the northern border realm of Egypt. Gripped by violence, cultural upheaval, and chaos of untold proportions, much of civilization was decimated. The aftermath left the ancient societies in ruin and poverty.[13] Even with such destruction, societies still valued the worship of a multiplicity of divine gods. What we find is that, "The Ugaritic mythological texts largely feature the deities **El**, the aged and divine patriarch of the pantheon; his consort and queen mother of the divine family, **Asherah**;[5] the young storm-god and divine warrior, **Baal**; [sometimes referred to as **Baal-Hadad** or just **Hadad** and] his sister, **Anat**, [...]"[6, 14] (bold-italics added). The Akkadians, Assyrians, and Babylonians also worshiped the fertility god **Dagon** and **Tammuz**, the god of food and vegetation. The Ammonites worshiped **Moloch** (having many different spellings). **All of these gods are featured in the Jewish Tanakh and Christian Old Testament.**

---

5. Asherah is believed to be the same goddess named **Athirat**. Asherah is linked to the Sumerian-Akkadian god **Anu** and the Ugartic god El as their female consort.

6. The goddess Anat is frequently written as Anath.

We have also learned that during the Iron Age I period that the cultures of the Israelites and Canaanites are nearly indistinguishable from a historical perspective. That is, while they could be different in actuality, we are lacking a degree of information that would enable us to clearly distinguish an Israelite settlement versus a Canaanite settlement. Even so, we come upon a truly startling concept that the ancient Israelites worshiped some of the same gods as the Canaanites. This assertion is partly supported by the discovery and excavation of Ugaritic clay tablets between 1930 – 1933 CE that tell the story of Hadad (i.e., Baal) and the lethal battle between several of the Ugaritic-Canaanite gods. The tablets are dated to 1400 – 1350 BCE. The textual narrative of the tablets is now referred to as the *Baal Cycle* and was comprehensively analyzed by Biblical scholar Mark S. Smith *et al.* in the seminal two-volume work entitled *The Ugaritic Baal Cycle (E. J. Brill, 1994)*. The importance of the *Baal Cycle* narrative is that it stands as the best comparative testament on polytheistic worship in contrast to Hebrew Scriptures. That is, it helped to decode the Old Testament by offering an unsanitized version of deity worship.

In his book *The Early History of God*, Smith advances that the "original god of Israel was El. [... and we find] early on, **Yahweh** is understood as Israel's god in distinction to El. Deuteronomy 32:8-9 casts Yahweh in the role of one of the sons of El, here called *'elyôn*."[15] (bold added) The term *'elyôn* is a Hebrew word meaning "Most High" and is found in both the Hebrew texts and the Christian Septuagiant (one of the earliest versions of the Christian Old Testament written in Greek). It is also found in a compounded form as *'el 'elyôn*—God Most High (see Genesis 14.18–20, Psalm 78:35). Deuteronomy 32:8 clearly depicts El as but one of many gods affirming that the ancient Israelites at the very least acknowledged the existence of multiple gods.

> When the **Most High** apportioned the nations, when he divided humankind,
> <u>he fixed the boundaries of the peoples according to the number of the **gods**</u>.

Deuteronomy 32:8

The short of it is that, in Ancient Judaism, the deity *El* was initially the chief god, not *Yahweh*.

Evidences point to the fact that the ancient Israelites worshiped Yahweh, El, Baal, Anat,[7] and Asherah. El was the supreme deity of the pantheon. In his New York Times Best Seller *The Evolution of God*, Robert Wright connects many elusive dots to explain how the

---

7. The so-called *Elephantine papyri* were discovered in Jewish temples located in Elephantine, Egypt and are dated to the 5th-century BCE. These documents refer to a deity named Anat-Yahu (or Anatyahu). It is thought that Anat was either combined with Yahweh (as often done in Egyptian mythology) or that Anat was the wife/consort of Yahweh.[46]

Israelite's Yahweh transitioned from being one of the many sons of El to become the chief God and ultimately the only God that should be worshipped. As ancient society changed, so too did its selection and arrangement of deities. There was much internal civil strife and intertribal conflict as well as regionalization of the tribal communities which led to an uneven theistic fabric. Some communities were more partial to the worship of one god versus another. Initially, the hierarchy remained intact, with El as the headmaster. Each god had a central area of dominance (e.g., war, fertility, love, etc.) though their dominions overlapped. Wright suggests that both foreign and domestic politics played an ongoing role in jockeying Yahweh to become the foremost deity. The continual upheaval and threats of being usurped or becoming a **VASSAL** (i.e., subordinate to) another foreign power necessitated the formation of alliances. And often, loyalties shifted. These changes were facilitated by alliance members being accepting of one another's gods.[47]

Yahweh seems to have emerged principally as a warrior-god. While this 'Ancient Judaism Yahweh' was not entirely the same god as the 'Modern Judaism Yahweh' we know of today, his war-like propensities would match well with Yahweh's sometimes vengeful nature described many times in the Old Testament. Smith comments that the Israelite cults began to differentiate themselves from the Canaanite cults. Note the use of the plural word 'cults' meaning that there was in actuality *sub-cults* within each of the main Israelite and Canaanite cults. It was not like the Catholic Church of today that has a capacity to project its unified orthodoxical influences across the entire world. Life back then consisted of small colonies each of which had concerns of their own. As a result, the concept of God was geopolitically regionalized.

Both Smith and Wright trace how the polytheistic traditions of the Israelites unsteadily give way to an initially tolerant **MONOLATRY** whereby one god is worshiped as the primal deity but readily accepts the existence of other deities. Smith's scholarship outlines how the god El begins to shift in meaning from pointing to a specific god to become a generic synonym for the word 'god'. **Yahweh assimilates the god El in piecewise fashion among the more southern Jewish settlements whereas both El and Baal retain their positions in the lands of Canaanite, Ugarit, and other areas of eastern and northern Mesopotamia. This is the start of early Jewish settlements altering their religious beliefs from polytheism into what is ostensibly called *pagan Yahwism*, a monolatrous belief system in an era I refer to as Early Judaism.** In time, the process of religious syncretism takes hold where religious beliefs from different traditions are mixed. The Israelite's Yahweh, who once was at peace with the ubiquitous Baal, starts to compete around the 9th-century BCE.[16]

In the Ugartic *Baal Cycle*, one of the stories depicts Baal killing **Lotan**, a seven-headed serpent-dragon. The Old Testament also tells the tale of Yahweh crushing the heads of a multiheaded dragron referred to as **Leviathan** (Psalm 74:13-14). Scholars generally believe that these beasts are one and the same and that the Israelites were harmonizing the actions of the two gods to demonstrate the strength of Yahweh. Similarly, Yahweh begins to accrete the same powers as Baal. In the pantheon of Ugaritic and Canaanite gods, Baal's primary authority was that of a storm-god. We see codified throughout the Old Testament that Yahweh adopts the same motif. Yahweh was a bringer of floods, storms, lightning, and "rode upon the clouds"—see Psalm 68:4.

Politically, geographically, and theologically, Yahweh becomes elevated in authority. Politically, Wright points to the evidence that Yahwism was transitioning in the $8^{th} – 6^{th}$-century BCE to focus more on Yahweh by the fact that roughly 50 percent of signatory seals (i.e., authorial instruments used to stamp official documents) referenced the name of a deity. Of those seals, fully 80 percent referenced Yahweh.[48] Geographically and theologically, an increasing number of Jewish temples were devoted to Yahweh at the expense of other gods in the divine council. At first, Yahweh's cohorts and deific family members are stigmatized and demoted in authority. These minor gods are then regarded as foreign deities—the gods of 'other people'. These non-Israelite gods were Baal, Dagon, and Moloch among others. In time, the Yahwistic cults vilify, then disempower, and ultimately banish the other gods altogether leaving Yahweh as the only emergent figure. Yahweh becomes the nationalized god of the Israelites, known by many biblical names—El, Elyon, Elohim, Eloah, Elohai, El Shaddai, Adonai, and Avinu. Today, many Jewish people consider these latter names as EPITHETS and that the true and proper name for Yahweh is the four-letter unspoken name *YHWH* (the original Hebrew alphabet does not contain vowels). This is also known as the *Tetragrammaton*.

While Smith and Wright in their own respects present a deeper analysis of the transition outlined above, the rationalization of the supernatural stage can be partially dissected from biblical sources. According to the Hebrew Bible and the Qur'an,[8] Moses was a former Egyptian prince who lived by various estimates in the timeframe of c. 1592 – 1271 BCE. He was rescued by Pharaoh's daughter and would later become an Israelite prophet. Moses took the Israelites out of Egypt—the Exodus—where each of the twelve tribes was gathered under its own banner illustrated with an icon (serpent, stag, wolf, lion, etc.). God directed that Moses to "Make a poisonous serpent of bronze, and put it upon a pole" (Numbers 21:8).[9] Time passed with other prophets, kings, and judges presiding over the Israelites. Approximately 650 years later

---

8. Moses is the most frequently cited individual in the Qur'an.

9. Some translations say, "Make a fiery serpent of bronze"

(c. 739 BCE) the prophet Isaiah had a vision from the Lord which was a plan to restore God's sovereignty across the world. As the authoritative successor to Moses and mediator between God and his people, Isaiah prompted King Hezekiah to destroy the image of the serpent named Nehushtan.[17]

> [Hezekiah's actions] He removed the high places, broke down the pillars, and cut down the sacred pole. He broke in pieces the bronze serpent that Moses had made, for until those days the people of Israel had made offerings to it; it was called **Nehushtan**.[10]   2 Kings 18:4

Hezekiah's actions to cleanse the kingdom was a particularly significant hallmark during the period of the kings whose activities are chronicled in the biblical books of 1 Kings and 2 Kings which were written in the mid-6th-century, c. 587/586 – 539 BCE.[18] This was a dramatic shift from the time of Moses and the wanderings of the Chosen People who embraced the power of the fire serpent sent forth by the Lord himself (refer to Numbers 21:5-9). It was deemed by Hezekiah and Isaiah that people had shifted focus away from the Lord and were idolizing a false god when they paid tribute to the serpent relics by burning incense to it. Seeking to disparage the serpent symbols, he called them "Nehushtan" which is translated as 'a thing of brass' which in those times had no particular value. So here we have a line of evidence that the Prophet Isaiah in the 8th-century BCE is missionizing the creation of a fully monotheistic vision for Judaism from the ashes of monolatrism.

We come to the realization that the modern-day English translations of the Jewish and Christian Old Testament would have us believe that Yahweh was always the only god deserving of worship and that all the other deities referred to were simply false gods idolized by pagans. It was the proud history of the Israelite prophets and kings to have freed the ancestral lands from the sinister imposters. But the historical discoveries of the *Baal Cycle* clay tablets, signatory seals, and other artifacts to be noted in the next section tell us a very different history. It is well-understood today that scribes had sanitized the Old Testament over the span of several centuries to parlay their emerging beliefs in a single God. A common tactic was to take advantage of the fact that the ancient Hebrew alphabet lacks capitalized letters. This introduces the challenge to understand whether nouns are proper nouns (e.g., names, places, etc.) or if they are meant to be common nouns (e.g., objects). Scribes would advantage themselves by translating words that clearly related to Yahweh (or his many names) to glorify him. Likewise, in instances where Yahweh might otherwise be interacting with another deity, they would render the god's name into something else. For instance, the storyline of 'Yahweh conquering the sea' was derived from Yahweh conquering

---

10. Nehushtan sounds like Hebrew for 'bronze' or 'snake'

Yam (also **Yamm**) the Sea God.[42] The scribes couldn't eliminate all references to other gods as that would have been a step too far, so they did what they could to minimize their stature in comparison to Yahweh.

DID YAHWEH HAVE A WIFE?

It was very much the norm in ancient polytheistic religions for gods to be arranged in families and for male gods to take on female consorts. Sometimes the goddesses would change affiliation with a different male deity in the pantheon. As more and more was being learned about the pagan gods and that Early Judaism had plausibly followed a path of monolatrism, a question arose whether Yahweh was always a bachelor given that the modern Old Testament paints Yahweh as asexual, being above the crass behavior of the pagan gods. The hypothesis that the Jewish god Yahweh had a wife was first forwarded in 1967 by historian Raphael Patai.[19, 20] It was proposed that Asherah, a pagan goddess, was married to Yahweh. At the time, this seemed so preposterous of a claim that it gained little attention in academic circles. But with the additional knowledge provided in the previous section on the merger between Yahweh and El, this theory gathers quite a bite of steam. Patai states,

> [bold added] Editorial revisions [of biblical texts and stories] were especially thorough when the subject matter pertained to the **non-monotheistic phases of early Hebrew religion. References felt to be offensive were toned down or abridged, and we have, of course, no way of knowing how many were excised altogether** [...] The temples, sanctuaries, high places, altars, and other religious structures which were unearthed from the early Hebrew period, contain, as a rule, no clear-cut evidence as to the identity of the deity to whom they were dedicated. From a comparison of Biblical references and archaeological discoveries we know that the rituals of both Yahweh and the Canaanite gods followed the same general pattern, and it is precisely this circumstance which makes the identification of the deity worshiped at any particular archaeological site extremely difficult [...] **Nevertheless, it is from Biblical sources that we know the names of the three goddesses who were worshiped by the ancient Hebrews down to the days of the Babylonian exile: Asherah, Astarte, and the Queen of Heaven, who was probably identical with Anath[11] [...] That Asherah was the chief goddess of the Canaanite pantheon we know from the rich mythical material unearthed a few decades ago at Ugarit [...]**[20]

---

11. The Queen of Heaven may instead be an epithet to Astarte (also Ashtoreth). The Semitic goddess Astarte is a cognate (i.e., linguistic equivalent) of the Canaanite goddess Ishtar.

The Old Testament offers some of the clues we need to evaluate Patai's theory. The life and times of the Prophet Elijah are detailed throughout 1 and 2 Kings. While Elijah lived during the mid-9th-century BCE, the historical sources indicate that his activities were not recorded until 300 years later which is quite a long time by anyone's standards. Elijah's prime focus is to warn the wicked King Ahab and his followers of their idolatry toward the Canaanite gods Baal and Asherah would lead to damnation and they were to leave their false idols in favor of the Almighty Yahweh. After Elijah, it would be Israelite King Jehu who lived in the early to mid-9th-century that exterminated the house of Ahab, the priests and prophets, and decimated all aspects of Baal worship. However, the Asherah temples, statues, worship poles were left unharmed and seemingly, so were the priests of Asherah. Patai observes that the opposition against all the other gods (Baal, Anat, Moloch, etc.) came relatively quickly, however, "Yahwist opposition to the Asherah worship [... was] much milder."[21] Asherah worship survived for roughly an additional two hundred years and both the pagan Canaanites and Jewish Israelites worshiped Asherah. As we see in 2 Kings (below), King Josiah of Judah finalized the Yahwist reform movement in 621 BCE with the elimination of Asherah. It is around this time that critical analysis of Hebrew texts demonstrates that polytheism/monolatry was wholly eliminated from Judaism.

> [v4]The king commanded the high priest Hilkiah, the priests of the second order, and the guardians of the threshold, **to bring out of the temple** of the Lord all the vessels made for Baal, for Asherah, and for all the host of heaven; he burned them outside Jerusalem in the fields of the Kidron, and carried their ashes to Bethel. [v5]He deposed the idolatrous priests whom the kings of Judah had ordained to make offerings in the high places at the cities of Judah and around Jerusalem; those also who made offerings to Baal, to the sun, the moon, the constellations, and all the host of the heavens. [v6]He brought out the image of Asherah from the house of the Lord,[12] outside Jerusalem, to the Wadi Kidron, burned it at the Wadi Kidron, beat it to dust and threw the dust of it upon the graves of the common people. [v7]He broke down the houses of the male temple prostitutes that were in the house of the Lord, where the women did weaving for Asherah.

2 Kings 23:4-7

---

12. The New English Translation of the Bible translates this as, "He removed the Asherah pole from the Lord's temple."

ARCHAEOLOGICAL EVIDENCE OF YAHWEH'S WIFE ... A DETECTIVE STORY

Patai's ideas found new footing with the excavation of archaeological artifacts that further confirm his thesis. In 1975, excavation began at a remote site called the Kuntillet 'Ajrud, located in the Sinai desert of Egypt. The site is dated to the late 9th- to early 8th-century BCE. It was not until the end of 2012, an astounding four decades later, that the final excavation report was published. The earliest artifacts found in 1975 – 1976 were preliminarily examined and what was revealed sent shockwaves throughout the academic world. Dr. Francesca Stavrakopoulou, Professor and Head of Hebrew Bible and Ancient Religion at the University of Exeter[22] and others[23-25] revived the claim that Asherah, goddess of motherhood and fertility, was the consort of Sumerian and Akkadian god **Anu** (as in, the Anunnaki people) as well as the Canaanite-Ugaritic god El. Because there is no definitive link literarily (e.g, in the Old Testament or in the *Baal Cycle*) or artifactually, it was always hypothetical that Yahweh absorbed the god El's sexuality and assumed El's deific relationship with Asherah. Until, that is, the discovery of two remarkable PITHOI (storage jars) at the dig site, referred to generally as Pithos A and Pithos B.[28]

The pithoi individually weigh approximately 30 pounds and are adorned with an array of illustrated deities, humans, and animals (refer to Figure 3-3, Top images). Joining the imagery are various painted inscriptions.[26] Several of the inscriptions refer to Yahweh and Asherah. One of the painted writings on Pithos A is in Hebrew is translated as "I have [b]lessed you to YHWH [Yahweh] of Shomron [Samaria] and to his *asherah*."[27] Pithos B has similar wording, "I bless you by Yahweh of Teman and by his asherah. May He bless you and may He keep you, and may He be with my lord [forever?]."[13, 28]

While the artifactual forensic evidence in conjunction with comparative biblical references present an exceptionally strong case for the Yahweh-Asherah pair theory, some scholars are less certain of this interpretation. The whole matter of the meaning behind the textual and graphical elements on the pithoi has deadlocked scholars resulting in *four decades* of back-and-forth debate. For instance, the word 'Asherah' is itself equivocal because there are many words that look similar to it in Hebrew. Furthermore, the word also refers to a sacred tree-like or pole-like symbol as described in the book of Judges: "When the men of the town rose early in the morning, behold, the altar of Ba'al was broken down, and the Ashe'rah beside it was cut down, and the second bull was offered upon the altar which had been built." (Judges 6:28 RSV). Because the Hebrew language does not contain capitalized letters, it can be difficult to discern whether 'asherah' is meant to be a proper noun or an object of a sentence.

---

13. The word 'Teman' has various ancient references, however, the most likely meaning is that Teman (along with Shomron—are the regions over which Yahweh either rules or where he dwells.

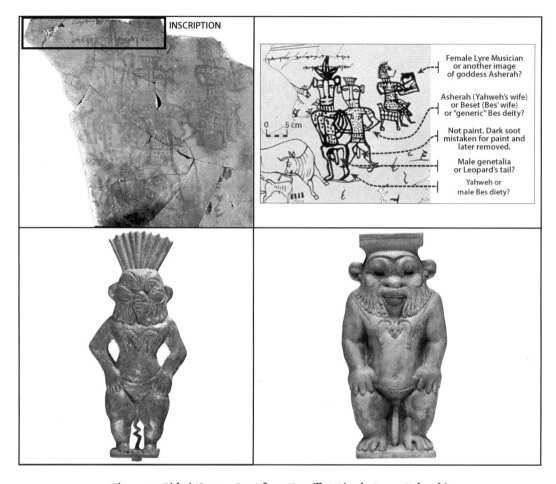

INSCRIPTION

Female Lyre Musician
or another image
of goddess Asherah?

Asherah (Yahweh's wife)
or Beset (Bes' wife)
or "generic" Bes deity?

Not paint. Dark soot
mistaken for paint and
later removed.

Male genetalia
or Leopard's tail?

Yahweh or
male Bes diety?

Figure 3-3. Pithoi (Storage Jars) from Kuntillet 'Ajrud – Bes or Yahweh?

[Top Left]   Actual photo of broken Pithos A with inscription (highlighted by the rectangle).

[Top Right]   An interpretive drawing of Pithos A (see image Top Left) made in 2012 clarifying image details from an earlier drawing created in 1982.[31] The 2012 image was further modified by the present author to add textual notes and locational arrows.

[Bottom Left] Bes statuette from Egypt.[29]

[Bottom Right] Copper Alloy Bes statuette found in Assur.
               Iraq. Egyptian Late Period (c. 664 – 332 BCE).[30]

INTRODUCING THE DEITIES BES AND HIS CONSORT BESET

A predominant number of scholars have indicated that the three painted figures on Pithos A resemble one of the most familiar **TUTELARY** Egyptian deities, ***Bes***, who is a minor god represented as a grotesque, **ITHYPHALLIC**, bow-legged dwarf that usually has a crown of tall straight feathers most often five in number, sometimes more, and very seldom four or less. Bes' arms are always akimbo (bent elbows with hands on the hips)—refer to Figure 3-3.[32]

According to Egyptologist and phonologist Christian de Vartavan, the deity Bes makes its initial appearance in the "Isin-Larsa period [...] which [...] coincides with the artistic, cultural and commercial revival which occurred during the XIIth dynasty in Egypt (circa 2000 – 1785 B.C.)."[33] Unlike most gods, Bes did not have temples or priests devoted to his worship. It is conjectured that Bes originated in the land of Punt (present-day Somalia) where there was active trade between this region and Egypt located over a thousand miles to the north.[34] Indeed, Bes' epithet was *The Lord of Punt*. The deity Bes was thoroughly integrated into the Egyptian and Mesopotamian cultures during the majority of Judaism's evolution to monotheism. What is well known is that Bes imagery changed dramatically over its long heritage of some two millennia which is a major complicating factor in determining whether the depictions on Pithos A might be one of the many morphologies of the Bes deity.

Some Bes iconographies feature the god wearing a leopard's pelt. The phallus-like depiction on the leftmost figure may represent the tail of a leopard pelt (refer to Figure 3-3, Top Right image). Closer to the Common Era and the Greco-Roman culture, the Bes figures changed in appearance with the leopard tail clearly being altered to visually represent male genitalia (refer to Figure 3-3, Bottom Right). As can be seen from the Top Left image of Figure 3-3, the original painted images on the pithoi are badly faded. When Pithos A was first discovered, it was believed that the second smaller middle figure had a leopard's tail (male genitalia according to some). This led scholars to opine that it was not the goddess Asherah, but another smaller male Bes deity. It was thought that a multitude of Bes more powerfully warded off evil. However, it was later discovered that this feature was actually dark soot that after its removal indicated that there was no tail/genitalia present on the middle figure (refer to Figure 3-3, Top Right). Once this discovery was made, this was like pouring gasoline onto the volatile fray of debate. The academic world was set ablaze as it were. Were these figures Yahweh and Asherah, Bes and his female consort Beset, or perhaps a troop of Bes (one male, two female)?

It is a question of special importance whether Bes is a single deity or whether Bes represents a troop of deities that are similar in form and appearance. As Véronique Dasen, a professor of classical archaeology and expert in Greek, Roman, and Egyptian iconography, alludes to in her book *Dwarfs in Ancient Egypt and Greece* (Oxford University Press, 2013), the history of Bes is deeply convoluted. Dasen's research clarifies that due to the paucity of literary evidence concerning Bes, what we know about the deity is chiefly garnered from studying physical artifacts. While artifacts are a powerful form of evidence, without some narrative to explain them, it can be difficult to reconstruct the purpose(s) for the object's existence. Compounding the challenge is that few Bes artifacts carry an inscription. She summarizes two possible theories about the Bes deity.

The first hypothesis is that Bes may have been called by many names over the deity's nearly two millennia history. In support of this idea is the fact that other Egyptian gods possessed multiple names as well as epithets. These epithets often described the god's power or functionary role. For instance, the god **Re** (sometimes spelled **Ra**) was the Egyptian Sun god who was usually depicted with the full power of the noon-time Sun above his falcon/hawk head. **Amun** was a self-created god who later merged with **Re** to become **Amun-Re** (or **Amun-Ra**). Ra was also associated with the god **Atum** (sometimes **Atem** or **Tem**). **Osiris** was another Egyptian god that was initially a singular deity who was later merged with two other gods to become **Ptah-Seker-Osiris**. As a tutelary god, Bes was well-known to be a protector of pregnant women and childbirth in general. Dasen highlights the second theory whereby the Bes deity may have been worshipped as a family of divine gods. It may have been the case that Bes was simply a generic name for multiple deities that were depicted with similar physical attributes but each of which had its own special role.[32]

The short of it is that the Bes god has at various times been represented as a single deity and multiple deities in male, female, and **ANDROGYNOUS** forms. One of the keys to solving the riddle lies with the history of the goddess Beset, the wife of Bes. Beset icons dating from about 2000 – 332 BCE are rare with the vast majority being of terracotta statuettes traced to the Ptolemaic Period (332 – 20 BCE).[35] Dasen further comments that prior to the Ptolemaic dynasty which coincides with the beginning of the greater Greco-Roman Period (332 BCE – 395 CE), Beset was presented with similar leonine features as Bes but had no tail and was sometimes somewhat smaller in overall physique. She also displayed a different body posture with gapless legs in contrast to Bes' knees being set apart. Whether Beset was shown beside Bes or was presented without him at her side, Beset's depiction changed in the Greco-Roman Period. Her head was altered to be distinctly human with hair and bulbous cheeks which accompanied her plump appearance. Atop her head was a feathery head-dress.[36] Figure 3-4 compares statuettes of Bes and Beset and it is quite evident how Beset's appearance changed in the general timeframe of the Ptolemaic dynasty. **Of major significance is that, prior to the Ptolemaic era, Bes and Beset are not depicted together.**[34] Rather, Bes was shown with the hippopotamus goddess **Taweret** or other male gods such as **Shu**—the god of light and air—as well as the youth **Horus** (son of the goddess **Isis**).[37-39] Figure 3-4 (Bottom Right) provides the archaeological evidence that Bes and Horus were strongly intertwined during the timeframe of when the Kuntillet 'Ajrud pithoi were made. The fact that Beset did not appear alongside her male partner until the early 4th-century BCE definitely raises considerable suspicion of the claim that the 8th-century BCE pithoi image was that of Beset.

Figure 3-4. Statuettes of deities Bes and Beset

[Top Left]   Terracotta Lamp with Bes and Beset (1st- to 3rd-century CE).

[Top Right]   Terracotta of the deities Bes and Beset.
                 Greco-Roman Period (1st- to 3rd-century CE -- date uncertain).[40]

[Bottom Left]   Bronze or Copper Alloy Statuette of Beset as found in Late Greco-Roman Period
                 (c. 664 – 332 BCE) through Ptolemaic period (332 – 20 BCE).

[Bottom Right]   Painted wooden cippus[14] of the head form of the god Bes with the god Horus standing
                 on crocodiles (c. 600 BCE). Possibly from Memphis (Egypt).[41]

---

14. A Cippus is a type of stela (an ancient upright stone bearing markings) that was used to protect against
    venomous animals. To invoke its healing and protection properties, water is poured over the Cippus. This
    Cippus depicts the head form of the tutelary god Bes. Cippi typically present the infant/youthful Horus
    standing tall on the backs of crocodiles while grasping dangerous animals in his hands.

There are many other supporting reasons to believe that the painted figures are not Bes figures. In 2015, Ryan Thomas, an independent researcher educated at the Harvard Divinity School and the Hebrew University of Jerusalem, provided a contemporary synoptic exposition of the state of affairs on the pithoi.[42] The two leftmost overlapping figures (refer to Figure 3-3, Top Right image) are illustrated with interlocked arms inferring a close relationship between the two gods. Thomas notes that the male figure is out in front in a dominant position and that the smaller figure is decidedly female. However, almost exclusively, "Bes symbols never overlap with their bodies [...] At the most they are found touching at the elbows so that the **APOTROPAIC** frontality of the image could have full effect."[42] By maintaining a degree of separation between individual Bes deities, Bes' protective powers are maximized. Thomas also forwards particularly strong evidence that the face of the male figure is more bovine/bullish in nature.[15] "We have ample archaeological and biblical evidence that bovine symbolism impacted ancient Israel's conceptualization of the divine and specifically that YHWH [Yahweh] was represented in the form of a young bull calf or '*egel*."[42] Thomas also states that we also have evidence that the "Canaanite El was commonly represented as a sexually mature bull."[42] The mature bull-versus-calf imagery supports the idea that at one point in time, El was the father of Yahweh. Strengthening the idea that male figure on Pithos A is *not* the Bes deity is the fact that the painted image lacks "the rounded and broad muscular face, high cheekbones, grimacing and wrinkled expression, and [a] protruding tongue [...] or shaggy-haired mane"[42] typical of most all Bes imagery (refer to Figure 3-3, Bottom images).

The third rightmost figure on Pithos A, the seated lyre musician, is obviously female. Given that she is seated on what appears to be a throne and is in the company of two other gods, it has been contended that she too is a deity. Thomas suggests that this figure is a reinterpretation of the same goddess as the middle figure.[42] Which, as he concludes, is the goddess Asherah.

There are additional parallels not previously drawn by examining an Ugaritic mottled stone relief of the god El dating anywhere between the 19th- and 12th-century BCE and the Kuntillet 'Ajrud Pithoi jars from the 8th-century BCE. A representational outline drawing of the stone artifact (not shown) is presented in Figure 3-5. One can note similarities in the general style of the waist-high, low-back, clawfoot throne that the god El is seated in and the ornamented musician's throne depicted on Pithos A. Both the god El and the musician are raised atop the throne (not set in) and are posed in side profile. These similarities in stylistic techniques could be loosely construed as another corroborating link that the Ugarit/Canaanite god El had become one and the same as the Israelite god Yahweh.

---

15. The term 'bovine' refers to the appearance of domestic cattle (cows) or oxen.

Figure 3-5. The deity El and the goddess Asherah

[Left]   An illustrative reproduction of the god 'El' being served food and drink by the King of Ugarit. The deity El is shown with bull horns protruding from his conical headdress and is seated in a clawfoot throne with his one hand raised in a gesture of welcoming.[16, 43]

[Right] Detail view of an interpretive drawing of the third figure painted on Pithos A (refer to Figure 3-3, Top Right).

Let us summarize all the knowledge that we have gleaned.

Accumulated Evidence of the Painted Figures on Pithos A

1. We have two distinct evidences in the form of two pithoi, both of which contain highly related inscriptions and paintings.

2. Judaism has been demonstrated to have originated as polytheistic and transitioned to monolatry before it became a monotheistic religion. Familial relationships among mythic gods were common. With this perspective, it takes no major shift of the mind to appreciate that Yahweh could have had a consort.

---

16. This illustration is an interpretation of a stone stele discovered from the ruins of the Acropolis at Ugarit (today called Ras Shamra)—modern-day Syria (c. 1300 – 1200 BCE). The actual stone stele is held at the Aleppo National Museum (Syria). A photograph of the actual stone stele can be accessed at *https://www.lessingimages.com*. Refer to ID 08-02-08/51. A direct link to the source is: *http://tinyurl.com/j6l3lx5*.

3. Bes, Beset, Yahweh, and Asherah all verifiably exist as deities during the timeframe of the fabrication of the pithoi (c. 8th-century BCE). By this point, Yahweh had already merged with El and the process of assimilation was underway for Yahweh to overtake Baal's position was nearing its finality.

4. When Bes and Beset are shown with a feathered headdress, the number of feathers is most often five in number and each feather usually rises straight from the base of the crown and then toward the top of the headpiece the feathers bend slight outward in somewhat of a plume shape. The leftmost painted figure only has three feathers and the outside feathers are directionally-oriented toward the lateral sides instead of rising straight and up from the base of the crown (refer to Figure 3-3). This would be a very uncharacteristic headdress arrangement for the deity Bes.

5. There are definite features consonant with Bes imagery in the two leftmost illustrations of Figure 3-3 (Top Right image) such as the depiction of leopard pelts, the feathery crowns, and arm positioning. "The amalgamation of Bes-like and bovine features is a local adaptation of the southern Levant, possibly unique to ancient Israel."[42]

6. The middle figure on Pithos A was first considered male. Now, it is universally considered female. The seated figure is sitting on a throne is indicative of her divinity. The likeness of the two female forms is strongly suggestive that they are one and the same goddess.

7. All the other pagan gods and the priests were removed from Judaism approximately 200 years before Asherah was removed. Asherah was still regarded as divine around the time the pottery was made.

8. There is a demonstrable fusion of deities between the pagan Canaanites and the Jewish Israelites. The Pithos A figures are likely to be hybridization between two or more of the male gods Bes/Yahweh/El/Horus and the female goddesses Beset/Asherah/Isis/Hathor. Gods were often symbolized as other objects such as animals or plants. In the case of El and Yahweh, they were depicted as bovine. Asherah was symbolized as a tree.

9. There are two hypotheses on the nature of Bes. The first hypothesis concludes that Bes is a single deity called by many names. This is supported by the fact that other Egyptian gods had multiple epithets. The other hypothesis suggests

that Bes was a family of deities appearing with dwarvish characteristics and came in both male and female form. This latter hypothesis is supported because other gods and minor deities are genericized in the sense that their name refers to a plurality of gods bearing similar appearance.

10. While the inscription on Pithos A is apparently added some time after the original painting, both Pithos A and B have similar inscriptions that essentially say, "Yahweh and his Asherah." It is plausible if not entirely logical that the inscriptions should reference the painted objects, though there is scholarly disagreement on this point.[28, 42]

11. There is some corroborating evidence that the throne depicted in the third figure (the musician, refer to Figure 3-3, Top Right image) bears similarity to a chair that the god El is seated in (refer to Figure 3-5). This is *not* to suggest that the musician is the god El, rather that the two chairs bear a similarity suggestive of a relationship in illustrative style that would have been commonly presented in concert with images of El. By 'commonly' I mean often performed during those ages and not to infer that we possess many comparative references in modern-day times. Finally, the methods of inscription differ, one is in stone and the other is a painting so an exact replication of features would not be easily possible.

12. All available evidence points to the fact that Beset is not shown together with Bes as a deity until the early 4th-century BCE. The construction of the pithoi date back to the 8th-century BCE.

Figure 3-6 illustrates a timeline of events to help put everything into perspective. **All things considered, the evidence decidedly favors the hypothesis that Yahweh and Asherah were worshiped by Israelite and Canaanite settlements as a divine couple for a relatively short period of history (i.e., one to several centuries in duration).**

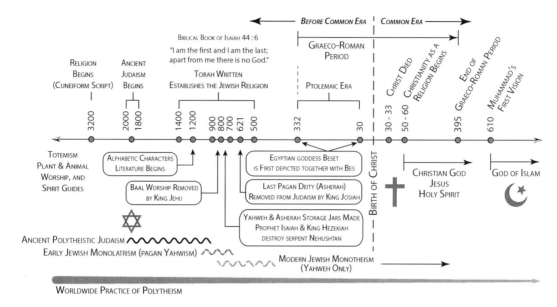

Figure 3-6. Development Timeline for Abrahamic Religions

ENLARGING THE PERSPECTIVE

The transitional prevalence of religious belief from the superstitious worship of totems, animals, and Spirit Guides to polytheism, coevolved by a period of fractious monolatrism, and finally to monotheism, even if exceedingly gradual, warrants concern. This winnowing and reshaping of the image of God to a single deity is of paramount importance. We are not saying what Abrahamic religious figureheads propound, that God holds his plans close to his chest and at his sole discretion incrementally reveals himself to us. No, what has transpired is that many dozens of mythical gods have been systematically eradicated in favor of a single most favored incarnation of the Creator-God Yahweh and that there is convincing physical evidence supporting this claim.

Before taking this point further, some points of clarification are required as it pertains to Christianity. Unlike Judaism and Islam, Christianity maintains that the Godhead is actually a divine trinity of three personages.[17] Canon 1 of the Fourth Lateran Council (1251 CE) of the Catholic Church declared the Father is self-generated, the Son is born, and the Holy Spirit proceeds from both the Father and the Son. The three are considered coequal, coeternal,

---

17. During the formation of Christian monotheism, some espoused *binitarianism*, that is, that God and Jesus are two distinct Gods, and the Holy Spirit is a living power that emanates and flows between them.

and **CONSUBSTANTIAL**.[18] This indwelling relationship whereby the three circulate their love and divinity in perfect fellowship is referred to as **PERICHORESIS**.[19] Traditional Christianity conceived the Second Person of the Trinity as the Word of God (oft referred to as the *Logos*). In this sense, the transcendent Father sent his Son to Earth as the embodiment of his Word so that his eternal Word would become the Word made flesh. However, this attempt at disambiguating how the three Persons of God exist as a Being of one substance is lacking thereby creating a perennial problem crying out for a well-reasoned clarification. We will explore the coherency of the Holy Trinity in later chapters. As an aside, the Fourth Lateran Council, convoked by Pope Innocent III, also proclaimed and canonized papal primacy[20] (Canon 5) and established procedures and penalties against heretics and their protectors (Canon 3).[44]

Figure 3-7 diagrammatically shows how the three personages of the Chalcedonian God[21] relate to one another in **HYPOSTATIC UNION**. Ancient groups that refuted the Holy Trinity practiced what is called *nontrinitarianism*. Modern-day nontrinitarian Christian groups include Christian Scientists, Jehovah's Witness, Judaism, Unitarianism, and The Church of Jesus Christ of Latter-day Saints (Mormons). Mormons believe in the Trinity to the extent that the three personages of the Godhead share the same attributes but are three distinct Beings (i.e., not consubstantial). Islam is considered *anti-trinitarian* because the Qur'an considers the Trinity blasphemous.

With this summary in hand, there exists a vast difference between the Common Man's understanding of the origin of the deity in Scriptures—the one, eternal, perfect-nature being —manifested as one Person in Judaism and Islam; in three Persons in *most* of Christendom—and the discordant, temporal, factious, and fictitious gods that were fabricated in the digressive imaginations of ancient Mesopotamians. **There are lines of evidence that demonstrate that the God of Scripture is a descendant of the Mesopotamian gods.**

---

18. The word consubstantial is equivalent to the Greek word *homoousios* which means "of the same being or substance."

19. This term first appears in the writings of Maximus the Confessor (b. c. 580 – d. 13 August 662 CE).

20. Note that *papal primacy* is NOT to be confused with the idea of *papal infallibility*. The former assigns the Pope as the successor to St. Peter's Church and rightful superior of all other bishops. Papal infallibility was not declared until the First Vatican Council (1869 – 1870 CE).

21. The term 'Chalcedonian God' refers to the view of the Christian God as decided at the Council of Chalcedon (451 CE). It marked a significant turning point in the Christological debates and provided a clear statement on the human and divine nature of Christ to wit Jesus was Man, Son, and God. The Fourth Lateran Council (1251 CE) further clarified the Trinity relationship between Son, God, and Holy Spirit.

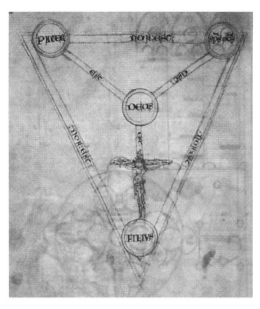
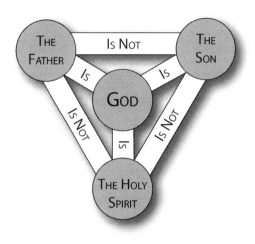

English Translation

Figure 3-7. The Christian Shield of the Trinity

[Left] Earliest attested version of the diagram[45]

[Right] Recreated image of the Christian Shield of the Trinity translated into English.

It is disarming that the Abrahamic religion's espousal of truth about God rest squarely on the Hebrew Bible which by evidences presented above has been sanitized in two highly salient ways. First, the Hebrew God is purported to have had a wife—not uncommon for polytheistic religions—as supported by the discovery of physical antique artifacts and by cross-referencing older and newer Scriptures. The second disquieting piece of evidence is that ancient humans started out worshiping totems, animals, and dozens of gods to subsequently dispel all these notions in favor of eradicating or consolidating them into a single Almighty Creator-God. **This process applies specifically to Judaism but owing to the adoption of legacies, it also applies to Christianity and Islam.** What is perplexing to me is the **INVETERATE** practice by theologians, biblical scholars, religious headmasters, or evangelicals to underrepresent or submerge this deep history as it forms the veritable bedrock on which the Great Religions sit upon.

An unbiased perspective mandates that we be mindful that while the accumulated data holds explanatory power and a considerable degree of plausibility, it is not proof positive. As we will find throughout our journey, proof positive is very simply an unachievable standard. History is and always will be a game of the gaps, requiring one to reconstruct the most plausible story with the available sources and assessing the authenticity thereof. In this case, we cannot interview those who made the pottery or be like primatologist Jane Goodall did with her chimpanzees and take notes on ancient society from behind a rock or tree. We will always be faced with architecting the past into an intelligible framework and testing these iteratively as new evidences become available. Some frameworks, however, are decidedly better than others.

Given our fuller understanding of archaeologically-backed history and that some scholars readily acknowledge that the Hebrew texts were continually edited to modify what were then codified Jewish beliefs, we have to question the historicity of what the Hebrew and Christian Bibles both say, starting with the very first verses.[22] As we know from the Bible, Judeo-Christian prehistory ignites with Genesis' proclamation (an implicit assumption) of a singular God creating the universe,

> [v1]In the beginning God created the heavens and the earth. [v2]The earth was without form, and void; and darkness was on the face of the deep. And the Spirit of God was hovering over the face of the waters. [v3]Then God said, "Let there be light"; and there was light.
>
> Genesis 1:1-3

Alas, if we only had the *Grand Observer's* telescopically-enabled knowledge to view true unadulterated reality and witness for ourselves whether or not this happened, we could put many questions to rest. Even so, our more feeble 'equipment' has elucidated that God may be, in one degree or another, a by-product of our imaginations caused by a myriad of environmental, physical, biological, and cultural influences. Such thoughts are tantalizing, if not provocative, and engender the need to explore these realms for evidences contrary or otherwise. In any case, I think it wrong-headed for people to become angry or thick-headed or worse mobilized to arms over the critical examination of information. People should be equally as critical of their beliefs and adopt an attitude of stewardship for questioning the knowledge they ingest.

We have to acknowledge that no person or group is the possessor of the vessel of all knowledge. Even so, as contingents of society, we are all called to be dominated by a spirit of respect and humility for the moral and ethical as well to favor pragmatism rather than overindulgence in ideology. Ultimately, in this book I am calling for people to move beyond fideistic or blind faith belief and **ATAVISTIC** behaviors to embrace all sources of knowledge

---

22.   The Qur'an does not have a Creation account like the Bible.

and evidences therein and to embrace literary free expression in general. For too long, the politically and religiously powerful have censored the world society. We only need recall Pope Urban VIII's Curia who condemned Galileo Galilei's science, hidden within the *Dialogue on the Two Great World Systems* (1632) that challenged the Catholic Church to update its position on the non-geocentricity of planet Earth. Or, in more modern times the reaction to Salman Rushdie's *The Satanic Verses* (1988) and Wendy Doniger's, *The Hindus: An Alternative History* which was written in 2009 and later withdrawn and copies destroyed in India in 2014.

For now, we must come to terms with how the crowded House of God went from many deities down to one and that at each step of the way our religious dogma and sacred texts were cultivated (redacted) to reflect these changing beliefs. Acknowledging this **RECONDITE** development for a progressive winnowing of the tribal community of gods with dispersed powers to one all-powerful God within a given belief system (or one that evolved from it) clearly hobbles arguments in favor of God's existence, at least in the form conceived by the Great Religions.

SUMMARY

In this chapter we explored the ignition point of religious belief by peeking back to the beginning of the human species to learn how these bipedal animals may have expressed religious experience. Jumping forward many thousands of years in time (as developments were extraordinarily slow by today's standards), we placed ourselves in the midst of ancient Mesopotamian society. Here we studied the evolution of religion from its primal beginnings of animal worship to belief in a pantheon of gods with domain-specific powers, often arranged in a succession of supremacy. At later times, evidences of societal dynamics of one cultic kingdom conquering another give plausibility to the idea that polytheism co-evolved in some geographic regions with monolatrism, a new belief that arose whereby many gods existed but only one of these gods is actually worthy of human worship. It is to be granted that ancient source materials are difficult to interpret. Nevertheless, it appears that it is plausible that the evolutionary course of Judaism transformed itself through the ages of many gods to a unitary deity. While the nature of God is different in certain respects, Christianity and Islam are inextricably tied to the Jewish deity through their acceptance of the God of Moses and Abraham.

CHAPTER 4

The Revealing Truth of Biblical Antiquities

The limitations of archaeology are galling. It collects phenomena, but hardly ever can isolate them so as to interpret scientifically; it can frame any number of hypotheses, but rarely, if ever, scientifically prove.

– David George Hogarth (b. 1862 – d. 1927)
Archaeologist, President of the Royal Geographical Society

When it comes to the Shroud, nearly everybody wanted to carbon date the Shroud "in the worst way" and that is precisely what happened. The protocols were supposed to map the way to the truth. Instead, the truncated protocols adopted led the carbon scientists over a cliff.[1]

– John Klotz
The Coming of the Quantum Christ, 2014

An unbelieved truth can hurt a man much more than a lie. It takes great courage to back truth unacceptable to our times. There's a punishment for it, and it's usually crucifixion.

– John Steinbeck
East of Eden, 1952
In his book East of Eden, Samuel Hamilton (Steinbeck's grandfather) speaks to his friend Adam Trask (the main character) about the incident where Samuel hit Adam in the face to knock some sense into him and to wake him from his despair. Essentially, Steinbeck is telling us that it is not always a pleasant experience to face the truth.

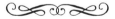

WHAT DO BIBLICAL ANTIQUITIES REVEAL ABOUT BIBLICAL CLAIMS?

WHEN ONE PONDERS THE HISTORY of mankind, one cannot help being disturbed by the tragic loss of a vastly sum of antiquities whether by erosive forces of time, neglect, indelicate handling, willful destruction or held distant from examination as they sit quietly in the shadows of private collections and a boisterous underground economy. We are left with a confounding and fragmentary set of relics with which to piece-together our human heritage. After centuries of painstaking effort, mankind has unearthed what we believe to be the veritable majority of the sacred texts which comprise the Hebrew and Christian Bible. Putting aside the many versions, translations, and interpretations, the Bible provides an ensemble of written stories that portend to reveal the divine interaction of the sovereign Lord and a battery of prophets and apostles. While a great many religious antiquities have been found, it is those artifacts associated with these major figures in the Bible that have provoked the greatest attention and source of intrigue. Among these is the great Ark that Noah built at the tender age of 600 (he purportedly lived to be 950 years old, some say centuries older), Moses' Ark of the Covenant that was ushered across the Holy Land, and the right hand of John the Baptist which he had placed upon Jesus' forehead during his baptism. Of even greater value would be anything that can be tied directly to Jesus of Nazareth or his immediate family. **However, we have not had a single artifact that can be authentically and directly affiliated with Jesus himself.**

When compared to literary sources and attendant theological and philosophical dialectical treatises, artifacts represent a common arena where believers and skeptics can more tangibly lock arms around theistic claims. They are innately powerful because they can either corroborate or refute theistically inspired scriptural revelations. However, this capacity can only be established if the artifact has a reliably known provenance or pedigree to understand the circumstances of its origin and its authenticity. For objects thousands of years old the task is usually arduous and fraught with uncertainty. This uncertainty breeds diverging hypotheses which scholars debate unendingly for decades, much as we learned in the story of the storage jars of Kuntillet 'Ajrud. As a result, these artifacts develop a convoluted deep history all their own, making a comprehensive examination herein too far out of scope. What is preserved is a capsule summary of the most recent research updates with a special emphasis on the most plausible assessments of their authenticity and value therein to support or detract from biblical claims.

Noah's Ark

One of the Bible's most fabled chronicles is that of the Noachian Ark whose three decks were crammed with matched creaturely pairs to ride out the worldwide watery inundation lasting some five to six months. The book of Genesis indicates that Noah's Ark measured 300 x 50 x 30 cubits in length, width, and height, respectively. The 'standard' measure for a cubit varied in different cultures of the world and changed across the time horizon. Assuming the use of Egyptian cubits, the size of the Ark translates to about 450 x 75 x 45 feet. That is approximately 25 percent longer than and about half as wide as an American football field. In alternate terms, it is just short of half as long as a modern American aircraft carrier. According to the Bible, the Ark "came to rest on the mountains of Ararat" in present-day Turkey (Genesis 8:4 NRSV). Explorers from across the globe have launched expeditions to find the Ark in these mountains. Former American astronaut James Irwin who walked on the moon in 1971 had become obsessed to find the Ark and led two expeditions in the 1980's. Confounded by his inability to locate any evidences of the Ark he is oft-quoted as saying, "It's easier to walk on the moon, [...] I've done all I possibly can, but the ark continues to elude us."[2] There have been numerous claims that petrified wood fragments and in-ground iron are testimony of the boat's existence. None of the wood samples have been authenticated and the iron deposits found within the mountain range, supposedly the nails used to fabricate the boat, were a red herring because iron nails did not exist at the time Noah is reported to have built the boat. A Hong Kong-based, evangelical Christian organization called *Noah's Ark Ministries International* claims to have found the Ark buried in a cave, but has never put forth any evidence to substantiate the claim and their claims are currently regarded as a hoax.[3] Scholars contend that the biblical account is an adaptation to **ANTEDILUVIAN** mythical flood pandemics found in Mesopotamian texts c. 1900 – c. 1600 BCE (i.e., *Epic of Ziusudra, Epic of Atra-Hasis*, and the *Epic of Gilgamesh*). It might also be noteworthy to mention that Noah's flood story is also featured twice in the Qur'an (Sura 11 and Sura 71).

In 1985, a collection of cuneiform tablets were brought to the British Museum by Douglas Simmonds. It was Simmonds' deceased father who was a hobbyist antiquities collector and had bequeathed his collection to his son. The tablets were permitted to be briefly inspected by Irving Finkel, the museum's curator for cuneiform inscriptions. Finkel noted that one of the tablets referred to a Babylonian flood narrative but that was all that could be ascertained. Simmonds was uncomfortable leaving the tablets in the possession of the museum so he took them away.

In 2009, some 25 years later, Finkel was granted permission to translate the tablet. The Ark Tablet as it is now called, is a 60-line text that outlines a dialogue between **Enki**, the Sumerian god of seawater and freshwater, and his earthly minion Atra-Hasis. Atra-Hasis is directed to build a huge circular basket-like boat known as a *coracle* constructed of coiled palm-fiber rope (reeds) and sealed with bitumen (pitch) to escape a planned flood by the god **Enlil**. In Finkel's book entitled *The Ark Before Noah: Decoding the Story of the Flood* (Hodder & Stoughton, 2014) he outlines that the physical dimensions denoted by the Ark Tablet suggest that the boat would be about 18 feet high and constitute an equivalent area of 4,300 square yards, to hold Atra-Hasis' family and the air-breathing menagerie. Not only would such a vessel be too short vertically to house giraffes, this watercraft would require an unduly amount of reed rope, approximately 340 miles worth. This is the distance from Los Angeles to San Francisco as the crow flies. A coracle of such a size would be quite unstable in rough seas and even more so if the boat's inhabitants were to be moving about the 'deck'. While there are three extant narratives that pre-date the biblical story, the Noachian account most closely mimics the flood myth provided in the Epic of Gilgamesh. The Ark Tablet has been dated to c. 1750 BCE—the middle of the First Babylonian Dynasty and coincident with the year King Hammurabi died. The first scripts of the Hebrew Bible were not written until the 11th- to the 10th-century BCE and took another thousand years for it to be fully written. In any case, Finkel and his collaborators have credibly ascertained that the Old Testament tale of Noah, his boat, and the flood is a re-work of prior fictional accounts, a clear indication that the Noachian flood never happened.

MOSES' ARK OF THE COVENANT

The book of Exodus recounts that approximately one year after the Israelites left behind enslavement by their Egyptian overlords they encamped at Mount Sinai (c. 15th-century BCE).[1] It was here that God informed Moses that he had appointed a man named Bezalel to craft a rectangular chest with four feet and four golden rings. Into the rings would be placed two poles made of acacia wood, never to be removed. All surfaces were to be gilded in gold. Affixed to the top of the box was the Kapporet (the 'Mercy Seat' or 'Atonement Piece')[2] and two solid gold winged cherubim figures,[3] one at each end, their wings swept forward (see Exodus 25:10-22; 37:1–9). Their wings support God's throne which is where the presence of God resides here on Earth. This is the Ark of the Covenant sensationalized in the movie *Raiders of the Lost Ark* and the one that most people think of when Moses' Ark is referred to. However, seldom remarked is that God gave a different set of instructions in Deuteronomy 10:1-6. Here, it is not Bezalel who makes the Ark, rather God tells Moses himself to make a much plainer Ark solely out of acacia wood (sans any gold embellishments, Cherubim, or Mercy Seat). These two different versions play into the final hypothesis concerning this relic as we will see a little later on.

According to Exodus and Deuteronomy, into this rectangular Ark were placed the two stone tablets inscribed with God's Ten Commandments. In another disagreement within the Bible, the New Testament states that the **RELIQUARY** also contained other holy articles in the form of a golden urn containing manna and the magical staff belonging to Moses' brother

---

1. The book of Deuteronomy places the Israelites at Mount Horeb, which may be another name for Mount Sinai or an entirely different mountain. There is no consensus on this point.

2. It is unclear from the translations if the Kapporet was the lid itself or an object on top of the lid. It is affiliated with Yom Kippur—the Jewish-affiliated Day of Atonement.

3. In the Hebrew Bible, Cherubim are not given status as angels but are supernatural beings. In contrast, in the Christian tradition, Cherubim are accorded as in the First Sphere but second highest order of angel behind the highest of angels, the Seraphim.

Aaron (see Hebrews 9:4). Like Moses' Ark, the stone tablets have never been found and the oldest written evidence of the Ten Commandments is from c. 30 – 1 BCE found among the Dead Sea Scroll collection (discussed in the next chapter).

By virtue of God's throneship situated at the top of the Ark of the Covenant, it is said to have been imbued with mystical energies that, if touched would instantly kill a man, and if opened, could radiate so powerfully it could level mountains and decimate armies. The Ark was moved from place to place for centuries and it eventually found its resting place in the back room of Solomon's Temple, the first Jewish temple located at Mount Zion, built in the 9th-century BCE. The only surviving artifact that attests that the temple ever existed is the Jehoash Tablet whose authenticity is generally considered genuine. The 12 x 10 x 3-inch black stone tablet contains a 15-line chiseled inscription detailing Jehoash making repairs to the temple in 800 BCE which strongly resembles the account provided in the Hebrew Bible (see 2 Kings 12:5-16). The temple was destroyed in the first Siege of Jerusalem by Assyrian King Nebuchadnezzar II in 587/586 BCE. It was at the time that the Ark mysteriously disappeared from recorded history and has remained so for some 2,500 years. The Bible suggests that, before Nebuchadnezzar razed the temple, the prophet Jeremiah received an oracle from God commanding him to hide the tabernacle and the Ark. Jeremiah and his acolytes placed it into a cave and had it sealed. God then erased their memories so that no one could find the Ark until God decided to make it known (see 2 Maccabees 2). Some have speculated otherwise to the effect that Nebuchadnezzar II, a worshiper of the god **Marduk** either stripped it of its gold and burned the wood or took it back with him as a trophy to Babylon.

Some believe the Ark was hidden by the Knights Templar—the secretive and wealthy Christian military order that operated from c. 1119 to 1312 CE—only to have spirited it away to Europe. Others have contended it is still buried in the tunnels under the Temple Mount (Jerusalem). In July 1981, Jewish Rabbis clandestinely excavated Temple Mount to search for religious artifacts, including the Lost Ark, but such efforts were short-lived as Muslim devotees discovered the activity and thwarted the advance. The tunnel was subsequently sealed with concrete.

Tudor Parfitt of the University of London's School of Oriental and African Studies forwarded an intriguing hypothesis in *The Lost Ark of the Covenant: Solving the 2,500 Year Old Mystery of the Fabled Biblical Ark* (Harper Collins, 2008). According to DNA testing, the *Buba Clan* of the African *Lemba* tribe was confirmed to be descendants of a guild of Jewish priests who had sojourned from oasis to oasis from the land of Jerusalem, through Yemen, to South Africa.[4] For centuries, the clan was the zealous guardian of a sacred drum called the *ngoma lungundu* (usually shortened as ngoma).[5] The ngoma is a wooden drum which would normally have animal skin pegged to its perimeter measuring about 2.5 feet. Like the biblical Lost Ark of the Covenant, it had two wooden rings on each side, was carried by two wooden poles, and served as a storage container for holy objects. While different in physical form, it shared a capacity with the Lost Ark in that it was regarded as divine (or nearly so) and could only be touched by the priestly order.[6] So too, the ngoma (also more colloquially referred to as the Lemba Ark) was purported to be used as an instrument of war. The ngoma lungundu translates as *'the drum that thunders'* because its drum beat was the voice of God which they supposed would intimidate the opposition. It was also called the *'Fire of God'* due to its functionary role as a vessel for primitive and lethal incendiary mixtures when used against the tribe's enemies—so say the Buba Clan.

In the 1940's, an authentic (but not necessarily the original) Lemba Ark was found buried in a cave near the arc-shaped Limpopo River located in the southern region of Africa. The drum had been photographed by a missionary by the name of Harald von Sicard. In time, the drum made its way to a museum in Bulawayo, Africa but was later untraceably removed. It was last seen in 1949.[7] Parfitt's inquisitiveness would yield that the drum was relocated to the Victoria Museum in Harare, Zimbabwe. Come 2007, in a dimly lit storeroom of the Zimbabwean Victoria Museum of Human Science, Parfitt re-discovered the lost Lemba Ark.[8] Shortly thereafter, a sliver of the ngoma was carbon-dated by the University of Oxford to the year 1350 CE $\pm$ 25 years.[9] This would make the Lemba Ark nearly two-thousand years younger than the biblical Ark. Parfitt advances the idea that the original Lemba Ark had probably deteriorated over time because of its use as a cauldron for militarily-oriented firework displays and other uses. The ngoma he found in the museum was a reproduction made by the Buba priests and is an artifactual descendant of the original Lemba Ark which he postulates is the biblical Ark of the Covenant. If it was not Moses' Ark of the Covenant, the Lemba Ark may have been a facsimile much in the way in modern times we place crosses/crucifixes in places of worship to remind us of the True Cross that Jesus was crucified upon. He explains that the differences in physical shape (rectangular versus circular), composition (i.e., one is overlaid in gold whereas the other is not), and the grandiosity of supernatural powers (supermassive radiative powers as compared to a relatively small chemically-induced fire) are due to embellishments made the author of the associated biblical accounts.[10]

While Parfitt's theory is indeed fascinating, there are gaps in his hypothesis. First, he simultaneously distrusts the biblical accounts as being accurate but at the same time he favorably compares all the shared virtues of both Arks. Second, a main function left unexplained is the Lemba Ark's SONOROUS capacity whereas the Jewish Ark has no such capacity. Third, the contention that the Lemba tribe actually protected a sacred drum is based on oral traditions of the Buba clan. So, the evidence we have to leverage that the Lemba Ark is the actual Ark of the Covenant are tribal stories and a supposed facsimile of the original Lemba Ark.

Around the time Parfitt discovered the ngoma lungundu and was publishing his theory, an archaeologist from the Hebrew University of Jerusalem, Yosef Garfinkel, was beginning an excavation of the ruins of the ancient walled city of Khirbet Qeiyafa (Elah Fortress) about 18 miles southwest of Jerusalem. Among the relics found were two small boxes, one made of clay (roughly 8 inches square) and the other of chalk stone (roughly 14 x 7 x 7 inches). They are believed to be miniature representations of portable shrines of Solomon's Temple because they share similar features (e.g., two pillars, two guardian lions, triple-recessed doorway). The fortress city is believed to have been erected around 1020 – 980 BCE (Iron 1 Age) which was about a century **before** the Solomon Temple was built. Amazingly, the physical similarities of the relics to depictions of the Solomon Temple suggest that the temple's design was based-off of these model shrines and not vice-versa. Garfinkel believes that these model shrines may also have contained models of the Ark of the Covenant (though none were actually found). Having such portable shrines allowed the ordinary people of the day to practice their Jewish faith in the presence of physical embodiment of Yahweh's sacred covenant.[11]

This new evidence provides corroboratory evidence to Parfitt's theory that it was customary for Jewish people to make artifacts that could be used in ritualistic practices to honor the Ark of the Covenant. Neither of the theories necessarily displaces the possibility that the Ark of the Covenant created during the time of Moses could have existed then or now. But, given that there are two different designs of the Ark reported in the Bible—one highly ornate, crafted with great precision and one a simple wooden box—and because other supposed facsimiles have been found are of simplistic design, it is more plausible that the highly ornate 'Exodus-version' never existed. What we can conclude is that original biblical Ark of the Covenant has never been found and if it existed, was never infused with God's earthly presence and destructive radiative powers. Rather, it was a sacred, but not supernatural, symbol for early Jews to offer worship to in remembrance of Yahweh's covenant to Moses.

THE BONES OF JOHN THE BAPTIST

As the Forerunner to Jesus, John the Baptist figures prominently in the New Testament Gospels and book of Acts. He is mentioned ninety times, more often than any other individual with the exception of his cousin Jesus of Nazareth and the Apostle Paul. John was an apocalyptic Jewish preacher that fervently evangelized that mankind must change their focus from worldly concerns in favor of returning to a pious and servile life honorific of the Jewish God. He, of course, is most notable for anointing Jesus in the Jordan River and for his decollation (beheading) by the decree of Roman Tetrarch Herod Antipas.

Because of John the Baptist's role in galvanizing Jesus as the new leader of the movement that John himself pioneered, he is revered as a prophet by Muslims, as a saint by Eastern Orthodox, Roman Catholic, and Protestant/Evangelical Christians and honored in many other traditions. Many have laid claim to possessing relics of the historical luminary, especially his skeletal remains which are highly prized. According to an estimate proffered by Oxford University archaeologist Georges Kazan in 2014, there are 36 skull fragments that are claimed to be those of John the Baptist. While it remains unclear how many of these fragments could be authentically attributed to a single individual, it is clear that they once belonged to a plurality of people.[12] Thus, some number of these bone fragments, if not all, are inauthentic.

Bulgarian archaeologists excavating the ruins of a 5th- or perhaps 6th-century CE monastery on St. Ivan Island—a small, rough-hewn coastal lump of land cresting a hundred feet out of the Black Sea just off of Sozòpol, Bulgaria—found an alabaster (marble) reliquary sarcophagus embedded beneath an altar. The box was small, about 8 x 4 x 4 inches,[13] and contained six human and three animal bone fragments.[14] The human remnants were of a cranium, a facial bone, a tooth, a rib, an ulna (forearm), and a knucklebone from a right hand.[14] Adjacent to the marble box was a smaller six-inch long box made of a type of volcanic rock called *tuff*[14] with a Greek inscription—"God, save your servant Thomas. To St. John. June 24."[13] The monastery's patron saint was St. John the Baptist, so this discovery on July 28, 2010 by archaeologists Kazimir Popkonstantinov and Rossina Kostova naturally led to the hypothesis that the bones were potentially those of the man who baptized Jesus of Nazareth. The date of June 24 is especially significant because it is the purported birth date of John the Baptist based upon the New Testament Lucan account that states that Jesus was born six months after John.

Kazan traces the sketchy serial relocation of the evangelist's remains from the hillside fortress of Machaerus (Jordan, east of the Dead Sea) where John the Baptist had been beheaded.[4] Disciples are said to have collected his remains and placed them in a tomb. The trail goes immediately cold for over 300 years until a claim is made that the bones resided in a monastery in the town of Sebaste (Palestine). In 361 CE the monastery was raided by

---

4. It should be clarified that while John the Baptist was an evangelist, he is not to be confused with John the Evangelist who some regard as the author of the Gospel of John. Though, it will be noted later in this book, that the Gospel of John was likely written by multiple authors in stages, one of whom could ostensibly have been John the Evangelist.

pagans and the bones were burned and scattered. What was left was ferreted away to be placed under the protection of the emerging Catholic Church Fathers (e.g., Athanasisus– Bishop of Alexandria who will be discussed in subsequent chapters) and various Roman emperors until they came to rest in Constantinople (present-day Istanbul, Turkey).[15] The bones were kept in a marble reliquary generally matching the type found in Sozòpol. With Constantinople being located only 125 miles away from Sozòpol, it is feasible that the bones could have been moved to the Black Sea island for safekeeping.

The bones were genetically and radiologically tested. Genetic tests performed by the University of Copenhagen enabled DNA extraction from three of the human bones. The radiocarbon C-14 dating of the bones was left to Oxford University archaeologist Thomas Higham who, in 2012, determined that only the knucklebone contained enough collagen to acquire a reliable result. These two sets of studies demonstrated with a high degree of certainty that at least three of the human bones were from the same person, a male, most likely of Middle Eastern descent, and of an age that is consistent with the time period of John the Baptist. However, because there is no comparative DNA profile for John the Baptist, it can never be confirmed that the bones are those of this historic and idolized man.[13, 14, 16]

Another unexplained oddity is that the three largest bones were much older and non-human. It was discerned that the bones were from livestock (a sheep, a cow, and a horse) and were approximately four centuries older than the human bones. Higham theorizes that the reason the animal bones were added to the collection of bones was to make the collection more visually substantive given that the human bone fragments were each very small in size.[14] Further complicating efforts to authenticate relics of this nature are that religious objects of all kinds were brought to the battlefield. Some artifacts were brought by individuals for simple worship much as people today would wear a crucifix around their neck. Other, more powerful talismans (e.g., sainted bones) were used to rally troops as conduits of God's power or to simply convince warriors that God was on their side. Because there was such a great demand for powerful religious objects, forgery of such objects was commonplace, particularly in the Middle Ages. The net result is that there is a line of evidence permitting a limited degree of plausibility that the Sozòpol bones are authentically those of John the Baptist but it is not something that could be considered a historical fact.

THE TRUE CROSS, CRUCIFIXION, AND THE (INITIAL) TOMB OF JESUS

Ostensibly, no biblically-oriented archaeological review would be considered complete without an obligatory mention of the True Cross, the actual cross upon which Jesus was crucified. History tells us that Helena, a very pious Christian who would later be venerated as a saint, and mother of the first Christian Emperor Constantine I, embarked on a pilgrimage across the Holy Land c. 325 CE to locate this all-important symbol of the Christian religion. The journey itself was an amazing feat in and of itself given that she was a woman in her late seventies. In 130 CE, the city of Jerusalem was laid to waste by Roman Emperor Hadrian. Hadrian changed the name of the city to Aelia Capitolina and erected the pagan Temple of Venus in 135 CE to cover the exact site where Jesus was crucified on the hill of Calvary—also called Golgatha—just outside the city's walls. Helena, accompanied by Macarius, the Bishop of Jerusalem, ordered the demolition of the Temple of Venus and is credited with having discovered Jesus' hillside tomb and the three crosses (the True Cross and those of the two thieves crucified with Jesus). The site is now home to the Church of the Holy Sepulchre which houses both Calvary and what is purported to be the initial rock-hewn tomb of Jesus from which his body disappeared.

What some today might perceive to be a sacrilegious act, Empress Helena is said to have had the True Cross divided into many pieces in the interest of dispersing them across the far reaches of the Roman realm so that all might share a more direct physical connection to the death and resurrection of Christ Jesus. Since then, many hundreds, perhaps a thousand, slivers and fragments are claimed to be authentic pieces of the Wood of the Cross. It has been reported that c. 326 CE Helena saved three special relics for herself which she brought back to Rome—a piece of the *Titulus Crucis*, three nails, and a fragment of the wooden cross.[17] The *Titulus Crucis* (Latin for 'Title of the Cross') was the tablet placed at the top of Jesus' cross which read "Jesus the Nazarene King of the Jews" (translated from Latin). Since the decline of the Roman empire, there were several reports that the tablet existed, however, a tablet matching the description did not physically appear until it was accidentally found during church renovations of The Basilica of the Holy Cross in Jerusalem in 1492.[18] Hidden behind a mosaic brick bearing the inscription "TITULUS CRUCIS" was a lead box containing a fragmented tablet made of walnut wood. On the wood are inscribed three successive lines of text, each line containing the word "Nazarene"—the top line in Hebrew, the middle line in Greek, and lower line Latin. Some have attempted to authenticate the tablet's date of fabrication by using comparative paleographic techniques,[17, 19, 20] which suggests a date between the 1st- and 4th-century. Some have identified "methodological holes" in such implementations saying that, "They base most of their argument on negative rather than positive evidence [... and] weave an imaginative narrative of the Titulus' history, to restore it to a 'spectrum of historical probability.' ",[21] among other more specific critiques. Radiocarbon C-14 testing indicates a date of 980 – 1146 CE with a 95.4 percent probability.[22] The greatest likelihood is that this tablet relic is not the authentic original from the True Cross but may be a replica or outright forgery.

Many supposed True Cross fragments are held by religious institutions and enshrined in churches. The relics attract a lot of visitors hoping to glimpse evidence associated with the human life of Jesus of Nazareth. However, few fragments have been independently validated by scientific dating methods or tested for speciation of the wood. Historians do not agree on what type of wood the True Cross was made from, but suggest it could be acacia, cedar, pine, cypress, or olive wood. In years past, radiocarbon dating was prohibitively expensive which would explain why claimants have not funded such measures to gain scientific validation. But this is no longer the case. The cost to conduct such test series is on the order of five hundred to a few thousand dollars depending on the institution accessed, along with a sacrifice of a few dozen milligrams of the wood fragment. It would seem to be a matter of economics (i.e., a loss of tourism) and the risk of embarrassment why the numerous articles are not being subjected to scientific assessment. In the end, even if the relics could be dated to the first-century, there is no feasible means to reliably determine if they were a constituent of the cross the Christian Savior died upon.

A related issue is that we are not even certain of the historical prevalence of crucifixion by the Romans in the 1st-century. In more ancient times, execution by impalement was enacted in various modalities by the Assyrians, Persians, Carthaginians, Greeks, Hasmoneans, Macedonians, and Phoenicians. Initially, people were run-through with a sharpened pole and then the pole and victim were vertically inclined. Seeking to extend the agony, the Romans are said to have evolved this torture technique into what we now call crucifixion.

Our knowledge of persecution by the Romans is gained almost exclusively from literary accounts. Many know of the bloodletting meted out by the Roman Army in the renowned story of Spartacus where in 71 BCE the Romans are said to have lined the 120-mile stretch of the Appian Way from Rome to Capua with the crucified remains of the 6,000 captured Spartans. Roman crucifixion is also featured in Christian literary sources such as the Bible and by Christian **APOLOGIST** Justin Martyr (*The First Apology*, c. 156 CE) as well as by the non-Christian writings of Mara bar Sarapion who was an Assyrian Stoic philosopher who was imprisoned by the Romans. It was in one of his letters he mentions the killing of a Jewish wise king. In the same general timeframe of Justin Martyr's work, Roman crucifixion is also noted by Romano-Syrian satirist and pagan, Lucian (*Death of Peregrinus*, c. 165 CE). These two latter references are further discussed in Chapter 6, but for now it is sufficient to point out that these specific narratives lack the backing of any physical evidence.

There are only three independent sources of archaeological evidence that validate the practice of Roman crucifixion. The most well-known source was the discovery in 1968 in Giv'at ha-Mivtar (Jerusalem) of an **OSSUARY** bearing the name *"Yohanan Ben Ha'galgol."*

Ossuaries are rectangular-shaped lidded storage receptacles for bones made from hard limestone or chalk (soft limestone). Inside was a 2,000 year-old heel bone of a man between 24-28 years of age that is pierced by a single 11.5 cm iron nail. The nail point itself contains fragments of olive wood. Between the bone and the head of the nail is a fragment of acacia wood which, in its full embodiment, was a slab of wood placed across the top of the feet to presumably prevent the condemned from freeing his foot by sliding it over the nail.

Film producer Simcha Jacobovici, of *Nails and the Cross, Biblical Conspiracies: Secrets of the Crucifixion, The Lost Tomb of Jesus,* and *Exodus Decoded* fame, documents that it is a rarity to find nails associated with burial sites. He notes that of 1,417 ossuaries sourced from hundreds of Jerusalem tombs, only 39 Roman nails have been found. Of the 39 nails, only two have been found inside an ossuary burial box.[23] One of these is the nail found in the heel bone discussed above and the other was found inside the ornately crafted Caiaphas ossuary. This latter ossuary, discovered in southern Jerusalem in 1990, was among six intact and six broken ossuaries and three lids—all found inside a single burial chamber. At this burial site two nails had been found, one inside the Caiaphas ossuary and the other lying outside of it in close proximity. It has been argued that the ossuary is that of none other than the Sadducee high priest Joseph Caiaphas who presided over the arrest and trial of Jesus and worked with Pontius Pilate to consign Jesus to death by crucifixion for his blasphemy and sedition. Because the inscription on the ossuary read *"Joseph bar* [son of] *Caiaphas,"* it is possible that it could be that of the high priest or that of his grandson or grandfather. Jacovobici and his collaborators spent five years investigating and scientifically verifying that the two nails were in fact unequivocally affiliated with the high priest Caiaphas himself.[24, 25] What is so astounding about the Caiaphas ossuary and its contents is that it is **the only archaeological evidence in existence that can be affirmatively tied to a specific person called-out in the New Testament Gospels**.

Studies using an electron microscope detected that traces of cedar wood were fused to one of the nails. This led to Jacobovici's hypothesis that the nails associated with the Caiaphas ossuary could be the very nails used to crucify Jesus of Nazareth on the True Cross. It is conjectured by Jacobovici that Caiaphas commanded that the nails be buried with his body because he was wracked with guilt over his involvement in Jesus' death.

Jacovobici and his fellow researchers were also afforded access to a different nail with Roman heritage. This third source of evidence for the practice of Roman crucifixion is a nail that is lodged into a hand bone and is the only evidence ever found of a nail driven through a hand.[26] The hand was determined to belong to Antigonus II Mattathias, the last King of Israel, who was tortured, crucified, and beheaded by the Romans in 37 BCE by

Marc Antony who was bribed by Roman King Herod I to have Antigonus executed. Contravening all prior thought, the evidence indicated that the nail was driven through the upper portion of the back of the hand and not through the wrist or front palm of the hand. This led Jacovobici to the conclusion that **most Roman crucifixions were conducted with the victim facing the cross**. Their studies showed this configuration would prolong the victim's agony while also proving to be expeditious for the Roman executioners to nail the victim on the cross and erect them with the least difficulty. Given that the hand was nailed with the palm contacting the wood and the nail through the back of the hand, they determined that the most tenable shape for the cross was X-shaped and not the T-shaped cross that has been emblematically displayed throughout Christendom. The X-cross would be presumably leaned against a vertical post already staked into the ground. *This startling evidence means that Jesus of Nazareth may well have been crucified on an X-shaped cross.*

While the sum total of evidence probably weighs in favor that crucifixions did actually occur at the hands of the Romans in the 1st-century, there is cumulatively no evidence that Jesus of Nazareth can be connected to the True Cross fragments. Furthermore, while there is a line of plausible rationale that the nails found in and around the Caiaphas ossuary *might* be those used to affix Jesus of Nazareth to his cross, there is no tangible evidence literarily, archaeologically, or otherwise that would support the notion that Caiaphas did indeed want to be buried with the nails from Jesus' crucifixion. In short, excluding literary narratives, we have no direct physical evidence for the long-presumed crucifixion of Jesus of Nazareth.

THE MYSTERIOUS BURIAL SHROUDS OF JESUS

Among the full compendium of discovered biblical artifacts, the most enigmatic and controversial is undoubtedly the Shroud of Turin, the purported burial cloth of Jesus Christ. As the most scientifically-investigated religious object of all time, this 14 foot long and three-and-a-half foot wide blood-stained linen cloth has garnered its own field of study entitled *Sindonology* and amounts to one of history's greatest unsolved mysteries. The feverish speculation is always high and only rises as 'fresh evidence' is brought forward. The woven linen cloth, determined to be manufactured in the Middle East, probably of Syrian heritage, bears a nearly imperceptible imprinted image of a naked, bearded, mustachioed, physically-tortured man whose back was laid to rest on top of the fabric with the loose end draped around the crown of the head and across the front side of the body. It is only when viewing a negative photographic image that the "Man of the Shroud" is instantly recognizable.[5] One of the most striking attributes is that the penetration depth of the brownish coloration forming the human outline extends superficially to the first two microfibers of the outermost surface. To provide an idea of how astonishingly thin this layer is it should be remarked that a single thread is constituted by some 200 microfibers. The coloration also displays a gradient in intensity which further suggests that the darkest regions are those that would have been in direct contact with the body and the lighter regions is where there is a lessening of such contact.[27]

Sindonology can be loosely segmented into disciplinary investigative techniques entailing historical, chemical, biological, medical, and image-based procedures. The greatest equivocation relates to the methods used to date the age of the Shroud. The radiological carbon-14 testing first performed in 1988 firmly concluded that the Turin Shroud was a medieval forgery estimating its date of production to c. 1260 – 1390 CE.[28] This claim has been regularly contested. The source of some of this debate revolves around the fact that the Shroud had suffered thermal damage in several fire-related incidents. In 1534 the Sisters of the Poor Clare nunnery at Chambéry (France) were asked by Cardinal Louis de Gorrevod to mend the Shroud by stitching the backside of fire-damaged areas with a material called Holland cloth. Further repairs were made throughout history in an attempt to conserve the cloth. A question was raised whether or not the 1988 C-14 sample was taken from a repaired section which may not at the time have been detected. Refuting this idea, the official report of the dating process plainly states that the sample was extracted from a single source location free from fire damage or prior repairs.[28] Various subsequent investigations and interpretations continued to inject doubt in the 1988 results. In 2010 researchers from the University of Arizona, the same institution where the original 1988 **ARCHAEOMETRY** was undertaken had re-examined unused fibers that had been retained by the university unbeknownst to many. They concluded that there was no evidence of dyes or coatings and that only minor contaminants could be observed, strongly suggesting that the 1988 C-14 sample was not derived from a repaired section of the cloth and that the original results were left untroubled.[29]

In *The Mystery of the Shroud* (Rizzoli, 2013)[30, 31] and *The Shroud of Turin: First Century after Christ!* (Pan Stanford, 2015)[32], Giulio Fanti *et al.* outline how three new tests have provided an alternative age to the Shroud. The source of the test material was trapped dust particles found in the vacuum filter when the Shroud samples were taken from buttock region on the backside of the Shroud in 1978.[33] Fanti used two spectroscopy methods—Attenuated Total

---

5. A negative photographic image is one where the lightest areas are made to appear as the darkest and vice-versa the dark areas made to appear to be the lightest.

Reflection Fourier Transform Infrared Spectroscopy (ATR-FTIR) and Raman Spectroscopy—to measure the amount of cellulose and particulates in the cellulose. This information combined with the degradation rate of cellulose could be used to date the Shroud. The ATR-FTIR method estimated the age of the Shroud to be 300 BCE ± 400 years. The Raman Spectroscopy tests provided a fairly similar result with a date of 200 BCE ± 500 years.

Fanti's third method of age estimation involved the measurement of multiple micro-mechanical properties of flax fibers (e.g., breaking strength, compressibility/stiffness, and energy efficiency of the fibers). He performed the same set of test protocols on nine ancient textile specimens of known provenance between 3000 BCE and 1000 CE and on two modern specimens to generate a calibration curve that characterized the degradation properties in relation to the age of the specimens. He then acquired the same characteristic data for the Shroud's fibers and compared it to the calibration curve. This series of tests provided a much more recent date of 400 CE ± 400 years indicating the cloth was manufactured as early as the birth of Jesus of Nazareth or about eight centuries later.[33] All the dates have a reported 95-percent confidence level. Taking the ATR-FTIR results as an example, this is to say that we can be 95-percent sure that the actual date lies between 700 BCE and 100 CE. Fanti points out that when all three methods are considered, the average date is 33 BCE ± 250 years.[32, 34, 35] While this average estimate brackets the time period of Jesus' death, this has to be viewed with an abundance of caution as it has very limited meaning in this context. What Fanti fails to point out is that one can also infer from the same data that the full range of potential dates—*all equally probable*—spans fifteen centuries from 700 BCE to 800 CE! Monsignor Cesare Nosiglia of Turin, the Archbishop of Turin and current Vatican curator of the Shroud, did not put much stock into Fanti's results because the source of the dust particles could not be validated that they had originated from the Shroud.

Among other key findings, the SEROLOGY of the stained fibers is suggestive that the blood is type AB (not type A, B, or O), though it is not certain if all the blood originates from the same source host. The only organisms known to possess the AB blood type are humans, gibbons, and orangutans. In 2010, a new serological test involving the characterization of the human antigen Glycophorin A was commercialized. This test is able to unequivocally distinguish human blood from animal blood.[36, 37] Such tests have not been performed because several milliliters worth of dried blood is necessary and access to the Shroud is currently prohibited. While immunological and DNA profiling has been performed, the testing is unable to discern wheter the DNA is from blood or some other type of DNA-bearing host cell. The testing is also stymied from the inability to follow good protocols to re-test the blood for repeatability purposes and because only a localized site was sampled.[38]

In spite of the many investigational approaches that the Shroud has been subjected to, just as in the case of John the Baptist's skeletal relics, most will agree that there is little hope of ever authenticating the cloth as belonging to the historical Jesus of Nazareth. Considering the tortured history of testing protocols and verification efforts from 1978 to the present, the contention that the Shroud was fabricated in the 14th-century CE can only be weakly attested to. The program of effort entailing the 1988 radiological tests is flawed in various ways. In terms of site selection, due to politically-oriented and conservation-oriented concerns, only a single location of the Shroud was examined. While the single sample was cut into multiple pieces so it could be tested by three independent labs, adjacently-located samples should also have been taken to increase the reliability of the results. And the most egregious error of all was that multi-site samples were not taken. This was due in large part to the insistence of the Vatican-appointed scientific advisor to constrain degradative investigative efforts (e.g., removal of material) to an absolute minimum. Without multiple samples from the same general site and from across the spread of the cloth, the reliability of the 1988 results lacks enough credibility to be considered scientifically valid. What can be said of the 1988 carbon-14 testing is that the data is suggestive of a medieval date for the Shroud, but it cannot be considered fully conclusive.

Furthermore, radiocarbon techniques have since improved. Even if dating of the Shroud by C-14 or spectroscopy methods could indisputably place its origin to Jesus' time, the historical traceability and efficacy to preserve its physical condition has been poor for the majority of its existence. And, should future serology and DNA testing confirm that the material on the cloth is the blood of a single human male, there is no current DNA profile for Jesus of Nazareth to match it to. Future DNA tests could compare the data with the DNA tests of genetic material from the bones found on St. Ivan Island to see if there is a familial connection. As we will learn in the next section, there is a chance that we already know where to obtain familial genetic traces of Jesus of Nazareth... and potentially, the actual skeletal remnants of Jesus himself!

Much could be learned in short order if the reticent Msgr. Cesare Nosiglia would authorize further scientific study of the cloth. It would appear that conservational concerns of a holy relic and the real risk of reinforcing the original findings of the 1988 commission are barriers enough to stonewall further investigations. The Catholic Church's official stance is neutral on whether the burial cloth is that of Jesus. In Easter comments alluding to Fanti's publication, Pope Francis remarked, "This image, impressed upon the cloth, speaks to our heart [...]

This disfigured face resembles all those faces of men and women marred by a life which does not respect their dignity, by war and violence which afflict the weakest... And yet, at the same time, the face in the shroud conveys a great peace; this tortured body expresses a sovereign majesty."[39, 40]

Long considered a forgery, the Oviedo Sudarium (Shroud of Oviedo), was the face cloth noted in John 20:6-7 that was placed atop the face of the deceased Nazarene. Over the course of history, the face cloth had been moved from Palestine, to various places in northern Africa, to multiple places in Spain, often to evade its loss to foreign invaders. New evidence has been gathered to attest to its authenticity. In 2015, a Spanish research group from the Catholic University of Murcia concluded that the face cloth contained a grain of plant pollen from the species *Helicrysum* which can also be found on the Turin Shroud. Use of this botanical is well known to have been used for cosmetic purposes in the Middle East for thousands of years and as a Jewish burial treatment in the first century of the Christian era. The face cloth also contains human blood stains as verified by mitochondrial DNA profiling. It is also determined that the blood on the face cloth had been deposited at the same time as the Helicrysum pollen and in a geometric pattern consistent with the stains found on the Turin Shroud (some 120 matching touch points) and is also of blood type AB.[41] The combination of these factors alter the calculus significantly to the effect that the face cloth is most likely the authentic companion cloth to the Turin Shroud. The Oviedo Sudarium is reliably placed to be made no later than 570 CE and could be of greater age. The scientific connection between the cloths indicates that the age of the Shroud of Turin would be at least as old as 570 CE going against the 1988 carbon dating findings. Further serology, genetic, and carbon testing could unequivocally determine the relationship between the two cloths. It is chiefly a matter of acquiring the necessary samples and the observance of strict scientific protocols. Alas, there are no plans to undertake this endeavor.

While much investigatory research has not been mentioned in regard to possible mechanism(s) of fabrication of the Shroud, some argue that no single result should be considered as fully authoritative. But who is to say whether all the evidences are equal or that one should be weighted more than another? More practically speaking, the history of the Shroud is undeniably dotted with improper care and handling right from the beginning. If only the Sheet (as it is commonly referred to in Sindonology) could have been the benefactor of the over-zealous protection that it enjoys from its current conservators, could there have been a better than even chance of deducing whether this artifact was the product of a phenomenal artist. The best opportunity to authenticate the Shroud would come about by the Vatican curator permitting multi-site testing for each of the present-day methodologies available in serology, carbon dating, and DNA profiling. It does not seem to me that, if careful protocols were to be observed, that the removal of a few fibers at each of a few dozen locations across the entire cloth would significantly degrade the preservation of the Shroud or the Oviedo Sudarium. This data would go far in clarifying the origins and authenticity of the burial cloths. For the time being, the wisest course of action is to take the neutral position until additional, more effectively managed, unbiased investigations can be undertaken.

THE TALPIOT TOMB, JAMES OSSUARY, AND LOST FAMILY TOMB OF JESUS THE NAZARENE

The familial relationships of Jesus are a source of continual disagreement. Roman Catholic doctrine teaches that Mary, the mother of Jesus, was a perpetual virgin making Jesus her sole child. On the other hand, the majority of non-Catholic biblical scholars and historians contend that Jesus did indeed have male and female blood siblings and/or half-siblings whether by Joseph or some other husband to Mary either pre- or post-Joseph. Enter the biblical figure *James the Just* who ecclesiastical Catholics say is the cousin of Jesus and others propound is a brother (or half-brother) of Jesus. He is also one of the contenders for having authored the New Testament book of James. James becomes prominent after the death of Jesus as the recognized successor of the Jewish movement sparked by John the Baptist and continued by Jesus. Until the last few decades, we have understood the familial structure of Jesus solely through fragmentary literary sources and have lacked *any* artifactual evidence to help deduce the truth or otherwise clarify the matter.

Fast-forward to the 1980 epic discovery of the Talpiot Tomb A (sometimes referred to as the "Garden Tomb") in East Jerusalem that upon excavation contained ten ossuaries.[6] A year later, about 45 meters away, seven additional ossuaries were discovered in an adjacent "patio" tomb (Talpiot Tomb B). It was a widespread funerary custom among Jews of Judaea from approximately 20 BCE (some sources put it at 30 BCE) to the Roman Siege of Jerusalem in 70 CE to practice *ossilegium* (secondary burial). Initially the deceased is placed into a temporary tomb and once the soft tissue had fully decomposed (roughly one year's time), the skeletal remains are relocated into an ossuary and the bone box is placed at its final resting place inside a family tomb.[42] It was also the case that the bones of multiple bodies could be placed into a single ossuary as a means to save space in the tomb and/or reduce the cost of burial. For individuals or families lacking the financial means, the deceased were buried in earthen field graves.

---

6. A second tomb was also discovered in the same general area in 1980 but it had largely been decimated by a dynamite blast by the Solel Boneh Construction company who was in the preparatory steps of constructing a new condominium complex.

According to the Israel Antiquities Authority (IAA), which at the time of the tomb's discovery was called the Israel Department of Antiquities, at least 35 bodies were interred in the Garden Tomb. Of these, 13 were located inside ossuaries[43] and the remainder were found lying in niches, shelves, or scattered on the floor. The disorderly nature of the Tomb A cave objects indicated that it was disturbed presumptively in the distant past.[44] All ten ossuaries in the Garden Tomb contained highly-degraded bones. **However, in accordance with standard practices, the Israeli government conveyed the bone matter found inside the ossuaries to Orthodox religious authorities for reburial in 1994.** At the time, ultra-Orthodox Jews believed it was a violation of Jewish law to tamper with ancestral remains, so no analysis of the bones was conducted. It is also the case that the bulk of the bone matter was probably placed into an unmarked grave making subsequent recovery and re-identification exceptionally unlikely.

Not long after the initial discovery of the Garden Tomb, the Tenth Ossuary (IAA catalogue #80-509) was stolen, discarded, or misplaced—no one knows for sure. All we know about the Tenth Ossuary is that it had a plain undecorated exterior façade with no inscriptions and measured 60 x 26 x 30-cm (roughly 24 x 10 x 12 inches).[45, 46] Six of the remaining nine ossuaries had EPIGRAPHS in the form of names, five of which were written in Hebrew or Aramaic and the other written in Greek. These names are provided in Table 4-1. Two epigraphs included reference to ancestral relationships, the first bearing the words *Yehudah bar Yeshua* (translated as '**Judah, son of Jesus**'–refer to Table 4-1–Ossuary 2) and the other ossuary inscribed with *Yeshua bar Yehoseph* (translated as '**Jesus, son of Joseph**' – refer to Table 4-1 – Ossuary 4). As one will recall, the Bible tells us that Jesus' father was named Joseph. Debated for some time was whether or not the inscribed Hebrew characters for "Yeshua" (translated as 'Jesus') were even present on Ossuary 4 due to the poor legibility of the inscription and if this word was in fact present, whether it was being correctly interpreted. Epigrapher Frank M. Cross of Harvard University among others have since provided their IMPRIMATUR that the characters are verifiably present and are to be interpreted as Yeshua (i.e., Jesus).[45] But does this specifically refer to Jesus the Nazarene?

This astounding connection of names has naturally led to the spectacular claim that the Talpiot Tomb A is that of Jesus of Nazareth and his family. Furthermore, it was hypothesized that Jesus may have had a son which has never been noted in any historical literary source. It would also suggest that his bones were moved sometime after Easter Sunday from the initial rock-cut tomb near Calvary. As noted earlier, a relocation of the bones to a second and final resting place would be entirely consistent with Jewish burial customs in the 1st-century CE. And, furthermore, such a claim would not by itself negate the claim that Jesus had been initially placed in a rock-hewn tomb. **If the skeletal remains were that of the**

Nazarene, then Jesus was not bodily resurrected, which sharply contrasts with Christian doctrine that fervently believes he was resurrected from the empty tomb—body, mind, and spirit—as reported in the four canonical gospels (i.e., Matthew, Mark, Luke, and John).

Table 4-1 provides a listing of the Talpiot ossuaries of the purported family of Jesus. There is little agreement on whether one of the ossuaries (Ossuary 1 / IAA #80-500) is that of Jesus' disciple Mary Magdalene. If this was her burial box, then it is postulated by some scholars that she may have been both a disciple *and* wife of Jesus. But, of the six inscribed ossuaries found in the cave, the epigraphical characters and their possible meanings remain hotly contested and there appears that there is no credible means to authoritatively determine an unequivocal truth to the matter. Alternative interpretations suggest that the inscribed characters on IAA #80-500 say "Mariam and Martha" or possibly "Mariamne and Martha" meaning that the ossuary contains two persons. A third possible translation of the Greek characters is "Mariamne's Mara" inferring that Mara (short for Martha) is the daughter of Mariamne.

With this newly found archaeological data, some have sought to characterize the statistical probability that the cluster of inscribed names on the six Garden Tomb ossuaries and the various interpretations therein could be the final resting place of Jesus and his family. Engineering professor Kevin Kilty and religious studies professor Mark Elliott conducted such an analysis utilizing Bayes' Theorem (this statistical approach is explained in later chapters). Their study concluded that the probability that the epigraphical names are that of the Jesus family is 47% if it is assumed that the name "Yoseh" (refer to Table 4-1 – Ossuary 5) is a rare Jewish name and that this individual is the brother of Jesus. However, if it is assumed that "Yoseh" is a variant of the common name Joseph, then the prediction outcome is only 3%.[48]

Given the uncertainties of the assumptions, their initial efforts were not all too convincing. It should also be noted that statistics by itself cannot yield the pivotal distinction that the names are those of a relational family. We could conjecture that the tomb belonged to multiple families. While this is probably less likely given burial customs of the day, it is still within the realm of possibility. As it turned out, some of the ossuaries contained small bone fragments, chips no larger than a pinky fingernail. In 2005, at the behest of Simcha Jacobovici and Jewish Studies professor James Tabor, Dr. Carney Matheson of the Paleo-DNA Lab at Lakehead University in Ontario conducted DNA tests on bone fragments from Ossuaries 1 and 4 (refer to Table 4-1). **It is profound to say the least that these skeletal remains could be the very bones of Jesus of Nazareth and Mary Magdalene.** Due to the degraded state of the bone material, nuclear DNA testing proved unsuccessful. However, reliable results were obtained from mitochondrial DNA testing

Table 4-1. The Talpiot "Tomb A" (Garden Tomb) Ossuaries and the James Ossuary

(Sources: Charlesworth[47] and Kloner[46])

Present Author's Numbering	IAA #	Exterior Façade	Native Inscription	English Translations and possible alternatives
1	80-500	Ornamented	Mariamene[1] kai Mara[2] or alternatively Mariamenou e Mara	One Person: Mary Magdalene Two Persons: Mariam[ne] and Martha Family Relation: Mariamne's [daughter] Mara
2	80-501	Ornamented	Yehudah bar Yeshua	Judah, son of Jesus
3	80-502	Plain	Matya [or Mata]	Matthew[3]
4	80-503	Plain	Yeshua bar Yehoseph	Jesus, son of Joseph
5	80-504	Plain	Yose [or Yoseh][4]	Joses[3] or alternatively, Joseph
6	80-505	Plain	Marya [or Maria]	Mary
7	80-506	Ornamented	—	
8	80-507	Ornamented	—	
9	80-508	Plain	—	
10 *Missing from Collection*	80-509	Plain	—	
11[5]	—	Plain	—	James, son of Joseph, brother of Jesus

(1) The name inscription could read "Mariamene", "Mariamne", "Mariame", "Mariam", "Maryam", or "Marya"

(2) "Mara" is translated as the contracted version of "Martha"

(3) Both Matthew and Joses are conjectured to be the brothers of Jesus

(4) "Yose" or "Yoseh" is either a rare name, or it might also mean "Joses". "Joses" might be a contracted version of Joseph, which is a very common name

(5) This is the Jame Ossuary that is allegedly a companion to the other ten Talpiot ossuaries listed in this table

which revealed that the deceased occupants were not blood related on the mother's side of the family. This presumes to an extent that there was only one occupant in Ossuary 1.

This added high-octane fuel to the fiery contention that Mary Magadalene (Ossuary 1) and Jesus (Ossuary 4) were married because why else would Mary Magdalene be buried inside Jesus' family tomb? Because nuclear DNA results could not be collected some scholars legitimately suggest an alternative idea that the deceased individual in Ossuary 4 might be the father or cousin of the deceased Mary or any number of different relations.[49] Therefore, there is an upfront limit to the probative value of such mathematically-directed endeavors. The predominant research has been focused on studying the patina created by the biological and environmental weathering of the ossuaries' interior and exterior surfaces.

Ongoing scientific research suggests that every tomb evolves into its own ecosystem whereby internal and external environmental factors and the constituent organic and inorganic materials within the tomb generate a unique geochemical signature. For the Talpiot Tomb A, it has been shown that in a given tomb there is low quantitative variability in elemental constituents (less than 5%) in the walls and ceilings, whereas adjoining tombs in the same rock formation and in close proximity demonstrate distinctly different geochemical profiles.[50] When the ossuaries were found in 1980, the cave and all the ossuaries were entombed in Rendzina soil. It is theorized that this was a result of subsidence associated with an earthquake that struck Jerusalem in 363 CE. Over time the Rendzina soil encrusted itself onto and even seeped into the porous surfaces of the ossuaries, including the interior surfaces of those where the lid was not secured.

Enter the **UNPROVENANCED** *James Ossuary* scrawled with the Aramaic words, "**James, son of Joseph, brother of Jesus**" (English translation). The bone box itself was dated by paleographer Andre Lemaire to 63 CE, so this would be the *first and only archaeological evidence in the historical record mentioning the name 'Jesus' during the time of Jesus*. Prior to this, the earliest known reference to Jesus was the Gospel fragment known as the *Rylands Papyrus* P^{52} (shortened by scholars as $\mathfrak{P}^{52}$) which dates to c. 125 – 175 CE.[51] The authenticity of the epigraph was contentiously debated ever since the ossuary publicly surfaced on October 21, 2002 (it was in circulation in the 1970's on the shadowy antiquities market) with many conjecturing that some or all characters of the epigraph was a forgery. However, in 2014, based on further archaeometric analysis of the patina and considerable pitting, researchers determined that the engraving is authentic after all.[52] However, the bigger question that remained unexplained is where this ossuary was being kept for the past two thousand years.

In an interesting twist, in 2006, archaeologist Shimon Gibson, co-Director of the 1980 Mount Zion dig of Talpiot Tomb A, hypothesized a missing eleventh ossuary.[47, 53] The dimensional size of the missing Tenth Ossuary and the James Ossuary are nearly identical with only a deviation in the length "by 3-4 cm."[50] By comparison, the dimensions of the James Ossuary are approximately 56.5 x 25.7 x 29.5 cm.[54] The variance could be attributed to the fact that the James Ossuary had been previously damaged and repaired in the length direction. The sides of the James Ossuary are not entirely parallel or even in length making it less rectangular and more trapezoidal in shape. Some have leveraged this asymmetry to say that the length dimension of the Tenth Ossuary may not have been measured in the same reference location thereby creating the disparity in measurements. However, during the well-publicized antiquities forgery trial of ossuary collector Oded Golan, he provided what would prove to be a highly pivotal photograph taken in 1976 of the James Ossuary as evidence to support his eventual acquittal. The photograph was determined by forensic investigators to be authentic. This would indicate that it would be extremely unlikely that the James Ossuary could be the one excavated in 1980 (a.k.a. the missing Tenth Ossuary) and may be in fact be the *eleventh* Talpiot ossuary hypothesized by Shimon Gibson (refer to Table 4-1 – Ossuary 11).

It should also be noted that the James Ossuary had contained significant bone matter which Golan removed and placed into a Tupperware container which, along with hundreds of other items, was also confiscated by the IAA. **The bone fragments could in theory contain genetic traces of Jesus of Nazareth** if in fact James the Just was a brother or a close enough familial relation. In late 2003, Shimon Gibson and James Tabor made an official request to conduct DNA testing on the bone fragments but it was denied based on the IAA's position that Oded Golan surreptitiously added them and that they believed they have no authentic connection to the ossuary. While the trial ended in 2012, the James Ossuary was not returned to Golan until the end of 2013 and it was not until May, 2014 that the IAA released 250-plus other confiscated items, including the Jehoash Tablet mentioned earlier in this chapter. There has been no specific mention whether the bones of the James Ossuary were returned to Golan, but one would presume that they are now back in his possession.

Both during and after the legal trial proceedings, analysis of outermost surface of the James Ossuary continued, adding strength to the theory that it could have been stored in the Talpiot Tomb A at the same time as the original ten ossuaries.[50, 55] In April of 2015, geologist Aryeh Shimron pronounced that new tests which examined the material *beneath the surface* patina provide "virtually unequivocal evidence"[56] that the James Ossuary had spent most of its existence in Talpiot Tomb A alongside the other ten ossuaries. To add credibility to his assertion he examined 25 ossuaries, 15 of which were sourced from unassociated tombs. From a battery of chemical tests, he concluded that the chemical profile of the James Ossuary and the Talpiot Tomb A possessed a comparable composition of iron, magnesium, and silicon.[57]

Tabor elaborates that Shimron also examined all nine of the Garden Tomb ossuaries along with the James Ossuary to bolster the fact the geochemical fingerprint was in fact unique to the tomb itself and the once concealed ossuaries.[56, 58] Tabor also points to the statistical work of Kilty and Elliott who modified their original statistical predictions working off of the idea that the James Ossuary was also entombed along with the other ten Talpiot Tomb A ossuaries. When making adjustments to include the seventh inscription of the James Ossuary, and assuming that "Yoseh" is a rarely-used name, the probability rises to 92% that the tomb of Jesus' family had been found.[48, 59] Likewise, if "Yoseh" is interpreted as a common variant for "Joseph," then the prediction is 32%. **By scientifically connecting the James and Talpiot ossuaries the evidences join to self-reinforce one another to effectively increase the collective explanatory power toward legitimizing the hypothesis that Jesus of Nazareth may in fact have had a family and was not resurrected bones and all**.

Some have suggested that to achieve an adequate threshold of statistical certainty that the James Ossuary could not have existed in some other tomb of a similar geochemical profile, a quarter to one-third of the 900 or so tombs built in the Herodian period and co-located in the Jerusalem area need to be examined. To achieve standard scientific measures, this is roughly suggesting that we need to randomly test between 225 to 300 tombs while stipulating a 95 percent confidence level with a margin of error of plus or minus five tombs. Because Shimron already tested 15 tombs we can knock this off the total. Scientists might also employ knowledge of soil types and other data that could further pinpoint the selection of tombs as potential candidates. By creating a sub-population of tombs, the requisite sample size decreases. However, as it turns out, such craftiness does not yield a very significant gain. Even if such tactics could rule out 600 tombs leaving a pool of 300 to consider, one would still need to examine about 170 to obtain the same 95 percent level of confidence in the results.

But all of this is somewhat conjectural because as of the printing of this book the academic world was still awaiting their opportunity to adjudicate Shimron's claims as he has not as yet published his work in a peer-reviewed periodical. His reluctance to get to press is likely related to the tsunami of scrutiny that will be applied to his work and because no one else has conducted this type of work eliminating any competitive pressure to be the first to publish his findings. It is important to keep in mind that the ossuaries *in toto* experienced a two-thousand year saga from being entombed, subject to probable looting and most definitely disarrangement, an earthquake, extensive erosive weathering, physical damage during transport, a court trial, physical damage to the patina caused by IAA forensics investigators who had used red silicon to take a mold of the James Ossuary inscription, a large number of physical tests, and 35 years of sometimes acrimonious debate.

The stakes for believer and skeptics have now eclipsed that of the awe-inspiring Turin Shroud by a wide margin. **The physical evidence is being held by some like a sword waiting to thrust mightily at the core of Christianity—calling into question Christ Jesus' celibacy, marital status, and most importantly, his resurrection and divinity. It may also lend credence to the oft-debated matter of whether Jesus the Nazarene was simply a myth or legend.**

Unless Shimron's results, if and when published, can otherwise demonstrate a sufficiently compelling case by itself, additional tomb/ossuary patina-related testing would be in order. So what if after scholars have scrutinized Shimron's work and/or more tests are performed and the verdict doesn't change? Even with substantiated geochemical data, I am very much inclined to believe two things will happen. First, it will take a decade or two at the soonest until this knowledge would become known. Second, no matter how convincing the evidence is, it will not be the same as proof positive. While all eleven ossuaries could be decisively demonstrated to have dwelled in the same tomb, the names and most importantly the relationships between the names will carry some measure of uncertainty that they belong to Jesus of Nazareth and his family.

Those skeptical of the aforementioned research forward the idea that there could be other 1st-century tombs and ossuaries that simply have not been found. These yet-to-be-found inscribed ossuaries might ostensibly contain names that would alter the statistical calculations of Kilty and Elliott. Others point to the Catholic Dominus Flevit **NECROPOLIS** located on the Mount of Olives (Jerusalem) as justification that other tomb sites have name clusters that contain the same names as that of the Talpiot Tomb. The cemetery was used for burials between 136 BCE to 300 CE and has 17 distinct tombs containing 122 ossuaries, 43 of which have inscriptions[60] bearing the (translated) names "[...] Jesus: Jonathan, Joseph, Jarius, Judah, Matthias, Menahem, Salome, Simon, and Zechariah. Many of these names appear in the New Testament records of the Early Church at Jerusalem. One ossuary contained the Greek inscription 'Iota, Chi and Beta,' which read 'Jesus Christ, the Redeemer.' "[61] This latter three-character monogram inscription (Iota-Chi-Beta) is akin in some respects to how we use the symbol of a cross or crucifix to symbolize faith in Christianity and scholars do not contend that this ossuary is that of Jesus of Nazareth.

Another interesting epigraph presents the words 'Martha and Mary' together validating the earlier statement that Jewish ossuaries sometimes contained the remains of multiple people. When all of the ossuaries of the necropolis are considered, we find among them the full collection of names that are found on the first six inscribed ossuaries (Ossuaries 1 – 6). However, none of the inscribed Dominus Flevit ossuaries contain a reference to the name 'James'. Importantly, the collection of Dominus Flevit ossuaries with the matching names are not found in the same cave site making it quite unlikely that cemetery contains the family tomb of Jesus. Of the 2,826 ossuaries discovered possessing provenance to 1st-century Jerusalem,[62] about 600 - 650 have inscriptions. However, *only three ossuaries* equating to 0.1 percent of all ossuaries that contain the combination of "Jesus, Son of Joseph" making this a rare expression.[63]

Others contend that Jesus was more likely to have been buried outside of Jerusalem. Renowned New Testament scholar and Christian apologist Craig A. Evans[7] posits that Galilee would be a more likely location for the Jesus' family tomb.[64] Of course, Galilee is where Jesus' life began, his ministry was started, and where he returned to after he learned of his John the Baptist's imprisonment. However, it is well established that his parents and siblings moved to Jerusalem prior to Jesus' death. Additionally, his brother James remained in the Jerusalem area to proselytize after his death. So, there is not a lot to grab onto here. Still others say there will never be evidence of Jesus' burial as he was treated as a political criminal and/or was poor and his body was given the rightful funerary treatment consistent with such circumstances which is an earthen trench grave. If this is true, the bones would be long since disintigrated by now.

The James Ossuary bone matter could be tested, presuming of course that it is the authentic material originally contained in the ossuary and that it is now in Oded Golan's possession. Assuming that the samples yield testable material and that testing protocols yield valid results, we may well be able to more clearly establish what relationships, if any, exist between the Talpiot Tomb occupants. This information could also be compared with the genetic data of the purported bones of John the Baptist to see if a connection exists. Furthermore, if additional serological testing of the Shroud of Turin would be permitted, it would yield more scientific data that would help adjudicate the various answers to the many open questions.

---

7. Craig A. Evans is an evangelical New Testament scholar and staunch Christian apologist. He is a distinguished Professor of New Testament at Acadia Divinity College in Nova Scotia having published works regarding early Christianity, the historicity of Jesus, and New Testament textual criticism.

Are the Eleven Talpiot Ossuaries the death knell of Jesus' divinity and final blow to the Christian conception of God!? When considered as a whole, the physical evidence in the form of the ancient bone boxes create a healthy plausibility that Jesus may well have lived and died as a human being and that his body was *not* resurrected. At the same time, it also lends support to the idea that he was not a mythic figure as some continue to contend. However, the current evidence is less conclusive about whether or not he was married and had a son or what relationship there is between the occupiers of the Talpiot Tomb A. Based on the ossuary information alone, namely the patina and statistical analyses; we cannot sit too comfortably that we have confirmed the burial container of Jesus of Nazareth. What is really holding things back is how the tomb occupants are genetically related and to a lesser degree the certainty of the epigraphical interpretations. All we can do for now is to move forward with a partially substantiated theory in hand. Having reviewed the most important religious relics from antiquity, we have arrived at a new transition point for the zetetic trek. We will now turn our full attention to the historical and literary origin of Christianity and how the three-Person Christian God arose from monotheistic Judaism, spiritual mysticism, polytheism, and an assortment of interpretations on the nature of a sociopolitcal revolutionary called Jesus Christ.

SUMMARY

Because of their tangible nature, biblical antiquities find themselves at the epicenter of the religion-science dialogue. When yoked with philology, archaeology, historiography, sociology, and other sciences, the authentication of these objects offer a lens piece to peer into our deep history. The image formed is rarely crisp as the past does not give up its secrets easily. The best we can realistically hope for is a shadowed outline that leads us step-by-step to a single hypothesis that stands above the rest.

After a great deal of investigative work, we have credibly ascertained plausible hypotheses for notable Old Testament relics, namely Noah's Ark and Moses' Lost Ark of the Covenant. In the case of the former, the evidence is quite compelling that the Genesis flood story is fictional. Somewhat less convincing but still plausible is that the Ark of the Covenant was most likely physically manifested as a simple wooden storage box or wooden drum as opposed to an ornate, golden chest. While the biblical narrative concerning the Ark of the Covenant is likely to have been a story passed down through generations until the Lemba tribe decided to build a make-shift mimic of Moses' Ark, there is no physical evidence that the golden Ark as described in Exodus ever existed.

Crossing into the Common Era, we find tangible evidence in the form of six bone fragments of a 1st-century, Middle Eastern male. While they were found in a monastery devoted to his worship, the related historical documentation is too thin to provide authoritative provenance that these belong to John the Baptist. A lack of provenance also haunts the multitude of True Cross remnants. This is also the case with the Turin Shroud and the Oviedo Sudarium but these also suffer from poorly conducted science chiefly as a result of restricted access to testable materials. In spite of 35 years of controversy, much of the nay-saying surrounding the authenticity of the Talpiot Tomb ossuaries have been put to rest. Archaeometric and statistical investigations have given a lot of weight to the idea that we may indeed have found the authentic family tomb of Jesus of Nazareth. Though, it is important to note that we have not yet closed the lid on the validity of this hypothesis.

We have the raw materials available this very instant—the Turin Shroud and its companion face cloth, access to other tombs and ossuaries, and bone matter of the James Ossuary—to rebalance the validity of the prevailing hypotheses. But, due to a general lack of will by central officiates that are able to facilitate the investigation, hopes remain dashed for those eager to catalog these long-standing mysteries as solved.

Our journey is set to take a major change in direction as we venture deeply into the philosophical and theological forest of Christian thinking and other alternative concepts. This is the province where testimonial evidence takes shape in the form of literary and oral works. There is no getting around the fact that this will be a much more difficult trek for the simple fact that the volume of information that needs to get parsed is nothing short of phenomenal. It is a land where chaos and confusion reigns supreme and there is no obvious path forward. Worry not. If you can remain focused, the underbrush will be pushed-aside and the canopy that darkens the trail will be opened-up. Together, let us take a few more steps in our journey to find what we may of God's potential existence.

CHAPTER 5

Rediscovering the Origins of Christianity

We live in a theistically inclined society. Religion preaches inviolable **CANONS** not the least of which that their God has the truest of form and that faith is the elder and wiser companion to reason, a dogma so persistent that it playfully overwhelms the unsharpened mind just as the angry wave motions the cork at its whim. The enlightened mind on the other hand swears fealty to be ever watchful—queued by each new invader, it presses into service a conscientious objector that banishes errancy before good knowledge settles into the creases of the mind.

– Present Author

The Church is not a gallery for the exhibition of eminent Christians, but a school for the education of imperfect ones.[1]

– Henry Ward Beecher
Protestant Clergyman, b. 1813 – d. 1887

Christianity is not a highly complicated collection of so many dogmas that it is impossible for anyone to know them all; it is not something exclusively for academicians who can study these things, but it is something simple: God exists and God is close in Jesus Christ.[2]

– Pope Benedict XVI
Remarks at Auronzo di Cadore (Italian Municipality), 24 July 2007

The little boat of St. Peter is beaten by many storms and tossed about upon the sea, but it grieves us most of all that, against the orthodox faith, there are now arising...more ministers of diabolical error who are ensnaring the souls of the simple and ruining them. With their superstitions and false inventions they are perverting the meaning of the Holy Scriptures and trying to destroy the unity of the catholic church. [...] And therefore by this present apostolic writing we give you a strict command that, by whatever means you can, you destroy all these heresies and expel from your diocese all who are polluted with them. You shall exercise the rigor of the ecclesiastical power against them and all those who have made themselves suspected by associating with them. They may not appeal from your judgements, and if necessary, you may cause the princes and people to suppress them with the sword.[3]

– Pope Innocent III
Letter to Archbishop of Auch (France), 1198

A Simple Belief in the Authority and Authenticity of the Bible

CHRISTIANITY HAS BEEN A BULWARK for many people and many nations, its fruit offering adherents moral guidance, a **TELLURIAN** purpose, and spiritual verve. As the source for rudimentary Christian convictions, the Christian Bible is the sacred text divided into the Old Testament, based largely on Hebrew Scriptures, and the New Testament.[1] While virtually all Christian denomination's New Testament contains the same 27 books, there is a variance in how many books are provided in the Old Testament. The Jewish Hebrew Bible (the Tanakh) contains 24 books whereas the Protestant and Catholic Old Testament contain 39 and 46 books, respectively. There are many reasons why the pedestrian Christian may feel that the Christian Bible is more or less true. The first and foremost reason is because it has withstood the test of time. The Bible also backs up Jesus' story by providing perspectives from multiple authors. There is no doubting that the message and themes are in every sense sensationally powerful. The thought that the Supreme Creator decided to become **INCARNATE** here on this one planet as it coasts around an unfathomably large universe to live among his creations is humbling. But, instead of receiving a universal love from humanity, he was humiliated and tortured to death at the hands of his creations. Add to this that billions of people have come to believe in the tenets of the faith, some so intensely that they followed his lead and martyred themselves as testament to their convictions. And then there is perhaps the greatest of reasons which is that God must be real for his existence was necessary to create our universe. Together these mutually reinforcing lines of evidence yield powerful justifications as to why we should believe in the existence of a divine Creator and that he briefly lived among us as Jesus of Nazareth.

In fact, the overwhelming majority take the arguments above as satisfactory support for their belief in the Bible. However, what we find is that the majority of people are lacking an appreciation for how the Bible and Christianity in general originated. So this sets the mark for the starting point of the next leg to our journey. In the next several chapters, we will critique the authenticity of the New Testament in an effort to understand who wrote it and why and under what social context it was written.

Interpretation of the Christian Bible and the Three Foundational Truth Claims

The Bible has been the subject of microscopic scholarly examination for many centuries and while much has been gleaned from these efforts it has done little to close the divide as

---

1. The Christian Bible is composed of the Greek Old Testament, also called the Septuagint (abbreviated as 'LXX'), and the New Testament. The Septuagint is a Greek translation of the Hebrew Bible (the Tanakh) but also includes additional texts called the Deuterocanonical books. The Deuterocanonical books are included in Orthodox and Catholic Bibles but not in most Protestant Bibles.

to how the Bible should be interpreted. Some believe the Bible to be the literal and **INERRANT** Word of God and is to be read in uncritical fashion. Others see it as a divinely inspired assemblage of texts that are authentic historical accounts. Alternatively, another contingent view it as a purely human production replete with politically **REDACTED** text consisting of a mix of mythological, allegorical, metaphorical, historical, and cultural references meant to bring unity to the congregation of the faithful. Whether any of these represent the reality of the Bible, the fact that some two billion faithful consider this a central conduit between man and God beckons us to confer judgment on the truth and utility of this book as a tool to access God's existence, nature, and intentions.

So, why is the Bible, or any set of literary sources for that matter, so difficult to figure out? Aren't the answers we seek sitting right there waiting to be lifted from the pages for us to read and understand? The short answer is that using literary sources from ages gone by to enlighten us of the *real truth* is like finding the proverbial needle in a haystack. Across the human scale of time, we have created a long list of deific agents which have been used to justify a great multitude of our individual and collective actions and to help us reason why we even exist at all. Religions are birthed to establish orthodoxy to orient us toward the correct depiction of God and are internally driven to expand and perpetuate themselves. **The inevitable clashes between other societal motivations and other religions profoundly affect the literature**. Just as in the case of biblical antiquities, literary works (original or otherwise) become lost, destroyed, damaged, altered, distorted, and forged. Writings can also be purposefully mistranslated. When literature is attributed with the intent to deceive or disguise the real author's name by attributing it to someone else or to an invented name, this is referred to as a **PSEUDONYMOUS** attribution. Literary works are also susceptible to redactions by later editors or they can be outright forgeries whereby there is an underlying intention to knowingly introduce false information. Forgers, for example, may adopt the style of a different author to pass off their work as that of the copied author.

One always has to question who the authentic author is, what their motivations are, and does their verbiage comport with what other authors have stated on the subject matter. And, every bit as important is to explain why they elected to *not* write about something central to the subject matter. Acquiring the answers turns out to be a daunting process. When examining multiple documents, typically written in different centuries, perhaps even different geographies, cultures, and languages, things get, shall we say, rather difficult to assess authenticity and **VERIDICALITY**. Hence, almost indubitably, disagreements arise as to a given text's proper interpretation and what intrinsic historical value is to be assigned to it.

Before proceeding further, a special comment may be in order. The forthcoming remarks on the Bible could presage anti-biblical or anti-Christian rebuke in the sense that some might claim there is an embedded attempt to malign the legitimacy of the Christian faith. As had been requested in Chapter 1, we need to put aside reactionary responses in favor of occupying a space of intellectual commitment to acquaint ourselves with the evidence to defend our beliefs with objectivity rather than blind faith. There is a clear difference between stating that something is not true and persecuting someone (verbally, emotionally, or physically) because of it. The first is a position of intellectual nonviolence and the latter crosses a moral boundary. Also, we need to appreciate the flip-side that injecting pro-Christian or more generally pro-religious thoughts outwardly could be perceived by nonbelievers as bias in the form discrimination against nontheists.

I recommend that we initiate our pursuit for God with the *a priori* proposition that God-by-whatever-name does not exist and to then to examine the legitimacy of religious beliefs on the basis of natural sources of evidentiary information. That is, to put aside miracles or theological suppositions as self-confirmatory evidence of a deity. The initial basis for this is two-fold. First, *Zeteo Alétheia* (the search for truth) starts with a blank slate, or as blank a slate as we humans can make it so. Second, most people will readily agree, and as much neuroscientific study supports, that it is a miscalculated assumption to suggest that our perceptive abilities yield a one-to-one correspondence with external reality. We no more have to think of a myriad of circumstances where two people seeing the same event at the exact same time (e.g., a crime in action) will have narratives of what transpired with varying degrees of accuracy. In the end, a miracle is a perceived event and much caution is warranted before we can equate miraculous events with the truth of reality. **Importantly, we evaluate Christian doctrine on its own terms**. That is, we take the beliefs as Christianity has presented it and critique the claims principally with the data disseminated by the Christian assembly to demonstrate its veracity or lack thereof.

In order to see things more clearly, we have to skin Christianity back to its purest form of unadulterated Christology in order to trace its growth from its various religious roots. To accomplish this task we must transport ourselves back 2,000 years to the beginning of the Common Era demarcation. In the next several chapters, we will take a compact tour of the vast arcane world of biblical scholarship. How vast is vast? According to Christian apologist Michael Licona's[2] assessment of the time period from 1975 to 2010 that there are 3,400

---

2. Michael Licona is an evangelical scholar regarded as a specialist in defending the resurrection. His PhD thesis is entitled *The historicity of the resurrection of Jesus: historiographical considerations in the light of recent debates.* (2009)

scholarly works[4] focused on the historicity of Jesus Christ's resurrection which does not take into account the innumerable source documents or non-academic mainstream publications. This amounts to a huge array of ideas being floated to explain how we might know that Jesus of Nazareth may or may not have been God incarnate. And this is but one of a great many topics in Christianity that is being literarily researched.

Biblical scholarship involves a mix of crafts under the umbrella term of textual scholarship.[5] Paleography is the study of ancient handwriting that seeks to decipher what a text says and to interpret it in the context of the culture. This is not to specifically interpret the textual content's meaning or how it relates to other texts, but to discern the form and the processes employed to create the text.[6] Philology is the study of language and seeks to establish the authenticity of the text in general and to restore the original meaning of the textual content itself.[7] Textual criticism is related to philology but is focused on identifying transcription/copying errors between various copies of the same text to discover what the original words were meant to be.[8] Then there is historical criticism which seeks to understand the broader meaning of the text as it relates to other pertinent texts, the authenticity of authorship and its contents, the audience to whom it was written for, the dating of the document, the text's sources, the historical context in which it was written including the culture and its location of where it was written.[9] Biblical hermeneutics is yet another area of study that generally follows in sequence relative to all the others. Hermeneutics owes its word-origin to Hermes, the Greek deity who could travel between the divine and mortal realms acting as the interpreter and messenger of the gods.

The hermeneutical (or exegetical) process applies a laundry list of principles or rules in which to interpret biblical texts. Some of these are given the names of their creators, for example, the Canons of Tischendorf, the Metzger Criteria of Internal and External Evidence, and the Twelve Basic Rules of Aland & Aland. Others are given descriptive titles such as the Law of First Mention, the Golden Rule of Interpretation, the Gap Principle, the Comparative Mention Principle, etc.[10] As is readily apparent, studying the authenticity of the Bible is a massive and meticulous endeavor. Because it is often up to the discretion of the individual scholar which principles are utilized and what relative importance they are to play it is easy to grasp why gaining consensus on historical truth is a messy affair. Scholars often seek to elevate their work, or the work of another colleague, by undermining the judgment of opposing scholars by criticizing their application of these principles. While this is fair enough, all too often the melee leaves things unresolved.

Because this book is not intended to replicate the full scope of biblical hermeneutical tools available to conduct biblical EXEGESIS, it is for the sake of convenience that I opt to call the general practice, implementation, and most importantly, the outcome of the various modalities of literary criticism as the catch-all term, *Literary Primacy*. This term shall connote in a broad sense that the text or passage of concern is to be considered as possessing the foremost authenticity and reliability.

It might also be mentioned that very little has been done in the way of scholarly criticism of the Qur'an because Muslims fundamentally believe that the sacred word of Allah should not be subjected to critique by human beings. This is to say that the Qur'an is *interpreted* by Muslim scholars, but the veracity and authenticity of Islamic Scripture is not questioned. Fundamentally, Muslims are expected by Islamic leaders to essentially maintain a fideistic or blind faith for their belief in Allah because his existence is not to be questioned and other than prophetic Scripture, no additional evidence is necessary.[3]

In the next several chapters it is my goal to employ some of the aforementioned critical techniques originating in large part from New Testament scholars to contrast the competitive visions of reality as it pertains to Christianity. Borrowing from the analogy in Chapter 1, we will be taking so thin a slice from the loaf of bread that drawing hot butter across it might tear it asunder. We will forego an interrogation of the Old Testament. This will allow us to expend our energies in the direction of the New Testament (hereafter, NT) and the many extra-biblical source materials written in the same timeframe. The goal is to gain an appreciation for the authenticity and historical reliability of the Christian Bible as a whole and to specifically burrow into the data set at hand to extricate the tiny kernels that lay bare after removal of the slice. The authenticity and reliability are most efficiently educed by directing our line of inquiry toward three essential truth claims proclaimed by Christian doctrine. The three Foundational Truth Claims of Christianity are presented in Table 5-1.

The resurrection, divinity, and position of Jesus in the Godhead represent the lodestone of Christianity. Our approach to study these claims is bidirectional whereby we will examine these claims using both the inside-out and outside-in perspectives. It may be that some readers, particularly those more interested in learning about what the latest advances of the physical sciences have to say about God, may find the rigor of EXEGETICAL study of biblical passages disinteresting or cumbersome. I implore such readers to steady themselves and bear through it as this forms one of the cornerstones of the overarching framework. For those not so disenchanted, this promises to be a journey of great enlightenment. Let us begin with some basic background concerning the Bible.

---

3. Muslims consider the Qur'an to be a divine revelation from Allah. It was transmitted orally to Muhammad through the angel Gabriel over a period of some 23 years. There is ongoing debate as to the authentic author(s) of the *written* compilation. In the standardized Qur'an, there are minor recensions to the original text.

Table 5-1. Foundational Truth Claims of Christianity
(Based on Biblical Interpretation)

1. Jesus died a natural death and was bodily resurrected.

2. Jesus is a divine Being who took human form.

3. Jesus is the Son of God, a constituent of the Holy Trinity that includes God the Father and the Holy Spirit.

CHRISTIAN AND QUASI-CHRISTIAN TEXTS

The contemporary **CANONICAL** New Testament is composed of 27 books—the four Gospels, The Acts of the Apostles, thirteen Pauline Epistles (letters), eight general epistles, and the book of Revelation to John. We have archived 5,686 Greek manuscripts which contain all, partial, or fragmentary portions of the NT. Also surviving are over 10,000 Latin manuscripts and on the order of 9,000 other writings in a variety of middle eastern and African languages[11] resulting in a massive collection of some 24,633 NT-related documents. This is astounding when one compares this to the second-most prevalent source of ancient writings, that of the great Greek poet Homer, who most famously authored the *Iliad* and the *Odyssey* whereby 643 copies of his works now survive.

Previously noted, the earliest **EXTANT** literary source of the NT is the Rylands Library *Papyrus P52* fragment containing a portion of John 18:31-33 and John 18:37-38 dated to c. 125 – 175 CE (refer to Figure 5-1).[12] An incidental side note is that scholars often abbreviate manuscripts sources using sigla, which for fragment P52 is represented as the siglum, $\mathfrak{P}^{52}$.

Figure 5-1. The Rylands Papyrus P^{52} ($\mathfrak{P}^{52}$)

The oldest source of the New Testament Gospel of John 18:31-33 (front side of fragment shown)

It is generally accepted that the original individual manuscripts of the New Testament were written between 50 – 150 CE. But, it would take another two centuries until the Bible was mostly formed, only being officially ratified at the tail-end of the third century. Importantly, we have not recovered the AUTOGRAPHIC CODEX of the Christian Bible, that is, 'The Original Bible', and are left with later replicas. The earliest *complete*

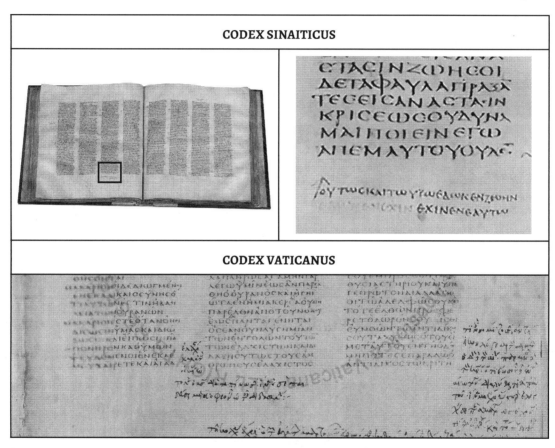

Figure 5-2. The Two Oldest Bibles

[Top] Codex Sinaiticus including Detail View. Note the handwritten annotations at the bottom of the page.

[Bottom] Codex Vaticanus – A page from the Gospel of Matthew. Note the handwritten annotations at the bottom of the page.

Christian Bible is called the handwritten *Codex Vaticanus* (c. 300 – 325 CE).[4] A second codex written close to the same time is *Codex Sinaiticus* (c. 330 – 360 CE)— refer to Figure 5-2.[13, 14]

These two codices are the closest thing to the original Catholic Bible, even though in their original form they each lack significant amounts of text. In both codices, the Old Testament is written in Greek, translated from Hebrew texts. There were a handful of Greek translations circulating in the 2nd- and early 3rd-century by multiple author-translators, but it was the *Septuagint* translation using Koine (common) Greek that was used for the Christian Bible. The Jewish Tanakh is formulated on the Hebrew Masoretic Text. Recent scholarship indicates that the Septuagint was not translated from this particular set of texts directly but from older Hebrew texts, some of which could have been the same or substantially similar source documents as used in constructing the Masoretic Text. While the Christian Old Testament contains more books than the Jewish Old Testament, the books shared in common are very similar to one another.

There are copies of entire books/manuscripts of the Bible older than the collected works contained within Vaticanus and Sinaiticus.[5] In fact, what is described herein is an incomplete narrative of how the Jewish Bible and Christian Bible came about, which is much more convoluted due in part because author-translators had different source documents, methods, personal capabilities, or goals in developing their respective translations. Almost all scholars maintain that somewhere between 98 – 99-plus percent of the canonical NT Gospels and 99.9 percent of the Pauline letters (the epistles) have been successfully reconstituted from the original texts. In historical vernacular, this infers that that New Testament passes the *Bibliographical Test* with flying colors.

The various biblical codices exhibit VERISIMILITUDE in that their contents cohere by place, people, periods, events, geography, topology, customs, and content. This consistency is a central argument for CHRISTIAN APOLOGISTS—the scholastic defenders of the Christian faith—to profess that we can confidently assert *historical* and *theological* truth to the Christian Bible, if not specifically in all cases, then generally. The historical truth is to be taken as that which can be reliably proven to be the case whereas theological statements are suppositional opinions that cannot be supported by natural sources of evidence. Going forward, we will rely heavily on these definitions.

---

4. The word 'complete' is a misnomer as it does not mean that 100 percent of the biblical text exists in any given codex. Often, words, phrases, or sections, and even entire books could be missing or contain errors or notes that another codex may not possess. Essentially 'complete' means it contains the beginning, the end, and most of the text in between.

5. Digital images of many biblical fragments can be found here: http://www.csntm.org/Manuscripts.aspx

It is the result of the assiduous labor of a large contingent of multi-lingual scholars and the decidedly fortunate discovery in modern-day times of ancient religious/spiritual texts that have accorded us with a vast improvement in our understanding of the historicity of the Bible. By integrating the translations of these texts with the historical, cultural, political, and spiritual climate at the time that they were written, we come to appreciate how the tide of religious diversity shaped the trajectory of the formation of the Bible over many centuries and in turn its yawning effect on Classical Christianity.

Nag Hammadi is an Egyptian town located about 300 miles south of Cairo and situated on the banks of the Nile River. Roughly six miles to the northeast of this town are the cliffs at Jabal al-Tarif. Indigenous farmers—three brothers—found 13 leather-bound papyrus codices sealed in earthenware jars in December of 1945.[6] The surviving 52 documents were Gnostic **TRACTATES** commonly referred to as the Nag Hammadi library (the term 'Gnostic' is discussed in more detail in this chapter).[15] Between 1946 – 1956 another trove of texts was found inside eleven caves, now called the Qumran Caves, located in the Judean Desert on dry plateaus about a mile inland from the western shore of the Dead Sea and 13 miles east of Jerusalem.[16] Over 900 manuscripts were eventually discovered of which 235 were of a biblical nature. These texts are eponymously referred to as the *Dead Sea Scrolls*. In February 2017, six decades after the last cave was identified, a twelfth Qumran cave was discovered. While scroll-binding paraphernalia were found along with 1940-vintage pick axes, additional scrolls were not found. The twelfth cave was very likely looted not long after the initial discovery of the caves.

The Qumranites, the probable authors of the scrolls, were an elitist Jewish sect that predated Jesus' life by a century and who existed in geographic proximity to Jesus and his post-death followers until their community was burned-down in 68 CE. It remains unclear how much longer the sect continued to operate until it completely disappeared. Some scholars are reticent to make the connection that Jesus himself and the 'Jesus Movement' in general were directly influenced by the Qumranites, but the Dead Sea Scrolls do make it clear that there were multiple Jewish sects that held different beliefs. This is to say, while Judaism was uniformly monotheistic at this point, there remained different doctrinal beliefs. There were sects who held more esoteric views (Jewish Mysticism) and some who were more influenced by Hellenism and others by Egyptian (e.g., Alexandrian and Carthagian) schools of thought.

The lines of evidence from the Dead Sea Scrolls in concert with how ancient religions developed through the borrowing of ideas from one another along with contemporary

---

6. Not aware of the significance of their discovery, one of the codices was almost immediately burned by the farmer's mother as was a part of a second codex.

historical perspectives of first century Judea are strongly suggestive of a dynamic and complex interplay of philosophical, cultural, political ingredients that were brewing for centuries. While it cannot be proven absolutely, the preponderance of evidence overwhelmingly leads one to conclude that early Christianity has its roots not only in what we today would consider mainstream Judaism, but also in Jewish Mysticism, **APOCALYPTICISM**, Hellenism, Egyptian, and an array of divergent quasi-Christian conceptions of the Godhead that stewed under the unrelenting pressure of Roman oppression. The term *quasi-Christian* is to refer to the early Christian-like sects generally in the first through the fifth century who maintained religious practices and theologies that resembled, but were sufficiently different from, what would eventually be called Roman Catholicism (or in other words orthodoxical Christianity).

We can only fathom guesses as to how many other primary sources of religious texts have met uncertain fates by accidental, willful, or forceful destruction over the intervening centuries, or have been anonymously secreted into private collections or passed about the clandestine antiquities black market. It is most unfortunate that mankind through its various weaknesses in mind and character have spirited away this knowledge for none to see. We can only hope that new treasures will be resurrected from the shadows through the diligent efforts of a cadre of knowledge seekers indubitably backed by benevolent financiers.

FILTERING INTERPRETATIONAL BIAS

No more so can we expect ourselves to reinvent the microprocessor to enable use of your e-reader device, we cannot expect of ourselves to engage in the art of **PHILOLOGY** for a quarter or half a lifetime learning Latin, Hebrew, Greek, Aramaic, and Syriac. We must summon forth the scholarly **HIEROPHANTIC** Dragons to reveal to us what they have learned through decades of self-education and unrelenting toil in **PALEOGRAPHIC** translations. As we will discuss at length in Chapter 12, scholars are human, subject to a range of internal and external influences that lead to unintentional as well as intentional bias. While the work of a scholar is generally adjudicated by peer review for accuracy and authenticity, this by no means confers the achievement of the these goals and certainly not the attainment of unanimity of community opinion on any given subject.

Furthermore, a few highly salient points have to be raised before we can begin interrogating the New Testament. Whenever one listens or reads the communiqué of biblical scholars as they defend their source materials and opinions, invariably you will encounter phrases akin to, "most critical biblical scholars believe this ... the majority of NT researchers agree that ... so and so <insert scholar's name> asserts that Jesus was never entombed in a rock-hewn tomb which is in contrast to the position of most critical scholars <insert long list

of scholars and their books> as the facts simply do not support so and so's position ... ", et cetera (mock quote). Immediately upon hearing words of this ilk one is to be wary of a biased viewpoint that is about to be espoused. If the point itself is not biased, then it still may emanate from a scholar or source that has an overarching agenda. **The overwhelming number of NT biblical scholars, theologians, and to a lesser extent religion historians are religiously affiliated and far outnumber skeptical or unaffiliated scholars. It stands to reason that the average trend is that affiliated scholars will tend to agree and disagree in unison on the general subject matter if not the specific point in question**.

A follow-on point is that when it comes to evaluating contradictory source materials the "majority does not rule; even if most sources relate events in one way, that version will not prevail unless it passes the test of critical textual analysis."[17] German theologian Wolfhart Pannenberg commented cogently, "A single judgment of a sober historian easily outweighs a majority vote, in my opinion. Historical judgment must remain a matter of argument. A majority vote may express the dominant mood of a group, possibly its prejudices, but it is not very helpful in judging claims to historical truth or authenticity."[18] In the end, *historical analysis is a game of measured speculation*.

When any biblical scholar imputes the majority opinion into their conjecture, we need to probe the scholar's affiliation to ascertain why it may be so that many scholars would attest to the point in question. It may be solely due to the numerical imbalance in disciplinary affiliation rather than the inherent power of the argument. Necessarily so, this situation arises to a far greater extent with Christian apologists. The reason is simply because the religious sources (texts, manuscripts, codices, scrolls, etc.) under examination are by their very nature making claims of a religious nature. Allow me to illustrate my point. It would be rather unlikely for a scholar with a skeptical affiliation to say something along the lines of, " ... when interpreting the Gospel of Mark where Jesus restores a demon-possessed man (Mk 5:1–19), most critical biblical scholars assert that this miracle is authentic evidence for the divinity of Christ." (mock quote). It would be more likely, however, to hear such statements from a religiously affiliated scholar as evidence to support Jesus' divinity. In these latter circumstances, it would then be a true—though potentially biased—statement that most critical biblical scholars would affirm Jesus' miracles. In reality the hypothetical statement should not be ascribed *any* historical power because no natural data have been presented. I bring this to the forefront because in reading apologetic literature from the last several decades, it is profusely perforated with such attestations and such language obfuscates what is factual versus what is non-factual, hypothetical, speculative, or even worse, untrue. Finally, a good number of scholars are professionally and/or contractually bound to the institutions for which they are employed. They are subject to much collegial pressure and in some circumstances may have signed statements that require them to comport with specific theological positions in all of their institutional-related affairs. This is a form of mandated bias.

Returning to the main point, we have to be ever so careful when analyzing this ancient body of work and those interpreting it on our behalf. It is all too easy for biblical scholars to trot out the conjecture that they retain academic neutrality and it requires painstaking work to filter-out their biases. What is closer to the truth is that apologetic scholars have been educated by or taught in seminaries, colleges of divinity, and religious institutions steeped in the aura of religiosity. One cannot help but be affected by so many years co-existing in this immersive environment.

Textual Criticisms of Ancient Documents

Touched on in the previous chapter was the fact that the earliest versions of the Hebrew Bible had been edited by later authors to reflect what the latter wanted it to say versus what it had originally said. The Codex Sinaiticus and Codex Vaticanus both have visible changes in its pages (refer to Figure 5-2) and both contain copious errors and serious re-editing by scribes over many centuries. Scholars gauge that the Greek New Testament manuscripts are replete with textual inconsistencies, numbering somewhere in the neighborhood 200,000 to 300,000 instances.[7, 19] For much of its history, both in its formative development and after, the Bible as a whole was very much a work-in-progress with the text being altered by scribal copyist error (intentional or otherwise), language translation mistakes or reinterpretations/misinterpretations, and the removal of entire books (e.g., Protestant versus Catholic versions).

Identification of textual inconsistencies is nothing new. Classical works that discuss textual inconsistencies were written by Spinoza (1677),[20] Voltaire (1764),[21] and Paine (c. 1794)[22] just to name a few. Professor Bart D. Ehrman[23] is a contemporary **DOYEN** in the field of NT scholarship and textual criticism. Talking of the New Testament, Ehrman states:

> Most changes are careless errors that are easily recognized and corrected. Christian scribes often made mistakes simply because they were tired or inattentive or, sometimes, inept. [...] Other kinds of changes are both more important and harder for modern scholars to detect. These are changes

---

7. It is important to state that this large number is subject to significant re-counting of the same error. That is, with some 5,686 documents if one contains an error and this error gets copied over into other documents this quickly multiplies the total number of errors. This author does not have substantiated insight on how many unique errors exist should this re-counting issue be accounted for.

that scribes appear to have made in their texts intentionally. I say that they "appear" to have made such changes intentionally simply because the scribes are no longer around for us to interview about their intentions. But some of the changes in our manuscripts can scarcely be attributed to fatigue, carelessness, or ineptitude; instead, they suggest intention and forethought.[24]

Ehrman concludes that even though the thicket of textual differences is immense, it has been through the rigor of scholastic endeavor that the New Testament has been reconstituted from the thousands of manuscripts to form what we believe to be a close approximation to a fully-accurate replica of the original.[24] **Even though the words of the New Testament have been largely recaptured from a troubled history, this by itself gives little footing to the historical accuracy of the events that are posed and whether they bolster central theological claims of Christianity**. We will explore this notion extensively, but first I want to discuss some counter-perspective to the former point of bounteous scriptural errors. Skeptics who are rude often latch onto the profuse number of errors to proclaim "A-ha! We told you the Bible was a contrivance of men, as by your own convictions, if God is the infallible source of all truth why would he allow his words to be so corrupted?" (mock quote). We needn't dwell for long on the volume of errors; rather we should only study those discrepancies and inconsistencies that critically address the Foundational Truth Claims presented earlier.

As a Christian-turned-Agnostic,[23] Ehrman has publicly debated NT HISTORICITY and indirectly theological inferences with apologists who oppose his central theses. In a public debate with Dr. Ehrman, esteemed evangelical NT scholar Craig A. Evans is not troubled with the myriad of said discrepancies. He explains that Jesus couched his teachings in a situational context of his present time and location. A seldom disputed fact is that Jesus' words were not dictated (as in recorded verbatim at the time he spoke the words) and the four canonical gospels were not written for many decades after Jesus died.[8] Evans suggests that in the intervening years the apostles and early Christians simply adapted Jesus' words to fit the circumstances to support their proselytizing of the Gentiles (non-Jewish people). For example, Apostle Paul wrote unique letters to different Gentile groups (e.g., the Thessalonians, the Galatians, the Corinthians, etc.) which to Evans suggests that we should not be surprised about the variations resulting from oral history being changed and influenced by needs of the time and place. Ultimately, he defends the position that it is perfectly acceptable to concede that all the identified forms of discrepancies and inconsistencies exist, but that they do not controvert the reality that the stories affiliated with Jesus are adequately

---

8. The four canonical gospels are Matthew, Mark, Luke, and John. The word 'Christianity' did not enter into the lexicon until approximately 30 years after Jesus died.

told in a larger context to convey God's overall inspired intentions. That is, there is sufficient verisimilitude that we can afford to believe as true the gist of what transpired.

THE UNEVEN CONTOURS OF EARLY CHRISTIANITY

It would be inappropriate to judge either Ehrman's or Evans' conjectures without first understanding the tumult of ideas and societal discord that existed after Jesus' death and how his life becomes immortalized in extant religious documents. As a result of modern-day normative Christian Church portrayals, the vast majorities of people have had, and continue to have, an erroneous understanding of Christianity's rise to prominence. Being mindful that there are variations to the theme presented, the following is a misrendering of history that is commonly believed by many Christians (refer to Box 2).

BOX 2 – COMMON MISCONCEPTION OF CHRISTIANITY'S ORIGIN

In the beginning God created the heavens and the Earth ... God was not always contented with his people's actions, some of whom were so wicked that the Almighty struck them down ... God wanted to set us on a straighter path so that we might one day join him in heaven. He chose the pious and virginal Mary to birth his essence as the Son of God, Jesus of Nazareth. ... After Jesus rode into Jerusalem on a donkey, his presence only exacerbated the contempt of the Jewish Sanhedrin lawgivers. The council became so inflamed they bribed the Apostle Judas Iscariot with 30 silver coins to betray his leader. After a farcical trial, Pontius Pilate reluctantly agreed to crucify Jesus even giving the Jewish crowd a second chance to save him.

Alas, those gathered jeered and Jesus was taken away and was soon after imprisoned, scourged, and crucified on a T-shaped cross. None of the apostles witnessed the crucifixion event. All the original Apostles, with the exception of Judas Iscariot who killed himself, went into hiding shortly after Jesus' betrayal. Jesus' body was wrapped in burial cloth and moved into a rock-hewn tomb from which he was miraculously bodily resurrected on the third day. This is verified by the fact that the Bible tells us that several of Jesus' women followers went to the tomb, rolled back the stone blocking the entrance, to find the tomb empty. During the next forty days, Jesus makes a number of appearances before he finally

(continued next page)

ascends into heaven. After a time, Jesus' disciples emerge to begin professing their belief in the risen Christ. They clandestinely proselytized small assemblies going from town to town spreading the Word of God.

A few centuries later, Roman Emperor Constantine the Great received a revelation from Jesus Christ that he would conquer his enemies if he adopted Christ. Constantine went to battle with the Cross of Christ emblazoned upon his army's shields and weapons easily vanquishing his opponents. Impressed with this outcome, Constantine converted to Christianity. Soon after he called the assembly of the First Council of Nicaea in 325 CE to formally indoctrinate Christianity as the official faith of the Imperial Realm.

Christianity henceforth swept the lands and the number of Christians swelled to overtake the old pagan gods. For those who professed unorthodox ideas about the Christian faith, they were deemed heretics, many of whom were punished severely, sometimes put to death. Then came the East-West Schism of 1054 CE that broke Christendom into the Western Church and the Eastern Orthodox Church. At the conclusion of the Middle Ages, Catholic priest Martin Luther began to vocally reject certain teachings and practices of the Roman Catholic Church, thereby sparking the Protestant Reformation (1517 – 1648 CE). This cleaved Western Christianity further into Roman Catholicism and Protestantism. Since that fateful turn, Protestantism proceeded to splinter itself into a great many denominations.

As a rough outline, this has been the general storyline engrained in the minds of many-a-Christian. While there are kernels of truth in this account, the *actual* history of Christianity runs far afield from this embodiment.

SETTING THE RECORD STRAIGHT – THE QUASI-CHRISTIANS AND PROTO-CHRISTIANS

The history of formational Christology is well known to present-day scholars, clergymen and their cohort ecclesiastical authorities, as well as a handful of the well-read public. Albeit, clergymen and their ilk are educated with a more sanitized history in seminary school and decidedly biased toward their line of faith. It is only after decades of decoding the extra-biblical sources (that is, sources outside of the Bible) along with the discovery of a grand raft of textual redactions interpreted through religious, cultural, and political lenses of the day, that an entirely new perspective on biblical formation has been elucidated. It is unequivocal that the first several centuries of the Common Era were a politically and religiously charged—even savage—time for the European continent. At the time of Jesus, paganism dominated most of the world which included pantheistic, polytheistic, and animistic religions. Monotheistic Jews and the emerging Christians, very much in the minority, shared the same pagan cities, towns, and villages. First-century society was very much entrenched in an age of fables and wonders where the Grecian gods of Mt. Olympus[9] and their Roman counterparts headlined the religious menu with Yahweh listed somewhere down below. But let us not forget that Jews and Christians held a belief in semi-divine creatures called angels and demons, delineated by a hierarchal power structure. These creatures were the divine correlates to the Greek gods (e.g., Apollo, Aphrodite, Ares, Athena, Hermes, and Prometheus). When combined with the personages of Christ and the Holy Spirit, Satan, and all the angels and demons, some have considered that both Judaism and Christianity have always been polytheistic theologies. This depends on how one wants to define polytheism. If it is defined strictly by the number of gods, then this position is less viable. If, however, one considers any Being that is classified as supernatural and co-existing in the realms of heaven and hell outside our normal construct of space and time, then this assessment would have more merit.

Society at this time was overflowing with deities and there was an entrenched ancient recipe that was recycled over and again. Step One: conquer a nation and control its populace. Step Two: steal or eliminate the conquered nation's gods. Step Three: conquerors change society to revere the new gods. To reduce the likelihood of insurrection (not always successfully), the **ROMAN PREFECTS** permitted Jews and Christians to quietly practice their faith. But without real Christian orthodoxy or written texts, there was a wide spectrum of what people espoused and believed about God, Jesus, the angels, and the demons. Not long after Jesus had died, many schools of interpretation materialized attempting to formalize dogmas. Counterfeit teachers popped-up to claim religious and spiritual authority. It was nothing short of a brewing cauldron of clashing creeds, doctrines, rituals, and ideologies and what one believed was the *soup du jour*. It would take the most influential man in all of human history—Saul of Tarsus—to hollow out what we know today as orthodoxical Christianity from this heterogeneous mix of beliefs.

---

9. The Greeks essentially assumed the Egyptian gods as their own, renaming them and changing their depictions and powers. Likewise, the Romans appropriated the Greek's gods doing the same thing the Greek's did to the Egyptian gods.

Understanding that the Christian God arose from the fertile soil of Zeus, Bes, Yahweh, and many other gods in the midst of an environment of great social, cultural, and political upheaval is of immense importance. Prior to Christianity, polytheistic and Judaic religions alike devoted themselves to appeasing the god(s). The new Christian God was antithetical to these ancient deities. Here we have an all-merciful God (as opposed to the wrathful Jewish God or the mercurial temperament of the Olympians) who offered for sacrifice his **PARAGON** Jesus Christ. He suffered and died for the sins of mankind to consummate the long foretold cosmic reconciliation. It was a role-reversal where God was sacrificing to his people so they may become more faithful. The Christian God accepted a person no matter what and did not demand homage in the form of ritualistic sacrifice or obedience to Jewish law.

This truly was a god for and of the common people. The affinity of nonbelievers toward Christian adherents greatly improved during the Crisis of the Third Century (235 – 284 CE) when the Roman Empire was under the threat of collapse from civil strife, invasions (Goths in modern-day Hungary 248 – 250 CE, Persians in Mesopotamia off-and-on from 237 – 284 CE), plague, and economic depression. In particular, it was the Antonine Plague (also called the Plague of Galen, 166 – 180 CE) and the Plague of Cypria (250 – 270 CE) that were brought back from Near East campaigns and by commodity traders that helped Christianity grow. These outbreaks (most likely small pox) killed 2,000 and 5,000 people a day, respectively. It was also conclusively confirmed by mitochondrial DNA testing in 2016 that malaria was a widespread lethal pathogen at the time of Christ and in subsequent centuries.[61] The Christians stood out as caregivers to the poor, sick, suffering, and the dying which garnered them friendships with non-Christians, many of whom became converts, and a measure of added tolerance by the Imperial Realm.

During this timeframe, the many Christian-like ideologies were still being principally passed around by oral tradition because widespread access to written documents did not exist. Whatever was in writing was in the hands of the educated elite. The most noteworthy of such distinction are the Apostolic Fathers (e.g., Clement of Rome (4th Pope), Ignatius of Antioch, Polycarp of Smyrna) and the Greek Fathers (e.g., Irenaeus of Lyons, Athanasius of Alexandria, Clement of Alexandria, Origen of Alexandria).[10] These thinkers collectively spent over three centuries studying and debating theologically oriented literature. Of some importance is the fact that nearly all Christian writers of the first two centuries hadn't met

---

10. Antioch is located in the southeastern corner of present-day Turkey. The city was a central hub for Hellenic Judaism and early Christianity. It is believed that the term 'Christian' was first used in Antioch. Smyrna was a metropolis on the western coast of present-day Turkey, an inlet port of the Aegean Sea. Lyon is a city in France and Alexandria is on the northern coast of Egypt.

in person or lived at the time of Jesus' apostles. Polycarp (b. c. 69 – d. 155 CE) is one of the few exceptions said to have personally known the then living apostles as he was a direct disciple of John the Apostle as he had ordained Polycarp as the Bishop of Smyrna. Polycarp's pupil, Irenaeus, may also have known John the Apostle.[25] It is also believed that Clement of Rome knew the Apostle's Paul and Simon Peter. Beyond these three figureheads, the knowledge of Jesus of Nazareth and the Apostles was passed to the Church Fathers by oral tradition and by handwritten texts passed down and/or copied from the original.

What we find is that the literary works emanating from the vast majority of early Christian figures are based upon secondary, tertiary, or quaternary sources. When evidence or conclusions rely upon such a long chain, one necessarily has to doubly question the authenticity and reliability of the work at hand and its ability to accurately reflect the original events being discussed. And yet, it was the Church Fathers who deciphered which texts to insert into the Bible and how to interpret the Bible to formulate what would become Catholic doctrine—the correct belief in the Christian God.

In 312 CE, as Augustus of the West, Co-Emperor Constantine I shared power with Licinius, Augustus of the East. Constantine I was a fervent devotee of the pagan sun god *Sol Invictus* (meaning *Unconquered Sun*).[26] More likely than not, Constantine I did not make a wholesale conversion to Christianity in 312 CE when he fought Emperor Maxentius at the Battle of the Milvian Bridge or in the ensuing years following his victory, contrary to what many have been led to believe. This is partially supported by the fact that Constantine wore an Apollonian sun-rayed diadem (an ornamental head band honorific of the god Apollo) at the dedication ceremony of Constantinople in 321 CE. Absent was any symbolism of Christianity. Furthermore, coinage continued to bear the image of the god Sol until c. 325/6 CE and Christian symbols never appeared on coins.[27] From 313 – 317 CE, Sol coinage comprised three-quarters of all coins in circulation.[26] There was also a colossal bronze statue of Sol (*Colossus Solis*) thought to be 125 feet tall built near the Colosseum. In 312 – 315 CE, Constantine built the Arch of Constantine to commemorate his victory over Maxentius.[28] It was purposefully positioned so that people entering the Colosseum Valley could view the dominating presence of the statue of Sol framed in the archway.[29] As Sol was an invincible anthropomorphized god, Constantine may have considered Christ Jesus as a parallel or new expression of Sol and in this sense his religion was a **SYNCRETISTIC** patronage of paganism and quasi-Christianity. We have to keep in mind that orthodox Catholicism had not yet been cemented as the correct dogma of Christianity during the lifetime of Constantine I. As will be covered later, the emperor converted to Arianism—one of the many quasi-Christian groups vying to displace the many other Christian-like sects—on his deathbed.

In any case, Constantine was a politician through and through, and in recognizing the social stability that the then peaceful ways of Christianity offered, he, along with his oft quarrelsome co-Emperor Licinius, authored the *Edict of Milan* in 313 CE.[11] This law forbade persecution of monotheistic worship of any kind throughout the Roman Empire, which included Christianity, and essentially legalized the practice of Christian worship. Constantine I died in 337 CE. Later, by the decree *Cunctos populos (Edict of Thessalonica)*[12] in 380 CE, the Nicene Trinitarian Christianity[13] was declared to be the only legitimate Imperial religion and the only one entitled to call itself Catholic. It was in this timeframe that the newly-formed Catholic Church wrestled with many internal conflicts. Perhaps the most prominent was the pre-orthodoxy of those who believed in the coequal nature of the Holy Trinity and the opposing theological faction of Arianism which believed in the rank ordering of the Father, Son, and Holy Spirit in descending order whereby Jesus was, in their view, neither coeternal nor consubstantial with the Father. Jesus was more than a man but was not in the same league as God the Father and was essentially regarded as semi-divine.

Prior to this institutionalized growth, Christian sects in the 1st-century proliferated to become contenders in the market of beliefs—Ebionites, Marcionites, Gnostics, and the Therapeutae and other belief systems joined the academy of quasi-Jewish/quasi-Christian religion. Montanism was founded in the late 2nd-century which was followed by other Christian-like beliefs in the late second through early 4th-century (e.g., Monarchianism, Novatianism, Arianism, Adamianism, Donatism, Audianism, and Nestorianism). These groups represented mixtures of pagan, Jewish, and *proto-Christian* doctrines and practices. Bart Ehrman coined the term "proto-orthodox Christians"[14,30] (or simply *proto-Christians*) as a **NEOLOGISM** to define the group of people whose Christian creed would ultimately rise above the fold of the quasi-Christian ideologies (i.e., non-Roman Catholic) to become orthodoxical Christianity (i.e., Roman Catholicism).

---

11. A year or so later (in either 314 or 316 CE), their relationship continued to deteriorate. What ensued was years of clashes that lead Licinius in 320 to renege on the Edict of Milan and to start oppressing Christians. The civil war continued until 324 CE when Constantine was victorious. A year later Constantine hanged Licinius and Licinius' son to make Constantine the sole Emperor.

12. The Edict of Thessalonica was jointly issued by Emperors Theodosius I, Valentinian II, and Gratian. Valentinian II and Gratian were half-brothers.

13. The Nicene Trinitarian Christianity is the newly-minted orthodox version of Christianity (i.e., Catholicism). The doctrine is encapsulated by the Nicene Creed which recognizes the Holy Trinity as being comprised by God the Father, God the Son (Jesus), and God the Holy Spirit, hence the word trinitarian.

14. *"Proto-orthodox"* are perspectives/beliefs that, at the time, may not have been dominant or the correct belief (that is, orthodox) but later become recognized as being the 'right belief'.

Ebionites were Jewish-Christians who followed Jewish religious customs but held Jesus in distinction as the Messiah. However, they thought Jesus was born of a sexual union between Mary and Joseph and was adopted by God as his best human representative. Theirs was a pure monotheistic religion. Marcionites were named after Marcion (b. c. 85 – d. c. 160 CE) who had broken away from the proto-orthodox Church Fathers. While he was a strong advocate for the ministerial writings of Paul the Apostle, Marcion believed in a two-god schema whereby the vengeful Hebrew God (which he referred to as the Demiurge and not as Yahweh) was lower in stature than the all-loving Christian God. He considered Jesus to be of an illusory construction who only appeared to be real but was hiding his divine nature.[15] Little is known about the Jewish Therapeutae community who congregated in lower Egypt. They were especially contemplative in prayer with some of their traditions resembling Christian worship practices. They appear to have led an **ASCETIC** lifestyle.[31]

The summary point according to Ehrman is there was no such a thing as "early Christianity," rather it was a time of "early *Christianities*"[32] —plural—which over centuries became orthodox Christianity after systematic purges and edicts from the first seven **ECUMENICAL COUNCILS** (325 – 787 CE) and fortified by Roman Imperialism. This creedal requirement for Christians to assert that their God was the one 'true God' was an alien concept because other Greco-Roman religions were tolerant of the notion that there were many forms and natures to be associated with deities. In fact, Jews around the time of Christ practiced **ORTHOPRAXY**,[16] focusing on doing right by God via ritual sacrifice and observance of laws rather than requiring strict adherence to belief, especially the rightness of beliefs.[30]

Christianity's origin began by swimming into a veritable sea of polyfaith and **SYNCRETISTIC**[17] traditions that over centuries stratified to become an orthodoxical and exclusionary religion in the 4th-century. It was by the societal health crises and the law of the land promulgated in 313 CE and 380 CE that led to the ballooning of Christianity to fill large swaths of greater Europe and its borderlands. This solidarity as it were would then galvanize Christians against their opponents who would later invade their lands time and again. Ehrman offers a cogent and enlightening dissertation—almost a resurrection if you will—on these long forgotten Christian groups whose competing ideologies proved absolutely pivotal in the formation of the Catholic Church in particular and for Christianity in general.

---

15. This belief is called *Docetism*. Docetism is defined as the doctrine that Jesus' body was not physically human but illusory/spiritual in form.

16. Orthopraxy is the correctness of the practices of religion. Orthodoxy, in contrast, is affiliated with the approved form of doctrine or ideology.

17. The word '*polyfaith*' means 'multiple faiths', whereas syncretism is the mixing of belief systems.

Suffice it to say that, after Jesus' death, Christianity's genesis was a multifaceted political, spiritual, philosophical, brutal, and bloody ideological war of ideas where in Ehrman's words; there were "winners and losers."[19] This portrait of Jesus' world does not bear much resemblance to anything taught in contemporary parochial education or society at large.

The Gnostics

Gnosticism is one of the more interesting sects of believers because, until the 1945 Nag Hammadi discoveries, there were no writings by the Gnostics themselves to describe who they were as a society. Our knowledge of this group was sourced mainly from Christianity's Church Fathers—Irenaeus, Tertullian, Clement of Alexandria, Epiphanius of Salamis, and Hippolytus of Rome—all noted heresiologists (i.e., 'heresy hunters'). These detractors of Gnosticism sought to cleanse unorthodox or otherwise distortionary systems by use of a host of spiritual weapons—by conversion, Imperial authority, **DEPOSITION**, confiscation of property, mockery and banishment.[33] In the late 4th-century death was added to the roster of punishments for heresy. Irenaeus denounced the Gnostic writings (what we now generally refer to as the Nag Hammadi library) as "an abyss of madness, and blasphemy against Christ."[34] The Church Father's mission was to define the structure and contents of the faith and to contemporaneously evangelize this 'truth' and decimate all **HETERODOXY** and the Gnostics were at the top of their 'hit list'. In full circle fashion, the once persecuted Christians became the persecutors of others.

Gnosticism is not a singular belief system rather it represents a spectrum of beliefs that were common to a diverse set of religions. Some have contended that a subset of the Gnostics were Christian ostensibly because they believed that Jesus was among the divine. However, apologists such as Craig A. Evans feel that Christian Gnosticism is an improper association of two belief systems because their precepts departed from core Christian beliefs.[35] To be certain, the Gnostics expressed various **EMANATIONISMS** (cosmological understandings of a religious or philosophical system) among the multitude of sects wherein cosmological beings are differently named, classified, and described.

Gnostics believed that *gnosis*, meaning knowledge or enlightenment, is necessary for salvation and spiritual regeneration because pieces of God known as divine 'sparks' had become trapped in the material world, specifically harbored within human bodies. According to certain Gnostic sects, these psychical humans were made by the **DEMIURGE**. The Demiurge was the fabricator of the material cosmos but was subservient and an antagonist to the unknowable Supreme God. Essentially, the Supreme God outsources the construction of the universe so that when things go wrong, the Demiurge takes the blame. Humans, according to the Gnostics, are lorded over by the Demiurge's servants, the Aeons and the Archons. The Aeons are beings of light and purity which are correlates to the Judeo-Christian angels.[18] Archons on the other hand are jailers of the soul and correspond to the Judeo-Christian demons. Because there are flaws in the universe, the Supreme God creates two ultra-powerful Aeons—Christ and The Holy Spirit—to save humanity from the Demiurge.

To liberate these sparks, the so-possessed humans needed to access secret knowledge to enable them to pass back from the material realm to the spiritual realm which was region of light where all the divine sparks could gather. This access was granted by the two powerful Aeons. We know that Jesus was considered an Aeon by the Gnostics because in John 8:31-32 Jesus states this plainly, "Then Jesus said to the Jews who had believed in him, 'If you continue in my word, you are truly my disciples; and you will know the truth, and the truth will make you free.'" Some Gnostics believed that humans were divided into three classes based upon their level of self-awareness. Material (*hylic*) persons were the lowest order of humans, essentially considered pure animals. Because they lacked the spark, they could never escape their fate as being forever outside of the spirit realm. The second echelon was those who also lacked the divine spark, but possessed a soul (*psyche*). Those who existed on this second rung could alter their eternal fate by being a good and faithful individual. If they achieved this, they had the opportunity to live in the spirit world. And finally, the third class of people contained a spirit (*pneuma*) and functioned as physical vessels for the divine spark.[36]

Most Gnostics are believed to have lived an ascetic life abstaining from sex, procreation, and indulgences. One particular Gnostic sect, the Carpocratians, deviated from this norm and were anything but ascetic.[19] Gnostics in general thought that the human body was an embodiment of evil because it trapped the divine spark and they engaged in debasing their bodies. The proto-orthodox Church Fathers thought these groups were completely wrong and condemnation became a centuries-long campaign to rein in nonbelievers. Before they perished, the persecuted Gnostics were able to ferret away the Codices of Nag Hammadi. Once decrypted, what they revealed was truly astonishing.

The Gnostic papyrus manuscripts contained **APOCRYPHA** that claimed apostolic authority. The origin of the word 'apocrypha' is the Greek verb to 'to hide away' so these apocryphal

---

18. As noted, the Nicene Creed was created in 325 CE. It was substantially revised in 381 CE (often called the Constantinopolitan Creed of 381 CE) and in this version it refers to word 'aeons'. Full versions of both creeds are presented in a separate future discussion about the Holy Trinity.

19. The Carpocratians were a unique and deviant Gnostic sect known for wild and lewd behavior because they believed they had power over all. They engaged in magic and Agape feasts (gluttonous religious, communal meals often followed by sexual orgies).

texts were revelations of secret spiritual knowledge. A subset of these texts are more commonly referred to as the noncanonical Secret Gospels because they offer a very different perspective on the lives and sayings of New Testament figureheads and because they are not included in the canonical Christian Bible. Some of the Gnostic gospels carried titles like, the Gospel of Truth, Gospel of Mary, the Gospel of Peter, the Gospel of Thomas, the Gospel of Philip, and the Gospel of Judas.

A Word about the Words 'Canonical', 'Apocrypha', and 'Pseudepigrapha'

Earlier the word 'canonical' was defined as being any book included in the Bible. To be a little more specific, one can refer to entire Bible as the biblical canon. Or, one can refer to Old Testament canon or the New Testament canon. Use of the words 'Old Testament canon' or 'canon of Scripture' when taken out of context is confusing as Jewish and Christian traditions include different books, so one has to use care by employing context or be more specific to avoid confusion. The Tanakh and the Christian Bible are considered 'closed canons' because addition or removal of books is not authorized (some Latter-day Saint sects have an open canon). This should not be confused with the steady practice of intentional and unintentional redactions within the canon itself. The word intentional can mean instances where there is an honest effort to alter text to reflect the original author's intent (i.e., emendations), which is why so many translations of the Bible have been created over the centuries. There are, of course, other purposeful efforts to alter the intent of the original author.

The word 'apocrypha' has taken on different meanings over the passage of time. In modern-day terms, apocrypha are noncanonical (extra-biblical) texts that, like the canonized texts, contain discussions about Jesus, the teachings of Jesus and his apostles, and the nature of God. Apocrypha are also so-named because the documents were either initially kept secret because of the esoteric knowledge was too profound or too sacred to expose to the uninitiated. Thus, there was no disparagement meant by their exclusion relative to their divine inspiration. Use of the word 'apocrypha' is also used to convey that the written work under discussion is of unknown authorship. There are both Jewish and Christian apocrypha pertaining to the Hebrew Old Testament, Greek Old Testament, and the New Testament.

Pseudepigrapha are texts written by author(s) that falsely attribute the writing to someone else. This is ostensibly done because during the age it was written, it might carry more weight if audiences thought it was written by a more prominent figure. Bart Ehrman provides a laundry list of other rationale in his book entitled *Forged: Writing* *in the Name of God—Why the Bible's Authors are Not Who We Think They Are* (HarperOne, 2011). In some cases, apocryphal texts can also be pseudepigrapha and the words can then be used interchangeably. While scholars are usually familiar among themselves when using the terminology in their academic expositions, the lay person can be easily confused by whether a text is strictly and simply pseudepigrapha or if it is also an apocryphal text. Like apocryphal texts, there are Jewish and Christian pseudepigrapha.

Gnostic Texts: The Coptic Gospel of Thomas

There is an abundance of books and scholarly papers that have surfaced on the interpretations of the Gnostic writings.[37-40] Among the corpus of Gnostic documents found, they fall into three genre—the Apocryphal Gospels, the Apocryphal Acts, and the Epistles. The New Testament is similarly arranged but also includes the Apocalypse of John (book of Revelation).

While exploration of the Gnostic texts offers many contradictions to the Christian Bible, for the sake of explanatory economy, commentary will be limited to a smattering of insights gleaned from the Coptic (Egyptian) *Gospel of Thomas* what is believed to be an alternative Gnostic version of the canonical Gospel of Mark referred to as *The Secret Gospel of Mark*. Because of their anti-orthodox message, the date of authorship of these texts is rather important. Had they been written right after Christ died, the information would likely have had a larger influence on what got inserted into the Bible. Unfortunately, it is unclear when the Gospel of Thomas was written. Ehrman submits that the literary work originated sometime between c. 100 – 150 CE.[41] That is, it is probably written several or more decades after the four canonical gospels and around a century after Christ lived.

The apocryphal Coptic Gospel of Thomas offers purported sayings from Jesus, many of which were previously unknown and bears some similarity to those found in the **Synoptic Gospels** (i.e., Matthew, Mark, and Luke) but with interesting twists of meaning. The nuclear idea of this gospel is that we humans are entrapped in a pitiful body in an evil world and the way to attain salvation is by accessing secret knowledge. It begins with, "These are the secret sayings which the living Jesus spoke and which Didymus Judas Thomas wrote down.[20] [Saying 1] And he said,[21] 'Whoever finds the interpretation of these

---

20. Didymus is a Greek word meaning 'twin'. There is much confusion as to what historical figure is being referenced as Didymus Judas Thomas because of differences in translations between the Greek and Syriac reference texts. Some scholars suggest he was Jesus' twin brother and others that he was simply a disciple.

21. In this book, text that is underlined with a wavy line is attributed to the words that Jesus spoke in noncanonical (extra-biblical) texts.

sayings will not taste death.' Due to the degraded state of the bone material, nuclear DNA testing proved unsuccessful. However, reliable results were obtained from mitochondrial DNA testing"[42] In Saying 108, "Jesus said, 'He who will drink from my mouth will become like me. I myself shall become he, and the things that are hidden will be revealed to him."[42] This has been interpreted to mean that those sparks who drink from *Aeon* Jesus' mouth (as in his words and knowledge) will be able to return to the divine Plemora (the heavenly region of fullness and light). Finally, in Saying 3, "Jesus said, 'When you come to know yourselves, then you will become known, and you will realize that it is you who are the sons of the living father. But if you will not know yourselves, you dwell in poverty and it is you who are that poverty.' "[42] From this we see that the Gnostics believed that personal salvation depended on one's self-awareness. This stands in stark contrast with the message from the Pauline ministry which indicates that the only way to eternal salvation is by one's acceptance of Jesus as the one true Lord and savior.

The Coptic Gospel of Thomas furthermore implies that divulgence of certain of Jesus' teachings were restricted to a select few. Was Christianity always meant to be so exclusive of a religion that the true knowledge of God and Jesus were to be kept a secret to a select cadre of believers? Titus Flavius Clemens, more commonly known as Clement of Alexandria (refer to Box 3, p. 169), is distinguished as a Church Father and as a saint, affirms this Gnostic belief in his *Miscellanies*:[22, 43]

> [bold-underline added] But since this tradition is not published alone for him who perceives the magnificence of the word; it is requisite, therefore, to hide in a mystery the wisdom spoken, which the Son of God taught. [...] For it is difficult to exhibit the really pure and transparent words respecting the true light, to swinish and untrained hearers. [...] But the natural man receives not the things of the Spirit of God; for they are foolishness to him. But the wise do not utter with their mouth what they reason in council. "But what ye hear in the ear," says the Lord, "proclaim upon the houses;" **bidding them receive the secret traditions of the true knowledge**, and expound them aloft and conspicuously; and as we have heard in the ear, so to deliver them to whom it is requisite; **but not enjoining us to communicate to all without distinction**, what is said to them in parables.[43]
>
> Stromata I.XII (Miscellanies)

---

22. Clement is credited with three major works referred to as the *Trilogy*. The Stromata (sometimes written Stromateis) is a part of these three works.

BOX 3 – CLEMENT OF ALEXANDRIA

Titus Flavius Clemens (Clement of Alexandria)
(born c. 150 - died c. 215 CE)
Image Credit: André Thevet, 1584 CE[44]

Clement of Alexandria is regarded as a Greek Church Father because he wrote in Greek. His contributions afforded him sainthood in Eastern Catholicism, Anglicanism, and Oriental Orthodoxy. While Clement was initially venerated as a saint in the Roman Catholic Church, Pope Sixtus V removed him from the *Roman Martyrology* in 1586 (the list of recognized saints was first published in 1583). As one of the earliest Church Fathers, that is living closer to Jesus' lifetime, Clement was deeply familiar with and influenced by Platonic and Stoic philosophy. He would be faulted centuries later for his merging of Greek, Jewish, and Gnostic thought systems which were deemed heretical once Catholic doctrine was formally established. Essentially all of his work has been lost to history. Beyond fragments, only a single surviving text (the Mar Saba Letter) exists. In this letter he comments on the apocryphal Secret Gospel of Mark, which had been stolen by the Gnostic Carpocratians and falsified to the effect that only the spiritually elite could be afforded access to the secret teachings of Jesus.[45]

Clement is saying that there is secret knowledge or what we would call mysteries that is to be delivered orally, not written down, and that it is to be communicated only to those of who are properly prepared with adequate background knowledge. Here we have a Christian Church Father, a heresiologist no less, who articulates in so many words that Christianity bears similarity to Jewish Mysticism, Gnostic Mysticism, and Egyptian beliefs to the extent that one has to undergo a disciplined preparation process to gain access to the higher sacred knowledge. To otherwise enter into these esoteric mysteries unprepared would risk psychological damage—hence the need for secrecy. His syncretic views of Christianity and mysticism originating in other faith traditions put him outside the fringe of acceptable orthodoxy which led Pope Sixtus V to remove him from the list of saints in 1586. This action made Clement a *de facto* heretic in the eyes of the Western (Latin) Catholic Church. Contrastingly, he is still revered today as a saint by other Christian groups. This was a major move by Sixtus because Clement of Alexandria is one of the earliest author-interpreters of biblical source documents making him closer in time to the life of Jesus and his apostles.

Often, however, what is important isn't what is said, but what is *not* said. The Coptic Gospel of Thomas makes no mention of the Creator-God—the God of Israel—or a need for the sinner to repent. **Another striking fact is that even though Jesus is hugely prominent in the entire text, any mention of the resurrection event is totally absent from this gospel**. Though, other Gnostic texts do refer to Jesus and the resurrection (i.e., the *Gospel of Truth* and *The Treatise on the Resurrection*).

Gnostic Texts: The Secret Gospel of Mark

In 1973, professor of ancient history Morton Smith of Columbia University published what has become to be known as the *Mar Saba Letter* as it was uncovered by Smith in the 1,500 year-old Mar Saba Monastery located just between Jerusalem and the Dead Sea on the southern bank of Palestine's Kidron Valley in 1958. Smith contended that it came from the hand of Clement of Alexandria. The letter is addressed to an individual named Theodore whereby Clement commends him on his polemical attacks against the Carpocratians, the Gnostic sect known for its LICENTIOUS lifestyle. This document has created considerable and ongoing controversy because of disagreement on how to interpret the meaning of his words, whether or not the document was written by the Clement of Alexandria (or by a different person by the same name), or whether it was a forgery or even a hoax.[46] It is important because, if properly understood, it sheds light on whether or not Clement as a Christian Church Father believed as the Gnostics did that higher spiritual knowledge of God, Jesus, and whatnot is to be revealed to only a select group of people. Putting aside its authenticity for a moment, this letter conveys Clement's knowledge of an alternative version to the Gospel of Mark. Recall that during Clement's life, the Bible did not yet exist. In the letter, Clement is cautioning Theodore that this Secret Version of the Gospel of Mark has been falsified by the LIBERTINE Gnostic named Carpocrates. Clement says to Theodore:

Excerpt of Clement of Alexandria's Letter to Theodore

[bold-underline added]

[...] But when Peter died a martyr, Mark came over to Alexandria, bringing both his own notes and those of Peter, from which he transferred to his former book the things suitable to whatever makes for progress toward knowledge. **Thus he composed a more spiritual Gospel for the use of those who were being perfected. Nevertheless, he yet did not divulge the things not to be uttered, nor did he write down the hierophantic teaching of the Lord**, but to the stories already written he added yet others and, moreover, brought in certain sayings of which he knew the interpretation would, as a mystagogue, lead the hearers into the innermost sanctuary of that truth hidden by seven veils. Thus, in sum, he prepared matters, neither grudgingly nor incautiously, in my opinion, and, dying, he left his composition to the church in Alexandria, where it even yet is most carefully guarded, **being read only to those who are being initiated into the great mysteries**.

But since the foul demons are always devising destruction for the race of men, Carpocrates, instructed by them and using deceitful arts, so enslaved a certain presbyter of the church in Alexandria that he got from him a copy of the secret Gospel, which he both interpreted according to his blasphemous and carnal doctrine and, moreover, polluted, mixing with the spotless and holy words utterly shameless lies. From this mixture is drawn off the teaching of the Carpocratians.

To them, therefore, as I said above, one must never give way; nor, when they put forward their falsifications, should one concede that the secret Gospel is by Mark, but should even deny it on oath. [...][47]

I will leave it to a laundry list of scholars who have proffered their divided opinions on Clement's letter and limit my comments to the underlined portions. The first underlined passage has been interpreted to mean that the unknown author of the Gospel of Mark wrote two versions, one of which contained secret knowledge that was only for those who are being perfected. Others contend that the words are simply to be taken as knowledge that would be given to any initiate advancing their knowledge of the Christian faith. In his book *Mark's Other Gospel: Rethinking Morton Smith's Controversial Discovery* religion scholar Scott Brown[23] sets up the two possibilities that either Clement, a patriarch of the

---

23. Scott G. Brown was the first person to have written a Ph.D. dissertation on the Secret Gospel of Mark (University of Toronto, 1999).

formative Catholic Church, withheld secret content concerning Jesus that was only to be disseminated in oral form or that Mark the Evangelist had simply authored two somewhat varying editions of his testimony.[48]

Morton Smith's book and Clement's letter generated a litany of academic debate regarding the authenticity of the existence and authorship of a second version of the Gospel of Mark as well as that of Clement's letter. Thirty-plus years into it, some conclusions can be reasonably drawn. First, there is near unanimous agreement that the Clement's letter is authentic. There also appears to be ***three versions of the Gospel of Mark***—(1) the canonical version which ends at Chapter 16, Verse 8 which may or may not include two additional sentences at the tail-end, (2) the Long version continues with Verse 9 and ends at Chapter 16–Verse 20, and (3) the 'Secret Version' highlighted by Clement. It is believed that the Secret Version is an expansion of the Shorter canonical version.[49] We will further review the Shorter and Longer versions later on in this chapter as the content of these two versions offer tantalizing insights regarding whether or not Jesus can be considered divine based on scriptural interpretation. It can also be cleanly stated that Clement disavows Gnostic ideology but does believe that certain higher knowledge of God is better transmitted orally versus literarily. Finally, it is fair to say that, in this particular instance, provocative author Michael Baigent in his book *The Jesus Papers: exposing the Greatest Cover-Up in History* takes too much license in his interpretation of some cherry-picked words from Clement to advance the legitimacy of his theory that Jesus Christ, existing as a normal human, survived his crucifixion—refer to Box 4, p. 173.

This examination of religious literature highlights the intricacies involved in interpreting what transpired over 1,800 years ago and validates that certain truths were '*managed*' by the elite Christian Fathers. Contemporarily, it is reminiscent of the incredulity Christians feel toward the secret rituals performed in Mormon temples and their adoption of their extra-biblical sacred canon, the Book of Mormon. Or, similarly, Scientology's secret documents, secret vaults, and bases of operation. Should one read the full (translated) library of the Gnostic texts, one is struck by both the similitude and utterly bizarre nature of the contents as compared to the Christian Bible. It is clear that there existed multiple interpretations,what might be considered legends[24] of many individual aspects of the Jesus Story. The Gnostics, for example, had different interpretations of the resurrection. Elaine Pagels, a renowned scholar of the Nag Hammadi library, tells us that some Gnostics believed that Jesus' resurrection was strictly a mental (nonphysical) experience that could

---

24. This comment about them being legends is especially important as it will come into play during discussions concerning the Legend Hypothesis for the resurrection (Chapter 6).

Box 4 – The Jesus Papers:
Exposing the Greatest Cover-Up in History

In his bestselling book *The Jesus Papers: Exposing the Greatest Cover-Up in History* (HarperCollins, 2006) Michael Baigent quotes Clement's words to Theodore ... *"being read only to those who are being initiated into the great mysteries"*[50] (italics added) to aide his thesis that the raising of Lazrus from the dead (see John 11:1-44) by Jesus is not to be taken literally. Rather, it is a reference to the Egyptian concept of the "Far World."[51] Baigent explains that the Far World is a mental journey that physically takes place in secret underground caves where one figuratively dies to oneself to be initiated in spirit by the infusion of new and secret knowledge. Therefore Lazrus does not die and come back to life in the traditional sense, he simply becomes enlightened.

More generally, Baigent's work has stirred great controversy with Christian apologist Dr. Craig A. Evans dismissing Baigent's book as seriously misguided in round terms.[52] Baigent's many conjectures decidedly make for interesting reading, if for no other reason than he presents a different perspective in which to interpret New Testament claims. I do, however, agree with at least one of Evans' primary criticisms about Baigent's book.

Baigent's overarching thesis is that Jesus survived the resurrection based on two papyri letters written in Aramaic and sourced from the antiquities black market that directly supported this claim.[52] The great weakness is that these letters were only in his hands for mere minutes and then spirited away by the possessor of the documents and therefore we have to believe such a great claim on his word alone. Furthermore, by his own admission, he has no reading proficiency of the Aramaic language.

be accessed in any number of modalities through contemplative mentation, psychical visions, or in an altered state of consciousness like a trance much as the Apostle Paul did (see Acts 22:17-21).[53] Keep this in your mind as we will soon broach the topic of Christ's resurrection and how he appeared to the people after his death as purported in the Christian Bible.

Why does this all matter? It matters greatly because the many early quasi-Jewish/ quasi-Christian groups differed on the resurrection and divinity of Jesus of Nazareth. If it weren't for the pestilence that embraced the regions near and far, Roman authoritarianism, and the influential power of certain Church Fathers (e.g., Athanasius of Alexandria), it may well have presented a clear opportunity for a different theology of Christianity to have emerged than what we now have in Catholicism in particular and in Christianity in general.

Construction of the Canonical Christian Bible

Unlike the Ten Commandments which God recites to Moses and later inscribes in stone (see Exodus 20:1-17 and Deuteronomy 5:4-20), God neither provided the New Testament in a quick nor clear fashion. It could not have been more different. So how did the Church Fathers decide which of the many available texts should be included? The reality was that it took decades that turned into centuries of unending debate and divisive argumentation among the proto-orthodox religious figureheads.[25] It was a time when many alterations to the original texts had been made prior to when 73 books were finally selected to form the Catholic Bible.

In one of more prominent examples, we gain insight how Church Father Irenaeus (c. 180 CE) makes the earliest defense we know of as to why the four gospels (Matthew, Mark, Luke, and John) are to be regarded as the only authentic gospels from among the many other gospels (e.g. the Gnostic Gospels of Mary, Peter, Thomas, and Philip, etc.). As he speaks out against the various heretical groups and their texts, he puts forth an entirely unconvincing even troubling set of analogies referencing the many examples of the four-part forms of God:

> It is not possible that the Gospels can be either more or fewer in number than they are. For, since there are four zones of the world in which we live, and four principal winds, [...] it is fitting that she should have four pillars, breathing out immortality on every side [...] it is evident that the Word, the Artificer of all, [...] has given us the Gospel under four aspects, but bound together by one Spirit. [...] For the cherubim, too, were four-faced [...] For this reason were four principal covenants given to the human race: one, prior to the deluge, under Adam; the second, that after the deluge, under Noah; the third, the giving of the law, under Moses; the fourth, that which renovates man, and sums up all things in itself by means of the Gospel, [...][54]
>
> Against Heresies 3.11.8

---

25. Ignatius, Polycarp, Tertullian, Irenaeus, Hippolytus, Origen, Eusebius, Athanasius, and Augustine to name the more familiar ones.

Today, we would deem his thinking as nothing but an absurd defense as to why the four gospels ought to be the only ones included into the Christian Bible. While there were many other theologians who entered their views as to which texts should be included in the New Testament, it would be Athanasius,[26] Bishop of Alexandria (Egypt), who was also a participant at the all-important First Council of Nicaea (325 CE), who would be the first person to nominate the 27 books of the New Testament. He did this in 367 CE, some 300-plus years after these religious texts had been written![27] According to Ehrman, the Church leaders used five criteria to decide what texts would become biblical canon. The text had to be (1) ancient, (2) contemporary with Jesus' death, (3) it must have been written by an apostle or one of their close associates, (4 and 5) it must be compatible with the orthodoxical views that had evolved. This meant that the texts selected were consistent with the beliefs that had been fully adopted or had represented the majority view of the proto-orthodox Christians.[55] A sixth criterion that could be added was the almost palpable fact that the selections should be sympathetic to Roman Imperialists in particular and the Roman audience in general.

These guidelines were used to identify what the Church Fathers believed were divergent claims, outright distortions, falsehoods, and fantasies, as well as the highly intractable esoteric mysteries of Jesus' miracles and resurrection. **It was not until the Synod of Hippo (393 CE) and Council of Carthage (397 CE) and after Athanasius had died in 373 CE when the biblical canon (a.k.a., the Catholic Bible) was finally solidified some three-and-a-half centuries after Christ died.** Athanasius had extraordinary influence as all of his initial 27 selections were to be cemented as the canonical Christian Bible for all time earning him the title *Father of Orthodoxy* as well as gaining him sainthood in most all Christian traditions. And, let us not forget, that Irenaeus got his way as well because his choice of gospels was among the chosen, though he would never know it because he died in 202 CE. This achievement would also draw a deep and permanent line for which heresy would be defined henceforth and further empowered a Roman leviathan on the march in its mission to eradicate heterodoxy. The first post-orthodox execution sanctioned by the Catholic Church on

---

26. Athanasius is venerated as a saint and also carries the epithets Athanasius the Great, Athanasius the Confessor, and Father of Orthodoxy. Also recall from the chapter on biblical antiquities, it was Athanasius who, for a time, oversaw the protection of the purported bones of John the Baptist.

27. Canonical Gospel composition dates: *Mark* c. 65 – 70 CE, *Matthew* c. 80 – 85 CE, *Luke* c. 80 – c. 110 CE, *John* c. 90 – 110 CE (the Gospel of John has no single date of composition as it was written in stages). The dating of the Acts of the Apostles is notoriously difficult. Dates range between 60 CE (provided by Norman Geisler/Colin J. Hemer) to 100 CE (provided by Steve Mason/Robert Eisenman) and others put it at 110 CE. These dates may affect or be affected by the date of authorship for Luke who may have authored both books. In 2012, Frank Dicken's analysis indicated the most probable date range is 75 – 90 CE.

the grounds of heresy was in 385 CE when Priscilliam, Bishop of A'vila, and four compatriots were beheaded.

All of the preceding knowledge begs the question, what would the Christian worldview be like if more of the apocryphal books had been included into the Bible or if those books now in the Bible were excluded? If, for example, in the ideological battles that ensued, what if the Gnostic gospels or Marcionite writings were deemed to be the more orthodoxical beliefs?[28] Did the Church Fathers get it right by selecting the most accurate portrayals of Jesus using the criteria noted above? Why would God be so terse and efficient in the handing down of the Ten Commandments but allow his inspired work of the NT to be vehemently argued by priestly men for over three-and-a-half centuries which would then lead to indescribable afflictions of suffering and continued doctrinal division for two thousand years after (e.g., the Protestant Reformation, Mormonism)? Can Protestants, Catholics, and Orthodox Christians take ease with the fact that the Bible was a literary transmutation by the hands of an untold number of men? Can the righteousness or divinity of the Bible as a whole be so comfortably proclaimed? The answers lie ahead.

Alternate Ways to Read the Bible to Ascertain Biblical Authenticity

Every scholar—biblical, theological, philosophical, and historical—will tell you that there are two major things to agree on when extracting truth from the Bible. First we have the *content* of the Bible, the raw data if you will, and the second thing is the *interpretation* of that information. The predominant acrimony arises from the latter. Roughly speaking, prior to the 20th-century, the Christian New Testament was almost exclusively read vertically, that is, the way it is organized when you buy it off the shelf (the canonical ordering—refer to Figure 5-3, shaded bottom). The vast majority of those who read the Christian Bible do so in this fashion. Some time ago, as dating of the biblical texts became somewhat more certain; some began to read the Bible chronologically to better understand temporal interrelationships (refer to Figure 5-3–top[56, 57]). This is now often done in non-collegiate Bible study groups that one might attend prior to or after their regular work-a-day jobs.

For those wanting to dissect the Bible in greater detail, it became popular to read the Bible *horizontally*. This side-by-side technique is designed to compare the wordings of the same events in terms of the exact words spoken and the chronology of when they are spoken

---

28. None of the writings of the Marcionites have survived and our knowledge of this group is chiefly through Tertullian, one of Marcion's foremost antagonists.

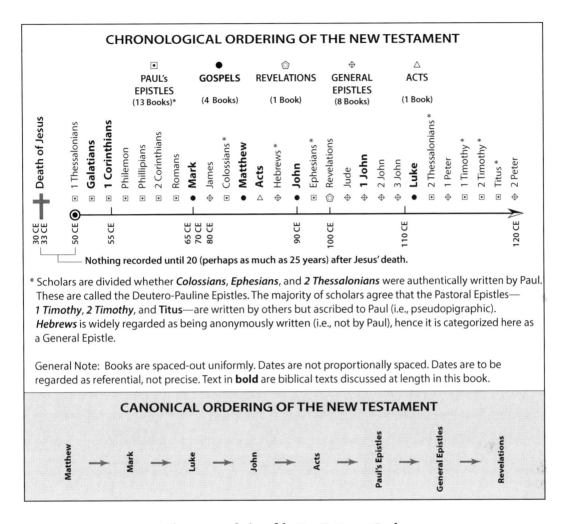

Figure 5-3. Ordering of the New Testament Books

and to see where gaps of information are present. At this point, things started to get interesting because the inscrutable inconsistencies literally leapt off of the pages, especially between the four canonical gospels. All the while, in the solitude of the bracing walls of universities and religious institutions, philologists minced over the possible permutations over and again of how to interpret the archaic languages and what to make of the Dead Sea Scrolls and Nag Hammadi texts. The findings punched a hole in the mountainside to spring a new geyser of PEEVISH disagreement between Christian apologists and skeptical scholars. Skeptical historians and New Atheists clamored that not only were there serious inconsistencies, but there lacked naturalistic support for the incarnate resurrection of Jesus and his ministry of miracles and exorcisms. That is to say, without appealing to God's providential action, there is insufficient natural data to establish the NT's credibility as a historical source. As expected, Christian apologists wishing to revalorize their religion doubled-down to more vigorously to defend the integrity of the Bible. We will put the claims and defenses of Christian apologists to the test and wring out whether their attestations reflect the best scenario of past reality.

Initially, it would appear to be truly astounding how an upstart religion originating from a band of chiefly Jewish reformers led a hardscrabble itinerant existence to gain adherents under the ruthless oppression of the Roman government. We might call to mind the three Jewish-Roman Wars (66 – 135 CE) in which by various estimates killed 350,000 people occupying the city of Jerusalem amounting to about 25 – 33 percent of the total population.[58] The Romans were indiscriminant about who got killed and many non-Jews were murdered, including one must think, some number of proto-Christian families who had lived in Jerusalem. We know this because James the Just, the brother of Jesus,[29] was the Bishop of Jerusalem until his execution by stoning in either c. 62 or c. 69 CE at the hands of Sadducee High Priest Hanan ben Hanan (recorded in *Antiquities of the Jews* 20.9.1).[59] Along with the Roman occupation of Antioch (Syria-Turkey border) and the newly-annexed Pontus region (northeastern Turkey), Jerusalem was among the first population centers of the proto-Christians and they were not very numerous at that time.

It is estimated that around the year 60 CE, just prior to the Jewish Great Revolt (c. 66 – 73 CE), there were only an estimated 800 Jewish-converts and 1,500 Gentile-converts in the entire Christian movement. By the end of 70 CE, after the first culling by the Romans in the locale of Jerusalem, there may have only been 400 Jewish-Christian converts left. **Christinity as a nascent religion was very much at risk of being exterminated**. This contrasts with an increase to 2,500 Gentile-converts outside Judea. By the end of the 1st-century there may only have been on the order of 7,500 Christians total, the overwheming number being Gentile-converts.[62] The early quasi-Christian and proto-Christian sects perpetuated under unforgiving circumstances for some two-and-a-half to three hundred years until the Edicts of Milan and Thessalonica (313 CE and 380 CE, respectively) were enforced to legalize and institutionalize Catholicism.

---

29. There were two apostles with the name James each of whom had monikers which help to distinguish them. *James the Just* is thought to be the Jesus' yonger brother who may also be the same individal in Christian literature as *James the Less* and *James, the son of Alphaeus*. The second apostle is *James the Great*, also referred to as *James, son of Zebedee*. James the Great was a brother to John the Apostle.

SUMMARY

The Hebrew and Christian Bibles have been sacred sources of inspiration for followers of their respective faiths. There is a spectrum of belief as to how to interpret these all-important religious literatures. For these reasons they have become a source of perpetual controversy for all concerned. After Jesus' death c. 30 – 33 CE, from the first to the third century, Christianity arose in the midst of a profound and intense ideological war. Judeans, Greeks, and the Egyptians were in a veritable fog of paganism, first-century Judaism, and a multitude of fractious Christian creeds. Jesus' life and sayings were recorded in dramatically different ways. Since the dating of their authorship, transcription, and publication, the Nag Hammadi codices and Dead Sea Scrolls have provided startlingly different accounts than that of the canonical books of the Christian Bible. The certainty of origin, authenticity, and authorship of these texts varies and has admittedly been highly controversial. However, it is widely accepted that the physical burial in earthen jars of these texts predated the canonization of the New Testament by three centuries.

What is known for certainty is that the Christian Church Fathers long considered unimpeachable prestigious theologians and teachers of their time recognized that the Church would be doomed with such great division of beliefs. Over the course of some three centuries the Church Fathers vehemently debated doctrinal choices as to what would constitute Christian orthodoxy. **Importantly, there were key doctrinal concepts that were not defined in the biblical manuscripts. Among these were the relationship between the members of the Holy Trinity and secondly whether the human soul is immortal/eternal.** This latter point is interesting because the Gnostics and Platonists clearly professed a belief in an immortal human soul and this idea was definitely in circulation prior to Christ Jesus' lifetime and was central to the Gnostics who were contemporaries of the proto-Christian sect. Ultimately, if the Bible is the inspired Word of God, then God vis-à-vis his athorial emissaries forgot to clarify how Jesus and the Holy Spirit fit into the Godhead and whether we humans can depend on an eternal afterlife.

In 367 CE, Athanasius of Alexandria is the first to propose the 27 books as the canonized New Testament to complete the Christian Bible. Athanasius insisted that, "The holy and inspired Scriptures are fully sufficient for the proclamation of the truth."[60] This assertion was met with decades more of contentious debate among Athanasius' contemporaries, but his influence was unstoppable and his proposal in full won the day for all history. While many of the non-Pauline beliefs were already considered heretical, this accord among the Church Fathers in conjunction with the adoption of the faith by the Roman Empire set the stage for a dogmatic effort to eliminate heterodox versions of the faith.

It should be reiterated that the autographic codex, that is, 'The Original' copy of the Bible has never been found and all of the extant codices, tractates, and writings have been heavily redacted. The canonical Christian Bible of today is to be contrasted with the fact that many other writings claiming apostolic authority have been excluded. The vast flock of Christians today is largely ignorant of how the concept of the Christian God evolved from the concept of the Jewish God, Yahweh (YHWH). And furthermore that there was a blurred transition period of monolatrism that sat between ancient polytheism and the Jewish monotheism that existed around the time of Christ. Similarly, most Christians today are not aware that Christianity was formulated in a time where there were many theologically oriented concepts in circulation as to what Christian doctrine ought to be. God did not simply give mankind the Bible in one tidy, complete package. It was instead assembled over several hundred years from a sea of individual manuscripts written in many cases by anonymous authors.

The Dead Sea Scrolls present us with great insights into an elitist Jewish sect that operated differently from other mainstream Jewish communities and that was in close proximity to Jesus and Jesus' post-death followers. Of special importance, these scrolls along with the Nag Hammadi library and other historical facts, paint a Near East culture swamped with many variations on the theme of God and how Jesus of Nazareth fit into the picture. There were many circulating beliefs in regard to Jesus. Some believed Jesus was only a human, albeit the chief apostle of God. Others maintained he was of a divine nature. Some believed that Christ Jesus was fully equal to the Supreme God, others thought of him as only semi-divine. Still others believed in a third entity, the Holy Spirit, and whether or not there was a hierarchy between God, Son and Holy Spirit created even more schisms. Some Christian sects centralized the resurrection in their doctrine whereas others were less certain of it. There were also wide differences of opinion whether Mary, the mother of Jesus, was a virgin at the time of Jesus' conception (that is, she birthed other children prior to Jesus) or whether she was a perpetual virgin. Some say that Jesus had biological siblings and others maintain that the individuals in question were either kinsmen or fraternal associations. The available evidence is contestable in any case.

These divisions culminated in a debate that lasted three centuries as to how to arrive at a ratified belief system called the Nicene Trinitarian Christianity, or what we call today, Catholicism. It is understandable why the early Christian leaders (i.e., Church Fathers) needed to solidify a single creed. But, we nevertheless must question the plausibility of the truthfulness of the Catholic creed when it took so long to agree on the 'correct' narrative of Jesus Christ when none of 'deciders' were alive during the life of Jesus of Nazareth, and with limited exceptions, never met with the apostles or writers of the texts from which the Bible was formed.

CHAPTER 6

The Historicity of the Resurrection... Did Jesus Rise from the Dead?

Could God have justified Himself before human history, so full of suffering, without placing Christ's Cross at the center of that history? Obviously, one response could be that God does not need to justify Himself to man. It is enough that He is omnipotent. From this perspective everything He does or allows must be accepted. This is the position of the biblical Job. But God, who besides being Omnipotence is Wisdom and-to repeat once again-Love, desires to justify Himself to mankind. He is not the Absolute that remains outside of the world, indifferent to human suffering. He is Emmanuel, God-with-us, a God who shares man's lot and participates in his destiny.[1]

– Pope John Paul II
Crossing the Threshold of Hope

Sometimes people approach me and say, "I really struggle with this aspect of Christian teaching. I like this part of Christian belief, but I don't think I can accept that part." I usually respond: "If Jesus rose from the dead, then you have to accept all that he said; if he didn't rise from the dead, then why worry about any of what he said? The issue on which everything hangs is not whether or not you like his teaching but whether or not he rose from the dead."[2]

– Timothy Keller
Theologian and Christian Apologist
The Reason for God: Belief in an Age of Skepticism

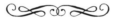

THIS IS A GOOD POINT to briefly reflect on where our journey has taken us thus far. In Chapter 1, in the interest to lay a foundation on which to build additional framework, I set out to define the concepts of faith, belief, and truth—something that is likely to be concordant with most people. We also contextualized contemporary religiously oriented beliefs and the rise of the unaffiliated and nonreligious (the "Nones"). It was offered that finding the truth about God-by-whatever-name could proceed under the banner of *Zeteo Alétheia*—a virginal origin that provides the space for an unbiased, rational pursuit. From here, to further orient ourselves, we recalled attributes commonly assigned to God and considered the very real issue that the general populace is generally unfamiliar with religious concepts, even for their home religion. We came to the vague conclusion that not all religions possess an accurate conception of God as a jumping off point.

Over many tens of thousands of years, superstitions led to the consignment of everyday workings of the world to a diverse ensemble of invisible agents. The human drive for self-preservation led to many cultural clashes that continually altered the membership and hierarchy of the Mesopotamian pantheon of gods. Ancient Judaism appears to have emerged out of well-healed polytheistic Egyptian concepts of multiple deities and was seemingly rooted in polytheism itself (c. 2000 BCE – 1800 BCE). The following millennia would see a transition from polytheism to monolatrism as a forerunner to its eventual conversion to monotheism. This sprouted yet two more religions that distanced itself from the wrathful, knowable, and selective Yahweh who focused on the Israelites to a more powerful but less accessible God named Allah and an all-loving, all-embracing Christian God comprised of three Persons.

Now that we have a more accurate conception how Judaic and Christian religions launched themselves and fought for their own survival, we find ourselves more cognitively prepared to examine their historicity from the literary and philosophical perspective. Going forward, the central thrust of our efforts will be directed at scrutinizing the Foundational Truth Claims of Christianity presented earlier (see Chapter 5, Box 3, p. 169). If we are to critically examine the resurrection based on literary narratives, then we need to depend on the insights of the many scholars who have opined their erudite thoughts in this direction. There is certainly a SURFEIT of argumentation on the matter. The difficulty then is parsing these sources to tease out the most likely explanation as to whether or not the resurrection can be historically proven to have occurred. Before we can study the biblical sources that discuss the resurrection, we must first develop an appreciation for the tools of the historian so that we can comprehend how they take fragments of information and put them together to make a cohesive hypothesis.

LITERARY PRIMACY AND THE HISTORICITY HYPOTHESIS TESTING ENGINE

Ancient history has always been and will always be an industry of studious patchwork owing to the paucity of both direct and indirect evidence. With each generation of historians missionizing themselves to assemble the next best hypothesis to frame history, we end up with a layered and convoluted 'progress' in the form of overwrought contrivances of the 'facts'. Unwinding each new theory is problematic even for those practicing in the same narrow discipline. Nowhere is this truer than in search of the truth of the resurrection. Biblical history is fraught with such a voluminous set of literature espousing this theory or that, it is no wonder we must view these with healthy skepticism when no one can be all too certain of the facts and every hypothesis is built upon a hillside of speculations one dumped on top of another.

In centuries past, when the populace was less educated, religion had it relatively easy because it did not have to defend itself too vigorously. As education and knowledge increased, previously taboo questions were raised (sometimes with grave consequences for the inquirer). Eventually, religion was on the defensive and it turned to historical methods to secure its footing. This was all the more important for exclusivist religions like Christianity that proclaimed theirs was the only true religion. In recent decades, the research and writings of theologians, philosophers, biblical scholars, historians, and archaeologists became much more focused on evolving a historical treatise for the validity of religious concepts and nowhere has this been more prevalent than for the Christian Bible. It turned into a tit-for-tat affair where Christian apologists would decimate woodland forests with all their publications now buttressed with 'historical facts'. Non-traditionalists would have to whittle away at the viral growth of new limbs and a thickened bark of the apologetic trunk of 'knowledge'. This only spurred apologists to produce even more defensive literature. Nowadays it is hard to find a book that focuses on a narrow resurrection topic of less than 500 pages with many hundreds of pages longer, crammed with quotes and a bulging section of end notes and bibliographic references in what appears to be a suggestive effort that the sheer volume of verbiage is reason enough to believe that the biblical events can be backed-up.

In establishing Literary Primacy historians impose core principles for source criticism such as the credibility relative to the type of evidence, originality of the source, indirect/direct eyewitness testimony, multiple/independent sources, motivations of the source and a raft of hermeneutical tools.[3, 4] But these apply to the minutia of understanding the historical value of a given text or contents therein. Ultimately, historians have to develop hypotheses that seek to explain central questions of interest and to this end evidences are collected that elevate or reduce the hypothesis' credibility. Historian C. Behan McCullagh explains that there are abductive criteria which his ilk use in testing historical descriptions.[5] This methodology can be applied to a single hypothesis or to contrast two or more hypotheses. If multiple hypotheses are being compared, then for each criterion, one is looking to understand which of the hypotheses performs better on a relative basis. The first step is to formulate the inquiry, that is, what is it that you want to know. The next step is to accumulate evidentiary information in the form of data, testimony, texts, and archaeological artifacts. I will simply refer to all of the material forms of evidence as 'the claims'. From the set of claims a hypothesis is formulated which seeks to explain the evidentiary information. The hypothesis and the associated facts are then weighed against McCullagh's abductive tests.[1]

Table 6-1. Historicity Tests

1. Explanatory Scope: This provides an assessment for the breadth of the hypothesis in terms of how many claims it can it explain, or conversely, whether and how many of the claims disconfirm the hypothesis.

2. Explanatory Power: How well does the hypothesis account for the observations or evidences? Or alternatively, are there evidences that the hypothesis does not fully explain?

3. *Ad hoc*-ness: In seeking to explain the claims, does the primary hypothesis rely on supplementary explanations/hypotheses to compensate for anomalies not anticipated by the primary theory in its unmodified form? Such adjustments may be more speculative nature, and to the degree this is true, would thereby reduce the likelihood that the primary hypothesis offers the best explanation. Often, as the number of supplemental arguments increase, the more contrived the whole becomes. It is easiest to think of the *ad hoc* criteria as the degree of speculation contained within a given hypothesis.

4. Plausibility: An honest assessment of how likely (statistically or otherwise) a hypothesis offers a rational (i.e., non-miraculous) explanation within specific claims and taken collectively given our general knowledge of the world. Events, ideas, relationships, 'things' that are unlikely, uncertain, illogical, or improbable are less plausible or outright implausible. This is to say there are degrees of plausibility.

5. Conformity with accepted beliefs: How well does the hypothesis comport with beliefs prior to, during, and after the (often estimated) date of the source information?

6. Superiority to rival hypotheses: Comparing this hypothesis and the outcome of the other tests above, how does this hypothesis rank in terms of providing the best overall explanation? This is less of a test per se as it is a conclusion of the five criteria above.

---

1. The list has been adapted and numerically reordered from McCullagh's arrangement.

I refer to this collection of abductive reasoning more conveniently as the Historicity Hypothesis Testing Engine (HHTE). While these tests permit us the opportunity to critique the quality of historical information, it must be admitted upfront that even in the most cautious application of these principles it can never be mistaken as an infallible mechanism. In conjunction with Literary Primacy, source criticism, and the many forms of textual and historical criticism (refer to p. 147), the HHTE allows historians to parse all the data that pertain to a given problem. By dumping the historical claims, suppositions, and raw data into the maw of this rubric, the grand hope is that an objective qualification of the hypothesis comes out the other end to allow us to formulate an *Inference to the Best Explanation*. As I have said before, we can seldom ever hope to obtain proof positive.

In practical terms, *reliable* knowledge from ancient times is not plentiful and what can be assembled may have embedded problems making the task of feeding the HHTE machine a challenge. We find that Explanatory Power and Plausibility are the most important of the tests, with Explanatory Scope, conformity with accepted belief, and *ad hoc*-ness of lesser importance. It is also to be acknowledged that plausibility is subjective to each person. As we all readily acknowledge, this is dependent on one's specific and overall knowledge, their set of beliefs, and their reasoning ability to synthesize and critique information. We will utilize the HHTE in the next chapter and the one following it. It is introduced now as we are to commence with assembling the information that will be injected into the HHTE.

A key question arises as to whether or not miracles are allowed to play an integral part in the argumentation and this is no more true than when it comes to discussing the resurrection of Jesus Christ. Prior to the turn of the 20th-century, Christian apologists had **GERRYMANDERED** the game simply because they controlled the vast majority of public mind share and volume of publications academically and otherwise. Skeptics were far fewer in number and scientific revelation hadn't hit its full stride so any contra-conjectures against the majority opinion were easily crowded out. As a result, there was limited need to be overly attached to miracles to defend the Bible and other extra-biblical texts.

As historical and scientific discoveries of importance increased and understanding of ancient texts progressed, skeptics gained a new foothold in religious debates. Back then, most Christian apologists were philosophers, theologians, and biblical scholars not necessarily well-trained in historical analysis. Christian apologist and resurrection specialist Michael Licona echoes this same line of thinking. He states, "Almost without exception, the literature pertaining to Jesus' resurrection has been written by biblical scholars and philosophers. Could a reason for the varied conclusions on the subject be that those writing on it are not equipped for the task? Have biblical scholars and philosophers received the same training in the philosophy of history and historical method as their cousins, that is, professional historians outside of the community of biblical scholars? Would an application of their approach lead us closer to solving the puzzle?"[6] The puzzle he is referring to are the historicity of Jesus' resurrection and divinity.

Historians require natural evidence that can be studied, reproduced, cross-referenced, et cetera, and further assert that imposing a bias upfront of barring miracle-claims is justified in the reckoning of true history. They outright discounted arguments that possessed any reliance on miracle-claims. With this pressure, apologists started getting uncomfortable because for every *historical* claim they put forward, an equal or more potent counter-claim would be lodged by historians that overturned, neutralized, or added another degree of uncertainty to the apologetic claim. Furthermore, some apologists became frustrated that the sharpest blade in their arsenal was being barred from the battlefield.

In an effort to intellectually pry open the locked door to unleash their banished weapon, Licona lectures on this point saying "we have observed that there are no sound reasons, *a priori* or **A POSTERIORI**, for prohibiting historians from investigating a miracle-claim. It is noteworthy that the climate is changing and professional historians are warming up to the notion of miracles[7] [...] If our assessments throughout this chapter are correct, historians are within their professional rights to give attention to miracle-claims. Moreover, there are signs from the community of professional historians that the epistemological ice age of antisupernaturalism appears to be coming to an end."[8] Licona's book *The Resurrection of Jesus: A New Historiographical Approach* (InterVarsity Press, 2010) is profusely littered with source citations but he offers nothing to back the claim for there being "signs" from "professional historians" backing away from their policy of historical analysis methodology. More to the point, I see no merits for this opinion. He continues on in a confident stride as if his ideological whims have come to pass to discuss what the burden of proof should be. "We are thus left with the conclusion that the paradigm provided by the [US] legal system in civil court is best suited for the investigation of miracle-claims."[9] By this he means that if the likelihood for a miracle exceeds fifty percent, then a miracle could be relied upon as a constituent of the best explanation of historical events.

Miracles are an intractable subject matter if for no other reason than defining and providing criteria toward identification of what constitutes a miracle is controversial. The delineation between human comprehension and the utterly stupefying is a shifting line. Prior to the 1800's it would have been thought impossible for man to set foot on the Moon, or to send a spacecraft beyond the outer reaches of our solar system, or for us to routinely physically manipulate individual atoms and yet all these things can be historically proven to have occurred. Resorting to miracles to explain history opens a can of slippery worms. What is the frequency with which God is intervening in our world? Was the resurrection the one and only time? And what about the Creation account of the universe and the many miracles stated in the Bible? And if we go by US polls, about a quarter of people believe that God is calling the outcomes of football, soccer, and basketball games,[10, 11] which goes against the philosophy of free will. Should we count these interventions as miracles too? When do we stop counting? Modern-day evangelicals famously believe that the Lord is prodigiously at work in our daily lives and that we just need to pray and God will listen, and sometimes, bless us in favorable ways.

This calls to mind the humorous movie *Bruce Almighty* (Universal Pictures, 2003) where actor Jim Carrey plays the character of down-on-his-luck Bruce Nolan. Nolan complains that God is not doing a good job of answering prayers very well so God, played by Morgan Freeman, endows Nolan with all his powers so that God can take a vacation. After more than a week of neglecting his duties, God pays Nolan a visit to goad him to start answering prayer requests. Nolan tries a few attempts to organize his efforts which turn out to be in vain. So, he digitizes all the incoming e-mail prayer requests using his newly created *"YAHWEH! Insta-Prayer"* account. The requests are so numerous he falls asleep while waiting for over a million and a half unread e-mail prayers to download. The next morning, he begins the work of answering the emails by typing at warp speed and finds that no matter how fast he types, he cannot keep pace with the volume of incoming prayer requests. While this scene is very comical, many people seriously believe that God is managing a perpetually renewing prayer list several hundred million strong, week-in and week-out.

Even though shocking events happen all the time and we have considerably more means today to qualify such events, we still cannot demonstrably show that God has intervened. Who is to be the arbiter of declaring such and such was a divine miracle versus something simply beyond our current comprehension? What threshold of evidence need be supplied to validate a **PUTATIVE** revelation? If we allow revelation, how are we to treat the disparate revelations among the various claimant world religions? I can assure you that there are a great many things that occur in the scientific realm that we do not really understand, but we can be certain it is not a process being directed actively by God.

Let us review the idea of Jesus walking on liquid sea water.[2,3] Historical analysis suggests that we should like to gather testimony by interviewing eyewitnesses, read any reports that might be available, review regional temperature charts, or adorn snorkeling gear to peer beneath the water to verify whether or not there are sub-surface rocks or outcroppings on which to step on. But we know from experience that self-levitation is not naturally possible and is confined to the imaginings of the mind. *Theologically*, however, we might say that God gave Jesus the power to alter the universe's properties in the immediate vicinity of his body to allow him walk on water. Alternatively, we might say that thousands of microscopic mystical pink- and purple-dotted dragons had teleported from a parallel dimension and fluttered their teeny-tiny wings to support Jesus' feet with each step and then just as rapidly teleported back to their original plane of existence. For all practical purposes these hypotheses are equally as plausible as they are equally unprovable. No one today has seen either of these things happen.

Licona and his cohorts are attempting to galvanize solidarity among the academic community by trying to rewrite historiographical methods as the once solid walls of Christendom are breaking daylight across its many faces due to the thudding blows of historical interrogation. Rather than seeking truth for the Christian God in an objective fashion, they see it as a re-balancing effort to cast off the unfair restrictions imposed by naturalism. For the purposes of objectively analyzing the Foundational Truth Claims, I shall follow the historian's tradition of relying on weighing physical evidence and testimony singly and collectively in fair-minded fashion while disallowing use of supernatural claims. Finally, I will appeal to my original assertion in Chapter 1 that we should adopt a sterilized position by assuming that God-by-whatever-name does not exist until evidence substantiates otherwise. We should call to mind the critical assumption that for Jesus to be resurrected, it presupposes that Jesus, the Holy Spirit, and God the Father existed at that pivotal moment in time.

New Testament Inconsistencies and Historical Qualifiers

There are those who wish to believe in the total inerrancy of the Bible, presumably because it represents the inspired Word of God. If the Bible were inerrant, then all the information presented in it is to be regarded as true. However, it does not take a lot of detective work

---

2. According to three Gospels (Matthew 14:22-36; Mark 6:45-56; John 6:16-24), Jesus walked across the Sea of Galilee. This sea was/is actually the largest fresh water lake in Israel and had many names over history—Lake of Gennesaret, Lake Chinnereth, Lake Tiberias, Lake Kinneret, and Sea of Ginosar.

3. We shall assume the real circumstances of the salinity of sea water, standard temperature, standard pressure, and normal Earth gravity at sea level and the normal body weight of healthy human male. We shall also assume that there is no exotic Einsteinian relativistic phenomenon at play!

to uncover inconsistencies. This is most readily apparent in the New Testament because the authors are more or less talking about the same events. It is where the stories cross paths that the purported facts do not mesh. While there are many disparities one can point to, only a sample will be provided herein. To this end, we can find incongruities with the bloodline of Jesus, the timing of the Passover relative to the anointing of Jesus, the day of Jesus' death, and multiple issues related the burial of Jesus.

It is safe to say that scholars on both sides of the divide believe that the genealogy of Jesus as written in the gospels of Matthew and Luke are radically different. Both gospels affirm that Jesus was born a virginal birth by Mary and God as opposed to being fathered by Joseph. While both gospels provide identical lineage from Abraham to King David, they branch away from each other after King David creating a stark inconsistency in the stories. The pedigree was vastly important to the ancient Jewish population as the Messiah was prophesied to come from the full and true line of David. In this respect, whether one gospel is true and the other is not in is by no means a death-blow to Christianity and as such I will not bother with examination of the various hypotheses that seeks to explain this particular discrepancy.

We also find inconsistencies between the gospels of Matthew and John as to where Jesus stayed the night after his second day in the Temple. In Matthew, the Passover is *two* days away as he takes respite at the home of Simon the Leper.

> [v1]When Jesus had finished saying all these things, he said to his disciples, [v2]"You know that after **two days the Passover is coming**, and the Son of Man will be handed over to be crucified." [...] [v6]Now while Jesus was at Bethany in the house of Simon the leper, [v7]a woman came to him with an alabaster jar of very costly ointment, and she poured it on his head as he sat at the table.

> Matthew 26:1-2, 6-7

John's account states that Jesus stayed at the home of Martha, Mary, and Lazarus in Bethany, *six* days before the Passover.

> **Six days before the Passover** Jesus came to Bethany, the home of Lazarus, whom he had raised from the dead. There they gave a dinner for him. Martha served, and Lazarus was one of those at the table with him. Mary took a pound of costly perfume made of pure nard, anointed Jesus' feet, and wiped them with her hair. The house was filled with the fragrance of the perfume.

> John 12:1-3

The difference in days is not an insignificant matter. Remember that Jesus cannot become the Jewish Messiah until he has been anointed per the Jewish tradition. In the Gospel of John, Jesus enters Jerusalem on a donkey already anointed as the Messiah, whereas in Matthew, he arrives *without* the sacred anointing. The crowds (which some contend were not there to begin with) may not have received him so positively if he had not been anointed as this had been long prophesied. Obviously at least one of these accounts is untrue. As before, this inconsistency is not going to crack the crucible of Christendom.

Other salient challenges to the historical accuracy of the NT arise in the gospels of Mark and John which clearly state that Jesus died on different days, with Mark saying that Jesus was crucified at 9 a.m. the day *after* Passover whereas John records Jesus' death as taking place in the afternoon, the day *before* Passover. It can be plainly shown that there are similar divergences on the burial narrative as to (1) who buried Jesus, (2) how many women went to Jesus' tomb, (3) whether or not the stone that barred entry was rolled back or not, and (4) what the women saw once they entered the tomb (men or angelic visitants).[4] I will leave it to the reader to establish the veracity of these claims as this is easily accomplished by reading the New Testament using the horizontal style.

These are by no means the only inconsistencies, but it is substantial enough to indicate that the New Testament is not wholly internally consistent and ***therefore the NT gospel accounts cannot be taken at face value***. This point cannot be overemphasized. Recall in Chapter 5 it was discussed that the Bible can be read vertically, chronologically, and horizontally. Reading the Bible at face value is reading the Bible vertically or chronologically whereby the words, phrases, and stories are accepted with no critical analysis of what motivated the authors to write what they did and how potential inconsistencies *were* reconciled (that is, redactions made to alter the original form) and how they *were not* reconciled within the Bible as shown above. Additionally, reading the Bible at face value ignores the great wealth of knowledge yielded by thousands of extra-biblical texts, some of which pre-date the NT, and how these influenced what texts were adopted as biblical canon. Those who are leaders or participants in non-academic Bible study classes often introduce a cultural, geographical, and historical backdrop of the ancient world to add context. This added context definitely improves the intended meaning of the Bible, but it falls very short of a deep introspection

---

4. Mark 16:5— Young man in white robe waiting for women. Matthew 28:2-6—As women approach, an angel descends from heaven and rolls back the stone. Luke 24:2-4—The stone was rolled back and the women did not find the body. Two men in dazzling clothes appeared suddenly. John 20:1-18—The stone was removed from the tomb and Mary Magdalene, Simon Peter, and a disciple (some suggest this was John the Evangelist) saw the empty tomb. After the two men left, two angels appeared before Mary. Then Jesus suddenly appeared which is the first of all the appearances that Jesus made.

of the kind we are considering herein. The considerable majority of biblical scholars (apologetic or otherwise) will readily admit that reading the Bible at face value glosses over a vast sea of textual and historical concerns and that what we understand today is in many pertinent aspects different than how we understood them decades ago.

Dr. Bart Ehrman goes a step further to conclude that the canonical NT Gospels simply cannot be trusted because they fail basic qualifications for being solid evidentiary sources for the historical record.

New Testament Presents Compromised Qualifications for Historical Evidence[12]

1. The NT accounts are chronologically distant in time from the events they are commenting on;

2. There were no eyewitnesses including the actual gospel writers (all of whom remain anonymous to this day);

3. The four gospels do not present related information in a factually consistent manner;

4. The writers were interested to persuade their audiences of their point of view concerning historical events and this view was not impartial.

So we have determined with no doubt whatsoever that the Christian Bible is *not* inerrant. But we cannot yet conclude that there are not aspects of the New Testament that offer some measure of truth. To reveal this insight we have to step onto the apologist–skeptic court to play some real hardball. At this point, we move onto the court with a demonstrable weakening of the canonical Bible as a reliable historical source. The aforementioned inconsistencies are not strong enough to hobble all of Christianity as it still rests on the TROIKA of Foundational Truth Claims—Jesus' resurrection, his divinity, and his coequal position with God and the Holy Spirit. Also, while the gospels suffer some problems, they of course are not the only books in the New Testament. We have the 13 Pauline Epistles some number of which is supposed to be written authentically by Paul, the eight general epistles, as well as the Acts of the Apostles and the book of Revelation. Let us now delve deeper to survey the authenticity of the first pillar of strength—the incarnate resurrection of Jesus.

HISTORICITY OF THE BODILY RESURRECTION OF JESUS FROM THE TOMB

The most central thesis in all of Christianity is that Jesus is God incarnate who was crucified and *bodily* resurrected from the sealed rock-hewn tomb, and by the power of the Holy Spirit, he ascended into heaven. The bodily resurrection of Jesus from the dead, if true, is the single most important event in world history. All four of the gospels attest that the tomb where Jesus was buried was empty and that Jesus was physically raised from the dead.[5] It is what I refer to as the Grand Intervention of God as it prevails above all other DEICTIC testimonials of God's presence in our world. If the resurrection cannot be reasonably supported, that is on balance between all the pro and con arguments, the bottom drops out from underneath Christianity.

Christian apologists mount a spirited multi-pronged defense that, to their mind, fortifies their position against successful counter-points. As this debate has raged for many decades and an astounding amount of material has been written on this topic. I have opted to select from the many potential sources the work of Professor Gary Habermas.[6] Habermas, who is an affable gentleman and a well-conversant evangelical biblical scholar, is regarded by many as the foremost authority and defender of the resurrection. Here I summarize an accreted list presented in *The Case for the Resurrection of Jesus* (Kregel Publications, 2004) which was authored by Habermas and his colleague Michael Licona who was mentioned earlier. This book compiles and distills the full scope of resurrection scholarship to form a *de facto* Christian handbook to defend the resurrection. So my contention is that if we can contrast this work with counter-evidences, we will have performed a fair analysis of the main components to proffer a decision on the historicity of Jesus' resurrection. And, to this point, Kris Komarnitsky, author of *Doubting Jesus' Resurrection: What Happened in the Black Box* (Stone Arrow Books, 2014) distills seven resurrection-related claims advanced by another leading apologetic luminary, William Lane Craig, along with his co-author, Michael Licona. Table 6-2 represents a harmonization of the central contentions of some of the most credentialed Christian apologists.[13, 14]

---

5. Empty tomb gospel accounts: Mark 16:1-8, Luke 24:1-11; 24, Matthew 28:1-10, John 20:1-18

6. Dr. Habermas is Chair, Department of Philosophy, at Liberty University, the largest Christian university in the world.

Table 6-2. Christian Evidence for the Resurrection

CLAIM 1: Jesus was buried in an honorable manner and in a rock-hewn tomb.

CLAIM 2: The discovery that the tomb was empty the following day. This is even attested to by Jesus' enemies (see Matthew 28:12-13).

CLAIM 3: Shortly after his crucifixion, Jesus' disciples believed he rose from the dead. His death and resurrection led to the conversions of Saul of Tarsus (Apostle Paul) and James the Just, the skeptical brother (some say half-brother) of Jesus.[7, 15, 16]

CLAIM 4: Many early disciples martyred themselves due to the strength of their convictions that the prophecy had been realized.

CLAIM 5:

(Part I) Post-death appearances of Jesus are reported by Paul, all four Gospel authors, and by the author of the book of Acts.

(Part II) Additionally, these events are commented on by non-Christian (detractor) sources.

CLAIM 6: The Bible contains contemporary writings about the resurrection.

CLAIM 7: Jesus' many posthumous appearances represent multiple independent eyewitnesses consisting of individuals and groups, under different circumstances, appearing to friends and foes.

CLAIM 8: Other naturalistic explanations presented to date are inferior.

---

7. There is much debate about the consanguinity (i.e., blood relationship) between Jesus and his siblings. It is unclear whether James the Just was part of Jesus' immediate nuclear family as a younger biological brother of Jesus, or a half-brother owing to a prior marriage by Joseph, or that the conversational use of the word 'brother' was intended to mean a kinsman or fraternal relationship. Catholics today espouse that Mary was a perpetual virgin and therefore deny James was a full blood brother of Jesus. However, in the first two centuries after Jesus died, there was significant controversy as to whether Mary was a virgin prior to or after the birth of Jesus. This position of perpetual virginity wouldn't be accepted until the third and fourth centuries when Hippolytus, Eusebius of Caesarea, Epiphanius, and Athanasius came to its defense.

CLAIM 1 – JESUS' HONORABLE BURIAL

Because Habermas and his compatriots extol that their claims are so abundantly and powerfully supported, they have outstretched their arms to clear the stakes from the table. Just as quickly, their counterparts wrap their knuckles saying, "Not so fast!" A number of erudite and astute refutations have been lodged by others against this supposed fortress of historical fact and logic, though I shall attempt to make quick work of the first four claims because in comparison to the latter points, they are relatively weak claims.

The first claim is made simply to assert that Jesus was given a respectable burial in accordance with Jewish law. This is to be interpreted to mean that after Jesus' death, mourners could lament for him in the presence of his body and that his body would be washed and anointed, followed by it being wrapped in a linen cloth and subsequently buried. While most everyone agrees that Pontius Pilate granted permission to Joseph of Arimathea[8] to remove the body from the cross, everything thereafter becomes a world of **AMARANTHINE** debate.

It is a well-supported from the archaeological examination of tombs from the associated period and from an array of literary sources how and under what conditions the 1st-century Jewish people buried the deceased and to what degree their Roman overlords allowed them to carry out their customs. Those who were poor were buried as individuals in shallow earthen pits, in so-called trench graves. The Jewish Sanhedrin apparently maintained two graveyards for criminals. One was reserved for criminals who were beheaded or strangled and the other for those that were executed by stoning or by fire.[17] Some have supposed that these two burial sites were rock-hewn tombs, however, there appears to be no hard evidence to support this contention and more than likely they were both field graveyards.[18] The body had to remain in this place of dishonor for at least one year. After that time expired, the remains could be relocated. However, only those with families of better than average means who could afford a rock-hewn tomb or cave-like structure and an ossuary to provide such an opportunity for relocation. These criminals had their skeletal remains placed as individuals or with other people's bones into an ossuary. The bones of poor criminals stayed buried in the graveyard cemeteries or possibly moved to a more honorable field plot. In either case, skeletal remains that have been buried 2,000 years ago would have long since decomposed leaving no traces of their existence.

According to Jewish custom, only those who died without a criminal conviction by the Jewish Sanhedrin could be honored in death by allowing people to openly mourn for

---

8. The has been no archaeological or other source evidence that can confirm the existence or location of a town called "Arimathea."

the deceased. However, mourning of the deceased was forbidden in any circumstance during Jewish festivals.[19] We infer from Deuteronomy 21 and the Temple Scroll (one of the Dead Sea Scrolls) that, for those criminals crucified in non-war times, deceased criminals must be buried prior to sunset to ensure the land is not defiled.[20] Furthermore, no one was permitted to visibly mourn for the deceased criminal. Their bodies were to be put into a place of dishonor, presumably into one of the reserved graveyards. Virtually everyone agrees that Jesus was punished as a criminal. We are told in John's gospel that Jesus' body was taken down on the eve of his death (see John 19:39). It is unlikely that any of his followers were present to mourn over Jesus' death because he died during the festival of Passover.[21] Since there is no information ever found that talks about who was in the presence of Jesus' corpse before Joseph of Arimathea and Nicodemus[9] prepared his body, we cannot really say that he had an honorable burial based on whether people openly mourned him or not. It really comes down to whether Jesus was initially put into a trench grave suited for the poor and criminally convicted or if he was put directly into a rock-hewn tomb which we would suppose would be honorable. This is discussed further in the following discussion of Claim 2.

But before we move onto the second claim, there is an 800-pound gorilla sitting in the room. We have to call to mind that all of Christendom believes that Jesus Christ was buried only one time and that it was in a rock-hewn tomb. Presuming for the moment that Jesus was buried as such, the rather striking fact is that there is nothing literarily or archaeologically in existence that speaks to the fact that Jesus' tomb was venerated by his early followers as a holy place where his miraculous resurrection took place. One would think that the original apostles, particularly his brother James, who resided in Jerusalem after Jesus' death and was the first Bishop of Jerusalem, would have made the tomb a primary site for worship. But, this apparently did not happen.

Beyond this, there are clues that (1) Jesus' *initial* burial place may have been an earthen field grave, (2) we are lacking robust information that Jesus' supposed rock tomb was empty on the third day, and (3) Jesus' bones may have been reburied following the common practice of secondary burial. We already explored the latter situation in discussing the ossuaries of Talpiot Tomb A and its potential status as the family tomb of Jesus of Nazareth. As to the first two clues, we will review these in due course in the investigation of the remaining claims.

---

9. In the canonical Bible, Nicodemus is only mentioned in the Gospel of John. He was a Pharisee and a member of the Sanhedrin Council.

CLAIM 2 – THE EMPTY TOMB

The second claim states that the lack of a body in the secured rock tomb is evidence that he was bodily (as well as mentally and spiritually) raised from the dead. While the four gospel accounts affirm Jesus was interred into a rock tomb and that it was later empty, this is not explicitly confirmed by the testimony provided directly from the Apostle Paul. All four gospel writers narrate that it was Jesus' female disciples (the identities of the women vary by account) who first witness the empty tomb. With the exception of Apostle Simon Peter (reported in Luke and John) and an unnamed disciple (noted only in John's gospel), these are prospectively the only apostolic witnesses to the empty tomb. The unnamed disciple is considered by some to be John the Evangelist, a candidate author of the Gospel of John. However, the contention that this disciple was in fact John or that it was the same person who may have contributed to the writing of the book of John is left as a relative uncertainty by scholars at-large. According to some of the gospels, the other apostles were within walking distance of the tomb but they apparently didn't go to view the empty tomb themselves. We also know that each gospel writer borrowed information from other source materials. Thus, with respect to the empty tomb, the actual written gospel testimony is most likely secondhand, if not third- or fourth-hand, information.

It is peculiar to say the least that the Apostle Paul himself never mentions the empty tomb in any of his epistles which are centrally geared toward converting people to Christianity. What does Paul himself say about this? The **only** words that Apostle Paul wrote about the burial is, *"that he was buried, and that he was raised on the third day"* (1 Corinthians 15:4). Paul *surely* would have brought everything to the table to argue the truth of the resurrection to the nonbelieving Gentiles. Alas, as to an explicit narrative on the empty tomb, Paul remained silent. Christian apologists commonly decree that Paul simply accepted the empty tomb as a matter-of-fact given that Jesus made post-death appearances. But this inference is not on stable ground either on Paul's exact testimony or even by the Acts of the Apostles which offers purported quotations from Paul.

In Acts 13:29-30, the author of Acts discusses that Paul presented a sermon in Antioch in Pisidia (southwest Turkey) where he extolled, "[...] they took him down from the tree and laid him in a tomb. But God raised him from the dead." Again, there is no confirmation that it was a rock tomb or that it was empty three days later. According to Komarnitsky's insights, the Greek word "tomb" as used in the context of this passage could either mean "tomb" or "grave."[22] A grave could be either a field grave or a structural tomb of some sort. It is sensible to conjecture that Jesus was either (1) initially laid to rest in a rock-hewn tomb, only to be buried in an earthen grave customary for criminals within a period of a few days afterwards, or (2) that he was straight away initially buried in a trench grave. Using literary sources as the sole basis, it is very challenging to say one way or another what type of initial burial Jesus was given and whether it was concordant with an honorable burial.

This second claim is most effectively countered by the argument regarding the posthumous appearances of Jesus (Claim 7). In fact, N. T. Wright, one of the most eminent Christian apologists and Bible scholars of the current generation confirms that, "Both the meetings [that is, the Jesus post-death appearances] and the empty tomb are therefore necessary if we are to explain the rise of the belief and the writing of the stories as we have them. Neither by itself was sufficient; put them together, though, and they provide a complete and coherent explanation for the rise of the early Christian belief."[23] Therefore, if the appearances can be shown to be untrue, then the circumstances of the empty tomb are moot.

CLAIM 3 – PAUL'S AND JAMES' CONVERSIONS TO CHRISTIANITY

According to Luke 10:1-24, prior to his death, Jesus sent out the Seventy disciples in pairs to evangelize his message.[10] Habermas contends that shortly after Jesus' death and miraculous resurrection that the disciples beliefs remained so strong that they would be willing to be adhere to them on pain of death. However, Matthew's gospel weakens this idea when, after the death of Jesus, "the eleven disciples went to Galilee, to the mountain to which Jesus had directed them. When they saw him, they worshiped him; *but some doubted.*" (Matthew 28:16-17). The book of Matthew concludes with three additional verses from Jesus, saying nothing about whether the doubting disciples ever became convinced.

Many are divided as to the exact motivations as to why the disciples James (the brother of Jesus) and Paul became devotees of Jesus. Many would point to the appearance accounts (discussed under the Claim 7 response) as the primary reason, but the Bible does not offer a lengthy discussion on the topic so it is largely left to speculation. In the case of James' conversion, one could speculate that his resistance/skepticism about his brother Jesus may have been appeased with his appointment as the leader of all the disciples (he became the first Bishop of Jerusalem). Maybe he was so psychologically affected by his brother Jesus being killed for what he believed in, he later felt remorse after he was gone and wanted to honor him by teaching his brother's message to the community. We know that Paul never met Jesus prior to his death. Furthermore, until his conversion three years later, Paul persecuted

---

10. Codex Sinaiticus states there were Seventy Disciples. In other texts the group is referred to as the Seventy-Two Disciples.

Christians (he consented as a bystander at the stoning of Stephen). It would be plausible that Paul had an epiphany that a life filled with persecuting people was no longer for him. In short, it comes down to speculation as to why these two biblical figures decided to become religious missionaries. While the evidence is not ironclad, James is thought to have towed the rites and customs of the Jews, much as John the Baptist did. Whereas Paul discarded these obligations and focused more on proselytizing people to see Jesus as the linchpin to accessing God. But, just because two people, only one of whom knew Jesus, decided to carry on Jesus' mission is not very convincing evidence that a man literally came back from the dead.

CLAIM 4 – Christian Martyrs

We are led to believe that ten of the original twelve apostles were martyred. The other two who escaped this fate were Judas Iscariot who committed suicide and John the Apostle who died of natural aging. Other disciples, including Paul, were also put to death. Would so many been so fervent in their belief that they would willingly die in the face of imminent death?

As a claim to support the resurrection, even if the disciples were martyred, such belief does not offer robust evidence that Jesus was actually resurrected. That is to say that the disciples may have believed in Jesus' teachings strongly enough to have died for them without Jesus actually being resurrected. We have far too many cultic examples in our history than I care to review. Let it suffice to bring to light the tragic incident in 1978 concerning cult leader James Warrant Jones, more commonly known as Jim Jones, and how he led himself and 909 members of the *Peoples Temple* to commit mass suicide in Jonestown, Guyana. Prior to the September 11, 2001 attacks, this tragedy had the dubious distinction as being the greatest non-accidental loss of American civilians.[24] The fact that some early Christians may have martyred themselves speak to their resolve in their belief, but it in no way validates that a human being died and came back to life. There are countless examples in other religions of people martyring themselves in the name of their religion (e.g., religiously-motivated suicide bombers). So it isn't that special of a thing, even in that particular time period, for people to die for what they believe in.

The Roman Imperialists had a long and well-accepted history of treating people equally. They had a considerable network of spies who were on the lookout for people committing infractions. They had no interest in incarcerating a large population of criminals and the maintenance required therein. Therefore, capital punishment was used with little regard to the severity of the offense. They killed Jews, Christians, or pagans with little to no discrimination. So, to whatever degree that Christians were being martyred, they were not necessarily being singled out from others. In fact, the Jewish people revolted against the Romans engaging them in three wars in an attempt to reclaim their religious heritage. The hundreds of thousands that died could well be considered martyrs.

The first four claims are leveraged to amass a larger cohort of evidences in the hope that multiple 'evidences' become additive to support the overall hypothesis. But, even if we are to be charitable and we allow the summation of all four sources of indirect evidence, it is woefully inadequate to validate that a human being actually rose from the dead. Let us now tackle the stronger claims.

CLAIM 5 – CHRISTIAN AND NON-CHRISTIANS WRITE ABOUT THE RESURRECTION

Habermas and many other apologists have long asserted that commentary by Christian and non-Christians confirms that Jesus was in fact a real person in human history and that these writers directly discuss the resurrection event. **The truth is that there is an overwhelming paucity of authenticated information of** *any kind,* **let alone textual information, about Jesus of Nazareth.** In our earlier review of biblical antiquities we considered the True Cross, the nails used in 1st-century crucifixion, the burial shrouds, and the Talpiot ossuaries as possible sources to confirm the basic claim that Jesus was a real person who lived and died in 1st-century Judea. We were unable to deduce with suitable historical reliability that any of these artifacts could be tied to Jesus of Nazareth. It was mentioned that we have the means at our disposal to add clarity to the matter, but the necessary steps have not as yet been taken. When we look to literary sources, we find a similar anemic supply of information.

Though his oratory is often quoted, we have found no literary works actually *written* by Jesus himself. The earliest known and authenticated textual references (not considering epigraphs written on physical objects) are the Pauline letters of which only seven of the thirteen are given full credence as being authentically authored by Paul himself. The first of these letters was written in the early 50's CE, some 20 – 25 years after Jesus died. It has been argued that the four canonical gospels were written anywhere between the 70 CE and 150 CE, about 40–120 years after the death of Jesus. **As best as can be ascertained, the actual authors of the four gospels are anonymous.** The original manuscripts do not exist and we only have copies. It would have been customary at the time for original papyrus scrolls to be marked or labeled with the author's name at the end of the document. Alas, the earliest copies of the gospels with the authorial attributions are but fragments that had been first created in the second century. There has been a torrent of scholarship attempting to solidify whether internal evidence (that is, information within the gospels) or external evidence could tie authorial attributions to Matthew, Mark, Luke, and John, but ultimately such efforts are speculative at best. Essentially, there was poor record-keeping in the first century in which to trace the authenticity of these particular documents. By the time the second century rolled around and commentators started writing about the Greek manuscripts and historians were recording history, the reliability of who wrote these documents was guesswork even then.

To add to the conundrum, biblical scholars have contended that the gospels were not simply written under the sole knowledge of each respective unknown authors. Rather, each gospel author used other written source materials to help develop their respective literary work. Mark is said to have used the pre-Marcan Passion Narrative that discusses Jesus' trial, crucifixion, and his burial in a rock-hewn tomb.[25] While this source purportedly references the name of Jesus, it does not mention the tomb being empty or the resurrection. This source has not been found and is conjectured to have been written between 30 – 60 CE. Scholars also theorize that three additional sources referred to individually as the L-source, M-source, and Q-source *may* have existed. These sources have a range of dates from the year Christ died (c. 30 – 33 CE) to after Paul wrote his first seven letters (c. 70 CE). This would mean that these writings could be the very first documents to reference Jesus, the empty tomb, and the resurrection. However, these sources remain strictly theoretical because they may never have existed, or if they did, they are not specifically mentioned by the Church Fathers or others who probably should have commented on their existence. The summary, if there is to be one, is that the Gospel of Mark is generally considered to be the first gospel written (referred to as the Marcan Priority), but some challenge this by asserting that Matthew was the earliest written gospel (Matthaean Priority).

There seems there will be uncertainty in the dating of these important literary works for some time to come. My studies favor the position of the Marcan Priority. While the reasons are numerous for this decision, I will suffice it to say that it can be shown that the author of Matthew actually corrects information in Mark's gospel. For instance, Mark misquotes the book of Isaiah in Mark 1:2-3 where he includes a quoted verse from Malachi 3:1 which should not be there at all (refer to Matthew 3:3 which corrects the testimony presented in Mark). Whether or not the gospels used earlier sources is of little interest here because their existence is highly uncertain and therefore there is no wish to create a framework to understand Christian claims on such a precarious set of assumptions. Beyond all this, the earliest textual evidence that we have in our possession in *physical* form that specifically uses the name Jesus, and that we know is authentically referring to Jesus of Nazareth, and that is part of the New Testament, is the Rylands Papyrus P[52] biblical fragment (c. 125 – 175 CE). Though the main interest at hand is to identify sources that discuss the empty tomb and the resurrection, there are a few earlier texts that mention names affiliated with Jesus as we will shortly explore.

The Christian Bible was assembled in part to address a Roman audience and that at its core was an appeal to the many-god pagan world of the exclusivist Christian way of thinking. Recall that prior to his conversion, the Apostle Paul was a Pharisee[11] and desired to coexist with Roman society. Having been a witness of how the Romans meted out imperial justice and specifically how the Jewish people were ill-treated, it did not make a lot of sense for Paul or the proto-Christians to revolt against or in any way antagonize Roman rulers in the early formational decades of the Jesus Movement. The earliest proto-Christians had to look no further than the heavy-handed Roman decimation of Jerusalem in 70 CE. Also, it is fairly clear that the early Church Fathers (well before Constantine's time) showed preference to texts that did not overtly upset the Roman establishment.

Athanasius, the foremost Church Father responsible for assembling the canonical Bible, was exiled five times by five different Roman Emperors (Constantine I, Constantius I, Constantius II, Julian the Apostate, and Valens) and his struggles with the power class earned him the moniker, *"Athanasius Contra Mundum"* (Latin for, Athanasius Against the World) for his apparent resolve to defend his views. In his second exile, he garnered a decree from Emperor Constantius I that he was to be put to death if he set foot in Alexandria which was induced by Athanasius' adversaries known as the Eusebians (the party that rooted for the Arian perspective of the Godhead and who carried forward the ideas of Eusebius of Nicomedia after his death).[26, 27] So, we see that the Roman politburo exerted palatable pressure onto those individuals responsible for debating and selecting the texts that would be included in the Bible. **Given the inherent bias, one has to ask if there are any other non-biblical sources around the time of Jesus that would serve as a testament that Jesus of Nazareth ever existed, and if so, was there any mention of the empty tomb or resurrection event.**

Beyond the four canonical NT Gospels, there are very few extra-biblical literary sources within two centuries of Jesus' death that make mention of the empty tomb of Jesus. These can be divided into writers sympathetic to the Christian movement and the one instance whereby the author campaigned against it. The two earliest proto-Christian commentaries are from Justin Martyr and Tertullian who indirectly infer that the tomb was empty.

---

11. According to Jewish-Roman historian Josephus, we know of five main Jewish sects; the Essenes, Pharisees, Sadducees, Essenes, Zealots and a sub-group of the Zealots, the Sicarii. Apostle Paul/Saul of Tarsus and Titus Flavius Josephus–or simply "Josephus"–were both Pharisees. The Pharisees followed both the Oral and Written Torah. The Pharisees would survive to become the basis for Rabbinic Judaism. Another important Jewish sect were the Qumranites comprised chiefly of ascetic males who believed their sect held the correct view of Judaism.

[bold-underline added]

[... speaking about Jesus] **his disciples stole him by night from the tomb**, where he was laid when unfastened from the cross, and now deceive men by asserting that **he has risen from the dead** and ascended to heaven.[91]

Justin Martyr, Dialogue with Trypho 108, c. 155 – 160 CE

This is He whom His disciples secretly stole away, that it might be said **He had risen again**, or the gardener abstracted, that his lettuces might come to no harm from the crowds of visitants![92]

Tertullian, De Spectaculis 30, c. 200 CE

Two other sources that possess a narrative that describe Jesus as having ascended to heaven from the tomb, body and all, thereby explaining the absence of the deceased Jesus are the apocryphal *Gospel of Peter* (c. 150 – 200 CE, see lines 38-42, 55-56) and the pseudopigraphic *Ascension of Isaiah* (c. 150 CE). Scholars have vetted these latter two documents and conclude with little counter debate that they do *not* have appreciable historical value. The reason for this is that they were written at least a century after the Gospel of Mark and were essentially legendized narratives. Furthermore, when compared to the NT gospels, their recounting of the events present important counter-doctrinal differences (i.e., certain elements are quasi-Christian in nature).

The earliest non-Christian commentary on the empty tomb was a sharply-worded barb from Celsus, a pagan philosopher, who pointed out that there were few primary sources who actually witnessed the missing body of Jesus (i.e., the women who fled and possibly two male disciples). This lack of historically-solid witnesses is the same point I was making in the discussion of Claim 2—The Empty Tomb (see p. 197). On the topic of the empty tomb, Celsus states:

When he was punished, everyone saw; yet risen from the tomb, almost no one.[93]

Celsus, On the True Doctrine, c. 177/8 CE

What is special about Celsus' rebuke in his *On the True Doctrine* is the breadth and depth of his exhortation. He scrutinizes every belief that Christians held sacred and demonstrates a deep knowledge of religious history and its many philosophic advocates. So, while many of his comments are caustic as represented above, he critiqued the Christian movement from a position of extensive knowledge.

To summarize, there is no authenticated extra-biblical literary work contemporary to Jesus' death that mirrors the empty tomb scenario consistent with the views of proto-orthodoxical Christianity. What we find is that, outside of the biblical texts, there is not a single authenticated *non-Christian* textual reference to Jesus of Nazareth in the first seven decades (and potentially double that) after Jesus died. This is an awfully long period of time for non-Christian society to go without saying *something* about this upstart religious community.

Most notable was that the Greek Jewish philosopher Philo-Judaeus of Alexandria (b. c. 15 - 25 BCE – d. c. 50 CE), never mentions Jesus. He was a prolific author writing on the order of 80 books all focused on Judaism[28] who endeavored to take Plato's work and merge it philosophically and theologically with Jewish Mosaic tradition.[29] His life's work was directed toward unifying Judaism, especially among Alexandrians, amidst a diversity of regional religions. His writings made reference to the fringe Jewish sects such as the Gnostic Jews, the Essenes, and the Therapeutae which he saw as heretical Judaism.[29] Philo was very aware of all the Jewish sects, however, in all his writings, he does not mention a sect that would be considered Jewish-Christian heretics which is what he would have considered Jesus and his followers. James, the brother of Jesus, was the leader of the Jewish-Christian converts at the time Philo was authoring his works. As there were two apostles named James, Jesus' brother (or half-brother) is referred to variously as *James the Just, James the Less,* and *James, the son of Alphaeus.*[12, 30] James the Just was put on trial by the Jewish Sanhedrin Council because of his ministry and was found guilty with a punishment of death. The main point is that the deviations from traditional Jewish practices certainly garnered them a reputation by the Sanhedrin. So, for Philo to omit a reference to this group of Jewish-Christians is noteworthy.

Neither Jesus nor his apostles are mentioned by the Qumranite Jewish sect in any of their Dead Sea Scrolls which are believed to be written *before* the original New Testament manuscripts somewhere between 250 BCE – 68 CE. Even so, the scrolls are eminently important because their discovery did two things. Firstly, they were not edited by the Romans, so we have a genuinely pure view of the attendant culture in the time and place of Jesus. Secondly, they are the evolutionary link that demonstrates how Christianity was a syncretic blending of Jewish Mysticism and many other religious concepts. An apocalyptic savior that went by the name *"Jesus"* is definitely mentioned in the Nag Hammadi library of texts, particularly the Gnostic gospels. However, no one is quite sure whether these

---

12. There was another of Jesus' apostles named James. He is referred to as *James the Great* or also as *James, the son of Zebedee.*

texts antedate or postdate the very beginnings of Christianity. There were various sects of Gnosticism, some being more closely affiliated with 1st-century Judaism (Gnostic Jews) and others more legitimately along the lines of proto-Christianity (Gnostic Christians), and still others that are distinctly not Christian. So, the Gnostic Nag Hammadi library may be the first documents that make mention of Jesus, but we cannot be certain of this.

The earliest *prospective* mention of a man named "Jesus" external to the Bible with a more certain date of authorship is by Titus Flavius Josephus. Josephus has notoriety because he was a Jewish Pharisee who initially fought against the Romans in the first Great Revolt (c. 66 – 73 CE) only to become a traitorous turncoat and play the, 'if you can't beat them, join them' card. Demonstrating his political deftness, he was able to change his fortunes to become an aide to Emperor Vespasian as well as a Jewish historian. In his writings, Josephus only references the name "Jesus" twice. The first time is in *Antiquities of the Jews* (see *Antiquities* 18:3:3, c. 93 – 94 CE) which directly mentions that Jesus the Messiah was crucified by Roman Prefect Pilate and came back from death on the third day. This passage is commonly referred to as the *Testimonium Flavianum*. While the authenticity of this text is broadly agreed to in terms of it specifically mentioning "Jesus, a wise man, [...] He was the Christ. [...],"[31] the sections which comment on the resurrection are believed to have been interpolated or outright inserted by someone else, perhaps by Eusebius of Caesarea,[13] the first Christian historian of the Christian Church.

The second instance that Josephus refers to Christ he says, "[...] and brought before them the brother of Jesus, who was called Christ, whose name was James, and some others; [...]" (*Antiquities of the Jews*, 20.9.1). Atheist activist David Fitzgerald articulates a line of thinking that reasonably suggests that this reference to Jesus is not the Jesus of Nazareth. Rather, Josephus may be talking about Jesus and James, the two sons of Damneus.[32] While there are other pro and con arguments, these two literary references in *Antiquities* simply cannot be regarded as reliable historical testimony given the inability to clearly authenticate whether Josephus was referring to Jesus of Nazareth.

As to other non-Christian sources, many point to the evocative letter written by Mara bar Sarapion to his son depicting his dramatic imprisonment after the Roman capture

---

13. Eusebius of Caesarea (b. 260/5 – d. 339/40 CE) wrote the first full-length historical narrative of the early Christian Church, though it wasn't complete or entirely accurate. The book, *Church History*, is written in the 4th-century from a Christian point of view and is inherently biased. Aspects of its accuracy and methods of development have been called into question. He was a contemporary of Eusebius of Nicomedia (d. 341), who was Bishop of Berytus and it was he who had baptized Emperor Constantine I as an Arian prior to his death.[93]

of Samosata (southern Turkey). Mara's letter contains a very brief reference alluding to Jesus where he states, "Or what did it avail the Jews to kill their wise king, since their kingdom was taken away from them from that time on?"[33] It has long been conjectured by apologists that Mara, a pagan, wrote this letter in 73 CE. However, there is no consensus among most scholars whether Mara was really a pagan at all. Some suggest that this writing could be "a fourth-century anti-Jewish polemic by a Christian posing as a pagan intellectual."[34] Because the author's motivations are uncertain as is the date of authorship, this cannot be considered a reliable early reference to Jesus or the resurrection.

We finally come to what is regarded as the earliest *authentic* mention of Jesus of Nazareth *and* the resurrection outside the biblical texts which is sourced from the *First Epistle of Clement to the Corinthians* (c. 95 CE). This was a letter sent from the nascent Church of Rome to the Church of Corinth (Greece) which had been founded by Apostle Paul (c. 51/52 CE). The missive was sent in response to dissension in the ranks of Church leaders at Corinth. The letter is anonymously written with no name of authorship. Though, it was Pope Clement who headed the Church of Rome, and is now commonly referred to as Clement of Rome, who is credited with the expressed content of the letter even though he did not write it. Clement repeatedly mentions Jesus and the resurrection as well as points to Paul's letters. *However, he makes no mention of the four gospels or the empty tomb. In fact, in none of Clement's attributed writings did he ever mention the gospels.* Many have speculated that the four gospel writings and the three other epistles of John were either (1) unknown at the time, or (2) were not well regarded by the Church. The first contention is harder to believe because the Apostle John, Ignatius of Antioch, and Polycarp of Smyrna were all still living. It appeared that Paul's views stood above the rest insofar as the formational Church was concerned.

The next mention of Jesus and the resurrection comes from another Christian source known as the *Didache* (Teaching of the Twelve Apostles). The date of authorship for the Didache had initially ranged from c. 50 CE to 120 CE, but it has since been conclusively determined that it had to have been written sometime in the second century.[35] In this general timeframe Ignatius, the Bishop of Antioch (b. c. 35 – d. c. 108 CE), wrote a series of 15 letters as one of the earliest records of Christian theology. In *The Epistle of St. Ignatius of Antioch to the Smyrnaeans* (c. 107 CE), Ignatius mentions the name *"Jesus Christ"* numerous times throughout. However, eight of the 15 letters are universally accepted as confirmed forgeries and the other seven (one being the letter to the Smyrnaeans) have an uncertain authenticity. A third literary reference dated to the mid-second century was by Justin Martyr. He mentions *"Jesus Christ"* by name in his literary defense of Christianity entitled *The First Apology* (c. 156 CE). While the Didache, a subset of Ignatius' letters, and Justin Martyr's literary work are the earliest non-biblical textual references, they are all quite clearly written by Christian authors.

It is not until the year c. 111 – 112 CE, some 80 years after Christ died, when we find the first non-Christian reference to an individual called Christ but not of the resurrection. Pliny the Younger, a Roman governor in present-day Turkey, had corresponded with Emperor Trajan about a conundrum he faced. In his letter, Pliny was faced with a contingent of Christians who were brought before him into his court. While it remains unclear what the chargeswere exactly, he was unsure whether he should or even had the legal authority to have them executed. After Pliny asked the group of Christians three times to recant their faith in this god they referred to as "Christ" and they refused to do so, he had them executed. There was no clarifying language that this was in fact Jesus of Nazareth.

Around the same time (c. 112 CE), we also find Roman historian Suetonius mentioning an instigator named "Chrestus" causing unrest within the Jewish community (*The Life of Claudius* 25:4). Scholars are divided whether this was a misspelling for "Christus" (meaning perhaps Christ) or a reference to an otherwise unknown individual. In any case, its historical value is tarnished. A third early reference to the Christians by a non-Christian is afforded by Roman Senator and historian Tacitus who refers to one "Christus" but with no mention of the resurrection (see *Annals* 15:44, c. 109 – 117 CE). As in Suetonius' case, it cannot be stated with certainty that Christus is the same individual as Jesus Christ the Nazarene, but Tacitus' narrative would suggest that there is a good chance that it was. The following passage is presented in the context of the six-day Great Fire of Rome that burned considerable portions of the city in July 64 CE:

[bold-underline added]

"Consequently, to get rid of the report, Nero fastened the guilt and inflicted the most exquisite tortures on a class hated for their abominations, called Christians by the populace. **Christus, from whom the name had its origin, suffered the extreme penalty during the reign of Tiberius at the hands of one of our procurators, Pontius Pilatus, and a most mischievous superstition, thus checked for the moment, again broke out not only in Judaea,** the first source of the evil, but even in Rome, where all things hideous and shameful from every part of the world find their centre and become popular.[36]

Tacitus, *Annals* 15.44, c. 109 – 117 CE

It would be five-and-a-half decades later when we encounter additional non-Christian commentary that refer to Christians worshipping a sage man that was crucified for his teachings. We find these words from Lucian of Samosata in his sarcastic play the *Death of Peregrinus* (c. 165 CE). Lucian was a satirical writer and was cynically inclined with the main objective to delight his audience by ridiculing this new religion called Christianity that was taking hold as he did with other religions and prominent figures. He wanted people to believe in the common sense of things and for his audience to apply logic and reason. He also affirms what I stated earlier that the Christians were noted for their communal charitable support which had raised their profile among the other religions of the time.

[bold-underline added]

The Christians, you know, worship **a man** to this day,--the distinguished personage who introduced their novel rites, and **was crucified** on that account. [...] In some of the Asiatic 13 cities, too, the Christian communities put themselves to the expense of sending deputations, with offers of sympathy, assistance, and legal advice. The activity of these people, in dealing with any matter that affects their community, is something extraordinary; they spare no trouble, no expense. [...] You see, these misguided creatures start with the general conviction that **they are immortal for all time**, which explains the contempt of death and voluntary self-devotion which are so common among them; and then it was impressed on them by their original lawgiver that they are all brothers, from the moment that they are converted, and deny the gods of Greece, and **worship the crucified sage**, and live after his laws. All this they take quite on trust, with the result that they despise all worldly goods alike, regarding them merely as common property.[37]

Lucian, *Death of Peregrinus*, c. 165 CE

The richest sources of ancient commentary that use the words, 'Jesus', 'Christ', 'raised himself up', 'immortality', and 'resurrection' were the Gnostics. Namely, we see these words used in the Gnostic *Gospel of Truth* (c. 140 – 180 CE), *Gospel of Thomas* (c. 100 – 150 CE), the *Apocryphon of John* (c. 120 – 180 CE) and most notably in *The Treatise on Resurrection* (c. 170 – 200 CE).[38] While the various Gnostic sects were deemed heretical by the proto-Christians, by and large the belief system embraced Jesus as a savior of human souls who lived beyond his earthly death. As such, they represent a midling group between the ortho-doxical Christians and those non-Christians who treated Christians offhandedly or that harsly attacked their views. However, we must recall that in the Gnostic context, resurrection did not mean a return to the conventional Christian understanding of heaven, rather the resurrection meant that the Aeon Jesus returned to the Plemora (the region of light).

Furthermore, Jesus was regarded as a separate deity alongside the Supreme God and the Demiurge god.

Earlier it was noted that Celsus was the first non-Christian we know of who wrote about Jesus' empty tomb. He also happens to be the first non-Christian to have unequivocally discussed the resurrection of Jesus. Celsus rebuked the Christians for concocting a new religion and who continually edited the original Greek manuscripts to better reflect their evolving beliefs. Unfortunately, his original text is no longer existent. It is a well-established fact that the Catholic Church in its formative and early history supressed heretical views. Often times this took the form of destroying pagan and anti-Christian literature. The Church burned copies of *Adversus Christianos* (Latin for, Against the Christians) authored by Porphyry of Tyre in 435 and 448 CE. Also in the fifth century, all copies of Celsus' *On the True Doctrine* were burned. At other points in time Christian authorities targeted the works of Hierocles the Stoic, Emperor Julian the Apostate, and the Gnostics, just to name a few.

We only know of Celsus' work because Origen of Alexandria authored *Contra Celsus* (Latin for, Against Celsus) in 248 CE which sought to vindicate Christianity by answering Celsus' challenge.

> [Origen responding to Celsus' *On the True Doctrine*, bold-underline added]
>
> And he [Celsus] goes on to say, that **"Jesus, while alive, was of no assistance to himself, but that he arose after death, and exhibited the marks of his punishment, and showed how his hands had been pierced by nails."** [...] Speaking next of the statements in the Gospels, that after **His** [Jesus'] **resurrection** He showed the marks of His punishment, and how His hands had been pierced, **he** [Celsus] **asks, "Who beheld this?"** And discrediting the narrative of Mary Magdalene, who is related to have seen Him, he replies, **"A half-frantic woman, as ye state."** And because she is not the only one who is recorded to have seen the Saviour after His resurrection, but others also are mentioned, this Jew of Celsus calumniates [meaning the spreading of falsities] these statements also in adding, **"And some one else of those engaged in the same system of deception!"** [90]
>
> Origen of Alexandria, *Contra Celsus*, 248 CE

If we take Clement of Rome's contribution and the earliest date for authorship of the applicable Gnostic writings, then the earliest authenticated extra-biblical reference from the Christian/quasi-Christian community to a man named "*Jesus*" and a resurrection-like event is between 95 – c. 100 CE—a full generation after Jesus died. It is not the

least bit surprising that Clement would affirm that Jesus was resurrected as it was the Apostle Simon Peter who ordained him and it was Simon Peter who was one of the few witnesses to have seen the empty tomb (according to the gospels of Luke and John). It was 80 years after Jesus died until a man referred to variously as *"Christ/Chrestus/Christus"* was mentioned in literary works by non-Christians (i.e., Pliny the Younger, Suetonius, and Tacitus). But it would be over *two centuries* until Christian detractors would remark on a man named *"Jesus"*, referring to Jesus of Nazareth, who was *"risen from the tomb."* With such aged commentary from both Christian and non-Christian writers, they cannot be considered as viable historical support that a resurrection actually took place.

In the end, chief apologist Habermas and his hailing of ancient non-Christian writers does not accomplish his original aim to find authentic support that a Judean man called Jesus was in fact resurrected. The most we can authentically say is that there was a religious holy man in the early first century whose personal activities attracted a band of followers that agitated the authorities to eventually get himself killed, possibly by crucifixion. They may have revered him as a god prior to his death or perhaps only after his human death. This latter point is much harder to argue. Nevertheless, none of these writings come close to establishing that a man was literally resurrected from the dead. To move further in our understanding of why people may have believed that a resurrection did actually happen, we have to evaluate the New Testament posthumous appearances of Jesus with a critical eye.

CLAIMS 5, 6, AND 7 – TIMING OF WRITTEN SOURCES AND THE POSTHUMOUS APPEARANCES BY JESUS

Claims 5, 6, and 7 present an interrelated set of claims (refer to p. 195). To summarize all three, they assert that there were many Christian writers and witnesses of the risen Jesus, some of them being contemporary to the timeframe of his human death. Taken at face value, the Christian Bible provides post-death encounters of Jesus in spades. There is commentary provided in all four gospels, two Pauline Epistles (Galatians and 1 Corinthians), the Acts of the Apostles, and the frequently ignored sole reference in the book of Revelation. A compiled list of the appearances is provided in Table 6-3. The first ten appearance accounts are pre-ascension accounts because they occur within the 40-day span between when Jesus was purportedly resurrected and ascended to heaven. **It should be noted that the post-death appearances of Jesus in the Gospel of Mark may not have occurred because the appearances are not described in Mark 16:1-8. Rather, the appearances are only described in the verses of Mark 16:9-20 which were not present in the original manuscript of Mark. These verses are highlighted in Table 6-3 with an asterisk (refer to rows 6 and 11).** This matter is taken up further on in our discussion.

Table 6-3. Biblical Post-death Jesus Appearances
Sequenced by the relative Time of Occurrence by Observers

(including auditory and psychical visions)

* May not have been attested to by gospel author

1	Mary Magdalene lingering at the tomb of Jesus	Mark 16:9-11*; John 20:11-18
2	The other woman returning from the tomb	Matthew 28:8-10
3	Cleopas and a companion, two of Jesus' followers, on the road to Emmaus	Mark 16:12-13*; Luke 24:31
4	Simon Peter (Cephas) in Jerusalem	Luke 24:34; 1 Corinthians 15:5 [a]
5	Ten apostles inside dwelling with doors locked in Jerusalem (Thomas (Didymus) was absent, Judas Iscariot was dead)	Luke 24:36-43; John 20:19-25
6	All eleven disciples while eating behind closed doors in Jerusalem (Thomas (Didymus) was absent, Judas Iscariot was dead)	**Mark 16:14***; John 20:26-31; 1 Corinthians 15:51
7	Seven disciples while fishing the Sea of Tiberias (Galilee)	John 21:1-14
8	A crowd (brethren) of 500	1 Corinthians 15:6
9	James the half-brother (some say full blood brother) of Jesus. [b]	1 Corinthians 15:7
10	Eleven disciples on a mountain in Galilee	Matthew 28:16-20
11	Those apostles near town of Bethany who watched Jesus ascend to heaven 40 days after the resurrection	**Mark 16:19-20***; Luke 24:44-51; Acts 1:6-11
12	The stoning of Stephen, two years after (c. 32 CE), but before Paul's first experience (c. 33-34 CE)	Acts 7:54-57

13	Paul, 3-4 years after the death of Jesus [(c)]	Galatians 1:12-16; 1 Corinthians 9:1; 15:8 Acts 9:1-16; 9:17-27; 18:9-10; 22:6-10; 22:17-21; 26:12-16, 26:19-23
14	To John of Patmos [(d)]	Revelations 1:9-18
15	Generic reference to the appearances	Acts 13:31

TABLE 6-3 NOTES	
(a)	In 1 Cor 15:5, the passage states the "and then to the twelve." This is intended as a general reference to the group to whom the apostles were associated and not a reference to the number of apostles present.
(b)	Appearance to James: This appearance is also mentioned in the apocryphal Gospel of the Hebrews and it claims this was the first of all the appearances. The apocrypha are documents that were not accepted into the biblical canon.
(c)	Scholars generally agree Paul's first appearance event, on the road to Damascus, took place between 3 – 8 years after the crucifixion. Most assert a timeframe of 3 – 4 years.
(d)	John of Patmos is considered the author of the book of Revelation and is not to be confused with John the Apostle or John the Evangelist. The latter two are more recently considered distinct individuals but some say they are the same individual.

GOSPEL TESTIMONY ON THE JESUS APPEARANCES

While by no means all-inclusive, it could be loosely suggested that between the years 1970 – 2008 the apologist-vs-skeptic debate had centered on the nature of the physical and spiritual embodiments of these various appearances. Dr. Habermas conducted an *ad hoc* count of scholastic writers encompassing 2,200 publications from 1975 – 2006 and found that 75 percent of biblical scholars would attest to the assertion that Jesus was corporeally resurrected.[39] The other 25 percent presumably side with the appearances being characterized as being phantasmal, intrapsychic, hallucinational, or that they never happened.

The Scriptures certainly do not make it easy to arrive at a consensus as to whether Jesus' appearances can affirm a *bodily resurrection* which is why the debate has gone on for so long. In some instances, Scripture presents Jesus in a body-like form that is immediately familiar to the observer. In other sightings, he is initially unrecognized—considered a gardener—then is suddenly recognized as the familiar Jesus. He also shows himself simply as a blinding flash of light and in other biblical narratives he suddenly metamorphoses from a traveler of no recognizable distinction to the recognizable Jesus. Other times he is a disembodied voice or makes himself present in the form of daytime intrapsychic (mental) visions and revelations in nocturnal dreams. How is it that the Christian Bible has the resurrected Jesus wearing mixed fabrics so to speak?

If we are to read the Bible at face value, then we might convince ourselves that God is well within his capabilities to freely transform the nature of his form from being fully human, to being phantasmal, to being a disembodied source of light and/or sound. But such a statement presupposes the conclusion to the question we are asking regarding the existence of God. Furthermore, the empty tomb of the gospels demands a *bodily resurrection.* If we categorize the nature of the appearances as they are described by each biblical writer, some interesting facts emerge.

Let us first review the following passages from three of the gospel writers—Matthew, Luke, and John—which portray Jesus in presumably human form.

> So they left the tomb quickly with fear and great joy, and ran to tell his disciples. **Suddenly Jesus met them** and said, "Greetings!" And they came to him, **took hold of his feet,** and worshiped him. Then Jesus said to them, "Do not be afraid; go and tell my brothers to go to Galilee; there they will see me."
>
> Matthew 28:8-10

> [v13] Now on that same day two of them were going to a village called Emmaus [...] [v15] **While they were talking and discussing, Jesus himself came near and went with them, but their eyes were kept from** recognizing him [...] [v29] "Stay with us, because it is almost evening and the day is now nearly over." So he went in to stay with them. **When he was at the table with them** [...] [v31] **Then their eyes were opened, and they recognized him; and he vanished from their sight.**
>
> Luke 24:13, 15, 29, 31

While they were talking about this [in their home, behind closed doors], **Jesus himself stood among them** and said to them, "Peace be with you." **They were startled and terrified, and thought that they were seeing a ghost.** He said to them, "Why are you frightened, and why do doubts arise in your hearts? **Look at my hands and my feet; see that it is I myself. Touch me and see; for a ghost does not have flesh and bones as you see that I have.**"

Luke 24:36-39

[v14] When she [Mary Magdelene] had said this, she turned around and **saw Jesus standing there, but she did not know that it was Jesus.** Jesus said to her, "Woman, why are you weeping? Whom are you looking for?" **Supposing him to be the gardener** [...] [v16] Jesus said to her, "Mary!" She turned and said to him in Hebrew, "Rabbouni!" (which means Teacher) [...] [v18] Mary Magdalene went and announced to the disciples, "I have seen the Lord"; and she told them that he had said these things to her.

John 20:14-18

As we can see, Jesus is described in a manner that he was of a solid human form. It is also rather apparent that details are severely lacking. The writing style is more akin to an abbreviated playwright's storyline than it is a well-constructed recording of history. The dialogue between the observers and Jesus is immensely sparse. What is of greatest importance historically is the amount of time that transpired between the actual event and the report. If we presume the dates as illustratively outlined in Chapter 5–Figure 5-3, then these accounts are written a half to three-quarters of a century after Jesus' death.

Another point to make is that just because we have located this ancient material and ascribed some particular date as to when it was written, it does not automatically convey that it has high historical value. Historically speaking, scholars are all but perfectly certain that these three gospels are not firsthand eyewitness accounts. Almost universally, scholars admit that the gospels of Matthew, Luke, and John employed source material from other people's writings; one such source was the Gospel of Mark. The author of Mark may well have used information from other authors. In short, as most scholars would agree, the gospels are at best second- or third-hand literary sources. This fact necessarily weakens their historical value for establishing the veracity of their content.

Let us think in analogical terms using a modern-day scenario. Let us imagine that a man named Joshua had lived in a city called Red Rock located 70 miles from where you currently live. Joshua was a renowned professional magician. Fifty years ago, Joshua put on a magic show where for his finale he levitated a Ford Model T automobile several feet off the ground and if that were not incredible enough, the car was then rotated so the car was **upside-down**, wheels pointing to the sky. He sadly passes away a week later. Pauline, an audience member and witness to the amazing Joshua wrote in a newspaper column, "Joshua the Magician put on a show that delighted his audience and whose remarkable talents were embodied by Joshua's ability to mysteriously levitate a Model T and **turn it in midair**." (mock quote). A different audience member, Mack, pens his experience and is more obscure saying, "the showman **lifted a vehicle** for his final act." (mock quote). Fifty or so years pass from the time of Joshua's death when another author, Marty, writes a book about the lore of famous magicians and cites Mack and Pauline as sources. Marty writes, "Joshua, the Magician of Red Rock, was a spellbinder extraordinaire. *He raised a half-ton car up in the air and* **twirled it** like it was on a BBQ spit. While Joshua took his secrets to the grave, we have since been able to recreate the props he may have used to spin the car." (mock quote). You, then, read Marty's book.

How would you respond if I were to ask you, did Joshua **actually** levitate and subsequently spin the Model T **upside-down**? You could reasonably attest to the fact that this man Joshua did exist by checking county birth records and that he was a practicing magician. However, it becomes a little more uncertain as to whether a car was lifted and rotated in midair and oriented upside-down. You were not there to see it for yourself and neither did Marty. Lifting a car is one thing, but also turning it is yet another. Furthermore, Marty's sources present words that are a little confusing. Pauline stated that Joshua levitated and **turned the Model T** and Mack's account implies that **Joshua himself lifted the car**. What did Pauline mean by turning the car? One could say that Joshua had spun the car in a circle with the wheels always pointing downwards. Mack's account does not yield any clarifications and furthermore is poorly worded because it makes it seem as though Joshua raised the car using his body strength.

Marty decided that Mack's report was lacking and he inferred that the magician used props to help him accomplish the feat based on modern-day techniques in the craft of magic. Using the reports, how does Marty arrive at his book comment that the Model T was rotated to a wheels-up orientation? All we can say is that perhaps he did not even think about the possibility when he consulted Pauline's article that she may have meant that the car had been rotated in midair with the wheels pointing downward. Utilizing only these two sources—Pauline and Mack—Marty would not know for sure in what manner the car was rotated. We see that each link of the chain makes the reality of what happened more and more uncertain. If we magnify this situation by projecting it back to ancient times some 2,000 years ago when fables, magic, alchemy, spirits, and multiple gods were ubiquitous and science was all but absent, our certainty wanes further.

The main point being driven at is that given the length of the chain of sources, the poor descriptions, and the ongoing uncertainty of who exactly wrote the gospels, we are forced to ascribe a low value to the historical reliability of these post-death appearance accounts regarding Jesus. Things become more worrisome when we examine the Gospel of Mark.

The Ending of the Canonical Gospel of Mark

I would forward that most people who read the New Testament at face value are probably not troubled with the fact that the sixteenth chapter of Mark, which also happens to be the final chapter, is presented with *three possible endings*.[14] The first alternative ends Mark's commentary with Verse 8 which tells of the women who were terrified upon discovery of Jesus' absence from the tomb. In Chapter 5 (see p. 172) this was referred to as the canonical version of Mark. As scholars have not given it a name, I will refer to this as the *Original Authentic Ending of Mark* (OAEM) for reasons to be covered. The second alternative ending, referred to in most Bibles as the "Short Ending" extends Mark 16:8 with two additional sentences (no verse numbers are assigned). The third alternative is called the "Long Ending" as it continues from Verse 8 of the OAEM to include the additional Verses 9-20. As you may recall, there is also the Gnostic-inspired Secret Gospel of Mark. This version is not part of the current discussion.

It is a mystery to solve whether or not either of the Short or Long endings were authentically a part of the original manuscript. *If it was the intention of the author of Mark to end his writings with Verse 8, then it would be quite significant because he will not have mentioned Jesus' posthumous appearances that would affirm his bodily resurrection.* **And, if the Gospel of Mark is the first gospel written, one would need to raise the question on what basis would the other three gospel authors, writing decades later, assert that Jesus appeared to people after his death.**

---

14. Earlier it was discussed that there may also have been a Secret Gospel of Mark which was potentially a Gnostic revisionist version of the gospel. However, we only know of this through the Mar Saba Letter and do not have a copy of the Secret Gospel of Mark to know its ending. As such, in the main body above, only the canonical versions of the ending of Mark are being considered.

ORIGINAL AUTHENTIC ENDING OF MARK (OAEM) TO THE GOSPEL OF MARK (CHAPTER 16, VERSE 8)

[v8] So they [referring to the women leaving the empty tomb where Jesus was buried] went out and fled from the tomb, for terror and amazement had seized them; and they said nothing to anyone, for they were afraid.

[The verse above is the concluding verse in the original Gospel of Mark per Codex Vaticanus and Codex Sinaiticus—refer to Figure 6-1]

SHORT ENDING OF MARK

[Continuing from Verse 8 above of the OAEM...] And all that had been commanded them they told briefly to those around Peter. And afterward Jesus himself sent out through them, from east to west, the sacred and imperishable proclamation of eternal salvation.

[The "Short Ending" is contained in a handful of Greek manuscripts and copies in other languages. The Short Ending is not ascribed with a verse number.]

LONG ENDING OF MARK (VERSES 9 – 20)

[Continuing from Verse 8 above of the OAEM...] [v9] Now after he rose early on the first day of the week, he appeared first to Mary Magdalene, from whom he had cast out seven demons. [v10] She went out and told those who had been with him, while they were mourning and weeping. [v11] But when they heard that he was alive and had been seen by her, they would not believe it.

[v12] After this he appeared in another form to two of them, as they were walking into the country. [v13] And they went back and told the rest, but they did not believe them.

[v14] Later he appeared to the eleven themselves as they were sitting at the table; and he upbraided them for their lack of faith and stubbornness, because they had not believed those who saw him after he had risen. [v15] And he said to them, "Go into all the world and proclaim the good news to the whole creation. [v16] The one who believes and is baptized will be saved; but the one who does not believe will be condemned. [v17] And these signs will accompany those who believe: by using my name they will cast out demons; they will speak in new tongues; [v18] they will pick up snakes in their hands, and if they drink any deadly thing, it will not hurt them; they will lay their hands on the sick, and they will recover."

ᵛ¹⁹So then the Lord Jesus, after he had spoken to them, was taken up into heaven and sat down at the right hand of God. ᵛ²⁰And they went out and proclaimed the good news everywhere, while the Lord worked with them and confirmed the message by the signs that accompanied it.

Recall that the canonical Gospel of Mark is thought to have been written c. 65 – 70 CE. As to what sources Mark may have used himself, oral and/or written, scholars concede that it is impossible to judge.[15] The earliest *copy* of the original Mark is on papyrus fragment P⁴⁵ that is highly damaged before the text of Mark 4 and after Mark 12 and is dated to 200 CE. As such it offers no useful insights as to the OAEM. The earliest *complete copies* of the Mark are provided in Codex Sinaiticus and Codex Vaticanus (c. 325 – 360 CE). Neither of these manuscripts contains Mark 16:9-20, however, both present an unusual blank column at the end of the text (Verse 8) which has stirred debate as to why scribes would do such a thing (there is no universally accepted reason to explain this). Figure 6-1 illustrates the blank space in Codex Sinaiticus.

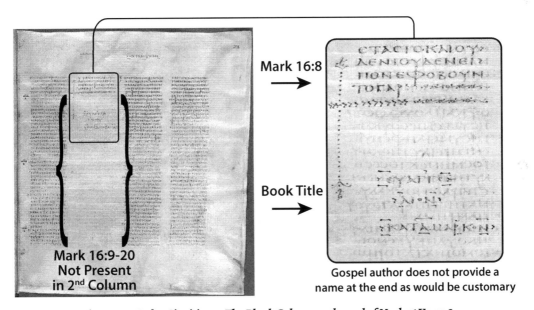

Mark 16:8

Book Title

Mark 16:9-20 Not Present in 2nd Column

Gospel author does not provide a name at the end as would be customary

Figure 6-1. Codex Sinaiticus – The Blank Column at the end of Mark 16 Verse 8

[Left] Full Page. Mark 16:1-8 (Columns 1-2); Luke 1:1-18 (Columns 3-4)

[Right] Magnified image of top of Column 2. Mark 16:8 ends at Line 4.

---

15. Some scholars believe that the author of Mark relied upon a well-informed source, possibly the Nazarenes, who lived in Jerusalem before Jesus had departed the city. This pre-Marcan Passion Narrative purportedly contains a narrative of Jesus' arrest, interrogation, and his crucifixion.

While many have attempted to explain this supposed anomaly that Mark could not have just ended his gospel at Verse 8, all of them are equally speculative and unconvincing. **Without the additional verses of the Long Ending, the Gospel of Mark gives no account of anyone seeing the postmortem Jesus as did Matthew, Luke, and John provide in their testaments**. In consulting other important ancient sources, Bruce Metzger, one of the 20th-century's most influential New Testament scholars and professor at the prestigious Princeton Theological Seminary notes that few of the major theologians and historians in first three centuries knew about the additional verses at the end of Mark. Metzger points out the neither Clement of Alexandria nor Origen[16] demonstrated any awareness and it would not be until after their deaths in the early to mid-second century that the historians Eusebius of Caesarea and Jerome[17] would later comment that these final verses were seldom encountered in the original Greek manuscripts that they knew of.[40]

Caesarea was an administrative capital for Roman interests located on the northern Mediterranean coast of Israel. As the Bishop of Caesarea and a well-known writer, Eusebius' (b. 260/265 – d. 339/340 CE) words became valued counsel for Constantine I. He played a large role at the First Council of Nicaea, convoked by Constantine himself, as the early Church leaders formulated the creed for what was becoming the orthodox Catholic Church. Eusebius is cognizant of the multiple endings associated with the Gospel of Mark. Below is a transcript of his interchange with a man called Marinus (c. 320 CE).

[bold-underline added]

[Eusebius writing in c. 320 CE ...] Your first question was:

[Eusebius repeats Marinus' question ...] How is it that the Saviour's resurrection evidently took place, in Matthew, "late on the Sabbath", but in Mark "early in the morning on the first day of the week"? (*sic*)

---

16. Origen of Alexandria—also called, Origen Adamantius—(b. 184/5 – d. 253/4 CE) was a scholar and theologian, allegedly having studied under Clement of Alexandria. Origen is a controversial figure because some of his beliefs were more speculative, not backed by Scripture. He maintained unorthodox views on the Holy Trinity which he maintained a hierarchical structure for the Father, Son and Holy Spirit. Like his teacher Clement of Alexandria, he wrote most of his works in the Greek language.

17. Jerome (b. c. 347 – d. 420 CE) added to Eusebius of Caesarea's work and he too presented erroneous facts. His writings were polemics assailing detractors of the orthodox doctrine of the Church which at the time was at a point of final solidification. Here, Metzger refers to Jerome's *Letter to Hedibia*, Epistle 120, Question #3 where, in reference to Mark 16:9-20 he says, "is carried in few gospels, almost all the books of Greece not having this passage at the end". Hedibia is a lady in Gaul (France). The letter is dated to c. 405 CE.

[Eusebius answers…] One who athetises [that is, marks the passage as spurious] that pericope [that is, this biblical passage, but he is referring more generally to the missing ending of the Gospel of Mark] would say that it is not found in all copies of the gospel according to Mark; **accurate copies end their text of the Marcan account with the words of the young man whom the women saw, and who said to them: "Do not be afraid" […] "because they were frightened."** [this refers to Mark 16 Verse 8] **That is where the text does end, in almost all copies of the gospel according to Mark**. What occasionally follows [that is, Verses 9-20] in some copies, not all, would be extraneous, most particularly if it contained something contradictory to the evidence of the other evangelists.[41]

Eusebius is confirming that to his knowledge that the majority of the copies available at that time in history end the Gospel of Mark with Verse 8. He further acknowledges that there were other copies, though fewer in number, which contained the Long Ending.

The earliest unequivocal source that comments on the ending of Mark comes from Irenaeus' *Against Heresies* (c. 180 CE) which is primarily written as an attack on the Gnostics. The underlined text must be considered a close reproduction of the essence of the Long Ending which contains Mark 16:19 as we cannot know Irenaeus' source.

[bold-underline added, italics by Irenaeus or by translator/publisher]

Again, **in the end of his Gospel Mark says, So the Lord Jesus, after He had spoken unto them, was taken up into Heaven, and sitteth at the right of God**: confirming what is said by the Prophet, *The Lord said unto my Lord, Sit on My right hand, until I make Thine enemies Thy footstool.*[42]

For comparison, Bible quote from the LONG ENDING of Mark 16:19

[v19]So then the Lord Jesus, after he had spoken to them, was taken up into heaven and sat down at the right hand of God.

There are other early Church writers—Tatian, Tertullian, Hippolytus, and Vicentius[18]—prior to the authorship of the Vaticanus and Sinaiticus codices that provide paraphrased statements of various Marcan endings. In any case, Irenaeus' commentary is the earliest undisputed textual reference to the Long Ending which would make it about 110 years after Mark's testament. Irenaeus as you will recall was in the midst of extraordinary doctrinal

---

18. Tatian the Assyrian (*The Diatessaron*, c. 170-175 CE), Tertullian of Carthage (*Scorpiace* 15, c. 212 CE), Hippolytus of Rome (*Apostolic Tradition* 36.1, c. 230 CE), Vincentius of Thibaris (7th Council of Carthage, c. 258 CE)

upheaval. As discussed in Chapter 5, many proto-Christian religions were vying for the hearts and minds of the populace. Irenaeus was on a crusade to establish a singular orthodoxical view and to denounce and marginalize heterodoxy. There were many conceptions of Jesus Christ, some seeing him as a normal human selected by God, some regarded him as only semi-divine, others holding that he was of lower order relative to God the Father or saying he was not eternal and had an origin to his existence, and yet others who saw him as a freer of the divine sparks (i.e., pieces of God).

At this point in time, debates were underway as to what texts should be accepted as orthodoxical. Irenaeus as we learned was the first to assert that Matthew, Mark, Luke, and John were the correct texts, which was a likely reaction to Marcion's (as in the originator of the Marcionism) claim that his edited version of Luke was the only true gospel. Both Irenaeus and his mentor Polycarp were sharp critics of Marcion. In short, there was no widespread consensus on the inclusion of the gospels into the Bible at the time and there was impetus for Irenaeus to harmonize the Marcan gospel with the other three to ensure that his selection of gospels would be retained as the orthodoxical treatise. We already discovered Irenaeus' poor logic in defending the four gospels where he said the four gospels must be the right ones to include because God presented his presence in groups of four (refer to Chapter 5, p. 174). Ultimately, it is only speculation what Irenaeus did or did not do in regard to editing the Gospel of Mark.

We can chase rabbit trails on this topic for quite a long time. What can be reasonably stated is that very few scholars believe that the Short Ending is authentic. Relative to the Original Authentic Ending of Mark, NT scholar Kelly Iverson summarizes thusly.

> "Though the majority of New Testament scholars believe that vv 9-20 are not original, virtually none come to this conclusion based purely on the external evidence. [...] Most text-critics appeal to the internal evidence in order to demonstrate that vv 9-20 are non-Marcan. [...] As is somewhat evident, the internal evidence raises significant problems with Mark 16:9-20. The awkward transition between vv 8 and 9 and the non-Marcan vocabulary has led the vast majority of New Testament scholars to conclude that the longer ending is inauthentic."[43]

Because the preponderance of evidence weighs in favor of the book of Mark ending at Mark 16:8, it has led the Vatican to declare that, "Catholics are not bound to hold that the verses [9 – 20] were written by St. Mark."[44]

Whereas Christian Bibles typically footnote that the Short and Long Endings were probably later additions by persons other than the original author, they completely sidestep the powerful significance of the original omission. That is, given that the book of Mark is the first written gospel testimony who does not affirm that Jesus was seen by others after his death, how is it that the other gospel writers comment that Jesus made an assortment of post-death appearances to confirm that he was reconstituted after his death so that people could be witnesses to the miraculous event?

Earlier I noted that the four gospel writers may have relied on the use of external sources apart from whatever knowledge they may have possessed themselves, namely the hypothetically-existent Passion Narrative, L-source, M-Source, and Q-source. *However, none of these sources are believed to have documented the resurrection event or the post-death appearances of Jesus.* Already noted is that the Passion Narrative does discuss the crucifixion and burial of Jesus but his resurrection. Comparatively, the L-source (used solely by the author of Luke) and the Q-source (used by both authors of Luke and Matthew) are thought to be devoid of a mention of either the crucifixion or the resurrection. Both of these sources principally contain parables. The M-source, used solely by the author of Matthew, is hypothesized to be drawn from multiple oral and written documents. But, like the other prospective sources, it too presents no mention of the resurrection or subsequent appearances by Jesus.[19]

As to the heritage of John's gospel, there is sizeable scholarly disagreement on who authored it and what the author's sources may have been. There is nothing in John that would lead to the conclusion that he used any of hypothetical texts or synoptic gospels as sources. Many think that John's gospel was written by multiple authors, in stages, using multiple oral and written sources, with the effort being completed c. 90 CE. Given that the gospel comes 35 years after Mark's and its authorship and source materials are so uncertain, its use as a historical instrument is substantially hobbled.

Let us regroup by considering Ehrman's synopsis regarding the overall historicity of the four gospels. What is found to be the case is that they are (1) not contemporary to the crucifixion event, (2) given the anonymity of the authors, the dates of authorship, and the content of their narrative, it is most unlikely that any of the gospels are providing firsthand eyewitness testimony, (3)) they are clearly not consistent when one considers the absent text regarding the post-death appearance of Jesus in the first-written Gospel of Mark and the

---

19. Refer to Chapter 4 (Van Voorst, Robert, *Jesus Outside the New Testament: An Introduction to the Ancient Evidence,* Wm. B. Eerdmans, 2000) for an exposition on the scholarly examination of the hypothetical sources of the canonical gospels.

different descriptions of how Jesus is manifested, and (4) the gospels are inherently biased as they are written to persuade people to become Christian adherents.

The insight of import is that neither Mark nor any of the hypothetical original source materials on which Matthew and Luke may be based upon, discuss the post-death appearances of Jesus. If the authors of Matthew, Luke, and John are not firsthand eye-witness accounts, then the writers most likely sourced their information through oral transmission. We have no idea about the frequency or accuracy with which the appearance stories would have been passed around. In the lens of a historian, the gospel testimony does not qualify as strong historical evidence that Jesus conquered his human death.

The next and last potential historical sources to evaluate whether Jesus came back from the dead would be either Apostle Paul's direct testimony as provided in his respective Letters to the Corinthians and the Galatians or the quoted testimony of Paul by others in the Acts of the Apostles. Let us review whether we can suss out any credible support for the claim that Jesus was resurrected as evidenced by his pre-ascension appearances.

St. Paul's Testimony on his Appearance Experience

Most every scholar will agree that the Apostle Paul presents the earliest authentic writings of any literary source on the resurrection. As it pertains to the Jesus appearances, Paul enumerates a list of those who had seen the risen Jesus in his *First Epistle to the Corinthians* (c. 54/5 CE).[20] By reviewing Paul's *Epistle to the Galatians* (c. 50 CE) it can be discerned that Paul received this list somewhere around 35 CE when he went to Jerusalem to see Cephas (the Aramaic name for Peter) and James the Just[21]—the brother of Jesus—three years after his conversion and five years after the crucifixion.

> For I handed on to you as of first importance what I in turn had received: that Christ died for our sins in accordance with the scriptures, and that he was buried, and that he was raised on the third day in accordance with the scriptures, and that **he appeared to Cephas**, then to **the twelve**. Then he appeared to more than **five hundred brothers and sisters** at one time, most of whom are still alive, though some have died. Then he **appeared to James**, then to **all the apostles**. Last of all, as to one untimely born, **he appeared also to me**.
>
> 1 Corinthians 15:3-8

---

20. First Corinthians was co-written by Paul and Sosthenes. Sosthenes was the ruler of the synagogue at Corinth.

21. James the Just is an epithet for James the brother of Jesus. As noted earlier, the nature of the brotherly relation is contested.

Then after three years I did go up to Jerusalem to visit Cephas and stayed with him fifteen days, but I did not see any other apostle except James the Lord's brother.

Galatians 1:18-19

In essence, Paul is writing about the post-death Jesus appearances 20 – 25 years after Christ died. Apologists latch onto this as being a most exceptional testament to the resurrection. According to them, (1) it meets all the qualification criteria for historical evidence as it is contemporary to the event (about 3 – 8 years after the crucifixion depending on what scholar one consults), (2) it is an eyewitness account (Paul and others witnesses), (3) the accounts are consistent, and (4) it is dispassionate in the sense that the various post-death appearance reports are from independent witnesses. As to this first point, it is a little bit of a stretch of the facts to say that the appearances are being reported only three (or so) years after the crucifixion when in reality Paul's writing takes place nearly a quarter-century after all this transpired. What Paul has done is akin to a middle-aged person recounting what transpired about a major event in their late teens. This is different than should he have reported it within weeks or months of the event taking place. Nevertheless, Paul only summarizes the list of appearances in First Corinthians and is not giving a long list of intricate details that could present mental recall problems so this is not too concerning. Thus, possessing a relatively early account is an ace in the pocket for the apologists and affirms, to a degree, Claim #6 (see p. 195).

For decades and probably a lot longer, apologetic writing has clung to this idea that the list of sources for those claiming to see the resurrected Jesus—the apostles, other disciples, the women at the tomb, and the crowd of 500—qualify as independent sources. Why this has persisted for so long is somewhat beguiling to me. An independent source must corroborate the same event using isolated sources of information. For example, if two people encamped in Antarctica see a pink polar bear and the next day twenty miles away a separate encampment also see a pink polar bear and the two camps are in no way connected, this qualifies as two independent sightings (it needn't be the same pink polar bear). During the decades that followed the death of Christ, the Seventy disciples, the fresh converts, and society in general intermixed and communicated principally by oral tradition and to a lesser extent by writing. This provides all the right alchemy for contamination of the truth. While it is likely these sources interacted in some form to coordinate messaging (Paul discusses talking about his ministry with others in Galatians 2:1-10 and travels with a few of the Seventy disciples), the fact is that they were evangelizing for years to anyone who would listen. It is far too speculative to suggest that these various sources Paul mentions in 1 Cor 15:3-8 could qualify as being independent. Nevertheless, it has only been in more recent times that apologists finally agree with this rationale and tend to refrain from using this in their argumentation.

What is almost unbelievable (and not oft stated) is that in all of Paul's testimony written by his hand is that he only mentions his Jesus appearance experience on three occasions in all of his letters.[22] As we see from Galatians and 1 Corinthians, Paul's report is executed with the greatest of economy of words.

The Complete Narrative of the Jesus Appearance Accounts as Reported Directly by Paul's Testimony

[v11]For I want you to know, brothers and sisters, **that the gospel that was proclaimed by me** is not of human origin; [v12]**for I did not receive it from a human source, nor was I taught it, but I received it through a revelation of Jesus Christ**. [...] [v15]But when God, who had set me apart before I was born and called me through his grace, **was pleased** [v16]**to reveal his Son to me**, so that I might proclaim him among the Gentiles [...]

Galatians 1:11-12; 15-16

Am I not free? Am I not an apostle? **Have I not seen Jesus our Lord?** Are you not my work in the Lord?

1 Corinthians 9:1

Last of all, as to one untimely born, **he appeared also to me.**"

1 Corinthians 15:8

---

22. As noted before, only seven of the epistles can be authentically linked to Paul. But, the comment still stands if all 13 epistles are considered as the only mention of the Jesus appearances comes from Galatians and 1 Corinthians who are firmly ascribed to come from the hand of Paul.

Of special interest here is that Paul does not specifically state in what form Jesus had manifested himself. Did Jesus reveal himself to Paul as a disembodied light or voice? Did Jesus appear as a human body in a mental vision? Could it be that Jesus' appearance looked more ghostly or phantasmal? Or, was Jesus looking like a normal human? From what is presented, it could be any or none of those. The only insights that permit us to discern the nature of Jesus' manifestations from Paul's point of view are presented in the Acts of the Apostle which will be discussed in the next section.

It is spectacularly remarkable that there is no other information authentically from Paul's hand that speaks to his personal appearance experience. What we have is what you see above. While Paul frequently mentions that Jesus was raised from the dead in his various sermons, the primary basis for him believing that Jesus came back from the dead was the personal appearance. One would think that Paul would elaborate extensively on what this experience was like in all of his letters. This cannot be chalked up to any physical or mental limitation of Paul, other than he felt it necessary to downplay it in his narrative. Paul does not talk about whether Jesus was clean or bloodied from his various tortures, or how he was clothed, or whether he looked gaunt like he must have at the hour of his death or if his body was that of a healthy male. Of course, nowhere in the New Testament do any of the authors physically describe Jesus prior to his death. **What we do know is that Paul never met Jesus. In summary, Paul never records that the tomb was empty and he only directly mentions his post-death encounter of Jesus three times in the vaguest terms possible.**

ACTS OF THE APOSTLES – QUOTING PAUL (SECONDHAND OR THIRDHAND EVIDENCE)

Before we review the appearance testimony provided in Acts, it is necessary to preface the interrogation. There is an ongoing controversy in regard to the author and date of authorship for the Acts of the Apostles. The range of dates places it anywhere from 60 CE to 110 CE which would put it before the Gospel of Mark or well after the Gospel of John. This makes it rather troublesome to gauge its interplay in the theological dynamics of the resurrection/appearance accounts. A more recent analysis by NT scholar Frank Dicken suggests that the most precise date that can be ascertained is between 75 – 90 CE.[45]

It was Church Father Irenaeus in the second century who first suggested the idea that Luke also wrote the Acts of the Apostles. Irenaeus intones, "Further: that this Luke was inseparable from Paul, and was his fellow-workman in the Gospel, he makes plain himself [...]."[46] Since then the most popular view was that Luke the Evangelist was a Gentile physician who traveled on occasion with Paul. Thus, the two books are often referred to as 'Luke-Acts' as Acts is considered an extension of the Lucan Gospel.[23]

Some scholars feel this acknowledgment does not go far enough to establish the historical truth of what Acts represents. These scholars wager that the historical soundness is to be called into question, substantiated in part by studying the author's usage of speech in what is now oft-cited as the "We" argument. Initially, the author of Acts writes in the third person, then abruptly switches to using the word 'we.' Some suggest that the author is pulling the reader, as in you and I, into the story[47] whereas others say that whoever the author is, is falsely leading the reader to believe that he was a traveling companion of Paul's.[48] Ehrman concludes that the disparities are too great between Acts and Paul's epistles and we should be wary given that Acts is pseudonymously written.[49] He further conjectures in essence that it is more likely that the author received his knowledge as second- or third-handed oral recollections. Ehrman lays out rationale concerning the noted discrepancies and compellingly concludes that the Acts of the Apostles is most likely a literary forgery. That is, it was not in fact written by Luke the Evangelist but by some unknown ancient evangelical writer. For the sake of brevity, I shall leave it to the reader to consult Ehrman's work to appreciate his thesis in full[50] or to review the myriad of alternative theories presented elsewhere.[51]

I will suffice it say here that the conclusion to be drawn is that the book of the Acts of the Apostles cannot be well-trusted insofar as the appearance accounts are concerned. Finally, owing to the hermeneutical Law of First Mention concerning the appearances, we should confer greater historical value in Paul's testimony (Galatians 1:11-12; 15-16 and 1 Corinthians 9:1; 15:8). With this preface in mind, let us be dutiful and quickly review what the author of Acts reports about the appearances to appreciate how Jesus' visitation was supposedly manifested.

Paul's conversion experience on the road to Damascus is the most widely recollected verse in perhaps all of the New Testament. It is repeated four times in Acts (Acts 9:3-8; 9:17, 22:6-10; 26:12-16). Below are the most relevant scriptural references from Acts that pertain to Paul's appearance experience.[24]

---

23. By saying that the author was a traveling companion, this therefore meets the Church Father's criteria for selecting it as a book to be inserted into the Bible.

24. There are other tangential references to Jesus being seen, but they do not offer any useful insights into how Jesus was manifested (refer to Acts 9:17; 9:27; 22:12-15; 1:6-11; 26:19-23).

Jesus Appearance Accounts Reported by the Unknown Author of Acts Talking About Paul's Experiences

Now as he was going along and approaching Damascus, **suddenly a light from heaven flashed around him**. He fell to the ground and heard a voice saying to him, "Saul, Saul, why do you persecute me?" He asked, "Who are you, Lord?" The reply came, "I am Jesus, whom you are persecuting. But get up and enter the city, and you will be told what you are to do." The men who were traveling with him stood speechless because they heard the voice but saw no one. **Saul got up from the ground, and though his eyes were open, he could see nothing**; so they led him by the hand and brought him into Damascus.

Acts 9:3-8

One night the Lord said to Paul in a vision, "Do not be afraid, but speak and do not be silent; for I am with you, and no one will lay a hand on you to harm you, for there are many in this city who are my people."

Acts 18:9-10

After I [Paul] had returned to Jerusalem and while I was praying in the temple, I fell into a trance and saw Jesus saying to me, 'Hurry and get out of Jerusalem quickly, because they will not accept your testimony about me.' And I said, 'Lord, they themselves know that in every synagogue I imprisoned and beat those who believed in you. And while the blood of your witness Stephen was shed, I myself was standing by, approving and keeping the coats of those who killed him.' Then he said to me, 'Go, for I will send you far away to the Gentiles.'"

Acts 22:17-21

If one reviews the full list of post-death appearance testimony in Acts (refer to Table 6-3, p. 212), one finds that the unknown author does not explicitly state that Jesus had manifested himself as a human corporeal body akin to his pre-death existence. Rather, one is induced to make an interpretational inference that Jesus returned as a physical human body. A post-death incarnate Jesus is perhaps the foremost of all Christian claims. Indeed, it is listed as the first claim in the list of Foundational Truth Claims of Christianity (refer to Table 5-1, p. 149). Why didn't the author of Acts simply make an unambiguous statement given the boldness of the claim in that day and age?

Let us also reflect again that according to Paul's direct testimony in Galatians and 1 Corinthians, Jesus had appeared as a blinding light and as a disembodied voice. *All told, whether or not you want to accept the authenticity of Acts, in none of Paul's direct or purported testimony in Acts does he explicitly attest to witnessing the post-death Jesus as a <u>corporeal body</u>! It is only toward the end of the chapters of Matthew, Luke, and John that we have the resurrected Jesus being seen in the form of a physically solid human body. Though, we call to mind the general unreliability of these particular gospels. And, as you will recall, the OAEM version of Mark, the first written gospel, does not present us with Jesus being seen after his death.*

To arrive at this discovery as it were, what have we assumed? As it pertains to the quoted material, we have assumed only a few things. First, we assume that the integrity of the texts used to perform the English translations is accurate. Second, we assume that the dating of the associated manuscripts to order Paul's comments as the first among all the other authors. Third, that Paul's letters were authentic and genuinely written by him. Mainly, this applies to Galatians and 1 Corinthians (the latter was co-written by Paul and Sosthenes). It was stated that Acts could not be suitably trusted as a source. We consulted the Acts testimony for the sole purpose to gather a few crumbs to better understand the nature of Jesus' appearance to Paul for without it we could say nothing using Paul's own words. The key takeaway is all that we had to do was to critically analyze the New Testament. Really, the only thing that was externally introduced was the notion, based on well-heeled historical and hermeneutical methods, to give maximum credence to the earliest testimonial sources. In this case it was Paul and the unknown author of the OAEM version of Mark who wrote about Jesus' final days on Earth.

Christian apologists naturally do not like it that we would only look to just two of the NT authors to critique the Jesus appearances. They would argue we should look at all the biblical testaments as being mutually corrobative. But this view overlooks the fact that these other texts do not measure-up when the historian's ruler is pressed against them. I will brandish the maxim—*Not all documents are created equal and they should be treated as such.* The common Christian mistakenly takes the New Testament at face value and treats its content as equally true.

So where does all this back-and-forth put us? It is time to frame the issue better by consulting Jewish traditions at the time of Jesus.

Inconsistencies with Established Jewish Traditions

1. Adherents of the Jewish religion, including the apostles, thought that the Messiah would be a great warrior, a great king, or a great judge, a harbinger for the establishment of the fifth kingdom (the previous four were pagan occupations by the Babylonians, Medes-Persians, Greco-Macedonia, and Rome—see Daniel 2). The fifth kingdom would defeat Israel's adversaries and restore the throne of David to the rightful heir, one who is of the line of David.

2. Jewish ethos did not hold that the Messiah would be someone who would be resurrected. They believed his work would be wholly of this Earth and when his mission started it would be fulfilled in its entirety, not cut short by the Messiah being put to death by their Roman ooppressors no less.

3. Nowhere in Ancient Judaism or even pre-Christianity in general was there record of a three-phased resurrection taking place wherein the resurrected person would first return to Earth and then subsequently disappear to exist in a non-earthly realm. Then, the individual would return once again to Earth at the **ESCHATOLOGICAL** end of the world. There is literary support for the dead being resuscitated back to life and deities being killed and being restored/reanimated/reincarnated into a different locale within the divine realm or as a new or combined character, but not at all like Jesus' resurrection.

   The first authentic mention by a non-Christian source for a resurrection was by the pagan philosopher Celsus (c. 177/8 CE), nearly a century-and-a-half after Jesus died.

4. Old Testament law dictated that anyone executed by hanging on a tree (or a cross) was under God's curse. This is well-documented in Deuteronomy 21:23; Ezekiel 39:11-16; Joshua 8:28-29; 10:25-27; John 19:31. External to the Bible there are attestations in the noncanonical Gospel of Peter 2:3; 5:1,[52] in Mishnah Sanhedrin 6:4-5,[53] and the Temple Scroll found in the Qumran Caves (refer to 11Q19 64:7 – 13a).

   > When someone is convicted of a crime punishable by death and is executed, and you hang him on a tree, his corpse must not remain all night upon the tree; you shall bury him that same day, for anyone

hung on a tree is under God's curse. You must not defile the land that the Lord your God is giving you for possession.

Deuteronomy 21:22-23

It was Jewish custom to also follow this tradition for those executed by crucifixion.

Remember, the Jewish people were very restless throughout the entirety of Jesus' life and beyond. The Jewish theocracy was weary of being under the foot of Rome and indeed this friction culminated in The Great Revolt, the first of three major uprisings in the land of Judea (66 – 73 CE). For people looking for a religion, worshiping the Greco-Roman gods or the Jewish God did not give them any freedom or advance their lives in any substantive way. So, planting roots in a new god that promised salvation found fertile soil. Even so, the Christian faith lacked a cohesive doctrine and there was not widespread access to pertinent publications among the common people. Additionally the followers of Jesus did not know what to make of Jesus' sudden death. Collectively, it explains why the tendrils of Christian faith went in so many different directions over the first several centuries.

As a point of clarification, while there is no record that resurrection events ever occurred before Christ in the Christian sense of the word, there was a belief in an afterlife. Nearly five hundred years before Christ, Plato describes the death and immortality of his teacher Socrates' soul in his book *Phaedo* (translated as, On The Soul) intoning that his spirit lives on. So, it is true that ancient peoples, even the most brilliant of men, were convinced that human beings possessed an immortal soul. Platonism is well understood to have had a major influence on Clement of Alexandria and on classical Christian doctrine as a whole.

All of the preceding argumentation makes it fairly plain to see that the evidence against Claims 5, 6, and 7 (and thereby Claim 2—the empty tomb) is rather staggering.

What we are coming to appreciate is that the overwhelming evidence puts into question the truth of the resurrection. This is not based on some contrivances because of an anti-Christian agenda. Rather, this is a synoptic compilation of sound exegetical and historical analysis of the source materials available for exposition.

What has been presented thus far regarding the authenticity of the New Testament is significantly affected by, (1) the dating and ordering of ancient texts, (2) the discernment of who wrote the NT texts which, other than Paul, most of whom are unknown or whose identity is much uncertain, (3) the interpretation of the motivations of the ancient unknown authors, (4) the success of adjudicating the utterly massive number of scholarly opinions across many topics, and (5) the fact that we fundamentally lack a continuous chain of evidence of unambiguous provenance. In the end, as a surgical tool to dissect the Bible at the microscopic level, biblical exegesis can only be so successful in our quest to understand the truth about God's existence. No single stroke is going to take down or bolster the Bible that much is certain.

We really have look at the field from afar. We already discerned with reasonable justification that (1) polytheism was the dominant form of religion for the majority of human history, (2) many different religions, including different Christianities, existed in the first several centuries of the Common Era, (3) the early quasi-Christian/proto-Christian sects vied to attract adherents, (4) it was realized by the proto-Christian leadership that the fragmented views about Jesus had to be consolidated into one-worldview, (5) there are unequivocal redactions and inconsistencies presented in both the Old and New Testament, (6) it took over three centuries for the Church Fathers to arrive at a singular doctrine, and (7) it was largely by the levitating support of the Roman Imperials and the sheer grit of determination and a sense of fellowship for mankind that the early proto-Christians rose above the fold. We also must appreciate the fact that the ancient writings were not written in detailed fashion resultantly leaving tremendous gaps in regard to important people and events and various interrelationships. They seldom wrote their compositions with the intention that their claims could be rigorously confirmed by others. Beyond that, as noted in Chapter 4, we only have a single piece of authenticated artifactual evidence for but **one** of all the New Testament people presented in the New Testament, namely the High Priest Joseph Caiaphas and the associated Caiaphas ossuary.

As a final comment on the appearances of Jesus, Ehrman calls to mind the intermixed culture of Judaism, Christianity, and paganism and how the cultural mentality of ancient peoples, who lived in close proximity to one another, had widely believed in phantasmal spirit gods that would take on human form. The Hebrew Bible offers a myriad of examples of angelic and demonic human-like beings. This representational characterization of human-like gods is also cemented in Hellenic Paganism in the opuses of Homer (i.e., The Odyssey, The Illiad, and The Homeric Hymns) and other pagan poets and philosophers. Ehrman also reminds us of a contemporary of Jesus, the Greek philosopher Apollonius of Tyana [c. 15 – c. 100 CE]. Apollonius' life had striking parallels to Jesus' life and he happened to live at approximately the same time as Jesus. Apollonius' birth was said to have been due to the intercession of God, he lived a sagely ascetic life surrounded by a bevy of itinerant disciples; he spoke in metaphors, healed the sick, cast out demons, was condemned by Roman authorities, and made a post-death appearance to one of his detractors. The primary difference is that Apollonius' life is confirmed by the Athenian writings of Philostratus (b. c. 170 - d. c. 250 CE) whereas the evidence for Jesus' existence remains relatively uncertain.[54]

We have not yet addressed Gary Habermas' final claim (Claim 8) that alternate hypotheses fail to rationally explain or otherwise dispel the resurrection. We also haven't 'run' the Resurrection Hypothesis—simply, that Jesus was raised from the dead—through the Hypothesis Historicity Testing Engine which is what we have been building up to. This will take some additional effort, but will round-out the discussion of the eight claims defending the Christian Doctrine of Incarnation and the first of the Foundational Truth Claims. It will be in the following two chapters that the second and third Foundational Truth Claims will receive our attention.

CLAIM 8 – ALTERNATE NATURALISTIC HYPOTHESES

In attempts to ascend to become the best explanation for the biblical accounts, rival naturalistic explanations for the resurrection have been crafted by scholars. The most widely recognized are the Conspiracy (Fraud) Theory, the Apparent Death Hypothesis, the Hallucination Hypothesis, Cognitive Dissonance Hypothesis, Mythological Hypothesis, and the Legend Hypothesis. Entire books have been dedicated to this subject matter and here I only seek to present touch points on each of them. The Conspiracy theories can be summed-up by saying that the Jesus' disciples lied and that they or someone else stole the body from the tomb. Probably the most well-articulated Apparent Death Hypothesis, albeit less scholarly than most, was given by Michael Baigent in his book *The Jesus Papers* (see Chapter 5, Box 4, p. 173) outlining a rather provocative thesis that Joseph of Arimathea, the Sanhedrin council member, was able to arrange for Jesus to be drugged into a state of unconsciousness while on the cross. Joseph tricked the Roman soldiers into thinking Jesus was dead and after Jesus was laid in the tomb he was given some form of medical triage. Under the cover of night, Jesus, in most dire medical straights, and Mary Magdalene were eventually taken to safety into Egypt.

N.T. Wright rebuts this line of thinking, "Jesus didn't really die; someone gave him a drug that made him look like dead, and he revived in the tomb. Answer: Roman soldiers knew how to kill people, and no disciple would have been fooled by a half-drugged, beat-up Jesus into thinking he'd defeated death and inaugurated the kingdom."[23]

In contrast, some have proposed that all of the appearances of Jesus were hallucinations brought on by the terrible grief for the loss of their beloved leader or due to their state of total bewilderedness. The Hallucination Hypothesis probably gained the most traction under the argumentation by Gerd Lüdemann who was resultantly ostracized by his professorial colleagues and others.[25, 55, 56] Briefly, Lüdemann proposed that the **CRESTFALLEN** followers of Jesus became susceptible to Marian-like apparitions, psychological grief hallucinations, and ecstatic experiences, which in some circumstances were experienced in mass. Later Christians then formulated narratives to reinforce these claims. One of the many difficulties with the theory is that the hallucinations would have had to affect the purported crowd of a half-thousand strong (see 1 Corinthians 15:6) and take place in different circumstances over 40 days after Jesus' resurrection.

A second challenge is that others were not so affected by this mass hallucination. St. Stephen[26] did not have his appearance experience for perhaps two years later (c. 32 CE) which occurred while he was being stoned to death (see Acts 7:55-56). Similarly, the Apostle Paul did not encounter the risen Jesus until some two years after Stephen's death. Michael Licona states in his 700-plus page analytical exhortation, *The Resurrection of Jesus: A New Historiographical Approach* (IVP Academic, 2010), a re-making of his PhD dissertation, that "collective hallucinations [...] are not supported by the professional literature in psychology and is implausible."[57] Kris Komarnitsky points to the most evident form of hallucination *en masse* by citing a news report filed a few weeks after the Indian Ocean tsunami of 2004 that had killed some 150,000 people.

Thai tsunami trauma sparks foreign ghost sightings

A second surge of tsunami terror is hitting southern Thailand, but this time it is a wave of foreign ghosts terrifying locals in what health experts described as an outpouring of delayed mass trauma.

Tales of ghost sightings in the six worst hit southern provinces have become endemic, with many locals saying they are too terrified to venture near the beach or into the ocean [...] "This is a type of mass hallucination [...]" Thai psychologist and media commentator Wallop Piyamanotham said [...] Mr. Wallop said widespread trauma began to set in about four days after the waves hit. "This is when people start seeing these farangs (foreigners) walking

---

25. Lüdemann is a German NT scholar at the University of Göttingen. As a result of his publications against the historical evidence for Christianity he came under heavy fire by the Confederation of Protestant Churches who called for his dismissal. While he wasn't formally dismissed, he was marginalized by his colleagues and cut-off from funding sources.

26. Saint Stephen is regarded as the Protomartyr (first martyr) of all Christianity. He was killed for his blasphemy which carried the punishment of stoning. Stephen was a deacon in the early Church who riled Jewish leaders. His death was witnessed and approved by Saul of Tarsus (refer to Acts 8:1), who later converted to become Apostle Paul.

on the sand or in the ocean," he said [...] Mr. Wallop said the reason almost all ghost sightings appear to involve foreign tourists stems from a belief that spirits can only be put to rest by relatives at the scene, such as was done to many Thai victims. "Thai people believe that when people die, a relative has to cremate them or bless them. If this is not done or the body is not found, people believe the person will appear over and over again to show where they are," he said.[58]

While this reporting may not meet Licona's standard for it being a peer reviewed academic study, I think it still carries sufficient merit to say that many people experienced ghostly visions while under a time of great duress associated with a singular commonly shared event. Putting aside the data collection and analysis standards, an equally relevant fact bears discussion. Beyond the biblical references to the crowd of 500, there is no other literature or artifactual evidence that repeats this same message. Lüdemann contends that it would have been rather unlikely that such a sizeable crowd would not have been elsewhere recorded in some fashion.[59] Considering what we now know of Christian origins where many forms of Christianity were vying for a toehold, such an event would have garnered extraordinary notoriety to help advance the credibility of Paul's new religion. Let us not forget the Marcionites, who believed that Jesus was always an illusion throughout his entire existence on Earth, still existed as a group until the fifth century.[60] Similarly, the Ebionites were also around at the time of Paul, believed that Jesus was always a mortal man, lacking divinity.[61] It would be almost expected that these and other non-Christian sources would have remarked about such a large assembly of people seeing a divine being. There is a possibility that these quasi-Christian sects may have written something, but so much of their literature is lost or destroyed.

This has led to the assertion that this appearance before the large crowd is literary fiction, inserted into the narrative by Paul and Sosthenes to help dramatize the resurrection and **PROPITIATE** recalcitrant Corinthian converts. If the large crowd account is untrue, then the plausibility of the Hallucination Hypothesis is upwardly increased quite significantly because it is far easier to say that a handful of individuals had a hallucinatory experience.

The Cognitive Dissonance theory, like the Hallucination Hypothesis, is a play to the properties of the human mind. In 1957, social psychologist Leon Festinger advanced this theory that suggests that humans have an inner drive to harmonize one's beliefs to achieve a cognitive consistency and importantly to avoid conflicting or otherwise disharmonious attitudes and beliefs. When an individual is exposed to information that is contradictory this creates a mental stress. The normative behavior is to seek a means to reduce or eliminate this inner tension or cognitive dissonance by altering a belief or a behavior or by creating new ones. Some individuals may be so beholden to a particular belief, that when they are presented with evidence that calls into question the veracity of this initial belief they will mentally discount this strong disconfirmatory evidence and become even more unyielding in their claims associated with their initial belief. As it applies to the biblical stories, Jesus' followers were distraught by the death of Jesus and this created a great tension with their belief that, as the Messiah, he was to reestablish the throne of David to the Jewish people.

This theory had never risen to any great height in the scholastic realm. Kris Komarnitsky has recast and reenergized this as a plausible explanation of what may have happened to Jesus' followers. He first notes that most scholars, apologetic and otherwise, doubt that Jesus actually foretold his own death (the so-called 'passion prediction') as stated in the four gospels.[62] While his followers were aware that Jesus was putting himself in harm's way while on his triumphant entry into Jerusalem, they would have been surprised that less than a week later he would be dead. Komarnitsky surmises that Jesus' followers immediately fled north to Galilee some seventy miles distant from Jerusalem (the women did not flee). Along the way, they would naturally have sought to find understanding in the unexpected outcome of their Messiah being killed. In their stress-filled minds, they encountered a cognitive dissonance between their belief that the Messiah would fulfill his mission on Earth and the fact that he was in fact killed before this occurred. The disciples invented a new belief that Jesus' death was necessary so that he could atone for humanity's sins against God and that he would later return to fulfill the messianic prophecy.

To connect these ideas, Jesus must be resurrected at some point. While the resurrection could have happened right after Jesus' death or anytime between then and his Second Coming (which hasn't yet happened), Komarnitsky argues that it made more sense that the resurrection take place shortly after Jesus' death. Many scholars have pointed to the fact that the resurrection event as embodied in Scripture was a foreign concept to Jewish people of the 1st-century. To defend the rationalization of Jesus' followers, however, Komarnitsky points to a host of evidence that supports the claim that this idea was not in fact new. He discusses that Jewish literature points to a belief in the concepts of "assumption" and "translation" which is where the body is translated/assumed up to heaven *prior* to death.[63] He also points to the apocryphal *Testament of Job* that talks about "the bodies of some children killed in the collapse of a house are portrayed as having been raised up to heaven alive."[64] Though the date of the *Testament of Job* is rather uncertain, anywhere between 100 BCE – 100 CE, this does describe a resurrection *after* the death of the individual. However, it is possible that it was written after Jesus died. Komarnitsky brings into view Greek culture which permeated the region where "beliefs that the bodies of special people were sometimes assumed or translated to the place of the gods before or right at the moment of death [...] According to Stephen Patterson: 'In the broader Hellenistic world, it was commonplace to speak of great heroic individuals who had been taken up to dwell among the gods as a reward for and the vindication of a life well lived. This tradition, too, would have been influential in the Hellenized Jewish environment of the first century, and it no doubt influenced the formulation of early Christian claims about Jesus.' "[65]

And finally, in Mark 6:14-16,

> Jesus' name had become known. Some were saying [of Jesus], "John the baptizer has been raised from the dead; and for this reason these powers are at work in him." But others said, "It is Elijah." And others said, "It is a prophet, like one of the prophets of old." **But when Herod heard of it, he said, "John, whom I beheaded, has been raised**."[27]

Mark 6:14-16

The content above purports that Herod Antipas was commenting about the concept of a resurrection within the short period after John the Baptist's execution and prior to Jesus' death.

While these various ideas are not precisely describing the resurrection imagined by Jesus' followers, they serve as stepping stones to the final belief. Furthermore, as noted earlier, there are prior historic examples in non-Christian contexts whereby people believed in gods appearing in visions. Ultimately, in a rational act of cognitive dissonance reduction, Christianity is kick-started by the beliefs that Jesus died for our sins, was bodily resurrected, and would someday return.

There have been other hypotheses forwarded following along the lines of psycho-social influence for which I will synopsize a few in the briefest manner possible which will not do them much justice. Michael Goulder, a scholar noted for his contributions in establishing Mark as being the first of the gospels written, reasoned that the appearances can be ascribed to psychological conditions of the witnesses. Geza Vermes, an authority on the Dead Sea Scrolls and historical Jesus, argued that the appearances were strictly visions/apparitions but that they, along with the empty tomb, were historical fact. NT scholar John Dominic Crossnan pegs Paul's experience as the only real appearance event and that it was a hallucination brought on by an altered state of conscious (i.e., trance-like state) and that Paul recognizes

---

27. This refers to Herod Antipas, the son of Herod the Great (King Herod I). It was Antipas' father who tried to kill Jesus by killing all boys aged two or less.

this as such. Paul, then, believes that the resurrection is a metaphor and does not believe in the literal bodily resurrection. **Crossnan's approach yields a result consistent with the outcome of what I had stated earlier whereby, if we consider Paul's account as the only historically reliable account as it pertains to the appearances, then Paul never attested to seeing a bodily resurrection.** There have been other hypotheses forwarded by Komarnitsky, Craffert, and co-authors Craffert & Botha. Add to these the Alien Theory that suggests Jesus was an extraterrestrial alien. I will not put forth additional energy to exposit these other theories.

The Mythological Hypothesis – Jesus as a Mythic Hero

This book started out discussing the myth of the Epic of Gilgamesh. Myths such as this have been with us in oral traditions well before recorded history and we find that as culture emerges, myths re-cycle wherein we create new myths to magnify and memorialize the glorious and inglorious human attributes important to our time in the form of imaginary stories that go beyond the frontiers of logic. Unlike legends, myths are a complete invention of the mind. Renowned folklorist Alan Dundes[28] defined a myth as a then-contemporary narrative of the world and mankind's relationship thereunto. He acknowledged that central truths of reality may be exposited under the guise of metaphors.[66] The best examples we have are the Egyptian, Greek, Roman, and Norse mythologies whereby the indigenous people created a cultural ecosystem of gods, demigods, heroes, and beasts. With interests in exploring the commonality of man, Nigerian professor Kingsley Okoro states that "Myths are an authentic epistemology that defines man and his place in the ordered universe. With [the] aim of teaching them values, responsibilities, privileges, and morality. It embodies the basic notion of common origin of humanity."[67]

Some skeptics have asserted that Jesus was never an actual person that lived; rather he was in the making of a mythical hero figure. Licona comments that those that would deny Jesus' existence as "extreme skeptics [who] assert he is a myth."[68] The basis some skeptics put forward are the mythic stories of the Egyptian god Osiris, the Babylonian/Sumerian gods Tammuz and Marduk, the Greek gods Adonis, Attis, Dionysus, and the Persian god Mithra that offer pagan parallels to gods who were revivified after their death. It is argued that the Jesus Story borrowed from these elements. Habermas and Licona maintain, with reasonable support, that these accounts (1) describe the resurrection-like events in highly vague terms, (2) do not suitably represent Jesus' resurrection in various ways (e.g., Jesus was willing to die to fulfill God's mission and would make an exalted return far greater than

---

28. Dr. Alan Dundes has been credited as being a central figure towards the establishment of folklore as an academic discipline.

his human life whereas others died unwillingly and did not rise as significantly), (3) the historical record indicates that it was the later revisions to the Adonis myth which were the first to clearly outline a dying god that rises back to life. The revisions that present this version of the myth *postdate* Christ's death, and (4) these pagan examples fail to explicate the positive evidence's for the incarnate resurrection of Jesus.[69] While tying Jesus' resurrection to mythical pagan gods is not all too successful of an endeavor, we can look more broadly at the entire Jesus Story to find mythical parallels at a different level.

British Major and 1st Baron FitzRoy Richard Somerset, was among many things, an independent scholar of mythology. In 1936 Lord Raglan (as Somerset was called) published a well-regarded book *The Hero: A Study in Tradition, Myth and Drama* which systematized hero myths of all sorts. Lord Raglan defined a dramatic ritual as a performance given before an audience of worshippers that possessed a magical quality owing to the mythic storyline. The storyline is an ensemble of dramatic elements that are not of a historical character but are circumstances seldom encountered in traditional life (e.g., a virginal birth, inhuman feats). A myth, according to Raglan, is not just the story but a story intimately tied to an acted-out ritual.[70] Just three years prior, anthropologist A. M. Hocart comments similarly, "We must always look for an explanation, not to the survival, but to the living custom or belief. If we turn to the living myth, that is the myth that is believed in, we find that it has no existence apart from the ritual. The ritual is always derived from someone, and its validity must be established by its derivation. The actors are merely impersonating the supposed inventors of the ritual, and this impersonation has to be expressed in words. Knowledge of the myth is essential to the ritual, because it has to be recited at the ritual."[71] Rituals are of course endemic to religion and as we well know both ritual and religion were culturally engrained in the earliest civilizations and persist today.

Raglan identifies a paradigm that befits the mythic hero as outlined in Table 6-4.

Table 6-4. Was Jesus a Mythic/Legendary Hero?
Lord Raglan's 22-Point Paradigm for Hero Archetypes[72]

(1)	The hero's mother is a royal virgin;	(12)	He marries a princess, often the daughter of his predecessor, and
(2)	His father is a king, and	(13)	Becomes king.
(3)	Often a near relative of his mother, but	(14)	For a time he reigns uneventfully, and
(4)	The circumstances of his conception are unusual, and	(15)	Prescribes laws, but
(5)	He is also reputed to be the son of a god.	(16)	Later he loses favor with the gods and/or his subjects, and
(6)	At birth an attempt is made, usually by his father or his maternal grandfather, to kill him, but	(17)	Is driven from the throne and city, after which
(7)	He is spirited away, and	(18)	He meets with a mysterious death,
(8)	Reared by foster-parents in a far country.	(19)	Often at the top of a hill.
(9)	We are told nothing of his childhood, but	(20)	His children, if any, do not succeed him.
(10)	On reaching manhood he returns or goes to his future kingdom.	(21)	His body is not buried, but nevertheless
(11)	After a victory over the king and/or a giant, dragon, or wild beast,	(22)	He has one or more holy sepulchres.

Alan Dundes leaned on Raglan's work in his 1990 book entitled *The Hero Pattern and the Life of Jesus* wherein he compared Raglan's hero archetypes to the life events of Jesus. His analysis determined that Jesus' life mirrored 19 or 20 out of the 22 elements listed in Table 6-4. What is more is that Dundes also compared the hero archetypes against other famous hero-type figures and found that Jesus' life mirrors the life of other heroes of history (refer to Figure 6-2, p. 242).[73]

The Greek myths of Zeus, Perseus, and Odysseus were precursors in many ways to The Jesus Story, though not specifically to the resurrection event. We can also refer back to what we learned about the Cognitive Dissonance theory where formational pseudo-resurrection ideas were entered into the conscience of society. The Jesus Story then could very well be a myth created by disenfranchised Jews and others who wanted a God that was less vengeful than Yahweh or who did not find themselves to be among the Chosen People. The myth was also directed to those wanting a new conception of humanity and a promise for personal salvation as well as those seeking palliative relief from their current situation that embodied misery, fear, brutality, and chaos promised them under Roman rule. The myth was a literary vehicle for people to become steeped in the folklore so much so that it became a way of life. Unlike any other myths before or since, it transformed into the largest religion there ever was. The myth evolved from being a mere story into a religious belief so fiercely held that some small number of adherents would martyr themselves.

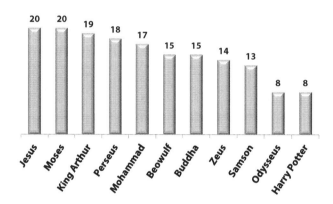

Figure 6-2. Attributes of Jesus' Life Compared to Other Legendary & Mythical Heroes

THE LEGEND HYPOTHESIS – JESUS AS A LEGENDARY HERO AND THE JESUS STORY AS AN ALLEGORY FOR OUR SPIRITUAL JOURNEY

The Legend Hypothesis is one of the oldest of the counter proposals against the Resurrection Hypothesis. While a myth is strictly fictional, a legend is an account that combines elements of myth and historical fact centered on a person or figure. In the legened framework, Jesus is considered a once living and breathing man revered as a Messiah. The word Messiah carried different meanings but centuries before Christ it usually referred to an anointed king or high priest that came from the lineage of King David. Renowned philosopher and theologian John Hick stated that Christians have misappropriated the poetry of God working through a normal man named Jesus by transposing "a metaphorical son of God to a metaphysical God the Son."[74] Hick's main contribution were his ideas regarding Religious Pluralism which makes the audacious attempt explain how most religions have credible insights on the existence and nature of God (his views are discussed principally in Chapter 10). Today, Christians synonymize Jesus Christ with the word Messiah without recognition of the fact that there were multiple Messiahs over the course of history. The Messiah was to come to free the Jewish people from their Roman overlords and to reclaim the throne of David for their people. Christians came to believe that Jesus' death was necessary to free people from Original Sin and that the **SUPERNAL** Father would willingly sacrifice his Son through the most horrendous means of human suffering in order to illustrate his commitment to mankind. The life of Jesus is construed as a compelling **ALLEGORY**, an extended metaphor, to transmit a message of hope and redemption. While Jesus was to be taken on a literal level, his parables conveyed abstract ideas about how to honor God by the way people lived their lives. The Bible was a tool to codify the legend while providing additional symbolism for people to interact with so that they may be fortified by ethical, moral, and spiritual direction.

John Warkwick Montgomery is by all accounts a highly accomplished individual. He is an attorney who has earned 11 degrees in the disciplines of philosophy, librarianship, theology, and law and has had a prodigious literary output creating more than 50 books and 100 scholastic journal articles. He was also a Lutheran apologist and public debater who in 1964 made an apropos remark regarding our inability to separate fact from legend regarding Jesus.[75]

[bold-underline added]

An accretion of legends grew up about this figure, was incorporated into the gospels by various devotees of the movement, was rapidly spread throughout the Mediterranean world by the ministry of St. Paul; and that because this is so, **it is impossible to separate those legendary elements in the purported descriptions of Jesus from those which in fact were true of him**.[76]

In 2010, Licona similarly admits "it can forthrightly be admitted that the data surrounding what happened to Jesus is fragmentary and could possibly be mixed with legend."[77]

With a weakening in their wall-front, Christian apologists raced to seal the leaks and to hurl yet another salvo against skeptics who pressed forward their Legendary Hypothesis. Apologists felt they aimed well by striking at the Achilles heel by calling to their defense a thesis by a well-regarded Oxford classical historian by the name of Adrian Nicholas Sherwin-White. The scholar studied the growth rate of myths, most especially in ancient societies.[29] While most everyone agrees that myths can grow quite rapidly, he wanted to understand

---

29. The analysis of the growth of myths and of legends is the same in this context.

how long it took to for a myth to displace the "hard core or basic layer of historical truth"[78] as it related to historical events. In 1961, he proposed the *two-generation rule* which implies that if a myth hadn't supplanted the core historical data within two generations, then one should regard the central information as an actual (real) phenomenon that occured. To his mind, the historical data of the Jesus Story were retained over the first two centuries which passes the two-generation criteria.

Sherwin-White's work apparently had great affect on some people. Atheist-turned-apologist Lee Strobel expressed why he ultimately switched from being an atheist to a staunch Christian apologist.

> [bold-underline added]

> The cumulative facts and data pointed unmistakably toward a conclusion that I wasn't entirely comfortable in reaching. Frankly, I had wanted to believe that the deification of Jesus was the result of legendary development in which well-meaning but misguided people slowly turned a wise sage into the mythical Son of God. That seemed safe and reassuring; after all, a roving apocalyptic preacher from the first century could make no demands on me. But while I went into my investigation thinking that this legendary explanation was intuitively obvious, I emerged convinced it was totally without basis. **What clinched it for me was the famous study by A.N. Sherwin-White, the great classical historian from Oxford University**, which William Lane Craig alluded to in our interview. **Sherwin-White meticulously examined the rate at which the legend accrued in the ancient world. His conclusion: not even two full generations was enough time for legend to develop to wipe out a solid core of historical truth.**[79]

Lee Strobel has managed to assemble a lucrative livelihood from his media empire. He has gone on to write a series of books, *The Case for Christ*, *The Case for Faith*, *The Case for a Creator*, *The Case for the Real Jesus*, *The Case for the Resurrection*, *The Case for Christmas*, *The Case for Easter* and many other books. However, a critical examination of how he used Sherwin-White's work indicates that Strobel appears to be either uninformed or has overlooked the fact that Sherwin-White's theory is no longer held in high regard.

Sherwin-White's work is predicated on the study of publicly significant historical figures (e.g., Alexander the Great) and the ancient writings of Greek historian Herodotus. Most will agree that during and shortly after Jesus' life, he was a person of little notoriety or social significance. Remember, his public ministry was a grass roots campaign only three years in the making and it would take time for the Jews of Judea and others to see him as a Messiah to which he never fulfilled his Jewish destiny. And while most current historical portraits of Jesus show him as a political revolutionary of sorts, he only raised real concern among the theocrats toward the end and with the Roman politicos not long before he was sentenced to death. And, his trial and punishment was meted out in less than a week. Ultimately, the majority of scholars have not embraced the two-generation rule as being anything other than a narrow judgment for the specific historical figures researched by Sherwin-White.

Unitarian Universalist[30] minister Rudolph Gelsey identifies the fatal fault in Sherwin-White's two-generation theory.

> The conclusion of Sherwin-White that, in general outline, the Gospel accounts of the trial are historic, appears unwarranted by the facts he cites. Sherwin-White argues, for instance, that the two generations between the actual events and the writing of the Gospels is too short a time-span for myth-making to occur. But does not the espousal by the evangelists of the virgin birth and the physical resurrection of Jesus contain the very stuff of myths, and yet these myths were also developed with the short time of two generations. If argumentation by analogy is allowed, then the analysis by Sherwin-White would militate against his own conclusions. [...] By concentrating on Roman law, Sherwin-White misses the inconsistencies that arise out of the trial before the Sanhedrin. [...] Sherwin-White makes a valiant effort to dispel the arguments against the Gospel version from the point of view of Roman law. The reasoning, however, is incomplete and unconvincing because it does not take into account the state of Jewish law in New Testament times. Considering this one-sidedness and the author's bias in favor of the Biblical story, the definitive work on the trial of Jesus still waits to be written.[80]

---

30. Unitarian Universalism is a highly diverse religion that holds that religion is a matter of individual experience and people are free to employ their own interrogative methods to understand the spirit of life. Its contemporary focus is spiritual growth and less so on deific agency. Thus, many types of believers are welcomed, including atheists, agnostics, deists, pantheists, and polytheists.

The Legend Hypothesis, for all its age and wisdom, has proven to be an unyielding foe for the Resurrection Hypothesis to contend with. Part of its strength lies in its straight-forwardness. It does not rely on the vagaries associated unprovable conspiracies or the validation of faked deaths. Nor does it rely on complex social constructs or hallucinations. All of these other approaches require extensive reliance of finding parallels throughout our history which are far more difficult to pin down. Legend-making on the other hand is an undeniable integral part of our human heritage.

THE MORTAL JESUS HYPOTHESIS — A PSILANTHROPIC VIEW

We are in a position to forward a somewhat different hypothesis that builds on the information amassed thus far. I refer to this as the *Mortal Jesus Hypothesis*. It goes as follows.

The Mortal Jesus Hypothesis

Without the aid of modern-day technology, ancient human life was an especially great hardship. Arising out of prehistoric superstition, tribal societies began to fashion adaptive frameworks to thrive against the odds and to define their place in the world. Having virtually no comprehension of natural planetary processes and being forcefully engaged in a never-ending effort to accrue vital resources to serve individual and tribal needs, to defend against would-be marauders, and to explain the cause of medical conditions, they found a source of understanding by the invention of spiritual Beings. These Beings were thought to be controlling and manipulating the destiny of men and by invoking the spirits, rulers effectively managed tribal life which over time centralized into societal structures. Conquering tribes would take possession of the gods of the defeated and the ruling class determined which gods would stay and which ones would go. Often, gods were combined and renamed. This was a circulating theme for millennia.

With the advent of writing (c. 3200 BCE), religion found firmer footing by the immortalizing power of the written word. Ancient Judaism arises out of the ancestry of Greek, Egyptian, Canaanite, Anatolian, and Persian pagan gods (c. 2000 BCE). Over the next 1,500 years, various factors came into play. First, the ancients became increasingly knowledgeable of their environs. Some probably questioned the whimsical response to their sacrificial offerings as well as the overlapping duties of so many gods which resulted, in part, from the continual consolidation of the deities. For reasons not well understood, some tribal colonies deescalated the importance of most gods to favor fewer and fewer gods. Upon delivery of revelatory insight, the Old Testament Great Prophets came to believe that most of the gods were false idols. Having command of the loyalty of Israelite Kings, the gods were demoted and ultimately expunged until the Supreme Yahweh and his consort Asherah ruled as a divine pair. Soon, even Asherah would meet the same fate as the others leaving Yahweh as the sole Supreme God. Under the Abrahamic and Davidic Covenants, Yahweh promised the Jewish people special treatment, land, and that the House of David would rule forever.

As centuries passed, the Jewish people would eventually come under the rule of the Egyptian dynasties and Roman Empire. This infringement of the Davidic Covenant brewed great animosity within the Jewish theocracy. It was foretold that a man of Davidic descent, a Messiah, would come to free them from this bondage. On cue, a human male of such noble ancestry named Jesus was born fully human with no divine qualities in the province of Galilee as a result of a *natural* sexual union (i.e., PSILANTHROPISM). Jesus was raised and lived in Galilee where he was educated in the Jewish tradition. In his adulthood, he fashioned himself to be a compassionate healer being unafraid of the sick, a gifted and prayerful teacher, and a political rebel of sorts. Though, for years he was of little relevance outside of his mostly motley, rag-tag followers. His theatrics, command of God's law, in concert with his noble heritage, made him a regional celebrity which gained him a loyal following and some, by oral tradition, would speak of his deeds in the context of miracles. His prominence among his followers sowed the first stitches of his legend. His reputation grew and he knew that to become the Messiah and to act as Yahweh's agent he must do certain things and ultimately challenge the theocrats who defiled God's ways. He was aware that his future actions would lead to unrest, and therefore carried great personal risks. Undeterred, he rode into Jerusalem upon the fabled donkey to become the Anointed One. The Jewish theocracy, hearing of his escapades, felt threatened enough by this man called Jesus that they induced Pontius Pilate to condemn him as a criminal. Feeling uneasy about the charges, Pilate granted the Sanhedrin their desires and had him put to death by crucifixion.

After his death, and in conformance with Jewish burial customs, he was taken down from the X-shaped cross before dawn of the following day. His apostles and closest disciples had already returned to their homes in Galilee out of fear for Roman reprisal and because it was already twilight, his body was hurriedly prepared for burial (a quick wash, anointment with oil, and wrapping in burial cloth). Like the majority of people who were not well-off financially or who were societally condemned, he was placed initially in an earthen grave. Following the custom of seconary burial, it is feasible that after one year had passed, his bones may have been placed into a bone box and reburied in a family-owned tomb in Jerusalem. His followers were dumbfounded, grief stricken, angry, and simply staggered with disbelief at how swiftly their teacher was killed and that their destiny to exit victorious over the Romans was nullified.

Over the next several weeks, Simon Peter and other individuals were psychologically affected and entered into alternative states of consciousness. Certainly, the disciples attempted to console one another in what would be emotionally charged events where they implored God to make things right and to help them understand what had happened. And, in some cases some would hear his voice or even see some visual figment of his body in a trance or nocturnal dreams. In more rationale moments, they sought meaning from their Jewish writings and this communal activity helped them over the ensuing months to remain banded together. James, Jesus' brother, reconsidered his skepticism in light of all that had happened and decided to pay tribute to his brother's memory by advancing his mission (he too was of the line of David) and by taking on the yoke of leadership of the new Jewish-Christians (not that they specifically referred to themselves as Christians as this moniker would not arise until decades later).

After overseeing the stoning of Stephen (the first Christian martyr) over his deeply engrained beliefs, Paul saw how the Christians behaved differently, even in the face of great adversity and atrocity. It dawned on Paul that there was a redemptive value to this new Jewish movement that was not present in then-normative Judaism and he thought that it would lead to a more wholesome life. His process toward full conversion was not instant; rather it took a good amount of time as he learned about this new faith from Jesus' disciples. He became so completely enthralled with it and realized that to make the faith grow, they needed greater leadership and organization. Paul was far more connected to higher society than the other disciples and being worldlier in view and otherwise more capable than others, became the leader of the Gentile discipleship outside of Judea. It was a deft move to make Apostle James (the brother of Jesus) his lieutenant with James assuming his position as leadership of the Jewish-Christian converts. Not only was this homage to the fallen leader but it served as an example that even hardline skeptics such as James could see new the truth. Up to this point, not a single word had been textually recorded about Jesus as it relates to his ministry or crucifixion.

Over the next two decades, they went far and wide to proclaim the good news of personal salvation. As most of those they encountered knew little to nothing of this new faith, facts began to fade in favor of fictional embellishments so beginning the legend accretion process. As cities and towns were separated by 50 to maybe 100 miles, the would-be converts could not easily confirm or deny the information passed onto them. To make his story seem a little more fantastical and interesting, Paul fictionally recounts how 500 brothers and sisters of Christ witnessed the risen Jesus. But, owing to the fact that he has to be on guard from being called the defender of a false god, he has to downplay this which explains why in his writings Paul vaguely and in a meagerly sum of words speaks about Jesus' post-death appearances.

The corpus of disciples begins to legendize the man using oral tradition. They spoke of his noble ancestry and noble burial within a hillside rock-hewn tomb. They painted him as a faithful servant of the Lord God who guided Jesus' hand on Earth. According to them, Jesus was imbued with the power to heal the sick and dying as well as being able to cast out demons among other extraordinary feats. His stock rises higher as he is now deified. Among themselves, some of the apostles admitted to having revelatory experiences where Jesus spoke to them. Some may have believed that Jesus was raised from the dead whereas others were less convinced but toed the line as it would add a sense of awe to their mission work and figured that the end justified the means.

Some converts, such as the unknown author of the Marcan Gospel, while knowledgeable of the claims that Jesus made appearances after his death, did not think these to be true. The writer therefore ends his evangelical gospel with the stone rolled back from the tomb entrance. When the three women went to anoint Jesus' body with spices, they saw an unnamed man in a white robe sitting in the tomb of Jesus who tells the women that Jesus was raised. The women were ecstatic, confused, and fearful as they departed from the tomb. Even though this mysterious robed man states that Jesus will make an appearance in Galilee, there is no mention of Jesus *actually* appearing to people after his death.

During this timeframe, people held varying beliefs about Jesus, God, Satan, angels, demons, and spirits. Also, paganism and esoteric mysticisms ruled the land with an entirely different divine council and mode of thought. The Ebionites claimed Jesus was just a mortal human who later became the most favored of God's prophet whereas the Marcionites contended that he was entirely illusory while others advanced the idea that Jesus was coequal with God. There was much division on whether Jesus was born naturally or was of virgin birth. Additionally, some felt that the Holy Spirit was a mechanism employed by God whereas others considered it as an equal part of the Godhead. Some Gnostics perceived Jesus as being conceived by the Supreme God to rectify cosmic mistakes committed by the Demiurge, and tasked with the job of coming to Earth to release trapped spirits so that they may return to the divine realm (the Plemora).

By the early second century, the Apostolic and Greek Church Fathers began a reckoning of what texts were to be considered as divinely inspired. Even at this time, it was extra-ordinarily difficult to acquire original texts and to make sense of the body of history from people who were no longer living. After some three centuries of contentious debate and a raft of textual redactions, a written orthodoxy of the Christian faith is assembled in the early 4th-century. Soon after, by stroke of good fortune, the Church Fathers and leading theologians fall into an uncomfortable alliance with the Roman power brokers who legalize Christianity in 313 CE and eventually indoctrinate the cannons of Catholicism as the singular official religion of the realm 67 years later. With Church and state having forged an alliance, the newly-formed Catholic Church, so emboldened, more strongly enforces its orthodoxy, in part, by suppressing/destroying counter-doctrinal literature and persecuting heretics. And the rest, as they say, is history.

• • •

THE PROBABILITY HYPOTHESIS: COMPUTING THE PROBABILITY FOR THE RESURRECTION

As is rather evident, historiographical methods will always be troubled by the relative ability to authenticate and weigh the value of ancient literary sources. This makes the process of discerning true history a ping-pong game between scholars. In 2003, Oxford analytical philosopher and Christian apologist Richard Swinburne (b. 1934 –) overturned the ping-pong table by changing the calculus of how to approach the truth of the resurrection.[31] In his book, *The Resurrection of God Incarnate* (Oxford University Press, 2003), Richard Swinburne essentially deemphasizes the dating, temporal ordering, and the minutia of inconsistencies of and between ancient documents by taking a wider view of the situation. He posited that it is feasible to collect the individual evidences both for and against the resurrection to generate a mathematical probability function to characterize the likelihood that Jesus existed and that the resurrection event happened. He also took stock of the probability for the existence of the Christian God in *The Existence of God* (Oxford University Press, 2004, 2nd ed.) where he updates his first edition to include this technique. We will cover this material in Chapter 9.

---

31. Swinburne is Emeritus Professor of Philosophy at Oxford University. Swinburne is affiliated with the Eastern Orthodox Church and is recognized as one of the foremost Christian apologists. Unlike so many of his compatriots who feel that God is principally beyond human reasoning, he believes that the Christian faith can be fully justified as being philosophically rational and coherent. Swinburne fathered the *Principle of Testimony* and the *Principle of Credulity*. The Principle of Credulity states that if certain circumstances appear to be true of reality, then we should accept it as true barring any reason not to believe it to be true. The Principle of Testimony is a correlate to the Principle of Credulity in that eyewitness accounts and personal testimony are valid statements of truth concerning religious experiences unless there are justified reasons to falsify or question the validity such statements.

Using mathematical probability was a fresh perspective that departed from the usual dialectical of deductive, reductive, and abductive treatments of the past (those we just reviewed). Swinburne says that we need to use those approaches but they alone are not adequate. According to his mind, one must also apply inductive reasoning. Inductive reasoning seeks to weigh hypotheses based on premises with varying degrees of uncertainty. Even though individual propositions may carry relatively low levels of certainty, taken collectively, abundant evidences can potentially lead to an unexpected strength in explanatory power. The method of combining these evidences in the form of evidentiary statements (as opposed to numerical data) is called *Bayesian epistemology*. This is an adaptation of Bayesian inference to the best explanation which is undergirded by the use of *Bayes' theorem*. This is the same theorem implemented by Kilty and Elliot who computed the probability that the names on the Talpiot Tomb were those of Jesus and his family. Whereas deductive logic characterizes reality as the necessity and full certainty of rational belief, **Bayesian induction depicts the likelihood of reality using the uncertainty of partially rational belief.** In applying *the Simple Rule*, the result is the ability to claim that a belief is justified when the final probability value passes an acceptable threshold.[81] This value is often taken to be greater than 50 percent, but circumstances may dictate that some other value ought to be utilized.

Bayes' theorem, named after its discoverer Thomas Bayes, is an elementary mathematical theorem referred to as conditional probability calculus and is a component of Decision Theory. The equation as we will see is surprisingly simple which belies it incredible power. The Bayesian interpretation of probability can be seen as an extension of regular propositional logic whereby a proposition's truth or falsity is uncertain. In other words, in contrast to interpreting probability as the *propensity* for some phenomenon to occur, what we think of as normal intrinsic probability (e.g., a coin toss), Bayesian probability is the quantification of a *state of knowledge*. We can use it to predict what may happen in the future or what may have happened in the past based on the accumulated evidences. Fundamentally, Bayesian analysis is all about coherently updating our beliefs based on evidence, and as new evidence is acquired, to subsequently re-update those beliefs. This process is called *Bayesian updating*.

Such methods have found wide application in medicine, science, and engineering. One such engineering application is in modern-day computer simulation models to estimate what is referred to as 'unknown parameters'. With the increasing competition in the automotive market, vehicle control and handling engineers are pressed harder and harder to eke out performance improvements. Engineers want to be able to predict in advance how the vehicle parameters (e.g., body roll rate, pitch rate) will respond to command inputs directed by the driver (e.g., a hard turn of the steering wheel during a crash avoidance situation) or indirectly from road conditions (e.g., hitting a pothole, slippery surfaces). Bayesian statistics can be used to forecast how a tire might respond milliseconds in the future after the driver cranks the steering wheel or a tire enters a pothole. The vehicle traction computer can take the current state of knowledge from sensor data (e.g., wheel speed, center of gravity of the vehicle, roll rate) to compute the probabilities of how each of these would change by doing performing some change in the system to maintain control of the car (e.g., alter the brake force, change engine speed, or change the absorption characteristics in the suspension). The computer can then decide based on the probability values what instructions to convey to the controllable aspects of the vehicle. Other applications for Bayes' theorem are used in digital e-mail spam filtering techniques, stock investing software, and law proceedings. It is now being used in the field of religious studies.

In the case of the resurrection, we can mirror the Bayesian process outlined above. Whereas the disciplines above typically compute probabilities based on numerical inputs, we can alternatively estimate the probability for the resurrection using premises and associated **EXPLANANS** (evidences). This knowledge emanates from our general background knowledge (truths of logic, analytic truths, mathematics, conceptual truths) and our specific evidences which might include scientific hypotheses, data, relevant sensory experience, and historical sources regarding the resurrection. We necessarily need to account for the reverse probability whereby there may exist counter-acting natural explanations that would support the negation of the main hypothesis. Armed with this insight, I will step you through how Swinburne setup the probability equation which may appear like a jumble of letters to those who are not mathematically inclined but I will do my best to break it down into comprehensible pieces. This same logic will be implemented in Chapter 9 so I will introduce you to some of the concepts here and save some for later so that you can absorb the implications in digestible pieces.

There are many ways to express Bayes' theorem, all of them are mathematically equivalent. I will start with the simplest referred to eponymously as Bayes' *Simple* form. The mathematical expression only contains three terms. When put into effect, the equation will produce a numeric value between zero and one. For example, if we computed the value 0.10 for $P(H|E)$, this would indicate that there is a 10% likelihood that the hypothesis is true based on all the information provided. After I explain what each of these terms mean, we will work through an example.

$$\mathbf{P}(H \mid E) = \mathbf{P}(E \mid H) \times \frac{\mathbf{P}(H)}{\mathbf{P}(E)} \qquad \text{Bayes' theorem} \atop \text{Simple Form}$$

$$\mathbf{P}(\text{Hypothesis} \mid \text{Evidence}) = \mathbf{P}(\text{Evidence} \mid \text{Hypothesis}) \times \frac{\mathbf{P}(\text{Hypothesis})}{\mathbf{P}(\text{Evidence})}$$

The left-hand side of this equation is read as: The probability (denoted as '$\mathbf{P}$') of a stated hypothesis or proposition ('H'), given (denoted by the vertical bar symbol, '|') the condition of all new evidences ('E'), is equal to the quantity provided on the right-hand side of the equation. The first term of the right-hand side, $\mathbf{P}(E|H)$, is the likelihood that the specific new evidences would explain the hypothesis given the assumption that the hypothesis is true. The numerator, $\mathbf{P}(H)$, is the probability of the hypothesis being true—using only background knowledge—before we consider any of the specific evidences. This is commonly called the 'prior probability'. What constitutes background knowledge is something that has to be considered on a case by case basis. As noted earlier, this might include things such as logical truths, conceptual truths, and mathematics. The bottom quantity, $\mathbf{P}(E)$, is the probability of the specific evidences being true without regard to the hypothesis. It is assumed that $\mathbf{P}(E)$ is always greater than zero.

An example will make this clearer. If we were to hypothesize that the sky was filled with a Blue Moon yesterday evening, what is the probability that this happened? To make it easier, let us assume that the only relevant background knowledge we have to consider is that the object that orbits our planet, something we call the Moon, actually exists. So, what is the intrinsic likelihood that the phenomenon of a *Blue* Moon exists? At this point we can neither appeal to any personal experiences on the Moon's color nor may we access scientific data that supports the notion that the Moon's coloration can change due to volcanic particulates trapped in the atmosphere. Therefore, only knowing that the Moon exists, $\mathbf{P}(H)$ is likely to be low because there are many hues it could be. Let us agree that the prior probability that the Moon's color could be blue, before considering specific evidences, is five percent (0.05). Now let us consider the specific evidences that would help us to understand what the probability is that a Blue Moon could have occurred last night.

Let's say a guy by the name of Harold wrote an internet blog that testifies that he saw the Blue Moon yesterday and that he posted a picture of it using his cell phone camera. A second piece of information is that when researching the Moon in an encyclopedia it states that the Moon is "usually white, yellow, or orange in color" (mock quote). There is no mention that it could be blue in color. Finally, we have literary evidence from a two thousand years ago that comments that, "God was angry and caused the volcano to erupt. The next ten Moons were blue." (mock quote). From this, we would think this evidence strongly favors the idea that the Moon changes color and that it can, on occasion, be blue. However, you hadn't heard of any active volcanoes that erupted in the last few weeks. Also, it could be that Harold edited the photo and applied a false color filter to make it look blue. Finally, we have to question whether the ancient text is authentic. Also, on the negative side, an encyclopedia is usually a pretty solid reference source and it did not mention that the Moon could be blue.

If we only look at the specific evidences above, what is the certainty that these evidences are trustworthy sources? We are uncertain of the authenticity of the ancient text and we are more certain that a volcano did not erupt as we may have heard about it in the news. We are certain that the Moon changes color given our confidence in the encyclopedic reference. The photo could be exceptionally strong if we were certain that Harold did not alter the photo, but we are lacking that critical information. We agree that that the evidence puts us at fifty-fifty, meaning that $\mathbf{P}(E)=0.50$.

Now, let us assume that a Blue Moon hypothesis is true, that a Blue Moon did indeed occur last night. How would this affect the probability that the accumulated evidences support the Blue Moon hypothesis? The evidences do seem to support the hypothesis fairly well. Let's agree that $\mathbf{P}(E|H)=0.60$.

$$\mathbf{P}(H_{Blue\ Moon}\,|\,E) = \mathbf{P}(E\,|\,H_{Blue\ Moon}) \times \frac{\mathbf{P}(H_{Blue\ Moon})}{\mathbf{P}(E)}$$

$$\mathbf{P}(H_{Blue\ Moon}\,|\,E) = 0.60 \times \frac{0.05}{0.50} = 0.06 = 6.0\%$$

We can now make a statement as follows: "Based on the hypothesis, the premises, the supporting evidence, and our relevant background knowledge about the Moon, we infer that it is highly *improbable* that a Blue Moon was present in the sky in the timeframe of interest." **While we are very certain that it did *not* happen, we can never express our position with absolute certainty with inductive techniques**. Notice that, even with the high probability (60 percent) of the evidences supporting the presumably true hypothesis, the end result was still low. This is because our prior knowledge lacked any notion as to the color of the Moon, and that all possible colors had to be considered, *and* that it had to be a specific color in the last 24 hours. This led to our very uncertain initial belief (5 percent).

The Simple form is not often used in Bayesian epistemology but it is less formidable in appearance so that is why it was presented. Let us now review the *Explicit* form of

Bayes' theorem. The reason for using this form is that it more clearly separates confirmatory information from the disconfirmatory information as will be evident below.

$$\text{Probability that Hypothesis is True} = \frac{\{\text{Quantity 1}\}}{\{\text{Quantity 1}\} + \{\text{Quantity 2}\}}$$

$$\mathbf{P}(H\,|\,E) = \frac{\{\mathbf{P}(H) \times \mathbf{P}(E\,|\,H)\}}{\{\mathbf{P}(H) \times \mathbf{P}(E\,|\,H)\} + \underbrace{\{\mathbf{P}(\sim H) \times \mathbf{P}(E\,|\,\sim H)\}}_{\text{Rival Hypothesis}}} \qquad \begin{array}{l}\text{Bayes' theorem}\\ \text{Explicit Form}\end{array}$$

Here we encounter the connective tilde symbol, ' ~ ', which confers the meaning 'not' or 'negation' or 'it is not the case that'.[32] In our context, the expression ' ~H ', is to be read as 'the negation of the hypothesis' or 'treating the hypothesis as untrue'. You will also note that the numerator and the denominator share a common quantity, $\mathbf{P}$(H) x $\mathbf{P}$(E|H). This quantity accounts for the prior probability with no specific evidence and the probability that the specific evidences affirm the hypothesis. The other term in the denominator, $\mathbf{P}$(~H) x $\mathbf{P}$(E|~H), speaks generally as to how well rival hypotheses are able to refute the stated hypothesis.

Let us now rewrite this equation to describe the Resurrection Hypothesis stated simply as, "Did the resurrection of Jesus occur?" To represent this hypothesis let us use the symbol, 'H_r'. Let us split the symbol 'E' into two pieces—'E_s' for specific evidences and 'B' for background knowledge. The equation then appears as follows:

$$\mathbf{P}(H_r\,|\,E_s\,\&\,B) = \frac{\{\mathbf{P}(H_r\,|\,B) \times \mathbf{P}(E_s\,|\,H_r\,\&\,B)\}}{\{\mathbf{P}(H_r\,|\,B) \times \mathbf{P}(E_s\,|\,H_r\,\&\,B)\} + \underbrace{\{\mathbf{P}(\sim H_r\,|\,B) \times \mathbf{P}(E_s\,|\,\sim H_r\,\&\,B)\}}_{\text{Rival Hypothesis}}}$$

The term on the left side of the equation is referred to as the ***posterior probability***. The first term in the numerator of this equation, $\mathbf{P}$(H$_r$|B), estimates the propensity for the resurrection to occur considering only our background knowledge. This is called the *intrinsic probability*. The second term that makes up the numerator is the probability that the specific evidences are true given background knowledge and that the resurrection did occur. Some quick examples of specific evidences would be the virginal birth of Jesus, that Jesus

---

32. Some statisticians prefer the ' ¬ ' symbol in front of the letter or the bar symbol ' ¯ ' above the letter to represent negation. Therefore, in some references you may see the negation of the hypothesis presented as ¬H or as $\bar{H}$.

was a prophet, that he was the Messiah, the empty tomb, and the post-death appearances. This second term characterizes the *Explanatory Power* of the hypothesis.

$$\overbrace{\mathbf{P}(H_r \mid B)}^{\text{Intrinsic Probability}} \times \overbrace{\mathbf{P}(E_s \mid H_r \,\&\, B)}^{\text{Explanatory Power}}$$

The final unexplained term, found in the denominator, seeks to account for the probabilities that the resurrection *did not* happen in light of the same evidences or altogether different evidences that favor rival hypotheses. It is defined as:

$$\overbrace{\mathbf{P}(\sim H_r \mid B)}^{\substack{\text{Intrinsic Probability that the} \\ \text{Resurrection \textbf{did not} happen} \\ \text{given only our Background knowledge}}} \times \overbrace{\mathbf{P}(E_s \mid \sim H_r \,\&\, B)}^{\substack{\text{Explanatory Power} - \text{the} \\ \text{probability that evidences} \\ \text{support rival hypotheses}}}$$

While Swinburne expends considerable effort describing what constitutes background evidences, he synopsizes that it can be ignored (he uses the symbol 'k' to represent background knowledge).

[underline added]

But when we are dealing with big theories of physics, <u>and above all theories of metaphysics</u>, there are no neighbouring fields of inquiry (since these theories purport to explain so much that there are no 'neighbouring fields' outside their scope), and so <u>we can ignore k</u>.[82]

Therefore, we can simplify the appearance of the equation as shown below.

$$\mathbf{P}(H_r \mid E_s) = \frac{\{\mathbf{P}(H_r) \times \mathbf{P}(E_s \mid H_r)\}}{\{\mathbf{P}(H_r) \times \mathbf{P}(E_s \mid H_r)\} + \underbrace{\{\mathbf{P}(\sim H_r) \times \mathbf{P}(E_s \mid \sim H_r)\}}_{\text{Rival Hypotheses}}}$$

Following the Simple Rule mentioned earlier, this implies the following:

if and only if: $\mathbf{P}(H_r \mid E_s) > \frac{1}{2} \overset{\text{inference}}{\Longrightarrow}$ Resurrection probably **did happen**

if and only if: $\mathbf{P}(H_r \mid E_s) < \frac{1}{2} \overset{\text{inference}}{\Longrightarrow}$ Ressurection is probably **untrue**

We can also discern that if the combination of all rival hypotheses is a large number, that this will weigh heavily against the probability that the resurrection is true. Note, we cannot say that just because the whole set of rival theories is highly probable, that this necessarily will infer that the resurrection did not happen. For if there are a few strong evidences or a large number of relatively weak evidences, these could tilt the posterior probability, $\mathbf{P}(H_r|E_s)$, in favor that the Resurrection Hypothesis. The probabilities for each rival hypothesis are additive as described below if there were three such theories to consider.

$$\overbrace{\mathbf{P}(\sim H_r) \times \mathbf{P}(E_s|\sim H_r)}^{\text{All Rival Hypotheses}} = \overbrace{\mathbf{P}(H_1) \times \mathbf{P}(E_{s_1}|H_1)}^{\text{Rival Hypothesis \#1}} + \overbrace{\mathbf{P}(H_2) \times \mathbf{P}(E_{s_2}|H_2)}^{\text{Rival Hypothesis \#2}} + \overbrace{\mathbf{P}(H_3) \times \mathbf{P}(E_{s_3}|H_3)}^{\text{Rival Hypothesis \#3}}$$

Swinburne's task is to identify the premises and supporting evidences and subsequently justify values for each of the necessary terms in the equation. In his work, he adopted different symbology to represent Bayes' theorem parameters which are described below and he rearranges his usage of Bayes' theorem which makes it less straightforward. In any case, his goal is to determine the posterior probability $\mathbf{P}(H_r|E_s)$—the left-hand side of the equation. The first step he takes toward computing the probability for Jeus' resurrection is to define the nature of God. He defines God by the terms adopted by the Council of Chalcedon (451 CE). The chief outcome of this ecumenical council was to clarify the perfection of Jesus' manhood and union with the Godhead.[33]

> The next several pages review the fine details of Swinburne's and my own assessment for the statistical likelihood that the resurrection actually occurred. This coverage admittedly requires a fair degree of focused review to comprehend it all.
>
> For those who would like to understand the intricacies of all the various considerations employed to arrive at the final probability, I encourage you to study the details. For those who would prefer to bypass this material and learn the final outcome, you may jump to the section entitled *"Final Synopsis for the Statistical Likelihood of Jesus' Resurrection"*—refer to p. 264.

---

33. As the Bible does not explain the interrelationship of the Holy Spirit with God and Jesus, the Catholic doctrine had to be created. This was largely performed by Athanasius late in his life during the late 4th-century and further debated by ecumenical councils for decades afterwards.[83]

Swinburne formulated his Bayesian Resurrection Hypothesis by the equation below (see p. 258).[84] The hypothesis is represented by Swinburne as $\mathbf{P}(c|e\&k)$, which, with the adoption of my terminology, is equivalent to $\mathbf{P}(H_r|E_s)$. Even though Swinburne concludes there is no background knowledge to consider, I have opted to leave the symbol 'k' in the equation to keep it consistent with how the equations are presented in his book. I have summarized how Swinburne arrived at his final probability (refer to Table 6-5 and the final calculation on p. 260); however, I cannot summarize the details of his convictions in such a short space.

The last two columns, Columns E and F, of Table 6-5 is my take. I provide a brief synopsis after the table (see p. 262) to aide in explaining how I arrived at values presented. In the table, I direct your attention to the grayed-out boxes rather than the uncolored boxes. The uncolored boxes are presented simply because they represent quantities that Swinburne had grouped together and are not explicitly shown in the equation below. Additionally, for each grayed-box, you may consult the table footnotes (see p. 260) to understand how the 'grayed values' are calculated using the uncolored box values.

$$\mathbf{P}(c\,|\,e\,\&\,k) = \frac{\{\mathbf{P}(c\,|\,k) \times \mathbf{P}(f\,|\,c\,\&\,k)\}}{\{\mathbf{P}(c\,|\,k) \times \mathbf{P}(f\,|\,c\,\&\,k)\} + \underbrace{\{\mathbf{P}(\sim c\,|\,k) \times \mathbf{P}(f\,|\sim c\,\&\,k)\}}_{\text{Rival Hypotheses}}}$$

Swinburne's setup of Bayes' theorem for the Resurrection Hypothesis

Table 6-5. Swinburne's Symbology and Probability Estimate for the Resurrection
(Refer to Column C and D for Swinburne's characterizations)

~ =	"not" or "negation" or "it is not the case that"
c =	the incarnation of God as defined by the Council of Chalcedon
e =	specific evidences (separate from background knowledge)
f =	claims that there is evidence supported by the strength attested to by Swinburne
k =	all relevant background knowledge (provided by natural theology)
t =	the claim that there is a God of the traditional kind (omnipotent, omniscient, etc.)

Line #	The Probability that ...	Swinburne's Nomenclature for Probabilities	Swinburne's Prescribed Probability	This Author's Prescribed Probability	
A	B	C	D	E	F
1	... God exists as validated by evidences given by traditional natural theological arguments (i.e., background knowledge).	$P(t\|k)$	0.50	Low	0.40
				Hi	0.50
2	... the Chalcedonian God exists AND that he would at some point become incarnate given that God exists and our background knowledge as provided by natural theology.	$P(c\|t\,\&\,k)$	0.50	Low	0.001
				Hi	0.05
3	... God becomes incarnate given the background knowledge provided by natural theology	$P(c\|k)$	0.25[a]	Low	0.0004[a]
				Hi	0.025[a]
4	... that the evidences (Jesus was a prophet, greater than any other prophet, lived a perfect morally-good life, and survived his death by the action of a "super-miracle") given that God had become incarnate on Earth as a human.	$P(f\|c\,\&\,k)$	0.10	Low	0.05
				Hi	0.10
5	... the claims and the Chalcedonian God incarnate are true given the background evidence provided by natural theology	$P(f\,\&\,c\|k)$	0.025[b]	Low	0.00002[b]
				Hi	0.0025[b]
6	... the incarnation of the Chalcedonian God did not happen given the background evidence provided by natural theology.	$P(\sim c\|k)$	0.75[c]	Low	0.9996[c]
				Hi	0.9750[c]
7	... that the claims and specific evidences are true given that there was no incarnation, either because there is no God or he chooses not to become incarnate but granting our background knowledge. Swinburne believes this can only happen if God were to commit a great deception and does so straight-forwardly or tacitly via other agents. He denies that a "good" Chalcedonian God is highly unlikely to do this.	$P(f\|\sim c\,\&\,k)$	0.001	Low	0.25
				Hi	0.60

Line #	The Probability that ...	Swinburne's Nomenclature for Probabilities	Swinburne's Prescribed Probability	This Author's Prescribed Probability	
A	**B**	**C**	**D**	**E**	**F**
8	... that the claims are true given our background knowledge provided by natural theology.	$P(f\|k)$	0.02575 [(d)]	Low	0.24992 [(d)]
				Hi	0.58750 [(d)]
9	... that the Chalcedonian God will become incarnate given the various claims – supported by specific evidences and our background knowledge of God provided by natural theology.	$P(c\|f\&k)$ ... or also ... $P(c\|e\&k)$	0.97 [(e)]	Low	8 / 100,000
				Hi	4.23 / 1,000
10	... that Jesus was the Chalcedonian God incarnate who died and was resurrected (same as Line 9).	$P(c\|e\&k)$	97%	Low	0.008%
				Hi	0.423%

TABLE 6-5 NOTES
(a) To obtain Line 3, multiply Lines 1 and 2.
(b) To obtain Line 5, multiply Lines 3 and 4. The resulting value is the numerator in Bayes' equation.
(c) To obtain Line 6, subtract Line 3 from the quantity "1" (as in, 1 – Line 3). This is dictated by probability axiom: $P(c\|k) + P(\sim c\|k) = 1$. Note that this results in the "Hi" value being lower than the "Low" value.
(d) To obtain Line 8, multiply Lines 6 and 7. Add this to the value in Line 5. This total is the sum of all the terms presented in the denominator of the Bayesian equation shown just above Table 6-5.
(e) To obtain Line 9, divide Line 5 by Line 8.

$$P(c \mid e \& k) = \frac{\{P(c \mid k) \times P(f \mid c \& k)\}}{\{P(c \mid k) \times P(f \mid c \& k)\} + \underbrace{\{P(\sim c \mid k) \times P(f \mid \sim c \& k)\}}_{\text{Rival Hypotheses}}}$$

$$P(c \mid e \& k) = \frac{\{0.25 \times 0.10\}}{\{0.25 \times 0.10\} + \underbrace{\{0.75 \times 0.001\}}_{\text{Rival Hypotheses}}} = \frac{0.025}{0.025 + \underbrace{0.00075}_{\substack{\text{Rival} \\ \text{Hypotheses}}}} \quad \underset{\text{for Rival Theories}}{\underbrace{\text{Almost Zero Probability}}}$$

$P(c \mid e \& k) \approx 97\%$ ⟵ Swinburne's Probability that the Resurrection actually occurred

It is immediately apparent that Richard Swinburne thinks that rival hypotheses are extremely weak as he arrives at a value close to zero. I will address his position on this by reviewing scholarly critiques of his proposal after I summarize my own estimates just below. Note that, because I elected to give a range of values (i.e., "Hi" and "Low"), some extra care is needed in selecting the appropriate value from the table. In computing the maximum probability for the resurrection, one seeks the largest numerator and smallest denominator of Bayes' equation, respectively. Likewise, in understanding the lowest probability, one is to use the values provided in Column F that yield the smallest numerator and largest denominator. To put it differently, in calculating the maximum probability of the resurrection using my Hi-Low approach, it would be erroneous to simply utilize all the "Hi" values.

Maximum & Minimum Probability Resurrection Occurred (present author's view):

$$P(c \mid e \& k)_{\max} = \frac{\{0.025 \times 0.10\}}{\{0.025 \times 0.10\} + \underbrace{\{0.975 \times 0.25\}}_{\text{Rival Hypotheses}}} = \frac{0.0025}{0.0025 + 0.244} \quad \underset{\text{about 25\% probable}}{\overset{\text{Rival theories}}{\longleftarrow}}$$

$P(c \mid e \& k)_{\max} \approx 1.0\%$ ⟵ Present Author's Assessment for the **Maximum Probability** that the Ressurection actually occurred

$$P(c \mid e \& k)_{\min} = \frac{\{0.0004 \times 0.05\}}{\{0.0004 \times 0.05\} + \underbrace{\{0.9996 \times 0.60\}}_{\text{Rival Hypotheses}}} = \frac{2.0 \times 10^{-5}}{2.0 \times 10^{-5} + 0.59} \quad \underset{\text{about 60\% probable}}{\overset{\text{Rival theories}}{\longleftarrow}}$$

$P(c \mid e \& k)_{\min} \approx 0.003\%$ ⟵ Present Author's Assessment for the **Minimum Probability** that the Resurrection actually occurred

Synopsis of The Present Author's Values (Table 6-5 – Columns E and F)

Here, I only discuss the **uncolored** rows from Table 6-5 as these are the basis for the values presented in the **colored** (grayed) rows of the table.

Row 1 – Given only background knowledge, it is generally agreed that there is about a 50/50 chance God-by-whatever-name exists. The lower value is in response to the fact that some scientific theories propound that God is not necessary to have created the universe. Admittedly, it is unclear if this qualifies as background knowledge or evidence. These theories use mathematical logic but also entail human interpretations. Whether these theories are true or not is not to be debated at this juncture, but to give it a small amount of credence I reduced the lower bound by ten points.

Row 2 – Here Swinburne and I disagree significantly. Given the origin and development of religion, in particular, the Judaic and Christocentric traditions, we elucidated that God was in effect the lone surviving descendant from a pantheon of many gods whose powers and character were morphed over hundreds and thousands of years. As such, the Chalcedonian God characterized by the human/divine nature of Jesus, born of the Virgin Mary, yet in perfect consubstantial union with the Triune Godhead, is rather unlikely given the revised appreciation of our background knowledge.

Row 4 – There are historical sources that claim that Jesus was an actual human being who was a prophet and a Messiah who performed amazing feats (e.g., healing the sick and cast-out demonic spirits). Some called him a god. I will agree with Swinburne's characterization that the value is to be no higher than 0.10. The lower bound of 0.05 is based on reducing the chances by half because the literary sources do not meet the metrics for historical reliability.

Row 7 – Probably the largest source of difference results from the lack of negative theology entertained by Swinburne (as noted by Cavin and Colombetti, discussed further below). The two were mostly discontented about the notion of whether or not God would be the author of or permit by agency deceptive practices to obfuscate the reality of the resurrection. Beyond that, I call into question Swinburne's reliance on both "Prior" and "Posterior" Historical Evidence as he puts it.

As to the Prior, Swinburne notes that Jesus implied his divinity. I have not yet addressed the divinity question (see Chapter 6), but suffice it to say here that justifications for Jesus' divinity are weakened. To a much greater degree, I disagree with Swinburne's Posterior judgments where he claims the Appearances of the Risen Jesus, the empty tomb, and that inferior rival hypotheses greatly strengthen his evidentiary claims. Never minding my reservations, these then go to supporting Swinburne's defense of why God would not permit deception to obscure the resurrection. It shall suffice that I have said my peace on the Jesus Appearances and the empty tomb. When one considers the rival hypothesis reviewed earlier, my lower bound appears to be more justified than Swinburne's prescription.

Swinburne's Bayesian calculations indicate that the resurrection is 97 percent likely to have occured. This is starkly different than the two assessments I provided. My lower bound estimate is 0.003 percent chance given an evaluation of the evidences provided by Swinburne and by those elucidated thusfar in the book. Granting certain uncertainties, my upper bound estimate increased the likelihood to 1.0 percent.

Ultimately, Bayesian analysis is a powerful means to determine the structural connection between causation and explanation. While the majority of the evidences are supposed to be backed by factual information or a solid rational basis for why a particular evidence has a level of justification for being considered a part of the evaluation, it has to be acknowledged that there is a measure of subjectivity and general uncertainty in the prescriptions, all of which contribute to the outcome.

I have not as yet delved into unresolved foundational structural principles of Bayesian confirmation theory which will further question its applicability toward useful enlightenment on problems in philosophy. Christian apologists are now implementing the technique widely to characterize the liklihood of God's existence, that Jesus was the Messiah, and that Jesus died by crucifixion. In conclusion, I shall provide more commentary on these issues and the increased reliance of Bayes' theorem by Christian apologists later in Chapter 9 when we discuss an outgrowth of Swinburne's approach referred to as Ramified Natural Theology.

SCHOLARS CRITICIZE SWINBURNE'S TREATMENT OF THE RESURRECTION HYPOTHESIS

Needless to say, when someone declares that we can be 97 percent certain that Jesus was divinely resurrected; people are going to raise an eyebrow ... or maybe two. Swinburne's prescriptions were critically assailed as being overly optimistic in favor of the resurrection effectively biasing the amount of pro-resurrection information. In a sign that just over ten years after his book was published it is still garnering much debate, Cavin and Colombetti[85] in 2013 published, in an evangelical Christian apologetics journal no less (*Philosophia Christi*), a critique that casts a very dim view indeed on the handling of the inputs. Essentially, Swinburne ignored theological assertions that would tend to disconfirm tenets of Christianity. They specifically point to the fact that his analysis did not suitably integrate the possibility that God might deceive us about his incarnation as Jesus or his subsequent resurrection, among other improperly handled evidences and assumptions.

While they point out additional criticisms of Swinburne's implementation, in an earlier critique, mathematics professor Andrew Wohlgemuth identifies another fundamental flaw in Swinburne's logic. He calls to mind Swinburne's statement, "It is a further fundamental epistemological principle additional to the principle that other things being equal we should trust our memories, that we should believe what others tell us that they have done or perceived—in the absence of counterevidence. I call this the principle of testimony."[86] Wohlgemuth adroitly forwards that our memories and the testimony of others is replete with misinformation. This sort of statement by Swinburne should worry anyone interested to discover the truth about God for it we could trust our memories so easily, finding God would be an open-and-shut case. Ultimately, Cavin and Colombetti conclude that Swinburne's Ramified Natural Theology[34] has in no way evinced the probable likelihood of Jesus of Nazareth's resurrection.[85]

Swinburne elevates the brinksmanship with counterstrokes against Cavin and Colombetti's characterization saying that they conflate two negative theological issues regarding God's deception. The first matter relates to God's permittance of unjustifiable deception. This conjecture is being confused with God allowing people to retain false beliefs and be otherwise deceived. Swinburne implies that the two author's position pertains to the latter category.[87] Swinburne states that God would never perform direct deception, but that he would allow people to develop erroneous beliefs.[88] When one considers Wohlgemuth's comment about the weakness of Swinburne's "principle of testimony" and what we have learned from the preceding discussion on the authenticity and reliability of Scriptures, the very source material used by Swinburne to formulate his positive propositions, Swinburne's analysis begins to crumble fast. Swinburne takes as bona fide evidence an array of biblical testimony about Jesus and human prophets. Reverend Rodney Holder,[35] an ordained minister and Oxford-educated astrophysicist who is on the national committee of Christians in Science, expressed his discomfort with Swinburne's presumptuous "claim to know *a priori* what God would do—even what God is morally obliged to do."[89]

Though he resolutely claims otherwise, it is my opinion that Swinburne considerably oversells his prescriptions for the various probabilities fundamentally because of his wedded commitment as a Christian apologist colors his view. In other words, his prior (and current) belief is solidly embedded in his countless narratives and arguments

---

34. Natural theology is theory of God based on our innate and developed ability to reason in conjunction with our ordinary experiences. That is to say, God is reasoned philosophically *without* appeals to supernatural revelation. Christian *Ramified* Natural Theology is an *extension* of this "bare" natural theology as it adds arguments from historical data. The term, "ramified", in this context is meant to further complexify, that is to enrich, natural theology.

35. Holder is an associate of the Faraday Institute for Science and Religion. He is an astrophysicist and ordained minister.

pre-dating his implementation of Bayesian epistemic probability. It goes against most people's intuition that there is such a remarkably high (97 percent) likelihood that the resurrection happened. Why? If it were so evident that it happened, why has this event been such a tremendous source of contention for two thousand years!? Why is it that we should expect God to become incarnate on planet Earth for a mere 30 to 33 years and then disappear for two thousand years and counting until the ESCHATON? There are a vast number of other things that that possess the same level of certainty such as the likelihood that you and I will live for another five minutes. Swinburne's examination just does not sync well with common intuition.

The next chapter will serve as a summary for this chapter.

WEIGHING THE EVIDENCE

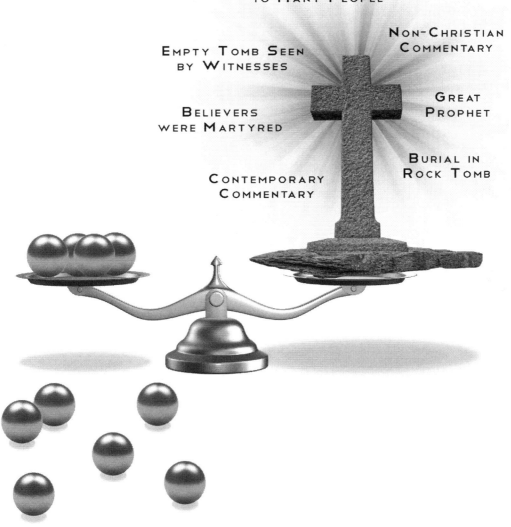

POST-DEATH APPEARANCES
TO MANY PEOPLE

NON-CHRISTIAN
COMMENTARY

EMPTY TOMB SEEN
BY WITNESSES

GREAT
PROPHET

BELIEVERS
WERE MARTYRED

BURIAL IN
ROCK TOMB

CONTEMPORARY
COMMENTARY

COUNTEREVIDENCE

CHAPTER 7

Testing the Truth
of the Resurrection

Unquestionably! No one can read the Gospels without feeling the actual presence of Jesus. His personality pulsates in every word. No myth is filled with such life. [...] No man can deny the fact that Jesus existed, nor that his sayings are beautiful.[1]

– Albert Einstein
Time Magazine, Einstein and Faith
Einstein's response when asked if he accepted the historical existence of Jesus.

On the other hand, we cannot leave history entirely to nonclinical observers and to professional historians who often all too nobly immerse themselves into the very disguises, rationalizations, and idealizations of the historical process from which it should be their business to separate themselves.[2]

– Erik Erikson
Young Man Luther: A Study in Psychoanalysis and History
A winner of the Pulitzer Prize and the National Book Award, Erik H. Erikson was a renowned worldwide teacher, clinician, and theorist in the field of psychoanalysis and human development.

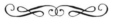

AFTER CONSIDERABLE EFFORT WE ARE finally in a position to circumscribe all of the evidence compiled thus far and dump it into the Historicity Hypothesis Testing Engine (HHTE). As a refresher, the HHTE reviews a historical hypothesis using six lenses: Explanatory Scope, Explanatory Power, Plausibility, *Ad Hoc* additions to the primary theory, and finally how the hypothesis compares to accepted beliefs and competing hypotheses. Taken together, they form the basis on which we are enabled to make an *Inference to the Best Explanation* for the hypothesis of interest. Employing this methodology, we can determine which of the Resurrection Hypothesis (RH) or the Mortal Jesus Hypothesis (MJH) better explains the eight claims of Christian Evidence and whether the resurrection was a historical event.

In preparing the exposition below, I have re-ordered the HHTE tests in the order of *least* to *greatest* importance as deemed by the going opinion of the historical society at large.

TESTING THE RESURRECTION HYPOTHESIS [RH]

The Resurrection Hypothesis asks the question, did Jesus rise from the dead—body, mind, and spirit? Christian apologists have assembled a laundry list of evidentiary support to answer this question in the affirmative. In the interest of reducing the scope of the task, I drew from the work of apologists seven key claims. These represent the strongest of the evidences they have assembled as it pertains directly to Jesus' resurrection. It is acknowledged that there are ancillary evidences that were left to the side, but such information is not going to alter the outcome of the analysis. If you do not wish to accept this statement, then you are given carte blanche to consult apologetic work of your choosing and apply it to the HHTE. With this disclaimer so noted, I will first provide a brief summary for each of the tests for the RH followed by the same process for the MJH. Then, the two hypotheses will be compared side-by-side to size-up which hypothesis is stronger.

HHTE: EXPLANATORY SCOPE (HOW MANY CLAIMS DOES IT EXPLAIN?)

The RH demonstrates a good deal of resiliency in terms of providing explanations for the full span of the eight Christian claims. There is an underlying assumption that many of the supporting facts are taken at face value which is a concerning matter, but on the whole, the RH covers all the bases.

HHTE: ACCORD WITH ACCEPTED BELIEFS (HOW WELL DOES IT CONFORM TO RELIGIOUS BELIEFS PRIOR TO, DURING, AND AFTER THE RESURRECTION?)

The RH is dependent on four anonymously-written gospel stories that offer conflicting accounts on how the resurrection story played out. It is to be granted that they exhibit verisimilitude, but there are specifics that require invalidation of those same specifics for at least one or more of the stories. Taking a wider view, the Jesus Story as told by the biblical accounts is definitely inconsistent with Jewish, pagan, and Gnostic beliefs. Recall that the Gnostics are not a single religious sect; rather this is a term that refers to a host of distinct belief systems. Relative to the Jewish beliefs, (1) Jesus did not restore David's throne to the Jewish people, (2) Jesus did not complete his work while a terrestrial, (3) the Jewish people had no prior concept of a bodily resurrection of a human being, and (4) Jesus died as a Jewish heretic. As pagan beliefs were dominate in Judea, Egypt, Greece, and elsewhere, the Christian beliefs were considered unusual. We also have to take into account that some pagan religions believed in reincarnation, so if the resurrection was true, one may have to concede that other people can also transcend death. Even among the many quasi-Christian sects, there was much divide on whether Jesus was even human. Recall the docetic belief of the Marcionites who saw a divine Jesus in the guise of a human male rather than being genuinely human. This belief survived for five centuries. Looking closer to modern-day times, we might also consider the visions of Jesus claimed by Latter-day Saints founder Joseph Smith. If those are true, then this falls in discord with the Christian belief that Jesus will not be seen until the Second Coming marking the eschatological end of the universe. In short, while mental visions were commonplace among other religions, these were not physical manifestations that could be equated to a physical body being reanimated after death.

In summary, the RH does not comport with accepted beliefs of the time.

HHTE: AD HOC SUPPORT (IDENTIFY SPECULATIVE ASSESSMENTS)

Assessing the level of speculation in hypothetical constructs is inherently a subjective activity. Often, the same information can lead to multiple rational conclusions. Nevertheless, it remains an informative step to identify what parts of a hypothesis are lacking evidence and to characterize the relative level of speculation.

Outside of the New Testament, there are no contemprary accounts describing the circumstances of the empty tomb of Jesus. There are no surviving copies of the Passion Narrative, which is the earliest text on the topic and may have been primary source. The earliest authentic mention is by the Christian defenders Tertullian and Justin Martyr who only vaguely reference the circumstances of the empty tomb. The other two quasi-Christian references—the Gospel of Peter and the Ascension of Isaiah—possess no historical merit. The clearest discussion on the empty tomb is given by Celsus who chastised everything about the upstart religion. Unfortunately, all his work was burned by Christian authorities. When considering the Acts of the Apostles, it surprising indeed that the author made no reference to the tomb being empty, only that Jesus was placed in a tomb. Relatedly, the original Greek terminology used in Acts in reference to the tomb could justifiably be translated as meaning a "grave" as in an earthen grave. And when we compare the inconsistent descriptions of the visitation of Jesus' empty tomb in the four gospels, it is out of necessity that we have to view these as historically speculative. Let us recall what apologist N.T. Wright said in the last chapter on the matter of the empty tomb and the appearance events. In order to establish a complete and coherent explanation for why a small number of Jewish people felt justified that their long-awaited savior had come, we need to validate the claim that the tomb was empty and that Jesus did in fact conquer death by visiting Earth after his human death over the course of forty days.[3]

Finally, there are highly essential implicit assumptions in the RH. It presumes that the Christian God and the Holy Spirit exist. Furthermore, the RH assumes that Jesus existed as a human and was divine. We shall explore the divinity of Jesus and the Holy Trinity in

Chapter 8. As I noted earlier, there is no artifactual evidence that can be authentically and firmly tied to Jesus. We only have access to primitive written texts and oral testimony passed down through the ages which are almost always weaker forms of historical evidence.

In conclusion, I agree with the following comment by Komarnitsky where he says, "I do not think even large differences of opinion about *ad hoc*-ness need to be settled. I think most people are willing to accept some conjecture as part of any explanation, as long as they feel that conjecture is plausible [...]"[4] Because *ad hoc* statements tie into plausibility and one's own sensibilities, no level of argumentation about speculative positions is going to change an **OBDURATE** mind. In consideration of the above argumentation, the RH is replete with speculative support. And, if for some reason one would wish to subscribe to a miracle-claim to the effect that God and the Holy Spirit came to reclaim their one-ness with the seating of Jesus in heaven, regardless of the poor quality of reporting by the apostles, then this would only increase the level of speculation associated with the RH.

HHTE: Explanatory Power (To what extent does the hypothesis explain the existence of the stated evidences?)

Regardless of whether one reads the biblical information at face value or with more critical thought, and without covering the ground again in unnecessary fashion, the RH offers an explanation for all facets of the eight claims regarding evidence for the resurrection. This is not to say that the RH explains all evidences we can amass. For example, the claims do not address the evidence that many gods have been manufactured by mankind over human history some of whom are said to have been reincarnated or killed only to live on in another realm. Additionally, our own experiences tell us that a resurrection would be considered an extremely rare occurrence and ostensibly has only occurred a single time in all of human history. The explanatory power is lacking in the sense that the evidences that we do have are not well corroborated when viewed from typical standards applied to scientific hypotheses. This situation motivates a need for exceedingly strong evidence that such an event occurred, which is not available. Nevertheless, in the context of the eight claims, the RH performs quite well.

HHTE: Plausibility (Given humanity's collective knowledge and experiences, does the resurrection cohere with our intellectual worldview and sensibilities?)

Let us remind ourselves that just over half (51 percent) of US adults firmly believe in miracles and another quarter (26 percent) believe that miracles may happen (refer to Chapter 2, Figure 3). With over three-quarters of people favoring the position that miracles are real, plausibility for the RH is veritably guaranteed at the outset without even adjusting for any positive evidentiary factors. The belief in miracles is an acquired belief based on one's own experiences and because people may opt to believe in the preachments of religion. Arguably, the belief in miracles may also be influenced by or be a manifestation of our biological neural programming. In any case, there is a very high mountain of preconception that must be overcome to change minds that the preeminent miracle of all time, happened (I will leave it to the reader to rank the birth of the universe). However, when we objectively grade the *historical plausibility*, miracles are not to be considered in the assessment. In scholarly public debate forums, Bart Ehrman argues that miracles are the *least* plausible explanation because any other naturalistically oriented explanation (e.g., Hallucination, Legend, Conspiracy theories) is more rational.[5]

The RH claims that Jesus was corporeally raised from the dead and that he made his continued earthly presence known to many people in different circumstances and different timeframes. When taking all the New Testament narratives that speak to Jesus' posthumous appearance at face value, the descriptions are tersely worded and in want of greater detail. Based on what is presented, Jesus' manifestations are varied from being the recognizable form of Jesus as well as being initially unrecognizable, yet also human. There are instances where he is embodied as a blinding light and a disembodied voice. And, at other times, he is a psychical vision or nocturnal dream. In most cases, Jesus appears instantaneously. That is, he is not in the nearby vicinity, and then all of a sudden, appears out of thin air. The suddenness of the supposedly corporeal appearances does not jive with the abilities of a normal human body. While we have experimentally confirmed that subatomic particles can and do teleport instantaneously from one location to another—one of a number of oddities associated with quantum mechanics—this has not been shown to be case for larger-scale complex atomic structures. This aspect of the Jesus post-death appearances is certainly historically implausible.

A further complication for the RH is that the Apostle Paul's account, prospectively the only firsthand eyewitness account, does not describe a corporeal posthumous Jesus. Furthermore, the testimony is 20 – 25 years after the event. All the other accounts are at best secondhand reports. The Gospel of Mark does not appear to have mentioned the appearances of Jesus, only that he was raised. This information is given to the women at the tomb by a mysterious young man who was dressed in a white robe. Could this man have taken the body out of the tomb before the women arrived? We also need to consider that the apostolic stories (e.g., Paul's conversion) are *beliefs* of people from 2,000 years ago that were untrained in the art of philosophic analysis or scientific assessment. Furthermore, all of the appearance accounts are provided by authors who are biased as they are seeking to gain adherents to their belief system. These issues significantly decrease the historical plausibility entailed in the RH. From a *historical perspective* the RH clearly ranks low on the plausibility scale.

HHTE: Superiority to Rival Hypotheses

By way of quick summary, it has been assessed that the Resurrection Hypothesis performs favorably in the Explanatory Scope and Explanatory Power tests but fails to perform well in the Acceptance with Accepted Beliefs, *Ad Hoc*, and Plausibility tests. Others have utilized the HHTE framework to weigh the Conspiracy, Apparent Death, Hallucination, Cognitive Dissonance, and Mythological Jesus-as-a-Hero hypotheses as well as those permutations by Goulder, Vermes, Crossnan, and Craffert/Botha. Each has its own strengths and weaknesses and in spite of a great deal of scholarly development, in my view, none are clearly better than the Resurrection Hypothesis. The traditional Legendary Jesus Hypothesis stands out as being more capable and is arguably superior to the RH. The Bayesian Probability analysis is said to have taken into account all the evidences both for and against the resurrection. By Richard Swinburne's assessment, the resurrection occurred beyond most any doubt. It was shown that his assessment was overly-biased and did not measure-up to an objective, historical accounting. In the assessment I provided, the resurrection event is very unlikely to have happened (a probability of one percent or less). The Mortal Jesus Hypothesis postulates that Jesus was a normal human who became subject to the processes of legend-making, is considered separately on its own terms.

Testing the Mortal Jesus Hypothesis [MJH]

HHTE: Explanatory Scope

The MJH, much like the RH, encapsulates the same facts surrounding the Jesus Story. Namely, that Jesus was a man who lived in the lands of Galilee and Judea who was crucified and buried in accordance to Jewish and Roman customs of the day. It furthermore offers an explanation why the disciples reported sightings and encounters of the posthumous Jesus as they missionized this new religion. In summary, it explains the historical claims equally as well as the RH in terms of the Explanatory Scope test.

HHTE: Accord with Accepted Beliefs

The ancients possessed vivid imaginations and belief in myths and legends were bountiful prior to and during the time of Jesus. Examples of legends around that timeframe can be found in the Pharaohs, Kings, and Emperors who were regarded as living deities. Another example we can draw on are the legendary Spartans whose valorous opposition to

Roman rule was heroicized. Relative to the number of gods, there were many at the time of Jesus. For a group of people to add one more deity to the menu of religions was not a new concept. In contrast, the idea of a bodily resurrection was a concept-in-formation. While there was no prior mention of a resurrection exactly like that of Jesus', there was a staircase of ideas that led up to this idea. The MJH offers historical support for the possible origin of the Christian God as a legend, whereas the RH starts with the all-important assumption that the Christian God (and Holy Spirit) has eternally existed.

In conclusion, the MJH reasonably comports with accepted beliefs of the time.

HHTE: Ad Hoc Support

There is a significant degree of speculation (*ad hoc*-ness) in this hypothesis for there is no historical document that would make comments to the effect that, "This is the legendary story of the life and times of Jesus ..." (mock quote). Likewise there are no physical artifacts that constitute direct or indirect evidence for this hypothesis as it applies to Jesus specifically. We do, however, have archaeological information that many gods had been worshiped hundreds and thousands of years earlier and during that the time of Jesus in the geographic region of interest. We know that these gods had their own storyline of how they interacted with humanity here on Earth and in the afterlife. The fact that these gods were being invented (now regarded as myth or legend) is an indisputable fact.

There is a small degree of speculation with respect to the ancient disciples entering into altered states of consciousness (e.g., trances, hallucinations) wherein they produced psychical experiences. The Apostle Paul himself says that on at least one occasion he saw Jesus while in a trance (see Acts 22:17). It is speculated that the crowd of 500 was a fictional appearance account made up by Paul and his co-writer Sosthenes, but there is no hard evidence to back this up other than to say that Paul's writings were highly biased toward recruiting adherents to the new faith.

All in all, the MJH does possess a level of speculative assessments that in my opinion are less than that required of the RH. However, because both hypotheses have a number of speculations, either skeptics or apologists could probably provide alternative views of the same information. Therefore, to limit argumentation to the more potent historical tests that follow, I will agree for the time being that the RH and MJH are in round terms equally speculative.

HHTE: Explanatory Power

The MJH has a high level of explanatory power because it highlights how the claims can be accounted for by naturalistic evidence. It does this not only in the context of what transpired in the months before and after the crucifixion event, but it also provides greater evidentiary support by looking at the resurrection issue in the much broader context of the history of non-Christian and quasi-Christian religion over a large expanse of time.

HHTE: Plausibility

Christian apologists have attempted to relegate the idea of a legendary Jesus to the dust bin with the argument that the growth rate of The Jesus Legend was not sufficient to destroy the historical core of the biblical accounts in the span of two centuries. This notion was put to sleep as a result of the fact that the analytical support for the two-generation rule is not supported by the majority of scholars because it cannot be extended beyond the narrow entailment of how the theory was constructed.

We should also revisit the fact that mythical gods were manufactured for thousands of years earlier by pagan religions. In the case of the Jewish deity, it would appear that Yahweh was initially something less than a supreme god who was later elevated to overtake the chief god El. This Yahweh is what the ancient Israelites called the God of Abraham. Yahweh eventually became the only god that was worshiped. Early Christians accreted ideas from many religions and mysticisms, the most prominent of which was the monotheistic Judaism. But all these other gods were often indifferent or sometimes greatly displeased with mankind. A new god that was fully engaged, interactive, benevolent, and wanting to be with his minions in life and in death was a concept that was an attractive alternative. It is plausible that mankind could create this type of a myth or better yet, affix it to a messianic figure that had the pedigree of coming from the Jewish line of King David.

We are lacking physical (non-literary) evidences that Jesus even existed on Earth. We only know of Jesus' likely existence from literary works and oral traditions. In fact, the only hard evidence we have for *any* individual noted in the New Testament is the Jewish Sanhedrin high priest Joseph Caiaphas in the form of his burial box. It is plausible that human beings would immortalize a messianic figure by adopting a storyline that would be relatively unique as compared to the storyline's of other gods. Rather than the gods hanging out in a heaven-like realm, controlling things from above, Jesus came down from heaven to live largely as a normal human, his exorcisms and miracles aside, to share in the best and worst of our experiences. Then, when he dies, he survives his human death he makes appearances over the course of forty days before he departs until the eschaton to confirm to his disciples that he really did conquer death. By putting a stop-watch on the amount of time human beings have to reform their ways before Jesus returns to sweep up the good souls provides a built-in sense of urgency. We are quite confident of the history of the Roman realm and the pagan and Jewish religions left many thirsting for something that would ameliorate their struggles. That the Christian God would sacrifice his only Son so that the lowly man could reap salvation was a welcome conception for their sorry souls.

In summary, the plausibility of the MJH is significantly stronger than that of the RH.

HHTE: SUPERIORITY TO RIVAL HYPOTHESES

It is to be granted that I have only provided a cursory review of some of the many rival theories that have been propounded by scholars. Without spending the time to rigorously cross-examine the MJH against all these other non-RH competing hypotheses, I will extend that the MJH offers the most compelling arguments amidst these other rivals. What is more important to determine is whether the MJH is a better explanation than the RH. This is summarized below.

Table 7-1. Resurrection Hypothesis vs. Mortal Jesus Hypothesis

HHTE Tests	Relative Importance	Resurrection Hypothesis	MJH Hypothesis	Result / Winner
Explanatory Scope	Lesser	👍	👍	Push
Conformity with Accepted Beliefs		👎	👍	MJH
Ad Hoc		👎	👎	Push
Explanatory Power		👍	👍	Push
Plausibility	Greater	👎	👍	MJH

What emerges from the Historicity Hypothesis Testing Engine presents a reasonably decisive verdict that disfavors the view that the resurrection is a historically authentic event. Furthermore, the Mortal Jesus Hypothesis is the Inference to the Best Explanation for how the resurrection legend came about and how it was propagated forward. It has been through the meticulous and systematic exegesis of biblical sources, a study of archaeological evidence, the implementation of a novel statistical technique (Bayes' epistemology), the study of the formation of legends, and an appreciation for psychological grieving processes that we have come upon the profound conclusion that the first of the Foundational Truth Claims of Christianity is nowhere near as certain as many present-day people believe it to be so. The resurrection of Jesus is, at the very least, historically unreliable and is apt to be the legendization of a man who met a terrible fate whose followers for reasons we can never know for certain, birthed a new faith from the folds of paganism, Ancient/Early Judaism, mysticism, and other quasi-Christian beliefs.

Thinking more broadly, if our quest ends with the idea that God himself, as in a supernatural Being (singular or multiple), does not or is not likely to exist, this would substantially embolden the MJH theory. **Of special importance is whether this supernatural Being (or Beings) would have to have the capacity to operate in our universe in order to bring about the resurrection or any other miracles for that matter. This issue is thoroughly examined later in the book. I bring this to your immediate attention because everything we have discussed about a divine Jesus is set on top of a platform that divine action in our realm of time and space is rationally feasible.**

While skeptics may feel a great sense of vindication about this assessment, I remain more reserved. With history being the game of the gaps that it is, we have to accept that absolute certitude will *always, always, always* be at least one plateau too high to access. Additionally, in utilizing the tools of abductive reasoning as well as the analytical methods of Bayes' theorem, neither informs us of how to judge whether the Inferred Best Explanation is in reality 'good enough'. Speaking hypothetically, let us assume a situation that we were to universally accept that the probability of the Resurrection Hypothesis (including all negative theology) is 0.4 percent. Secondly, let us assume that the Bayesian probability of the MJH is shown to be 1.2 percent. This in no way is saying that these are the correct values, only that we are simply assuming this to be a justified conclusion for the sake of argument. Should we be so convinced that the MJH is all that more probable because it is three times stronger relative to its counter proposition? In such circumstances, we should not because in the grand scheme, *both are weak explanations*.

We live in a single-metric-society. We attempt to encapsulate our understanding for anything of interest, no matter how complex, into a single metric. For example, we look at the GDP (Gross Domestic Product) number to summarily judge our hugely complex national productivity. We look to the Dow Jones Industrial Average® index to give us a snapshot glimpse of how the financial markets have performed. Then we have the National Unemployment Rate which in reality represents nothing because useful unemployment figures only become apparent when we drill down into various factors (by sector, industry, gender, race, ethnicity, geographic region, etc.). In sports, we look to the win-loss record or the final game score. For religion, we want a simple 'Yes' or 'No' as to whether God-by-whatever-name exists or whether this religion or that religion is true.

After all that has been said, should we not form our beliefs based on the preponderance of evidence? Given what we have just learned, let's examine what choices we have to choose from to consider revising our beliefs:

Synopsis of Choices Given the Resurrection Event is Not Historically Credible

1. Because of the superiority of alternative hypotheses, chiefly the MJH, and the preponderance of evidence therein, we can reasonably declare that the resurrection is not a historically authentic event. Jesus was not God incarnate.

2. Heedless of the historical data as to whether or not Jesus Christ was raised in bodily or spiritual form or made appearances, Jesus' divinity is assured by his entrance into heaven and his reuniting with the Godhead by the ***miraculous*** intervention of the Christian God and Holy Spirit. The nature of this Godhead was cemented for Christianity by the Council of Chalcedon.

3. If you are a believer in a non-Christian religion, then the argumentation for the Foundational Truth Claims set forth herein may not adequately address the truth claims of your faith tradition.

4. Based on the summation of evidence and lack therein and/or because of our limited intellect, we must adopt some form of agnostic position. This is to say that we are unsure of whether or not God exists and we are similarly uncertain that he manifested himself as a human being some two thousand years ago.

5. By outright disavowal of the existence of any God, Jesus could not have been resurrected. It is therefore pointless to discuss these other possibilities.

If the historical record denies the likelihood of the resurrection ever occurred, Christian apologists and Christians more generally may implore the over-tired *God-of-the-Gaps* **argument** wherein they attempt to explain their personal experiences (which might include miracles for some) as a result of the unknowable divinity of God, his Son, and the Holy Spirit. That is, **whenever we face the unknowable or the uncertain, God fills the gap**. In the next chapter we shall explore what we can evince about Jesus' divinity as well as this ephemeral concept of the Holy Spirit. In later chapters, we will tackle the ever-present dilemma of obtaining a coherent and rational explanation for the three-Person Godhead of Christianity. And, after that, we will examine a range of issues concerning the existence of deities in general and the challenges inherent to deific action in our physical universe.

SUMMARY

We have brought to bear all the relevant historical evidences, principally in literary form, but also useful archaeological references, regarding the *historicity* of Jesus' incarnate resurrection. The Resurrection Hypothesis provides satisfactory support relative to Explanatory Scope and Explanatory Power historical test criteria but does not perform well under the other historical lenses relative to discordance with accepted beliefs of the time, its level of speculation, and most importantly, its plausibility.

Notwithstanding these deficiencies, in contrast to the Conspiracy, Apparent Death, Cognitive Dissonance, and Mythological Jesus hypotheses, none are overwhelmingly convincing. The Legend Hypothesis and the Probability Hypothesis offer intriguing viewpoints wherein it could be argued are individually more superior as compared to the Resurrection Hypothesis. Interestingly, the Probability Hypothesis was initially forwarded by a preeminent Christian apologist (Richard Swinburne), which in his estimation, provided that the evidences he considered demonstrated a high probability that the resurrection did occur. Several critiques of Swinburne's hypothesis rather clearly show numerous fault lines in his rationale in applying the Bayesian statistical methods. When corrected, the Probability Hypothesis soundly rejects favoring the idea that the resurrection was a historical event.

The Mortal Jesus Hypothesis was forwarded by the present author. It entails a mosaic of elements from the Hallucination, Myth, Legend, and Probability hypotheses. This hypothesis also leans on prior documentary and archaeological evidences on the ancient origin and development of religious traditions, namely that of paganism and Ancient/Early Judaism. When compared to the Resurrection Hypothesis using the tools of the historian, the evidences favor the Mortal Jesus Hypothesis. It is to be acknowledged that there may be important additional revelations that may affect this hypothesis once certain scientific disciplines are consulted and how we answer two broader questions. Firstly, do deities exist and secondly, if they do exist, how are they capable of operating in our physical realm so visibly but so undetectably? This is explored in later chapters.

CHAPTER 8

Jesus' Divinity and Position in the Godhead

We are to admit no more causes of natural things than such as are both true and sufficient to explain their appearances.

– Isaac Newton

I seriously doubt that Jesus himself said that he was God, for he was too much a Jew to violate that great commandment: 'Hear O Israel, the Eternal is our God and He is one!' and not two or three.[1]

– Albert Einstein
Einstein and the Poet: In Search of the Cosmic Man

ON THE DIVINITY OF JESUS

WITH THE CORPOREAL RE-ANIMATION OF Jesus cast into doubt, a key link in the chain of evidence that Jesus was a supernatural Being is damaged. One has to wonder how much credence can be given to the NT authors' commentary on the miracles performed by Jesus if the greatest of them is so questionable. There is to be no question that the NT authors speak to Jesus' miracles which by themselves would affirm his divinity insofar as the authors believed or wanted others to believe. There are many biblical references that espouse Jesus' holiness and that he was the "Son" but these are said *about* Jesus by others, not *by* Jesus himself. It is only in Matthew 19:7 that Jesus is *indirectly* said to have claimed that he was the Son of God. This occurred when Pontius Pilate was speaking to the crowd of Jews about Jesus' innocence. The Jews shouted to Pilate, "We have a law, and according to that law he ought to die because he has claimed to be the Son of God."

The fact is, throughout the New Testament, Jesus never *explicitly* refers to himself as God or more generally as a supernatural Being. His divinity is only implicitly revealed through his words and more so from his purported miraculous deeds. The Gospel of John is credited as the one author who most forthrightly affirms the notion of his divine authority.

Jesus said to them, "Very truly, I tell you, before Abraham was, I am."

John 8:58

[Author(s) of John's gospel comment] In the beginning was the Word,[1] and the Word was with God, and the Word was God.

John 1:1

[Jesus speaking] "All that the Father has is mine ... "

John 16:15

[v5]Thomas said to him, "Lord, we do not know where you are going. How can we know the way?" [v6]Jesus said to him, "I am the way, and the truth, and the life. No one comes to the Father except through me. [v7]If you know me, you will know my Father also. [...] [v9]Whoever has seen me has seen the Father.

John 14:5-9

The Gospel of John was written in stages and probably by multiple authors, one of which may have been Apostle John, over a number of years and was completed around 90 CE.[2] We have to insert ourselves mentally into the context of the end of the 1st-century. Jesus was long dead, having been killed some six decades prior. The growth of Christianity was just getting a toehold in the Roman occupied territories of Antioch, Jerusalem, and the region of Pontus situated along the south-eastern coast of present-day Turkey. Many of the relatively few proto-Christians living in Jerusalem could well have been slaughtered in the First Jewish-Roman War. While the apostles had already left Jerusalem before the war set in to evangelize other cities and nations,[3] by the time the Gospel of John was completed, all the original apostles were dead other than the Apostle John.

---

1. One of Jesus' titles was 'The Word' or in Greek, 'Logos'. Other biblical epithets were Lamb of God, King of the Jews, Bread of Life, Light of the World, Lord, Son of God, and Second/Last Adam.

Interestingly, this was the same time that the fourth Pope, Clement of Rome, had assumed the papacy. As you will recall, he was the first extra-biblical author to have unmistakably mentioned Jesus by name, the resurrection, and the Apostle Paul, though he did not mention the writings of the four gospel authors in his writings. Recall that the Christian Bible wouldn't be canonized for two more centuries. Some have conjectured that after the fall of Jerusalem in 70 CE that the respect for the apostles by Jewish-Christians, particluarly that of John, declined. John lhelped build the Christian congregation in Jerusalem after Jesus' death but relocated to Ephesus (Turkey) around 67 CE, fortuitously prior to Rome's successful sacking of the city. While the final manuscript edition for *The Revelation to John* (i.e., what would become the biblical book of Revelation) may not have been completed until c. 100 CE (refer to Figure 5-3, p. 177), early drafts may have been in circulation four decades earlier. Revelations presents many prophecies (e.g., Jesus' Second Coming, see Revelation 1:7). These prophecies were not coming true which jeopardized the credibility of John in the eyes of Jewish-Christians and perhaps that of the Church in that timeframe.

It was important to John to emphasize that Jesus was the Son of God and that it was only through Jesus that we could access God the Father. This gospel is written in a notably different style when compared to the Synoptic Gospels. We are not certain why it was especially important for the collection of Johannine authors to focus so much more on Jesus' relationship to God. Perhaps this was a message that needed reinforcing because the other gospels and other oral evangelical efforts were not having the desired effect recruiting adherents. Or, just as likely is that there were many quasi-Christians/proto-Christians circulating ideas about the Godhead and the authors felt obliged to assert their opinions. John's writings would tend to support the idea that Jesus was positioned as something less than coequal with God. This is rather vividly identified in John 14:28 where Jesus states, "You heard me say to you, 'I am going away, and I am coming to you.' If you loved me, you would rejoice that I am going to the Father, *because the Father is greater than I.*" This passage would have great effect in history because some two hundred years later, Arius, the chief proclaimer of Arianism, in the late 3rd-/early 4th-century used this as evidence to claim a rank ordering of the Godhead because Jesus was created by God and was neither coequal nor consubstantial.[4]

Some are quick to point out that John actually does affirm that Jesus is coequal and consubstantial because Jesus plainly says, "[...] The works that I do in my Father's name testify to me; [...] What my Father has given me is greater than all else, and no one can snatch it out of the Father's hand. The Father and I are one." (see John 10:25, 29-30). However, the preceding text in John 10 needs to be consulted to provide the context that what Jesus was really saying is that he shares a common missionary purpose of God the Father and his role is that of a messenger (i.e., a prophet). He is neither claiming to be of the same substance nor equivalent in power or knowledge as God.

There may be another reason why the Gospel of John was more focused on defending Jesus' divinity. The authors may have felt the need to fend off what they saw as competitors to Jesus. As a contemporary of the authors of John, Apollonius of Tyana (b. c. 15 – d. c. 100 CE—dates uncertain) was a Greek philosopher and world traveler who commanded a following. He was said to have had extra-sensory perception and performed works of wonder making him out to be a parallel of Jesus.[5] Ultimately, because John is written so late, it can be ventured that the majority of modern-day biblical scholars view it as inferior to the Synoptic Gospels in terms of giving us an accurate portrayal of the historical Jesus.[2]

In order to understand Jesus' divinity from the perspective of earlier commentators, we will study the following passages, one each from Matthew, Mark, and Luke. **These are the only clear attestations that provide insights on Jesus' divinity in terms of his omniscience and omnipotence.**

<u>Immediately aware that power had gone forth from him</u>, Jesus turned about in the crowd and said, "Who touched my clothes?"

Mark 5:30

But about that day or hour **<u>no one knows</u>**, neither the angels in heaven, **<u>nor the Son, but only the Father</u>**. Beware, keep alert; for you do not know when the time will come.

Mark 13:32-33

<u>All things have been delivered to Me by My Father, and no one knows the Son except the Father. Nor does anyone know the Father except the Son, and the one to whom the Son wills to reveal Him</u>.

Matthew 11:27 KJV

When Jesus heard him, **<u>he was amazed</u>** and said to those who followed him, "Truly I tell you, in no one in Israel have I found such faith."

Matthew 8:10

And <u>Jesus increased in wisdom</u> and in years, and in divine and human favor.

Luke 2:52

The underlined words of the foregoing NT passages created quite a stir among theologians from the third century forward, most striking was this idea revealed in Luke 2:52 that Jesus "increased in wisdom" and in Mark 13:32 "no one knows." Generally supportive of this same theme, the gospels also say Jesus "was amazed" and became "aware" as in he previously was unaware. Are we to impugn Christ's divinity because of his intellectual limitations or lack in perceptual awareness? Since the third century and for some 1,700 years after, erudite theologians and biblical scholars have grappled with this issue and have decidedly come up empty-handed.

The finest of arguments was proposed by Thomas Aquinas[2] in *Summa Theologica III* wherein he argues that Jesus took on three modes of knowledge—beatific, infused, and acquired.[6] The *Summa Theologica* led, in part, to Aquinas being elevated as the greatest of the medieval theologians. The beatific knowledge, also referred to as the *beatific vision*, is to say that Jesus had seen the essence of God firsthand. If he did not have this knowledge, then Jesus would necessarily require faith like all other humans do where we must believe in the unseen. The second mode of knowledge is perfect in nature and represented by the totality of all possible human knowledge (past, present, and future). This is infused or imprinted instantaneously into Jesus by the supernatural power of God in which he unites his human and divine soul. Finally, Jesus' third mode is *acquired* or experiential knowledge as obtained through his human senses and rational thoughts. This is by definition of finite capacity.[7] This Thomistic interpretation allows the intellect of Jesus to know reality in three ways—tripartite embodiments of intellect as it were—which is problematic because if any one mode is considered perfect, the other two modes are superfluous. Some come to the aid of Aquinas and suggest that Jesus does not need to acquire experiential knowledge as a human because he already possesses this knowledge as a result of the infused knowledge. However, if this were true, then Jesus would have to deny his humanity and associated sensory faculties.

If in fact one posits that Jesus acquires experiential knowledge progressively, we are confronted with formidable problems that require full reconciliation. Firstly, a progressive increase in knowledge leads directly to the notion that Jesus was not at some point fully

2. There are numerous treatises on the subject which cannot be easily synopsized because they reference too many arcane and scholarly concepts to meet this author's expositional needs while also doing them justice. As such, I only summarize one of the stronger testaments by Thomas Aquinas.

omniscient. A second tension arises if Jesus possessed even the slightest of ignorance's; this mortally imperils the Christological mystery of the hypostatic union whereby God's knowledge is identically Jesus' knowledge. The concept of this union was first referenced in Chapter 3. The hypostatic union requires that God the Father, God the Son, and God the Holy Spirit are three Persons sharing themselves, which include a perfect sharing of all knowledge. Additionally, Aquinas' tripartite formulation introduces yet a third tragedy in that Jesus somehow retains faculties that offer both infinite and finite knowledge.

As Harvard University Christian historian Kevin Madigan points out, for much of his life, Aquinas actually believed that Jesus did *not* increase in knowledge. Of Jesus, Aquinas said that he "knew all things from the first instant of his conception."[8] But after many years of toiling over this problem and debating this with his contemporaries, Aquinas changed his opinion as represented in *Summa Theologica III*—that is, Jesus *did increase* in knowledge. What's more, in repudiating his former belief, he went against the tide of the majority opinion.[9] But, neither Aquinas nor his contemporaries, or any theologian since has neatly worked out the kinks as it relates to Jesus' divine omniscience and unity with God against the fact that during his human life he was lacking in awareness and knowledge.

This is but one of the many trappings of accepting the views as presented by the New Testament authors. Alone, the New Testament does not yield a full explication of the Holy Trinity. This doctrine evolved over hundreds of years. And, as we will come to understand, it has never yet been fully resolved. Christians have been pigeon-holed into a belief that Jesus (hence God) must necessarily be omniscient, omnipotent, etc. (the *omni-perfections* noted in Chapter 2). This creates an extraordinary burden so weighty that it buckles the columns of Christianity. This will be better explained in later chapters.

Unfortunately, none of the other canonical (or even the noncanonical) gospels repeat the essence of the Luke 2:52 message. The only way to explain the passage provided is to wave the ready wand of the theologian to say that we are too feeble a creature to comprehend how God works. Can we stake Jesus' divinity on so few biblical passages? It is somewhat like what we found in Paul's own testimony where we learn that Paul did not mention the empty tomb or see the corporeally resurrected Jesus. It is painfully clear that Jesus skirts the issue of coming right out and proclaiming his divinity in any of his orations. All told, the four NT gospels identify 37 instances of miraculous deeds though, according to John's gospel, these were just a few among many—"Jesus did many other things as well. If every one of them were written down, I suppose that even the whole world would not have room for the books that would be written." (John 21:25 NIV). That is, if miracles were somehow demonstrated to be permissible occurrences in reality as theologians, Christian apologists, and others would suggest is the case, then the biblical miracles *sans the resurrection* would appear to be the only lifeline to support Jesus' divinity as narrated in the Bible.

Geza Vermes, a Roman Catholic priest who left the Church to become a Jewish scholar, postulates why Jesus never made any avowals of his godliness. In Vermes' concluding remarks in his book *Jesus the Jew* he says, "A final word must be said about the bridging of the gulf between *son of God* and God. None of the Synoptic Gospels try to do this. Indeed, it is no exaggeration to contend that the identification of a contemporary historical figure with God would have been inconceivable to a 1st-century AD Palestinian Jew. It could certainly not have been expressed in public, in the presence of men conditioned by centuries of biblical monotheistic religion."[10] This is essentially what Albert Einstein also surmised (refer to his quote at the beginning of this chapter).

Vermes' assertion may possess merit. As he says, it may have been blasphemous for a 1st-century common follower of Judaism, priest or otherwise, to proclaim himself, or any other human, to be divine. But recall that Jerusalem was taken by Pompey the Great, a military commander of the Roman Republic in 65 BCE. The Romans maintained an iron-grip on the region until 313 CE. The Jewish people hadn't had a Jewish prophet since Prophet Malachi last prophesied c. 420 BCE. Along came Jesus, a Messianic figure. Jesus interpreted Jewish laws in his own way which were at odds with Jewish officiates. We also know that there were multiple sects of Judaism who practiced the religion in differing ways. The region was blanketed with practioners of paganism, magic, sorcery, and alchemy. Josephus, the Jewish historian, records a particular instance of a Jewish magician named Atomus in *Antiquities of the Jews* (see *Antiquities* 7:2). These soothsayers and healers, some of whom apparently were Jewish, were displacing the Jewish Temple Priests. Jesus himself was well aware that there were other exorcists and healers in his locale (refer to Matthew 12:27; Mark 9:38–41; 6:7). A central difference was that Jesus claimed his performance of miracles was manifested by the Spirit of God (see Matthew 12:28; Luke 11:20). All we can say for certain is that Jesus expressly claimed to be a conduit for God's power. We can argue against Verme's comment rather easily by saying that Jesus didn't explicity claim to be the Son of God because he himself didn't believe that he was such. We have zero written testimony by Jesus himself, only words from Jewish converts, who other than Paul, wrote anonymously. Ultimately, I don't think we can adjudicate whether or not Jesus stated he was the Son of God based on 1st-century Jewish norms.

Suffice it to say; based on the aforementioned rationale, Jesus' resurrection and divinity cannot be historically validated by the bespoken words of Jesus or that of the NT authors. In fact, the NT presents literary evidence that generates deeply penetrating problems for Christology.

ON THE HOLY TRINITY

Some may be surprised to learn that the Holy Trinity is *not* explicitly described in Christian Scriptures. Certainly there is mention of the Father, Son, and the Holy Spirit, but beyond the familial tie, there is no discussion of how they exist as three intertwined entities. Rather, it is up to the inferential conclusions of early Christian thinkers to surmise how the three Persons of the Trinity relate to one another. It is not clear exactly when the concept of the Triune God was originated. The earliest extant text that implements the usage of the word 'Trinity' is accorded to Theophilus, the Patriarch of Antioch, in his writings to his pagan friend Autolycum. His three-series compilation called *Ad Autolycum* (translation, *To Autolycus*) is estimated to be written c. 169 CE the purpose of which was Theophilus' attempt to convert Autolycum to Christianity. In Book II of the series, Theophilus refers to the Trinity as "God and his Logos [Jesus] and his sophia [wisdom]."[11]

The formalization of trinitarian thought was by Tertullian, credited as the founder of Western theology.[3] Tertullian was initially a North African pagan who in midlife became a fervent Christian apologist c. 197 CE writing against Gnosticism and other heretical beliefs. Strikingly, c. 206 CE he renounced Catholicism and adopted a heterodox offshoot of proto-Christianity called Montanism which focused on prophecy and the Johannine literature.[12] It was as a Montanist that he authored his definitive *Adversus Praxean* (translation, Against Praxeas) adopted by the nascent Roman Catholic Church because "he coined formulas that would be of great importance in later trinitarian and Christological debates."[13] As a Monarchian, Praxeas believed that God was one Person, not three.

For the first 300 years, the trinitarian concept sparred with a range of disparate views such as Monarchianism (God as one Person), Arianism (multiple divine entities arranged hierarchically), Modalism (God as one Being who operates in three modes), and binitarianism where God and Jesus were considered consubstantial and the Holy Spirit simply linked the two Persons. To help the early Christian Church sort out how to define the Godhead, the teachings of the first and second century Apostolic Fathers[4] were appealed to by the Church Fathers at the First Council of Nicaea (325 CE). In adopting the Nicene Creed, the council

---

3. Refer to *On Modesty* (XXI, 16) c. 200 CE and the first comprehensive treatise in *Adversus Praxean* (c. 213 - 222 CE).

4. The Apostolic Fathers included Clement of Rome (Pope Clement I, the 4th Pope), Ignatious of Antioch, and Polycarp of Smyrna and lived within two generations of the Twelve Apostles. The Church Fathers were those that filled the gap between the Apostolic Fathers and the end of the Patristic period (749 CE) which coincides with the death of St. John of Damascus. As I refer to the Church Fathers above, I refer to the subset that filled the gap between the Apostolic Fathers and the end of the fourth century.

affirmed that Jesus was "God of God, Light of Light, very God of very God, **begotten, not made, being of one substance with the Father**"[14] (emphasis added). If we go by Athanasius' accounting of how the council meetings went, it was a raucous debate.[15]

On the council was Arius who believed mightily, among other things, that Jesus had an origin in time whereby he was created by God the Father (refer to Box 5, p. 292). He scoffed at the other council members because the phrasing above (in bold italics) was to his mind a false understanding of this most central doctrinal precept. He was furious because it was clear that the council had manufactured the Trinity concept for the very fact that it had no basis in Scripture. "Athanasius, who was present at the Council as one of the Bishop of Alexandria's assistants, stated that the bishops were forced to use this terminology [referring to the description of Jesus as part of the Trinity in the Nicene Creed was] not found in Scripture, because the biblical phrases that they would have preferred to use were claimed by the Arians to be capable of being interpreted in what the bishops considered to be a heretical sense."[16] In the end, Arius lost the dispute and because Arius refused to accept the Nicene Creed, Constantine the Great (i.e., Constantine I) had him exiled. This is a clear case of how the relationship of the early Church with the imperial backing of Rome was being leveraged to encourage people to adopt the still evolving orthodoxy being decided by the Church Fathers.

It would be 400 years after Christ died until the Nicene Creed orthodoxy is firmly cemented.[5] The Nicene Creed was amended to become the Niceno-Constantinopolitan Creed in 381 CE. In the late 6th-century some Latin churches wanting to embolden the consubstantiality claim of the Holy Trinity added *"and the Son"* to the creed as shown below.[19]

> [Italicized text is changed to bold-underline from the original source by the present Author to better highlight the three added words.]

> [...] And in the Holy Ghost, the Lord and Giver of life, who proceedeth from the Father **and the Son**, who with the Father and the Son together is worshiped and glorified, who spake by the prophets. [...]

> Excerpt from the Constantinopolitan Creed of 381 CE[14]

This added text is called the **filioque**. By this time the Oriental Orthodox Church had already broken-away from the Roman Catholic Church regarding the nature of Jesus' divinity and humanity.

---

5. Ecumenical Councils that debated the doctrine of the Holy Trinity: First Council of Nicaea (325 CE), Council of Constantinople (360 CE), First Council of Constantinople (381 CE), and First Council of Ephesus (431 CE)

> ### Box 5 – Arianism
>
> Arianism is the eponymous attribution of Arius (250 – 336 CE), a local Christian Church leader in Alexandria, Egypt. Arius believed that the nature of the Godhead was one where only the divine Father is eternal and it is he who created the Son as a separate Being. Similarly, "Arius considered the Holy Spirit to be a person or a high-ranking angel, which had a beginning as a creature."[4] This belief arose decades before Arius, but the theory is attributed to him because of his vocal advocacy brought this to the theological forefront at the First Council of Nicaea (325 CE). None of his writings exist as they were either suppressed or destroyed by the edict of Constantine I.[4]
>
> While Arianism was deemed heretical it was better tolerated than other heterodoxies as it survived ages of intolerance, even the Middle Age Inquisitions, re-surfacing after the Protestant Reformation in the 16th- and 17th-century. Post-Reformation Movement, Sir Isaac Newton (1642 – 1727 CE), one of the greatest minds, if not *the* greatest minds to ever have lived, is generally considered to have adopted *Arian-like* Christianity.[4] In recent times, the Jehovah's Witnesses are often regarded as Arian[17] as are beliefs of American Unitarianism. Interestingly, it was just over a decade ago when The Holy Catholic and Apostolic Church of Arian Catholicism canonized Arius as a saint in 2006.[18]

With this new supposition that the Holy Spirit proceeded from both God and Jesus, it created a deep division between the Catholic Church and both the Oriental and the Eastern Orthodox Churches. They felt that the Western Church had critically altered the fundamental orthodoxy and it seemingly lowered the Holy Spirit hierarchically relative to the other two. Furthermore, it was the Eastern Church's position that the Holy Spirit only emanated from God, not Jesus. In spite of their dissension, Pope Benedict VIII formally indoctrinated the *filioque* into the doctrinal creed in 1014 CE. The Vatican's power-play drove a wedge between the Eastern and Western churches leading to the Great Schism in 1054 CE. This was an ongoing conflict between the Eastern and Western churches all the way to 2002 – 2003 CE when the Catholic Church agreed to remove the three words.[19]

Arianism would continue to survive outside of the steadfast march of Christian ortho-doxy. In fact, Constantine the Great, the first Christian Emperor, was baptized just prior to his death in May of 337 CE by Eusebius of Nicomedia[6] as a convert to Arianism.[20] Christians are so vocal about Constantine I's backing of Catholicism but few are aware that he ultimately converted to become a heretic! Paradoxically, Constantine had exiled Eusebius of Nicomedia a few months after the First Council of Nicaea (325 CE) for his strong defense of Arius' position and even though he signed the creed. At the time of his signing, Eusebius of Nicomedia extolled that he would "subscribe with hand only, not heart."[21] He was absolved of his heresy and reinstated to the Church in 329 CE and eight years later he would baptize the emperor that originally exiled him into the faith of Arianism.[20] It was under heavy peer pressure and the insertion of text into the Nicene Creed that the three-Person Catholic God was solidified as being comprised of a singular substance.

Other major commentators on the Trinity were Augustine of Hippo (354 – 430 CE), Boethius (c. 480 – 524/525 CE), Alcuin of York (c. 735 – 804 CE), Anselm of Canterbury (1033 – 1109 CE), and Thomas Aquinas (1225 – 1274 CE).

The Inimitable Sir Isaac Newton Weighs In on the Holy Trinity

Sir Isaac Newton was an intellectual luminary bar none, though he was much more than a mathematical and scientific genius; he was a quintessential **POLYMATH**. In addition to his technical prowess he was a prodigious writer and an erudite theologian, philosopher, and dabbler in biblical numerology. "His theological writings take up millions of words"[22] which far exceed any of his other writings scientific or otherwise.[22]

Newton was the second individual to ever have been awarded the most illustrious academic position in the world as the Lucasian Professor of Mathematics at Trinity College (University of Cambridge at London, England) in 1669.[7] In 1673, he was required by the college's charter to become an ordained minister in the Church of England (i.e., the Anglican Church).[23] Newton, in his usual incomparable style, prodigiously studied the entire literary history of the Church with cloistered fervor. He absorbed the knowledge found within the **PATRISTIC** tomes written by the entire lineage of Christian theologians from antiquity to then modern-day times. He even scrutinized the Greek-to-Latin translations. He took copious notes which lead to the towering theological word count noted above.

---

6. Eusebius of Nicomedia is not to be confused with the great Church historian Eusebius of Caesarea. They both participated in the First Council of Nicaea and died only a year or so apart. Eusebius of Nicomedia was a strong advocate of Arius. So too, Eusebius of Caesarea is thought to have been an Arian sympathizer. Whereas the former had been exiled temporarily by Constantine I, Eusebius of Caesarea was protected by the emperor from such a fate.

7. The full proper name of Trinity College is *College of the Holy and Undivided Trinity*.

"Newton was perhaps the greatest biblical scholar of his age"[24] in terms of his historical and doctrinal knowledge of the Christian faith.

In the course of his enlightenment he practiced what we might call today a horizontal reading of all the literature where he dissected what one literary source said about a topic matter versus another, much as we have done in this book but amplified manyfold. He educed a number of serious inconsistencies in the texts which he never publicly professed, but he did record them in his notes and shared some of his findings with trusted contemporaries. Newton had written a letter to John Locke entitled *An historical account of two notable corruptions.*[25] In it, he identifies two short biblical passages, one in the book of 1 John and the other in the book of 1 Timothy that may have been purposely doctored.[26] These discoveries set him at great unease because for him to become an ordained minister of the Church, he had to take a vow of chastity, vow of clerical celibacy, and assent to the 39 Articles of Faith in accordance with the Act of Uniformity instituted in 1662.[27]

This was a serious matter in the time of Newton. Upon installation of this Act, over 2,000 clergyman were expelled from the Church of England for non-conformity in what is referred to as the Great Ejection.[28] These Articles were biblically derived summations of Christian doctrine that sought to draw a clear line between Catholicism and what was then viewed as dissident Protestantism. "The first five articles articulate the Catholic credal statements concerning the nature of God [and how he manifests himself] in the Holy Trinity."[29] He was so unnerved that he seriously contemplated ceasing his ordination preparations which would have resulted in him being ineligible for the esteemed post. It required an intervention by university officials and by Isaac Barrow (the first recipient of the Lucasian professorship) whereby they sought out an exemption from the binding statute. It was the Secretary of State who acquiesced to the request and removed the requirement for Newton and future chair holders.[30] This was only made possible because the university wanted so badly for Newton to be awarded the prestigious Lucasian chair.

We do not know precisely what Newton may have conveyed to the university and Secretary of State but he never publicly published his findings. You see, the Parliament of England enacted the Blasphemy Act of 1697 whereby denial of the Holy Trinity by writing, preaching, teaching, or advised speaking was a punishable offense.[8] In 1697, 18-year old student Thomas Aikenhead was hanged in Scotland for publicly denying the trinity. Newton therefore remanded his writings to his own safekeeping and only cautiously shared aspects

---

8. Punishments remitted for violations of the Blasphemy Act of 1697. The first offense would have the person removed from any office or place of trust. The second offense led to additional legal ramifications, and a third offense would be rewarded with three years of imprisonment without bail.

of them with trusted cohorts. His works were posthumously published in 1754, 27 years after Newton's death.[31] It is understandable that Newton would reveal his thoughts privately because there was a virulent controversy concerning the Trinity within the Anglican Church theocrats in the 1690's[32, 33] though denying it publicly outside the Church would have resulted in punishment.

On November 14, 1690 Newton issued his "Two Corruptions" letter to John Locke,[9] the great philosopher, empiricist, political theorist, and most influential thinker in the Age of Enlightenment movement. Locke was a believer in Socinian Christology[34] which was one of numerous anti-trinitarian (yet Christian) sects and derives its name from Italian reformer Lelio Sozinni and his nephew and theologian Fausto Sozzini.[10] Locke sent the letter to Jean Le Clerc, a Swiss theologian and biblical scholar, for possible publication. Le Clerc was famous for promoting critical interpretation of the Bible which made him out to be a radical of his age.[35] After Le Clerc offered Newton a literary source to polish his findings, Newton revised his letter in preparation for publication. However, at the last minute, he permanently forestalled its publication.[36, 37]

The letter brazenly begins with Newton accusing the Roman Church for being "pious frauds."[25, 31] As his lengthy dissertation continues, he identifies alterations to the book of 1 John.[11] He noted that the following words were in the King James Version but were not present in the original Greek texts and were surreptitiously inserted—"in heaven, the Father, the Word, and the Holy Ghost: and these three are one." Newton's research demonstrated that 1 John 5:7-8 was a marginal note in Latin translations of the Greek text and that in 1515 CE, Cardinal Ximenes de Cisneros had elevated the margin note into the main body of the original text.[31] The matter goes even deeper.

Below are two biblical translations of 1 John 5:6-8. The first passage is taken from one of the very first Christian Bibles, Codex Sinaiticus, as it is translated from Koine Greek. The second passage is from the King James Version that Newton had referred to.

---

9. Newton's original manuscript is held at New College, Oxford and is now digitally available from The Newton Project (http://www.newtonproject.sussex.ac.uk/). The specific letter is provided at: http://www.newtonproject.sussex.ac.uk/prism.php?id=73.

10. A brief review of the doctrine of Socinianism can be found here: http://www.newadvent.org/cathen/14113a.htm

11. There is no discussion presented herein on Newton's discontents with 1 Timothy 3:16. Here he refutes an alteration to the word 'God' in the passage and it involves exegetical minutia that does not sufficiently add to our discussion.

[Koine Greek translated to Modern English]

[v6]This is he that came through water and blood, Jesus Christ: not in the water only, but in the water and in the blood; and it is the Spirit that testifies, because the Spirit is the truth. [v7]**For they that testify are three, [v8]the Spirit, and the water, and the blood, and the three are one.**

1 John 5:6-8

from *Codex Sinaiticus*, c. 330 – 360[38]

[To reiterate, Newton states that the underlined words presented below were **not** present in original Greek texts. These words were added from the Latin translation into Early Modern English]

For there are three that bear record **in heaven, the Father, the Word, and the Holy Ghost: and these three are one.**

1 John 5:6-8

from King James Version, 1611[39]

An important contextual note is that Newton died in 1727, over a century before the first cache of documents would be discovered of what would be called Codex Sinaiticus in 1844.[12] Therefore, Newton was not consulting Codex Sinaiticus because of its lost status during his lifetime. In the passage from Codex Sinaiticus, the words "Jesus" and "blood" are to be treated synonymously whereby the usage of the word 'blood' refers to Jesus being of human form. The words "Spirit" and "water" are to be connoted as being synonymous. Elsewhere in the book of 1 John of Codex Sinaiticus, God is referred to as "God" and "Father." *It is therefore clear from the translation of Codex Sinaiticus, the second if not the earliest of all Bibles, that the original passage of 1 John 5:6-8 does not equate Jesus or the Holy Spirit to being the same as God the Father.* Recall that Codex Sinaiticus was written entirely in Koine Greek, the same language as the original Greek source materials. It can be unequivocally stated that the intent of the original passage was only meant to affirm that Jesus is both human and divine. **This fact preserves the notion that the original Greek texts and the canonical Bible, constructed over three centuries, never entailed a definitive description of the relationship between God, Jesus, and the Holy Spirit.**

More generally, "Newton blamed both Athanasius *and* Arius for distorting Scriptures when, in the fourth century, they 'introduced metaphysical subtleties into their disputes and corrupted plain language of Scripture.' "[26] Newton, according to most scholars, was

---

12. The history of the discovery of Codex Sinaiticus is highly convoluted. Refer to the following site for a historical brief: http://codexsinaiticus.org/en/codex/history.aspx

affiliated with Arian theology, though he himself never explicitly admitted as such. Some have said that it would be most accurate to say that Newton's Christology paralleled aspects of Socinianism.[34, 40] Ultimately, his beliefs were a syncretic formulation of both Arianism and Socinianism. Science historian Richard Westfall's book *The Life of Isaac Newton* clarifies that, "In Newton's eyes, worshiping Christ as God was idolatry, to him the fundamental sin."[41] Disavowal of the Holy Trinity was the central dissent of Arianism's view. "We know, however, that Newton believed in the divinity of Christ and the Holy Spirit; he also believed that Jesus was the Messiah and through him gave infinite atonement for our sins with his death on the cross. Newton even believed, contrary to Arianism (of which he is usually accused), in the eternality of the Son. He also embraced the straightforwardly biblical position that the Father and the Son are one. What Newton did not believe, however, was that the Father and Son were one in the sense that they were *consubstantial* or of the same substance. According to Newton, the Father and Son were one, but this unity was not a metaphysical unity; rather, it was one of dominions and purpose."[26]

So beyond the profundity of his mathematical and scientific endowments, through laborious and attentive study, Newton made a shrewd observation that the political elite of the Catholic Church were still tweaking the New Testament well into the 1500's—some 1,200 years after the Church published Codex Sinaiticus. **And these perturbations to the Latin translations of the Greek manuscripts were not minor adjustments; they affected the cornerstone of Catholic Christianity by injecting meaning that was never there. It had been recognized that the Christian Bible had lacked adequate support for the then institutionalized belief of the coequal union between Jesus and God. Sometimes it only takes a minor adjustment to a text for it to become immortalized as powerful evidence.**

THE INCOHERENT HYPOSTATIC UNION OF THE TRINITY

There has always existed an enigma surrounding the idea of the three in one being-ness of God, one that has never been satisfactorily explained by any of the Christian traditions. The hypostatic union describes the three-Person God as consubstantial (same substance) and perfectly coequal in knowledge, power, eternality, and love. This confers that they are mutually indwelling and interpenetrating, that is, living and existing as one Being. St. Augustine of Hippo's interpretation was that the Spirit is the love, fellowship, and communion between the Father and the Son and that, while on Earth, Jesus' power is generated from the Father to the Son through the Holy Spirit. On the face of it, this sounds like a harmonious enough description. It is when one pricks at the loose threads that logical incoherencies begin to be exposed in this union.

The consubstantiality of the three-Person God is a troubling concept, even for the well-equipped theologian to deal with. If the three Persons are different manifestations of the same divine substance, then it begs the question how can the same substance exist with different fundamental properties? Stated in other terms, how can the three ONTOLOGICAL manifestations exist simultaneously? If we use water as an analogy, we know that this material substance can exist in three phase states (i.e., solid, liquid, and gas). At what is called the triple point, water can coexist in all three states simultaneously as a result of thermal equilibrium. Chemically, the water is made of the same atomic elements regardless of the phase state. When water is not at its triple point, ice, liquid water, and water vapor have different physical properties because the arrangement and energy of the atoms is altered. However, at the triple point, the physical properties become identical. While this is a close analogy, it does not go far enough.

In Classical Christianity, God is presented as three Persons that have the same properties in all respects. When Jesus was flesh and bone in our universe, he was made of physical materials (i.e., atoms). God on the other hand is considered by Christian doctrine to be eternally immaterial and transcendently external to the physical and temporal universe. **How can a single unified substance be both material/temporal and immaterial/atemporal?** In the section of reality that we call our universe, this is impossible. It would be akin to saying that the immaterial abstraction of the number '4' has precisely the same properties as a common ice cube. Likewise, the atoms that comprise Jesus the Son would be subject to the natural laws of physics, chemistry, and biology whereas God the Father is not apparently so affected. The Holy Spirit, also of the same substance, somehow exists as an ephemeral and immaterial essence somewhere beyond the borders of our consciousness and aptitudes presents yet another quandary. Finally, if Jesus did ascend to join God in his realm, are we to take this as he has left the universe thereby transforming his atomic body into immaterialness? Or, is he still here in some invisible, nonphysical spirit form? How does anything cross into or exit from our physical universe? **The only way Classical Christianity can answer this is to call it a mystery well beyond our comprehension. Therefore, one must apply a fideistic faith because no amount of existent evidences can be supplied that would coherently explicate the Trinity.** Christian Panentheists believe they can provide a better answer which is to be explored in Chapter 11. Also in this same chapter, I will highlight the seven outstanding challenges to trinitarianism.

Going back to the mid-second century, the Marcionites believed that Jesus was so divine that his presence on Earth was illusory. To Marcion's way of thinking, Jesus was God but "How far Marcion admitted a Trinity of persons in the supreme Godhead is not known."[42]

As you may recall, Marcion also believed that Yahweh also existed as a lower-order divine entity making his beliefs a polytheistic religion. While Marcionism carried on beyond his death c. 160 CE, the idea of the Trinity was being interpreted by Sabellius, a 3rd-century theologian, in a way that led to his excommunication by Pope Callixtus I (Callistus) in 220 CE.[43] Sabellius preached a schismatic view that the three aspects of God were three unique *modes* or *forms* of a singular **MONADIC** divine Person.[13] This came to be known as Modalism.[14] While Modalism was regarded as a heretical interpretation, it does offer a distinct advantage because it eliminates the need for an ill-defined relationship between three different divine Persons as well as the pitfalls of a hierarchical arrangement to the Godhead. Sabellius, however, did not adequately explain how Jesus was manifested as a divine Being who was also a human who suffered pain and death. About a half-century later, Arianism re-opened the door to polytheism by maintaining that Jesus was both subordinate and distinct from God. To the credit of Arianism, it avoids many of the trappings of Classical Christianity's hypostatic union. Nevertheless, it is still weighted with the lack of evidence that Jesus was a divine Being that was resurrected.

The Holy Spirit plays a vital role in Christian theology as it was responsible for the virginal conception of Jesus. It is an invisible operator that presumably exists within the confines of our universe that helps Christians understand God's will. Indeed, it was the Holy Spirit who inspired the authors of the Bible to write what they did. While the divine functions of the Holy Spirit are understood, the **PNEUMATOLOGY**, or the study of the Holy Spirit, has always been less developed in comparison to the other two personages of the Trinity. For example, there is little defense offered for the way in which this invisible entity is existent in the universe. It would be for all intents and purposes a perpetual miracle in action.

The Ever-Evolving Doctrine of Christianity

To the best of our knowledge, there was no one who had chronicled the life and death of Jesus during his life, or for decades after. It would take centuries for theologians to iron out what they felt was the correct view of a singular God that lived on Earth for three decades. This 'ironing-out' process was supported by debates many of which were highly contentious. Virtually none of the debaters had ever met Jesus or the original apostles. Teaching of the quasi-Christian and proto-Christian views were largely passed on orally through teacher-student relationships. In larger towns and cities across the Near East and

---

13. A schism is an offense that generates a division with the Catholic Church which is generally significant enough in scope and nature as to become formally labeled as a schism. [Code of Canon Law c.751]

14. This form of modalism is also referred to as Sabellianism, Patripassianism, or modalistic monarchianism.

Northern Africa, academies were setup. This naturally led to divergent schools of thought. These differences came to the fore as debates took place. These debates were polluted, just as most debates are, by biased opinions and if the religious texts were not altogether aligned with their thinking, the texts were redacted to become more harmonious with their teacher's and/or institutional logic. It is understandable why there was an intense interest in the 4th-century to solidify a core doctrine as the 'correct' doctrine. It is difficult for a religious sect to make progress when off-shoots are sapping momentum by creating confusion or contempt and by attracting adherents from the sect's mainline theology.

Even though the Catholic Church's dogma of the Niceno-Constantinopolitan Trinitarian system was the official Roman religion by the end of the 4th-century, there were still central questions on Jesus' divinity that created division in the mostly orthodox Christian ranks. In the fifth century, the First Council of Ephesus (431 CE) disputed the arguments of Nestorius who was newly installed as Archbishop of Constantinople in 428 CE. He argued that Christ's human and divine natures were distinct (*two Persons* in *one body*) which ultimately got him deposed and exiled. This created the first major rupture in the newly-formed Catholic Church and the first new Christian sect called the Nestorian Church.[44]

Later, the Council of Chalcedon was convoked in 451 CE to clarify that Christ Jesus is *one Person* consisting of *two natures*, one human and one divine (this is referred to as dyophysitism). This viewpoint was rejected by many churches who called themselves *miaphysites*. These churches maintained a Christology that Jesus' divinity and humanity were united in a *single nature* and never separate, constituted in a *single Person*.[15] The resulting schism created a communion of churches referred to as the Oriental Orthodoxy. Then the Great Schism in the early 11th-century cleaved the Church further into the Eastern Greek Orthodox and Western Latin Catholic branches. The principal differences were the Pope's assumption of universal jurisdiction (Papal Primacy) and the issues concerning the addition of the filioque into the Niceno-Constantinopolitan Creed mentioned earlier. And, of course, there was the most major rift of all when the Protest Reformation precipitated a total break from Rome only for Protestants to splinter into a great number of denominations (refer to Figure 8-1).

---

15. The Council of Chalcedon also reached agreement on disciplinary canons. Canon 16 stated that monks and nuns could not marry, lest they be excommunicated.

DISUNITY WITHIN CHRISTIANITY

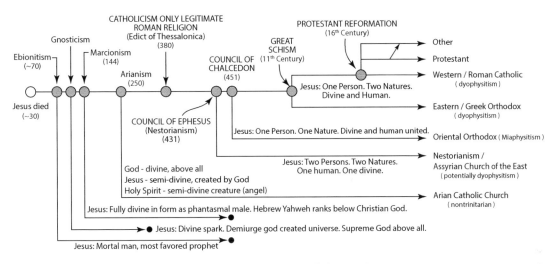

Figure 8-1. Major Schisms of Christianity

Not only was Christianity struggling to remain unified regarding the nature of Jesus, but it also foundered over other central issues such as the virginity of Mary, the role of Satan, the definition of the **TRANSUBSTANTIATION** of the Eucharist and the wine, and among many other theological trouble spots, the doctrine of purgatory. The founders of the concept of purgatory (the state of final purification) were 1st-century Greek theologians who never fully developed the doctrine. In the late second century, Clement of Alexandria used a term called "apokatastasis" which referred to the restoration of the Gnostic Christians but it was not used in the sense of universal salvation.[45] The concept of universal salvation was furthered by Augustine of Hippo (modern-day Algeria) in the early fifth century. The greatest emphasis on the matter of purgatory arose in the four ecumenical councils that took place from 1274 – 1563 CE.[16]

When one takes into account the fact that central dogmas were so uncertain for so many centuries, even millennia, this scarcely inspires confidence that the correct perspectives were achieved with so many divisional outlooks at hand. It seems that what was chosen to be orthodoxical was more related to which sect and figureheads had the most influence at the time any given doctrine was debated.

---

16. First Council of Lyon (1245) – initial definition of purgatory, Second Council of Lyon (1274) – purgatory officially consecrated and institutionalized, the Council of Florence (1438–1445) which was originally called the Council of Basel and later named the Council of Ferrara reaffirmed the doctrine of purgatory, and the Council of Trent (1545–1563).

Moving Beyond The New Testament

The Christian Bible is an **ANTHOLOGY** whose point of origin was smeared out over roughly 350 years from the time Apostle Paul wrote his letters until the canon was accepted by the Council of Carthage in 397 CE. This historical fact is little known to the throngs of Christians worldwide and fewer comprehend how proto-Christianity trampled over other Christian-like sects to rise from the fold to become orthodoxical Christianity (i.e., Catholicism). And, even when a sense of orthodoxy was achieved, there was still great division on the nature of Jesus himself, how the Godhead was arranged, and other concepts of heaven, hell, and purgatory. It is ventured that few are aware of the original autographic copy of the Bible has never been found and that Christians worship a version of the Bible that contains a great multitude of culturally and politically influenced redactions that served to reinforce a developing storyline. It has been through the extraordinary exegetical work by biblical scholars, historians, archaeologists, and other tradesmen that we have learned that great care must be at hand in reading the Bible because the authenticity of the English translations is problematic.

Many Christians I fear are being defrauded because Christian educators are not being intellectually honest with people. Overwhelmingly, they teach people to read the Bible at face value and seldom point out the inconsistencies. They also do not point out how orthodoxical Christianity developed in the midst of many quasi-Christian and polytheistic ideas that crept into the interpretational thought of the first several generations of theologians. These were the very individuals responsible for fashioning the Christian Bible and for creating the concepts of the Holy Trinity, purgatory, and other doctrinal developments. In contemporary times, the most egregious sources of disingenuous education are brought on by televangelists, who I refer to as spiritual entrepreneurs. These faith dealers rake in fortunes while extolling information as truth though they have not obviously not done their due diligence.[17] All these televangelists really do is to recite biblical verses in such rapid succession that they would give the bid calling of a hog auctioneer a run for his money. I want to make clear that I am not saying the Bible's message cannot be inspiring, indeed it is heartening and motivating to many millions of people. In some senses, it serves real human needs. What I am saying is that these pontifical peddlers are not honest in **EDIFYING** their flock (i.e., their customers) as they do not talk about the things that are represented in this book thus far. I would tend to believe that it would prove disastrous to their pocketbooks if they were to provide such information in a matter-of-fact way as I have

---

17. Estimated Net Worth as of 2015: Joel Osteen ($40M), Billy Graham ($25M), Toufik Benedictus "Benny" Hinn ($42M), Robert Schuller ($5M), Pat Robertson (Not known, but estimates in the hundreds of millions).

done here. Everything thus far is ultimately traceable to the original Greek manuscripts from which the Bible has been created and the historical writings of the various religious leaders in ancient society. These television preachers take their seed from a redacted version of the Bible and even worse, take the words at face value and/or profess that the Bible is inerrant when it is clearly not the case. Ultimately, the New Testament, the gospels in particular, should not be read literally. Rather they should be read as an apocalypse, that is, a revealing of information that tells the inspirational legend of Jesus the Nazarene.

Barring the possibility of divinely-sourced miracles, the evidence amassed thus far indicates that there is next to nothing in terms of supportable historical evidence in regard to Foundational Truth Claims. However, none of what has been said negates the possibility that a god(s) or god-like entities exist in the natural universe or transcends its boundaries. Such Beings would then exist in a form that is completely foreign to our frail metaphors

SUMMARY

We entered into a discourse on the divinity of Jesus. The heavenly ascription comes under heavy doubt when one studies various passages in the NT, particularly those verses in the Synoptic Gospels (Mark 5:30; 12:32-33; Matthew 8:10, and Luke 2:52) which put into question the omniscience of Jesus and his union in the Holy Trinity. We sought counsel from Thomas Aquinas who is regarded as one of the greatest theological minds to evince meaning from these troubling words. Even he was challenged how to interpret the Bible and make it cohesive with doctrine that was developed outside of the Bible. Aquinas initially towed the line of most theologians who asserted that Jesus' knowledge was perfect and complete. He later recanted his position to favor the position that Jesus' knowledge did grow while living his human life. The tripartite proposition tendered by Aquinas was beset by not one, but three mortal flaws in logic. First we have the acknowledgment Jesus 'progressed' in knowledge damaging his claim to omniscience. The second problem descends from the first in that without omniscience, the all-important hypostatic union between God the Father, God the Son, and God the Holy Spirit is fatally compromised. Lastly, there is no way to reconcile that Jesus possessed both infinite and finite knowledge as a consequence of his dualistic nature (divine and human).

The Holy Trinity is arguably one of the most hotly debated creedal concepts to ever have faced Christianity. How Jesus fits into the triumvirate and how to reconcile his humanness with his divine self has led to permanent schisms that fostered the growth of different Christian sects. After the extraordinary examination of Christian biblical texts, Isaac Newton identified a particular redaction (1 John 5:7) that was inserted in the year 1515 CE to buttress the notion that Jesus was coequal with God the Father and God the Holy Ghost. It is one of many redactions that have been made over the centuries that have sought to make the Bible as a whole more cohesive with the evolving orthodoxy professed by the Catholic Church.

The final point to be made is that we will not be able to solve our theological problem to validate God's existence through use of the Hebrew or Christian Bible. These tomes represent an assembly of individual manuscripts that often lack substantive detail. Many of the writings were not firsthand accounts and were synopsized based on unreliable oral transmission. For some of the more important texts, the authors are unknown or are highly uncertain.

The selection and canonization of the 27 books of the New Testament took three full centuries to decide upon. And, even after an exceptional amount of scholarly attention, there is no consensus when the Hebrew Bible was cemented as a closed canon (dates range from 450 BCE – 2nd-century CE). It is also a fact that many of the texts were serially edited by scribes over the intervening centuries from when the original was written (principally in Greek or Hebrew) and translated into Latin and English. In some circumstances, the original meaning was altered to bolster doctrinal views developed at a much later date. For the Jewish Bible, polytheistic and monolatrous worship narratives were sanitized to diminish the validity of the pagan gods in preference to pure Yahwism. Christian biblical texts and creedal doctrine were changed to embolden a Godhead of three Persons because the concept was not stated with any clarity in the original biblical sources. Lastly, the ecclesiastical proto-Christian authories were under pressure from Roman imperialists and once the biblical canon was finalized, the newly-elevated Church fortified its position by eliminating existing literature and suppressing those who might write against its orthodoxy. This silencing of the populace has made it especially difficult to appreciate the full societal debate on how Jesus was to be idolized.

CHAPTER 9

The Probability for God's Existence & Is God Still Alive?

The simple believes every word, but the prudent considers well his steps.
— Proverbs 14:15 (NKJV)

I cannot conceive of a personal God who would directly influence the actions of individuals. . . . My religion consists of a humble admiration of the illimitable superior spirit who reveals himself in the slight details we are able to perceive with our frail and feeble mind. That deeply emotional conviction of the presence of a superior reasoning power, which is revealed in the incomprehensible universe, forms my idea of God.[1]

— Albert Einstein
A letter to Milton M. Schayer, an American businessman and politician in Denver, August 1, 1927

The theory of Induction is the despair of philosophy—and yet all our activities are based upon it.[2]

— Alfred North Whitehead
Lowell Lectures, 1925

ONE MAY HAVE NOTED THAT our trek to discover the existence (or nonexistence) for God-by-whatever-name has conspicuously avoided the great battlefield filled with the shrill cries of prior philosophical, theological, and atheistic debates to answer the question of God's existence and any truths thereof. For the uninitiated, I am predominantly referring to the seriously developed formal treatises that have been placed upon the warrior's chariot and raced around the coliseum of ideologies in the wider religion-science debate forum. Some will recognize their banners as **"The Arguments"**—Cosmological, Ontological, **Teleological**, Axiological (i.e., Morality), Intelligent Designer, Scientism, Personal Religious Experience, Problem of Evil (i.e., theodicy), Consciousness, Degrees of Perfection, Efficient Causality, Time and Contingency, Change, Desire, Transcendence, Truth, and of course, the Argument from Miracles. There are additional derivative and unique treatises left unmentioned. Any number of these may find varying levels of appeal in some quarters of this readership. There is a shared characteristic among most, if not all, of these arguments.

Alone, none can define with sufficient specificity the God of traditional religion. That is, these arguments only depict the existence (or not) of a *generic* God. As a result, such arguments have witnessed limited success in enshrining any particular religion as being unquestionably true. This is why traditional religions have developed particularisms that more clearly define what they see as the truth of God. It is the qualification of these particularisms on which we have focused much of our attention. To remind us once more, the zetetic approach requires that we initiate without theological attachments until such a time it might require us to do so. In a practical sense, it was acknowledged upfront that this may be difficult, perhaps even impossible, for many to release such attachments. Let us renew this agreement as we continue along our zetetic campaign.

In Chapter 1, it was suggested that the zetetic pilgrimage would share certain characteristics of Ramified Natural Theology. It is time now to make final remarks about the success of RNT. As a matter of course, we will be entering the fray of some of The Arguments listed above while also addressing the particularities associated with the Abrahamic religions. The Philosophy of Religion as a discipline has been reinvigorated as of late to reshape worldview contours with RNT and other contemporary attempts to clarify and complexify the classic foundational Arguments. Also introduced into the religious dialogue is a freshened version of Religious Pluralism and altogether new approaches hailed by Continental Philosophy under the visages of **Phenomenology** and **Deconstructionism**. A relatively brief review of contemporary Pluralism will be presented in Chapter 10 but no depositions will be given in regard to the latter two philosophies.

Ramified (Extended) Natural Theology

Natural theology is any inquiry to explain the existence and nature of God using information (e.g., knowledge and reason) derived from the universe so long as divine revelation (e.g., personal revelatory experience, direct contact from God, miracles, or supernaturally-inspired Scripture) is precluded. The ancient Greeks were responsible for the inception of natural theology and this program of inquiry is available to both theists *and* nontheists (i.e., atheists/agnostics).

There are many formulations of natural theology, all of which are to be classified as 'generic', 'traditional', or 'bare' (pick your adjective). Herein, I will refer to it as Bare Natural Theology (BNT) because this is how philosopher Richard Swinburne refers to it in his work. In the last decade or so, the Oxford Professor Emeritus is principally responsible for re-energizing the use of BNT—but with the added twist of confirmation theory (vis-à-vis Bayes' theorem). He calls this new formulation *Ramified Natural Theology* (RNT). In Chapter 6,

I held back a full-throttled assessment of this epistemic philosophy to make the entire concept more digestible. In its original conception, **RNT (or if you like, extended Natural Theology) integrates what is knowable from sensory perception, reason (i.e., deductive, inductive, reductive, abductive), and special knowledge sourced from history, science, and mathematics**. RNT can be applied to Judaism, Christianity, and Islam as well as other traditions. As a matter of practice, it has been overwhelmingly been used to circumscribe Christianity. Christian apologists David Baggett and Ronnie Campbell, the latter a former student of resurrection-specialist Gary Habermas, take this a step further to refer to the argumentative strategy for Christian RNT as *doubly ramified natural theology* (DRNT). DRNT argues that RNT can be leveraged to differentiate and ultimately isolate from the fold of the many Christian denominations the best representation of God.[3] Because DRNT builds upon the framework of RNT, any structural weaknesses found in RNT will by and large apply in full force to DRNT.

In what follows, I will only refer to RNT as it is principally conceived by Richard Swinburne as he has developed what some might consider to be the best and certainly impressive case to demonstrate the likelihood for the existence of a singular, eternally-existent deity that is omniscient, omnipotent, and acts unhindered by anything, in his book *The Existence of God*.[1,4] He goes on to clarify that his arguments are only valid to the extent that they describe a singular diving Being consistent with the view of the three Abrahamic religions.[5] He argues more forcefully the case for the Triune Christian God in his namesake book *The Christian God*.[6]

This is a great period to find oneself to be alive because until the publication of his two books, theism was circumscribed by mostly tortured philosophical/theological constructions that relied on far too little objectified and systematized evidentiary support, many of which have been (or will be) ultimately relegated to the stockpile of *philos terminus* (dead-ended philosophy). I refer to them as such because they need to be retired to history and laid to rest once and for all. RNT has, for reasons better and worse, added desperately needed arrows to the quiver of Christian apologists.

Using a similar approach to how he explicated the probability for the Resurrection, Swinburne offers a systematic, cumulative case, leveraging the power of confirmation theory vis-à-vis Bayes' theorem, to inductively infer the mathematical probability for God's existence. His cumulative work is widely regarded as one of the most thorough and effective

---

1. Swinburne originally published this book in 1979 and a later revision with added appendices in 1991. His most recent edition, published in 2004, is substantially modified wherein he explicates the probability for God via confirmation theory.

defenses of Christian theology. While the inductive cosmological argument presented in *The Existence of God* is highly commendable and germane to our task of elucidating whether God-by-whatever-name exists, in the interest of explanatory economy I shall take the course of addressing only the weaknesses of his argumentation.

A BRIEF OVERVIEW: THE CLASSICAL COSMOLOGICAL ARGUMENT FOR THE EXISTENCE OF GOD

The cosmological argument is an age-old argument to explicate why, in the universe, there is *something rather than nothing*. It seeks to identify a First Cause (or depending on your viewpoint, an uncaused cause) to the universe. This argument has been revised into multiple variations and has been exhaustively critiqued by others; accordingly I will keep my commentary short and to the point. The most familiar rendition is the Kalam cosmological argument originally developed by Sunni Muslim theologian Al-Ghazali.[2]

> "Every being which begins has a cause for its beginning; now the world is a being which begins; therefore, it possesses a cause for its beginning."[2]
>
> Al-Ghazali, (b. c. 1055/1058 – d. 1111 CE)
> from *The Middle Path in Theology*

This rationale generates three considerations in need of explication. The first musing is whether every event must possess a cause, especially prior to the universe. The second notion is whether the universe had a beginning or is temporally infinite to the past. And thirdly, if there was a cause, then what is the nature of this (presumably) First Cause or uncaused cause? To gather the requisite insights, a *very* large can of worms has to be opened-up to appreciate such things as whether the Causal Principle even applies, whether the Big Bang is the right hypothesis for the genesis of the universe, and if so, can it be considered to be a causal event in what we define as the property of time. This requires that we carefully study what the property of time is as well as the full definition of the phenomena we call 'reality'. Beyond all this, we need a determination as to whether an actual infinity of anything even exists. Can the puzzling world of **QUANTUM MECHANICS** give us any insights? For the moment, we will keep the lid on these vital matters until later chapters. What is to be investigated now is the intrinsic power, even beauty, of inductive logic. For it is inductive logic in the form of probability calculus in which Swinburne formulates his cosmological argument.

---

2. Initial attribution is afforded to Al-Ghazali who lived c. 1058–1111 CE and is considered by many as the second-most influential Muslim (after Muhammad).

Troubles-a-Brew for the Swinburnian World of Metaphysics

Swinburne's cosmological argument is designed to show that the known universe requires an explanation and that God is the sole and most probable source to explicate the universe's existence. *His aim is to show that the likelihood of the universe's existence is greater if God were to exist than if he did not exist.* This can be interpreted in the language of conditional probability that, given theism and our background knowledge, the evidences for God are better explained than an atheistic position. In Bayesian terms, the expression is posed as: $\mathbf{P}(E_s \mid H_g \,\&\, B) > \mathbf{P}(E_s \mid {\sim}H_g \,\&\, B)$ where '$\mathbf{P}$' is the probability, 'H_g' is the hypothesis that God exists (i.e., theism), '${\sim}H_g$' is the negation of this hypothesis (i.e., theism is untrue/God does not exist), 'E_s' is the specific evidence—namely the existence of our universe, and 'B' is our relevant background knowledge (e.g., analytic **TAUTOLOGIES** and deductive logic).

Inherent to the use of this inferential logic is that, assuming theism is true; it cannot distinguish how many deities might exist. Furthermore, we cannot be assured whether the Being(s) are 'good God(s)' or 'evil God(s)'. The latter could be discerned with appropriate premises and evidences but the disposition cannot necessarily be automatically guaranteed just because we are hypothesizing God exists. As we will discuss, in defending the Christian view, Swinburne must appeal to a supplemental argument to claim that *only one god* is necessary and to other arguments that God is comprised of *exactly three Persons* (i.e., the Holy Trinity). In fact, he appeals to many different arguments beyond the cosmological argument such as the argument from personal experience, the Problem of Evil, a **TELEOLOGICAL** argument, an argument from human consciousness, and an argument from miracles. For a comprehensive analysis of all these arguments, I point you to an exquisite critique given by philosopher Emma Beckman.[8] While I will refrain from dissecting these additional arguments for brevity's sake, where I see considerable merit for what Swinburne has done is to touch on a bedrock principle of this book. **In attempting to circumscribe God-by-whatever-name, the only way to accomplish the task is via** *cumulatius indicium*— **by way of cumulative evidence. That is, we cannot look solely from a religious lens (e.g., via faith or Scripture). We have to seek truth from every source of knowledge accessible to humans—sensory, reason, history, literature, science, mathematics, probability, and to a limited extent personal experience to assemble a systematic framework to synthesize belief upon the preponderance of** *objectified evidence*. **What I stress and Swinburne does not is the criticality of plumbing from the inside-out, outside-in, top-down, bottoms-up, and holistically and to do so with a zetetic mentality maximally focused on objectivity.**

Swinburne readily admits that it is *conceivable* and **COHERENT** that there is *no explanation* for the universe whatsoever, though his framework demonstrates this to be an improbable position (that is, $\mathbf{P}(E_s|B)$ is very low). Given that he has systematically built a case upon a set of cumulative evidence and arrived at a theistic determination, the zetetic process demands that we probe the underpinnings of his analytical framework to give it a strong shake and dressing down to appreciate whatever weaknesses may exist, beyond those Swinburne adroitly attempts to head off.

SWINBURNE'S GOD THEORY – NEITHER SCIENCE NOR QUASI-SCIENCE

In defense of his thesis, Swinburne attempts to persuade the unwary reader by his analogical reference of his work being coequal with that of scientific hypotheses. He maintains that his God-theory parallels the storied histories of the development of Isaac Newton's laws of motion, and 277 years later, the idea that the ubiquitous subatomic protons and neutrons were made of even smaller undetectable matter called quarks. *However, the foundational principle of what differentiates what we call scientific enterprise from metaphysics is that any scientific hypothesis must be testable.* There is a parade of physicists (typically those in the dominant discipline of condensed matter physics) that regard astrophysical cosmogony (the study or the origins of the universe)[3] as metaphysics or pseudoscience and not a bona fide science.[4] The reason is that many of its theories are untestable. Take, for example, the multiverse proposition (often referred to as 'M-theory')[5] that suggests that a vast sea of unique universes must exist in greater reality. While development of this theory implicitly involves an intense reliance on the use of some of the most complex mathematics known and the application of advanced physical principles including the probabilistic realm of quantum theory, the fact that it appears that no test can be conceived to evaluate the proposal pushes it to the fringes of science and possibly beyond. If such theories of cosmogony for all its worth are questionably scientific, then Swinburne is very off-base with his preoccupation of raising the credibility of his hypothesis to that of serious scientific introspection. Regardless of how it compares to astrophysical cosmology theories, Swinburne's God-theory is *not* empirically testable.

GOD AS THE SIMPLEST EXPLANATION

In *The Existence of God*, it is argued that theism is the simplest of all rival explanations for the existence of the universe. It is in fact, the underlying slab of Swinburne's intuitive

---

3. *Cosmology* is the study of the universe at large in all respects whereas *Cosmogony* solely focuses on the early universe, particularly the origin of the universe.

4. This is called the Demarcation Problem in the Philosophy of Science

5. The Multiverse theory implies an atheistic position

approach. As it goes, the universe (a.k.a. naturalism) is intrinsically a highly complex structure where galaxies, black holes, humans, and even pebbles serve as testamentary phenomena. Something very powerful, Swinburne maintains, is needed to have the extraordinary wherewithal to pull off the creation of the universe. He posits that there is no requirement for the Creator itself to be complex and argues it would be more rational that it was a simple Being.

Swinburne presses into service the presumption that there is an operational and apparently inviolable principle at work that, all things being equal, the most compelling argument is one that is the simplest. This argument by Swinburne is in essence an attempt to conflate simplicity with the well-worn Ockham's razor which is the law of parsimony wherein a hypothesis with the *fewest assumptions* should be selected. Circa 1960 Ray Solomonoff, an information theorist and the father of the theory of universal inductive inference, confirmed that *shorter (**COMPUTABLE**) theories do in fact offer greater predictive power*. However, we must keep separate the concept of *simplicity* from the idea of *enumeration*. Is unity really simpler than two? Or, are two circles more complex than three circles? All else aside, this is not the case. The attribute of being enumerable must be joined by additional properties before complexity can arise.

Let us conduct a thought experiment by bringing to our minds two rectangular masonry bricks that are identical in all respects. The bricks have the exact same properties (e.g., color, size, shape, mass, chemical composition, intrinsic energy, etc.), but do not share the same atoms of material or physical space. Place one of the bricks so that one of its large faces mates-up with the flat surface of a table. Now take the other brick and place it atop the bottom brick to form a shape analogous to an upside-down 'T'. We can agree that this organizational structure is more complex than if there was simply a singular brick sitting motionless on the table top. However, if there were two identical masonry bricks that existed, each located on table tops in different galaxies having absolutely nothing to do with one another; do the two unassociated bricks entailing the same innate capabilities possess any more complexity than a single brick? No, they do not. A substance that is a single substance that is divided into two does not add complexity. It is through the addition of relationships and properties other than plurality wherein complexity can develop.

Zero, on the other hand, is a very special number. It denotes the absence, negation, or nonexistence of 'things'. If we were to enumerate something as being zero and compare it to something of unity (or any other number), then relative complexity is generated. *Something* is more complex than *nothing*. Therefore, having a God as the First Cause to the universe would be more complex than if nothing whatsoever existed prior to Creation. Such a statement presumes that the universe is not eternally existent to the past. This idea of an eternally-existent universe is examined in Chapter 13.

This idea that a perfect god is the simplest of all rival conceptions is disputed by Keith Parsons[6] who illuminates thusly,

> God's omnipotence is, **PRIMA FACIE**, a rather complex property. Divine omnipotence entails not simply the ability to deploy unlimited amounts of energy, but the logically independent abilities to create, arrange, sustain, or annihilate matter and energy, or, indeed, to actualize all sorts of possible worlds that contain nothing like the matter and energy that constitute our universe. In fact, the hypothesis of theism seems to add considerable complexity to our overall view of reality [...] (indeed, the Christian God, if you accept the identity of the Son and the Father and the doctrine of the Incarnation, had to be at one time both corporeal and incorporeal) [...] Even if we assume that all of these postulated divine properties are intelligible – a very big assumption – theism clearly is a hypothesis that carries a large amount of weighty metaphysical baggage. A worldview that carries such baggage appears **IPSO FACTO** less simple than [bare] naturalism, which simply discards the baggage.[11]

Swinburne defines the nature of God with ten critically necessary *and* inseparable attributes that this Being *must* possess in order for his arguments to be philosophically consistent:

> [bold-underline added]

> How is the claim that there is a God to be understood? I suggest-provisionally --in this way: there exists **necessarily and eternally a person essentially bodiless, omnipresent, creator and sustainer of any universe there may be, perfectly free, omnipotent, omniscient, perfectly good, and a source of moral obligation**. The claim that the person 'necessarily' has the properties of being essentially bodiless, omnipresent, etc., is to be read as the claim that **these properties are inseparable from him; if he were to cease to be omniscient or whatever, he would cease to exist**.[2]

---

6. Keith M. Parsons is a Professor of Philosophy at the University of Houston–Clear Lake. He is a self-professed atheist, who in an open letter September 1, 2010 decided to quit the academic field of Philosophy of Religion principally because of boredom and frustration arising from the fact that in spite of the many well-argued philosophical/theological treaties, no consensus view has appreciably altered mindsets. He maintains that atheism has provided the strongest arguments across many aspects of the debate spectrum and that pretty much all that can be said, has been said.

It is paramount to qualify Swinburne's godly attributes relative to the concepts of omnipotence and omniscience. In his view, God possesses these qualities in a strictly logical sense to avoid situations of logical incoherency. Swinburne acknowledges that the two God-powers are restricted in certain respects to ensure that God is not forced into a paradox of *doing or knowing something* and *not doing or not knowing something* at the same time (e.g., God causes the Earth to be formed and he also causes it *not* to be formed). Oddly, such restrictions will come to violate a cornerstone requirement of Swinburne's argument that God *cannot* be considered a *logically necessary Being*. We will explore what a logically necessary Being is in the upcoming section entitled *The Holy Trinity*. For now, let us appreciate this theistic logical condition in Swinburne's own words.

> [underline added]

> God is omnipotent in the sense (roughly) that he can do whatever it is logically possible that he do. The qualification in the last clause is important. There are some apparent states of affairs, the description of which involves a logical contradiction—for example, me existing and not existing at the same time. God cannot bring about such apparent states, not because he is weak, but because the description 'me existing and not existing at the same time' does not really describe a state of affairs at all, in the sense of something that it is coherent to suppose could occur. There are also states of affairs that it is coherent to suppose could occur, but that it is not coherent to suppose God could bring about, because the very description of him bringing them about does not really describe an action. An example would be 'an uncaused state of affairs'. It is logically possible that such a state occurs, but it is not coherent to suppose that God could bring about, that is cause, an uncaused state. He is omniscient, at any rate in the sense that he knows at any time whatever it is logically possible that he know at that time.[10]

To summarize Swinburne's position, for it to be possible for God to exist, God **_must_** possess ten inseparable characteristics.[7] Furthermore, God's properties must obey logic restrictions to avoid being trapped by irresolvable paradoxes. Swinburne's theism grows more complex by his prescription of an exacting set of attributes God **_must_** have, for if God is deficient in these qualities, Swinburne's logic collapses like a house of cards.

---

7. According to Swinburne, the ten properties God MUST possess are that God is: (1) Necessary, (2) Eternal, (3) Bodiless, (4) Omnipresent, (5) the Creator and Sustainer of the universe, (6) Perfectly free, (7) Omnipotent, (8) Omniscient, (9) Perfectly good, and (10) a source for absolute morality.

The Universe is Complex ... or is it?

Another assumption made by Swinburne is that the universe evolved into complex structures and that this has in effect been curated by a divine entity. I would suggest that complexity in this sense is a matter of timing. While I freely admit that our universe as it exists today is comprised of highly complex structures and processes, this was not the case in the early universe. If (and I do mean if) the model of the Inflationary Big Bang hypothesis is accurate, then in the first moment of Creation there was an ultra-short duration SUPRALUMINAL expansion of spacetime. There existed during this tinniest fraction of time only pure energy. After the expansion ended and after the first few hundred thousand years, the universe was essentially nothing more than a fairly uniform, hot but completely dark (to human eyes) expanding bulk of subatomic matter and energy. That is, nature was fundamentally simple in both constitution and organization. It would not be for some 380,000 years after the Big Bang for electrons to be trapped in orbits around nuclei, forming the first hydrogen and helium atoms. If we humans could travel back in time to say 200,000 years after the Big Bang and we could ask ourselves the very same questions about God's existence, would the claim that the universe is complex be given strong credence? While things back then were no doubt the epitome of chaos with energetic particles furiously buzzing about absorbing and exchanging energy, the universe was structureless and highly uniform.

This leads us to another insight that now becomes obvious. We have a different set of knowledge in the cosmic year 200,000 as we do in the year 13.82 billion (today). This situation points to a disturbing fact that when Bayes' theorem is implemented that there is a good possibility that the specific evidences and background knowledge are dependent on *when* we identify this set of data *and by whom*. That is, you and I may have the same views on specific evidences in the year 200,000, but in the year 13.82 billion, you may have generated a repository of specific evidence and background knowledge that is significantly different than my own. Therefore, when one performs a Bayesian analysis; a different Inference to the Best Explanation could materialize. This is disregarding the level of intellectual objectivity that may be at work to select and assess the information selected from these two different repositories which itself could be a factor in the outcome.

We can go a step further with the question as to why it is that the observable universe[8] contains immutable and supremely fine-tuned universal physical constants (e.g., the speed

---

8. It is generally accepted that the observable universe is a subset of a much larger universe. As such, what is testable is confined to the smaller confines of what we can access.

of light in vacuum, Planck's constant) that if they were even the slightest bit different than what they are, our cosmos would be radically different and perhaps not even exist at all.[9] In his book *Superforce: The Search for a Grand Unified Theory of Nature* (Simon & Schuster, 1984) and in numerous other works of his, theoretical astrophysicist Paul Davies discusses the supreme precision inherent in the set of cosmic universal parameters. He points to the example that if the respective forces of gravity and electromagnetism were different in the tiniest amount (10^{-40}), all stars like our Sun would fail to exist.[10, 12] It is completely logically coherent to postulate that these cosmic parameters exist for absolutely no reason other than they must take on the respective properties they are imbued with. That is, their properties are **MONADIC**—irreducibly innate and are uncaused by a deity. If we were to insist that a deity caused these parameters to have the properties they have, this inherently requires an additional cause to exist.

To be fair, what I have passed over is that while the parameter values of matter and space are relatively simple, their interrelationships *could be* extraordinarily complex. Einstein's famous mass-energy relationship is provided below which involves the universal constant for the speed of light in vacuum. The second relationship is the momentum of light photons (i.e., radiation) which depend on Planck's constant and the photon's wavelength.

Einstein's Mass-Energy Relationship
(c = speed of light in vacuum)

$$E = \frac{mc^2}{\sqrt{\left(1 - \frac{v^2}{c^2}\right)}} \approx mc^2$$

(for lower relativistic velocities, v)

Photon Momentum (p)
h = Planck's constant, λ = wavelength

$$p = \frac{h}{\lambda}$$

These are very simple relationships; however, we cannot be completely certain these are exactly true of reality. It may be that these happen to be very good approximations. For example, as I will later comment on, there may be conditions in which the speed of light in a vacuum is different than what we have previously believed to be a never-changing constant.

---

9. There is no consensus among physicists how many fundamental parameters there are. Some say there are 26 and others say there are only two which can be selected from a list of three (speed of light in vacuum, the strength of gravity, and Planck's constant). Also, some have conjectured that the parameters may not be constant across the entire universe, though verifying this is beyond the current state of technology.

10. This means to say that if either constant were different by a single digit located forty places after the decimal point; many stars like the Sun would fail to exist. To make this easier to understand let us say for explanatory purposes that the gravitational constant was exactly equal to 1.0. If this value were increased it by one part in 10^{40}, the value would be... 1.**00000** 00000 **00000** 00000 **00000** 00000 **00000** 00001.

For now, we have to go with the preponderance of evidence that suggests these cosmic universal parameters and their interrelationships do represent true reality.

The main point to be made is that a brute existence to the universe—one without deities or prior causes—is in fact simpler than a universe requiring a god. This is the essence of what physicists Stephen Hawking and Leonard Mlodinow advance in *The Grand Design* (Bantam Books, 2010) whereby they suggest that the universe must necessarily have been spontaneously created as a result of the fundamental nature of quantum mechanics.[13] Their quantum cosmology extends the idea that quantum particle properties (e.g., spin, momentum, position) are not single-valued but are represented as a superposition of many possible values. Among the viable states is a state of nothingness. Thus, creation of the universe was nucleated by the virtue of quantum states spontaneously arising from *nothingness* into *something-ness*. We will leave this for now, but pick up on the topic of scientific theories of Creation in Chapter 13.

THE HOLY TRINITY

For all the work Swinburne puts forth to convince us of the simplicity of a single God, he is forced to deal with the central doctrine of the Holy Trinity. In his treatise, he makes it appear as though he is presenting us with a bottom-up logical and intuitional progression of why God exists and furthermore must be comprised of three Persons and that this vision is coherent and philosophically sound in all respects. To wit, it will be shown that this is not the case.

Swinburne's Perfect Being Theology is leveraged to derive whether God's existence is any or all of the following: (1) *logically necessary*, (2) *ontologically necessary*, and/or (3) *metaphysically necessary*. I will explain these shortly. Here, the abstract metaphysical waters get deep very quickly and I shall do what I can to prevent the reader from being drowned by the extensive and highly nuanced debates about the various understandings that can arise from such contemplations. Herein we are trying to source the zetetic truth and not to find a perch to wax philosophic.

To be *logically necessary* the statement "God exists" or "God does not exist" must be coherent (i.e., self-consistent). Recollect that this condition falls squarely onto the fabric of our accepted Coherency of Truth Condition (refer to Chapter 1, see TC-8, p. 52). Furthermore, if God exists, then with the exception of God, the existence of all else must depend on God (that is, it would be illogical for an apple, a human, or a galaxy to exist independent of God). In other words, **God must be shown to be the necessary cause**

for the creation of the universe. *Ontological necessity* is the condition that God must exist without an *a priori* cause (i.e., God exists as an uncaused cause). Finally, Swinburne defines a *metaphysical necessity* as either of two options. The first option is that God is ontologically necessary and the second option is that God brought the universe into being by virtue of God's own properties.[14]

Before moving into a deeper discussion, understand that if something is ontologically necessary then it *must also be logically necessary*. That is, if God is uncaused, then we also need to be able to logically assert that God exists. If God is ontologically and logically necessary, then we must conclude that he is also metaphysically necessary, for if something is required to exist in reality, then it intrinsically meets the looser constraint of this 'thing' existing metaphysically.[15]

It is useful to understand ahead of time that Swinburne's cosmological argument requires an outcome that God is only metaphysically necessary by virtue of his ten properties and cannot be ontologically or logically necessary. This is for the simple fact that if God is also either of logical or ontological necessity, then only a singular divine Being can be permitted which would leave Jesus and the Holy Spirit out in the cold so to speak. Also, were God to be ontologically necessary, this would impute his existence causa sui, that is, his self-existence as an uncaused cause. If this were to be the case, then there is nothing to compel God to take the action of creating the universe. God could simply sit around his 'eternity' of nonspatial timeless existence and never bring the cosmos into being. However, because something (e.g., the aforementioned apple, human, or galaxy) rather than nothing does come into existence, then according to Swinburne, this action is solely dependent on God's perfection (his virtuous properties) to bring it all about. In creating and sustaining the universe, the Swinburnian God becomes metaphysically necessary.

Swinburne is on the hook to explain why God is neither ontologically or logically necessary. He reasons that ontological necessity has an additional onus by the intrinsic relational aspect between an uncaused cause and all else that exists. In his mind this is added complexity. The professor's discomfort with such a relationship is not in the least a satisfying explanation as to why God is not an uncaused ontological necessity. It is to be acknowledged that ontological necessity is an *a priori* argument that presumes as true the uncaused existence of God. Swinburne denounces the reality of *a priori* arguments (which also happens to jive with the zetetic approach) as well as the reasonableness of *a posteriori* arguments by saying, "I do not believe that there is any force in *a priori* arguments for the existence of God [...]. Worthwhile arguments are *a posteriori* [...] I do not think that there are any sound deductive *a posteriori* arguments for the existence of God."[16]

Swinburne believes that a metaphysical prescription is simpler because God exists as a result of his array of necessary and perfect monadic properties and not because he is ontologically uncaused or that it would be a logical imperative. This is a very weak argument and I can only comprehend this in the context of his self-imposed requirement for simplicity and the fact that Swinburne needs to have God solely metaphysically necessary to carry out the Christological demands for the existence of a Triune God. I would further proffer that if Swinburne were not theologically committed and aiming for a particular outcome he would probably see the wisdom of *not* going down this path. But, his confessional attachments compel his footwork to parallel the path of Christian doctrine rather than to take the zetetic path to objectively source the most probable truth to reality. In total, his argumentative support for his position that God is not ontologically necessary enjoys virtually no credible support whatsoever.

Beyond this ontological necessity issue, Swinburne's wisdom fails catastrophically when he argues that God is not logically necessary because if God's existence were dependent on the application of logic, then he could not be totally independent (that is, perfectly free and omnipotent). However, earlier I noted that Swinburne emphatically requires that God *must* be restricted by logic to prevent his omnipotent and omniscient powers from trapping him in a logic paradox whereby God could be forced to be doing or knowing something while simultaneously *not* doing or *not* knowing the same thing. Swinburne confusingly feels that we cannot impute God's existence as being subject to logical necessity but on the otherhand he suggests that God's powers are constrained by logic laws.

I see no way for Swinburne to escape this bondage of illogic other than for Swinburne to admit that God is ontologically, logically, *and* metaphysically necessary. This would allow him to have a basis for a coherent claim that God exists. Unfortunately, this step dooms any prospects for his thesis because it would annihilate the chance to successfully argue the Christian claim that God consists of three personages.

Let's further appreciate Swinburne's theological assertions by traveling further down the Swinburnian road because he has as yet to explain how in reality that the singular divine cause consists of three indivisible Persons—no fewer and no greater in number. He initiates by imagining three divine Persons—G_1, G_2, and G_3.[17] He argues that due to its perfect goodness, G_1 causes G_2 to come into existence so that it may share its love and to have another being capable of cooperating with G_1 and sharing its love. Swinburne then posits that the necessity for G_1 and G_2 to cause (we might say metaphysically birthed) G_3 so that the love between G_1 and G_2 can be fully expressed. But once the third is caused, there is no more necessity to create a G_4 as now the three can perfectly love, share, and cooperate. Each of these gods is endowed with the same divine properties though they have formulated a cooperative arrangement to prevent irreconcilable conflicts from occurring. In the interest of economy, I have leapt over many of the confusing scenarios that can create conflicts with things such as the (1) existence of multiple gods with the same- or varying-level of powers, (2) gods that might have separate and unique powers, and (3) whether any or all of the so-identified powers are ultimate in capacity.

In the case of three *independent* gods, we would have a state of *tritheism* (i.e., polytheism) which presents a strong potential for creating a colossal mess of conflicting divine powers and actions therein. The early Church Fathers cogitated on this for many decades (in particular Athanasius) and determined that greater coherence would be achieved if the three gods were actually only one substance but were of three personages who exist in hypostatic union. This is the thinking that was commented on in Chapter 8 when the idea of God's consubstantiality with Jesus and the Holy Spirit was promulgated into the conciliar narratives of the Nicene Creed (325 CE), its follow-on revision the Niceno-Constantinopolitan Creed (381 CE), and the Athanasian Creed (c. 500 – 600 CE).[11]

Reflecting once again, the Bible itself cannot be used as a source to conclude that God, Jesus, and the Holy Spirit are made of the same substance or that their collective nature as three Persons is the same singular God. This is because the Bible simply does not provide any information on how their existence as individual Persons is intertwined. This is apart from the various instances in the Bible where Jesus' affiliation to God is mentioned in oblique terms that require inferences to be made that he might be God's son. What we are interested in is how the earthly Jesus can be the same deity made of the same 'divine material' as a bodiless, all-powerful God. However, Swinburne does not digest the wording of these creeds as most all prior theologians have where it pertains to God's three-part union. He postulates that these three documents in their original Greek and Latin language ambiguously define the Godhead and ultimately lead toward the idea that there are effectively three deities. In his essay *Trinity or Tritheism?* Christian philosopher Kelly James Clarke concludes that, while Swinburne himself believes in the long-held trinitarian concept, the argumentation he presents is better interpreted that he ultimately depicts a tritheistic Godhead which further crumbles Swinburne's overall thesis.[18]

What is especially worrisome is how his linchpin strategy employs the anthro-pomorphization of the relationship between G_1, G_2, and G_3 much as a human married couple

---

11. The authorship of the Athanasian Creed is widely disputed as to when it was written, but it is widely agreed that Athanasius did not write it. It probably originated in southern France around the middle of the 5th-century (see Krueger, "The Origin And Terminology Of The Athanasian Creed", Oct 5-6, 1976)

might complete their union by bearing a child. Assuming God-by-whatever-name exists, I have always wondered whether he would experience loneliness. But, I would never go so far as Swinburne to apply my pitiful human cognition onto God in such a way as to require him to cause into existence two other Beings. Similarly dodgy is how each of these Persons in the Godhead is interdependent for the other's existence and must strike up an accord to prevent any of the omnipotent personages from annihilating the other(s) and to share duties in the way Swinburne describes this. Collectively, his reasoning cries out for a copious injection of coherency. Finally, what are we to make of Swinburne's list of ten critical attributes for God? I am dubious of Swinburne's thought processes that allow him to effectively dictate what powers God *must* have and how he *must* implement these powers. He puts too fine a point on the matter to be credible.

Ultimately, in *The Existence of God* (1979 and 1991 editions) and *The Christian God* (1994), Swinburne does an extraordinary job of trying to authenticate Christian theology in light of the criticisms that were assailing the tradition at that time and since. He attempts to make a solid chain with strong links but fails to connect them in proper fashion. It is, for all intents and purposes, a limp and nearly useless chain. A tireless apologist, he comes back to revise *The Existence of God* with his 2004 edition to authenticate Christianity through confirmation theory, a year after he first employs this new weapon in 2003 to craft his defense of the resurrection event in *The Resurrection of God Incarnate*. We will briefly examine his findings regarding confirmation theory a little further on.

At this point, I would like to conclude this discussion to come full circle on Swinburne's defense of simplicity and why this is a particular treacherous idea and that it must be excised from metaphysical argumentation. Keith Parsons sums up these notions of simplicity and parallelism to scientific theorization in his incisive dissection of Swinburne's *The Existence of God* (its first-run publication in 1979).

[bold emphasis added]

Once untestable hypotheses become entrenched they are very difficult to dislodge, even when better (albeit somewhat more complex) hypotheses are available. The extreme tenacity of superstitious explanations in the face of conflicting, and more productive, scientific accounts is sufficient evidence of this claim. Explanations in terms of demons, poltergeists, mental telepathy, magic, and other such occult entities and processes frequently possess a greater simplicity, as Swinburne defines the term, than rival scientific explanations [...] The simplicity and untestability [...] of such hypotheses gives them great obscurantist potential. [...]

> **Virtually *any* phenomenon that we currently think possesses an adequate scientific explanation could be explained more simply in nonscientific terms. Occult powers wielded by disembodied agents could be invoked to cover just about any occurrence.**[19]

Parsons has really pegged a critical issue. A large contingent of the world society assigns, with relative ease, deific agency as the genesis for many phenomena that are not well understood. Many of these same individuals go further to do the same for things that are understood by scientists, but they are simply unaware or steeped too deeply in their beliefs to consider well-substantiated counter evidence.

THE META-TRANSIGNIFICATION AND THE ORIGIN OF THE UNIVERSE HYPOTHESIS

I see in the theism-versus-nontheism debate constrained binary thinking which only leads to an intractable dead-lock that so frustrated Keith Parsons that he left the field of Philosophy of Religion altogether. I suggest that there is an intermediate possibility that bridges the incompatible visions of theism and its nontheistic counterpart.[12] I shall call this approach the *Meta-Transignification and the Origin of the Universe Hypothesis* which I shall coarsely outline and offer an incomplete defense thereof. It initiates with the *a priori* assumption that our universe had a beginning and that God exists. By assuming the latter, I depart from the zetetic process which I justify doing so for the simple purpose to introduce a new perspective. We will discuss in a later chapter various scientific hypotheses of both beginningless (eternal) theories of Creation as well as those that support a universe with a temporal origin.

The Meta-Transignification and the Origin of the Universe Hypothesis

It could be that an inconceivably powerful (though not necessarily omnipotent) divine essence or Being actually *did* exist prior to the conception of the universe in perfect **ASEITY** (i.e., uncaused) or caused by some means completely alien to us, even *ex nihilo*. We will not presuppose that the pre-universe was devoid of character or medium (i.e., timeless, non-spatial, or immaterial) as we cannot know. Employing its unconditioned freedom and incomprehensible intellect (which needn't necessarily infer omniscience), the entity—what we

---

12. I purposefully refrain from using the word "atheist" because of the many forms of atheism may cloud the issue. *Nontheism* is an umbrella term encapsulating distinct and potentially mutually exclusive positions that confederate under a common naturalistic approach.

will henceforth call the *Cosmic Creator*—determined to alter its manifestation by repurposing its existence.[13]

The Cosmic Creator conceived of a generalized plan for his universe starting with the crafting of a physically dimensionless reality consisting of a **QUANTUM STATE**, what I will call the Primal Quantum Dot.[14] After this quantum nucleation event, the property of physical time is conceived as the Cosmic Creator irreversibly converts the totality of his essence into a **FERMENT** of pure energy as quantum foam.[15] This quantum nucleation is the seed material for the universe (or multiverse). The Cosmic Creator is keenly aware of the high degree of precision entailed in the tuning of the physical universal constants necessary to lead to a causal course that would ensure its long-term survival and ability to develop interesting patterns of creation. He is also aware that much is left to chance. The Cosmic Creator selects the initial conditions in such a way as to maximize the odds that growth of the nascent universe (or some number of the multiverse membership) would survive its tumultuous beginnings. The Primal Quantum Dot is inherently unstable and instantaneously transitions, taking on dimensional attributes creating what we now call spacetime (which could be a continuous or **QUANTIZED** substance, we do not yet know which it is).

The Cosmic Creator's scale of benevolence is not measured by any emotional scale of love, but rather by the abiding interest in the cosmic good that arises from the universe's survival and longevity which yields a mystifying artistry of a continually emergent creation. This might be referred to as a cosmic love which is not to be confused with an interpersonal love for human kind (or any specific form of life) per se. An analogy can be drawn with mankind who is also capable of producing things of great beauty that are admired by those that come after. Upon expiration, our mind-body becomes completely and absolutely divorced of whatever knowledge, power, and emotion it previously possessed. We give back to the cosmos all the borrowed atomic

---

13. Use of the word "repurposed" is a convenience. This is not to infer that we have any knowledge of the Cosmic Creator's purposes prior to the final act of creating the universe.

14. Within our universe, quantum states exist as wave-like entities that can be infinitely superimposed physically and temporally on top of one another. However, prior to the universe, physical time does not exist for the Primal Quantum Dot.

15. This is not to be confused with the notion of self-annihilation or self-termination.

matter used to compose our essence. Accordingly, there is no disembodied soul or corresponding afterlife.

We mistakenly **ANTHROPOMORPHIZE** and **REIFY** the Cosmic Creator with our own conception of good and evil. Rather, human beings whose existence is owed to an innumerable number of fortuitous causal events come to possess a limited free will to define civility/incivility and morality/immorality. That is, there exists moral relativism. Hence, we are left to judge our own **ANTHROPODICY**. Our existence is limited to the individual capacities and frailties of the human mind-body. While we can freely choose between reading a book and driving a car, humans have many physical limitations. For example, we cannot process all of the information that can be perceived in reality. We have evolved brains that filter-out the vast majority of sensory information. There is also oodles more information present in the electromagnetic spectrum (e.g., x-rays, microwaves, radio waves) or the trillions of neutrinos speeding through our bodies at any given moment that we cannot directly sense.

Once set in motion, the emergent universe(s), now devoid of its Cosmic Creator, grows in beauty, richness, complexity, order, including spontaneous self-ordering, that generates a new domain of reality subject to natural law and chance (i.e., statistical) events. Importantly, given that the majority of the universe unveils itself as frigid (-455 °F) empty space and much of the condensed matter is ultra-hot (e.g., stars); it is not all too conducive to the perfuse formation and sustainment of intelligent life. Due solely to causal connectedness that pervades the universe—and not good and evil—misfortune arises unendingly. Among the trillions upon trillions of planets that come to exist, a complement becomes the domicile for sentient life, indeed civilizations of intellectual awe. A number fail to reach their zenith because their planet becomes totally sterilized as it sat unwittingly in the path of the jets of a **GAMMA-RAY BURST**. Other civilizations are snuffed out due to their proximity to their binary star system, one of which goes supernova. While they are forewarned of their imminent demise well in advance, even their spaceship galleons cannot provide them safe harbor from the oncoming blast wave rippling through space at high fractions of the speed of light. The supernova will reap its due, obliterating anything within the **HELIOSPHERE** and beyond. From afar, we humans are in awe of the majesty and artistry of the death throes of one of the exploding celestial dots in the sky, completely unaware of what tragedy that may have befallen other intelligent life-forms.

God, then, is not the divine transcendent 'existing on the other side' or the **IMMANENT** interventionist (or personal savior) that religion would have him be, rather, his essence found what we might call bliss in the creation of the grand cosmos. By altering the Cosmic Creator's own significance in this incomprehensible, magnanimous, and transformative way, the divine essence achieves its full and complete Meta-Transignification.

This hypothesis is clearly more plausible than Swinburne's installation in terms of the relaxation of monadic properties of the Cosmic Creator. In doing so, it gets around the major problems of Perfect Being Theology encountered in arguments that rely on such godly attributes. Ontological arguments usually call forth the idea that God is a "maximally great being" which is to say that there is nothing greater than can be conceived. I hesitate to borrow this description because the Cosmic Creator's 'reality' transcends our comprehension of what *we* call reality. And, because when we use the word "great" many will immediately begin to humanize the language. Furthermore, we do not have a unified, let alone useful, barometer on what "maximal" means. The Meta-Transignification hypothesis only requires that the Cosmic Creator possesses an adequate amount of capability to accomplish the feat of Transignification.

We also have to consider the notion that the amount of capability required to create the universe might be forever masked and furthermore, that it might be much less than we might otherwise think. For example, it may be that the total amount of energy needed to start the universe may have been sizably less than what the universe contains now. It is strongly (perhaps universally) held that the total energy content of the visible and nonvisible universe always was, is, and will always be a constant. This is a compulsory fact due to the Law of Conservation of Energy for an isolated system which emanated at the origin of or some (very short) time after the Big Bang. However, *before* the formation of the natural laws, it may be that the energy required of the Cosmic Creator was considerably lower because it could be exponentially increased outside of the infant universe by principles unknown to us and which may no longer exist.

While the Cosmic Creator presumably once existed beyond our four known dimensions and its natural laws, it was always logically, ontologically, and metaphysically necessary. This hypothesis is also simpler because it only requires one deity. Could there have been more than one deity? Strictly speaking, it is possible that multiple divine entities co-existed prior to the Big Bang. Though, it would be presumably unlikely that there was a family of divine Beings. What might be more convincing is that the Cosmic Creator created (caused) other lesser beings. Though this begins to complicate things because one would have to explain what happened to any additional entities after the act of the Creator's Transignification. We furthermore may have to question the idea of whether the Cosmic Creator possessed unconditioned freedom or would be required to obtain ascent from his brethren (or perhaps he simply forced or tricked them). Or, maybe, these other entities were not affected by the Cosmic Creator's actions because of their existence outside of the spacetime. That is, everything is happening within the 'bubble' of the Big Bang. Conceivably then, these other entities may also follow suit and create their own unique universes playing with different parameters and relationships. While multiple divine essences cannot be ruled-out entirely, their actions are apparently totally divorced from our universe. In short, a single deity is the only relevant concern and perhaps the most rationally reasonable option.

This overall hypothesis would more than likely sit well with the majority of nontheists because to them, the natural universe is freed from all the things they rail against. It furthermore solves the vexing Problem of Evil (theodicy) and the free will-vs-determinism dilemma by their simple nullification. We are no longer bound by the intractable problem of why an all-loving God would willingly permit the suffering and death of organic life for billions of years because he simply no longer exists to function as a cosmic curator/arbitrator. This then vanquishes any need for any conception of heaven, hell, angels, or demons. It also releases us from the Axiological (Moral) argument for God's existence because humans have full control over what defines morality. We define our own anthropodicy. The hypothesis also releases us from a need for an everlasting or eternal God. Ultimately, the prosperity and intrinsic beauty of the universe defines the Cosmic Creator's cosmic good at a universal-scale. The Meta-Transignification hypothesis also eliminates the need for any of the pantheistic and panentheistic explications for God's immanence or ongoing action in the world (we will examine Panentheism in Chapter 11).

It is fully acknowledged that the Meta-Transignification hypothesis will forever remain speculative and untestable. In this respect, it shares kinship with many of the age-old philosophical arguments and their modern improvements because they too postulate many things about God-by-whatever-name prior to the advent of the universe. Even so, beyond the many issues it addresses, it accomplishes something keenly important, something missing from our interpretation of religion—a *de-emphasis* of our human chauvinistic perspective to properly place us on the sliding scale of cosmic significance. Religion bespeaks our position as being nothing in comparison to God but at the same time our own self-aggrandizement reinforces a belief that we are the valued creations of God-by-whatever-name.

Let us now set this theory aside and return to the Swinburnian God to further investigate if uncertainty theory in the form of Bayes' theorem can reasonably offer insights on the Abrahamic God.

Is God's Existence Favored by Inferential Probability?

Swinburne concludes his book *The Existence of God* with the summation that Bayesian probability calculus, when injected with the total evidences both pro and con, favors the God Hypothesis (i.e., theism) as the most justified view.[20, 21] Recalling that Swinburne suggests that there is no applicable background knowledge leaving only evidences such as scriptural information, pertinent literary works, and oral beliefs passed down across generations, his conclusion is stated very simply in Bayesian terms as:

$$\mathbf{P}\left(H_g \mid E\right) > \tfrac{1}{2}$$

Whereby all his argumentation that led to the conclusion above comes about because

$$\mathbf{P}\left(E_s \mid H_g\right) > \mathbf{P}\left(E_s \mid {\sim}H_g\right)$$

This is to say that assuming in the first place that theism is true; the specific evidences are better explained by Swinburne's hypothesis in contrast to the case that these specific evidences are explained when considering the accumulation of all rival hypotheses.

He goes further to say that the Resurrection Hypothesis (H_r), which was not used in his God Hypothesis (H_g), greatly bolsters this conclusion. Reflecting on what is presented in Chapters 6 and 7 it is rather more likely the case that the Resurrection Hypothesis actually works to *detract* from Swinburne's case for theism, that is $\mathbf{P}(E_s \mid H_r) < \mathbf{P}(E_s \mid {\sim}H_r)$, where 'r' denotes the Resurrection Hypothesis. However, if we step outside of Swinburne's realm of argumentation, the fact that the Resurrection Hypothesis is untrue would cripple the case solely for the Christian conception of God and not necessarily the Hebrew God, the God of Islam, or any other conception for God-by-whatever-name.

Up to this point, we have focused our attention on sorting through the most powerful arguments to date for the case for God and to a greater extent the Christian/Abrahamic God. What remains to be said is to critique the going assumption that Bayes' theorem is even an appropriate tool to investigate epistemic problems of a divine nature. This has been largely or completely lost in contemporary apologetic or skeptical literature. Let us review one more time Bayes' theorem to come to appreciate this concern.

As I noted in Chapter 6, there are multiple ways to express Bayes' theorem. Each form of the theorem offers a utility that is better used in some circumstances relative to others. In contrast to the Explicit form which provides the *probability* of a hypothesis being true, the Odds form provides the *odds* that the hypothesis is true relative to its negation. So one might say, "Tell me the odds that favor the hypothesis." The response would be, "Given all that we can ascertain, there is a three-to-one likelihood that the hypothesis is true." (mock quote).

$$\underbrace{\frac{\mathbf{P}(H\,|\,E\,\&\,B)}{\mathbf{P}(\sim H\,|\,E\,\&\,B)}}_{\text{Posterior Odds}} = \underbrace{\frac{\mathbf{P}(H\,|\,B)}{\mathbf{P}(\sim H\,|\,B)}}_{\text{Prior Odds}} \times \underbrace{\frac{\mathbf{P}(E\,|\,H\,\&\,B)}{\mathbf{P}(E\,|\sim H\,\&\,B)}}_{\text{Likelihood Ratio}} \qquad \begin{array}{l}\text{Bayes' theorem}\\ \text{Odds Form}\end{array}$$

The prior odds is the ratio of prior probability of *a priori* propositions derived purely by deductive reasoning whereas the posterior odds is the probability ratio of *a posteriori* propositions derived from sensory experience and empirical evidence. The Likelihood Ratio, then, is just the odds that the evidence would be observed if the hypothesis were assumed to be true versus that it was not. Let's review this again in a different manner.

Starting with the first term on the right-hand side of the equation we have the ratio of prior probability of the hypothesis being true to that of its negation (i.e., its falsification). Said another way, it is the prior odds that favor the hypothesis *before* the presentation of specific evidence while relying only on background knowledge (i.e., sourced from reason/logic alone). This is commonly referred to as simply 'the prior'.

$$\frac{\mathbf{P}(H\,|\,B)}{\mathbf{P}(\sim H\,|\,B)} \qquad \text{the prior}$$

The last term on the right-hand side of the equation is called the *Likelihood Ratio*. Also referred to as the *Bayes' factors*, it serves to quantify the evidence in relation to the acceptance of the hypothesis as well as its negation. If it is likely that the evidence will be observed when the hypothesis is assumed to be true, then the Likelihood Ratio will be large.

$$\frac{\mathbf{P}(E\,|\,H\,\&\,B)}{\mathbf{P}(E\,|\sim H\,\&\,B)} \qquad \begin{array}{l}\text{The Likelihood Ratio}\\ \text{(Bayes' factor)}\end{array}$$

The term on the left-hand side of is called the posterior odds which are the odds that the hypothesis is true relative to it not being true *after* inclusion of the evidence.

$$\frac{\mathbf{P}(H \mid E \,\&\, B)}{\mathbf{P}(\sim H \mid E \,\&\, B)} \quad \text{the posterior}$$

If there were multiple *independent* evidences, the equation would take the form as shown below where the subscript 'n' is the total number of independent evidences.

$$\overbrace{\frac{\mathbf{P}(H \mid E_1 \,\&\, E_2 \,\&\, \dots E_n \,\&\, B)}{\mathbf{P}(\sim H \mid E_1 \,\&\, E_2 \,\&\, \dots E_n \,\&\, B)}}^{\text{the posterior}} = \overbrace{\frac{\mathbf{P}(H \mid B)}{\mathbf{P}(\sim H \mid B)}}^{\text{the prior}} \times \overbrace{\left[\frac{\mathbf{P}(E_1 \mid H \,\&\, B)}{\mathbf{P}(E_1 \mid \sim H \,\&\, B)} \times \frac{\mathbf{P}(E_2 \mid H \,\&\, B)}{\mathbf{P}(E_2 \mid \sim H \,\&\, B)} \times \dots \times \frac{\mathbf{P}(E_n \mid H \,\&\, B)}{\mathbf{P}(E_n \mid \sim H \,\&\, B)} \right]}^{\text{Likelihood Ratio / Bayes' factors}}$$

It would be instructive at this point to provide an example to appreciate the mechanics of how this relationship works when put to use. Let us consider the very real situation in modern day times of the very worrisome matter of Iran's (presumed) intent to build a nuclear weapon arsenal. The hypothesis we put forth is a belief that Iran does in fact possess a nuclear warhead which we shall call 'H_{nw}'. We have at our disposal certain specific evidences and background information to qualify the probability that our hypothesis is true. This information carries varying levels of certainty (refer to Table 9-1).

Table 9-1. Belief / Knowledge of Iran's Militarized Nuclear Ambitions

E_1	We possess satellite surveillance imagery of nuclear production sites that suggest that several hundred centrifuges have been delivered. Centrifuges are used to enrich uranium yellow-cake (mostly U-238). About 5,000 centrifuges are needed to produce enough material for a nuclear weapon.
E_2	Iran has not conducted any tests that would infer that it was of an origin consistent with a nuclear detonation.
E_3	Iran possesses a large repository of low-enriched, non-weapons grade uranium yellow cake. This seed material has the potential of being further enriched to be fissile material for use in nuclear warhead.
E_4	The Iranian ruling class testifies vehemently that they have not and are not seeking to enrich the yellow cake to weapons-grade level.
B	Countries that possess nuclear weapons are among the most powerful countries in the world. It has been the historical policy of Iran to preserve and further strengthen its influence in the Middle East. Logically, Iran would pursue nuclear weapons. We will assume that this is a well-regarded true fact by all people.

Recalling that this is a strictly instructional exercise and that it is not intended to reflect current reality necessarily, let us now prescribe numerical values to the probabilities. Beyond this figurative example, these are not arbitrary values but are based on supporting rationale. However, to get to the main point, we will simply assume that we have already laid out all this rationale in comprehensive fashion in advance. Let us begin with the *prior odds*, $\mathbf{P}(H_{nw}|B) / \mathbf{P}(\sim H_{nw}|B)$, which is what the probabilities are for the nuclear weapon hypothesis to be true *without* consideration of the specific evidences (E_1, E_2, E_3, E_4) but given our background knowledge (B). Iran would be motivated to use all means necessary to increase their influence, especially those that have historically been shown to be effective. Therefore, let us prescribe the $\mathbf{P}(H_{nw}|B)$ a value of 0.75 and $\mathbf{P}(\sim H_{nw}|B)$ a value of 0.375. The value of the prior odds is therefore 2.0. **Note, that the *probabilities* must be between zero and one. And, because we are rarely perfectly certain or perfectly uncertain of anything, probabilities are generally never zero or one. Furthermore, the *odds* can be most any number in theory.** However, even if the prior odds are high, this does not necessarily convey that the posterior odds are high. The Likelihood Ratio (alternatively known as *Bayes' factors*) help to decide the ultimate outcome. In the interest of expediency, allow me to assume the Bayes' factors without supplementary rationale or agitation so that we can appreciate more important implications of Bayes' theorem.

$$\frac{\mathbf{P}(E_1 \mid H_{nw} \& B)}{\mathbf{P}(E_1 \mid \sim H_{nw} \& B)} = 2.0 \qquad \frac{\mathbf{P}(E_2 \mid H_{nw} \& B)}{\mathbf{P}(E_2 \mid \sim H_{nw} \& B)} = 0.10$$

$$\frac{\mathbf{P}(E_3 \mid H_{nw} \& B)}{\mathbf{P}(E_3 \mid \sim H_{nw} \& B)} = 10.0 \qquad \frac{\mathbf{P}(E_4 \mid H_{nw} \& B)}{\mathbf{P}(E_4 \mid \sim H_{nw} \& B)} = 0.10$$

$$\underbrace{\frac{P(H_{nw} \mid E \& B)}{P(\sim H_{nw} \mid E \& B)}}_{posterior} = \overbrace{2.0}^{prior} \times \overbrace{[2.0 \times 0.1 \times 10.0 \times 0.1]}^{Bayes' \; factors} = 2.0 \times 0.2 = 0.40$$

Here we see that the prior odds fairly strongly suggest that our hypothesis is true (a value of 2.0), but once all the probability of the evidence was accounted for, the posterior odds were significantly reduced (a value of 0.40). Effectively, the odds are significantly suggestive that Iran is <u>not</u> seeking to build nuclear warheads and one ought maintain that Iran is *not* engaged in building nuclear warheads by better than 2.5-to-1 odds (the inverse of 0.40). If continual monitoring were to be undertaken and it was discovered that a large number of centrifuges were brought on site or by some means that highly-enriched uranium were to be detected, the equation would be updated to reflect this new information.

Let us suppose two different sets of Bayes' factors whereby all the evidences are uniformly weak or uniformly strong. Additionally, let's look at a case where there were, say 10 pieces of uniformly strong evidence but the prior odds are low (e.g., 10%).

Posterior Odds: $\dfrac{\mathbf{P}\left(H_{nw} \mid E \,\&\, B\right)}{\mathbf{P}\left(\sim H_{nw} \mid E \,\&\, B\right)}$

Uniformly **Weak** Evidences: $= 3. \times \left[0.2 \times 0.2 \times 0.2 \times 0.2\right] = 3. \times \left[0.2\right]^4 = 3. \times 0.0016 = \mathbf{0.0048}$

Uniformly **Strong** Evidences: $= 3. \times \left[2.0 \times 2.0 \times 2.0 \times 2.0\right] = 3. \times \left[2.0\right]^4 = 3. \times 16.0 = \mathbf{48.0}$

Many Strong Evidences: $= 0.1 \times \left[2.0\right]^{10} = 0.1 \times 1,024 = \mathbf{102.4}$

From this we can see that a series of weak evidences can seriously weaken the truth of a hypothesis and contrastingly that strong evidences substantially bolster it. The final case demonstrates that if a larger set of evidences whose probability ratio is even modestly greater than one, the *posterior* result can counteract a hypothesis with pessimistic prior odds. These principles are similarly illustrated by the work of philosophers McGrew and Depoe, both of whom favor the validity of inferential probability for theistic hypotheses.[22] It is the utilization of the such insights as identified by McGrew and Depoe that apologists have glommed onto this idea to elucidate as many specific evidences as possible due to the multiplicative power of probability ratios that exceed the value of unity. Hypothetically, if it were to be agreed that the prior odds of God existing is low, let's assume a value of 0.1, then one would only need six independent specific evidences that, individually, would have a Bayes' factor of 1.5 to provide posterior odds slightly greater than unity, thereby allowing one to conclude that theism is the more probable reality.

BAYESIANISM – FINAL COMMENTS

The general theory of Bayesianism has often split adherents into two camps where reconciliation between the two has been very uneven. There are those that swear by *Frequentism*, which is what the lay person might understand as the standard interpretation of probability methodology that draws conclusions from a collection of sample data and on the frequency or proportion of the data. Bayesians on the other hand draw conclusions not on empirical data, rather on the rationalizations of evidentiary sources using mathematical and reasoned intuition. Epistemic Bayesianism functions with a *degree of belief* that is quasi-logical yet reliant on subjective intuition.

A major challenge with the Bayesian approach is the so-called *Problem of the Priors*, a well-known issue whereby it is difficult to assign what the probability should be for something that we are to take as *a priori* knowledge—that is *the prior*. Sometimes this can be rather arbitrary and certainly subject to the biases of those prescribing the values. As philosopher William Talbott summarizes, "Because there is no generally agreed upon solution to the Problem of the Priors, it is an open question whether Bayesian Confirmation Theory has inductive content, or whether it merely translates the framework for rational belief provided by deductive logic into a corresponding framework for rational degrees of belief."[23] On the plus side, as the number of independent evidences increases, the relative effects of the prior become somewhat diminished.

When applied to philosophic hypotheses, a key attribute of Bayesianism seldom called to our attention is that our background knowledge and specific evidences on which we assign our "degree of belief" is dependent on our individual knowledge of the totality of reality. Furthermore, this assignment is time-specific. Expanding on these two comments, we collectively often do not operate with a common reference frame when it comes to assessing background knowledge or specific evidences. It is very much a matter of argument as much as it is a matter of fact. We only need look at how hard it is for everyone to come to agree on universal truths to appreciate this situation. Additionally, an individual's beliefs might change if we take in information at different points along the time continuum. That is, what is true in the past may not be true of the present. I also wish to differentiate the changing of one's beliefs based on new information and the implementation of the technique of Bayesian Updating. The former is subject to various cognitive biases and the latter is intended to update beliefs based on well-objectified information. These range of issues put into question the validity of the posterior results (i.e., final outcome) of Bayes' theorem.

After examining aspects of Swinburne's rationalizations both in terms of what other scholars have said and what I have surmised, it is clear that we must come to terms with numerous catastrophic flaws. We also come to the conclusion that statistical inferential analysis is a poor choice of tool. This is not to be confused with concluding that God exists or that he does not exist. Rather, what we are saying here is that *we cannot reasonably infer whether or not God exists based on Bayes' theorem*. This will not stop philosophers and apologists from developing probability computations in the future, but on the whole, the underlayment is constructed from the weak fabric of personal intuition, differing knowledge sets, differing abilities to objectively qualify evidences, and the ever-so uncertain valuation of the prior probability. The specific evidences would have to be cumulatively overwhelming and essentially uncontestable for inferential probability to be of much utility. But, *if* we were to accept Bayes' theorem as a proper tool, then the evidence and rival hypotheses reviewed herein would suggest that the odds do not favor the existence of the Abrahamic God regardless of whether one adopts or declines the Triune nature of this Being.

While other inductive methods exist to model reducible epistemic uncertainty,[16] these are very unlikely to alter the calculus appreciably nor will it affect the final outcome. If none of these paradigms are apt to enlighten us on the truth of the Abrahamic God, then by extension, it cannot offer anything for the truth of God-by-whatever-name. Stepping away from uncertainty theory altogether, using deductive top-down inference alone, we *are able* to determine that God is possible or impossible, but we *are unable* to determine with certainty that he exists. Emma Beckman puts it thusly:

> [emphasis Beckman's]

> The deductive method allows merely for conclusions concerning what is possible or impossible. Propositions claiming something to exist are contingent. The fact that it is *possible* that God exists does not imply that he *does* exist, but if it is *impossible* that God exists, he *cannot* and *does not exist*. In other words: it may be proved by deductive inference that God *does not* exist, but never that God *does* exist.[24]

Let me break down this powerful conclusion. Beckman is telling us that we are free to generally theorize about God's existence and collect observations and evidence. And, should this effort affirms God's existence, then such an existence is dependent on the data and all the assumptions thereunder. Some of these assumptions necessarily are rooted in understanding what the fundamental nature of reality is in concert with and apart from our human conceptions. **Given that what comprises reality is uncertain, *God can never be reasoned to exist with certainty*. In contrast, and speaking hypothetically, if God needed to breathe air to survive, and he were to live in outer space where air does not exist, we could deductively infer that it would be impossible for God to exist.**

Contemporary Mystical Theology – The Last Anchor Point for the Abrahamic God

In Chapter 2, we discussed the metaphysical mysteries of *cataphaticism* (positive theology) and *apophaticism* (negative theology). It is now necessary to return to this discussion to

---

16. It is called reducible because the uncertainty can be reduced. Other uncertainty theories include the Dempster-Shafer Theory, Coherent Upper and Lower Previsions Theory, Possibility Theory, Evidence Theory, Transferable Belief Model, and Gap-Decision Theory.

further unwind these two theological ideas because whether or not we will ever be in a position to clarify God's existence, we must appreciate the rationality that theologians would have us understand about the supposed nature of God.[17] Cataphaticism attempts to affirmatively describe the nature of God using reason and revelation. The success of this endeavor is best depicted as an imperfect tracing of the outline of God rather than the filling of the canvas. In constrast, apophaticism conjectures that God is ineffable and therefore we possess a total (but learned) ignorance of this divine essence. Recall that negative theology is *not* the inverse or negation of positive theology. Rather, apophaticism suggests that, try as we might to scale the full height of our intellect, now or for generations to come, it will always be a fruitless endeavor. Apophasis is in some comparative sense akin to the inexpressible Jewish theonym for God (i.e., the Tetragrammaton transliterated as YHWH). In their view, it is beyond the ability of humans to pronounce or verbalize the true name of the Hebrew God and to do so would be **PEJORATIVE**. A foremost proponent of natural theology, Thomas Aquinas saw the opposites of positive and negative theology as working together, very much paralleling the Chinese philosophy of yin and the yang—polar dualities working in tandem. Ultimately, these constructs are the very essence that underwrites the faith of billions. The zetetic process has muscled the two mighty chains of positive and negative theology taut as they strain to anchor the Abrahamic conception of God to solid ground.

Let us first refresh our memory that Christianity is divided into Western and Eastern traditions. Western Latin traditions include Roman Catholicism and Protestantism accounting for about 90% of all Christians. Eastern Orthodox (Greek) Christianity was created by doctrinal differences arising out of the East-West Schism that arose around 1054 CE.[18] Western traditions, as defended by the majority of Christian apologists, lean to a great extent toward the superiority of cataphatic theology whereas Eastern traditions lean decidedly in the other direction. Eastern Christianity shares similar thoughts about the Triune God existing in hypostasis and in the revealed knowledge of Scripture. It is believed that the Second Person (i.e., Jesus) was a presence of this Earth who was 100% human and 100% divine (at all times). This is a challenge unto itself because a human being, who also possesses characteristics befitting a deity, is not truly human, but something more than human. Eastern Christian theology believes that God is an uncreated, immaterial, eternal, and incomprehensible essence (even to angels) that possesses inseparable divine energies. He is regarded as an **APODICTIC** truth and not subject to philosophical speculation. And yet,

---

17. As noted in Chapter 1, Judaism and Islam have correlates to Christian apophatic and cataphatic theology. Kabbalism is form of Jewish mysticism, whereas Sufism is the counterpart in Islamic doctrine.

18. These differences, in part, include the interpretations of apostolic succession, the seven sacraments, and the transubstantiation of the Eucharistic bread and wine into a divine substance.

it is believed that human beings are connected to God through these divine energies even though we cannot comprehend the divine essence. This is logically troublesome because if God's Second Person did become an earthly Being, it means that there is *something* we can understand about the nature of God during his thirty-some years on Earth.

Regardless of affectation, all flavors of Christianity profess a belief in both theological mysticisms to some degree. The question before us is whether or not this dual position is rationally coherent. By definition, a theology is a construct that analyzes the existence (or otherness), nature, and relationships associated with God from which religious truth claims are promulgated. Recalling our working definition of truth that if a theology is not fundamentally coherent, then its legitimacy is undermined (refer again to TC-8 – Coherency of Reality, p. 52). If we were to abandon this truth condition, then we would wedge ourselves into the corner of fideism—a place where our questioning of God ends and the Many-Faced God Conundrum rears-up (refer to Chapter 1, p. 18). We already identified two concerning incoherencies above. Namely, it is incoherent to claim that Jesus was both 100 percent human and 100 percent divine. Secondly, it makes little sense to claim that human beings have no ability to comprehend God if in the same theology one also claims that Jesus the Nazarene was God incarnate who walked the sands of Judea and who ate, drank, bled, and died in human form. At the very least, people back then knew his nature to some degree.

Cataphatic theology is considerably easier to understand because we possess a language set that can ostensibly describe what God's nature is to some appreciable extent. While no human truly understands the unboundedness of omnipotence (power far in excess of that needed to create the universe), omniscience, or eternity, we have at least a vague sense of what these mean. Christianity professes that the Almighty God is in our midst and we access him through prayer and that God may elect to intercede to fulfill these prayers.[19] Indeed, the doctrine affirms that God works mysteriously through his performance of miracles that at times may appear **NUGATORY** and at other times genuinely wondrous.

In several of his homilies, Pope Francis proclaims Jesus as the deified Savior and that God is real and concrete:

> Christianity, [...] is not a philosophical doctrine, it is not a programme of life that enables one to be well formed and to make peace. These are its consequences. Christianity is a person, a person lifted up on the Cross. A person who emptied himself to save us. He took on sin. And so just as in

---

19. Protestants only pray to God or Jesus, but not to saints or Mary, Jesus' mother.

the desert sin was lifted up, here God made man was lifted up for us. And all of our sins were there. [...] one cannot understand Christianity without understanding this profound humiliation of the Son of God who humbled himself and made himself a servant unto death on the Cross. To serve.[25]

(below, the introductory comment is provided by a reporter summarizing Pope Francis's remarks. These are followed by actual quoted words by the Pontiff himself)

[...] many people say they believe in God, but what kind of God do they believe in exactly? God is a real person -- a father -- and faith springs forth from a tangible experience of an encounter with him, the pope told his listeners. [...] "We believe in God who is Father, who is Son, who is Holy Spirit" [...] "We believe in persons and when we talk to God we speak with persons" who are concrete and tangible, not some misty, diffused god-like " 'god-spray,' that's a little bit everywhere but who knows what it is."[26]

Pope Francis's remarks make God out to be a distinct Being made presumptively of material substance that is a divine Person accessible to humanity. He also clearly delineates that God is not a dispersed substance which is the central belief of pantheists.

The doctrine of the Catholic Church, as professed in the authoritative book *Catechism of The Catholic Church* affirms that God is predominantly a mystery, but aspects of him are knowable. The following excerpts highlight Catholicism's doctrinal attachment to both apophaticism and cataphaticism.[27]

Table 9-2. Catholic Doctrine – Apophatic & Cataphatic Mysticism

Apophatic Statement	**42** God transcends all creatures. We must therefore continually purify our language of everything in it that is limited, image bound or imperfect, if we are not to confuse our image of God—"the inexpressible, the incomprehensible, the invisible, the ungraspable"—with our human representations. Our human words always fall short of the mystery of God.
Cataphatic Statement	**48** We really can name God, starting from the manifold perfections of his creatures, which are likenesses of the infinitely perfect God, even if our limited language cannot exhaust the mystery.
Cataphatic Statement	**51** "It pleased God, in his goodness and wisdom, to reveal himself and to make known the mystery of his will. His will was that men should have access to the Father, through Christ, the Word made flesh, in the Holy Spirit, and thus become sharers in the divine nature."

God's activity, whether confined to the creation of the universe and the Resurrection or daily interaction or something in between poses philosophical problems as to whether this impinges on our free will. The various problems that arise have already been extensively debated in the Philosophy of Religion so I will not articulate them here. Suffice it to say that one has to wrestle with God's supposed omniscience in the context of there being a past, present, future, and the potentiality for an eternal existence and the dilemma of a timeless knowledge all the while we humans go about making decisions and forge our future. It becomes quite unclear as to who ultimately is in control of our destiny, if any such thing even exists.

There is to be no doubt that cataphatic theology is now being recognized by Christian (or once Christian) societies as a highly unstable belief system, even if few understand the mechanics of philosophy at work. With the changing landscape from traditional religiosity to a de-traditionalized Europe and United States, there is a very tangible culturally motivated drive toward apophaticism. The undercurrent is so strong that Catholic theologian Lieven Boeve questions if "negative theology [is] the future of all Christian theology?"[28,29] Of course, whether or not general society's beliefs change, it does not usually alter the actual theological doctrine. Though, this is how religious schisms and sects often come about.

After all that has been said, it would be fair to suggest that cataphatic belief is buckling under its own weight of misconceptions arising from the particularities of Scripture, the incarnate and resurrected Christ, the divinity of Christ, and the incoherencies of the Holy Trinity. If there is no Resurrection, there is no divine Christ. If there is no divine Christ, there is no logical, ontological, or metaphysical use for a Holy Spirit who is envisioned as a mediating entity between God and Son. We are then left with one prospective God of a single identity, not three. We also find no empirical or natural proof that God is represented by some or all of the hyperbolic terminologies we tend to ascribe. This theology is also seriously weakened because, whether or not one wants to apply Bayes' theorem to estimate the probability of God, we have either determined that God is unlikely to exist or we cannot say anything at all about the likelihood of his existence. **At best, the cataphatic nature of God is left unexplained. At worst, cataphatic mysticism is a misguided, even fallacious attempt to comprehend the great essence that is God. Under the strain of all that has been discussed thus far, the chain jerks and is severed loose from its irrational grounding.**

Given that such conclusions lead us to an **APORETIC** state on positive theology, Christianity is left with the lone chain of negative theology to hold it fast. On apophaticism, Wesleyan University Professor of Religion Mary-Jane Rubenstein reckons that "*definition* in this case counteracts the work of that which it defines."[30] What is often stated is that God's essence cannot be described as being existent or nonexistent. Additionally, he is also not of our material realm physically or in any transitive sense. He is simply beyond our linguistic capabilities, our sensory abilities, and our intellect. Strong apophaticism[20] (regardless of the Christian, Jewish, or Islamic interpretation) offers no grounding point whatsoever to comprehend God. The Strong version even negates the concept of atheism because the latter relies on a statement of belief that God does not exist. While atheism might be on firm footing to say that God does not exist *in this universe*, it does not address the **ETIOLOGICAL** concerns of what created the universe.

What is most important to understand is that if God is truly beyond comprehension, then he is also beyond any human-developed theology. That is, there is no such thing as a valid religious (i.e., theologically-oriented) truth claim! [21] This is a very important conclusion for which we will revisit at the end of the book.

This final point is precisely why both Eastern and Western Christianity are in an intractable bind. Neither tradition seems to wholly accept the Strong form of apophatic theology; rather they describe the connection between positive and negative theology in extra-ordinarily cryptic fashion. Christianity, regardless of tradition or denomination, levitates somewhere between the two positions of Weak apophaticism[22] and cataphaticism. Frankly, Christian orthodoxy, Eastern or Western, is very unclear where its rests in concrete terms. Christian headmasters want to claim everyone has personal access to an all-loving, perfect, and singular God but in the same sentence they maintain he is beyond most all comprehension. It is believed by Christians that God visited Earth in human form for a very short span of time and at all other times is a completely enigmatic entity existing everywhere but is in no way detectable. We only infer his existence through spontaneous miraculous events that unfold repeatedly across human history.

If Christianity adopts the Strong form of apophasis, then they have killed themselves by their own hand by making themselves completely irrelevant because such a divorce of comprehension renders all theology inoperative. Therefore, they only 'lean toward'

---

20. I take the liberty of calling Strong apophaticism (or equally, Strong negative theology) the position where God is ineffable in totality and is therefore beyond theological circumscription. As such, it is not compatible with cataphaticism which makes affirmative truth claims via scriptural and sacred referents.

21. Buddhism is not a technically a theology. According to Catholic theologian and philosopher Raimundo Panikkar, Buddha's orientation is best described as transcendental apophaticism. (*The Silence of God: the Answer of the Buddha*, Orbis Books; June 1989, ISBN 0-88344-446-1)

22. Weak (or diluted) apophaticism is the position that incoherently posits God's ineffability while also retaining some attachment to cataphaticism. Weak apophaticism is essentially the position of Eastern Christianity.

apophatic belief of an extra-cosmic Father as they grasp in one hand the now flailing chain of cataphatic beliefs entailing revelatory Scripture, the incarnation and Resurrection of Jesus, and the Holy Trinity. **So, as it were, there has always existed, but rarely recognized as such, an irresolvable tension leading to an incoherency of truth. The mastheads of Christianity have managed to maneuver around this obstacle because they would prefer to leave their understanding of God as a 'great mystery', a 'mystery within a mystery', or to say that 'by unknowing him, we come to know him'. By occupying this position, they have successfully confused everyone by intoning that God is a continuous loop wherein closure is always beyond reach as they go about their business proselytizing the endless love of this enigmatic God and herding ignorant lambs into their stable. The combinatorial approach of positive theology and Weak (diluted) negative theology is thusly unmoored from its final anchor to endlessly spin about in the realm of incoherency.**

Strong apophasis does have a flaw in its attempt to clear the table on the nature of God, because it admits to having knowledge of the table. That is, it affirms knowledge of its very existence. In the words of acclaimed French philosopher Jacques Derrida (the father of Deconstructionism), "all negative theologies ultimately posit a hyperessence beyond essence."[31] If we can describe God in this ephemeral way, as possessing a hyperessentiality, then he is in effect *within* the limits of our intellect, even if it is at the most distant periphery of such limits.

A final point regarding Strong apophaticism may be in order. With the inability to effectively describe God-by-whatever-name's existence in terms other than a hyperessence, we travel perilously close to a lesser known ideology called *theological noncognitivism* (also synonymously referred to as Ignosticism and Igtheism).[23] This ideology denies the meaningfulness of religious, or more accurately, theological language and argumentation (i.e., apologetics) considering them as completely irrelevant. That is, because there is no coherent definition for God-by-whatever-name, entering into a dialogue is nonsensical. An example of a grammatically correct but meaningless sentence would be: "The circular triangles jump quickly as ideas sleep forcefully in linear closed holes." Analogically, this is how a conversation on the topic of God or theism would go. If all we can know about God is that he is a hyperessence with no quantifiable or intelligible characteristics this is very close to having no language that would describe him. If this is the right way to conceive God, then given the entrenched position of religion in society both

---

23. The word *"ignosticism"* was coined in the 1960's by Rabbi Sherwin Wine, a founding figure of Humanistic Judaism. Some have also equated ignosticism with *"igtheism"* which was coined by Paul Kurtz, a secular humanist, in his book *The New Skepticism: Inquiry and Reliable Knowledge*, 1992, p. 188

ancient and contemporary and all that has ever been written in the name of religion, it would be hard to forecast when Ignostic ideology could be embraced as a universal position.

In the end, both positive and negative theology offer highly speculative postulations about the Abrahamic God. But because these serve as the veritable pillars to support central religious truth claims, this is truly a concerning affair. Christianity and its Abrahamic cousins sit upon an unbalanced fulcrum. With positive theology torn asunder and Strong apophaticism telling us virtually nothing at all about the nature of God, the only thing resting upon the mantle of prospective truth is an Otherness we describe as an enigmatic hyperessence. This hyperessence is ostensibly the creative force responsible for originating the universe, so I will refer to this characterization of God as the '**Source**' in honor of Wayne Dyer, the preeminent self-improvement guru who I must credit as having introduced me to this terminology. While I would not consider Dyer's views as my own, he embraced this transcendent Source as the *Infinite Source*—an unintelligible, eternal, life-giving resevoir of energy pervading the universe that any person can connect to, to fulfill one's needs and wants.

Stepping past how we might term this hyperessence, Christianity is disrobed of all its weighty vestments and sits as equals with all similarly denuded religions. Theistic faith, then, is universally distilled (some might say deconstructed) to a singular belief in a Source that is forever beyond our reach **in all ways. We might even go so far as to say that what we have arrived at is a *Deconstructed Pluralism* whereby the complexities and incoherencies of Religious Pluralism (discussed in the next chapter) simply evaporate to become a singular signature—a unifying rally point if you will. Under such provisions, any and all connection to God is lost. This effectively eliminates the need for any theological doctrine whatsoever thereby coring out the heart of virtually all religion.** But this doesn't necessarily mean the end to religion. It would, however, indicate a need for a seismic shift away from claiming that one vision of God is better than any other. Religious institutions could universally celebrate the same ineffable God with all related tensions, language, and symbology falling away. Religious institutions could still maintain ownership over the necessary changes of their own unique rituals to be consistent with adoption this new outlook.

There is, however, one particularly sticky issue that sticks out like a sore thumb. While the zetetic approach has dismantled a host of traditional religious embodiments of God, we have not discerned whether or not the nature of this Source's existence is immanent, transcendent, or some combination thereof relative to our universe. More to the point, can this indiscernible and enigmatic Source act upon or within the universe? This matter will be taken up in forthcoming chapters.

THE SHRINKING SPACE FOR GOD-BY-WHATEVER-NAME

Our heroic journey has taken us far. We have reached a major milestone in our zetetic approach where we have re-marked, sharpened, and reduced the perimeter of God. In fact, if theological noncognitivism prevails, we find ourselves flattened up-against an impermeable wall seperating our mind-based universe from God. The assumptions that have carried us this far is that we have stayed true to the path we set out upon by resisting invocation of deific actions (i.e., miracles, revelation), the paraintellect, and personal revelatory experiences. **We have traveled through a veritable forest of philosophy, theology, archaeology, history, and science to arrive at a compelling realization. Should he exist at all, the Abrahamic conception—the God of some 62 percent of the world's population—is highly unlikely to be an accurate portrayal of God.**

Because the Abrahamic truth claims are so severely weakened, some have sought to reconcile the gaps by looking at religion and faith with the wide lens of Religious Pluralism or by re-defining classical theism by re-tooling panentheistic ideas in the form of Christian Panentheism. This will be our next step forward to understand whether we can better affirm God's existence or to zero-in on his modal qualities to give any form to the now shapeless Source.

SUMMARY

Up and until this chapter, our expedition took us on an odyssey that examined the critical underpinnings of religious belief from ancient times, focusing predominantly on Judaism and Christianity which are in central respects precursors to Islam. These three traditions share a common origin as all three claim a direct lineage to Abraham (originally called Abram) a patriarch believed to have lived c. 2000 BCE. There is, however, an important difference between the Abrahamic faiths. Judaism maintains their connection to Abraham through the lineage of generations, that is, by birthright whereas Christianity claims Abraham as the patriarch of all prophets as an article of faith. Islam on the other hand sees ancestral heritage as unimportant. While Abraham himself is important, he is one of many prophets who came after Adam and before the most important prophet, Muhammad.[32]

Theologically-speaking, there are greater differences in the understanding of God. The Hebrew God and the God of Islam is a singular Being that is both a wrathful and benevolent God. The Christian God sheds most traces of choleric temperament[24] of the Old Testament God and is painted as a Being of perfect love, comprised of three indivisible Persons existing in consubstantial hypostatic union. The God of Islam is formulated from the Qur'an and Hadith[25] and is regarded as a singular entity attributed with largely the same capabilities as ascribed by Christianity and Judaism (e.g., omnipotence, omniscience, all-merciful, creator, sustainer, ordainer, and judge of the universe). God is likewise considered eternally existent. A central difference between Christianity and Islam is that the former has Jesus as a divine savior for people whereas Islam's **SOTERIOLOGY** is that people themselves are responsible for saving their own soul.

The zetetic march had also largely maneuvered around the crowded village of philosophical/theistic Arguments that have been registered and tweaked for millennia (e.g., the Cosmological, Ontological, Teleological, Axiological, etc. ... Arguments). While many of these have been masterfully massaged by the greatest of minds that ever lived, it is questionable how these efforts have had a measurable effect on determining the existence or nature of God. In their efforts to clarify the positions of any given treatise, the scholarly dragons have effectively made it more complex and therefore intractable to the

---

24. Jesus, as an indivisible person of the Holy Trinity, does show anger toward his people. For example, Jesus throws out the moneylenders in the Temple (Mark 11:15; Matthew 21:12; John 2:15-19). Jesus also is angered by the Pharisees' lack of faith (Mark 3:5).

25. The Hadith is a compilation of the life, conduct, and sayings of Muhammad.

Common Man. Even conscientious students of philosophy and theology are challenged by such encounters.

After re-committing to the zetetic approach, we engaged one of, if not *the* most effective, contemporary attempts to validate God's existence. By employing methods of epistemic philosophy, specifically Bayes' theorem, we critiqued the prolific body of work by Oxford Philosopher and Christian apologist Richard Swinburne. While his approach is portable to each of the Abrahamic religions, his intent was to defend the Christian conception. The initial focus was directed at Swinburne's argumentation for the definition of God's monadic properties and how this relates to the conditionality of God being any or all of metaphysically, ontologically, and logically necessary. In order to arrive at the pre-established Christian conception of the Holy Trinity, God can neither be ontologically or logically necessary. His argumentation to denounce these latter conditions possessed little to no merit. So too we find that his reliance on God's supposed simplicity as an adequate justification is equally as problematic. While putting aside his claims, when further reviewing the rationale he puts forward to justify the three personages of God (Father, Son, and Holy Spirit), he creates even more fault lines of incoherency.

In an effort to turn the tables, he parries with an avant-garde move with his use of inferential probability. He employs an array of arguments to generate his propositions—Cosmological, Teleological, Problem of Evil, Consciousness, and Miracles. Due to spatial limitations and because it was the strongest of the positions offered, we only reviewed Swinburne's cosmological argument. In applying Bayes' theorem, he arrives at the conclusion that God exists is more likely than not (in probability terms, that $\mathbf{P}(H_g|E) > \frac{1}{2}$) which follows from the fact that specific evidences are best explained by his hypothesis than by rival hypotheses, that is, $\mathbf{P}(E_s|H_g) > \mathbf{P}(E_s|\sim H_g)$. It is after all of his exhaustive elaboration that he ultimately resorts to applying his own intuition on implicitly characterizing the prior probability and Bayes' factors.

In examining a hypothetical example regarding a hypothesis that Iran is seeking a nuclear weapon, we discerned the mechanics of Bayes' theorem (using the Odds form) and that this informs certain strategies to shape the probabilities. Christian apologists have been hard at work trying to identify additional evidences that would favor the Resurrection (H_r) and Theistic (H_g) hypotheses. So too, they argue for higher valuations of the Bayesian prior and additional evidence that might lower valuations for the probability of rival hypotheses.

Arriving at the *best* inference is wholly reliant on capturing all relevant knowledge for both the initiating hypothesis and its rivals. Foundational weaknesses of using Bayes' theorem for epistemic problems of a divine nature are exposed. The probability (or odds) is inextricably linked to the (1) the knowledge set of the operator(s) of the analysis, (2) the objectivity applied in processing this information, (3) the timing of when the knowledge is accumulated, and finally (4) the caliber of intellectual and intuitional capability of the individual. If any of these are in any way lacking, the inference is indelibly affected. So too we always encounter the unresolved *Problem of the Priors* and how we are to assign a probability in the absence of all existing rationalizations. While initially very enticing, we come to the practical conclusion that the application of uncertainty theory (Bayes' theorem or other competitive theoretical constructs) is not a particularly useful approach for this type of metaphysical introspection.

With inferential probability theory put aside and a greater appreciation for the particularities of the Abrahamic God, vis-à-vis the Christian God, we waded back into the dark waters of esoteric mysticism. In an attempt to sketch the **WHORLS** and **ARCHES** for the thumb print of God, positive theology marks out a list of monadic properties that are ultimately unsupportable. It was also deemed unlikely that God could be the great interventionist that Christian doctrine would have us believe (though, this will be more deeply investigated in our discussion on Christian Panentheism). Because of scientific **POSITIVISM** and rationalizations such as those recorded in this book, modern theologians have gravitated toward negative theology as a better stronghold to stage a last line of defense.

In order to bring clarity to the utter confusion surrounding apophaticism, negative theology was segmented into Strong and Weak (diluted) forms. The combinatory position of positive theology mixed with Weak negative theology, the effective position of both Eastern and Western Christianity, was shown to be incoherently unstable. Strong apophaticism is essentially the same position as ignosticism because both ideologies maintain that human language and cognition are incapable of describing God's nature making God unknowable. In spite of this limitation, Strong apophaticism signals that we can vaguely access God through his benevolence in the form of his grace, the gift of human life, the gift of our consciousness to be self-contemplative, the beauty in the cosmos, and by the initial presumption that a divine essence exists in the first place. On the other hand, ignosticism sidesteps these esoteric claims, because if God is so ineffable then the most rational course of action is to abandon *all* discourse on the topic of God.

We closed this chapter by conjecturing that Strong apophaticism and ignosticism share a great deal of commonality that has not been previously discussed in the scholarly literature. This may be in part be because the definition of apophaticism in relation to the various Christian religions are not unanimous on what the term means and where exactly in the spectrum of apophaticism they respecitvely sit. Christian doctrine likes to present God as beyond comprehension and yet somehow ascribes many characteristics of God. The situation is best captured by Winston Churchill's famous expression, "It is a riddle, wrapped in a mystery, inside an enigma; [...]."[33] When we finally pierce and force open the petals of this flowery construct, there is almost nothing on the inside. Assuming that God exists at all—something we could never verify with complete certainty—we arrive at the RADICAL, and perhaps for some, disappointing one-dimensional statement. **The Source is forever to be a perfectly mysterious hyperessence that may have created all of reality ... and nothing more ... which is to confer that we cannot go further to describe its ontology in any way whatsoever.**

Since its inception, theism has been gripped by a restless internal struggle. Initially, polytheistic pantheons of gods were humanized and anthropomorphized by their familial relationships, hierarchy, cooperation, treachery, love, and hate. Over time the pantheons overcame and/or intermixed with pantheons from other cultures. Over millennia, the number of gods dwindled from polytheism into monolatrism which gave way to monotheism. Atheistic notions began filtering in around 600 BCE which proffered a disbelief in the existence of some deities. This created another source of robust rivalry for theism in general. The inter- and intra-religious tension has made for a society at continual unease with itself.

The admittedly speculative Meta-Transignification hypothesis was put forward to demonstrate a plausible alternative construction for the Cosmic Creator's one-time existence. While one may be troubled by a God that would re-purpose his existence in a way that his essence is no longer a living presence (within or outside of the universe), this is not to be thought of as self-termination. Rather, this can be thought in analogous human terms of a human being giving one's own life to save the life of another where the one yielding their life believes he/she does so for a greater good and that their soul will be in a better place for all eternity. Or, alternatively, much like a painter creates a work of art which may have aesthetic value well beyond his or her own death. The Cosmic Creator achieves bliss with his final act of significance—the creation of this wondrous cosmos.

In an odd sort of way, the Meta-Transignification Hypothesis is compatible with Strong apophaticism because we can find no useful words that would describe the nature of the Source. The only serious difference between the two ideas is that apophaticism attests to the position that God still exists to this day whereas the other counters this notion.

CHAPTER 10

Pluralism & the New Sciences of Religion

Religion is important for humanity, but it should evolve with humanity. The first priority is to establish and develop the principle of pluralism in all religious traditions. If we, the religious leaders, cultivate a sincere pluralistic attitude, then everything will be more simple. It is good that most religious leaders are at least beginning to recognize other traditions, even though they may not approve of them. The next step is to accept that the idea of propagating religion is outdated. It no longer suits the times.[1]

> – Dalai Lama XIV (Tenzin Gyatso), Tibetan Buddhist Monk
> A Conversation with The Dalai Lama

Do not be idolatrous about or bound to any doctrine, theory, or ideology, even Buddhist ones. All systems of thought are guiding means; they are not absolute truth.[2]

> – Thich Nhat Hanh, Vietnamese Zen Buddhist Monk
> Founder of Engaged Buddhism
> The quotation is the first of fourteen precepts of Engaged Buddhism

There will be no peace among the nations without peace among the religions. There will be no peace among the religions without dialogue among the religions.[3]

> – Hans Küng, Roman Catholic Theologian
> "Living Buddha, Living Christ"
> A progressive Roman Catholic theologian seeking church reform, he notably argued for the rejection of papal infallibility in his book "Infallible? An Inquiry" (1971). This resulted in the Vatican rescinding Hans Küng's authority to teach Catholic theology in 1979.

The Growth of World Population, World Religion, and Irreligion

IN THE DECADE THAT SPANNED 2000 – 2010, the world population increased annually by about 1.20%. Islam was the fastest growing religion at 1.86%/year. Christianity came in a close second averaging 1.31%/year. In contrast, while the number of agnostics and atheists also grew, their rate of growth was tepid at just 0.32%/year and 0.05%/year, respectively.[4] The long-term worldwide religious trends are depicted in Figure 10-1[5] and Figure 10-2[6].

It is clear from Figure 10-1 that religious growth is being driven by the Christian and Muslim faith traditions. All other religions in aggregate are falling as a share of the population. While exact figures for 2050 are not reported for US adults in Figure 10-3,[7, 8] the general trends will continue as shown going from 2014 to 2050 wherein Christianity will decline and the Nones (i.e., the unaffiliated) will grow.[1] When comparing Figure 10-1, Figure 10-2, and Figure 10-3, the trends in the United States are the *reverse* of that seen worldwide. Whereas Protestantism and Catholicism will tend to grow elsewhere, in the United States it will decline as a percentage of the population. And conversely, Agnosticism/Atheism will decrease outside the US but will conversely increase within the US. **What seems clear is that the United States will become more and more religiously unaffiliated but not necessarily less theistic. The reason is that many of the disaffiliated will retain some degree of theistic belief resulting in a personalized and syncretistic conception of God.**

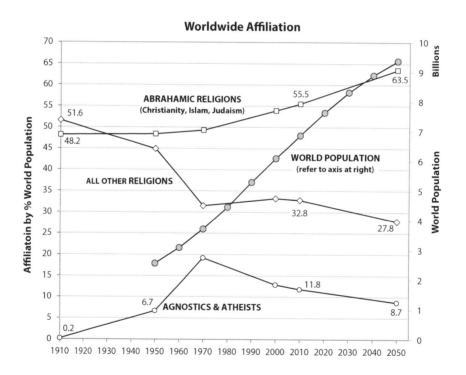

Figure 10-1. Summary of Worldwide Affiliation

---

1. In this same time frame, Muslims will double to a little more than two percent of the total US population. Hindus will grow to less than two percent and those of the Jewish religion will decrease to around one percent of the total population.

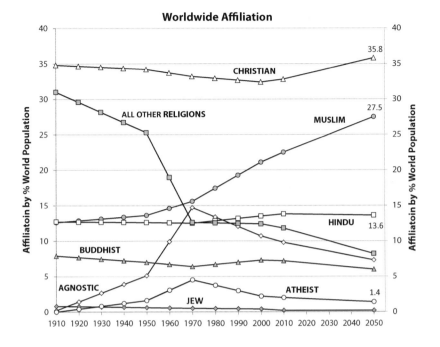

Figure 10-2. Worldwide Affiliation by Major Groups

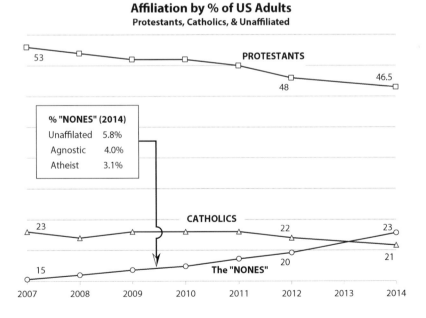

Figure 10-3. Affiliation by Adults (United States)

These charts partially represent how religious and irreligious affiliation is always in a state of flux due to population growth (the net between births and deaths), population migration, religious transmittance by conversion or upbringing, cultural and political evolution, an increase in our set of knowledge and capability to extend that knowledge, and a subtle yet powerful undercurrent of the relative level of fear or peace present in a given society. While a change in affiliation is an understandable human phenomenon, the more intriguing matter is the proliferation of unique theologies via syncretic combinations to create a vast and complex landscape that entertain many thousands of different ways to name, interpret, and honor God-by-whatever-name.

THE CONTINUAL REVAMPING OF RELIGION

In the garden of religion, it is the case that some never reach maturity and among those that do, the majority eventually wither or stagnate. Others mushroom to great heights only to splinter into schismatic off-shoots. We see this prominently in the 2,400 Protestant denominations in the United States[2] along with the 43,000 Christian denominations globally.[2,10] This continual evolution of new religious movements comes about because of the unwillingness of 'Tradition X's' ecclesiastical authorities to alter what they see as their righteous and essentially immutable theology. Regardless of the particularities of all these denominations, the prior chapters outlined the fractured foundations of fundamental doctrine shared by all of them.

These failings stirred a renaissance for other religious and philosophical concepts to take root. This tension had an interesting effect when, in the 1820's, Mormonism was founded. In 1838, by supposed revelations from God to its founder Joseph Smith, the movement was given the official name *The Church of Jesus Christ of Latter-day Saints*. Rather than to introduce some new twist to existing Christian doctrine like the thousands of other Christian denominations before and since, Mormonism is better thought of as a restorational movement to return to the primitive apostolic ways and to rely more so on more recent revelations (i.e., those given to founder Joseph Smith). So much so, an entirely new sacred text was created by Smith in 1830—the *Book of Mormon*. The book is essentially a compilation of prophetic narratives by ancient peoples who had inhabited the American Continent, which is unlike the Abrahamic religions which were founded in the Middle East.

---

2. The tremendous diversity of Christian belief may surprise many. Some are annoyed, considering the figures outlandish. They point out that those who assembled the data separated sects by minor differences in rites or over-counted because a sect whose borders spanned more than one country was counted for each country the religion was practiced. Nevertheless, it is fair to say that many hundreds to many thousands of Christian beliefs are practiced.

The creation of Mormonism did little to alter the course of the deterioration of the discipline of Philosophy of Religion. It would take an appeal to a much more grandiose thesis, that of *Religious Pluralism* (hereafter pluralism), to inject new vitality into the veins of philosophical dialectics. The ideas of pluralism have been around for centuries, but these ideas were revamped to renew its initial intrigue to understand God-by-whatever-name, or more aptly, *God-by-most-names* as we shall soon observe.

Religious Pluralism (Religious Diversity)

The origin of the majority of wars over history have centered on the preservation and accumulation of physical, monetary, and personnel resources as well as to fulfill the needs of egoists whose ethos is directed at amassing power and influence and the institutionalization of one cultural viewpoint over another. Thematically, religion was much more seldom the rationale for war. In more recent times, societal forces have accelerated change across many facets of life. There are religious factions that do not welcome such change and self-justify radicalized militarism to reinforce their dogma. Societal change for them translates to the demise and potential annihilation of their belief system. With the ready access to arms and the inability of world powers to engage every incident of religious oppression or extremism, certain religions with a self-righteous theology successfully **FOMENT** violence in the name of the sacred.

With the expectant friction generated by each religion claiming to possess the superior vision of truth, religious pluralism emerged as a social lubricant. Pluralism acknowledges that many, but importantly not all, faith traditions can *concurrently* conceive and experience reality and are *more or less equivalent* in veridical access to the ineffable God, *even in spite of fundamental contradictions*. In this way, an entirely new level of religious respect and tolerance might be achieved by various religious traditions while preserving the uniqueness of their orthodoxy. It was hoped that it would engender interfaith dialogue between different religions and foster cooperation.

Like many religious traditions, pluralism has been something of an intrigue to philosophers because it provides ample ground to bandy about endless philosophic inquiries. It has taken on many interpretive approaches. At the concluding remarks of Chapter 1 to this book, I quoted a phrase from Katherine Tingley, a chief proponent of Theosophy here in America in the late 19th-/early 20th-century (see p. 61). This pluralistic movement was initially founded in 1875 by Madame Helena Petrovna Blavatsky, the first Russian woman ever naturalized as a US citizen. The word *theosophy* in Greek essentially means 'divine wisdom'. It is a form of pluralism still in practice today, managed by the Theosophical Society.

Pluralism is like most other religious ideologies in the sense that there have been numerous variations to its theme making the literature surrounding it quite extensive. It is generally observed in the Philosophy of Religion that the most robust development came from John Hick (b. 1922 – d. 2012), a revered British analytic philosopher and the chief architect and advocate of modern pluralism. His views have been both celebrated and heavily criticized. Hick proposed that *Ultimate Reality*, most often referred to as the '*Real*' or the '*Ultimate*' in the context of his work, is "infinite" and "ineffable."[11] In his book *The Fifth Dimension: An Exploration of the Spiritual Realm* he adds that the *Real* is also *transcategorical*.[12] This is to say that God is vaguely accessible through our experiences and other modalities, but these glimpses and insights poorly cognize him.[13] Hick elaborates, where he states that "the Transcendent surpasses all discourse and all knowledge. It abides beyond the realm of mind and of being. […] escaping from any perception, imagination, opinion, discourse, apprehension, or understanding […]."[14]

He analogizes his sense of pluralism to the wave-particle duality of light in physics.[15] While not directly observable, due to the quirkiness of quantum mechanics and the Heisenberg **UNCERTAINTY PRINCIPLE**, light can be physically manifested as a succession of waves or as a cloud of discrete particles. Whether it is a wave or a particle depends on how it is interacted with by the observer (or more accurately, the physical instrument processing a sensory detection).[3, 16] So too in the tradition of pluralism many religions are true at the same time, neither being superior to the other, and may be considered to describe a different human experience of God. The contradictions are not seen as opposing when juxtaposed, rather they are complimentary when viewed with the perspective that multiple human realities can coexist in the transcendent *Ultimate Reality*.

Hick's pluralist manifesto served as a meta-interpretation that introduced religious diversity by effectively leveling Abrahamic religions (especially Christianity) with other (but not all) world religions. He viewed religion as an attempt to deepen our awareness of the *Real* and was especially disenchanted with the idea that access to such awareness required

---

3. Since the early 1900s, it was believed that the physical structure of light (indeed, all electromagnetic radiation) manifested itself in the dual wave-particle modality whereby light was thought to have existed in two forms. In a major break-out scientific discovery in 2014, physicists determined that light waves and light particles are in fact different manifestations of identically the same phenomena. In the past physicists had utilized two different sets of relationships (equations)—one to describe wave-particle duality and a second set to describe quantum uncertainty relationships pertaining to Heisenberg's uncertainty principle. The researchers mathematically demonstrated using a different formulation altogether that the prior relationships, once thought to define light as operating in two modes, could be unified. This signified that waves and particles are physically the same thing. It was the earlier relationships that obscured this fact making it 'appear' as though light could take on dual forms.

an orthodoxical set of beliefs. While pluralism is a very accepting theology, it contends that Christian dogma is not entirely compatible with pluralistic ideology given its policy on personal salvation being reserved to a select few.[4] Hick viewed the Jesus Story as mythical and his divine nature as only metaphorical to support the themes of the story.[17] Given Hick's position, it is easy to understand why Christian apologists and the ecclesiastical bureaucracy at large have held a disapproving stance on Hick's pluralism.

Hick was notably criticized by then-Cardinal Joseph Ratzinger who was at the time Prefect of the Congregation for the Doctrine of the Faith (CDF). This office was originally called the Supreme Sacred Congregation of the Roman and Universal Inquisition and was responsible for the control of heresy and the infamous Roman Inquisition tribunals of the 16th-century as well as for condemning both Copernicus and Galileo for their views on the arrangement of the universe. Cardinal Ratzinger, who is now referred to as His Holiness Benedict XVI, Pope-Emeritus, had examined the works of several theologians accused of relativism and found that they were philosophically inspired by Hick. In the year 2000, to invigorate the Catholic Church's doctrine, *Dominus Iesus*[18] was published. Authored by the CDF with the full endorsement and ratification by Pope John Paul II, this decree sought to clarify the **UNICITY** and salvificity of the Catholic faith. It was a broad-brush condemnation of Hick's ideas and theories. An unusually large legion of additional detractors came out to **PILLORY** Hick, though it would seem that many had misunderstood his initial ideology. Hick was able to correct an array of misinterpretations and seemingly successfully won over many of his critics. He clarified that his ideas were to be construed as a *conjectural hypothesis* not as a factual account of reality, open to modification or outright supplantation in the face of a better explanation for God.[19]

Over the course of time, the strength of Hick's religious pluralism rebuffed its many detractors because it rested on the immortalized bedrock of the philosophic forefathers Immanuel Kant, St. Thomas Aquinas, Ludwig Wittgenstein, Alvin Plantinga[5], as well as key concepts from Buddhism and Hinduism. Also, it remains attractive for those religions whose faith traditions do not require God's unicity. Hick reasons in like manner to Thomas Aquinas (see *Summa Theologica*) that there is a distinction to be made between faith

---

4. John Hick is referring to the Catholic doctrine *Extra Ecclesiam Nulla Salus* which means "no salvation outside the Church."

5. Plantinga is a leading Protestant philosopher and is the 2017 Templeton Prize Laureate. The prize is awarded by The John Templeton Foundation. The award honors distinguished contributions that expand mankind's understanding of ultimate reality *and* that also affirm the spiritual dimension. The monetary prize amount is the richest award for achievement in any field, always set to be greater than the amount awarded for the Nobel Prize.

and knowledge. The latter necessitates interpretation by the individual whereas faith can be interpreted *uniquely, unextraordinarily*, or *not at all*.[20] Importantly, Hick's notions force one to accept that Naturalism (i.e., a world reality sans spirits and deities) and religious views that include supernatural existents are equally acceptable as neither can be conclusively argued to be true or untrue because of inherent levels of human interpretation are woefully inadequate. To explicate this position, Hick borrows from Immanuel Kant to describe the *Real* as all but entirely external to mankind.

Immanuel Kant conceived the central ideas that reality is both *phenomenal* and *noumenal*. The phenomenal are objects or events that we detect using our senses. The noumenon is an object or event that we know without use of our sensory interrogation. This noumenal world may exist, but it is completely unknowable to human beings. Hick extended this concept with the notion that we are exposed to pre-programmed thought schemas introduced by our cultural environs and this shapes our experiences of the unknowable *Ultimate*. A simpler way of putting this is that it is through the combination of our cognitive abilities and societal influences that predominantly shape how we see God. In Hick's view, the *Real* is the divine noumenon and is an ontological reality. With God's nature being defined as transcategorical, Hick neatly steps over the thorny issues that arise in the distinctions of (Strong or Weak) apophatic and cataphatic mysticism.[21] To this end, we cannot ascribe to God *positive or negative* statements (love, compassion, just, unjust, partisan, etc.), "For the *Ultimate Reality*, the *Real*, is beyond the personal/impersonal duality."[22] (italics added) He arrives at essentially the same conclusion as discussed in the last chapter, but in a very different way. That is, God can only be described as a completely inaccessible hyperessence (or *Source* as I called it). Interestingly, this view also aligns with the Meta-Transignification hypothesis described earlier where God did not create the universe out of love and benevolence for the benefit of a species of organic life (a.k.a. mankind). Rather, as the Cosmic Creator (or Source), he brought the universe into being to perpetuate and immortalize his imprint across the cosmic sea. While there is some kinship among the zetetic framework that is beginning to take shape, there are major fault lines racking across the full width of Hick's philosophy.

According to Hick's doctrine, an authentic religion is gauged by whether or not it meets pluralism's *Golden Rule*. This rule is to be equated to the oft stated maxim, '*Do unto others as you would do yourself*'. In other words, if a religion professes kindness and love for all and has no opposing tenets to this cardinal precept, then the religion in question passes the minimum requirement to validly convey partial meaning to the *Ultimate*. In its final form, Hick's pluralism is a philosophical manifesto for which the Golden Rule forms the only two supports of a four-legged altar. It is by Hick's own admission that his Golden Rule cannot be proven empirically.[23] The zetetic approach thusly requires that we kick-out both legs from Hick's altar due to the intrinsic weakness of his argumentation. If there is no feasible way to demonstrate such a central principle is a valid yardstick to measure the veracity of a religion, then all it amounts to is a philosopher's musing that authentic religious systems should be a positive force in society. While that is all well and good, the rule is effectively impotent because it does not move us a foot toward the truth of the ontology, etiology, or metaphysical nature of God.

Many philosophers and theologians have criticized that on the whole, his philosophy results in circular logic. Hick readily agreed with this critique.[24] He noted that because the *Real* exists external to us, one must resort to faith which is something that cannot be independently verified.[25] Probably the greatest problem with pluralism is that it collapses under the weight of its own incoherency. Fundamentally, it is an exclusivist religion because it effectively posits that the truth claims of each admissible religion on its own cannot explain the *Real in toto*, only when all the admissible religions are added-in (that is, the pluralistic view) can the best appreciation for God be attained, even if unsatisfactorily so. Thus, if you don't subscribe to pluralism, then your particular theological views are at least partially invalid.

In the end, in spite of whatever philosophical artifice that might exist, pluralism is intrinsically incoherent, is bedeviled with circular reasoning, and critically depends on blind faith. Because the *Ultimate* is beyond our abilities, we are wholly and naturally incapable of grounding this faith with evidence of any kind, even our experiences. Even though Hickian pluralism accepts the combination of conceptions of God, unitary or otherwise, it ultimately triggers the the Many-Faced God Conundrum in a rather unique manner. As explored earlier, fideistic/blind faith compels the individual to logically allow *any* singular conception of god(s) to be valid. Contrastingly, the Hickian worldview suggests that *no* singular conception is genuinely valid. It equally allows for fideistic faiths and justified faiths to live under the same umbrella. Because pluralism holds that God is ineffable and offers quarters for fideistic beliefs, the philosophy runs smack into the Many-Faced God Conundrum. Finally, in practical terms, pluralism has at best been weakly successful in repairing religious rifts.

There is, however, a redeeming kernel of wisdom that can be extracted from the nutshell of pluralism. While the philosophical rationalizations that were used to erect Hick's house of cards prove to be improper, when we perch upon its apex, a new vista is revealed. But to get a clear understanding of what this horizon looks like, we have to erect an entirely new and philosophically sound structure. It is only after it is erected and we have ascended its full height that we will gain the requisite vantage point to see how God could be legitimately defined. As a hint, God may be absolutely transcendent in which he is totally external to not only human mentation but also physical time and the entire cosmos. While this is nothing prophetic to say or imagine in our minds, the difficulty arises when one is tasked with convincingly encapsulating how this could be the case. Hick, a great philosopher, came up short. **But Hick realized something very important that if God was purely transcendent or inaccessible, then all religious orthodoxy is necessarily nonsensical.** He concludes, "We cannot rationally hold both that the ineffable, or transcategorical, *Ultimate Reality* is indescribable in human terms and also that it is correctly describable in the terms provided by one's own religious tradition. We are, it seems to me, driven instead to distinguish between the *Ultimate Reality* in itself, beyond human description, and the describable mental images of it which we can comprehend and to which we can respond."[26] (Italics and capitalization added)

As we follow this zetetic path to its logical conclusion, it will become more evident how the zetetic framework differs from Hick's depiction of *Ultimate Reality*. For now, we need to keep the following insight in our back pocket. *__If God as the Source or the Ultimate is purely transcendent or is inaccessible making him ineffable, then all religious orthodoxy is to be regarded as irrational belief.__*

The New Sciences of Religion (NSoR)

Fast-forward to the year 2010 and we come upon a jog in the zetetic path to explore a very recent development in the great religion-science debate. Akin to the efforts herein though by somewhat different means, religion scholar William Grassie[6] decries a need to reconcile these two Arch Dragons (the latter is my terminology). In his book *The New Sciences of Religion*, shortened herein as NSoR, he exquisitely articulates a new boundary, he may prefer to say pathway, for *God-by-whatever-name* (a term I had attributed to him in Chapter 1) to enable all religions to learn from both the content and interpretation of science and vice-versa. Grassie believes that "Yoking science and religion together in a mutually constructive manner may hold the greatest promise for advancing truth and goodness in the twenty-first century."[27] He puts forward five concepts that acknowledge the challenges to and tentative solution for his *telos* of achieving a peaceful journey toward the enlightenment of God-by-whatever-name. We are to be sober to the idea that Grassie's viewpoint is an

---

6. William Grassie is a religion scholar and is an affiliate of the Quaker society (also referred to as the Religious Society of Friends). Grassie founded *The Philadelphia Center for Religions and Science* in 1998 which subsequently changed its name to the *Metanexus Institute* (http://www.metanexus.net/).

unending path with no terminus, meaning that religion and science continually evolve and with it our understanding of God-by-whatever-name.

His first premise is that religious and spiritual phenomena are inherently complex consisting of various levels and parameters. In understanding this complexity, he refers to his scientific approach as "nonreductive functionalism" which is an expansion upon the concept of the same name put forward by renowned philosopher and cognitive scientist David Chalmers (see *The Conscious Mind: In Search of a Fundamental Theory*, Oxford University Press, 1996).[28]

> By "nonreductive," I mean that there is no single scientific paradigm or analytic framework from which to understand the complex phenomena [...] An adequate philosophy of science today recognizes that there are emergent phenomena and that different methodologies need to be employed to account for different levels of complexity. Religion is also a complex and emergent phenomena [...] In employing the term "functionalism," I mean that religions exist and persist in part because they serve diverse human purposes. These functions work on the level of both individuals and groups. [...] to say that religions can be functional also implies that they can be dysfunctional [...][29]

He indicates that the various scriptural or story-based religious narratives are untrue in a literal sense, but he leaves it as open-ended whether the central theological truth claims of world religions can be preserved as he believes that in some way they may "transcend their specificity and establish universal profundities."[30] He proceeds to his second point wherein he acknowledges that the combination of religious worldviews present a daunting set of "entangled narratives"[31] in many ways at odds with one another. Grassie suggests that the best way to disentangle these narratives toward useful ends is to adopt a position of intellectual nonviolence which he defines as *"noncoercive habits of thought."*[32]

> The greatest untruth's will always be the unconscious lies that we tell ourselves, the mistaking of our own limited perspectives for the Absolute. [...] the goal of intellectual nonviolence is to set out in as many different directions as possible and to be converted multiple times to diverse metanarratives, inhabiting their truths, forgiving their failures, taking the best, and leaving the rest.[32]

In his third conjecture, he stakes out that there is a difference between the *content* and the *interpretation* of science. He postulates that cumulative sciences are out of its depth when it attempts to define God-by-whatever-name without some level of reliance on the broad-based (yet highly entangled) metanarratives religion has to offer. To his fourth point, Grassie reckons that, once we disentangle the narrative of a particular religion by removing the untrue or ancillary elements, we can then take the next step of gathering any remaining seeds of "universal verities"[33] that may survive this process. He coins the term *Particularist Universalism* to encapsulate this idea. He comments that, like the great diversity of languages which change and interact, there is an interreligious exchange that works to evolve all religions. This drives a universal need for multireligious fluency for all peoples. This exchange of ignorance for knowledge breeds, he hopes a useful interchange where knowledge begets comprehension, comprehension begets community, community begets empathy, and empathy bears the fruit of both tolerance and acceptance. Together then, we may work together to understand God-by-whatever-name vis-à-vis the unending coevolution of science and religion.[34]

Grassie's fifth and final contention is that both religion and science are to be considered emergent phenomenon. The concept of emergence is deserving of a comprehensive unpacking which we will address later. For now, we can think of emergence simply as a larger entity (usually something of greater complexity) or that a new property arises that is more than the combination of its individual components or lower properties. A biological example of emergence in nature is manifested by ant colonies. A single ant's purpose is derived by its gender and its role within a caste system (e.g., egg creation, workers, drones, soldiers). This division of labor allows the group as a whole to solve complex problems that are not present among the lower entities of a single ant as the intellect of the individual ant is rather benign. However, as a society of social animals they act as a unified intelligent super-organism whereby individuals will sacrifice their bodies by working tirelessly and martyr themselves to benefit the many. Their collective intelligence goes well beyond the capability of the individual. Different species exhibit varying behavioral traits. For instance, if fire ants are washed away by rains into a stream of water, fire ant workers will immediately form a porous raft-like structure by interlocking themselves together leg-to-leg, leg-to-mandible, mandible-to-mandible, body-to-body and in any which-way possible. They usually form a large mass of non-stratified layers. While ant bodies are hydrophobic (water repellant) by nature, they are nevertheless air-breathing (via spiracles—tiny holes on their skin) and therefore those ants on the bottom are likely to drown if the safety of a plant, stick, outcropping, or land is not accessible. The ant eggs, as will the queen ant, will be saved by keeping them on the top-most layer of the flotilla. This porous structure offers emergent self-healing properties whereby the ants self-organize to adjust their spacing (i.e., communal density) of their bodies to ensure maximum buoyancy of the collective raft whereby no single ant is in charge.

In the immediate context of science and religion, Grassie suggests that there is a "logical possibility space"[35] for what one might generally characterize as *qualified miracles*. In this sense, he warms us to the idea that we ought to treat personal experiences of the supernatural kind (e.g., miracles, paranormal encounters, epiphanies, and otherwise) as valid expressions of our intuition and personality. He would separate out general hearsay or the mentally or medicinally impaired person as being an unreliable source and that some supernatural experiences could be investigated scientifically. However, he generally concludes that science has little to nothing to say in regard to many of these phenomena.[36]

These five points lead to '*Grassie's God*' to be conceived as an impersonal, abstract, transcendent yet immanent force of nature. In identifying the locus of a more personal God he suggests that the sacred is revealed by the very fact that human beings are but one of many emergent phenomena in the cosmos, a part of God's overarching **TELEOLOGY**. In NSoR, we gaze indirectly into the eyes of God by recognizing the brilliant features of cosmic complexity and by employing our collective abilities to make use of our evolving capacities to seek out universal profundities.

A Zetetic Deconstruction of the New Sciences of Religion

Grassie's paradigm parallels our zetetic approach in several ways. Grassie calls for the need to adopt an inside-out, outside-in, and bottom-up framework. The New Sciences of Religion supports the need to evaluate God-by-whatever-name holistically by working to reconcile all world religions via dialogue and by other means of historical, philosophical, anthropological, societal, archaeological, and scientific introspection. NSoR's deep embrace with the idea of emergence is also testament to its holistic perspective, though this is not something that we have yet explicitly adopted in our zetetic process. Grassie does not comment on the need to also look at science-religion from a top-down perspective, but this might be implied via reference to accessing philosophy and science which can be employed to achieve these ends.[7] It is also agreed that the scientific approach is ultimately incapable of completely circumscribing the sphere of human experience, cosmic complexity, and proving absolutely the existence or nonexistence of God.

There is also strong agreement on the topic of religion and science being a vastly complex phenomena and that this complexity exists at many different levels. Grassie also questions the verities of foundational truth claims of religion with a cogent overview of hermeneutics

---

7. Grassie does refer to top-down causation which is referential to processes associated with the development of complexity in the "mind-brain-body." (Palgrave Macmillan, 2010)

and historical criticism,[8] but in his book he largely avoids delving deeply into such efforts on a tradition-by-tradition basis. On Christianity he concludes that,

> It seems more likely that Jesus is a composite personality, even as Christianity is a mixed movement, drawing from multiple cultural sources including Jewish mythological and Greek philosophical overlays in the context of first- and second-century Roman civilization. [...] In terms of traditional trinitarian theology, the historical Jesus is not all that essential and in any case can only be known through the Holy Spirit. The Father is too transcendent to be known directly. Jesus, the incarnation of God, came to bridge that gap and effect a cosmic reconciliation between the transcendent Father and humanity.[37]

Another point of unification is that both approaches agree that religions are rich in splendor and are virtually inseparable from the human drama. Additionally, miracle-claims based on hearsay are to be viewed with great skepticism. This brings us to some points of departure.

The ultimate goal for the zetetic process is to ascertain the best characterization for the existence and nature of God and does not preoccupy itself with reconciling world religions, at least not in the sense of mandating that religions successfully disentangle their narratives. NSoR and zetetics *may* agree on the idea of the pursuit of universal profundities but this deserves clarification. The ideal of zetetics is to zealously proceed by inquiry until the truth is found. To wit, we may, with perseverance, source certain universal profundities. NSoR on the other hand may also identify universal truths (perhaps the same ones) but whether it will achieve its aims of convincing existent religions with their current theologies mostly intact to converge is an entirely different prescriptive course. The logical coherency of any given religion, assuming that a particular religion is even coherent to begin with, could potentially be lost by adopting one or more of NSoR's universal truths.

There is a strong air of Hick's pluralism in the ideas forwarded by Grassie that both philosophical systems separate out religions that advance a sense of love, compassion, and mercy for the human community at large (i.e., Hick's Golden Rule). It is reasonable to say that this trio of principles is already shared by the majority of religious dogmas. We also see that the majority of individual adherents tend to believe that there are multiple ways to interpret their own faith tradition and that many religions permit differentiated believers access to an eternal life afforded by God-by-whatever-name

---

8. Refer to *The New Sciences of Religion*, Chapter 7 (Palgrave Macmillan, 2010)

(refer to United States poll results provided in Chapter 2–Figure 2-4). But this profession of love and communal appreciation of a life hereafter has not been a sufficiently motivating force to nudge religions to abandon their narratives or even to peacefully coexist. There remains much interreligious friction, friction between believers and nonbelievers, friction with the scientific community, and friction with pseudo-religious fanatics.

This being said, Grassie will find great solidarity from me on the notion that individuals must become religiously literate in multiple religions which will lead humanity toward comprehension and compassion. But I go further to say that the religious must also study atheistic and agnostic arguments to put their worldview into perspective. This would require a seismic shift in our K-12 educational system and the post-education study by adults. Meaningful interreligious dialogue must be fostered to a far greater degree than history has thus far recorded for the simple purpose of achieving peace between the denizens of Earth and to support the rights to life, liberty, and self-determination.

However, I do not see it as a requirement that one religion must be reconciled to another, at least not quite in the sense that Grassie envisions it. Recall from Chapter 2 that religion is "designed to formulate, encode, organize, protect, transmit and cyclically perpetuate information in the form of beliefs, values, worship practices, rituals, symbols, culture, language, and truth claims that accede to the primacy and allegiance to a sacred or transcendent being(s)." **Nowhere in this definition is there a mandate for religion to self-challenge or revamp their theological positions based on new enlightenments. Rather, a religion adopts a central orthodoxy and perpetuates it**. Major deviations are rare and when they occur they risk cleaving the original into two orthodoxies effectively birthing a new religious sect. Grassie finds further agreement with the zetetic approach in that he too foresees the dire need for religious systems to more quickly update their doctrinal tenets where well-performed science has introduced clarity on things vaguely or incorrectly intuited by religion.[38]

In so many words, NSoR attempts to broker a deal to allow religious adherents to hold onto their traditions (worship practices, language, stories, religious experiences, etc.) but to re-catalog their sacred texts from the shelf of truth to the fiction section that houses legendary stories and myths. The religious headmasters and adherents can re-deploy these thematic stories as sources for inspiration and motivation for good moral human behavior. Unfortunately, Grassie leaves the massive surgical task of disentangling core doctrine from the as-yet-to-be-determined universal verities in what must be an absolutely dreadful hand-wringing affair for the future as he sets us on our way with a highly vague instruction set. Fortunately, the zetetic method does provide a rather clear solution which will be elucidated in forthcoming chapters.

Zetetics must be above all else a light in the crowded darkness. NSoR proceeds forward stern to stern with the zetetic way, passing under many of the same shadows and sunlit bayous on an uncertain journey but forks in another direction due to the repelling force incurred by NSoR's granting of subjective experience protective asylum as a valid modality to know God. Grassie does not seem to recognize the Pandora's Box he is opening which is the domicile of the Many-Faced God Conundrum. If we allow one individual's epiphany or miraculous encounter with God to claim his existence and nature, then we have to be willing to accept someone else's claims, and those two must be willing to accept a third view, and so on. At some point in the chain, there will invariably be a clash of ideas that can't be reconciled, most of which are ultimately to be crowned as irrational beliefs once they are pursued to their fullest extent.

Zetetics and NSoR are also wedged apart by the fact that NSoR operates with the *a priori* assumption that God or something of this ilk exists. The reasoning Grassie offers for why we should accept his model of both deific and personal agency is probably one the most uncompelling aspects of his overall proposition. He essentially believes that recognizing an impersonal God would be a limiting factor in our desire to praise and worship this type of God. His concerns may be well warranted, however, this deficiency for God to choose to be inaccessible is in no way a valid justification that God is, should, or must be reachable through our subjective experience. He works to close this gap by invoking the premise that humans, like science and religion, are emergent phenomena. To his mind, this unfolding tapestry of ever-increasing complexity to ultimately create from lower-order entities an intelligent and sentient species, generates a cosmic imperative that God *must* be personal. Grassie describes this in terms that people experience transformative events and that God permeates all cosmic things (past, present, and future), at all levels of reality, inclusive of our minds and personalities. In short, he does not provide any means to substantiate that such a mechanism or medium exists. Rather, it is best described as a subjective ungrounded interpretive metaphysical conjecture.

This criticism does not necessarily outright reject the possibility of cosmic emergence or that this panentheistic (i.e., immanent plus transcendent) "God-ing-Universe"[39] view is patently wrong. The God-ing-Universe is Grassie's view that that God transcends the universe making him an abstract Being but that he is also actively present by continually evolving/complexifying the universe. While we cannot directly access God we see him indirectly through his continual act of creation. It is through God's teleology we intuit his purpose for mankind to respect one another. The criticism here is that the rationale provided by Grassie is not sufficiently developed to take his thesis as the best explanation for the ontological reality of God or that divine teleology exists as a real thing. While I applaud Grassie and his NSoR for taking serious the need to forge in the cauldron of society a more realistic interpretation of God-by-whatever-name, I wish I could be more hopeful that his ZYGONIC approach would provide a ladder tall enough to reach this envisioned dangling fruit.

Up until this point, the zetetic approach has yielded a possibility for a generic deistic *Source* that ostensibly created the universe. We have not as yet explored whether and how this Source exists in present-day times as a TRANSCENDENT or IMMANENT entity. In taking another glance back at theological mysticism, we might ask if this analysis is too condemning of God's immanence. Could it be that God works outside of the natural laws of the cosmos yet be *within* our physical realm operating in some undetectable modality or dimension? Could the idea of a panentheistic, non-anthropomorphic, formless yet form-full everywhereness presence in the universe hold some countenance with the zetetic process? In the next chapter, we shall explore the possibility of a God who occupies both a transcendent and immanent position and assess the relative plausibility of such a construct. While the zetetic process has provided little hope for the Christian conception of God, and more generally the Abrahamic God, Christian theologians and philosophers alike are actively working toward healing the doctrinal deficits of Classical Theism to appeal to the demands of evolutionary biology and the exquisite complexity of our cosmic neighborhood.

SUMMARY

While there is a much needed salve to heal the rifts between religious divides, as a philosophical project, religious pluralism is not the ointment to accomplish this task. This is not to say that its central goals are unworthy; quite the contrary. Hans Küng is exactly right in saying that the pursuit of world peace will be a forlorn effort without constructive dialogue between national governments and religious leaders (refer to the quoted words of Küng at the introduction to this chapter). However, while this goal may be universally accepted, this approach throws into the pit a group of decision makers who have incongruous agendas where it is difficult to see how the whole assembly will be able to see the forest through the dense thicket of entrenched ideological 'trees'. There is much hard-mindedness and acrimony to overcome when attempting to alter generations of belief and corresponding behavior. It is an extremely rare event where vast multitudes of leaders and their congregations can come together to solve deeply challenging problems. We need look no further at the uneven record of governance at the United Nations to forecast how difficult of a task this will be.

We found that Hick's philosophy painted a God who is wholly transcendent making him absolutely indescribable, an *Ultimate Reality* outside our own. This would logically permit one to adopt ignosticism, the position that it is meaningless to contemplate God. Hick himself would not be on board with this because he believed that our experiences permit an indirect, albeit extremely vague, means to comprehend God. He furthermore felt that those religions that were aligned with Golden Rule are more or less equally assistive in guiding us toward this minor plateau to envision God.

Perhaps one could differentiate between a strong version of ignosticism that views it as totally meaningless to converse about God and a weak form of ignosticism that maintains that we can derive some value from God's ultimate existence via our meager interpretations. On such a view, one could believe that God exists as a hyperessence external to all physical and mental reality. And, all that we can ascertain is that he created a universe with the implied intention that its inhabitants are to respect all his creations. While additional justification is required, this is at least a sketch of at least one option as to how God might be circumscribed. This matter will be picked-up again at the tail end of this book.

William Grassie and his Metanexus Institute's multi-perspective New Sciences of Religion is a valiant attempt to change the religious landscape by leveraging scientific insights to correct religious narratives. Recognizing that the NSoR is a nascent effort attempting to gain a foothold in the religion-science dialogue, my sense is that its approach is not traveling upon firm bedrock. NSoR argues that there exists a "God-ing-Universe" whereby God must be a personal force in the universe; however it does not offer effective grounding that would help one to accept this as a universal truth. As we will see in Chapter 11, Grassie's reliance on the notion of complexity and emergence will not take him as far as he would like.

Grassie is moving in the right direction where he suggests that we must embrace nonviolence as the immutable core of our advance and that it is incumbent on everyone to examine many faith traditions. The Christian should understand the religious tenants and traditions of the Catholic, the Protestant, the Anglican, and the Orthodox. Likewise, the Christian needs to do the same for the Jew, the Muslim, the Jainist, the Hinduist, and the Buddhist. And these adherents must in turn understand the Christian. Finally, the theist must seek community with the nontheist. Dialogue unto itself is a mute agent without underscoring such efforts with a similar intensity of learning the inner workings of religious belief. Such learning is made critically difficult when one generation after another bequeaths knowledge of the parental faith to their offspring without putting it into the context of other faith traditions or contemporary scientific knowledge.

If the vast majority of adults are religiously and scientifically illiterate, and such things are only becoming increasingly complex, how can we expect a more universal perspective to ever get properly conveyed to a new generation of youths who will one day be required to bring into effect a peaceful society? How are we to combat the zealous religious militant whose poison glistens across the long blade of violence? Will this zetetic endeavor we are undertaking produce a simpler wisdom while also disencumbering our world-body of the nearly impossible task of mincing the great many theological doctrinal concerns as NSoR would have us do?

To gain purchase of the answers to these questions, let us continue the promising enterprise of *Zeteo Alétheia*. Our forward path is set to take yet another turn. While our former footsteps have tread the width and length of major traditional religion from a predominately theological, philosophical, and historical approach, the road ahead will integrate contemporary scientific perspectives entailing evolutionary biology, origins-of-life research, physics, neuroscience, quantum biology, and cosmogony. We will use these tools to investigate and discover what we may of God's existence as an immanent Source and/or as a transcendent Source and whether this Source ought to be called a deity or something else altogether.

The next chapter tackles the ideas of complexity, emergence, and teleology set against the claims of Christian Panentheism. This ideology attempts to re-work underlying theological constructs to overcome the poorly supported, and in some cases, irrational tenets of traditional/classical Christianity, namely, those issues concerning the resurrection, the Trinity, transcendence, immanence, and Perfect Being Theology.

PART III

SCIENCE ON GOD

CHAPTER 11

Teleology and Emergence – Evidence of God's Hand Strokes at Work in the Universe?

One's ideas must be as broad as Nature if they are to interpret Nature.[53]

– Sir Arthur Conan Doyle
Fictional character Detective Sherlock Holmes speaking to his friend and assistant, Dr. Watson.

The establishment of a cosmic temperature gradient is the essential point. Such a thermal gradient is the patent signature of a heat engine, and it is this ever-widening gradient that has rendered environmental conditions suitable for the growth of complexity. The result is a grand flow of energy between the two differentiated fields, and with it a concomitant availability of energy (for use in work) over and above that extant in the early, equilibrated Universe. Hence, the Matter Era has become increasingly unequilibrated over the course of time; the expansion of the Universe guarantees it. Such non-equilibrium states are suitable, indeed apparently necessary, for the emergence of structure, form, or organization—of order! Thus we reason that *cosmic expansion itself is the prime mover for the construction of a hierarchy of complex entities through the Universe.*[1] [...] Thus we confirm the seemingly paradoxical yet wholly significant result for the scenarios of cosmic evolution: In an expanding Universe both the disorder [...] and the order [...] can increase simultaneously —a fundamental duality, strange but true.[2]

– Eric J. Chaisson
Cosmic Evolution: The Rise of Complexity in Nature (2001)
Astrophysicist and Astronomer

The humble approach rejects all self-centered philosophies, especially those brands of humanism teaching that man is the end purpose of evolution. In humility let us admit that God's awesome creative process is likely to continue even if humans should disappear from the face of the earth. Humanism is egotistical because it encourages men to think that mankind is, itself, the ultimate concern.[3]

– Sir John Marks Templeton (b. 1912 – d. 2008)
Founder of the philanthropic Templeton Foundation whose mission is the pursuit of the Big Questions concerning human purpose and ultimate reality.

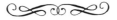

Teleology and Downward Causation

ARISTOTLE, A GOLIATH AMONG PHILOSOPHERS—PERHAPS the greatest—and the First Scientist, observed that everything has a purpose and its existence requires an agency of operative efficient causes. In his greatest work *Metaphysics*, he outlines that these causes can be traced to the *Final Cause*, the immaterial *Prime Mover*, and the first of all substances, who he himself is unmoved. Aristotle (b. 384 – d. 322 BCE) believed there to be multiple divine movers and hence was a polytheist. Aristotle is also credited as the father of **TELEOLOGY** (a term not invented until the 18th-century) whereby he pointed to natural organisms (e.g., plants and animals) that have aims which ultimately benefit their intrinsic functioning and hence their survival.

Aristotle believed that the Prime Mover had to be a living Being and his only logic why the Prime Mover should be equated with God is because he also regarded the Prime Mover as an eternally existent Being.[4] He specifically did not believe that the hand of God was upon the plow moving earthly happenings toward some final **ANTHROPOCENTRIC** causation or moving his creaturely assets about as chess pieces. God, in Aristotle's mind, is a transcendent Being of impersonal pure spirit and thought, acting immaterially as the final *attractive* cause in a long chain of causation where things trended toward a state of divine perfection. This God was immutable and unchanging (hence why he was also called the Unmoved Mover) as well as apathetic toward our world because God only thought about himself and not lesser things. His philosophic treatise was effectively coopted by others some 2,000 years later when teleology came to entail the notion of causal events possessing intrinsic purpose which effectively push one another toward an intentional end-directed outcome. This was, by some people's reckoning, a way to explain why human beings came to possess a mind, spirit, and soul that are separate from our physicality (i.e., mind-body dualism).

Irrespective of his endowment of being the finest of philosophers, the **CORPUS ARISTOTELICUM** is filled with ideas that have now become disfavored. For example, Aristotle believed that the human intellect was harbored in the heart which heated the blood. The brain radiated away this heat to cool the blood.[5] Aristotle was also a geocentrist believing Earth to be positioned at the center of the universe and that the heavens were interconnected by 47 or possibly 55 concentric crystalline spheres made of celestial aether (also referred to as ether, quintessence, or the fifth element). Each planet was attached to a unique sphere and the stars affixed to the second-outermost sphere. The outermost sphere contains the Prime Mover (and is correspondingly what the biblical book of Genesis refers to as the *firmament*). This belief of Aristotle's was articulated and reinforced by Claudius Ptolemy in the *Almagest* (c. 150 CE), the only comprehensive extant treatise on Babylonian and Hellenic cosmology which has proved to be one of the most influential scientific documents of all time as the idea of geocentrism persisted as the prevailing belief for 1,500 years. Is Aristotle wrong on yet another account to the effect that God is waiting for all things to become divinely perfected?

Teleologically-minded ideas have been steadily gathering since the late 19th-century to buttress the notion of anthropocentric emergence (i.e., man's centrality amidst cosmic evolution) under the broader umbrella of cosmic emergence. Since the dawn of the scientific age, the prevailing caricature is that all etiological causation was of the bottom-up kind. That is, complex things are generated inexorably in response to actions attributed to simpler, lower-order entities. Our bodies, for example, are composed of a system of individual organs. Each organ is made of tissues comprised of cells. Cells are made from molecules and molecules from atoms. Atoms are the smallest units that define the chemical elements (and their ISOTOPES). Atoms of course are made of even smaller particles—protons, neutrons, and electrons. These three entities are composed of elementary particles (or composite particles made of two or more elementary particles) which are generally classified as fermions or bosons. Fermions include all matter (e.g., quarks, electrons, neutrinos) and their antimatter counterparts. Bosons are referred to as force carrier particles (e.g., photons, gluons, Higgs bosons, hypothetical gravitons) which transact the four fundamental forces of nature.

More generally, scientists apply reductionist methods to break complexity further and further into its rudimentary parts (the basis of the theory of reductionism). Roger Sperry was a neuropsychologist and neurobiologist who became a Nobel laureate for his work on split-brain research and its relation to the causation of epilepsy, a brain disorder marked by whole-body convulsive seizures. Sperry is also credited with articulating the idea of downward (top-down) causation (c. 1965). He likened downward causal control to that of a wheel rolling downhill. As it applied to his neuroscientific work he suggested that while atoms and molecules were ultimately responsible for the constitutive and operative nature of the brain, the brain's higher properties worked to exercise authority over these lower elements. His work led him to believe that mind-body dualism (that is, that the two are of distinct natures) is a fallacious interpretation and that the events of the higher mind SUPERVENE upon the lower-order physical brain cells, molecules, and atoms. The inner experience then is an emergent property of a myriad of brain processes, generated initially by lower properties but become the causal constructs that work at the higher level that in turn acts upon the lower-level properties. This power of the mind-brain to supervene over matter essentially confers that our thoughts and physicality are ultimately of a singular nature thereby affirming the view of monism.

We will return to this discussion on the monistic or dualistic nature and hierarchy of the mind in the next chapter. For now, let us maintain our focus on teleology and how it relates to emergence.

TELEOLOGY, NATURAL TELOS VS. DIVINE TELOS, AND ORIGINS OF LIFE

The concept of emergence of higher-ordered entities possessing a whole nature whose sum is greater than its parts stoked the discipline of Complexity Theory and a somewhat related one, that of Chaos Theory, to explicate dynamical systems which are systems whose state (or variables) evolve over time. The interrelationships of such systems are inherently nonlinear by nature in that a particular input is not simply directly proportional to the output. Often, such systems may be said to exist in *far-from-equilibrium* conditions and such disequilibrium is a fundamental driver for the evolution of the system. This often leads to a progression toward unpredictable characteristics even though the system may yet contain both order and structure. Concepts of emergence and Complexity Theory have settled in many areas of the hard and soft sciences most especially in mathematics, biomedicine, and the biological sciences.

In Thomas Aquinas' *The Five Ways*, he articulates his five philosophical proofs on the existence of God. In his fourth way, what he calls "The Argument from Gradation,"[6] he suggests there are different degrees of goodness of things and for this to be so there must be gradations to both form and matter where God is of pure form. His ideas were extensions of his grounding of Aristotelianism as well as Plato's and Plotinus' concepts regarding levels of reality. It is here we must make a clear distinction between emergent phenomena existing as real mechanisms at work in the natural universe and those that are, until demonstrated otherwise, of only conjectural qualities. Naturalistic *telos* then are those natural phenomena that exhibit mechanistic causation in an end-directed process. Transcendental *telos* are phenomena that would be attributed to some otherworldly cause that is in some way coaxing the causal chain of natural events toward some final end by means that will in and of themselves require explication.[7] This otherworldly cause at first blush might be a transcendent God (a Being or essence outside the universe), a cosmic God (a physical Being or pervasive physical essence within the universe), a combined transcendent and immanent cosmic God, or some nondescript mechanism working outside the natural laws of the universe (perhaps in an undetectable fifth or higher dimension of reality).

Beyond the metaphysical contrivances fathered by philosophers and theologians, it remains to be the case that no one has been able to find to **any** empirical evidence that could explain how complex, sentient life could arise from the cosmic soup of inorganic (nonliving) matter. In fact, it was not even fundamentally comprehended whether teleological phenomena were compatible with physical phenomena. Ever since the famous Miller-Urey experiments[1] over six decades ago (early 1950's), Origins-of-Life researchers have been stymied to pinpoint any naturalistic process that could spontaneously create even the simplest life-form from inanimate matter. It was later recognized that going from nonliving material to unicellular life capable of metabolism, homeostasis, growth, reproduction, adaptation, evolution, and also be responsive to external stimuli was too great a leap. The focus shifted toward identifying a mechanism to formulate pre-cellular life using **PREBIOTIC** materials as a stepping stone to the subsequent generation of lipid-based *protocells* that were capable of spontaneous self-organization.[8] Not only has there been no substantive success in creating a single protocell from **ABIOGENIC** processes, there is no consensus as to whether genes in the form of **RNA**, or alternatively proteins, were the first necessary ingredient to have formed or whether the two came to exist contemporaneously.

There have been many competing theories for the origin of life on Earth. The fundamental reason why we are stymied to identify the essential precursors to life is that the primary sources of evidence are trapped within ancient rocks and are potentially harbored by inaccessible space bodies (e.g., comets, asteroids, moons, and planets). Rocks contain chemical signatures of ages gone by. In many cases, the rock relics are no longer in pristine condition as they have been subjected to the destructive forces of heat and pressure (principally from plate tectonics) and the weathering forces of time. Additionally, rocks that may have contained important clues could now be submerged at the bottom of the sea. Compounding these challenging conditions is that no one has fingered whether life is the result of a code (i.e., by a recipe or specific design) or whether it occurs as a random event. In either case, in some fashion, chemical constituents once entered into an extended dance of chemical and environmental processes that somehow converted inanimate substances into organic life. While there is some contention to the authenticity of the discovery, the oldest biological residue (i.e., biological rot) and microfossils found thus far date back to between 3.77 billion to 4.28 billion years old. The Earth is thought to be 4.54 billions years old.[56]

---

1. The Miller–Urey experiment sought to test the hypothesis for the chemical origins of life and specifically whether simple precursor chemicals and environmental factors thought to be present during the formative years of the early Earth could be synthesized into more complex organic compounds. The tests ultimately successfully produced 25 unique amino acids whereas all known life is composed of 20 "standard" amino acids. Amino acids are precursors to the formation of protein molecules but are not themselves considered biotic life. Source: Miller–Urey experiment, http://tinyurl.com/q2dkwka, *Wikipedia, The Free Encyclopedia*, accessed 27 October 2014.

One of the prevailing ideas that has garnered a contingent of followers is that early life was formed in concert with the dynamic action of deep-sea hydrothermal vents. Fissures in the sea bed's crust permitted superheated gas and mineral-rich alkaline materials to escape. These mixed with the acidic sea water to form 'mineral pillars' comprised of sulfur and iron. These porous structures became host to thousands of tiny openings that collected and protected ingredients from the surrounding environment. Hydrogen gas was available in plentiful supply and is thought to be the primary source of 'food energy' to support molecular and cellular activities.[57]

A second theory suggests that life came about through stretches of volcanism. Volcanoes created fields of geothermal ponds and geysers. At the periphery of these hot spring were zones of roughened land features (e.g., mounds of craggy rocks). These areas possessed features akin to the pores in the ocean-based mineral pillars having pockets and crevices that offered small protected 'laboratories'. The ponds and surrounding terrain provided a microenvironment suitable for amino acids to coalesce to form compounds and lipids (simple fatty molecules and cells). The geothermal fields were exposed to repeated cycles of being wetted and dried. At different points the materials would become a gelatinous biofilm, a glue-like state that allowed for greater proximity and exchange of molecules. Over time, perhaps only several hundred thousand to a few million years, the conjugated materials dispersed and underwent adaptation, eventually evolving into more complex primitive structures that in ways yet to be determined became organic life forms.[57]

A common theme among some renditions of these two theories is that a portion, or perhaps all, of the source materials were 'delivered' from outer space. These source materials are believed to be amino acids that were either present during the formation of our planet or were in-falling material from leftover primal dust and debris in orbit after the planet formed which eventually fell to the ground. The amino acids could also have been deposited from direct collisions with asteroids and comets. Alternatively, the amino acids could have arrived indirectly as the result of these objects impacting other planet/moon bodies. The combination of immense impact forces, lower surface gravity, and thinner atmosphere setup a scenario whereby surface materials were ejected from the planet (or moon) with velocities large enough to escape the planet/moon body and travel to Earth.

It is postulated that prebiotic chemical reactions utilized the once spaceborne materials to synthesize nucleobase materials here on Earth. Nucleobase pairs are created through the formation of molecular bonds between two chemical compounds. In mid-2016, researchers demonstrated the ability to form proto-RNA supramolecular assemblies from the nucleobases *melamine* and *barbituric acid*, both of which were in great supply on early-Earth.

Of special importance is that these chemical reactions can take place in environments of moderate temperatures and in moist environments (e.g., beachheads or cooled/temperate geothermal ponds). While the molecular structures that were generated in laboratory conditions are not representative of modern RNA we see in all life forms, it is conjectured that these molecules could have been precursors to other nucleobases materials such as *uracil* and *adenine*, both of which are necessary for the production of modern RNA and DNA.[54] Earlier, in 2009, scientists at NASA's Ames Astrochemistry Laboratory showed that the *pyrimidine* molecule could survive in space-like conditions (e.g., high vacuum, very low temperatures, and high radiation) if it is entrapped in water-ice. When exposed to ultraviolet radiation, the pyrimidine was converted into other chemical forms, one such form being uracil.[55] Thus, the uracil on Earth could have originally come from interstellar space.

Prior to these advances, it was the groundbreaking theoretic discovery of *autocells* forwarded by biological anthropologist Terrence Deacon in 2006 that shook loose the decades of stalemated research against this vexing problem of how life may have started.[9] Since then, there has been a veritable explosion of inquiry surrounding this because it has been seen as the best hope to appreciate in a detailed mechanistic way how biologic life may have formed. The idea has created such an enormous self-gravity to it that it has drawn in many from the theological and philosophical community to analyze how this idea could be leveraged to understand its relevancy to the comprehension of God. The autocell construct is an amazingly simple principle that demonstrates in a rudimentary way how teleological naturalistic phenomena vis-à-vis emergence could be compatible with the generation of 'life-like' entities. That is, entities that possess some, but not all, aspects of living matter. A year later, Deacon and his cohort Jeremy Sherman, further developed the autocell concept through a conjectural explanation using notional chemical catalytic processes and related this work to prospective theological implications.[10]

The Creation of Autocellular "Life"

A normal chemical reaction occurs between two or more distinct reactants. Catalysis is simply the situation where the rate of a chemical reaction is increased due to the introduction of an additional substance called the *catalyst*. The interesting effect is that the catalyst itself is not consumed in the chemical transactions it stimulates. It only acts to lower the free energy required for the reactants to reach their transition state. Deacon, basing his work off of the renowned theoretical biologist/biophysicist Stuart Kauffman (a pioneer and advocate of

Complexity Theory) and others[2] posed the situation where there are two reactants, R_1 and R_2, which react to form catalyst, C_A. It is feasible to introduce a second unique set of different reactants, R_3 and R_4, for which the newly-generated catalyst C_A catalyzes the reaction between the new reactants thereby producing a second catalyst, C_B. By design, Catalyst C_B is also a catalyst for the first set of reactants, R_1 and R_2 which will react to generate more catalyst C_A. Assuming that there is a sufficient amount of unreacted reactants available, the cycle will auto-repeat until the reactants R_1, R_2, R_3, and R_4 are depleted. Each time a cycle is completed, the number of catalysts doubles. This process is referred to as an *autocatalytic set* and is characterized as possessing spontaneous self-assembly behavior. This is shown generically in Figure 11-1.[3] We see that the minimum conditions for the autocatalytic process requires four unique reactants (sometimes called substrates) and two distinct catalytics.

Process 1: $$R_1 + R_2 \xrightarrow{\text{yields}} C_A$$

Process 2: $$C_A \text{ catalyzes } (R_3 + R_4) \xrightarrow{\text{yields}} C_B$$

Process 3: $$C_B \text{ catalyzes } (R_1 + R_2) \xrightarrow{\text{yields}} C_A \text{ and self-assembly}$$

Figure 11-1. The Autocatalytic Process

Based on the discussion of autocatalysis outlined in Deacon (2006)[11]

Deacon and Sherman suggest that either the synthesized catalysts (e.g., C_A, C_B) or reaction byproducts (non-catalysts that are not explicitly depicted in Figure 11-1) could clump or crystallize into molecular structures in the form of sheets, filaments, hollow polyhedrals, and even open-ended tubes. It can be further imagined that sheets can become layered or curved to create enclosed voids, or in analogous fashion, filaments might curl like a spring to form an open-ended tube to form a containerized space. Such hollow structures are referred to as shells. During their formation, shells are apt to entrap entire autocatalytic sets creating a closed microcosm separate from their local and global environment. Deacon refers to these self-enclosing autocatalytic sets that resemble unicellular life-forms as *autocells* which, in theory, could be envisioned as a general model for **PROTOBIOTIC** life.

---

2. Other contemporary pioneers and colleagues in the field of autocatalysis: J.D. Farmer, N.H. Packard, I. Prigogine, and I. Stengers.

3. Here I implement different symbology than what Deacon presented in his original publication. Deacon assigned the reactants as symbols A, B, D, and E and the catalysts as C and F.

Autocells are self-stopping because of the limited amount of autocatalytic material contained within them which, if left undisturbed, will eventually dissipate. However, because autocells form during the energetic reaction process, the shells can be damaged or destroyed by molecular impacts emanating from the surrounding chemical bath of particles and with other autocells.[4] This creates a two-state feature of autocells of being either open or closed. Full or partial rupture of the autocell releases the captured materials which can subsequently restart the autocatalytic cycle energizing several potentialities: (1) create a new autocell (essentially 'offspring' that could through processes outlined herein have the potential to create their own progeny), and/or (2) if close enough in proximity, repair/reconstitute the original autocell shell structure thereby closing it and entrapping materials, and/or (3) create a multi-shell complex around the original autocell which may be reconstituted (closed/repaired) or open creating a speciation of different types of autocells. At this point, autocells take on the emergent properties of living things. Taken as a whole, (1) they are dynamic, (2) can operate in two states (closed and open) like a cell, (3) are spontaneous, (4) self-organizing, (5) can self-generate their own protection to continue its functioning within the shell structure, (6) are capable of self-repair and reconstitution, (7) have the capacity for self-replication, (8) demonstrate the capacity for variation akin to speciation of autocell lineages, (9) are self-benefiting, (10) possess primitive adaptation through blind variation and selective retention, and (11) they have their own (intermittent) internal energy flow that allow them to persist without external energy inputs, and finally (12) they have a lifespan. As a result of these combined properties, it can be said that autocells exhibit primitive evolution that is both emergent and end-directed (i.e., natural *telos*).[12]

In spite of their amazing properties, autocells fall short of being classifiable as living entities. Living things employ **ENDOTHERMIC** and **EXOTHERMIC** reactions through the exchange of energy. Contrastingly, autocells rely on the internal energy of the catalyst-reactant mixture. And unlike genetic material, they have no capacity for precise pattern replication and do not possess the metabolism we would associate with cellular organisms. As Deacon and Sherman observe, it would be appropriate to categorize autocells as a form of protolife. Autocells also lack an ability for information transmission or to interpret their environment to generate any sense of meaning for their functionality. It should also be said that autocells are themselves limited in their complexity and evolvability and if life did arise from some autocellular process, the original autocell colonies would likely have been replaced leaving little to no trace of their existence which would mean we may never learn with certainty or precision how life originated.[13]

---

4. The autocatalytic process can potentially occur between substances in their solid, liquid, or gas phase. To my mind, it is easier to conceptually understand the process in a liquid phase.

Deacon and Sherman go on to say that the autocell approach is potentially indicative of a protracted evolutionary process that may have originated protolife which contrasts with the notion that life abruptly and accidentally came into existence. They sketch out a speculative means by which simple autocells could be the initiation point for a series of stepping stones toward the formation of genetic-based material. Even though autocells are theoretic in nature, the underlying implications of autocellularity are profound, not unlike that of the **RECONDITE** theoretic discovery of subatomic quarks which have forever transformed our views of the universe. The authors adroitly observe that **autocellularity exposes a hidden truth concerning the inherent nature of transformation from inorganic-to-organic life which is that the intrinsic capacity for self-automation emanates from within its own host domain indicating that an external (i.e., transcendental) telos is unnecessary.**[14]

While it was recognized at the time that autocells were a proof-of-principle mind experiment, it is possible to employ present-day scientific methods to empirically study the feasibility of creating autocells. In studying the general feasibility of Deacon's proposal, Bruce Weber, Emeritus Professor of Biochemistry, averred that it would be feasible to develop computer algorithms to generate the mechanics of autocellularity.[15] Indeed, in 2010 Christopher Southgate and Andrew Robinson, both traditional Christian theologians, report that they and their colleagues had succeeded in computationally simulating autocells.[16] But, even if real laboratory experiments failed to produce the physicality of **MORPHODYNAMIC** 'autocell-like' constructs, the theory and computer simulations by themselves demonstrate a plausible means for naturalistic telos to emerge from a state of non-telos.[17] Deacon and Sherman conclude that during the tiny spec of cosmic time that humans have existed, there has been only the most meager of natural evidence suggestive of a master plan to the universe's intrinsic clock-work which is to say that the overwhelming odds show that the idea of transcendental telos is fundamentally unsound.[17]

Autocells are suggestive that teleological properties can emerge from naturalistic *telos* without the need of transcendental *telos*. While this does not *necessarily* negate the presence of a providentially active, immanent and/or interpenetrating God working behind the scenes, this plausible scenario heavily weighs against such metaphysical claims in probabilistic terms. Recall, that the zetetic journey asks that we seek plausible naturalistic explanations before we resort to weighing the plausibility of non-provable inductive claims formulated by metaphysics. However, just because a plausible natural explanation exists does not mean we *automatically* accept it as the best explanation. That is, if a plausible naturalistic explanation and a metaphysical explanation are equiprobable, or the naturalistic explanation is weak, then a better answer may be that neither provides a suitable explanation.

It is also important to highlight from above that I referred explicitly to an immanent and/or interpenetrating God and left out reference to a **purely transcendent God**. A purely transcendent God is totally outside our universe—including any higher or other hidden dimensions. That is, God's reality is perfectly divorced from our reality. Thus, a purely transcendental deity is by definition an apathetic God (much like Aristotle's Prime Mover-God) in the sense that such a Being does not, indeed cannot, meddle in cosmically-bounded affairs. If God were to be **dimensionally transcendent**—existent within our universe but existing in some other dimension(s) which some might call the spirit realm—he might retain some capacity to operate within or upon our four-dimensional universe. But, if this were to be the case, we're still on the hook to find tangible evidence as to how transcendental *telos* operates.

One might conjecture that the autocell and its implication for biological and naturalistic teleological emergence would sound the bell for the demise of many teleological arguments that favor the existence of some metaphysical entity acting as a cosmic steward. However, it has accomplished nothing of the sort and has in fact done just the opposite by reinvigorating new treatises on how to fix ailing theologies. Before we delve into what this last comment means, let us take a step backward to a critical junction in time in the development of modern Panentheism as this will provide an underlayment for our future work of understanding how and whether teleological emergence can provide further insight on God.

It may serve as a helpful reminder to briefly review the following theistic concepts originally presented in Chapter 3 which will be referenced to a significant extent going forward (refer to Box 6, p. 382).

A CHRISTIAN REVIVAL VIA PANENTHEISM

Classical Theism has been the principal property of the Abrahamic religions. As we have seen in prior chapters, these schools of thought are bedeviled with irreconcilable philosophical incoherencies (e.g., the omni-perfections of God). There have been many who have sought to correct these problematical concerns. Of particular note, Georg Wilhelm Friedrich Hegel (b. 1770 – d. 1831) and Friedrich Wilhelm Joseph von Schelling (b. 1775 – d. 1854) were academic colleagues who later became rivals had each developed philosophical systems that can best be considered as modernist versions of Christianity. The two are considered the godfathers of modern Panentheism.

Box 6 – A Brief Refresher of Theisms

Monotheism	A belief in a single deity existent as a single, distinct, separate entity, Being, or essence outside (i.e., transcendent) of the four dimensions of the physical universe.
Classical Theism	A belief in a single deity existent as a single, distinct, separate Being that is absolutely and maximally ultimate and perfect possessing five attributes—transcendence, omnipotence, omniscience, omnipresence, and omnibenevolence. Aquinas maintains that God is ontologically simple, immutable, timeless (atemporal), impassible, and sovereign (God ordains all to occur). Additionally, some contend that God is also perpetually immanent and omnipresent in our physical realm though this position creates philosophical dilemmas as to how he exists as an undetectable cosmic Being, why evil is prevalent, and to what degree God is controlling events of the universe.
Pantheism	The belief that 'Everything is God' or God is identically the world-universe. God exists not as a single Being / distinct Entity, but persists as a pervasive indwelling Essence in and of the universe, often referred to as an immanent God. Importantly, God does not transcend the universe. Pantheists can believe in one or more gods.
Panentheism	The belief that 'Everything is *in* God' whereby he is both transcendent *and* immanent. Unlike pantheism (above) whereby God is diffused throughout all the cosmos, panentheism understands God as interpenetrating nature's four dimensions but is a distinct, separate Entity from the universe. Panentheists can believe in one or more gods.

Other transformative figures include Theosophy advocate Helena Petrovna Blavatsky (b. 1831 – d. 1891), mathematician and philosopher Alfred North Whitehead (b. 1861 – d. 1947), Roman Catholic Jesuit priest Pierre Teilhard de Chardin (b. 1881 – d. 1955), and Christian philosopher and theologian Paul Tillich (b. 1886 – d. 1965), and a cadre of others who also challenged the wisdom of the normative theological views of the time.

Teilhard was notably condemned by some within the ecclesiastical Catholic community for his views. When Teilhard finished his opus *The Human Phenomenon* (translated from French) in the 1930s, its publication was prohibited by the Church until after his death in 1955 (it was re-published in English in 1959). While the *Supreme Authority of the Holy Office* did not officially place this book and his other works onto the list of heretical publications banned by the Church (officially referred to as the *Index Librorum Prohibitorum*, translated as *List of Prohibited Books*), they forbade all libraries religious and otherwise to retain copies or to translate it. Interestingly, Pope John Paul II and Pope Benedict XVI later came to warmly embrace his theological undertaking as they saw promise in reconciling Catholic theology with scientific hegemony. Later, the above-mentioned philosophical luminaries were joined by contemporary philosophers William Lane Craig and Richard Swinburne to echo the arguments that God is temporally attached to the goings-on of the universe (i.e., God is affected by the property of time).

These notions went beyond the classical Christian view that God is utterly transcendent aside from the brief encounter by God's Second Person who walked among the living for some three decades as the Incarnate Jesus.[5] These newer conceptions placed God front-and-center as being personally active on an ongoing basis in a process of active Creation throughout our spatiotemporal existence. The Abrahamic religions have always had a belief that God was personally accessible (though to varying degrees), but the explication of *how* this is plausibly realized is fraught with difficulties that we have already wrestled with. Unbeknownst to virtually all Christian adherents worldwide, over the last two centuries, their theology has been unrested from its aged position upon the mantle to become refashioned with Panentheistic undertones. This project continues to this very day. By no act of formality, Christian theology has slowly released their grip on the classical monotheistic inclinations and is gravitating instead toward a Christian interpretation of generic Panentheistic ideology. However, this transition is slowed by the need for Christian orthodoxy to explicate the mechanism by which God is either nucleated or diffused in

---

5. Catholic theology holds that God intercedes not only in miracles, but through the performance of the sacrament of the Eucharist whereby the liturgical bread and wine is consecrated by the Priest leading to its transubstantiation (change of substance from ordinary matter to that of the unified body and blood of Jesus Christ)

the universe and how it is he acts to sustain and continually create the universe. If God is immanent and perpetually acting, then his worldly existence must be squared-off against the twin antagonists of free will-vs-determinism and the Problem of Evil which have proven to be philosophically and theologically intractable when one subscribes to an omnipotent, omniscient, omnibenevolent, omnipresent, maximally perfect God. If Christianity is to make this shift, the weathered dictum *something's gotta give* must be invoked.

Like monotheism, Panentheism is not a single monolithic theology. Rather, there is a plurality of perspectives, Christian and non-Christian, that represents mixtures of aspects of philosophy and theology. It is principally founded on views fostered by Plato himself (early 4th-century BCE) and seminal Neoplatonic ideas emanating thereafter (e.g., by Plotinus, b. 204 – d. 270 CE). Plotinus ironed-out some of the kinks in Plato's proposals, extending his concept of the *World-Soul* and believed God to be of purely transcendent *One Form*, undivided in all ways. Plotinus believed that the world-universe emanated from God in a timeless fashion[18] and is beyond our intellectual capacities and is therefore characterless (i.e., absent of attributes) and indescribable (i.e., another version of apophaticism). This purist simplicity of One Form does not allow room for the Trinity and is therefore a non-Christian form of Panentheism. Presently, we will focus on the junction whereby certain Christian-affiliated thinkers made a radical push to clothe God in the vestments of the physical universe vis-à-vis modern Panentheism and the closely affiliated and soon to be discussed *Process Theology*.

Teilhard de Chardin was not only a priest but was also a trained paleontologist and geologist. Like many who chose to widen their base of knowledge, his education profoundly affected his worldview. Specifically, he became conflicted by the Catholic views of his day and the special evidences arising out of evolutionary biology. Recall, Charles Darwin published his first edition of *On the Origin of Species* in 1859 but it took many decades until scientists started to take his ruminations seriously and many more to refine it to a well-accepted theory. Darwin's theory was finally taking root in the late 1930's, roughly in the same timeframe that Teilhard had completed *The Human Phenomenon*.

In her magnum opus *The Secret Doctrine-The Synthesis of Science, Religion, and Philosophy* (1888), Helena Blavatsky animated a movement toward the reconciliation of these three towers of knowledge. This work was composed of two volumes, the first of which was entitled *Cosmogenesis*. Her highly esoteric cosmology made God out to be an impersonal primordial essence that infuses itself with all physical matter in the manner of a divine spark (of no specific relation to the Gnostic belief of divine sparks discussed in Chapter 5). In a similar vein, Theilhard, while using the term 'cosmogenesis' differently, endeavored to heal the rift between the dichotomous views of science and religion in a manner mostly consistent with Catholic dogma. In *The Human Phenomenon*, Teilhard analogizes that cosmic evolution is shaped like a pyramidal funnel. At the base of the pyramidal architecture he postulated that the evolution of the universe is driven by an end-directed force. At its beginning, the cosmos was pervaded by non-life. Life-bearing entities eventually came to exist. Over time, organic life generated humanity and its conscious mind. Moving further into the funnel, mankind developed into a community filled with love and empathy that marshalled us toward a union with Christ. He called this event the Omega point.[19] The Omega point is the apex of complexity and consciousness for which the universe is have been converging toward since the dawn of cosmic Creation. The ultimate summit (i.e., the end of the funnel) will be realized with the eschatological return of Christ (the Second Coming which heralds the **MILLENARIAN** Age).

Teilhard is generally credited with the origination of the term *noosphere* which was co-developed by his contemporaries Édouard Le Roy and Vladimir Vernadsky.[20] The noosphere refers to the sphere of the human mind resulting from Anthropo-Cosmogenesis—the genesis of the human mind, soul, and spirit. Teilhard believed that cosmogenesis lead to biogenesis (creation of the biosphere of our world), which then leads to psychogenesis and the creation of man's intellect and capacity for conscious reflection, which in turn leads to the noosphere (genesis of mind) which creates our sense of personhood that has the capacity to recognize a self-reflective universe. The noosphere ultimately leads to the pinnacle of Christogenesis and the unity of the Holy Trinity connected by love propagating through the process of cosmic evolution. This supreme consciousness was Teilhard's Omega point. Along with human evolution, we encounter the complexification of culture and language.

Teilhard also maintained that God is a Being that not only interacts with the world but crucially that he *needs* the world and is changed by it, that is, *God co-evolves with us*. While God remains unchangeably good and wise, this is a clear departure from prior Christian conceptions that call for God's immutability in all ways and why his Catholic brethren were quite discomforted by his views. He forwards the idea that cosmic matter and cosmic spirit is the same thing but is essentially divided into two states of psychic energy, itself comprised of *radial* and *tangential energies*. Tangential energy is represented by the commonplace things we see outside of ourselves whereas radial energy is that which the spirit is composed.[21] But most important to our zetetic project at hand is his postulation that, in addition to his transcendence, God is immanent in the sense that the Cosmic Christ (that is, the resurrected and ascendant Christ) is manifested as the divine soul whereby the physical world is his body. Teilhard's point of view imagines a singular God of three Persons being in complete union with but wholly distinct from the universe. It is through the two psychic energies that we sense and commune with God.

Even though he identified himself to be a Christian Pantheist, Teilhard's views disqualify him from being such. He believed that all living creatures existed as distinct entities separate from God which is a dualistic view. This directly opposes the primary thesis of Pantheism in which God is identically the whole entire universe, inclusive of all creatures and otherwise. Teilhard's philosophy is better branded as *Christocentric Panentheism.*[22] He is nevertheless, one of the harbingers of change that would alter doctrinal inclinations at the highest levels of the Catholic Church and Christianity in general. Teilhard explicitly desired *The Human Phenomenon* to be regarded as a scientific work and not a metaphysical one.[23] However, he falls short in scientifically demonstrating the mechanisms of how it is that God is continually creating the universe. And, aside from the Incarnate Jesus of Scripture, he also does not provide evidences of how the Transcendent Father and the Cosmic Christ are manifested in the ways he outlines. His attempts to describe the immanent Christian God are more akin to a subjective airy hypothesis (indeed mysticism) versus the provision of clear hand holds to grasp the nature of God as a scientific description would require.

This overall schema where God is temporally interacting with the universe through event-driven dynamic processes is referred to as *Process Metaphysics* or equivalently *Process Theology.* This may seem like odd terminology to the uninitiated, but the words are well-paired. Theology is literally defined as the study of God and in Process Theology one attempts to demonstrate how the complex processes of the universe are caused by divine forces. The origins of Process Philosophy are traced back 2,500 years to the Greek philosopher Heraclitus (b. c. 535 – d. c. 475 BCE), a predecessor of the great Socrates. Heraclitus viewed reality as a continual flow of change and becoming, as opposed to a stationary state of being. In Process Theology the focus is shifted away from the things or substances of the universe (e.g., a stone, animals, people, stars, atoms, etc.) to the events and processes that create and complexify the universe which is the cornerstone of reality. These stratifications in complexity are voiced differently by commentators as degrees, levels, layers, gradations, or hierarchies. Today, the lines that separate Process Theology and Process Philosophy are blurred.

Process Philosophy evades the ability to concisely define it but can be loosely characterized as a position that favors the idea that dynamic processes and their interrelationships is what fundamentally drives the existence and evolution of objects, states of affairs, and the creation and interaction of substances. The paradigms which attempt to harness this general idea are highly diverse.[24] While many well-respected academicians have contributed expositions seeking to elevate and clarify the discipline, the result is a blurred line of thinking that is too intricate to parse in our relatively brief zetetic undertaking.

By way of feeble synopsis, Alfred North Whitehead is regarded as offering the most comprehensive and most explored philosophical framework as explicated in the prestigious Gifford Lectures at the University of Edinburgh (1927 – 1928) and his follow-on authorship of *Process and Reality* (1929). His work has been used and extended across a broad array of disciplines and its ubiquitous construal is due to the fact that it describes the world as a vast, tangled, interdependent web of ever evolving relationality.

In the present-day, this concept maps well to the burgeoning wavefront of technology and scientific advancement. A. N. Whitehead's work is closely affiliated with that of Charles Hartshorne, who is eminent in his own right. Hartshorne was Whitehead's assistant for a semester during Whitehead's post as a professor of philosophy at Harvard University. He had also functioned as the editor of another academic celebrity, Charles S. Peirce, whom we shall refer to later. Hartshorne and Whitehead developed their conceptions of God at relatively the same time, but the former, a liberally-minded Christian with Quaker influences, more robustly formulated the theological implications of Process Philosophy which catalyzed a reinvigoration of Process Theology.[25] In the prior chapter, it was footnoted that William Grassie is a Quaker. One finds in his New Sciences of Religion a deep connection with Process Philosophy.

Whitehead-Hartshorne's embodiment effectively loosen the strictures of ultimacy on God's power, his knowledge, his immutability, as well as his status as a master-controller seeing reality as an uncertain unfolding of possibilities in which God cooperates and participates in and is himself affected by. They defined God as being of one substance in that everything in the universe is locatable within God which eliminates difficulties associated with the various philosophical dualisms (e.g., mind-matter). Reality is therefore is a temporal succession of actualizations in which all of reality, even God himself, continually changes along with it, though his core essence remains unchanged.[26] According to them, God can apply his massive persuasive powers to affect in some fashion future opportunities and possibilities; however, God is not in full control of the future.

The two philosophers were cognizant of the development of quantum mechanics that was taking the hard sciences by storm at the time. This then burgeoning theory revealed that there is an inherent indeterminacy associated with subatomic matter which is to say that we are incapable of precisely knowing all the physical properties of fundamental matter at any given instant of time. We will take up the topic of quantum mechanics in later chapters.

Simply put, nature at the smallest of scales is stochastic (non-deterministic), always containing randomness. The philosophers capitalized on this new conception of reality to conjecture that the future is not indelibly written; rather it unfolds with a degree of uncertainty under the auspices of God loading the dice to preference certain outcomes but never being able to perfectly dictate the future.

This curbing of God's maximal monadic properties offers some enticing benefits. Recall, Classical Theists face the dual challenges of resolving the Problem of Evil and the free will-vs-determinism dilemma. They also have to figure out how a God living in the spirit realm is able to act in the material world without breaking the laws of physics. The best explication Classical Theism can offer is that justice will be served to the perpetrators of evil acts in the eschatological end of the universe whereby God will only then be victorious over evil in accordance with God's will and his own timeframe. Between the present time and this summary point, God allows his creatures to freely choose between good acts or evil acts under the proviso that they will be judged in the afterlife. I think even hard-over Christian apologists have a great deal of angst in being anything but unsettled by this account when we can point to the millions upon millions of heinous acts repeated over and again and the tremendous suffering that exists in our world. The Panentheistic model with its abolishment of a perfect God cleanly eradicates the problems of theodicy and the free will-vs-determinism quandry because God's authority is no longer considered limitless. This is the attractive force driving modern-day efforts to develop a Christian model of Panentheism and why modern-day Popes are intrigued. These efforts need to contend with the fact that, with the exception of the universe's initial creation, the majority of contemporary Panentheists, Process philosophers/Process theists *do not* believe in supernatural miracles or revelatory Scripture.

Since the patriarchal figures of Panentheism (i.e., Hegel and Schelling) proffered their initial thoughts of a cooperative God, and the subsequent embodiment of Process Philosophy by A. N. Whitehead, their treatise came to reside upon the single spear tip of *strong cosmological emergence* (to be discussed shortly). It was up to others to bind the dominant perspectives of Christian theology to reinvigorate the struggling incoherency of Classical Theism to fashion a new model of Christian thinking with empirically-justified scientific theories about cosmological evolution and complexification therein. Seeing a promising franchise in Christian Panentheism, there have been many attempts, one often leaning on the other, by Ian Barbour[*], Arthur Peacocke[*], John Polkinghorne[*], Philip Clayton, Joseph Bracken, and Jürgen Moltmann.[6] These individuals had evolved concepts that have sought to reconcile

---

6. The names with an asterisk following their name are Templeton Prize Laureates.

science with Christian theology. In general terms, they employ the dynamics of emergent evolution of the living and universal processes to rationalize the idea that an immanent God is tirelessly at the forefront of the production line, pressing buttons, pulling levers, turning knobs so to speak, guiding the course of the unfolding universe. The underlying belief is that there is a transcendental *telos* actualizing a continual process of Creation.

It is here we find it necessary to call attention to two schools of thought divided as *strong* and *weak* theories of emergence. Both theories acknowledge that the functioning of high-level phenomenon that arises from low-level constituents can be deduced from the phenomena imbued at the low-level. This means that such high-level emergent properties are computable—addressable by logical algorithms to develop the properties and relationships. Resultantly, high-level phenomena are not always examples of strong emergence. Strong emergence arises when high-level phenomena are irreducible from its low-level constituents creating properties that are ontologically new. The adage one calls to mind to encapsulate the concept of strong emergence is that the sum is greater than its parts.[27] In this sense, complex systems exhibit characteristics or perform functions that the components themselves cannot.

It is on the principle of strong cosmological emergence that Process Theology is inextricably dependent. Because cosmological emergence is quite challenging to study by direct observational means, let alone along theoretic lines of thought, we generally turn to studying naturalistic emergent processes either historically or in present-day times. If the mechanisms of naturalistic emergence cannot be properly circumscribed, then we might be on good grounds to say that there must be transcendent prime movers (borrowing Aristotle's terminology) operating the clock-work of the universe. If, however, we can pinpoint the mechanisms of strong emergence, then this weakens Christian Panentheistic claims that some 'God-like force' is at work.

Until Terrence Deacon proposed his autocell concept, the effort to Christianize the ideas of generic Panentheism was the veritable equivalent of a philosopher's Lego® set whereby there were few constraints on the mental creativity to meld God's postulated efforts to connect with his kingdom of creatures. However, emergentism does not in and of itself motivate a preference or priority to any form of agency or effort to hierarchically define a system (e.g., as being 'higher' or 'lower'). Rather, emergence is about the relational dynamics between and among phenomena and how disequilibrium can bring about changes that may not be generally or specifically predictable. There is nothing 'personal' about emergence. Therefore, if one seeks to employ Process Metaphysics to claim a personal God, one must appeal to other arguments to develop a rationale as to why a continually creating God is engaged in a dialogue with humanity. Some have argued that emergence is in fact 'personal' by calling to mind that the human mind-body mirrors the God-World relationship.[28] Such a position is not rationally defensible as all this amounts to saying is that our evolved intelligence is emblematic of God's intelligence. When one reviews the chapter and verse of the many philosophical wonderings and metaphysical reflections of academic Process Theologians over the last forty-to-fifty years, it doesn't engender much confidence that any have pegged the tell-tale signs of transcendental *telos*. I admit that striking them down so curtly is a harsh move, but I suffice it to say that their systematic theologies do not adequately address the free will dilemma, the pivotal concepts of eternity and infinity, or the incoherencies of the Holy Trinity. To its credit, the philosophical system does manage to successfully evade the thorns presented by the Problem of Evil.

It is scientist Terrence Deacon and his colleagues who have stood on the most authoritative ground when it comes to defining naturalistic emergence and how complexity arises from less complex components. We reviewed an entry-level definition of strong emergence that implied that high-level phenomena exert efficient causation onto lower-level components. On such a view, our intelligence can engage in nonlinear thought (e.g., creative writing) and direct the atoms in our fingertips to press computer keys to record them. This is rather simplistic and does not go far enough to tackle deeply-complex physical phenomena. Deacon has conceived what seems to be the most compelling thesis of how the principle of strong emergence mechanistically works in reality.

The first principle of Deacon's is that complex phenomena possess intrinsic potentiality. For instance, a tree has the potential to become a house, but does not ordinarily self-assemble itself thusly. This is because complex systems are imbued with limitations on potential relationships which introduce tendencies or biases into what might emerge in the dynamic process of transitioning from a set of low-level components into a high-level system or conversely the causal action of a high-level system onto low-level subsystems. This is what scientists generally refer to as a *selection effect to reduce variation*. What's more is that Deacon posits that these constraints can amplify or reduce the development of relationships among the whole and parts thereby propagating them throughout the system.[29] Using the tree example once again, a tree generally grows toward the direction of sunlight, but it must develop limbs. The main branches tend to be of similar thickness because the water supply, internal water delivery system, and structural properties of the wood constrain how thick the branches can get. These constraining relationships propagate throughout the tree. The variation is reduced in that branches develop having very similar properties (e.g., shape). For instance, the tree favors branches of one or a few shapes, perhaps they are straight, crooked, or smoothly bowed, but none are coil-shaped.

This process of spreading constraints works to establish patterns, regularity, and self-order throughout the system over time. This is to say that constraints in general have causal powers.[30] Furthermore, as constraints multiply they generate dynamic relationships. It becomes a fluid cycle whereby the high-level generates constraints to define how the low-level components function and these in turn affect the macro-level functioning. For instance, a tree's branches sprout leaves, which individually do not block significant sunlight, but collectively they fully shade the ground illustrating how the low-level components (i.e., individual leaves) affect the tree's macroscale capabilities (i.e., ability to block-out the sunlight from reaching ground-level). But beyond this relationship, a maxim exists that only high-level complex units, as opposed to low-level phenomena, are capable of admitting certain possibilities to occur.[31] In our tree example, the leaves, branches, tree trunk, or individual trees as a whole cannot influence a large ecosystem, but a rainforest system consisting of interlocking canopies greatly affects the ecosystem close to the ground. This higher-order system permits some things to happen while also locking-out other possibilities from occurring. Deacon adroitly observes that as much as a complex system can be defined by the relational dynamics, high-level phenomena are intrinsically defined by the incompleteness associated with unrealized potentialities.[32] Leaning on the tree analogy yet again, this is to say that we can define the rainforest, in part, by the interlocking trees, but the density of vegetation both of the trees themselves and of other plant life, could become extremely dense or relatively sparse. In a manner of speaking, the system sort of 'chooses' a particular density pattern and relegates other possible density patterns as unrealized potentialities.

Strong emergence is characterized by high-level phenomena initially exercising constraints on its low-level components which can be classified as efficient or inefficient top-down causation. Over time, the subsystem's behavior is to increase its orderliness (i.e., internal simplification as opposed to complexification) while the overall macro-system remains in a constant state of transition (increasing complexification).[33] A useful analogy might be found in our 4.5 billion year-old stellar host, the Sun. When the Sun was first forming out of the cloud of interstellar dust, the individual hydrogen atoms seldom bumped into each other. But at a critical point, gravity coalesced the atoms enough whereby atomic collisions greatly intensified, heating the gas to 13 million degrees above absolute zero, or equivalently 23.4 million degrees Fahrenheit. At this temperature, the repulsive atomic Coulomb force keeping individual particles apart is exceeded and the particles of hydrogen fuse together to create a new substance (helium). This process was outright violent. Not long after, a sense of order came about. Hydrogen and helium formed loosely defined zones of activity where certain physics dominate. At the core, fusion processes continued to occur. Further from the core, in the radiative zone, light photons insanely flit about, zigging and zagging every which way. In the next layer, the convective zone, the super-heated gas circulates into loosely-shaped cellular structures. The Sun went from a simple, essentially disordered cloud of free-floating, virtually pure hydrogen gas to become a complexly structured dynamic system made of 67 chemical elements. At the subsystem level, the stratification of regions increases orderliness of the system but at the global level, the structure is extremely dynamic.

Deacon coins the term *teleodynamics* to describe the most advanced form of strong emergence which signifies systems whose complexity, relational dynamics, and cyclical self-reconstitution, having evolved over time, now exhibits a robust self-sustainability and end-directedness.[34, 35] According to him, organic life and human consciousness are the preeminent example of teleodynamics. Deacon goes further to suggest that for highly complex systems, these limitations in themselves constitute a means for novel causal powers. That is, not only is there bottom-up and top-down causation presented by the components and their sum, but as the system evolves, new constraints can form which is a separate power unto itself. This understanding elevates our comprehension from what were once just physical materiality and the trivial interaction therein to a formalized, yet dynamically fluid framework of inefficient causality and statistical chance created by far-from-equilibrium actions and evolving constraints.

This is where the project of Christian Process Theology (i.e., Christian Panentheism) begins to become unsteady. As a proponent for this line of thinking, philosopher of science and religion Philip Clayton (b. 1956 –) proposes the anthropocentric view that human beings arose from inanimate matter which, under the physical laws of world, operated upon chemistry of internally available ingredients. In time, as complex processes were able to interact with themselves and potentially other complex processes, macromolecular information-bearing living organisms came into being. These continuing dynamics later led from simple forms of life to sentient organisms with rudimentary awareness. As sentient organisms evolved so did social culture and language. His line of thought thus far parallels that of evolutionary biology. Clayton pushes the boundary further by his belief that at some indistinct time, human beings developed *Consciousness* which represented another stratum of complexity, importantly, one that goes beyond the highest level of organization embodied by Deacon's teleodynamics. It is at this level that our personhood comes into existence. Beyond the level of consciousness, the higher tier of *Spirit* came into existence which Clayton intuits is the origin of both consciousness and nature.[36]

Clayton's Consciousness and Spirit are two modes of emergent higher complexity that beckon for rationalization. In a paper entitled *Emergence and Non-Personal Theology* it is Zachary Simpson, a philosopher of religion whose graduate academic advisor was none other than Philip Clayton, who points out that for his mentor to be successful in such a claim, that he must demonstrate the causal mechanisms of how these two modes operate and that they are in fact unique and are not due to other possible phenomena. He concludes that Clayton's mentation fails to explicate the underlying naturalistic mechanisms that motivate the development of Consciousness and Spirit and that the only way that his ideas could be supported is by adopting metaphysics which means that we would have to crossover into the territory where *any* conjecture can be made but never proven.[37] One further dent in Clayton's construction is that he positions human cognition at the second highest tier among **all** Creation (next to Spirit). However, there is a strong possibility that there is alien intelligence that supersedes our own somewhere in the cosmos and he falls prey to mankind's tendency to anthropocentrize human beings as the apex construct of the universe which is, in my opinion, an overindulgence of the drunkard's ale.

The uncertain future associated with strong dynamical processes of biological emergence lead us to a quandary as to why *Homo sapiens sapiens* (the human species of today and throughout the entire timeline of polytheism to monolatrism to monotheism) is the object of God's interest. We suppose that God loves us creatures so much so that he imbues us with cognitive abilities to question the meaning of why we exist and to contemplate and explore a relationship with him. Why would God spend the totality of 13.82 billion years to reach this milestone? While this span of time may seem trivial to a deity, it nevertheless is an important question to advance given that trillions of life-forms that have suffered and/or died, many due to our own foibles and moral privations, for us to evolve into what we are at this immediate point in cosmic history. Furthermore, if we rewound history as did our cosmic Grand Observer (harkening back to Chapter 1), and then restarted evolution all over again, we would with near perfect certainty witness a history completely different than what we now understand it to be.

This idea of alternate evolutionary paths is easily accepted by most everyone with the exception of those who would believe that God micro-manages every event there ever was or ever will be to recreate the world exactly as it is. We can imagine alternative realities with a simple scenario. If, during the physical formation of planet Earth, an additional 50 percent more mass was accreted—all else being the same—organisms would have to withstand gravitational forces half-again as strong. Organisms would adapt to such a dramatic change in this environmental factor in a number of ways. For example, many organisms would not be as tall as they might otherwise be for the simple fact that pumping bodily fluids upwards against gravity would require 1.5 times more force (or equivalently, energy). Giraffes, for instance, may be much shorter in overall height or have significantly thicker necks. Additionally, complex life-forms would be more prone to developing structures to distribute their body weight more evenly (e.g., many more legs). Notwithstanding any objections, history would change so radically in almost any scenario that *Homo sapiens sapiens*—you and me—would not emerge in a physical or mental form anything resembling what we are today.

Given this curiosity for the nonexistence of our kind, there is the associated problem that arises in the Abrahamic religions in regard to our postulated immortal soul, which according to these traditions is reserved only for human beings.[7] The Catholic Church affirms the creation and immortality of the human soul in the *Catechism* in which we humans are unified from two substances, spirit and body, into a singular nature.[38] If our immortal soul is affixed to our personhood, then we must tangle with the conundrum as to what would happen in some alternative historical reality where human beings (you and me) never came to exist, but perhaps some other organism came to develop consciousness. We will talk more of the concept of the human soul in the next chapter.

THE SEVEN CHALLENGES TO CHRISTIAN TRINITARIANISM

It is this type of interaction between science and theology where wedge issues develop that are very difficult to close. Within the last decade, traditional Christian apologists Christopher Southgate and Andrew Robinson, acknowledge that our current understandings of evolutionary biology introduce serious challenges to Christian theology.[39] The duo has occupied their time with an intriguing project to develop an adaptation to traditional Christian theology via a new theology of nature to theorize an explication of our reality. It is hoped, by them, that their proposal offers a more coherent synthesis between the tensions between evolutionary biology and Classical Theism. The discussion to follow will assess the success of this project.

Southgate and Robinson use the motivating force of Deacon's autocell revelation and that of philosopher Charles S. Peirce's (b. 1839 – d. 1914) insights to ground their thesis. Peirce was an innovator extraordinaire making highly important contributions in logic, mathematics, semiotics, and was the father of philosophical Pragmatism (later renamed Pragmaticism) which is a theory of Truth (recall in Chapter 1 we discussed how to discern theories of truth). As the founder of Pragmatism, Peirce did not believe in the concept of absolute truth. Rather, he felt that it was up to people to settle differences of opinions to determine what is most practical (i.e., pragmatic) for a given society of peoples, furthermore believing that the scientific method was a superior method to other alternative means to accomplish this task.

---

7. Jainism and Hinduism believe that all living organisms have souls.

His theological leanings were very much in the outline of the shadow of Schelling and therefore he was a Panentheist through and through but with some tinge of Christian sentiments though he was not particularly trinitarian in his thinking. It is his development of **SEMIOTICS** in which we are most interested in dwelling on.

Semiotics is the discipline of studying signs, symbols, and signification and how meaning is created. A sign (e.g., an image, a page of text, a facial expression) is something that can be interpreted as having a meaning and has the capacity to communicate information to the interpretant which is defined as something, conscious or not, who interprets or decodes the product of an interpretive process. Within semiotics, Peirce created the technique of triadic analysis-synthesis he referred to as *Trichotomics* where objects of study are composed of three-fold divisions. In this vein, he suggested that three primal categories exist—Firstness, Secondness, and Thirdness. Firstness is a grouping of abstract qualities that are irreducible monadic properties (e.g., color, ideas, probability, potentiality, and self-relation). Secondness is the solidification of abstraction into brute facts and actualization brought about by the reaction or resistance presented by the world (e.g., the resistance of gravity, correction of falsities, the perceptual awareness of things, and the discretization or distinction among things). Finally, Thirdness is characterized as mediation between things (e.g., physical laws acting between objects, continuity, and connections between things).[40]

The point of invoking Peirce's work by Southgate and Robinson is that it prospectively addresses three divisional matters between science and Christian theology. Firstly, they appeal to his Trichotomic system to better rationalize the relationships of the three Persons of the Holy Trinity.[41] Secondly, they speculate that semiotic processes and God's apparent action on the world stage share parallels. Thirdly, by leveraging biosemiotics, a derivative of semiotics as applied to biological systems, they interpret Deacon's work and that of evolutionary biology more generally. Together, they hope to fabricate an enduring cord between at one least one frontier of science and Christian theology.

As we have discussed on several prior occasions, Christian trinitarian thought has always presented a mystifying relationship between the Father, Son, and Holy Spirit, one that even theologians standing one behind the other have never crisply articulated in a coherent paradigm. And to be clear, I am not referring to the familial relationship but their intrinsic nature as one or more Beings, their identity and purpose for existing as a member of the Trinity, their respective attributes, and how all these interrelate. Past explications have delivered intricately nuanced and often forced arguments that falter to simultaneously address **in a rational fashion** the Seven Challenges to Trinitarianism (see below). For core Christian doctrine to be wholly rational, all of the challenges have to be answered without resorting to miracle claims, faith, or divine revelation. We already covered the ground that biblical Scripture does not provide the necessary clarification on these issues, so for those who believe that Scripture is inherently divinely inspired; we can check the box that resorting to divine revelation is a dead-end avenue right from the start.

The Seven Challenges to Christian Trinitarianism

1. Number of Personages in the Trinity

Does the Trinity encompass three distinct gods (tritheism) or is the Trinity a singular deity comprised of three Personages as unity (monotheistic trinitarianism)? Why is the divine realm necessarily comprised of *three and only three* Persons which are ontologically a single deity? If one is to suppose that God is a Being comprised of more than one Person, then what logic could be put forward that would justify limiting the number of Persons to three and only three?

2. Modality versus Identity

Is God existent as three distinct modes of a single entity (i.e., Modalism[8]) where God the Father was initially the Old Testament God, later incarnated as the Son, and after the resurrection changing modes to be the Holy Spirit? That is, God is not coexistent in his three modes; rather they are successive modalities or identities. Using water as an analogy, we can envisage a container of pure water. It can change between a gaseous, liquid, and solid phase (i.e., modalities). In such a case, there is no individuation of chemical identity as all three phases are still considered water (H_2O) but each phase is characterized with varying levels of solidity. In this context, God is therefore a singular entity, revealed in three ways, but not all three at the same time.[9]

In contrast to Modalism, is the notion that the three Persons possess their own identity (i.e., the transcendent Father, the cosmic Son, and the mediating spirit). This is standard trinitarianism as believed by most Western traditions of Christianity. Eastern Orthodox Christians are nontrinitarian because they view God as an incomprehensible substance—an apophatic position—thus, how can one identify three separate identities?

---

8. Modalism is also referred to as Sabellianism, Patripassianism, or modalistic monarchianism.

9. Here, I ignore the reality of multiple Triple Points of water whereby all three phases can coexist simultaneously.

3. Relationality of Knowledge

When God took human form, was Jesus' knowledge perfect, complete, and identical to God's knowledge? Or did Jesus acquire and continue to increase his knowledge successively over time using his human perceptual abilities? Thomas Aquinas, one of, if not the greatest, of all theologians was unable to suitably rectify this matter in a wholly consistent manner.

A second related issue to God's knowledge is whether or not he is omniscient. If God is omniscient then this state of affairs generates a laundry list of hairy philosophical issues to be dealt with concerning God's property of changelessness, his temporal or atemporal existence, the infallibility of God's knowledge across all time scales, and whether human free will exists.[42]

4. Relationality of Divine Substance

Do the three Persons constitute one substance (consubstantial) or are the three Persons composed of three unique substances? If the three Persons are of exactly the same substance, then there is dissolution of relational lines between them. Let us consider a small pool of perfectly uniform, pure liquid water. We now remove three samples of water by dipping a soup ladle into the pool three different times. We would find that each sample is identical and totally undifferentiated (other than each is comprised of a different set of atoms). We then return the three ladles of water to the pool where the atoms can freely intermix. The substance has never changed its manifestation or intrinsic properties and is the same no matter where the ladle draws from the pool. How then can pure liquid water in one part of the pool have different attributes than two other locations in the pool? Aside from physical location and different atoms, there is no differentiation in the relationship of the three quantities of water. There is no need to make distinctions between water in one place versus another because it is perfectly the same substance. The Holy Trinity disturbs the water so to speak by affirming the idea that this same substance Being consists of three different Persons (we might call these entities distinct consciousness's).

5. Spatiotemporal Location of Divine Substance

If the Trinity is a singular, indivisible substance, how can it be the case that the substance can simultaneously straddle the boundary of the physical realm where he is subject to the universal property of time and the natural physical laws while also being ungoverned by such strictures existing transcendently outside the four-dimensional universe? If the divine is within the physical realm in an immanent sense, how is this entity manifested and where it is located? Does God possess UBIETY wherein he is localized as a distinct entity somewhere in the universe? Or is it the case that God is a perfused substance knitted into the fabric of universe? Some would describe this condition as God *interpenetrating* our reality. If it is none of the former, does he exist in some other hidden dimension attached to our universe (i.e., dimensionally transcendent) or is he entirely external to the universe (i.e, purely transcendent)?

It bears reminding that the Second and Third Persons of the Trinity are considered "begotten, not made" according to the Nicene Creed—that is, they flow from but are not created by—the First. Additionally, the three are considered coeternal where one could not precede another. So as substances of the same manifestation that have eternally existed together, the delineation of "Father, Son, and Holy Spirit" is trivialized to the point of being tautological. If, on the other hand, we are to contend that the Father exists as a transcendent Being unaffected by the physical laws of our universe, but also was a human being (totally affected by all physical laws of the universe and the property of time), then how could the two substances be identically the same?

6. Coexistence Between Maximally Capable Persons

Is there an ontological ordering between the three Persons in the sense that one Person is subordinate to the other?

If they are perfectly coequal and maximally capable, then an assortment of potential conflicts arises. Even though the Catholic Catechism firmly holds that they are inseparable in what they do, that is they have a unified mission, it is still feasible that any given task can be accomplished in multiple ways. How are duties distributed between the three Persons? Would it not be redundant to have more than one Person acting in the ecosystem? Being maximally powerful, could one Person intentionally do harm to another Person? What if there is no way to ascertain the number of gods (refer to Challenge #1, p. 396), there could be many gods vying to participate in the Creation and sustainment of the universe. Can we be certain enough that all these gods are wholly good, with no tendency to do ill will?

7. How does God mechanistically interact in the physical realm?

Beyond God's location within or outside of three-dimensional space and his maximal powers, how is it that he could impose his will to affect the natural world without continually violating the physical laws and general limitations of material existence (e.g., eventual degradation of molecular structures)? How does God relate to the property of time?

● ● ●

Southgate and Robinson bring forward Peirce's metaphysics of triadic relationships to address the first five Challenges. The Southgate-Robinson-Peirce (S-R-P) approach describes a three-dimensional perspective employing the principles of Firstness, Secondness, and Thirdness. Within this taxonomy, Firstness is embodied by the Trinity being abstract and monadic. What this means is that the Trinity is fundamentally the most elemental and non-separable substance consisting of one divine property. While the three Persons are of the same divine essence and have the same capacity, the three Persons are distinct. By his incarnation, Jesus is a brute actuality disseminating some but not all of the divine capacities. Likewise, the Father chooses among other capacities in a different but not opposing manner to love his creatures and his cosmos. This embodies the Trinity's attribute of Secondness. The third leg of the triad is recognized through a fellowship of perfect love between the three Persons that is non-hierarchical. And, because they are of unified purpose there is no internal struggle for dominion over another. The Holy Spirit is what mediates between the Father and the Son to maintain the three in perfect union.[43] Southgate and Robinson also argue that if this semiotic understanding holds for the Trinity, then they suggest it is plausible to believe that an analogous triadic relationship or orderliness must also be manifested between the otherworld (i.e., the spirit realm) and nature. If creatures do operate in ways defined by biosemiotics, then this would suggest a pathway of how humans can participate in the divine life.[44]

In some ways, the S-R-P proposal smooths-out some of the wrinkles in explaining how the Trinity operates as a unified Being, but it does not satisfactorily iron out all the kinks. There is no robust logic put forward to defend why exactly three Persons are necessary and not some other number (two, four, five, six, …). Southgate and Robinson prop up the idea that the Son was made flesh and blood and was resurrected to become the Cosmic Christ. The New Testament tells us of Jesus' ascension into heaven whereby the Son is seated at the right hand of the Father. One could argue that this is to be interpreted as the Son joining the Father in his everlasting transcendence. But, Christian theology more strongly recommends that Jesus becomes the Cosmic Living Christ, an ephemeral Being that still lives among us and is accessible to us in word and thought. It leaves one wanting additional clarity on the mechanics of the Cosmic Christ's tangible manifestations (i.e., Challenge #5 and #7 above).

Returning to the autocell concept, Southgate and Robinson leverage this and other Origins-of-Life proposals in conjunction with the continuation of Peirce's philosophy. Recognizing that the autocell is deprived of an ability to interpret its environment or to project meanings, they opine that the act of interpretation is an emergent property which is irreducible and is the most probable next step in the evolution of autocell-like prebiotic phenomena.[45] While the pair of theologians are bent on demonstrating that naturalistic emergence and biosemiotics is tied to cosmological emergence and the semiotics of the Trinity, others are more skeptical. Anglican[10] theologian Jeremy T. Law undercuts Deacon, Sherman, Southgate, and Robinson by stating that the theological implications of the autocell's natural *telos* are essentially circular logic. According to Law, if the autocell or a construct like it can completely describe our own reality, it is foundationally an introspection of science and therefore its authority is bounded to the natural realm. It therefore cannot pronounce final judgment on whether transcendental *telos* exists or not.[46]

Law makes a valid point. Thus far, we have come along the path carrying along a presumption that biological emergence and its supposed teleological properties can in fact be used to ratify God's existence, his nature, and how he interacts with his Creation and the creatures within it. But is this really the case? Panentheists (here I mostly refer to the Christian variety) developed an interesting paradigm for divine causality that rid us from wringing our hands over theodicy and free will concerns. By conceiving God as the perpetual co-creator of future uncertain possibilities that tend toward ever-greater complexity, God could become a full-fledged actor on the stage of the universe without violating its natural laws or disrupting the flow of temporal causality. Accordingly, God interpenetrates the universe essentially resulting in a singular substance, what we might call the God-World substance.

---

10. The Anglican Communion has an estimated membership estimated of around 85 million members making it the fourth largest Christian communion in the world (after the Catholic, Eastern Orthodox, and Oriental Orthodox Churches, respectively).
   Source: http://www.anglicancommunion.org/structures/member-churches.aspx

Mikael Leidenhag, a philosopher of religion, reiterates a central tenant of Classical Theism is its insistence that the universe is dualistic whereby the divine spirit is separate from nature (i.e., physical matter). Such a conviction draws a fault line that, for the gap to be filled, demands empirical evidence that this is the case. Is there only God as one substance and the universe the only other substance of ultimate reality? If we just rely on metaphysics to answer this question, then we could just as easily conjecture that the world consists of yet a third, fourth, or fifth substance existing outside of the universe and the spirit realm. Leidenhag goes on to say that yoking Panentheistic worldviews with emergence theories attempts to define a state of monism (i.e., a singular God-World substance). This has been a central principle behind the models espoused by philosopher Philip Clayton and theologian/biochemist Arthur Peacocke. In a sense, the natural realm is the blacksmith's anvil and the spiritual divine force is the hammer. Together they work together to forge a singular reality of matter-energy transactions.

As you will recall, embedded in Panentheism is the precept that God is *in* the universe and must be comprised of the common stuff of the physical universe (interchangeable matter and energy). If God is indistinguishable from this elementary substance, then God is identically the universe which is precisely what Panentheism's competing theology calls for (i.e., Pantheism).[47] **Basically, Christian Panentheism is presenting an internally incompatible system of thought. If God is to be able to intervene as a creator (or more accurately, a co-creator) whether by persuading certain potentialities or more directly at distinct points in the form of miracles, then he can only do so by breaking the natural laws of the universe to achieve his divine purpose.[48] If this is the case, then there must be at least two substances which is ontological dualism.[49] If God's nature is dualistic, then how can he also be regarded as interpenetrating physical nature? Otherwise, if God were to be prohibited from acting in this universe, then we would have to adopt the Deistic view of a transcendent engineer who is a totally apathetic God. This would never be acceptable to Christian theology. Essentially, Christian Panentheists are trapped in a logical loop that once a position is selected—monism or dualism—it leads to a cardinal unresolved challenge.**

Leidenhag also critiques the Panentheistic contention that reality is fundamentally made up of different levels. This strikes at the heart of Panentheism, emergence, and the use of semiotics to defend the existence of transcendental *telos* (i.e., divine causality). He pins both Panentheists and scientists alike to the mat by stating that we have not decisively determined that strong emergence truly exists as a physical phenomenon much less as a transcendent phenomenon. He furthermore wraps the knuckles of Panentheists Philip Clayton and

Stuart Kauffman for not fully revealing hidden assumptions and for drafting metaphysical propositions to reinforce their theoretical framework.[50]

The preceding enlightenments dim the prospects for Southgate and Robinson's project to reconcile evolutionary biology with Christian theology and to offer a robust, coherent defense of the Holy Trinity. It similarly closes the gate to Panentheism's ability to logically rationalize that God is likely to be a perpetual cosmic creator of our known universe. It should also be made clear that, by itself, divinely-influenced cosmic emergence, even if true, would not provide any knowledge as to which conception of God he might be. That is, there is no way to claim that this perpetual Creator-God was the Abrahamic God or any other speculated supreme entity.

The eminent polymath Paul Davies,[11] a self-described Uniformitarian[12] Panentheist, is freed from the ancient encumbrances of Christian theology. As a result, his treatise may escape some of the criticisms levied above. He subscribes to a belief that there is a transcendent Creator-Sustainer God that selected the finely-tuned universal parameters, governing natural laws, and organizational rules—an intelligent design—that would guarantee the generation of a universe that would be suitably stable. This set of circumstances "encourage or facilitate rich and interesting patterns of behavior (e.g., by making some laws nonlinear, inherently statistical, etc.). On the other hand, details of the actual evolution of the universe are left open to the 'whims' of the players (including chance operating at the quantum or chaos level, the actions of human minds, etc.). I will call this proposed mode of divine action 'modified uniformitarianism.' I believe it has a number of appealing features. First, God need never suspend, manipulate, bend, or violate God's own laws since their statistical character allows for the action of divine—and perhaps human—agency. There are no miracles, save for the miracle of existence itself. Second, God does not exercise an overbearing influence on the evolution of the universe, thus reducing it to a pointless charade. There is room for human freedom, and room for even inanimate systems to explore unforeseen pathways into the future."[51]

In essence, Davies blends his finely-tuned universe treatise thoroughly discussed in many of his other works with a tinge of divine immanence, just enough to breach the edges of Panentheistic thought. I used the word 'tinge' because other models of Panentheism are

---

11. Paul Davies is a Templeton Prize winner.

12. Not to be confused with Unitarian Universalism (see p. 245), Uniformitarianism is the view that all the laws and processes of nature are the same everywhere throughout the cosmos. There is some division about whether these laws are invariant (i.e., unchanging) across cosmic timescales or whether they might be variation.

more assertive in postulating that God is cosmically present as a Being, essence, spirit, or active co-creator, whereas Davies essentially confers a divinity to the work product of a transcendent God via the perfectly balanced natural laws, universal properties, and organizational rules. These give rise to and support continual Creation, spontaneous emergence, self-organization, semi-transparent rules for cosmic organization, complexity, nonlinearity, and ordered chaos. Ultimately it leads to an **ANTHROPIC** destiny inclusive of the evolution of humanity (man, culture, and language) imbued with a freedom to act and with some likelihood, the existence of intelligent alien life-forms. Davies conjectures that this reality is the hand print of "an ingenious—even loving—designer."[52] In short, Davies' affirms a **DIPOLAR** Creator-Sustainer God who exists completely outside of the universe. We and the entire universe are essentially the after-effects of his initial handiwork. If we thought of the universe as an apple pie, God created the recipe, the ingredients, the oven, and the physics to bake the pie into the proper round shape, texture, consistency, and color but once he put the pie into the oven, he lets it cook without further direct intervention.

Davies admits that his worldview offers a deity that is less personal than most theists would prefer. Where Davie's pitch is somewhat weakened is his defense of a loving God that engineered such a supremely accommodating universe for life-forms to emerge. He offers little explication for why the bad things that beset mankind and the universe as a whole are allowed to happen as a loving God sits on the sidelines watching his finely-tuned universe indiscriminately annihilate and harm life of every sort. As such, I do not think his worldview neatly sidestep the perils brought by the existence of evil as well as other models of Panentheism. Using his rationale, one could equally maintain that God does not express love for his human creations per se, at least not in the human sense of the word. He could love his Creation in a more global sense for all its beauty, diversity, and complexity but is accepting of the path of destruction that occurs to achieve this desirable state of affairs. In other words, while the natural laws are a highly creative force, they also work to transmute both animate and inanimate objects via methods that involve the death/destruction of other things.

As Davies recognizes himself, his case for divinely inspired natural laws may not be wholly convincing to those that believe that Creation, evolution, and the laws therein are simply brute facts and do not require a divine ascription to their nature. This, then, boils down to a Deistic view of God, which was Davies' original position before he transitioned to his modification of Uniformitarian Panentheistic system of belief. In the end, Davies' mentation on God sits upon a fulcrum created by his fundamental metaphysical assertion that an intelligent designer exists and that this wondrous deity caused the universe to come into being and sustain itself against great odds. Davies, a distinguished cosmologist, is an advocate for a non-eternal universe whereby the universe came into existence at a distinct point. In Chapter 13, we'll further examine the temporal state of the universe.

WHERE DOES THIS LEAVE GOD?

Our etiological efforts to understand the causation of (or not) and the existence of (or not) for God has being skinnied-down to a choice between one of several constructs. The zetetic process started out by claiming nothing whatsoever about God-by-whatever-name and moved incrementally forward in step-wise fashion to critique fundamental aspects of theological concern while moving to the side any claims of miraculous intervention or personal revelatory or intuitive experience. With much effort, it has been elucidated that Classical Theism, monotheism, monolatrism, polytheism, pluralism, Panentheism, and Pantheism (the latter via arguments against a worldly God presented in Panentheism) are seriously troubled with a generous lack of evidence and catastrophic incoherencies.

Given that none of the God-concepts are rationally satisfactory, there are five options available for us to consider. The first possibility is that the God-Source could be a purely transcendent and totally unknowable Being. This falls in line to some extent with the untouchable and impersonal views of Deism. A second alternative, albeit unprovable, is the idea that God once existed to create the universe but exists no longer. This is the Meta-Transignification Hypothesis which is in some sense the conjoining of Deism *and* nontheism. A third option is that the universe is caused by something other than a living Being, that is, some form of inanimate substance and corresponding process or event. This option might produce a fourth possibility whereby this substance not only creates our universe but is responsible for creating many universes (i.e., the multiverse hypothesis). Perhaps all four of these possible realities are wrong. Maybe the fifth possibility is the case that the universe is eternally existed, never having had a First Cause. This would alleviate the necessity for God to exist. And, as crazy as it may sound, a sixth concept to consider is that we live in a simulated world created by some form of alien super-intelligence. To amuse the aliens, we are left to endlessly query about things we call God and reality when in fact we are essentially fictional (non-real) constructs of super-advanced programming. The zetetic process demands that we pursue these other options, which is the direction we shall head after we consider neuroscientific perspectives which is the subject of the next chapter.

SUMMARY

Aristotle contemplated, among many things, that God was a purely transcendent attractive Unmoved Mover that was unconcerned with our worldly affairs making him in the mold of a polytheistic Deist though the term was not in circulation during his time. He originated the concept of teleology (but not the word itself) which in modern-day times is now used to define end-directed processes in nature (natural *telos*) and end-directed divine purpose (transcendental *telos*). The theories of weak and strong emergence were reviewed as means to describe the apparent increase in cosmic and biologic complexity. This complexity, some believe, leads to a hierarchical structure to nature. Contemporary Origins-of-Life research has revealed the intriguing theoretic concept of catalytic autocells as a promising means to give rise to protolife. The morphodynamics (i.e., self-organization) of autocellular processes have been computationally simulated in virtual environments. Scientific investigations have further revealed plausible mechanisms regarding the formation of proto-RNA supramolecules as a potential precursor to modern RNA and DNA structures.

Borrowing the concept of strong emergence and transcendental *telos*, modern Panentheism seeks to explain how it is that some divine force is actively participating in the universe. While there have been many models of non-Christian Panentheism, the more prominent models and those most rigorously articulated in contemporary times are arguments for a Christian Panentheism that depend much on the ideas promulgated in Process Theology. Process Theology trades the focus on things or substances of the universe for event-driven processes which better account for the complexification we see around us. Classical Theism has long been plagued with the Problems of Evil, free will-vs-determinism, and how their transcendent God can exist and act in the cosmic realm without continually violating the natural laws and its temporality. Panentheism has the highly attractive features of resolving all of these problems by describing God with less than perfect monadic properties. By relinquishing the demands of Perfect Being Theology and imbuing God with a more limited capability we are freed as human beings to act in accordance with our own will and to release God of any responsibilities for the evil that embraces world affairs. God plies his preferences by influencing possible future outcomes to enrich the cosmos as a whole as well as the position and evolution of his creaturely creations.

The most recent theological efforts have been complemented by the introduction of the relatively new science of semiotics—the study of meaning-making—which is itself is in some respects still justifying itself as legitimate field of scientific endeavor. By combining the ideas of complexity, emergence, Process Philosophy/Process Theology, semiotics/biosemiotics, and generic Panentheism, Christian apologists have attempted to inflate a deflated Christian theology. While theologians Christopher Southgate and Andrew Robinson recognize that the findings of evolutionary biology pose a significant threat to the reality of transcendental *telos*, their commendable attempt to leverage the aforementioned thought systems and theoretical paradigms to achieve some level of reconciliation between religion and science has not yielded the fruits they so desire. As a final commentary on the trinitarian paradigm, the Seven Challenges were presented. While limited clarity was garnered from Southgate and Robinson's proposal about how perichoresis (i.e., the relationship between the three divine Persons) might be effectuated, most of the challenges remained defiant of any coherent explication.

Two years before Terrence Deacon proposed the autocell construct; Paul Davies levied his Panentheistic-oriented opinion that God is a transcendent Creator-Sustainer God who designed a universe that is outfitted with governing laws and universal parameters that promote the emergence of ever-increasing complexity. In particular, the parameters are supremely precise for even the slightest change would radically alter the universe. He suggests that our universe may also possess organizational rules that work to support the teleological complexification process. Davies argues that God is also the divine, immanent, and loving sustainer of the universe by way of these laws, parameters, and rules which tirelessly work to perpetually create the universe. However, God himself is not present within the universe. His God is much less personal than many theists would have him be as God only works through the natural ingredients that come about through cosmic emergence. Therefore, to his mind, God is not a miracle-worker but loves his creation of sentient and conscious life-forms from afar.

This chapter was concluded with an appraisal of where the zetetic process has led us. It was summarized that the major religious schools of thought are not altogether successful in providing a rational basis for their interpretations of God. Even if we allow such theologies to resort to mysticism to explain his nature and existence, such efforts come up short on supplying the Common Man with anything that is digestible wisdom, let alone a coherent framework. Presuming God's existence, what remains is an impersonal purely transcendent deity. It would be difficult to conceive this Source as a form-full Being anything akin to our comprehension. As such, referring to this hyperessence simply as the Source` of which any description is strictly symbolic is as far as we can go. Another hypothesis is that God once existed but chose to convert his existence into a living cosmos filled with beauty, life, and enigma. If we do not presume God's existence, there are ideas (yet to be reviewed) that suggest that the universe has always and forever been a godless reality.

The primary conclusion of this chapter is that teleological arguments, of which there are many more than we can review here, are ultimately unsuccessful in affirming the existence of God as the active Sustainer of the universe. If we are thus far unable to find anything definitive in defense of a God that sustains and interacts with the universe, we are left to question did a living deity even have a hand in creating the universe? This question is pursued following the next chapter which puts our human capabilities front and center. Is it not necessary to understand how our onboard instruments—our physical senses and the mind-brain—could affect how we are to understand external reality? The zetetic path swerves once more so that we can develop an appreciation for the science of the mind-brain and what can be learned about how our brains function to interpret the world around us and to reveal what we may about human consciousness as well as the concept of the human soul.

CHAPTER 12

The Cognitive Science of Religion

At its core, science is a human endeavor. Its strengths and flaws mirror our own.[1]

— Alan Lightman
Astrophysicist and novelist

For the mind of man is far from the nature of a clear and equal glass, wherein the beams of things should reflect according to their true incidence; nay, it is rather like an enchanted glass, full of superstition and imposture, if it be not delivered and reduced.

— Francis Bacon
Novum Organum Scientiarum (trans. New Instrument of Science), 1620
Francis Bacon is credited as the father of Empiricism and early developer of the scientific method. He was also Baron of Verulam and Lord Chancellor of England.

The first principle is that you must not fool yourself—and you are the easiest person to fool.[2]

— Richard Feynman
"Surely You're Joking, Mr. Feynman!", 1977
Adapted from the Caltech University commencement address given in 1974. Feynman is discussing mysticism, UFOs, astrology, ESP, and pseudoscience in general and instructing the graduates on how to conduct quality scientific investigations to discover the truth.

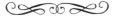

THE PERILS OF ROMANTICIZING SCIENCE

AFTER THE SUM OF A great many careful steps, we have progressed far on our zetetic odyssey to separate the substantive wheat from the philosophical and theological chaff in the search for the existence and nature of God. To reach this precipice, we have leveraged many footholds in our ascent; specifically we have applied our cognitive dialectical capacities (abductive, reductive, inductive, and deductive reasoning) and the tools of historiography, scriptural exegesis, archaeology, comparative mythology, and evolutionary biology. It was alluded to in Chapter 1 that we might also consult the disciplines of neuroscience, neurotheology, evolutionary psychology, quantum biology, physics, and cosmogony. These will be the final ports of call as we move forward. However, before we change our tack to reorient ourselves toward these scientific perspectives, it is of paramount importance that we level with the might and wit of science for there is an onslaught of weaknesses that beleaguer the process of scientific inquiry, indeed it affects most any scholastic endeavor scientific, philosophical, or otherwise.

While scholars are generally aware of the trappings of academic research, even with the best of intentions and well-resourced projects, the outcomes of scientific research must be met with a strong sense of skepticism. The Common Man is often skeptical of what science has to say on any given topic, but perhaps not for all the right reasons. Most individuals have encountered on more than one occasion the situation whereby a new scientific discovery heralds research outcomes demanding a new world order. Then months, perhaps years later, another study comes along that discounts the findings hailing instead the earlier view or some other view altogether. This process goes on *ad nauseum* and all too often people become tone deaf and disinterested in changing their beliefs deciding consciously or not to settle on what suits them best. It ends up being a case of 'crying wolf' once too often. As a result people lose confidence in scientific research. While this scenario rather closely reflects the relationship between science and the Common Man, there are many more profound problems that pervade the truss-work of scientific investigation that we need to be aware of as we consider its value in deciphering the reality of God.

Dollars and Science

In 2016, the world nations spent just short of $2 trillion for research and development (R&D) investment activities. The United States accounts for 26.5%, or $514 billion of this total, or in alternate terms, 2.8% of national GDP. A quarter of this amount is used to fund spending activities of the Department of Defense ($60B), National Institute of Health ($31B), NASA ($12B), the Department of Energy ($12B), and the balance used for the other federal agencies engaged in R&D.[2] While these dollar amounts may be considered by the unacquainted as staggeringly large numbers, when they are traced back to the funding of individual projects, most federally- and academically-funded researchers operate their affairs on what might be referred to as a 'shoe-string budget'. One has to be cognizant of the fact that a considerable amount of dollars spent go toward facilities, very expensive laboratory equipment, and the fabrication of one-off (or very low quantity) materials or products which consistently cost an order of magnitude or two more than the same product made in large volumes. The amounts allocated to salaries (that is, the time to do the work) and administrative costs can be a small portion of the total. The available funding is often so meager, that *offset funding* is usually accessed by other means.

The main point is that ambitious researchers must aggressively compete for their project funding. This is most often accomplished via the submission of proposals, the success rate of which is typically 10–20 percent, but can be much lower. This means that the average researcher must submit between four to seven proposals to succeed in capitalizing their endeavors. This can easily translate to a period of one or two years for some applicants to win an actual award for funding. And, quite frequently, a decision to award a proposal will take three to four months, with an additional month to solidify a contract making the funding accessible. Many projects may be in the making for several years even before there is an official sponsorship in place. This long cycle to 'first dollar earned' is what keeps researchers up at night combined with the fact that most projects have multiple phases. In most cases, at the conclusion of one phase there is a period of consideration by the funding authority as to whether or not the next phase will be given permission to proceed. The powers that be may think that the outcomes do not merit further investment and the research stops dead in its tracks. It is also the case that more experienced and/or prominent researchers garner the lion's share of research dollars. This tends to leave younger, less experienced or less well-known academics out in the cold. Without a steady stream of funding, it becomes impossibly difficult to launch a scholar's career from the dregs of the bottom-dwellers. It also creates great angst, envy, and resentment in the community of scholars because of the relative ease for senior researchers to gather up the scarce bounty. While collaboration is widely practiced, there always exists this undercurrent of divisive allocation of resources.

Because R&D funding is always and forever a carousel of annual budgeting, this set of environmental factors produces an alchemy which produces perennial winners and losers. And, even the winners are hard-pressed to deliver on their promised bill of goods given the general limitations of all monies to be had. Those that can bring in the money year after year will be rewarded with promotions and tenure and in non-academic settings a title of *Fellow* or *Senior Fellow* and all its accoutrements. Tenure is the academic equivalent of a bulletproof vest that permits professors to advance controversial, non-conformist viewpoints without the threat of being dismissed from their faculty positions. Continued success will attract further prestige via an 'endowed chair' or distinguished professorship that essentially pays for the researcher's (usually enhanced) salary and other supporting personnel. This prestige becomes an overwhelming advantage that overshadows otherwise promising approaches presented by other peers which get sidelined with no hope of seeing the light of day. It is a vicious and interminably-so dog-eat-dog world—a fight for the survival for the career academician.

Scholars and researchers, especially university-supported academicians, operate under a zombied credo of *'publish or perish'*. If professors are not tenured and are not publishing frequently enough or in widely respected literary venues, they will not be granted tenure and in many cases are released from their academic appointment or their career-growth is otherwise severely stunted. When combined with the publishing industry's standard for the restriction on dual submission (also called simultaneous submission),[1] duplicate publication,[2] and their long review processes, this mantle of pressure leads to the larding of their *curriculum vitae* by various methods. The primary technique is to split hypotheses and their related conclusions into 'chunks' so that it yields a series of papers whereas in many cases all the work could have been otherwise contained within a single paper. With ideas narrowed and finely parsed, it is often difficult to impossible to see the 'bigger picture'. Thus, scholarly publishing misses its aim of effectively communicating revelations in human knowledge in the greater context. Academic publishing shares greater kinship with *The Rifleman* TV character Lucas McCain whose rapid-levering of his Winchester rifle authors the release of as many pieces of lead as possible. The fact that many 'literary bullets' miss their mark is beside the point.

While there is competition for dollars among researchers, research institutions have their own pressures to churn out research that will offer a monetary return for its investments. Similarly, they are very much interested in projects that attract celebrity figures or offer a 'prestige factor'. This pressure cascades down to the individual researcher to publish as many papers as possible and to have them published in journals of distinction (rated by high **IMPACT FACTORS** and **ALTMETRICS**). These internal stresses create opportunities to run afoul of the "Seven Sins of Academic Behavior"[4] which include, but are not limited to, bias toward reporting favorable results, a neglect in correcting errors identified post-publication, plagiarism, and falsification/fabrication of data. A *Los Angeles Times* news article entitled "Science has lost its way, at a big cost to humanity" echoes these concerns. "The journals want the papers that make the sexiest claims [...] and scientists believe that the way you succeed is having splashy papers in Science or Nature – it's not bad for them if a paper turns out to be wrong, if it's gotten a lot of attention."[5]

Published at nearly the same time, *The Economist* magazine reported that publications that portrayed negative results, as in not affirming the researcher's initial hypothesis, has decreased over the last twenty years by nearly a third. Today, only three out of every

---

1. Dual (or simultaneous) submission is when an author submits an article to more than one publisher for consideration.

2. Duplicate submission is when the author submits an article that is the same, or substantially similar, to an already published paper to a publisher.

twenty reports present negative results. They also found that the peer review process to verify the legitimacy of the information in scientific reports is lacking which leads to the publication of false or misleading information.[6] This is not all too surprising really. Performing proper peer reviews are time intensive endeavors and if academicians are spending time on this activity it is time they are not doing their own research or writing publications. The peer review process often includes one or more anonymous reviewers to encourage open criticism. Sometimes the biases of the anonymous reviewer or the editor-in-charge will creep in to delay or reject the publication of an otherwise worthy piece of literature. Careerism and the paucity of public/private funding are largely to blame for these outcomes. If the funding of projects were made at a level more commensurate with the need, it would ostensibly lessen pressures and facilitate higher quality research and better protocols for publishing both positive and negative findings.

In the last decade, it has become abundantly clear that the biomedical research industry has created an alarming epidemic all its own. Richard Harris, a science correspondent at NPR News and author of *Rigor Mortis: How Sloppy Science Creates Worthless Cures, Crushes Hope and Wastes Billions* (Basic Books, 2017) affirms that the bulk of biomedical research cannot be validated, is partially flawed, or is patently wrong. He cites that a myriad of underlying issues are to blame including the systemic use of contaminated or improperly identified base samples (e.g., cancer cell cultures) that were initially not known to be contaminated or misidentified, but nevertheless proliferated throughout the R&D community. Another industry-wide problem is the inability for the majority of resesearch studies to meet the basic standard of good science, that is, reproducibility of experimental results. Contributing factors are poor experimental design, lack of proper training, basic mistakes in analyzing results, and biased interpretations. Serial reductions in R&D investment and perverse professional incentives has stimulated the production of an endemic hypercompetitive culture that values authors to be the first to publish positive results. This was further exacerbated on March 16, 2013 after the enactment of the *America Invents Act* which awards patent rights to the first entity to apply for a patent in contrast to the former system whereby U.S. patents were awarded on a first-to-invent basis.

A global-scale example where such a competitive dance has played out for all the public to see is in the harrowing five decade long search for the elusive elementary particle, the Higgs boson—or better known by its popularized name—the "God particle." The Higgs boson (noted in Chapter 1, see pp. 9, 45, and 54) was theorized to exist by multiple researchers in the timeframe of 1960 – 1972. The Standard Model is an incomplete scientific theory that represents our best understanding of how the three fundamental forces of nature—

electromagnetism, the atomic nuclear force, and the weak force associated with radioactive decay—fundamentally interact with particle matter. It is an incomplete model because it does not describe how these three forces interact with the gravity, the fourth fundamental force. Prior to the theorization of the Higgs boson, it was unknown what was physically responsible for certain elementary particles (e.g., the proton, neutron, and electron)—all the matter we see in the universe—to become imbued with their intrinsic property of mass.[3] The Higgs mechanism is a mathematical model that describes the laws of nature of the *why* and the *how* particle symmetries come about and how such symmetries, under certain conditions, may not be obeyed. The model loftily predicted that an entirely new structure (a field) permeates the entirety of the spatial realm of the universe.

The Higgs field is a uniform field of energy which is not directly detectable. It does not transfer any force, acceleration, or its own energy into matter. Rather, each class of matter interacts with the field at different strengths. The greater the strength of the interaction (excitation) that exists, the more massive that particular type of matter is. Therefore all fermions[4] (i.e., particle matter) interact with the field to varying degrees resulting in different rest masses. Some particles do not interact at all which explains their lack of mass (e.g., photons have zero rest mass). While protons and neutrons are physically made up of quark particles, the quarks, vis-à-vis the Higgs field interaction, are only responsible for about one percent of the proton or neutron mass. The other 99 percent comes from the binding energy to keep the quarks together. One may then question why the discovery of the Higgs field was so momentous if we are only talking about a measly one percent of something. Simply put, without this tiny one percent of mass, atomic matter would not be the same and the universe would fail to exist as it does.

The theory also predicted the existence of a distinct companion to the Higgs field in the form of a mediating particle—the Higgs boson.[5] The Higgs particle's existence arises from the existence of the Higgs field, but not vice-versa. Because the field itself is directly undetectable, if the Higgs particle could be detected, then the field's existence would be indirectly proven to exist. However, it turns out that among all other particles, the Higgs particle excitation is one of the weakest which means that it too is immensely difficult to detect.

---

3. Usually, one refers to the "rest mass" of the particle.

4. Fermions are one of two classes of elementary particles that include leptons (e.g., electrons, neutrinos) and quarks (e.g., protons, neutrons). Bosons are the other class of elementary particles.

5. Bosons are the second elementary counterpart to fermions. They are called 'force carrier' particles that give rise to the interactive forces between individual and composite particles.

To prove the existence of the Higgs particle, the most powerful particle accelerator/collider ('atom smasher') was needed. This massive piece of equipment uses electromagnetic fields to contain and propel charged particles to speeds of 99.999 percent of the speed of light (186,282 miles per second/299,792 kilometers per second) and then impact the particles to break them apart into their decay signatures. Because it was expected to be a rare event, hundreds of trillions of collisions were necessary which generated dozens of petabytes of information (a million gigabytes, or 10^{15} bytes, equals one petabyte). This colossal amount of information required massive computing power. There were only two facilities in the world that might be capable of producing the extreme impact energies and parse the information to produce a signature of the Higgs boson—the United States' Fermilab Tevatron 4-mile circular collider located in Batavia, Illinois and Europe's more powerful, but under-construction, CERN Large Hadron Collider located in Geneva, Switzerland.

The race was on between the two nation teams. CERN's facility, a 17-mile circular collider, would not be inaugurated until 2008 giving Fermilab a sizable upfront time advantage. Less than four years later, on July 4, 2012, CERN broadcasted that its ATLAS and CMS experiments had made a verifiable observation of the Higgs boson that met the so-called 5σ—five-sigma—criterion. The five-sigma metric is the statistical likelihood that what they observed was in fact a particle having the necessary characteristics and not one of the many other particles that possess features similar to it. Stated another way, researchers were confident that the data was exceptionally unlikely to be a statistical anomaly from an oddball random result occurring only once in 3.5 million chances. Knowing that the CERN collider out-matched Fermilab's collider capabilities, the Tevatron was shutdown permanently on September 30, 2011 even before the particle was officially detected by CERN. This was a sad day for America's supremacy as the epicenter of particle physics. This was writ large well before 2011 as the US Congress cancelled funding in 1993 to produce a collider powerful enough to compete with CERN's atom smasher. As the CERN facility came online, scientists from the United States steadily flocked to CERN because where the money flows, scientists must necessarily follow.

The lesson here is the what, where, who, and how of research very much swears fealty to ambiguous policy makers who decide which projects to fund, de-fund, or not fund at all. In its wake, troves of promising research, some with great potential value, is left behind. Researchers pile behind one another like lemmings looking for the next fist waving cash in the air. However, money has a much deeper effect than the selection, duration, and quantity of research projects. It affects how research is fundamentally performed in terms of its breadth, depth, and the quality therein. By way of simplified example, a $250,000 grant in psychological research may entail the use of twenty human subjects to investigate several hypothetical phenomena of interest. Such a study may produce certain findings that can offer a statistical significance that suggest that there is an 85 percent chance that the observations collected reflect the actual characteristics of the study population (i.e., the statistical sample) and is not due to sampling error. This leaves open a fairly large margin (15 percent chance) that the results could in fact be attributed to sampling error. That is, that the sample results for the twenty subjects do not represent the characteristics for the population of human beings at large. Additional certainty in the results could be had by reducing this type of error if the funding was increased to support a greater number of human subjects.

But, there are much deeper concerns associated with research protocols than measurement-type errors. The greatest of which are the *a priori* assumptions employed in the theoretical framework and the general experimental setup. Science, for example, always initiates with the assumption that the world (reality) is as how we measure or analyze it. Furthermore, it is assumed that the assessment will remain stable over time. And, thirdly, we assume that scientists are free to make inferences to affirm our knowledge. Whether or not science has this inductive authority to begin with is at the heart of what is referred to as the Problem of Induction. A superlative example of how scientific assumptions can lead us terribly awry for great lengths of time is when, in the latter part of the 1600's, Isaac Newton's law of universal gravity took firm hold in the scientific community. It was agreed that it completely and accurately described the mutual attraction of any and all bodies (i.e., physical matter) throughout the universe.[6] Its validity remained unquestioned for over two centuries until Einstein made known his stunning observations in the early 1900s. Until that time, all experiments and theories assumed the perfect exactness of Newton's reality.

Another assumption that is often overlooked is the reliance on approximations. It is very often the case that mathematical relationships which describe a particular phenomenon or principle are represented by a highly complex set of equations. Such relationships are quite often nonlinear in that one parameter may change disproportionately relative to other parameters (recall from the previous chapter the nonlinearity of emergent dynamics). To illustrate this point more concretely, consider a simple nonlinear function as shown below. When the value of '*x*' is specified equal to 0.1, the function value is only slightly nonlinear. The exact value of this expression is a one with ten ones after the decimal point. This series of numbers would often be abbreviated (approximated) in the realms of science, mathematics, or

---

6. The origination of Newton's second law of motion was contested by his contemporary, Robert Hooke, who believed he was the first to have discovered the relationship.

engineering as being a value of 1.1 to simplify the representation. This would be called a linear approximation.

$$\sum_{n=0}^{10} x^n = \overbrace{x^0 + x^1}^{\text{Linearity}} + \overbrace{x^2 + x^3 + x^4 + x^5 + \ldots + x^{10}}^{\text{Nonlinearity}}$$

Let us assume that $x = 0.1$

$$\sum_{n=0}^{10} (0.1^n) = \overbrace{(0.1^0) + (0.1^1)}^{\text{Linear}} + (0.1^2) + (0.1^3) + (0.1^4) + (0.1^5) + \ldots + (0.1^{10})$$

$$\sum_{n=0}^{10} (0.1^n) = \overbrace{1.0 + 0.1}^{\text{Linear}} + .01 + .001 + .0001 + .00001 + \ldots + 1 \times 10^{-10}$$

$$\sum_{n=0}^{10} (0.1^n) = \underbrace{\overbrace{1.1}^{\text{Linear}} \; 1111 \cdots 1}_{\text{Exact Value}} \approx \mathbf{1.1} \longleftarrow \text{Approximate Value}$$

This type of assumption is generally referred to as taking into account first-order effects. In many cases this would provide sufficiently accurate data for whatever this expression might relate to. However, if this value were being used in a time-keeping system requiring high precision, for example, in an internal clock of a communication satellite, a timing system for a spacecraft rocket thruster, or for high volume production equipment, then this approximation may well prove to have highly adverse repercussions. Sometimes it is easily recognized when it is prudent to make approximations and in other instances, it is not at all clear. Nevertheless, linearization of nonlinear phenomena is routinely performed, warranted or not. Seldom is there any verification undertaken until 'things go wrong'. The fact remains that reality is nonlinear in most things. Needing to make things more amenable to our cognitive abilities, we very frequently fall into a state of repeated **SIMPLISM**—reducing things to a state of affairs by ignoring salient information leading to a situation of false simplicity.

Science is not sacred. The 20th-century Duhem–Quine thesis gives us an essential insight that any single scientific hypothesis is always reliant on other auxiliary hypotheses.[7] This is to say that we cannot take individual theoretic claims and confirm or falsify them in isolation. Scientific theories are built upon the prior framework of other theories, so-called conjoined hypotheses or conjoined beliefs, some of which are considered **AXIOMATIC**. Scientific theories are therefore susceptible to what I metaphorically refer to as the *Leaning Tower of Pisa Effect*. Initially, the bell tower was a marvel of medieval engineering.

At eight stories high it may have been the tallest of its ilk throughout Europe. However, it was built upon unstable soil which caused it to start leaning during construction of its second story. As each new story was fabricated there is a corresponding increase in the building's weight and center of gravity which added uncertainty to the overall stability of the architecture.

A scientific correlate of the Leaning Tower of Pisa Effect can be found in the theory concerning the multigenerational habits of the migratory Monarch butterfly. The phenomena of this butterfly's annual migration of some three thousand miles to the exact same destination are a mixture of innate and learned behavior. But, due to the short lifespan of a given individual, the large distances involved, and the energy required making such an epic journey, it takes four generations of adult butterflies to complete one migration. What is truly astounding is that *none* of the four generations of butterflies had ever previously visited the end destination. It is thought that the brains of the Monarch butterfly contain two different photoreceptor proteins called *cryptochromes* that, through an unconventional photochemical mechanism, allows the creatures to see ultraviolet light and detect the Earth's geomagnetic field.[8]

Of course, such biochemical processes and the internal magnetic forces of the Earth are assumed to be subject to a number of universal laws of nature. Along the same lines, the Monarch's flight is subject to the gravitational effects of the Earth which seeks to pull the butterfly toward the planet's center of mass. The butterfly is able to oppose this force by rhythmically beating its wings and using the physics of aerodynamics to lift its body upward and forward. The migration theory also presupposes that the laws of nature are the same throughout our worldly environment. We automatically assume that the quirkiness of quantum dynamics and endemic randomness and spontaneity whereby the individual subatomic particles that make up the body of the Monarch's body will not appreciably alter the integrity of the animal given the imprecise movement and position of its subatomic structure. We generally understand (assume) that matter at scales larger than the **PLANCK SCALE** behave statistically. We also fundamentally assume that the butterfly is a real physical 'thing' and not the sole product of our mind. So, we see there are many layers of theories that create an interconnected network.

Since we have no absolute Archimedean point of reference, the stability of our grounding of scientific introspection is always a little uncertain and never absolute.

Cognitive Bias and Beliefs

While use of *a priori* assumptions is a sizable concern, cognitive biases are phenomena that persistently threaten the quality of research. Cognitive biases are by no means confined to the conduct of investigators but apply to people in general. It turns out that the human brain is quite skilled at deceiving itself. In the basement of our minds lie many cognitive biases that work in the darkness that is our subconscious that can lead to identifying false patterns or to introduce deviations or distortions in judgment that lead toward irrationality and the development of a subjective social reality that may not comport with 'real reality'.

In 2016, two curious and enterprising gentlemen by the names of Buster Benson and John Manoogian III decided that it was necessary to better highlight the sheer number of documented cognitive biases. They organized the biases by segmenting them into four generalized groups associated with the following decision-making circumstances: (1) memory recall, (2) information overload, (3) inadequate information or meaning, and (4) the need to decide or act quickly. These four groupings are parsed into a total of 22 sub-categories which then splinter further into the **188 documented cognitive biases and distortions**. Whereas Benson performed the arrangement of the groupings, Manoogian developed a visually stunning color-coded chart illustrating the connectivity of the groupings called the *Cognitive Bias Codex, 2016*.[7] Due to the volume of information presented and its use of color-coding, the chart cannot be legibly reproduced herein; however, it is enough to consider that our mind-brains are awash in dozens and dozens of biases and distortions of reality and that these are routinely employed day-in and day-out. We can only feel slack-jawed when we consider how it is we human beings function on a daily basis with such a staggering number of deep-seated nonobjective decision-making aptitudes. It ought to make us feel a deep sense of humility of how erroneous each of us can be when we compare our inner thoughts to objective reality. To offer a sense of appreciation for what some of these biases are, seven are selected from the fold for brief discussion whereas others are more generally touched upon throughout this book directly and indirectly.

Probably one of the most recognized and repeated sources of cognitive bias is *Confirmation bias* which is the tendency to seek, interpret, focus, and recall information that supports established beliefs and to furthermore ignore, discount, or reinterpret disconfirming information. While Confirmation bias is often thought of in the context of a singular incident, it can also be embodied in the entire scholastic careers of many an

---

7. The *Cognitive Bias Codex, 2016* can be accessed here: http://tinyurl.com/jp45dm3. Last accessed 30 Sep 2016.

academician. As a given philosopher, historian, religionist, or scientist meditates day after day, year after year, and decade after decade on a particular subject matter, they become conditioned to see reality through the specific lens of their pet theory that they have matured over those long stretches of time. Some will persist in belief of their paradigm even in the face of stark evidence to the contrary. If there was ever a bias that could be justifiably levied against a multitude of prominent religious apologists, this would be it.

In a renowned study by cognitive psychologists Hasher, Goldstein, and Toppino (1977),[2] it was demonstrated that when people receive repeated information, they are more apt to consider it as true in comparison to new (i.e., unrepeated) information that is presented. They called this the *Illusory-truth effect*. Researchers have also discovered a parallel phenomenon that people who receive *repeated false information* are more apt to more intensely believe the information to be more plausibly true. This is due to the repetition as well as a secondary effect of them erroneously believing that their knowledge has been supplemented from other external sources apart from the original source.[10] This bias is used by evangelical theists by repeatedly drumming the many themes and facets of religion into the unwitting and essentially receptive individual. This is the central purpose of regularized religious gatherings which are essentially spiritual conduits for a captive audience to be subjected to repeated exposure of one-sided religious messages. This is to say that these social gatherings are geared toward one-way dissemination of pre-programmed ideas and are not analytical dissections of truth and falsity of the disseminated information. **This comment may seem biased in and of itself, however, in achieving an objective view, it is generally required that we be exposed to multiple perspectives that we may disagree with a lot or a little.**

I take my life story as an example. When I was in parochial elementary school, I was taught by priests, nuns, and teachers the many themes of Catholicism. It was all new to me. This was only reinforced by my parents and to a lesser extent, my school friends. I attended religion classes during the school day and special ones at night, prayed in school, performed hands-on projects, read the children's Bible, took paper quizzes, constructed a stole[8] for the Confirmation process, and attended weekly mass as well as during the school days of religious commemoration. I cannot recount a single instance when *any* of my educators ever offered alternative views. With old and new information being repeatedly 'given' to my still maturing mind, for better or worse, I was certainly affected by Confirmation bias and the Illusory-truth effect.

---

8. A long, narrow strip of cloth draped around the neck. Attached to it are stitched-in or bonded symbols of the Catholic faith (e.g., Christ's cross, chalice, Eucharist, candles).

Anchoring bias is the tendency to rely too heavily on an existent piece of information when making decisions, which is often the first piece of information acquired. In a sense, we weigh this prior information more than is justifiable to do so. One example that everyone can relate to is that the older generation in society had paid 10 cents for a cup of coffee and these same individuals five decades later contend it should still cost 10 cents. In the case of religious education, we tend to retain the initial installment of religious ideas concerning God. As illustrated in Chapter 1–Figure 2, a Christian convert is most likely to be anchored to some other denomination of Christianity or to become religiously unaffiliated before they would choose to select a radically different conception of God. Likewise, a convert from Judaism will remain in the larger circle of Jewish sects or become unaffiliated rather than to cross the boundary of Christianity or Islam. And, similarly, a Muslim is more likely than not to remain within his or her own tradition or to overwhelmingly choose to become unaffiliated than to convert to the Christian or Jewish faith.

Given the sheer breadth, depth, and overall complexity of religion and science, we often defer to authorities in areas that we are unfamiliar with. We therefore tend to weight the opinions of authority figures more highly whether or not such authorities actually convey truthful, rational, or otherwise valid information. This tendency to allocate greater value to authoritative figures is not surprisingly referred to as *Authority bias*. As the content of this book has so firmly revealed, intellectual agreement on ideas by so-called authorities both between and within science and religion, respectively, is hard to come by.

A fifth type of cognitive bias is introduced when one is given a choice between a simple (or more general) set of conditions versus a complex (or specific) set of conditions. For instance, if presented with the question, "What is more likely to occur—A fox is running at top speed across a field, or, a fox running across a field at top speed chasing after a rabbit?" In this *Conjunction fallacy*, one will tend to select the fox chasing a rabbit, though in reality, this may be the more improbable choice because two things need to be true for the entire statement to be true. In essence, people tend to believe choices that have a greater quantity of information. This technique is often exploited by religious apologists who put forth a massive trove of arguments and supposed data to support their ideas about God-by-whatever-name. The sheer volume of purported evidence impresses upon one that such a mass of information must be true. In reality, it is incumbent upon us to examine each and every detail on its own terms to assess the overall validity to avoid being caught-up in a Conjunction fallacy.

Yet another bias found all too commonly is *Herd bias* (or *Bandwagon Effect*) where the tendency is for people to adopt or otherwise follow the behaviors or beliefs of the majority of the group members as a means to fit in and avoid conflict. Andrew Newberg (b. 1966 –), an eminent neuroscientist, psychiatrist, and pioneer of the nascent field of neurotheology, indicates that religious rituals operate on this principle when a subgroup of people's behavior influences the behavior of those around them.[11] For example, if the customary ritual for a religious group is to have a religious congregation encircle a bride and groom as they then extend their arms upward and outward as they pray for the couple, a nonreligious person may tend to follow the rest of the group in playing out the ritual by also extending their own arms. This might be explained in part on a neuronal level as the brain contains *mirror neurons* whose specific duty is to replicate our perceptions presumably as a means to achieve cognitive consonance (as opposed to dissonance) as the brain interprets worldly externalities.

A prominently employed bias affecting an individual, group, or society is the situation whereby different conclusions are derived from the same set of information based solely on how the information is presented. This *Framing effect* is an incredibly effective means for the communicator to inculcate the receiver of the information. An example that ties in political, cultural, and religious sentiments into a single context was vividly provided in September 2014, when both U.S. President Barack Obama[12] and U.K. Prime Minister David Cameron televised words to the effect that the Islamist militants of ISIL are politically-motivated and specifically are not religiously affiliated with the Sunni Islamic faith. These **ANODYNE** statements were made not long after ISIL's front man, known by the pseudonymous moniker "Jihadi John," later identified as Mohammed Emwazi, executed American's James Foley and Steven Sotloff by beheading them while alive. Such statements were intended to prevent backlash from Islamic people worldwide. Jihadi John went on to execute Peter Kassig, David Haines, Alan Henning, Haruna Yukawa, Kenji Goto while also leading a group of ISIL members to kill 21 Syrian soldiers simultaneously in the same way. Jihadi John's rampage was ended after he was killed by a drone strike in November 2015.

The reality is that ISIL represents a relatively small band of disenfranchised and oppressed Sunni Muslims who were inspired by predecessor values of **WAHHABISM** who came to believe that the only way they could practice their faith without external influences was to carve out geography by whatever means possible. This so-called caliphate is an Islamic political-religious sovereign state—a theocracy—that is governed by the caliph, the modern-day successor to the prophet Muhammad. Their economic, political, and cultural desperation along with their interpretations of Quranic Scripture and Islamic law have self-justified their barbaric actions. While ISIL terrorism is not strictly a religious holy war, it is highly evident that Islamic doctrinal beliefs are a driving force. One such example was in July of 2014 when Syrian Christians of Mosul were told by ISIL to convert to their radicalized religious ideology and pay a religious tax or be killed.[13] Whether or not ISIL's religious claims and actions distort those of the Islamic faith is to be determined by the Imams, Grand Imam, the Mujtahid, and Grand Mufti who all interpret and adjudicate the Islamic doctrine.

HEURISTICS – SHORTCUTTING THE MENTAL ANALYTICAL PROCESS

Beyond cognitive bias, the human brain is predisposed to employing heuristics which are experience-based short-cut techniques or rules-of-thumb that we develop through trial-and-error, intuition, and other informal learning and discovery methods. More worrisome is that heuristics are quite often generated using a subset of the would-be available information. The level of care and ability of how well any given individual parses what is important or not varies considerably. For example, a Harvard University study found that 4.4 percent of young to median-aged adults express symptoms of Attention Deficit Hyperactivity Disorder (ADHD) which is correlated with decision-making deficits when processing detailed information.[14] Left untreated such individuals are more apt to rely on cognitive heuristics with a reduced set of information for decision-making purposes which are partly responsible for the prevalence in making mistakes or otherwise sub-optimal choices.

More generally, brain imaging studies of general population subjects have shown that supervisory attentional systems within the brain become more active when heuristic responses are bypassed. When these cognitive control centers are engaged, the individual consciously and unconsciously becomes more attentive to the outcomes of corresponding actions and how they compare with internal thought processes. In contrast, for more automatic responses driven by heuristic programming, the individual is often less aware of the relationship between the outcome and the decision-making process.[15] All else being equal, those individuals who may be considered to have a stronger knowledge drive and are more deliberate in their thinking are more apt to develop a perception of reality (i.e., beliefs) that is more representative of the actual state of affairs than those who rely to a higher degree on heuristic mental processing.

Leonid Perlovsky is a renowned theoretical physicist of wide-ranging expertise, but most notably in the area of computational intelligence and neural networks. In 2001, and later developed in 2006, he conceived of the notion that human beings innately generate mental models of reality and that there is a drive to maximize knowledge content and its consistency therein across the hierarchal levels of the brain. He refers to this as our Knowledge Instinct (KI). The KI motivates our efforts to enhance the clarity and specificity of our mental models and for them to be more accessible to memory retrieval. However, for things that are either complex, new to the framework, that involve retrieval of many or poorly recollected memories, or may radically contravene or harken forth core beliefs, then a higher cognitive effort is required. Before these items are fully-processed, the mental model is intrinsically vague. An example of the KI process in action is when we deeply contemplate art forms (e.g., a painting, a lyric, poetry) and we try to create meaning out of embedded abstract ideas.[16]

The more often we rely on using the KI to function in our lives; our thinking becomes more diverse and capable at managing high cognitive load situations. Conversely, the more often we rely on heuristics, the less likely we are to mature our cognitive abilities and use them when warranted.

In our local external reality, the amount of information available for observation is staggering. Our sensory modalities take in only a small fraction of this information, but the amount is nevertheless a king's treasure-load of information. Perlovsky synopsizes that the amount of information we receive is for all practical purposes an infinite set.[17] According to Newberg, our brains are awash in a continual flood of information on the order of 400 billion bits/second. This is equivalent to 50 gigabytes, which is roughly equivalent to two full-length Blu-ray high definition movies being watched every second. **However, our brains filter-out all but 2,000 bits/second leading to the fact that the overwhelming proportion of reality is not being integrated.**[18] Of the relatively miniscule 2,000 bits of information, our brains work furiously to interpret and synthesize this data by making models of the data and comparing them with existing models. When there is a match, the cognitive load is lessened by accessing pre-programmed models of behavior. When there is no match, then the brain has to work harder which can induce a state of cognitive dissonance. This is often the point at which heuristics are employed to make decisions easier.

Perlovsky posits that an individual can rectify the state of dissonance by changing their behaviors, beliefs, or a hybrid synthesis of the two. By and large, individuals will select behavioral changes because these are often easy or comfortable changes and can be temporarily shifted versus a whole-sale change to their ongoing belief system.[19] Of course, with time, people will either forget entirely or the memory will become more and more vague of the circumstances, outcomes, and how they may have responded. Often, the individual can slip back to their original 'more hardened' belief at some future point. It usually requires significant cognitive effort sustained over significant periods of time for the KI to make significant alterations to one's mental model of reality.

It is interesting, if not somewhat disheartening, that people become overly entrenched in their beliefs. According to a 2006 poll conducted by TIME Magazine, when asked whether or not they would change something doctrinally professed by their religion should scientists demonstrably disproved the particular belief, nearly two out of every three people (64%) would choose to retain their religious belief. A 2007 Gallup poll showed that between 16%-19% of people reject Darwin's theory of evolution based upon their religious convictions.[20] In a more recent Gallup poll conducted in May 2014, 42% of Americans believe that the homo sapiens species is no older than 10,000 years because that was when God created our kind. This is the Creationist view of human origins. Nearly a third of those polled held a somewhat looser belief that God only *guided* human evolution from its more primitive forms. Only an average of 19% of respondents believe that God played no part in the human evolutionary process. Interestingly, the percentage for the first grouping where humans are believed to be recently created has remained essentially flat since 1982 when this survey was first administered. There was a strong correlation between the respondent's age and level of education and their stated belief. Approximately half of those who were 65-plus years old or who had a high school education or less, believed that humans were created in the last 10,000 years. In comparison, the Creationist belief for those who were aged 18-29 or who had a college degree dropped by roughly half to 27%-28%. The highest percentage of people who believed that God played no part in the origin of human kind was among college graduates (41%).[21]

The lesson here is that changing encoded belief within any given person's brain is difficult regardless of whether or not that particular model of belief is representative of general reality. Often, when it comes to religion, we require a traumatic event in our life to begin questioning our existential beliefs in a higher power. For example, a nonreligious person may begin to believe in a divine providence when a loved one survives a would-be terminal illness or when they themselves require an external source for hope to alleviate despair. Whereas a religious person may question the existence of a benevolent God when their loved one passes in a way they consider unfair.

Perlovsky adds that targeting central beliefs, what he refers to as high-value concepts, on any given topic, are particularly challenging because our emotions often stifle our ability to effectively engage our supervisory control centers in the brain. The KI is essentially bypassed in favor of resorting to heuristically-programmed knowledge.[22] **In summary, understanding of religion and theological constructs of God ranks as one of the most cognitively demanding tasks that we can undertake.** This theory concerning the interplay between knowledge maximization (KI) and effort minimization (heuristics) goes a long way in explaining why organized 'ready-made' religion is as attractive as it is in the sense that it reduces the cognitive load to grapple with a huge number of abstract concepts. Religious headmasters take advantage of the fact that few will undertake an exhaustive investigation of its all-too-fuzzy origins or general veracity. **It is my opinion that we are better off being uncertain of our beliefs and to allow room for challenging and changing what we think we know. A strong corollary to this is that, regardless of chronological age, we need to *actively* and *continually* seek out a wide range of perspectives in developing our mental models of reality.**

Evolutionary psychologists have been endeavoring to decipher how the mind-brain is organized. For a long time, the mind-brain was thought to act as a unitary general-purpose supercomputer. This paradigm shifted to a Darwinian-inspired view that described the mind-brain as massively modular with the modules numbering in the hundreds or thousands.[23] Each module was optimized and largely dedicated to manage specific types of sensory information and in this way acted as a command center to communicate with other modules that acted in a supportive but subordinate role. The most contemporary view of mind-brain organization eschews both of these ideas. Harvard University Professor of Psychology Elizabeth Spelke *et al.* is credited with having demonstrated that humans and a variety of animal species appear to share similar cognitive processes. Specifically, the cognitive capacities of human infants, children, adults, and non-human primates can be grouped into four or potentially five distinct knowledge systems that are the byproduct of phylogeny (human evolution) and ontogeny (in-life development).[24]

The first system manages the representation within the mind of spatiotemporal relationships of inanimate objects and their associated mechanical interactions. This system deals with identifying physical boundaries, shapes, and sizes and how their constraints permit movement, connection, disconnection, or are totally separate (non-interacting) from other objects. The second system Spelke *et al.* outlines has to do with external agents, for example, a person, an animal, the wind, the ocean, flames of a fire, anything that can be represented as a causal agent within the environment. The components of the brain that process the actions of agents also diagnoses their goal-seeking purposes as to their efficiency of action, whether or not they decide to perform an expected action (contingent actions), and whether the agent reciprocates the behavior of other agents or that of the observing individual.

A third distinct core system embodies the use of sensory modalities (sight, sound, scent, etc.) to understand the numbering of objects and their relationships (e.g., addition, subtraction, ordering, and sequencing of actions). The fourth knowledge system pertains to the geometrical relationships of the surrounding environment to help the individual with proper orientation of objects as well as their own orientation relative to the objects. This system develops our sense of the three-dimensional environment and how things are located at varying distances relative to one another.[23]

The researchers propose the possible existence of a fifth system that is adapted to discern social relationships. This aids the individual to appreciate social group membership (who is within or outside of a group). It is the in-group of the individual which helps to evolve an understanding of cooperation, language, and culture.[25] It is the full collection of these four or five systems that enables the individual to learn language and symbology and acquire skill sets from these cooperative social networks.[26] Ultimately, these core systems work to define their sense of rationality and reality. I would further suggest that these are essentially utilitarian tools to help construct and adapt the mental models/mental maps forwarded by Perlovsky.

Various studies conducted by Berkley psychologist and philosopher Alison Gopnik demonstrate that human infant brains are cognitively more adaptable than the average adult brain. As compared to the latter, infant brains possess more neuronal connections and have relatively larger amounts of chemicals necessary to connect neurons. While these connections are initially inefficient, as the infant matures, there is a pruning and growth-stimulation process to make them increasingly efficient.[27] In essence the neural activity (cognitive load) of a baby's brain far exceeds that of an adult human. Unlike adult humans, babies do not have a database of models to compare their experiences with, and certainly no heuristics. Relatively speaking, as we progressively age toward adulthood, our brain becomes neurologically lazy for the simple reason that much of reality has already been mapped and modeled albeit with many fallibilities. Unlike babies who have essentially no control over the insatiable drive to absorb environmental data, adults have a level of conscious control as to whether to engage their Knowledge Instinct or let heuristics perform the job. In many domains of adult life we have more or less successfully created a state of relative consonance with the world. This is very much the meaning behind the phrase that we 'get set in our ways' as we get older and learning new things are viewed by some as a tiresome nuisance or altogether unnecessary.

One of the things that I find especially worrisome is the propensity for people to perceive reality as dyadic, comprised of two oppositional elements. Some prominent examples are our assignment of good–evil, right–wrong, just–unjust, heaven–hell, conservative–liberal, rich–poor, us–them. **I also refer to this as *compartmental minimalism* because of our tendency to force our understanding of reality into as few categories as possible. Essentially, by perceiving reality in this way, we intentionally and unintentionally, reduce the cognitive load. We do not want the hassle of too many details or abstractions; however, this convenience comes at a cost that goes unacknowledged. We essentially build a false reality bit-by-bit.**

Newberg's neuroscientific research affirms that people have come to heavily rely upon this dyadic mental-ordering of reality as we formulate our *ad hoc* assumptions of how reality works.[28] It is here where religion takes center stage to reconcile the various dyadic pairings. In a sense, a formalized religion reduces the cognitive load as it has already performed the hard work of reconciling these challenges on behalf of its adherents.

Patternicity, Agenticity, and Genetic Predisposition

The human brain has evolved to become highly attuned to and affected by patterns or the absence thereof in our local environments. For instance, we are very sensitive to acoustic signatures (sound waves) that are harmonious (consonant) or discordant (dissonant) in quality. Music that is regarded as pleasant to the human ear possesses tonal frequencies that are neither too loud (large wave amplitude) nor too high-pitched (high frequency). And when singular tones are sounded together, then the wavelengths are synchronized in specific patterns. An octave is the interval between two points where the frequency at the second point is half the frequency of the first. This is a sonic frequency interval ratio of 2:1. When musical notes are played in unison that are separated by any multiple of octaves, the sound will be perceived as harmonious. Likewise, there are other interval ratios that provide harmonious so-called pure tonal qualities such as the 1:1 (unison), 3:2 (perfect fifth), and the 4:3 (perfect fourth).

When consonant chordal progressions are played in succession, as in a musical arrangement, the sound is apt to make us feel relatively at ease. If, however, the intervals become dissonant (i.e., a lack of pattern), then the brain reacts in a sense of alarm. Musical composers often use this effect to create tension in their music. The animal kingdom uses sounds in a similar manner. For example, when felids—cats, lions, tigers, leopards, etc.—purr, they purr at 20 to 30 Hertz, a low frequency that has a calming effect. However, when humans or animals become provoked to anger, their vocalizations become shrill and evoke a very different response because the frequencies emitted do not obey harmonious interval frequencies. The point is that human brains are poised to respond to acoustic patterns.

In his book *The Believing Brain* prominent skeptic Michael Shermer outlines two neural processing modalities called *patternicity* and *agenticity*. Patternicity is the evolutionarily-developed capacity of the mind-brain to create mental meaning and connections based on patterns from external data sources (i.e., our external environment) which possess both meaningful and meaningless information.[29] This is closely affiliated with an earlier concept called *apophenia* which is the tendency to find patterns within random data. Patternicity is an evolutionary development found throughout the animal kingdom.

Whether a praying mantis is studying the movement of a potential prey item in contrast to a nearby leaf wafting back-and-forth in the wind or when we humans study the face of another person, our animal brains are using sensory input to identify whether the external patterns match-up with our internal models. The result of this evaluation process is our behavioral response to the external stimuli.

Shermer points out that our brains are not equipped with any inherent neural mechanism to detect the truth or falsity of these cognitively-developed patterns.[29] In responding to stimuli, we may do so 'correctly' or we may commit one of two cognitive errors. Borrowing statistical terminology, Shermer calls a *Type I* cognitive error the situation when a person generates a pattern which does not really exist (i.e., a false positive identification). Correspondingly, a *Type II* error is failing to identify a pattern that actually exists (i.e., a false negative identification).[30] Because our environment presents an extreme amount of information for us to process, and because our brains filter-out much of the sensory information we receive, we often falter in our ability to clearly identify all possible causal associations. In certain situations, we may make erroneous assessments because we improperly connect or group non-causal associations with causal associations.

Let us explore this notion of Type I and Type II errors with the following scenarios. Conjure in your mind the situation where a child is in bed at night and suddenly hears repetitive creaking noises outside his bedroom. The child, thinking the sound is probably from his parents walking on the wooden floor in the hallway, gets out of bed and walks over to the door. Unknowingly, the child is on the verge of committing a Type II error by failing to connect the creaking sound with other possible phenomena of why there would be creaking noises in the dead of night. Essentially, the child had a pre-programmed pattern that leads to an action to open the door because he feels it is safe to do so. As the door opens, the child sees a burglar trying to pry something open with a crow bar (hence the creaking noise). The burglar, wearing a monster mask, turns his head to lock eyes with the instantly mortified child. The burglar then binds the child with rope further engraining the horrible event into child's memory (i.e., a new pattern has been generated).

Two weeks later, the child is awoken by irregular creaking noises in the adjacent room. Terrified, he screams because the monster is back in the house. In reality, the window in the hallway was ajar and the wind was strong enough to cycle the shutters back-and-forth on its rusty hinges. Because the wind strength varies randomly, there is no particular pattern to the sound pattern to the creaky shutters. This is a case where the child's brain had encoded a new mental pattern of 'creaky noises means bad things'. In reality, it is due to a different stimulus, the creaky window shutters. This time the child has committed a Type I error by using the new pattern that falsely identifies a nonexistent pattern.

What we find is that both animals and humans program their brains using associative learning. In associative learning we use patterns (often false ones) to guide our cognitive behavior. Above, the child learned several patterns from prior experiences and later used those patterns to interpret similar circumstances. Essentially, in the second instance, the child's brain decided that it was better for his well-being if he risked making a Type I error versus his brain's perception of the more unsafe option of repeating a Type II error.

Evolution has programmed our minds to favor strategies that will ensure our self-protection and survival (as well as reproductive success) by making, on occasion, incorrect causal associations. This then, is the fundamental mind-brain basis for superstition learning. By rationalizing our environment, we consciously and unconsciously, make errors in assigning causation. Magicians employ this technique to fool our senses by levitating a coin leading us to believe that the magician wields supernatural power over matter when in reality it is suspended by a very thin thread. **Because the brain does not possess functionary components to regulate patternicity we cannot differentiate normal learning from superstition learning. Therefore, we draw the unavoidable conclusion that it is a normal instinct for human beings to develop and maintain superstitious beliefs!**[29] This is a rather astounding fact given how often in American society we make *other* superstitious people out to be PARIAHS.

The second cognitive processing modality Shermer brings forward is called agenticity. Agenticity is the bias to attribute external agents (e.g., spirits, deities, supernatural beings, etc.) to the causes of phenomena when it would be more appropriate to rationalize the circumstances as a result of natural causes or randomness.[31] His central thesis is that patternicity and agenticity are chiefly responsible for human beings inventing all manner of gods and spirits—good, bad, and otherwise—and that we are evolutionarily- and biologically-driven to do so. He does not intend to infer that we are robotically-inclined to come to such conclusions rather this is to be thought of as a natural tendency. We can overcome these natural tendencies by developing a skeptical mindset that 'scrubs' the information we take in to examine it critically and to routinely question the models (patterns) of belief. This is in keeping with the zetetic method.

The great empiricist Francis Bacon (b. 1561 – d. 1626) is accorded with saying that "**Man prefers to believe what he prefers to be true.**" Following in his footsteps, the 17th-century Dutch philosopher and excommunicated Jew, Baruch Spinoza (b. 1632 – d. 1677 CE), postulated his *Spinoza's conjecture* which asserts that the initial act of comprehending a written or verbal statement leads to a level of acceptance that the inherent content and meaning is truthful, whereas the act of rejecting the truthfulness of the statement requires additional cognitive effort. This operates on the basis of the Illusory-truth bias confirmed some three centuries later. Shermer adapts Spinoza's hypothesis to suggest that we are evolutionarily adapted to take in sensorial information and expend minimal efforts to process this information. **When it comes to our embedded beliefs, our relative intolerance to ambiguous and contrary information leads us in many instances to ignore or less thoroughly process incoming data for its actual truth value.[32] It is for this reason that society at large is so prone to religiosity because taking a skeptical stance is the difficult path; it is the path of greatest cognitive load.** The cognitive load is high because we have to conscientiously work to continually question the information we receive and often re-program our subconscious for a subject matter that is both complex and abstract. **More simply stated, it is cognitively easy for people to attribute perplexing phenomena to an abstract, all-powerful deity than it is to engage in a rigorous examination to discern potential explanatory data.**

There are those that believe biological evolution underpins all religious belief. It is the foundational platform of the New Atheist movement led by Sam Harris, Richard Dawkins, Daniel Dennett, and the late Christopher Hitchens (d. 2011). In 2004, molecular biologist Dean Hamer claimed in his book *The God Gene: How Faith Is Hardwired into Our Genes* to have found a heritable genetic basis that predisposes the traits of self-transcendence. Self-transcendence is expressed in three primary modes of spirituality. The first is *self-forgetfulness* which is the aptness to become so engrossed in something that the individual disregards all other things (often referred to being in a 'flow state' or 'in the zone'). The second component is *transpersonal identification* which is the sense of a deep emotional connectedness to the greater universe outside of ourselves. Finally, *mysticism* is the relative acceptance of the supernatural or something superior to our known reality that cannot be rationally proved.[33, 34] His research identifies the vesicular monoamine transporter 2 (VMAT2) protein encoded into the human genome as the "God Gene," but readily acknowledges that there are likely to be many more genes that could be cumulatively responsible for people's proneness toward a spiritual orientation.[35] However, we have to be careful that just because we may be predisposed toward having feelings of some form of transcendence, this in no way guarantees it will parlay into an organized belief system. In any case, whether true or not, the theory as it stands is not the primary force motivating the large-scale adoption of spiritual or religious beliefs.

One of the main takeaways is that the purpose of our brain and its related cognitive processes is not to necessarily determine what is real in reality with high accuracy. Rather, its manifest is to ensure safety and survival of the host body, inclusive of the mind-brain. To this end, in addition to managing internal organ function, it instinctively engages the environment to develop a general sense of reality, at times focusing attentional aptitudes on some details at the cost of losing others. In spite of encoded patterns, there is no perfectly set way in which new and previously memorized information is processed by the same individual. That is, the brain is not like a computer that rigidly and precisely follows algorithms the same way, one-hundred percent of the time. Often, the exact same information can be processed differently depending on many factors. For instance, in walking across a street, when the light signals that it is safe to cross, we might immediately cross without looking around to see if there are oncoming cars. Other times, we are more vigilant and actively search the environment to see if it really is safe to cross the street. Analogically, this is in part why people (with healthy brains) are so different from one another.

Because the brain does not possess robust 'fault detectors', the brain will just as easily encode irrational thoughts and beliefs just as it will rational ones. To root-out irrational thoughts, it is often the case that a great deal of effort is required to take into account prospective biases and to collect and objectively analyze multiple sources of relevant information from different points of view. And, once a prospective belief is developed, one has to test it and adjust it accordingly. This is often made difficult when one considers the prevalence of attentional conditions which interfere with cognitive processing such as anxiety, depression, information overload, and tiredness to name a few in the gamut of distractors.

Neurotheology – Combining Neuroscience and Theology

One of the world's most acclaimed neuroscientists of the 20th-century was Yale professor of physiology, José Delgado. He was famed for his pioneering work in mind control via implantation into the brains of cats, monkeys, and humans his invention he called a *stimoceiver*. The stimoceiver is a radio-based device that stimulates the brain electrically and records the response signals received with an EEG (electroencephalography) while allowing the subject full freedom of movement. Delgado demonstrated that he could elicit specific emotions (e.g., euphoria, sadness) and specific physical responses (e.g., movement of a limb). In one of his most famous experiments, he implanted a stimoceiver into the brain of a bull in an area of the brain called the caudate nucleus which regulates the animal's instinct for aggression. In 1963, Delgado got into the bull ring and waited for the bull to charge him. With a press of remote control button, the bull immediately stopped his charge.[9, 36]

Some two decades later, in the 1980's, neurotheology experimentalist Michael Persinger created the "God Helmet" which artificially stimulated the temporal lobes of test subjects with a weak magnetic field. Persinger claimed that his device possessed the capability to induce an experience within the mind of the subject such that they would sense an ethereal presence in the room. He also believed that strong electromagnetic fields can generate hallucinations in the human brain theorizing that geophysical electromagnetic phenomena (e.g., seismic faults, buried high voltage cables) could be responsible for all types of superstitious phenomena (e.g., UFO's, Marian apparitions). His results remain contested to this day which leads us to the question, can neuroscience offer a portal into the reality of God? Let us see where this question leads us.

First, this is not as well-posed question as one might initially think. Understanding that neuroscience and spiritual phenomena are inherently complex, the better question to ask is, can neuroscientific and theological insights—together—offer an integrated understanding into the reality of God? In some ways, we find ourselves tripped-up as soon as we exit the gate. As Andrew Newberg points out in his *Principles of Neurotheology*, consciousness in general and self-reflexive consciousness in particular remain an unresolved problem across all scientific perspectives in philosophy, theology, and neuroscience.[37] As of 2017, while research has largely demonstrated that the mind-brain is 'one-thing' (monism) and not 'two-things' (dualism), we only have an abstract sense of what consciousness is and an even vaguer sense of how it might arise from the mind-brain. As to the efficacy of neurotheology, Newberg advocates that to efficaciously advance the field, scientists and theologians need to cross-train themselves to develop a comprehensive understanding of the other's discipline to mitigate errors in judgment and to maximize overall enlightenment.[38] Notwithstanding the problems associated with dual competencies, there is a more fundamental issue pertaining to the lack of study protocols for all investigators to follow.[39] This set of challenges, according to the neuroscientist, will take decades to work through.[38]

When someone with the credentials of Newberg, who himself is a nontheist, and who has authored a number of books outlining how spiritual phenomenon are most likely to be figments of our evolutionarily-created brains, waves the cautionary yellow flag, this is a major deal. While patternicity, agenticity, and 'model-making' are authentic phenomena of

---

9. A YouTube™ video of Delgado's bull experiment can be found at the web link: http://tinyurl.com/jb67dp2. Last accessed 03 March 2017.

the human brain, when it comes to electrically, magnetically, or chemically stimulating the brain to monitor its output (e.g., through EEGs or functional brain imaging studies) to induce or investigate spiritual states of mind, it is much too soon for us to draw too many definitive conclusions from the current database of neuroscientific research. This also goes for most behavioral and cognitive psychological studies of religious and spiritual experience because they too suffer from the unavailability of subjective and objective measurement tools that can accurately distinguish the many complex phenomena at work.

This is not to say that we are defeated to circumscribe certain aspects of the human brain. Newberg submits that the brain has natural, biological functional limitations on how we experience what we call physical reality and the supposed spiritual reality. **Resultantly, the ways in which we embody God are fundamentally shaped by our evolutionarily-developed brain. That is, theological arguments are always and forever framed by the combination of endemic cultural influences at the time they are conceived and the biological capacities and limitations of the brain.**[40] **This is a very powerful statement!** To put this into perspective, if we were to assume for the moment that Neanderthals from nearly a quarter of a million years ago were to have maintained a conception of God, what Newberg is essentially saying, is that due to biological variation, the Neanderthal's vision of God would invariably be different than what modern man could conceive God as. Likewise, 250,000 or a million years from now, our species and any evolved offshoot species will almost certainly see God quite differently. We also see this over the course of the last five or six millennia whereby world religions have framed God in thousands of ways. *God is therefore a malleable construct that will necessarily follow in step with the changes to our underlying neurobiology and cultural constructs.*

Ultimately, for most things, reality is a continuum of possibilities and very seldom is it absolute. We need not look further than what quantum mechanics tells us of the behavior of fundamental matter where reality is rarely a choice between dyads. If the preponderance of non-human reality is non-dyadic, does this not behoove us to become more considerate in our dualistic judgments? **I truly believe that this over-reliance on binary thinking, simplism, and mental biases are epically major counter-forces for our progress as a species and is seated at the core of many pandemic issues between men and nations.**

Based on the aforementioned discussions, we can now see why in Chapter 1, it was commented that the unreliability of the human mind warrants a cautious advance in following the way of *Zeteo Alétheia*. And, given that we are only now on the verge of understanding how our brains create our perceptions of reality via biases, heuristics, model-making, and instinctual processing we might better accept why the use of our paraintellect (i.e., our intuition) to make claims of supernatural phenomena cannot be a trustworthy source of information when it comes to affirming or disconfirming God-by-whatever-name.

THE HUMAN SOUL AND QUANTUM CONSCIOUSNESS

Well before the Christian Church Fathers laid claim to explication of the immortal human soul, our Greek forebears articulated their philosophy on the afterlife. Socrates (b. c. 469 – d. 399 BCE) defined death as the separation of the soul and the body. Much of what we know about Socrates' philosophy comes from his students. In Plato's *Phaedo* (trans. *On the Soul*, c. 360 BCE) he conveys Socrates' belief that when the soul is freed from its bodily encasement, it received its just due in accordance with the person's earthly deeds. Plato himself had a conflicted understanding of the soul whereby he seemingly believed in its immortality but never comes to a cogent explication as did other philosophers. He tacitly suggests that the number of souls in existence was fixed, never to be diminished or augmented. In his *Republic*, he portrays the soul as eternal and tripartite where it consisted of logical (reason, knowledge, truth), high-spirited (emotions, spirit, ambition), and appetitive (cravings for food, carnal desires, wealth) components. Plato adopted the theory that the soul transmigrated from the spirit realm to the individual upon birth and then back to the spirit realm upon death.

To Aristotle's mind, Plato's finest pupil, all beings are a compound of form and matter. In contrast to his predecessors and contemporaries who maintained that the soul was wholly separate from the human body, Aristotle's theory advocated that all living matter—plants, animals, and humans—possessed an incorporeal soul that could be differentiated into distinct, hierarchical categories. The soul was a source for *capacity*, the drive for the being to enable self-nourishment, intellect, growth, degeneration, and movement. In this way, the soul was causally responsible for the behavior of the animated being. Furthermore, his idea of the soul links it more directly to the material body in the sense it was necessary for the body to survive. There has been no reconciliation whether Aristotle believed that the human soul was ultimately separable from the body or whether it was immortal.

Some six centuries later, during the formational years of proto-Christianity, Origen (b. c. 185 – d. c. 253/4 CE) became the first Christian Church Father to attempt to prepare a systematic theology. As a Greek Neoplatonist, he was sympathetic to Plato's views on the existence of an immortal soul that would separate from the body and be judged according to worldly deeds. It was very much in keeping with Jesus' exhortations to live a faithful life in honor of God or face eternal damnation. Origen stated that "The soul, having a substance and life of its own, shall after its departure from the world, be rewarded according to its deserts, being destined to obtain either an inheritance of eternal life and blessedness, if its actions shall have procured this for it, or to be delivered up to eternal fire and punishments, if the guilt of its crimes shall have brought it down to this." (*Origen De Principiis*, c. 231 CE)[41] Origen's cosmology maintained that human souls preexisted the creation of the world, and interestingly, had the same belief as certain Gnostic sects insofar as the soul being trapped in the insufferable physical domain to endure torment and that the purpose of a human life is to be wholly-directed toward redemption to purchase an afterlife. The Gnostics and Origen differed on what constituted this afterlife and the divine realm. Recall, that the concept of the physical size of the "world" at that time was immeasurably smaller. It was only in 2016 that humans have discerned that the world-universe contains some two trillion galaxies and that our significance as living beings is almost certainly to be unexceptional in the grand scheme of things.

In Augustine's[10] *City of God* (426 CE) he articulates that that the soul would depart upon death to find the eternal bliss of living with God or be relegated to an eternity of separation from God. In his *Summa Theologica–Part I* (1265 – 1274 CE), Thomas Aquinas solidifies Catholic doctrine where he affirms that man consists of an indivisible, immaterial, indestructible soul connected to a body, the latter possessing a conscious intellect and will. Another way to think about this is that it took 12 centuries to develop a doctrine on the human soul, which can only make one feel discomforted why it took theologians so long to cement a central doctrine of Christianity.

The concept of immortality certainly predated the Greeks and likely extends back to the emergence of proto-human consciousness. From this vantage point, it is easy to understand how this concept has settled deeply into the minds of the considerable majority of people worldwide. People have a natural inclination to want to be immortal, if not bodily, then spiritually. The spirit realm is purportedly where an all-encompassing bliss happens and we are freed from the toils and drudgery of earthly life. This is reminiscent of certain Gnostic beliefs. We must nevertheless ask if the immortal soul is real and what evidence exists to support this claim. **While the Bible offers a clear distinction that the soul is separate from the body and discusses the idea of eternal life in a general context, it may come as a surprise that *the Bible does not specifically indicate that the human soul is immortal*. The postulation that we have an immortal soul is an extrapolation or 'a reading between the**

---

10. Augustine of Hippo (b. 354 – d. 430 CE) lived at the same time as Jerome, both of whom were Church Fathers, was an apologist who wrote against heretical views of his day. He helped shape the development of the Holy Trinity in his treatise, *On the Trinity*. He also provided significant contributions on the doctrine of Original Sin and justifications for war.

lines' made by the Church Fathers. Even though the Bible itself cannot affirm the eternal soul, this has been the prevailing thought for billions of people.

In an effort to produce a level of scientific credibility to the existence of the soul, physician Duncan MacDougall weighed the body of six tuberculosis patients at the moment of their death. The hypothesis was that the soul had mass and therefore, when it departed the body, the body would weigh less. His results were published in 1907, oddly taking six years to post his findings. He reported that one of the patients' data indicated that the soul weighs "three-fourths of an ounce."[42] MacDougall did not rely on the data of the other five patients which presented contravening evidence to his hypothesis. His work was summarily discredited as unscientific due, in part, to the reliance of a single data point and by failing to fully consider the other data.

In modern-day times, people point to those who have had near-death experiences (NDEs) or shared-death experiences (SDEs). The NDE is where a person has existed in the border realm of clinical death as evidence for an afterlife where the human consciousness may glimpse a spiritual, transcendental existence outside of our normal spatiotemporal existence. Notwithstanding medical interventions that place the body in stasis (e.g., chilling the core body temperature to a point where brain waves are nearly nil), it is generally regarded that consciousness begins to die after 10 seconds of oxygen deprivation and clinical death ensues within five minutes and no longer than 10 minutes. Therefore, NDEs occur in this general timeframe. Those who have entered this state of semi-consciousness report a variety of experiences from feeling a sense of peace or clarity, separation from the body ('out of body experience'), seeing and/or entering a light source, experiencing a 'Being of Light' radiating love, or some other vivid mentation. Often, while the person is in this state, the body is comatose, undergoing major physical trauma either due to internal issues (e.g., cardiac arrest, electrical shock, drowning, and catatonia), or from related resuscitative efforts (e.g., surgery, defibrillation, thermal ice bath, intravenous hypercooling of the blood, chemical intervention). About the only constant with NDEs is that there is no singular signature profile experienced by people; rather it is composed of a mixture of elements.

Shared-death experiences have been documented since the late 1800s by the Society of Psychical Research (London). The term was first coined only recently in 2009 by psychiatrist Dr. Raymond Moody in his book *Glimpses of Eternity*. The SDE is a more infrequently encountered phenomenon that involves two persons, a living person and one who is in the process of dying. The living person, usually someone very close in both relationship and local proximity, shares in the initial transition of the dying person's death. The SDE of the living person presents similar experiences to those who have had NDEs where the living person sees mystical lights, encounters an unparalleled sense of peace, and even a strong upward pull on the body or the spirit. While having an out of body experience, the individual may also look into the eyes or 'feel at one' with the individual who is dying. In terms of definitively qualifying NDEs and SDEs, all neurophysiological and psychological models remain aimlessly at sea relegating the direct causation of such events substantially unknown.[43] All we can really say is that NDEs and SDEs are subjective human experiences and are relatively common in frequency.

What can be objectively known about the existence of a soul is indirectly investigated through the understanding of human consciousness. The problem is that there is a huge explanatory gap about what we currently know about consciousness. In the 17th-century, the father of modern western philosophy, René Descartes, conjectured that the seat of the soul and locus of consciousness was inside the brain's centrally-located pineal gland. Today we regard this as an erroneous conjecture. And, while general anesthesia was first introduced in 1842, we remain quite uncertain how it specifically acts to permanently erase certain aspects of conscious awareness yet not interfere with vital functions of the brain.

It has long been the consideration that neurons and neuronal assemblies along with their 'integrate-and-fire' mechanisms were the fundamental source for brain computing, that in ways yet to be fully understood, produced consciousness.[11] Since the early 20th-century, a handful of theories surfaced postulating a connection between quantum theory and consciousness. Initially these were philosophical in nature, contemplating that quantum indeterminism and randomness might provide insight into the unresolved problem of free will-versus-determinism. By the late 20th-century, as quantum mechanisms became understandable to a wider audience, theories began to circulate about quantum field theory at work at the neuronal and neuronal assembly level. The most provocative, heavily derided, yet enduring theory that has risen in prominence is the Orchestrated Objective Reduction (Orch OR) model of consciousness which suggests that consciousness is a biologically orchestrated phenomena governed by quantum computational processes that regulate neuronal synaptic and membrane activities.[44-54]

In order to understand the inner workings of this theory at a top level, a condensed synopsis of relevant aspects of quantum theory is necessary to be comprehended. In due

---

11. A typical neuron possesses a cell body called a soma (refer to Figure 12-1 on page 442). The soma contains a nucleus and other things (organelles) to keep the cell living and functional. On one end of the neuron there are branching structures called dendrites and on the other end are the axon terminals. A neuron's dendrites connect with other neurons at their axon terminals. The gap (junction) between the dendrite and axon is called a synapse. Information is sent across the synapse by electrochemical stimulation.

course, the origin of the ungainly name of this theory of consciousness—one that is not at all obvious—will be fleshed-out, but only after pushing you through the quantum 'meat grinder'. If you keep your wits about you and work to understand what is said, you will be rewarded with an intriguing hypothesis about how the source of the soul can be located. This next discourse on quantum mechanics is also important because chapters further on will reflect on the concepts discussed here.

The quantum state of a physical system (a subatomic particle, an atom, a molecule, or even macroscopic matter) can be described by the mathematical Schrödinger equation which entails the concept of what is called its wave function.[12] To those in the theoretical physical sciences, the Schrödinger equation is nearly as famous as Einstein's equation for matter-energy equivalency (i.e., $E = mc^2$). Schrödinger's discovery is an equally profound statement that essentially encodes a complete description of a quantum system. Using a single particle as a referent (e.g., an electron), the wave function is a mathematical abstraction about the particle's quantum state (e.g., energy, position, momentum, spin, etc.). This information is probabilistic in nature and is characterized by the Heisenberg uncertainty principle which tells us that we can only assign a probability for what the numerical value of the particle's properties might be. We can think of it as a cloud of possible values for each of its properties at any given point in time. Furthermore, it is perfectly impossible for us to simultaneously determine all the information about a particle at a distinct point in time with total certainty. The realm of the subatomic world is a perpetual state of randomness and uncertainty.

This runs counter to the intuition of our everyday macroscopic reality whereby we can measure multiple properties of things precisely. For instance, we could spin a basketball on a fingertip and use measurement devices to determine the position of any point on the surface as well as its rotational spin velocity, rotational spin direction, angular momentum, mass, and energy. And with enough information, we can accurately predict its past history and future history. Contrastingly, in the quantum realm, if we measure one property, say the position of the particle, with extreme precision then the precision associated with the most likely value for a different property, for example the particle's momentum, is instantaneously *decreased* and becomes *less certain*. We should think of the position of the particle not as a discrete, singular position, but as a state where the position is smeared out across a range of possible positions. Let us consider a mechanical analogy whereby the momentum and position

---

12. It should be noted that physicists are still debating whether things such as 'particles' or even 'fields' exist in nature. Some maintain an 'all-fields' view and others say that both fields and particles can be reduced to relationships and properties (e.g., mass, charge, spin).

properties of this particle are linked to their own push-button. If we press the 'momentum push-button' to acquire a precise value for the particle's momentum, the size of its 'smear' decreases. However, as the 'momentum smear' decreases in size, the 'position smear' is correspondingly and instantaneously larger and we are less certain of the particles most likely position. This phenomenon is referred to as the *Observer Effect* of quantum mechanics.

Ultimately, each particle property consists of a multitude of physically possible states at any given time which are collectively called its quantum state. When the quantum states of two or more particles interact, each having their own wave function, they are said to interfere with one another. This means that their 'smears' (i.e., all permissible values for property parameters) have become *superimposed* where the wave function of one particle is added to the wave function of the other particle to generate a new, combined wave function and associated quantum state. The smears of possible values are referred to mathematically as the wave function's *eigenstate*.

It is known that when individual quantum states interfere, they can add together in such a manner that they are in phase with one another enabling them to better 'communicate' and 'cooperate' with one another to produce a coherent symbiosis. When this occurs, the quantum system is said to have achieved quantum coherence, or equally, quantum resonance. It is believed by Orch OR consciousness theorists that there exists a physical criterion (i.e., condition) that defines a threshold, that when and if attained, the wave function *collapses*. Wave function collapse is a focusing process whereby the actual value (i.e., the eigenvalue) for the intrinsic property is determined. For instance, if we were attempting to measure the position of an electron, the actual position is said to have been 'reduced' from the many possibilities into the number displayed on the instrument panel's display screen as a single-valued parameter.[13] This distillation process essentially interrupts the coherent quantum state and hence it is why physicists call it *decoherence*. Decoherence is simply a descriptive metaphor of what is apparently happening to the quantum state and by itself is an abstraction. Some physicists, however, believe that wave function collapse is a physically-real transition process.

Suffice it to say that physicists are still in a quandary as to whether and how wave function collapse exactly comes about in terms of what the physical criterion threshold is and how the many possibilities are suddenly sieved to produce observable reality. Various theories have been put forward as to how this objective threshold criterion works

---

13. At the quantum level, it is possible for particles to take on more than one value at a given time. Hence, a particle could be momentarily in two places at exactly the same time. Wave function collapse is also synonymously called wave function reduction.

but none have been fully accepted. Whether and how wave function reduction *actually* happens is referred to in quantum physics as the **MEASUREMENT PROBLEM**. This problem is oft envisaged as the "Schrödinger cat" thought experiment proffered by Erwin Schrödinger himself in 1935. The thought experiment places a cat, a radioactive source, a flask of poison, a hammer, and radioactivity sensor (e.g., a Geiger counter) into an environmentally-isolated box. The hammer is rigged in such a way that should the sensor detect any radiation (generally presumed to be a 50-50 chance), the hammer will drop to strike and shatter the flask of poison thereby killing the cat.

In a quantum system, the cat can be represented as a wave function of possibilities where the cat is a superposition of both possibilities of being simultaneously alive *and* dead. It is only when we perform the act of observing the inside of the box that we determine whether the cat is actually alive *or* dead, but not both. Prior to looking in the box, the 'quantum cat' is simultaneously alive *and* dead. Not only does this highlight the issue of how the existence of multiple simultaneous states get reduced to a single state, but it also illustrates the confounding issue of where to draw the line between the quantum realm and the realm we understand as everyday life. While there are several theories which seek to address the associated phenomena, for now, it is an operative assumption in the Orch OR model of consciousness that the quantum wave function collapse process actually occurs as a real, non-abstract process.[14]

This quantum state reduction process has been conjectured to occur internal to brain neurons. This is a very different model from traditional models of consciousness which contend that consciousness somehow arises outside the neuron, from one neuron to another. Brain neurons are composed of a scaffolding of microtubule nanowires (refer to Figure 12-1).[55] Nanowires are hollow tubes 25 nanometers (~ 0.1 micro inches) in diameter and range from 200 nanometers (~0.000008 inches) to 25 micrometers (~0.001 inches) in length. Dimensionally, one could fit between two to four nanowires laid lengthwise, end-to-end, across the width of a human hair. A single microtubule may be constructed from 30,000 to 40,000 tubulin protein subunits and number as many as a billion for a single neuron. The hollow core of the nanowire is filled with a special arrangement of monomolecular water creating a biological symbiosis between the water core column and the tubulin proteins. It is believed by Orch OR advocates that the entrapped water and tubulin proteins work

---

14. At the present time, the leading candidate theory to describe the threshold criterion to initiate wave function collapse is the Diósi-Penrose Criterion. This theory insinuates that the quantum collapse is due to gravitational self-energy between the mass distributions of the eigenstates which requires an unproven extension of standard quantum field theory. The idea of quantum gravity is briefly touched upon in the next chapter.

together through a mechanism of electromagnetic resonant oscillations (i.e., they vibrate in a coherent manner due to quantum coherence). The combined resonance controls the macroscopic electronic and optical properties of the individual microtubule. **These microtubule quantum vibrations are thought to be the fundamental embodiment of consciousness.**

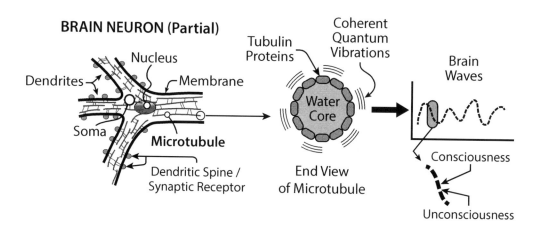

Figure 12-1. Microtubules inside Neuron

When many microtubules are in a state of quantum coherence, all the individual microtubule's resonant frequencies interfere constructively (i.e., they cooperate) to generate what is known as a composite beat frequency. At the quantum level, the beat frequencies are extremely fast when considering the phenomena is occurring in a biological system. Microtubules resonate in the kilohertz (10^{-3} seconds) range, whereas the protein-based tubulins are three orders of magnitude faster, in the megahertz range (10^{-6} seconds). The water core itself oscillates nearly two or three orders of magnitude greater, in the sub-gigahertz range (10^{-8}–10^{-9} seconds). This high frequency provides for a quantum computational capacity for trillions of operations per second per neuron! Hence we have the notion that our brains function as a quantum computer.

It is believed that only 0.1 percent of the microtubules that exist in a given neuron are involved in consciousness. The preponderance of microtubules that resonate are located at the end the neuron at the dendrites and in the soma. The other 99.9 percent of the microtubules also vibrate, but not in a coherent manner. Even with the low participation rate of 0.1 percent per neuron, there are some 86 billion neurons that comprise the neuronal forest contained in the brain. This would mean perhaps as many as 86 million microtubules are posited to self-organize into a chain of resonance that enters into coherent quantum states. This is to say that a stream of consciousness is produced by a continual cascading series of orchestrated rhythmic 'pulsing' of these microscopic and sub-microscopic structures that have attained quantum coherence that reach the objective threshold condition to then be subsequently reduced/collapsed (i.e., decohered).

Until this theory emerged, there was no organized comprehension of the underlying mechanisms of how EEG signals were originated in the brain.[56] The Orch OR theory suggests that this composite beat frequency (the combination of all the resonances) is what we detect as the origin of electro-encephalographic ('EEG') signals when we monitor brain waves. Elevated production of gamma waves is associated with a heightened intellectual acuity and the sense of bliss as developed in the practice of meditation. Gamma synchrony EEG brain waves range from 25 – 100 Hertz with the norm being closer to 40 Hertz. To develop brain waves at 40 Hertz, hundreds of thousands of neurons would be necessary to be undergoing quantum resonance. Ultimately, it is the grand orchestration of the chain of resonances of the water core-tubulins, microtubules, neurons, and indeed supraneuronal structures across the brain that create consciousness and capacity for mentation. Because these 'orchestrated' resonances depend so highly on the quantum system cohering to enable the 'objective' threshold to be reached and to lead to wave function 'reduction', the authors of this theory decided to call it the *Orchestrated Objective Reduction* (Orch OR) theory.

An interesting artifact of this process is that because of the oscillations, normal consciousness occurs as discrete moments of conscious awareness linked together with moments of unawareness (refer to the brain wave illustration, Figure 12-1—rightmost figure). The founding developers of the Orch OR model, renowned mathematical physicist Roger Penrose and anesthesiologist Stuart Hameroff, state that their construct of the mind parallels the thinking of Process philosopher A.N. Whitehead. Whitehead considered consciousness as a process constituted by discrete instances that were repetitious and monotonous.[45] These moments of dullness correspond to the events wherein there is a lack of orchestration existing among the microtubules. In referring back to the discussion on heuristics, it may be that this dullness correlates to instances of using heuristic methods of decision-making. These often random non-cognitive elements (i.e., decoherent states) are what Penrose and Hameroff refer to as proto-consciousness.

It may now be apparent that quantum processes are not strictly a biological phenomenon. It happens for any kind of quantum system—animate or inanimate. And more strikingly, quantum processes have been occurring throughout the entire lifetime of the universe. According to the Penrose-Hameroff interpretation, non-cognitive proto-consciousness is embedded into the fabric and functioning of the universe.[45] This view that there is a universal consciousness is a rendition of panpsychism put forth by pre-Socratic Greek philosopher Thales of Miletus (one of the Seven Sages of Ancient Greece, c. 550 BCE) where he proffers that "all things are full of gods."[57] Thales lived and died in the same region of modern-day Western Turkey (then called Ionia) as did Heraclitus who was born about a decade after Thales died. As you may recall, Heraclitus is considered the founder of Process Philosophy.

We come then to Hameroff's conception of the immortal soul. He conjectures that after the heart stops pumping blood to the brain, cellular processes degrade to the point that the quantum state of the microtubules is destabilized, in essence it becomes unorchestrated. Hameroff points to the well-known fundamental fact that matter and energy cannot be created or destroyed, only transferred or changed from one form to another. This is the essence of the First Law of Thermodynamics (also called the Law of Conservation of Energy). Therefore the quantum information still exists and reverts to random resonances (proto-consciousness), rejoining the rest of such events taking place throughout the cosmic quantum ocean. The human conscious essentially mirrors the cosmic conscious. Drawing close parallels to Platonian thought, the soul has always existed in the universe, first as proto-consciousness (unorchestrated) quantum information, then as consciousness (orchestrated resonance), followed by its recycling back to proto-consciousness. These ideas are also similar to those of the ancient Vedic *Brihadaranyaka Upanishad* (refer to Chapter 1, p. 12) which contemplates that consciousness is not separate from reality, rather consciousness is integral to reality, as in a single reality-consciousness. Hameroff postulates that after death, the person's essence is diffused as intra-cosmic information,[15] potentially forever. In the case of NDEs, Hameroff signals that, for a short time, the quantum information is able to return back into the body's microtubules enabling the person to be reanimated.

In yet another quirk of the quantum realm, the two phenomena of **QUANTUM NONLOCALITY AND ENTANGLEMENT** have been empircally verified. Pairs or groups of particles can become entangled such that their quantum states are interdepedent and cannot be described independently for each particle involved. Normally, two non-interacting particles 'A' and 'B' possess their own properties unaffected by the other. However, if 'A' and 'B' are entangled and we measured the uncertainty of the value for a property for 'A', this would immediately determine the uncertainty for the same property of 'B'. The term nonlocal means that the particles can be separated by relatively large distances (i.e., many miles). While it it had been known for a very long time that quantum non-local entanglement and quantum coherence

---

15. Information is neither matter nor energy but requires both to exist. Recall, matter and energy are ultimately interchangeable quantities.

were closely related, the precise relationship was not understood. In 2015, physicists discovered that they are operationally equivalent in the sense that any degree of coherence within a quantum system can be converted into the entanglement of properties between the system and some other incoherent system.[58]

Hameroff's ideas have been extended to serve as a possible explanation for paranormal experiences, premonitions, and mental connectedness to other people. The latter is the notion that we are thinking the same thoughts of someone else, especially loved ones, who may be proximal or distant from us. Could this phenomenon be described in terms of quantum mechanical processes such as quantum nonlocality, entanglement, and coherence?

As it stands today, Orch OR remains an unproven theory. As of early 2015, the Penrose-Hameroff Orch OR model is moving toward the state of being a testable hypothesis. In 2013/2014, Japanese researchers were able to experimentally measure coherent quantum resonance in a single brain-neuron extracted microtubule which is a highly significant step in its favor.[44] While very meaningful, it must be demonstrated that this process can scale-up to the neuronal and supraneuronal level within a living brain. As to Hameroff's comments on the relationship of proto-consciousness, human consciousness, panpsychism, and indeed the human soul, this must be categorized as mere speculation. We are a very far cry from being able to claim that our individual consciousness' survive beyond our physical death.

So what are we to do with the Abrahamic conceptions of the immortal soul and this idea of an ever-present universal consciousness that is closely affiliated with virtually all Eastern thought traditions? The fear of mortal death, the fear of eternal damnation, the yearning for salvation, and the need for personal meaning have, at a minimum, propelled mankind to a deep-seated belief in a much-hoped-for afterlife. In proving that there is an afterlife, we certainly cannot hang our hat on the uncountable subjective accounts of NDEs/SDEs. There are numerous factors that cloak our ability to elicit much of anything we would consider useful. This is not to say that many of those who experienced what they claim to have experienced and whose life was changed for the better is to be wholly discounted. But, we cannot give such stories any *scientific credence* until neuroscientific protocols and religious phenomena are understood to a far greater degree.

Are we then nothing more than a mere biological extension of some soul-less apelike ancestor? We should call to mind that there are a significant number of other creatures in the animal kingdom that possess near-human levels of consciousness and self-consciousness. While Jainists and Hindus would contend that animals have souls, this is not widely believed in the Abrahamic traditions. When we look at the accumulated evidences for and against the idea of a soul, much less an immortal one, it would seem that there is no unbiased, scientific data or theories that sufficiently support such a claim. Can the existence of a soul be ruled-out? If we look strictly at the NDE/SDE data, personal experiences, and current status of theories of consciousness, we should probably take a guarded position on what these experiences tell us of post-death phenomena. But, we also have to take into account what we have learned on the zetetic path about tracking down the existence of God. If there never was a God, or there is no longer a living God, or if God is 'trapped' in a transcendent realm blocked by an impermeable barrier to our physical, mental, or soulful reality, then what is the utility of having a soul? The answer is none, as far as I can see. The summary point here is that if one is to choose to believe in a human soul, immortal or otherwise, then it will require one to adopt a metaphysical position, one that cannot be demonstrated to be a factual state of reality. If Penrose and Hameroff are correct in their assertions about a quantum soul, then this is not the least bit comforting to exist in the afterlife as dispersed, disassociated quantum information. This state of affairs would be make our afterlife devoid of our human personality, memories, or connections to loved ones.

If we choose to side with the zetetic approach, then we should tell ourselves that we do not know enough one way or another if a soul truly exists, though the odds weigh heavily against it. Is there any other evidence that might add some clarity to this situation? That is, is there something we haven't yet considered that might sway the probability that human beings do or do not have a soul? Perhaps there is. In the next two chapters we will explore the scientific origins of the universe and whether or not the universe had a beginning, or whether the property of time and the grand universe itself extends infinitely into the past. If the universe did have a beginning, then we have to inquire what caused the universe to come into existence. Was it produced under the auspices of God or did it suddenly burst into existence out of nothingness (*ex nihilo*) or some nondivine substance? If we can find a compelling reason to believe that God created the universe, then this idea of a soul and an afterlife might gain new footing. If the universe is more likely to have existed for all eternity, then God is not necessary to create or sustain the universe because it always existed. While God could still exist in the context of a universe with no beginning, we have to admit that it is much less plausible that such a Being would exist. The eternal universe would therefore favor the idea that human beings are soul-less organisms.

Reflections by Sages on the Immortal Soul

All men's souls are immortal,
but the souls of the righteous are immortal and divine.

Socrates (b. c. 469 – d. 399 BCE)

• •

The soul of man is immortal and imperishable.

Plato (b. c. 428 – d. 348 BCE)

• •

Four thousand volumes of metaphysics will not teach us what the soul is.[59]

Voltaire (1764 CE)

SUMMARY

Just as there is with foundational religious doctrine, scientific inquiry is beset with its own set of problems. While scientific discovery and engineering innovation has been a powerful engine to uplift humanity in a great many aspects, the practice of science does not always rise to the standards of excellence it could otherwise attain. As a resource-intensive endeavor, scientific progress is influenced by money which heavily governs what gets investigated and what does not and who will be doing the investigating. While the discipline of science and engineering can be collegial it is more often competitive in the larger scheme. While competition offers many prospective positive benefits, it also generates a list of ills from bad science to fraudulent science. The preponderance of research is under fantastic pressure to provide positive or affirmatory results and the majority of the dollars spent are tagged for a relatively small segment of the community. We find that research studies that yields no appreciable effects, that generate negative results, or that disconfirm the majority opinion is not given anything close to equal weight. Science, given the inherent and unresolved Problem of Induction and the associated Duhem-Quine thesis, will always be beleaguered with an inability to be pinpoint reality with absolute certainty. Here, we are to be cautious not to say absolute truth, for philosophers haven't been able to unequivocally determine what truth is. But, even with these terrible hindrances, when performed properly, science can correct for many of our inherent fallibilities in discerning reality.

The community of scientists and engineers worrisomely fall subject to the spell of simplism as does the general populace. While we should not do away with Ockham's razor completely, we are overlooking the sophistication of the universe through the use of too many *a priori* assumptions and simplifications. We are also susceptible to many conscious and subconscious biases which sometimes act contemporaneously on our thinking processes. Mentioned here were just a few of the 188 mental biases—Confirmation, Anchor, Authority, and Herd bias, along with Conjunction fallacy, Framing effect, and the Illusory-truth effect. Neuroscientists and physicists are working to understand the inner workings of our mind. An intriguing perspective is the notion that we are driven by a Knowledge Instinct whereby we are continually developing and matching models of reality. In support of this general idea is that the human brain is programmed both biologically and socially to identify patterns in our environment (i.e., patternicity) and to fallaciously give external agents casual powers when other, more mundane phenomena may be the root cause (i.e., agenticity). When we engage in higher-order thinking, such as the meaning of our own existence or the existence of a deity, the models are intrinsically more vague and difficult to wrap our minds around. This situation points to the fact that if we as individuals have a desire to better understand reality, we have to systematically, dynamically, and continually re-examine and adapt our world views. **It is a primary purpose of this book to facilitate more rationally justified model-making.**

These primal model-making and pattern recognition modalities are simply recursive programs that run and re-run through our mind but are susceptible to the creation of erroneous conclusions. We learned that we are instinctually programmed toward superstition learning. This, in concert with agenticity and tangentially genetic pre-dispositions, are at the very least a partial explanation for why our early ancestors may have conceived deific agents in the first place. The deific agents came in many incarnations which would aid in our current understanding of how polytheism was deeply rooted for millennia and why, even today, we both consciously and unconsciously seek active agents outside of ourselves to explain what we do not readily understand.

When we look at the frailties of the human mind and the apparent disinterest by the multitude to do the very hard work of consistently thinking deeply to actively and carefully construct well-hewn models of reality, it is only a small wonder why major leaps in societal progress remain elusive. Rather, we are afflicted with our biases that lead naturally to the development and enduring sustainment of irrational beliefs. It is partly due to the profusion of differing irrational beliefs that it is so difficult to find common ground to confront major social issues which include how God's existence and nature might be best represented.

We then ventured to appreciate what we might know about the reality of the human soul and prevailing models of human consciousness. As to the latter, we reviewed the provocative

Orch OR model that views the source of consciousness as quantum mechanical resonance processes taking place in neuronal microtubules. The number of such resonators is astonishingly small, less than 0.1 percent of all neurons in the brain. It also suggests that our human existence is based on long chains of ultra-short states of alternating consciousness and unconsciousness. More tenuously speculated is that our entire universe is a sea of proto-consciousness with an innumerable number of eroded quantum states pervading the universe inasmuch as the Higgs field does. While the 20 year-old Orch OR model has been badgered with criticism throughout its continued refinement, there haven't been other rival theories advanced that go as far as it has in concretely explaining the physical mechanisms of consciousness. And while there has been recent success toward experimental confirmation of the theory, there is quite a ways to go before the theory would be accepted as the actual description of human consciousness.

Even though we have no decisive theory for human consciousness, there is a general consensus that consciousness is a phenomenon that supervenes onto the brain. That is, that our human experience is fundamentally monistic and materialistic and not some distinct ethereal dualistic mind-physical body apparatus.

Finally, there has been much philosophical and theological rumination for the existence of a human soul, immortal or otherwise. However, when the sciences are consulted, there isn't much to support the supposition that this thing we call a soul actually exists. All that we have are anecdotal, unscientific, and widely-varying personal accounts regarding encounters with the afterlife in the context of Near-Death and Shared-Death Experiences. If the Orch OR model were to be correct wherein our afterlife is strictly a dispersal of quantum wave functions, this hardly satisfies our earthly appetites for a meaningful immortal life. And for whatever it is worth, the Bible is silent on the actuality of a distinct immortal soul belonging to each individual. The Christian conception is simply a 12-century long extrapolation based on the notions that human beings can live eternally in heaven or hell.

The zetetic pilgrimage soldiers forward to wade more deeply into astronomical and astrophysical investigations to attempt to explicate the origin of our utterly awesome universe and what this may tell us about the possible existence of a generic God. What will be learned in the next chapter will be leaned on in the following chapter to help us understand the possibilities of God's existence as a purely transcendent Being, a dimensionally transcendent Being, an immanent Being, or some combination thereof. We will then have covered all the shadowy kingdoms of wisdom and knowledge and will be ready to circumscribe God's existence as best as we possibly can.

CHAPTER 13

The Scientific Theories of Creation –
Viewing God from the Cosmic Keyhole

[Elegance] goes directly to the question of how the laws of nature are constructed. Nobody knows the answer to that. Nobody! It's a perfectly legitimate hypothesis, in my view, to say that some extremely elegant creator made those laws. But I think if you go down that road, you must have the courage to ask the next question, which is: Where did that creator come from? And where did his, her, or its elegance come from? And if you say it was always there, then why not say that the laws of nature were always there and save a step?[1]

– Carl Sagan, 1996

Renowned cosmologist and prolific science and science-fiction author and host of the most widely watched series aired on American public television, *Cosmos*

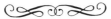

MODELS OF THE UNIVERSE

We have arrived at the frontier of the science-religion dialogue where modern cosmology is entranced with the cosmic quest to determine how our material reality first originated and evolved into what it is today or whether our universe is eternally existent. If science can decipher the truth of the finitude or lack thereof for reality, it will more tightly circumscribe the potentiality for the existence of a Master Creator. If it is determined that we live in an eternal universe (as in one that has existed for all past time), all of reality would be a brute fact making a Master Creator superfluous. While an eternal universe would not absolutely negate the existence of a deity, it would raise a host of tough questions, the answers to which would substantially diminish this likelihood. To sidestep these questions altogether, Christian apologists in particular are advocates for a temporally finite universe and the philosophical Cosmological Argument (CA).

Earlier I made passing mention of the Kalam CA and subsequently interrogated the Bayesian-based CA by Richard Swinburne (see Chapter 9). We will review the Kalam CA in depth in the following chapter as it has been held up high as a testament to the existence of God. If cosmology research validates once and for all that our universe had a solitary beginning, then we are left to posit what came before or at the instant of Creation. While it would be a crowning scientific achievement of the human mind to check the box on the truth behind the temporal nature of the universe, it can never answer *why* the universe exists. Theology would like to claim the latter as belonging to its sole purview; however, as a prelude of what is to come, there will be an idiomatic grasping of the straws for all involved.

It was the emergence of quantum theory and the publication of Einstein's special relativity and general relativity theories in the early 20th-century that sparked the world of physics to more fervently rationalize the processes of material reality. This chapter will review a constrained set of foundational concepts regarding the current reach of contemporary cosmology to accomplish this task. Cosmologists generally proceed to address this great challenge with the development of theoretic models. Of special interest here are **COSMOGONIC** models that seek to replicate how our universe came into being. *Cosmogony* is the cosmological study to discern how, from a scientific perspective, the universe came into existence. These models typically rely on highly sophisticated mathematical maneuvers that treat the various laws of physics as immutable. Sometimes, however, there is a purposeful alteration or outright abandonment of any number of the parameters found in the governing equations to test whether these constructs are really as firm as we think them to be. As a given model matures, the fidelity in terms of predictive power involving many factors is compared against astronomical observations, physical test data, computer simulation data, as well as other competing models. Theories also ought to be *a priori* intrinsically plausible without reliance on observations.

There are many hundreds of differentiated cosmogonic models under development worldwide. New ones are being created all the time and a contingent become disregarded and are unceremoniously consigned to the proverbial dust bin. Most, however, just creep along interminably under the stewardship of a cadre of physicists wedded to their theory. Herein we must restrict the exploration to a lightning quick review of a handful of cosmogonic models. To do these models the justice they deserve we would have to immerse ourselves in high-powered mathematics, however, we shall eschew taking that line in favor of a topical summary to consider the relative advantages and disadvantages for a subset of the approaches.

Behind the veneer of so-called scientific progress is a hugely competitive environment that tends to favor certain ideologies over others. This favoritism morphs over periods of decades as the bulk of scientists behave like a pack of lemmings pursuing in their wisdom more promising avenues along certain theoretic directions only for them to turn on their heels after hitting a dead end. Those scientists who pursue a non-congruous path by proposing what are seen as fluky theories face a range of troubling difficulties advancing their ideas as the lemming pack trod over them or avoid them altogether. And yet, most scientists readily admit that great discoveries often arise in unexpected places. At the heart of science, which is otherwise fixated on meticulous discipline and elimination of bias, lays an estranged business model that does not always compliment high ideals of fairness. It is to say that the predilection of science is to get in its own way.

Cosmological "Knowledge"

If we are to assume that the universe is temporally finite as the current wave of 'lemming cosmologists' suggest is the case, then the universe must have had a beginning. It is at this moment of Creation where we are confronted with a boundary between philosophy/theology and science. So say theorists who postulate that the universe had a beginning, after the first trillionth (10^{-12}) of a second from the inception of Creation, the physics of material reality are pretty well understood. Any earlier than this ultra-tiny fraction of time and our knowledge turns into speculation of the highest order. The bifurcation results from the fundamental fact that all available theories fail to describe gravitational effects in this timeframe and we are moreover uncertain of whether some, none, or all the laws of physics apply.

Not long after Einstein's theory of general relativity was still sending shockwaves into the scientific community, in the late 1920's, astronomers Edwin Hubble, Hubble's assistant Milton Humason, and Vesto Slipher generated the first observational data that revealed that the Milky Way was not the full extent of our universe, but it was but one among a great many galaxies. Hubble demonstrated that our universe appears to be expanding at a roughly constant rate in what is called the Hubble Flow. The numerical value for the Hubble Flow is called the Hubble constant or also the Hubble parameter whereby a positive value (i.e., greater than zero) represents an outward expansion and a negative value (i.e., less than zero) represents an inward contraction. The Hubble telescope, eponymously named after the Edwin Hubble, enabled astronomers[1] to discover that the universe's expansion is actually growing at a rate of 70 km/second (~44 miles/second) for every 3.26 million light-years.

Further study indicates that the universe evolved over its chronology of 13.8 billion years in four major eras. The first epoch is punctuated by an inconceivably short burst of **SUPRALUMINAL** expansion starting at the very first 10^{-36} second of the universe's existence

---

1. The three astronomers were Saul Perlmutter, Adam Riess and Brian Schmidt. Their work from 1988 – 1994 garnered them the 2011 Nobel Prize in Physics.

and ending around the first 10^{-33} second (one decillionth of a second). Depending on which astrophysicist you ask, some will give different durations for this initial phase of cosmic expansion, but we will not get hung up on that here. A decillionth is to one second, as one second is to 31.7 trillion-trillion years. The expansion process inflated the size of the universe from the size of a proton to the size of a slow-pitch softball. To give you an idea of how fast of an expansion this is, let us call to mind that the diameter of a proton is about one femtometer (10^{-15} m). If the expansion of spacetime was at exactly the speed of light, spacetime would only have increased by 10^{-24} meters—only one billionth the distance across the diameter of a proton! Instead, spacetime expanded to a diameter of about 0.1 meters indicating that it expanded many times faster than lightspeed. Because it mimics the process of a balloon that so-rapidly expands when pressurized helium is blown into its cavity, this blindingly fast process is referred to as *cosmic inflation*, which we will discuss throughout this chapter.

In the second epoch, the universe was dominated by unimaginably intense radiation lasting approximately 47,000 years which transitioned into the third major phase, a long matter-dominated period of acceleration. After 9.8 billion years of matter domination the universe apparently gave itself a fantastic boost in acceleration in what astronomers call the *cosmic jerk*. It is postulated that this boost is due to an enigmatic repulsive and pervasive force called **DARK ENERGY**. If real, dark energy dominates the universe comprising 68.3% of the entire observable universe, hence the name of the fourth and current epoch, the Dark Energy Era.

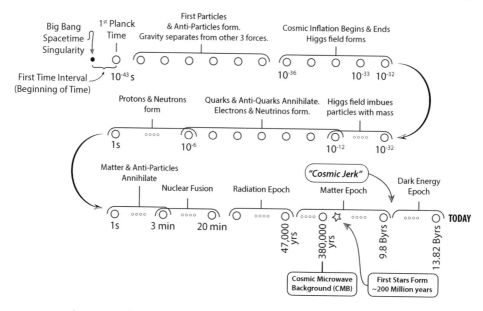

Figure 13-1. Chronology of the Universe (Hot Inflationary Big Bang Model)

The whole universe is of unknown size and potentially is boundless. The observable part that we can see is some 92 – 93 billion light-years across. This defines our light horizon. This figure may strike some as rather curious. How can the observable universe be that large when the age of the universe is 13.8 billion years old? This would seem to suggest that ordinary matter (the stuff we can see and detect) exhibits a sustained law-breaking supraluminal expansion. Even if we accepted matter spread out at 'only' lightspeed, the universe would be 27.6 billion light-years across (obtained by doubling the radial dimension of 13.8). This perspective would be generally accurate if the spacetime fabric was absolutely flat and physical matter (e.g., planets, stars, and galaxies) expanded within a stationary medium of 'static space'. However, the majority of physicists believe that *spacetime itself* is dynamically expanding at an accelerated rate, so the cosmic medium that light travels 'upon' is continually stretching faster and faster. This means that the size of space will necessarily be larger. Furthermore, Einstein's relativity theory only places restrictions on things that exist *within* spacetime, but not spacetime itself. Thus, spacetime could expand in supraluminal fashion. This is not presently happening in the observable universe, but it might be occurring well beyond our light horizon. Because this dynamic scenario has galaxies and galaxy clusters moving distally apart, there are large swaths of bulk spacetime that can no longer communicate with one another due to the maximal limit associated with the speed of light.

But does this commonly accepted narrative faithfully represent reality? In measuring extragalactic distances, there are a host of problems. Because every physical *thing* in the cosmos is in perpetual relative motion (linearly and rotationally) and subject to varying amounts of acceleration through time, computing proper and true distances is exceedingly challenging. The Earth revolves on its axis while rotating about the Sun while the Sun orbits the Milky Way. The Milky Way, 0.1 million light-years in size, turns on its own axis while spinning around the axis of the larger Virgo Supercluster of galaxies. The Virgo Supercluster is itself an 'arm' of the four-part Laniakea Supercluster which encompasses 100,000 galaxies spanning 520 million light-years (Laniakea means "immeasurable heaven" in Hawaiian). The Milky Way is located at the outer 'edges' of the Laniakea boundary. The Laniakea gravitationally interacts with the Shapely Supercluster and other major clusters. This behemoth bulk of mass swirls around a focal point. In late-2016, a massive but sparsely-populated region of space was identified which has been named the Dipole Repeller. The combination of this hugely-sized but low-density zone and the high mass density of the 'supercluster bulk' creates a gradient of gravitational potential. This essentially generates a system of flow and anti-flow properties whereby there is a flow of mass that pulls the bulk toward the focal point and an 'anti-flow' that effectively adds to the the motion because of the defect in 'attractive power' associated with the Dipole Repeller. Collectively, the combined system revolves around the Great Attractor which is an ever-moving point of space.[20] While all this rotation is going on, everything is, by prevailing cosmological perspectives, being stretched apart in linear fashion by the expansion of spacetime. All this relative motion in conjunction with various physical phenomena affecting electromagnetic signals challenge our abilities to comprehend which objects are moving closer and which are speeding away from us.

Measuring distances to objects on Earth is a relatively straightforward process. Contrastingly, measuring cosmic distances is incomparably more difficult. The astronomer's yard stick relies on a host of different methods to ascertain distance which often times need to be used in concert with one another. Most heavily used is a technique entailing the use of a special class of stars that pulsate in temperature and circular diameter called Cepheid variable stars. There is a relationship between the individual Cepheid star's pulsations and its luminosity which determine how far it is from Earth. When the Cepheid's distance from Earth is established, it can be used as a benchmark to gauge distances to other objects. But there are unresolved uncertainties in these measurements. Because Hubble's flow parameter is principally derived from observational data of Cepheid variable stars, this introduces a source of measurement error that affects many cosmological equations.

Another primary means to calculate astronomical distances is through the use of *Type Ia supernovae* which are produced by a binary star system whereby one of the stellar pair is a white dwarf star. A white dwarf is an end stage for low-to-medium mass stars whose nuclear fusion processes have stopped because its supply of stellar fuel has been exhausted. Resultantly, the outer layers are expelled leaving only its extremely hot and dense stellar core. The white dwarf siphons gas from its companion star until it builds to an unsustainable mass and the star collapses bursting into a supernova. It is believed that all white dwarf stars contain a similar amount of the isotope nickel-56. Because there is a uniform amount of this isotope in all Type Ia supernovae, or so goes the thinking, then all supernovae of this type will have uniform peak brightness in the isotopes' spectral data which can be used to compute its distance from Earth. Thus, it can be used as a milepost to compute distances to other objects. In fact, Hubble's flow parameter can also be derived from Type Ia Supernovae just as it can be determined using Cepheid variable stars.[2] We will revisit this assumption of luminal peak uniformity of Type IA supernovae later in this chapter.

There are other distortions associated with the use of light measurement techniques such as atmospheric effects, Doppler REDSHIFT / Doppler BLUESHIFT, cosmological redshift, GRAVITATIONAL REDSHIFT (the so-called Einstein Effect), the FINGERS OF GOD EFFECT, the **PANCAKE OF GOD EFFECT**, the **MALMQUIST BIAS**, and the relativistic gravitational effects known as **GRAVITATIONAL LENSING**. Another photometric problem still under study arises from a long-contemplated anomaly discovered on February 24, 1987. Astronomers working in the southern Atacama Desert of Chile detected the tell-tale signature of a supernova. The oddity was that the neutrino particles expelled from the stellar destruction of SN 1987a arrived to Earth 7.7 hours *before* the first stream of photons (particles of light).[3] Because photons move at exactly the speed of light through free space and neutrinos a hair less than the speed of light, the photons should have arrived first. In 2014, through the interpretation of SN 1987a data, physicist James Franson illuminated that light may self-interfere with itself thereby reducing the theoretical maximum speed of light traveling in the vacuum of space to something less.[3, 4] If this proves to be correct, this could have a major impact on photometric calculations which in turn would lead to profound alterations of our understanding of how matter is distributed in the universe and its proximity to Earth. Worsening the overall measurement situation is that errors are cumulative in general and are further amplified for more distantly located objects. Suffice it to say that in spite of our knowing of these issues, distance calculations are a serious issue confronting the cosmological sciences. As a prelude, we will review an enterprising cosmogonic model that may turn our understanding of the universe on its head when it comes to appreciating additional factors that affect distance calculations and whether the universe is truly expanding.

COSMOGONIC MODELS (SCIENTIFIC THEORIES TO EXPLAIN HOW UNIVERSE CAME TO EXIST)

Up to this point, we have proceeded with the assumption that our material universe: (1) is *the* solitary realm of all reality (i.e., no multiverse), (2) it had a single temporal beginning arising from a **SINGULARITY** (defined and discussed later), (3) it has always been in a state of positive cosmic expansion (i.e., a positive-valued Hubble parameter), (4) it is comprised of spacetime represented by a total of four dimensions—three spatial and one temporal—not more, not less, (5) all cosmic events are causally connected, (6) the arrow of natural time always points forward, never backward, (7) the concept of natural time is meaningless prior to the instant of Creation (this is to be reviewed in the next chapter), (8) the physical laws of the universe apply everywhere for all time with the three possible exceptions of (a) the first moments of the beginning of Creation, (b) inside black holes,[2] and more tenuously,

---

2. It remains an open question if black holes conform to known physical laws or if such phenomena break such laws. It largely comes down to whether such objects contain a singularity condition where all the black hole's mass is concentrated into a single point of no physical dimension, a prevailing thought by most cosmologists. Some physicists have argued that there is no singularity associated with a black hole which may in fact be an ultra-dense crystal made of nuclear matter or some other phenomena related to plasma and electro-magnetic fields.

(c) far beyond the observable universe (i.e., beyond the light horizon), and that (9) the fundamental parameters of the observable universe are finely-tuned (for reasons yet to be explicated) and are unchanging which permit the existence of sustained biologic life. Some would go further to suggest that (10) the mass-energy balance for the observable universe is disproportionately divided as follows: 4.9% ordinary (baryonic) matter,[3] 26.8% COLD DARK MATTER, and 68.3% dark energy. By such measures, it is a sobering indeed to think of the barrenness of the universe as it is almost entirely inanimate being made up of a lifeless distribution of particles and molecules. In spite of the predictions for the proliferation of intelligent civilizations (see Chapter 1), relatively speaking, life is a rarity to the extreme as it is comprised of the tiniest fraction of all ordinary matter.

The narrative above describes the Standard Hot Big Bang (HBB) model of the universe. The central assumption of the framework is that a physical *singularity* existed at the genesis of Creation. A physical singularity is also referred to by a number of different names: a curvature singularity, a conical singularity, a geometric singularity, a cosmological singularity, a gravitational singularity, a spacetime singularity, or more plainly as just a singularity. They are all the same thing for the purposes of this discussion. It is a circumstance where the 'fabric' of four-dimensional spacetime finds itself so extremely stretched, compacted, or knotted-up that physical matter can no longer travel smoothly from one point in space to an adjacent location. This singularity condition is a feature in the overwhelming majority of cosmogonic models.

In lieu of describing the complexity of curvature knotting of spacetime, let us look to the simpler case of conical singularities involving an over-stretching of spacetime. If you can imagine spacetime as a super-thin flat cloth lying on a table with a hole cut into it and you push a super sharp-tipped pencil into the cloth to push the 'spacetime cloth' through the hole, you get close to forming an analogous geometry of a singularity (refer to Figure 13-2). The cloth material forms a conical structure that comes to a point and is no longer smooth and flat nearest the tip. If you were to traverse the pinnacle of the point, there is no preferred direction to advance when you reach the absolute tip. This is called path incompleteness. Because nothing is ever absolutely motionless in the universe, you will 'fall off the face of the universe', literally disappearing from spacetime the instant you reach the sharpened tip. One moment you exist and the next you don't. If this were to happen, matter and energy would be destroyed, violating the universal bedrock principle that matter

---

3. Baryonic matter is made of baryon particles. Protons and neutrons are baryons because each is made entirely of quarks. Because each is made up of more than one quark, baryons are called Composite Particles instead of Elementary Particles. Quarks are elementary particles.

and energy cannot be destroyed. Mathematically, the local area around the tip is insufficiently flat and is said to be no longer 'differentiable' which violates the mathematical assumptions behind Einstein's greatest work.

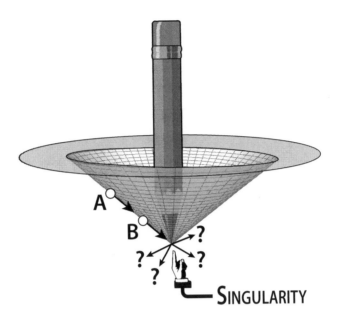

Figure 13-2. A Conical Singularity

It is Einstein's famous field equations which form the basis of his namesake theory of gravity (general relativity). His equations describe how spacetime and matter-energy interact. We can envision what this means with an analogy. Perhaps you played the following game when you were a child. A bunch of kids would form a ring and hold onto the edges of a large sheet of very thin and very light cloth (a bed sheet or parachute cloth). Then, into the center, someone threw a bunch of balls. When someone shouted a command, everyone started moving their arms up and down to create waves and ripples in the fabric. If the kids moved the cloth gently enough, the balls would all stay in contact with the cloth and under each ball the cloth would be dimpled due to the shape and weight of the ball. The dimple would follow wherever the ball went. This is very much what spacetime looks like with all the planets, stars, and galaxies moving around though they do not move as haphazardly as the balls on the parachute cloth do. A key difference is that in 3D-space, the planets, etc. warp space all around the object, not just underneath it.

The Einstein field equations contain parameters (namely, the Einstein tensor) that describe the shape of every location of spacetime (the parachute cloth) as it responds to the presence of matter (the balls). When matter is exceptionally heavy, the 'dimple' hugely distorts spacetime. If other matter comes close then the dimples interact. If we put two bowling balls onto the fabric, the dimples would be quite a bit more noticeable than if we put in two volleyballs. Now, if the two bowling bowls rolled into close proximity, the fabric would be dimpled even more.

Einstein discovered that gravity is not a physical force per se; rather it is a consequence of spacetime curvature resulting from nonuniform distributions of mass-energy. The dimples created by the presence of matter and their co-interaction with other matter are what we see as an attractive force where two (or more) bodies appear to move toward their collective center of mass. However, if enough mass centralizes to a single point as in the table cloth-sharpened-tip pencil example, then the conditions of a spacetime singularity will develop. When we apply Einstein's theory to the spatial scales present at the early moments of the Big Bang, Einstein's equations 'break down' because the resulting predictions become nonsensical (e.g., spacetime of zero volume, curvature without limit, matter-energy can disappear from the universe). It should also be mentioned that gravitational spacetime singularities are also thought to exist at the innermost recesses of cosmic black holes, though we will not discuss this matter further.

The ramifications of an initial singularity thought to exist at the moment of Creation, what I will now refer to as the *Great Cosmological Singularity*, has been cosmology's single greatest headache of all time.

Einstein himself was for most of his career uninterested in the mathematical oddity of the spacetime singularities his equations produced. He was much more interested in physical or real cosmology figuring that something in nature would smooth-over this problem and would be described by some other theory that would supersede his own. In 1917, Einstein initially advocated for a stationary universe. His universe was a singular, past-eternal and future-eternal cosmos. It was also spatially curved and of finite size, neither contracting nor expanding. This is referred to as the *Einstein Static State*. He later realized that this was untenable because his mathematical insights would suggest that these conditions would be unstable.

It was here he introduced his **Cosmological Constant**, represented by the Greek symbol lamda (Λ), which he later regretted as a monumental mistake and removed it by assigning it a zero value in his field equations. His mathematical treatise presumed that gravity was the only force holding the universe together, and if this was the case, the universe would eventually collapse or that the spatial curvature would lead to a runaway universe with never-ending acceleration. The instability of his static universe would eventually motivate him in 1931 to formally change his mind and adopt a model of an eternally expanding universe. A year later, he and his colleague, Willem de Sitter, published a new cosmological model that proposed a homogeneous (highly uniform distribution, irrespective of vantage point), **ISOTROPIC** universe (i.e., the universe is made of the same stuff in every direction) with no curvature (i.e., spatially flat). The universe and the property of natural time began with the Big Bang and spacetime would expand forever forward. And to Einstein's satisfaction, the Cosmological Constant was set to zero ($\Lambda=0$).[5] The Einstein-de Sitter universe concept would become the dominant cosmological model for the next sixty years. However, they never addressed the origin to the universe and the pernicious issues of a spacetime singularity that beleaguers all Big Bang models.

Another venerable model proposed by cosmologists is the Big Bounce model which postulates that our universe is the result of the total collapse of a previous universe that contracted to near-zero size destroying everything within it other than energy or entropy (the latter term is discussed at length later in this chapter). No sooner had this universe collapsed; it suddenly reversed direction and rapidly ballooned in size (the Big Bang). Physicists like to amuse themselves by calling this the Big Crunch followed by the Big Bang. This was joined by other cyclic (also referred to as oscillating) models whereby the universe is in an indefinite, self-sustaining, sequence of Big Crunches (re-collapse) and Big Bangs (re-expansion). This is a destiny of total annihilation followed by a period of reconstitution.

An outgrowth of the HBB (Standard Hot Big Bang) theory is a large number of inflation-based cosmologies that paint Creation as a super-accelerative expansion just after natural time came into being. An oft-cited analogy is if we were to take a rubber balloon and mark it with dots using a permanent marker representing the Earth, stars, galaxies, etc., and then rapidly inject it with gas, all the dots would rush away from each other. The speed of inflation is extremely fast. Depending on the model, inflationary expansion rates can be subluminal, match the speed of light, or be supraluminal (refer to Figure 13-3). In any case, it is far speedier than regular Hubble Flow expansion that is ostensibly caused by dark energy. Astrophysicists who study the process of inflation are undecided whether the Big Bang was initially hot temperature-wise, followed by a relatively cooler period of inflation, which subsequently became re-heated, or, if the Big Bang started off at a cooler temperature prior to the start of inflation and became orders of magnitude hotter after inflationary processes subsided. In any case, the Big Bang models that rely on some form of inflationary process are to be referred to as Hot Inflationary Big Bang (HIBB) models because in the first minute of the Big Bang, temperatures were the most extreme to have ever been produced in cosmic history.

There are eternal and non-eternal inflation theories. Eternal inflation is exactly what it says it is—a never-ending unbridled accelerative expansion of spacetime that never stops or slows down. This could be occurring beyond our light horizon which defines the 'edges' of the observable universe. If that were to be the case, the observable portion of the universe would be utterly tiny in size relative to the total (and ever-increasing) size of the total universe. In non-eternal inflation models, phenomena-to-be-ascertained put the brakes on the speed of inflation. Whatever its cause, inflation may slow to attain speeds closer to that of regular Hubble expansion.

Initially, eternal inflation theories were thought to operate in both past and future eternity. However, due to the *Borde-Guth-Vilenkin theorem* (discussed a little further on), it is believed that upon commencement of inflation, the process can only be eternal in the forward direction. We can also distinguish between the physics acting at the very beginning of inflation (primordial inflation) and the physics of inflationary processes that apply well downstream. The main point of departure is the former has to explain how inflation started out of nothingness (a.k.a., the pre-universe and whatever that means) whereas the latter has to explain how any braking mechanisms might develop to quash an infinite sprint of future-eternal inflation.

An important ramification of cosmic inflation is that everywhere inside the 'field of inflation' exist quantum fluctuations. What this means is that the energy of the inflation field will, according to the rules of quantum mechanics, randomly and radically increase or decrease. And because this can happen differently in disparate locations within the field, what may well happen is that *pocket universes*, also called *bubble* or *baby* universes, are created. If we think of this situation as a marathon race, the group of faster more energetic runners will pull away from the rest of the pack. Then other packs form. Within each pack, sub-groups split-off. What has happened is that the main race has dispersed into dozens of what we might call mini-races. This happens repeatedly in the inflation field and is how a great many universes are created. If inflation lasts a long time, an incomprehensibly large number of pocket universes end up generating a frothy sea of multitudinous worlds. This many-worlds scenario is called the multiverse.

So we see why it has become vitally important to understand the physics underlying cosmic inflation as it will help us to characterize the legitimacy of the various multiverse hypotheses. The HIBB model suggests that primordial cosmic inflation started and ended within the first one decillionth of a second that the universe existed. In round terms this is the same as starting, ramping to top speed and then ramping down within one billionth-trillionth-trillionth of a second! It is presumed in this theory that the duration was short enough to prevent pocket universes from forming (i.e., no multiverse). If this cosmic inflation phenomenon is true, it is absolutely dumbfounding to think how greatly this inconceivably short duration event affected the entire history of the universe thereafter.

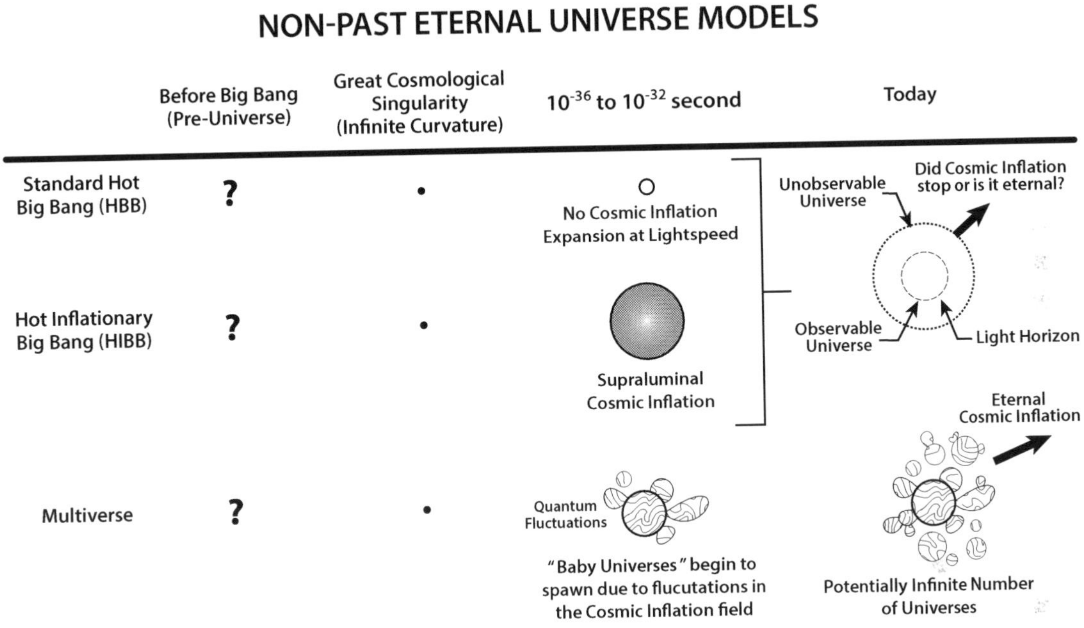

NON-PAST ETERNAL UNIVERSE MODELS

Figure 13-3. Big Bang with and without Cosmic Inflation

Beyond inflationary paradigms are a broad range of Superstring theories whereby most of them have since been culled and the remaining unified under the banner of M-theory which proposes that the universe is comprised of a total of 11 (some say 10) dimensions—ten spatial and one temporal. It was the brilliant theoretical physicist and mathematician Ed Whitten who in 1995 amazed the physics community by demonstrating that the major String theories in circulation at the time were specialized cases of the same general mathematical construct. It is this more general construction that we call M-theory. There are many ideas within M-theory of what constitutes these other dimensions and the physics that should exist which will not be explored here.

Another type of cosmogenesis conceived is the Ekpyrotic model (meaning "conversion into fire") that uses Superstring theory where the eleventh dimension is a hyperspace called the *bulk*. The bulk is imagined as two parallel three-dimensional 'hyperspace slabs' in co-proximity that are unimaginably large, dwarfing our own universe, and perpetually inflating in size. The bulk slabs undulate and with some frequency come into contact and stick to each other. At the point of contact, the high kinetic energy generates a massive burst of heated particles (hence, the reference to fire) used to birth a new universe or infuse an existing universe with new energy.

The last type of cosmogonic model I will briefly mention is the Vacuum Fluctuation model that portends that spontaneous creation of the universe came about by large-scale quantum fluctuations associated with **VACUUM ENERGY** taking place in a 'background space' that preexisted our spacetime continuum. Such theories posit that the net energy of the universe is identically zero whereby the positive mass-energy is balanced exactly with the negative gravitational potential energy. This does not strike the non-cosmologist as intuitive whatsoever because we see huge sums of energy being expended on Earth, by the Sun, and all the stars in the Milky Way galaxy.

Why are there so many scientific theories of Creation? Simply stated, for a theory to be successful it must match-up with observational astronomical data and to a lesser extent theoretic data. To this end, the universe presents a battery of formidable *Cosmological Problems* that need to be resolved before a theory can be considered a good fit to represent cosmic reality. A partial list of these cosmological challenges go by the names of the Flatness Problem, the Fine-Tuning Problem, the Horizon Problem, the Structure Problem, the Large-Scale Structure Problem, the Measure Problem, the Matter-Antimatter Asymmetry Problem, the Metallicity Problem, the Lithium Problem, the Cosmological Constant Problem, the Monopole Problem, and for certain cosmogonic models, the Boltzmann Brain Problem. These will be curtly introduced to help you appreciate where leading-edge cosmology is heading and the relative success in describing how our cosmic reality came to be from a scientific point of view.

Philosophers and scientists alike have wondered what the shape of our universe is for thousands of years. Aristotle thought that it was made of concentric spheres and many have followed in his thinking in the sense that the universe is spheroidal, much like the Earth is. The Flatness Problem is troublesome because in recent years there has been convincing experimental data that affirms that the **TOPOLOGY** of the observable universe is flat (i.e., zero curvature) as opposed to being closed (i.e., positive curvature implying a spherical universe) or open (i.e., negative curvature implying a hyperbolic shape). Current data tell us that the universe is flat to within 0.4% margin of error. This small uncertainty implies that there could be a very slight curvature.[4] The fact that the universe could be perfectly flat makes physicists wince because of the exactitude that it implies and that virtually nothing is ever perfect especially when it comes to highly complex, dynamic things. The advocates of quantum theory maintain that the universe *should* be curved. This is because the vacuum of space is filled with weak fields that sponsor something called vacuum energy. Due to the fundamental random nature of anything quantum, these weak field must necessarily fluctuate. This fluctuation should cause spacetime to curve. Since the predicted curvature should be well in excess of what is observed, physicists remain baffled as to what would suppress quantum-induced curvature.[6] The Flatness Problem is closely connected to the Fine-Tuning Problem. This latter issue was broached earlier which is to ask why a handful of cosmic parameters are imbued with the precise values they have. If the parameter values were even the tiniest bit different, the effect on the universe would be extraordinary, one such thing would be the shape of the universe.

Theories must also explain the Horizon Problem. When astronomers perform mapping surveys of the universe, the furthest they can see correlates to a time when the universe was about 380,000 years old, presuming that the Big Bang coincided with the origination of natural time. What these satellite-based surveys have found is that early into the matter-dominated epoch the entire universe became opaque with the latent heat (often referred to as the afterglow) generated by the Big Bang event. This energy forever blocks our ability to gather any observational information earlier in the cosmic timeline.

Today, this heat signature falls into the microwave portion of the electromagnetic spectrum; hence it is called the **COSMIC MICROWAVE BACKGROUND** (CMB). Scientists studying the data were amazed at how homogenous and isotropic the universe is at the largest of scales from one horizon to another. This primordial source of electromagnetic radiation encodes many clues about what the universe may have been like before and during the CMB's creation. Given that some regions of space in the CMB are so far apart, they are causally disconnected. This is to say that nothing in one sector could have affected in any way the events in another sector. It would be far more likely in such circumstance that the various regions would have evolved with greater differentiation—hence, the Horizon Problem. The only way this could have happened was by some mechanism operating within a fraction of the first second of

---

4. It is feasible that the universe is so incredibly large that the greater undetectable universe is non-flat. Imagine a huge circle; say the diametric size of the Earth. Now imagine that you are standing at the top of the circle at one end of a football field. If you look at an object at the other end zone, the connecting line would appear perfectly straight. But, if you zoom way out, you will see that in reality there is an imperceptible continuous curvature existing between you and another object on the circle.

the Big Bang. This is because no information can travel faster than lightspeed, so whatever evened-out the entire universe must have occurred right then. This is why cosmologists conceived of the cosmic inflation process which could smooth-out irregularities in supraluminal fashion. Whether or not the homogeneity and isotropy of the universe are accurate depictions will be discussed a little further on. Then there is the Matter-Antimatter Asymmetry Problem which presents us with the quandary of the asymmetry between the billion-to-one ratio of matter-versus-antimatter in the universe.

A fourth issue that theories have to contend with are the lumps and bumps or 'texture' of the universe in the form of galaxies and galactic groups (the clumping of galaxies) more commonly known as the Structure Problem. This is not at all trivial because all matter in the early universe was both diffuse and being accelerated apart. Gravitational effects decrease by the square of the separation distance between an object, so for every hundred paces apart, the strength of mutual attraction decreases ten-thousand fold. Computations indicate there is not enough mass in individual galaxies or galactic groups to keep them gravitationally bound without some additional 'gravity-like phenomena' at play. And when we look at large-scale images of the current universe, there are concentrations of matter in the shape of filamentary structures and huge areas of relatively little matter. Viewed as a whole, the universe appears to be very unlike what gravity by itself would make. Gravity likes to clump things into spherical balls, not stringy filaments.

All cosmological models must confront the Metallicity Problem which is the dual-sided issue of the three-to-one ratio of hydrogen and helium balance and the fact that the two elements constitute 98% of all matter. That means the metallicity (i.e., all other chemical elements) of the universe is exceptionally low. If the universe existed for a great deal longer than the suspected age of 13.8 billion years, stars would have converted most of the hydrogen to helium and a good portion of stars would have expired in supernovae explosions significantly increasing the metallicity of the universe.

Because it cumulatively addresses the Cosmological Problems associated with flatness, uniformity of the cosmic horizon, matter-antimatter ratio, texture, and hydrogen-helium content, the prevailing cosmogonic theory has been the HIBB model with some form of initial supraluminal cosmic inflation lasting on the order of a billionth-trillionth-trillionth seconds (10^{-33}). In this scenario, initially developed by MIT astrophysicist Alan Guth in 1978 – 1980, following the instant of Creation, the universe expanded from the initial singularity at supraluminal speed for an exceptionally short (but sufficient) amount of time. Finding direct physical evidence that this theorized cosmic inflation did actually occur has been at the top of the agenda for astrophysicists and astronomers ever since. It has long been conjectured that there may still exist a trail of bread crumbs in the form of primordial (sometimes referred to as relic) gravitational waves.

As a phenomenon in general, gravitational waves were first predicted by Albert Einstein in 1916 arising out his then recently proposed theory of gravity (i.e., general relativity) published six months prior. His idea was that spacetime is physically distorted when large amounts of physical matter (mass) are propelled through the cosmic medium. These disturbances, a series of contractions and expansions, are often analogized to the undulating ripples a stone or moving boat makes within a body of quiescent water. It is postulated that cosmic inflation would have been accompanied by the creation of primordial gravitational waves and density waves[5] that to this very day punctuate all of spacetime. Even though they are theorized to exist everywhere, they are supremely difficult to detect for multiple reasons. A key point here is that gravitational waves can be produced by a myriad of phenomena, not just cosmic inflation.

The first *indirect* physical proof that gravitational waves in general existed was by J. Taylor and R. Hulse in 1978 when the pair of physicists measured the energy dissipated between binary **PULSARS** spinning around one another was due to gravitational pulsations (what they called gravitational radiation). These insights earned them the 1993 Nobel Prize in Physics. However, these gravitational waves are not at all associated with the primordial (relic) gravitational waves from the creation of the universe. On March 17, 2014 a group of scientists at Harvard made headlines with the first direct detection of the ultra-elusive primordial gravitational waves.[7] This was an epic day for cosmology for sure. Ten months later it all got scuttled when on January 30, 2015 it was announced that upon further analysis of the data what was thought to be the imprint of gravitational waves was actually common interstellar dust.[8]

This was a major setback to those backing the inflationary/singularity theory of Creation. On September 14, 2015, the LIGO (Laser Interferometer Gravitational-Wave Observatory) experiment, a system requiring an unprecedented level of instrumental precision and sensitivity, made the first-ever *direct* detection of gravitational waves. The phenomena was generated by a pair of relatively small, colliding black holes—one 36 and the other 29 solar masses. Interestingly, the merger resulted in a single black hole with a combined mass of 62 solar masses, with three solar masses of cosmic material being radiated away into space. This evidence has since been confirmed with the highest standard of scientific certainty

---

5. Primordial **density waves** are fluctuations of compressed and elongated matter which had a sizeable effect on the structural architecture of the universe. Primordial **gravitational waves** are associated with the rippling of spacetime itself as opposed to the matter which 'rides upon it'. Both types would have been produced as a result of cosmic inflation.

(five-sigma confidence). Further evidence was gathered on December 26, 2015 when LIGO detected a different black hole merger generating gravitational waves.[2] A third, and more massive, binary black hole merger event was detected on January 4, 2017.[621] The conclusion is that, while it took 100 years to confirm the existence that gravitational wave phenomenon is real, we have yet to detect primordial gravitational waves and thus cosmic inflation remains a theoretical construct with many approaches vying for how it would operate.

THE GREAT (AND VEXING) COSMOLOGICAL SINGULARITY SUBDUES GENERAL RELATIVITY AND QUANTUM THEORY

Virtually all cosmogonic models with only a few exceptions (e.g., the Steady State, Ekpyrotic, and Vacuum Fluctuation models) involve the origination of the universe from the Great Cosmological Singularity. The crux is that the entirety of the universe—all the stars and galaxies of stars and everything else—is compacted into this single 'patch of space' vastly smaller than a single atom. But, for singularity accounts to hold any water, theorists have to rectify the fiendishly difficult mechanisms in the first decillionth (10^{-33}) second or so. While the theory of quantum mechanics is amazingly successful in predicting the interactive behavior of subatomic particles subject to the other three fundamental forces, it does not entail any descriptive nature of gravity.[7] Gravity is believed to have existed prior to the beginning of cosmic inflation either at the first Planck time (10^{-43} second) or as one of the first events to occur within the first 10^{-36} second of the universe's existence. When the entire mass of the universe is crunched together in such a tight space, the force of gravity becomes highly influential on the shape of spacetime. This is why for many decades physicists have been dauntlessly working to unify quantum mechanics with general relativity. However, to this day, they remain fundamentally incompatible. With no bridging theory of gravity, we have no effective means to understand how the universe evolved from a singularity. The situation throws a major wrench into the HIBB model because we do not have an indirect, let alone direct, confirmation of cosmic inflation.

---

6. The principal architects of the LIGO experiement were Drs. Rainer Weiss, Barry Barish, Kip Thorne, and Ron Drever. The first three physicists were awarded the 2017 Nobel Prize in physics. Ron Drever died on March 7, 2017 before the award was made. In accordance with the *Statutes of the Nobel Foundation*, the prize cannot be shared between more than three persons or awarded posthumously. The LIGO project was 40 years in the making and funded by the National Science Foundation at a total of cost $1.1 billion dollars.

7. A basis to ascertain if a system is better described quantum mechanically is to compute the multiplicative product of the typical mass, velocity, and distance. If the resulting value has the same order of magnitude as Planck's constant (h), then treating it as a quantum system is most valid. If, however, the product value exceeds Planck's constant, then classical physics provides a better tool to describe the system. (Victor Stenger, *The Unconscious Quantum*, Prometheus Books, 1995, p. 284)

Physicists are furiously working on a range of **QUANTUM GRAVITY** theories to address this hugely major conundrum. Some theories treat gravity as being continuously smooth just as general relativity does whereas other theories present gravity as existing as a dynamic granular texture, or foamy structure, or sometimes as a network of spidery strands that form loops. In the quantum gravity theory called *Loop Quantum Gravity* these loops define a minimum unit of permissible area for any structure. By virtue of this property, the geometric area is always greater than zero which prohibits the condition of infinite curvature from occurring thereby avoiding the development of singularities. All quantum gravity theories run into multiple intractable problems. It is important to understand that quantum gravity is built upon the framework of **QUANTUM FIELD THEORY** which conceives the universe as being comprised solely of physical fields. How many fields and what they are, is a subject of much debate. In quantum field theory, what we think of as particles are essentially energy states that emerge from the field (i.e., excitations). This is notably different from quantum mechanics that views reality as a bunch of distinct spherical particles jostling around the fabric of spacetime.

In quantum gravity, the property of time exists only in the sense of the evolution of quantum states. There is no corollary of 'quantum time' in general relativity. This is what is known as the Problem of Time which has needled theoretical physicists for decades. A breakthrough came forth in 2014 when the tough nut was cracked for one of quantum gravity theories called the *Canonical Quantum Gravity* approach which seeks to extend Einstein's general relativity theory through the invention of a new, not-yet-discovered, *graviton* particle.[10] Nevertheless, many tall problems still exist for all quantum gravity theories.

The practical upshot is that we are in a quandary of all quandaries. With no viable overarching theory for quantum gravity, we come up empty-handed in terms of having a coherent cosmogonic model that suitably describes matter-energy interactions taking place after the Great Cosmological Singularity spews forth spacetime. But how do we know whether a singularity even existed in the first place? This question was answered authoritatively in 2001 and revised in 2003 with the introduction of the *Borde-Guth-Vilenkin* (BGV) theorem noted earlier which is an eponym for the physicists who discovered it.[11]

The BGV theorem is elegant in both its general conclusion and the underlying mathematical simplicity supporting the conclusion. In short it states that for *any expanding universe*, there *must* be a cosmic beginning. This revelation presents strong implications for inflationary cosmogonic models that a singularity is likely to have existed. The primary assumption of the BGV theorem is that the cosmic expansion rate is on average positive (that is, it does not stop or reverse for any appreciable amount of time). This is asserted mathematically as the Hubble parameter being greater than zero on average.

It is salient for now to appreciate that the BGV theorem neither conjectures that a singularity *must* exist unconditionally nor does it presume that the *something-ness* we see all around us came from absolutely *nothingness*. That is, the BGV theorem says nothing about the existence or nature of a singularity or what came before it. It only affirms that an always-expanding universe must have beginning to the expansion. It furthermore only applies to a universe that is expanding sufficiently fast. That is, if the Hubble parameter were small in value, zero, or negative, the BGV theorem would not apply. Therefore, it remains feasible to avoid the problems associated with a singularity if the universe was either: (1) infinitely contracting (Hubble parameter less than zero), (2) infinitely cyclic (interminable Crunches and Bangs), (3) **ASYMPTOTICALLY** (progressively) static whereby the expansion rate slows to a halt (Hubble parameter is almost equal to zero) or (4) a situation where spacetime expands eternally to the past and to the future. The architecture of this latter universe is comprised of two distinct 'flows to time'. One time-flow moves forward to the future just as we customarily understand it. The other flow of time is reversed so to speak, moving away in the opposite direction. This 'reverse-time' is not to be thought of as the temporal past. Rather, it would be a totally divorced evolution of reality where there is a completely inaccessible second flow of time going in the opposite direction to what we consider to be normal construct of natural time. We would have absolutely no physical or causal connection to this other realm. This model is called the Aguirre-Gratton proposal after the physicists who conceived it. Finally, (5) one can differentiate between a physical, geometric, curvature singularity and a newly developed concept of a *field singularity*.

I will postpone further discussion of the third, fourth, and fifth options to a later section that tackles the various cosmogonic models predicting an eternal universe. The first option—an infinitely contracting universe—presents an infinite regress (compaction) of spacetime. Theories of this ilk fail to explain how the initial conditions were established in an acausal manner. Meaning, what were the conditions at the start of the universe? Once compaction begins on a grand scale, some physical mechanism is required to stop the process before total collapse occurs. Such mechanisms are hard to come by. If compaction goes too far, utter chaos would reign where gravitational effects would whip things around in increasingly violent ways. Lastly, contraction models struggle to explain how our universe is suitably settled to generate sentient life-forms.

The second type of model that avoids the singularity condition are infinitely cyclic models (an ongoing series of Big Crunches/Big Bangs) which are infinite to the future, but not to the past. Because the property of entropy for closed universes must always increase, it means that at some point the entropy must have been zero indicating an origin to the universe. We will later discuss why the presumption of a zero value for entropy is problematic. Cyclic models present a range of intractable challenges, one of which is a lack of a scientific explanation how the universe contracts to a singularity-like condition that is ultra-condensed and then re-expands. Another key detractor of cyclic models is that entropy should cumulatively increase cycle-to-cycle which would suggest our universe would have extremely high or even maximal entropy at the present time. Such a high (or maximal value) would ostensibly mean that we would be closer to the heat death of the universe. This is a state of perfect thermal equilibrium whereby the entire universe achieves a unified temperature. Without temperature differences, all energy-consuming processes stop. There are other reasons cyclic models fall into disfavor which we will refrain from reviewing.

Turning our attention back to inflationary models which are built using quantum theory, there is reason just on the basis of statistical probability alone but for other reasons as well to believe that other universes would exist because there is no real mechanism we know of whereby quantum fluctuations would only produce a single self-contained universe. From M-theory we can strongly infer that the other universes would have different sets of physical properties and associated laws that govern them. The overwhelming majority of universes would not be life-giving and those that might be otherwise would produce unimaginable things. Many universes would simply be outright unstable and fail to survive. Ostensibly they would self-contract into a singularity or meet some other impossible to discern fate.

It is here that we have to consider the especially important notion whether cosmic inflation is a relatively smooth and very low entropy process or one that is chaotic and random thereby producing high entropy. At first blush this seems like a trivial matter, but as we will see, the distinction holds deterministic power over the general plausibility of M-theory. Inflation-based models have to explain the Entropy Problem which is to answer how it is we have arrived in our current state of relatively high entropy (estimates vary widely, $\sim 10^{90} - \sim 10^{104}$ Joules/Kelvin). If entropy is too high then we human beings as relatively ordered biochemical beings could not possibly evolve into physical form as embodied conscious agents. We would otherwise have to be what is referred to in the jargon as Boltzmann Brains which are defined as unembodied self-aware entities (observers) coming into existence (sometimes only briefly) due to the chaotic/random fluctuations of the Creation process. The Boltzmann Brain is one of the several implications of the **MEASURE PROBLEM** in quantum cosmology which must rationalize biting ambiguities such as ratios of infinity (e.g., ∞/∞) which has no intelligible meaning. These nonphysical brains would ostensibly have the exact same organization as our own or other architecture for consciousness to arise. Multiverse hypotheses are undergirded with a large amount of randomization which inexorably leads to the creation of an exceptionally large, perhaps infinite, number of universes and simultaneous realities, all packed with unembodied conscious entities.

While philosophers like to argue about the expected ratio of Boltzmann Brain Observers-to-Embodied Conscious Agent Observers, all that needs to be said is that the statistical probability invariably prescribes that the multiverse in general will be chocked full of unembodied Boltzmann Brains. Relatively speaking nothing much gets done in the multiverse because Boltzmann Brains are unable to physically act upon their environments. The fact that M-theory posits so many chaotic universes must exist, ends up refuting the **ANTHROPIC PRINCIPLE** wherein evolutionary processes take hold to create complex cosmic inanimate structures as well as organized animate matter (e.g., humans). It is for this reason that M-theory is often regarded as an atheistic outlook on the world. Some philosophers have made attempts to salvage God as viably existent in the multiverse but none are too convincing.

To tamp down the number of Boltzmann Brains, physicist Sean Carroll *et al.* hypothesized that the actual process of inflation must have been free of dynamical quantum fluctuations.[12, 13] They suggest that existent during inflation was a quiescent vacuum where the quantum state was unchanging with respect to time which also means that entropy was not being produced. This would greatly diminish but not eliminate the eventual creation of Boltzmann Brains and neither would it negate the possible existence of a multiverse.

Their proposal relies heavily on the 1957 Many-Worlds Interpretation of quantum mechanics by Hugh Everett (the Everett Interpretation) which posits the existence of a fundamental entity called the universal wave function (refer to Chapter 12 regarding wave functions and the Schrödinger equation) that extends throughout the totality of the universe. However, according to this view, the universal wave function never collapses because if such a mechanism existed to cause this to happen, there would be in effect no way for all quantum outcomes to be realized thereby nullifying the need for the Many-Worlds Interpretation hypothesis. The Everett Interpretation implies that quantum events are not random but are smooth, deterministic, unitary transitions between quantum states that permit all outcomes to exist but not interfere with one another.

The Everett Interpretation is but one of a multitude of quantum mechanics interpretations so whether or not this proposal truly deals with the Boltzmann Brain dilemma is very much an open question. Carroll *et al.* admits this highly relevant issue where he acknowledges that one's choice of quantum mechanical interpretation prejudices how they would expect the universe to evolve.[12] Ultimately, while this new theory presented by Carroll dramatically cuts down the Boltzmann Brain Problem to something more plausible, and deals effectively with the Horizon Problem, it is highly vulnerable to a selection effect because of its inherent dependence on which quantum mechanics interpretation one decides to choose thereby relegating the overall theory into a sort of a 'no man's land'.

Inflation theories typically predict the existence of the as-yet hypothetical *inflaton particle* and associated *inflaton scalar field*.[8] Scalar fields are described by one-dimensional physical properties (a single numeric value and a dimensional unit for any given point in spacetime) that are coordinate invariant (i.e., same for all observers). Examples of a scalar property are mass, temperature, and charge. A scalar field is a distribution of scalar properties (e.g., a temperature distribution). Cosmologically speaking, the only fundamental scientifically confirmed scalar field is the Higgs field. Inflaton particles are not normal matter and are thought to have existed only during the ultra-short burst of inflation. These source particles must have undergone some mechanistic process which converts (or decays) the particles into forms of matter we know of or may theoretically exist but we have not observed yet. Physicists have imagined two rapidly-acting principle processes called *preheating* and *reheating* which result from the out-of-equilibrium conditions in the inflaton field leading to high rates of entropy production to explain the current level of entropy.[14] Such disequilibrium is also thought to have generated primordial gravitational waves, which is why astronomers have been working hard to detect them.

Beyond the challenges to primordial inflation, eternal inflation, and the multiverse, the HBB/HIBB models have additional challenges. On the order of three minutes after primordial inflation and continuing for 17 more minutes, the temperature of the universe dropped sizably to about 10 billion degrees Celsius to enable the process of primordial nucleosynthesis to begin forming isotopes of hydrogen (^2H), helium (^3He, ^4He), and lithium (^6Li, ^7Li). After 20 minutes, the temperature cooled to the point that the nucleosynthesis process totally shutdown until some 200 million years later when stellar nucleosynthesis processes formed the first stars. While astronomical observations confirm the amounts of Deuterium (^2H) and Helium-4 (^4He) predicted by the theory, there is a very large disparity with the amounts of Lithium-6 (^6Li) and Lithium-7 (^7Li).[15-17]

---

8. Note, one can speak of a csomic **inflation** field and separately, a highly-related **inflaton** field. The former refers to the general phenomena for the hyperexpansion of space. The inflaton scalar field, or simply the inflaton field, specifically refers to a physical field that operates as a component of space during the initial phases of cosmic inflation.

Big Bang theory predicts that more Lithium-7 (about two to four times higher) and far less Lithium-6 (three orders of magnitude less) should exist than what we actually observe.[16] With several recent observational studies confirming this problem, it is an indication that there is a fundamental correction needed for the generalized Big Bang theory or that there is a misunderstanding of stellar processes. The former would be more probable than the latter.

An altogether different challenge for Big Bang theory is that ever since the early 1980s, astronomers began collecting data that indicated that the universe was marked with astronomical structures of absolutely gargantuan size.[18] The further we probe the observable universe, the more we find structures so large that it would be infeasible they could have formed in the 13.8 billion years that the Big Bang theory attests to. In 1989 the largest cosmic structure ever found is the Great Coma Wall, some 550 million lights years long and 200 million light-years wide.[19] Estimates suggest that this would have taken 100 billion years or seven times the presumed age of the universe to form. In 2003, an even larger galactic filament—2.5 times greater in size—called the Great Sloan Wall was detected.

In 2012, a colossal 4 billion light-year sized-structure containing 73 quasars (supermassive black holes) was discovered which is equivalent to about 4% of the size of the known universe.[20] In 2012/2013, the king of all cosmic structures in the form of an unusual concentration of gamma-ray bursts was detected. A gamma-ray burst is a tell-tale signature of a supernova or hypernova being created by the death of a very large star. As the most energetic events in the universe, they release more energy in ten seconds than the accumulated energy our Sun will emit in its lifetime (about 10-11 billion years). This amazing structure is called the Hercules–Corona Borealis Great Wall and is estimated to be somewhere between 6–10 billion light-years in size which is roughly six times larger than the Great Sloan Wall.[21-23] The enormity of these structures cannot be explained by prevailing Big Bang models (HBB/HIBB) and for this reason the enigma is known as the Large-Scale Structure Problem. The existence of such enormous structures are evidence that the Big Bang theory is wrong. The universe is either much older than 13.82 billion years or our distance measurement techniques are way off the mark, or both. These structures also mean that the universe is heterogeneous and not homogeneous. This informs us that cosmic inflation may never have occurred.

Yet another curiosity that haunts inflation theories, as if they need any more problems to contend with, relate to two asymmetries in the CMB and several other not-to-be-discussed anomalies. One of the foremost operating principles for invoking inflationary processes in the first place was to address the Horizon Problem. The fundamental premise of inflation is that it would smooth-out any irregularities. It was mentioned earlier that the CMB data indicated that the early universe was homogeneous and isotropic. However, there exist two unexplained anomalies. Because of scanning methods employed to create the CMB map, the map is 'split' into a northern and southern ecliptic hemispheres.

The first oddity is that the average temperatures are slightly lower in the northern region and cooler in the southern region. The second irregularity is the CMB Cold Spot located in the southern galactic region in the constellation Eridanus. A recent study indicates that the Cold Spot is due to a large-sized, low-density region called a supervoid.[24] The Cold Spot may be the largest individual structure in the observable universe. The more widespread north-south anomaly has garnered a handful of hypotheses. One approach entails a new particle called the *curvaton* and an associated *curvaton scalar field*. The curvaton field would arise during the inflation process, much as the inflaton field, but it would outlast inflation before it too would decay away.[25-28] An alternative theory is that the CMB asymmetry results from one of the bubble universes in the multiverse colliding with our own universe which ignite the inflationary process or sends a shockwave through it.[29, 30] Many cosmologists would prefer to chalk it up to statistical randomness. None of these explanations have proven to be very satisfactory in explaining the **ANISOTROPY**, so it remains a chink in the credibility of the HIBB cosmological model.

All told, the Big Bang singularity and cosmic inflation theories are badly suffering in want of totally new physics or a new interpretation.[31] Stated in more basic terms, the Big Bang theory of Creation is very much in question as the best explanation for how the universe came to be.

ENTROPY

The property denoted as *entropy* figures prominently into the cosmological discussion because it is a signature for matter-energy transactions. Cosmologists employ it widely to build and characterize the validity of cosmological theories. It is also a property of the universe that religious apologists use in their scholarly arguments to favor cosmological models that predict a non-past-eternal universe, hence why we must explore this **RECONDITE** property of the universe. A discussion on entropy was delayed until now because, while the terms 'matter' and 'energy' are easily grasped, entropy is difficult to define in concise, accurate, and easy to understand terms that would be suitably clear to a layman. Often parroted is that entropy is the level of disorder of a **THERMODYNAMIC** system. This is what I was taught thirty years ago in undergraduate physics class. However, this definition for entropy has been abandoned in contemporary science in part because the term 'disorder' is rather fuzzy and subjective. Let us move forward to understand how entropy is comprehended in the present-day.

In the thermal sciences, a system is defined as a collection of processes that are contained within a global boundary that separate the internal processes from the surrounding external environment. As a thermal property, entropy is calculated mathematically as a surprisingly simple function of internal heat energy and temperature. Mathematically, it is the amount of heat transferred in a thermodynamic process divided by the absolute temperature at which that heat is exchanged. When thermodynamic processes occur, there is a transfer or exchange of energy. While the total energy is always conserved (i.e., matter-energy cannot be created or destroyed in an isolated system), there is a price to be paid when an object of higher temperature transfers its heat to an object with lower temperature. This price is called entropy. If we think of this transfer as a pay-per-use highway, then as one uses the 'temperature highway', a toll will have to be paid. Importantly, because you pay as you go, and because there are only very special instances when one might be able to avoid payment, the vault of entropy 'dollars' is always increasing in the universe.

Entropy, however, is not something tangible like the paper US dollar. Rather, it is essentially abstract information about the state of the universe; sort of like a large set of numbers on a billboard that continually update, counting-up our national debt. The numbers rapidly change and provide us with a gauge that something is changing. Because we can never truly collect or locate entropy, it reveals itself to us as missing information that we know is there, but we cannot manipulate it in any way. Entropy is also something that characterizes future possibility. In this sense, we have a car, a point of origin, a highway, and a destination. We could pick a number of different destinations, getting off the highway at different exits or by changing highways altogether. Therefore, there are many possibilities for the future of thermal energy transactions. The only thing we know for sure is that we will have to pay at the universe's toll booth. Thus, the more contemporary understanding is that entropy is a measure of uncertainty, missing information, or possibility—all of them synonymous. To my mind, the technical definition of entropy is best understood as the quantitative cost demanded by nature to permit the physical activity of internal energy as it (1) transitions from an initial state to a final state inside a defined system, or (2) interchanges energy with its surrounding external environment. Entropy is ultimately a *thermal and temporal* property, each of which gives us information about the universe.

A finer point on entropy is that while internal energy exchanges within a system boundary can result in a *decrease* in entropy, it can only do so with a simultaneous counter-balance of *equal or greater* entropy in the external environment. While there are theoretical processes whereby entropy is unchanged, in physically real processes, the entropy for the combined system-environment must always increase.

We can classify thermodynamic systems as open, closed, or isolated. The reason this is pertinent to the discussion is that our universe is a thermodynamic system and it has to be one of these three options. If we can know which one it is, it will provide important clues about the past, current, and future amounts of entropy. Open systems allow transfer of both energy and matter to its external environs (i.e., outside the system boundary). Closed systems are differentiated by permitting the exchange of energy, but the amount of matter is fixed within the boundary. Finally, an isolated system disallows exchange of anything to its external environs.

The second law of thermodynamics holds that for *isolated* systems, the total (global) system entropy can *stay the same or increase* and never decrease. To reiterate from above, an important caveat is that entropy can theoretically decrease anywhere locally for isolated systems if the system is suitably large enough to balance-out with a simultaneous and commensurate or greater increase elsewhere in the system. There are two main takeaway points on entropy. For many decades cosmologists have been focused on developing models that provide for a continual increase in total entropy. The other major insight is that the second law of thermodynamics does not establish what the *initial* value of entropy ought to be.[9] Assuming the universe had a beginning, did entropy start out at zero or low entropy, or was the entropy relatively high (e.g., due to a chaotic inflation process)? We have no way of knowing for sure, especially since we are not even sure if the universe had a beginning or was past-eternal.

Thermodynamic processes are exquisitely unique in that they always proceed in one direction and it is this property that leads to the *thermodynamic arrow of time*. Equally astonishing is that, unlike the second law of thermodynamics, all other physical laws possess *time-reversal symmetry*. This is to say they are theoretically temporally reversible (or equivalently, temporally invariant) permitting natural time to operate in forward or reverse direction to equal effect. Imagine a glass of milk that falls over, spilling the liquid contents onto the table. All other physical laws permit the reversal of the sequence (i.e., un-spilling of the milk) such that the laws are not violated. This is to say, the total energy of the event is the same regardless of whether it was spilt or the glass filled back up. It is therefore tempting to equate the thermodynamic arrow of time with the **COSMOLOGICAL**

---

9. As an aside, the current value of entropy is overwhelmingly generated by the combination of stellar black holes and super-massive black holes. Stars as we all know are roiling balls of energy fluctuation which generate huge amounts of entropy. If we added up all the entropy for all the stars in the universe, we would have to multiply this compounded entropy a billion, billion, billion times to equate to the entropy stored inside black holes.

ARROW OF TIME (i.e., natural time moving forever forward), though for well over a century there has not been an adequately justified scientific reason for doing so.

But this may have changed. Initially conceived by physicist Seth Lloyd in his 1988 PhD thesis, he suggested that using a then obscure and nascent field called quantum information theory in conjunction with the well-known process of progressive quantum nonlocality and entanglement may lead to a directionality to the property of time. But his idea was met with stone cold silence, even scorn, in the scientific community.[32] This notion settled into the darkness for twenty years until quantum information theory swelled in popularity and his ideas were resurrected by a set of physicists[33] whose ideas were independently developed by an altogether different physicist.[34] This stimulated others still to further mature the concept.[35-37] In short, we may well have a second means, in addition to the Second Law, for why macroscopic events travel in one direction only. And it could lend further credence to the cosmological arrow of time whereby cosmologists are integrating these new findings into their cosmogonic theories.

The universe is a thermodynamic system for the simple fact that it contains both matter and heat energy that are not in equilibrium. When speaking of the universe, the terms 'isolated' and 'closed' systems are often confused or carelessly used in the literature as being synonymous with one another. However, in strict terms, the total entropy *inside* closed systems can in actuality decrease. It is often presumed that the entire universe (not just the observable universe) is an isolated system and that the entropy of the pre-Big Bang state of reality was zero. For a very long time, Big Bang/inflationary cosmologists were constrained with the belief that as a result of being locked within our cosmic system boundary, that entropy would forever increase toward its maximal value.

However, the role of entropy and quantum dynamics is changing the landscape of our cosmic worldview. Firstly, we do not know how much entropy there was at the supposed beginning of the universe, if in fact there was a beginning. Secondly, as Seth Lloyd noted, the Second Law may not have been applicable for preexistent states of low entropy in the very early universe.[38] So, we cannot determine whether the Big Bang did or did not violate the second law of thermodynamics or consequently whether inflation was chaotic (high entropy) or smooth (low entropy). Also, it may be as some physicists suggest that there was a maximal value of entropy at the beginning of the universe, but that as the cosmos expands, the maximum value continually increases at a faster rate than the rate of production inside the universe and that there is no such thing as a maximal quantity of entropy. In this case, the universe might never achieve a state of thermal equilibrium (i.e., heat death).

Another cosmological issue concerning entropy is whether there exists a maximally-global thermodynamic boundary at all. If the universe were to be spatially infinite, there would be no system boundary to separate it from something outside itself because there would be nothing that would not also be part of the system. If, however, spacetime is finite and inflation theory is to be true, what then is the 'edge of spacetime' expanding into? Is spacetime expanding into a void of absolute nothingness? Or is there a transitional physical *something* that was pushed out of the Great Cosmological Singularity ahead of the Creation of spacetime? Could it be that we are expanding into a pre-Big Bang energy field (or energy bubble) so that as spacetime expands it sops up additional energy well outside of our visible universe making the Second Law–isolated universe combo a moot issue altogether? This last conjecture bears similarity to others who postulate that other universes in the multiverse may come into contact with our own thereby injecting ours with energy. Because these aforementioned ideas are non-testable, they are fundamentally unscientific conjectures that cosmologists do not get too wrapped-up about. Nevertheless, the question of cosmological initial conditions remains of paramount importance.

The summary point regarding entropy is that we do not know (1) what kind of thermodynamic system the universe finds itself in, (2) what the initial entropy value is or whether entropy as a property was established before, during, or after inflation (assuming inflation was a real phenomenon), (3) whether the common assumption of a very low value of entropy at the beginning of Creation is valid, or (4) whether there is a maximal entropy value to our universe. We also do not know (5) what range of entropy values would define sufficient orderliness to support biospheres (i.e., biologic life). Finally, (6) it remains unclear whether the universe could be receiving influxes of energy from whatever might exist outside of it. It would be therefore natural to question the reasonableness of the untold ruminations by cosmologists, philosophers, and religious apologists to use entropy as a tool to differentiate between the viability of cosmogonic theories as is often done.

THE ETERNAL UNIVERSE

If singularity/inflationary-based models are in such tatters, what about non-singularity or eternal models of the universe? The most prominent non-singularity proposals are the Steady State Eternal Inflation model and the Hartle-Hawking No-Boundary proposal (of Stephen Hawking fame). To start with, we need to differentiate between speaking of an eternal past, eternal future, or both (perfectly eternal). Here we are principally concerned with past-eternal models. Past-eternal models are faced with the daunting matter of observational data regarding the metallicity of the universe. If the past were indeed infinite or far older than the estimated 13.8 billion years, then on the face of things, the net entropy would be considerably higher than it is now.[10] Celestial objects that are now bright lights in our sky would be dark as they would have expended all their heat energy and the balance between hydrogen-helium and all other elements would shift away from the former in favor of the latter.

The Steady State Eternal Inflation model is typified by the Aguirre-Gratton proposal referred to earlier, though other adaptations have been proposed by others. It is essentially a double Big Bang creating a *biverse* where the cosmological arrow of time would be bidirectional with natural time in one universe flowing much like it does in our usual spacetime, but in a second mirror universe, time would likely operate in some alien manner. This is not to suggest that the realities would mirror one another as they almost certainly would not because they are physically and causally disconnected. Rather, the two realities will evolve in their own way. The biverse would experience eternal inflation in both time directions and would either originate from a 'classical singularity' or originate out of a non-classical quantum-dominated "minisuperspace" as defined by the Hartle-Hawking state where space exists but not natural time.[39, 40]

The Hartle-Hawking No-Boundary model gained a huge amount of press and fanfare in 1983 for the simple fact that it authentically produces a universe with an absence of a Great Cosmological Singularity. The theory posits that our universe is finite in the temporal past when we define the term 'past' in terms of normal natural time and that this property originated with the Big Bang. However, by incorporating what is referred to in mathematics as complex imaginary numbers (e.g., $i=\sqrt{(-1)}$) into the universal wave equation, the two physicists introduce a second form of time reference called, unsurprisingly, imaginary time. Imaginary time according to the physicists existed before the first Planck time (10^{-43} second) and is needed to support quantum tunneling processes which are causators of the Big Bang. While natural time is finite looking in the direction of the past, imaginary time is eternal to the past and to the future. The would-be singularity, instead of suffering the mathematical dilemmas of infinite curvature, is smoothed-out into what we can think of as a geometric sphere where any point on the surface is an arbitrary position for the beginning to our universe. The "No-Boundary" aspect of the model's title comes into play to say that there were no boundaries to our natural realm either in terms of natural time or space due to the absence of a true singularity condition.

---

10. Distinguishing between eternal and non-eternal models may be the most appropriate use of entropy as a metric, if it is to be used at all.

This model avoids all the troubles of a singularity while providing to us what we observe as normal time and all the trimmings of Big Bang cosmology while establishing a new construct for eternality. Therefore, the no-boundary universe is wholly self-contained with our universe emanating from a primordial sphere made of four-dimensional spacetime (imaginary time plus three spatial dimensions). Also, because there is an absence of a boundary, there is nothing external to the universe that could affect it. While not outright disproving the existence of God, Hawking's *et al.* stance is that God or other laws needed to establish the initial conditions for the universe are unnecessary. This primordial 4D-sphere is, according to their construct, something that had no origin and has always existed.[41, 42] The Hartle-Hawking theory has not enjoyed a great deal of momentum in recent times in large part because of its need for a second wholly separate and eternal domain of imaginary time. Another criticism is that it predicts a closed universe which some day would be expected to stop expanding. This would mean that it would necessarily subsequently collapse. Finally, the model must contend with the related and unresolved challenges confronting multiverse theories (e.g., cosmic inflation, Boltzmann Brains, etc.).

Another class of singularity-free models that are not beholden to the BGV theorem is referred to as Emergent Universe models which are derived on the basis of asymptotically (progressively) static past-eternality. This is to say that over the entire past history of the universe, the average expansion rate is essentially nil. One can conceive that there may be some point(s) in history where spatial expansion (or a series of expansions) might occur, but when one averages any amount of finitude over the span of past-infinity, the expansion will asymptotically tend toward zero. With such flexibility, one can envision various forms of a 'convulsing' universe where the magnitude of expansion and contractions are much less what happens in cyclical models but would be more frequent. In one scenario, a two-stage process is envisioned whereby in the first phase, the universe is eternal to the past but of a finite initial size (i.e., Einstein's Static State).[43, 44] This immediately defeats the Horizon Problem. Also, with an eternal past, the model already escapes all the troubles of a singularity. Furthermore, if one goes further to assume certain special fine-tuned conditions,[ii] it is feasible to bypass the need for an epoch dominated by quantum gravity alleviating the need to reconcile the incompatibilities between quantum mechanics and general relativity, a major advantage for sure.

---

ii. These conditions are specified by the authors George Ellis and Roy Maartens as choosing the initial radius to be greater than the Planck Scale, or equivalently that the Einstein's cosmological constant takes on an initial special value (meaning it would change in the second phase). A second condition is that certain kinetic energy conditions are upheld.

The second stage is initiated with density perturbations which become unstable igniting a finite period of inflation (a Big Bang) brought to an end by a reheating process leading to stable everlasting expansion much as we see today. As the authors note, the theory is also attractive because it does not require highly elaborate physics or invention of new forms of matter (e.g., particles such as inflatons, curvatons, and gravitons). One of the problems for this model is that the Einstein Static State is **METASTABLE** and is asymptotic toward negative infinity which means it is not truly eternal, but is exponentially long-lived. Since publication of the Emergent Universe proposal, there has been continued efforts to find some satisfactory curative approach to allow the metastable conditions to extend into the eternal past, but as yet it appears to be generally infeasible.[45]

A NEW FRAMEWORK FOR UNIVERSE-BUILDING – IS VARIABLE GRAVITY THE COSMIC KEY TO UNLOCKING THE SECRET TO THE UNIVERSE?

After reviewing a broad range of cosmogonic models, cosmology finds itself playing with a Chinese finger trap. Each time they poke their fingers in this direction or that, they get bound-up in problems that they cannot get out of. Inflationary-based HIBB cosmologies, our so-called 'best bet', have become increasingly mathematically and phenomenologically complex to overcome intrinsic failures. Without a theory of quantum gravity to unify quantum mechanics with general relativity or an effective means to winnow an infinity of universes and the dizzying number of unembodied consciousness's, inflationary physics is wedged into a crevasse so deep the only assurance to be claimed is that it will take a miraculous effort to extricate itself. It becomes rather obvious that without dependable knowledge of the initial conditions of an inflationary universe or when and what physical laws apply as spacetime transitions from the singularity to a well-formed state, singularity and inflationary paradigms are aggrieved with a good number of long-fanged problems that tear monstrously at their cosmogonic plausibility.

For the last three decades, German physicist Christof Wetterich (b. 1952 –) has been capably engineering a new cosmology that promises to break past many of the stalemated solutions conceived thus far. In broad terms, his idea centers on the notion that the exact same reality can be described differently by multiple choices of fields, in what he calls *field relativity—* an analogy to Einstein's general relativity.[46] Unlike most other cosmological theories of Creation, his is unusually flexible.

For example, in one frame of reference, today's universe is expansionary in character, whereas, in a different field choice, the same reality will be observed as contracting. This may come off as totally irrational at first, but it is made less so when one thinks about how in everyday life people can see the exact same event and yet have altogether different descriptions. For example, let us imagine a baseball game where a batter has just hit a pop-fly to center field. If we were spectators sitting behind the batter, the ball would appear as though it was moving away from us. If we were positioned in the stands on the opposite side of the stadium, then the ball would look like it was getting closer to us. If we were sitting to the side, say at third base, the ball would appear to move from right to left. And, if we were somehow riding along with the ball (let's assume the baseball does not spin), the ball would not seem to be moving relative to us at all. Regardless of where we sat, the same physics would apply, but we would have a different description of the motion of the ball. Therefore, there is a single reality where the physical observables are the same regardless of the frame of reference. This is what Wetterich refers to as *frame invariance*.

While there are many frames one could consider for the universe, Wetterich offers that the current cosmic state of affairs associated with the HBB and HIBB models can be referred to as the Einstein frame. In the Einstein frame, gravity and the Cosmological Constant are essentially unchanging in magnitude across the expanse of the universe and across timescales dating from the Big Bang origin to today. So too, the Planck Mass, the fundamental value of mass in the natural system of Planck units, is also constant. From the Einstein frame, the evolution of the universe begins with the Great Cosmological Singularity followed by cosmic expansion. In the HBB model, this is a form of rapid but regular expansion whereas in the HIBB model it is the much faster inflationary process followed by regular expansion. This produces the aforementioned radiation, matter, and dark energy epochs just as astronomical data suggests. In this frame, when we look at the Big Bang event, a curvature singularity exists. But this singularity, Wetterich postulates, is not a *physical* singularity; rather, it is a *field singularity*.

He mathematically demonstrates that his governing equations (analogous to Einstein's field equations) can be transformed vis-à-vis a mathematical construction called Weyl scaling (or also, Weyl field transformation) to represent an equivalent (invariant) frame called the Jordan frame, named in honor of theoretical physicist Ernst Pascual Jordan (b. 1902 – d. 1980). In the Jordan frame, gravity, dark energy, and the Planck Mass can be non-constant (i.e., variable). **The key point is that when the Einsteinian cosmological singularity is scaled into the Jordan frame, *the curvature singularity does not develop!*** The primary difference is that Einstein's field equations 'break down' at the singularity condition, whereas, there is no such breakdown of Wetterich's field equations. Therefore, it is believed that the Great Cosmological Singularity is nonphysical, as in, it never existed! And, because of frame invariance, Wetterich's model describes all the same physics and observables seen in the Einstein frame. The cosmic arrangement of the Hot Inflationary Big Bang Model is illustratively compared to the **Cosmon Field Model**, the name of Wetterich's cosmogonic model (refer to Figure 13-4).[47]

Once one recognizes that the Great Cosmological Singularity never truly existed, it should queue the mind to ask whether the universe had a beginning or is past-eternal. In Wetterich's view, the Jordan frame perspective indicates that it took on the order of *50 trillion years* for physical processes to play out to generate the observable universe, with the entire universe continuing into past eternity.[48, 49] But this past eternity is not the same static ever-existent universe conceived by Einstein. Rather, the universe was in a deep freeze, or *freeze frame* as Wetterich puts it, that took trillions of years to 'thaw'. The Cosmon Field Model predicts that the universe was in absolute darkness for nearly all past time because matter interactions were not occurring to produce concentrations of photons to any appreciable extent.

Another way to look at this is if the universe were to have thawed over the course of one Gregorian year, then the Big Bang period of rapid expansion and subsequent epochs would comprise the last 14-½ minutes on December 31st and we would be ringing in the New Year in present-day times. Wetterich's field equations permit time to extend to past-infinity without any inconsistencies developing, which differs from the Emergent Universe's troubled asymptotic formulation. He sees relevant changes evolving in large chunks of time, on the order of 10 billion years.

While traditionally applied to Big Bang models (e.g., HBB or HIBB), any cosmological model that includes dark energy and dark matter to help explain how the universe evolved can be grouped under the catch-all term of being a Lambda Cold Dark Matter model (ΛCDM). In such models, dark energy is a phenomena that generates repulsive negative pressure, or conversely a positive vacuum energy, that is directly responsible for pushing all objects apart whereas the mass attributed to dark matter has a hugely significant role in holding things together. Because dark matter and dark energy combine to enact a net expansion of the universe at a nonrelativistic speed, it is said to be a relatively 'cold' expansion as compared to the ultra-hot expansion due to cosmic inflation. The 'Λ' symbol refers to the cosmological constant parameter which Einstein had devised. The two preeminent questions in cosmology today is why the value of Λ is so incredibly tiny and whether its value is an unchanging constant or changes with time. To the first question, the value of Lamda in Planck units is believed to be nearly zero, but not quite ($\Lambda = 3.34 \times 10^{-122}$). It seems unnatural that some physical phenomena that came to dominate our entire universe would be so close to being numerically zero and that it remained so for all past time. This is called the

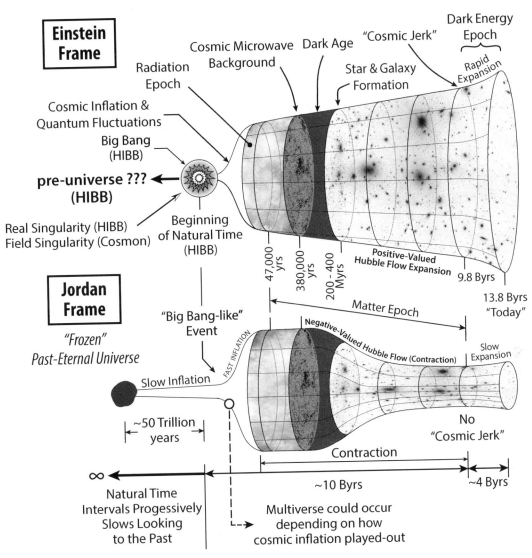

Figure 13-4. Hot Inflationary Big Bang Universe Model vs. the Cosmon Field Model

cosmological Smallness Problem. Highly related is the Cosmological Constant Problem because the Standard Model of particle physics and general relativity prescribe that the Cosmological Constant should be 60 to 120 orders of magnitude larger.[50]

The HBB/HIBB models had Big Bang physicists scratching their heads. How could something that had little to no effect for the first 10 billion years or so lead to an abrupt runaway process—they call it the cosmic jerk—that is threatening to make our universe dark once again due to objects being accelerated faster and faster apart? In 1987, in what may eventually be considered a watershed moment of human ingenuity, it was first conjectured that the Cosmological Constant actually varies across the cosmological timescale and this new time-varying phenomenon was called Quintessence (Latin meaning 'fifth element'). Wetterich was among the first physicists to have developed a theory of variable gravity.[51-54] He postulated the existence of a pervading universal and homogeneous scalar field akin to the Higgs field called the cosmon field along with its corollary cosmon particle.

Quintessence is referred to as dynamical dark energy because it is what we see in the Einstein frame as the underlying cause of both primordial inflation and what we call dark energy in the current epoch that is represented as an invariant (static) Cosmological Constant. To reiterate, what we call dark energy in the Einstein frame is the scaled equivalent to dynamical dark energy (Quintessence) in the Jordan frame. One primary difference between Quintessence (Jordan frame) and dark energy (Einstein frame) is that the former acts over trillions of years whereas the latter is a phenomenon cornered to the timeframe after the Big Bang (refer to Figure 13-5[55]).

As a theory of modified gravity, the cosmon field acts across large cosmological distance scales, whereas regular gravity acts at smaller distance scales and is depicted to be quantized into graviton particles. The cosmon particles and the graviton particles couple to dynamically affect the characteristic Planck Mass over the course of time. The cosmon field is itself nearly massless but it alters the mass of all mass-bearing particles. This relationship between a supposed reality of changing fundamental mass properties and the associated variable strength of gravity carries a wide range of ramifications that we'll discuss in turn.

Wetterich's theory postulates that in the extremely ancient past (~50 trillion years ago) all particles started out in a massless photon-like state. Photons are massless at all times past and present, regardless of frame. Far into the past, the Planck Mass was exponentially lower than it is today (but never zero). Conversely, the Planck length and Planck time were exponentially higher. This immediately infers that our understanding of physical time runs slower such that the intervals between the 'ticks' and 'tocks' of a clock increase the further back in natural time you go. Wetterich theorizes that proper natural time is no longer a useful metric because time intervals were so large in the ancient past (i.e., trillions of years ago). When particle masses were closer to their original massless or near massless states, the construct of physical time could be better measured using a sort of quantum clock. This cogent maneuver leverages the fact that as a quantum wave function oscillates, it will necessarily pass through the same "zero-point" time and again which is analogous to the ticking of a clock.

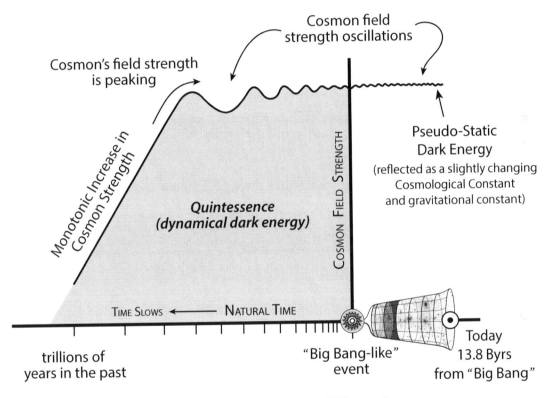

Figure 13-5. Evolution of cosmon field strength

Central to the theory is that the cosmon field dynamically evolves by growing in strength which leads to a growing mass of all mass-bearing particles in the universe. This continual change drives large-scale phenomena to alter the behavior of the universe with one phase transition leading to another in what Wetterich calls *crossover points*. This change in state is mathematically afforded by the selection of the value for a small number of free parameters in the field equations which are different from, but no larger in number than, what is ingrained in Big Bang theory. This is relevant because it essentially means that, other than the cosmon field, there is no need to postulate a larger set of physical parameters which is what many competing theories do. For the majority of cosmic history, the cosmon field grows in strength which directly increases the Planck Mass (and by extension the Planck Density and energy density). This naturally leads to a proportionate interaction with all particles to negotiate a simultaneous increase in their respective particle masses. This happens with the lone exception of neutrino matter which has a unique relationship with the cosmon field wherein the neutrino mass grows much faster as compared to all other particles. We will discuss the general issue of neutrino mass further on.

In a highly intriguing twist, Wetterich's field equations allow for a *family of initial states* which permit a multitude of ways for the current state of our universe to come about![56] It would seem from his mathematics that there are many distinct sets of initial conditions at the time of the ancient universe that, over great expanses of time, would eventually converge such that the same (or substantially similar) universe would result downstream. Using cooking terminology, we can use recipes stipulating significantly different amounts of brown sugar, egg, salt, and pepper, but by some stroke of luck, the meatloaf will look and taste exactly the same.

While one may be tempted to argue that these circumstances appear to support the idea of a teleological end-directed outcome, the reality is that it actually decimates any philosophical or scientific notion of teleology or fated existence. While it may well still be the case that the individual values of universal parameters need to be exact to sustain a universe, the circumstances are such that there are many ways to generate a life-filled universe like our own employing the collective universal parameters. This is not to say that life is inevitable; rather there is a broad range of factors that produce and evolve a universe to ultimately produce life in one form or another. Furthermore, the field equations specify how matter, energy, and gravity operate, but the entire universe is also governed by quantum chance. Thus, the universe could be subtly different or wildly different. Quantum chance may be chiefly responsible for our universe to be somewhat hospitable to life. For instance, there would be a distinct possibility that the star we call the Sun would not come into existence as it did as a relatively average star. Perhaps, six or seven billion years ago, matter could have distributed in a slightly different way and the material that would otherwise been used to create the Sun had more material to work with and the alternate-Sun became 50 times larger. Earth as we know it would not exist and human beings would not have come into existence. Nevertheless, the universe looks the same from a global perspective.

Nature, it seems, isn't the rigid mother we think she to be. Rather, she is a beautiful swan—flexible, adaptable, and migratory toward a most favored, but not necessarily exact, destination. There is, however, a ruffling of the feathers so to speak. Because there are multiple recipes to the universe and they all converge to the same or similar set of circumstances well downstream to generate a 'Big Bang-like' event and because these events are forever unobservable, **it means that we will never be certain which set of conditions were responsible for the initial changes that primed the universe to become what it is today**. I use the term 'Big Bang-like' because Wetterich generally sees cosmic inflation as an extremely long-lived and relatively slow process in the grand scheme of the cosmon field, but he acknowledges that it is viable that primordial cosmic inflation similar to what is posed by the HIBB model—sans the Great Cosmological Singularity—could have occurred.

It is as a result of quantum fluctuations that regions in the cosmic inflation field could experience different expansionary characteristics from slow-and-smooth expansion, to smooth inflation, or even chaotic inflation.[49] At the initiation of the Big Bang-like event, the German physicist equates the cosmon field with the inflaton scalar field theorized by others whereby the cosmon particle is is synonymous with the inflaton particle. After inflationary processes ebb, regular expansion takes over. After a period of time, the smooth MONOTONIC progression that characterized the prior history of the cosmon field strength begins to peak (refer to Figure 13-5). While the field strength continues to increase overall, it begins to oscillate. This oscillation eventually flattens-out in asymptotic fashion to its present-day strength which is relatively constant. Because the cosmon and graviton particles strongly interact, the two together are the reason why the Cosmological Constant is essentially invariant in the Einstein frame or in other words in the timeframe after the Big Bang-like event.

In the Jordan frame, the field equations predict that the *absolute value* of the Hubble parameter which is mathematically expressed as, '$|H|$', is essentially constant throughout the entire history of the Big Bang-like event and for all time forward to the present. Recall, that the mathematical procedure of taking the absolute value of any non-zero quantity means that the result will always be positive. During inflation, the Hubble parameter is positive but it flips sign to become negative for the radiation- and matter-dominated epochs. That is, the universe contracts in the Jordan frame while it is simultaneously expanding in the Einstein frame. If we bring back the baseball field analogy, in the Einstein frame, the fly ball is moving out and away from the batter whereas in the Jordan frame, the crowd in the bleacher seats located behind second base sees the ball coming right at them because of the shrinking distance between them and the ball.

After the universe is approximately 10 billion years old (using the Einstein frame as a reference), the sign on the Hubble parameter flips again marking the start of spatial expansion. This is the Dark Energy Era which, in the Einstein frame is an accelerative expansion according to the prevailing position of the veritable majority of physicists.[12] However, in the Jordan frame, the universe is undergoing much slower expansion or no expansion whatsoever. As we move closer in history to present-day times, the cosmon's field strength is cresting in overall strength, but still fluctuating, making the value of the Cosmological Constant change slightly up and down. Along with it, the growing neutrino mass forces them to slow to non-relativistic speeds. Thus, dynamical Quintessence during the last 10-plus billion years becomes essentially equivalent to the static Einsteinian Cosmological Constant in the Einstein frame.[46] Saliently, the universe's contraction-expansion profile of Wetterich's cosmology escapes any violation of the BGV theorem as well as the existence of a true spacetime singularity.

Neutrinos exist everywhere in huge quantities and collectively are among the most numerous type of particle matter in the universe. The Sun emits enough neutrinos that by the time they reach the Earth there are 65 billion solar neutrinos per second rushing past a square centimeter of space (this includes the human body). Our bodies are penetrated by approximately 100 trillion neutrinos at any given time! Because of the interplay between the cosmon field and the gravitational field induces a significant reduction in neutrino speeds, the coupling mediates forces that would tend to clump neutrinos together. Wetterich *et al.* believes that the combinatorial influences of cold dark matter and dark energy are the result of this clumping, in what he calls a *neutrino lump fluid.*[57]

In spite of their ubiquity, we know very little factual information about neutrinos, in large part because they are infamously difficult to detect owing to their lack of an electrical charge and because of their tiny mass. These properties give way to the fact that they only very weakly interact with other forms of matter. In fact, only in the last few years have we even developed decent mass estimates of the three species (often referred to as 'flavors') of neutrinos believed to exist—the electron, muon, and tau neutrino. In 2010, a study showed that the upper bound for neutrino mass was 0.28 **eV** (electron volts).[58] In 2014, studies put it between 0.18 eV [59] and 0.32 eV.[60, 61] Since then, the actual number has been shown to be no more than 0.12 eV with a confidence level of 95-percent.[62] However, it is believed that neutrinos are unique among all other known mass-bearing particles in that each neutrino flavor exists as a mixture of three possible mass states. For instance, the tau neutrino can exist in a purely tau mass state having a precise singular mass value. It can also transition

---

12. There are recent scientific investigations that highlight that the universe may not be expanding as fast as it has been commonly believed for many decades and may not be expanding appreciably at all (i.e., pseudo-static). This is highlighted further on. Nevertheless, it takes times for scientists to consider the merits of bold scientific statements and there is often a slow and uneven adoption of new research outcomes.

from being a purely tau neutrino into either a purely muon neutrino or a purely electron neutrino, each having a different mass value. Even stranger is that as a neutrino travels through space, a transitioning (one might say 'mutating') neutrino can exist as a mixture of all three mass states at the same time. This transitional process is referred to as *neutrino oscillation.*[92]

Though we do not know the precise values for any of the three neutrino species, it is thought that the three mass states cause the particle to travel at slightly different velocities. This extraordinary ability is a consequence of quantum mechanical principles and Einstein's special theory of relativity which governs the velocity of mass-bearing particles traveling near the speed of light.[92] To put the mass of neutrinos into context, the **REST MASS** of the miniscule electron is on the order of a half-million times more massive than the present-day mass of known neutrinos.

Physicists hypothesize that an even more ghostly particle, the *sterile neutrino*, exists which is expected to interact with the other species of neutrinos. No one is sure how heavy these particles are. Estimates between four times (~0.5 eV) and seven-thousand times heavier (7 keV) than the other three types has been postulated, though researchers have considered much higher values (up to 100 MeV). They are roughly categorized as *light-*, *intermediate-*, *and heavy sterile neutrinos*, respectively. The Cosmon Model suggests that neutrino masses in general were nearly massless trillions of years ago, but that their mass dramatically increased in concert with the growth of the cosmon field strength. Comparatively, most all other mass-bearing particles were not affected nearly as much by the increasing strength of the cosmon field.

In 2014 astronomers claimed to have found the first tangible evidence of dark matter particles. By studying the Perseus Cluster, a monstrously-sized structure containing thousands of galaxies enshrouded in a superheated gas cloud, astronomers detected an anomalous photon emission. The signature was inconsistent with currently-known matter and was very weak necessitating further investigation. However, the strongest candidate for the properties identified according to the researchers is the sterile neutrino which would add some credence to Wetterich's proposal.[63, 64]

Scientists the world over have set up various experiments to detect neutrinos. The most well-known of the experiments is the IceCube Neutrino Observatory located at the South Pole in which 48 institutions from 12 countries have collaborated to detect these elusive particles. The search involves an array of 5,160 detectors placed about a mile deep into a block of Antarctic ice measuring one cubic kilometer.[65] First published in May 2016, the IceCube Collaboration reported with high statistical certainty (99%) that light sterile neutrinos are highly **unlikely** to exist.[66] While this is an exceptional result, it is widely-acknowledged that this does not absolutely exclude the existence of sterile neutrinos because it is possible that scientists could be looking at the wrong clues, in part because we do not have a full-enough understanding of neutrino behavior. Not too long after, Wetterich *et al.* published their findings that if sterile neutrinos were on the lighter side, they would *not* be apt to clump in sufficient concentrations for long enough to be detectable. Conversely, if sterile neutrinos were of the so-called heavy variety, then stable clumps would arise. However, their concentration would grow so much that their behavior would no longer match what we have deduced from astronomical observations. Thus, if the sterile neutrino mass was more intermediate, they would be in a 'Goldilocks sweet spot' of sorts by which clumps would be stable enough, and concentrated enough to be detectable.[67] It would appear that if sterile neutrinos exist, the greater likelihood is that they are of intermediate or somewhat heavier in mass.

A past-eternal universe that experiences phases of contraction and expansion, changing particle masses, and variable gravity, does not come easy to a lot of physicists, not when Einstein's theories have been so well tested. But, as Wetterich notes, the thing he is changing the reality of is the removal of the curvature singularity from Big Bang cosmology. The rest comes with a change of perspective (field relativity) and the imposition of frame invariance. So, how does he explain Edwin Hubble's *et al.* observations that everything is racing away from everything else due to a rapidly accelerating spacetime expansion in the Einstein frame?

Hubble expressed his cosmological expansion hypothesis in terms of *cosmological redshift*. When self-luminous or illuminated objects are moved apart by the expansion of space itself, light is stretched-out. This stretching effect acts to increase the light's wavelength, and correspondingly, decrease its frequency. This shifts the light to the red end of the electromagnetic light spectrum. Thus, it is believed by Big Bang advocates that, when we observe cosmically-distant light-emitting objects, the emitted light leaves the object at a particular frequency. On its cosmic journey toward Earth, the frequency is decreased (refer to Figure 13-6). It is also pertinent to recall that the frequency and wavelength can also be affected by the relative motion between objects as they move through the medium of space. This Doppler effect can either add to or subtract from cosmological redshift. Astronomers correct their measurements and calculations by adjusting for, among other things, both cosmolological redshift and the Doppler effect.

Wetterich forwards an alternative interpretation for the celestial electromagnetic wave data collected by spectroscopic instruments. For those light sources now billions of light-years distant—emitted billions of years ago—the masses of protons and electrons at such times were smaller owing to a slightly weaker cosmon field. Also, the frequencies of the light emissions back then were lower as compared to light that is emitted by the same type of atoms in present-day times.[46] What we think we observe in deep space as the accelerated expansion of spacetime is not actually the physical process of the stretching of space so much as it is a result of two phenomena from ages ago—lower particle masses and potentially smaller atomic radii.[49] **In short, what is being said is that the redshift phenomenon laced into nearly every cosmological discussion and research paper for the last one hundred years is a red herring. This is utterly profound to say the least. It is important to note that Wetterich is not refuting that cosmological redshift exists. Rather, he feels it is a secondary-level contributor. He agrees that the universe experiences spatial expansion. However, he believes that the actual expansion rate of the universe over the last 13.8 billion years is considerably less than what the majority of the cosmological community suggests is the case.**

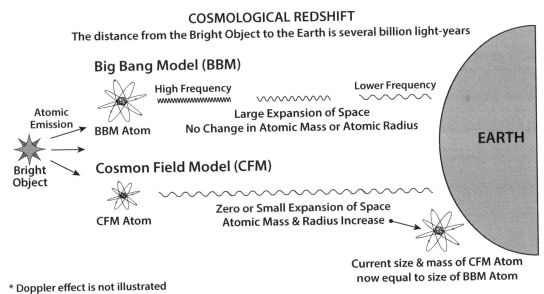

COSMOLOGICAL REDSHIFT
The distance from the Bright Object to the Earth is several billion light-years

Big Bang Model (BBM)

High Frequency   Lower Frequency
Atomic Emission
BBM Atom   Large Expansion of Space
No Change in Atomic Mass or Atomic Radius

Bright Object

Cosmon Field Model (CFM)

EARTH

Zero or Small Expansion of Space
Atomic Mass & Radius Increase
CFM Atom

Current size & mass of CFM Atom
now equal to size of BBM Atom

* Doppler effect is not illustrated

Figure 13-6. Source of Cosmological Redshift

Much of what has been discussed of Wetterich's cosmology is theoretical. The question that is at the tip of the tongue is how can his hypothesis be physically tested? Because dynamical dark energy interacts with many species of particles one can look to effects in the early universe when dark energy was far less influential (and when neutrino masses were smaller and the particles moved at relativistic speed). One could also look at certain aspects of the CMB as well as the formation of large cosmic structures. But, the most promising avenue is to search for the physical clumping of neutrinos because their mutual attractive force is 2,500 times stronger than gravity. And, as it turns out, the best place to look for neutrino clumps is in galactic superclusters in the scale range of 30 – 300 million light-years in size.[68-70] Another prominent feature of the neutrino lump fluid is that it is predicted to pulsate due to the fact that the cosmon field strength is not entirely constant which leads to small oscillations in dark energy.[71]

Wetterich is not presenting his variable gravity theory as a final grand unified theory of Creation, or at least not as yet. Rather, he views his contribution as a new framework on which cosmologists can build improved models that could result from tinkering with parameters that define the dynamism of the cosmon field. He acknowledges that the parameters of the equations can be alternatively selected to produce different expansion-contraction histories.[72] His model is one of a very few that successfully overcomes the many thorny Cosmological Problems while also finding a way to develop a more plausible conception for the property of physical time. In other proposals, the concept of time had to take on many tenuous characteristics from time running in two directions simultaneously (the Aguirre-Gratton model), or having two unique measures—one real and one imaginary (the Hartle-Hawking model), or a total divorce of a relationship between macroscopic physical time and quantum time as defined in many quantum gravity models (recall the quantum field theory's Problem of Time).

While we didn't discuss it, Wetterich's model of quantum gravity (called Dilaton Quantum Gravity [73, 74]) is simpler than other quantum gravity models trying to describe inflationary physics in large part because it does not have to reconcile the incompatible theories of quantum mechanics and general relativity. Let us recount that his framework does not require that cosmic inflation was an actual physical event. This is in large part due to two reasons. First, we have no physical evidence that cosmic inflation happened in the first place. It is hoped by mainstream astrophysicists that primordial gravitational waves will be detected in the near future to help confirm cosmic inflation as they would immediately crow that it supports the HIBB model. Such a discovery equally validates the Cosmon Model as it too can accommodate cosmic inflation. The other reason is that, even if cosmic inflation did happen, it is unclear how smooth or chaotic it was. Relatedly, physicists are still trying to ascertain what physical mechanisms might have existed to moderate quantum fluctuations within the cosmon/inflation field. If cosmic inflation was chaotic and/or long-lived, then this lends support to the existence of a multiverse. If it was smooth and/or short-lived, then the multiverse would be appreciably reduced, potentially constrained to just one universe.

There is another highly relevant feature to the Cosmon Model that may never have been considered. The vast majority of cosmogonic models rely heavily on presuppositions about events occurring prior to the beginning of natural spacetime or otherwise outside of it altogether. When proposals take on such initiatives it crosses a threshold between the physical into the metaphysical. Some of these theories are embroidered in elaborate mathematical treatments that belie the fact that such treatments are no longer proper science because they cannot be empirically tested and are therefore speculative pseudoscience. Furthermore, it can only be regarded as highly uncertain if logic or mathematical relationships exist in the same manner or even at all in models that conceive the existence of a pre-universe. The Cosmon Model does not suffer under these weighty assumptions because there was no pre-universe, at least not in the same context as these other models. In the Cosmon Model, there was a pre-Big Bang universe but it was the very same universe undergoing new physical phenomena.

Wetterich's theory may have received a boost of credibility from an unexpected source. In 2014, astronomers confirmed constancy in the average surface brightness—brightness per unit area—of galaxies both near and far that varied only 2.5%. Big Bang theory predicts that that the surface brightness should decrease the further the source is. There are two reasons why this should be the case according to Big Bang theory. First, as light rays from a source are emitted, they spread out over an increasingly larger area the further they travel, making the object appear larger. But because the number of light rays emitted at a given time is the same and the distance between the rays spreads out, the average brightness per unit area is smaller. An additional contributor to the dimming effect also comes from the fact that the light signal is getting stretched-out by the expansion of spacetime making it weaker in strength. To reiterate, according to Big Bang theory, far away objects should appear to be larger, but dimmer. **However, in direct contrast to Big Bang theory, the observations indicated that more distant objects were fainter—*and smaller*—which is consistent with a pseudo-static (i.e., non-expanding or slowly expanding) flat universe.**[75] Critically, the methods employed to come to this conclusion relied on physical phenomenon that permitted the researchers to circumvent the need to process the data with complex distance corrections which inherently makes the data less susceptible to being falsified. This is particularly important because, if you will recall, the way astronomers typically calculate distance measurements in an expanding universe is replete with corrections and uncertainties.

Additional support for an eternal universe is that the concept ably explains the Large-Scale Structure Problem in cosmology and why it is that large-scale structures, such as the Great Coma Wall noted earlier, could have formed 100 billion years ago. The HBB and HIBB models have no feasible means to explain how such massive structures could come to exist without a major reconstruction of its theoretical foundations.

In 2015, as a sign of some level of acceptance, other cosmologists are beginning to extend Wetterich's ideas on field relativity to conceive new mechanisms for smooth, non-chaotic inflation to occur which would avoid a multiverse from being created and the concomitant creation of Boltzmann Brains.[76] While it may be too early to accept Wetterich's Cosmon Model lock-stock-and-barrel (most physicists have not as most physicists remain well-glued to other theories), it appears to model the physics of an eternal universe with no messy singularity involved and with total mathematical consistency. It furthermore replicates many significant features of the observable universe and offers a plausible explanation for mass-energy balance between normal matter, dark matter, and dark energy.

Ultimately, in my estimation, the theory is considerably more plausible than the problem-riddled Hot Inflationary Big Bang model physicists have become so enamored with as well as the many offshoot M-theories that abound. Yes, I would agree that it is hard to comprehend in our mind's eye a frozen block of spacetime for the majority of past eternity and it leads one to naturally wonder how the frozen block of spacetime could have come about. Back then, because of how slow proper time trespassed on the continuum, it might be fairer to look at the universe as only a three-dimensional space field where time was all but inconsequential versus the usual four-dimensional spacetime. If the universe only started to un-freeze over 50 trillion years ago, then the state that existed prior to this was for all intents and purposes was *changeless* and *timeless*. This has important ramifications for the philosophical cosmological argument (the Kalam CA) which we will take up in the next chapter.

A Recent Update on the Expansion Rate of the Universe

Several recent astronomical discoveries have helped to better understand both the cosmic scale and expansion rate of the universe as viewed from the usual Einstein frame of reference (that is, the one astronomers typically use to measure such quantities). Earlier in this chapter, it was commented that astronomical distances could be characterized by Type Ia supernovae because of their uniform peak luminosity in the spectra of the element nickel-56. In 2014, astronomers confirmed that this is a mistaken view stemming from the fact that the luminosity values had been characterized using the optical light spectrum. When studying ultraviolet data from the Swift satellite, it became clear that there were variations in Type Ia supernovae explosions throughout the time history of the universe. There are in fact essentially two different populations of Type Ia supernovae that differ by their color signature.[77-81] When correcting for the previous erroneous assumption, it was determined that Einstein's Cosmological Constant is just that—constant. **That is, the universe *did not* experience a cosmic jerk (accelerated-acceleration), rather the acceleration has been essentially constant throughout cosmic time.** Thus, in the top illustration of Figure 13-4, the 'swooped curve' at the far right of the top image is inaccurate. The entire line should be straight (i.e., no swoop). Using the ground-based Sloan Foundation telescope in New Mexico, in 2013/2014 researchers mapped our universe as far out as six billion light-years with an unprecedented accuracy of one-percent. The data lends credence to the constancy of the Cosmological Constant and that the universe is flat and infinite in size.[82, 83] All three features are completely compatible with Wetterich's Cosmon Field Model.

Naturally, these new revelations mean that an awful lot of astronomical data and related theories that leveraged the erroneous distance computations are in need of updating. The main takeaway is that our scientific advancements in the last 25 years tend to confirm a universe many orders of magnitude larger than the observable universe. **The detectable universe is essentially the size of a grain of sand relative to the ultimate cosmos. Additionally, the age of this gargantuan reality may be eternal-to-the-past and probably eternal-to-the-future as well.**

A Short Note on Two Other Singularity-Free Cosmologies

Initially advanced in 2014 and published in 2015, an entirely different approach from Wetterich's was advanced by physicists also showed that a singularity-free cosmology would also infer a past-eternal universe.[84] This formulation will be referred to as the Cosmology from Quantum Potential (CQP) approach. This newer approach illustrates how quantum corrections can be leveraged to generate a new solution to Einstein's field equations assuming the condition that the expansion of the universe is homogeneous and isotropic.

In the interest of avoiding the need to explain many more quantum mechanical concepts, I will only cover a few aspects of the idea. Einstein's equations are founded on the basis of geodesic geometry. If we think of the universe as a sphere, then the shortest line between two points that lie on a curved surface is a geodesic line. We can think of this analogically in regular two-dimensional planar geometry as the shortest straight line between two points.

In regular spacetime, the curved geodesics lines are continuous, facilitating the uninterrupted travel of particles from one position in space to another. However, when one considers the over-curvature conditions associated with a singularity, the continuity of geodesic lines is disrupted and the path becomes incomplete.

The physicists employ one of the many interpretations of quantum mechanics called Bohm's Interpretation.[85] Like the Everett Interpretation, the Bohm Interpretation views the wave function as a physical field in contrast to other interpretations that view the wave function as nonphysical (abstract). In the Bohmian view, a physical wave function exists for the entire universe, but unlike other theories, it never actually collapses. Thus, all particles in the universe are defined by the wave function and are guided along their trajectories. Unlike geodesic trajectories in general relativity theory, the quantum equivalent called quantal Bohmian trajectories never become incomplete. Therefore, the mathematical description they arrive at avoids the existence of the initial Great Cosmological Singularity. Consistent with the mathematical development, the property of time extends to an infinite past.

The CQP model is very much in its infancy and has yet to be subjected to extensive scientific criticism. But, there are fundamental issues that are immediately apparent. First, it relies on a specific interpretation of quantum mechanics (i.e., Bohm's Interpretation) and physicists are far from determining which of the many interpretations ought to be favored. It also assumes that gravitational expansion is always and forever homogeneous and isotropic. From our prior discussion of the CMB anomalies, some of which were left unmentioned, this assumption is not built on the most solid foundation. Like many contemporary models, it relies on the existence of a hypothetical particle either the graviton or the quasi-scalar *axion* particle. Finally, the model focuses on describing the mechanics for the geometric expansion of spacetime but it does not speak to what physical evolutionary processes are underway prior to the radiation-dominated era going back to past-infinity. The one potentially favorable aspect of this model over the Cosmon Model is that the Cosmological Constant is treated as being constant over time. Therefore, it does not have to explain how the intrinsic mass of all mass-bearing particles increase across cosmic history because in the CQP model the particle masses never change.

In 2000, yet another set of theorists put forward a different singularity-free cosmology to the effect that reality is comprised of five dimensions—four spatial and one temporal dimension.[86] Their view is that our 3D-universe exists in a four-dimensional bulk hyperspace and that our universe was birthed as the result of the death of a four-dimensional star located in the bulk which collapsed to become a four-dimensional black hole. Our universe then is the ejecta from the explosion of the 4D-star. What we perceive with our instrumentation as expansion of the 3D-universe is actually growth of the 4D-bulk hyperspace.[87, 88] According to the authors, the Big Bang event is simply a mirage. This would be yet another singularity-free cosmological model that mimics that basic precept of Wetterich's notion that the so-called 'Creation Event' was not the absolute temporal beginning. Both theories posit the existence of a pre-Big Bang universe. The main difference is that Wetterich's cosmology is rooted in 4D-spacetime and this other concept requires an extra spatial dimension, a hyperspace, which is forever beyond our abilities to directly observe. This model has not as yet managed to suitably match physical observations of the temperature and density patterns in the CMB, so the theory's creators are hard at work trying to modify it to see if this can be resolved.

Concluding Remarks

Before we started this leg of the journey, the considerable majority of us would have had little reason to doubt that there was a temporal and physical origin to the universe. For many theistic believers, this 'fact' has been a stalwart **RAMPART** to defend the ontological status of God-by-whatever-name. Namely, that God exists because his existence is necessary to bring about the universe. The eternality of our universe simply goes against the grain of our intuition. When one contemplates the utter profundity of our universe—its size, extremities of mass and temperature, complexity, and aesthetic beauty—in contrast with our puny humanity, the prima facie case for a supremely powerful deity is rather striking. But, after a century of study under the stewardship of a legion of scientists and mathematicians, a universe springing-forth from an impossibly ultra-compact physical state (a.k.a. the Great Cosmological Singularity) presents us with a large host of **MULISH** problems that refute the viability of such a cosmic beginning. So, it may come with chagrin to ardent 'Inflationary Big Bangers' that the evidentiary tide is turning against such a conception and that the universe may well be past-eternal. The cadre of M-theory advocates and their ilk are more comfortable with the notions of infinite space, infinite time, and infinite realities, so a past-eternal reality is more digestible in their minds. Wetterich's Cosmon Model does in principle make room for a possible multiverse, so this may offer the M-theorists some opportunity for **REPOSE.**

Now that there is a far more robust eternal cosmology on hand that has so far been able to escape the common trappings afflicting other cosmologies, we should be more wary of cosmological arguments (scientific or philosophical) for God-by-whatever-name.

This is to say, with an increase in the plausibility of an eternal universe, the ontological, logical, and metaphysical necessity of a God is accordingly diminished. God would then be contingent on the universe, not the other way around.

In the next chapter, we will revisit the Kalam CA in light of the current status of scientific theories of Creation, and by other means as well, to make some determination on the Kalam CA's future philosophic viability.

SUMMARY

In the 20th- and 21st-century, the disciplines of physical and theoretical cosmology have immensely benefited from a great many leaps in technological advances in the form of super-computing clusters, greatly enhanced ground-based and space-based telescopes, massive increases in digital storage capacity, generation of new informational processing algorithms, information sharing platforms, and fundamental advances in theoretical mathematics. We are able to detect minutely weak signals from many billions of light-years away, record cosmic transactions around the clock in all directions, and physically recreate the blistering tempest of conditions close to the initiation of the Big Bang (presuming a Big Bang even occurred in the first place). With all this firepower at our disposal, one may be nonplussed by the astoundingly large number and diversity of theories that have been conceived to explain whether or not there was a cosmic origin. Ostensibly we would have hoped for a narrowing of viable explanations, not an explosion of alternatives. This unsettling divergence gives us pause as to how confident we can be of natural explanans for how this one great universe we reside in, is the way it is.

For many decades, cosmologists have pedaled a broad mix of theories to support every manner of universe including static, pseudo-static, contracting, expanding, oscillating, and hyperexpanding states of evolution. They paint reality arising from a one-time Big Bang event forming a singular four-dimensional continuum of colossal yawning breadth that may expand forever. Others go further to suggest that we are but one of an unimaginably large number of universes that continue to multiply interminably. This multiverse condition yields a mind-boggling situation where every possible permutation of reality either has, is, or will happen along with a raft of conscious unembodied observers popping into and out of existence.

Interestingly, the Cosmon Model propped-up by Christof Wetterich in some respects depicts the cosmos as a chameleon of many types. Initially, it was static for most of past eternity. This phase was followed by a thawing process lasting eons of time and as it thawed it transitioned into a pseudo-static state (i.e., a very slow expansion). The dynamic play between fundamental physical parameters lead to circumstances whereby a much more rapid expansion occurred. The likelihood is that it was a very fast expansion (i.e., subluminal speed) but not ultra-fast (i.e., light speed or supraluminal). The expansion phenomenon is generally a reframing of what has been called the Hot Inflationary Big Bang. In the Jordan frame, the expansion gives way to a ten-billion-year steady *contraction*. The universe reverts to a new state of relatively slow expansion starting about four billion years ago. The fact that his field equations are able to comprehensively map the entire evolution of the universe with total mathematical consistency as it alters greatly in character from one phase to another is a breathtaking achievement unto itself. And furthermore, it is able to gracefully leap frog over the terribly messy situation of a curvature singularity and the need to reconcile quantum mechanics with general relativity while presenting a relatively reasonable conception for how the property of natural time works. The fact that time is not of rigid, changeless 'tick-tock' construction, much slower in past times, is easier to accept when we consider Einstein's finding that time runs more slowly for objects moving at relativistic speeds relative to objects that move a great deal more slowly (i.e., **TIME DILATION**). The theory also offers a tentative explanation for both dark matter and dark energy—two of the most pressing questions in cosmology today. Another fascinating side benefit to the Cosmon Model is that it quashes the tower of the many 'fine-tuning arguments' by virtue of the universe being more forgiving on the parameters that have come to define the initial conditions of our universe.

Lemming cosmologists continue to this day to harbor favoritism for the singularity-driven HIBB model with either smooth or chaotic inflation while sometimes admittedly down-playing highly significant anomalies. A large contingent of physicists also continues to toy with many variations of M-theory, looking for ways to tame chaotic inflation, devise viable quantum gravity formulations, and terminate a proliferation of Boltzmann Brains. But because all these cosmogonic models are weighed down with numerous onerous factors, the present outcome is that their individual plausibility suffers greatly. The Cosmon Model has its own blemishes that must be dealt with. Namely, it is no small feat to validate that atomic or neutrino masses are increasing because mass is a relative property. Thus, the best line of evidence gathering will be to directly identify large-scale, pulsating groups of non-relativistic neutrinos or perhaps indirect effects of phenomena that could be tied exclusively to clumping neutrinos. If such a thing can be observationally-confirmed, this would be tantamount to validating that the cosmon field exists.

While I can broad brush some of the advantages and disadvantages of some cosmogonic models, I am not qualified to authoritatively judge the validity of the full gamut of cosmogonic models. There are too many, each is richly complex, and all have warts and beauty marks of some kind. However, given that cosmologists associate themselves into different camps, I do not know who would be a valid adjudicator. The rather clear sense one gets from the community of scientists is that no one is claiming they have a final theory of everything. At the time of this writing, Wetterich and his colleagues are initiating a search for gigantic clumps of neutrinos which may arise because of their relatively strong self-attractive properties. However, these particles are not sitting idle in space; instead they are zipping all about at subluminal speeds. It is therefore unclear what the outcome of such efforts will be because it is not clear if large-scale congregation of such particles would come about.[89]

The final point to be made is that there is building evidence for the idea that the universe may not have had a beginning in time or space. The universe may have always existed into the past in a timeless and changeless state. Then, perhaps due to mathematical probability, something started to change 50 trillion years ago. This initial change marks the true origin of natural time, but early on, each interval of time are separated by what today would be many eons of time. Slowly, but steadily, the syncopation of time increases. This provocative enlightenment infers that the universe may be past-eternal and possibly future-eternal. If the Cosmon Model accurately traces pre-Big Bang history, then there were many viable sets of initial conditions for how the universe unthawed to evolve into the universe we know. The kicker is that the *actual* set of initial conditions will be forever masked from our questioning minds.

CHAPTER 14

Time, Infinity, and the Cosmological Argument

In the first place, though people had talked glibly about infinity ever since the beginnings of Greek thought, nobody had ever thought of asking, What is infinity? If any philosopher had been asked for a definition of infinity, he might have produced some unintelligible rigmarole, but he would certainly not have been able to give a definition that had any meaning at all.[1]

– Bertrand Russell
British philosopher, logician, mathematician, and Nobel laureate, 1901

That great mystery of TIME, were there no other; the illimitable, silent, never-resting thing called Time, rolling, rushing on, swift, silent, like an all-embracing ocean-tide, on which we and all the universe swim like exhalations, like apparitions which *are*, and then *are not*: this is forever very literally a miracle; a thing to strike us dumb,—for we have no word to speak about it.[2]

– Thomas Carlyle
British historian and essayist, 1840

What really interests me is whether God had any choice in the creation of the world.[3]

– Albert Einstein
An undocumented, but oft-attributed expression of Einstein's which he made while musing with Ernst G. Straus, his assistant at Princeton University from 1944 – 1948.

THE COSMOLOGICAL ARGUMENT

AFTER A LONG AND ARDUOUS trek, we have arrived at the final defense for the existence of an almighty deity. In Chapter 9, we broached the 12th-century contemplation of Al-Ghazali, the Sunni Muslim scholar who put forth a disarmingly simple but effective intellectualization for the existence of a First Cause for the world at large. Repeating the philosophical muse's words (next page):

Original Kalam Cosmological Argument (translated)

Every being which begins has a cause for its beginning;

now the world is a being which begins;

therefore, it possesses a cause for its beginning.[4]

As testament to its implacability, the Kalam Cosmological Argument (KCA) is a towering pillar of theistic philosophy surviving nine centuries of scrutiny.[1] We should further recognize that, while the argument has its origin in Islamic history, the argument is applied equally to the Judeo-Christian milieu. If the argument were to be successful, it would not validate the God of Abraham (i.e., Theism); rather it can only confirm the necessary existence of a generic deity (i.e., Deism). Furthermore, it does not distinguish whether there is a singular god or a plurality of gods or if any such Beings are 'good gods' or 'evil gods'. Contrastingly, if the argument is proven to be false or less plausible than alternatives then this would not by itself negate the potential existence of God. It would simply mean that this particular argument fails to demonstrate of its own accord that a deity (or deities) existed at the time the 'First Cause event' was under way.

The most prominent contemporary advocate of the KCA is the literarily prolific Christian apologist William Lane Craig (b. 1949 –). Craig has been pedaling this deductive **SYLLOGISM** in one fashion or another ever since he obtained his doctorate in philosophy in 1977 while studying under the tutelage of the foremost pluralist John Hick (see Chapter 10). Craig's wide-ranging influence is testified by the fact that, as of 2007, more scholastic philosophical articles have been published regarding his defense of the KCA than all other arguments pertaining to God's existence combined.[5] We have before us his rendition of the KCA.

W. L. Craig's Version of the Kalam Cosmological Argument

Whatever begins to exist has a cause. [Premise 1]

The universe began to exist.   [Premise 2]

Therefore, the universe has a cause.[6] [Conclusion]

---

1. *Kalam* is the Arabic word for medieval theology.

To comprehend Craig's steadfast viewpoint that this piece of propositional logic powerfully evinces the reality for the existence of a deity, it may serve us best to work backward from his conclusions knowing at the outset he is a proponent of the Big Bang model of the universe. Given the conclusion in the form of the third line of the KCA, Craig argues that the cause to the universe is the first of all causes. This First Cause is itself uncaused (or self-caused) and according to his ruminations must have always existed in a timeless, spaceless, and immaterial state. As natural time did not exist prior to the universe's creation, the First Cause was also necessarily unchanging. And, because it is responsible for the creation of this magnificent universe, it was incomprehensibly powerful.[7] He maintains that God (synonymous with the First Cause according to Craig) was a singular and lone Being who had existed in a state of timelessness prior to the universe and by the necessity of his logic, God left behind the properties of changelessness, timelessness, spacelessness, and immateriality to become changeful and bound to the strictures of natural time at the conception of the universe.

This is a logical imperative because God cannot be simultaneously timeless (atemporal) *and* subject to time (temporal). This is to say that God existed in two sequential non-overlapping phases—one timeless and one temporal. Therefore, while God has always existed everlastingly, he has not lived for an infinite amount of natural time.[8] Craig's view introduces a philosophical question. If God was timeless and omniscient (or maximally intelligent), how could God know prior to Creation about things in a temporal domain of reality that hadn't yet existed (such as you reading this book)? Craig forwards that because time was not yet a real property it is not subject to his need for intellectual awareness. God conjured his plan for the universe in his timeless state, and once the universe and time came into being, God knows all things concerning the past, present, and future. Such a position strikes me as one that is too close to Christian mysticism and the reading of the mind of God rather than a robust rationalization.

Figure 14-1 provides a snapshot overview of the 'Craigian worldview' which will be further examined throughout this chapter.

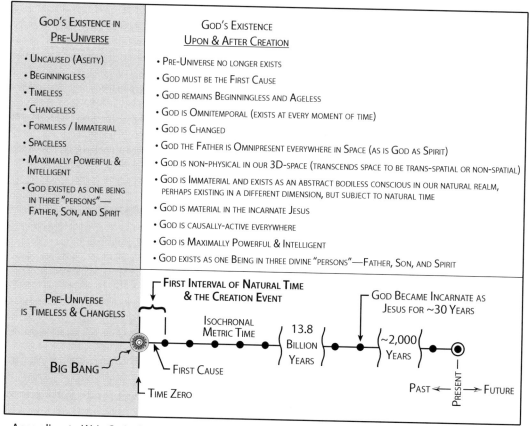

According to W. L. Craig, it is axiomatic that infinities do not exist in nature or anywhere in reality. As such, the universe cannot be past-eternal and there must be a First Cause since an infinite regress of time or causation is impossible. Resultantly, it was God who, as the First Cause, acted in the first interval of natural time to bring the universe into being.

Figure 14-1. William Lane Craig's—"Craigian"—Worldview

As a stronghold for religious apologists, many skeptics have hurled a gamut of academic and non-academic criticisms against the KCA. Craig has released an equal number of arrows from his quiver fatalistically removing them from contention as **DEFEATERS** or otherwise weakening their plausibility. Rather than to review the vast compendium of past treatises that have more or less failed to effectively counter this argument, we will chiefly center attention on those ideas that may evade the wrath of Craig's nocked bow. We can smoothly sidestep a great deal of the debate by agreeing with Craig on two points upfront. First, the syllogism's logical construction is undeniably totally consistent. Second, there is no serious **ANTIMONY** between the premises. Therefore, if one is to negate the verity of the KCA, one has to find falsity or implausibility in at least one of the three lines independently or to demonstrate that it is an empty formalism rendering it a moot argument. The third and fourth option is to demonstrate that the universe is beginningless or that the construction of the property of time in some way defeats the argument. Let us begin a line of inquiry employing the first method.

Craig maintains that the first premise of the KCA is bulletproof for the simple fact that *something*—matter, energy, spacetime, quantum virtual particles popping into existence out of the vacuum of empty space, the universe, or any 'thing'—cannot arise causally from *nothing*. He goes on to say that if this were to happen even once then there would be no constraints from this happening time and again. And, furthermore, we have experiential confirmation from our common, everyday experience that all material effects that come into existence must have an antecedent or simultaneous cause. He forwards the notion that Premise 1 carries an authority greater than that associated with the laws of nature because the principle of causality supervenes on all of reality, inclusive of the pre-universe.[2]

To further elucidate whether or not the universe came from nothing or if it was dependent on a First Cause, we need to become familiar with the origin and nature of the property of time as well as the concept of infinity. Understanding the nature of time turns out to be a devilish problem. Much like the concept of truth encountered in Chapter 1, how we interpret reality is intertwined with how we define the nature of time. It is for this reason I have attempted to be clear what theory of time is being assumed when we parse analytic arguments.

CAUSALITY AND THE ORIGIN AND NATURE OF TIME

Twenty-five hundred years ago, Buddhism was taking root which sought to free the human spirit in anticipation of Nirvana, a state of liberation from time and space. Time was a concept of great importance to Gautama Buddha for he quipped that, "The trouble is, you think you have time," meaning that we never know when we as individuals will run out of time before we die. He also intonated that the present moment is a virtue far greater than the past or the future—"Every morning we are born again. What we do today is what matters most." The Buddha rejected the notion of a deific Creator, but he did believe in the steady march of time but also that we as spiritual beings could transcend its limitations.

In his autobiography entitled *Confessions in Thirteen Books*, written between 397 – 400 CE, Augustine of Hippo carefully reasoned the nature of time. *Confessions* was one of the most profound works of medieval philosophy and Augustine's views in general had an enduring impact on Western society for a great many generations. In defending the Christian God,

Augustine recognized the need to define God's relationship with respect to time. In the quote below he is deliberating on the reality of time.

> What then is time? If no one asks me, I know: if I wish to explain it to one that asketh, I know not: yet I say boldly that I know, that if nothing passed away, time past were not; and if nothing were coming, a time to come were not; and if nothing were, time present were not. Those two times then, past and to come, how are they, seeing the past now is not, and that to come is not yet? But the present, should it always be present, and never pass into time past, verily it should not be time, but eternity. If time present (if it is to be time) only cometh into existence, because it passeth into time past, how can we say that either this is, whose cause of being is, that it shall not be; so, namely, that we cannot truly say that time is, but because it is tending not to be?[30]

Augustine of Hippo, Confessions, 397 – 400 CE

Augustine concludes that the property of time is fundamentally tied to human perception and cognition as a "distention" of the mind. Distention captures the notion that time extends into the past and the future but is principally about the present. Furthermore, that there is a mental tension, a torment and continual confusion of sorts, for the mind to comprehend the passing of natural time. Indeed, he feels that the full concept may well defy human language. God, he determines, occupies a timeless eternity, a realm in which God is external to natural time.

Our conception of time has morphed between then and now, however, we continue to puzzle over the deep challenges associated with the ontology of time. Did natural time begin at some finite point in reality or is it beginningless? Does time flow CONTIGUOUSLY and continually in intervals of time whereby the duration from one 'tick' to the next 'tock' is equal? Is time the same everywhere throughout the universe or can time run fast or slow at different places? Is time spatially global in the sense that time uniquely exists at every point in space or are there parts of the universe (or multiverse) where time does not exist? Does time exhibit irreversibility, always moving directionally forward or could it move backward or operate in loops? Does time possess a relational property between past, present, and future? Which of these three states—past, present, and future—are actually real? Some say only the present exists, others argue the past and the present but not the future exist, and yet another contingent espouse that all three exist. A portion of the adherents who say that all three partitions of time exist go one step fuFrther to posit that time is static (i.e., it does not flow) and that the past, present, and actual future are undifferentiable.

It should be no surprise that questions such as these have sparked a multitude of theories of time by philosophers and scientists alike.

If Craig is right and the universe did *not* appear out of absolute nothingness and had a beginning, then there is a First Cause and that First Cause, whatever that might be, *must have acted in natural time*, **and specifically in the very first interval of natural time** (refer to Figure 14-1). As an operative assumption, Craig stipulates that the KCA is predicated on the *A-theory* formulation of time.[10] A-theory conceives time as being temporally ordered into three partitions which we refer to as past, present, and future. Because of this arrangement, it is called a relational, *tensed* theory of time because we can use language about whether events happened prior to or after the present moment. A-theory is also referred to as *A-series* and is what we customarily think of as natural time.

There are alternative theories of time which, if true, would up-end the KCA entirely, but we will put this aside for now and revisit the matter at a later point in the chapter. Given the operating assumption that A-series is the correct view, then the past is always prior to the present and the present is prior to the future. We can conclude that if the universe were temporally past-eternal whereby time flows at all times into the infinite past, never ceasing to exist; there would be no First Cause to consider. Because such a situation would imperil the necessity for a deity, determining whether attainment of infinity is possible becomes critically germane to the KCA.

Do Infinities Exist?

The concept of infinity has been lectured on incessantly since Aristotle opined on the differences between a *potential* infinity and an *actual* infinity. The former is such that things continue on without termination or no recognizable end point but that we can observe or capture a subset as being finite. A potential infinity is technically-termed an *incomplete* series. In contrast, an actual infinity is defined as a *completed* series that has no end point. There has been no universally accepted determination whether actual infinities can or do exist for actual objects, but Craig has in large part persuasively argued that actual infinities *cannot* exist.

To appreciate the potentiality of actual or possible infinities, we need to consider the nuances of *subjunctive possibility*. Subjunctive possibility can be conceived as three concentric rings (refer to Figure 14-2).[11] The outermost ring contains all things that are *logically possible*. Going inward, the qualification of what is deemed possible becomes more restrictive. The middle ring contains all things that are *metaphysically possible* which is to be taken as anything that has the potential to be manifested as real or the capacity of being actualized though is not necessarily true of the natural realm. The innermost ring is reserved for all things that are nomologically possible (i.e., true of nature/reality, physically possible).

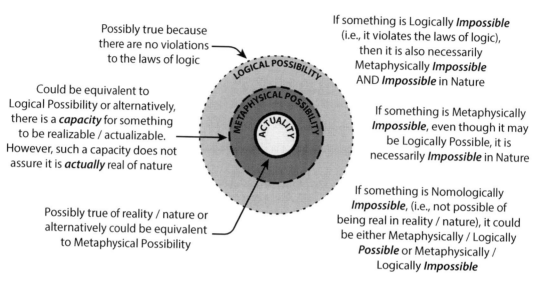

Possibly true because there are no violations to the laws of logic

If something is Logically *Impossible* (i.e., it violates the laws of logic), then it is also necessarily Metaphysically *Impossible* AND *Impossible* in Nature

Could be equivalent to Logical Possibility or alternatively, there is a *capacity* for something to be realizable / actualizable. However, such a capacity does not assure it is *actually* real of nature

If something is Metaphysically *Impossible*, even though it may be Logically Possible, it is necessarily *Impossible* in Nature

Possibly true of reality / nature or alternatively could be equivalent to Metaphysical Possibility

If something is Nomologically *Impossible*, (i.e., not possible of being real in reality / nature), it could be either Metaphysically / Logically *Possible* or Metaphysically / Logically *Impossible*

Figure 14-2. Subjunctive Possibility

Let us consider that it is logically possible that a colony of all-red Emperor penguins is also simultaneously all-blue in color. This is logically possible because there is no violation of logic laws. However, such a circumstance is neither metaphysically nor nomologically possible because we cannot conceive how penguins would have the capacity to be completely red or blue and we certainly do not see that in nature.

It is metaphysically possible (and therefore also logically possible) that Emperor penguins of the traditional black and white feathered variety could at some distant future point in time evolve to have four (instead of two) flippers to effectuate enhanced aquatic performance. However, this is nomologically impossible in the next 24 hours. Likewise, it is currently nomologically impossible for contemporary Emperor penguins to fly under their own power because their body mass far exceeds the capacity of their vestigial wings to lift them into the air. While the earliest penguins in the fossil record date back to about 60 million years ago did not exhibit the capacity for flight, it is metaphysically possible that flighted penguin ancestors could fly when their bone structures were thinner and had lower density.

Craig holds to the belief that neither *actual* nor *metaphysical infinities* formally exist anywhere in reality as it applies to things that are spatial and temporal (i.e., material objects).

While infinities do exist for abstract objects (e.g., mathematical numbers and sets), this has no special impact on the viability of a deity. Even God, in Craig's view, is absent of being infinite in virtually any capacity. God is neither omnipotent nor omniscient. Rather he ambiguously defines God as a maximally great being.[12] **Should his musings be correct, then there can be no infinite regress of events, and therefore, an eternal-to-the-past universe cannot have been so existent.**[13] Resultantly, the First Cause must be uncaused and beginningless to prevent an infinite regress of causes, time, or events. With Premise 1 of the KCA tightly locked-in, Craig is comforted that Premise 2 must also be true because the universe, according to his ruminations, must have had a beginning constituted by the property of natural time coming into existence and correspondingly the first interval of time. And out of logical necessity and the inability to form an infinite series of time, the First Cause was preceded by a state of absolute timelessness.

With an open-and-shut case, one might wonder whether we should toss our boxing gloves into our duffel bag, take a cold shower to sober us up, and call it a day. Collect our wits we must, but so too we need be the tireless PUGILIST, tighten the laces, and put up our dukes to counter Craig's able blows until a winner emerges from the ring. Let us re-enter the fray by revisiting Premise 1—*Whatever begins to exist has a cause*. Recall that we are led to believe that causality is a metaphysical principle governing all being and all reality, greatly more INSTANTIATED than the physical laws of the universe. Let us remind ourselves that what we call 'reality' is the framework of *all things both within our universe and everything external to it*—if anything else exists—including all materiality, immateriality, God, and the multiverse. Reality also includes immateriality as represented by abstract objects and a state of abstractness in general. Saliently, reality *excludes* a state of primal nothingness because this is a condition in which materiality, immateriality, and abstractness are *perfectly nonexistent*. In such a state of affairs, God could not exist. This is why some theologians posit that God neither exists nor does he not exist, rather his state of Being-ness is 'other', meaning his status is absolutely undefinable by human cognition.

Before we continue this line of discourse, I would like to make a few remarks about a reality containing multiple universes. If the multiverse were physically manifested, then **it** would be the cause to our universe's existence. Some raise a finger to say that the Borde-Guth-Vilenkin theorem ostensibly requires that the energetically expanding inflation field which is actively creating the multiverse must have had a beginning (see Chapter 13). However, this can only be regarded as a weak contention. While the parcel of cosmic inflation that led to the generation of *our* bubble universe may be subject to this BGV constraint condition, we cannot say with any certainty that the rest of the inflation field running amok outside of our universe is thusly compliant for the simple fact that we can never be certain how things operate outside this universe.

Regardless of the applicability of the BGV theorem to the multiverse, Craig's negation for the actual infinite regress of events would stake the multiverse to some initial point of origin in time. If the multiverse were to exist, then by the power of statistical probability alone, our bubble universe was not the first among the *gazillion* other universes. In which case, it would be almost impossible for the Time Zero for our universe to have been the true origin of time (let's call this Absolute Time Zero). Therefore, there would be some span of finite time from when the First Cause brought the multiverse into existence and when our bubble universe came into being. We also need to consider that time may not exist as a global property of the multiverse or could operate differently in each bubble universe or indeed within the inflation field itself. Some universes may become failed universes when they are birthed with relatively low energies. They may suffer a quick heat death and become essentially frozen and changeless. With no events taking place, this is a state of timelessness. Reality would then contain an ensemble of time-bound universes and some number of timeless universes. Craig is not in favor of the multiverse hypothesis but suggests that even it were to exist, that it would require a transcendent intelligent Creator and designer to kickoff Creation and to organize the finely-tuned parameters of our universe.

While we needn't trouble ourselves over the multiverse any further, we have struck philosophic bedrock concerning the properties of time and we need to explore A-series terrain further. It is seldom philosophically contentious that 'change' is a process that necessarily requires the property of time to exist. It has been proffered by a small contingent of philosophers that the reverse is not true, that time does not strictly have to involve change. This is to say that intervals of changeless (eventless) time could exist.[14] However, most regard it as axiomatic that time must necessarily involve change and that absolute changeless time is logically, physically, and conceptually impossible.[15] Therefore, any state in which there are no events occurring is considered timeless (atemporal). We proceed forward with the A-series truisms that (T1) change necessitates time, (T2) time necessitates change, (T3) changeless (eventless) time does not exist in nature (i.e., it is a nomological and metaphysical impossibility), (T4) as a corollary to the preceding remark is that there is no such thing as 'empty time' in nature, and (T5) a changeless state is a timeless state. We shall also agree that (T6) abstract objects are timeless across all reality.

The next foundational principle that needs discussing is the actual measurement of time. Here again, we are operating on A-theory principles. On the face of things, time appears to exhibit continuity and uniformity as a perfectly smooth, indivisible continuum in which we assign a unit a measure (e.g., seconds, minutes, hours) for the convenience of communication. This view is flawed because in such a reality we could never determine when the present of 'now' happens for we could divide time into an ever-greater number of smaller slices and still not arrive at 'now'. Therefore, while applying the A-theory of time, it must be **SUBSUMED** that time must be differentiable into distinct intervals of time. This is to say that we can measure the length (i.e., magnitude or duration) of one moment of time as it transitions to a contiguously connected and non-overlapping subsequent moment of time. Physicists **IMPUTE** the Planck time (5.39×10^{-44} seconds) as the smallest discretization of time, however, this particular ascription is not especially relevant here because a particular 'duration of time' needn't be measureable in specific quantities. It is, however, important that there exist distinct finite intervals that elapse successively.

A further insight to consider is that an interval of zero duration would be called a *degenerate interval* which by definition is identically a zero amount of time.[16] A zero amount of something is by definition nothing and if we are talking about the very first instant of time—Time Zero—then this would mean that this 'point of time' did not exist. This is why we need to speak of *the first interval of time* as opposed to Time Zero which does not formally exist as a real construct.

A series of time intervals can be categorized as **equal** (i.e., **isochronal**—constant in length), **unequal** (i.e., **irregular**—non-constant length whereby, beyond the first of all intervals, intervals strictly increase or decrease in length), or **amorphous** (intervals vary in length with any amount of frequency)—refer to Figure 14-3. Isochronal and irregular time qualify as what is referred to as *metric time* which is also called *differentiated time* because distinct intervals can be identified. Amorphous time is a bit of an odd duck because time could become *undifferentiated* to such an extent that there is no distinction between any accumulation of time whether it were 20 seconds or a million years. Amorphous time implies that intervals progressively grow longer into the past.[17] All the categories of time are *time-bearing*, meaning that events are able to shift from one moment to next, regardless of whether the durations of intervals are altogether different. It is also important to point out that all of these definitional concepts presented in the preceding three paragraphs would, I think, be perfectly agreeable to Dr. Craig as we are only attempting to establish common ground in his theoretic framework.

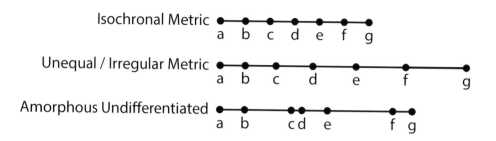

Figure 14-3. Concepts of Different Types of Time Intervals

In specifying the A-theory of time, Craig holds to an isochronal perspective for our universe. But, in the pre-universe, as it was already noted, it is out of necessity that the 'Craigian Christian God' was existent in a timeless, eventless state. While other philosophers have argued that God might have existed in the pre-universe in an amorphous state of time, and Craig is sympathetic to this idea, he counters that undifferentiated time would infer that intervals would be increasingly lengthened into the past. Furthermore, it would require past time to be infinite which he fundamentally refutes because of his assertion that actual or metaphysical infinities do not exist.[18] Undifferentiated amorphous time not only permits, but requires, events to occur which infers God changes (refer to truism T2, p. 514). And because God would be subject to time he would either have to be past-eternal, thereby violating the Craigian rule concerning an infinite temporal regress to the past, or God would have a beginning to his existence.

So now we have a clear understanding why Craig believes God must have existed in two phases. Prior to Creation, God was atemporal (eventless, changeless, and timeless) and upon the creation of the universe and natural time he became fully temporal. Therefore, on Craig's view the First Cause has in coherent fashion been demonstrated to be beginningless and everlasting. And, because of his view that an infinite regress of causes is neither metaphysically or nomologically possible, the First Cause must be self-caused.[19] So, where are the flies in the ointment hiding?

Chipping Away at the KCA

The first metaphorical fly is found in contesting the legitimacy of Craig's pronouncement that causality is factually a metaphysical constant across all reality. Causality is usually understood as a sequential mechanism where the material effect follows the cause, but it could also be executed in a manner whereby the cause and the effect occur at the same instant (Craig would tell us the Big Bang is such an example). According to such logic, the First Cause did *not* precede the Big Bang in time, or even did the First Cause act *at* Time Zero, rather it occurred *during the first interval of time* after Time Zero for we cannot define Time Zero without the first interval (refer to Figure 14-1). If we are to abide by the A-series truisms outlined earlier, the cause-effect relationship insists on a condition of temporality. If the pre-universe existed as a state of timelessness, then causation does not necessarily exist in reality prior to when Creation was put into motion. It is a safer assumption by far to say that causality, like time, came into existence at exactly the first interval of metric time.

Craig wants us to believe causality has always existed in all of reality as a matter of brute fact. However, it is mere speculation (of the highest order) how things might function in the pre-universe. Our capacity to reason, imagine, experience, or explore scientifically is bound to nature, time, and space. Therefore, we cannot affirm the existence of time (or timelessness), causality (or acausality), energy, space, governing laws, materiality, immateriality, mathematical constructs, or even logic in the pre-universe, should it exist. This last point is of particular interest. Even if the KCA syllogism were convincingly powerful in *our* plot of reality, it may have no force of effect external to our cosmic perimeter.

We can argue all we like about the power of logic as being inviolable in our universe, but it may not be an intrinsic property outside of this realm. This would in some senses make the KCA a fallacy of composition whereby the parts, in this case the individual premises, retain certain properties and we improperly infer that the whole (i.e., the entire syllogism) also has the same properties. The central point here is that the KCA carries a presupposition that we are to know exactly what causality is and that logic prevails as an interpretive mechanism, because otherwise, the original stanza of three lines would simply be three completely disconnected, independent sentences and nothing more.

This insight uncovers additional fundamental concerns in how the argument is simplistically encapsulated in the formalized 3-line structure of a syllogism. It creates a sense of confusion as to what the meaning of the individual words is intended to be and what they might otherwise be interpreted as. Referring back to W. L. Craig's version of the KCA, it is unclear if "a cause" in the conclusion is to be interpreted as a single cause or that a cause could be derived from multiple sources. The words "universe" used in Premise 2 might be ambiguous to someone believing in a multiverse. Adding to the quandary is that in Premise 1, use of the word "begin" is used in the present tense and in Premise 2 the past tense is used ("began"). This implies a relationship that necessitates an explanation outside of the syllogism. We can square some of the jagged edges of the W. L. Craig KCA by departing from the 3-line structure to enhance the overall clarity of the logical argument as follows:

The (Clarified) W. L. Craig Kalam Cosmological Argument

Reality is the universe and all that is apart from it. [Premise 1]

All of reality fully abides by the same laws of logic and logical inference. [Premise 2]

All of reality fully abides by the same rules of causality. [Premise 3]

Whatever exists is real. [Premise 4]

Whatever does not exist is not real. [Premise 5]

The property of natural time exists at the beginning of the universe and thereafter. [Premise 6]

Whatever begins to exist has a cause (or causes). [Premise 7]

The universe began to exist. [Premise 8]

Therefore, the universe has a cause (or causes). [Conclusion]

It is important to note that the added premises do not favor a particular outcome or alter Craig's original intent. They only seek to frame the ground rules on which to interpret the original three lines (bolded for emphasis). The revised KCA clarifies what is meant by the concepts of the universe, causality, and existence and that there could be a plurality of causes. What is still open to interpretation is how the property of natural time relates to use of the words "begins" and "began" and whether time exists prior to or outside of the universe. Additionally, left unclarified is whether time flows, and in what direction(s), and whether past time and future time are real constructs. With these newly added premises (1 – 6, above), it does add a greater burden to the interpreter because now one has to justify that logic and causality exist globally in all of reality. As noted earlier, any justification forwarded about these concepts outside of our universe is on feeble grounds. There is also an additional onus to explain why there would exist a particular number of causes. All these issues were always embedded in the 3-line syllogism; it just was made opaque by the simplistic arrangement and the verbiage employed.

It was already mentioned, but not yet explored, that there are different theories of physical time that run counter to the A-series tensed theory of time. For all we know, in the pre-universe, time may have existed as a circular (closed) construct which would avoid the problem with infinities. At some point, some may say at the origin of the Big Bang, time 'broke free' to become either a single unified linear stream or a branching of time into a circular component and a linear stream. An altogether different construct of time was already reviewed when we considered how the nonphysical quantum wave function possesses time-like qualities permitting one to progressively count 'time-like' intervals. This might be more appropriately labeled quasi-time for as you may recollect from our earlier discussion concerning the Problem of Time, the wave function associated with quantum mechanics does not involve natural time. As a third outstanding alternative, it was already mentioned that time in the multiverse could have started well before Time Zero of our universe. And more interestingly, reality as a whole could simultaneously contain pockets of time (which might operate differently) *and* pockets of timelessness. None of these concepts of time would necessarily violate the obdurate "infinite regress" axiom posed by W. L. Craig. We will briefly review a few other contemplations concerning the ontology of time a little further on.

Craig's thesis is further **VITIATED** by inadequately explaining why, after acknowledging that simultaneous causes factually exist, that the First Cause must be the result of a singular cause. He rallies a defense behind the use of Ockham's razor which is to say it would simply be unnecessary for multiple uncaused First Causes to exist.[20] To my mind, this amounts to an occupational offense of the first-order for a philosopher to take such an intrinsically weak principle of *this* realm and extend it so mightily across the border of rationality into the pre-universe. But, he can be partially forgiven because having discharged his philosophic mentation; he no longer dons the hat of an analytical philosopher but rather the feathered **FEDORA** of a theological metaphysician. Ockham's razor asserts if all things can be treated equal, we should apply the well-worn heuristic and show deference to the parsimonious option. This is only a guiding principle, not a natural law. The fact of the matter is that the First Cause could just as well be a multiplicity of causes (a.k.a. gods) acting to create the first interval of time. This is further emboldened because Craig only considers God as "enormously powerful" and "maximally great" but not omnipotent. God's prospective omnipotence was already discounted in earlier chapters, so why should one presuppose that a single deity had all the necessary power to create the universe? Ignoring any temperamental issues between multitudinous gods, it could be more plausible to think that some number of deities with lesser powers could combine their capacities to be sufficiently powerful.

We also have no clue how much energy is required to start a universe because the laws of physics, or in acknowledgment of our limited understanding thereof, the real laws of nature, do not necessarily apply in the pre-universe or even in the first interval of time.

Energy in the pre-universe may not have existed or may not have obeyed conservational principles which hold that the energy of an isolated system must be constant. If conservational laws were nonexistent but energy did exist, then perhaps energy could be created and/or destroyed. This could also mean that energy could beget more energy. Therefore, the universe could be created with a very minute amount of initial energy and be magnified manyfold in a runaway effect conceptually analogous to the thermal runaway nuclear fusion reaction in stars.

The final monadic property that Craig assigns to the First Cause is that, by virtue of it being both timeless and spaceless, is that it must also be an immaterial Being lacking in form or substance. Therefore the First Cause must be an unembodied conscious that intrinsically possesses a will (i.e., intentional purpose) and a great store of power. If the First Cause had form or substance, then Craig forwards that the substance would necessarily change in some fashion at the micro-level, macro-level, or both, which then necessitates the existence of time, and if time existed in the pre-universe then there must have been a beginning. If there was a beginning, then there would be something existent earlier than the First Cause. Furthermore, if the First Cause was made of an inanimate material substance (formless or otherwise) then it would be absent of an intentional will to cause Creation. Craig overreaches yet again with his presumption that materiality and associated laws function in the same or similar manner in the pre-universe as we are accustomed to on our side of reality.

Let us reflect for a moment on the topic of material substances. There are five known low-energy states of matter: solid, liquid, gas, plasma, and Bose-Einstein condensate. The primary difference between each state is in the densities of the particles. But there are many other exotic high-energy states of matter such as degenerate matter principally found in neutron stars and white dwarf stars. There are also supercritical fluids where the division between the gaseous and liquid states no longer exists and a supersolid state whereby material is rigid in form but flows without friction. While other states exist, one final example to be given is the quark-gluon plasma which is a hypothetical state of matter in the presence of ultra-high temperatures, ultra-high densities, or both. Such a state is thought to have occurred during the Quark Epoch of the Big Bang beginning at the first trillionth of a second (10^{-12}) and ending in the first few microseconds (10^{-6}). The point is that physical matter exists in a wide plurality of forms.

While we could conceive of a large multiplicity of substances and states having existed in the pre-universe, let us consider two 'will-deficient' substances I will arbitrarily call

Adamite and *Eveitite*.[2] Neither of these substances is constituted by the same type of atomic or fundamental quantum matter existent in our universe, but are of totally alien composition and amorphous in shape (gravity or gravity-like forces presumably do not exist in the pre-universe). Adamite and Eveitite are peripherally adjacent but not mixed with one another and possess a property of equal and opposite charge (analogous to electrical charge, though are not necessary mutually attractive). Let us also presume that the two substances fill the total volume of 'pre-space' however small or large that might be. If the two charged materials were to intermix even in the slightest, they would become instantly unstable and generate a source of energy sufficient to create a universe.

As a result of Craig's infinite regress axiom, assuming that it is true of reality for the sake of discussion, change and time are not options in the pre-universe. The only way material substances like Adamite and Eveitite could exist would be in a totally frozen state (i.e., zero change). However, we bring to the fore that there is something even more inviolable than the infinite regress axiom which is the absolute and timeless existence of mathematical probability. Probability exists simply because we know numbers and sets exist timelessly (refer to truism T6, p. 514). Whether one wishes to believe in the absence of an actual infinity or not, the probability would be exceptionally high ($\mathbf{P} = \overline{0.9999}$) that at least one change in a non-abstract object (presuming its existence) would randomly occur in the pre-universe. The probability would even be quite high for multiple changes to randomly occur. A random event may be one such that Adamite and Eveitite come into contact which sets off the creation of the universe and the existence of metric (natural) time. Just as in Craig's application of logic, the First Cause acts during the first interval of time.

We therefore have conceived of a logically coherent alternative of two conscious-less substances lacking any purpose whatsoever which, under the irrepressible demands of mathematical probability, could have created our universe without violating the antagonistic infinite regress axiom. As a quick **RIPOSTE**, I tend to agree with Craig that, assuming that the universe had a beginning and that the A-theory of time holds, I see no way how the universe could arise from a state of *absolute nothingness*. The validity of this concept has been publicly debated between Craig and noted theoretical physicist and cosmologist, Lawrence M. Krauss. Krauss is an ardent advocate for the Big Bang theory to explain cosmic origins and generally believes that the multiverse idea is sufficiently evidenced. He defends his position in his namesake book *A Universe from Nothing—Why There Is Something Rather than Nothing* (Atria/Simon & Schuster, 2012). As noted earlier, absolute nothingness is a state devoid of materiality and immateriality. This would ostensibly include

---

2. Adamite is not to be confused with the colorless mineral named adamite (zinc arsenate hydroxide).

even abstract objects such as mathematical constructs and consciousness of any sort. Let us recall that mathematical probability is only a construct that quantifies the frequency of occurence for chance events. By itself, it is not imbued with causal powers and thereby has no intrinsic ability to 'do' anything. And, we can probably all agree on the truism that material things do not materialize out of abstract objects. For instance, it would be impossible for the number '6' to create or have any effect on a hydrogen atom. The probability value for such an event is identically zero ($\mathbf{P} = 0$).

Given the particulars of A-series time, a beginning to the universe, and the infinite regress axiom, the upshot is that there is a choice in the First Cause which acted as the Creator to the universe. The first choice is the Craigian worldview which attributes the act of Creation as the willful act of a living, maximally powerful, immaterial, changeless, timeless, spaceless, everlasting, self-caused, solemn conscious source (a.k.a. God). The second option for the First Cause is the existence in the pre-universe of inanimate, unconscious, amorphous blobs of reactive material (e.g., Adamite and Eveitite). There would be more latitude if we discarded the strictures of Craig's timeless, changeless, and immateriality features of the preuniverse, which I have said are only a philosopher's postulations and not a matter of fact as Craig would have it. The third option is almost too obvious. It may be that the universe self-caused its own beginning. The universe as such did not require externally-derived motive powers from animate or inanimate sources to come into being. It inexplicably came into being under its own causal capacity. This third option is difficult to swallow because this essentially posits that the universe arose from a state of absolute nothingness which is logically, metaphysically, and actually impossible. But then again, logic, possibility, or probability ostensibly would not have existed. In such a circumstance, we could never fathom how the seed-universe came to be.

But let us not be too hasty in coming to final conclusions for the ontological or metaphysical status of a deity for we have two more reasons to reject the KCA. In an interesting coincidence, Louis J. Swingrover authored a paper in 2014 that was put into service as a writing sample for admission to a master's degree in philosophy presumably submitted to his alma mater Biola University's Talbot School of Theology, the very same institution where Dr. Craig is employed. The paper, entitled *Difficulties with William Lane Craig's Arguments for Finitism,*[21] challenges Craig's basic precept that an actual infinity is nomologically and metaphysically impossible. While I shall demur on exploring the details herein, Swingrover convincingly tears down Craig's various illustrative examples generated by Craig intending to show the absurdity that manifests when we attempt to find examples of actual or metaphysical infinities. By precisely pinpointing the fault lines in Craig's argumentation in this regard,

Swingrover severs the Achilles tendon of Craig's thesis. In light of the fact that Craig is unable to clearly identify the metaphysical impossibility of an actual infinity and because Swingrover doesn't push the counter argument to locate sources of metaphysical or actual infinities, rather he contends that the prudent position to take is one of neutrality. That is, until a better argument for or against is erected, the concept of infinity should not be used to weigh-in on the past-finitude or lack thereof for the universe.[22] In short, Craig's KCA should be shelved indefinitely if not persuasively denied by other means as provided herein.

Against Swingrover's recommendation, if we were to unjustly preference the notion that actual and/or metaphysical infinities are possible, then Craig's applecart is overturned with apples spilling everywhere. The pre-universe could then be governed by metric or non-metric time and it could be eternal to the past. Time could pass smoothly from the pre-universe into the created universe. The pre-universe could be filled with causality and materiality. Ultimately, while there still ought to be a cause or causes to the beginning of our universe, there needn't be a First Cause in the pre-universe. However, since we are not warranted to take such a position we can find further weakness in Craig's KCA by additional questioning of Premise 2—*The universe began to exist.*

Going back to the previous chapter, we explored the inner workings of Christof Wetterich's Cosmon Field Model. His field equations are unique in that they gracefully avoid the problems of the initial curvature singularity that wreaks havoc with the ability of the prevailing Hot Inflationary Big Bang model to explain how the universe came into being. It also offers at least a potential explanation of how dark matter and dark energy have evolved over cosmic history. Of greatest relevance here is that his equations predict that the universe may in fact be past-eternal and that the syncopated beat of natural time continually slows the further one delves into the past (or alternatively speeds up going from the past to the present). In the very deep past, the universe 'awoke' from a frozen state (changeless and timeless) perhaps due to the same reasons I noted about Adamite and Eveitite to the effect that it was statistically necessary that material changes would occur leading to the natural emergence of time and causation.

For Wetterich's theory, it is unclear how to describe the frozen state with respect to the interaction of time and causality. Prior to 50 trillion years ago, when the universe was frozen, was this a state of true timelessness and changelessness or was it the case that intervals of time were extremely large whereby each tick-tock cycle could be the equivalent of billions of years? Did any changes occur during these intervals or were there instances of eventless time? The Cosmon Field Model would probably require rejecting some number of the first five A-series truisms earlier in the chapter. As the unfreezing ensued it begs the question whether time would be considered irregular or amorphous. In one sense, because intervals of time successively shorten as one proceeds from the deep past to the present, it would be considered irregular time. However, as the cosmon field strength flattens-out, it oscillates. Such oscillations would affect time whereby it would continually alternate between shorter and longer time intervals in the recent past and present. Whether this variation could be detectable by instrumentation is an outstanding question. Nevertheless, this looks a lot like amorphous time. The main point is that in Wetterich's model of the universe, there is no First Cause to the beginning of the universe unless one wants to pin this title to mathematical probability. It may be as the early 20th-century British philosopher and Nobel laureate Bertrand Russell explained in *Why I Am Not a Christian* (1948), "I should say that the universe is just there, and that's all."[23]

ALTERNATE STRUCTURES OF TIME

It was noted earlier that the structure of time could be strictly linear, circular, or branched (circularity followed by linearity or both linearity and circularity simultaneously). The latter two options were presented as potential means to escape the infinite regress axiom. There are many more competing ideas on what the true nature of time may happen to be which are deserving of some mention. However, synopsizing the corpus of the Philosophy of Time is too great a task to tackle here and therefore what is to be presented is akin to tasting of a cake's frosting that sits upon the finger after drawing through its full goodness. With this disclaimer in mind, let's skate through the alternative topologies of time.

Relationism, as we have seen in A-series, supposes that time is defined by how objects relate to one another as they undergo change. *Substantivalism* treats time as a substance that exists as a self-governing quantity with its own properties that are totally independent of three-dimensional space and materiality. A notable distinction is that substantivalism permits eventless empty time, a violation of the adopted truism T4 for A-series time (see p. 514), whereas relationism does not. The battle lines could not appear any more formidable when one considers how the juggernauts of science and philosophy have lined-up. In the relationism camp, the ranks are filled with the likes of Aristotle, Gottfried Wilhelm Leibniz, Albert Einstein, and Christof Wetterich. On the substantivalist side, there was Isaac Newton, Immanuel Kant, Christiaan Huygens, W.V.O. Quine (of the Duhem–Quine thesis noted earlier), and Ernst Mach.[31] Then we have a newer theory advanced in the year 2000 called *Structural Spacetime Realism* which attempts to relieve the great tension between these two rival theories by supporting the relational nature of time but declaring that aspects of spacetime do exist independent of objects and events.[24-26]

The substantivalist perspective affirming eventless time would not particularly fluster Dr. Craig's thesis because time, according to him, did not exist in the pre-universe. And, even if time did exist and substantivalism held sway, the fact that eventless time might come to pass in any frequency, would not damage his thesis appreciably.

In opposition to A-theory tensed time is the *B-theory* of *tenseless time*. Whereas in A-theory events are intrinsically objective enabling temporal progress from the past to the present and the present to the future, B-series time offers no such objectivity. This is to say that, in spite of our human sense on the flow of time behaving like that of water in a river, in absolute reality, there is no temporal ordering between the past, present, or actual future (here we delineate the actual future from all possible futures). Furthermore, there is no dynamical relationship between objects and how they change. In short, the past, present, and actual future all coexist, there is no privileged location in time, and the indexing of time is a strictly a subjective experience. While B-series is bereft of a flow of time, it still permits causality to act. One of the consequences of B-series is that the actual future is essentially locked-in which means that free will must be tossed aside in favor of a wholly deterministic reality. It would also put into question what the beginning of the universe even means. Let us explore A- and B-theory just a little further.

The mish-mashing of time, such as it were, puts into question what partitions of time are actually real. One can view only the present time as real in what is called *Presentism* or *Nowism*. This means that the past and the future are not real constructs of reality. *Possibilism*, more frequently referred to as the *Growing Block Universe* or 'the growing past', is a second perspective which considers both the past and present as real with the actual future to be determined. Eternalism (also called the '*Block Universe*' or '*Static Block Universe*') is a third way to conceive time. On this view, the past, present, and actual future are each regarded as segments of time that are equally real. Both Presentism and the Growing Block Universe are two varieties of A-series time and the Block Universe is squarely a B-theory of time.

The term 'Block Universe' is the conception that spacetime is an unchanging four-dimensional block which is to be contrasted with our usual notion of a dynamical interplay between three-dimensional space and the passage of time. In the Block Universe, time does not flow (hence the reference to a block), but one can cleave planes of simultaneously occurring events in so-called '*time slices*'. Time slices are ordered by event sequences where one set of causes leads to another (often stated as the "happens-before relation"). In the Growing Block Universe theory, the past continues to build as the present moment gives way to the next moment of time and in this way the block of spacetime continually increases.

The general notion of the universe existing as as a static block of time as conceived in the Block Universe strikes one as a cockamamie conception. It seems to go against all our senses of what natural time is. However, one is to be sobered to the fact that Einstein's vaunted special theory of relativity informs us that there are no absolute frames of reference in spacetime. Motion (and therefore time) is relative to the frames of reference being considered. Given the apparent validity of this scientific theory, the Block Universe concept cannot be easily dismissed. The upshot is that efforts to validate A-theory or B-theory time remain in a contested domain rankling philosophers and scientists alike.

There are yet other theories physicists have been working on since the 1990's whereby time and space is an illusion and what we see as reality is more akin to a **HOLOGRAPHIC** projection. Such theories presume the existence of a fifth space-like dimension. More recently, the idea of *tensor networks* that run off of quantum entanglement principles is being researched. Tensor networks in the context of cosmology envision spacetime as a complex of interlinked nodes. These nodes are comprised of quantum information such that all information is ultimately linked together. This is analogous to what was described in earlier chapters as quantum nonlocality and entanglement whereby information is shared instantaneously and without respect for separation distances between two subatomic particles. In the tensor network all information is quantum-connected. Accordingly, the quantum tensor network is what we have traditionally referred to as the *'fabric of spacetime'*. The holographic principle comes into play because this insight suggests that it is possible to describe the contents inside the volume of an object by studying only the boundary circumscribing the volume. This is a fascinating idea made possible because the contents of the internal volume are spatially and informatically linked to the bounding surface. This overall approach stems from String Theory/M-Theory and the search to elucidate a tenable theory of quantum gravity.[27, 28] Other intellectuals pursue a different line of thinking that conceives the world-universe as a holographic-like illusory reality much akin to a grand computer-like simulation.

Suffice it to say, that like the problem of human consciousness, we are similarly perplexed by what the true ontological nature of time is. With the exact nature of time still under dispute, and the status of the infinite regress axiom just as indefinite, the determinative authority of the KCA is mooted but not irrefutably defeated. However, even without a First Cause hanging over our heads, the universe could nevertheless still have had a beginning. If so, we can still ask the question what constituted the Potter's hand and his clay. Did the universe come into being by self-causation, inanimate substance(s), animate Being(s) in material form, or via animated immaterial Being(s) or, do we find ourselves in a grand cosmic simulation?

The answer to this all-important question comes down to a plausibility argument which is almost entirely obscured by our inability to adjudicate what did or did not exist in the pre-universe in terms of time, causality, energy, space, governing laws, materiality, immateriality, logic, etc. let alone the existence of material or immaterial Beings. We might all agree that abstract objects may have existed along with mathematical probability, but that might be the full extent of mutual agreement. A self-caused universe containing ostensibly only abstract objects with mathematical probability or absolute nothingness whatsoever possesses no operative functionality. It is not hot or cold, dense or diffuse, light or dark, moving or still, thinking or unthinking, purposeful or purposeless. There is no causal capacity to alter this state of reality. Thus, this appears to be the most implausible option. If there was something animate or inanimate in the pre-universe, then we would have something to grab onto. The main question would be whether this animate or inanimate 'thing' existing in the pre-universe is material or immaterial which we will soon understand why this is so important.

Materiality, as in material objects, is fundamentally tied to the coexistence of a *substrates*. In the natural world we have the 'spacetime fabric' and fields (e.g., the Higgs scalar field) as substrates to host the existence and properties of material objects. I will contend that our mind-brain consciousness is also similarly hosted by these substrates and that our conscious minds cannot exist without these substrates. Furthermore, our minds are intrinsically tethered to our physical bodies because they are unable to exist separately whether this means in another room, down a city street, or elsewhere in the galaxy. At best, the extent of the mind's reach is limited to its host organism. For instance, it has never been authentically demonstrated that our individual minds are empowered with the ability to move or manipulate external objects through mental thought alone (i.e., telekinesis).

Without materiality, pure thought alone accomplishes nothing in the physical world. This is the same problem faced by Boltzmann Brains in the multiverse scenario. It is therefore highly implausible from a rational perspective that a Being of pure thought has the capacity to manipulate or create a state of materiality out of a state of nothingness or immateriality. However, this is the very definition of what the majority of religionists believe God to be—an immaterial Being who created the material universe out of his immaterial self. When we pause to reflect on this a little further, we come to a rather befuddling observation. Many people would prefer to believe that an undetectable, inconceivably powerful, indescribable, and abstract entity exists over the idea that we have a staggering unawareness of how physical reality or our human consciousness truly works. So, rather than chalking-up bizarre phenomena to our vast ignorances and leave

it at that, many would assign, often with unwavering conviction, full responsibility to this living and inexplicable deific agent. On the whole, there isn't a large difference from the ancients who believed in multiple gods in control of the various aspects of nature and human destiny and the contemporary view of a singular god. It is true that we no longer ascribe the health of our crops or abundance of water supply to the gods. We also are aware that viruses and bacteria are often the cause of disease and not the action of an angry deity. However, what remains the same is that many still believe that God is very much involved in mankind's daily activities and life destiny, but instead of many gods with distributed powers at the helm of the universe, it is a solitary all-powerful god.

Let us consider further how materiality works in our universe. Experiential knowledge affirms that, with the exception of the noble metals and noble gases, all other chemical elements are chemically reactive materials. A vivid example is when Fluorine, the most reactive of all the elements, is put into contact with Cesium, the most reactive metal; the two materials will combust violently into a ball of intense heat and light. Granting that materiality (i.e., substances, substrates, non-abstract objects) in the pre-universe may be totally alien in their composition as compared to materials in our world, is it not more plausible that material substance(s) in the pre-universe begets material substance in the natural realm versus the idea that an unembodied, immaterial, unchanging, timeless Being acted to transform a state of perfect immateriality into an incomprehensibly vast material-filled universe? I think it is potently clear that the existence of pre-universe inanimate materiality (e.g., materials like Adamite and Eveitite) would be undeniably more plausible given our scientifically confirmed knowledge of elemental interactivity. In any case, if the universe had a beginning, it is to be admitted that the Adamite-Eveitite arrangement as a representative schema for pre-universe still suffers under the same complaints for all the other explanations. Namely, that it is an improper action of un-shackling ourselves from the **ADAMANTINE** constraints to rationally conclude anything outside the natural realm.

There is a final card to be laid down onto the table. What if we were to accept Craig's KCA with a few alterations to his interpretation of the syllogism? Let us consider that God alone (or in concert with other Beings) created the universe along with the property of time but God himself always remained in his abode of the pre-universe whatever that might entail. God would only have one phase to his life whereby he would live a perfectly transcendent life, never being subject to time or anything else our universe might throw at him. **From the first interval of time onwards, God would lack the ability to enter into or interact with our universe. This is a state of pure transcendence.** Alternatively, if we revisited the *Meta-Transignification and the Origin of the Universe Hypothesis*, we could surmise that if W. L. Craig was right after all, it could be suggested that the maximally powerful Being that was lacking in omniscience and immutability, ceased to exist as a singular living Being upon the act of Creation. Both of these scenarios would fully respect the force of logic embodied in the KCA, the primary difference of course is that God, aside from creating the universe, has nothing to do with our natural realm whatsoever. **It also highlights that, even if the W. L. Craig KCA or its revision thereunto were left standing, it says nothing about the continued existence of a First Cause (a.k.a. God).**

But then again, it is under the force of arguments of the Cosmon Field Model already laid out that the universe may in fact be eternal to the past. Not only does this make the KCA a moot argument, but it also vanquishes the teleological fine-tuning argument. While the cosmon field theory has been shown to possess exceptionally strong mathematical viability and closely corroborates many salient cosmological phenomena, it admittedly has yet to clinch much needed validation of certain fundamental premises. Given this state of affairs, what can be reasonably forwarded is that the Cosmon Field Model of the universe presents us with a plausible arrangement of physical reality and one in which a First Cause for the brute existence of the cosmos is unnecessary.

Where Does the "Craigian God of Christianity" Live to Enact His Will?

While the corpus of William Lane Craig's work discusses *ad nauseam* God's temporal and personal nature, his articulations on how God exists in the natural realm are comparatively nonexistent. Craig maintains that God changed into his new phase of life in our universe to exist as a bodiless, ageless, immaterial, consciousness whose presence is simultaneously everywhere in the universe. It is necessary for Craig to assert that God is a part of this universe and not wholly transcendent because his Christian affiliation subsumes that God is a personal agent to mankind. Also, his omnipresence permits him to causally act everywhere at all times. He demurs on explaining how such a nonphysical Being can so dramatically affect all physical substance other than to say that God's divinity is trademarked by his transcendence of the universe's spatial dimensions. He cautions that God is not to be thought of as ethereal spirit-matter or as an essence disbursed throughout all of space. Rather, the Craigian Christian God is viewed as an omnipresent, immaterial conscious that is external to our 3D-space making him "trans-spatial" or "non-spatial."[29] However, for all intents and purposes, Craig's view makes God the 'unseen ghost in the machine' who is a singular Being who is maneuvering the universe along some divine chord to ultimately reach the eschatological end of things. While such an immaterial existence by itself would not cause physicists to lose sleep, a kerfuffle arises because Craig leaves unexplained how God could be affecting the course of events and all materiality without disrupting natural laws.

This side-stepping of God's manifestation and more importantly God's ability to act in and upon the physical realm is the metaphorical axe that cleaves in two the philosopher's worldview. He is undoubtedly aware of these shortcomings in addition to the various attempts by Christian Panentheists to resolve how God could be dynamically interacting within our realm. He leaves this 800-pound gorilla sitting in the room unattended apparently contented that revealed theology (as opposed to natural theology) holds the answer. To this end, God only partially reveals his mysterious powers upon his choosing. The most prominent example is that God chose to provide insights into his existence, nature, and intentions for mankind by inspiring the authors of the Bible to write what they did. It is on faith then that we must take God as a mysterious consciousness and that God was always (even in the pre-universe) a Being of three Persons—Father, Son, and Spirit. Why God needed to be a singular Being comprised of three Persons in the pre-universe is set-off as yet another unanswered question by Craig. According to the Craigian view, it was after 13.8 billion years (the going estimate by Big Bang theory) that God decided to physically manifest himself on Earth in the same physical form as the evolved Homo sapiens. **In the end, it remains an article of faith in the Craigian Christian worldview that God pervades and intervenes in the world society.**

SUMMARY

Until the emergence of the use of Bayesian inference, cosmological arguments, especially the Kalam variant, have been considered the most powerful naturally-based logic that can be singly marshaled to rationally justify belief in a deific Creator. Under the able protection of William Lane Craig, the KCA has successfully rebuffed many efforts over the last four decades attempting to take down the elegantly simple and stalwart syllogism. As is all too often the case, the many complexities and nuances defy the ability to defeat the KCA with absolute certainty. Nevertheless, if we are to adopt rationality as the basis of our understanding of God's potential existence, then we are PEREMPTORILY obligated to accept that the counter-arguments negating the KCA are significantly more plausible than those provided by the many defenses erected by Craig.

If we were to contemplate for a moment the demise of Swingrover's conclusions to the effect that a nomological or metaphysical infinity was in fact impossible as Craig would have it, and if Wetterich's cosmon field theory were to be someday discredited, or that the Adamite-Eveitite proposal outlined in this chapter is found to be lacking, we are still left with the matter that Craig has overdetermined the monadic properties of what exists in the metaphysical pre-universe realm. The over-prescription was already brought to heel in the context of Swinburnian metaphysics as was the likelihood that a deity could be operative in the past or on an ongoing basis (i.e., Process Theology).

Craig also fails to provide the mechanisms by which God could act in our universe without disrupting the natural flow of events that operate by physical laws and rules. And, even if all these things could be dismissed, the KCA, if true, would at its very best only tell us that a powerful 'something' once existed. It cannot tell us if there is a sole deity or a colony of deities or what physical form, if any, they might be. It furthermore cannot affirm if such deities exist in the present time for all that the KCA can say is that they were the operators of the First Cause. It may be that the perpetrators of the First Cause did not survive the act of Creation or that they have everlastingly existed outside of our universe with no ability to enter into our natural domain. If God manifests himself as a supreme consciousness in this realm, then the burden of proof is on those who maintain such a claim. The only way I see this happening is if we are able to definitively determine what human consciousness is and what it is not. This would be the first stepping stone one would have to find firm footing and we appear to be a long ways from such a sure-footed maneuver. If God's essence is additionally extra-dimensional, then he will forever remain inaccessible to us unless God himself makes it possible to overcome our inherent limitations.

Ultimately, the KCA fails to defend a deity that lives in our universe and is interacting in our worldly affairs. If it were to be a valid argument, it would only tell us that *something*—a Source—created the universe. It does not tell us what it is, whether this 'thing' was alive or inanimate, or material or immaterial, when it created the universe. It is also mute as to whether this 'thing' still exists. It does not tell us anything itself about the pre-universe and neither can we rationally conclude much of anything about this other parcel of reality. When it comes down to the brass tacks, we only have what we have inside our universe. And when we look to our universe, it seems far more plausible that materiality begets materiality rather than something immaterial creating materiality out of immateriality or absolute nothingness. And, it may well be that the great Kalam Cosmological Argument is nothing more than an empty argument to begin with should the universe be past-eternal.

All things considered, the existence of a God(s) living within the borders of our universe—whether reality is comprised of a pre-universe, a multiverse, extra dimensions, or just a solitary four-dimensional cosmos—is not affirmed by the KCA or by W. L. Craig's extensive efforts to portray God as the First Cause.

Part IV

The
Six Towers
of God

Sea
of
Irrationality

CHAPTER 15

The Six Towers of God

I suppose therefore that all things I see are illusions; I believe that nothing has ever existed of everything my lying memory tells me. I think I have no senses. I believe that body, shape, extension, motion, location are functions. What is there then that can be taken as true? Perhaps only this one thing, that nothing at all is certain.

– René Descartes
Father of Modern Philosophy, b. 1596 – d. 1650

The truth is rarely pure and never simple.[1]

For what is Truth? In matters of religion, it is simply the opinion that has survived. In matters of science it is the ultimate sensation. In matters of art it is one's last mood.[2]

– Oscar Wilde
Excerpts from his play "The Importance of Being Earnest" (1895)
and his essay "The Critic as Artist" (1891)

Reality can be beaten with enough imagination.[3]

– Mark Twain
Actual name: Samuel Langhorne Clemens.
Author and humorist, b. 1835 – d. 1910

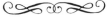

THE VALIDITY OF BUNDLING ARGUMENTS

In spite of our sure-footedness and conservational efforts to limit our attention to tackle the mightiest of evidences for God, the zetetic venture has been long and difficult leaving us a little tuckered and drawn. In light of the fact that deities have followed us as far as the species of man can be traced back, it was an **INELUCTABLE** destiny from the start that progress would only come in measured paces. It was as Einstein forewarned, finding an understanding of the truly significant involves a painful search.

Because undeniable proof of a deity or absolute negation thereof has always been out of reach, the principled approach of *Zeteo Alétheia* (Greek: *to seek out or to proceed by inquiry to find the truth*) was employed to probe the scholastic **INTELLIGENTSIA** to gather the strongest evidences that have been accumulated over thousands of years. We can say with a good measure of confidence, and I think most philosophers, theologians, and scientists would tend to agree, that there exists no singular naturalistic argument that clearly distinguishes itself from others as having a convincingly high relative degree of plausibility for the existence of a deity. Apologists such as William Lane Craig and many others of his ilk have advanced the idea that bundling the ensemble of Ontological, Teleological, Cosmological, Axiological, Scriptural, Experiential, etc. "Arguments" for the existence of God is the best of all possible defenses. However, one is never instructed on how this is to be performed. To my mind, this conviction is very much allied with the strategy of using Bayesian updating methods (refer to Chapter 6 and Chapter 9) to continually add more and more evidences to raise the conditional probability of theism. The belief is that if legions of hypotheses are intrinsically endowed with varying degrees of plausibility, then this will bolster the case for the existence of God.

Prima facie, this looks all good and well, but is in fact quite misleading. Firstly, it is not statistically justified to simply combine all these conditional probabilities in additive fashion as we are not dealing with frequentist probability of dependent events (i.e., use of frequency distributions often associated with data sets) whereby this is permissible. Secondly, it is not sufficient for any given hypothesis to simply be plausible, rather it has to be *more* plausible than all alternative explanations. Thirdly, rules for Bayesian updating involve the accounting of new *conditionally independent* evidences for the stated hypothesis and its associated contravening proposals. What is really being talked about here is something more akin to *Bayesian Model Averaging* whereby ensembles of hypotheses are conjoined. This approach is leveraged in the context of computer simulation tasks related to neural networks and machine learning (e.g., email spam filtering) which fundamentally involves numerical operations of data-centric considerations. There are various techniques that have been devised to successfully combine multiple data-centric models. However, we are dealing with the probability of something that is brokered through epistemic inferences (i.e., statements of knowledge that may be certain or uncertain), not numerical data, so the applicability of model averaging is speculative. When multiple hypotheses (let's call them 'sub-hypotheses') that relate to a broader hypothesis of the epistemic variety are combined, what we find is that the broader hypothesis is not bolstered. Instead, when Bayesian Model Averaging is utilized, what happens is that just one of the sub-hypotheses with the greatest likelihood of being correct is identified from among all of the sub-hypotheses.[4]

A simple example is in order. Let us hypothetically presume the posterior probabilities of the Ontological, Teleological, and Cosmological arguments as being 0.1, 0.3, and 0.4, respectively. Comparatively speaking, the Cosmological argument would have the greatest probability of being correct. However, when the combined posterior probability of all three is performed, model averaging techniques would be apt to produce a probability tending toward a value of 0.4 (and not 0.8 that arises from adding the three together). There is yet another detail to contend with. Bayes' theorem requires the use of conditionally independent evidences so there can be no dependent evidences cross-pollinating to another model hypothesis. As such, any dependent evidences that might exist across all the arguments would have to be eliminated to construct a set of independent evidences.

The final synopsis is that a 'clean' aggregation method to somehow build-up, let alone properly balance, the array of probabilities associated with the bundle of arguments does not exist. **Therefore, to maintain coherency, the various Arguments must stand alone using the weight of their own evidences if we are to characterize plausibility in terms of epistemic probability.**

Re-Tracing Our Footsteps to Etch the Perimeter of God

We started the zetetic undertaking by ascertaining the first insight that only a subset of the thousands of differentiated religious theologies that mankind has conceived might properly characterize God. Fideistic and blind faith were shown to lead to the Many-Faced God Conundrum whereby any kind of god or gods would be equally legitimate. To avoid this unsettling problem, those wanting to employ faith or intuition had to bring some added measures of rationality to the table. We ran headlong into one of several theological camps that portray God as unknowable (apophatic mysticism/negative theology), knowable to a limited extent (cataphatic mysticism/positive theology), or a combination of the two. Eastern Orthodox Christian, Jewish Kabbalistic, Islamic, and pluralistic doctrines initially stood by apophaticism whereas Western Christianity, Christian Panentheism (i.e., Process Theology), and Modern Judaism adopted cataphaticism. But this positioning delivered unavoidable, uncomfortable, and irresolvable dilemmas. With apophaticism disaffirming any means for humans to rationalize God, there is literally no reason to justify if God is a singular Being or many Beings, or whether he was an all-good or all-evil entity. God, as a purely transcendent Being, divorces us from having a personal relationship with him. It also puts into question how this transcendent God delivered to us inspirations in the form of Scriptures which describe God in human language which goes directly against the core tenant of apophaticism that God is ineffable and therefore beyond language. The Qur'an, for example, gives 99 names and attributes for God. Eastern Christians have an additional problem to explain how God became incarnate in the physical realm where Jesus revealed information about the nature of God.

Cataphatic mysticism gets around this by telling us that God is accessible and personal, but it then becomes incumbent to describe God using language. He is thusly described by most traditions as a Being with omni-perfections, a weight so heavy, that the very viability of God suffers greatly. We run into the well-worn and as yet unresolved Problems of Evil and free will-vs-determinism. Perfect Being Theology and theologies that decree God has maximal capacities overdetermine what the properties of an enigmatic God must be when the best that we can do is to provide a highly uncertain metaphysical estimate. It is the ana-logical act of pushing a large God and a camel through the eye of a seamstress' needle.

To ameliorate this condition, some of these traditions have edged-away in modern times from the extreme positions of the two mysticisms to adopt aspects of each maintaining that they complement one another. But this mixing of mysticisms—the seeing of vagueness through the concealment of a mystical veil—only pushes them into a different pool of illogic. What makes one religious mystery truer than another? As soon as one conjectures that our human faculties can access God through language then he is open to the full complement of rationalization methods at our disposal.

From here, evidence from our Homo sapiens, Homo naledi, and Neandethalic forebears indicated reverence for the deceased via earthen burials. More recent ancestors created rock art in the form of rock carvings (petroglyphs) and rock paintings (pictograms) that depicted plants, animals, humans, and god-like creatures of cultural and religious significance. As 'civilized' society began to take hold it became clear that people universally worshiped multiple god-like idols that came in many animalistic, humanistic, and hybrid forms. Gods and goddesses came and went as one cultic kingdom conquered another. Sometimes particular gods disappeared altogether or were otherwise morphed with existing gods.

Arising from the fold was ancient Judaism where lines of evidence indicate that the ancient inhabitants who would much later become the Israelites of the Hebrew Bible were intermixed with their Canaanite brethren and who later became their foes. These Mesopotamian settlements were difficult to separate on an archaeological basis but they seem to have worshiped similar gods (El, Baal-Hadad, Asherah, Anat, and Yahweh). There were other regional gods as well (Moloch, Dagon, Amun-Re, and Osiris, etc.). Religion was geographically localized and some gods were emphasized over others based on the preference of the ruler de jour. Over time, polytheism among the would-be Israelites shifts to monolatry worship where, ultimately, Yahweh and El compete and combine with the theonym of Yahweh prevailing as the chief deity. The pantheon of 'other gods' were forcibly phased-out, though Yahweh seems to have retained Asherah as a deific consort until she too was removed. Her affiliation with Yahweh was summarily redacted from early Hebrew texts.

Christianity and Islam share in the provenance of the once pluralistic God of Abraham. Judaism and Islam worship a God who is both a loving and a wrathful deity. Christianity holds that God is an all-good God, though this is more than a little conspicuous when one considers that the Christian Bible's Old Testament contains the Genesis flood story and Exodus's ten plagues sponsored by God himself. So while the theonym is different and some of his properties are somewhat different, the Abrahamic God is in all three religions the one who speaks to Abraham and his descendant prophets as detailed in their respective Scriptures. Because theological expositions of the Christian God overwhelmingly represent the share of treatises on the ontological and metaphysical status of this deity, primary attention was shifted to focus on Christianity.

In examining the array of religious archaeological relics, it was the discovery of ancient tablets that illuminated that the Old Testament tale of Noah's Ark was just that, a fictional rendition of earlier mythical stories. Other archaeological discoveries provide plausible reasoning that the Ark of the Covenant was unlikely to be of the gold-laden design and construction stated in the Bible (see Exodus 25 and 37). Furthermore, it is conceivable that followers of the Jewish tradition made facsimiles of the Ark as worship objects. This is construed on the basis that these peoples fabricated hand-held models of the worship temple that housed the Ark. The Turin Sheet left us in a neutral position as to whether the burial shroud can be authentically tied to the time of Christ's death until improved protocols vis-à-vis multi-site blood assays, genetic evaluations, and radiometric dating can be conducted. Relative to the evidence garnered from 1st-century tombs and Jewish ossuaries, it is suggestive that Jesus' bodily remains and those of his family members may have been found. This lends credence to those who argue that Jesus was not a mythic figure, but it also means that he was not bodily resurrected in accordance with New Testament Scripture. While the Talpiot tomb, the Talpiot ossuaries (including the James ossuary), and the bone matter found inside the ossuaries exists to this very day, due to an array of intransigent circumstances, the data that could be collected to further validate (or invalidate) these claims remains elusive.

Delving into the first three-and-a-half centuries after Christ died, quasi-Christian cults were found to be in abundant supply amidst the influence of other Greco-Roman polytheistic dogmas, esoteric philosophies, as well as magic and alchemy. All of these co-existed alongside monotheistic Early Judaism and the proto-Christians. Syncretistic beliefs pervaded the full breadth of the broader Middle East and surrounding territories. During this general timeframe the identity of Jesus Christ as part of the Holy Trinity was much in contention. Arians, a quasi-Christian group, vouched that as the Son of God, he ranked below God the Father, and the Holy Spirit existed behind him. Some adhered to binitarianism whereby the Holy Spirit is a flow of power between Father and Son and not a distinct personage. Marcionites believed Jesus to be a fully-grown man who was hiding his divinity in the illusory guise of a human male. Ebionites cast Jesus as God's most favored mortal. Some Gnostic cults saw Jesus and the Holy Spirit as purely divine entities (sparks) sent to Earth as Aeons to wrest our souls from the ills of humanity and bring only the deserved to the region of light called the Plemora.

It was persistent plague and illness, the threat of invasion, the rise of monotheism against a backdrop of polytheism, and percolating political unrest that were the ever-present tendrils that gripped the whole of Roman Society. After hearing of Christianity and how its followers provided aid to the suffering, Emperor Constantine the Great became curious about this new religion and adopted elements of it into his polytheistic worship, ostensibly merging Sol the Sun God with the resurrected Jesus. It was in 325 CE that Constantine helped to bring about the Council of Nicaea which produced the Nicene Creed which was later altered to become the Niceno-Constantinopolitan Creed in 381 CE. This was followed by a series of councils that debated Christian biblical canon. The Bible's final content was finally ratified by Rome shortly after the Council of Carthage (397 CE) some 367 years after Christ's death. It was only a handful of years earlier that Christianity was made the law of the land by the Edict of Thessalonica (380 CE).

There were many texts written by proto-Christians in the centuries following the crucifixion of a man purported to be Jesus of Nazareth. The formative Roman Catholic Church selected texts that were ostensibly chosen on the basis of direct or indirect prophetic or apostolic authority. However, the proto-Catholic Church Fathers were in tenuous league with Emperor Constantine I. Proto-Christians had been persecuted by Roman rulers after Jesus of Nazareth was crucified, so the Church Fathers and their flock of adherents were likely be wary of upsetting Constantine with their contingent arrangement. While speculative, it is plausible that Roman magistrates overseeing the church leaders in their area of governance may have applied influence to ensure that the selected texts would not create unrest in the populace for their Emperor to deal with. As the canonization process neared finality and for times thereafter, an unknown number of religious texts were hidden away, lost, or otherwise destroyed as heretical proclamations. It was the Dead Sea Scrolls and the Nag Hammadi library that revealed the diversity of religious belief in the two-or-so centuries that bookend the demarcation of the Common Era. One has to ask themselves whether it is reasonable that the correct doctrinal nature for the almighty God arose from the teaming market of religious cults when the final 'winner' was by no small margin by decree of a political ruler.

And, that this ruler committed apostasy by his conversion from Catholicism to Arianism on his death bed.

Ultimately, after critical scholarly examination, the New Testament presents us with many questions as to the authenticity of the various authors. Not only is the authorship either unknown or questionable, the relationship between the content of the Scripture authors is problematic. It is here we put to the test the three Foundational Truth Claims—Jesus' resurrection, his divinity, and his coequal union with God and the Holy Spirit. The plausibility of the bodily resurrection of Jesus of Nazareth was investigated to great depths operating under the assumption that miracles are precluded as a viable explanation. Applying Bayesian methodology, it was demonstrated that evidences forwarded by Christian apologists defending the resurrection hypothesis fell critically short of their goal. In regard to Jesus' divinity, there was no way to reconcile God's monadic properties of omnipotence and omniscience with an array of pertinent scriptural content. If Jesus is part of the Holy Trinity, he was, according to doctrine, omniscient. But based on Scripture, it becomes clear that Jesus was not fully aware. Also, Jesus himself never explicitly refers to his own divinity and the implicit references are themselves ambiguous.

Sir Isaac Newton, known as a prodigy of science and mathematics, was in equal proportion a great theologian. His sharp mind and vast knowledge catches in red-handed fashion a Roman Catholic Cardinal purposively corrupting the translation of a key passage of the Bible (1 John 5:7). The verse was altered to embolden the relationship of a three-Person God—the Father, the Son, and the Holy Spirit—in opposition to the original meaning of Jesus being represented as blood and water. This is only the tip of the iceberg as it pertains to how the three are interrelated (i.e., perichoresis). In recognition of the fact that the coherency of the Holy Trinity requires further exposition, Oxford philosopher-theologian Richard Swinburne attempts to show how the three-Person God concept is intelligible as a singular Being but his argumentation more strongly bolsters the case for a godhead comprised of three distinct deities (i.e., tritheism). With Swinburne's efforts proving ineffective, I laid out the Seven Challenges to Trinitarianism to highlight that after two thousand years of contemplation, there is still no crisply coherent paradigm that describes how God can exist in the union espoused by trinitarian Christianity (Western Christianity and Eastern Orthodox Christianity).

Bayesian inferential probability has become in the last ten years a central tool for Christian apologists to advocate for the likely existence of the Christian God in light of epistemic uncertainties. Richard Swinburne is the one credited as kicking-off this trend. While he is to be commended for his exhaustive consideration of the evidences, his Ramified

Natural Theology suffers because of his presumptive prescription of what God's properties *must* be and his inappropriate application of his intuitions that adulterate his Bayesian calculations. Invocation of Bayes' theorem should carry with it a cautionary moniker of 'Not all Bayesian inferences are created equal'. This is justified by the insight first outlined in Chapter 1 which noted that truth can take on a transitory character. What is true at one point in time may not be true in the future, or vice-versa. For example, if we were raised four thousand years ago, we might very well believe with no doubt whatsoever that people cannot physically transport themselves into the sky above, but we now accept that flying around in airplanes makes for a different truth. Therefore, when appraising the Bayesian priors and the evidences assuming the truth and negation of the hypothesis, this bias (among others) may come into play. A follow-on issue is that the Bayes computation is also reliant on one's own bucket of knowledge concerning the evidences whereby the range of information considered is greater or lesser than someone else's computation.

Philosophical religious pluralism entered the world stage to assuage the many tensions underlying doctrinal choices staked out by the many world religions. We found in John Hick's pluralism that his essentially circular explication of the *Real* (*Ultimate Reality*) as being absolutely unknowable and his definition of the Golden Rule—loving your neighbor as yourself—left us malnourished to distinguish religion's ability to know God's nature or existence. Not only that, but in its attempt to embrace most all religions, pluralism rejects them out of hand for the simple fact that no singular religion can satisfactorily explain the *Real*, except in the context of the pluralistic framework. Which, paradoxically is by its own admission is wholly deficient because of the *Real's* intrinsic nature of being inaccessible.

Panentheism in the context of Process Philosophy/Process Theology was given a turn at the table. Prompted in part by Roman Catholic priest Teilhard de Chardin, but moved by many others before and since (Hegel, Schelling, A. N. Whitehead, C. S. Peirce, Hartshorne, Barbour, Peacocke, Pannenberg, Clayton, Polkinghorne, Bracken, and Moltmann), the scholars sought to leverage the apparent emergence and growth in the complexity of the universe as teleological movement drawn toward some purposive end. Some of these scholars were more strongly affiliated with the tenants of classical Christian theism than others. A core component of Christian Panentheism was the abandonment of God's omni-perfections which permitted the classical concept of a transcendent deity to additionally encompass the machinations of the natural realm. This permitted the heavy burdens of explaining the existence of evil and solving the free will-vs-determinism dilemma to fall off the shoulders of God. However, such ruminations did little to address the particularities of Jesus Christ's resurrection and the troubled perichoresis of the Holy Trinity. In fact, the emergent process by itself is impersonal. To give God its Christian-like attributes or those affiliated with any other religion's prescriptions, additional arguments are necessary.

The most stimulating work arises from Christian apologists Southgate and Robinson who attempt to leverage biological evolutionary mechanisms to align with Christian doctrine and the idea that God is the cosmic Creator-Sustainer. The main challenge for these theists is to explain how this mysterious God exists as a transcendent and immanent Being but can operate without issue in the physical realm and yet maintain a consistent and coherent perichoresis for a triune God. They represent God as an immensely powerful Being that exists outside of spacetime but is able to influence the general course of spacetime reality but not dictate every event with precision.

The two theologians brought forth Terrence Deacon's concept of autocellularity as a mechanism for biological evolution. The going thought of the duo was to suggest that if natural telos could be identified in the process of biological evolution, it would lend credence to the notion that divine telos might also exist. To their mind, divine telos would be the ultimate sponsor of natural telos. Deacon and his cohort Jeremy Sherman took a sharply different stance. They conjectured that if a natural end-directedness could be identified, then there would simply be no need for a divine telos. Even if Southgate and Robinson had been successful in their endeavor, they side-stepped how and where God exists as an immaterial spirit. They conveniently did not tackle the issue head-on as to where God exists as spirit. Is God in his own transcendent realm totally separated from spacetime or is he in some other dimension attached to spacetime? If God is a bodiless immaterial consciousness, does he live outside of spacetime and project his intentions into our universe or does God's consciousness live inside of spacetime proper? Regardless of which one God is supposed to be, the reasoning was lacking. In short, there is no difference between the two realities of (1) asserting that God is real—existing in some nether region of reality—and able to directly engage with our universe or (2) that we simply use our imaginations to think this to be the case. *When imaginary reality and real reality cannot be distinguished from each other, what have we gained?*

In round terms, Southgate and Robinson's efforts to embolden a Christian Panentheistic worldview into a coherent philosophy is fundamentally an effort to pull the full dead weight of Christianity's doctrine out of slope-less quicksand. Christian Panentheism starts with the *a priori* belief in scriptural revelation and an incarnate God and then tries to work backward using natural theology as a basis to forecast the operative action of an enigmatic, transcendent Creator-Sustainer deity. This is in many ways the *reverse* of the zetetic process of inquiry!

Another argument for the existence of a transcendent or worldly God is the argument from personal experience. Here we called to mind the great multitude of cognitively-developed biases and the reliance on heuristics that affect our reasoning faculties. So too there are innate operations of the mind-brain (e.g., patternicity and agenticity) that play into our awareness and our response to external reality. We only have the most tenuous grasp on what consciousness is. Does consciousness dualistically exist independent of neuronal activity and sensory stimulus such that they are ontologically distinct substances or is consciousness EPIPHENOMENAL, an artifact of brain functioning but having no direct causal efficacy on physical function? Because monistic EPIPHENOMENALISM does not explain how consciousness is generated we must ask what anchors our action potential for our knowledge and memories. Then, of course, we have the more generic and well-accepted view of monism where the mind-brain is ontologically substance-based. The problem here is whether consciousness is explained by mechanistic psychological states and processes or is it the case that the mind itself has the capacity to supervene onto the physical brain. In this latter view, the principle of strong emergence is appealed to whereby the mind-brain is thought to be hierarchically organized into lower properties (e.g., chemical and biological substrates) that generate the higher properties (e.g., psychological states) and these higher properties can in turn affect higher and lower properties. We also have the view of panpsychism in which all matter in the universe is infused with some form of mental or conscious property, primitive or otherwise. The greatest consensus in modern times is that the mind-brain is essentially a monistic pairing.

The Philosophy of Mind has experienced resurgence with a proliferation of theories of consciousness whose ontology ranges from purely physical to the nonphysical and metaphysical. We reviewed the provocative Orch OR quantum model for brain function which is a physical theory but there are other quantum-based theories of consciousness whose features are best described as nonphysical. All of the theories must tussle with monistic and dualistic views of reality and furthermore find some route through the free will-vs-determinism debate and describe what consciousness is, how it works, and whether or not it has causal capacities. The safe bet is that we really do not know anything substantively certain about consciousness.

Lacking any solid platform to work off of to comprehend human consciousness as a physical or nonphysical phenomenon, we are crippled to project how our experiences might relate to an embodied or unembodied conscious deity. If, for example, it could be definitively shown that our human consciousness exists independently from our physical bodies, then, this would give us a leg to stand on to say the God could sustain his existence as an unembodied consciousness in the dimensional realm of spacetime and perhaps, more feebly, extra-dimensionally. On the other hand, if our consciousness is a by-product of functioning brains, then it raises the evidentiary support needed to claim that God is floating within or outside the universe as a bodiless consciousness.

In any case, we can resolutely conclude and hopefully universally agree that human beings possess an imaginative capacity that far surpasses our potential to actualize our thoughts or could so many notions constitute reality. It is as Mark Twain remarked, "Reality can be beaten with enough imagination."[3] There are a limitless number of examples one can bring to bear to exemplify this idea. Imagine that you wish to be transported to another planet in an altogether different galaxy than our own Milky Way. In your mind, you could easily accomplish this by teleporting instantaneously or by building a mental vision of a colossal faster-than-light spacefaring vehicle. We would quickly come to grips that this will not happen in our lifetime and the likelihood is high that the human species will not set foot (or whatever appendage we might evolve to have) in some distant galaxy—ever. When our perceptive capacities and our model-making brains confront puzzling phenomenon, we can conjure-up a long list of possible and impossible explanations. Differentiating the possible from the impossible often puts matters into a gray area. Sometimes we reach the limits of our capacities to understand phenomena—real or imagined. We are then left to choose to leave it as totally unexplainable by naturally-based principles or to chalk it up to deific agency.

Explaining the existence and purpose to the universe is one such enigmatic phenomenon that tests our collective capacities. This is where metaphysicians, using their imaginative powers, pick up the ball and make conjectures about the ontological, metaphysical, and logical existence of a deity that possesses 'X, Y, and Z' properties. Initially, it seems very easy to make proposals that God must be omnipotent, omniscient, transcendent, immanent, etc., but, as we have seen from the lore, this is akin to traversing a minefield while running at full speed. **I hope it is fulsomely clear that should one wish to believe that God is an almighty Being with incomprehensible capacities of power, knowledge, wisdom, benevolence, and aseity, etc., whether or not these attributes adequately circumscribe God in totality, that the act of saying such and such is true only qualifies this statement as a *personal* belief or if under the umbrella of formalized religion, a *doctrinal* belief. If left standing by itself, it is not, however, a *justified* belief.** As the zetetic process has vividly made clear, finding ironclad reasoning for specific theistic beliefs or a systematic all-encompassing theology is much harder to come by than what we might originally think would be the case. **Without credible justification, personal and doctrinal theistic beliefs become *de facto* fideistic statements. This positions the individual to confront the**

Many-Faced God Conundrum or to thrash wildly in the forbidding *Sea of Irrationality*. The full significance of this statement will be more evident later in this chapter.

GETTING TO THE BOTTOM OF GODLY TRANSCENDENCE AND IMMANENCE

Probably the most pervasive statement concerning theistic belief is the contention that God-by-whatever-name is both a transcendent and immanent Being who is so powerful that he can defy the strictures of the four dimensions of spacetime and associated physical laws by fiat. That is, God can exist in both parcels of reality because he wills it to be so—he is just **THAT** powerful. Those who believe this are standing on a trap door and pulling the lever with both hands. This trap door, however, has remained un-sprung because of the web of many faulty doctrines have kept it stuck shut and the believer is left unware of their irrational or otherwise logically-impaired beliefs.

When we export ontological and epistemological statements into a transcendent domain that resides external to the natural four-dimensional realm, it is always to be ranked with the highest order of uncertainty. Religions that espouse belief in a transcendent God tend to use words of the following ilk—'God transcends the human brain's capacity to comprehend him'. However this self-proclaimed ignorance does not prevent these same believers from describing God's temperament, embodiment, locality, extent of power and knowledge, plans for humanity, the answering of one's prayers, his physical appearance, etc. Such believers typically point to a combination of our imaginative faculties, knowledge, experience, reasoning, intuition, our basal instincts, and some contend revelation, that these resources are a sufficiently potent force able to punch peep-holes through the **INSUPERABLE** barrier separating our universe and the transcendent realm. However, there is the stubborn fact that there is no force within our universe capable enough to prove the existence of logic, mathematical relationships, causality (including self-causation), infinity, simplicity (as in Ockham's razor), spatiality, materiality, temporality, or the existence of living things outside 4D-spacetime. Therefore bantering about the plausibility of how things operate in an inaccessible region of reality is simply inappropriate if we are to be seriously engaged. **When it comes down to it, a transcendent realm only yields unanswered questions and meritless conjectures. That is all.**

In light of our human blindness of a transcendent branch to reality, could it be that the transcendent barrier is a one-way looking glass permitting only God to see through? This is a moot question for we have no way of knowing since an answer infers knowledge of the transcendent realm. Even so, challenges do not arise from a deity watching us. It is how a deity would be an active and immanent agent within the universe where things get complicated. Is God enacting his intentions from an outpost within the transcendent realm that are then projected into our universe or is it that he is simultaneously existent in both his realm and ours? While this is an interesting question to ask, it too is largely moot because the transcendent aspect of his life is totally inaccessible to us.

The two main issues to tackle are God's materiality (or lack thereof) inside the four-dimensional universe and whether God is able to routinely influence worldly outcomes. Both raise the same concern that God cannot be continuously evading natural laws (e.g., time, causality, gravity, thermodynamics, quantum mechanics, etc.) to impose his actions. If God is an immaterial conscious Being, free of any physical host, perhaps he himself could be immutable to the laws of nature, but this has no bearing on his capacity to freely manipulate spacetime physics or the materiality of the universe. But let it also be said that it is an unsettled question whether human consciousness is dualistic (mind separate from body) or monistic (the mind-body as one). While the latter view is probably more justified, we can't yet consider it absolutely true. This leaves open the related question whether consciousness is imbued with the ability to influence physical processes or not. Until this human-centered conundrum is resolved, it is more difficult to make forceful conjectures about God floating around as an immaterial consciousness influencing worldly outcomes. **If we are to be rational, should we not first acquire a fuller understanding of human consciousness before we take the larger step of assigning a deific signature to events in reality?**

I think most individuals would readily discount the idea that God survives this universe in material form contained in some sort of 'bubble of invulnerability' that neutralizes any ill-effect or restriction on his capacities due to the properties and processes of the universe. Rather, God is described as a Being that is amply capable of waving aside any limitations because he was the author of the universe underscoring his raw power and intellect. With such awesome power we should be easily convinced that he effortlessly works his divine will (a.k.a. miracles) inside our universe. But, if he were so powerful, then we immediately face the problems of free will-vs-determinism and why God permits bad things to happen. We also need to justify why it is God was needed to form the universe.

Because of the intractable issues with God existing as a transcendent Being or existing immanently as a material Being or immaterial consciousness, some posit that God has taken up residence in some other dimension(s) tucked away from our prying minds and technological capacities (i.e., he is dimensionally transcendent). In this way, God is still living within the *greater universe,*[1] but is outside of 4D-spacetime proper. Esoteric cosmologies postulate that the universe is comprised of extra dimensions or hidden planes of reality that exist separately from the four known dimensions. Aristotle imagined the universe to be a nested hierarchy of celestial spheres though his was hardly the only alluring notion to argue for a larger reality. It has been forwarded that reality may be comprised of other domains that contain the divine planes of heaven and hell, or a realm between the living and the dead which is inhabited by souls, ghosts, and phantasms, or possibly where consciousness resides. It has even been said that this extra-dimensional neighborhood is a backdoor for super-advanced aliens to traverse great cosmic distances. A common theme is to organize these planes in a hierarchical pattern as higher or lower or that the planes interpenetrate one another.

It is rather apparent why religion and their theistic foundations are so difficult to grasp. They offer esoterically knotted explications of how God exists transcendentally and/or immanently. The confusion starts with the fact that religions as a group characterize the quality of transcendence and immanence differently. Therefore, we find ourselves running on a treadmill if we do not use care in the use of these terms because each unique definition potentially poses a different set of challenges to rationalize God. As illustrated in Figure 15-1–Box A (see p. 550), a purely transcendent God imposes the condition that God is forever and completely divorced from our domain of 4D-spacetime including extra so-called *hyperdimensions* (i.e., any fifth or greater dimension to 3D-space or time). As such, God has no ability to act upon our universe in any manner whatsoever. This sort of transcendence is generally what Deism holds to be true, though, as will be discussed later; there are several key misalignments between Deism and a purely transcendent Being.

The traditional versions of the Abrahamic religions view God as a domain-piercing transcendent distinct Being that exists in total self-solemnity in his own domain but is able to act upon both realms of reality (refer to Figure 15-1–Box B). This represents a dimensionally transcendent God. Some adherents of these religions may have a slightly altered construction whereby God's transcendent realm is actually located in a hyperdimension(s) attached to normal 4D-spacetime (refer to Figure 15-1–Box C). Often, this is referred to as the fifth dimension. Both pagan Panentheism and Christian

---

1. The phrase *'greater universe'* denotes the combination of our observable 4D-universe (consisting of natural time and three spatial dimensions), the unobservable universe (consisting of the same), and any hyperdimensions beyond the 4D-realm that might otherwise exist. It remains a point of discussion whether a transcendent deity would exist in these hyperdimensions attached to 4D-spacetime or in some completely external domain. This external domain could ostensibly be the pre-universe or some distinct portion of reality detached from the greater universe.

Panentheism present God in more nebulous terms in that God exists transcendentally but is also immanent because he 'interpenetrates' the totality of our universe (refer to Figure 15-1–Box D). The frequently cited moniker is that God is *in* the universe but is distinct from and greater than the universe.

Three of the fundamental beliefs in Christian theological doctrine are that God is solely responsible for the creation of the universe and that he is part of our universe. God was also incarnated as an immanent presence in the form of a human being. These tenants brings forth many thorny issues, one of which is how could God be transcendentally outside of natural time prior to the universe but also acting and living within natural time. It would be totally illogical for God to be simultaneously atemporal and temporal. William Lane Craig poses the notion that God lived successively as an atemporal Being followed by a temporal existence upon creation of the universe.

Craig largely demurs on defining the realm in which God presently lives, suggesting that God is a distinct, singular, abstract unembodied living consciousness in the greater universe, being omnipresent, but is non-spatial (refer to Figure 15-2–Box A). Einstein showed that space and time are integrally connected and while Craig is quite aware of this, it is left unexplained how God is bound only to natural time. Ultimately, Christian doctrine is a confused mix of a domain-piercing, transcendent, totally abstract, eternally existent God who is able to immanently act upon our universe (refer to Figure 15-1–Box B). So too, he became incorporeally immanent on Earth vis-à-vis a voice from the sky or a speaking from a burning bush later to become fully corporeal to walk amongst humanity in human form (refer to Figure 15-2–Box A).

Mormons envision their deity as a Being existing in a distinct location in the cosmos but whose power is distributed through all things (as opposed to God's divine power acting on things). God, therefore, does not exist transcendently apart from the 4D-universe (refer to Figure 15-2–Box B). Finally, the pantheistic view that God is identically the universe and all that exists is of divine nature (refer to Figure 15-2–Box C).

Mormonism differs from pantheism in that God is viewed as a distinct Being that exists apart from the universe. With these delineations marked-out we come to the foremost challenge facing theology. Presuming God's existence, whether this is an immanent or transcendent existence or some combination thereof, by what mechanisms is God able to act within 4D-spacetime without upsetting natural laws? It is tangential that God may have created the universe eons ago. The core question is how do we know he exists in present-day times? It has already been covered that it is not enough to pin this entirely on scriptural or

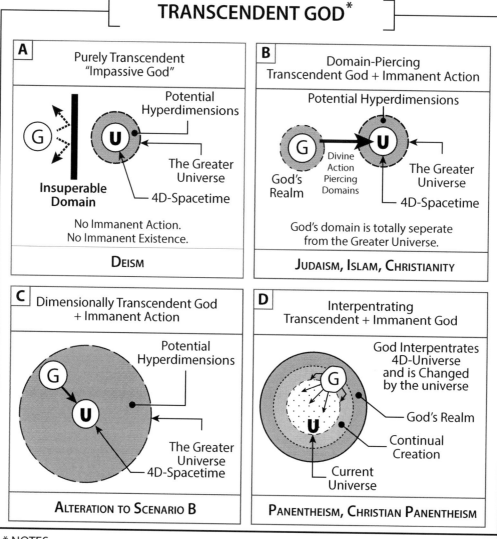

Figure 15-1. Ontological Propositions for a Transcendent God

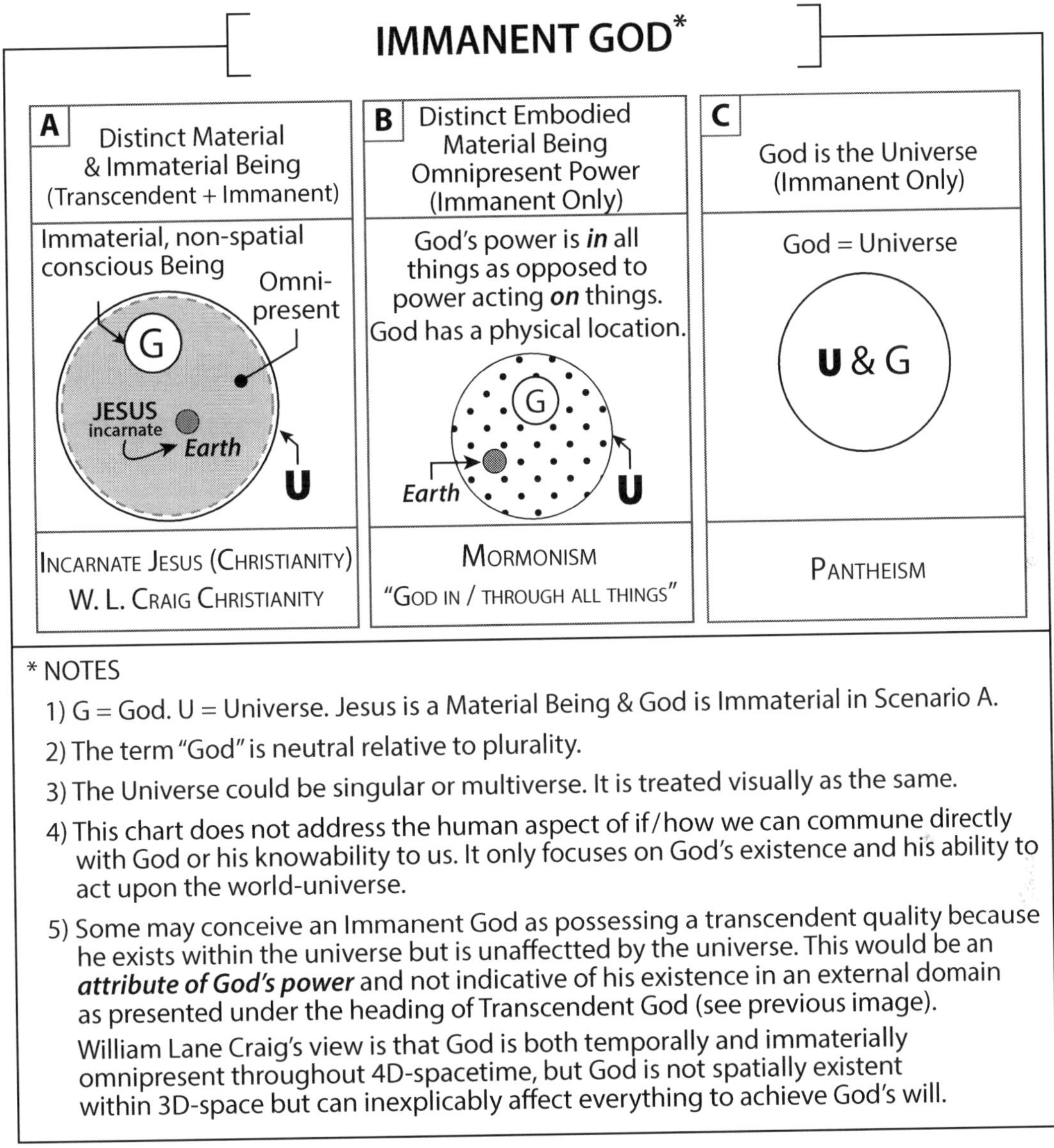

IMMANENT GOD*

A Distinct Material & Immaterial Being (Transcendent + Immanent)	**B** Distinct Embodied Material Being Omnipresent Power (Immanent Only)	**C** God is the Universe (Immanent Only)
Immaterial, non-spatial conscious Being Omnipresent	God's power is *in* all things as opposed to power acting *on* things. God has a physical location.	God = Universe
INCARNATE JESUS (CHRISTIANITY) W. L. CRAIG CHRISTIANITY	MORMONISM "GOD IN / THROUGH ALL THINGS"	PANTHEISM

* NOTES

1) G = God. U = Universe. Jesus is a Material Being & God is Immaterial in Scenario A.

2) The term "God" is neutral relative to plurality.

3) The Universe could be singular or multiverse. It is treated visually as the same.

4) This chart does not address the human aspect of if/how we can commune directly with God or his knowability to us. It only focuses on God's existence and his ability to act upon the world-universe.

5) Some may conceive an Immanent God as possessing a transcendent quality because he exists within the universe but is unaffectted by the universe. This would be an *attribute of God's power* and not indicative of his existence in an external domain as presented under the heading of Transcendent God (see previous image).

William Lane Craig's view is that God is both temporally and immaterially omnipresent throughout 4D-spacetime, but God is not spatially existent within 3D-space but can inexplicably affect everything to achieve God's will.

Figure 15-2. Ontological Propositions for an Immanent God

experiential divine revelation. If we were to accept for the sake of argument that God-inspired miracles could be authentic features of reality and that God is continually performing miracles to keep the course of the universe on his divine track, we are immediately confronted with a tremendously sticky situation.

Because God acts so mysteriously and does not advertise in any unequivocal format that he is the author of any particular miracle, we are left to the devices of human judgment to adjudicate whether a particular set of circumstances meets the qualifications for a miracle. There is so much happenstance in the universe it is incredibly hard to see when a miracle could be considered authentic. For instance, we hear of a car accident involving a mother and her child who were driving down the road. They skid off the roadway and the car is jettisoned off a 100-foot sheer cliff wall and crashes down below. Both occupants survive beyond all normative odds. Many will say that this event qualifies as a miracle.

But how would we characterize the following circumstance? In recent times, the public has become more aware that the number of Near-Earth objects is considerable (NEOs are comprised of asteroids and comets). NEOs now number over 14,000 with nearly 1,700 of them being labeled potentially hazardous.[5] Of course, there are many more 'dark NEOs' that have not yet been discovered and by some estimates there may be as many as 25,000 NEOs. The feasibility that the trajectory and timing of that one of these objects or a more distant astronomical object could intersect with the Earth's orbit is much higher than we previously considered. If the Earth were to be suddenly struck by a large NEO that wiped out half of civilization, what would we attribute this to? Would it be dumb luck or would it be God's interpretation for **ARMAGEDDON**? Or, has God designed the universe so that the Earth is forever nagged by ominous objects that hover dangerously close to our planet that threaten to annihilate life as we know it?

Because divine intervention is so difficult to arbitrate, it is why theologians and apologists have appealed to natural theology that undergirds the various Arguments (e.g., Teleological, Ontological, Cosmological, Axiological, etc.). **With the possible exception of a purely transcendent God, all other portrayals of God involve his immanent action upon the universe and/or his immanent existence within the greater universe. It is therefore the duty of the claimant to rationally explain the operative mechanisms God employs to act upon our worldly existence.** If a believer contends that there needn't be any evidence given to demonstrate God's existence and divine action, then they run afoul of the Many-Faced God Conundrum. Likewise, if in defense of an immanent God one stipulates that human beings are simply unable to comprehend God's nature (i.e., his capacities, temperament, location, plurality, materiality or lack thereof, etc.)

then those who take this position must also shoulder the same weighty mantle of the Many-Faced God Conundrum as no proper evidence is presented.

The two aforementioned scenarios are purist forms of blind faith. However, the cousin to blind faith is a *partially-justified faith*. Partially-justified faith is a catch-all term representing a spectrum of scenarios in which forms of evidence are provided in various proportions and of varying quality. This could be exemplified by fairly well-established religions with systematic theologies to situations where evidences are relatively few or are loosely-connected. The main test to determine whether partially-justified beliefs place one into the kingdom of the Many-Faced God is whether the evidences singly and collectively are implausible, incoherent, or irrational.

It is not an unfair action to demand a rational account of how God can manipulate universal processes. When theoretical physicists first proposed the existence of an invisible, all-pervasive scalar field (i.e., the Higgs field), the community of scientists did not simply take it on faith that such a thing was genuinely real. One reason why they were skeptical is that scalar fields of any kind had never previously been shown to exist. It was only after physical observations that left very little room for doubt that the Higgs field existed that it was formally recognized as a real phenomenon of our universe. Likewise, the cadre of M-theorists who tinker around with cosmic models, all of which require extra spatial dimensions (i.e., hyperdimensions) to exist, are subjected to extensive critical audits. In yet another example, astronomers and astrophysicists have extensively documented the existence of objects we call quasars. Quasars are believed to be supermassive black holes located at the center of some galaxies that emit fantastical sums of energy, on the order of a thousand times the output of billions of stars. These enigmatic objects were first detected in 1963. While this amount of energy is virtually inconceivable to us today, just as it was then, scientists never theorized that this immense source of raw energy was God. Rather, scientists spent decades deducing how such an extreme physical phenomena could arise.

Despite the mighty efforts by theologians and philosphers alike to explicate otherwise, we have deduced no overarching divine purpose to the universe. When you add the above facts together, and consider that we have not been able to find the indelible evidence for God's UBIETY (i.e., distinct physical location) or his physical embodiment (corporeally or incorporeally), or how in such form he could evade natural laws, it is understandable why *God as a material immanent Being is the least rationally plausible option.*

If God is an *immaterially immanent* Being floating around as a localized unembodied entity or as an omnipresent consciousness, then this entity might be immune to the laws of nature because these only apply to physical things. However, we are left holding the bag as to how the immaterial can affect materiality without upsetting the balance of universal processes. It would be fideistic or blind faith to simply claim that God's abilities are above these limitations. We go back to the idea presented earlier in this chapter that there is no way to separate this supposed reality from our amazing imaginations (refer to p. 543 and Mark Twain's aphorism on p. 545).

This is why conceiving God as a fully generic, purely transcendent Being—existing in his own realm insuperably distinct from our own—may be the most defensible theistic option. In light of prior discussion on apophatic mysticism which makes similar claims, such a statement requires further qualification. As a purely transcendent deity, God is nothing short of an impenetrable mystery as he would forever evade all efforts to access him through logic, knowledge-seeking, language, sensorial perception, or revelatory communication. And, counter to most all apophatic beliefs proffered by religious traditions, God can in no way manifest himself inside our universe or act upon our realm of reality. We should therefore expect that divinely-sourced miracles are not real phenomena and that there will be many things that humanity will not be able to explain. A purely transcendent deity in this context places all religious conceptions of God on the same plateau which is not to suggest that their theological suppositions are equally or partially true. Rather, they are all equally uncertain of the highest order.

Furthermore, if one wishes to posit that this purely transcendent God is responsible for the creation of our universe, then it is encumbent upon the claimant to provide the framework to justify such a position. We found that even the greatest philosophic mentations by Christian apologists (e.g., W. L. Craig's efforts to define causality in the pre-universe and the finitude of all reality) along with scientific theories (e.g., Big Bang cosmology) have been unable to support the claim that God's existence is necessary for the universe to exist. We must therefore surmise that belief in a purely transcendent deity is fundamentally irrational because we are not presently able to rationally differentiate between a deity possessing such an existence and one conjured by human imagination. It could be made rational if one were to identify God's fingerprints on the universe in ways not explored herein. Ultimately, we are unable to absolutely negate the possibility that a purely transcendent deity might exist.

The perimeter of God is finally taking shape. Before we summarize the zetetic process with a new circumscription of God, a few miscellaneous remarks are needed.

Some Miscellaneous Remarks Before Final Conclusions are Drawn

In considering the property of time operating in the modality of B-Theory (Block Universe), time only exists as relational between successive events (i.e., changes) but it does not flow per se. What exists is a series of events whereby God could in theory exist outside of this series in a timeless state. This idea parallels Augustine of Hippo's line of thinking insofar as God being existent in an eternal state of timelessness. If such a state is true, then God's mentation is dynamic in the sense that thoughts progress from one thought to another without consuming any quantity of time. When God chooses to apply his will, then events in our realm take place. The obvious drawback to this situation is that our world is fully determined eliminating any liberties for us to make any decisions of our own volition and God is the ultimate sponsor of all societal ills. God would also be responsible for making 'believers' have faith in him and for 'nonbelievers' to discount his existence. In short, God would be responsible for all associated discords.

On the view that time is but an illusion, we would be for all intents and purposes living in a timeless reality. This would not feel too much different than an A-Theory existence because human beings just plug-along thinking that time is progressing forward. But the reality is that we would be in something akin to a dream-like state, or worse, a computer simulation as proffered by others.[6] Everything that we are aware of and beyond, including our bodies and our minds, could be a virtual creation by some advanced alien civilization. This is not as absurd as it initially sounds. We human beings can use our 'mind's eye' to create a virtual world right this minute. It could be a universe where spacetime is pink and purple swirls of color everywhere, planets are pyramidal in shape, and inhabitants resemble the characters in the cantina scene of the theatrical production of *Star Wars Episode IV: A New Hope* (1977). We could even program a game where these inhabitants dynamically interact in their environment according to strictures enforced by computer algorithms. The simulation could also include virtualized deific entities of all sorts to exist. The crux of the issue is whether such an advanced simulation could produce conscious beings. The mind-brain possesses emergent features for intellect and self-awareness and this is not so easily reproduced by means of an algorithm. Additionally, if we are to accept that our conscious states could be simulated, we would automatically concede that consciousness must be fundamentally a physical phenomenon (i.e., monism) as opposed to a separate abstraction (i.e., dualism).

In more recent years, given the successes of the *Kepler* satellite to identify the existence of habitable planets in the nearby region of our own galaxy, it has been more supportable to conjecture that alien life must exist elsewhere that is extraordinarily more advanced than we are. In Paul Davies' *The Eerie Silence: Renewing Our Search for Alien Intelligence* (Mariner Books, 2011) he comments that alien life might exist that is so advanced that it may not itself have definitive shape or size, possibly existing in immaterial 'form' or in some unobservable medium, with the ability to organize regular matter. Their technology would appear to be miraculous to us. In any case, while such a 'reality' is ostensibly possible, there is no way of gaining an Archimedean vantage point to know that we exist as virtualized components in a simulation or that aliens exist in an unobservable medium. That is, unless the aliens living at the periphery of our existence somehow informed us. In short, no matter how unsettling this scenario might be, there is no way to rule out this possibility. We find ourselves in a capital aporetic state. You must be wondering by now if we disaffirm the doctrinal theology and philosophical inquests consistent with those discussed, are we then obliged to adopt a nontheistic view of the world? Or, is there still space available in which we could reasonably affirm God's existence and his qualities? The answer lies ahead.

Redrawing the Perimeter of God

For millennia much of mankind has professed a belief in deific agency. The prehistoric Mesopotamian and Egyptian societies adhered to a plurality of gods and to the best of our knowledge accepted their existence in unquestioning fashion. Vedic philosophers are thought to have offered the first documented intelligent speculations about the universe. Greek philosophers presented a broad range of contemplations building off the ideas of their fellow Grecian predecessors. The trek toward large-scale adoption of monotheistic worship took many generations to purchase a foothold. Romanization of large swaths of civilization was ultimately responsible for dramatically increasing the footprint of monotheism. While orthodoxification led to the systematic demise or diminishment of certain dogmas, especially polytheistic traditions, many rifts fissured under the weight of unification efforts. The pressure became so pointed that monolithic orthodoxy shattered into disparate orthodoxies.

Following the principles of *Zeteo Alétheia*, we shook the strongest of these architectures to ascertain if any of them yielded the much sought after fruit that might bear true knowledge of God. All doctrinal traditions suffered catastrophic injuries that took them out of contention for presenting a case that stood up to the variety of fundamental truth conditions and truth tests set forth. Barring miracles, the cumulative positive evidence and its associated level of certainty is insufficient to justify God's existence in comparison to the contrary evidence and its certainty. Nevertheless, one cannot on good grounds absolutely negate the existence of God.

We are now able to squat knee to ground and redraw the 'rational perimeter' for the potential existence and nature of God. If, after all the considerations made herein, anyone wishes to differ on the size or shape of the line, then the burden is on them to justify why and how the line needs to be shifted. We have several permissible options to rationally and coherently delineate God's potential existence which entail an underlying (1) acceptance of the truth criteria presented at the outset (see Chapter 1) and the contention that (2) divinely-authored miraculous events that would affect our universe as a going concern are impossible. In accounts where God might exist, (3) the act of creation of the universe could be considered the sole miracle. Furthermore, (4) we are unable to discern the level of benevolence that God maintains toward living things or (5) whether there is a singular or multiplicity of deity-like Beings. For the purposes of convenience, any reference to a deific agent is stated arbitrarily as a singular entity, but is to be understood that the plurality is fundamentally unknown. A final disclaimer is issued to say that (6) while the most powerful evidences have been considered, there may be other justified evidences that may arise.

Given the above, and after much effort on our part, the skyline of **The Six Towers of God** can finally be illuminated. As philosophers, theologians, and scientists are always eager to brand their ideologies, it would seem apropos to follow this particular tradition. Given that we have employed the zetetic process—proceeding to the truth by rigorous inquiry with all the stated assumptions (i.e., the Truth Criteria)—this new worldview that encapsulates the possibilities for God's existence and inexistence is to be called **Zeteticism.**

Each tower is architected by the collection of positive and negative evidences that have been studied throughout this book. A brief summary for each tower is presented is presented on the next seven pages.[2] Figure 15-3 illustratively encapsulates the full landscape of the **Six Towers of God worldview** (refer to p. 565).

---

2. Only a minimal explication for each category of the individual scenarios is provided. To gain a finer appreciation for the underpinnings for why these ascriptions are made, one must consider the material discussed throughout this book.

Table 15-1. God's Nature: Categories for
The Six Towers of God Paradigm

[U]   Temporal origin of the universe (beginning or beginningless)

[T]   The permissible ontology(ies) of time in the universe

[O]   Ontological status of God relative to the universe
       (transcendence, immanence, or some combination thereof)

[E]   Eternality of God (alive, no longer or never existent, unknown)

[K]   Knowability of God by mankind in the present or future

[M]   Materiality of God (embodied, unembodied, unknown)

[C]   Capacities of power and knowledge of God

[S]   Special notes

The Six Towers of God

Tower 1 – The Purely Transcendent God

[U]   The singular universe had a beginning. Additional justification is required to claim that God was the originator of our universe.

[T]   The universe could operate on the A-series or B-series Block Universe conception of time. However, if the universe does operate according to the Block Universe concept of time, then all of reality is fully-determined and human beings have no free will.

[O]   God is absolutely transcendent to human reality and all of 4D-spacetime (including would-be extra hyperdimensions)—meaning the greater universe. This entity is unable to act as an immanent sustainer or active agent. At best, from the human point of view, God would be an Impassive Observer.

[E]   Eternality is unknown. God's current existence is also unkown.

[K]   Due to the insuperable barrier, God and humanity are mutually and absolutely inaccessible to the other and no real relationship can exist between the two.

[M]   Materiality is unknown in the transcendent realm. God cannot be materially or immaterially present in our universe.

[C]   God's abilities are/were limited.

[S]   Dimensional transcendence is essentially equivalent to pure transcendence because extra-dimensional reality has not been suitably rationalized to exist as a feature apart from 4D-spacetime.

Consistent with the Kalam Cosmological Argument whereby a wholly transcendent God could have been the First Cause.

The Six Towers of God (continued)

Tower 2 – The Meta-Transignification Creator

[U]   The singular universe had a beginning.

[T]   The universe could operate on the A-series or B-series Block Universe conception of time.

[O]   God was once existent, but is no longer existent. Since God is not existent in our reality, he can be considered a transcendent Creator. The materiality of the universe is of God, but is not imbued with intrinsic divine power or consciousness.

[E]   God's life was finite.

[K]   God's focal intent was to employ his abilities to create a masterpiece of dynamic artistry. We have no ability to know what may have existed in the pre-universe.

[M]   God may have materialized himself as seed material to initiate Creation of the universe.

[C]   God's abilities are/were limited.

[S]   Consistent with the Kalam Cosmological Argument whereby God could have been the First Cause.

The Six Towers of God (continued)

Tower 3 – The Adamite-Eveitite Universe

[U] The universe had a temporal beginning as the result of the combination of mathematical probability and the dynamic action of substances which co-acted to produce the universe. The highly reactive substance called Adamite and Eveitite were exemplars of how materiality could be the cause to the universe (or multiverse – refer to Tower 4). Beyond this, the features of the pre-universe are unknowable. Furthermore, we are unable to know if the pre-universe vanished from reality at the time of Creation or if currently exists external to our universe.

[T] The universe could operate on A-series or B-series Block Universe conception of time.

[O] The universe's existence is not contingent on God and therefore God is not necessarily the Creator or Sustainer. The odds are significantly against the existence of a deity-like Being in the pre-universe or in this universe, but it cannot be ruled-out in an absolute sense. If such a Being was to have existed and had survived the Creation process, then the greater likelihood is that God is transcendent. If existent within the universe as a material or immaterial Being, evidence is lacking to explain how this would be the case.

[E] If existent, God's eternality is unknown.

[K] God would be unknowable in the preferred context. If God survived the Creation event and resides in our universe in some sense materially or immaterially, we lack evidence that humanity has engaged with him or vice-versa.

[M] If existent, God's materiality is unknown, past or present.

[C] If existent, God's abilities are/were limited.

[S] Consistent with the Kalam Cosmological Argument whereby inanimate, non-abstract substances could have been the First Cause.

The Six Towers of God (continued)

TOWER 4 – THE BRANCHING MULTIVERSE

[U]   The multiverse and our universe had distinct beginnings. That is, the multiverse is not eternal to the past. The cause to the universe/multiverse follows the line of thinking presented in the Adamite-Eveitite Universe (refer to Tower 3).

[T]   The universe could operate on A-series or B-series Block Universe conception of time.

[O]   The multiverse/universe is not contingent on God. The odds are significantly against the existence of a Being in the pre-universe or that this Being continues to survive transcendentally and potentially within the ever-increasing number of bubble universes. God's existence cannot be negated in an absolute sense.

[E]   If existent, God's eternality is unknown.

[K]   God would be unknowable in the preferred context. If God survived the Creation event and resides in our universe in some sense materially or immaterially, we lack evidence that humanity has engaged with him or vice-versa.

[M]   If existent, God's materiality is unknown, past or present.

[C]   If existent, God's abilities are/were limited.

[S]   This paradigm is also consistent with the Kalam Cosmological Argument whereby inanimate, non-abstract substances could have been the First Cause.
Refer to Notes (1) and (2) below.

(1) Recently published is the book *God and the Multiverse: Scientific, Philosophical, and Theological Perspectives* (Oct 2014, Routledge). The book aggregates twelve papers authored by a variety of authors that discuss the compatibility of theism and the multiverse proposal. Individually and collectively the motivating support for the treatises are bound-up in an array of assumptions that are not thoroughly wrought-out. It is the general opinion of this author that these position papers do not go far enough to firmly establish a complete, compatible, and/or coherent and therefore credible prescription for a theistic brand of the multiverse. Nevertheless, it remains this author's viewpoint that a generic deity (or deities) cannot be absolutely negated.

(2) Some have suggested that the multiverse would, out of the sheer force of probability, contain simulated universes—refer to Reality as a Simulation (Tower 6). Others go further to say that simulated universes would outnumber real universes because it would be easier to simulate a universe than it would be to create a real universe.

The Six Towers of God (continued)

TOWER 5 – THE UNCAUSED TEMPORALLY ETERNAL UNIVERSE

[U] In accordance with the contemporary cosmogonic theories (e.g., the Cosmon Field Model), the universe is eternal to the past and possibly to the future. It is most likely to be the sole universe, but a multiverse would be remotely feasible.

[T] The universe operates on A-series time, and potentially, time intervals have shortened since the distant past. In the very ancient past, the universe may have existed in a timeless state.

[O] The universe's existence is not contingent on God and therefore God is not necessary. Neither is God the universe's Sustainer as we have devised no argument by which this would be credibly the case. God's existence cannot be negated in an absolute sense.

[E] If existent, God's eternality is unknown.

[K] Since God is not the Prime Mover of the universe, it would be unclear what God's nature is since we have inadequate sources of credible evidence to inform us.

[M] If existent, God's materiality is unknown, past or present.

[C] If existent, God's abilities are/were limited.

[S] The Kalam Cosmological Argument is rendered moot.

The Six Towers of God (continued)

Tower 6 – Reality as a Simulation / Ultra-Advanced "Aliens"

[U]   The reality we perceive is an illusion and we are essentially virtualized entities in an incomprehensible simulation. An external-to-the-simulation universe potentially exists to serve as a host to the simulation and the Simulator Creators/Operators. The universe may or may not have had a beginning. The simulation would have had a beginning.

[T]   Time within the simulation would appear to consistent with A-series time, however, we could not know if time as a property exists outside the simulation, and if it did, what its nature would be.

[O]   The Simulator Creators/Operators would not be deities in the common sense of the word, but would be better described ultra-capable Beings that have the necessary wherewithal to build and operate a massively complex simulation. Such Beings would not be immanent or transcendent in the traditional sense. God's existence cannot be negated in an absolute sense.

[E]   The lifespan of the Simulator Creators/Operators would ostensibly be finite.

[K]   We would only know God to the extent the Simulator Creators/Operators programmed that into the simulation.

[M]   The materiality of reality external to the simulation is unknowable. One could suppose that the Simulator Creators/Operators are material Beings. Alternatively, one could suppose that all of reality, including the Beings, is a construct of pure consciousness. In this sense, the intentional consciousness creates a virtual realm in which to operate the simulation.

[C]   The ultra-capable Beings would possess extraordinary but limited power and knowledge.

[S]   This paradigm is consistent with the Kalam Cosmological Argument in the context of an alien simulation that made it appear that the universe had a beginning to time and space. That is, the simulation contains certain simulated astronomical/astrophysical phenomena that are suggestive that the universe had a temporal and spatial origin.

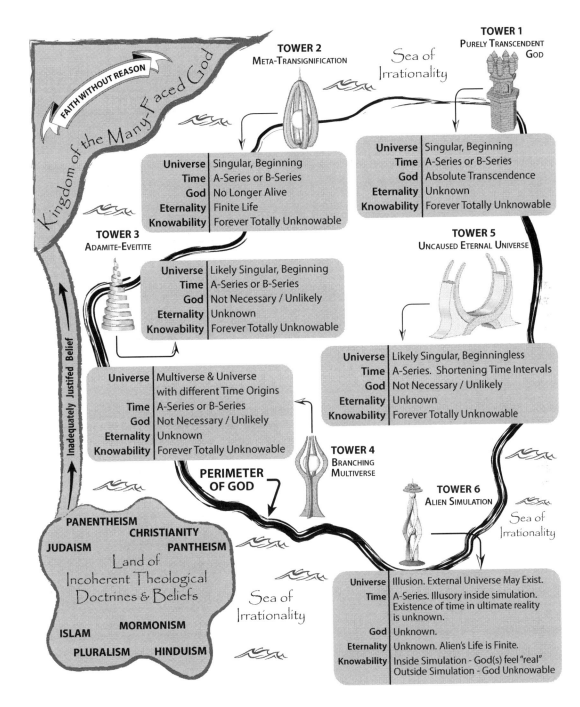

Figure 15-3. The Six Towers of God Worldview and the Perimeter of God (Zeteticism)

The Plausibility for God's Existence among the Six Towers

The single most important insight to glean from the Six Towers paradigm is that we are free to affiliate ourselves with _any_ of the towers in the six-fold constellation for we have bounded God the best we can and do not have license to eliminate any of the towers as a possible state of reality. We are constrained from making changes to the landscape principally because of (1) the relative uncertainties in our knowledge of how the universe came to exist and how it operates, (2) a lack of comprehension of what consciousness is, (3) the adoption of truth criteria stated in Chapter 1, and finally, (4) we can never access an Archimedian point of view. As to the latter, this is to say that we cannot purchase a vantage point to conclusively judge whether or not all of 'reality' is a simulation or if God is stationed in some divorced realm.

If one is theistically inclined toward a living God, the greatest consolation would be found by aligning oneself with Tower 1, albeit this God is totally alienated from our universe. The second tower might appeal to those who remain attached to the idea that God had a plan for the universe and human kind. Tower 2 might also be attractive to those who are enamored with the profound beauty of the world-universe, or who are spiritual, and you are comfortable with the idea that God is not an eternal Being. It is important to keep in mind that Tower 2 poses the possibility that the world-universe is _of_ God, meaning that it was generated from a great _Source_ of some sort. However, it should not be construed that the physical universe is imbued with any special divine qualities or consciousness. If you are of a scientific or mathematical bent, lean toward nontheism, are comfortable with the notion of a universe that sprang into existence via nondivine causation or via inanimate material action, favor the existence of many universes, or are willing to accept the idea of an eternal universe, then the third, fourth, or fifth tower would be choices of interest. The sixth tower would be a draw for those who contend that many billions of years of time have passed and the structures of the universe were stable enough to have produced environments suitable to the evolution of creatures that have since mastered manipulation of universal processes. It would also be captivating to the contingent of pseudoscientific 'ancient astronaut theorists' who believe that alien species visited our planet in the distant past.

It should be further observed that the Six Towers are not to be thought of as a fixed construct embedded into the reality-universe as some form of unalterable, infallible absolute truth. Rather, the paradigm is fundamentally a construction of human reasoning and discovery. The reasoning process was guided by the Truth Criteria established in Chapter 1 as well as by a variety of domain-specific principles and adjudication of many theoretical concepts. Through a combinatorial process of elimination and synthesis initiating from a null state, the Six Towers took shape.

While eliminating any of the towers with our present state of knowledge is not rationally feasible, it is to be acknowledged that the individual towers are not equiprobable. We could take another step and rank each tower based on plausibility. This is admittedly a tenuous maneuver because it relies on the sensibilities, overall knowledge, life experiences, and biases held by the individual. Nevertheless, **some of the architectures must be inferior relative to the others.**

It might be useful to further organize the Six Tower landscape by grouping them on some appropriate basis. Given that the first two towers house the notion of a transcendent God, they will be enjoined under the label of *Theistic Transcendency*. Because they all assert that the cosmos most likely exists from nondivine causes and arises from nonliving, non-abstract substances, let us collectively refer to Towers 3, 4, and 5 as representing an ideology of *Inanimate Substantialism*. This appellation is given as a subtle reference to the philosophical theories of *substance*. The idea and meaning of what a substance ultimately is, has been a source of philosophical controversy since pre-Socratic times. Many giants of Philosophy have weighed-in on this topic including Plato, Aristotle, Descartes, Leibniz, Spinoza, Hume, and Kant. They debated whether objects and properties depended on one another as well as postulated that God was made of a distinct metaphysical substance. The term 'substantialism' arose to account for the sense that substances were imbued with a sense of permanence. In the current context, for Towers 3, 4, and 5, the genesis of reality was borne out of nonliving substance(s). For Towers 3 and 4, it isn't precisely detailed whether the source substances were metaphysical materials (i.e., objects not of our universe) or were made of physical materials of our universe. Tower 5 more explicitly suggests that the source materials were native to our universe. The sixth tower is its own category entitled *Pseudorealism* as it encapsulates a faux-reality which completely masks what might constitute true reality.

On the whole, the Inanimate Substantialist perspective is generally more plausible than the others for the simple reason that they do not involve the miraculous action of a living Being. They comport with our sensibilities that materiality begets materiality and that we are absent any evidence where immaterial abstract thoughts are capable of creating material objects separate from its host. If we wish to do so, we can employ Ockham's razor to suggest that it appears to be a more economical approach than stipulating a living, immaterial solemn Being existing in perpetuity prior to the universe in a realm that is impenetrable to our reasoning capacities. Though, a caveat should be invoked in regard to Tower 4. In spite of its mathematical prowess and the many tantalizing oddities that result from quantum randomness and hyperspatial dimensions, the multiverse idea (i.e., M-theory) is very far from consideration as a valid theory. It is held down with many intractable endemic problems ranging from mathematical, astrophysical and astronomical deviances, an inability to select a correct interpretation for quantum theory, whether reality is fundamentally made of fields or particles, and philosophical challenges (e.g., all realities are true and there are infinite possibilities). This merits de-escalation in its rank relative to the other Inanimate Substantialist constructions. It cannot be entirely winnowed from the possible worldviews because there are many cosmological questions that have yet to be answered. A primary concern is the proper relationship of quantum theory to general relativity.

Tower 5 is considered the most plausible arrangement of reality. From 2014 and continuing to today, astronomical observations are more certain than ever that the universe is spatially flat, slightly expanding, and is essentially infinite in size. There has been no physical evidence for the existence of hyperdimensions. Well-founded scientific (not pseudoscientific) models that circumvent the catastrophic circumstances of a spacetime singularity that also avoid the need for an additional time stream are gaining the attention of cosmologists. An ultra-ancient universe that 'unfroze' at an incomprehensibly slow rate, offers a far more coherent explanation for the large-scale astronomical structures we observe and why all the stars haven't already died-out. Physicists are generally favoring the notion that the property of natural time might well be a malleable construct. To the extent the aforementioned are true, it becomes plausible that our universe has existed eternally. Even though God's existence in an eternal universe would be unnecessary, we cannot rule out his potential existence.

If the universe had a beginning as Tower 3 suggests, then the pre-universe causal actions between inanimate objects is more rational than self-existent, animated (living), immaterial, missionized Being(s). This is particularly so when we think about the essentially infinite size of the universe and why such a Being(s) would have any interest in human animals. The universe itself is a reflection of the dominance of inanimate objects given that, on a volume-basis, such material substances dominate the cosmos.

The Meta-Transignification of God, represented by Tower 2, is a thoughtful way to answer the perennial question of how the now godless-universe first originated. It is more sympathetic to a universe that required a beginning. However, its plausibility suffers because it is occupied with the idea that a magnificent Being of considerable power lived and subsequently altered its status. There is no evidence whatsoever that this God or Source created the universe and neither is there concrete evidence that he survived for any particular period of time. All that we have to consider is the majestic beauty of the universe. I would advance that it is arguable whether Tower 2 is more or less plausible than Towers 4 and 6.

As for an advanced alien species engaged in operating a grand-scale simulation, the texture, continuity, and seamlessness of the tapestry we call reality appears to flow so well, it does strike one as a rather preposterous idea. How could the entire simulation be so perfectly choreographed? Although, when we look to state-of-the-art computer animation, 3D-visualization, and holographic technologies and how they have advanced in recent decades and project how human technology might evolve thousands of years from now, the idea that we ourselves could create a convincing simulation is not all that unbelievable. Countering this is the very real fact that we have not yet confirmed extraterrestrial life exists, let alone ultra-capable life forms. From a statistical point of view, pockets of sentient, complex, intelligent life almost certainly exist *somewhere* in the universe. All things considered, the plausibility of Tower 6 should be ascribed with a low rank. Given the above, the Six Towers are ordered as shown in Figure 15-4.

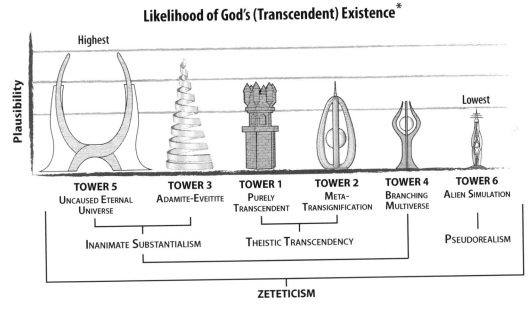

Likelihood of God's (Transcendent) Existence[*]

*Owing to the lack of tangible and well-justified affirmative evidence for the **_Immanent_** existence of God, a deity that lives or interacts within our 4D-universe realm is **_maximally unlikely_** among any of the Towers. Therefore, this illustration principally considers God as a transcendent entity. A trascendent deity (or deities) is most strongly affiliated with Tower 1 and Tower 2.

Figure 15-4. Level of Plausibility for God's Existence Among the Six Towers

It is a result of putting aside deific intercession (a.k.a. miracles) and canvassing many potential artifacts, historical transformations of deific embodiments, physical and mathematical processes, as well as a myriad of philosophical musings that we arrive at the conclusion that *a materially immanent God is the least plausible option. An immaterially immanent God is almost as implausible because we haven't rationalized the mechanisms of how immateriality might exert control over the material realm.* This position is somewhat presumptuous because we haven't conclusively established whether human consciousness is innately a substance-based phenomena.

If existent, God is purely transcendent relative to our natural realm, occupying his own domain which is insuperable for both God and us. If one wishes to posit God's existence as dimensionally transcendent, living in some hyperdimension(s), then one must deliver quality evidence to attest to this state of affairs. While the zetetic process has been unable to delineate whether or not God is a necessary Being or continues to exist in present-day times, these issues are relatively moot given the more plausible scenario that he is locked away in a separate domain.

Is this the God of Deism? Deism is a formalization of theism that has been defined in various terms since its inception. In order to centralize an orthodoxy for the tradition, the World Union of Deists states that "Deism is the recognition of a universal creative force greater than that demonstrated by mankind, supported by personal observation of laws and designs in nature and the universe, perpetuated and validated by the innate ability of human reason coupled with the rejection of claims made by individuals and organized religions of having received special divine revelation."[2] Deism further holds the view that God is a singular, eternal, impersonal, Intelligent Designer-Creator to the universe (a teleological viewpoint) believing God exists in a seperated spirit world. It is not specified if this spirit world is a hyperdimension or is outside the greater universe. Deists further believe that God is not a providential deity who is actively tending to the universe. Thus, to a deist, God is not immanent in any way, which is what Tower 1 affirms. Whereas Deism favors the idea that we can expand our knowledge of God's nature through our reasoning capacities and by studying nature, Tower 1 generally precludes this notion. The first tower only affirms God as a totally disconnected entity whose plurality and continued existence we cannot know. It also does not intrinsically assert that God created the universe because we would need additional evidence to make that leap. Whether God left us clues to his existence is an open possibility for Tower 1 believers. But, to date, we haven't identified any solid clues.

If it was not already abundantly clear, because the zetetic process is unable to draw the perimeter small enough to absolutely negate the existence of a deity-like entity, the position of strong / hard atheism is not a credible viewpoint to hold. We then come to the fact that there exists a spectrum of agnosticism and atheism which asserts a level of uncertainty toward the nonexistence of God. As famed evolutionary biologist and self-asserted atheist Richard Dawkins frames it, there are two types of agnosticism.[3] "TAP, or Temporary Agnosticism in Practice, is the legitimate fence-sitting where there really is a definite answer, one way or the other, but we so far lack the evidence to reach it (or don't understand the evidence, or haven't time to read the evidence, etc.). [...] But there is also a deeply inescapable kind of fence-sitting, which I shall call PAP (Permanent Agnosticism in Principle)."[8] "PAP agnostics aver that we cannot say anything, one way or the other, on the question of whether or not God exists."[9] PAP mirrors the purist form of blind faith as it too holds that we can never know God.

Overall, I think Dawkins' view is an impoverished characterization of the available options.[4] Zetetics as a methodology has demonstrated six options that circumscribe God's potential existence. Dawkins would have us choose between the interminable incapability of knowing (i.e., PAP) or the position that it is inevitable that at some point in the future we will possess unambiguous justification to declare the ontological status of God (i.e., TAP). **Dawkins' "fence" is an oversimplification of the situation because the Six Towers tells us that it is improper to take either of the two positions as superior to the other.** *Zeteo Alétheia* binds us to the course of continual seeking of evidence that might alter the character (or number) of the towers in some as yet indiscernible way. This does not guarantee that we will eventually come to know with certainty which Tower is the correct one and therefore the TAP orientation may or may not be the appropriate view. Likewise, because we can affirmatively state that we cannot absolutely negate God's existence; it partially goes against PAP principles. Furthermore, we may never gain substantially greater insights than the present form of the Six Towers which would leave us in the current situation with an unsatisfying force of conviction that God may exist with unknowable properties and apparently little affinity for mankind. But then again, he may not exist at all.

---

3. Dawkins orients himself between agnosticism and hard atheism in which he attests that we cannot know with certainty that God does not exist, but that it is very improbable. He calls this position "de facto atheism" which is one notch above strong atheism. (*The God Delusion*, p. 50-51, Hougton Mifflin, 2006, Hardcover)

4. The term "impoverished" is a play on Dawkins' titling of his discussion on agnosticism—"The Poverty of Agnosticism." (*The God Delusion*, p. 46, Hougton Mifflin, 2006, Hardcover)

Alteration of the Six Towers may come about if, for example, it came to light that mathematical infinities are clearly demonstrated to be nomologically or metaphysically impossible. Science may someday determine that four-dimensional spacetime exists alongside sister hyperdimensions. Or, perhaps some version of Christof Wetterich's theory for an eternal universe will be validated with astronomical observations (e.g., the clumping of intermediate-mass sterile neutrinos). We may finally develop a comprehensive understanding of regular and altered states of consciousness that would inform us if consciousness can exist independent of a physical host. Might we ever find a 1st-century text that is demonstrably authored by Jesus of Nazareth which discloses his full humanity and lack of divinity? Perhaps God will show himself to be existent in some unequivocal documentable **THEOPHANIC** manifestation. However, we could accumulate all the evidences we like and it may ultimately prove to be a fool's errand. Dawkins' proposition only makes sense if God were an immanently-acting God within 4D-spacetime, which the Six Towers indicates is an extremely low probability.

Have we ventured headlong into an ignostic worldview whereby there is no coherent concept of God to be had? Individually, all six towers permit to varying degrees the existence of a deity but none paint God's attribute with defining brush strokes. When we zoom-out of the picture frame, the zetetic process defines a coherent outline of what God could be and what he is not. The question to ask is, presuming the existence of a transcendental realm that possesses attributes and contents beyond our ability to define with any certainty whatsoever, is the concept of God undefinable? A noncognitivist (i.e., ignostic) would surmise that because God is not empirically testable he is undefinable and therefore it is meaningless to carry on about God. It is reminiscent of a quip by the renowned linguist, philosopher, and atheist Noam Chomsky which he intoned at a conference held at the Salk Institute for Biological Studies, "Like everyone participating, I'm what's called here a 'secular atheist,' except that I can't even call myself an 'atheist' because it is not at all clear what I'm being asked to deny."[10]

I do not wholly embrace the logic that just because God lacks a description that it is therefore meaningless to discuss God. On one hand, if God is beyond all comprehension and is purely transcendent, I tend to believe that given the Six Towers as they are, it makes little sense to commit ourselves too deeply to something that has no transactional effect on us or us on him either in our lifetimes or thereafter. Notwithstanding this remark, there is meaning to be found in at least two important senses. While life seems to have proliferated on this tiny spheroidal rock by the whimsy of spatiotemporal processes,[5, 11, 12] we can be unified by our shared human condition and become an active steward to care for and respect the environment which sustains us. This could be facilitated by unshackling ourselves from the many incoherent doctrines that guarantee to cut many lines of division between kin and neighbor. The second sense that God is meaningful is that, just because God may not be real or is eternally inaccessible and undefinable, God is not going to instantaneously disappear from our social lexicon and interpersonal dialogue.

If you were among those who came to this venue embracing an interactive God, one that could be connected with in personal terms, now or in the afterlife, then you would be subscribing to the least plausible notion found within the perimeter. The zetetic process of inquiry demonstrated that the boldest of attempts by philosophers, theologians, or critical thinkers in general—ancient or contemporary—simply falter in their attempt to present humanity with a sufficiently coherent, logical, probable, and/or plausible discernment. In the absence of new data, the interactive God is strongly disfavored from the evidentiary point of view, but still a remote possibility. Having been a believer in a personal God for the majority of my own life, this is a visceral punch in the gut. This will not be easy or quick to digest for many. Personal and widespread acceptance of the Six Tower framework will require deep contemplation for each and every individual.

Will people in general adopt this new Six Tower worldview? That depends in part on whether you find God to be a positive force in your life. In 2011, neuroscientist Tali Sharot penned her research findings in her book *The Optimism Bias*[13] which were also featured in a TED2012 film production. Sharot identified that human beings are innately programmed with a positive bias toward optimism and a negative bias toward negative information. This is presumably to help immunize us against excessive stress and anxiety while also staying motivated to survive life's many difficulties. When people receive negative information that detracts from their current state of well-being, they will cognitively diminish or completely disregard its importance to the individual. In this sense, we remain optimistic that we'll escape or overcome the negative consequences. This happens even if the negative outcome is highly certain to arise or even if such negative outcomes may be highly injurious in some way.

Sharot advances that cognitive scientists have identified our brain's proclivity to process new incoming information by contrasting it to existing beliefs. Central to this process is

---

5. A recent biodiversity study estimates that the Earth may host up to one trillion species of unique microbes (i.e., prokaryotic life) [Locey, K.J. and Lennon, J.T., May 2016] and approximately 8.7 million eukaryotic species (plants, animals, fungi, algae, and lichens) [Mora, et. al. 2011].

that the brain has evolutionarily optimized the process to generate a *valence* condition. That is, in order to process things expediently, it quickly characterizes new information as a valent choice between it being congruent (i.e., affirmatory) or incongruent (i.e., contradictory) with existing beliefs. This is largely irrespective of the truth, correctness, factuality, or rightness of the new information. Thus, the brain's initial inclination is to more easily accept things that are conforming (i.e., agreeable) to our existing belief and conversely, to disavow those things that do not align with currently-held beliefs. For example, it would be fair to say that you believe with a high degree of confidence that Gray whales can only live in large bodies of water (e.g., seas or oceans). If I were to tell you that, "Earlier today I saw a Gray whale living in the forest and it was eating marshmallows" (mock quote), your brain will immediately engage this optimal strategy to conclude using existing knowledge and experiences that this could not be true and that I'm probably a bit crazy to suggest such a thing.[14-17]

Sharot also observes that, if we are to be given a choice to believe 'A', 'B', or 'C', whichever we decide is correct, our brain's are apt to subsequently reinforce the selection we made as being the best or correct choice later on. This is a sort of a self-reward for the brain to reduce cognitive dissonance by reducing any anxiety or troubled feelings that may have accompanied the decision to process the favored choice.[14-17]

What her work shows, and that of many other neuroscientists, is that such research findings are consistent with well-established cognitive biases. In particular, it affirms several of the cognitive biases already discussed (i.e., Confirmation bias, Illusory-truth effect, and Anchoring bias). We should understand that such responses are not automatic or robotic in nature for there are many things that affect our decisions, particularly our emotional state and our state of alertness at the time we are receiving new information which can profoundly change how we process information.

The main point being conveyed is that for people who retain especially strong convictions on a given topic, that unless they themselves are engaged in a very careful examination, they are most apt to quickly locate and ingest information that fortifies their prevailing beliefs. Such actions assist in satisfying the brain's inherent desire to feel like it is in a state of control. which is much more important than it being an accurate reflection of reality. Basically, it is for the above reasons, why it is so difficult for an individual to change one's existing beliefs of the world, even when better, more accurate, information is presented to them.

And, so it is with God. If people who find peace and contentment with God are disenchanted with this more restricted view on what God could be or that he may not even exist at all, their brains will work unconsciously and consciously to find a way to retain or alter their view of reality in a manner to minimize distress and/or the need to re-map their mental models. It is not enough that I simply tell you about the Six Towers of God. Hence, why I noted above that you the reader will need to deeply contemplate this new perimeter on God. When we contemplate things in a rigorous, critical, and thoughtful manner, we are more apt to see past our inherent and learned biases. If we fail to do this, we are apt to develop irrational thoughts and beliefs about reality. Human beings are far from being consistently logical. Irrationality is so prevalent, it can be considered normal brain functioning. Nevertheless, reality is reality, irrespective of our individual or collective perceptions, irrational or otherwise. It is the ultimate human condition to parse what is real versus what is perceived or imagined.

If you wish to retain the interactive God as our guide, guardian, or savior, at a minimum you need to concretely intellectualize how the hand and mind of God mechanistically operates in our realm. For reasons already discussed, concocted mentation based on metaphysics and mysticism is almost certainly doomed to be unintelligible. Some will become frustrated or otherwise be tempted to retreat to a position of quasi-blind faith maintaining that God is so far beyond our puny intellect that we could not possibly comprehend his abilities to freely mix with our 4D-reality. There is, in the mind of such an individual, no explanation for God other than that which is provided via miraculous revelations or intercessions (scriptural or experiential). Such individuals have just jumped onto a boat that will take them full circle to the beginning of this venture. They will enter the harbor of the Many-Faced God Conundrum. Either that or they will have sailed waywardly into the insensible and shoreless *Sea of Irrationality* (refer to Figure 15-3 on page 565).

There will be those who will simply ignore or reject the treatment of the evidences presented herein for whatever off-handed or seemingly justified reason. Many who hold countenance to the actuality of miracles or personal revelatory experiences will be loathe to release their commitment to the embodiment of some external agent. I would ask of one who retains this attachment to develop a rational framework to precisely and systematically define what constitutes a miracle and why a particular belief must require a divine-like source and cannot be attributed to known or unknown operative physical mechanisms intrinsic to our universe. The individual should also conscientiously ask themselves whether they are retaining a belief in divine events and entities because it offers them a measure of peace and comfort or that it would require too much work to qualify the event or circumstances as a consequence of natural phenomena. Scientists and mathematicians are held to a high standard when they make claims about the difficult-to-understand inner-workings of reality. We should therefore require the same for those making divinity claims. It behooves us to frame the problem in the context that Earth is but one of some 40 billion or so Earth-like planets hosted by our galaxy.

Some will proffer cries of rebuke that their home religion is not amongst the Six Towers. It is the normative reaction when entrenched ideas of the day are challenged. Whether you have engaged this book as a philosopher, theologian, scientist, or Common Man, the challenge is the same. When one posits the existence of God, there is an onus upon the claimant to deliver a systematic worldview to justify the position. One has to come to the table with alternatives that systematically address (1) What is reality?, (2) What constitutes truth in reality?, (3) What is the property of time and how does God's existence relate to time?, (4) What is consciousness?, (5) What is the form and materiality of God (i.e., localized or diffuse, material or immaterial, embodied or unembodied)?, (6) What are God's powers, attributes, and limitations?, (7) How and where does God reside (i.e., transcendent or immanent, single location or everywhere)?, (8) How is God able to act upon the universe and/or humanity?, (9) Is God responsible for the creation of our universe?, (10) How many divine-like entities exist and how do they interrelate?, (11) What are the evidences and assumptions for the aforementioned questions, and finally (12) How are the answers to the aforementioned items affected by the array of cognitive biases and mind-brain processes? Of course, the Zetetic worldview must be open to validly-constructed criticisms to any aspect of its foundational principles, assumptions, specific evidences, or conclusions. If the Six Towers of God are to be the most defensible fortress for God's potential existence, what now are we to do with this knowledge? The Grand Observer's telescopic information recording system is poised in anticipation of our next steps.

SUMMARY

After enduring a long and difficult journey, beset with many jogs in the path, we managed to canvass a huge swath of human activity to understand how God has been conceived throughout the ages. This chapter recapped the zetetic effort to unwind this astoundingly complex history. After 'lifting the hood' and inspecting the major theological tenants and philosophical interpretations, we found that none were sufficiently convincing. The justification for this conclusion is that, in each case, there are serious faultlines that prevent us from ratifying them as being representative of reality. Too often, metaphysical statements are conjectured with too great a force to support the underlying claim. It is analogous to fitting a square peg in a round hole. Whenever this happens, it is a clue that something isn't quite right. The *Six Towers of God* paradigm essentially tosses any square pegs to the side and whatever remains must embody the truth. What we found, however, is that we are incapable of identifying ultimate reality at the present time. Effectively, we are left with multiple possibilities because we are not suitably equipped to make a finer discernment.

A major theme of this chapter also entailed the delineation of the ontology of God as a transcendent and/or immanent phenomena. This is admittedly a challenging topic to parse because there are so many perspectives and defintions to manage. Not to mention the fact that we have to wage a battle between rationality and pseudo-rational metaphysics. Here I am being charitable to associate metaphysics with rationality. If our journey was arranged such that we did not cover all the pre-history of religion, neuroscience, and cosmology before tackling the subject matter of God's ontology, it would have been all too easy to be satisfied with the idea that God must exist because he was necessary to create our universe, and ultimately, mankind. We would be unchallenged if we avoided the call to produce evidence for the following:

- God was the spark of Creation (i.e., cosmogenesis or eternal cosmic existence);

- God is actively sustaining the universe (i.e., overcoming physical laws, the illogic of omni-perfection attributes, the responsibility for suffering and evil acts, the allowance of free will);

- the universe is moving teleologically toward an Omega point (borrowing this terminology from Teilhard de Chardin);

- qualifying whether consciousness can exist external to a physical host.

When we are not required to answer these intractably difficult questions with proper evidence, God easily fills the space for what we call reality. When reason is vacuumed from the room of discourse, God can sit comfortably in the chair of immanence or fill the air of transcendence.

When we applied the zetetic filter to consider the immanence of God, material or immaterial, it was determined that this ontological status is the least likely embodiment for God. If God exists as a dimensionally transcendent Being, we have no evidence for that. This would mean that God's 'house' is not located in our zip code, our planet, at a galactic outpost, or within the greater universe. If God is in anyway involved with the universe, then mankind will need to redouble its efforts to identity additional evidences. In the absence of evidence, while we cannot deny God's potential existence, though he may as well be a purely transcendent entity. Otherwise, if he really does have a local cosmic address, we would have to content ourselves with an impassive entity that distances himself from the countless tragedies that befall human life.

CHAPTER 16

Chiseling the Stone of History

The Age of Nations is past. The task before us now, if we would not perish, is to shake off our ancient prejudices and build the earth.[1]

– Pierre Teilhard de Chardin
Construire la Terre (trans. *Building the Earth*), 1958
French Jesuit Priest and Paleontologist

This is my simple religion. There is no need for temples; no need for complicated philosophy. Our own brain, our own heart is our temple; the philosophy is kindness.[2]

– Dalai Lama XIV (Tenzin Gyatso)

As for the various religions, there's no doubt that they are very meaningful to adherents, and allow them to delude themselves into thinking there is some meaning to their lives beyond what we agree is the case. I'd never try to talk them out of the delusions, which are necessary for them to live a life that makes some sense to them. These beliefs can provide a framework for deeds that are noble or savage, and anywhere in between, and there's every reason to focus attention on the deeds and the background for them, to the extent that we can grasp it.[3]

– Noam Chomsky
Atheist, linguist, philosopher, and socio-political activist

At this present moment, the human race, even after thousands of years of historical development, is still at the dawn of a new creation. This is a tremendous, awe-inspiring responsibility. It should humble us.[4]

– Sir John Marks Templeton

HUMANITY'S MAGNIFICENCE AND RELATIVE INSIGNIFICANCE

When we look into the night sky, all that we see is a depthless black sea punctuated by the silvery moon and a sprinkling of hovering white dots. The unaided eye can only see about 9,000 stars of the several hundred billion in the Milky Way. If we strain hard enough, we just might glimpse the Andromeda galaxy (M31) or possibly the Triangulum galaxy (M33) some 2.5 million and 2.9 million light-years distant, respectively. The many billions of stars in these galaxies appear to us but as single smudges of light. In 2008, the Swift satellite detected a fantastically-bright gamma-ray burst (GRB 080319B). The cosmic wonder was the most intrinsically luminous object ever catalogued and the most distant light source ever visible to the naked eye at a staggering distance of 7.5 billion light-years.[5] If at that time in 2008 we were to instantly teleport to the original location of this gamma-ray burst and look back toward Earth, we would only see darkness in the line of sight because the final light trails would be several billion light-years away and moving farther away.[1] Situated at this remote location in 2008, our perceived reality would be that this intensely powerful and long-lasting event never happened for this 'light data' would be forever lost to us. This is a naked example of how true reality and perceived reality can be radically different. One perspective holds that nothing existed and the other has evidence in hand that affirms that something of a grand scale transpired. We can quite rightly say that truth is in the eye of the beholder.

When one meditates on the cosmic wonders that are happening all around us, it diminishes the sum total of humanity to a state of insignificance on the global stage. However, what is remarkable is the fact that we are able to contemplate this at all. Unlike any other species, we have been able to prove to ourselves that there are far grander things than the Earth. If distance calculations hold, we live in a 90-plus billion light-year sprawling cosmos chock-full of planetary systems many of which almost certainly have had biologic life at one time or another. More than likely, the full size of the universe is immensely larger and possibly infinite. We appreciate the amazing fluidity and sometimes delicacy of natural processes but are aware of the destructive savagery of supernovae which may well be responsible for the annihilation of an uncountable number of life-forms. We spy in our telescopes the inconceivable sums of raw energy spewing out of quasars—trillions of degrees hot—ripping through the frozen stillness of deep space. After much debate, we can affirm the existence of obsidian globes—'black holes'—that pepper the cloth of spacetime. These awesome and enigmatic objects have played a pivotal role in the construction of the panoramic tapestry of galaxies. Our tinkering minds have uncovered how matter and energy are transmuted and that all things cower to the pitiless laws of nature. They are handmaidens to nothing.

The story of terrestrial life here on Earth is just as humbling when one considers that it arose out of the maximally chaotic events of planetary formation. Our Earth formed out of a once frigid molecular gas cloud that came to be influenced by the combinatorial effects of gravity, electromagnetism, and potentially by the radiative pressure generated by then-nearby stars. The giant blob of solar gas eventually accreted into a messy roundish ball

---

1. The longevity of quasar events is unknown, but estimates suggest they could last tens of millions of years, even several billion years.

of solidified rock. We were very fortunate that the gas contained the crucial element of iron because this material eventually leeched into the interior of the young Earth. The iron became molten allowing it to churn. This action generated a magnetic field that prevented both then and now the solar wind's trillions of particles from irradiating away the Earth's atmosphere and water resources. Fossilized *microbial mats*—short layered pillars of microorganisms called stromatolites—appear to be the earliest forms of life that came into existence 3.7 billion years ago[6] after the relative cessation of 300 million years of meteoritic bombardment. While there are terrestrial and extraterrestrial hypotheses, we have not as yet determined how biologic life originated from carbon-based compounds. Carbon-based life had cycled through periods of proliferation and ruinous decline through a panoply of volcanism, watery inundation, extreme atmospheric changes in chemical composition that at one point became lethally toxic to the majority of life-forms. The planet also experienced global glaciation leading to an encasement in ice and snow, massive earthquakes which must have generated terrifically-sized tsunamis, continued meteoritic bombardment, and a more rapidly spinning Earth.

The many forces at work serendipitously shaped humanity into a sentient, self-aware bipedal animal equal parts human and microbial.[7,8] Humanity, along with a small menagerie of self-aware animals, is for all intents and purposes alone in their cognitive existence as we collectively whirl about our host star. In a very stark sense, the brotherhood of mankind is all that we have. If we as neighbors struggle so mightily in this relatively quiescent period of geologic history, I fear for how our species will fare when the ecosystem has become less hospitable. We need to shift to a coexistence rooted on greater mutual cooperation and a bearable standard of equality and global prosperity.

Neuroscientists tell us that the overwhelming majority of our existence is mediated by unconscious processes. What becomes conscious is a minute portion of reality as a result of the severe limits of our perceptual abilities or because what is received by the brain is mostly filtered-out well before the information can be processed against our mental models. The smattering of decipherable information that the brain decides is important is sieved by deep-seated preconceptions. What happens next is dependent on many factors.

Social scientists tell us that we are far more swayed by our personal and societal values than any well-demonstrated line of rational thinking. Values often conflict with and even outrank entrenched moral and ethical standards. For instance, a person's ethos may hold that capital punishment is immoral. However, this same person may value justice strongly enough to also believe that those who commit terrible crimes are deserving of mutilation by removal of a hand, foot, eye, or tongue. The democratic republic that is the United

States values competition and free market principles so staunchly that capitalism has spun out of control bifurcating society into the 'few haves-and-the-many-have-nots' relative to financial wealth and facilities to accumulate societal influence. These values are gauged to be more important than efficaciously institutionalizing some basis to ground how low the 'lowest citizens' are afforded an equitable share in the various aspects of our society. When inequity becomes overly deep and the lower of the classes is beaten down one too many times, it can instigate major societal upheaval. Aside from wealth and power, in many places around the world, we have established borderless principles to sanctify liberty and self-determination. Unfortunately, as is widely apparent, this is all too frequently unenforced for pragmatic and/or political reasons. It is an understatement to say that advancing toward a common good given the intrinsic power of the *status quo* is indubitably problematic. Substantial progress will only come with the grist of sacrifice and the passionate pushing of the millstone of justice and equality.

The crux of the episodic struggle of society comes down to values. What values are we to support and among those which is to be elevated and which is to be subjugated? Systems of governance, codified as law or otherwise instituted, are aimed at organizing the mayhem of contrasting values as a means to establish fairness and stability. But the serviceability of such efforts often falls short of ideals. In no small part is this failure due to the implementation of many forms of boundaries. What is valued highly in one place is not in another. If one region asserts their value system onto another, it is most often unwelcome. Our values have been too misaligned for far too long. What we see in ancient times, we see today ... the patchwork of society trudges along in uneven paces. There is no shortage of calls to action to do better, but they soon become hollow echoes of the past. Our present is freighted with our past. Can we unyoke ourselves from the chronic unpleasantness and habilitate society? The interplay of religion is but one of many cogs in the wheel of society.

A SIMPLE WISDOM FOR THE COMMON MAN

We have come to the Everest of rationalizing the best circumscription of God, all things considered. Reflecting once again on Einstein's prolific words from the first **EPIGRAPH** of Chapter 1, taking reliable steps toward the truth has been epically difficult as we have had to traverse the uneven ground of a dozen or more distinct domains of knowledge. The zetetic inquiry however does not necessarily end. It has only been temporarily paused. New knowledge might arise that, after appropriate scrutiny, could alter the landscape of the Six Towers. Such knowledge is more apt to come from scientific discoveries in cosmology, physics, mathematics, and consciousness studies rather than the domains of philosophy and theology, but we are to remain open to all possibilities. Nevertheless, we need to leverage the wisdom of the Six Tower paradigm as it currently stands. The insights from the Six Towers tell us that we are not being watched-over by a mighty cosmic steward, personal redeemer, or divine counselor. Ironically enough, after assiduous labor, lifting every weighty stone, should he exist at all, he is unknowable and inaccessible in the most absolute sense. For all that can be reasonably discerned, we are but small potatoes to this would-be Source in the great cosmic garden! It is well recognized that a great many people find solace in a personal God with whom they can partner to receive guidance to navigate the heady waters of life. By going to the river of God, they hope and pray their pains will be washed away and they will be revitalized. So it is no wonder why such a stalwart life companion is an attractive, powerful, and empowering motivator in many people's lives. The zetetic worldview may be relatively less comforting in a direct sense, but it potentially offers equally powerful benefits by placing the locus of control within one's own self and shifting within the mind the ways in which we cogitate reality to facilitate self-empowerment and a new clarity of thinking.

The central precept of Buddhism is the attainment of enlightenment, or in other words, a revealing of the truth of the self. As with any religious or spiritual tradition there are different branches of Buddhism with different designs as to how to achieve such liberation. But in all cases, there is a reverence for contemplative mindfulness that distills what is important. The Dalai Lama[2] says that "Buddhism is a science of mind."[9] Remarking on the compatibility of science and Buddhism, Zen Buddhist monk Thich Nhat Hanh's center for international practice professes that, "The practice of mindfulness and concentration always brings insight. [...] It is our belief that in this 21st Century, Buddhism and science can go hand in hand to promote more insight for us all and bring more liberation, reducing discrimination, separation, fear, anger, and despair in the world."[10]

What can be derived from the Buddhist tradition is that we need to be engaged in our lives by harnessing the clarity of *deliberate thought*. This does not mean we need to enter into a preserved state of self-transcendence or become a BLISS NINNY. Rather, we attain this mental state by being thirsty for knowledge and by equipping ourselves with an abiding gratitude and immersive altruism. When we do these things consistently, the desert of ignorance, complacency, and selfishness is left behind. We come into a new relationship with the world consisting of a never-ending grooming of our persona while concurrently availing ourselves to others. Transcendentalist and abolitionist Henry David Thoreau averred,

---

2. The 14th Dalai Lama (Tenzin Gyatso) is a Templeton Prize Laureate.

"If one advances confidently in the direction of his dreams, and endeavors to live the life which he has imagined, he will meet with a success unexpected in common hours." This wisdom dually applies when we work toward common purposes, neighbor helping neighbor.

Expounding on this idea of deliberate thought, **the need is for us to develop a greater self-awareness of our mental programming in terms of cognitive biases and interpersonal prejudices.** This awareness comes naturally when we first understand how our brains function to interpret incoming data. We are then eminently more prepared to critically inspect the knowledge we consume while being on guard against patterned biases or an overdependence on heuristics which allow us to mentally 'check-out'. **I think this point is so vitally important it bears repeating. We, as individuals, have to become much more attuned to our multitude of patterned bias before we will make any substantial strides in developing a truer understanding of external reality.** It should be recognized that, at times, this is likely to come at a cost of internal feelings of uncomfortableness or vulnerability as we become more practiced in critiquing how we think and process the world around us.

So too our introspective thoughts must lead to contemplative action in a spirit of charity, discovery, and a strong sense of brotherhood. These are the essential core values that need to be emboldened throughout world society. It is to be granted that we are all prospectors trying to lay claim to a stake in the world. This pressures us to sometimes mistakenly build a moat around ourselves when the structure of necessity is of another sort. When we over-insulate ourselves whether individually or by forming exclusive in-groups, as time passes, our understanding of 'the other' dissipates. This separation can become so potent it becomes institutionalized and even legalized. This can lead to bigotry in its various forms—racial, religious, sexual, and ideological. If instead, we embrace the aforementioned values, bigotry withers and in its place grows an invigorated desire to assure liberty, a safeguarding of life, and self-determination for all.

Just as light takes time to travel to the distant reaches of the cosmos, the enlightenment of Zetetics and the Six Towers paradigm will take time to disseminate into this world. Meanwhile, as a practical consideration, religion will continue to exist as part of the fabric of society far into the future. As noted early on, religion is personal and communal. We must therefore respect the right for an individual's choice of religion so long as it is peacefully manifested *and* it is not foisted unduly upon others. Any animus toward an individual's freedom of choice should be resisted by society. However, there is a distinction to be made between encouraging another person to become educated about religious/spiritual choices and a directed effort to guide, persuade, or otherwise pressure another to follow a particular course. This applies to youths and adults alike. Positive values can always be instilled without religious narrative.

In his book *The Great Partnership: Science, Religion, and the Search for Meaning*, Rabbi Lord Jonathan Sacks[3] offers a parallel ideology to that of the Six Towers paradigm where he intones, "We need moderates, that is, people who understand that there can be a clash of right and right, not just right and wrong. We need people capable of understanding cognitive pluralism, that is, that there is more than one way of looking at the world. [...] The way is always long and hard. But the only way is together. Religion and science, believer and sceptic, agnostic and atheist. For, whatever our view of God, our humanity is at stake, and our future, and how that will affect our grandchildren not yet born."[11] The Six Towers perspective is cognitively pluralistic because it offers both believers and nonbelievers a set of alternative worldviews to choose from, though some are considerably more justified than others. While Sacks is passionately supportive of an ongoing dialogue between religion and science, given the challenges to theological foundations outlined herein, we have to redirect the dialogue in a number of ways. This can be summarized as follows:

Table 16-1. Religious and Scientific Institutional Change

1. Religious institutions are overly-reserved, lagging, or completely neglecting the adoption and dissemination of credible relevant knowledge. They also falter in educating adherents about alternative religions and worldviews. This only emboldens isolation of the in-group from those outside. A concerted effort to overturn these trends, preferably by the institutions themselves, is vitally necessary.

2. Theistic mysticism as a framework to discuss God is a confused and digressive alchemy of pseudo-rationality and imagination to the absolutely unknowable. It acts to cover-up the incoherencies of foundational theological doctrine rather than being a coherent circumscription for God's nature to which it attests to. Almost all mysticisms claim that God is a Being that yields little to our faculties and yet a massive architecture is built-up claiming knowledge of God's many attributes. Mysticism needs to be excised from the dialogue in favor of plain speak. God is either unknowable or knowable. If the latter is chosen, then new evidence beyond what has been studied herein has to be presented. This might come in the form of demonstrating

---

3. Jonathan Sacks is the 2016 Templeton Prize Laureate.

consciousness can exist separate from a physical host, or by determining whether or not there is an origin to the universe's existence, or by a clear demonstration of what constitutes a miracle and providing evidence that can meet a high threshold of scrutiny.

3. Religious and scientific scholasticism needs a wholesale improvement in identifying, reporting, and eliminating bias in it many forms.

4. Scientific and engineering research (theoretical and applied) are grossly underfunded endeavors. Dollar for dollar, science and engineering irrefutably yields an unparalleled high return on investment, much of which can be directly measured in human benefit. Nation states need to invest far more capital in the short term to gain in the long run.

5. Scientists and engineers are particularly subjected to excessive pressures to produce positive results in typically short timeframes. Enhanced funding will help ameliorate some of this. Grant monies should be more evenly distributed among researchers. Research that provides negative results need to be given stronger consideration as valid research. Also, a stronger emphasis on coordination, cooperation, and knowledge dissemination over data-hording and competition is necessary.

6. Public and private educational curriculums need to provide classes and/or programs suited to the audience's cognitive capacities to convey religious, spiritual, and scientific viewpoints in an effort to promote community and critical thinking. This should be a compulsory element to formalized education and be provided throughout the progression of one's educational career.

7. A national/global center, or network of centers, committed to apolitical, **zetetically-motivated** (that is, truth-oriented) ideals, could facilitate knowledge sharing, dialogue, and implementation of effective policies. There are numerous centers for religion-science studies already operational, but they produce works and platforms that are categorical or thematic. They are not integrative in a grander sense. This center's primary mission is to keep the Common Man abreast of contemporary developments and integrate these in intelligible and accessible ways.

8. There is a desperate need among the majority of citizens to increase the capacity and application of critical/analytical thinking skills and to become more acutely aware of the cognitive biases that influence our individualistic and collective thinking. This former concern is partially substantiated by a 2017 Wall Street Journal report that found that more than one-third of graduating seniors from U.S. colleges hadn't increased their critical thinking skills from when they first entered college. In a separate assessment, 50% of employers identify that college graduates are unprepared for the workplace citing a deficiency in critical thinking skills as the primary factor.[13]

9. Beyond the need to become familiar with the specifics of the large assembly of biases, we have to move away from dyadic thought structures where we compartmentalize life into two or a few constructs. Rather, things are intrinscially more complex than we would like them to be. If we want a more refined appreciation, more often than not, we have to expend an extra effort to gain purchase of this enlightenment.We also need to be continuosly aware that 'others' are apt to view life issues differently because their exposure to, and perception of, reality can be significantly different than our own. This is but one reason how values can become differentiated from one group to another. Ultimately, greater vigilance in how we collect and critique knowledge is called for. Prior to forming final conclusions, we have to factor-in as much raw knowledge as feasible, give proper weight to our own ignorances, and to apply our adopted values thoughtfully.

MARKING THE STONE: A PRESCRIPTION FOR HARMONIZING HUMANITY

The Six Towers paradigm presents an **IRENICAL** solution to the multiple millennia of religious sectarian discord. We have before us an arresting thought. Could we imagine the greater good that could come about if religious dogmatists unshackled themselves from their peculiar notions of God so that the many houses of God could find common dwelling under the sanctuary of Tower 1 and the simple unknowable purely transcendent God!? Sunni, Shiite, Catholic, Protestant, and Jew all become theologically allied as the divisional walls disappear. Because scriptural revelation and personal revelatory experience is antithetical to a purely transcendent deity, the focus of religious customs could be realigned to center wholly on the noble values that embody compassion toward all. Atheists, agnostics, and **SECULAR HUMANISTS** (generally, the irreligious) would be appeased as they no longer need to fret about the provincialism of this-or-that religion. They, along with Buddhists and other spiritualists, can find peaceful coexistence among any of the Six Towers.

We are all potters created from the same primordial cosmic clay. But a potter's inspiration *doth not maketh* a better world just because he works the clay to fit his vision. He needs the perspective of others to appreciate his art. Thus, it is only when we place the yeoman's yoke upon our neck that our heads become level with our neighbor's eyes. Even then, inspiration, mutual consideration, and work ethic are not enough. We need the sage's wit to make intelligent choices. Together, when each man and woman becomes the potter, the yeoman, and the sage, we become thirsty to forge an imprint on mankind that propels our ascension to a new zenith in our collective humanity. It is as our beloved Einstein has told us, and many since, that every individual must contribute to positively transform the spirit of our times.[4]

This is not a hopelessly QUIXOTIC utopian prescription. **It is a simple philosophy of oneness in the daily practice of mutual compassion, humility, and intellectual curiosity. Additionally, it is a commitment to the self and to society to make an earnest effort to become acutely aware of mind-brain function as it applies to our capacity and peculiar propensities to interpret reality.** In the next millennium, the human species seems apt to be the sole 'prime mover' to guide the destiny of Planet Earth. If we were to exchange ego for humility, bigotry for compassion, self-interest for conjoined interest, ignorance for intellectual curiosity, so many of our moral and societal dilemmas would dissipate, would they not? We can start down this path by greatly minimizing religiously-oriented tensions by engraining the Six Towers of God worldview which gives safe harbor to hardened theists and nontheists alike, as well as to those who had positioned themselves somewhere in between.

The Grand Observer's PLEXUS of telescopes have journaled your intrepid footsteps to discover the six well-obscured towers. From his distant outpost, he spies the blurred arc of the hammer-head strike true against the cold, hardened steel chisel ... the piercing echoes ring-out as the stone of history is scribed for all eternity, ending a repeating chapter for humanity. The hammer lifts once more, rising swiftly to its apogee; its next impulse becomes frozen as we individual cosmic authors recalibrate our minds and reset our footwork to ennoble the quest for a more just, secure, enlightened, free, and balanced world.

---

4. Refer to the last sentence of the second epigraph presented at the introduction to Chapter 1.

Rubáiyát of Omar Khayyám

(Translation: The Quatrains of Omar Khayyám)

[Quatrain XXIV - 24]

Ah, make the most of what we yet may spend,
Before we too into the Dust descend;
Dust into Dust, and under Dust to lie,
Sans Wine, sans Song, sans Singer, and--sans End!

[Quatrain LXIII - 63]

Of threats of Hell and Hopes of Paradise!
One thing at least is certain--This Life flies;
One thing is certain and the rest is Lies;
The Flower that once has blown for ever dies.

[Quatrain LXVI - 66]

I sent my Soul through the Invisible,
Some letter of that After-life to spell:
And by and by my Soul return'd to me,
And answer'd "I Myself am Heav'n and Hell:"

[Quatrain LXXI - 71]

The moving finger writes; and having writ,
Moves on: Nor all thy Piety nor Wit,
Shall lure it back to cancel half a Line,
Nor all thy Tears wash a Word of it.

(continued next page)

Quatrain LXXIII - 73]

With Earth's first Clay They did the Last Man knead,

And there of the Last Harvest sow'd the Seed:

And the first Morning of Creation wrote

What the Last Dawn of Reckoning shall read.[12]

• • •

The Rubáiyát is a sprawling poem of 110 quatrains written by Persian poet, philosopher, and and astronomer Omar Khayyám c. 1120 CE. Among other themes, it is about self-realization, following our inner path, and the spirit of *CARPE DIEM (Latin for 'pluck the day')*.

The poet beseeches us to focus on the self and then move beyond our self-centeredness to join the communion of mankind to use the time we have to advance the common good.

APPENDIX

COPYRIGHT FAIR USE PROVISIONS, USES REQUIRING PERMISSION, AND PREFERRED CITATIONS

Fair use legal doctrine is provided in Section 107 of the United States Copyright Act (17 CFR 1.107). The U.S. Copyright Office also provides an index of legal decisions which are interpretations of the principals and applications of fair use policy (see http://www.copyright.gov/fair-use/fair-index.html).

Any use of the copyrighted material herein, regardless of whether it is considered Fair Use or not, requires the proper attribution of the source material. *Please use the appropriate Preferred Citation* (see p. 595).

The following Fair Use provisions are interpretations by the Author/Publisher to delineate circumstances that will require the permission of the Author/Publisher from those uses which do not. The Author/Brian Goedken and Publisher/Arkenstone Media are not liable for inappropriate or illegal uses of copyrighted materials owned by third parties presented herein.

Special Material

Permission is required to use, reproduce, or transmit in any form, any portion of text or imagery from any of the following:

(1) **the List—numbered "Tower 1" through "Tower 6"—denoted with the headline text "The Six Towers of God" which appears in Chapter 15, pp. 558 – 564;**

(2) **any of the text presented in Chapter 15, pp. 566 – 576, under the section heading entitled "The Plausibility for God's Existence among the Six Towers" which further explicates the List;**

(3) **the image presented in Chapter 15, p. 565, following the List with the caption entitled "The Six Towers of God Worldview and the Perimeter of God (Zeteticism)";**

(4) **the image presented in Chapter 15, p. 569, with the caption entitled "Level of Plausibility for God's Existence Among the Six Towers."**

This material (above) constitutes, in part, the 'heart of the book'. Please contact the publisher for permissions to reproduce these items.

Text-Based Material

Use of copyrighted material of third parties must be secured by contacting the rightful owner(s) of the material(s) of interest. Consult the Works Cited section which may provide copyright-related information. This is generally stated at the end of the citation in the **Notes**.

Permission is required to use, reproduce, or transmit in any form any text that is to be used as an epigraph (i.e., text used at the beginning or ending chapter of a chapter) or as a prominent heading. The book title by itself is not subject to US copyright law.

The epigraphical quotes presented in this book at the beginning of each chapter are generally the property of third parties. Some survive under copyright law and others have since expired. The two exceptions are (1) the last epigraph presented in Chapter 1, and (2) the first epigraph in Chapter 5, which are attributed to the present Author. Unless in the Public Domain, epigraphical material requires permission to use.

Exclusive of (1), (2), (3), and (4) noted in the Special Material section above and epigraphical material, the following permissions are granted for text-based material as Fair Use.

Criticism, Comment, or Parody: For book reviews and other comparable forms of criticism, comment, or parody, up to 1,000 total words may be used for direct quotation without permission.

Non-Commercial Research, Scholarship and Nonprofit Educational, Electronic Course Materials, Printed Course Materials, Thesis/Dissertation, Non-Commercial Scholarly Book: Up to 750 total words may be used for direct quotation without permission.

News Reporting: Up to 500 total words may be used for direct quotation without permission.

Commercial, For-Profit — Book, Journal, Magazine, Promotional Materials, or Educational use: Up to 500 total words may be used for direct quotation without permission.

Imagery-Based Materials

Use of copyrighted material of third parties must be secured by contacting the rightful owner(s) of the material(s) of interest.

Imagery is defined as graphic elements constituted in the form of photographs, illustrations, drawings, charts, tables, or stylized symbols (e.g., flourishes, text separators).

Refer to Special Material section, Items (3) and (4). The identified imagery requires permission.

The imagery presented on the front cover requires permission unless it is used (1) by book distributors, (2) to promote this book or, (3) is used in support of a book review.

With regard to Imagery and its Fair Use, exclusive of (3) and (4) (see Special Material section), up to two images can be used without permission at the image resolution provided in the book for a single project per organization/per individual (i.e., a book, an article, a paper, etc.). Higher resolution images require permission (if available). Imagery that is generated by the present Author may also require the additional attribution to third parties (e.g., in cases whereby external source data or source images were relied upon to create the Imagery).

Consult the *Photo and Illustration Credits* section (see p. 683) to aid in understanding copyright ownership assignments for imagery.

PREFERRED CITATION

Text-Based Material

For uses that meet Text-Based Fair Use Provisions above. Specify page references as needed.

Goedken, B. D., *The Naked Truth about God — The Quest to Find Evidence for Whether God Exists Reveals an Epic Discovery that has Eluded Religion and Science*, 1ˢᵗ ed., Arkenstone Media, 2018, ISBN: 978-0-9984898-6-5. Copyright © 2018 by Brian D. Goedken. Reproduced under Fair Use provisions.

For uses granted _outside_ of Text-Based Fair Use provisions. Specify page references as needed.

Goedken, B. D., *The Naked Truth about God — The Quest to Find Evidence for Whether God Exists Reveals an Epic Discovery that has Eluded Religion and Science*, 1ˢᵗ ed., Arkenstone Media, 2018, ISBN: 978-0-9984898-6-5. Copyright © 2018 by Brian D. Goedken. Reproduced with permission of Brian D. Goedken.

Imagery-Based Material

For uses that meet Imagery Fair Use Provisions stated above.

Image Copyright © 2018 by Brian D. Goedken. Reproduced under Fair Use provisions.

For uses granted _outside_ of Imagery Fair Use provisions.

Image Copyright © 2018 by Brian D. Goedken. Reproduced with permission of Brian D. Goedken.

GLOSSARY

note on source materials[1]

❦ A ❧

a posteriori: Involving reasoning derived from observed facts (e.g., from sensory experience and/or empirical evidence).

a priori: Derived by deductive reasoning or logic without reliance on observed facts.

Abductive (Abduction): Abductive logic may be considered an inference to the best explanation. It is a compromise between deductive and inductive reasoning.

Abiogenesis: A hypothetical organic phenomenon by which living organisms are created from nonliving matter.[1]

Abrahamic religion: The group of monotheistic religions sharing a common origin with the God's first prophet Abraham (or also Abram). The principle religions that adopt this position are Judaism, Christianity, and Islam.

Abstruse: Deep, recondite, difficult to penetrate; incomprehensible to one of ordinary understanding or knowledge.[1]

Adamantine: Utterly impervious or unyielding, intransigent or impenetrable.

Adjudicate: Decide, settle, resolve.[1]

Agency: A general term indicating the capacity of a unit system (agent) to act in this world to generate end-directed behaviors. An agent may be an entity or essence such as God (transcendent and/or immanent), an otherworldly Being, or a human being and/or its conscious mind depending on the context it is used.

Agnosticism: A [theological] orientation of doubt; a denial of ultimate knowledge of the existence of God[s].[1] Agnosticism is represented by a spectrum of beliefs. Some agnostics contend that it is impossible for us to know whether a deity(ies) exist. There are agnostics who maintain that it may be possible to determine that deity(ies) exist but hold varying degrees of uncertainty. Secularists are a group of non-religionists who could be affiliated with agnosticism. Generally, agnostics are uncertain of God's existence and can lean toward theism or nonthesim, but do not reject God completely (i.e., atheism—see entry). While agnostics could self-identity as

---

1. Terms sourced from Princeton University's dictionary—WordNet®—are identified by citation. Otherwise the definitions provided are this author's.

leaning toward a particular formalized religion, agnostics generally are not affiliated with a specific religion and therefore are generally considered nonreligious.

Alétheia: (*Greek*) Translated as the state of being revealed as in the truth or factuality of reality. See Zeteo Alétheia and Zetetic entries.

Allegory: An expressive style of writing or illustration that uses fictional characters and events as a device for an extended metaphor to reveal a hidden meaning.

Altmetrics: Alternative metrics to the Impact Factor to assess the level of influence a specific journal or article has based on various factors (e.g., frequency of views, discussion, saves, citations, recommendations, and Tweets—sometimes called Twimpact Factor).

Amaranthine: Constancy, perennial, unceasing, everlasting.

Amity: A state of friendship, peace, and cordiality, especially the political relationship between nations.

Androgynous: Relating to or exhibiting both masculine and feminine characteristics; ambiguous appearance or sexual identity.

Anisotropy: The property of being anisotropic; having a different value when measured in different directions.[1] Compare Isotropy entry.

Anodyne: A way to impute a level of criticism to something that is not going to be perceived as offensive or would provoke a negative reaction from others.

Antediluvian: Of or belonging to the period before the biblical Flood.[1]

Anthology: A book or of selected literary passages or writings composed by different authors, commonly consisting of material from the same subject matter, time period, and/or literary form.

Anthropic (Cosmological) Principle: The philosophical, but unproven, notion that the finely-tuned parameters of the physical Universe are such that they are conducive with the origination and sustainment of conscious and sapient life that observes it.

Anthropocentric: To ascribe human beings as the focal point for causal purposes.

Anthropodicy: An argument to justify the fundamental goodness of human nature in spite of the wickedness originating from humans. This is to be contrasted with Theodicy (see entry).

Anthropomorphize: Ascribe human features to something.[1]

Antimony: A real or apparent contradiction or mutual incompatibility between two logical statements, both apparently obtained by correct reasoning.

Antipode: A direct, exact, or diametrically opposite.

Apathetic: Indifferent, unconcerned, showing little or no emotion.

Apocalypticism: The religious belief that there will be an apocalypse, a series of events that will bring the world to an end, especially within one's own lifetime. See Eschaton entry.

Apocrypha: (Greek) Meaning "hidden books." Books considered to be Scripture but were excluded from biblical canon. There are Jewish apocrypha and Christian apocrypha.

Apodictic: Necessarily true or logically certain.[1]

Apologetics: The branch of theology that is concerned with the defense of Christian doctrines.[1] See Christian Apologetics entry.

Apologist: A practitioner of apologetics wherein they defend the beliefs or ideas concerning religious doctrine. See Apologetics and Christian Apologetics entries.

Apophatic Mysticism (Apophasis): The theological approach that God is ineffable (see Ineffable entry). Any knowledge or intuition that generates an understanding of God is gained through statements of what he is not (i.e., so-called "negative statements") even though such statements are always lacking because God is beyond all definitional attempts. Even labeling God as "existent" is lacking in comprehension. Compare Cataphatic Mysticism entry.

Aporetic: Puzzlement or doubt arising from the lack of solutions to a philosophical dilemma.

Apostasy: The formal or informal act of abandonment or rejection of one's religion or religious beliefs.

Apotropaic: Having the power to prevent or ward off evil or bad luck.[1]

Archaeometry: the discipline within archaeology that uses science or technology to examine and interpret archaeological specimens, often to determine their age.

Arches: The sloped shapes of a fingerprint. Compare Whorls entry.

Archimedean Point: A hypothetical vantage point from which an observer can objectively remove oneself from the subject of inquiry such that the observer's view is independent and provides a total view of all relations to all other things.

Argot: A characteristic lexicon associated with a particular profession.

Armageddon: The final and complete destruction of the world-universe.

Ascetic: A person who is strict with either their practice of self-denial or who adopts an austerely simple life that rejects materialism usually undertaken to attain a high spiritual state.

Aseity: In metaphysics, it is the existence originating from and having no source other than itself (i.e., self-caused).

Asymptotic: A line or curve that approaches, but does not attain, a value because it is tangent at infinity.

Atavistic: Reverting to or a reappearance of characteristics of an ancestor or primitive form of an organism whereby those characteristics had disappeared in the intervening timeframe.

Atemporal: Independent of, free from limitations of, or unaffected by time; timeless.

Atheism: The doctrine or rejection of belief in the existence of God(s), deity(ies), or Supreme Being(s). Like Agnostics (see entry), there is a spectrum of beliefs that are categorized as atheistic. There are those whose uncertainty registers so high that they rate the existence of a deity(ies) as being highly improbable or nearly zero probability. Then there are so-called 'strong atheists' who are completely certain that a deity(ies) does not exist.

Augur: A person, usually a religious official that predicts events from signs or omens; to foretell or prognosticate.

Autographic Codex: The original physical document, usually an assembly of ancient manuscripts (as in Bible/Scripture). The term 'autographic text' refers only to the original words of the Bible.

Axiom: A proposition that is not susceptible of proof or disproof; its truth is assumed to be self-evident.[1]

❧ B ☙

BCE: Before the Common (or Christian) Era.

Black hole: A mathematically defined region located in spacetime exhibiting an attractive gravitational pull stronger than any other object in the universe and under which no particle of matter or electromagnetic radiation (energy) can escape. Black holes vary greatly in size/mass. Stellar black holes are those having masses equivalent to several to dozens of solar masses. Supermassive black holes can be hundreds of thousands to many millions of solar masses. The centrally-located black hole located at of our Milky Way galaxy is between 4 – 5 million solar masses. The most massive black hole yet detected (as of 2015) is 12 billion solar masses.

Blind Faith: A religious belief that God's existence and nature are real and in some ways knowable. However, it is acceptable that these beliefs can remain unexamined and/or poorly qualified. Often blind faith is fundamentally an incomplete, incoherent, or irrational belief system, even though this may not be evident because the belief system only provides superficial statements and answers to questions that demand greater qualification. Compare Fideistic Faith entry.

Bliss ninny (also Blissninny): A person who is unrealistically or is obsessively optimistic.

Blueshift: A shift in the spectral lines of a stellar spectrum whereby there is a decrease in the wavelength (or conversely an increase in frequency) in electromagnetic waves resulting in the light waves being perceived as more blue when compared to the visible light spectrum. This most often refers to Doppler Blueshift which is the relative motion of an object moving toward another object (as in the Earth). However, there is also Cosmological Blueshift for instances when spacetime contracts. A third type is Gravitational Blueshift when light becomes more energetic in a gravity well. Compare Redshift entry.

Brobdingnagian: Unusually great in size or amount or degree or especially extent or scope.[1]

∞ C ∞

Canon: A collection of books accepted as Holy Scripture especially the books of the Bible recognized by any Christian church as genuine and inspired.[1] Especially, as it refers to biblical canon or scriptural canon.

Canonical: A religious text that is authorized, recognized, accepted, and conforms to the orthodoxical view and is included within sacred Scripture, as in the Bible. See Orthodoxical entry.

Captious: The tendency to find fault or to entrap the opponent in argumentation.

Cataphatic Mysticism (Cataphasis): While emphasizing revelation (scriptural or experiential), cataphasis is the theological approach that affirms our ability to learn facts about God. This is to say we can make so-called "positive statements" about God. Also commonly spelled *kataphatic/ kataphasis*. Compare Apophatic Mysticism entry.

Causa Sui: (Latin) A self-caused cause. A cause that is not the result of prior causes.

CE: The Common (or Christian) Era

Changeless: As it pertains to God, it is an attribute of God whereby God is not changed (affected by) anything or any events in the universe. This is a weaker form of immutability. God, however, can intrinsically change his conscious thoughts, emotions, or will.

Christian Apologetics: A field of Christian theology aimed to defend the faith against objections through the use of rational arguments. See Apologetics and Apologist entries.

Christology: The branch of theology concerned with the person and attributes and deeds of Jesus Christ.[1]

Cognitive Bias: A cognitive bias is a pattern of judgment in which the inferences relied upon may be illogical themselves or, when combined, lead to illogical conclusions.

Coherent: Logically consistent.

Cold Dark Matter: See Dark Matter entry.

Colloquy: a conversational exchange typically formal in nature.

Computable: Capable of being computed, as in the ability to solve a problem algorithmically.

Consubstantial: Identically the same in substance, essence, or nature.

Consubstantiality: A doctrinal term associated with Christianity that describes one of the Monadic (see entry) properties of God. Accordingly, the three-Person God (Father, Son, and Spirit) is comprised of a singular divine substance. See Perichoresis entry.

Contiguously: (as in the property of time) One instant of time followed immediately adjacent, subsequent, and different instant of time.

Corpus Aristotelicum: Aristotle's collective body of work.

Cosmic Inflation: In physical cosmology, this is often referred to simply as 'inflation'. Inflation represents a class of theoretical paradigms that postulate the physical mechanisms and mathematical description for the exponential expansion of space occurring almost immediately after the universe came into being. Relative to our own universe, inflation was ultra-brief in duration. Some theories contend that inflationary processes could have continued to propagate external to our universe thereby creating the multiverse.

Cosmic Microwave Background: The vestigial thermal radiation that pervades the universe (hence the use of "background") as a result of the successive cooling (loss of energy) following the Big Bang event which is the supposed origin of the universe. The predominant signature is in the microwave region of the electromagnetic spectrum.

Cosmogony: The branch of astrophysics that studies the origin and evolution and structure of the universe.[1]

Cosmological arrow of time: Pointing in the direction of the (presumed) expansion of the universe.

Cosmological Constant: A concept first introduced by Albert Einstein which is referred to symbolically as the Greek letter lambda (Λ). It is a parameter in his field equations to account for the Vacuum Energy Density (see Vacuum Energy entry) of space. It acts like an anti-gravity phenomenon that is an outward pressure versus an inwardly attractive 'force'. It is often thought to represent hypothetical Dark Energy (see entry) which is the accelerative expansion of spacetime. There is ongoing debate whether or not the value of the Cosmological Constant is unchanging (i.e., constant) over cosmic history or whether it has changed. A changing Cosmological Constant is often referred to as Dynamical Dark Energy or Quintessence (see entry).

Creatio ex nihilo: (Latin) Creation from nothing. This usually implies that God created the universe out of nothing other than his own divine self. The word "nothing" in this context is to mean that God did use preexisting material or anything external to his divine self. Whether or not there was any material or reality external to God before or at the conception of the universe is essentially considered inconsequential.

Credulity: (1) As it pertains to John Hick's Golden Rule, credulity is a principle of acceptance or truth found within religious experience. (2) Tendency to believe something too readily, that is, without proper evidence.

Crestfallen: Brought low in spirit.[1] Also, a feeling of being dispirited or discouraged.

ങ **D** ೲ

Damoclesian: An allusion to the imminent peril presented by the large sword that was held above Damocles' head by a single strand of hair. Damocles is a fictional character in a legendary Greek story—The Sword of Damocles—that had him switching positions with his king, Dionysius II of Syracuse. The king had a sword dangle precariously above Damocles' head to make him aware that the assumption of power invites both responsibility and danger.

Dark Energy: A hypothetical phenomena that behaves like a repulsive anti-gravity responsible for accelerating spacetime and all things inside the universe apart from one another. See Cosmological Constant entry.

Dark Matter (Hot and Cold): A hypothetical form of matter that, if real, constitutes the majority of all physical matter in the observable (and presumably the unobservable) universe. Because there has been no means identified to directly detect it, the existence and natural properties are inferred from its influence (presumably gravitational in nature) on visible matter (e.g., stars, nebulae, galaxies, and galactic superclusters). Hot Dark Matter is composed of particles (e.g., neutrinos) that have zero or near-zero mass which move at or close to the speed of light, respectively. Because of the high velocities, it must be extremely hot eliminating the possibility that small-scale structures could form. Cold Dark Matter is matter that moves more slowly relative to the speed of light. This permits structures to grow hierarchically whereby small objects collapse under their self-gravity which cyclically continues to form larger and more massive objects. The majority of cosmologists favor the Cold Dark Matter theory.

Deconstructionsim (also Deconstruction): A philosophy founded by Jacques Derrida in the 1960s, and based in part on the thoughts of Friedrich Nietzsche, that later took on a variety of meanings. In some interpretations, Deconstructionism (meaning 'to take apart') analyzes and questions the utility of literary works of any kind to ascertain the truth of philosophy, religion or reality generally because words only refer to other words producing only abstract ideas. This is an ongoing process such that there is no final or ultimate meaning to be ascertained. Thus history is always to be subjugated to present time concrete experience which holds more truth.

Deductive: A mental process entailing the use of logic or reasoning to analyze a set of information (often in the form of premises or propositions) from which a conclusion is generated.

Defeater: a line of evidence, argument, hypothesis, or theory that is sufficiently is more compelling than a competing theory.

Deictic: A term of logic to indicate direct proof; to prove directly.

Deism: The belief that the existence of God can be ascertained solely by reason and observation of the natural world. It specifically rejects things of a supernatural nature (e.g., divine Scripture, miracles, personal revelatory experience). Deism generally considers God to be a singular, transcendent Being. See Transcendence entry.

Demiurge: Often affiliated with the Gnostic religious system, the demiurge was a supernatural Being who was responsible for creating the world-universe who is also considered the progenitor of evil. The demiurge was the chief antagonist of a greater Supreme Being. This is also referred to in an earlier form in Platonism where Plato discusses an artificer of the universe.

Denude: To strip or divest of all coverings to become bare or free.

Deposition: Removing a powerful person from a position or office.[1]

Desideratum (pl. Desiderata): Something desired as a necessity.[1]

Dialectic (Dialectical): Any formal system of reasoning that arrives at the truth by the exchange of logical arguments.[1]

Dipolar Theism: The position that a perfect God must be conceived as sometimes opposing and dichotomous terms. For example, the One and the Many, Mutable-Immutable, Simple-Complex, Atemporal-Temporal, and Transcendent-Immanent.

Disabuse: To free someone from deception or an erroneous belief.

Doctrine: A system of beliefs or a body of principles accepted as authoritative, usually formally codified.

Doyen: The most senior, respected, or prominent person in a particular profession.

Dyadic (Dyad): Two items of the same kind.[1]

❦ E ❧

Ecclesiastical: Of or associated with a church (especially a Christian Church).[1]

Ecumenical Council: (early Christian church) one of seven gatherings of bishops from around the known world under the presidency of the Pope to regulate matters of faith and morals and discipline.[1]

Edify: To enlighten the mind (intellect) or character (morality) by instruction.

Emanationisms: A cosmological theory that all things flow from an initial source (often called the Absolute or The One). However, reality has always existed and was not created by the Absolute out of nothingness.

Empiricism: The philosophical doctrine that knowledge is sourced from experience. It is a position within the field of Epistemology (the study of knowledge—see entry) which uses rationalism (an appeal to reasoning faculties) and skepticism (a questioning of the certainty of knowledge). It is often affiliated with scientific introspection as empirical study is a fundamental concept in the scientific method of discovery. Compare Positivism entry.

Encyclical: A letter authored by the Roman Catholic Pope, addressed to all the bishops of the church.

Endogenous: Something synthesized, originating, or derived from within a person, organism, or system.

Endothermic: Of a chemical reaction or compound occurring or formed with absorption of heat.[1] Compare Exothermic entry.

Epic of Gilgamesh: An epic poem written in cuneiform script by the Sumerian peoples of Ancient Mesopotamia (c. early 3rd – late 2nd-century BCE). It is one of the earliest surviving works of literary fiction.

Epigraph: An inscription, especially an engraving on a physical artifact (coin, statue, box, etc.). It also can mean a quotation presented at the introduction of a book or book chapter that is related to the narrative's theme.

Epiphenomenalism: A mind-body philosophical view that mental thoughts do not exist independent of the physical body and that mental thoughts have no causal capacity affect the physical body or other mental thoughts. It is physical events within the body that cause mentation to occur.

Epiphenomenon: A secondary phenomenon that accompanies and is a by-product of another phenomenon.[1] This secondary phenomenon cannot affect the primary phenomenon. As it applies to cognition, see Epiphenomenalism entry.

Epistemology: The philosophy of knowledge which examines the origin, nature, scope, and validity of knowledge with the chief aim to distinguish justified belief from opinion.

Epithet: Any word, phrase or title used to describe an actual or attributed quality of someone or something: "Zeus the god of sky and thunder" is an epithet of Zeus.

Eschatological: Of or relating to or dealing with or regarding the ultimate destiny of mankind and the world.[1]

Eschaton: The final climax event in the divine plan of God; the end of the world. See Apocalypticism entry.

Eternal: The absolute lack of a beginning, end, or sequence. Compare Everlasting entry.

Etiological: Of or relating to the philosophical study of causation.[1]

eV: An abbreviation for electron volt. A unit of energy equal to the work done by an electron accelerated through a potential difference of 1 volt.[1]

Event Horizon: The spherical boundary or surface surrounding a Black Hole (see entry) whereby the gravitational attractional property prevents any matter (light or otherwise) from escaping. It is colloquially termed the point of no return.

Everlasting: The absolute lack of a beginning or end but implies a sequential aspect of time. Compare Eternal entry.

Ex nihilo: (Latin) Meaning "from nothing." See Creatio ex nihilo entry.

Exegesis (or Exegetical): An analytical explanation or interpretation of a text, especially a religious text such as the Bible.

Exigent: Requiring or calling for urgent or immediate action.

Existential Nihilism: The philosophical theory that life is intrinsically senseless and without value and that it is pointless to construct a reality to avoid such a condition. Compare Moral Nihilism entry.

Exothermic: Of a chemical reaction or compound occurring or formed with the liberation of heat. Compare Endothermic entry.[1]

Explanan: Explanations are composed of two parts: the explanandum and the explanans. The explanandum is the proposition, event, or phenomenon that is to be explained. The explanans are the set of statements, propositions, or hypothesis that perform the actual task of explaining. In this book's context, explanans are considered specific evidences.

Extant: Still in existence; not extinct or destroyed or lost.[1]

ೞ F ೲ

Fedora: A hat made of soft felt hat with a curled brim and a lengthwise creased crown.

Fiat: An authoritative command, determination, or decree.

Fideism: See Fideistic Faith entry.

Fideistic Faith: A religious belief system that asserts that its beliefs in God are certain and true and do not require rational justification by appeals to logic, reason, science, or philosophy. It is often an absolutist position ideologically and in practice. Commonly, fideistic faith is fundamentally an incomplete, incoherent, or irrational belief system, even though this may not be discernible because evidence is not forthcoming in response to queries concerning God's existence or nature. Compare Blind Faith entry.

Finger of God Effect: A Redshift (see entry) space distortion. For grouped or clustered galaxies of a similar physical distance from an observer that are in the line of sight, some galaxies will have different redshift values. This makes the galaxies appear elongated when in fact they are the same distance from the observer. This occurs because galaxies have their own velocities relative to each other (called peculiar velocities).

Foment: To incite agitation or excitement, especially as in public opinion.

⚙ G ⚙

Gamma-Ray Burst (GRB): Usually extremely distant and energetic explosions so intense they are, for a few milliseconds to as long as several minutes, the brightest astronomical source of cosmic gamma-ray photons in the observable universe. It is believed that the source of GRBs are rapidly spinning hypernovae (exploding ultra-high mass stars) whose stellar core collapses to become a black hole many times faster than a typical supernova core collapses. This generates a momentary void and the inward swirling and highly magnetically-charged gas becomes so superheated it cannot be contained. The entangled magnetic ropes of energy act like cannons to slingshot bi-directional jets of gas through the poles of the star on the order of a million trillion times brighter than our Sun.

General Relativity Theory: See the end of Special Relativity entry.

Geocentrism: Introduced by Aristotle and expounded on by Claudius Ptolemy, it is the theory that subscribes to the notion that the Earth maintains the preferred location as the center of the universe. This view was also embraced by the Catholic Church's most beloved and respected theologian, St. Thomas Aquinas. It would not be until 1543 CE that Copernicus published his idea that the Sun, not the Earth, was the center of the universe igniting the Copernican Revolution.

Gerrymander: Divide unfairly and to one's advantage.[1]

Gravitational Lensing: The "fabric" of spacetime is sufficiently warped near massive objects (e.g., large galaxies, supermassive black holes, galaxy clusters) that passing electromagnetic rays become bent to follow the underlying geometry. As we observe the incoming light, it creates a lensing effect that distorts, magnifies, and/or splits the background source. When the electromagnetic rays are split with enough intensity, multiple images of the same source are perceived.

Gravitational Redshift: A change in the electromagnetic radiation whereby the frequency is reduced (or conversely the wavelength increased) because the source is within a strong gravitational field and the observer is in a weaker gravitational field. Gravitational redshift is called Einstein Shift (or Einstein Effect) because it is a direct result of Einstein's discovery of gravitationally-induced Time Dilation (see entry) whereby the time passes more slowly nearer the source of a strong gravity field and relatively faster in a weak gravity field. There is also a related phenomenon called Gravitational Blueshift.

∝ H ∾

Hegemony: Dominance, influence, or leadership of or over a group.

Heliosphere: The heliosphere is the roughly spherical region of space surrounding the Sun (and any 'living star') whereby space is influenced by the solar wind and magnetic field. The terminus of the heliosphere is transitional region called the heliopause which separates it from interstellar space.

Hermeneutics: The branch of theology that deals with principles of Exegesis (see Entry), especially as it applies to biblical Scripture. [1]

Hermetic: Completely sealed; completely airtight.[1]

Heterodoxy: Any opinions or doctrines at variance with the official or orthodox position.[1] Compare Orthodoxy entry.

Hierophant: An interpreter, expositor, promoter of sacred mysteries or arcane principles or knowledge.

Historicity: Historical actuality or authenticity.

Homogeneous: Parts, components, elements, or aspect of the same or similar kind or nature.

Homologous: Having a common origin, often in reference to an evolutionary characteristic.

Hot Dark Matter: See Dark Matter entry.

Hyperbolic: an extravagant or exaggerated figure of speech.

Hypostatic union (Hypostasis): The word hypostasis means essential nature or underlying reality. In Christian theology, the hypostatic union is the doctrinal belief that the holy trinity comprised of God, Jesus Christ, and the Holy Spirit is a perfect union. How this union is actually effectuated is called Perichoresis (see entry).

ଓ | ଙ

Iconography: The images and symbolic representations that are traditionally associated with a person or a subject.[1]

Ideogram: A graphic character or symbol that is a representative of an idea directly used in replacement for a word or sound (e.g., the symbology often used for "No Smoking" in the form of a cigarette and a red circle with a red diagonal line).

Ignosticism: The belief that we lack any coherent concept of God regarding his existence and nature. Therefore, it is meaningless to contemplate God in any manner. Ignosticism is generally considered synonymous with Theological Noncognitivism.

Igtheism: Another term of Ignosticism. See entry.

Immanence: The state of being within or not going beyond a given domain.[1] As it pertains to God, this is the philosophical or metaphysical conception that God is manifested inside the world-universe. This manifestation may be as a singular or localized Being, corporeal or incorporeal. It may contrastingly confer that God is globally manifested as all materiality or in some transcendent modality that permits action within the physical world-universe. Compare Transcendence entry.

Immanent: Existing and/or acting within the universe, often considered as pervading and sustaining the universe. See Immanence entry.

Immortal: Not subject to death.[1]

Immutable: Not subject or susceptible to change or variation in form or quality or nature.[1] As it pertains to God, this means that nothing in the natural world can have any effect on God.

Impact Factor: A metric used to rank the frequency articles are cited in scholastic journals. The larger the number, the more often a journal is being cited.

Impassible: As it pertains to God, he is incapable of experiencing pain or to be moved emotionally by others.

Impassive: As it pertains to God, he is unmoved and is without emotion. God is apathetic. Also, the same as Impassible. See entry.

Imprimatur: Usually someone of import who confers an endorsement, approval, or warrant that something meets a good standard.

Impute: To attribute or credit to.[1]

Incarnate: Possessing or existing in bodily form[1] (usually human).

Inculcate: Teach and impress by frequent repetitions or admonitions[1]

Indubitably (indubitable): Too obvious to be doubted;[1] patently evident.

Inductive (Induction): Inductive reasoning utilizes information in the form of analogical examples, personal experiences and observations, facts, and other theories or propositions to reach a conclusion which inherently contains a degree of uncertainty. Thus, one can never be certain whether or not a truth has been elucidated as a result of this process. Mathematical induction can be best appreciated through the use of statistical methods wherein all results are subject to a degree of inaccuracy.

Ineffable (Ineffability): Defying the ability to be expressed or described or something too sacred to be uttered.

Ineluctable: Impossible to avoid or evade[1]; inescapable.

Inerrant: Not liable to error.[1] Biblical inerrancy is the doctrine that religious Scriptures, particularly in the original manuscript form, is free from error of any kind. Some add to this that the Scriptures are also infallible referring to the idea that the no fault can be found in its meaning.

Inimical: Unfriendly, in opposition to, or to be adverse in effect.

Instantiate: To find the instance or evidence to favor a theory, idea, or claim.

Insuperable: Insurmountable; incapable of being surmounted or overcome.

Intelligentsia: Those regarded as, or who regard themselves, to be the intellectual or enlightened elite of a society.

Interlocution: A conversation, discourse, or dialogue.

Interstitial (Interstice): A small structural or physical space between things.

Inveterate: An ingrained or long-established habit.

Ionized Plasma: A gas in which the atoms that have lost all or some of their electrons. Plasma is the most abundant form in the universe barring the potential existence of Dark Matter (see entry). It is highly electrically conductive.

Ipso facto: (Latin) by the fact itself;[1]

Irenic: Aimed at promoting peace; reconciliation.

Irreligion (Irreligious): The absence or indifference to religion; having no adherence to religious beliefs. This circumscribes the group of nontheists which include atheists, agnostics, ignostics, secular humanists, and religious dissenters.

Isotope: One of two or more atoms with the same atomic number but with different numbers of neutrons.[1]

Isotropy: Having the same value when measured in different directions.[1]

Ithyphallic: A statue of a deity, sculpture, carving, or graphic art form depicting an erect penis.

ೞ K ೲ

Kaiser Effect: A related phenomenon to the Finger of God Effect (see entry), but instead of an elongation effect, it is an apparent flattening of the galactic cluster structures along the line of sight. This gives it the name the Pancake of God Effect. This effect is attributed to the coherent, inward-falling motions during cluster formation as they collectively rotate about the cluster's center of rotation.

ೞ L ೲ

Libertine: A dissolute person; usually a man who is morally unrestrained;[1] especially sexually.

Licentious: Lacking moral discipline; especially sexually unrestrained.[1]

Light horizon: Due to the absolute limit of the speed of light two phenomena generate the circumstance that highly distant objects can never be observed from our vantage point (namely, our Earth). *This effectively creates an "edge" or physical barrier that separates the observable and unobservable universe.* As light travels, the signal becomes weaker the further it travels. Over a period of time, the light will become so weak as to be undetectable. A cut-off region of spherical shape is thereby created from the 'seeable' to the 'unseeable'. A second phenomenon is the accelerative expansion of spacetime itself in the past, present, and future. This faster-and-faster expansion of the universe, while very widely accepted as a factual phenomenon, is still at its core a hypothetical phenomenon. Presuming that accelerated cosmic expansion is real, then objects are increasingly separated from one another. Consider and object 'O' existing at two distinct points in time 'A' and 'B', where 'B' occurs a great deal later than 'A'. If at time 'A' the object 'O' is close enough to Earth, that light emitted from 'O' will eventually be detectable, even though this light was transmitted say two billions of years ago. Let's call this time 'C'. Thus, we are seeing the state of this object as it existed 2 billion years ago but we have to wait until time 'C' to acknowledge its existence. Given that spacetime is continually expanding faster and faster, then light essentially 'loses ground'. For every year it travels, spacetime essentially drags the light stream with it making it take longer to reach observation points. Thus, there is a point in time we'll call 'B' at which spacetime has expanded so fast for long enough that the light will never reach Earth. This is a cumulative effect to the first phenomenon. Ultimately, we can be rather certain that the universe is physically larger than what we can empirically determine.

Light-year: A light-year is the distance that light travels in vacuum for the duration of one year. A light-year is about six trillion miles (~9.5 trillion km). The closest star to Earth is Alpha Centauri at 4.4 light-years (excluding the Sun).

Liminal: A position of being at the transitional threshold or boundary of something.

Lithic Technology: Methods to produce tools made from stone; archaeological tool and weapon-making from stone.

Locution: A word or phrase that particular people use in particular situations.[1]

❧ M ☙

Magnum Opus: (Latin) The greatest work or masterpiece, especially of a writer or artist.

Malmquist Bias: The accurate determination of stellar luminosities remains a major challenge in modern astronomy. The Malmquist Bias is due to statistical sampling bias. When astronomers define a group of stars to study, they generally do not want to study all the stars in the group. Instead, they eliminate from the sample those stars whose apparent brightness would characterize them to be more distant. This is the cutoff distance. However, intrinsically brighter objects that are more distant will make it into the sample as well as particularly fainter stars that are closer than the cutoff distance. The statistical properties of the sample will then be something other than what the statistics imply which leads to errors for conclusions based on this data.

Measure Problem: For essentially all cosmologies that include cosmic inflation as a real phenomenon, the multiverse predicts a regime whereby properties and events tend toward infinity in number. This generates a problem when one considers the measurement ratio of one event occurring versus that of another (e.g., infinity divided by infinity). There exist "regularization" hypotheses and the "Causal Diamond" hypothesis that attempt to make these ratios finite but there as yet is no known way to select which of these may be correct.

Measurement Problem: The quantum mechanical issue as to whether and how the wave function of a quantum system collapses (or is reduced). Some quantum theorists posit that there is a process of decoherence and others postulate a physical criterion (an objective collapse). Others say the wave function never collapses and yet other physicists say that there is an "apparent collapse" but it isn't a physically real collapse.

Metaphysics: The branch of philosophy that studies the abstract concepts related to the fundamental nature of reality (Ontology–see entry), the origin of the universe (Cosmogony–see entry), and the nature of knowledge (Epistemology–see entry). This involves answering questions concerning what is reality, what does it mean to know something, how do we know something is true, what is causality, substance, time, and space.

Metastable: (of physical systems) Continuing in its present state of equilibrium unless sufficiently disturbed to pass to a more stable state of equilibrium.[1]

Metastasize: To spread throughout; to grow; to transform.

Milieu: A social environment or cultural setting.

Millenarian Age: An "End of Times" belief where Christ will return in his Second Coming to reign on Earth for a period of one thousand years (hence the reference to "millennia"). Christ will gather the just and send the chosen people's souls and saints to rise into the full glory of God's eternal kingdom and damn the wicked for all eternity.

Monad (Monadic): An indivisible, simple, elementary, irreducible entity, property, or characteristic. For instance, two monadic properties of God are that he is all-knowing and is immaterial (i.e., abstract).

Monolatry: The worship of a single god but without claiming that it is the only god,[1] or acknowledging that other god or god-like beings do exist but are not venerated.

Monotheism: The doctrine or belief that there only one God exists.

Monotonic: Of a sequence or function; consistently increasing and never decreasing or consistently decreasing and never increasing in value.[1]

Moral Nihilism (also Ethical Nihilism): The view that reality is neither intrinsically moral nor immoral. For instance, there is no such thing as "absolute good" and "absolute evil." Such things are the byproducts of cultural norms (i.e., one might adopt relative moralism or the stronger position that morals do not exist at all). Compare Existential Nihilism entry.

Morphodynamic: A process characterized by spontaneous self-organization.

Mosaic Law: The ancient law of the Hebrews, ascribed to Moses, as provided in the Pentateuch. The Pentateuch is the group of five biblical books—Genesis, Exodus, Leviticus, Numbers, and Deuteronomy.

Mulish: Unreasonably rigid in the face of argument or entreaty or attack.[1]

Mysticism: Mysticism is a spiritual belief stating that a connection (union or communion) can be obtained with God or 'spirits' by transcending the physical via thought and meditation. It generally relies on intuitive "knowledge." As mysticism is about experiencing the mysterious, logic cannot be applied, thus, mysticism is an irrational belief.

∝ N ∞

Naturalistic Telos: Natural phenomena that exhibit mechanistic causation in an end-directed process. See Teleology and Telos entries. Compare Transcendental Telos entry.

Necessary: God is a necessary Being because he could not fail to exist as he was needed to create the universe and ostensibly for other divine and naturalistic purposes.

Necropolis: A large tract of land used for burials; a cemetery of an ancient city.

Neolithic: Pertaining to the last phase of the Stone Age (also called the New Stone Age). This time period is marked by the domestication of animals, agricultural crops, and the production of pottery and textiles. The New Stone Age period varied geographically, in some areas of the Middle East it began as early as c. 10,200 BCE and in other parts of the world perhaps as late as 2,000 BCE.

Neologism: The invention or use of new words or introduction of new meanings of previously established words.

Neutrinos: A fundamental particle with no electrical charge and a rest mass close to zero. As a result of these two intrinsic properties, neutrinos seldom interact with normal matter. Neutrinos are known to exist in three states: the electron, muon, and tau neutrino. Each can change into the other two types. A fourth type of neutrino—the sterile neutrino—is theorized to also exist.

Nihilism: An extreme form of skepticism: the denial that there is any formal basis for objective knowledge or truth; a rejection that reality exists. Compare Existential Nihilism and Moral Nihilism entries.

Noetic: Originating with the use of the mind.

Nugatory: Of no real value;[1] inconsequential.

∝ O ∞

Obdurate: Stubbornly persistent in wrongdoing.[1]

Omnibenevolent: A conception of God's Monadic (see entry) property of having unlimited or infinite benevolence (goodwill or love).

Omnipotent: A conception of God's Monadic (see entry) property of having unlimited or infinite power.

Omnipresent: A conception of God's Monadic (see entry) property of being everywhere at the same time.

Omniscient: A conception of God's Monadic (see entry) property of having complete or unlimited awareness, knowledge, or wisdom.

Omnitemporal: A conception of God's Monadic (see entry) property of being existent for all past, present, and future time. According to the characterization of Christian philosopher and theologian William Lane Craig, God existed in two phases. God existed in a timeless phase *prior* to Creation of the universe in which he has no beginning or end and then an omnitemporal phase *upon and after* Creation. Compare Eternal, Everlasting, Timeless, Atemporal entries.

Ontology (Ontological): The domain of metaphysical philosophy that studies the nature and relationships of being, becoming, existence, or reality. To refer to something as ontological is to discuss its quality or status of being real or existent.

Orthodoxy (Orthodoxical): A belief or orientation of conforming to the approved form of any doctrine (especially religious doctrine), philosophy, ideology, etc. See Doctrine entry. Compare Heterodoxy entry.

Orthopraxy: the correctness in following the practices outlined by orthodoxical doctrine. Specifically, it is not to be confused with the orthodoxy of *belief*. Compare Orthodoxy.

Ossuary: Any receptacle for the burial of human bones,[1] usually box-like and manufactured of stone (e.g., chalk, limestone).

☙ P ❧

Paleographer: An archaeologist skilled in paleography, the study of ancient forms of writing and the deciphering of them.[1] The aim is often to date the authorship of manuscripts.

Pancake of God Effect: See Kaiser Effect entry.

Panentheism: A doctrine that conceives God as interpenetrating the universe (i.e., his spirit is everywhere, in everything, and in everyone), but is more and greater than just the universe. Thus, there is a distinction between divine and nondivine. God is the transcendent Creator and an immanent Sustainer of the cosmos. See Immanence, Immanent, Transcendent entries.

Papyrus: Paper made from the papyrus plant by cutting it in strips and pressing it flat; used by ancient Egyptians and Greeks and Romans.[1]

Paragon: A model of excellence or perfection of a kind; one having no equal.[1]

Parahuman: A human-animal hybrid in which physical characteristics of both are apparent.

Paraintellect: The cognitive-based ability to vaguely understand something because only a limited set of consciousness-related faculties are involved, the amount, type, and level of familiarity of knowledge the individual retains, and potentially because the subject matter itself may be abstract or not well understood outside of the individual's own mental faculties.

Pariah: A person who is rejected from society.[1]

Patristic: Of or relating to the writings of the early church fathers.[1]

Pavlovian: Of or relating to Ivan Pavlov or his experiments; "Pavlovian conditioning."[1] Pavlov was a Russian physiologist.

Pedagogue (Pedagoguery): A teacher or educator that is especially a strict, dogmatic, formal, or pedantic. See Pedantic entry.

Pedantic: Marked by a narrow focus on or display of learning especially its trivial aspects.[1]

Peevish: Easily irritated or annoyed.[1] Querulous from being discontented.

Pejorative: Using words of a disparaging or derogatory character.

Pericope (pl. pericopae): A selection or extract from a book, especially the Bible.

Perduring: To continue indefinitely, last permanently, or endure forever.

Peremptory: Peremptory not allowing contradiction or refusal; putting an end to all debate or action.[1]

Perichoresis: A Greek term that describes the relationship between each person of the triune Godhead. The three are indwelling (living as one), co-inhere (share an interpersonal relationship), and experience mutual interpenetration (their essence is the same). The term "circumincession" is also used to convey the same idea. Compare Consubstantiality entry.

Perpetuity: The property of being perpetual. Continuing forever or indefinitely; uninterrupted in time.[1]

Petroglyph: A drawing, inscription, or carving on rock formations/surfaces produced by prehistoric man. The term petroglyph should not be confused with a "petrograph," which is a drawn or painted image on rock surfaces.

Phenomenology: A 20th-century philosophy attributed to initially to Edmund Husserl and expanded upon by Martin Heidegger. It broke into three types: Realist, Transcendental, and Existential Phenomenology. Generally, it is a unique method to explain the nature of human experience through a first person point of view. Thus we give meaning to experiences, objects, events, the flow of time arising from our various aptitudes (e.g., sensory perception, memory, emotion, imagination, language). The description of how this happens is wide-ranging. It essentially describes what and how things achieve meaning, but a chief criticism of Phenomenology is that it does not offer rationale on causal explanations.

Philology: the scientific study of written source materials, especially of a historical nature, to characterize their authenticity and whether they are original or copies. Specifically, its goal is to establish the meaning of the words in the context of the language(s) used and how those words were initially developed and how their use may have evolved.

Pillory: Criticize harshly or violently.[1]

Pithos (pl. Pithoi): A large ceramic earthenware jar or container, often having a wide mouth, used for storage of food, oils, water, or other liquids.

Planck Scale: The point at which measurements of length, time, mass or interactions of gravity, electromagnetism, and strong/weak nuclear forces can no longer be described by classical (non-quantum) approaches.

Plexus: Any arrangement or structure containing an intricate network of elements.

Pneumatology: the study of spiritual beings, especially the theological doctrine concerning the Holy Spirit (or Holy Ghost).

Polemic: Disputing or criticizing beliefs or doctrinal positions by use of writing or speech, often in a harsh manner.

Polymath: A person who has achieved advanced learning in several fields of study.

Polysemism: The ambiguity that exists between multiple religious traditions that have become blended. The blended tradition share two (or more) foundation which share similarities with each individual constituent tradition but also has new differences. The polysemic belief may differ in its use of Scriptures, worship of a deity(ies), or religious rituals performed. Compare Syncretism entry. The main difference between polysemism and syncretism is that the latter specifically involves the merging of traditions that are more unrelated having stronger incompatibility of beliefs.

Polytheism: The doctrine of or belief in multiple gods.

Positivism: A philosophical system that is a strong form of Empiricism (see entry) which views that positive (true) knowledge can only be authoritatively derived by the rational justification evinced exclusively from natural phenomena (science, mathematics, logic, and sensory experience). Positivism rejects metaphysics, theism, revelation, and intuition. This system was founded by French philosopher Auguste Comte.

Prebiotic: Pertaining to the chemical or environmental precursors existing prior to the emergence of life.

Prescient: Perceiving the significance of events before they occur.[1]

Prescind: To isolate, separate, cutoff, terminate or withdraw consideration or attention.

Prevenient grace: A Christian theological concept in which divine grace predisposes people to make a conscious and justified decision to conversion which leads to salvation. Christian denominations are not uniform in the existence and meaning of prevenient grace.

Prima facie: As it seems at first sight;[1] before investigation.

Problem of Evil: The epistemic question of how to reconcile the pervasive existence and enactment of evil and related suffering of human beings with the theistic belief of a perfect God (one that is absolutely or relatively Omnipotent, Omniscient, and Omnibenevolent—see entries). This is sometimes referred to as the Logical Problem of Evil and invariably concerns a discussion on whether there the universe and/or God permits the freedom of choice (i.e., free will) or is deterministic, or some in between conception of the two. Compare Theodicy entry.

Profusion: The property of being extremely abundant.[1]

Prolepsis (Proleptic): The anticipation and act of rebutting objections prior to them being raised.

Propitiate: To make peace with.[1] To conciliate or appease.

Protobiotic: A construct or modality that resembles certain facets of living things but is not necessarily prebiotic itself. It may be a building block or component to prebiotic life. Compare Prebiotic entry.

Provenance: The physical location or source of where something originated.

Pseudepigrapha: Literary works, commonly the ancient noncanonical Jewish and Christian literary texts, which were written Pseudonymously (see entry). That is, the true author is someone other than the claimant author. Some of these are also biblical Apocrypha (see entry) and therefore the words are sometimes used interchangeably. This often creates confusion whether an apocryphal text is also pseudopigraphic. One has to become knowledge of the history of the text to discern this.

Pseudonymous: A literary or written document that is identified by an assumed fictitious name (i.e., a pen name). As it generally applies to ancient texts, it means that the text was written by someone other than the author claiming to have written it.

Psilanthropism: The Christological view that Jesus was entirely human, conceived from human parents. Therefore, Jesus is not divine or the Son of God.

Pugilist: Someone who fights with his fists.[1]

Pugnacious: Easily poised and ready to be argumentative or to engage in a fight.

Pulsar: A highly-magnetized, rapidly rotating neutron star that periodically emits continuous and extremely powerful beams of electromagnetic radiation. Because of the orientation of the beam relative to earthly observers, the beam appears to pulsate in an on-and-off manner as it sweeps into and out of our line of sight. Neutron stars are the smallest and densest stars known to exist in the universe. The gravitational field at the star's surface is on the order of 100 - 200 billion times stronger than on Earth.

Putative: Commonly put forth or accepted as true on inconclusive grounds.[1] Something supposed to be true.

ೞ Q ಹ

Quantize: A reference to Quantum Mechanics (see entry) in which physical things are discretized (separated) into unitary structures.

Quantum Coupling: A physical phenomena in Quantum Mechanics (see entry) whereby two or more quantum systems interact such that the respective quantum states become interdependent. The coupled (entangled) system can only be described by the whole system. Thus, when any physical change occurs to one of the quantum systems, the others instantaneously change in the other bound systems. The Quantum Coupling phenomenon is limited to quantum scales. Compare Quantum nonlocality and entanglement entry.

Quantum Electrodynamics (abbr. QED): The Quantum Field Theory (see entry) that describes electrodynamics—the interactions between light (electromagnetic waves) and matter (specifically, charged fundamental particles, e.g., electrons, positrons). Notably, it is the first theory which achieved full mathematical agreement between Quantum Mechanics and Einstein's Special Relativity Theory (see entry).

Quantum nonlocality and entanglement: The same as Quantum Coupling (see entry) with the exception that this phenomena is theoretically unaffected by the physical distance between the bound quantum systems. Thus, the respective distances can be arbitrarily large.

Quantum Mechanics (abbr. QM): The branch of quantum physics that mathematically describes the motion and interaction of matter at very small physical scales. It presumes that the basic form of matter is comprised of particles. A quantum system is one that is governed by the conceptions of Heisenberg's Uncertainty Principle, Pauli's Exclusion Principle, wave-particle duality, the correspondence principle, and the quantization of energy. In general, it is used to describe a relatively small number of particles. Importantly, it is not reconciled with Special Relativity Theory (see entry).

Quantum Theory: A non-specific term referring to a range of different theories related to Quantum Mechanics, Quantum Field Theory, and Quantum Gravity (see entries) and their underlying principles. Sometimes the term Quantum Theory is used interchangeably with the term Quantum Mechanics.

Quantum Gravity: A general term for theories attempting to explain the gravitational interaction as a quantization of General Relativity Theory in accordance with the principles of Quantum Mechanics (see entry).

Quantum Field Theory (abbr. QFT): There is no canonical definition of what QFT is. In some senses, it is a contemporary extension of Quantum Mechanics (see entry) in which quantum particles are not so much viewed as particulate matter but as energy signatures embedded within an underlying physical field. In contrast to Quantum Mechanics, QFT can be used to analyze large systems of particles. QFT differs from QM in that QFT can be reconciled with Special Relatively Theory (e.g. refer to Quantum Electrodynamics entry).

Quantum State: In the present context of the Meta-Transignification and the Origin of the Universe theory, the quantum state is defined by a Quantum Wave Function (see entry) describing information for all of reality. Generally, a quantum state is a quantum system describable by quantum numbers and a specific energy level.

Quantum Tunneling: A quantum mechanical phenomenon whereby a particle is able to transition through energy states that are not permissible under classical physics. In this way, the particle is said to have tunneled through a barrier.

Quantum Wave Function: A complete mathematical description of a Quantum State (see entry). According to the superposition principle, wave functions can be added and multiplied together. Wave functions have eigenstates which are coexistent and represent the permissible energy states of a quantum system. It is thought that when the act of measurement of physical properties (e.g., momentum, spin, position) is undertaken by an observer, there is an as yet to be understood mechanism which causes the wave function to 'collapse' or 'reduce' to a single eigenstate from the many coexistent eigenstates. It is not agreed that wave function collapse is a real phenomenon.

Quark: An elementary particle of matter. Composite particles such as protons and neutrons are constituted through the combination of quarks. Composite particles made of quarkian matter are called hadrons of which there are two types—baryons and mesons.

Quasar: A shortening of the words quasi-stellar radio sources. A term that refers to the phenomena of Active Galactic Nuclei that consist of the region of space surrounding the supermassive black holes found to exist in many galaxies. Quasars are among the most energetic and luminous structures in the entire universe, powered by the accretion of material influenced by the presence of the black hole.

Quintessence: In cosmology, it is a scalar field that acts as an anti-gravity phenomena pushing outwardly in spacetime. It is the underlying explanation for the accelerative expansion of spacetime due to Dark Energy (see entry). However, in contrast to a constant value of the Cosmological Constant (see entry), it espouses that the value has changed over the course of cosmic time; hence it is differentiated by calling it Dynamical Dark Energy. Compare Cosmological Constant entry.

Quixotic: Unrealistic; impractical.

Quotidian: Found in the ordinary course of events.[1]

෫ R ഔ

Radical: Arising from or going to the root.[1]

Rampart: A fortification used for defensive barrier.

Recondite: Difficult to penetrate; incomprehensible to one of ordinary understanding or knowledge.[1]

Redaction: To revise or edit a literary work.

Redshift: An increase in wavelength with a corresponding decrease in frequency in electromagnetic waves. There are three types of redshift. One is called Doppler Redshift and is affiliated with the relative motion of an object moving away from another (as in the Earth). The other is called Cosmological Redshift which is caused by the fact that light travels upon the expanding cosmic fabric of spacetime. Unfortunately, in the literature, the two are seldom made distinct. Hubble's Law (as in Hubble Flow) is based upon cosmological redshift. The third type is Gravitational Redshift (see entry). Also, compare Blueshift entry.

Reductionism: A theory that all complex systems can be completely understood in terms of their components.[1]

Reify: To consider an abstract concept to be real.[1]

Relativism: The philosophical doctrine that all criteria of judgment are relative to the individuals, language, culture, and situations involved.[1] Relativism holds that there are no absolute truths.

Religious Exclusivism: A doctrine that claims that only one particular religion, generally the claimants, is authentically true.

Reliquary: A storage container or receptacle for religious relics.

Repose: A disposition of having the sensation or experience of peacefulness; tranquility.

Rest mass: The observed mass of a physical body of matter that is not moving with respect to the observer. In Newtonian mechanics, this is the usual mass value we measure. However, in Einsteinian relativity, the rest mass of a body can differ from the same mass when in motion. The rest mass is also called by other names—invariant mass, intrinsic mass, or proper mass.

Riposte: A quick reply to a question or remark, especially a witty or critical one.[1]

RNA: Ribonucleic acid (RNA) is a biological molecule. It plays a central role in coding/decoding genes and whether the genes are expressed or suppressed.

Roman Prefect: An appointed magistrate of ancient Rome conferring to the individual authority over military and civil governance matters.

᎛ S ᏂᎨ

Salvific: Intending to admit to salvation;[1] redemptive power.

Secular humanism: A philosophical position that rejects the use of religious dogma or supernaturalism as the foundational basis for morality and its attendant application to personal and societal decision-making.

Semiotics: The discipline of studying signs, symbols, and signification and how meaning is created. A related discipline is biosemiotics which is the study of the same phenomena applied to biological systems.

Serology: Dealing with serums; commonly blood serums; especially associated with diagnostics thereof.

Shaman: A person who is said to be empowered with the ability to transact between the visible and spirit worlds. Shamanism is frequently associated with sorcery and practiced by tribal groups.

Sharia law: The moral code and religious canon law derived from Koranic (Qur'anic) Scripture. It generally describes responsibilities and penalties for members of the Islamic faith. Human interpretations and strictness of sharia vary between Islamic sects.

Simplism: An act of excessive simplification; the act of making something seem simpler than it really is[1] by ignoring complicating factors.

Singularity: A hypothetical phenomena whereby the geometric structure of spacetime is over-stretched or over-compacted whereby the localized volume becomes infinitesimally small and the mass density becomes infinitely large. Mathematically, the geometry of spacetime becomes undifferentiable (i.e., it does not exist).

Sisyphus: Sisyphus, king of Ephyra, was a conniving, greedy, and murderous man. He was punished with an eternal task by the Greek god Zeus by being compelled to roll an immense enchanted boulder up a hill. As Sisyphus reached the top, the rock would roll back down hill.

Socratic method: A method of teaching by question and answer; used by Socrates to elicit truths from his students.[1] The technique aims to identify hypotheses that contradictory or false to incrementally move toward the best hypothesis.

Sonorific: A characteristically deep or full sound; a sound so loud it is imposing.

Sophistry (Sophism): a deliberately invalid argument displaying ingenuity in reasoning in the hope of deceiving someone.[1]

Soteriology: The theological doctrine that deals with the concept of post-life salvation resulting from the authorship of a divine source. Christian theology maintains that personal salvation is given by the grace of God.

Spacetime: Also called the spacetime continuum. The four-dimensional continuum is constituted by three spatial coordinates and one temporal coordinate. It is the underlayment of nature and all physical events and all physical quantities are realized.

Special Relativity Theory: Einstein presented his paper entitled *On the Electrodynamics of Moving Bodies* in 1905. This became to be called Special Relativity Theory. It mathematically describes the relationships between cosmic space and natural time under certain special conditions. The conditional assumptions are that there exist uniform frames of reference which are stationary or in constant motion, but never accelerating. This is to say that the frames of reference are inertial. It is further assumed that these frames of reference are flat (i.e., non-curved). The outcome is that the laws of physics are invariant (identical) and quantities such as speed, distance, and time is relative for all observers with the lone of exception of the speed of electromagnetic radiation (e.g., visible light) in vacuum which is identically the same everywhere. Einstein's other theory of General Relativity, published in 1915, addresses nonuniform frames of reference.

Subsume: To incorporate an idea as a subordinate or component element under a more comprehensive context.

Supraluminal: Referring to a speed in excess of the speed of electromagnetic radiation (e.g., light) in vacuum.

Supernal: Something existent, belonging to, or emanating from heaven (e.g., happiness, punishment, spirits).

Supervene: To come after a prior event or action.

Surfeit: The state of being more than full;[1] overindulgence; overabundant.

Syllogism: A formal logical argument consisting of two premises and a conclusion. If both premises are true, then the conclusion must also be true.

Syncretism (Syncretic, Syncretistic): The merger or unification of different religious belief systems, particularly theological, mystical, or mythological tenants that are contradictory, that effectively create a unique religious belief system. Compare Polysemism entry.

Synod: A Christian church council convened to discuss ecclesiastical business.[1]

Synoptic Gospels: The biblical Gospels of Matthew, Mark and Luke, which describe the events of Christ's life using a similar literary style and purpose.

Systematic theology: The discipline to formulate a theological system of belief in a categorical, coherent, and rational manner. This works hand-in-hand to undergird religious doctrine.

≈ T ≈

Tautology: A repetitive statement or two or more ideas in which the second statement imparts no additional clarity. In formal logic it is a proposition that is necessarily true by definition. For instance, "The Earth is round in shape or it is not round." Such a statement requires no empirical testing to validate its truth value.

Teleology (teleological): The philosophical doctrine that asserts that phenomena are designed or intrinsically imbued with end-directed purpose(s). One can distinguish between Naturalistic Telos and Transcendental Telos (see respective entries). Also see Telos entry.

Tellurian: Of or relating to or inhabiting the land or the Earth.[1]

Telos: (Latin) The ultimate aim of a goal-directed process; often affiliated with Aristotle.

Theism: The doctrine or belief in the existence of a God or gods.[1]

Theistic mysticism: The theory of the unknowable nature, or mysteries, pertaining to God.

Theocracy: A political unit governed by a deity (or by officials thought to be divinely guided).[1]

Theodicy: The theological defense of the attributes of God, especially his goodness, justness, and omnipotence, given the manifestation of physical and moral evil.

Theonym: The proper name of a deity as it pertains to a given theological belief system.

Theophany (Theophanic): A visible (but not necessarily material) manifestation of a deity to a human person.[1]

Theriomorphism: The use of animal characteristics to describe deities or supernatural beings.

Thermodynamic: Thermodynamics is the domains of physics that studies and describes the physical properties of heat and temperature and their relation to energy and how changes in energy affect the internal (to the system) environment and the external environment. It is often defined by macroscopic properties such as internal energy and entropy but can also be describe the behavior of a system from a statistical point of view.

Timeless (or Timelessness): Unaffected by time. A hypothetical property of reality wherein the natural property of time does not exist. Compare Eternity, Everlasting, and Omnitemporal entries.

Time dilation: A principle of the theory of relativity which predicts that time intervals (that is, elapsed time) will differ between two observers if they are moving relative to each other or if they are stationed differently from a gravitational source mass such that the strength (induced by the curvature of spacetime) is different. The latter is sometimes referred to as gravitational time dilation. The elapsed time will be shorter (i.e., time slows) for the observer who is moving faster or for the observer located closer to the gravitation potential where the gravitational effects are stronger.

Topology: The structure of how contiguously connected constituent parts are arranged.

Totemism: An animistic system of belief in which humans are able to be mystically or spiritually connected to animals or plants.

Tractate: A short treatise or essay.

Transcategorical: An idea associated chiefly with Pluralism that suggests Ultimate Reality is completely transcendent and the divine is unknowable. A sense of God is only accessible through metaphor or narrative.

Transcendent: As it pertains to God, transcendence is any phenomenon—a thing, an object, a process, an abstraction—real or imagined—that is beyond the current (and probably future) perceptive or cognitive abilities of humans to detect or know directly or indirectly its existence.

Transcendental Telos: Phenomena that would be attributed to some otherworldly (divine) cause that is in some way coaxing the causal chain of natural events toward some final end. See Teleology and Telos entries. Compare Naturalistic Telos entry.

Transubstantiation: An act that changes the form or character or substance of something. The Roman Catholic doctrine that the whole substance of the bread and the wine changes into the substance of the body and blood of Christ when consecrated in the Eucharist.[1]

Triune: Being three in one.[1] In Christianity, it is view of the Holy Trinity—Father, Son, and Holy Spirit—as unity.

Troika: An association of three things (i.e., a triumvirate) that coordinate their actions in order to influence something.

Tutelary: Providing protective supervision or guardianship; watching over or safeguarding.[1]

♂ U ♀

Ubiety: The state of existing and being localized in space.[1]

Uncertainty Principle (Heisenberg Uncertainty Principle): The indeterminacy principle of quantum theory discovered by Werner Heisenberg. Because of the intrinsic probabilistic nature of reality at the quantum scale, there is a fundamental limit to the precision of measurement of physical properties.

Unchangeable: Nothing in the universe can affect; forever constant.

Unicity: The state of unification of an entity to be comprised as a whole.

Unprovenanced: An undetermined or unknown source of origin; lacking in provenance.

❧ V ❧

Vacuum Energy: Sometimes referred to as Zero-Point Energy because it the lowest energy (or ground) state of a quantum system. It pervades the entire universe and at any given location in space it is the ground state of all existent fields (e.g., electromagnetic field, Higgs field). There is no agreement on how much total energy exists in the universe ranging from exactly zero to infinity. Vacuum energy exists as a direct consequence of the Uncertainty Principle (see entry). Some physicists believe that a contributing source to vacuum energy is virtual particles that are perpetually blinking into and out of existence in exceptionally short time intervals. Some physicists believe that vacuum energy is the source of Cosmological Constant & Dark Energy.

Variegated: Make something more diverse and varied.[1]

Vassal: a person (or country) who owes allegiance and service to a feudal lord.[1]

Vedic: Of or relating to the Hindu Vedas or to the ancient Sanskrit language of India in which they were written.[1]

Veridicality: Something that appears to be true because of its correspondence with the facts.

Verisimilitude: The appearance of truth; the quality of seeming to be true.[1]

Vitiate: To make imperfect[1] or less effective.

❧ W ❧

Wahhabism: A conservative and intolerant form of Islam[1] chiefly associated with Sunnism.

Whorls: A pattern of spirals or concentric circles as found in a fingerprint. Compare Arches entry.

❧ Z ❧

Zeteo Alétheia: (Greek) To seek or strive to find by thinking or reasoning the truth (of reality).

Zetetic: The process of seeking or proceeding by inquiry; investigating; as in the truth of reality. It is a blended translation from Greek to English of the two words Zeteo and Alétheia.

Zygon: The harnessing of religion and science as a means to unify our understanding toward an ultimate meaning.

WORKS CITED

Introduction

1. ARDA, *U.S. Congregational Membership: County Reports (1980 Report)*, The Association of Religion Data Archives, 1980, Accessed 24 May 2016, http://www.thearda.com/RCMS2010/selectCounty.asp.

Chapter 1

1. Einstein, A., *Albert Einstein, The Human Side: Glimpses from His Archives*, Eds. Dukas and Hoffmann, Princeton University Press, 2013, No., p. 18: Original Pub. 1979, ISBN 978-0691160238, **Notes:** Copyright © 1982 The Hebrew University of Jerusalem. Reprinted by permission.

2. Einstein, A., *The World As I See It*, Citadel Press / Kensington Publishing Corp., 2006, No., pp. 7-8, ISBN 978-0806527901.

3. Baltasar Gracián y Morales, *The Art of Wordly Wisdom (Oráculo manual y arte de prudencia)*, London and New York, Macmillian and Co., Ltd, 1647; Translation 1892, No., p. 86, Trans. by Jacobs, https://archive.org/details/artworldlywisd001jacogoog, **Notes:** See aphorism entitled, "cxlvi *Look into the Interior of Things.*" The page number (p. 86) refers to the PDF copy (see URL). In the Public Domain.

4. Lemaître, G., *The Beginning of the World from the Point of View of Quantum Theory*, Nature, 9 May 1931, No 127, p. 706, DOI: 10.1038/127706b0.

5. Sarma, K.V., *Acyuta Pisārati*, in Book: Encyclopaedia of the History of Science, Technology, and Medicine in Non-Western Cultures, Ed. Selin, Springer, 2007, Vol. 1 (A-K), No., pp. 317-320, ISBN 978-1402045592, See Also: http://dx.doi.org/10.1007/978-1-4020-4425-0_9546, **Notes:** Refer to p. 317, second column.

6. Swami Nikhilananda, *The Upanishads: Aitareya and Brihadaranyaka*, New York City, New York, Harper & Brothers, 1956, Vol 3 of 4, No., p. 215, Trans. by Nikhilananda, ISBN 0-91120617-5.

7. Aschwanden, C., *The Irrationalist in You*, Discover Magazine (Special Issue: The Science You Don't See), Vol 36, No 6, pp. 46-49, Kalmbach Publishing Co., ISSN 0274-7529, http://discovermagazine.com/2015/july-aug.

8. Paine, T., *The Political Writings of Thomas Paine*, Printed and published by G. Davidson, 1830, Vol 2 of 2, No., p. 284.

9. Pope John Paul II, *Encylical Letter, Fides et Ratio, Of the Supreme Pontiff John Paul II to the Bishops of the Catholic Church on the Relationship Between Faith and Reason*, Libreria Editrice Vaticana (*trans.* The Vatican Publishing House), 14 September 1998, Accessed 13 Sep 2014, http://tinyurl.com/qfqndk3.

10. Aquinas, T., *Summa Theologica - Part I (Prima Pars). From the Complete American Edition*, The Project Gutenberg, 1265-1274, Series Ed(s). Perry and McClamrock, http://www.gutenberg.org/ebooks/17611, **Notes:** Refer to Part 1, Question 12, Article 13.

11. Aquinas, T., *Summa Theologica - Part II-II (Secunda Secundae)*. *Translated by Fathers of the English Dominican Province*, The Project Gutenberg, 1265-1274, Series Ed(s). Perry and McClamrock, http://www.gutenberg.org/ebooks/18755, **Notes:** Refer to Part II-II, Question 2, Article 1. Originally sourced from: http://en.wikipedia.org/wiki/Faith_and_rationality#cite_note-8/. Note that this Wikipedia source is a paraphrasing and not an exact quote.

12. Grassie, W., *The New Sciences of Religion: Exploring Spirituality from the Outside In and Bottom Up*, New York, NY, Palgrave Macmillan, 2010, No., p. 6, ISBN 978-0230108776, **Notes:** "God-by-whatever-name", first referenced on P. 22. Reproduced with permission of Palgrave Macmillan.

13. Pope John Paul II, *Letter of His Holiness John Paul II to Reverend George V. Coyne, S. J. Director of the Vatican Observatory*, 1987, http://tinyurl.com/ouxn3ht, **Notes:** Published as the preface to the papers from the Study Week at Castel Gandolfo, Sept. 21-26, 1987. Reprinted with permission. Libreria Editrice Vaticana.

14. Campbell, J., *The Hero with a Thousand Faces (The Collected Works of Joseph Campbell)*, 3rd ed., Novato, CA, New World Library, 2008, No., pp. 133-134, ISBN 978-1577315933.

15. Johnson, T.M. and B.J. Grim, *The World's Religions in Figures: An Introduction to International Religious Demography*, 1st ed., Wiley-Blackwell, 2013, No., p. 9, ISBN 978-0470674543.

16. Baylor University, *The Baylor Religion Survey, Wave II*, 2007, Baylor Institute for Studies of Religion, Waco, TX.

17. Lugo, L., et al., *Faith in Flux: Changes in Religious Affiliation in the U.S.*, 2009, Pew Research Center, p. 3, Pew Research Center's Forum on Religion & Public Life, http://www.pewforum.org/, **Notes:** The study margin of error for this statistic was 44 ±0.6%.

18. Bengston, V.L., N.M. Putney, and S. Harris, *Families and Faith: How Religion is Passed Down across Generations*, Oxford University Press, 2013, No., p. 57, ISBN 978-0199948659.

19. Lugo, L., et al., *Faith in Flux: Changes in Religious Affiliation in the U.S.*, 2009, Pew Research Center, p. 13, Pew Research Center's Forum on Religion & Public Life, http://www.pewforum.org/, **Notes:** Refer to Table entitled, "Views of Religion and Becoming Unaffiliated". The reported margin of error was 75 ±6.5% and 66 ±6.5%, respectively. The margin of error for those who believe that modern science proves religion is superstition was not reported but can be reasonably estimated to be between 32 ±6.0% and 32 ±8.0%.

20. Lugo, L., et al., *"Nones" on the Rise: One-in-Five Adults Have No Religious Affiliation*, 2012, Pew Research Center, p. 13, Pew Research Center's Forum on Religion & Public Life, http://www.pewforum.org/, **Notes:** The sample populations for 2007 and 2012 were 9,443 and 17,010, respectively.

21. Lugo, L., et al., *"Nones" on the Rise: One-in-Five Adults Have No Religious Affiliation*, 2012, Pew Research Center, p. 42, Pew Research Center's Forum on Religion & Public Life, http://www.pewforum.org/, **Notes:** Aggregated data. No statistical information reported.

22. Lugo, L., et al., *"Nones" on the Rise: One-in-Five Adults Have No Religious Affiliation*, 2012, Pew Research Center, p. 48, Pew Research Center's Forum on Religion & Public Life, http://www.pewforum.org/, **Notes:** The sample size was 631 individuals.

23. Cooperman, A., G. Smith, and K. Ritchey, *America's Changing Religious Landscape: Christians Decline Sharply as Share of Population; Unaffiliated and Other Faiths Continue to Grow*, 2015, Pew Research Center, pp. 3-4, http://www.pewforum.org/files/2015/05/RLS-05-08-full-report.pdf.

24. Robert J. Barro, J.H., *Religious Conversion in 40 Countries*, National Bureau of Economic Research, 2007, DOI: 10.3386/w13689, http://www.nber.org/papers/w13689, **Notes:** The graphic was produced using data from Table 2, pp. 33-34.

25. Johnson, T.M. and B.J. Grim, *The World's Religions in Figures: An Introduction to International Religious Demography*, 1st ed., Wiley-Blackwell, 2013, No., p. 10, ISBN 978-0470674543, **Notes:** Refer to Table 1.1 entitled, "World religions by adherents, 1910-2010". See the fifth column heading "% 2010". The source database is the World Religion Database (Leiden/Boston: Brill).

26. Altemeyer, B. and B. Hunsberger, *Amazing conversions: Why some turn to faith and others abandon religion.*, Amherst, NY, Prometheus Books, 1997, No., ISBN (ASIN) B00ZLW7Z7S.

27. Hunsberger, B., *Swimming against the current: Exceptional cases of apostates and converts.*, in Book: Joining and leaving religion: Research perspectives, Eds. Francis and Katz, Leominster, England, Gracewing, 2000, No., pp. 233-248, ISBN 978-0852445174.

28. Berger, P.L., *The Sacred Canopy: Elements of a Sociological Theory of Religion*, New York, NY, Anchor Books/Doubleday, 1990, No., p. 107, ISBN 978-0385073059.

29. ARDA, *Secularization Theory*, The Association of Religion Data Archives, Accessed 20 Jan 2014, http://wiki.thearda.com/tcm/theories/secularization/.

30. Lambert, Y., *A Turning Point in Religious Evolution in Europe*, Journal of Contemporary Religion 2004, Vol 19, No 1, pp. 29-45.

31. Gorski, P.S., *Remaking Modernity*, in Book: The Return of the Repressed: Religion and the Political Unconscious of Historical Sociology, Series Ed(s). Adams, Clemens, and Orloff, Durham, NC, Duke University Press, 2005, No., pp. 161-189, ISBN 978-0822333630, **Notes:** Refer to p. 180.

32. Boeve, L., *Negative Theology and Theological Hermeneutics: The Particularlity of Naming God*, Journal of Philosophy & Scripture, 2006, Vol 3, No 2 (Spring), pp. 1-13, ISSN 1555-5100, http://www.philosophyandscripture.org/Issue3-2/Boeve/Boeve2.html, **Notes:** Quote is on p.1 and p.2, respectively. This article was originally pre-published by the Journal of Philosophy & Scripture. The copyright owner (Mohr Siebeck) later published the article in a book entitled *Gott Nennen: Gottes Namen und Gott als Name*, eds. Dalferth and Stoellger, 2008, Mohr Siebeck. Reproduced with permission of copyright owner Mohr Siebeck Tübingen.

33. Boeve, L., *Negative Theology and Theological Hermeneutics. The Particularity of Naming God*, in Book: Gott Nennen: Gottes Namen und Gott als Name (trans. God Name: God Name and God as Name), Eds. Dalferth and Stoellger, Mohr Siebeck, 2008, No., pp. 189-207, ISBN 978-3161497926, **Notes:** Quotes are to be found on p.190 and p. 191. Article is published in English. Book content is generally in German. Reproduced with permission of copyright owner Mohr Siebeck Tübingen.

34. Lugo, L., *et al.*, *"Nones" on the Rise: One-in-Five Adults Have No Religious Affiliation*, 2012, Pew Research Center, p. 56, Pew Research Center's Forum on Religion & Public Life, http://www.pewforum.org/, **Notes:** The total sample size was 2,973 individuals. The reported margin of error for the total population was ±2.1% . The margin of error was ±6.3% for Atheist/Agnostic (n=327) and ±4.5% for "Nothing in particular" (n=631).

35. Smith, D., *Discovery: Nearby star hosts closest alien planet in the "habitable zone"*, University of New South Wales, 16 Dec 2015, Accessed 28 Feb 2016, https://www.science.unsw.edu.au/news/discovery-nearby-star-hosts-closest-alien-planet-in-habitable-zone, **Notes:** The paper supporting this news articles can be found here: http://newt.phys.unsw.edu.au/~duncanw/Wolf1061.pdf.

36. Wright, D.J., *et al.*, *Three Planets Orbiting Wolf 1061*, The Astrophysical Journal Letters, 2016, Vol 817, No 2, p. L20, ISSN 2041-8205, http://stacks.iop.org/2041-8205/817/i=2/a=L20.

37. Lendon, B., *Tens of billions of planets out there are like Earth, study finds*, CNN, 2013, Accessed 05 Nov 2013, http://www.cnn.com/2013/11/05/tech/innovation/billions-of-planets/.

38. Petigura, E.A., A.W. Howard, and G.W. Marcy, *Prevalence of Earth-size planets orbiting Sun-like stars*, Proceedings of the National Academy of Sciences, 4 Nov 2013, DOI: 10.1073/pnas.1319909110, http://www.pnas.org/content/early/2013/10/31/1319909110.abstract, **Notes:** This journal paper does not explicitly state that there are tens of billions of planets in the Milky Way Galaxy, but it can be inferred using computational techniques broadly outlined in the CNN article (Lendon, B., *"Tens of billions of planets out there are like Earth, study finds"*, 05 Nov 2013, http://www.cnn.com/2013/11/05/tech/innovation/billions-of-planets/).

39. Daily Galaxy, *500 Billion --A Universe of Galaxies: Some Older than Milky Way*, The Daily Galaxy via Cfa and ESA/Hubble Information Center, 2013, Accessed 5 Nov 2013, http://tinyurl.com/ka9ug65.

40. Campbell, J., *The Hero with a Thousand Faces (The Collected Works of Joseph Campbell)*, 3rd ed., Novato, CA, New World Library, 2008, No., p. 101, ISBN 978-1577315933.

41. Behroozi, P. and M.S. Peeples, *On the history and future of cosmic planet formation*, Monthly Notices of the Royal Astronomical Society, Vol 454, No 2, 1 Dec 2015, pp. 1811-1817, DOI: 10.1093/mnras/stv1817, http://mnras.oxfordjournals.org/content/454/2/1811.abstract.

42. Daily Galaxy, *30 Supernovas Per Second in the Universe*, The Daily Galaxy via University of Colorado at Boulder, 2013, Accessed 19 May 2016, http://tinyurl.com/nstav29.

43. Mora, C., *et al.*, *How Many Species Are There on Earth and in the Ocean?*, 2011, PLOS Biology, DOI: 10.1371/journal.pbio.1001127, http://journals.plos.org/plosbiology/article?id=10.1371/journal.pbio.1001127.

44. Behroozi, P. and M.S. Peeples, *On the history and future of cosmic planet formation*, Monthly Notices of the Royal Astronomical Society, Vol 454, No 2, 1 Dec 2015, p. 1813, DOI: 10.1093/mnras/stv1817, http://mnras.oxfordjournals.org/content/454/2/1811.abstract.

45. Wooden, C., *Homily by Pope Francis at Papal Mass*, Catholic News Service/USCCB, 22 Oct 2013, http://tinyurl.com/jmg5ajg. Also See: http://www.catholicnews.com/data/stories/cns/1304440.htm.

46. Christian Web Foundation, Accessed 04 Jun 2016, http://www.theopedia.com/Knowability_of_God.

47. Public Religion Research Institute, *Half of American Fans See Supernatural Forces at Play in Sports*, 16 Jan 2014, Accessed 28 June 2014, http://publicreligion.org/research/2014/01/jan-2014-sports-poll/, **Notes:** Number polled: 1,011. Poll taken January 8-12 2014. Margin of error is +/- 3.1 percent at 95% confidence level.

48. Public Religion Research Institute, *Nearly 3-in-10 Americans Say God Plays a Role in Outcomes of Sports Events*, 29 Jan 2013, Accessed 28 June 2014, http://publicreligion.org/research/2013/01/january-2013-tracking-poll-2/, **Notes:** Number polled: 1,033. Poll taken 16-20 Jan. 2013.

49. Newberg, A.B., *Principles of Neurotheology*, Ashgate Publishing Limited, 2010, No., p. 218, ISBN 978-0754669944.

50. Glanzberg, M., *"Truth"*, The Stanford Encyclopedia of Philosophy (Fall 2014 Edition), Series Ed(s). Zalta, Accessed 18 Sep 2014, http://plato.stanford.edu/archives/fall2014/entries/truth/.

51. Wikipedia contributors, *Criteria of truth*, Wikipedia, The Free Encyclopedia, Accessed 25 Nov 2015, https://en.wikipedia.org/wiki/Criteria_of_truth.

52. Wikipedia contributors, *Correspondence theory of truth*, Wikipedia, The Free Encyclopedia, Accessed 25 Nov 2015, https://en.wikipedia.org/wiki/Correspondence_theory_of_truth.

53. Sahakian, W.S. and M.L. Sahakian, *Ideas of the Great Philosophers*, Barnes & Noble, 1993, No., p. 8, ISBN 978-1566192712, **Notes:** Originally sourced from https://en.wikipedia.org/wiki/Criteria_of_truth. Refer to section entitled, "Correspondence", Footnotes 1 and 8. Accessed 18 Sep 2014.

54. Wikipedia contributors, *Coherence theory of truth*, Wikipedia, The Free Encyclopedia, Accessed 25 Nov 2015, https://en.wikipedia.org/wiki/Coherence_theory_of_truth.

55. Carroll, L., *Alice's Adventures in Wonderland*, The Project Gutenberg, Series Ed(s). Arthur DiBianca, Accessed 19 Sep 2014, http://www.gutenberg.org/ebooks/11/, **Notes:** See Chapter VII: A Mad Tea-Party. Copyright has expired.

56. Young, J.O., *"The Coherence Theory of Truth"*, *The Stanford Encyclopedia of Philosophy (Summer 2013 Edition)*, Series Ed(s). Zalta, Accessed 18 Sep 2014, http://plato.stanford.edu/archives/sum2013/entries/truth-coherence/.

57. Vatican Secret Archive, Accessed 4 Feb 2014, http://www.archiviosegretovaticano.va/content/archiviosegretovaticano/en/l_archivio.html.

58. Vatican Library, *Vatican Library History*, Accessed 25 Nov 2015, https://www.vatlib.it/home.php?pag=storia.

59. Campbell, J., *The Hero with a Thousand Faces (The Collected Works of Joseph Campbell)*, 3rd ed., Novato, CA, New World Library, 2008, No., p. 23, ISBN 978-1577315933, **Notes:** For quote, see inset image (page center).

60. Tingley, K., *Greater Than We Seem*, Theosophical University Press, Nov 1952, Series Title: Sunrise Magazine, Accessed 04 Aug 2014, **Notes:** Refer to Volume 2. No longer in print. The essay can be accessed at the following web address: http://tinyurl.com/jmg5ajg.

61. Doyle, A.C., *The Complete Sherlock Holmes*, Series Title: Knickerbocker Classics, Race Point Publishing, 2013, p. 17, ISBN 978-1937994303, Notes: From *A Study in Scarlet*, Part I, Ch. III. First published in the magazine entitled *Beeton's Christmas Annual* (November, 1887). It is distinguished as the first story in which the characters of Sherlock Holmes and Dr. John H. Watson are introduced. Copyright expired. In the public domain.

62. Conselice, C.J., et al., *The Evolution of Galaxy Number Density at z < 8 and its Implications*, arXiv.org, 09 Oct 2016, https://arxiv.org/abs/1607.03909, **Notes:** The paper has been accepted for publication in The Astrophysical Journal.

63. Atran, S., et al., *The devoted actor's will to fight and the spiritual dimension of human conflict*, Nature Human Behaviour, 2017, Vol 1, No 9, 09 Sept 2017, pp. 673-679, ISSN 2397-3374, DOI: 10.1038/s41562-017-0193-3, https://doi.org/10.1038/s41562-017-0193-3.

Chapter 2

1. Einstein, A., *The World As I See It*, Citadel Press / Kensington Publishing Corp., 2006, pp. 7-8, ISBN 978-0806527901.

2. Pope John Paul II, *Apostolic Journey to Ireland, Holy Mass in Drogheda, Homily of His Holiness John Paul II*, Libreria Editrice Vaticana (*trans.* The Vatican Publishing House), 29 September 1979, Accessed 02 June 2014, http://tinyurl.com/zpn7tt8, **Notes:** Reprinted with permission. Libreria Editrice Vaticana.

3. Toft, M.D., *Religion, Civil War, and International Order: BCSIA Discussion Paper 2006-03, Kennedy School of Government*, Belfer Center for Science and International Affairs (Harvard University), 2006, p. 9.

4. Lord Tennyson, A., *Idylls of the King: The Last Tournament*, 1871

5. Spilka, B., *et al.*, *The Psychology of Religion: An Empirical Approach*, 3rd ed., New York, NY, The Guilford Press, 2003, p. 45, ISBN 978-1572309012.

6. Pew Research Center, *Eastern, New Age Beliefs Widespread: Many Americans Mix Multiple Faiths*, 2009, p. 19, http://www.pewforum.org/, **Notes:** Refer to Question Q.291b, p. 19. Also refer to table, "Supernatural Experiences and Beliefs", p. 2.

7. Pew Research Center, *Eastern, New Age Beliefs Widespread: Many Americans Mix Multiple Faiths*, 2009, pp. 1-2, Pew Research Center's Forum on Religion & Public Life, http://www.pewforum.org/, **Notes:** The reported margin of error was ±2.5% (n=2,003).

8. Cooperman, A., G. Smith, and K. Ritchey, *America's Changing Religious Landscape: Christians Decline Sharply as Share of Population; Unaffiliated and Other Faiths Continue to Grow*, 2015, Pew Research Center's Forum on Religion & Public Life, p. 4, http://www.pewforum.org/2015/05/12/americas-changing-religious-landscape/, **Notes:** Refer to Table entitled, "Christians Decline as Share of U.S. Population; Other Faiths and the Unaffiliated Are Growing". Data utilized is from Year 2014.

9. Heath, E.A., *The Mystic Way of Evangelism: A Contemplative Vision for Christian Outreach*, Baker Publishing Group, 2008, pp. 16-19, ISBN 9781441201843.

10. Egan, H.D., *Christian Apophatic and Kataphatic Mysticisms*, Theological Studies, Vol 39, No 3, September 1978, pp. 399-426.

11. Boeve, L., *Negative Theology and Theological Hermeneutics: The Particularlity of Naming God*, Journal of Philosophy & Scripture, 2006, Vol 3, No 2 (Spring), pp. 1-13, ISSN 1555-5100, http://www.philosophyandscripture.org/Issue3-2/Boeve/Boeve2.html, **Notes:** Quote is on p.1 and p.2, respectively. This article was originally pre-published by the Journal of Philosophy & Scripture. The copyright owner (Mohr Siebeck) later published the article in a book entitled *Gott Nennen: Gottes Namen und Gott als Name*, eds. Dalferth and Stoellger, 2008, Mohr Siebeck. Reproduced with permission of copyright owner Mohr Siebeck Tübingen.

12. Berkhof, L., *Systematic Theology*, W.B. Eerdmans Publishing Company, 1996, ISBN 978-0802838209.

13. Pew Research Center, *U.S. Religious Landscape Survey: Religious Beliefs and Practices: Diverse and Politically Relevant*, 2008, p. 5, Pew Research Center's Forum on Religion & Public Life, http://tinyurl.com/lgo2xhs, **Notes:** The reported margin of error was ±0.6% (sample population=35,556). Refer to Appendix 4, Table 2, p. 177 for additional breakdown of the population numbers and margin of error for sub-populations.

14. Smith, T.W., *Beliefs about God across Time and Countries*, 2008, p. 9, **Notes:** Refer to Table 3: Believing in a Personal God.

15. The Holy See, *Catechism of the Catholic Church*, 2nd ed., Libreria Editrice Vaticana (*trans.* The Vatican Publishing House), 1997, ISBN 978-1574551105, **Notes:** A free online English translation of the Cathechism of the Catholic Church is provided by the United States Conference of Catholic Bishiops at the following URL: http://tinyurl.com/h6ljlnx (full URL: http://ccc.usccb.org/flipbooks/catechism/).

16. Pew Research Center, *U.S. Religious Knowledge Survey*, 2010, pp. 6, 16, 17, Pew Research Center's Forum on Religion & Public Life, http://www.pewforum.org/, **Notes:** The reported margin of error is individually reported for each religious group (p. 57). The margin of error varied between ±2.5 % to ±11.0% and varies because the sample size for each group varied considerably from as low as 334 individuals to as many as 2,528 individuals. Data reflects knowledge in the United States only. Quiz can be taken at http://www.pewforum.org/quiz/u-s-religious-knowledge/.

17. Smith, T.W., M. Hout, and P.V. Marsden, *General Social Survey, 1972-2012 [Cumulative File]* ICPSR34801-v1, 2013, http://doi.org/10.3886/ICPSR34802.v1, http://www.icpsr.umich.edu/icpsrweb/ICPSR/studies/34802. Access Online Database here: http://sda.berkeley.edu/sdaweb/analysis/?dataset=gss12, **Notes:** Online databse used to compile data.

18. Pew Research Center, *U.S. Religious Landscape Survey: Religious Beliefs and Practices: Diverse and Politically Relevant*, 2008, pp. 58-59, Pew Research Center's Forum on Religion & Public Life, http://tinyurl.com/lg02xhs, **Notes:** The reported margin of error was ±0.6% (sample population=35,556). Refer to Appendix 4, Table 2, p. 177 for additional breakdown of the population numbers and margin of error for sub-populations.

19. Moser, P.K., *The Evidence For God: Religious KnowledgeReexamined* New York, NY, Cabridge University Press, 2010, p. 234, ISBN 978-0521736282.

20. Larrimore, M., *The Problem of Evil: A Reader*, 2000, p. XX, ISBN 978-0631220145.

21. Einstein, A., *Albert Einstein, The Human Side: Glimpses from His Archives*, Eds. Dukas and Hoffmann, Princeton University Press, 2013, p. 18: Original Pub. 1979, ISBN 978-0691160238, **Notes:** Copyright © 1982 The Hebrew University of Jerusalem. Reprinted by permission.

CHAPTER 3

1. Russell, B., *The Basic Writings of Bertrand Russell*, Taylor & Francis, 2009, p. 348, ISBN 978-1134028672.

2. Camus, A., *The Myth of Sisyphus: And Other Essays*, Knopf Doubleday Publishing Group, 2012, p. 41, ISBN 978-0307827821.

3. Richards, G., *Dingr*, Accessed 20 Nov 2014, https://en.wikipedia.org/wiki/Dingir, **Notes:** Last modified 03 February 2015. Copyright: Public domain; use without restriction.

4. Hammurabi, *Hammurabi's Code of Laws*, c. 1780 BCE, Series Title: Internet Ancient History Sourcebook, Ed. Paul Halsall, Accessed 09 Oct 2015, http://legacy.fordham.edu/halsall/ancient/hamcode.asp, **Notes:** Translated by L. W. King, 1915. Copyright expired.

5. Pettitt, P., *When Burial Begins*, British Archaeology, No 66, Aug 2002, ISSN 1357-4442, http://www.archaeologyuk.org/ba/ba66/.

6. Tattersall, I., *Once We Were Not Alone*, Scientific American, Vol 282, pp. 56-62, ISSN 0036-8733, DOI: 10.1038/scientificamerican0100-56.

7. Klein, R.G., *The Human Career: Human Biological and Cultural Origins*, 3rd ed., University of Chicago Press, 2009, p. 469, ISBN 978-0226027524.

8. Shermer, M., *The Believing Brain: From Ghosts and Gods to Politics and Conspiracies---How We Construct Beliefs and Reinforce Them as Truths*, Henry Holt and Company, 2011, pp. 198-202, ISBN 978-1429972611.

9. Shreeve, J., *This Face Changes the Human Story. But How?*, National Geographic, 10 Sept 2015, http://tinyurl.com/oyf3fwn, **Notes:** A full story is to be published in the October 2015 issue of National Geographic.

10. McKenzie, D. and H. Wende, *Homo naledi: New species of human ancestor discovered in South Africa*, CNN, 10 Sept 2015, Accessed 10 Sept 2015, http://tinyurl.com/nalowv4, **Notes:** A full story is to be published in the October 2015 issue of National Geographic.

11. Mellars, P., *Why did modern human populations disperse from Africa ca. 60,000 years ago? A new model*, Proceedings of the National Academy of Sciences of the United States of America, 2006, Vol 103, No 25, pp. 9381-9386, National Academy of Sciences, DOI: 10.1073/pnas.0510792103, http://tinyurl.com/jbdfhu2, **Notes:** Refer to Footnote 17, https://en.wikipedia.org/wiki/Human_evolution#cite_note-17.

12. University of Texas, *Perry-Castañeda Library Map Collection*, Accessed 09 Oct 2015, http://www.lib.utexas.edu/maps/middle_east_and_asia/middleeast_ref00.pdf, **Notes:** Base Map: Middle East (Reference Map) 1999 (339K) [larger jpeg]. The present author imported the Base Map image into Adobe Illustrator and traced a rough outline of the geography. Annotations by present author. The Base Map is public domain; use is without restriction.

13. Bertonneau, T.F., *"The Catastrophe" - Part 1: What the End of Bronze-Age Civilization Means for Modern Times*, The Brussels Journal: Society for the Advancement of Freedom in Europe, 15 Sept 2009, Accessed 12 Aug 2015, http://www.brusselsjournal.com/node/4095.

14. Smith, M.S., *The Early History of God: Yahweh and the Other Deities in Ancient Israel*, 2nd ed., Eerdmans Publishing Company, 2002, pp. 1-14, ISBN 978-0802839725.

15. Smith, M.S., *The Early History of God: Yahweh and the Other Deities in Ancient Israel*, 2nd ed., Eerdmans Publishing Company, 2002, p. 32, ISBN 978-0802839725.

16. Smith, M.S., *The Early History of God: Yahweh and the Other Deities in Ancient Israel*, 2nd ed., Eerdmans Publishing Company, 2002, pp. 74-78, ISBN 978-0802839725.

17. Arbel, I., *"Yahweh"*, Encyclopedia Mythica, Encyclopedia Mythica Online, Accessed 25 Feb 2014, http://www.pantheon.org/articles/y/yahweh.html.

18. Kirby, P., *Early Jewish Writings: 1Kings*, 2015, Series Ed(s). Kirby, Accessed 06 Oct 2015, http://www.earlyjewishwritings.com/1kings.html, **Notes:** The dates are extracted from *A Survey of the Old Testament*, Hill, A.E., Walton J. H., p. 204, Harper Collins, 2010.

19. Viegas, J., *God's Wife Edited Out of the Bible -- Almost*, Discovery News, 2012, Accessed 25 Feb 2014, http://tinyurl.com/ht6cdty.

20. Patai, R., *The Hebrew Goddess*, Wayne State University Press, 1990, pp. 35-36, ISBN 978-0814322710.

21. Patai, R., *The Hebrew Goddess*, Wayne State University Press, 1990, p. 46, ISBN 978-0814322710.

22. Podcast Title: *Did God Have a Wife?*, Show Title: *The Bible's Buried Secrets*, Narrator: Stavrakopoulou, Episode No. 2, Series Title: Did God Have a Wife?, Producer(s): Davis and Bragard, British Broadcasting Company (BBC), 22 March 2011, Run time 01:44, http://www.bbc.co.uk/programmes/b00zw3fl.

23. Day, J., *Yahweh and the Gods and Goddesses of Canaan*, 1st ed., New York, NY, Sheffield Academic Press, 2002, pp. 42-67, ISBN 978-0826468307.

24. Dever, W.G., *Did God Have a Wife? Archaeology and Folk Religion in Ancient Israel*, Wm. B. Eerdmans Publishing Company, 2005, ISBN 978-0802828521.

25. Kosnik, D., *History's Vanquished Goddess ASHERAH: God's Wife: the Goddess Asherah, Wife of Yahweh*, Emergent Press LLC, 2014, pp. 141-196, ISBN 978-0985609573.

26. Shanks, H., *The Persisting Uncertainties of Kuntillet 'Ajrud*, Biblical Archaeology Review, Vol 38, No 6, pp. 28-37, ISSN 0098-9444, http://tinyurl.com/hncgowf.

27. Shanks, H., *The Persisting Uncertainties of Kuntillet 'Ajrud*, Biblical Archaeology Review, Vol 38, No 6, p. 31, ISSN 0098-9444, http://tinyurl.com/hncgowf.

28. Shanks, H., *The Persisting Uncertainties of Kuntillet 'Ajrud*, Biblical Archaeology Review, Vol 38, No 6, p. 32, ISSN 0098-9444, http://tinyurl.com/hncgowf.

29. Decamps, C., *The god Bes*, Art Resource, Inc., Musée du Louvre, Paris, France, http://www.artres.com/, **Notes:** Museum System ID: 13-566188, Inv No. E25948, Art Resource, Inc. ID #: ART525308. Used with permission.

30. Liepe, J., *Copper Alloy Statuette of the god Bes found in Assur, Iraq*, c. 664 - 332 BCE, Size 16.8 x 8.2 x 2.2 cm, Neues Museum - Egyptian Museum and Papyrus Exhibit, Berlin, Germany, http://www.artres.com/, **Notes:** Museum System ID: 04-502572, Museum Inventory No. AM22200, Art Resource, Inc. ID #: ART525310. Used with permission.

31. Shanks, H., *The Persisting Uncertainties of Kuntillet 'Ajrud*, Biblical Archaeology Review, Vol 38, No 6, p. 33, ISSN 0098-9444, http://tinyurl.com/hncgowf.

32. Dasen, V., *Dwarfs in Ancient Egypt and Greece*, Series Title: Oxford Monographs on Classical Archaeology, Oxford Universy Press, 2013, pp. 55-83, ISBN 978-0199680863, **Notes:** The quoted material is to be found on pp. 55-57.

33. Vartavan, C.T.d., *Bes, The Bow-Legged Dwarf or the Ladie's Companion: A Revised Unpublished Study*, Bulletin of Parthian and Mixed Oriental Studies 1, 2005, pp. 81-95, http://tinyurl.com/zo6bk5n, **Notes:** In personal communications with the author (22 Dec 2015), Dr. de Vartavan noted that the reason the title says "unpublished" is because it was originally hand-distributed in 1986. The journal article cited herein is considered published.

34. Seawright, C., Accessed 23 May 2014, http://tinyurl.com/joup7ek.

35. Török, L. and L. Torok, *Hellenizing Art in Ancient Nubia 300 B.C. - AD 250 and Its Egyptian Models: A Study in "Acculturation"*, Brill, 2011, pp. 88, 93, ISBN 978-9004211285.

36. Dasen, V., *Dwarfs in Ancient Egypt and Greece*, Series Title: Oxford Monographs on Classical Archaeology, Oxford Universy Press, 2013, pp. 59-60, ISBN 978-0199680863.

37. Pinch, G., *Egyptian Mythology: A Guide to the Gods, Goddesses, and Traditions of Ancient Egypt*, Oxford University Press, 2002, p. 119, ISBN 978-0195170245.

38. Stevens, A., *Domestic Religious Practices*, Series Title: UCLA Encyclopedia of Egyptology, Eds. Wendrich, et al., Los Angeles, 2009, pp. 2, 11, 17, 18, http://tinyurl.com/zg7xssa (full URL: http://www.escholarship.org/uc/item/7s07628w), Notes: Online book. A PDF copy can be downloaded at the URL provided.

39. Weingarten, J., *The Arrival of Egyptian Taweret and Bes[et] on Minoan Crete: Contact and Choice*, in the proceedings of *SOMA 2012, Identity and Connectivity, Proceedings of the 16th Symposium on Mediterranean Archaeology*, Eds. Bombardieri, *et al.*, 1-3 March 2012, Florence, Italy, Archaeopress.

40. Heilig, M., *Around the god Bes*, 2003, http://archeographe.net/Autour-du-dieu-Bes/, **Notes:** Reprinted with permission. This artifact resided at the Museum of Egyptian Antiquities in Cairo.

41. The Trustees of the British Museum, *Painted wooden cippus of the head form of the god Bes with the god Horus standing on crocodiles*, Late Period (c. 600 BCE), British Museum, London, Great Britain, http://www.artres.com/, **Notes:** This artifact may have been found in Memphis, Egypt. Museum System ID: 12-552097, Museum Inventory No. 60958, Art Resource, Inc. ID #: ART306030. Used with permission.

42. Thomas, R., *The Identity of the Standing Figures on Pithos A from Kuntillet 'Ajrud: A Reassessment*, 26 Feb 2015, Feb 2015, Weblog: Religion and Literature of Ancient Palestine, Accessed 31 Dec 2015, http://tinyurl.com/hqsfs8h or https://ryansthomas.wordpress.com/religion-of-ancient-israel/, **Notes:** In private conversations with this author on 31 Dec 2015 and on 08 Aug 2016, it was indicated that this research paper had been submitted to the *Journal of Ancient Near Eastern Religions* for publication, Vol 16, No. 2, ISSN 1569-2116, Brill. This journal issue had not printed when the present book was in press. The pre-publication is reprinted by permission of Ryan Thomas.

43. Camocon, *El (deity)*, Wikipedia, The Free Encyclopedia, 28 Nov 2011, Accessed 30 Nov 2015, https://en.wikipedia.org/wiki/El_%28deity%29, **Notes:** This item is in the public domain. The filename was listed as "Canaanite_God_El.png". This image was deleted from Wikipedia in 2015. This image was subsequently located at the following two URLs (both accessed 05 Jun 2016): http://tinyurl.com/gqmkyz4, or see p. 6 of the pdf file provided here: http://tinyurl.com/j9gyx9l.

44. Fourth Lateran Council of the Roman Catholic Church, *Medieval Sourcebook: Twelfth Ecumenical Council: Lateran IV 1215*, Fordham University, 1996, Ed. Paul Halsall, Accessed 28 Feb 2014, http://legacy.fordham.edu/halsall/basis/lateran4.asp, **Notes:** From H. J. Schroeder, Disciplinary Decrees of the General Councils: Text, Translation and Commentary, (St. Louis: B. Herder, 1937, pp. 236-296).

45. Unknown, A., *Scutum Fidei (Shield of the Trinity)*, c. 1210 CE, Accessed 05 Jun 2016, http://tinyurl.com/z5sbe07, **Notes:** This is part of a manuscript c. 1210 that included this illustration to the Compendium Historiae in Genealogia Christi by Peter of Poitiers (or Petrus Pictaviensis). This artwork is considered public domain by US copyright law.

46. Gnuse, R.K., *No Other Gods: Emergent Monotheism in Israel*, Bloomsbury Publishing (T&T Clark), 1997, p. 185, ISBN 978-1850756576.

47. Wright, R., *The Evolution of God*, Little, Brown and Company, 2009, pp. 140-160, ISBN 978-0316053273, **Notes:** See p. 160 where Wright concludes that the FP (Foreign Policy) and DP (Domestic Policy) hypotheses explain the transition of Judaism from polytheism to monolatry.

48. Wright, R., *The Evolution of God*, Little, Brown and Company, 2009, pp. 148-149, ISBN 978-0316053273.

49. Wright, R., *The Evolution of God*, Little, Brown and Company, 2009, pp. 120-121, ISBN 978-0316053273.

50. Hawks, J., et al., *New fossil remains of Homo naledi from the Lesedi Chamber, South Africa*, eLife, Vol 6, 09 May 2017, p. e24232, eLife Sciences Publications, Ltd, ISSN 2050-084X, DOI: 10.7554/eLife.24232, https://dx.doi.org/10.7554/eLife.24232.

51. Dirks, P.H.G.M., et al., *The age of Homo naledi and associated sediments in the Rising Star Cave, South Africa*, eLife, Vol 6, 09 May 2017, p. e24231, eLife Sciences Publications, Ltd, ISSN 2050-084X, DOI: 10.7554/eLife.24231, http://dx.doi.org/10.7554/eLife.24231.

CHAPTER 4

1. Klotz, J.C. and M.R. Lanzarone, *The Coming of the Quantum Christ: The Shroud of Turin and the Apocalypse of Selfishess*, 1st ed., John C. Klotz, 2014 ISBN 978-1505468410, **Notes:** The quote is also provided on Klotz's blog: The article is entitled, "Ebola, Protocols and the Shroud of Turin", 17 Oct 2014, http://quantumchrist-jck.blogspot.com/2014/10/ebola-protocols-and-shroud-of-turin.html.

2. Wilford, J.N., *James B. Irwin, 61, Ex-Astronaut; Founded Religious Organization*, New York Times, 10 Aug 1991, http://tinyurl.com/jdt7xat.

3. Kurczy, S., *Chinese explorers stand by claim of Noah's Ark find in Turkey*, 30 April 2010, Accessed 15 Jun 2015, http://tinyurl.com/kbz8k8p.

4. Parfitt, T., *The Lost Ark of the Covenant: Solving the 2,5000 Year Old Mystery of the Fabled Biblical Ark*, e-book, HarperCollins e-books, 2009: ISBN (ASIN) B0014H32AI, **Notes:** Refer to Chapter 10.

5. Parfitt, T., *The Lost Ark of the Covenant: Solving the 2,5000 Year Old Mystery of the Fabled Biblical Ark*, HarperCollins e-books, 2009, p. 230: ISBN (ASIN) B0014H32AI.

6. Parfitt, T., *The Lost Ark of the Covenant: Solving the 2,5000 Year Old Mystery of the Fabled Biblical Ark*, HarperCollins e-books, 2009, p. 12: ISBN (ASIN) B0014H32AI.

7. Parfitt, T., *The Lost Ark of the Covenant: Solving the 2,5000 Year Old Mystery of the Fabled Biblical Ark*, HarperCollins e-books, 2009, pp. 13, 252, 254, 335-336, 341-342, 354: ISBN (ASIN) B0014H32AI.

8. Parfitt, T., *The Lost Ark of the Covenant: Solving the 2,5000 Year Old Mystery of the Fabled Biblical Ark*, HarperCollins e-books, 2009, p. 356: ISBN (ASIN) B0014H32AI.

9. Parfitt, T., *The Lost Ark of the Covenant: Solving the 2,5000 Year Old Mystery of the Fabled Biblical Ark*, HarperCollins e-books, 2009, p. 370: ISBN (ASIN) B0014H32AI.

10. Parfitt, T., *The Lost Ark of the Covenant: Solving the 2,5000 Year Old Mystery of the Fabled Biblical Ark*, HarperCollins e-books, 2009, pp. 370-372: ISBN (ASIN) B0014H32AI.

11. Boyle, A., *3,000-year-old artifacts reveal history behind biblical David and Goliath*, NBC News, 8 May 2012, Accessed 15 Jun 2015, http://tinyurl.com/j3lthnr.

12. Kazan, G., *The Head of St John the Baptist: Byzantium and the Circulation of Relics in the Early Middle Ages*, in the proceedings of *Institute of Historical Research*, 14 May 2014, Bedford Room G37, Senate House, University of London, **Notes:** Dr. Kazan presented a lecture with Microsoft Powerpoint slides that detailed the number of skull fragments claimed to be those of John the Baptist. In a private email dated 05-Jan-2016 between Mr. Kazan and this author (B. Goedken), he clarified that he has not as yet published this work. In this same correspondence, he outlined that he had reported in the lecture that of the 36 skulls, 9 were jaw fragments, 9 were teeth, 2 face/cheek, and 16 were unidentifed skull parts. He also noted that since the lecture, several more skull fragments came to to his atttention. Beyond this, Dr. Kazan noted that there were 37 finger/arm fragments which are from at least four individuals.

13. O'Connor, A., *An Early Christian Reliquary in the Shape of a Sarcophagus in the University of Wisconsin-Milwaukee Art Collection*, M.A. - Art History, University of Wisconsin-Milwaukee, Advisor: Leson, Dec 2013, http://dc.uwm.edu/etd/300/, **Notes** Refer to *Theses and Dissertations*. Paper 300.

14. Pappas, S., *Mysterious Bones May Belong to John the Baptist*, Purch, 14 Jun 2014, Series Title: LiveScience, Accessed 10 Oct 2015, http://www.livescience.com/20975-bones-reliquary-john-baptist.html, **Notes:** Editor's Note: This article was updated on June 15 to correct the nationality of Kazimir Popkonstantinov and Rossina Kostova. They are Bulgarian, not Romanian.

15. Kazan, G., *The Head of St John the Baptist – the Early Evidence*, 2011, Accessed 15 May 2015, https://oxford.academia.edu/GeorgesKazan/Papers

16. Gibson, D. and M. McKinley, *Finding Jesus: Faith. Fact. Forgery.: Six Holy Objects That Tell the Remarkable Story of the Gospels*, St. Martin's Press, 2015, pp. 13-16, ISBN 978-1466877900.

17. Davidson, N., *Myth Hunters: The Quest for the True Cross*, Season 1, Episode 13, 8 Feb 2013, Perfomer(s): Boregehammar and Hesemann, Director(s): Davidson, N., Prod.(s) Barett, *et al*.

18. Lombatti, A., *The Relics of Jesus: The Case of the Titulus Crucis*, Eds. Elliott and Landy, 2014, http://www.bibleinterp.com/articles/2014/02/lom388011.shtml.

19. Thiede, C.P. and M. D'Ancona, *The Quest for the True Cross*, Palgrave Macmillan, 2003 ISBN 978-1403962126.

20. Hesemann, M., *Titulus Crucis*, Michael Hesemann, Official Webpage: Michael Hesemann, Historian and Author, http://michaelhesemann.info/12_8.html.

21. Forgacs, T., *The History of a Relic: The Titulus Crucis from the Church of Santa Croce in Gerusalemme, Rome*, Contrapposto, 2002, Vol 1, pp. 6-17, Graduate Union of the Students of Art in the Department of Art at the University of Toronto, http://groups.chass.utoronto.ca/gradart/journal/journal.2002.html.

22. Bella, F. and C. Azzi, *14C Dating of the 'Titulus Crucis'*, Radiocarbon, 2002, Vol 44, No 3, pp. 685-689, ISSN 0033-8222, http://tinyurl.com/z328534.

23. Jacobovici, S., *The Nails of the Cross: A Response to the Criticisms of the Film*, 22 June 2011, Weblog: TaborBlog, http://jamestabor.com/2011/06/22/simcha-jacobovici-responds-to-critics-of-his-nails-of-the-cross-film/.

24. Jacovobici, S., *Nails of the Cross (Episode 1)*, Biblical Conspiracies, 14 Dec 2014, Director(s): Jacovobici, S., Prod.(s) Jacovobici and Golubev, Distr. Discovery Science Channel.

25. Shimron, A., *et al.*, *The Caiaphas Tomb in Jerusalem: Petrochemistry of ossuary bones, two nails and their implications*, Nature, 2014, http://www.geoarch-tours.com/articles.html, **Notes:** In preparation as of 02 October 2015.

26. Jacovobici, S. and G. Ball, *Secrets of the Crucifixion (Episode 3)*, Biblical Conspiracies, 15 Dec 2014, Director(s): Jacovobici, S. and G. Ball, Prod.(s) Jacovobici and Golubev, Distr. Discovery Science Channel.

27. Breault, R., *The Shroud of Turin: The most analyzed artifact in the world*, Shroud of Turin Education Project Accessed 11 Oct 2015, www.shrouduniversity.com/Fact_Sheet.doc.

28. Damon, P.E., *et al.*, *Radiocarbon dating of the Shroud of Turin*, Nature, 1989, Vol 337, No 6208, pp. 611-615, DOI: http://dx.doi.org/10.1038/337611a0, Freely available at http://www.shroud.com/nature.htm/.

29. Freer-Waters, R.A. and A.J.T. Jull, *Investigating a Dated Piece of the Shroud of Turin*, Radiocarbon, 2010, Vol 52, No 4, pp. 1521-1527, https://journals.uair.arizona.edu/index.php/radiocarbon/article/view/3419.

30. Giulio Fanti, S.G., *Il Mistero della sindone [trans. The Mystery of the Shroud]*, Rizzoli, 2013 ISBN 978-8817065580, **Notes:** This book is written in Italian.

31. Gryboski, M., *Uncertainty Abounds Regarding Latest Turin Shroud Claims*, The Christian Post, 29 March 2013, Accessed 8 July 2014, http://www.christianpost.com/news/uncertainty-abounds-regarding-latest-turin-shroud-claims-92925/.

32. Fanti, G. and P. Malfi, *The Shroud of Turin: First Century after Christ!*, Pan Stanford, 2015 ISBN 978-9814669139.

33. Fanti, G. and P. Malfi, *A New Cyclic-Loads Machine for the Measurement of Micro-Mechanical Properties of Single Flax Fibers Coming from the Turin Shroud*, in the proceedings of *Italian Association of Theoretical and Applied Mechanics (AIMETA) Congress*, September 17-20, 2013, Turin, Italy, https://shroudofturin.files.wordpress.com/2013/09/aimeta-fanti.pdf/.

34. Tornielli, A., *New experiments on Shroud show it's not medieval*, La Stampa, 2013, Series Title: Vatican Insider, Accessed 19 May 2015, http://vaticaninsider.lastampa.it/en/inquiries-and-interviews/detail/articolo/sindone-23579/.

35. Shafer Parker, J., *Science Shines New Light on Shroud of Turin's Age*, National Catholic Register, 2013, Accessed 19 May 2015, http://www.ncregister.com/daily-news/science-shines-new-light-on-shroud-of-turins-age/.

36. Kearse, K.P., *Empirical evidence that the blood on the Shroud of Turin is of human origin: Is the current data sufficient?*, Shroud of Turin Education and Research Association, Inc. (STERA, Inc.), 2012, Accessed 12 Oct 2015, http://www.shroud.com/pdfs/kearse1.pdf, **Notes:** Refer to section entitled, "Serological testing for human glycophorin A", p. 9.

37. Anonymous, *Developmental Validation of a Novel Lateral Flow Strip Test for Rapid Identification of Human Blood, Rapid Stain Identification, RSID(tm)-Blood*, Independent Forensics, Inc., 2010, Accessed 12 Oct 2015, http://www.ifi-test.com/wp-content/uploads/2014/02/BloodValid.pdf.

38. Kearse, K.P., *DNA Analysis and the Shroud of Turin: Development of a Shroud CODIS*, Shroud of Turin Education and Research Association, Inc. (STERA, Inc.), Jan 2014, Accessed 12 Oct 2015, https://www.shroud.com/pdfs/kearse3.pdf.

39. Pope Francis, *Exposition of the Holy Shroud: Video Message of His Holiness Pope Francis (Holy Saturday, 30 March 2013)*, Libreria Editrice Vaticana (*trans. The Vatican Publishing House*), 30 March 2013, Accessed 8 July 2014, http://tinyurl.com/juel3wk, **Notes:** Reprinted with permission. Libreria Editrice Vaticana.

40. Zaimov, S., *Pope Francis Comments on Shroud of Turin After New Research Upholds Authenticity*, The Christian Post, 01 April 2013, Accessed 8 July 2014, http://www.christianpost.com/news/pope-francis-comments-on-shroud-of-turin-after-new-research-upholds-authenticity-93047/.

41. Hermosilla, A.S., *UCAM's researchers have found scientific evidence that places the Shroud of Oviedo and the Shroud of Turin in the same scenario*, Catholic University of Murcia http://tinyurl.com/jgcorlk.

42. Lemaire, A., *Burial Box of James the Brother of Jesus: Earliest Archaeological Evidence of Jesus Found in Jerusalem*, Biblical Archaeology Review, 2002, Vol 28, No 6, pp. 24-33.

43. Bock, D., *What evidence causes problems for those who claim this is Jesus' family tomb?* , Ankerberg Theological Research Institute, 2007, Accessed 12 Oct 2015, https://www.jashow.org/articles/uncategorized/response-to-the-lost-tomb-of-jesusprogram-2/, **Notes:** An interview with Darrel Bock on the John Ankerberg Show. Bock corrects statements made by Craig A. Evans in which he stated there were 17 bodies inside ossuaries (source: http://www.craigaevans.com/tombofjesus.htm).

44. Charlesworth, J.H., *The Tomb of Jesus and His Family?: Exploring Ancient Jewish Tombs Near Jerusalem's Walls*, Eerdmans Publishing Company, 2013 p. 230, ISBN 978-0802867452.

45. Tabor, J., *The Talpiot Jesus Tomb: Sorting Through the Facts and the Fictions*, 02 April 2014, James Tabor, 2014, Weblog: TablorBlog, http://tabortemp.com/category/talpiot-jesus-family-tomb/page/3/, **Notes:** The URL link may not function correctly. The TaborBlog website was under construction and this appears to be a temporary link. Accessed 05 Sep 2016.

46. Kloner, A., *A Tomb with Inscribed Ossuaries in East Talpiot, Jerusalem*, Antiquot, 1996, Vol 29, pp. 15-22.

47. Charlesworth, J.H., *The Tomb of Jesus and His Family?: Exploring Ancient Jewish Tombs Near Jerusalem's Walls*, Eerdmans Publishing Company, 2013 p. 167, ISBN 978-0802867452, **Notes:** Refer to Table 1, p. 167.

48. Kilty, K. and M. Elliott, *The James Ossuary in Talpiot*, The Bible and Interpretation, May 2011, Accessed 01 June 2015, http://bibleinterp.com/articles/kilell358029.shtml/, **Notes:** Website Sponsors: Paul V.M. Flesher -- University of Wyoming, Religious Studies Department; J.E. Wright -- University of Arizona, Center for Judaic Studies; Jennie Ebeling -- Department of Religious Studies and Art History, University of Evansville.

49. Rollston, C.A., *Prosopography and the Talpiyot Yeshua Family Tomb: Pensées of a Palaeographer*, Society of Biblical Literature, 2007, Accessed 12 Oct 2015, http://www.sbl-site.org/publications/article.aspx?articleId=649, **Notes:** See SBL Forum 5.3 (2007).

50. Rosenfeld, A., et al., *The Connection of the James Ossuary to the Talpiot (Jesus Family Tomb) Ossuaries*, 2011, http://www.bibleinterp.com/articles/JOT.shtml/.

51. Orsini, P. and W. Clarysse, *Early New Testament Manuscripts and Their Dates: A Critique of Theological Palaeography*, Ephemerides Theologicae Lovanienses, 2012, Vol 88, No 4, pp. 443-474, DOI: 10.2143/ETL.88.4.2957937, **Notes:** See p. 470 for Table 1, Siglum 52.

52. Rosenfeld, A., H.R. Feldman, and W.E. Krumbein, *The Authenticity of the James Ossuary*, Open Journal of Geology, Vol 4, No 3, Mar 2014, pp. 69-78, DOI: 10.4236/ojg.2014.43007 http://www.scirp.org/journal/PaperInformation.aspx?PaperID=43671#.VV_GrEbxh-c/.

53. Shimon, G., *Is the Talpiot Tomb Really the Family Tomb of Jesus?*, Near Eastern Archaeology, 2006, Vol 69, No 3/4, pp. 118-124, The American Schools of Oriental Research, ISSN 10942076, DOI: 10.2307/25067661, http://www.jstor.org/stable/25067661.

54. Tabor, J., *What's What Regarding the Controversial James Ossuary?*, 13 Feb 2016, Weblog: TaborBlog, http://tinyurl.com/zduwyuf.

55. Kronfeld, J., A. Rosenfeld, and H.R. Feldman, *Determining the Authenticity of Artifacts by Oxygen Isotope Analysis*, Open Journal of Geology, 2013, Vol 3, No 4, pp. 313-321, DOI: 10.4236/ojg.2013.34036.

56. Kershner, I., *Findings Reignite Debate on Claim of Jesus' Bones*, The New York Times, 04 April 2015, The New York Times Company, http://nyti.ms/1C1QagI, **Notes:** Article appeared in print on 05 April 2015, p. A4 of the New York Times under the headline,"Finding Reignite Debate on Claim of Jesus' Bones.".

57. Griffiths, S., *Geologist claims Jesus was married... and had a SON: Expert says he has proof son of God was buried in 'family tomb' along with wife Mary and his brother*, DailyMail.com, 07 April 2015, Accessed 25 May 2015, http://tinyurl.com/ldfz92w.

58. Tabor, J., *Ben Witherington on the James Ossuary and the Talpiot "Jesus" Tomb*, 07 April 2015, Weblog: TaborBlog, Accessed 25 May 2015, http://tinyurl.com/zhlljbw, **Notes:** The blog was a rebuttal to another blog posted on the same date by Ben Witherington in which he interviewed New Testament Scholar Craig Evans. This can be accessed at http://tinyurl.com/zj69y7f.

59. Tabor, J., *The Case for a "Jesus Family Tomb" in East Talpiot: A Comprehensive Summary of the Evidence*, 13 Feb 2016, Weblog: TaborBlog, Accessed 05 May 2016, http://tinyurl.com/gw3se00.

60. Feissel, D., *et al.*, *Volume 1 Jerusalem, Part 1: 1-704*, Eds. Cotton, *et al.*, Berlin, Boston, De Gruyter, 2010, pp. 200-201, ISBN 978-3110222203, http://www.degruyter.com/view/product/42384.

61. Jeffrey, G., *Rapture: Three Fascinating Discoveries! - The Discovery of the Tombs of Mary, Martha, and Lazarus*, Todd Strandberg, Weblog: Rapture Ready, http://www.raptureme.com/terry/james27.html.

62. Elliott, M. and K. Kilty, *Inside the Numbers of the Talpiot Tomb*, The Bible and Interpretation, 20 Mar 2008, Accessed 12 Oct 2015, http://www.bibleinterp.com/PDFs/tomb2.pdf, **Notes:** Website Sponsors: Paul V.M. Flesher -- University of Wyoming, Religious Studies Department; J.E. Wright -- University of Arizona, Center for Judaic Studies; Jennie Ebeling -- Department of Archaeology and Art History, University of Evansville.

63. Charlesworth, J.H., *The Tomb of Jesus and His Family?: Exploring Ancient Jewish Tombs Near Jerusalem's Walls*, Eerdmans Publishing Company, 2013, pp. 364-365, ISBN 978-0802867452.

64. Evans, C.A., *The Tomb of Jesus and Family? Second Thoughts*, 2015, Accessed 23 May 2015, http://craigaevans.com/tombofjesus.htm.

CHAPTER 5

1. Lloyd, J.T., *Life of Henry Ward Beecher*, 1881, p. 170.

2. Pope Benedict XVI, *Meeting of the Holy Father Benedict XVI with the Clergy of the Dioceses of Belluno-Feltre and Treviso*, Libreria Editrice Vaticana (*trans.* The Vatican Publishing House), 24 Jul 2007, Accessed 01 Dec 2015, http://tinyurl.com/hjy5nwa, **Notes:** A speech given at the Church of St. Justin Martyer, Auronzo di Cadore (Italian Municipality). Reprinted with permission. Libreria Editrice Vaticana.

3. Pope Innocent III, *Medieval Source Book, Letter on Papal Policies: On Heresy: Letter to the Archbishop of Auch*, 1198, Fordham University, 1998, Ed. Paul Halsall, Accessed 28 May 2014, http://tinyurl.com/j2w76jm.

4. Licona, M.R., *The Resurrection of Jesus: A New Historiographical Approach*, InterVarsity Press, 2010, pp. 19, 278, 611, ISBN 978-0830827190, **Notes:** Within fair use policy of InterVarsity Press.

5. Wikipedia contributors, *Textual scholarship*, Wikipedia, The Free Encyclopedia, Accessed 11 Nov 2015, https://en.wikipedia.org/wiki/Textual_scholarship.

6. Wikipedia contributors, *Palaeography*, Wikipedia, The Free Encyclopedia, Accessed 11 Nov 2015, https://en.wikipedia.org/wiki/Palaeography.

7. Wikipedia contributors, *Philology*, Wikipedia, The Free Encyclopedia, Accessed 11 Nov 2015, https://en.wikipedia.org/wiki/Philology.

8. Wikipedia contributors, *Textual criticism*, Wikipedia, The Free Encyclopedia, Accessed 11 Nov 2015, https://en.wikipedia.org/wiki/Textual_criticism.

9. Theopedia.com, *Biblical criticism: Higher criticism*, Christian Web Foundation, Accessed 11 Nov 2015, http://www.theopedia.com/biblical-criticism, **Notes:** The publishers have acknowledged that the website's content is biased toward the Protestant point of view. In regard to the quote, the definition of Historical (Higher) criticism accurately portrays the field of study relative to most definitional sources.

10. Hartill, J.E., *Principles of Biblical Hermeneutics*, Zondervan, 1960 ISBN 978-0310259008.

11. Geisler, N. and, p. Bocchino, *Unshakeable Foundations*, Minneapolis, MN, Bethany House Publishers, 2001, p. 256, ISBN 978-0764224089.

12. Orsini,, p. and W. Clarysse, *Early New Testament Manuscripts and Their Dates: A Critique of Theological Palaeography*, Ephemerides Theologicae Lovanienses, 2012, Vol 88, No 4, pp. 443-474, DOI: 10.2143/ETL.88.4.2957937, **Notes:** See, p. 470 for Table 1, Siglum 52.

13. Refer to Notes, *Photo of Codex Sinaiticus*, Accessed 03 Dec 2015, http://www.bl.uk/collection-items/codex-sinaiticus, **Notes:** Shelfmark: Add. MS 43725. This photo has been sourced from the British Library website. To the extent possible under law, Getty Images has waived all copyright and related or neighbouring rights to this work dedicating it to the public domain. The photo was altered by changing the color scheme to grayscale and by adding a black rectangular outline to signify the region of print that is magnified to make the text more legible.

14. Unknown, *Codex Vaticanus*, Manuscript No. Vat.gr.1209, Folio No. Section IV,, p. 1239, Library, Vatican Library- Manuscripts Catalogue, http://digi.vatlib.it/view/MSS_Vat.gr.1209/1243, **Notes:** Image is a segment of the Gospel of Matthew. Notice the handwritten text in the margins. Also note that the URL refers to "1243". This is a reference ID to catalogue the images of each page. The actual page number of the Codex is, p. 1239.

15. The Gnostic Society Library, *The Nag Hammadi Library*, Accessed 11 May 2014, Desc.: A free online digital site that contains all the gnostic texts., http://www.gnosis.org/naghamm/nhl.html.

16. Israel Antiquities Authority, *The Leon Levy Dead Sea Scrolls Library*, Accessed 11 May 2014, Desc.: A free online digitized virtual library of the Dead Sea Scrolls, http://www.deadseascrolls.org.il/home/.

17. Howell, M.C. and W. Prevenier, *From Reliable Sources: An Introduction to Historical Methods*, Cornell University Press, 2001, p. 70, ISBN 978-0801485602, **Notes:** The source of the 7-Step procedure for evaluating contradictory sources was originated by (1) E. Bernheim (Lehrbuch der historischen Methode und der Geschichtsphilosophie [*trans.* Guidebook for Historical Method and the Philosophy of History], 1889); and by (2) Charles Langlois & Charles Seignobos (Introduction aux etudes historiques [*trans.* Introduction to the Study of History], 1898).

18. Licona, M.R., *The Resurrection of Jesus: A New Historiographical Approach*, InterVarsity Press, 2010, p. 279, ISBN 978-0830827190, **Notes:** Licona quotes Wolfhart Pannenberg, "The Historical Jesus as a Challenge to Christology", Dialog 37 (1998), pp. 22-27. Quote on, pp. 22-23. Within fair use policy of InterVarsity Press.

19. Ehrman, B.D., *Lost Christianities: The Battles for Scripture and the Faiths We Never Knew*, Oxford University Press 2003, p. 219, ISBN 978-0195182491.

20. Spinoza, B., *Spinoza: Theological-Political Treatise*, 1st ed., Ed. Jonathan Israel, Cambridge University Press, 28 May 2007 Trans. by Michael Silverthorne, ISBN 978-0521530972.

21. Voltaire, *Dictionnaire philosophique (trans. Philosophical Dictionary)*, 1674 **Notes:** Voltaire is the pen name of François-Marie Arouet.

22. Paine, T., *The Age of Reason - Part I and II - Volume 4 (1794-1796): The Age of Reason by Paine*, Ed. Conway, The Project Gutenberg, 15 Nov 2012, No.: Original Pub. 1796, http://tinyurl.com/zvzymhw, **Notes:** This is a collected work of Paine's, "The Age of Reason", Part 1 and Part 2. Part 1 was published in 1794 and Part 2 was published in 1795. He also wrote a Part 3 around 1800.

23. Podcast Title: *Unbelievable?*, Show Title: *Bart Ehrman on his loss of faith*, Narrator: Brierley, Premier Christian Radio, 27 Aug 2011, Run time 1:20:46, http://tinyurl.com/gu3z7an, **Notes:** Justin Bierly interviews guests apologist Michael Licona and New Testament Scholar/Agnostic Bart Ehrman. Bart Ehrman discusses his early faith and "born again" experience (@ 3:44 min) and his later conversion from being a Christian to an Agnotic beginning at 40:24 minutes into the program. He describes his personal difficulties in changing long-held, deeply entrenched Christian beliefs to adopting what later believed to be the truth (a disbelief in Christ Jesus and Christian God).

24. Ehrman, B.D., *Lost Christianities: The Battles for Scripture and the Faiths We Never Knew*, Oxford University Press, 2003, pp. 220-221, ISBN 978-0195182491, **Notes:** The quoted text is to be found on p. 220. The second citation referring to Ehrman's assertion that the New Testament is nearly fully reconstituted from an accuracy perspective is provided on p. 221.

25. Wikipedia contributors, *Apostolic Fathers*, Wikipedia, The Free Encyclopedia, Accessed 15 Oct 2015, https://en.wikipedia.org/wiki/Apostolic_Fathers, **Notes:** Refer to section entitled, "*Polycarp of Smyrna*".

26. Marlowe, E., *Framing the Sun: The Arch of Constantine and the Roman Cityscape*, The Art Bulletin, 2006, Vol 88, No 2,, p. 225, College Art Association, ISSN 00043079, DOI: 10.2307/25067243, http://www.jstor.org/stable/25067243.

27. Wikipedia contributors, *Constantine the Great*, Wikipedia, The Free Encyclopedia, Accessed 26 Oct 2015, https://simple.wikipedia.org/wiki/Constantine_the_Great, **Notes:** Refer to section entitled, "*Religious rules*".

28. Marlowe, E., *Framing the Sun: The Arch of Constantine and the Roman Cityscape*, The Art Bulletin, 2006, Vol 88, No 2,, p. 226, College Art Association, ISSN 00043079, DOI: 10.2307/25067243, http://www.jstor.org/stable/25067243.

29. Marlowe, E., *Framing the Sun: The Arch of Constantine and the Roman Cityscape*, The Art Bulletin, 2006, Vol 88, No 2, pp. 223-242, College Art Association, ISSN 00043079, DOI: 10.2307/25067243, http://www.jstor.org/stable/25067243.

30. Ehrman, B.D., *Transcript: Lost Christianities: Christian Scriptures and the Battles over Authentification*, The Great Courses, Course #6593, 2002, pp. 2, 20, 27-28, 390, http://tinyurl.com/p35c552, **Notes:** Refer to Course No. 6593.

31. Ferguson, E., *Backgrounds of Early Christianity*, William B. Eerdmans Pub., 2003 ISBN 978-0802822215.

32. Ehrman, B.D., *Transcript: Lost Christianities: Christian Scriptures and the Battles over Authentification*, The Great Courses, Course #6593, 2002, p. 366, http://tinyurl.com/p35c552, **Notes:** Refer to Course No. 6593.

33. Ehrman, B.D., *Transcript: Lost Christianities: Christian Scriptures and the Battles over Authentification*, The Great Courses, Course #6593, 2002, p. 53, http://tinyurl.com/p35c552, **Notes:** Refer to Course No. 6593.

34. Irenaeus, *Adversus Haereses (trans. Against Heresies)*, Book I, 180 CE, Accessed 11 June 2015, http://www.earlychristianwritings.com/text/irenaeus-book1.html, **Notes:** See Book I, Preface, No. 2.

35. Podcast Title: *Refuting the New Controversial Theories About Jesus*, Show Title: *The John Ankerberg Show*, Narrator: Ankerberg, http://tinyurl.com/hmnzedw, **Notes:** Refer to Program 5, Heading -"Did Jesus Need to Hide the Fact of His Marriage?" Refer to the middle of the 8th paragraph by Craig Evans in which he comments that he does not believe there is such a thing as Christian Gnosticism or Gnostic Christians.

36. Freke, T. and, p. Gandy, *Jesus and the Lost Goddess: The Secret Teachings of the Original Christians*, Three Rivers Press, 2002 ISBN 978-1400045945.

37. King, K.L., *What is Gnosticism?*, Belknap Press, 2005 ISBN 978-0674017627.

38. Meyer, M., *Secret Gospels: Essays on Thomas and the Secret Gospel of Mark*, Bloomsbury T&T Clark, 2003 ISBN 978-1563384097.

39. Pagels, E., *Beyond Belief: The Secret Gospel of Thomas*, New York, Vintage, 2004 ISBN 978-0375703164.

40. Marvin W. Meyer, J.M.R., *The Nag Hammadi Scriptures: The Revised and Updated Translation of Sacred Gnostic Texts Complete in One Volume*, HarperOne, 2009 ISBN 978-0061626005.

41. Ehrman, B.D., *Transcript: Lost Christianities: Christian Scriptures and the Battles over Authentification*, The Great Courses, Course #6593, 2002, p. 117, http://tinyurl.com/p35c552, **Notes:** Refer to Course No. 6593.

42. Claremont University, *The Gospel of Thomas (translated by Thomas O. Lambdin)*, Coptic Gnostic Library Project of the Institute for Antiquity and Christianity (Claremont University), Accessed 27 Oct 2015, http://www.gnosis.org/naghamm/gthlamb.html.

43. Clemens, T.F., *The Stromata, or Miscellanies: Clement of Alexandria*, c. 198 – c. 203 CE, http://www.earlychristianwritings.com/text/clement-stromata-book1.html, **Notes:** See Book 1, Chapter 12.

44. Thévet, A., *Portrait of Clement of Alexandria*, 1584, https://commons.wikimedia.org/wiki/File:Clement_alexandrin.jpg, **Notes:** Copyright is expired making this image accessible to the public domain. The original image was altered by (1) removing the background, (2) adding a monochromatic light gray background, and (3) changing the color scheme of the central image to grayscale. Photo taken from book 1, folio 5 recto of Les vrais pourtraits et vies des hommes illustres grecz, latins et payens

45. Wikipedia contributors, *Clement of Alexandria*, Wikipedia, The Free Encyclopedia, Accessed 18 Nov 2015, https://en.wikipedia.org/wiki/Clement_of_Alexandria.

46. Carlson, S.C., *The Gospel Hoax: Morton Smith's Invention of Secret Mark*, Baylor University Press 2005 ISBN 978-1932792485.

47. Smith, M., *Clement of Alexandria and a Secret Gospel of Mark*, Cambridge, Mass., Harvard University Press, 1973, pp. 446–447, **Notes:** Copyright © 1973 by the President and Fellows of Harvard College. Used with permission. Also cited in Brown, S., *Mark's Other Gospel: Rethinking Morton Smith's Controversial Discovery*, 2005, Wilfrid Laurier University Press, pp. xviii - xx, ISBN 0889204616. Refer to paragraphs II.8 - II.12.

48. Brown, S.G., *Mark's Other Gospel: Rethinking Morton Smith's Controversial Discovery*, Wilfrid Laurier University Press, 2005, p. 62, **Notes:** Refer to last paragraph.

49. Anonymous, *Secret Mark*, Early Christian Writings, Series Ed(s). Kirby, Accessed 08 Jun 2016, http://www.earlychristianwritings.com/secretmark.html, **Notes:** Refer to the section entitled "Information on Secret Mark". The referenced information concerning the three versions of the Gospel of Mark is at the end of this discussion.

50. Baigent, M., *The Jesus Papers: Exposing the Greatest Cover-Up in History*, HarperCollins, 2006, pp. 231-233, ISBN 978-0061146602, **Notes:** Quote is on, p. 231.

51. Baigent, M., *The Jesus Papers: Exposing the Greatest Cover-Up in History*, HarperCollins, 2006, pp. 160-163, 166-171, 173-175, ISBN 978-0061146602.

52. Podcast Title: *Refuting the New Controversial Theories About Jesus*, Show Title: *The John Ankerberg Show*, Narrator: Ankerberg, http://tinyurl.com/h9hhpk2, **Notes:** Refer to Program 1, Heading - "*New View of Jesus: Five Books Reveal a Jesus We Never Knew*". Refer to the 3rd set of commentary by Craig Evans where he gives his opinion of Michael Baigent's book, "*The Jesus Papers*", 1st ed., Harper San Francisco, 2006, ISBN 978-0061214745.

53. Pagels, E., *The Gnostic Gospels*, Vintage; Reissue edition 1989, p. 5, ISBN 978-0679724537.

54. Irenaeus, *Adversus Haereses (trans. Against Heresies)*, Book III, 180 CE, Accessed 11 June 2015, http://www.earlychristianwritings.com/text/irenaeus-book3.html, **Notes:** See Book III, Ch. 11, No. 8.

55. Ehrman, B.D., *Transcript: Lost Christianities: Christian Scriptures and the Battles over Authentification*, The Great Courses, Course #6593, 2002, p. 321, http://tinyurl.com/p35c552, **Notes:** Refer to Course No. 6593.

56. Borg, M.J., *Evolution of the Word: The New Testament in the Order the Books Were Written*, 1st ed., New York, NY, Harper One, 2012 ISBN 978-0062082107.

57. Borg, M.J., *A Chronological New Testament*, Huffington Post, Accessed 22 Apr 2014, http://tinyurl.com/grl5x6w, **Notes:** The web page has an Adobe Flash-based interactive that offers a fairly brief summary of Borg's book, "*Evolution of the Word: The New Testament in the Order the Books Were Written*". The dates from Borg's book are utilized as general reference. A special note is that the date for the Acts of the Apostles is altered to be between 75 - 90 CE instead of Borg's placement of around 110 CE in which Borg places after/ with the Gospel of Luke).

58. White, M., *Body Count of the Roman Empire*, 2011, Accessed 15 Oct 2015, http://necrometrics.com/romestat.htm, **Notes:** Refer to heading entitled "Jewish Wars (between 66 and 135 CE)".

59. Josephus, F., *Antiquities of the Jews*, 93 CE, Series Ed(s). Whiston, Accessed 15 Oct 2015, http://tinyurl.com/jkhbtqh (full URL: http://data.perseus.org/citations/urn:cts:greekLit:tlg0526.tlg001.perseus-eng1:20.197), **Notes:** Translated by William Whiston, A.M. Auburn and Buffalo. John E. Beardsley. 1895. Sourced from the Pereus Digital Library Project. Refer to Book 20, Section [197] - 203.

60. Kelly, J.N.D., *Early Christian Doctrine: Revised Edition*, HarperOne, 1978, p. 44, ISBN 978-0060643348, **Notes:** See Reference 7, Athanasius C. Gent. I:cf. de syn. 6.

61. Marciniak, S., *et al.*, *Plasmodium falciparum malaria in 1st–2nd century CE southern Italy*, Current Biology, 5 Dec 2016, Vol 26, No 23, pp. R1220-R1222, Elsevier, ISSN 0960-9822, DOI: 10.1016/j.cub.2016.10.016, http://tinyurl.com/h25f4n5.

62. Sim, D.C., *How many Jews became Christians in the first century? The failure of the Christian mission to the Jews*, HTS Teologiese Studies/Theological Studies, 09 Oct 2005, Vol 61, No 1/2, pp. 417-440, ISSN 2072-8050 (online) / 0259-9422 (print), DOI: 10.4102/hts.v61i1/2.430. **Notes:** See p. 435-436 for the referenced numerical figures.

CHAPTER 6

1. Pope John Paul II, *Crossing the Threshold of Hope*, Ed. Messori, Alfred A. Knopf (Random House), 1994, p. 60, ISBN 0679440585 / 978-0679440581, **Notes:** Translated from Italian by Jenny McPhee and Martha McPhee. Credit: Excerpt(s) from CROSSING THE THRESHOLD OF HOPE by Pope John Paul II, translation copyright © 1994 by Alfred A. Knopf, a division of Penguin Random House LLC. Used by permission of Alfred A. Knopf, an imprint of the Knopf Doubleday Publishing Group, a division of Penguin Random House LLC. All rights reserved.

2. Keller, T., *The Reason for God: Belief in an Age of Skepticism*, Penguin Group US, 2008, p. 202, ISBN 978-1101217658.

3. Olden-Jorgensen, S., *Til Kilderne! Introduktion til Historisk Kildekritik (in Danish) [trans. Introduction to Historical Source Criticism]*, Gads Forlag, 1998 ISBN 978-8712037781.

4. Thurén, T., *Källkritik*, Stockholm, Almqvist & Wiksell, 1997, No.

5. McCullagh, C.B., *Justifying Historical Descriptions*, 1984, p. 19, ISBN 978-0521318303.

6. Licona, M.R., *The Resurrection of Jesus: A New Historiographical Approach*, InterVarsity Press, 2010, pp. 611-612, ISBN 978-0830827190, **Notes:** Within fair use policy of InterVarsity Press.

7. Licona, M.R., *The Resurrection of Jesus: A New Historiographical Approach*, InterVarsity Press, 2010, p. 189, ISBN 978-0830827190, **Notes:** Within fair use policy of InterVarsity Press.

8. Licona, M.R., *The Resurrection of Jesus: A New Historiographical Approach*, InterVarsity Press, 2010, p. 191, ISBN 978-0830827190, **Notes:** Within fair use policy of InterVarsity Press.

9. Licona, M.R., *The Resurrection of Jesus: A New Historiographical Approach*, InterVarsity Press, 2010, p. 197, ISBN 9780830827190, **Notes:** Within fair use policy of InterVarsity Press.

10. Public Religion Research Institute, *Nearly 3-in-10 Americans Say God Plays a Role in Outcomes of Sports Events*, 29 Jan 2013, Accessed 28 June 2014, http://publicreligion.org/research/2013/01/january-2013-tracking-poll-2/, **Notes:** Number polled: 1,033. Poll taken 16-20 Jan. 2013.

11. Public Religion Research Institute, *Half of American Fans See Supernatural Forces at Play in Sports*, 16 Jan 2014, Accessed 28 June 2014, http://publicreligion.org/research/2014/01/jan-2014-sports-poll/, **Notes:** Number polled: 1,011. Poll taken January 8-12 2014. Margin of error is +/- 3.1 percent at 95% confidence level.

12. *Is There Historical Evidence for the Resurrection of Jesus? (A Debate between William Lane Craig and Bart D. Ehrman)*, Interviewee(s): Craig, W.L., B.D. Ehrman, and College of the Holy Cross, 28 Mar 2006, Debate Transcripts: http://tinyurl.com/7gc3fpc (full URL: http://www.reasonablefaith.org/is-there-historical-evidence-for-the-resurrection-of-jesus-the-craig-ehrman), **Notes:** Refer to Bart Ehrman's Opening Statement remarks. Copyright belongs to Bart Ehrman and William Lane Craig.

13. Habermas, G.R. and M.R. Licona, *The Case for the Resurrection of Jesus*, Grand Rapids, MI, Kregel Publications, 2004, pp. 48-80, ISBN 978-0825427886, **Notes:** Refer to (1) Chapter Three - A Quintet of Facts (4 + 1): The First Two items and (2) Chapter Four - A Quintet of Facts (4 + 1): The Last Three items. Refer to the Appendix for a complete synopsis of all the author's arguments, pro and con.

14. Komarnitsky, K., *Doubting Jesus' Resurrection: What Happened in the Black Box*, 2nd ed., Stone Arrow Books, 2014, pp. 159-162, ISBN 978-0982552896.

15. Brown, R.E., *Mary in the New Testament*, Eds. Brown, *et al.*, 1978, pp. 267-277, ISBN 978-0809121687.

16. Rahner, K., *Encyclopedia of Theology: A Concise Sacramentum Mundi*, Burns & Oates, 2004, pp. 896-897, ISBN 978-0860120063.

17. Komarnitsky, K., *Doubting Jesus' Resurrection: What Happened in the Black Box*, 2nd ed., Stone Arrow Books, 2014, p. 27, ISBN 978-0982552896, **Notes:** Original source for two graveyards for criminals is presented in Mishnah, Sanhedrin 6:5-6.

18. Komarnitsky, K., *Doubting Jesus' Resurrection: What Happened in the Black Box*, 2nd ed., Stone Arrow Books, 2014, p. 28, ISBN 978-0982552896.

19. Komarnitsky, K., *Doubting Jesus' Resurrection: What Happened in the Black Box*, 2nd ed., Stone Arrow Books, 2014, pp. 30-31, ISBN 978-0982552896.

20. Josephus, F., *The Wars of the Jews*, 78 CE, Series Ed(s). Whiston, http://tinyurl.com/hyobpaj (full URL: http://data.perseus.org/citations/urn:cts:greekLit:tlg0526.tlg004.perseus-eng1:4.314), **Notes:** Translated by William Whiston, A.M. Auburn and Buffalo. John E. Beardsley. 1895. Sourced from the Perseus Digital Library Project. Refer to Book 4 Section 317: "Nay, they proceeded to that degree of impiety, as to cast away their dead bodies without burial, although the Jews used to take so much care of the burial of men, that they took down those that were condemned and crucified, and buried them before the going down of the sun.".

21. Komarnitsky, K., *Doubting Jesus' Resurrection: What Happened in the Black Box*, 2nd ed., Stone Arrow Books, 2014, p. 31, ISBN 978-0982552896.

22. Komarnitsky, K., *Doubting Jesus' Resurrection: What Happened in the Black Box*, 2nd ed., Stone Arrow Books, 2014, pp. 145-146, ISBN 978-0982552896.

23. Wright, N.T., *Surprised by Hope: Rethinking Heaven, the Resurrection, and the Mission of the Church*, 1 ed., HarperCollins, 5 Feb 2008, pp. 59, 61, ISBN 978-0061551826, **Notes:** Copyright (c) 2008 by Nicholas Thomas Wright. Courtesy of HarperCollins Publishers.

24. Rapaport, R., *Jonestown and City Hall slayings eerily linked in time and memory*, San Francisco Chronicle, 16 Nov 2003.

25. Unknown, *The Pre-Markan Passion Narrative*, Accessed 01 Nov 2015, http://www.earlychristianwritings.com/passion-young.html, **Notes:** The Passion Narrative text is from Young's Literal Translation of the Bible.

26. Wikipedia contributors, *Athanasius of Alexandria*, Wikipedia, The Free Encyclopedia, Accessed 12 Nov 2015, https://en.wikipedia.org/wiki/Athanasius_of_Alexandria.

27. Clifford, C., *St. Athanasius*, Series Title: New Advent: The Catholic Encyclopedia, Series Ed(s). Knight, New York, Robert Appleton Company, 1907, Vol 2 http://www.newadvent.org/cathen/02035a.htm.

28. Bentwich, N., *Philo-Judæus of Alexandria*, The Project Gutenberg, 2005, p. 74, http://tinyurl.com/hzk5nqu (full URL: http://www.gutenberg.org/files/14657/14657-h/14657-h.htm), **Notes:** Refer to Section III - Philo's Works and Methods.

29. Bentwich, N., *Philo-Judæus of Alexandria*, The Project Gutenberg, 2005 http://tinyurl.com/hzk5nqu (full URL: http://www.gutenberg.org/files/14657/14657-h/14657-h.htm), **Notes:** Refer to Section VI - Philo as a Philosopher.

30. Wikipedia contributors, *James (brother of Jesus)*, Wikipedia, The Free Encyclopedia, Accessed 12 Nov 2015, https://en.wikipedia.org/wiki/James_%28brother_of_Jesus%29.

31. Wikipedia contributors, *Josephus on Jesus*, Wikipedia, The Free Encyclopedia, https://en.wikipedia.org/wiki/Josephus_on_Jesus#Testimonium_Flavianum, **Notes:** Refer to section entitled, "*Testimonium Flavianum*".

32. Fitzgerald, D., *Nailed: Ten Christian Myths That Show Jesus Never Existed at All*, Lulu.com, 2010, pp. 22-30, ISBN 978-0557709915.

33. Theissen, G. and A. Merz, *Historical Jesus: A Comprehensive Guide*, Minneapolis, Fortress Press, 1998, p. 77, **Notes:** Quote sourced from: Schulthess, 'Mara bar Sarapion', 371. Cf. W. Cureton, Spicilegium Syriacum, London, 1855, 43-48.

34. Speidel, M.A., *Making Use of History beyond the Euphrates: Political Views, Cultural Traditions, and Historical Contexts in the Letter of Mara bar Sarapion*, in the proceedings of *The Letter of Mara bar Sarapion in Context: Proceedings of the Symposium*, Ed. Annette Merz, 10-12 Dec 2009, Utrecht University, Brill.

35. Richardson, C.C., *The Library of Christian Classics: Volume 1 - Early Christian Fathers*, The Westminster Press, 1953, http://tinyurl.com/gnlvt9a (full URL: http://www.ccel.org/ccel/richardson/fathers.viii.i.i.html), **Notes:** Refer to the commentary in the Introduction.

36. Publius Cornelius Tacitus, *Annals*, 116/117 CE, p. 15:44, **Notes:** See Theissen & Merz, Historical Jesus: A Comprehensive Guide, 1998, pp. 81-83.

37. Samosata, L.o., *The Death of Peregrine in The Works of Lucian of Samosata*, 2012, Vol 4, pp. 82-83, Trans. by Fowler, ISBN 978-1420945362, **Notes:** A copy of *The Death of Peregrine* can also be found at http://sacred-texts.com/cla/luc/wl4/.

38. Claremont University, *The Treatise on the Resurrection (translated by Malcom L. Peel)*, Coptic Gnostic Library Project of the Institute for Antiquity and Christianity (Claremont University), Accessed 27 Oct 2015, http://gnosis.org/naghamm/res.html.

39. Habermas, G.R., *Experiences of the Risen Jesus: The Foundational Historical Issue in the Early Proclamation of the Resurrection*, Dialog, 2006, Vol 45, No 3, pp. 288-297, Blackwell Publishing Ltd, ISSN 1540-6385, DOI: 10.1111/j.1540-6385.2006.00279.x, http://tinyurl.com/hw6xfcp (full URL: http://dx.doi.org/10.1111/j.1540-6385.2006.00279.x), **Notes:** Refer to, p. 292 for Habermas' assertion that 75 percent of biblical scholars accept the discovery of Jesus was boidly resurrected due to the empty tomb scenario and the various post-death appearances.

40. Metzger, B., *A Textual Commentary on the Greek New Testament*, 2nd ed., Hendrickson Publishers, 2005, p. 103, ISBN 978-1598561647.

41. Eusebius of Caesarea, *Eusebius of Caesarea: Gospel Problems and Solutions (Ancient Texts in Translation)*, Ed. Pearse, Ipswich, UK, Chieftain Publishing Ltd, 2011, p. 97, Trans. by David J. D. Miller, ISBN 978-0956654014, **Notes:** Eusebius' text is generally referred to as *Questions to Marinus* (Latin - *Quaestiones Ad Marinum*).

42. Saint Irenaeus, *Five Books of S. Irenaeus: Bishop of Lyons, Against Heresies*, J. Parker, 1872, p. 229, http://tinyurl.com/hqfzbln, **Notes:** See Book 3, Section 6, S. Mark xvi. 19.

43. Iverson, K.R., *Irony in the End: A Textual and Literary Analysis of Mark 16:8*, in the proceedings of *Southwestern Regional Conference of the Evangelical Theological Society*, April 2001, www.bible.org, http://tinyurl.com/hzhvpkb (full URL: https://bible.org/article/irony-end-textual-and-literary-analysis-mark-168). Reprinted with permission., **Notes:** Also See: https://en.wikipedia.org/wiki/Mark_16#cite_ref-38. Last accessed 20 Sep 2016.

44. MacRory, J., *Gospel of Saint Mark*, Series Title: New Advent: The Catholic Encyclopedia, Series Ed(s). Knight, New York, Robert Appleton Company, 1910, Vol 9 http://www.newadvent.org/cathen/09674b.htm#IV, **Notes:** Refer to section entitled, *State of text and integrity*.

45. Dicken, F.E., *Issues in Luke-Acts*, Series Ed(s). Sean A. Adams, Gorgias Pr Llc, 2012, Vol 26 of Gorgias handbooks, p. 25, ISBN 978-1607241607, **Notes:** A copy of the paper may be obtained here: https://www.academia.edu/6818602/Issues_in_Luke-Acts_Selected_Essays.

46. Saint Irenaeus, *Five Books of S. Irenaeus: Bishop of Lyons, Against Heresies*, J. Parker, 1872, p. 256, **Notes:** See Book 3, Section 6, S. Mark xvi. 19.

47. Marília, p. Futre Pinheiro, J.P.R.P., *The Ancient Novel and Early Christian and Jewish Narrative: Fictional Intersections*, Barkhuis, 2013, pp. 171-188, ISBN 978-9491431210, **Notes:** This section is written by Warren S. Smith and is entitled, "We-Passages in Acts as Mission Narrative".

48. Ehrman, B.D., *Forged: Writing in the Name of God--Why the Bible's Authors Are Not Who We Think They Are*, New York, HarperOne HarperCollins, 2011, p. 209, ISBN 978-0062012616.

49. Ehrman, B.D., *Forged: Writing in the Name of God--Why the Bible's Authors Are Not Who We Think They Are*, New York, HarperOne HarperCollins, 2011, p. 206, ISBN 978-0062012616.

50. Ehrman, B.D., *Forged: Writing in the Name of God--Why the Bible's Authors Are Not Who We Think They Are*, New York, HarperOne HarperCollins, 2011, pp. 202-209, ISBN 978-0062012616.

51. Kirby, p., *Gospel of Luke*, Early Christian Writings, 2015, Series Ed(s). Kirby, Accessed 02 Nov 2015, http://www.earlychristianwritings.com/luke.html, **Notes:** Refer to Section entitled, *Information on the Gospel of Luke*.

52. Kirby, p., *Apocryphal Gospel of Peter*, Early Christian Writings, 2015, Series Ed(s). Kirby, Accessed 10 June 2014, http://www.earlychristianwritings.com/text/gospelpeter-andrewbernhard.html/, **Notes:** English translation by Andrew Bernhard.

53. Tannaim, T., *Mishnah Sanhedrin Chapter 6*, Accessed 10 June 2014, http://www.sefaria.org/Mishnah_Sanhedrin.6, **Notes:** Edited by: Emily Fishman, Translated by Yael Klausner. The authors (the Tannaim) were a group of approximately 120 Rabbinic thinkers.

54. *Is There Historical Evidence for the Resurrection of Jesus? (A Debate between William Lane Craig and Bart D. Ehrman)*, Interviewee(s): Craig, W.L., B.D. Ehrman, and College of the Holy Cross, Format: Debate, 28 Mar 2006, Debate Transcripts: http://tinyurl.com/7gc3fpc (full URL: http://www.reasonablefaith.org/is-there-historical-evidence-for-the-resurrection-of-jesus-the-craig-ehrman), **Notes:** Refer to transcript-"Bart D. Ehrman-First Rebuttal", see his fourth point (see URL). Copyright belongs to Bart Ehrman and William Lane Craig.

55. Craig, W.L., *Visions of Jesus: A Critical Assessment of Gerd Lüdemann's Hallucination Hypothesis*, Undated, Accessed 30 March 2014, http://tinyurl.com/jlgdw6x (full URL: http://www.reasonablefaith.org/visions-of-jesus-a-critical-assessment-of-gerd-ludemanns/).

56. Lüdemann, G., *Resurrection of Jesus: History, Experience, Theology*, Ed. Bowden, Minneapolis, Fortress Press, 1994 ISBN 978-0800627928.

57. Licona, M.R., *The Resurrection of Jesus: A New Historiographical Approach*, InterVarsity Press, 2010, p. 517, ISBN 9780830827190, **Notes:** Within fair use policy of InterVarsity Press.

58. Komarnitsky, K., *Doubting Jesus' Resurrection: What Happened in the Black Box*, 2nd ed., Stone Arrow Books, 2014, p. 87, ISBN 978-0982552896, http://tinyurl.com/zpb79cp, Accessed 12 June 2014. A printable version can be accessed at: http://tinyurl.com/zu7j9uq, **Notes:** As cited by Komarnitsky in Chapter 4, p. 87 (refer to Reference 13). Original source: Australian Broadcasting Corporation News Online, "*Thai Tsunami Trauma Sparks Foreign Ghost Sightings*", reported on 14 Jan 2005. Copyright owner: Agence France Presse. Reprinted with permission of AFP.

59. Lüdemann, G., *Resurrection of Christ: A Historical Inquiry*, Prometheus Books 2004, pp. 73-74, ISBN 978-1591022459.

60. Wikipedia contributors, *Marcionism*, Wikipedia, The Free Encyclopedia, 2015, Accessed 08 Nov 2015, https://en.wikipedia.org/wiki/Marcionism, **Notes:** Refer to section entitled, "*Marcionism in Modern history*" where it states that Marcionism survived until the fifth century.

61. Wikipedia contributors, *Ebionites*, Wikipedia, The Free Encyclopedia, 2015, Accessed 08 Nov 2015, https://en.wikipedia.org/wiki/Ebionites, **Notes:** Refer to sections entitled, "*History*" and "*Last days of the Ebionite sect*" which indicate that the Ebionites existed in the late fourth century but may have disappeared by the fifth century. Other scholars say Ebionitism may have survived much longer, as long as 11th- or 12th-century.

62. Komarnitsky, K., *Doubting Jesus' Resurrection: What Happened in the Black Box*, 2nd ed., Stone Arrow Books, 2014, p. 59, ISBN 978-0982552896.

63. Komarnitsky, K., *Doubting Jesus' Resurrection: What Happened in the Black Box*, 2nd ed., Stone Arrow Books, 2014, pp. 61-62, ISBN 978-0982552896.

64. Komarnitsky, K., *Doubting Jesus' Resurrection: What Happened in the Black Box*, 2nd ed., Stone Arrow Books, 2014, p. 67, ISBN 978-0982552896.

65. Komarnitsky, K., *Doubting Jesus' Resurrection: What Happened in the Black Box*, 2nd ed., Stone Arrow Books, 2014, pp. 68-69, ISBN 978-0982552896, **Notes:** The excerpted quote is taken from Stephen J. Patterson, *The God of Jesus* (Harrisburg, PA: Trinity, 1998), p.222.

66. Dundes, A., *Introduction, Sacred Narrative: Readings in the Theory of Myth*, Ed. Dundes, 1987, p. 1, ISBN 978-0520051928

67. Okoro, K., *An Inquest into Common Humanity through Myths and Mythologies: Joseph Campbell's Paradigm*, Scholars Journal of Art, Humanities and Social Sciences, 2014, Vol 2, No 1, p. 92, ISSN 2347-5374, 2347-9493 **Notes:** A copy can be obtained here: http://saspjournals.com/sjahss or here: http://tinyurl.com/jghknnl (full URL: http://www.academia.edu/6336921/An_Inquest_into_Common_Humanity_through_Myths_and_Mythologies_Joseph_Campbells_Paradigm).

68. Licona, M., *The Resurrection of Jesus: A New Historiographical Approach*, InterVarsity Press, 2010, p. 611, ISBN 978-0830827190, **Notes:** Within fair use policy of InterVarsity Press.

69. Habermas, G.R. and M.R. Licona, *The Case for the Resurrection of Jesus*, Grand Rapids, MI, Kregel Publications, 2004, pp. 89-92, ISBN 978-0825427886.

70. Somerset, F.R.B.R., *The Hero: A Study in Tradition, Myth and Drama*, Dover Publications, 2011, pp. 189, 221, ISBN 978-0486427089, **Notes:** his material is now in the public domain (former copyright owner Penguin Publishing Group).

71. Hocart, A.M., *The Progress of Man*, Methuen & Co, 1933, p. 223, ISBN (ASIN) B00110FG4I, **Notes:** This quote is cited in *In Quest of the Hero*, 1990, pp. 95-96, Princeton University Press.

72. Somerset, F.R.B.R., *The Hero: A Study in Tradition, Myth and Drama*, Dover Publications, 2011, pp. 174-175, ISBN 978-0486427089, **Notes:** This material is now in the public domain (former copyright owner Penguin Publishing Group).

73. Dundes, A., O. Rank, and L. Raglan, *In Quest of the Hero*, Princeton University Press, 1990, pp. 179-223, ISBN 978-0691020624, **Notes:** Alan Dundes' book "The Hero Pattern and the Life of Jesus" is contained in this book.

74. Hick, J., *The Myth of God Incarnate*, SCM Press, 1977, p. 176, ISBN 978-0334010654, **Notes:** Hick's concept is more fully explored in "The Metaphor of God Incarnate, Second Edition: Christology in a Pluralistic Age" (1st ed. 1993, 2nd ed. 2005).

75. Wikipedia contributors, *John Warwick Montgomery*, Wikipedia, The Free Encyclopedia, Accessed 12 Nov 2015, John Warwick Montgomery, **Notes:** Refer to section entitled, "*Literary output*".

76. Montgomery, J.W., *History and Christianity*, Minneapolois, Bethany House, 1964, p. 14, **Notes:** See also Geisler & Bocchino, Unshakable Foundations, 2001, p. 255.

77. Licona, M.R., *The Resurrection of Jesus: A New Historiographical Approach*, InterVarsity Press, 2010, p. 185, ISBN 978-0830827190, **Notes:** Within fair use policy of InterVarsity Press.

78. Sherwin-White, A.N., *Roman Society and Roman Law in the New Testament: The Sarum Lectures 1960-1961*, Eugene, OR, Wipf & Stock Pub 2004, p. 186, ISBN 978-1592447473.

79. Strobel, L., *The Case for Christ*, Grand Rapids, MI, Zondervan, 2013, pp. 284-285, ISBN 978-0310339304, **Notes:** This quote is cited by Komarnitsky, *Doubting Jesus' Resurrection: What Happened in the Black Box?*, 2014, pp. 188-189. He cites Strobel's work as, p. 357 for the Aug. 18, 1998 printing and, p. 264 in the Sept. 1, 1998 printing. My source is the 2013 paperback version and this quote is found on, p. 285.

80. Gelsey, R.C., *Roman Society and Roman Law in the New Testament (The Sarum Lectures)*, The American Journal of Legal History, 1964, Vol 8, No 4, pp. 348-351, Oxford University Press on behalf of Temple University American Society for Legal History, ISSN 00029319, DOI: 10.2307/844459, http://www.jstor.org/stable/844459, **Notes:** Refer to, p. 351 for the quotation. Used with permission of Temple University American Society for Legal History.

81. Pollock, J.L. and J. Cruz, *Contemporary Theories of Knowledge*, Rowman & Littlefield Publishers, 1999, p. 101, ISBN 978-0847689378.

82. Swinburne, R., *The Resurrection of God Incarnate*, Oxford University Press, 2003, p. 207, ISBN 978-0199257461.

83. Hornblower, S., A. Spawforth, and E. Eidinow, *On Athanasius: The Oxford Classical Dictionary*, 4th ed., OUP Oxford, 2012, p. 193, ISBN 978-0199545568.

84. Swinburne, R., *The Resurrection of God Incarnate*, Oxford University Press, 2003, pp. 204-216, ISBN 978-0199257461.

85. Cavin, R.G. and C.A. Colombetti, *Swinburne on the Resurrection: Negative verus Christian Ramified Natural Theology*, Series Title: Philosophia Christi, Series Ed(s). Hazen, Evangelical Philosophical Society/Biola University, 2013, Vol 15, No. 2, pp. 253-264.

86. Wohlgemuth, A., *The Resurrection of God Incarnate by Richard Swinburne*, Ars Disputandi, Vol 4, 13 May 2004, ISSN 1556-5399, **Notes:** The original quote is from, Richard Swinburne, *The Resurrection of God Incarnate*, pp. 12-13, 1 ed., 2003, Clarendon Press, 978-0199257461.

87. Swinburne, R., *The Probability of the Resurrection of Jesus*, Series Title: Philosophia Christi, Series Ed(s). Hazen, Evangelical Philosophical Society/Biola University, 2013, Vol 15, No. 2, pp. 239-252.

88. Swinburne, R., *Does God Permit Massive Deception*, Series Title: Philosophia Christi, Series Ed(s). Hazen, Evangelical Philosophical Society/Biola University, 2013, Vol 15, No. 2, pp. 265-270.

89. Holder, R., *Why We Need Ramified Natural Theology*, Series Title: Philosophia Christi, Series Ed(s). Hazen, Evangelical Philosophical Society/Biola University, 2013, Vol 15, No. 2, p. 276.

90. Origen of Alexandria, *Contra Celsus*, c. 177/8 CE, Series Title: Early Christian Writings: Church Fathers: Origen, Series Ed(s). Kirby, Accessed 28 April 2017, http://www.earlychristianwritings.com/text/origen162.html, **Notes:** Refer to Book II, Chapter LIX (59). Translated by Roberts-Donaldson.

91. Justin Martyr, *Dialogue with Trypho*, Christian Classics Ethereal Library, c. 155 - 160 CE, Series Title: Ante-Nicene Fathers, Volume 1 – The Apostolic Fathers, Justin Martyr, Irenaeus, Series Ed(s). Schaff, Robertson, and Donaldson, http://www.ccel.org/ccel/schaff/anf01.viii.iv.cviii.html, **Notes:** Refer to Chapter CVIII (108) – The resurrection of Christ did not convert the Jews. But through the whole world they have sent men to accuse Christ.

92. Tertullian, *De Spectaculis*, Christian Classics Ethereal Library, c. 200 CE, Series Title: Anti-Nicene Fathers, Volume 3 – Latin Christianity: Its Founder, Tertullian, Series Ed(s). Schaff and Menzies, http://www.ccel.org/ccel/schaff/anf03.iv.v.xxx.html, Notes: Refer to Chapter XXX (30).

92. Celsus, *On the True Doctrine*, New York, Oxford University Press, c. 177/8 CE, p. 68, Trans. by Hoffmann.

93. Kaatz, K., *Early Controversies and the Growth of Christianity*, Praeger, 2012, pp. 112-113, ISBN 9780313383595, **Notes:** Kaatz points out that Eusebius of Caesarea wrote the *Life of Constantine* which talks of Constantine I's baptism but he does not state who had performed the baptismal rite. Similarly, Socrates Scholasticus, Sozmen, and Theodoret—all Christian historians—refrained from stating who baptized Constantine I in the interest to supress such an epic embarassment. It was a scholarly monk named Jerome who recorded that Constantine I was baptized as an Arian by Eusebius of Nicomedia.

CHAPTER 7

1. Viereck, G.S., *What Life Means to Einstein*, The Saturday Evening Post, 26 Oct 1929, pp. 17, 110-117, Newspaper article: http://tinyurl.com/ca3myrz, **Notes:** This quote is believed to be in the public domain. A copyright renewal could not be ascertained from the *Catalogue of Copyright* Entries, Part 1, Books, Group 2 which catalogues newspaper articles in the last half of 1929. This catalogue can be found at this URL: http://tinyurl.com/hk22ose.

2. Erikson, E.H., *Young Man Luther: A Study in Psychoanalysis and History*, W. W. Norton, 1993, p. 20, ISBN 978-0393347418.

3. Wright, N.T., *Surprised by Hope: Rethinking Heaven, the Resurrection, and the Mission of the Church*, 1 ed., HarperCollins, 5 Feb 2008, pp. 59, 61, ISBN 978-0061551826.

4. Komarnitsky, K., *Doubting Jesus' Resurrection: What Happened in the Black Box*, 2nd ed., Stone Arrow Books, 2014, p. 171, ISBN 978-0982552896.

5. *Is There Historical Evidence for the Resurrection of Jesus? (A Debate between William Lane Craig and Bart D. Ehrman)*, Interviewee(s): Craig, W.L., B.D. Ehrman, and College of the Holy Cross, 28 Mar 2006, Debate Transcripts: http://tinyurl.com/7gc3fpc (full URL: http://www.reasonablefaith.org/is-there-historical-evidence-for-the-resurrection-of-jesus-the-craig-ehrman), **Notes:** Refer to Bart Ehrman's Opening Statement remarks. Copyright belongs to Bart Ehrman and William Lane Craig.

CHAPTER 8

1. Hermanns, W., *Einstein and the Poet: In Search of the Cosmic Man*, 1st ed., Brookline Village, MA, Branden Books, 1983, p. 69, ISBN 978-0828318518.

2. Wikipedia contributors, *Gospel of John*, Wikipedia, The Free Encyclopedia, Accessed 16 Nov 2015, https://en.wikipedia.org/wiki/Gospel_of_John, **Notes:** Refer to sections entitled, "*Authorship, date, and origin*" and "*Historical reliability*".

3. McBirnie, W.S., *The Search for the Twelve Apostles*, Tyndale House Publishers, 2013, ISBN 978-1414385358, **Notes:** Refer to Chapter 2.

4. Wikipedia contributors, *Arianism*, Wikipedia, The Free Encyclopedia, Accessed 17 Nov 2015, https://en.wikipedia.org/wiki/Arianism.

5. Wikipedia contributors, *Apollonius of Tyana*, Wikipedia, The Free Encyclopedia, Accessed 17 Nov 2015, https://en.wikipedia.org/wiki/Apollonius_of_Tyana.

6. Aquinas, T., *Summa Theologica - Part III (Tertia Pars). From the Complete American Edition*, The Project Gutenberg, 1265-1274, Series Ed(s). Perry and McClamrock, Desc.: QQ. 10, http://www.gutenberg.org/ebooks/19950, **Notes:** Refer to the Part III, Question 10, introductory information.

7. Madigan, K., *Did Jesus "Progress in Wisdom"? Thomas Aquinas on Luke 2:52 in Ancient and High-Medieval Context*, Traditio, 1997, Vol 52, pp. 179-200, **Notes:** Refer to p. 191. This paper was republished in 2007, "*The Passions of Christ in High-Medieval Thought : An Essay on Christological Development: An Essay on Christological Development*", Ch. 3, pp. 23-38, ISBN: 978-0195322743.

8. Madigan, K., *Did Jesus "Progress in Wisdom"? Thomas Aquinas on Luke 2:52 in Ancient and High-Medieval Context*, Traditio, 1997, Vol 52, pp. 179-200, **Notes:** Refer to p. 190. This paper was republished in 2007, *"The Passions of Christ in High-Medieval Thought : An Essay on Christological Development: An Essay on Christological Development"*, Ch. 3, pp. 23-38, ISBN: 978-0195322743.

9. Madigan, K., *Did Jesus "Progress in Wisdom"? Thomas Aquinas on Luke 2:52 in Ancient and High-Medieval Context*, Traditio, 1997, Vol 52, pp. 179-200, **Notes:** Refer to p. 180. This paper was republished in 2007, *"The Passions of Christ in High-Medieval Thought : An Essay on Christological Development: An Essay on Christological Development"*, Ch. 3, pp. 23-38, ISBN: 978-0195322743.

10. Vermes, G., *Jesus the Jew*, Fortress Press, 1981, p. 212, ISBN 978-0800614430.

11. Rogers, R., *Theophilus of Antioch: The Life and Thought of a Second-century Bishop*, Lexington Books, 2000, pp. 7, 75, ISBN 978-0739101322, **Notes:** Refer to p. 7 for the authorship date of 169 CE for Ad Autolycum. Refer to p. 75 for the quotation.

12. Chapman, J., *Tertullian*, Series Title: New Advent: The Catholic Encyclopedia, Series Ed(s). Knight, New York, Robert Appleton Company, 1912, Vol 14, No. 18 Nov 2015, http://www.newadvent.org/cathen/14520c.htm.

13. Gonzalez, J.L., *The Story of Christianity: Volume 1: The Early Church to the Dawn of the Reformation*, HarperCollins, 2010, pp. 91-93, ISBN 978-0061855887.

14. Wikipedia contributors, *Nicene Creed*, Wikipedia, The Free Encyclopedia, Accessed 18 Nov 2015, http://tinyurl.com/hceo2u8 (full URL: https://en.wikipedia.org/wiki/Nicene_Creed#Niceno. E2.80.93Constantinopolitan_Creed), **Notes:** Refer to section entitled, *"Comparison between Creed of 325 and Creed of 381"*.

15. Saint Athanasius, *Athanasius: De Decretis or Defence of the Nicene Definition*, Christian Classics Ethereal library, 06 Aug 2004, Series Title: Nicene and Post-Nice Fathers, Series II, Volume 4, Series Ed(s). Schaff and Wace, **Notes:** Refer to Chapter V. - Defence of the Council's Phrases, "From the Essence," And "One in Essence.", No. 19., pp. 513-515, http://www.ccel.org/ccel/schaff/npnf204.pdf/.

16. Wikipedia contributors, *Trinity*, Wikipedia, The Free Encyclopedia, Accessed 18 Nov 2015, http://tinyurl.com/hydemfp (full URL: https://en.wikipedia.org/wiki/Trinity#cite_ref-dedecretis_40-0), **Notes:** Refer to section entitled, *"History for quotation"*.

17. Hunt, S., *Alternative Religions: A Sociological Introduction*, 2003, p. 48, **Notes:** Refer to the first full paragraph (p. 48) and the third paragraph (p. 48).

18. Wikipedia contributors, *Arius*, Wikipedia, The Free Encyclopedia, Accessed 18 Nov 2015, https://en.wikipedia.org/wiki/Arius, **Notes:** Refer to section entitled, *"Arianism today"*.

19. Wikipedia contributors, *Filioque*, Wikipedia, The Free Encyclopedia, Accessed 18 Nov 2015, https://en.wikipedia.org/wiki/Filioque.

20. Wikipedia contributors, *Eusebius of Nicomedia*, Wikipedia, The Free Encyclopedia, Accessed 18 Nov 2015, https://en.wikipedia.org/wiki/Eusebius_of_Nicomedia.

21. Rufinus, T., *The Church History of Rufinus of Aquileia: Books 10 and 11*, p. 13, Trans. by Amidon, **Notes:** See Book 10, Section 5.

22. Stokes, M., *Isaac Newton*, Series Title: Christian Encounters Series, Nashville, TN, Thomas Nelson, 2010, p. 83, ISBN 978-1595553034, **Notes:** Taken from *Isaac Newton (Christian Encounter Series)* by Mitch Stokes. Copyright © 2010 by Mitch Stokes. Used by permission of Thomas Nelson. www.thomasnelson.com.

23. Barnes, T.G., *Science and Biblical Faith: A Science Documentary*, T.G. Barnes, 1993, ISBN 978-0963755001.

24. Barnes, T.G., *Science and Biblical Faith: A Science Documentary*, T.G. Barnes, 1993, p. 44, ISBN 978-0963755001.

25. Newton, I., *No 30 An historical account of two notable corruptions of Scripture, in a Letter to a Friend.*, The Newton Project, Series Ed(s). Iliffe, Accessed 18 Nov 2015, http://tinyurl.com/3yq5qa3 (full URL: http://www.newtonproject.sussex.ac.uk/view/texts/normalized/THEM00261).

26. Stokes, M., *Isaac Newton*, Series Title: Christian Encounters Series, Nashville, TN, Thomas Nelson, 2010, pp. 85-86, ISBN 978-1595553034, **Notes:** Taken from *Isaac Newton (Christian Encounter Series)* by Mitch Stokes. Copyright © 2010 by Mitch Stokes. Used by permission of Thomas Nelson. www.thomasnelson.com. The inside quote (Stokes, p. 86) is sourced from Manuel, Frank E., *The Religion of Isaac Newton: Freemantle Lectures*, p. 58, 1973 (Oxford: Clarendon Press).

27. Cantlay, A.S., *English history analysed*, Longmans, Green and Company, 1875, pp. 12-13.

28. Wikipedia contributors, *Act of Uniformity 1662*, Wikipedia, The Free Encyclopedia, Accessed 19 Nov 2015, https://en.wikipedia.org/wiki/Act_of_Uniformity_1662, **Notes:** Refer to section entitled, "*Great Ejection*".

29. Wikipedia contributors, *Thirty-Nine Articles*, Wikipedia, The Free Encyclopedia, Accessed 19 Nov 2015, https://en.wikipedia.org/wiki/Thirty-Nine_Articles, **Notes:** Refer to section entitled, "*Thirty-Nine Articles (1563)*".

30. Iliffe, R., *The Newton Project*, University of Sussex, Series Ed(s). Arts and Humanities Research Council, Accessed 1 May 2014, http://tinyurl.com/2k83m5 (full URL: http://www.newtonproject.sussex.ac.uk/prism.php?id=1).

31. Wikipedia contributors, *An Historical Account of Two Notable Corruptions of Scripture*, Wikipedia, The Free Encyclopedia, 2015, Accessed 15 Sept 2015, http://tinyurl.com/a8cpkks (full URL: https://en.wikipedia.org/wiki/An_Historical_Account_of_Two_Notable_Corruptions_of_Scripture).

32. Champion, J.A.I., *The Pillars of Priestcraft Shaken: The Church of England and its Enemies, 1660-1730 (Cambridge Studies in Early Modern British History)*, Cambridge University Press 1992, pp. 116-120, ISBN 978-0521405362.

33. Spurr, J., *The Restoration Church of England, 1646-1689*, Yale University Press, 1991, ISBN 978-0300050714.

34. Mulsow, M. and J. Rohls, *Socinianism And Arminianism: Antitrinitarians, Calvinists, And Cultural Exchange in Seventeenth-century Europe*, Brill, 2005, pp. 247, 258, 262, ISBN 978-9004147157.

35. Wikipedia contributors, *Jean Leclerc (theologian)*, Wikipedia, The Free Encyclopedia, Accessed 18 Nov 2015, http://tinyurl.com/zvavkfe (full URL: https://en.wikipedia.org/wiki/Jean_Leclerc_%28theologian%29).

36. Westfall, R.S., *The Life of Isaac Newton (Canto original series)*, Cambridge University Press, 1994, pp. 199-200, ISBN 978-0521477376.

37. Jorink, E. and A. Maas, *Newton and the Netherlands: How Isaac Newton Was Fashioned in the Dutch Republic*, University of Chicago Press, 2012, pp. 24-26, ISBN 978-9087281373.

38. The Codex Sinaiticus Project, Accessed 18 Nov 2015, http://codexsinaiticus.org/en/manuscript.aspx, **Notes:** Refer to passage for 1 John 5:6-8.

39. Unknown, *Book of 1 John*, The Zondervan Corporation, L.L.C., https://www.biblegateway.com/, **Notes:** Refer to 1 John 5:6-8 using the King James Version selection.

40. Snobelen, S.D., *Isaac Newton, Socianianism and "the one supreme God"*, in Book: Socinianism and cultural exchange: the European dimension of Antitrinitarian and Arminian Networks, 1650-1720, Eds. Mulsow and Rohls, Brill, 2005, pp. 241-293, **Notes:** A copy of the paper is provided here: http://tinyurl.com/h6zlfr3 (full URL: https://isaacnewtonstheology.files.wordpress.com/2013/06/newton-and-socinianism.pdf).

41. Westfall, R.S., *The Life of Isaac Newton (Canto original series)*, Cambridge University Press, 1994, p. 124, ISBN 978-0521477376.

42. Arendzen, J., *Marcionites*, Robert Appleton Company, 1910, Series Title: The Catholic Encyclopedia, Series Ed(s). Knight, Accessed 20 Nov 2015, http://www.newadvent.org/cathen/09645c.htm, **Notes:** Refer to section, Doctrine and discipline.

43. Wikipedia contributors, *Sabellius*, Wikipedia, The Free Encyclopedia, 2014, Accessed 04 Nov 2014, http://en.wikipedia.org/wiki/Sabellius/, **Notes:** For a historical synopsis on Sabellianism refer to the Christian Classics Ethereal Library: http://tinyurl.com/j55jhaw.

44. Wikipedia contributors, *Nestorius*, Wikipedia, The Free Encyclopedia, Accessed 20 Nov 2015, https://en.wikipedia.org/wiki/Nestorius.

45. Wikipedia contributors, *Apocatastasis*, Wikipedia, The Free Encyclopedia, Accessed 23 Nov 2015, https://en.wikipedia.org/wiki/Apocatastasis, **Notes:** Refer to section entitled, *"Early Christianity"*.

CHAPTER 9

1. Einstein, A., A. Calaprice, and F. Dyson, *The Ultimate Quotable Einstein*, Princeton University Press, 2010, p. 325, ISBN 978-1400835966, **Notes:** Original source is a letter to Milton M. Schayer, August 1, 1927 which is quoted in *Albert Einstein, The Human Side: Glimpses from His Archives*, eds. Dukas and Hoffman, p. 66, Einstein Archives 48-380, ISBN 978-0691160238. Copyright © 1982 The Hebrew University of Jerusalem. Published by Princeton University Press. Reprinted by permission.

2. Whitehead, A.N., *Science and the Modern World*, Cambridge University Press, 2011, p. 30, ISBN 978-0521237789, **Notes:** Also cited in Grassie, The New Sciences of Religion, Palgrave Macmillan, 2010, p. 194.

3. David Baggett, R.C., *Omnibenevolence, Moral Apologetics, and Doubly Ramified Natural Theology*, Series Title: Philosophia Christi, Series Ed(s). Hazen, Evangelical Philosophical Society/Biola University, 2013, Vol 15, No. 2, p. 337, **Notes:** See original abstract posted in the footer.

4. Swinburne, R., *The Existence of God*, 2nd ed., Oxford University Press, 2004, p. 343, ISBN 978-0199271689.

5. Swinburne, R., *The Existence of God*, 2nd ed., Oxford University Press, 2004, p. 344, ISBN 978-0199271689.

6. Swinburne, R., *The Christian God*, Oxford University Press, 1994, ISBN 978-0198235125.

7. Craig, W.L., *On Guard: Defending Your Faith with Reason and Precision*, David C. Cook, 2010, p. 74, ISBN 978-1434701886, **Notes:** Refer to Chapter 4, Citation 1. Al-Ghazali, Kitab al-Iqtisad fi'l-I'tiqad (The Moderate Path in Theology), cited in S. de Beaurecueil, "Gazzali et S. Thomas d'Aquin: Essai sur la preuve de l'existence de Dieu proposée dans l'Iqtisad et sa comparaison avec les 'voies' Thomiste", Bulletin de l'Institut Francais d'Archaeologie Orientale 46 (1947): 203. This former citation is translated as folloows: S. de Beaurecueil, "*Ghazzali and St Thomas Aquinas : An Essay on the evidence of the existence of God proposed in Iqtisad and its comparison with the 'pathways' Thomiste*", Bulletin of the French Institute of Oriental Archaeologie, 46 (1947): 203.

8. Beckman, E., *Richard Swinburne's Inductive Argument for the Existence of God – A Critical Analysis*, Masters - Culture and Communication, Linköping University (Sweden), Advisor: Petersson, 80 p., 28 Nov 2008, Doc. No: ISRN: LIU-IKK/PF-A-09/001--SE, http://tinyurl.com/h63tehl (full URL: http://urn.kb.se/resolve?urn=urn:nbn:se:liu:diva-17319).

9. Swinburne, R., *The Christian God*, Clarendon Press, 1994, p. 125, ISBN 978-0198235125.

10. Swinburne, R., *The Existence of God*, 2nd ed., Oxford University Press, 2004, pp. 94-95, ISBN 978-0199271689.

11. Parsons, K.M., *The Problem of Theistic Arguments*, Series Title: Routledge Companion to Philosophy of Religion, Series Ed(s). Meister and Copan, Taylor & Francis, 2013, p. 494, ISBN 978-1136696855.

12. Davies, P., *Superforce*, Simon & Schuster, 1984, p. 242, ISBN 978-0671476854.

13. Stephen Hawking, L.M., *The Grand Design*, Bantam Books, 2011, p. 180, ISBN 978-0553840919.

14. Swinburne, R., *The Christian God*, Clarendon Press, 1994, p. 146, ISBN 978-0198235125, **Notes:** This is paraphrased to reduce potential confusion stemming from Swinburne's original words where he mentions other concepts.

15. Clark, K.J., *Trinity or Tritheism?*, Religious Studies, 1996, Vol 32, No 4, p. 466, Cambridge University Press, ISSN 00344125, 1469901X, http://www.jstor.org/stable/20008053.

16. Beckman, E., *Richard Swinburne's Inductive Argument for the Existence of God – A Critical Analysis*, Masters - Culture and Communication, Linköping University (Sweden), 80 p., 28 Nov 2008, Doc. No: ISRN: LIU-IKK/PF-A-09/001--SE, **Notes** For quote, refer to p. 13. Op. cit. Swinburne, "*Arguments for the Existence of God*", Milltown Studies, Vol. 33, 1994, p.24-36. Her citation references p. 22 as the source of this quote which appears to be outside the range in this Milltown Studies document. A copy of Beckman's thesis can be found here: http://tinyurl.com/zn4m2v7 (full URL: http://www.diva-portal.org/smash/get/diva2:208388/FULLTEXT01.pdf). Also, a permanent link is posted: http://tinyurl.com/h63tehl (full URL: http://urn.kb.se/resolve?urn=urn:nbn:se:liu:diva-17319).

17. Swinburne, R., *The Christian God*, Clarendon Press, 1994, pp. 172-191, ISBN 978-0198235125.

18. Clark, K.J., *Trinity or Tritheism?*, Religious Studies, 1996, Vol 32, No 4, pp. 463-476, Cambridge University Press, ISSN 00344125, 1469901X, http://www.jstor.org/stable/20008053.

19. Parsons, K.M., *Science, Confirmation, and the Theistic Hypothesis*, Ph.D. - Philosophy, Queen's University (Kingston, Ontario), Advisor: Prado, 218 p., 1986, Accession Number: 682714, Call Number: Thesis PhD .P2684 (see also Microfiche no. 390), ISBN 978-0315320789, **Notes** A copy of this material can also be sourced from: http://tinyurl.com/jyu8tjy (full URL: http://infidels.org/library/modern/keith_parsons/theistic/3.html). Refer to Chapter 3 - Swinburne and the Inductive Cosmological Argument.

20. Swinburne, R., *The Existence of God*, 2nd ed., Oxford University Press, 2004, p. 342, ISBN 978-0199271689.

21. Swinburne, R., *The Existence of God*, 2nd ed., Oxford University Press, 2004, p. 341, ISBN 978-0199271689.

22. Timothy McGrew, J.M.D., *Natural Theology and the Uses of Argument*, Series Title: Philosophia Christi, Series Ed(s). Hazen, Evangelical Philosophical Society/Biola University, 2013, Vol 15, No. 2, pp. 299-309, **Notes:** See original abstract posted in the footer.

23. Talbott, W., *"Bayesian Epistemology"*, The Stanford Encyclopedia of Philosophy (Summer 2015 Edition), Series Ed(s). Zalta, Accessed 06 Jun 2016, http://plato.stanford.edu/archives/fall2013/entries/epistemology-bayesian/.

24. Beckman, E., *Richard Swinburne's Inductive Argument for the Existence of God – A Critical Analysis*, Masters - Culture and Communication, Linköping University (Sweden), 80 p., 28 Nov 2008, Doc. No: ISRN: LIU-IKK/PF-A-09/001--SE, http://tinyurl.com/h63tehl (full URL: http://urn.kb.se/resolve?urn=urn:nbn:se:liu:diva-17319), **Notes** For quote, refer to p. 15.

25. Pope Francis, *Morning Meditation in the Chapel of the Domus Sanctae Marthae: Misery and Glory*, 8 Apr 2014, http://w2.vatican.va/content/francesco/en/cotidie/2014/documents/papa-francesco-cotidie_20140408_misery-glory.html, **Notes:** Used with permission. Libreria Editrice Vaticana.

26. Pope Francis, *Homily at St. Martha's House: Pope: God is real, concrete person, not mysterious, intangible mist*, Catholic News Service, 18 April 2013, Accessed 11 Sep 2014, http://www.catholicnews.com/data/stories/cns/1301739.htm/. See Also: http://www.catholicnews.com/services/englishnews/2013/pope-god-is-real-concrete-person-not-mysterious-intangible-mist.cfm, **Notes:** Web article headline: "Pope: "God is real, concrete person, not mysterious, intangible mist", Carol Glatz, Reporter for Catholic News Service.

27. Church, C., *Catechism of the Catholic Church: With Modifications from the Editio Typica*, Doubleday, 2003, pp. 22-24, ISBN 978-0385508193, **Notes:** A free online English translation of the Cathechism of the Catholic Church is provided by the United States Conference of Catholic Bishiops at the following URL: http://tinyurl.com/h6ljlnx (full URL: http://ccc.usccb.org/flipbooks/catechism/). Refer to p. 16, 18-19 for the quoted text.

28. Boeve, L., *Negative Theology and Theological Hermeneutics. The Particularity of Naming God*, in Book: Gott Nennen: Gottes Namen und Gott als Name (trans. God Name: God Name and God as Name), Eds. Dalferth and Stoellger, Mohr Siebeck, 2008, pp. 189-207, ISBN 978-3161497926, **Notes:** Quotes are to be found on p.189. Article is published in English. Book content is generally in German. Reproduced with permission of copyright owner Mohr Siebeck Tübingen.

29. Boeve, L., *Negative Theology and Theological Hermeneutics: The Particularlity of Naming God*, Journal of Philosophy & Scripture, 2006, Vol 3, No 2 (Spring), pp. 1-13, ISSN 1555-5100, http://www.philosophyandscripture.org/Issue3-2/Boeve/Boeve2.html, **Notes:** Quote is on p.1. This article was originally pre-published by the Journal of Philosophy & Scripture. The copyright owner (Mohr Siebeck) later published the article in a book entitled *Gott Nennen: Gottes Namen und Gott als Name*, eds. Dalferth and Stoellger, 2008, Mohr Siebeck. Reproduced with permission of copyright owner Mohr Siebeck Tübingen.

30. Rubenstein, M.-J., *Unknow Thyself: Apophaticism, Deconstruction, and Theology After Ontotheology*, Modern Theology, 2003, Vol 19, No 3, p. 394, ISSN 0266-07177 (Print); 1468-0225 (Online).

31. Rubenstein, M.-J., *Unknow Thyself: Apophaticism, Deconstruction, and Theology After Ontotheology*, Modern Theology, 2003, Vol 19, No 3, p. 391, ISSN 0266-07177 (Print); 1468-0225 (Online).

32. Levenson, J.D., *Inheriting Abraham: The Legacy of the Patriarch in Judaism, Christianity, and Islam*, Princeton University Press, 2012, p. 8, ISBN 978-0691155692, **Notes:** The source for this reference was originally obtained from Wikipedia "Abraham", Heading: "Abraham in religious traditions", Sub-Heading: "Islam", Footnote 25, http://tinyurl.com/jca3o6y (full URL: http://en.wikipedia.org/wiki/Abraham#CITEREFLevenson2012/), Access date: 03 September 2016.

33. Churchill, W., *"The Russian Enigma"*, We Will Deal in Performances, Not Promises: *IT IS NOT FOR HITLER TO SAY WHEN "THE WAR WILL END*, BBC Radio Broadcast, 1 Oct 1939, http://tinyurl.com/je6x6p5 (full URL: http://www.ibiblio.org/pha/policy/1939/1939-10-01a.html), **Notes:** This quote is from a radio address in London. ibiblio.org is a collaboration of the School of Information and Library Science, the School of Journalism and Mass Communication, and Information Technology Services at the University of North Carolina at Chapel Hill.

CHAPTER 10

1. Ouaki, F. and A. Benson, *Imagine All the People: A Conversation with the Dalai Lama on Money, Politics, and Life As It Could Be*, Wisdom, 1999, p. 59, ISBN 978-0861711505.

2. Hanh, T.N., *Interbeing: Fourteen Guidelines for Engaged Buddhism*, Ed. Eppsteiner, Parallax Press, 1987, ISBN 978-1888375084.

3. Küng, H., *The World's Religions: Common Ethical Values*, 2005, Accessed 23 Nov 2014, http://tinyurl.com/zn8v8vk (full URL: http://www.oneworlduv.com/wp-content/uploads/2011/06/hkung_santaclara_univ_global_ethic_human_resp_2005.pdf). Last accessed 27 Sep 2016. Refer to the Conclusion, **Notes:** Presented on March 31, 2005 at the opening Exhibit on the World's Religions at Santa Clara University. Introduction by Paul Locatelli. The exhibit was prepared by the Global Ethic Foundation, of which Kung is co-founder and president. A similarly worded quote is also cited earlier (1995) in *Living Buddha, Living Christ* (Thich Nhat Hanh and Elaine Pagels, 2007, p. 2, Riverhead Books, 978-1594482397, First printed 1995).

4. Johnson, T.M. and B.J. Grim, *The World's Religions in Figures: An Introduction to International Religious Demography*, 1st ed., Wiley-Blackwell, 2013, p. 11, ISBN 978-0470674543.

5. Johnson, T.M. and B.J. Grim, *The World's Religions in Figures: An Introduction to International Religious Demography*, 1st ed., Wiley-Blackwell, 2013, pp. 10, 12, 112, ISBN 978-0470674543, **Notes:** Refer to Table 1.2 (Percentage of the world's population belonging to no religion or religion, 1910-2010). Data is reported for 1910, 1950, 1970, 2000, 2010. For intervening years, the data was linearly interpolated. This dataset was additionally supplemented by data sourced from Table 1.1 (World religions by adherents, 1910-2010) for the group entitled "Jews". The data associated with the "Other Religionists" group in Table 1.2 was further adjusted by subtracting-out the associated data of the "Jews" group (Table 1.1 - Jews) to properly balance the overall data. Also, the "Jew" data group only contained data on Jews for the years 1910 and 2010. The data for the Jewish tradition was interpolated as follows in the following format YEAR : % Population ... 1910 : 0.80 / 1950 : 0.60 / 1970 : 0.50 / 2000 : 0.40 / 2010 : 0.20 (end). This interpolation is expected to be very close to actual data because the the summation of annual data adds up to 100.0% which is what is to be expected. The data used for the Year 2050 is from Table 4.1. The original source data for all three Tables 1.1, 1.2, and 4.1 is: Todd M. Johnson and Brian J. Grim, eds, *World Religion Database* (Leiden/Boston: Brill, accessed January 2012). All adjustments of the data were performed by Brian Goedken (present author). The data for the World Population is from the US Census Bureau, International Database, 1950-2050. Figures are Total Midyear Population.

6. Johnson, T.M. and B.J. Grim, *The World's Religions in Figures: An Introduction to International Religious Demography*, 1st ed., Wiley-Blackwell, 2013, pp. 10, 12, ISBN 978-0470674543, **Notes:** Refer to Table 1.2 (Percentage of the world's population belonging to no religion or religion, 1910-2010). This dataset was supplemented by data sourced from Table 1.1 (World religions by adherents, 1910-2010) for the Jewish tradition. The data associated with the "Other Religionists" group in Table 1.2 was modified by subtracting the associated data for the "Jews" group presented in Table 1.1. Also, the "Jew" data group only contained data on Jews for the years 1910 and 2010. The data for the Jewish tradition was interpolated by the present author as follows in the following format YEAR : % Population ... 1910 : 0.80 / 1950 : 0.60 / 1970 : 0.50 / 2000 : 0.40 / 2010 : 0.20 (end). This interpolation is expected to be very close to actual data because the the summation of annual data adds up to 100.0% which is what is to be expected. The original source data for Tables 1.1 and Table 1.2 is: Todd M. Johnson and Brian J. Grim, eds, *World Religion Database* (Leiden/Boston: Brill, accessed January 2012).

7. Pew Research Center, *"Nones" on the Rise: One-in-Five Adults Have No Religious Affiliation*, 2012, p. 13, Pew Research Center's Forum on Religion & Public Life, http://www.pewforum.org/, **Notes:** Refer to Table entitled "Trends in Religious Affiliation, 2007 - 2012". This data was supplmented data for 2013 and 2014. The data for 2014 is sourced from Pew Research Center's report, *America's Changing Religious Landscape*, 12 May 2015. The data for 2013 is a linear interpolation of the respective 2012 and 2014 data.

8. Cooperman, A., G. Smith, and K. Ritchey, *America's Changing Religious Landscape: Christians Decline Sharply as Share of Population; Unaffiliated and Other Faiths Continue to Grow*, 2015, Pew Research Center's Forum on Religion & Public Life, p. 4, http://tinyurl.com/ldnxabw (full URL: http://www.pewforum.org/2015/05/12/americas-changing-religious-landscape/), **Notes:** Refer to Table entitled, "Christians Decline as Share of U.S. Population; Other Faiths and the Unaffiliated Are Growing". Data utilized is from Year 2014.

9. Johnson, T.M. and B.J. Grim, *The World's Religions in Figures: An Introduction to International Religious Demography*, 1st ed., Wiley-Blackwell, 2013, p. 104, ISBN 978-0470674543.

10. Johnson, T.M. and B.J. Grim, *The World's Religions in Figures: An Introduction to International Religious Demography*, 1st ed., Wiley-Blackwell, 2013, p. 171, ISBN 978-0470674543.

11. Hick, J., *A Christian Theology of Religions: The Rainbow of Faiths*, Louisville, KY, Westminster John Knox Press, 1995, p. 27, ISBN 978-0664255961.

12. Hick, J., *The Fifth Dimension: An Exploration of the Spiritual Realm*, 2nd ed., Oxford, England, Oneworld Publications, 1999, ISBN 978-1851681914.

13. Peters, R., *John Hick: Man of Many Mysticisms*, 2005, Accessed 08 Jan 2016, http://people.bu.edu/wwildman/bce/mwt_themes_875_hick.htm, **Notes:** Refer to heading entitled, *"Transcategorial reality"*.

14. Hick, J., *Exclusivism vs. Pluralism: A Response to Kevin Meeker*, Religious Studies, 2006, Vol 45, No 2, pp. 207-212, ISSN 00344125, 1469901X, http://www.jstor.org/stable/20008645, **Notes:** Cited in "Hick's Philosophical Advocacy of Religious Pluralism: Exposition and Evaluation", Bradley Cochran, 2012, p. 7, refer to footnote 25, https://udayton.academia.edu/BradleyCochran. Cochran notes that Hick's primary source for the quote is from: Dionysius, The Divine Names, in The Complete Works of Pseudo-Dionusius, translated by Colm Luibheid, New York: Paulist Press, 1987, p. 53, 978-0809128389.

15. Hick, J., *A Christian Theology of Religions: The Rainbow of Faiths*, Louisville, KY, Westminster John Knox Press, 1995, pp. 25-26, ISBN 978-0664255961.

16. Coles, P.J., J. Kaniewski, and S. Wehner, *Equivalence of wave–particle duality to entropic uncertainty*, Nat Commun, Vol 5, 19 Dec 2014, Nature Publishing Group, a division of Macmillan Publishers Limited. All Rights Reserved., DOI: 10.1038/ncomms6814, http://dx.doi.org/10.1038/ncomms6814.

17. Hick, J., *An Interpretation of Religion: Human Responses to the Transcendent*, Yale University Press, 2004, pp. 101-103, ISBN 978-0300106688.

18. The Holy See, Cardinal Joseph Ratzinger, *Declaration "Dominus Iesus" On the Unicity and Salvific Universality of Jesus Christ and the Church*, Roman Curia, The Vatican, 2000, Accessed 08 Jan 20016, In English: http://tinyurl.com/81n1. Also if link is broken, try locating in the list of documents provided here: http://tinyurl.com/zuq6she, **Notes:** This is also officially archived in the Acta Apostolicae Sedis, AAS 92 (2000) pp. 742-765 (in Italian), http://www.vatican.va/archive/aas/documents/AAS-92-2000-ocr.pdf.

19. Hick, J., *A Christian Theology of Religions: The Rainbow of Faiths*, Louisville, KY, Westminster John Knox Press, 1995, p. 51, ISBN 978-0664255961.

20. Cochran, B., *Hick's Philosophical Advocacy of Religious Pluralism: Exposition and Evaluation*, Bradley Cochran's website: T h e o • p h i l o g u e, 2012, https://theophilogue.com/pdf-catalogue/. Also try: https://theophilogue.wordpress.com/. The paper is also provided at: https://udayton.academia.edu/BradleyCochran, and at, https://www.researchgate.net/profile/Bradley_Cochran.

21. Hick, J., *An Interpretation of Religion: Human Responses to the Transcendent*, Yale University Press, 2004, pp. xx-xxi, ISBN 978-0300106688.

22. Hick, J., *An Interpretation of Religion: Human Responses to the Transcendent*, Yale University Press, 2004, p. xxv, ISBN 978-0300106688.

23. Hick, J., *Exclusivism versus pluralism in religion: A response to Kevin Meeker*, Religious Studies, 2006, Vol 42, No 2, p. 211, **Notes:** Article is to be found on pp. 207-212.

24. Hick, J., *Exclusivism versus pluralism in religion: A response to Kevin Meeker*, Religious Studies, 2006, Vol 42, No 2, pp. 207-212, ISSN 00344125, 1469901X, http://www.jstor.org/stable/20008645, **Notes:** Refer to p. 211.

25. Hick, J., *A Christian Theology of Religions: The Rainbow of Faiths*, Westminster John Knox Press, 1995, p. 78, ISBN 978-0664255961.

26. Hick, J., *An Interpretation of Religion: Human Responses to the Transcendent*, Yale University Press, 2004, p. xx, ISBN 978-0300106688.

27. Grassie, W., *The New Sciences of Religion: Exploring Spirituality from the Outside In and Bottom Up*, New York, NY, Palgrave Macmillan 2010, p. 209, ISBN 978-0230108776, **Notes:** Reproduced with permission of Palgrave Macmillan.

28. Grassie, W., *The New Sciences of Religion: Exploring Spirituality from the Outside In and Bottom Up*, New York, NY, Palgrave Macmillan 2010, p. 221, ISBN 978-0230108776, **Notes:** Refer to endnotes: see Introduction - Note 3.

29. Grassie, W., *The New Sciences of Religion: Exploring Spirituality from the Outside In and Bottom Up*, New York, NY, Palgrave Macmillan 2010, pp. 3-4, ISBN 978-0230108776, **Notes:** Reproduced with permission of Palgrave Macmillan.

30. Grassie, W., *The New Sciences of Religion: Exploring Spirituality from the Outside In and Bottom Up*, New York, NY, Palgrave Macmillan 2010, p. 6, ISBN 978-0230108776, **Notes:** Reproduced with permission of Palgrave Macmillan.

31. Grassie, W., *The New Sciences of Religion: Exploring Spirituality from the Outside In and Bottom Up*, New York, NY, Palgrave Macmillan 2010, pp. 181, 212, ISBN 978-0230108776, **Notes:** Reproduced with permission of Palgrave Macmillan.

32. Grassie, W., *The New Sciences of Religion: Exploring Spirituality from the Outside In and Bottom Up*, New York, NY, Palgrave Macmillan 2010, p. 154, ISBN 978-0230108776, **Notes:** Reproduced with permission of Palgrave Macmillan.

33. Grassie, W., *The New Sciences of Religion: Exploring Spirituality from the Outside In and Bottom Up*, New York, NY, Palgrave Macmillan 2010, p. 215, ISBN 978-0230108776, **Notes:** Reproduced with permission of Palgrave Macmillan.

34. Grassie, W., *The New Sciences of Religion: Exploring Spirituality from the Outside In and Bottom Up*, New York, NY, Palgrave Macmillan 2010, pp. 214-216, ISBN 978-0230108776, **Notes:** Reproduced with permission of Palgrave Macmillan.

35. Grassie, W., *The New Sciences of Religion: Exploring Spirituality from the Outside In and Bottom Up*, New York, NY, Palgrave Macmillan 2010, p. 200, ISBN 978-0230108776, **Notes:** Reproduced with permission of Palgrave Macmillan.

36. Grassie, W., *The New Sciences of Religion: Exploring Spirituality from the Outside In and Bottom Up*, New York, NY, Palgrave Macmillan 2010, pp. 200-201, ISBN 978-0230108776, **Notes:** Reproduced with permission of Palgrave Macmillan.

37. Grassie, W., *The New Sciences of Religion: Exploring Spirituality from the Outside In and Bottom Up*, New York, NY, Palgrave Macmillan 2010, p. 136, ISBN 978-0230108776, **Notes:** Reproduced with permission of Palgrave Macmillan.

38. Grassie, W., *The New Sciences of Religion: Exploring Spirituality from the Outside In and Bottom Up*, New York, NY, Palgrave Macmillan 2010, p. 159, ISBN 978-0230108776.

39. Grassie, W., *The New Sciences of Religion: Exploring Spirituality from the Outside In and Bottom Up*, New York, NY, Palgrave Macmillan 2010, p. 214, ISBN 978-0230108776, **Notes:** Reproduced with permission of Palgrave Macmillan.

CHAPTER 11

1. Chaisson, E.J., *COSMIC EVOLUTION: THE RISE OF COMPLEXITY IN NATURE*, Cambridge, Mass., Harvard University Press, Copyright © 2001 by the President and Fellows of Harvard College, p. 126, ISBN 978-0674003422.

2. Chaisson, E.J., *COSMIC EVOLUTION: THE RISE OF COMPLEXITY IN NATURE*, Cambridge, Mass., Harvard University Press, Copyright © 2001 by the President and Fellows of Harvard College, p. 129, ISBN 978-0674003422.

3. Sir John Marks Templeton, *The Humble Approach: Scientists Discover God*, Revised ed., Radnor, Pennsylvania, Templeton Foundation Press, p. 114, ISBN 978-1890151171, **Notes:** Reprinted by permission from Templeton Press.

4. Defilippo, J.G., *Aristotle's Identification of the Prime Mover as God*, The Classical Quarterly, 1994, Vol 44, No 2, p. 394, Cambridge University Press, ISSN 00098388, 14716844, http://www.jstor.org/stable/639643, **Notes:** Full article is on pp. 393-409.

5. Bear, M.F., B.W. Connors, and M.A. Paradiso, *Neuroscience*, Lippincott Williams & Wilkins, 2007, p. 5, ISBN 978-0781760034.

6. Aquinas, T., *Summa Theologica - Part I (Prima Pars). From the Complete American Edition*, The Project Gutenberg, 1265-1274, Series Ed(s). Perry and McClamrock, http://www.gutenberg.org/ebooks/17611, **Notes:** Refer to Part 1, Question 2, Article 3.

7. Sherman, J. and T.W. Deacon, *Teleology for the Perplexed: How Matter Began to Matter*, Zygon: Journal of Religion & Science, 2007, Vol 42, No 4, pp. 878, 897, 900, Blackwell Publishing Ltd, ISSN 1467-9744, DOI: 10.1111/j.1467-9744.2007.00878.x, http://tinyurl.com/jdj7z69.

8. Deacon, T.W., *Reciprocal Linkage between Self-organizing Processes is Sufficient for Self-reproduction and Evolvability*, Biological Theory, 2006, Vol 1, No 2, p. 138.

9. Deacon, T.W., *Reciprocal Linkage between Self-organizing Processes is Sufficient for Self-reproduction and Evolvability*, Biological Theory, 2006, Vol 1, No 2, pp. 136-149.

10. Sherman, J. and T.W. Deacon, *Teleology for the Perplexed: How Matter Began to Matter*, Zygon: Journal of Religion & Science, 2007, Vol 42, No 4, pp. 873-901, Blackwell Publishing Ltd, ISSN 1467-9744, DOI: 10.1111/j.1467-9744.2007.00878.x, http://tinyurl.com/jdj7z69.

11. Deacon, T.W., *Reciprocal Linkage between Self-organizing Processes is Sufficient for Self-reproduction and Evolvability*, Biological Theory, 2006, Vol 1, No 2, pp. 139-141.

12. Sherman, J. and T.W. Deacon, *Teleology for the Perplexed: How Matter Began to Matter*, Zygon: Journal of Religion & Science, 2007, Vol 42, No 4, pp. 884-895, Blackwell Publishing Ltd, ISSN 1467-9744, DOI: 10.1111/j.1467-9744.2007.00878.x, http://tinyurl.com/jdj7z69.

13. Sherman, J. and T.W. Deacon, *Teleology for the Perplexed: How Matter Began to Matter*, Zygon: Journal of Religion & Science, 2007, Vol 42, No 4, p. 893, Blackwell Publishing Ltd, ISSN 1467-9744, DOI: 10.1111/j.1467-9744.2007.00878.x, http://tinyurl.com/jdj7z69.

14. Sherman, J. and T.W. Deacon, *Teleology for the Perplexed: How Matter Began to Matter*, Zygon: Journal of Religion & Science, 2007, Vol 42, No 4, p. 896, Blackwell Publishing Ltd, ISSN 1467-9744, DOI: 10.1111/j.1467-9744.2007.00878.x, http://tinyurl.com/jdj7z69.

15. Weber, B.H., *Selection, Interpretation, and the Emergence of Living Systems*, Zygon: Journal of Religion & Science, 2010, Vol 45, No 2, pp. 361-366, Wiley-Blackwell, ISSN 05912385, DOI: 10.1111/j.1467-9744.2010.01086.x.

16. Southgate, C. and A. Robinson, *Intrepretation and the Origin of Life*, Zygon: Journal of Religion & Science, 2010, Vol 45, No 2, p. 354, Wiley-Blackwell, ISSN 05912385, DOI: 10.1111/j.1467-9744.2010.01085.x.

17. Sherman, J. and T.W. Deacon, *Teleology for the Perplexed: How Matter Began to Matter*, Zygon: Journal of Religion & Science, 2007, Vol 42, No 4, p. 897, Blackwell Publishing Ltd, ISSN 1467-9744, DOI: 10.1111/j.1467-9744.2007.00878.x, http://tinyurl.com/jdj7z69.

18. Morley, B., *Internet Encyclopedia of Philosophy: Western Concepts of God*, Series Ed(s). Fieser and Dowden, ISSN 2161-0002, Accessed 12 Nov 2014, http://www.iep.utm.edu/god-west/.

19. Cooper, J.W., *Panentheism The Other God of the Philosophers: From Plato to Present*, Grand Rapids, MI, Baker Academic, 2006, p. 149, ISBN 978-0801049316.

20. Wikipedia contributors, *Noosphere*, Wikipedia, The Free Encyclopedia, Accessed 28 Oct 2014, http://en.wikipedia.org/wiki/Noosphere/.

21. Cooper, J.W., *Panentheism The Other God of the Philosophers: From Plato to Present*, Grand Rapids, MI, Baker Academic, 2006, p. 150, ISBN 978-0801049316, **Notes:** This is a paraphrasing of Cooper's comments under the heading *Evolution from Energy to Humanity*.

22. Cooper, J.W., *Panentheism The Other God of the Philosophers: From Plato to Present*, Grand Rapids, MI, Baker Academic, 2006, pp. 160-161, ISBN 978-0801049316.

23. Cooper, J.W., *Panentheism The Other God of the Philosophers: From Plato to Present*, Grand Rapids, MI, Baker Academic, 2006, pp. 149-150, ISBN 978-0801049316.

24. Seibt, J., *"Process Philosophy"*, The Stanford Encyclopedia of Philosophy (Spring 2016 Edition), Series Ed(s). Zalta, Accessed 06 Jun 2016, http://tinyurl.com/hpytvwk.

25. Viney, D., *"Process Theism"*, The Stanford Encyclopedia of Philosophy (Spring 2014 Edition), Series Ed(s). Zalta, Accessed 29 Oct 2014, http://tinyurl.com/z57ukqh, **Notes:** Paraphrased commentary about C. Hartshorne assisting A. N. Whitehead and that they wrote about God in the same general timeframe.

26. Cooper, J.W., *Panentheism The Other God of the Philosophers: From Plato to Present*, Grand Rapids, MI, Baker Academic, 2006, p. 167, ISBN 978-0801049316, **Notes:** As cited in Footnote 10 - "A preliminary overview of his system is in Whitehead, "The Categorical Scheme," and "Some Derivative Notions," chaps. 2-3 in part 1 of *Process and Reality*.

27. Chalmers, D.J., *Strong and Weak Emergence*, in Book: The re-emergence of emergence : the emergentist hypothesis from science to religion, Eds. Clayton and Davies, Oxford, University Press, 2008, No., Ch. 11, p. 244, ISBN 978-0199544318.

28. Cooper, J.W., *Panentheism The Other God of the Philosophers: From Plato to Present*, Grand Rapids, MI, Baker Academic, 2006, p. 311, ISBN 978-0801049316.

29. Deacon, T.W., *Incomplete Nature: How Mind Emerged from Matter*, W. W. Norton, 2011, pp. 303,427, ISBN 978-0393080834.

30. Deacon, T.W., J. Haag, and J. Ogilvy, *The Emergence of Self*, in Book: *In Search of Self: Interdisciplinary Perspectives on Personhood*, Eds. Huyssteen and Wiebe, Grand Rapids, MI, William B. Eerdmans, 2011, No., Ch. 16, ISBN 978-0802863867, http://anthropology.berkeley.edu/people/terrence-w-deacon, **Notes:** Deacon presents a copy of this paper on his website. Accessed 15 Jan 2016. The reference page for this discussion on regularity and patterns in complex systems is page 10 of the paper (see URL).

31. Simpson, Z., *Emergence and Non-Personal Theology*, Zygon: Journal of Religion & Science, 2013, Vol 48, No 2, p. 408, Wiley-Blackwell, ISSN 05912385.

32. Deacon, T.W., *Incomplete Nature: How Mind Emerged from Matter*, W. W. Norton, 2011, p. 23, ISBN 978-0393080834.

33. Simpson, Z., *Emergence and Non-Personal Theology*, Zygon: Journal of Religion & Science, 2013, Vol 48, No 2, p. 409, Wiley-Blackwell, ISSN 05912385.

34. Deacon, T.W., *Incomplete Nature: How Mind Emerged from Matter*, W. W. Norton, 2011, pp. 270-271, ISBN 978-0393080834.

35. Simpson, Z., *Emergence and Non-Personal Theology*, Zygon: Journal of Religion & Science, 2013, Vol 48, No 2, p. 410, Wiley-Blackwell, ISSN 05912385.

36. Simpson, Z., *Emergence and Non-Personal Theology*, Zygon: Journal of Religion & Science, 2013, Vol 48, No 2, pp. 414-416, Wiley-Blackwell, ISSN 05912385.

37. Simpson, Z., *Emergence and Non-Personal Theology*, Zygon: Journal of Religion & Science, 2013, Vol 48, No 2, p. 420, Wiley-Blackwell, ISSN 05912385.

38. Church, C., *Catechism of the Catholic Church: With Modifications from the Editio Typica*, Doubleday, 2003, p. 104, ISBN 978-0385508193, **Notes:** Refer to Paragraph 6-Man, Section II, Number 365 and 366. A free online English translation of the Cathechism of the Catholic Church is provided by the United States Conference of Catholic Bishiops at the following URL: http://tinyurl.com/h6ljlnx (full URL: http://ccc.usccb.org/flipbooks/catechism/).

39. Robinson, A. and C. Southgate, *Semiotics as a Metaphysical Framework for Christian Theology*, Zygon: Journal of Religion & Science, 2010, Vol 45, No 3, p. 706, Wiley-Blackwell, ISSN 05912385, DOI: 10.1111/j.1467-9744.2010.01122.x.

40. Wikipedia contributors, *Charles Sanders Peirce*, Wikipedia, The Free Encyclopedia, Accessed 08 Mar 2016, https://en.wikipedia.org/wiki/Charles_Sanders_Peirce, **Notes:** Refer to section entitled, *"Theory of categories"*.

41. Robinson, A. and C. Southgate, *Semiotics as a Metaphysical Framework for Christian Theology*, Zygon: Journal of Religion & Science, 2010, Vol 45, No 3, p. 707, Wiley-Blackwell, ISSN 05912385, DOI: 10.1111/j.1467-9744.2010.01122.x.

42. Borland, T.A., *Internet Encyclopedia of Philosophy: Omniscience and Divine Foreknowledge*, Summer 2006 Edition, Series Ed(s). Fieser and Dowden, ISSN 2161-0002, Accessed 13 Jul 2016, http://www.iep.utm.edu/o/omnisci.htm.

43. Robinson, A. and C. Southgate, *Semiotics as a Metaphysical Framework for Christian Theology*, Zygon: Journal of Religion & Science, 2010, Vol 45, No 3, Wiley-Blackwell, ISSN 05912385, DOI: 10.1111/j.1467-9744.2010.01122.x.

44. Robinson, A. and C. Southgate, *Semiotics as a Metaphysical Framework for Christian Theology*, Zygon: Journal of Religion & Science, 2010, Vol 45, No 3, pp. 708-709, Wiley-Blackwell, ISSN 05912385, DOI: 10.1111/j.1467-9744.2010.01122.x.

45. Robinson, A. and C. Southgate, *Interpretation and the Origin of Life*, Zygon: Journal of Religion & Science, 2010, Vol 45, No 2, p. 346, Wiley-Blackwell, ISSN 05912385.

46. Law, J.T., *Toward a Theology of Boundary*, Zygon: Journal of Religion & Science, 2010, Vol 45, No 3, pp. 758-759, Wiley-Blackwell, ISSN 05912385, DOI: 10.1111/j.1467-9744.2010.01125.x.

47. Leidenhag, M., *The Relevance of Emergence Theory in the Science-Religion Dialogue*, Zygon: Journal of Religion & Science, 2013, Vol 48, No 4, p. 977, ISSN 1467-9744, DOI: 10.1111/zygo.12046, http://tinyurl.com/zmftpth.

48. Leidenhag, M., *The Relevance of Emergence Theory in the Science-Religion Dialogue*, Zygon: Journal of Religion & Science, 2013, Vol 48, No 4, p. 973, ISSN 1467-9744, DOI: 10.1111/zygo.12046, http://tinyurl.com/zmftpth.

49. Leidenhag, M., *The Relevance of Emergence Theory in the Science-Religion Dialogue*, Zygon: Journal of Religion & Science, 2013, Vol 48, No 4, pp. 977-979, ISSN 1467-9744, DOI: 10.1111/zygo.12046, http://tinyurl.com/zmftpth.

50. Leidenhag, M., *The Relevance of Emergence Theory in the Science-Religion Dialogue*, Zygon: Journal of Religion & Science, 2013, Vol 48, No 4, p. 980, ISSN 1467-9744, DOI: 10.1111/zygo.12046, http://tinyurl.com/zmftpth.

51. Davies, P., *Teleology without Teleology: Purpose through Emergent Complexity*, in Book: In Whom We Live and Move and Have Our Being, Eds. Clayton and Peacocke, Wm B. Eerdmans, 2004, No., p. 100, ISBN 978-0802809780.

52. Davies, P., *Teleology without Teleology: Purpose through Emergent Complexity*, in Book: In Whom We Live and Move and Have Our Being, Eds. Clayton and Peacocke, Wm B. Eerdmans, 2004, No., p. 101, ISBN 978-0802809780.

53. Doyle, A.C., *The Complete Sherlock Holmes*, Series Title: Knickerbocker Classics, Race Point Publishing, 2013, p. 28, ISBN 978-1937994303, Notes: From *A Study in Scarlet*, Part I, Ch. V. First published in the magazine entitled *Beeton's Christmas Annual* (November, 1887). It is distinguished as the first story in which the characters of Sherlock Holmes and Dr. John H. Watson are introduced. Copyright expired. In the public domain.

54. Cafferty, B.J., *et al.*, *Spontaneous formation and base pairing of plausible prebiotic nucleotides in water*, Nature Communications, 2016, Vol 7, 25 Apr 2016, p. 11328, DOI: 10.1038/ncomms11328, http://dx.doi.org/10.1038/ncomms11328.

55. Nuevo, M., *et al.*, *Formation of Uracil from the Ultraviolet Photo-Irradiation of Pyrimidine in Pure H2O Ices*, Astrobiology, Vol 9, No 7, 01 Sep 2009, pp. 683-695, Mary Ann Liebert, Inc., publishers, ISSN 1531-1074, DOI: 10.1089/ast.2008.0324, http://dx.doi.org/10.1089/ast.2008.0324.

56. McGowan, K., *Where did it all Begin?*, Popular Science, 2017, Vol 5/6, pp. 38-44, 90, Bonnier Publishing, Harlan, IA, ISSN 0161-7370.

57. Kranendonk, M.J.V., D.W. Deamer, and T. Djokic, *Life Springs*, Scientific American, 2017, Vol 317, No 2, pp. 28-35, Scientific American, ISSN 00368733.

Chapter 12

1. Lightman, A., *Nothing but the Truth: Science's Greatest Weakness is also its Greatest Strength*, Popular Science, May, 2015, pp. 50-51, Bonnier Publishing, Harlan, IA, ISSN 0161-7370.

2. Feynman, R.P., From "SURELY YOU'RE JOKING, MR. FEYNMAN!": ADVENTURES OF A CURIOUS CHARACTER by Richard Feynman as Told to Raplph Leighton, W. W. Norton, 1985, p. 343, ISBN 978-0393316049., **Notes:** Copyright © 1985 by Richard P. Feynman and Ralph Leighton. Used by permission of W. W. Norton & Company, Inc.

3. Industrial Research Institute, *2016 Global R&D Funding Forecast*, 2016, Winter, Industrial Research Institute, Advantage Busines Medial, , **Notes:** A PDF report can be directly accessed here: http://tinyurl.com/hylav38. Another link to access the report: http://tinyurl.com/hghvx73.

4. van Gunsteren, W.F., *The Seven Sins in Academic Behavior in the Natural Sciences*, Angewandte Chemie International Edition, 2013, Vol 52, No 1, pp. 118-122, WILEY-VCH Verlag, ISSN 1521-3773, DOI: 10.1002/anie.201204076, http://tinyurl.com/hx38tq8.

5. Hilzik, M., *Science has lost its way, at a big cost to humanity*, Los Angeles Times, 27 Oct 2013.

6. Anonymous, *How Science Goes Wrong*, The Economist, 19 Oct 2013, The Economist Newspaper Limited, London, ISSN 0013-0613.

7. Wikipedia contributors, *Duhem-Quine thesis*, Wikipedia, The Free Encyclopedia, 2015, http://tinyurl.com/l2pazm8.

8. Gegear, R.J., *et al.*, *Animal Cryptochromes Mediate Magnetoreception by an Unconventional Photochemical Mechanism*, Nature, 2010, No 463, pp. 804-807, DOI: 10.1038/nature08719.

9. Hasher, L., D. Goldstein, and T. Toppino, *Frequency and the conference of referential validity*, Journal of Verbal Learning and Verbal Behavior, 1977, Vol 16, No 1, 1977/02/01, pp. 107-112, ISSN 0022-5371, DOI: 10.1016/S0022-5371(77)80012-1, http://tinyurl.com/j8nvdgd.

10. Polage, D.C., *Making up History: False Memories of Fake News Stories*, Europe's Journal of Psychology, 2012, Vol 8, No 2, pp. 245-250, DOI: 10.5964/ejop.v8i2.456.

11. Newberg, A.B., *Principles of Neurotheology*, Ashgate Publishing Limited, 2010, p. 155, ISBN 978-0754669944.

12. Obama, B., *Statement by the President on ISIL*, 10 Sep 2014, http://tinyurl.com/jjmst79 (full URL: https://www.whitehouse.gov/the-press-office/2014/09/10/statement-president-isil-1), **Notes:** This speech is archived under The White House's Office of the Press Secretary Briefing Room, categorized under "Speeches & Remarks".

13. Alkhshali, H. and J. Berlinger, *Facing fines, conversion or death, Christian families flee Mosul*, Cable News Network/Turner Broadcasting Systems, Inc., 20 July 2014, Accessed 03 Aug 2016, http://tinyurl.com/kk4xc6c (full URL: http://www.cnn.com/2014/07/19/world/meast/christians-flee-mosul-iraq/).

14. Kessler, R., *et al.*, *The prevalence and correlates of adult ADHD in the United States: results from the National Comorbidity Survey Replication*, American Journal of Psychiatry, 2006, Vol 163, No 4, pp. 716-723.

15. Levine, D.S. and L.I. Perlovsky, *Simplifying Heuristics Versus Careful Thinking: Scientific Analysis of Millennial Spiritual Issues*, Zygon: Journal of Religion & Science, 2008, Vol 43, No 4, pp. 814-815, Wiley-Blackwell, ISSN 05912385, DOI: 10.1111/j.1467-9744.2008.00961.x.

16. Levine, D.S. and L.I. Perlovsky, *Simplifying Heuristics Versus Careful Thinking: Scientific Analysis of Millennial Spiritual Issues*, Zygon: Journal of Religion & Science, 2008, Vol 43, No 4, pp. 803-804, Wiley-Blackwell, ISSN 05912385, DOI: 10.1111/j.1467-9744.2008.00961.x.

17. Levine, D.S. and L.I. Perlovsky, *Simplifying Heuristics Versus Careful Thinking: Scientific Analysis of Millennial Spiritual Issues*, Zygon: Journal of Religion & Science, 2008, Vol 43, No 4, p. 804, Wiley-Blackwell, ISSN 05912385, DOI: 10.1111/j.1467-9744.2008.00961.x.

18. Arntz, W., B. Chasse, and M. Vicente, *What the Bleep Do We Know?*, 23 April 2004, Director(s): Arntz, W., B. Chasse, and M. Vicente, Prod.(s) Arntz, Chasse, and Vicente, Distr. Roadside Attractions, **Notes:** The quote is from Neuroscientist and Psychiatrist Andrew B. Newberg.

19. Levine, D.S. and L.I. Perlovsky, *Simplifying Heuristics Versus Careful Thinking: Scientific Analysis of Millennial Spiritual Issues*, Zygon: Journal of Religion & Science, 2008, Vol 43, No 4, p. 798, Wiley-Blackwell, ISSN 05912385, DOI: 10.1111/j.1467-9744.2008.00961.x.

20. Masci, D., *How the Public Resolves Conflicts Between Faith and Science*, 2007, Pew Research Religion & Public Life Project, **Notes:** The Pew Reserach Center article can be accessed here: http://tinyurl.com/hud5pcl. The author refers to a Gallup poll by *TIME* magazine (May 2007), conducted by Schulman, Ronca, & Bucuvalas. A data chart can be viewed here: http://tinyurl.com/zpavxfo.

21. Newport, F., *In U.S., 42% Believe Creationist View of Human Origins*, Gallup, Inc., 2014, Accessed 02 Jan 2015, http://tinyurl.com/msz3ujq (full URL: http://www.gallup.com/poll/170822/believe-creationist-view-human-origins.aspx), **Notes:** Results for this Gallup poll are based on telephone interviews conducted May 8-11, 2014, with a random sample of 1,028 adults, aged 18 and older, living in all 50 U.S. states and the District of Columbia. For results based on the total sample of national adults, the margin of sampling error is ±4 percentage points at the 95% confidence level.

22. Levine, D.S. and L.I. Perlovsky, *Simplifying Heuristics Versus Careful Thinking: Scientific Analysis of Millennial Spiritual Issues*, Zygon: Journal of Religion & Science, 2008, Vol 43, No 4, p. 812, Wiley-Blackwell, ISSN 05912385, DOI: 10.1111/j.1467-9744.2008.00961.x.

23. Spelke, E.S. and K.D. Kinzler, *Core Knowledge*, Developmental Science, 2007, Vol 10, No 1, p. 89, Developmental Science, ISSN 1363-755X, DOI: 10.1111/j.1467-7687.2007.00569.x, **Notes:** As cited in Skeptic Magazine, Vol 15, No 3, pp. 50-55, 2010, Leonid Perlovsky, *"The Mind is Not a Kludge"*.

24. Kinzler, K.D. and E.S. Spelke, *Core systems in human cognition*, in Book: Progress in Brain Research, Eds. Hofsten and Rosander, Elsevier, 2007, Vol. Volume 164, No., pp. 257-264, ISBN 0079-6123, http://tinyurl.com/hcobq6r, **Notes:** A PDF copy of the paper can be accessed here: http://tinyurl.com/hahs62b (full URL: https://software.rc.fas.harvard.edu/lds/wp-content/uploads/2010/07/Kinzler_CoreSystemsHumanCog.pdf).

25. Spelke, E.S. and K.D. Kinzler, *Core Knowledge*, Developmental Science, 2007, Vol 10, No 1, p. 91, Developmental Science, ISSN 1363-755X, DOI: 10.1111/j.1467-7687.2007.00569.x, **Notes:** As cited in Skeptic Magazine, Vol 15, No 3, pp. 50-55, 2010, Leonid Perlovsky, *"The Mind is Not a Kludge"*.

26. Spelke, E.S. and K.D. Kinzler, *Core Knowledge*, Developmental Science, 2007, Vol 10, No 1, p. 92, Developmental Science, ISSN 1363-755X, DOI: 10.1111/j.1467-7687.2007.00569.x, **Notes:** As cited in Skeptic Magazine, Vol 15, No 3, pp. 50-55, 2010, Leonid Perlovsky, *"The Mind is Not a Kludge"*.

27. Gopnik, A., *How Babies Think*, Scientific American, 2010, Vol 303, No 1, pp. 76-81, Scientific American, ISSN 00368733.

28. Newberg, A.B., *Principles of Neurotheology*, Ashgate Publishing Limited, 2010, p. 76, ISBN 978-0754669944.

29. Shermer, M., *The Believing Brain: From Ghosts and Gods to Politics and Conspiracies---How We Construct Beliefs and Reinforce Them as Truths*, Henry Holt and Company, 2011, p. 60, ISBN 978-1429972611.

30. Shermer, M., *The Believing Brain: From Ghosts and Gods to Politics and Conspiracies---How We Construct Beliefs and Reinforce Them as Truths*, Henry Holt and Company, 2011, p. 59, ISBN 978-1429972611.

31. Shermer, M., *The Believing Brain: From Ghosts and Gods to Politics and Conspiracies---How We Construct Beliefs and Reinforce Them as Truths*, Henry Holt and Company, 2011, p. 87, ISBN 978-1429972611.

32. Shermer, M., *The Believing Brain: From Ghosts and Gods to Politics and Conspiracies---How We Construct Beliefs and Reinforce Them as Truths*, Henry Holt and Company, 2011, p. 135, ISBN 978-1429972611.

33. Kluger, J., *Is God in Our Genes? A provocative study asks whether religion is a product of evolution. Inside a quest for the roots of faith.*, TIME, p. 66, Time, Inc., ISSN 0040-781X, http://tinyurl.com/j8kcpta (full URL: http://www.time.com/time/magazine/article/0,9171,995465-1,00.html), **Notes:** Cover Story. United States edition.

34. Hamer, D.H., *The God Gene: How Faith is Hardwired into our Genes*, 1 ed., Doubleday, 14 Sep 2004, pp. 23-30, ISBN 978-0385500586.

35. Hamer, D.H., *The God Gene: How Faith Is Hardwired into Our Genes*, Knopf Doubleday Publishing Group, 2005, ISBN 978-0307276933.

36. Horgan, J. and H. J, *The Forgotten Era of Brain Chips*, Scientific American, 2005, Vol 293, No 4, pp. 66-73, Springer Nature, ISSN 00368733.

37. Newberg, A.B., *Principles of Neurotheology*, Ashgate Publishing Limited, 2010, p. 186, ISBN 978-0754669944.

38. Newberg, A.B., *Principles of Neurotheology*, Ashgate Publishing Limited, 2010, p. 68, ISBN 978-0754669944.

39. Newberg, A.B., *Principles of Neurotheology*, Ashgate Publishing Limited, 2010, p. 2, ISBN 978-0754669944.

40. Newberg, A.B., *Principles of Neurotheology*, Ashgate Publishing Limited, 2010, pp. 84-85, ISBN 978-0754669944.

41. Schaff, P., *Ante-Nicene Fathers: Volume 4 - The Writings of the Fathers Down to A.D. 325*, Grand Rapids,MI, Wm. B. Eerdman's Publishing Company, 1995, p. 240, Trans. by Crombie, http://tinyurl.com/jbscbaw (full URL: http://www.ccel.org/ccel/schaff/anf04.vi.v.i.html).

42. MacDougall, D., *Hypothesis Concerning Soul Substance Together with Experimental Evidence of the Existence of such Substance*, Journal of the American Society for Psychical Research, Vol 1, No 5, May 1907, p. 239, http://tinyurl.com/z6zq6y8 (full URL: http://vesmir.cz/wp-content/uploads/2016/01/duncan_macdougall_1907.pdf), **Notes:** The article was also simultaneously published in the journal *American Medicine*.

43. Kelly, E.F., et al., *Irreducible Mind: Toward a Psychology for the 21st Century*, Rowman & Littlefield, 2009, pp. 367-421, ISBN 978-1442202061.

44. Sahu, S., et al., *Atomic water channel controlling remarkable properties of a single brain microtubule: Correlating single protein to its supramolecular assembly*, Biosensors and Bioelectronics, Vol 47, No 0, 15 Sep 2013, pp. 141-148, ISSN 0956-5663, DOI: http://dx.doi.org/10.1016/j.bios.2013.02.050, http://tinyurl.com/gtrug5w.

45. Hameroff, S. and R. Penrose, *Consciousness in the universe: A review of the 'Orch OR' theory*, Physics of Life Reviews, 2014, Vol 11, No 1, pp. 39-78, ISSN 1571-0645, DOI: http://dx.doi.org/10.1016/j.plrev.2013.08.002, http://tinyurl.com/norepj8.

46. Tuszynski, J.A., *The need for a physical basis of cognitive process: Comment on "Consciousness in the universe. A review of the 'Orch OR' theory" by Hameroff and Penrose*, Physics of Life Reviews, 2014, Vol 11, No 1, pp. 79-80, ISSN 1571-0645, DOI: http://dx.doi.org/10.1016/j.plrev.2013.10.009, http://tinyurl.com/haoqvon.

47. Hameroff, S. and R. Penrose, *Reply to seven commentaries on "Consciousness in the universe: Review of the 'Orch OR' theory"*, Physics of Life Reviews, 2014, Vol 11, No 1, pp. 94-100, ISSN 1571-0645, DOI: http://dx.doi.org/10.1016/j.plrev.2013.11.013, http://tinyurl.com/hlre4go.

48. Chopra, D., *Reality and consciousness: A view from the East: Comment on "Consciousness in the universe: A review of the 'Orch OR' theory" by Stuart Hameroff and Roger Penrose*, Physics of Life Reviews, Vol 11, No 1, Mar 2014, pp. 81-82, ISSN 1571-0645, DOI: http://dx.doi.org/10.1016/j.plrev.2013.11.001, http://tinyurl.com/z8ct6ms.

49. Ghosh, S., S. Sahu, and A. Bandyopadhyay, *Evidence of massive global synchronization and the consciousness: Comment on "Consciousness in the universe: A review of the 'Orch OR' theory" by Hameroff and Penrose*, Physics of Life Reviews, Vol 11, No 1, Mar 2014, pp. 83-84, ISSN 1571-0645, DOI: http://dx.doi.org/10.1016/j.plrev.2013.10.007, http://tinyurl.com/zcboztb.

50. Jumper, C.C. and G.D. Scholes, *Life—Warm, wet and noisy?: Comment on "Consciousness in the universe: A review of the 'Orch OR' theory" by Hameroff and Penrose*, Physics of Life Reviews, 2014, Vol 11, No 1, pp. 85-86, ISSN 1571-0645, DOI: http://dx.doi.org/10.1016/j.plrev.2013.10.008, http://tinyurl.com/j97k7p4.

51. Lucas, J., *The face of freedom: Comment on "Consciousness in the universe. A review of the 'Orch OR' theory" by Stuart Hameroff and Roger Penrose*, Physics of Life Reviews, 2014, Vol 11, No 1, pp. 87-88, ISSN 1571-0645, DOI: http://dx.doi.org/10.1016/j.plrev.2013.11.008, http://tinyurl.com/jefu562.

52. Sahu, S., et al., *Multi-level memory-switching properties of a single brain microtubule*, Applied Physics Letters, Vol 102, No 12, 25 March 2013, DOI: http://dx.doi.org/10.1063/1.4793995, http://tinyurl.com/ztlncf5.

53. Reimers, J.R., et al., *The revised Penrose–Hameroff orchestrated objective-reduction proposal for human consciousness is not scientifically justified: Comment on "Consciousness in the universe: A review of the 'Orch OR' theory" by Hameroff and Penrose*, Physics of Life Reviews, Vol 11, No 1, Mar 2014, pp. 101-103, ISSN 1571-0645, DOI: http://dx.doi.org/10.1016/j.plrev.2013.11.003, http://tinyurl.com/jgztyqe.

54. Hameroff, S. and R. Penrose, *Reply to criticism of the 'Orch OR qubit' – 'Orchestrated objective reduction' is scientifically justified*, Physics of Life Reviews, Vol 11, No 1, Mar 2014, pp. 104-112, ISSN 1571-0645, DOI: http://dx.doi.org/10.1016/j.plrev.2013.11.014, http://tinyurl.com/j2q65u3.

55. Hameroff, S. and R. Penrose, *Conscious Events as Orchestrated Space-Time Selections*, 2007, Vol 1, No. 1, ISBN 1303-5150, http://tinyurl.com/htstt4j, **Notes:** Refer to Figure 2.

56. Angelica, A.D., *Discovery of quantum vibrations in microtubules inside brain neurons corroborates controversial 20-year-old theory of consciousness*, KurzweilAINetwork, Inc., Accessed 02 Jan 2015, http://tinyurl.com/ksu6u2o.

57. Blowers, P.M., *Drama of the Divine Economy: Creator and Creation in Early Christian Theology and Piety*, OUP Oxford, 2012, p. 25, ISBN 978-0199660414, **Notes:** Originally cited in Physica (meaning "Studies of Nature") (DK 59B12), translated by Richard D. McKirahan, *Philosophy before Socrates: An Introduction with Texts and Commentary*, Hackett Publishing, 1st ed., 1994, p. 198. This quote by Thales is also identified in McKirahan's 2nd edition (same book) on p.30 (see 4.11) and p. 31. The "DK" is the Diels-Kranz number system for referencing the works of pre-Socratic philosophers developed by H. Diels and revised by W. Kranz. The "59" refers to the Chapter called Anaxagoras 59. Anaxagoras of Clazomenae was a pre-Socratic philosopher. The "B12" refers to Fragment Number B12.

58. Streltsov, A., *et al.*, *Measuring Quantum Coherence with Entanglement*, Physical Review Letters, Vol 115, No 2, 08 July 2015, p. 020403, American Physical Society, DOI: http://dx.doi.org/10.1103/PhysRevLett.115.020403, http://tinyurl.com/z7oxyds.

59. University of North Dakota, *The Quarterly Journal of the University of North Dakota*, 1922, No. v. 12, p. 150, **Notes:** See footnote 84. Voltaire, Oeuvres, Dict. philo., Ame. (trans. Philosophical Dictionary, 1st Edition published in 1974). A second edition was expanded and published in two volumes.

CHAPTER 13

1. Sagan, C. and T. Head, *Conversations with Carl Sagan*, Series Title: Literary Conversation Series, University Press of Mississippi, 2006, p. xiv, ISBN 978-1578067367, **Notes:** The quote is only cited as "Obst." (see Citation 13 in this source). The original source is uncertain, however, it is thought that the quote stems from an interview by Lynda Obst, "*Valentine to Science. Interview with Carl Sagan*", Interview Magazine, February 1996.

2. Ngeow, C. and S.M. Kanbur, *The Hubble Constant from Type Ia Supernovae Calibrated with the Linear and Nonlinear Cepheid Period-Luminosity Relations*, The Astrophysical Journal Letters, 2006, Vol 642, No 1, p. L29, ISSN 1538-4357, http://tinyurl.com/zgpysq9. See Also: http://arxiv.org/abs/astro-ph/0603643.

3. Franson, J.D., *Apparent correction to the speed of light in a gravitational potential*, New Journal of Physics, 2014, Vol 16, No 6, p. 065008, ISSN 1367-2630, DOI: 10.1088/1367-2630/16/6/065008, http://tinyurl.com/zbxd539. See Also: http://arxiv.org/abs/1111.6986.

4. Templeton, G., *Einsteinian error: The 25-year old supernova that could change the speed of light forever*, ExtremeTech.com, 24 June 2014, Series Ed(s). Lendino, Accessed 02 Jul 2015, http://tinyurl.com/qjnhz47.

5. Nussbaumer, H., *Einstein's conversion from his static to an expanding universe*, The European Physical Journal H, 2014, Vol 39, No 1, pp. 37-62, ISSN 2102-6467, DOI: 10.1140/epjh/e2013-40037-6, http://tinyurl.com/znepfl7.

6. Daily Galaxy, *"Curvature of the Universe" --New Cosmology Reveals "the Future of Particle Physics"*, The Daily Galaxy Blog. Posted by The Perimeter Institute, 20 March 2016, Accessed 23 March 2016, http://tinyurl.com/jujofqu, **Notes:** The paper by N. Ashfordi and E. Nelson referenced in The Daily Galaxy article can be found here: http://arxiv.org/abs/1504.00012.

7. Wall, M., *Major Discovery: 'Smoking Gun' for Universe's Incredible Big Bang Expansion Found*, Space.com, 17 Mar 2014, Accessed 10 Jul 2015, http://tinyurl.com/q99c79k (full URL: http://www.space.com/25078-universe-inflation-gravitational-waves-discovery.html/), **Notes:** A news conference can be viewed at: http://www.cfa.harvard.edu/news/news_conferences.html. The video is entitled, "First Direct Evidence of Cosmic Inflation".

8. Cofield, C., *Evidence for Cosmic Inflation Theory Bites the (Space) Dust*, Space.com, 30 Jan 2015, Accessed 10 Jul 2015, http://tinyurl.com/gq4evrd.

9. LIGO Scientific and Virgo Collaboration, *et al.*, *GW151226: Observation of Gravitational Waves from a 22-Solar-Mass Binary Black Hole Coalescence*, Physical Review Letters, 2016, Vol 116, No 24, 15 Jun 2016, p. 241103, American Physical Society, http://tinyurl.com/h4nte75.

10. Shlaer, B., *Solution to the problem of time*, arXiv.org, 18 May 2015, http://arxiv.org/abs/1411.8006/.

11. Borde, A., A.H. Guth, and A. Vilenkin, *Inflationary Spacetimes Are Incomplete in Past Directions*, Physical Review Letters, Vol 90, No 15, 11 Jan 2003, p. 151301, American Physical Society, DOI: 10.1103/PhysRevLett.90.151301, http://tinyurl.com/hvqmshe.

12. Carroll, S.M., K.K. Boddy, and J. Pollack, *De Sitter Space Without Dynamical Quantum Fluctuations*, Foundations of Physics, 2016, Vol 46, No 6, 10 Mar 2016, pp. 702-735, ISSN 1572-9516, DOI: 10.1007/s10701-016-9996-8, http://tinyurl.com/hp3ga3h. See Also: http://arxiv.org/abs/1405.0298v2/.

13. Grossman, L., *Quantum Twist Could Kill Off the Multiverse*, New Scientist, No 2969, http://tinyurl.com/zv4uayd. See Also: https://www.newscientist.com/issue/2969/.

14. Allahverdi, R., *et al.*, *Reheating in Inflationary Cosmology: Theory and Applications*, Annual Review of Nuclear and Particle Science, 2010, Vol 60, No 1, pp. 27-51, DOI: 10.1146/annurev.nucl.012809.104511, http://tinyurl.com/grwrgs9.

15. Helmholtz-Zentrum-Dresden-Rossendorf, *Measurement at Big Bang Conditions Confirms Lithium Problem*, 27 August 2014, http://tinyurl.com/h4uexqx.

16. Luna Collaboration, *et al.*, *First Direct Measurement of the 2H(α;γ)6Li Cross Section at Big Bang Energies and teh Primordial Lithium Problem*, Physical Review Letters, Vol 113, No 4, 21 Jul 2014, p. 042501, American Physical Society, http://tinyurl.com/hrwyzyr.

17. Mucciarelli, A., *et al.*, *The cosmological lithium problem outside the Galaxy: the Sagittarius globular cluster M54*, Monthly Notices of the Royal Astronomical Society, Vol 444, No 2, 09 Sept 2014, pp. 1812-1820, DOI: 10.1093/mnras/stu1522, http://tinyurl.com/zv4uayd.

18. Clowes, R.G., *et al.*, *Two close Large Quasar Groups of size ~ 350 Mpc at z ~ 1.2*, Monthly Notices of the Royal Astronomical Society, 2012, Vol 419, No 1, pp. 556-565, DOI: 10.1111/j.1365-2966.2011.19719.x, http://tinyurl.com/zg7369w. See Also: http://arxiv.org/abs/1108.6221.

19. Geller, M.J. and J.P. Huchra, *Mapping the Universe*, Science, 1989, Vol 246, No 4932, November 17, 1989, pp. 897-903, DOI: 10.1126/science.246.4932.897, http://tinyurl.com/zu56apt.

20. Clowes, R.G., *et al.*, *A structure in the early Universe at z ~1.3 that exceeds the homogeneity scale of the R-W concordance cosmology*, Monthly Notices of the Royal Astronomical Society, Vol 429, 11 Jan 2013, pp. 2910-2916, DOI: 10.1093/mnras/sts497, http://tinyurl.com/gunzl3c.

21. Horváth, I., J. Hakkila, and Z. Bagoly, *The largest structure of the Universe, defined by Gamma-Ray Bursts*, arXiv.org, 05 Nov 2013, http://arxiv.org/abs/1311.1104/.

22. Horváth, I., J. Hakkila, and Z. Bagoly, *Possible structure in the GRB sky distribution at redshift two*, Astronomy & Astrophysics, Vol 561, Jan 2014, p. L12, EDP Sciences, ISSN 0004-6361, DOI: http://dx.doi.org/10.1051/0004-6361/201323020, http://tinyurl.com/zkoh9w3.

23. Horváth, I., *et al.*, *New data support the existence of the Hercules-Corona Borealis Great Wall*, Astronomy & Astrophysics, Vol 584, Dec 2015, p. A48, EDP Sciences, ISSN 0004-6361, DOI: http://dx.doi.org/10.1051/0004-6361/201424829, http://tinyurl.com/has82z8.

24. Szapudi, I., *et al.*, *Detection of a supervoid aligned with the cold spot of the cosmic microwave background*, Monthly Notes of the Astronomical Society of South Africa, Vol 450, No 1, 11 Jun 2015, pp. 288-294, DOI: 10.1093/mnras/stv488, http://tinyurl.com/jh85xwa. See Also: http://arxiv.org/abs/1405.1566/.

25. Enqvist, K. and M.S. Sloth, *Adiabatic CMB perturbations in pre-big bang string cosmology*, arXiv.org, 30 Jan 2002, DOI: 10.1016/S0550-3213(02)00043-3, http://arxiv.org/abs/hep-ph/0109214.

26. Lyth, D.H. and D. Wands, *Generating the curvature perturbation without an inflaton*, arXiv.org, 06 Mar 2002, DOI: 10.1016/S0370-2693(01)01366-1, http://arxiv.org/abs/hep-ph/0110002/.

27. Moroi, T. and T. Takahashi, *Effects of cosmological moduli fields on cosmic microwave background*, Physics Letters B, 2001, Vol 522, No 3–4, 13 Dec 2001, pp. 215-221, ISSN 0370-2693, DOI: http://dx.doi.org/10.1016/S0370-2693(01)01295-3, http://tinyurl.com/jba37er, **Notes:** The authors published a followup paper to correct an erroneous calculation. See the corrected paper here: http://tinyurl.com/jcharfn.

28. Moroi, T. and T. Takahashi, *Erratum to: "Effects of cosmological moduli fields on cosmic microwave background": [Phys. Lett. B 522 (2001) 215]*, Physics Letters B, 2002, Vol 539, No 3–4, 7/18/, p. 303, ISSN 0370-2693, DOI: http://dx.doi.org/10.1016/S0370-2693(02)02070-1, http://www.sciencedirect.com/science/article/pii/S0370269302020701.

29. Kleban, M., T.S. Levi, and K. Sigurdson, *Observing the multiverse with cosmic wakes*, Physical Review D, Vol 87, No 4, 21 Feb 2013, p. 041301, American Physical Society, http://tinyurl.com/h3e58by. See Also: http://arxiv.org/abs/1109.3473.

30. Wolchover, N., *In Lopsided Map of the Cosmos, a Glimmer of Its Origins*, Quanta Magazine, 24 Jun 2013, quantamagazine.org / Simons Foundation, http://tinyurl.com/goaq9lh (full URL: https://www.quantamagazine.org/20130624-in-lopsided-map-of-the-cosmos-a-glimmer-of-its-origins/).

31. Ratcliffe, H., *Monthly Notes of the Alternative Cosmology Group – May 2014*, http://www.cosmology.info/, Alternative Cosmology Group, May 2014, http://www.cosmology.info/newsletter/2014.05.pdf, **Notes:** This newsletter, and the Alternative Cosmology Group in general, advocate that the Big Bang theory has too many gaps between the theory and astronomical observations and that alternative ideas ought be considered by the community of cosmologists. The newsletters discusses problems of Big Bang theory, namely, the Lithium problem, large-scale structures, CMB asymmetry, surface brightness, and that dark matter may not exist.

32. Wolchover, N., *Time's Arrow Traced to Quantum Source*, Quanta Magazine, 16 April 2014, quantamagazine.org / Simons Foundation, http://tinyurl.com/gtocmwc (full URL: https://www.quantamagazine.org/20140416-times-arrow-traced-to-quantum-source/).

33. Linden, N., *et al.*, *Quantum Mechanical Evolution Towards Thermal Equilibrium*, Physical Review E, Vol 79, No 6, 4 Jun 2009, p. 061103, DOI: http://dx.doi.org/10.1103/PhysRevE.79.061103, http://tinyurl.com/j3m6lyj.

34. Reimann, P., *Foundation of Statistical Mechanics under Experimentally Realistic Conditions*, Physical Review Letters, Vol 101, No 19, 07 Nov 2008, p. 190403, American Physical Society, http://tinyurl.com/zzs75ye.

35. Short, A.J. and T.C. Farrelly, *Quantum equilibration in finite time*, New Journal of Physics, 2012, Vol 14, No 1, p. 013063, ISSN 1367-2630, http://tinyurl.com/hj6l5g7.

36. Malabarba, A.S.L., *et al.*, *Quantum systems equilibrate rapidly for most observables*, Physical Review E, Vol 90, No 1, 22 Jul 2014, p. 012121, American Physical Society, http://tinyurl.com/h73mt58.

37. Goldstein, S., T. Hara, and H. Tasaki, *Extremely quick thermalization in a macroscopic quantum system for a typical nonequilibrium subspace*, arXiv.org, 03 Feb 2014, DOI: 10.1088/1367-2630/17/4/045002, http://arxiv.org/abs/1402.0324.

38. Lloyd, S., *Black Holes, Demons and the Loss of Coherence: How complex systems get information, and what they do with it.*, Ph. D. - Theoretical Physics, The Rockefeller University, Advisor: Pagels, 122 p., 1988, **Notes** See pp. 8-9.

39. Hartle, J. and T. Hertog, *Arrows of Time in the Bouncing Universes of the No-boundary Quantum State*, Physical Review D, Vol 85, No 10, 22 May 2012, p. 103524, American Physical Society, DOI: http://dx.doi.org/10.1103/PhysRevD.85.103524, http://tinyurl.com/hnehn3q. See Also: http://arxiv.org/abs/1104.1733v3/.

40. Vilenkin, A., *Arrows of time and the beginning of the universe*, arXiv.org, 2013, http://arxiv.org/abs/1305.3836.

41. Hawking, S., *A Brief History of Time: From the Big Bang to Black Holes*, Bantam, 1988, p. 136, ISBN (ASIN) B002C994OU.

42. Pickover, C.A., *Archimedes to Hawking: Laws of Science and the Great Minds Behind Them*, Oxford University Press, USA, 2008, p. 483, ISBN 978-0199792689, **Notes:** Original source, *Der Spiegel*, 17 Oct 1988.

43. Ellis, G.F.R. and R. Maartens, *The emergent universe: inflationary cosmology with no singularity*, Classical and Quantum Gravity, 2004, Vol 21, No 1, p. 223, ISSN 0264-9381, http://tinyurl.com/gp2rs7z. See Also: http://arxiv.org/pdf/gr-qc/0211082.pdf.

44. Ellis, G.F.R., J. Murugan, and C.G. Tsagas, *The emergent universe: an explicit construction*, Classical and Quantum Gravity, 2004, Vol 21, No 1, p. 233, ISSN 0264-9381, http://tinyurl.com/jggw67r. See Also: http://arxiv.org/abs/gr-qc/0307112/.

45. Mithani, A.T. and A. Vilenkin, *Instability of an emergent universe*, Journal of Cosmology and Astroparticle Physics, 2014, Vol 2014, No 05, p. 006, ISSN 1475-7516, http://tinyurl.com/z9n2dwq. See Also: http://arxiv.org/abs/1403.0818/.

46. Wetterich, C., *A Universe without expansion*, arXiv.org, 12 Nov 2013, Cornell University Library, DOI: 10.1016/j.dark.2013.10.002, http://arxiv.org/abs/1303.6878v4/.

47. Wetterich, C., *Universe without Expansion*, 2013, Paris, PDF: http://tinyurl.com/hbolbk3, Powerpoint: http://tinyurl.com/hbolbk3 (full URL: http://www.thphys.uni-heidelberg.de/%7Ewetteric/Talks/Cosmo/Y1214/Universe_without_expansion_Paris1113.ppt)

Notes: Refer to Slide 3 of the presentation. This is a companion Microsoft Powerpoint presentation to Wetterich's paper entitled, "*Universe without expansion*", http://arxiv.org/pdf/1303.6878.pdf. The paper does not contain this image.

48. Heidelberg University, *How did the universe begin: Hot Big Bang or slow thaw?*, Nanowerk News, 2014, 25 Feb 2014, Nanowerk.com, http://tinyurl.com/jyllwbz (full URL: http://www.nanowerk.com/news2/space/newsid=34525.php).

49. Wetterich, C., *Hot big bang or slow freeze?*, Physics Letters B, Vol 736, 07 Sep 2014, pp. 506-514, ISSN 0370-2693, DOI: http://dx.doi.org/10.1016/j.physletb.2014.08.013, http://tinyurl.com/hylu4ku. See Also: http://arxiv.org/abs/1401.5313v2/.

50. Bousso, R., *The Cosmological Constant Problem, Dark Energy, and the Landscape of String Theory*, arXiv.org, Mar 2012, p. 5, http://arxiv.org/abs/1203.0307.

51. Wetterich, C., *Cosmologies with variable Newton's "constant"*, Nuclear Physics B, Vol 302, No 4, 13 Jun 1988, pp. 645-667, ISSN 0550-3213, DOI: http://dx.doi.org/10.1016/0550-3213(88)90192-7, http://tinyurl.com/jv3sonr.

52. Reuter, M. and C. Wetterich, *Time evolution of the cosmological "constant"*, Physics Letters B, Vol 188, No 1, 02 Apr 1987, pp. 38-43, ISSN 0370-2693, DOI: http://dx.doi.org/10.1016/0370-2693(87)90702-7, http://tinyurl.com/gt4c73k.

53. Peccei, R.D., J. Solà, and C. Wetterich, *Adjusting the cosmological constant dynamically: Cosmons and a new force weaker than gravity*, Physics Letters B, Vol 195, No 2, 03 Sep 1987, pp. 183-190, ISSN 0370-2693, DOI: http://dx.doi.org/10.1016/0370-2693(87)91191-9, http://tinyurl.com/z5v9uty.

54. Wetterich, C., *The cosmon model for an asymptotically vanishing time-dependent cosmological ``constant"*, arXiv.org, 1994, http://arxiv.org/abs/hep-th/9408025/, **Notes:** See Also: Astronomy & Astrophysics, Vol. 301, pp. 321-328, September 1995.

55. Wetterich, C., *Universe without Expansion*, 2013, Paris, PDF: http://tinyurl.com/hbolbk3, Powerpoint: http://tinyurl.com/hbolbk3 (full URL: http://www.thphys.uni-heidelberg.de/%7Ewetteric/Talks/Cosmo/Y1214/Universe_without_expansion_Paris1113.ppt), **Notes:** Refer to Slide 58 of the presentation entitled "cosmon evolution". This is a companion presentation to Wetterich's paper entitled, "*Universe without expansion*", http://arxiv.org/pdf/1303.6878.pdf. The paper does not contain this image.

56. Wetterich, C., *Eternal Universe*, Physical Review D, Vol 90, No 4, 18 Aug 2014, p. 043520, American Physical Society, DOI: 10.1103/PhysRevD.90.043520, http://tinyurl.com/zeywknf. See Also: http://arxiv.org/abs/1404.0535v2/, **Notes:** Refer to p. 4-5 and Figure 1 of the arXiv.org print (see second URL listed).

57. Ayaita, Y., M. Weber, and C. Wetterich, *Neutrino lump fluid in growing neutrino quintessence*, Physical Review D, Vol 87, No 4, 08 Feb 2013, p. 043519, American Physical Society, http://tinyurl.com/zue7g6w. See Also: http://arxiv.org/abs/1211.6589/.

58. Thomas, S.A., F.B. Abdalla, and O. Lahav, *Upper Bound of 0.28 eV on the Neutrino Masses from the Largest Photometric Redshift Survey*, Physical Review Letters, Vol 105, No 3, 12 Jul 2010, p. 031301, American Physical Society, DOI: 10.1103/PhysRevLett.105.031301, http://tinyurl.com/jgwmzd3. See Also: http://arxiv.org/abs/0911.5291/.

59. Riemer-Sørensen, S., D. Parkinson, and T.M. Davis, *Combining Planck data with large scale structure information gives a strong neutrino mass constraint*, Physical Review D, Vol 89, No 10, 05 May 2014, p. 103505, American Physical Society, http://tinyurl.com/hcf2xzr. See Also: http://arxiv.org/abs/1306.4153.

60. Battye, R.A. and A. Moss, *Evidence for Massive Neutrinos from Cosmic Microwave Background and Lensing Observations*, Physical Review Letters, Vol 112, No 5, 06 Feb 2014, p. 051303, American Physical Society, http://tinyurl.com/zypjec2. See Also: http://arxiv.org/abs/1308.5870/.

61. Foley, J.A., *Mass of Neutrinos Accurately Calculated for First Time, Physicists Report*, Nature World News, 2014, Accessed 21 Jul 2015, http://tinyurl.com/hrw3ujb.

62. Nathalie, P.-D., et al., *Neutrino masses and cosmology with Lyman-alpha forest power spectrum*, Journal of Cosmology and Astroparticle Physics, 2015, Vol 2015, No 11, p. 011, ISSN 1475-7516, http://tinyurl.com/jet8k90. See Also: http://arxiv.org/abs/1506.05976.

63. Boyarsky, A., et al., *Unidentified Line in X-Ray Spectra of the Andromeda Galaxy and Perseus Galaxy Cluster*, Physical Review Letters, Vol 113, No 25, 15 Dec 2014, p. 251301, American Physical Society, http://tinyurl.com/hpwtutp. See Also: http://arxiv.org/abs/1402.4119/.

64. Cooper-White, M., *Dark Matter Signal May Have Been Found In Mysterious X-Ray Data*, The Huffington Post, 2014, Accessed 21 Jul 2015, http://tinyurl.com/zftx35l (full URL: http://www.huffingtonpost.com/2014/12/15/dark-matter-signal_n_6316174.html/).

65. No Author Specified, *IceCube Quick Facts*, IceCube headquarters, Accessed 13 Aug 2016, https://icecube.wisc.edu/about/facts.

66. IceCube, C., et al., *Searches for Sterile Neutrinos with the IceCube Detector*, Physical Review Letters, 2016, Vol 117, No 7, 08 Aug 2016, p. 071801, American Physical Society, http://tinyurl.com/jhqhwpb. See Also: http://arxiv.org/abs/1605.01990.

67. Casas, S., V. Pettorino, and C. Wetterich, *Dynamics of neutrino lumps in growing neutrino quintessence*, arXiv.org, 08 Aug 2016, Cornell University Library, http://arxiv.org/abs/1608.02358.

68. Brouzakis, N., et al., *Nonlinear matter spectra in growing neutrino quintessence*, arXiv.org, 2014, DOI: 10.1088/1475-7516/2011/03/049, http://arxiv.org/abs/1012.5255/.

69. Pettorino, V., et al., *Growing neutrino quintessence: large scale structures and CMB*, in the proceedings of *The Nature of Dark Energy*, 2011, Madrid, Spain, Institute for Theoretical Physics (University of Madrid & Spanish National Research Council), http://tinyurl.com/hauz727 (full URL: http://members.ift.uam-csic.es/W15/talks/madrid_110603_pettorino.pdf), **Notes:** Access to presentation may be restricted to members only.

70. Wintergerst, N., et al., *Very large scale structures in growing neutrino quintessence*, Physical Review D, Vol 81, No 6, 18 Mar 2010, p. 063525, American Physical Society, DOI: 10.1103/PhysRevD.81.063525, http://tinyurl.com/jjy7yby. See Also: http://arxiv.org/abs/0910.4985/.

71. Baldi, M., et al., *Oscillating nonlinear large scale structure in growing neutrino quintessence*, arXiv.org, 2011, DOI: 10.1111/j.1365-2966.2011.19477.x, http://arxiv.org/abs/1106.2161/.

72. Wetterich, C., *Variable gravity Universe*, Physical Review D, Vol 89, No 2, 06 Jan 2014, p. 024005, American Physical Society, http://tinyurl.com/hee58je. See Also: http://arxiv.org/abs/1308.1019/.

73. Henz, T., et al., *Dilaton Quantum Gravity*, arXiv.org, 2013, DOI: 10.1016/j.physletb.2013.10.015, http://arxiv.org/abs/1304.7743/.

74. Wetterich, C., *Dilaton quantum gravity and cosmology (lecture)*, University of Heidleberg, 2014, Accessed 22 Jul 2015, http://tinyurl.com/zmhrkel, **Notes:** Powerpoint presentation entitled, "Dilaton quantum gravity and cosmology" (pdf): http://tinyurl.com/jh3elv2.

75. Lerner, E.J., R. Falomo, and R. Scarpa, *UV surface brightness of galaxies from the local universe to z ~ 5*, International Journal of Modern Physics D, 2014, Vol 23, No 06, p. 1450058, World Scientific Publishing Co Pte Ltd, DOI: 10.1142/S0218271814500588, http://tinyurl.com/m37ac84. See Also: http://arxiv.org/abs/1405.0275/.

76. Ijjas, A. and P.J. Steinhardt, *The anamorphic universe*, arXiv.org, 2015, http://arxiv.org/abs/1507.03875/.

77. Daily Galaxy, *New Light on Our Accelerating Universe --"Not as Fast as We Thought"*, 11 Apr 2015, http://tinyurl.com/hl9he4p.

78. Milne, P.A., et al., *The Changing Fractions of Type Ia Supernova NUV--Optical Subclasses with Redshift*, The Astrophysical Journal, 2015, Vol 803, No 1, p. 20, ISSN 0004-637X, http://tinyurl.com/ze6d224. See Also: http://arxiv.org/abs/1408.1706.

79. Semiz, İ. and A.K. Çamlıbel, *What do the cosmological supernova data really tell us?*, Journal of Cosmology and Astroparticle Physics, 2015, Vol 2015, No 12, p. 038, ISSN 1475-7516, http://tinyurl.com/jamxyof. See Also: http://arxiv.org/abs/1505.04043.

80. Brown, P.J., *et al.*, *Theoretical Clues to the Ultraviolet Diversity of Type Ia Supernovae*, The Astrophysical Journal, 2015, Vol 809, No 1, p. 37, ISSN 0004-637X, http://tinyurl.com/znpg8zf. See Also: http://arxiv.org/abs/1504.05237.

81. Pierre, A., *The expansion of the universe observed with supernovae*, Reports on Progress in Physics, 2012, Vol 75, No 11, p. 116901, ISSN 0034-4885, http://tinyurl.com/z7cqqke.

82. Kramer, M., *Scale of Universe Measured with 1-Percent Accuracy*, 08 Jan 2014, Accessed 09 Jan 2014, http://tinyurl.com/p2j99vl (full URL: http://www.space.com/24207-dark-energy-galaxy-map-aas223.html).

83. Anderson, L., *et al.*, *The clustering of galaxies in the SDSS-III Baryon Oscillation Spectroscopic Survey: baryon acoustic oscillations in the Data Releases 10 and 11 Galaxy samples*, Monthly Notices of the Royal Astronomical Society, Vol 441, No 1, 11 Jun 2014, pp. 24-62, DOI: 10.1093/mnras/stu523, http://tinyurl.com/jqro6yk. See Also: http://arxiv.org/abs/1312.4877.

84. Zyga, L., *No Big Bang? Quantum equation predicts universe has no beginning*, Omicron Technology Limited, 2015, Series Ed(s). Benson, *et al.*, Accessed 25 Sept 2015, http://tinyurl.com/ob37h8g (full URL: http://phys.org/news/2015-02-big-quantum-equation-universe.html).

85. Farag Ali, A. and S. Das, *Cosmology from quantum potential*, Physics Letters B, Vol 741, 04 Feb 2015, pp. 276-279, ISSN 0370-2693, DOI: http://dx.doi.org/10.1016/j.physletb.2014.12.057, http://tinyurl.com/p6sfcwx. See Also: http://arxiv.org/abs/1404.3093v3.

86. Dvali, G., G. Gabadadze, and M. Porrati, *4D gravity on a brane in 5D Minkowski space*, Physics Letters B, Vol 485, No 1–3, 13 Jul 2000, pp. 208-214, ISSN 0370-2693, DOI: http://dx.doi.org/10.1016/S0370-2693(00)00669-9, http://tinyurl.com/hhheqo8.

87. Razieh, P., A. Niayesh, and B.M. Robert, *Out of the white hole: a holographic origin for the Big Bang*, Journal of Cosmology and Astroparticle Physics, 2014, Vol 2014, No 04, p. 005, ISSN 1475-7516, http://tinyurl.com/hw3joq2. See Also: http://arxiv.org/abs/1309.1487.

88. Merali, Z., *Did a hyper-black hole spawn the Universe*, 2013, Accessed 27 Feb 2016, http://tinyurl.com/p6xu5g6 (full URL: http://www.nature.com/news/did-a-hyper-black-hole-spawn-the-universe-1.13743).

89. Führer, F. and C. Wetterich, *Backreaction in growing neutrino quintessence*, Physical Review D, Vol 91, No 12, 30 Jun 2015, p. 123542 DOI: http://dx.doi.org/10.1103/PhysRevD.91.123542, http://tinyurl.com/zf4mmwa. See Also: http://arxiv.org/abs/1503.07995.

90. Hoffman, Y., *et al.*, *The dipole repeller*, Nature Astronomy, 30 Jan 2017, Vol 1, p. 0036, Macmillan Publishers Limited, part of Springer Nature., DOI: 10.1038/s41550-016-0036, http://www.nature.com/articles/s41550-016-0036#supplementary-information, http://dx.doi.org/10.1038/s41550-016-0036.

91. LIGO Scientific and Virgo Collaboration, *et al.*, *GW170104: Observation of a 50-Solar-Mass Binary Black Hole Coalescence at Redshift 0.2*, Physical Review Letters, 2017, Vol 118, No 22, 01 Jun 2017, p. 221101, American Physical Society, http://tinyurl.com/ybpqla3v.

92. Moskowitz, C., *The Neutrino Puzzle*, Scientific American, 2017, Vol 317, No 4, pp. 34-39, Scientific American, ISSN 00368733.

CHAPTER 14

1. Russell, B., *Mathematics and the Metaphysicians*, in Book: Mysticism and Logic: And Other Essays, 3rd ed., New York, Longmans, Green and Co., 1919, No., Ch. V, p. 85, **Notes:** The essay on "Mathematics and the Metaphysicians" was written in 1901, and appeared in an American magazine, *The International Monthly*, Vol 4, pp. 83-101, under the title "Recent Work in the Philosophy of Mathematics." It was reprinted under the title, "Mathematics and the metaphysicians," Ch.5, in Mysticism and logic and other essays, Longmans, Green and Co., New York, 1918.

2. Carlyle, T., *On Heroes, Hero-Worship, and the Heroic in History*, The Project Gutenberg, 1893, http://www.gutenberg.org/ebooks/1091, **Notes:** The following online Book source is better formated than the Gutenberg source (see URL). The original publication: Carlyle, T., *"Lecture 1. The Hero As Divinity. Odin. Paganism : Scandinavian Mythology."*, 5 May 1840, http://tinyurl.com/hmay8fz (full URL: https://ebooks.adelaide.edu.au/c/carlyle/thomas/on_heroes/chapter1.html). Published in Australia.

3. Holton, G.J. and Y. Elkana, *Albert Einstein: Historical and Cultural Perspectives*, Dover Publications, 1997, p. 238, ISBN 978-0486298795, **Notes:** The original expression is undocumented and therefore copyright status is unassignable. Refer to bibliographical reference number 84 (p. 249). Partial reference provided here: One of the many versions is given by B. Kuznetzov in *Einstein and Dostoyevsky*, Hutchinson Educational, 1972, p. 39, ISBN 978-0091066604. There we find: "What interests me: could God have made the world differently?" Does the requirement of logical simplicity leave any lattitude?".

4. Craig, W.L., *On Guard: Defending Your Faith with Reason and Precision*, David C. Cook, 2010, p. 74, ISBN 978-1434701886, **Notes:** Refer to Chapter 4, Citation 1. Al-Ghazali, Kitab al-Iqtisad fi'l-I'tiqad (The Moderate Path in Theology), cited in S. de Beaurecueil, *"Gazzali et S. Thomas d'Aquin: Essai sur la preuve de l'existence de Dieu proposée dans l'Iqtisad et sa comparaison avec les 'voies' Thomiste"*, Bulletin de l'Institut Francais d'Archaeologie Orientale 46 (1947): 203. This former citation is translated as follows: S. de Beaurecueil, "*Ghazzali and St Thomas Aquinas : An Essay on the evidence of the existence of God proposed in Iqtisad and its comparison with the 'pathways' Thomiste*", Bulletin of the French Institute of Oriental Archaeologie, 46 (1947): 203.

5. Martin, M., *The Cambridge Companion to Atheism*, Cambridge University Press, 2006, p. 183, ISBN 978-1139827393.

6. Moreland, J.P. and W.L. Craig, *Philosophical Foundations for a Christian Worldview*, InterVarsity Press, 2003, p. 468, ISBN 978-0830826940.

7. Craig, W.L. and J.D. Sinclair, *The Blackwell Companion to Natural Theology*, Wiley, 2012, p. 194, ISBN 978-1444350852.

8. Craig, W.L., *Time and Eternity: Exploring God's Relationship to Time*, Crossway Books, 2001, p. 233, ISBN 978-1581342413.

9. Craig, W.L., *On Guard: Defending Your Faith with Reason and Precision*, David C. Cook, 2010, p. 77, ISBN 978-1434701886.

10. Craig, W.L. and J.D. Sinclair, *The Blackwell Companion to Natural Theology*, Wiley, 2012, p. 183, ISBN 978-1444350852.

11. Swingrover, L.J., *Difficulties With William Lane Craig's Arguments for Finitism*, Academia.edu, 2014, Accessed 20 Aug 2015, http://tinyurl.com/zeborwt (full URL: https://www.academia.edu/7068171/Difficulties_With_William_Lane_Craigs_Arguments_for_Finitism), **Notes:** See page 5.

12. Craig, W.L., *Pantheists in Spite of Themselves? Pannenberg, Clayton, and Shults on Divine Infinity*, Reasonable Faith, Undated, Accessed 19 Aug 2015, http://tinyurl.com/zlnxmy6.

13. Craig, W.L., *Time and Eternity: Exploring God's Relationship to Time*, Crossway Books, 2001, pp. 221-229, ISBN 978-1581342413.

14. Shoemaker, S., *Time Without Change*, The Journal of Philosophy, 1969, Vol 66, No 12, pp. 363-381, Journal of Philosophy, Inc., ISSN 0022362X, DOI: 10.2307/2023892, http://www.jstor.org/stable/2023892.

15. Altuna, E.E., *Time without Change: A Challenge to Sydney Shoemaker's Argument*, 2012, Vol 3, No 1 (Article 21), pp. 148-153, Res Cogitans, http://tinyurl.com/hjxnunb (full URL: http://commons.pacificu.edu/rescogitans/vol3/iss1/21/).

16. Craig, W.L., *Time and Eternity: Exploring God's Relationship to Time*, Crossway Books, 2001, p. 157, ISBN 978-1581342413.

17. Craig, W.L., *God, Time, and Eternity: The Coherence of Theism II: Eternity*, Springer Netherlands, 2013, p. 269, ISBN 978-9401717151.

18. Craig, W.L., *Time and Eternity: Exploring God's Relationship to Time*, Crossway Books, 2001, p. 235, ISBN 978-1581342413.

19. Craig, W.L. and J.D. Sinclair, *The Blackwell Companion to Natural Theology*, Wiley, 2012, pp. 191-192, ISBN 978-1444350852.

20. Craig, W.L. and J.D. Sinclair, *The Blackwell Companion to Natural Theology*, Wiley, 2012, p. 192, ISBN 978-1444350852.

21. Swingrover, L.J., *Difficulties With William Lane Craig's Arguments for Finitism*, Academia.edu, 2014, Accessed 20 Aug 2015, http://tinyurl.com/zeborwt (full URL: https://www.academia.edu/7068171/Difficulties_With_William_Lane_Craigs_Arguments_for_Finitism).

22. Swingrover, L.J., *Difficulties With William Lane Craig's Arguments for Finitism*, Academia.edu, 2014, Accessed 20 Aug 2015, http://tinyurl.com/zeborwt (full URL: https://www.academia.edu/7068171/Difficulties_With_William_Lane_Craigs_Arguments_for_Finitism), **Notes:** See Abstract.

23. Podcast Title: *Debate on the Existence of God: Betrand Russel v. Fr. Frederick Copleston*, Narrator: Brown, Run time 19 minutes, http://tinyurl.com/j7rzroh, **Notes:** BBC Recording Number T7324W. This is an excerpt from the full broadcast from cassette tape A303/5 Open University Course, Problems of Philosophy Units 7-8. This quote is excerpted from "A Debate on the Argument from Contingency: Father F. C. Copleston and Bertrand Russell", broadcast in 1948 on the Third Program of the British Broadcasting Corporation. This was published in Humanitas (Manchester) and reprinted in Bertrand Russell's, *"Why I Am Not a Christian"* (© 1957, 1985, George Allen & Unwin Ltd.). This note is cited from URL: http://www.ditext.com/russell/debate.html/. The audio program can be accessed on YouTube: Part 1: http://tinyurl.com/zr5kw32 and Part 2: http://tinyurl.com/jzbrzom. The original radio broadcast source material is no longer in UK/BBC copyright.

24. Dorato, M., *Substantivalism, Relationism, and Structural Spacetime Realism*, Foundations of Physics, Vol 30, No 10, Oct 2000, pp. 1605-1628, Kluwer Academic Publishers-Plenum Publishers, ISSN 0015-9018, DOI: 10.1023/A:1026442015519, http://tinyurl.com/hggv434.

25. Dorato, M., *Chapter 2 Is Structural Spacetime Realism Relationism in Disguise? The Supererogatory Nature of the Substantivalism/Relationism Debate*, in Book: Philosophy and Foundations of Physics, Ed. Dennis, Elsevier, 2008, Vol. Volume 4, No., pp. 17-37, ISBN 1871-1774, http://tinyurl.com/zp36ld5.

26. Grant, S.K., *The Metaphysics of Space-time Substantivalism: A Methodological Study of the Structure of Space-time in the Context of General Relativity*, Ph.D. - Philosophy, University of Otago (Dunedin, New Zealand), Advisor: Dyke, 201 p., 2013, http://tinyurl.com/zl8p5jr (full URL: http://hdl.handle.net/10523/4176).

27. Siegfried, T., *Part 1: Tensor networks get entangled with quantum gravity*, Science News: Magazine of the Society for Science & the Public, 02 Sept 2014, Accessed 08 Sept 2015, http://tinyurl.com/j4qpbmw, **Notes:** The quote is to be found in Part 2 of this article, Siegfried, *Holography entangles quantum physics with gravity*, Science News, 08 Sept 2015.

28. Siegfried, T., *Part 2: Holography entangles quantum physics with gravity*, Science News: Magazine of the Society for Science & the Public, 08 Sept 2014, Accessed 08 Sept 2015, http://tinyurl.com/lseot7f.

29. Craig, W.L., *Defenders Podcast - Series 2*, 2014, **Notes:** This is a transcript of a lecture. The relevant portion of the lecture is "Doctrine of God"-Part 8-"Infinite: Omnipresence". Refer to section entitled "Systematic Summary". Access Transcript: http://tinyurl.com/jdetlha (full URL: http://www.reasonablefaith.org/defenders-2-podcast/transcript/s3-8). Access Audio Podcast: http://tinyurl.com/jbzzjgm (full URL: http://www.reasonablefaith.org/defenders-2-podcast/s3).

30. Augustine of Hippo, *Confessions in Thirteen Books* (also frequently translated as *The Confessions of Saint Augustine*), The Project Gutenberg, 397 - 400 CE, http://tinyurl.com/n6gt5qm, **Notes:** Translated by E. B. Pusey. Refer to Book XI (11).

31 Huggett, N. and C. Hoefer, *"Absolute and Relational Theories of Space and Motion"*, The Stanford Encyclopedia of Philosophy (Spring 2017 Edition), Series Ed(s). Zalta, Accessed 02 Jun 2017, http://tinyurl.com/y8aav3yw.

CHAPTER 15

1. Wilde, O., *Play: The Importance of Being Earnest, A Trivial Comedy for Serious People.*, 1895.

2. Wilde, O., *Intentions*, London, Methuen & Co., LTD., 1891, http://www.gutenberg.org/ebooks/887, **Notes:** The quote is from the essay within Oscar Wilde's publication of Intentions. The essay is entitled as, *"The Critic as Artist"*. See Part II - A conversation between Gilbert and Ernest.

3. Coenn, D., *Mark Twain: His Words*, BookRix, 2014, ISBN 978-3736818613.

4. Martinez, T., *Ensembles, Model Combination and Bayesian Combination*, 2015, Accessed 14 Sep 2015, **Notes:** A Microsoft Powerpoint slide presentation from Course 678:Advanced Machine Learning and Neural Networks, Brigham Young University. See Powerpoint slide pp. 22-26 from course: http://axon.cs.byu.edu/~martinez/classes/678/Slides/BMC-Ensembles.pptx.

5. NASA, P.C., *Jet Propulsion Labratory's Near Earth Object Program*, NASA, 2016, Accessed 16 May 2016, http://neo.jpl.nasa.gov/stats/, **Notes:** This data is as of May 16, 2016.

6. Bostrom, N., *Are We Living in a Computer Simulation?*, The Philosophical Quarterly, 2003, Vol 53, No 211, April 1, 2003, pp. 243-255, DOI: 10.1111/1467-9213.00309, http://tinyurl.com/gmyhnqz.

7. World Union of Deists, *Deist Glossary*, World Union of Deists, L.L.C., 2015, Accessed 21 Sep 2015, http://www.deism.com/deismdefined.htm. See also the "Deist Glossary": http://www.deism.com/deism_defined.htm, **Notes:** Refer to glossary term for "Deism".

8. Dawkins, R., *The God Delusion*, 1st ed., Houghton Mifflin Harcourt, 2006, p. 47, ISBN 978-0618680009.

9. Dawkins, R., *The God Delusion*, 1st ed., Houghton Mifflin Harcourt, 2006, p. 51, ISBN 978-0618680009.

10. Chomsky, N., *Beyond Belief: Science, Religion, Reason, and Survival*, Edge Foundation, Inc., 2006, Series Ed(s). Brockman and Weinberger, Accessed 22 Sept 2015, http://edge.org/discourse/bb.html#chomsky, **Notes:** A discussion hosted by Edge - The Reality Club (www.edge.org) that took place at the Salk Institute, La Jolla November 5-7, 2006

11. Locey, K.J. and J.T. Lennon, *Scaling laws predict global microbial diversity*, Proceedings of the National Academy of Sciences, May 2, 2016, DOI: 10.1073/pnas.1521291113, http://tinyurl.com/ju9ypcr.

12. Camilo Mora, D.P.T., Sinda Adl, Alastair G. B. Simpson, Boris Worm, *How Many Species Are There on Earth and in the Ocean?*, PLOS Biolog, 23 Aug 2011, http://tinyurl.com/qylk3sn.

13. Sharot, T., *The Optimism Bias: A Tour of the Irrationally Positive Brain*, Knopf Doubleday Publishing Group, 2011, ISBN 978-0307379832.

14. Sharot, T., *Why dont' facts matter?*, CNN / Turner Broadcasting System, Inc, 14 Sept 2017, Accessed 02 October 2017, http://tinyurl.com/y8wrrx2f, Notes: This article is Part 1 of a two-part series.

15. Sharot, T., *Want to change minds? Try this*, CNN / Turner Broadcasting System, Inc, 14 Sept 2017, Accessed 02 October 2017, http://tinyurl.com/ybl7cahy, Notes: This article is Part 2 of a two-part series.

16. Sharot, T., B. De Martino, and R.J. Dolan, *How Choice Reveals and Shapes Expected Hedonic Outcome*, The Journal of Neuroscience, 2009, Vol 29, No 12, pp. 3760-3765, DOI: https://doi.org/10.1523/JNEUROSCI.4972-08.2009, http://tinyurl.com/y722e8qk.

17. Sharot, T., T. Shiner, and R.J. Dolan, *Experience and Choice Shape Expected Aversive Outcomes*, The Journal of Neuroscience, 2010, Vol 30, No 27, pp. 9209-9215, DOI: https://doi.org/10.1523/JNEUROSCI.4770-09.2010, http://tinyurl.com/y7fqj2ll.

CHAPTER 16

1. Chardin, P.T.d., *Building the Earth*, Wilkes-Barre, PA, Dimension Books, 1965, p. 54, Trans. by Lindsay, ISBN 978-0871930781, **Notes:** The original French text was called, Construire la Terre (*trans.* Building the Earth), published 1958.

2. Piburn, S., *Dalai Lama, A Policy of Kindness: An Anthology of Writings by and about the Dalai Lama*, 2nd ed., Snow Lion Publications, 1990, p. 52, ISBN 978-1559390224, **Notes:** Reprinted by arrangement with Shambhala Publications, Inc., Boston, MA. www.shambhala.com. Fair Use.

3. Chomsky, N., *Beyond Belief: Science, Religion, Reason, and Survival*, Edge Foundation, Inc., 2006, Series Ed(s). Brockman and Weinberger, Accessed 22 Sept 2015, http://edge.org/discourse/bb.html#chomsky, **Notes:** A discussion hosted by Edge - The Reality Club (www.edge.org) that took place at the Salk Institute, La Jolla November 5-7, 2006

4. Sir John Marks Templeton, *The Humble Approach: Scientists Discover God*, Revised ed., Radnor, Pennsylvania, Templeton Foundation Press, p. 3, ISBN 978-1890151171, **Notes:** Reprinted by permission from Templeton Press.

5. Space.com, *Stellar Explosion Is Most Distant Object Visible to Naked Eye*, Space.com, 21 Mar 2008, Accessed 01 Oct 2010, http://tinyurl.com/zejxco4 (full URL: http://www.space.com/5153-stellar-explosion-distant-object-visible-naked-eye.html).

6. Nutman, A.P., et al., *Rapid emergence of life shown by discovery of 3,700-million-year-old microbial structures*, Nature, 2016, 08 Aug 2016, Macmillan Publishers Limited, part of Springer Nature., ISSN 1476-4687, DOI: 10.1038/nature19355, http://tinyurl.com/glk4h76, **Notes:** The earliest fossilized life form ever found as of 2016 is in the form of a layered microbial community called stromatolites.

7. Sender, R., S. Fuchs, and R. Milo, *Revised estimates for the number of human and bacteria cells in the body*, bioRxiv, 06 Jan 2016, DOI: 10.1101/036103, http://tinyurl.com/jqwk6jb.

8. Abbott, A., *Scientists bust myth that our bodies have more bacteria than human cells*, Nature Publishing Group/ Macmillan Publishers, 2016, Accessed 18 May 2016, http://tinyurl.com/jflqy7c.

9. Piburn, S., *Dalai Lama, A Policy of Kindness: An Anthology of Writings by and about the Dalai Lama*, 2nd ed., Snow Lion Publications, 1990, p. 101, ISBN 978-1559390224, **Notes:** Reprinted by arrangement with Shambhala Publications, Inc., Boston, MA. www.shambhala.com. Fair Use.

10. Hanh, T.N., *The Science of the Buddha: A collection of Sutras and Articles for reference*, Series Ed(s). Plum Village Mindfulness Practice Centre, 2012, p. 9, **Notes:** Plum Village is founded by Zen Master Thich Nhat Hanh who lives in residence. This is a booklet created for a 21 day retreat organized by the Plum Village Practice Center (Dieulivol, France). Document was accessed from the website of the European Institute of Applied Buddhism on 29 Sept 2015. Refer to https://www.eiab.eu/index.php?index=88. A second source is a PDF document provided here - click on the hyperlink under the heading "Letter to a Young Scientist": http://tinyurl.com/hpu57dq (full URL: http://mindfulnessacademy.org/images/docs/manifestationonly/2012%20-21-DayRetreat-TheScienceOfTheBuddha-Booklet.pdf).

11. Sacks, J., *The Great Partnership: Science, Religion, and the Search for Meaning*, Schocken Books, 2012, p. 296, ISBN 978-0805212501.

12. Khayyam, O., *Rubaiyat of Omar Khayyam (Translated by Edward Fitzgerald)*, Series Ed(s). Judy Boss, The Project Gutenberg, No. 20 May 2016, http://www.gutenberg.org/ebooks/246, **Notes:** Refer to Fifth Edition which contains 110 quatrains. Rendered into English by Edward Fitzgerald (1879).The First edition was translated in 1868 and conatined 75 quatrains. Refer to *Rubaiyat of Omar Khayyam*, edited by Daniel Karlin, Oxford University Press (2009) for an extensive discussion on the various versions.

13 Belkin, D., *Many Colleges Fail in Teaching How to Think–A test finds students often gain little ability to assess evidence, make a cohesive argument*, Wall Street Journal, 06 Jun 2017, Dow Jones & Company, p. A1 (front page) and A10, http://tinyurl.com/ydcwt3zk.

Glossary

1. Princeton University, *"About WordNet"*, 2010, http://wordnet.princeton.edu, **Notes:** Version 2.1 (Windows). WordNet is a registered trademark of Princeton University. Reprinted with permission.

PHOTO AND ILLUSTRATION CREDITS

P = Photo   I = Illustration   T = Top   B = Bottom   C = Center   L = Left   R = Right

#	Reference	Page	Type	Position	Credit
–	Front Cover	–	I	—	Image Copyright © 2017 by Brian D. Goedken. A derivative work of the following:
					The graphic of the naked man with glyphs and text on his back in addition to the primary background is credited to Bruce Rolff / Shutterstock.com, Image ID: 111979028 and Image ID: 90072934.
					The punch-through effect is credited to Grishankov/ Shutterstock.com, Image ID: 385875220.
–	Back Cover	–	I	—	The abstract wave graphic is credited to Unscrew/Shutterstock.com, Image ID: 258949361. Modifications by Brian D. Goedken.
–	–	–	I	—	The "traveling footprint" graphic presented at the introduction of each chapter is credited to/ copyrighted by iStock.com/blackred. Stock photo ID: 19768616. Modifications by Brian D. Goedken.
–	Dedication	vii	I	—	The "Dove of Peace" graphic presented on the Dedication page is credited to KsanasK/Shutterstock.com. Image ID:193449032.
–	End Intro.	–	I	—	Head with maze pondering the Big Questions. Copyright: Bruce Rolff / 123rf.com. Image ID: 9772333.
–	Partition I	–	I	—	The Zetetic Path. Image Copyright © 2017 by Brian D. Goedken.
					A derivative work of the following:
					The "traveling footprint" Copyright iStock.com/blackred. Stock photo ID: 19768616.
–	Partition II	–	I	—	The Puzzle of Scripture. Image Copyright © 2017 by Brian D. Goedken.

#	Reference	Page	Type	Position	Credit
–	Partition III	–	I	—	Image Copyright © 2017 by Brian D. Goedken. A derivative work of the following: Gears, Copyright: enki / 123rf.com. Image ID : 18708252, Man's Illuminated Mind Copyright: Agsandrew / Shutterstock.com Image ID:229039786 Deep Space, Copyright: Bruce Rolff / Shutterstock.com. Image ID:64210054
–	Partition IV	–	I	—	Image Copyright © 2017 by Brian D. Goedken. A derivative work of the following: Moon, Clouds, Flock of Birds Copyright: mexitographer / 123RF.com. Image ID: 49269062 Doonagore castle, (Round Castle) Co Clare, Ireland Copyright: Alberto Loyo / 123RF.com. Image ID: 15470408 Twin Pillar Arch Copyright: Ievgenii Slivin / 123RF.com. Image ID: 57224078 Castle (Single Spire) Copyright: Elena Duvernay / 123RF.com. Image ID: 30237454 Stormy Sea. Copyright: PÃ©ter Gudella / 123RF.com. Image ID: 22490595 Jaws of the Devil (Boca do Inferno) sea cliff located at Cascais, Portugal. Copyright: Ievgenii Fesenko / 123RF.com. Image ID: 62284669
1	Figure 1-1	29	I	—	The "Mysterious power - open palm with a glowing light" graphic is credited to Mopic/Shutterstock.com. Image ID:105943679. Modified by Brian Goedken. Source data from Baylor Institute for Studies of Religion, *The Baylor Religion Survey – Wave II*, 2007.
2	Figure 1-1	31	I	—	Image Copyright © 2017 by Brian D. Goedken. Source data from Barro R., Hwang, J., *Religious Conversion in 40 Countries*, National Bureau of Economic Research.

#	Reference	Page	Type	Position	Credit
3	Chapter End	61	I	—	Stylistic flourish. Image Copyright © 2017 by Brian D. Goedken.
4	Figure 2-1	68	I	—	Image Copyright © 2017 by Brian D. Goedken. Source data from *America's Changing Religious Landscape* (Pew Research Center, 12 May 2015).
5	Figure 2-2	74	I	—	Image Copyright © 2017 by Brian D. Goedken. Source data from *U.S. Religious Knowledge Survey* (Pew Research Center, 28 Sep 2010).
6	Figure 2-3	75	I	—	Image Copyright © 2017 by Brian D. Goedken. Source data from *General Social Survey, 1972 – 2012 Cumulative.*
7	Figure 2-4	75	I	—	Image Copyright © 2017 by Brian D. Goedken. Source data from *U.S. Religious Landscape Survey* (Pew Research Center, June 2008).
8	Figure 3-1	84	I	—	Geoff Richards. Public Domain.
9	Figure 3-2	89	I	—	Image Copyright © 2017 by Brian D. Goedken. Source Base geography from University of Texas Perry-Castañeda Map Library. Middle East Map 1999. Used with permission.
10	Figure 3-3	98	P	TL	BibleLandPictures.com. Modified by the present author to highlight the location of the inscription.
11	Figure 3-3	98	P	TR	BibleLandPictures.com. Modified by the present author to highlight features in the drawing for discussional purposes.
12	Figure 3-3	98	P	BL	© Musée du Louvre, Dist. RMN-Grand Palais / Christian Decamps / Art Resource, NY.
13	Figure 3-3	98	P	BR	© BPK, Berlin, Neues Museum - Egyptian Museum and Papyrus / Jürgen Liepe / Art Resource, NY.
14	Figure 3-4	101	P	TL	KM 6573 Terracotta lamp, Fayum, Egypt, Kelsey Museum of Archaeology, University of Michigan.
15	Figure 3-4	101	P	TR	Marc Heilig, Archeographe (2003). Museum of Egyptian Antiquities (Cairo).
16	Figure 3-4	101	P	BL	Image copyright © The Metropolitan Museum of Art. Image source: Art Resource, NY.
17	Figure 3-4	101	P	BR	© The Trustees of the British Museum / Art Resource, NY.

#	Reference	Page	Type	Position	Credit
18	Figure 3-5	103	I	L	Camocon (2011). Public Domain.
19	Figure 3-5	103	I	R	BibleLandPictures.com. Modified by the present author to extract the image from the context of the full picture (refer to # 11 in this listing).
20	Figure 3-6	106	I	—	Image Copyright © 2017 by Brian D. Goedken.
21	Figure 3-7	108	P	L	Image Credit: By unknown 13th-century scribe. Public domain via Wikimedia Commons.
22	Figure 3-7	108	I	R	Image Copyright © 2017 by Brian D. Goedken.
23	Figure 5-1	149	P	—	BibleLandPictures.com.
24	Figure 5-2	150	P	T	Getty Images. All copyright rights waived. Public domain. The photo was altered by Brian Goedken by changing the color scheme to grayscale and by adding a black rectangular outline to signify the region of print that is magnified to make the text more legible.
25	Figure 5-2	150	P	B	The Vatican Library.
26	Figure 5-3	177	I	—	Image Copyright © 2017 by Brian D. Goedken.
27	Ch. 6, Ch. 8	—	I	—	Horizontal bar to separate biblical references are illustrated by Brian Goedken.
28	Figure 6-1	219	P	L, R	© The British Library Board, Add. 43725, Mark, 16:1 - 16:8 / Luke, 1:1 - 1:18 28 scribe: D. Modifications including the rounded square, large bold braces, bolded text, and the graphic excerpt are added by Brian Goedken to enhance features elucidated in the narrative of the book.
29	Chapter End (continued nex page)	261	I	—	Image Copyright © 2017 by Brian D. Goedken. All modifications by Brian D. Goedken A derivative work of the following: Pre-1900 granite cross in Milltown Cemetery (Belfast, Ireland).By Fine Art Imagery/Shutterstock.com, Image ID: 84109207. Large stone. Dolmen in Burren, Ireland. Stephanie Zaccaria/Shutterstock.com, Image Id: 516110941 continued on next page ...

#	Reference	Page	Type	Position	Credit
29	Continuation		I	—	Silver metal spheres. Copyright iStock.com/Ravitaliy, Stock photo ID: 594022228
					Scale. Copyright iStock.com/ISerg, Stock photo ID: 513806380
30	Figure 6-2	242	I	—	Image Copyright © 2017 by Brian D. Goedken. Source data from Dundes, A., Rank, O., and Lord Raglan, *In Quest of the Hero*, Princeton University Press, 1990, p. 179-223.
31	Table 7-1	277	I	—	Thumbs Up and Thumbs Down figures are illustrations by Brian Goedken.
32	Figure 8-1	301	I	—	Image Copyright © 2017 by Brian D. Goedken.
33	Figure 10-1	350	I	—	Image Copyright © 2017 by Brian D. Goedken. Source data from *The World's Religions in Figures* (Wiley-Blackwell, 2013) and the *World Religion Database* (Brill, 2012).
34	Figure 10-2	351	I	—	Image Copyright © 2017 by Brian D. Goedken. Source data from *The World's Religions in Figures* (Wiley-Blackwell, 2013) and the *World Religion Database* (Brill, 2012).
35	Figure 10-3	351	I	—	Image Copyright © 2017 by Brian D. Goedken. Source data from *"Nones" on the Rise* (2012) and *America's Changing Religious Landscape* (2015) by the Pew Research Center.
36	Figure 11-1	378	I	—	Image Copyright © 2017 by Brian D. Goedken. Based on source material from Deacon, T., *Reciprocal Linkage between Self-organizing Processes is Sufficient for Self-reproduction and Evolvability*, Biological Theory, 2006, Vol 1, No 2, pp. 139-141.
37	Figure 12-1	442	I	—	Image Copyright © 2017 by Brian D. Goedken. Based on source material from Hameroff, S., Penrose, R., *Conscious Events as Orchestrated Space-Time Selections*, 2007, Vol 1, No. 1.
38	Figure 13-1	454	I	—	Image Copyright © 2017 by Brian D. Goedken.
39	Figure 13-2	459	I	—	Image Copyright © 2017 by Brian D. Goedken.
40	Figure 13-3	463	I	—	Image Copyright © 2017 by Brian D. Goedken.

#	Reference	Page	Type	Position	Credit
41	Figure 13-4	459	I	—	Image Copyright © 2017 by Brian D. Goedken. Adapted from an image by Dr. Christof Wetterich in a Powerpoint presentation in Paris, France (2013) to explain his research paper, *Universe without Expansion*. Refer to citation for additional bibliographical information.
42	Figure 13-5	487	I	—	Image Copyright © 2017 by Brian D. Goedken. Adapted from an image by Dr. Christof Wetterich in a Powerpoint presentation in Paris, France (2013) to explain his research paper, *Universe without Expansion*. Refer to citation for additional bibliographical information.
43	Figure 13-6	493	I	—	Image Copyright © 2017 by Brian D. Goedken.
44	Figure 14-1	508	I	—	Image Copyright © 2017 by Brian D. Goedken. W. L. Craig's worldview is principally assembled from his book *Time and Eternity: Exploring God's Relationship to Time* (Crossway Books, 2001).
45	Figure 14-2	512	I	—	Image Copyright © 2017 by Brian D. Goedken. Adapted from Swingrover, L.J., *Difficulties With William Lane Craig's Arguments for Finitism*, 2014, p. 5. Refer to Figure 1: Modes of Possibility.
46	Figure 14-3	516	I	—	Image Copyright © 2017 by Brian D. Goedken.
47	Figure 15-1	550	I	—	Image Copyright © 20 17 by Brian D. Goedken.
48	Figure 15-2	551	I	—	Image Copyright © 2017 by Brian D. Goedken.
49	Figure 15-3	565	I	—	Image Copyright © 2017 by Brian D. Goedken.
50	Figure 15-4	569	I	—	Image Copyright © 2017 by Brian D. Goedken.

INDEX

A posteriori 188, 319, 329

A priori 19, 43, 68, 146, 188, 265, 319, 323, 329, 333, 364, 416, 419, 448, 452, 543

A-theory (A-series) time

    A-series 511, 514-518, 521-526, 555, 559-564

    truisms T1 - T6 514, 517, 523

Abductive reasoning

    abduction 15

    collection of 187

    tools of 278

    use of 54

Abraham (Abram), prophet of Islam and of the Bible 57, 111, 191, 276, 284, 343, 506, 539

Absence (of evidence) 15

Absolute objective truth 47, 50, 51, 349, 394, 447, 566

Acausality 517

Accepted beliefs 186, 269-271, 274, 275, 277, 281

Achilles tendon (of W. L. Craig's 'infinity argument'). *See* Craig, William Lane

Acts of the Apostles (canonical)

    Acts, a literary forgery 228

    Apocryphal Acts. *See* Gnostic, genre of Gnostic literature

    authenticity of 230

    author of, unknown 229

    authorial attribution, Luke the Evangelist 198, 227-229

    canonical text (book) in Christian New Testament 149

    dates of authorship 175, 177, 227

    description of Jesus' post-death manifestations 228, 229

    Jesus' post-death appearances (*See Also* Gospels, list of post-death...) 211, 224, 228, 229

    quoting Apostle Paul's words and deeds 227, 228

    "We" argument increases unreliability of Act's testimony 228

Ad Autolycum (Greek, To Autolycus by Theophilus) 290

Ad hoc / Ad hoc-ness 186, 187, 213, 269, 271, 272, 274, 275, 277, 428

Adamianism 162

Adamite (metaphysical material). *See Also* Eveitite 521-523, 528, 561

Adenine (nucleobase molecule) 377

ADHD (Attention Deficit Hyperactivity Disorder) 423

Adonis, deity 239, 240

Adversus Praxean (Against Praxeas)—literary work 290

Aeons

    divine sparks take wisdom from Jesus 168

    two powerful aeons (Jesus and Holy Spirit) 165

Aether, celestial. *See* Aristotle, aether, celestial

Affiliation

    irreligious affiliation 352

    summary of religious affiliation (charts) 350, 351

Afterlife

    eternal 179

    much-hoped-for 16, 445

    survey results (U.S.), adult belief in an afterlife 74

Agape (feast) 165

Age

    Age of Enlightenment 25, 32, 35, 295

    Age of fables 159

    antisupernaturalism 188

    Axial Age 86

    Bronze Age 86, 90

    Bronze-Iron Age 90

    dawn of the scientific age 373

    Iron Age 86, 90, 91

    Middle Ages 121, 158

    Millenarian Age 385

    Stone Age 85

Agency

    agency to causality 372

    divine (deific) agency 32, 34, 41, 47, 245, 323, 402, 545, 556

    in the context of emergence of complexity 389

    personal agency 364, 402

Agenticity. *See* Bias, types of

Aggregated belief 74, 75

Agnosticism

    and Atheism 32, 44, 350, 571

    PAP (Permanent Agnosticism in Principle) 571

    the poverty of 571

Agnosticism (*continued*)

 TAP (Temporary Agnosticism in Practice) 571

Agnostic 30, 31, 45, 68, 72, 73, 245, 279, 308, 349, 363, 571, 585, 587

Aguirre-Gratton Proposal (cosmic biverse). *See* Cosmogonic models

Ahab, King 96

Akkadians, people of the Akkadia kingdom 89, 90, 97

Al-Ghazali (Sunni Muslim theologian)

 Al-Ghazali

 The Middle Path in Theology (literary work) 310

Al-Nusra, Jabat (terror organization) 27

Al-Qaeda (terror organization) 26, 27, 63

Alcubierre (warp engine) 38

Alcuin of York 293

Alétheia. *See* Zeto Alétheia

Alice's Adventures in Wonderland 49

Alien

 alien civilizations 37, 39, 555

 alien intelligence 393, 556

 alien simulator operators 564

 aliens (extraterrestrial) 20, 37, 39, 43, 65, 239, 393, 403, 404, 548, 555, 556, 564, 566, 569, 581

Allah, God of Islam. *See* Islam, Allah, God of Islam

Almagest (book on ancient cosmology)—literary work 372

Ammonites (people of Ammon kingdom) 89, 90

Amorites (people of Amorite kingdom) 89

Amorphous time. *See* Time, amorphous time

Amun, deity (Amun-Ra, Amun-Re, Ra) 100, 538

Analogy

 automobile, Model T (levitation by magician) 216

 bb, shotgun (defense of God) 76

 baseball field (cosmon model, frame invariance) 489

 brain surgery (applying scrutiny to religious beliefs) 33

 bricks, masonry (enumeration, simplicity vs. complexity) 313

 balloon (cosmic inflation) 454

 car (religion versus theology) 67

 Chinese finger trap (difficulties, cosmogonic models) 482

 eye of needle (difficulties with Perfect Being Theology) 538

 prayer, answering by YAHWEH! Insta-Prayer 189

 proton-to-softball size (cosmic inflation) 454

 Star Wars Episode IV (imagining a virtualized world) 555

 tree (emergence, teleology, autocell) 391

Anat, deity 90, 91, 96, 538

Anat-Yahu (Anatyahu), deity 91

Anath, deity 90, 95

Anchoring bias. *See* Bias, types of

Andromeda Galaxy (M31) 37, 38, 78, 579

Anesthesia, general 438

Angels

 divine creatures 74, 159, 165, 249, 286, 327, 335

 hierarchy 116

 two at empty tomb (Gospel of John) 192

Anglicanism (Anglican Church) 169, 293, 295

Animism 86

Anisotropy 475

Annals (literary work, Tacitus) 208

Anomaly (anomalies)

 light signal from supernova SN 1987a 457

 not-to-be-discussed, Cosmic Microwave Background 474

 statistical (certainy of LHC analysis of Higgs Boson) 415

 widespread north-south, Cosmic Microwave Background 475

Anselm of Canterbury 15, 293

Anthropo-Cosmogenesis 385

Anthropodicy 325, 327

Anti-trinitarian 295

Antigonus II Mattathias, King 124, 125

Antigravity. *See* Gravity, antigravity

Antimatter / Matter

 positron 10

 Problem. *See* Problems in cosmology, Matter-Antimatter Asymmetry Problem

Antipas (Herod Antipater)

 decree of Roman Tetrarch Herod 120

 Roman Tetrarch Herod 238

Antony, Marc 125

Ants (emergent properties) 360

Anu, deity 97

Aphrodite, deity 159

Apocalypse 303

Apocalypse of John (literary work). *See* Johannine, book of Revelation

Apocalypticism 153

Apocrypha

 Apocryphal Acts. *See* Gnostic, Gnostic apocrypha

 Apocryphal Epistles. *See* Gnostic, Gnostic apocrypha

 Christian and Jewish 166

 definition of 166

Apocrypha (*continued*)

    Gospel of Judas. *See* Gnostic, Gnostic apocrypha

    Gospel of Mary. *See* Gnostic, Gnostic apocrypha

    Gospel of Peter. *See* Gnostic, Gnostic apocrypha

    Gospel of Philip. *See* Gnostic, Gnostic apocrypha

    Gospel of the Hebrews 213

    Gospel of Thomas 167

    Gospel of Truth. *See* Gnostic, Gnostic apocrypha

    Secret Gospel of Mark. *See* Gnostic, Secret Gospel of Mark

    Testament of Job (Old Testament) 237

    The Treatise on the Resurrection. *See* Gnostic, Gnostic apocrypha

Apokatastasis (restoration of Gnostic Christians) 301

Apollo, deity 161

Apollonian diadem (jeweled crown) 161

Apollonius of Tyana (Jesus-like figure) 233, 234, 286

Apologetics 264, 340

Apophaticism (apophasis, apophatic)

    Catholic doctrine affirming 337

    Christian, Judaism, Islam 335

    core tenant of 537

    difficulty in defining, Mary-Jane Rubenstein 338

    likeness to the Jewish Tetragrammaton 335

    negative theology 69-71, 79, 262, 278, 334, 335, 338-341, 345, 537

    Strong apophaticism 339-341, 345-347

    summarizing God's perimeter of existence 537

    trend toward, in the U.S. & Europe 338

    unknowingness of God 70

    view of Greek philosopher Plotinus 384

    Weak apophaticism 339

Apostasy (apostates) 26, 31, 203, 210, 541

Apostles

    original 157, 197, 284, 299

    ten of the original twelve 200

    Twelve 200, 207, 290

Apparitions, Marian 235, 433

Apparent Death Hypothesis (resurrection) 234, 274, 281

Approach (es)

    bottom-up 318, 334, 373, 392

    bottom-up, top-down, outside-in, holistic 53, 54, 311, 361

    Canonical Quantum Gravity 469

    cognitive (zetetic process) 42

    combinatorial, (positive and negative theology) 340

    inside-out 34, 53, 148, 311, 361

    new historiographical 188, 235

    outside-in (and inside-out) 148

    top-down 334, 361, 373, 391, 392

    use constellation of (science, mathematics, philosophy, theology) 41

    zygonic (William Grassie & the New Sciences of Religion) 365

Aquinas, Thomas

    defending whether Jesus' knowledge grew (three modes) 287, 304

    Holy Trinity, major commentator 293

    influenced by Aristotle, Plato, & Plotinus 374

    The Five Ways (literary work) 374

    Summa Theologica (five volume literary work) 23, 287, 288, 355, 436

    Thomism 87, 382

Ararat, Mountains of (proposed site for Ark of God) 114

Archaeologists 85, 113, 119-121, 135, 185, 302

Archimedean vantage point 8, 418, 556

Archons (angelic / demonic servants) 165

Ares, deity 159

Arguments

    a priori / a posteriori (Richard Swinburne's view) 319

    against W. L. Craig's 'infinity axioms' 522

    against Sherwin-White's "two-generation rule" 245

    Axiological Argument. *See* Axiological Argument

    belief in God affected by culture and brain 434

    bundling, validity of 535-537

    cherry-picking of information 58

    circular arguments (example) 49

    complexity of arguments for God 74

    Cosmological Argument. *See* Cosmological Arguments

    cumulative evidence necessary to 'prove' God's existence 311

    common but oversimplified arguments for God's existence 144

    fine-tuning (of cosmos). *See* Fine-tuning (of the universe), teleological

    for and against God 64

    historians discount miracle-based arguments 188

    if the resurrection argument fails 194

    Josephus, argument whether he referred to Jesus of Nazareth 206

    Kalam. *See* Kalam Cosmological Argument

    Meta-Transignification Hypothesis. *See* Meta-Transignification Hypothesis

    Mortal Jesus Hypotheis. *See* Mortal Jesus Hypothesis

Arguments (*continued*)

Nestorius, on Jesus' human and divine nature 300

Ontological. *See* Ontological Argument

Personal Religious Experience (argument for God's existence). *See* Personal Religious Experience Argument

R. Swinburne & W. L. Craig, God is subject to time 383

Richard Swinburne's defense of a generic god 309, 344

Richard Swinburne's defense of the Christian God 309

Richard Swinburne's necessary features of God 314

resurrection-vs-mortal Jesus hyptotheses 277

scholarly dragons 24

speculative / supplemental (ad hoc-ness) 186

The Arguments (list of major defenses for God's existence) 307, 308, 343

Teleological Argument. *See* Teleology / Teleological Argument

theistic arguments for God's existence are weakened 404

whether or not Jesus progressed in knowledge 287

winnowing worship of polytheistic gods 110

Arianism

Arian 203, 206, 291-293, 297, 539

Arius, chief proclaimer 285, 291-293, 296

avoids incoherencies of God's hypostatic union 299

denial of Holy Trinity 297

of the many quasi-Christian groups vying 161

opposing theological faction of 162

Aristotelianism (influence on Thomas Aquinas). *See* Aquinas, Thomas

Aristotle

aether, celestial 372

beginning of religion-science debate 2

concept of infinity, potential and actual 511

corpus of 372

downward causation 372

influence on Thomas Aquinas 374

Metaphysics (literary work) 372

on the human soul 435

Prime Mover (teleological concept) 371, 372, 563, 588

Relationism-vs-Substantivalism 524

universe made of concentric crystalline spheres 372, 464, 548

Unmoved Mover 372, 405

Ark of God's Covenant

Atonement Piece / Mercy Seat. *See* Atonement, Piece

contents of the Ark, biblical disagreement 116

Jewish Ark 118

Lemba Ark 118, 119

models of the Ark of God 119

movie, Raiders of the Lost Ark 116

two different designs, plain wood or gold embellishment 116

who made the Ark, Bezalel or Moses? 116

Ark, Noah's. *See* Noah

Armageddon 552

Arrow of time. *See* Time, arrow of time...

Aseity (God's action of self-creation) 71, 79, 323, 545

Asherah, deity

Ashe'rah (spelling in RSV version of the Bible) 97

consort of Yahweh (also the deity El) 90, 247

elimination of 96

goddess 99, 102, 103

image of (2 Kings 23:6) 96

Israelite worship of 91

priests of 96

Assur, deity 98

Assyrians, people of Assyrian kingdom 89, 90, 117, 123, 221

Astarte, deity 95

Atem, deity 100

Atemporal. *See* Time, atemporal

Athanasius (Bishop of Alexandria)

Against the World 203

adversaries 203

Athanasian Creed. *See* Creed, Athanasian

defense of Mary as a perpetual virgin 195

development of doctrine on Holy Spirit 257

epithets 175

exiled by Roman Emperors 203

Greek Church Father 160

hotly debated addition to Nicene Creed 291

selected the 27 books of New Testament 175, 179

timing of his death relative to canonization of the Bible 175

Atheism

atheism and agnosticism 32, 44, 350, 571

atheistic 30, 88, 307, 311, 312, 346, 363, 472

concept of atheism 339

does not address how universe exists 339

many forms of 323

New Atheists 64, 177

rare for conversion to if reared as religious 31

Atheism (*continued*)

    Richard Dawkins' "de facto" atheism 571

    Strong / hard view not credible 571

    versus nontheism 323

    worldwide affiliation 350, 351

Athena, deity 159

Athirat, deity 90

ATLAS (CERN LHC experiment) 415

Atom

    Primeval 10

    smasher. *See* Particle collider

Atonement

    infinite atonement by Jesus 297

    Piece (Kapporet or Mercy Seat of God's Ark) 116

Attis, deity 239

Atum, deity 100

Audianism 162

Augustine of Hippo

    Church Father 174

    City of God (literary work) 27, 436

    Confessions in 13 Books (literary work) 509, 510

    on the hypostatic union of God 297

    on God existing in an eternal timeless state 510, 555

    on the Trinity 293, 436

    on universal salvation 301

Authority bias. *See* Bias, types of

Autocatalysis, discussion of 378

Autocells

    feasibility of creating 377, 380

    discovery of 377

    morphodynamics 380

    emergent qualities resembling organic life and natural telos 379

    two-state feature of 379

Autocellularity

    concept of 543

    processes 379, 405

    underlying implications of 380

    validation of natural telos, negation of transcental telos 380

Axiological Argument 307, 327, 343, 536, 552

Axiom

    always question assumptions & fewer the better 3

    infinite regress 519, 521, 522, 524, 526

    scientific hypotheses 417

    Many-Faced God Conundrum) 17

    mathematical and statistical 50

Axon (neuronal structure) 438

B-theory / B-series time 525, 526, 555, 559-562

Baal (Ba'al, Baal-Hadad, Hadad), deity

    Baal 90-94, 96, 97, 104, 538

    Israelite worship of 91

Baal Cycle (literary work) 91, 93, 94, 97

Babylonia (ian) 84, 95, 115, 116, 239, 372

Bacon, Francis (epigraph) 409, 430

Baggett, David 309

Baigent, Michael 172, 173, 234

Baltasar Gracián y Morales (epigraph) 7

barbituric acid (nucleobase molecule) 376

Barbour, Ian 388

Bare Natural Theology (BNT) 265, 308

Barrier

    impenetrable, to all human discernment 10

    impermeable, God unable to act upon our realm 446

    insuperable 546, 559

    transcendent 546

Barrow, Isaac 294

Baryons (baryonic matter) 458

Battle of the Milvian Bridge 161

Bayes, Thomas 251

Bayes' theorem (Bayesian / Bayesianism)

    an interpretation of probability 251

    Bayes' factors 329, 331, 332, 344

    Bayesian epistemology 251, 254

    Bayesian induction 251

    Bayesian inference 251, 530

    Bayesian updating 251, 536

    epistemic probability 266, 537

    estimated probability that ossuaries belong to Jesus' family 132

    example, design of automobile traction computer 252

    example, Iran nuclear stockpile 330, 331

    Explict form of equation 255

    list of fundamental weaknesses 345, 542

    likelihood ratio 331

    model averaging technique 536

    Odds form of equation 329, 344

    posterior probability 329, 331, 332, 536

    power of 264, 530

    prior probability 253, 255, 329, 331-333, 344

    probabililty for the existences of a generic God 309, 311, 328, 338

    Problem of the Priors 333, 345

    problems / concerns of 316, 333, 345

    Richard Swinburne's probability estimate for a generic

Bayes' theorem (*continued***)**
  God   328, 344
  Simple form of equation   252
  use of in Ramified Natural Theology   308
  viability as a tool to define the probability of God's existence   328, 338, 345

Beat frequency. *See* **Frequency, composite beat frequency**

Beckman, Emma   311, 334

Beecher, Henry Ward (epigraph)   143

Behroozi, Peter   35-37

Benson, Buster. *See* **Bias, map of biases**

Berger, Peter   32

Bes, deity
  date of initial appearance in human culture   99
  geographic location first worshipped   99
  typical physical features   98
  change in physical appearance over time   99
  convoluted history of   99
  deity   98, 99, 101, 102, 104
  single deity or multiple deities   100
  not shown with Beset (wife of Bes) prior to Ptolemaic Period   100
  lack of literature on Bes deity   99
  leopard tail changed to male genetalia over time   99
  protective powers   100, 102
  statuettes of   98
  troop of   99

Beset, deity
  appearance compared to Bes   100
  varying representational images   101
  female consort of Bes   99
  history of the goddess   100

Bezalel (fabricator of Ark of God)   116

BGV. *See* **Borde-Guth-Vilenkin (BGV) theorem**

Bias
  elimination of by scientists   453
  errors in assigning human experience as religious   66
  filtering bias in biblical interpretations   153
  map of biases   419
  number of biases   419

Bias, types of
  Agenticity   428, 430, 433, 448, 544
  Anchoring   421, 574
  Authority   421
  Cognitive   65, 419, 421, 423
  Confirmation   419
  Conjunction fallacy   421, 448

  favorable results (publishing)   412
  Framing effect   422
  Illusory-truth effect   420, 431, 448, 574
  Herd (or Bandwagon effect)   421, 448
  number of known cognitive biases (188 biases)   419, 448
  negative results (publishing)   412, 413, 447, 586
  Patternicity   428, 430, 433, 448, 544
  Optimism   573
  Type I. *See* Type I cognitive error
  Type II. *See* Type II cognitive error

Bible (general)
  apocrypha. *See* Apocrypha
  belief it is divine word of God (survey results)   74
  continually edited   109, 155, 176, 297
  difficulties in authentication of   145, 147
  first official Bible (never found). *See* Codex, autographic
  Foundational Truth Claims of Christianity   148
  God did not provide Bible as a single package   174
  interpretation of (inerrancy, divinely-inspired, metaphorical)   145
  method to read Bible, chronologically   176
  method to read Bible, horizontally   176
  method to read Bible, vertically   176
  pseudepigrapha. *See* Pseudepigrapha

Bible (Christian). *See Also* **New Testament**
  apocrypha. *See* Apocrypha
  closed canon   166
  compared to Hebrew Bible   144, 151
  continually edited   155, 159, 176, 297
  does not clarify triune nature of godhead   295
  does not clarify eternality of the soul   436, 437, 449
  first official Bible. *See* Codex, autographic
  Foundational Truth Claims of Christianity   148
  Joseph, Jesus' father   131
  number of Books (Catholic)   174
  reasons why some may choose to believe Bible is authentic   144
  official ratification date of biblical canon (the Bible)   150, 175, 540
  oldest copies of 'complete' Bible   150

Bible (Hebrew Tanakh)
  apocrypha. *See* Apocrypha
  cherubim, nature of   116
  closed canon   166
  compared to Christian Bible / Old Testament   144, 151
  completeness of   113

Bible (Hebrew Tanakh) (*continued*)

continually edited 109

date of first written Hebrew texts 116

Masoretic Text 151

Moses 69, 93, 94, 111, 114, 116-119, 140, 174

Solomon's Temple. *See* Solomon's Temple

Tanakh 90, 144, 151, 166

Torah 84, 203

Bible (Greek)

apocrypha. *See* Apocrypha

continually edited 155, 159, 176, 297

New Testament 155

reliability of 202

Septuagint (LXX) 144, 151

Ending of Gospel of Mark (Greek manuscripts) 218, 220

filioque (Constantinopolitan Creed). *See Also* Filioque 291

Isaac Newton identified improper addition to biblical Greek text 295

Isaac Newton studied Greek texts 293

Bible (New Testament). *See* New Testament

Bible (Old Testament)

apocrypha. *See* Apocrypha

cherubim, nature of 116

chief deity El (ʿelyôn) and Yahweh 91

compared to Hebrew Bible 144, 151

Moses' Ark (*See Also* Ark of God's Covenant) 116-119

completeness of 113

continually edited 109

"eye for an eye" system of justice 84

goddess Asherah (also found in Hebrew Bible) 97

Noah's Ark. *See* Noah

number of books (Tanakh vs. Protestant vs Catholic) 144

prophets believed other gods were false idols 246

Big Bang (*See Also* Cosmogonic models, HBB and HIBB)

and the Law of Energy Conservation 326

central assumption, existence of a singularity 458

coexistence of multiple deities before / external to Big Bang 326, 327

Einstein's Big Bang predicts eternal expansion of spacetime 461

Einstein's relativity theory breaks down 460

Horizon Problem (*See Also* Problems in cosmology) 464, 465

initial expansion of universe hot or cold? 461

introduces many difficult-to-answer questions 310

isolated system and zero initial entropy 478

Large-Scale Structure Problem 464, 474, 496

Lithium Problem (too much and too little) 464, 473, 474

snap of God's fingers 8

thunderclap of God ignites Big Bang 10

cosmic complexity a function of timeframe 316

countdown to time zero 8-10

violation of Second Law of Thermodynamics? 478

Big Bounce. *See* Cosmogonic models

Big Crunch. *See* Cosmogonic models

Big Questions

the Big Questions 1, 2

how to answer the Big Questions 3, 4

Binitarianism 106, 290, 539

Biogenesis 385

Biology

evolutionary biology 4, 42, 59, 365, 367, 384, 392, 394, 395, 402, 406, 409

quantum biology 42, 367, 409

Biosemiotics 395, 399, 400, 405

Biverse. *See* Cosmogonic models, Aguirre-Gratton Proposal

Blasphemy Act of England 294

Blavatsky, Helena Petrovna 353, 383

Block Universe

Static Block Universe (Eternalism) 525

Growing Block Universe (Possibilism) 525

BNT. *See* Bare Natural Theology

Boethius 293

Boeve, Lieven 32, 338

Bohm's Interpretation. *See* Quantum mechanics

Bohmian trajectories. *See* Quantal Bohmian trajectories

Boko Haram (terrorist organization) 26, 27

Boltzmann Brains. *See* Problems in cosmology, Boltzmann Brain Problem

Bones

DNA of Jesus via James' and John's bones 128

Homo naledi human species 85

James Ossuary, bone matter 135

Jesus' bones reburied in 1994? 131

John the Baptist's, history of relocation 120

dating of purported bones of John the Baptist 121

hand bone with nail 124

heel bone with nail 123

relocation of Jesus' bones from rock-tomb? 131

Book of Revelation (Christian Bible). *See* Johannine
Books
    list of prohibited books (by the Vatican). *See* Index Librorum Prohibitorum
    New Testament, ordering of 177
Borde-Guth-Vilenkin (BGV) theorem
    conditions in which it does not apply 470
    definition of 462, 469, 470, 481, 513, 514
    Cosmon Field Model does not violate BGV 490
Bose-Einstein condensate 520
Boson (Higgs). *See* Higgs boson
Boson, definition of 373
Bottom-up. *See* Approach (es)
Bovine symbolism (Bes / Yahweh) 102
Bracken, Joseph 388
Brain
    authentic phenomena of the human 433, 434
    average adult verus infant 427
    The Believing Brain (literary work) 428
    Boltzmann. *See* Boltzman Brains
    unembodied. *See* Boltzman Brains
    EEG (electroencephalography) 443
    evolution and brain developement 426, 430, 431, 433
    function, consciousness, and anesthesia 438
    genetic predisposition of the human 431, 448
    hierarchal levels of the 423
    higher properties of the 373
    model-making (mental maps) 545
    nonphysical. *See* Boltzmann Brains
Brightness
    average surface brightness of a star 495
    luminosity 456, 496, 497
    peak brightness (Type Ia supernovae) 456
Bronze Age. *See* Age
Brotherhood of mankind 56, 581, 584
Brown, Scott G. 171
Brute (actuality, existence, or fact) 318, 395, 399, 403, 451, 517, 529
Buba Clan 117-119
Bubble
    bubble of the Big Bang 327
    bubble universes 475, 513, 514, 562
    universe expanding into an energy bubble 479
    warp bubble 38
Buddha
    Gautama (quotes of) 509
    Buddha's philosophical orientation regarding God 339

Buddhism (Buddhist)
    central precept of 583
    Dalai Lama. *See* Dalai Lama
    different branches of 583
    persepctive on science 583
    Thich Nhat Hanh. *See* Hanh, Thich Nhat
    transcendental apophaticism 339
Bulk, the (hyperspace) 498
Burial
    first emergence of protohuman burials 85
    cloth. *See* Shroud, Shroud of Turin and Shroud of Oviedo
    Christian belief, Jesus buried one-time 197
    customs, first-century Judea 129-132
    necropolis (cemetery) 137, 138
    royal 85
    secondary (ossilegium) 130, 197
    shroud. *See* Shroud, Shroud of Turin and Shroud of Oviedo
C-14 (carbon-14) dating 118, 121-123, 126, 128
Caiaphas, Joseph (high priest) 124, 233, 276
Caliphate (Caliph) 422
Calvary
    hill of Calvary 122
    initial rock-tomb of Jesus 131
Cavin, Robert G. 262, 264, 265
Cameron, David 422
Campbell
    Joseph 27, 35, 61
    Ronnie 309
Camus, Albert (epigraph) 83
Canaanites 89, 91-93, 95, 96, 102, 104, 105, 246, 538
Canon
    biblical canon 166, 175, 192, 213, 305, 540
    canon of Fourth Lateran Council 106, 107
    Canons of Tischendorf 147
    closed canon 166
    extra-biblical 172
    New Testament canon (canonical NT) 149, 166
    Old Testament canon 166
    open canon 166
Canonical Bible, ordering of 177
Canonical Gospel. *See Also* Noncanonical 132, 151, 156, 166, 167, 172, 174, 175, 177, 180, 193, 197, 201, 203, 217, 219, 223, 296
Canonization of the Christian Bible 179, 540
Carlyle, Thomas (epigraph) 505
Carneades 77

Carpocrates 170, 171
Carpocratians 165, 169-171
Carrey, Jim 189
Carroll, Sean 472
Cat
    Cheshire Cat 49
    Schrödinger's cat experiment. *See* Schrödinger, Erwin
Catalysis 377
Catalyst 63, 377, 378
Cataphaticism (Cataphasis, positive theology) 69-71, 79, 334-341, 345, 356, 537, 538
Catechism (Catholic) 72, 337, 394, 398
Causality (cause, causation)
    Adamite and Eveitite 521-523
    additional cause needed to explain cosmic fine-tuning 317
    all material effects have antecedent or simultaneous cause 509, 516
    and the pre-universe 517
    and the transcendent realm 546
    and transcendental telos 401
    attractive toward divine state 372
    autocells and teleodynamics 392
    Bayesian statistics as a means to find causal connections 264
    bottom-up and top-down 392
    bottom-up causality, commonly held belief 373
    causal priority, zetetic process 43
    Causal Principle 310
    cause and uncaused state 315
    cause-effect relationship requires temporality to exist 517
    efficient causality 307, 372, 390, 391
    everyday natural causation 69
    existence of causality outside 4D-spacetime 546
    Final Cause (final attractive cause) 372
    First Cause could be singular or multiple causes 517
    First Cause might lack intentional will 520
    First Cause 310, 313, 404, 505-507, 509, 511, 513, 514, 516, 517, 519-524, 526, 529, 531, 559-562
    for beginning of universe (Kalam argument) 310, 506
    for beginning of universe (W. L. Craig argument) 506, 513, 518
    God as a necessary cause 318
    God, natural law, and causality 547
    in relation to SDEs and NDEs 438
    in the context of B-series theory of time 525
    in the context of the Cosmon Field Model 523, 524
    inefficient causality 391, 392

    infinite regress (axiom, causality, events) 513, 516, 519, 521, 522, 524, 526
    initial idea of downward (top-down) causation 373
    KCA, clarification of potential multiple causes (refer to Premises 3 & 7) 518
    making errors in attributing causation 430
    multiverse as First Cause to our universe 513
    naturalistic telos 374
    Panentheism, divine causality 400, 401
    Panentheism, God able to act without violation natural laws 400
    principle of causality 509, 513
    reducing the potential options for God 404
    self-causation of universe 526
    simultaneous cause and effect 509, 519
    uncaused cause 310, 319
    what if actual/metaphysical infinities were possible? 523
    W. L. Craig's assumption that metaphysical causality is a valid construct 516, 517
    why must divine First Cause be three Persons? 320
Caves
    Ark of God buried in a cave 115, 117
    burial option, first-century Judea 196
    Lemba Ark found in 118
    ossuaries, Dominus Flevit 138
    Qumran caves 152, 231
    secret knowledge, ancient Egyptian worship 173
    South African Rising Star cave 85
Cavin, Robert G. 262, 264, 265
CDM (cold dark matter) 458, 484, 490
Celsus 204, 210, 231, 271
Cepheid variable star 456
CERN. *See* Particle collider
Chaisson, Eric J. (epigraph) 371
Chalcedonian 107, 259, 260, 262
Chalmers, David 359
Changeless, related to unchanging universe—truism T5 496, 514, 523
Changeless, pre-universe (W. L. Craig's view and alternatives to) 522
Changeless, related to property of time. *See* Time, changeless
Changeless, unchanging property of God 72, 397, 507, 508, 516, 522
Charlesworth, J. H. 133
Cherubim 116, 174
Chinese finger trap. *See* Analogy, Chinese finger trap
Chomsky, Noam (epigraph) 572, 579

Church of Jesus Christ of Latter-Day Saints. *See* Mormonism

Chrestus / Christus (potential reference to (Jesus) Christ) 208, 211

Christ (*See Also* Jesus of Nazareth)

Cosmic. *See* Cosmic Christ and Cosmic Creator

Cross of Christ (Constantine the Great) 158

eschatological return of Christ. *See Also* Second Coming 385

Christianities (multiple) 163, 233

Christianity

Christian beliefs (summary chart) 75

Christian-like sects 153, 160-162, 302, 543

Christain Truth Claims. *See* Foundational Truth Claims of Christianity

Christianity as a polytheistic faith 159

Church Fathers. *See* Church Fathers

Common Misconception of Christianity's Origin 157

conversion to / from (illustration) 31, 421

Craigian Christian God. *See* Craig, William Lane—Craigian Worldview of God

development timeline for Abrahamic religions (illustration) 106

early Christians / early Christianity 69, 138, 153, 157, 160, 161, 163, 180, 199, 206, 238, 290

Eastern (Greek) Orthodox. *See* Orthodox, Eastern (Greek)

eight evidence claims for the resurrection 195

inquisitions and crusades 222, 355

major schisms (illustration) 301

Nicene Trinitarian Christianity (Roman Catholicism) 162, 180

number of Christians in first century 178

Orthodox Christianity, major divisions. *See* Orthodox

Orthodoxical Christianity (Roman Catholicism) 153, 159, 162, 302

Six Towers of God worldview, placement 565

Western (Latin). *See* Orthodox, Western (Latin)

Christogenesis 385

Christological 107, 290, 320

Christology 146, 158, 289, 295, 297, 300

Christus / Chrestus (potential reference to (Jesus) Christ) 208, 211

Church Fathers

Athanasius of Alexandria. *See* Athanasius (Bishop of Alexandria)

Augustine of Hippo. *See* Augustine of Hippo

Clement of Alexandria. *See* Clement of Alexandria

Clement of Rome. *See* Pope, Clement I

Epiphanius of Salamis 164, 195

Hippolytus of Rome 164, 174, 195, 221

Ignatious of Antioch 290

Irenaeus of Lyons. *See* Irenaeus of Lyons

Origen of Alexandria. *See* Origen of Alexandria

Polycarp of Smyrna 160, 161, 174, 207, 222, 290

Tertullian of Carthage 164, 174, 176, 203, 204, 221, 271, 290

Church of the Holy Sepulchre 122

Churchill, Winston 346

Circularity (argument). *See* Arguments, circular arguments

Claims, Foundational Christian. *See* Foundational Truth Claims of Christianity

Clarke, Kelly James 321

Clayton, Philip 388, 392, 393, 401, 542

Clemens, Samuel Langhorne (Mark Twain) (epigraph) 535

Clement of Alexandria

Clement 69, 160, 164, 168-171, 220, 232, 301

Letter to Theodore (literary work) 170, 173

Stromata (literary work) 168

truth of God hidden by seven veils 171

Cleopas (traveling companion of Jesus) 212

Closed system. *See* Thermodynamics

CMB. *See* Cosmic Microwave Background

CMS (CERN LHC experiment) 415

Co-Essential Faith. *See* Faith, Co-Essential Faith

Code of Hammurabi (*See Also* Hammurabi, King Hammurabi) 84, 89

Codex

autographic 150, 180

Sinaiticus 150, 151, 155, 199, 218, 219, 221, 295-297

Vaticanus 150, 151, 155, 218, 219, 221

Codices, Nag Hammadi library 152, 164, 165, 172, 177, 179, 180, 205, 206, 540

Cognition

general unreliability of human 43

requiring God to create two new Beings 19

limited level of 19

pitiful human 322

second tier of reality 393

God is undefinable by human cognition 513

Cognitive bias. *See* Bias, types of, Cognitive

Cognitive Dissonance

Cognitive Dissonance Hypothesis (resurrection) 234, 236-238, 241, 274, 281, 574

mental overload in discerning reality 424

Cognitive load 424, 425, 427, 428, 431

Cognitive pluralism 585

Coherence

degree of coherence 445

Church Fathers belief that it was more coherent if God was one substance 321

logical coherence / coherency 52, 53, 362

quantum. *See* quantum coherence

Coherency

Coherency of Truth theory 49, 52, 318

relative coherency of religion on its own terms 28

validity of coherency (circularity) 49

Cold dark matter. *See* CDM

Cold Spot (of the CMB) 475

Collaboration

among scientists 411

IceCube collaboration 492

Planck collaboration 9

Collapse, wave function. *See* Quantum, wave function collapse

Collider, CERN Large Hadron 415

Collision, galactic 78

Colombetti, Carlos A. 262, 264, 265

Commandments, Ten 116, 117, 174, 176

Common Man, the 2, 12, 13, 24, 25, 28, 39, 50, 59, 60, 74, 107, 344, 406, 410, 576, 582, 586

Complementary faith. *See* Faith, Complementary Faith

Complexification

culture and language 385

of the cosmos and our surrounds 388, 405

strong emergence 391

teleology and complexification 406

Complexify 265, 308, 386

Complexity

advancement in knowledge, hyper-specialization 59

amount affected by selected timeframe 316

an argument to defend Christian theology 405

an argument to defend the existence of a supreme deity 499

autocells, limited complexity 379

Complexity of Reality. *See* Truth Criteria, [TC-5]

Complexity Theory 374, 378

complexity versus simplicity (enumeration of objects) 313

Consciousness and Spirit, Philip Clayton 392

environmental conditions of the cosmos to support 371

God as a perpetaul co-creator of complexity (Panentheism) 400

natural emergence 390

NSoR, emergence, and cosmic complexity 361, 364

of religion and science 421

of religious / spiritual phenomena, nonreductive functionalism (NSoR) 359

of the cosmos, Meta-Transignification hypothesis 325

Omega point, the apex of complexity 385

ontological necessity increases complexity 319

panentheist's teleological movement 542

Paul Davies' panentheistic view 403, 406

promote use of psychological heuristics 74

reduce complexity of concepts of religion and science 56

scientific methodology of reductionism 373

'something' more complex than 'nothing' 313

stratifications in complexity 386

teleodynamics and the property of complexity 392

theism is more complex than nontheism 314

Confidence. *See* Five-sigma statistical confidence

Confirmation bias. *See* Bias, types of

Confirmation theory. *See* Bayes' theorem

Conformity with accepted belief 187

Confucianism 67

Conjunction fallacy. *See* Bias, types of

Consanguinity 195

Consciousness

altered state of 173, 275, 572

alternating betwen consciousness / unconsciousness 449

animals, near-human levels of consciousness 445

comparably difficult problem—human consciousness and property of time 526

cosmic consciousness. *See* Cosmic consciousness

cosmic proto-consciousness. *See* Proto-consciousness

Consciousness and Spirit (Philip Clayton) 392

fundamental embodiment of 442

God as a mysterious consciousness (W. L. Craig view) 530

God as a supreme consciousness 531

God as an immaterial consciousness 529, 543, 547, 549

microtubule quantum vibrations. *See* Orch OR model of consciousness

Orch OR. *See* Orch OR model of consciousness

self-reflexive consciousness an unsolved problem 433

universal consciousness. *See* Panpsychism

Conservation of Energy, Law of. *See* Thermodynamics

Constantine I (Constantine the Great)
    Arch of Constantine 161
    Church Fathers influenced by Roman governance 540
    co-Emperor with Licinius 161
    committed apostasy 541
    conversion to (pre-orthodox) Christianity 158
    conversion / baptism to Arianism by Eusebius of Nicomedia 161, 292
    convoked First Council of Nicaea 220, 540
    date of death 292
    destroyed / supressed all writings of Arius 292
    devotee of the pagan sun god Sol Invictus 161
    Emperor Constantine I's backing of Catholicism 293
    exiled Arius, patriarch of Arianism 291
    exiled Athanasius of Alexandria 203
    exiled Eusebius of Nicomedia 293
    Helena, mother of the first Christian Roman Emperor 122
    revelation from Jesus Christ 158
    syncretic belief mixed paganism and Christianity 540
Constantinopolitan Creed. *See* Creed, Constantinopolitan
Constantius I and II, Roman Emperors 203
Consubstantiality 291, 298, 321
Contingency (Argument for God's existence) 307
Conundrum. *See* Many-Faced-God-Conundrum
Conversions, religious 236
Copernicus 355
Coptic 69, 167, 168, 170
Coptic Gospel of Thomas. *See* Apocrypha, Gospel of Thomas
Corinthians, people of Corinth (Greece) 156, 207, 224, 236
Corinthians, First (book, Christian Bible) 198, 211-213, 224-226, 228, 230, 235
Correspondence Theory of Truth 48
Cosmic Christ (Teilhard de Chardin) 385, 386
Cosmic Christ (Southgate-Robinson-Peirce) 400
Cosmic consciousness 13, 444
Cosmic Creator (Meta-Transignification hypothesis) 324-327, 346, 356
Cosmic expansion. *See* Inflation, cosmic and Hubble, Hubble expansion
Cosmic inflation. *See* Inflation, cosmic
Cosmic jerk 454, 486, 497
Cosmic Microwave Bacground (CMB) 465, 474, 475, 494, 498, 499
Cosmic mistakes (the Demiurge) 249
Cosmic simulation 526, 555

Cosmogenesis
    Helena Blavatsky 384
    Teilhard de Chardin 385
    cosmic origin (Ekpyrotic model) 463
Cosmogonic models
    Aguirre-Gratton Proposal (cosmic biverse) 470, 480, 494
    Big Bang model. *See* HBB and HIBB (below). *See Also* Big Bang
    Cosmology from Quantum Potential (CQP) model 497, 498
    Cosmon Field Model 484, 485, 497, 523, 529, 563
    Cyclic or Oscillating model 461, 470, 471, 481, 501
    Einstein-de Sitter universe 461
    Ekpyrotic model 463, 468
    Emergent Universe model 481, 482, 484
    Hartle-Hawking No-Boundary proposal. *See* below, No-Boundary proposal
    Hot Big Bang model (HBB) 458, 461, 473, 474, 483, 484, 486, 496
    Hot Inflationary Big Bang model (HIBB) 454, 462, 466, 468, 473-475, 482-486, 489, 494, 496, 501, 502, 523
    Lamda-Cold Dark Matter (ΛCDM) 484
    M-theory 11, 312, 463, 471, 472, 499, 502, 526, 568
    Multiverse model 11, 312, 324, 404, 457, 462, 463, 472, 473, 475, 479, 481, 495, 496, 499, 501, 510, 513, 514, 517, 519, 521, 527, 531, 561-563, 568
    No-Boundary proposal (Hartle-Hawking model) 479, 480, 494
    Steady State Eternal Inflation 479, 480
    String Theory 11, 526
    Superstring theories 11, 463
    Vacuum Fluctuation model 464, 468
Cosmogony
    contrasted with cosmology 312
    definition of 42, 312
Cosmological Arguments. *See Also* Kalam Cosmological Argument 310, 311, 319, 344, 451, 499, 505, 530, 536
Cosmological Constant (Λ)
    Cosmological Constant Problem. *See* Problems in cosmology
    time-varying / dynamic Cosmological Constant 486, 487, 490
    invariant (static) Cosmological Constant 483, 486, 489, 490, 497
    value of the Cosmological Constant 461, 484, 486, 489

Cosmological singularity. *See* Singularity, cosmological

Cosmology from Quantum Potential model (CQP). *See* Cosmogonic models

Cosmon particle 486, 489

Cosmon field 486-491, 493, 494, 502, 524, 529, 530

Cosmon Field Model
    contrasted with HIBB (Big Bang universe) model, illustration 485
    cosmon field, nearly massless 486
    cosmon field strength, illustration of 487, 489, 491, 494, 524
    Cosmon Field Model 484, 485, 497, 523, 529, 563
    family of initial states to ancient universe 488
    mass of mass-bearing particles increases 487
    redshift phenomena explained 493
    scalar field, shared characteristic with Higgs field 486
    validation of theory 491, 492, 494, 495
    Wetterich's field equations 483, 484, 487-489, 496, 502, 523

Cosmos. *See* Universe

Councils. *See* Ecumenical councils

Covenants (*See Also* Commandment, Ten and Ark of God's Covenant)
    four principal (given by God) 174
    infringement of the Davidic 247

CQP. *See* Cosmogonic models

Craig, William Lane (W. L. Craig)
    Achilles tendon (of W. L. Craig's 'infinity argument') 523
    belief in A-series isochronal property of time 516
    belief in physical and metaphysical causality across all reality 517
    belief that neither actual nor metaphysical infinities exist 512
    bundling of The Arguments 536
    concepts of time that may not violate infinite regress axiom 519
    Craigian Christian God 516, 529
    Craigian Worldview of God,synopsis 508
    Craigian KCA and the Meta-Transignification Hypothesis 529
    eight claims of evidence for the resurrection 194, 195
    difficulties with William Lane Craig's Arguments for Finitism (literary work) 522
    evidence for the existence of Craigian God not supported by KCA 531
    failure to explain how God acts without disrespecting natural laws 530
    failure to identify impossibility of actual or

    metaphysical infinities 523
    interview of A.N. Sherwin-White (with Lee Strobel) 244
    KCA, clarified version 518
    KCA, Craig's version of 506
    KCA, confusion single or multiple causes 517
    KCA, problem with logical construction 517
    metaphysical claims are overreaching 520
    on God changing his nature 520
    on God creating the universe in first interval of time 511
    on God not being wholly transcendent 529
    on God's properties in his first phase of existence 516
    on God's properties in his second phase of existence 529
    on God's omnipotence (maximally powerful) 519
    on God's omniscience 507
    on God's two phases to his existence (timeless & temporal) 549
    on God's immanance 549
    on God's spatiality within the universe 529, 549
    overdetermination of God's monadic qualities 531
    wide-ranging influence of 506
    W. L. Craig and Richard Swinburne, God is a temporal Being inside universe 383

Creator
    deific 509, 530
    elegant 451
    existence of a divine 144
    existence of a Master 451
    Meta-Transignification 560
    monadic properties of the Cosmic 326
    perpetual cosmic 402
    Purely Transcendent God (Tower 1) 559
    supreme 144
    transcendent intelligent 514

Creators, Simulator. *See* Simulator Creators / Operators

Creed
    Athanasian 321
    Constantinopolitan 165, 291
    Nicene 46, 162, 165, 290, 291, 293, 321, 398, 540
    Niceno-Constantinopolitan 291, 300, 321, 540
    multitude of fractious Christian creeds 179

Criteria
    historical. *See* Historicity Tests
    internal and external evidence (Metzger) 147
    Truth. *See* Truth Criteria
    two-generation. *See* Two-generation rule

Criterion (Orch OR model)
    Diósi-Penrose 441
    objective threshold 440, 441
Criticism
    cherry-picking information 58
    of the Qur'an 148
    peer review process of literary works 153, 413
    source criticism 185, 187
    textual criticism 138, 147, 155
Cross
    T-shaped cross 125, 157
    True Cross 118, 121-125, 140, 201
    X-shaped cross 125, 247
Crossnan, John Dominic 238
Crowd of 500. See Jesus' post-death appearances, crowd of 500
Crucifixion
    artifactual evidence, nail in Caiaphas ossuary 124
    artifactual evidence, nail in hand bone 124
    artifactual evidence, nail in heel bone 124
    early literary reference by Lucian 123
    historical prevalence of, first-century 123
    Spartacus 123
    T-shaped cross 125, 157
    X-shaped cross 125, 247
Crusades 26, 222
Cult (cultism)
    ancient cults, removal / merging of gods 538
    deviant cults (e.g., Satanism) 77
    differentiation, Israelite from Canaanite cults 92
    Peoples Temple cult (James W. Jones) 200
    Judaic polytheistic cultism 90
    Gnostic 540
    cults, Joseph Campbell's view 27
    many cults existed within a couple centuries of Jesus' time 540
    quasi-Christian cults abundant 539
    Yahwistic cults. See Yahwism
Cunctos populos. See Edict of Thessalonica
Curvaton particle 475, 482
Curvature
    closed (positive) curvature (spherical universe) 464
    condition of infinite curvature (Loop Quantum Gravity) 469
    consequence of spacetime 460
    gravity due to curvature of spacetime (not a physical force) 460
    imperceptible continuous 465

    knotting and over-stretching of spacetime 458
    no (zero) curvature (flat universe) 464
    open (negative) curvature (hyperbolic universe) 464
    singularity. See Singularity, cosmological
Cyclic (oscillating) model. See Cosmogonic models
Dagon, deity 90, 93, 538
Dalai Lama XIV (Tenzin Gyatso)
    no need for complicated philosophy (epigraph) 579
    on Buddhism and science 583
    religion needs to evolve with humanity (epigraph) 349
Damascus (Apostle Paul's travel to) 213, 228, 229
Damneus 206
Damoclesian 8, 11
Dark
    energy 454, 458, 461, 483, 484, 486, 489, 490, 494, 496, 502, 523
    matter (See Also CDM) 9, 458, 484, 490, 491, 496, 502, 523
    NEOs (Near-Earth Objects) 552
Darwin, Charles 384, 425, 426
Dasen, Véronique 99
David
    House of David 247
    King David 90, 191, 242, 276
    lineage of King David 191, 231, 242, 248, 276
    throne of David 231, 237, 243
Davidic Covenants 247
Davies, Paul
    cosmos as a divine product of God 402
    fine-tuning of cosmic parameters 317
    God as an intelligent designer 403
    impersonal God 403
    Panentheism, Paul Davies' version of 383, 402, 403, 406
    Uniformitarian Panentheist (personal worldview) 402
    universe not eternal 403, 404
Dawkins, Richard 64, 431, 571, 572
de Chardin, Teilhard
    death of 383
    Omega point. See Omega point
    Teilhard de Chardin 383-386, 542, 577, 579
    The Human Phenomenon (literary work) 383
    theological views aligned with Christocentric Panentheism 386
Deacon, Terrence
    autocells as a form of protolife 379
    autocells infer transcendental telos is unnecessary 380

Deacon, Terrence (*continued*)
  best defense of strong emergence 390
  complexity and naturalistic emergence 390
  complexity and principle of potentiality 390
  Deacon's work as basis for biosemiotics 395
  discoverer of autocells 377
  example of autocatalysis 378
  forms (shapes) of autocells / autocatalytic sets 378
  incompleteness of unrealized potentialities 391
  prospective theological implications of autocells 377
  teleodynamics, term coined by 392
  teleodynamics, lower-order phenomenon compared to consciousness 392
  teleogical properties of autocells as evidence of natural telos 380
  theological implications of autocell concept, circular logic 400
  transcendental telos is unevidenced 380
Dead Sea Scrolls 117, 152, 177, 179, 180, 197, 205, 238, 540
Death of Peregrinus (literary work) 123, 209
Death
  death / destruction caused by natural laws of the universe 403
  death of Christ. *See* Jesus of Nazareth, date of death
  death of Constantine I. *See* Constantine I, date of death
  death of Isaac Newton. *See* Newton, Isaac
  death of Marcion. *See* Marcion of Sinope 299
  Death of Peregrinus (literary work) 123, 209
  death of Saint Stephen. *See* Martyr, first Christian martyr
  death of stars 474, 498
  death of Teilhard de Chardin. *See* de Chardin, Teilhard
  death of the universe. *See* Universe, heat death
  definition of death (by Socrates, Plato, Aristotle, Origen, Augustine) 435, 436
  fear of death a justification for existence of a soul 445
  idea of assumption / translation of body 237
  martyr. *See* Martyr
  NDE. *See* Near-death experience
  organic life 327
  penalty for Athanasius if he returned to Alexandria after exile 203
  penalty of, Code of Hammurabi 84
  penalty of, Sharia Law 31
  population growth 352
  punishment for heresy 158, 175

  ritual sacrifice (ancient Mesopotamia) 84, 85
  SDE. *See* Shared-death experience
  trampled to death, Hajj 35
  transcend death. *See* Reincarnation
  upon death, human consciousness becomes quantum information 444
Decision-making, heuristic methods of 443
Decoherence. *See* Quantum, decoherence
Deconstructionism, Father of. *See* Derrida, Jacques
Degree of Perfection (Argument for God's existence) 307
Deism
  conundrum for Christian Panentheism 401
  definition of 570
  general reference 44, 87, 404, 506, 548, 550
  World Union of Deists 87, 570
Deist
  Aristotle, polytheistic deist 405
  Paul Davies (former position) 403
  The Source 365
  Thomas Paine 22
Deity, generic 365, 506, 562
Delgado, José 432
Demigods 85, 239
Demiurge's servants 165
Demons (*See Also* Devil) 74, 85, 159, 165, 171, 218, 233, 249, 322, 327
Dendrites (neuronal structure) 438, 442
Dennett, Daniel 431
Denominations, Christian 74, 76, 144, 158, 300, 309, 339, 352, 421
Depoe, John M. 332
Derrida, Jacques 340
de Sitter, Willem 461
Descartes, René (epigraph) 438, 535, 567
Determinism. *See* Free will and Determinism
Detraditionalisation of Europe, processes of 32
Deuterocanonical 144
Deuteronomy 91, 116, 174, 197, 231, 232
Devil 74
Dialogue. *See* Religion-science
Diatessaron, The (literary work) 221
Dicken, Frank 175, 227
Didache (literary work) 207
Didymus Thomas. *See* Thomas, Thomas the Apostle
Differentiable (mathematical concept) 459
Dilaton Quantum Gravity 494

Dimensions (*See Also* Four dimensions)
  extra-dimensional (extra-dimensions) 499, 531, 545, 548, 553, 559
  fifth space-like dimension (reality as a holographic projection) 526
  fifth dimension 45, 354, 548
  ten or eleven dimensions (multiverse) 463
  hyperdimension 548, 553, 559, 568, 570, 572
  hyperspace 463, 464, 498, 499
Dimensional transcedence. *See* Transcendence, dimensional transcendence
Dingir (Sumerian symbol for 'deity') 84
Dionysus, deity 239
Diósi-Penrose criterion 441
Disaffiliated, disaffiliation (religious) 29-31, 350
Disciples, Seventy 199, 225, 226
Distances (calculation of cosmic distances)
  discovery, multiple classes of Type Ia supernova 497
  estimated size of the universe 10, 455, 580
  list of sources of measurement distortion 456
  most distant object visible to naked eye 580
  serious challenges measuring cosmic distances 455, 457
  use of average surface brightness 495
  use of Type Ia supernovae 456
Ditto, Peter 20
Divine
  entity / entities 290, 299, 316, 326, 540
  essence 323, 326, 335, 336, 345, 399
  natures 107, 163, 180, 262, 300, 328, 337, 345, 355, 549
  property / properties 314, 321, 399
  purpose 50, 401, 405, 553
  sparks 164, 165, 222, 384
DNA (DNA-based dating) 24, 48, 117, 121, 127-130, 132, 134, 135, 160, 168, 377, 405
Docetism 163
Domain-piercing transcendence. *See* Transcendence, domain-piercing transcendence
Dominus Flevit Church necropolis. *See* Necropolis
Dominus Iesus (declaration of unified Catholic Church) 355
Donatism 162
Doniger, Wendy 110
Doppler redshift / Doppler blueshift 456
Doyle, Sir Arthur Conan (epigraph) 7, 371
Dragons 8, 24-26, 40, 60, 74, 85, 153, 190, 241, 343, 358
Drum, sacred. *See* Ngoma lungundu

Dualism (*See Also* Monism) 372, 373, 387, 401, 433, 544, 555
Duality. *See* Wave-particle duality
Duhem, Pierre. *See* Duhem-Quine thesis
Duhem-Quine thesis 47, 417, 524
Dundes, Alan 239, 241
Dwarf
  Bes (deity) 98, 99, 105, 456, 520
  white dwarf stars 456
Dyads 11, 427, 428, 434, 587
Dyophysitism (dual nature of Jesus) 300
Earliest complete Christian Bible. *See* Bible (Christian), first official Bible
Earth-like (or -sized) planet. *See* Exoplanet
Easter 128, 131, 244
East of Eden (literary work) 113
Eastern (Greek) Orthodox. *See* Orthodox
Ebionite (Ebionitism)
  beliefs about Jesus and Holy Trinity 222, 540
  Ebionites 162, 163, 236, 249, 540
Ecumenical councils
  Basel 301
  Carthage (synod) 175, 221, 302, 540
  Chalcedon. *See Also* Chalcedonian 107, 257, 258, 279, 300
  Constantinople I 291
  Ephesus I 291, 300
  Ferrara 301
  first seven ecumenical 163
  Florence 301
  four ecumenical (concept of purgatory) 301
  Nicaea I 158, 175, 220, 290-293, 540
  Vatican I 107
  Lateran IV 106, 107
  Lyon I and II 301
  Trent 301
Edict of Milan 162
Edict of Thessalonica (Cunctos populos) 162, 178, 540
EEG 432, 434, 443
Efficient causality. *See* Causality, efficient causality
'egel (Hebrew, young bull calf) 102
Egyptian (Coptic). *See* Coptic
Ehrman, Bart
  canonical New Testament not reliable 193, 223
  Christian-turned-Agnostic 156
  coined term "proto-orthodox Christians" 162
  Coptic Gospel of Thomas (dating of) 167
  early Christian sects, winners and losers 164

Ehrman, Bart (*continued*)
 early Christianities, not early Christianity 163
 five criteria to select texts as biblical canon 175
 Forged: Writing in the Name of God (literary work) 166, 167
 on biblical errors 155, 156
 on miracles as least plausible explanation for resurrection 273
 on post-death appearances of Jesus 233
 on reliability of Gospel of Luke and Acts of the Apostles 228

Eigenstate 440, 441

Eigenvalue 440

Einstein
 author's idol 55
 Bose-Einstein condensate 520
 comparing Einstein and Newton's concept of gravity 416
 cosmological constant. *See Also* Cosmological Constant (Λ) 484
 Einstein tensor 459
 quote (epigraph), affirming Jesus' existence 269
 quote (epigraph), did God have a choice in creating universe 505
 quote (epigraph), everyone needs to contribute 7, 588
 quote (epigraph), God beyond human thought 63
 quote (epigraph), God wouldn't directly influence mankind 307
 quote (epigraph), Jesus wouldn't call himself God 283, 289
 quote (epigraph), search for the truth 7, 535
 Einstein Effect. *See* Gravitational redshift
 Einstein frame (Cosmon Field Model) 483, 484, 486, 489, 490, 492, 496
 field equations 65, 459, 460, 483, 497
 gravitational waves 467
 gravity is not a force 460
 matter-energy equivalency 439
 relationism (concept of time) 524
 singularity predicted by Einstein does not exist 483
 spacetime as integral 549
 spacetime (mathematical) singularities 460, 461
 stationary (static / steady state) universe 460, 482, 484

Ekpyrotic. *See* **Cosmogonic models, Ekpyrotic model**

El, deity
 deity 90, 92, 97, 102, 103, 105, 276
 depiction of (illustration) 103
 Elyon or 'elyôn 91, 93
 Israelite worship of 91
 Yahweh, a son of El 91, 92

Electroencephalography 432

Electromagnetism 10, 317, 414, 580

Electron particle, rest mass 491

Electron volt (eV) 490

Elephantine (papryi) 91

Elijah, biblical prophet 96, 238

Elliott, Mark 132

'Elyôn. *See* El, deity

Emanationism 164

Emergence (emergentism)
 advanced definition of (*See Also* basic, entry-level definition subheading) 390
 autocell, emergent properties 379, 381
 basic, entry-level definition of (*See Also* advanced definition subheading) 360
 biological emergence and why would God care about humanity 393
 biological example (ants) 360
 cosmic emergence (general). (*See Also* strong and weak cosmological emergence subheading) 364, 406
 does emergence / emergentism infer existence of God? 389, 400
 emergence and New Sciences of Religion 361, 366
 emergence and states of non-equilibrium (epigraph) 371
 emergence and states of dynamic disequilibrium 389
 emergence applied to scientific disciplines 374
 emergence, by itself, does not defend concept of a God that communes with mankind 389
 emergence, Complexity Theory, Chaos Theory 374
 natural emergence and biosemiotics 400
 naturalistic emergence 389, 390
 natural (naturalistic) telos. *See* Telos, natural (naturalistic telos)
 Panentheism and strong emergence 401
 Process Theology inherent assumption strong emergence 389
 strong (cosmological) emergence 388, 389, 391
 teleodyanmics and strong emergence 392
 transcendental telos. *See* Telos, transcendental (divine) telos
 weak cosmological emergence 389, 405

Empiricism
 empiricist 295, 430
 theory 44
 Father of Empiricism 409

Empty time. *See* Time, changeless (eventless, empty) time

Empty tomb

Apostle Paul does not mention the empty tomb 198, 288

evidence for Claims 5, 6, and 7 make empty tomb claim moot 232

first literary referance to the empty tomb 202

mentioned in all four NT Gospels 132

N. T. Wright, without empty tomb and appearances, Christianity 199

only three extra-biblical sources mention the empty tomb 204, 271

Emwazi, Mohammed (a.k.a. Jihadi John) 422

End-directed process 374, 405

Ending of Gospel of Mark (chapter 16 of Christian Bible)

Long Ending 217, 218, 220-223

Original Authentic Ending of Mark (OAEM) 217-219, 222, 230

Short Ending 217, 218, 222, 223

Secret Gospel of Mark, ending unknown 217

validation of Original ending (OAEM) 219, 220

Vatican's official position 222

Energy

binding energy 414

dark energy. *See* Dark, energy

energy density 488

Law, Conservation of Energy. *See* Thermodynamics

mass-energy (*See Also* matter-energy, below) 317, 458, 460, 464, 496

matter-energy (*See Also* mass-energy, above) 9, 401, 439, 459, 460, 469, 475, 476

mystical energies 117

psychic energy 385, 386

radial and tangential energy 385

spiritual energy 67

vacuum. *See* Vacuum, energy

Enki, deity 115

Enlightenment, Age of. *See* Age, Enlightenment

Enlil, deity 115

Entanglement. *See* Quantum, nonlocality and entanglement

Enumeration, idea of 313

Entropy 461, 471-473, 475-480

Epic of (literary work)

Atra-Hasis 115

Gilgamesh 25, 115, 116, 239

Ziusudra 115

Epigraph (epigraphical) 131, 132, 134, 138, 139, 201, 582, 588

Epiphanius, Bishop of Salamis 164, 195

Epiphenomenalism 544

Epistemology

definition of 46

Bayesian epistemology. *See Also* Bayes' theorem 251, 254, 278

Epistles (books, Christian Bible)

eight general epistles 149, 176, 193

Gnostic epistles. *See* Gnostic, Gnostic apocrypha

Pauline epistles 149, 151, 176, 193, 198, 211, 226, 228

Epithets 93, 95, 99, 100, 104, 175, 224, 284

Epoch (cosmology)

current epoch (Dark Energy Era) 454, 489

first epoch (cosmic inflation) 453

third epoch (matter-dominated) 465

quark epoch 520

second epoch (radiation) 454

radiation- and matter-dominated 454, 465

Equation (mathematical formula)

Bayes' Explicit form 255

Bayes' Odds form 329

Bayes' Simple form 252

Einstein's matter-equivalency 439

Schrödinger equation 439, 472

Personal belief 21

Equilibrium, state of thermal 478

Equivalency, matter-energy 439

Erikson, Erik H. (epigraph) 269

Eschaton (eschatological) 231, 266, 271, 276, 385, 388, 529

Essence, divine. *See* Divine, essence

Essenes 203, 205

Eternal

compare—atemporal, timeless, everlasting, eternal, omintemporal 71

God is unnecessary if universe is eternal 446

eternal cosmic inflation. *See* Inflation, cosmic

Eternal to the past, reality or universe 480, 481, 523, 529, 562, 563

Eternalism. *See* Block Universe, Static Block Universe

Eternality

of Jesus. *See* Jesus of Nazareth, eternality of Jesus

of God (Six Towers of God worldview) 557, 559-565, 588

of the Holy Trinity. *See* Holy Trinity, eternality of

of the universe inconsistent with our intuition (*See Also* Eternity, human inability...) 499

Eternality (*continued*)

    past-eternality. *See* Cosmogonic models, Emergent Universe model

Eternity

    compare—atemporal, timeless, everlasting, eternal, omintemporal 71

    final judgment of humanity 57

    God existing in a nonspatial, timeless state 319

    human inability to comprehend (*See Also* Eternity, of the universe...) 336

    past eternity. *See* Past eternity (Cosmon Field Model) Process Theology, doesn't address concept of eternity 390

    stone of history inscribed for eternity 588

Etiology 357

Europe, changing religiosity 32, 338

Eusebians 203

Eusebius of Caesarea 195, 206, 220, 293

Eusebius of Nicomedia (Bishop of Berytus) 203, 206, 293

eV. *See* Electron volt

Evans, Craig 138, 156, 157, 164, 173

Eveitite (metaphysical material). *See Also* Adamite 521-523, 528, 561

Event horizon 78

Eventless time. *See* Time, changeless (eventless, empty) time

Everett, Hugh (*See Also* Quantum mechanics, Everett Interpretation) 472

Everett Interpretation. *See* Quantum mechanics

Everlasting (ness) 71, 79, 327, 400, 482, 516, 522

Evil

    general, God and existence of evil 77, 78, 405

    good and evil are relative, defined by mankind 77, 325, 427

    inability to adjudicate if God is a good or evil Being 18, 311, 506

    man and world inherently evil (Gnostic view) 165, 167

    Problem of Evil 77, 79, 87, 307, 311, 327, 344, 382, 384, 388, 390

    theodicy 77, 307, 327, 388, 400

Evolution, of the mind / brain 22, 430, 431, 433

Evolutionary biology 431, 543

Exclusivism (religious) 63, 76, 185, 357

Execution (first post-orthodox Catholic) 175

Exegesis. *See Also* Hermeneutics 147, 233, 278, 409

Exodus 69, 84, 93, 116, 124, 140, 174, 539

Exoplanet 34-37, 576

Exorcisms (by Jesus) 178, 276

Expansion

    chaotic expansion 471, 472, 477, 478, 489, 495, 502

    Hubble expansion. *See* Hubble, Hubble expansion

    Hubble Flow. *See* Hubble, Hubble Flow

    inflationary expansion. *See* Inflation, cosmic

    negative expansion (contraction) 453, 470, 492, 501

    no (zero) expansion, Einstein Static State 460, 481, 482

    no (zero) expansion on average, Emergent Universe model 481

    positive (outward) expansion 453, 457

    slow-and-smooth expansion 489

    smooth expansion 471, 478, 489, 495, 496, 502

    supraluminal expansion 316, 453, 455, 461, 466, 501

Explanatory Power 41, 108, 136, 186, 187, 251, 256, 269, 272, 274, 276, 277, 281

Explanatory Scope 186, 187, 269, 270, 274, 277, 281

Explicit form. *See* Bayes' theorem, Explicit form of equation

Extinctions, mass 36

Extra-biblical. *See* Noncanonical

Extra-dimensional. *See* Dimensions

Extraterrestrial. *See* Aliens

Extremism. Radicalism, religious

Eyewitness, testimony / account. *See Also* Oral testimony / transmission 185, 190, 193, 195, 215, 223-225, 250, 273

Ezekiel, biblical prophet 231

Faith

    Co-Essential Faith 23, 55

    Complementary faith 23

    fideism (fideistic) 16-18, 21, 23, 109, 148, 298, 336, 357, 537, 545, 554

    Many-Faced God Conundrum 18, 23, 336, 357, 364, 537, 546, 552, 553, 575

    partially-justified beliefs / faith 553

Fallacy, Conjunction. *See* Bias, types of, Conjunction fallacy

Fallacy of Composition 517

False negative identification. *See* Type II cognitive error

False positive identification. *See* Type I cognitive error

Familial relationships 103, 130, 346, 395

Fanaticism, violent religious (Terrorism, Radicalism, Fundamentalism) (*See Also* Zealots) 16, 17, 28, 63, 353, 422

Fanti, Giulio 126

Fermilab. *See* Particle collider

Fermions 373, 414

Festinger, Leon 236

Feynman, Richard (epigraph) 409

Fideism. *See* Faith, fideism

Fides et ratio (Latin) 23

Fides quaerens intellectum (Latin) 15

Field singularity. *See* Singularity, cosmological, field singularity

Field

Cosmon field. *See* Cosmon Field Model

Curvaton field 475

field equations (Einstein's). *See* Einstein, field equations

field equations (Wetterich's). *See* Cosmon Field Model, Wetterich's...

gravitational field 78, 490

Higgs field. *See* Higgs field

inflation field 462, 473, 489, 495, 513, 514

scalar field. *See* Scalar field

Field graves. *See* Graveyards

Fifth dimension. *See* Dimensions, fifth dimension

Filioque 291, 292, 300

Fine-tuning (of the universe), teleological 402, 403, 514

Fingerprint, geochemical. *See* Geochemical fingerprint

Finitism (rejection of infinity) 522

Finkel, Irving 115

Firmament. *See* Heaven, Firmament

First Cause. *See* Causality, First Cause

First interval, of time 511, 513, 515, 517, 519, 521, 528

First Law of Thermodynamics. *See* Thermodynamics

Firstness, Principle of. *See* Principle, principle of Firstness...

Fitzgerald, David 206

Five-sigma statistical confidence 45, 415, 468

Flat Earth hypothesis 43

Flatness Problem. *See* Problems in cosmology, Flatness Problem

Foley, James 422

Forerunner (John the Baptist) 119, 184

Forgery 121, 122, 126, 129, 134, 135, 170, 228

Formless, an attribute of God 18, 365, 520

Fossilized microbial mats 581

Foundational Truth Claims of Christianity 144, 148, 149, 156, 184, 190, 193, 229, 234, 278, 279, 303, 361, 541

Foundational Truth Claims of Christianity (list of three claims) 148

Four dimensions (*See Also* Dimensions)

4D black hole 498

4D bulk hyperspace 498

4D spacetime singularity 458

4D universe, No Boundary Proposal 481

external domains (5D+) highly uncertain 546

four dimensions of physical universe (time and space) 50, 87, 88, 381, 382, 398, 457

God as unembodied consciousness 520, 544, 545

God can defy 4D spacetime 546

space, but no time (Cosmon Field Model) 496

Fourier Transform Infrared Spectroscopy (FTIR). *See* Spectroscopy

Fragments

bone 120, 121, 124, 132, 135, 140

digital image library of biblical fragments 151

fragments of literary works 130, 134, 149, 169, 202, 219

True Cross 122, 123, 125

wood (Noah's Ark) 115

Framing effect. *See* Bias, types of, Framing effect

Free will and Determinism

Free Will and Determinism dilemma 39, 77, 79, 189, 325, 338, 390, 397, 400, 525, 559, 577

Process Theology doesn't explain free will 390

Freeman, Morgan 189

Freeze. *See* Frozen

Frequencies

composite beat frequency 442

observation of lower frequency of cosmic light (Cosmon Field Model) 493

resonant frequency 442

statistical frequency 332, 536

tonal quality to human ear 428

Frequentist probability (frequentism) 332, 536

Frozen

frozen universe, current state 580

frozen universe, initial state (Cosmon Field Model) 484, 496, 521, 523, 588

frozen unvierse, final state 514

FT-IR. *See* Spectroscopy

Fundamental questions. *See* Big Questions

Fundamental forces of the physical universe 10, 373, 413, 468

Fundamentalism, violent religious. *See* Fanaticism, violent religious

Future-eternal

future-eternal cosmos 460, 503

future-eternal cosmic inflation 462

Galatians (book, Christian Bible) 156, 211, 213, 224-226, 228, 230

Galilei, Galileo 110

Gamma-ray burst 325, 474, 580

Garden Tomb. *See* Talpiot Tomb A

Garfinkel, Yosef 119

Gelsey, Rudolph 245

Geochemical fingerprint 136

Gene, The God 431

General relativity theory. *See Also* Special relativity theory 65, 452, 453, 455, 459, 467-469, 481, 482, 486, 494, 498, 502, 568

Generic God (deity). *See* Deity, generic

Genesis, book of Hebrew / Christian Bible
  flood story 140, 539
  biblical quote, beginning of all (Genesis 1:1-3) 157
  biblical quote, Ark of God (Genesis 8:4) 114
  firmament, the. *See Also* Firmament 372
  on Noah's Ark 114

Gentiles 156, 198, 226, 227, 229, 248

Geocentrism (geocentrist and non-geocentricity) 70, 110, 372, 373

Geodesic line 497

Geometric singularity. *See* Singularity, cosmological

Ghosts, visions (sightings) of 235

Gibson, Shimon 135

Glanzberg, Michael 46

Glass Bead Game 24

Gluons (elementary particle) 373

Gnosis 164

Gnostic (Gnostics, Gnosticism)
  "apokatastasis"—restoration of Gnostic Christians 301
  Against Heresies (literary work, attack on the Gnostics) 174, 221
  Archons and Aeons (servants of the Demiurge god) 165, 540
  ascetic lifestyle 165
  belief, self-awareness key to salvation 168
  Carpocratians (deviant Gnostic sect) 165, 169-171
  Christian, quasi-Christian, Jewish, and non-Christian sects 164, 206, 270
  Clement of Alexandria on secret knowledge about the divine 169, 170, 172
  Coptic Gospel of Thomas. *See* Apocrypha, Gospel of Thomas
  Demiurge, fabricator of the universe 164
  Church Fathers, accurate portrayals of Jesus? 176
  disappearance of Gnostic sects 165
  genre of Gnostic literature 167
  Gnosis, need knowledge for personal redemption 164
  Gnostic apocrypha (Gnostic gospels) 167, 174
  Gnostic belief in an immortal soul 179
  Gnostic literature, earliest references to Jesus, resurrection, and immortality 210
  Gnostic view of Jesus' resurrection 172
  Gnostics affirm Jesus as a savior 205
  Godhead, Gnostic view of 249
  heresiologists against the Gnostics 164
  humans inherently evil 165
  lack of historical knowledge about the Gnostics 164
  list of early quasi-Christian sects 162
  Nag Hammadi library 152
  Origen, different views on afterlife and heaven 436
  Origen, similar views on trapped human soul 436
  Philo-Judaeus of Alexandria commented on the Gnostics 205
  Secret Gospel of Mark (apocrypha) 167, 169-171, 217
  sparks (divine). *See* Sparks, Gnostic
  Tertullian, writing against 290
  three classes of humans 165

God-by-most-names 353

God-by-whatever-name
  first usage, a neutral, respectful name for "God" 23
  other usages 24, 26, 28, 33, 41, 42, 46, 56, 57, 59, 60, 64, 67, 86, 146, 183, 190, 262, 279, 307, 310, 311, 322, 327, 328, 334, 340, 342, 352, 353, 358-362, 365, 404, 421, 435, 499, 546

God-concepts 404

God-ing-Universe (concept of God, New Sciences of Religion) 364, 366

God-of-the-Gaps argument 280

God-World 390, 400, 401

Godhead
  Arianism, view of 203, 285
  Chalcedonian (orthodox Christianity), views of 257, 262
  Ebionite, Marionite, and Gnostic, views of 249
  general Christianity, view of 179, 279, 280, 290, 292
  Marcionite, view of 299
  Modalism (also Sebellianism, Patripassianism, and modalistic monarchianism) 299
  Mormonism, view of 107
  orthodox Christianty, view of 148, 302
  quasi-Christianity, views of 153
  quasi-Christianity / proto-Christianity, views of 285
  Richard Swinburne, view of (critique by Kelly James Clarke) 321, 322, 541

Golan, Oded 135, 138

Golden Rule. *See* Hick, John, Golden Rule

Goldstein, D. 420

Golgatha 122

Goodall, Jane 109

Gopnik, Alison 427

Gorski, Phil 32

Gospel of John (*See Also* Gospels)

    affirmation of Jesus' divinity 283-286

    authored by multiple authors 120, 175, 223

    canonical text (book) in Christian New Testament 149

    date of authorship. *See* Gospels, dates of authorship

    earliest fragment of New Testament. *See* Rylands Papyrus P52

    empty tomb (*See Also* Gospels, empty tomb...) 194

    Jesus became angered 343

    Jesus in human form (post-death) 214, 215

    Jesus' post-death appearances (*See Also* Gospels, list of post-death...) 211, 215, 224

    Jesus, subordinate to God 285

    Jesus walks on water 190

    Jews did not want Jesus left on cross overnight / religious days 231

    Johannine (literary works). *See* Johannine

    John the Apostle / John the Evangelist 120, 161, 178, 192, 198, 200, 207, 213, 284

    John's testimony affirms Gnostic belief that Jesus was an Aeon 165

    Mark and John disagree on day of Jesus' death 192

    Matthew and John disagree as to when Jesus was annointed 192

    Matthew and John disagree on where Jesus stayed 191

    Polycarp, a disciple of John the Apostle 161

    Shroud of Oviedo (burial face cloth). *See* Shroud, Shroud of Oviedo

    source materials for. *See* Gospels, primary source materials...

Gospel of Luke (Lucan) (*See Also* Gospels)

    author of Luke, also wrote Acts of the Apostles? 227

    author of, unknown 228

    canonical text (book) in Christian New Testament 149

    date of authorship. *See* Gospels, dates of authorship

    empty tomb. (*See Also* Gospels, empty tomb...) 132, 194

    family lineage, different from Matthew 191

    Jesus in human form (post-death) 214, 215

Jesus increased in wisdom 287, 288

Jesus' post-death appearances (*See Also* Gospels, list of post-death...) 211, 214, 224

Marcion's edited version of Luke 222

on Jesus' omniscience and omnipotence 286, 287, 304

seventy disciples sent by Jesus (*See Also* Seventy disciples) 199

source materials for. *See* Gospels, primary source materials...

Gospel of Mark (Marcan) (*See Also* Gospels)

    author of, unknown 171, 249

    canonical text (book) in Christian New Testament 149

    date of authorship. *See* Gospels, dates of authorship

    does not affirm Jesus' post-death appearances (*See Also* Ending of Gospel of Mark) 224, 273

    earliest complete copies of Mark 219

    earliest copy of (fragment P45) 219

    empty tomb (*See Also* Gospels, empty tomb...) 194

    ending of chapter 16 (Short, Long, Original). *See* Ending of Gospel of Mark

    first canonical gospel written. *See* Gospel of Mark, Marcan Priority

    Jesus became angered 343

    Jesus in human form (post-death). *See* Ending of Gospel of Mark, Long Ending

    on Jesus' omniscience and omnipotence 286, 287, 304

    Jesus' post-death appearances (*See Also* Gospels, list of post-death... and Ending of Gospel of Mark, Long Ending) 211, 224

    Jesus walks on water 190

    Marcan Priority 202, 223, 238

    Mark and John disagree on day of Jesus' death 192

    Secret Gospel of Mark. *See* Gnostic, Secret Gospel of Mark

    source materials for. *See* Gospels, primary source materials...

    three possible endings to Mark's gospel (*See Also* Ending of Gospel of Mark) 217

    three versions of Marcan gosepl 172

Gospel of Matthew (Mattthaean) (*See Also* Gospels)

    author corrects information found in Gospel of Mark (*See Also* Marcan Priority) 202

    canonical text (book) in Christian New Testament 149

    date of authorship. *See* Gospels, dates of authorship

    disciples doubted Jesus 199

    empty tomb (*See Also* Gospels, empty tomb...) 194

    empty tomb, Claim 2 – Christian evidence for the Resurrection 195

Gospel of Matthew (*continued*)

    family lineage, different from Luke 191

    Jesus became angered 343

    Jesus himself indirectly says he is the Son of God 283

    Jesus in human form (post-death) 214, 215

    on Jesus' omniscience and omnipotence 286, 287, 304

    Jesus' post-death appearances (*See Also* Gospels, list of post-death...) 199, 211, 214, 224

    Jesus walks on water 190

    Matthaean Priority 202

    Matthew and John disagree as to when Jesus was annointed 192

    Matthew and John disagree on where Jesus stayed 191

    source materials for. *See* Gospels, primary source materials...

Gospels (canonical / biblical)

    angelic visitation at empty tomb, different narratives 192

    authorship of, speculative and unknown 171, 201, 228, 249

    canonical gospels (Christian Bible), names of 156

    dates of authorship 175, 177

    empty tomb, list of passages in the Bible 194

    empty tomb, indirect testimony 132

    gospels, second- or third-hand evidence 215

    list of post-death appearances of Jesus 212

    number of miracles by Jesus 288

    primary source materials do not mention post-death appearances of Jesus 224

    primary source materials used by gospel authors. *See* Passion Narrative, L-Source, M-Source, and Q-source

    Synoptic Gospels (Matthew, Mark, Luke) 167, 223, 285, 286, 289, 304

    Irenaeus, earliest defense of four gospels 174, 222

Goulder, Michael 238

Grace, prevenient 23

Gracián, Baltasar (epigraph) 7

Grand Observer 8-11, 26, 46, 61, 109, 393, 576, 588

Grassie, William 23, 358-366, 387

Graveyards (*See Also* Tombs)

    graves, earthen field 130

    reserved graveyards 197

Gravitational field and cosmon field 490

Gravitational lensing 457

Gravitational redshift 456

Gravitational singularity. *See* Singularity, cosmological

Gravitational waves (*See Also* Observatory, LIGO) 467, 468, 473, 494

Graviton particle 373, 469, 482, 486, 489, 498

Gravity

    antigravity 18

    Canonical Quantum Gravity 469

    cause for creation of the Earth 580

    cause for creation of the Sun 391

    creation of gravity (Big Bang model) 454

    Dilaton Quantum Gravity 494

    effect of increased Earth gravity 393

    Einstein's field equations, describe effect of gravity 488

    finely-tuned parameter 317

    fundamental parameter of the universe 10, 317, 414

    gravity and Cosmological Constant 483

    gravity and the Structure Problem of cosmology 466

    gravity as quantized graviton particles 486

    gravity is not a physical force 460

    how does God evade natural laws (gravity, etc.)? 547

    incompatibility between quantum mechanics and general relativity 468

    influence of at origin of universe (Big Bang model) 468

    instability of Einstein's initial model of gravity 460

    Isaac Newton's law of gravity 416

    Leaning Tower of Pisa 418

    Loop Quantum Gravity 469

    quantum gravity 468, 469, 481, 482, 494, 502, 526

    quantum mechanics does not describe gravity 468

    relativity theory. *See* General relativity theory and Special relativity theory

    variable gravity 482, 483, 486, 492, 494

Gray, Thomas (idiom—**ignorance is bliss**) 53

GRB. *See* Gamma-ray burst

Great Attractor 456

Great Cosmological Singularity. *See* Singularity cosmological

Great Revolt (Jewish revolutions) 178, 206, 232

Greater universe 431, 548, 549, 552, 559, 570, 577

Greco-Roman (Graeco-Roman) 72, 99-101, 163, 232, 539

Growing Block Universe. *See* Block universe

Guth, Alan. *See Also* BGV 466

Gyatso, Tenzin. *See* Dalai Lama XIV

Habermas, Gary 194, 196, 199, 201, 211, 213, 234, 239, 309

Hadith (Islamic literature) 343

Hadrian, Roman Emperor 122

Haines, David 422

Hajj (Islamic pilgrimage) 35

Hallucination

electromagnetic fields cause hallucinations 433

survey of scholars, Jesus appearances 213

Hallucination Hypothesis (resurrection) 234-236, 238, 246, 273-275, 281

Hamer, Dean 431

Hameroff, Stuart 443

Hammurabi

Code. *See* Code of Hammurabi

King Hammurabi 84, 89, 116

Hanan ben Hanan (also called Ananus ben Ananus) 178

Hanh, Thich Nhat (epigraph) 349, 583

Harris, Sam 431

Hartle-Hawking No-Boundary proposal. *See* Cosmogonic models

Hartshorne, Charles 387

Hasher, L. 420

Hathor, deity 104

Hawking, Stephen 318, 479

HBB. *See* Cosmogonic models, Hot Big Bang model

Heat death. *See* Universe, heat death

Heaven (*See Also* Purgatory)

belief in, U.S. survey results 75

Firmament 45, 372

Gnostic conception of heaven. *See* Plemora

Jesus, ascension (pre-ascension) to 66, 158, 194, 204, 211, 271, 357, 385, 400, 588

various names for 45

Hedibia, Letter to (literary work by Jerome) 220

Hegel, Georg Wilhelm Friedrich 381

Heisenberg's uncertainty principle. *See* Quantum mechanics, uncertainty principle

Helena, Roman Empress 121, 122

Helicrysum (plant pollen) 129

Heliosphere 325

Helium-4 473

Hellenism 1, 152, 153, 238

Hemer, Colin J. 175

Henotheism 87, 88

Heraclitus 386, 444

Hercules–Corona Borealis Great Wall 474

Herd bias. *See* Bias, types of

Heresy

Against Heresies (literary work) 174, 221

as canonization/orthodoxification of Christianity advanced, heretical literature disappeared 540

early Arianism deemed heretical 291, 292

Church Father Irenaeus, identifies heretical gospels 174

heresiologists, list of 164

Catholicism, punishment of 107, 158

Clement of Alexandria, some views heretical 169, 170

Constantine the Great became a heretic after emboldening orthodox Christianity 293

Jesus died as a heretic in the eyes of 1st-century Jews 270

Philo-Judaeus of Alexandria, viewed Gnostic cults as heretics 205

Modalism, a heretical view of Sabellius 299

Teilhard de Chardin, writings not officially heretical 383

Tertullian of Carthage wrote against heretical cults 290

violent religious fanatics, expunge heretics 26

Hermeneutics (Hermeneutical) 3, 42, 147, 185, 228, 230, 361

Hermes, deity 147, 159

Hero

hero's journey 61

legendary 241-245

mythic hero 239, 240

Herod Antipas, Roman Tetrarch 120, 238

Herod I, King (Herod the Great) 125, 238

Herodian 136

Herodotus 244

Hesse, Hermann 24

Heterodoxy 164, 175, 222

Heuristics 74, 423-425, 427, 434, 443, 544, 584

Hezekiah, King 94

HHTE (Historicity Hypothesis Testing Engine). *See* Historicity Tests

HIBB. *See* Cosmogonic models, Hot Inflationary Big Bang model

Hick, John

distinction between faith and knowledge 355

fundamental incoherency with pluralism 357

God, an ineffable, inaccessible hyperessence 356

Golden Rule, unprovable and ineffective 147, 356, 357, 362, 366, 542

important discovery, religious orthodoxy is irrational 358

Jesus was soley human, a metaphor for God 242, 355

modern pluralism 354-357, 362, 542

philosophy circumvents problems with religious mysticism 356

Hick, John (*continued*)

philosophy shares similarities with New Sciences of Religion 362

pluralistic ideas escape Many-Faced God Conundrum 552

Ultimate Reality (the Real), concept for God 354, 356-358, 366, 542

worldview, borrows from Immanuel Kant 356

Higgs

boson (elementary particle) 45, 55, 413-415

field 9, 45, 54, 414, 449, 473, 486, 553

mechanism 414

High-level 45, 276, 373, 389-391

Higher-order 19, 391, 448

Higham, Thomas 121

Hinduism (Hinduist)

Hinduism 366

Six Towers of God worldview, placement 565

Hippolytus of Rome 164, 174, 195, 221

Historicity Tests (HHTE – Historicity Hypothesis Testing Engine)

Ad hoc-ness 186

Conformity with accepted beliefs 186

Explanatory Power 186

Explanatory Scope 186

HHTE 187, 269-272, 274-277

Plausibility 186

Superiority to rival hypotheses 186

Historicity 109, 138, 146, 147, 152, 156, 184, 186-188, 194, 223, 234, 269, 278, 281

Historiography 140, 409

History, true 8, 11, 188, 250

Hitchens, Christopher 431

Hittites, people of the Hittite kingdom 89

Hocart, A. M. 240

Hogarth, David George (epigraph) 113

Holder, Rodney, Reverend 265

Holistic (paradigm). *See* Approach (es), bottom-up, top-down...

Holland cloth 126

Holmes, Detective Sherlock 7, 371

Holographic principle 526

Holy Ghost (1 John 5:6-8) (*See Also* Holy Spirit) 291, 295, 296, 304

Holy Sepulchre 122, 241

Holy Spirit (*See Also* Consubstantiality, Holy Ghost, Hypostatic Union, and Perichoresis)

falsifications added to Bible to enance relationship. *See* Holy Ghost

Aeon and a divine spark (Gnostic) 165, 540

Arius, Holy Spirit a high-ranking angel 292

Arianism, Holy Spirit subordinate to God and Jesus 162, 539

Athanasius, chief developer of doctrine of Holy Spirit 257

Augustine of Hippo, Holy Spirit embues earthly Jesus with power 297

binitarianism 106, 290, 539

Catholic Doctrine on Holy Spirit (cataphatic belief) 337

Christianity, a polytheistic religion? 159

co-equal with God and Jesus 193

eternality of 297

filioque, subordinated Holy Spirit (*See Also* Filioque) 292

Foundational Truth Claim of Christianity (Claim 3) 149

Fourth Lateran Council 106, 107

if Jesus not divine, no need for Holy Spirit 338

if God is a logical or ontological necessity, Holy Spirit is illogical and unnecessary 319, 344

loss of uniqueness relative to God and Jesus 398

modalism, is Holy Spirit a successive mode of God? 396

Origen of Alexandria, a hierarchical view 220

pneumatology, the study of the Holy Spirit 299

Pope Francis, on the Holy Spirit 337

relationship of the Spirit with God and Jesus unclarified in Christian Bible 179, 290, 321

responsible for inspiring biblical authors 299

responsible for Jesus' ascension into heaven 279

responsible for virginal conception of Jesus 299

Holy Trinity (*See Also* Consubstantiality, Hypostatic Union, Perichoresis, Trinitarian, and Triune)

Arianism, Holy Spirit subordinate to God and Jesus 162, 539

coherency (incoherency) of the Holy Trinity 107, 338, 390, 541

filioque, subordinated Holy Spirit (*See Also* Filioque) 292

Foundational Truth Claims of Christianity (Claim 3) 149

hotly debated, Holy Trinity 304, 539

if Jesus is part of the Trinity, he must be omniscient 541

Isaac Newton, corruption of Scripture and views on Holy Trinity 294-297

list of Ecumenical Councils that debated the Holy Trinity 291

Holy Trinity (*continued*)

Nicene Creed, the creed of the Holy Trinity 162

omniscience of Jesus, logical concerns on how he fits within the Holy Trinity 304, 541

Origen of Alexandria, a hierarchical view 220

Process Theology, doesn't address concept of Holy Trinity 390

relationship between Persons of the Holy Trinity unclarified in Christian Bible 179, 288, 290, 321

Richard Swinburne, defense of exactly three divine entities 311, 318, 541

Richard Swinburne, for Trinity to be coherent, God cannot be ontologically or logically necessary 344

Southgate-Robinson, Trichotomic view to argue coherency of the Trinity 395, 402

trinitarianism 298, 394-396, 541

Homer (Greek poet) 149, 233

Homo naledi 85, 538

Homo sapiens sapiens 64, 393, 394

Homo neanderthalensis (Neanderthal) 64, 85, 86, 434

Homoousios (Greek) 107

Hooke, Robert 416

Horizon Problem. *See* Problems in cosmology, Horizon Problem

Horus, deity 100, 101, 104

Hot Big Bang (HBB) model. *See* Cosmogonic models, Hot Big Bang model

Hot Inflationary Big Bang (HIBB) model. *See* Cosmogonic models, Hot Inflationary Big Bang model

Hubble

Hubble constant (parameter) 453, 457, 470, 489

Edwin Hubble 453, 492

Hubble expansion (same as Hubble Flow) 462

Hubble Flow 453, 461

Hubble space telescope 35, 453

Hulse, Russell A. 467

Humason, Milton 453

Hurrians, people of the Hurrian kingdom 89

Huygens, Christiaan 524

Hydrogen-helium ratio 466, 480

Hyperdimension. *See* Dimensions, hyperdimensions

Hyperessence (hyperessentiality) 340, 341, 346, 356, 366, 406

Hyperspace. *See* Dimensions, hyperspace

Hypostatic union (hypostasis) 107, 288, 297, 299, 304, 321, 343

IAA. *See* Israelite, Israel Antiquities Authority

Ian Barbour 388

Ignatius of Antioch 160, 174, 207

Ignostic (Ignosticism)

ignostic 341, 572

Strong form of ignosticism 366

Weak form of ignosticism 366

Igtheism. *See* Ignostic, ignostic

Illusory-truth effect. *See* Bias, types of, Illusory-truth effect

Imagination (imaginary, imaginative)

Christian mysticism, a product of human imagination 70, 585

God as a by-product of human imagination 109

if Truth Criteria not met 53

imaginary gods of ancient Mesopotmians 107

imaginary gods of 1st-century civilization 274

imaginary numbers (mathematical concept) 480

imaginary time. *See* Time, imaginary time

imagination as a defense for reality of God 546

inability to separate reality from imagination / power of imagination 20, 21, 545

John Hick, God is beyond the human imagination 354

Mark Twain / Samuel Clemens quote about reality / imagination 535, 545

metaphysicians abuse imaginative abilities to define God's properties 545

Mythological hypothesis / myths 239

Southgate-Robinson, do not address hard question regarding God as a spirit Being 543

Imam. *See Also* Mufti and Mujtahid 31, 423

Immanent (immanence)

definition of 72

materiality / immateriality of God. *See* Six Towers of God worldview, Towers 1-6

potential ways God could be immanent (illustration) 551

Immaterial (ity) 50, 66, 70, 298, 323, 335, 372, 436, 507, 513, 517, 520-522, 526-529, 531, 543, 547, 554, 556, 561, 567, 568, 570, 576, 577

Immoral (ity) 77, 325, 581

Immortal (Immortality)

of God 71, 79

of humans 209

of the human soul 179, 232, 394, 435, 436, 444, 445, 447, 449

of Jesus 157, 209, 276

Immutable (Immutability) 72, 79, 87, 316, 352, 366, 372, 382, 385, 387, 452, 529, 547

Impersonal (attribute of God) 72, 79, 87, 356, 361, 364, 372, 384, 404, 406, 543, 570

Inanimate Substantialism. *See* Six Towers of God worldview, Inanimate Substantialism

In-group 17, 21, 27, 427, 584, 585

Incoherent (incoherencies, incoherency)

author's incoherencies 55

Christianity incoherent (apophatic and cataphatic mysticism) 345

Classical Theism 381, 388

examples, logical coherence and incoherence 52

fideism / blind faith 17

Jesus, 100 percent human and divine 336

hypostatic union of Holy Trinity 297-299

improving human condition, abandon incoherent beliefs / faiths 573

partially-justified beliefs 553

Process Theology, incoherencies of 390

religious mysticism, eliminate from science-religion narrative 585

Religious Pluralism, incoherencies 341, 357

Richard Swinburne, God's properties 315, 344

theism (many forms of), lack of coherency 404

weak (diluted) apophaticism 339

weakly justified faith 17

Incompleteness

of natural emergence. *See* Emergence

path of. *See* Path incompleteness

Indeterminism, quantum. *See* Quantum, indeterminism

Index Librorum Prohibitorum (List of Prohibited Books) 383

Indivisible (non-separable)

property of God 320, 343, 398, 399, 436

property of time 514

Induction

Bayesian. *See* Bayesian, induction

beyond Bayesian methods, alternative inductive methodologies 334

faculty of human reasoning / definition of 19, 42, 54, 409

father of inductive logic 313

ramified natural theology, reliance on induction 309

Richard Swinburne, defining God's nature / existence, need inductive reasoning 251

Richard Swinburne, inductive cosmological argument 310

unresolved Problem of Induction 416, 447

zetetics, plausible naturalistic evidence vs. inductive evidence 380

Ineffability 71, 339

Inefficient causality. *See* Causality, inefficient causality

Inerrancy (of the Bible) 145, 190, 193, 303

Infallibility

papal infallibility 107, 349

infallibility of God's knowledge 156, 397

Inference

adding logical inference to W. L. Craig Kalam Cosmological Argument 518

Bayesian. *See* Bayes' theorem, Bayesian inference

deductive, top-down inference to determine possibility / impossibility of God 334

existence of Higgs boson infers existence of Higgs field 45

Inference to the Best Explanation 54, 187, 251, 269, 278, 316, 345

intuition vs. logical inference / reason 19

science and inferential assumptions 416

Infinity (infinities)

amorphous / undifferentiated time, infinite to the past 516

Aristotle, potential vs. actual infinity 511

Bertrand Russell, on infinity (epigraph) 505

circular time, avoids infinite regress problem 518

cosmic inflation troubled by an infinite number of universes 482

importance of infinity to validity of the Kalam Cosmological Argument 511

infinity does exist for abstract objects 513

plausibility and the existence of infinity in pre-universe 546

Process Theology, doesn't address concept of infinity 390

ratios of infinity, Measure Problem, cosmology 471

Six Towers of God worldview, altered by future discovery of infinities 572

statistical probability more certain than actual infinities (Adamite / Eveitite) 521

understanding causality to origin of universe (First Cause) requires understanding infinity 310, 509

W. L. Craig, actual or metaphysical infinities do not exist 512

W. L. Craig's infinite regress axiom, neutralized indefinitely 522, 523, 530

Wetterich's field equations mathematically valid in temporal past-infinity 484

Inflation, cosmic (*See Also* Expansion)

analogy to describe cosmic inflation 454, 461

BGV theorem, applies only in our universe 513

chaotic inflation 477, 478, 489, 495, 502

Inflation, cosmic (*continued*)

Cosmon Field Model, view of cosmic inflation 489, 494, 501

definition of 10

did cosmic inflation stop or is it future-eternal? 462

Ekpyrotic model, eternal inflation 464

Emergent Universe model, finite period of inflation 482

eternal / non-eternal inflation 462

gravity created before inflation 468

HBB / HIBB model, hot inflation contrasted with cold expansion 484

HIBB model, nature of inflation 462, 466, 468

Hubble parameter, positive-valued during inflation 489

inflation and the Entropy Problem 471

inflation theory, in need of new physics 475

inflation, existence of curvaton field and particles 475

inflation, existence of inflaton field and particles 473

inflation, free of quantum fluctuations 472

multiverse theory, challenged by need to understand cosmic inflation 481, 495

primordial gravitational waves, evidence of inflation 467, 468

primordial inflation 462, 473, 486

problem with inflation theory, Horizon Problem 474

problem with inflation theory, Structure Problem 474

problems with inflation theory, Lithium Problem 473

property of time could vary inside inflation field 514

responsible for creating the multiverse 462

smooth inflation 489, 495, 502

smooth or chaotic? 471

smooths-out irregularities in infant universe 466

Steady State Eternal Inflation model 470, 479, 480, 494

temperature of, hot or cold? 461

what is edge of universe expanding into? 479

Inflaton particle / field 473, 475, 482, 489

Inquisitions 26, 292, 355

Inscriptions

Ark Tablet 115

evidences for God, sources of 15

Jehoash Tablet 117

ossuaries 124, 131, 133, 136-138

pithoi jars from Kuntillet 'Ajrud 97, 100, 103, 105

reliquary, John the Baptist's bones 120

stone tablet, gods 'El' and 'Asherah' 105

Titulis Crucis, lead box 122

Inside-out (paradigm). *See* Approach (es)

Intellectual nonviolence 146, 359

Intelligent Designer 1, 307, 403

Intelligent civilization 37, 38, 458

International Bill of Human Rights (literary work) 27

Intrapsychic 213, 214

Intuition (intuit, intuitive, paraintellect)

Bayesianism based on reasoned intuition 332

definition of 19

eternality of the universe goes against intuition 499

God is simple, Richard Swinburne's primary argument 318

heuristics, learning based on intuition 423

paraintellect 19, 20, 342, 434

people's intuition, dependent on timeframe in history 333

Philip Clayton, Spirit responsible for consciousness 392

quantum uncertainty principle, goes against intuition 439

results of Bayesian analysis, dependent on personal intuition 345

Richard Swinburne's probability estimate for existence of God 344, 542

Richard Swinburne's probability estimate for resurrection 266

unreliabile faculty, invalid to use as evidence for God 19, 20, 48, 333, 404, 537

use of intuition etc. to predict properties of the pre-universe 546

William Grassie (NSoR), intuiting God's plan for humanity 364, 365

William Grassie (NSoR), miracles as expressions of intuition 361

William Grassie (NSoR), religion needs to correct incorrect intuitions 363

Irenaeus of Lyons

Against Heresies (literary work) 221

denounced the Gnostics 164

first person to select the four canonized Gospels 175

Greek Church Father 160, 164

knew John the Apostle 161

poor logic in choosing the four Gospels 222

Iron Age. *See* Age, Iron

Irrational (irrationality) of belief / faith

all religious orthodoxy 358

belief in miracles 364

belief in unseen God 2

brain, encoding of irrational thoughts 432

cataphatic mysticism (positive theology) 338

Irrational (irrationality) of belief / faith (*continued*)
cognitive bias 419
faith-based belief in God (Many-Faced God Conundrum) 18
faith in God without reason 21
fideistic faith 16
frustration of scientists 66
human nature to be irrational 20, 575
partially-justified belief / faith in God 553
personal beliefs, irrationality of 13
prevent ability to find common ground 448
Sea of Irrationality 546, 575
Six Towers of God worldview 575
Temporal Relativity of Reality (Truth Criteria [TC-7]) 51
Truth Criteria, in relation to 53
Irregular time. *See* Time, irregular time
Irreligious. *See Also* nonreligious 352, 587
Irwin, James 115
Isaiah
biblical prophet 94
book of Hebrew / Christian Bible 202
Judas Iscariot the Apostle 157, 200, 212
ISIL (Islamic State of Iraq and the Levant) 3, 26, 27, 63, 422
Isin-Larsa period 99
Isis, deity 100
Islam (Islamic)
Allah, God of Islam 148, 184
an Abrahamic religion (See footnote) 18
anti-trinitarian 107
conversion to / from (illustration) 31, 421
development timeline for Abrahamic religions (illustration) 106
doctrinal commonality with Christianity and Judaism on properties of God 57, 343
doctrinal affiliation / disaffiliation with ISIL / violence determined by Islam's adjudicators 423
exclusivist religion 76
fastest growing religion 349
fideistic / blind faith 148
God as a transcendent Being (illustration) 550
God's omnibenevolence, doctrinal difference with Christianity 72
Islamic State of Iraq and the Levant (ISIL) / Islamist militants. *See* ISIL
Jesus of Nazareth is / was not divine 76
Kalam Cosmological Argument generated by Al-Ghazali 310, 505, 506
monotheistic religion 87, 382
natural theology by itself does not defend the Abrahamic God 44
Qur'anic scripture. *See* Qur'an
relative importance of the prophet Abraham 343
relative validity of Resurrection Hypothesis does not affect Judaism or Islam 328
shared legacy of Abraham connects change from polytheism to monotheism 108, 539
Sharia law. *See* Law, Islamic law
Shiite Islam 587
Six Towers of God worldview, placement 565
soteriology (doctrine of salvation) 343
Strong apophaticism and Islamic thought 339
Sufism (Islamic mysticism) 335
Sunni Islam 63, 310, 422, 505, 587
temperament of God 343
Wahhabism. *See* Wahhabism
worldwide affiliation (charts) 350, 351
Isochronal (property of time) 515, 516
Isolated system. *See* Thermodynamics
Israelite (*See Also*** Yahweh)**
ancient settlements, archaeology / culture 91, 92
ancient worship, bronze serpent Nehustan 94
ancient worship, fusion of deity El to Yahwism 93, 102, 104
ancient worship, list of gods 91
ancient worship, polytheism to monolatrism 92
exodus from Egypt 116
Israel Antiquities Authority (IAA) 131-133, 135, 137
Kings of Israel 96, 124
Iverson, Kelly 222
Jacobovici, Simcha 124, 132
Jainism 88, 366, 394, 445
James the Apostle (James the Just, brother of Jesus)
book of James (Christian Bible) 130, 177
distinction between James the Just and James, the son of Zebedee 178
James' conversion 199
James the Just, brother of Jesus 130, 132, 135, 138, 178, 195, 197, 199, 205, 206, 212, 213, 224, 248
James Ossuary 130, 133-138, 140, 539
Jars, storage. *See* Pithoi, Pithos A, and Pithos B
Johoash Tablet 117, 135
Jehovah's Witnesses 107, 292
Jehu, Israelite King 96
John of Patmos 213
Jeremiah, biblical prophet 117
Jerome 220, 436

Jesus of Nazareth (*See Also* Christ)

Arianism, view of Jesus 162, 285

birth (virginal). *See* Mary, virginity of Mary / virginal birth of Jesus

bloodline (geneaology) of 191, 195

burial cloth of Jesus. *See* Shroud of Turin and Shroud of Oviedo

burial tomb of Jesus. *See* Empty Tomb and Tombs

crucifixion on X-shaped cross. *See* Cross, X-shaped cross

date of death 106, 179, 202

earliest authentic literary mention of Jesus 207

earliest prospective literary mention of Jesus 206

Ebionite, view of Jesus. *See* Ebionite, beliefs about Jesus and Holy Trinity

eternality of Jesus 297

evidence of death, nails of the cross. *See* Nail

evidence of death, True Cross. *See* Cross, True Cross

evidence of death, burial shrouds. *See* Shroud of Turin and Shroud of Oviedo

evidence of death, burial tomb. *See* Empty Tomb and Tombs

evidence (literary) of a man named Jesus / Christ. *See* earliest... (above)

Genealogy (bloodline) of Jesus 191

Gnostic, view of Jesus. *See* Gnosticism, view of Jesus

Jesus as an Aeon. *See* Aeons

Jesus as a legend (Legend Hypothesis) 242-245

Jesus as a mythic hero (Mythological Hypothesis) 239-242

Jesus as solely mortal. *See* Arguments, Mortal Jesus Hypothesis

Jesus' life compared to mythological heroes (chart) 242

Marcionite, view of Jesus. *See* Marcionism

mother of Jesus. *See* Mary

post-death appearances of Jesus (biblical) 212

progressed in knowledge / wisdom 287, 288

skeletal remnants of Jesus 128

wife of Jesus 132

Jesus' post-death appearances

compiled list of all 15 in Bible 211-213

pre-ascension accounts 211

crowd of 500 236

Jewish (Jews) (*See Also* Judaism)

Antiquities of the Jews (literary work) 178, 206, 289

Gnostic Jews 205, 206

Inconsistencies with Established Jewish Traditions (list) 231

King of the Jews 122, 284

Sanhedrin Council. *See* Sanhedrin

"Jihadi John" (Mohammed Emwazi) 422

Johannine (*See Also* Gospel of John)

1 John 5:7-8 113, 294-296, 304, 541

book of Revelation (Revelation to John) 149, 167, 177, 193, 211, 213, 285

Johannine 285, 290

John the Apostle / John the Evangelist. *See* Gospel of John and Johannine

John the Baptist

baptism of Jesus 114

bones of 119-121, 138, 175

imprisonment and execution 138, 238

ministry of 119, 120, 130, 140, 200

Jones, James Warrant 200

Jordan

Ernst Pascual Jordan 483

Jordan frame (Cosmon Field Model) 483, 484, 486, 489, 490, 501

Joseph

father of Jesus 130, 131, 133, 138, 163, 191, 195

Joseph of Arimathea 196, 197, 234

name variant for the name Yoseh 132, 136

ossuary with the name Joseph 131, 133, 137, 138

Josephus. *See* Titus Flavius Josephus

Joses 133

Joshua (book, Hebrew / Christian Bible) 231

Josiah, King 106

Judah

ossuary with the name Judah 137

"Judah, son of Jesus" inscription 131, 133

Judaism

Ancient Judaism (polytheism) 87, 88, 90-92, 103, 159, 184, 231, 246, 538

conversion to / from (illustration) 31, 421

development timeline for Abrahamic religions (illustration) 106

Early Judaism (monolatrism) 87, 88, 90, 92, 95, 103, 278, 281, 539

Modern Judaism (monotheism) 87, 90, 92, 103, 537

Six Towers of God worldview, placement 565

timeline, development of Judaism (illustration) 106

Julian the Apostate, Roman Emperor 203, 210

Kabbalism 537

Kalam Cosmological Argument (KCA)

clarified version of the KCA 518

KCA, most powerful singular argument for God's existence 530

Kalam Cosmological Argument (*continued*)
original version of KCA (Al-Ghazali) 310, 506
Six Towers of God paradigm, compared with KCA 559-564
William Lane Craig version of KCA. *See* Craig, William Lane
Kant, Immanuel 25, 44, 45, 355, 356, 524, 567
Kataphatic. *See* Cataphatic mysticism
Kathenoism 88
Kauffman, Stuart 377, 402
Kazan, Georges 120
KCA. *See* Kalam Cosmological Argument
Kepler Mission 34
Keller, Timothy (epigraph) 183
Kepler Mission / satellite 34, 555
KI. *See* Knowlege Instinct
Kilty, Kevin 132, 136, 137, 251
Kloner, A. 133
Klotz, John (epigraph) 113
Knights Templar 117
Knowledge Instinct (KI) 423-425, 427, 448
Koine Greek (language) 151, 295, 296
Komarnitsky, Kris 194, 198, 235, 237, 239, 272
Kostova, Rossina 120
Küng, Hans (epigraph) 349, 365
Kuntillet 'Ajrud 97, 98, 100, 102, 114
Kur (first dragon) 25
Kurtz, Paul 340
L-source (Gospels) 202, 223
Laniakea Supercluster 455
Large Hadron Collider. *See* Particle collider
Latter-day Saints. *See* Mormonism
Law, Jeremy T. 400
Law (Laws)
Code of Canon Law 299
Conservation of Energy. *See* Thermodynamics
First Law, Thermodyanics. *See* Thermodynamics
Islamic law (Sharia) 31, 422
Jewish law 131, 160, 196, 245
law of First Mention (hermeneutic) 147, 228
laws (truths) of logic 252, 518
laws of motion. *See* Newton, Isaac
laws of nature (natural law) 51, 298, 325, 326, 365, 374, 400-403, 405, 414, 418, 451, 509, 519, 530, 547, 549, 553, 580
law of parsimony. *See Also* Ockham's razor 313
Second Law, Newton's 416
Second Law, Thermodynamics. *See* Thermodynamics

Lazrus, raising of 173
Le Clerc, Jean 295
Leaning Tower of Pisa Effect 417, 418
Lectures
Gifford Lectures 387
Lowell Lectures 307
Legends 137, 172, 234, 239, 242-244, 246-248, 273-276, 278, 281, 303
Legend Hypothesis (resurrection) 172, 234, 242-244, 246, 281
Leibniz, Gottfried Wilhelm von 55, 524
Leidenhag, Mikael 401
Lemaire, Andre 134
Lemaître, Georges, Fr. 10
Lemba
Ark. *See* Ark of God's Covenant, Lemba Ark
tribe 117, 119, 140
Lemming cosmologists 415, 452, 453, 502
Letter to Hedibia (literary work) 220
Level, Higher (high-level). *See* High-level
Leviticus (book, Hebrew / Christian Bible) 84
Licinius, Roman Emperor 161, 162
Licona, Michael
Michael Licona 146, 187, 194, 235
The Case for the Resurrection of Jesus (literary work) 194
The historicity of the resurrection of Jesus: historiographical considerations in the light of recent debates (literary work) 146
The Resurrection of Jesus: A New Historiographical Approach (literary work) 188, 235
Life
alien. *See* Alien 39, 555, 556
earliest forms of 581
meaning of life 2, 33
Origins-of-Life research 367, 375, 400, 405
prebiotic 375, 376, 400
prokaryotic 573
protobiotic 378
sentient 11, 325, 374
Light, wave-particle duality of. *See* Wave-particle duality
Lightman, Alan (epigraph) 409
LIGO. *See* Observatory, LIGO
Likelihood ratio. *See* Bayes' theorem, likelihood ratio
Linearity (linear approximation) 524
List of Prohibited Books. *See* Index Librorum Prohibitorum
Literary primacy 148, 184, 185, 187

Lithium Problem. *See* Problems in cosmology, Lithium Problem

Lithium-6 473, 474

Lithium-7 473, 474

Lloyd, Seth 478

Locke, John 294, 295

Locus of control 583

Logic

circular 49, 51, 115, 118, 340, 357, 400, 415, 456, 518, 519, 524, 542

deductive 19, 42, 44, 54, 251, 309, 311, 319, 329, 333, 334, 409, 506

existence of logic, impossible to prove outside of 4D-spacetime 546

inductive 54, 310

inferential logic 311

laws (truths) of logic. *See* Law, laws of logic

logical loop 401

mathematical 546

propositional logic 251, 507

syllogism 506, 508, 517, 518, 528, 530

Logical coherencies 4, 16, 28, 49, 52, 53, 65, 107, 199, 250, 271, 280, 311, 315, 317, 318, 320, 322, 334, 336, 340, 362, 394, 395, 402, 406, 440, 442, 445, 469, 516, 521, 537, 541, 562, 568, 572, 573, 585

Logical incoherencies 17, 53, 55, 297, 315, 336, 338, 340, 341, 344, 357, 381, 388, 390, 404, 445, 553, 573, 585

Logos (Greek) 46, 107, 284, 290

Loop

God as a continuous loop 340

Loop quantum gravity. *See* Gravity, Loop Quantum Gravity

Low-level 19, 373, 389-391

Lower-order 222, 299, 364, 373

Lucian of Samosata (*See Also* Death of Peregrinus) 123, 209

Lüdemann, Gerd 235

Luke. *See* Gospel of Luke

Luminosity. *See* Brightness, luminosity

Luther, Martin 158

M-source (Gospels) 202, 223

M-theory. *See* Multiverse

M31. *See* Andromeda Galaxy

M33. *See* Triangulum Galaxy

Macarius, Bishop of Jerusalem 122

MacDougall, Duncan 437

Mach, Ernst 524

Madigan, Kevin 288

Malachi, biblical prophet 202, 289

Malmquist bias 457

Manoogian, John III. *See* Bias, map of

Many-Faced God Conundrum 18, 23, 336, 357, 364, 537, 546, 552, 553, 575

Mara bar Sarapion 123, 206

Mar Saba Letter (literary work) 169, 170, 217

Marcion of Sinope 163, 176, 222, 298, 299

Marcionism (Docetism) 222, 299

Marcionites 162, 163, 176, 236, 249, 270, 298, 540

Marduk, deity 117, 239

Marinus 220

Mark the Evangelist. *See* Gospel of Mark

Martyr

apostles / disciples of Jesus 171, 195, 200

first Christian martyr (*See Also* Stephen) 203, 235, 248

general context 144, 200, 242

list of Christian marytrs recgonized as saints 169

members of ant colony 360

Martyr, Justin 123, 203, 204, 207, 271

Mary Magdalene (also Gospel of Mary) 132-134, 166, 192, 210, 212, 215, 218, 234

Mary

mother of Jesus 130, 133, 134, 138, 157, 163, 174, 180, 191, 192, 195, 215, 262, 301, 336

virginity of Mary / virginal birth of Jesus 130, 157, 180, 191, 195, 245, 249, 255, 262, 299, 301

Mary, name on Talpiot ossuary, uncertain who this Mary is 133, 134, 138

Masoretic text 151

Mass-energy. *See* Energy, mass-energy

Material Beings 527, 547, 564

Matter-energy. *See* Energy, matter-energy

Matter-antimatter ratio 466

Matthew the Apostle. *See* Gospel of Matthew

Maxentius, Roman Emperor 161

McCullagh, C. Behan 185, 186

McGrew, Timothy 332

Measure Problem. *See* Problems in cosmology, Measure Problem

Mecca 35

Melamine (nucleobase molecule) 376

Mental models 423, 424, 426, 427, 575, 581

Messiah (messianic)

Jewish Messiah 192

meaning of the word 242, 243

messianic figure 276, 289

messianic prophecy 237

Messiah (*continued*)

   multiple Messiahs 243

Meta-synthesis 3, 42

Meta-Transignification hypothesis 323, 325

Metallicity Problem. *See* Problems in cosmology, Metallicity Problem

Metaphysical

   impossibility 512, 514, 523

   infinity 512, 516, 522, 523, 530

   possibility 511, 512

   necessity 318-320, 326, 344, 500

Metaphysics (literary work) 372

Metric time. *See* Time, metric (differentiated) time

Metzger, Bruce (*See Also* Criteria, internal and external evidence) 220

Miaphysites 300

Microtubules (illustration) 442

Microtubules (tubulins) 441-445, 449

Milky Way 11, 34, 35, 37, 39, 78, 453, 455, 464, 545, 579

Milky Way-Andromeda merger 37

Miller–Urey experiment 375

Mind-body 324, 325, 372, 373, 390, 547

Mind-brain (mind-brain consciousness) 33, 373, 407, 426, 428, 430, 432, 433, 527, 544, 555, 576, 588

Mind-matter 387

Miracle-claim (miracle-making) 41, 44, 77, 188, 272, 362

Mithra, deity 239

MJH. *See* Arguments, Mortal Jesus Hypotheis

Mlodinow, Leonard 318

Modalism (also called Sabellianism, Monarchianism, Patripassianism)

   290, 299, 396

Model-making 433, 434, 448, 545

Moloch, deity 90, 93, 96, 538

Moltmann, Jürgen 388

Monadic (property or attribute of God) 299, 317, 320, 326, 344, 345, 388, 395, 399, 405, 520, 531, 541

Modal monarchianism. *See* Modalism

Monism (*See Also* Dualism) 373, 374, 401, 433, 449, 544, 547, 555

Monolatrism

   definition of 87, 88

   definition (Table: Types of Theism) 87

   Jewish monolatrism (monolatry, monolatrous) 87, 88, 90, 92, 94-96, 103, 106, 111, 180, 184, 305, 346, 393, 404, 538

Monopole Problem. *See* Problems in cosmology, Monopole Problem

Monotheism 83, 87, 88, 90, 99, 106, 180, 184, 346, 382, 384, 393, 404, 540, 556

Monotheism, definition of (Table: Types of Theism) 87

Monotonic progression 489

Montanism 162, 290

Montgomery, John Warkwick 243

Moody, Raymond 437

Moral relativism 77, 325

Morals (Morality) 11, 17, 18, 23, 26-28, 55, 56, 63, 77, 109, 144, 146, 239, 243, 307, 314, 315, 325, 327, 363, 393, 581, 588

Mormonism

   Book of Mormon (literary work) 172, 352

   compared to Pantheism 549

   immanent God, concept of 72

   Mormonism 72, 76, 87, 172, 176, 352, 353

   Six Towers of God worldview, placement 565

   The Church of Jesus Christ of Latter-day Saints 107, 166, 271, 352

Morphodynamics. *See* Autocells, morphodynamics

Mortal Jesus Hypothesis (MJH) 246-249

Moser, Paul 76

Moses, biblical prophet 69, 93, 94, 111, 114, 116-119, 140, 174

Mount

   Mount Horeb 116

   Mount of Olives 137

   Mount Sinai 116

   Mount Zion 117, 135

   Mt. Olympus 159

   Temple Mount 117

Movement

   Jesus Movement 152, 203

   Jewish movement 130, 248

   jihadist movement 26

   New Sciences of Religion movement. *See* New Sciences of Religion

   Pluralism, movement 353

   Post-Reformation movement 292

   Protestant Reformation movement 158, 176, 300

   Restorational (Mormonism) movement 352

Mufti (Grand). *See Also* Imam and Mujtahid 423

Muhammad, prophet of Islam 148, 310, 343, 422

Mujtahid. *See Also* Imam and Mufti 423

Multiverse (M-theory)

an atheistic position 312

as used in the context of Meta-Transignification hypothesis 324

BGV theorem, applicability to the multiverse 513

Cosmon Field Model, is compatible with or altogether avoids creation of multiverse 485, 494, 496, 499

chaotic cosmic inflation, responsible for creating multiverse 495

cosmic inflation, responsible for creating multiverse 462

cosmic inflation, short-lived indicates no multiverse 463

created by quantum randomness 472

definition of 11

inanimate substance responsible for creation of multiverse 404

KCA 506-509, 511, 513, 516-518, 522, 523, 526, 528-531

m-theory contrasted against Richard Swinburne's assertion his ideas are scientific 312

multiverse as an explanation for the Cold Spot of the CMB 475, 479

multiverse filled with Boltzmann Brains 472, 501

multiverse, a precursor to the creation of our universe and property of time 513, 514, 519

possibilities within Tower 3, 4, and 5 — Six Towers of God paradigm 561-563

possibility of multiverse in definition of a Trascendant or Immanent God (illustrations) 550, 551

property of time may not exist as a global property 514

W. L. Craig, not in favor of multiverse idea 514

W. L. Craig, ambiguity of words 'universe' and 'multiverse' in KCA 517

Muon (elementary particle) 490, 491

Mysticism

Apophatic. *See* Apophaticism

Cataphatic (Kataphatic). *See* Cataphaticsim

Christian mysticism (*See Also* Apophaticism and Cataphaticism) 70, 71, 507

esoteric mysticism 345

Gnostic Mysticism 169

Jewish Mysticism 152, 153, 169, 205, 335

Theistic (theological) mysticism 23, 365, 585

Mythological Hypothesis (resurrection) 234, 239, 240, 242

Mythology

Egyptian 91, 239

Greek 239, 241

Norse 239

Roman 87, 239

Sumerian 85

Nag Hammadi library. *See* Codices, Nag Hammadi library

Nail (Nails)

Noah's Ark 115

number of Roman nails found 124

one, in hand bone 124

one, in heel bone 124

rusty (Jesus' crucifixion) 15

three, retained by Emperess Helena 122

two, in / near the Caiaphas ossuary 124

NASA

Ames Astrochemistry Laboratory 377

Exoplanet Archive 34

Hubble Space Telescope 35

Natural theology (*See Also* Ramified Natural Theology and Bare Natural Theology)

definition of 44, 265

general references to 44, 258-260, 265, 308, 335, 530, 543, 552

prohibits supernatural claims 44, 265

underpins most arguments favoring God's existence 552

Naturalism

Religious 44

Traditional 44

NDE. *See* Near-death experience

Neanderthal 64, 85, 86, 434

Near-death experience (NDE) 437, 438, 444-446

Near-Earth object (NEO) 552

Nebuchadnezzar II, King 117

Necropolis, Dominus Flevit 137

Nehushtan 94

Negative theology. *See* Apophaticism

NEO. *See* Near-Earth object

Nero, Roman Emperor 208

Nestorian Church 300

Nestorianism 162

Nestorius 300

Neurobiology (and God) 434

Neuron (illusration) 442

Neurons 422, 427, 438, 441-443, 449

Neuronal 422, 427, 438, 442, 445, 449, 544

Neuroscience (neuroscientific) 4, 41, 42, 58, 146, 367, 373, 404, 409, 428, 432-434, 445, 577

Neurotheology 4, 41, 42, 59, 409, 422, 432, 433

Neutrino

clumping of neutrinos (neutrino lump fluid) 490, 492, 494, 502

electron neutrino 490, 491

growing mass, slows speed of neutrinos 487, 488, 490

light, intermediate, heavy mass 491

mass of 491

muon neutrino 490, 491

neutrino particles (general) 19, 325, 373, 414, 457, 488, 490-492, 494, 502, 572

supernova SN 1987a, neutrino / photon conundrum 457

sterile neutrino 491, 492, 572

tau neutrino 490, 491

time in history first neutrino created 454

Neutron particle 10, 312, 373, 414, 458, 520

New Atheists 64, 177, 431

New Scienes of Religion (NSoR) 59, 349, 358, 361-367, 387

New Testament

1 Corinthians. *See* Corinthians, First

1 John. *See* Johannine

1 Timothy 294, 295

Acts. *See* Acts of the Apostles

completeness of 151

epistles. *See* Epistles

Galatians. *See* Galatians

Gospel of John. *See* Gospel of John

Gospel of Luke. *See* Gospel of Luke

Gospel of Mark. *See* Gospel of Mark

Gospel of Matthew. *See* Gospel of Matthew

gospels. *See* Gospels (canonical / biblical)

number of books in New Testament 175, 304

Revelation, book of. *See* Johannine

Newberg, Andrew 41, 42, 421, 424, 428, 433, 434

Newton, Isaac

Arian-like views 292

author's idol 55

death of 295

quote (epigraph), attribution of causality to natural things 283

law of universal gravity 416

laws of motion 312, 416

Newton's Christology (Arianism and Socinianism) 297

Holy Trinity 293

Isaac Newton 55, 283, 292-297, 304, 312, 416, 524, 541

The Newton Project 295

Ngoma lungundu (sacred wooden drum) 118, 119

Nicene Creed. *See* Creed, Nicene

Niceno-Constantinopolitan Creed. *See* Creed, Niceno-Constantinopolitan

Nicodemus 197

Nihilism 23

Nirvana 509

No-Boundary Proposal (Hartle-Hawking). *See* Cosmogonic models

Noachian 114, 116

Noah

Noah's Ark (boat) 114-116, 140, 539

Noah's Ark Ministries International 115

flood story 115

size of Noah's Ark 114

Nobel Prize 355, 453, 467, 468

Nolan, Bruce (movie Bruce Almighty) 189

Nomological 512, 514, 516, 522, 530, 572

Non-spatial 323, 508, 529, 549

Noncanonical (extra-biblical) 148, 158, 166, 167, 172, 187, 192, 203, 205, 210, 231, 285, 288

Nonbelievers 1, 146, 160, 165, 363, 555, 585

Noncognitivism, theological 340, 342

Noncognitivist 572

Nones, the (group of the unaffiliated / irreligious) 30, 183, 350

Nonexistence 70, 307, 313, 361, 394, 557, 571

Nonlinearity 374, 390, 402, 403, 416, 417

Nonreductive functionalism 359

Nonreligious. *See Also* Irreligious 13, 31, 33, 57, 183, 422, 425

Nontheism (nontheistic, nontheist) 46, 146, 308, 323, 327, 366, 404, 433, 556, 566, 588

Nontrinitarian (-ism) 107, 396

Nonviolence. *See* Intellectual nonviolence

Noosphere 385

Nothingness 11, 318, 446, 462, 470, 479, 511, 513, 521, 522, 527, 531

Noumenon (noumenal) 356

Novatianism 162

NSoR. *See* New Sciences of Religion

Nucleosynthesis (primordial) 473

OAEM. *See* Ending of Gospel of Mark, Original Authentic Ending of Mark

Oath Against Modernism (literary work) 25

Obama, Barack 422

objective truth. *See* Truth, objective truth

Observable universe 9, 34, 35, 316, 454, 455, 458, 462, 464, 474, 475, 478, 484, 496, 497

Observatory
    Grand Observer's. *See* Grand Observer
    IceCube Neutrino 491
    LIGO (Laser Interferometer Gravitational-Wave) 467, 468
    Vatican 25
Ockham's razor 313, 447, 519, 546, 567
Odds, posterior or prior. *See* Bayes' theorem, Odds form of equation
Okoro, Kingsley 239
Old Testament. *See* Bible (Old Testament)
Omega point 385, 577
Omni-perfections 72, 288, 381, 538, 542
Omnibenevolence 71, 72, 79, 87, 382, 384
Omnipotence (omnipotent)
    Abrahamic theologies believe in God's omnipotence 343
    biblical claims of Jesus' omnipotence 286-288, 541
    challenges of a multi-Person / multiple gods 322
    Classical theism defend's God's omnipotence 87, 382
    definition of (as a property of God) 70, 71
    God's omnipotence challenges free will 384
    God's omnipotence is complex not simple 314
    Metatransignification hypothesis, God may not be omnipotent 323
    Perfect Being Theology 72
    personal / doctrinal belief versus justified belief 545
    Pope John Paul II espouses God's omnipotence (epigraph) 183
    R. Swinburne's Bayesian analysis, a claim of the "traditional kind" 258
    Richard Swinburne, one of God's necessary properties 309, 314, 315, 320
    W. L. Craig, Christian God is not omnipotent 513, 519
Omnipresence 71, 72, 79, 87, 314, 315, 382, 384, 529, 549, 553
Omnitemporal 71, 79
Ontogeny 426
Ontological Argument 307, 326, 343
Ontology 19, 50, 346, 357, 510, 519, 544, 558, 577
Optimism bias. *See* Bias, types of, Optimism
Oral testimony / transmission 15, 119, 141, 156, 160, 161, 172, 203, 219, 223-225, 228, 239, 247, 249, 272, 276, 285, 304, 328
Orch OR (Orchestrated Objective Reduction) model of consciousness
    objective threshold 440, 443
    founding developers of the Orch OR model 443

Orch OR 438, 440, 441, 443, 445, 449, 544
    orchestrated resonance 443
    orchestration, lack of 443
Oral tradition 119, 160, 161, 225, 239, 247, 249, 276
Origen of Alexandria (also called Origen Adamantius)
    Contra Celsus—Against Celsus—(literary work) 210
    first to prepare a (Christian) systematic theology 435
    Greek Church Father 160, 174
    no awareness of final ending to Gospel of Mark 220
    on the human soul 436
    Origen De Principiis (literary work) 436
Original Bible. *See* Codex, autographic
Origins-of-Life. *See* Life, Origins-of-Life
Orthodox
    Eastern (Greek) Orthodox 70, 120, 158, 250, 292, 300, 335, 339, 345, 396, 400, 537, 541
    Oriental Orthodox 70, 169, 291, 300, 400
    Orthodox Christian 70, 176, 300, 396, 537
    Western (Latin) Orthodox 70, 71, 90, 152, 158, 160, 170, 290, 292, 300, 335, 339, 345, 396, 438, 444, 509, 537, 541
Orthodoxification, elimination of some religions, creation of new ones 556
Orthopraxy 163
Oscillating (Cyclic) model. *See* Cosmogonic models, Cyclic...
Oscillations
    Orch OR model of consciousness, oscillations 442, 443
    Cosmon Field Model 489
    oscillations in dark energy 494
Osiris, deity 100, 239, 538
Ossilegium. *See* Burial, secondary
Ossuary
    Caiaphas ossuary (*See Also* Caiaphas, Joseph) 124, 125, 233
    Dominus Flevit ossuaries 138
    James Ossuary. *See* James the Apostle, James Ossuary
    list of eleven ossuaries 133
    Talpiot ossuaries. *See* Talpiot Tomb A and Talpiot Tomb B
Otherness (nature of God) 336, 341
Otherworld 399
Out-group 17
Outside-in (paradigm). *See* Approach (es)
Over-curvature. *See* Singularity, cosmological, curvature / over-curvature

Pagan (paganism) 88, 89, 92, 95, 96, 104, 122, 123, 158, 159, 161, 162, 179, 203, 204, 207, 210, 231, 233, 239, 240, 246, 249, 270, 276-278, 281, 289, 290, 305, 548

Pagels, Elaine 172

Paine, Thomas (epigraph) 22, 63

Panentheism (panentheistic)

    Christian and non-Christian 384, 405, 542

    definition of (Table: Types of Theism) 88, 382

    general Panentheism 388, 389, 401-403, 405

    Meta-Transignification hypothesis 327

    Modern Christian Panentheism 59, 342, 345, 367, 381, 386, 388, 392, 401, 537, 542, 543

    New Sciences of Religion, panentheistic ideas 364

    NSoR and zetetics, compatible with Panentheism? 365

    Paul Davies' version 383, 402, 403, 406

    Six Towers of God worldview, placement 565

    summary, Panentheism lack of coherency 404

    zetetic journey outline, review of Panentheism 57

Pannenberg, Wolfhart 154

Panpsychism 444, 445, 544

Pantheism (Pantheistic)

    definition of (Table: Types of Theism) 88, 382

    Pantheism 25, 72, 88, 159, 327, 382, 386, 401, 404, 549

    Six Towers of God worldview, placement 565

PAP. *See* Agnosticism, PAP

Papal primacy 107, 300

Papal universal jurisdiction 300

Paraintellect. *See* Intution

Parameters

    fundamental parameters of the universe 317, 318, 402, 406, 458, 488, 514

    Hubble parameter. *See* Hubble, Hubble constant

Paranormal 361, 445

Parfitt, Tudor 117-119

Parsons, Keith M. 314, 322, 323

Partially-justified beliefs / faith. *See* Faith, partially-justified

Particle collider 415

Particles

    anti-particles 454

    axion 498

    baryons 458

    charged particles 415

    composite particles 373, 414, 458

    cosmon. *See* Cosmon particle

    electron. *See* Electron particle, rest mass

    elementary 413

    fermions 373, 414

    free particles 19

    gluon 373, 520

    graviton. *See* Graviton particle

    Higgs boson. *See* Higgs, boson

    inflaton. *See* Inflaton particle / field

    leptons 414

    muons 490, 491

    neutrino. *See* Neutrino

    neutron. *See* Neutron particle

    photon. *See* Photon particle

    proton 10, 312, 373, 414, 454, 458, 493

    positron 10

    quarks. *See* Quark particle

    subatomic particles. *See* Subatomic particles

    virtual particles 509

Particularist Universalism (NSoR) 360

Passion Narrative 202, 219, 223, 271

Passover 191, 192, 197

Past-eternal 71, 460, 477, 479, 484, 492, 497, 499, 503, 511, 516, 523, 531

Past eternity (Cosmon Field Model) 484, 496, 501

Past-eternality (static, Emergent Universe model) 481

Past-finitude 523

Past-infinity 481, 484, 498

Patai, Raphael 95

Path incompleteness 458

Patina 134, 135, 137, 139

Patio Tomb. *See* Talpiot Tomb B

Patripassianism. *See Also* Modalism 299, 396

Patternicity. *See* Bias, types of, Patternicity

Patterson, Stephen 238

Paul the Apostle (Saul of Tarsus)

    alive at time of Marcionites & Ebionites 236

    appearance of Jesus to Paul as a metaphor 239

    appearance of Jesus to Paul as a legend 243

    biblical quotes of. *See* Paul the Apostle, biblical quotations

    Christian claim, post-death appearance of Jesus to 195

    conversion of 195, 203, 235, 273

    coexistence with Roman rulers 203

    date of first letter (1 Thessalonians) 201

    did not report seeing Jesus as a corporeal body 239, 273, 288

    earliest testimony of Jesus' resurrection 224

    first appearance of Jesus 213

    Jesus' burial & empty tomb 198, 227, 288

Paul the Apostle (*continued*)

never met Jesus 199, 227

number of instances Paul directly mentions Jesus' appearance 226

ordering of Paul's letters in Bible 177

Paul's death 200

Pauline ministry 168

Pauline Epistles (letters) 156, 163

persecution of Christians 248

purpose of writing letters 275

rank, historical value of testimony 228

Saul of Tarsus 159, 203, 229, 235

testimony of Jesus' resurrection 224

timing of written testimony after Jesus' death 225

timing of when Jesus appeared to Paul / Saul 235

trance state (Jesus appearance) 173, 275

traveling companion, Luke the Evangelist? 228

Paul the Apostle, biblical quotations

direct from Paul, 1 Corinthians 224, 226

direct from Paul, Galatians 225, 226

indirectly, Acts of the Apostles 229

Pavlovian 34

Peace (Peaceful, Peacefully)

man's need for a comforting philosophy 13

no peace between religious institutions without dialogue (epigraph) 349, 365

NSoR and Hick's pluralistic ideals lack achievement of peaceful co-existence 363

religious and scientific ignorance challenge future peace 367

religious zealots (violent) versus peace-giving faithful 16

respecting individual choice in religion 66, 584

responsibilities of a peaceful religion to deal with violent adherents 28

Six Towers of God offer peace by releasing sectarian discord 587

Peacocke, Arthur 388, 401

Peeples, Molly 35

Peirce, Charles S. 387, 394, 395, 399, 400, 542

Penrose, Roger 443

Perfect Being Theology 72, 318, 326, 367, 405, 538

Perichoresis 107, 406, 541-543

Perimeter of God's existence 79, 342, 537, 554, 556, 557, 565, 571, 573, 575

Perlovsky, Leonid 423

Persinger, Michael 433

Personal Religious (Revelatory) Experience (Argument for God's existence) 307

Phaedo (literary work) 232, 435

Pharisee 197, 203, 206, 343

Phenomenology 308

Philo-Judaeus of Alexandria 205

Philology 140, 147, 153

Philosophy

beginnings of philosophy 86

closed-minded philosophy 14

Continental Philosophy 308

dead-ended philosophy 309

Father of modern philosophy 438, 535

Philosophy of Mind 3, 19, 544

Philosophy of Science 312, 359

Philosphy of Religion 3, 69, 308, 314, 323, 338, 353, 354

Process Philosophy. *See* Process Theology

simple philosophy (wisdom), what the Common Man wants 2, 4, 56, 367, 582, 588

systematic philosophy 4

unenlightened personal philosophy 2

Vedic philosophy 12

Philostratus the Athenian 234

Photon particle 9, 19, 317, 373, 391, 414, 457, 484, 486, 491

Phylogeny 426

Physical singularity. *See* **Singularity, cosmological**

Pithoi 97-100, 102-105

Pithos A 97-99, 102-105

Pithos B 97

Piyamanotham, Wallop 235, 236

Plague

Antonine Plague (Plague of Galen) 160

Plauge of Cypria 160

Planck

constant 317, 468

density 488

length 486

mass 483, 486, 488

scale 418, 481

space observatory / collaboration 9

temperature 10

time 10, 468, 480, 486, 515

units 483, 484

Planets

Earth-like / Earth-sized. *See* Exoplanet

habitable 34, 36, 555

number of Earth-like planets in universe 35

number of intelligence-bearing planets in Milky Way

Planets (*continued*)

    from birth to after it combines with Andromeda 37

    number of intelligenec-bearing planets in universe 37

Plantinga, Alvin 355

Plato (Platonism, Platonian, Platonists)

    birth and death 447

    Gnostics and Platonists, belief in immortal soul 179

    influence on Penrose-Hameroff Orch OR model 444

    influenced Clement of Alexandria 169, 232

    influenced Origen of Alexandria 435

    influenced Philo-Judeas of Alexandria 205

    influenced Plotonus 384

    influenced Thomas Aquinas 374

    Phaedo (On the Soul) -- literary work 232, 435

    Plato's view of the soul 435

Plausibility test. *See* Historicity Tests, Plausibility

Plemora (divine place) 168, 209, 249, 540

Pliny the Younger 208, 211

Plotinus 374, 384

Pluralism (pluralistic)

    cognitive pluralism. *See* Cognitive pluralism

    Dalai Lama XIV (epigraph) 349

    incoherency of pluralism 341, 404

    John Hick's Pluralism 353-357

    John Hick's view, Jesus is a metaphor 242

    methodical pluralism, the zetetic approach 41, 42

    NSoR, shares pluralistic ideas 362

    potential refuge from incoherent Abrahamic concepts 342, 353

    summary, effectiveness of John Hick's pluralism 366, 542

    William Lane Craig, student of John Hick 506

Plurality, number of deities

    Kalam Cosmological Argument 506

    major religions believe in multiple deities 556

    Many-Faced God Conundrum 552

    multiple Bes (Egyptian) deities 105

    neutral perspective 550, 551

    Six Towers of God paradigm, plurality unknown 557, 570

    Six Towers of God worldview, placement 565

Pneuma (Gnostic spirit) 165

Pneumatology 299

Polkinghorne, John 388

Poltergeists 322

Polycarp, Bishop of Smyrna (knew John the Apostle) 160, 161, 174, 207, 222, 290

Polyfaith. Compare with Syncretism and Polysemism 163

Polysemism 32

Polytheism

    Christianity and Judaism as polytheistic religions 159

    definition of 87

    definition of (Table: Types of Theism) 87

    most dominant view of God across human history 86, 233

    orthodoxification eliminated many forms of polytheism 556

Pontius Pilate (Pontius Pilatus) 124, 157, 196, 208, 247, 283

Pope

    Benedict XVI (epigraph) 143, 292, 383

    Callixtus I (Callistus I) 299

    Clement I (Clement of Rome) 160, 161, 207, 210, 285, 290

    Francis 40, 41, 128, 336, 337

    Innocent III (epigraph) 107, 143

    John Paul II (epigraph) 23, 25, 26, 63, 183, 355, 383

    Pius IX 25

    Sixtus V 169, 170

Popkonstantinov, Kazimir 120

Population

    ancient Jewish population 191

    world population (charts) 68, 349, 350

Positive theology. *See* Cataphaticism

Positivism, scientific 345

Possibilism. *See* Block Universe, Growing Block Universe

Post-death appearances (list of all biblical accounts) 212

Post-death appearances of Jesus 195, 198, 199, 211, 217, 223-225, 229, 233, 249, 256, 273

Posterior odds. *See* Bayes' theorem, posterior probability

Posterior probability. *See* Bayes' theorem, posterior probability

Pragmaticism (Pragmatism) 49, 109, 394

Pre-universe 323, 462, 495, 509, 516-523, 525, 527, 528, 530, 531, 548, 554, 560-562, 568

Preheating (cosmic inflation) 473

Preponderance of evidence 42, 153, 222, 279, 318

Presentism (Nowism). Compare to Block Universe 525

Prime Mover (Unmoved Mover) 371, 372, 381, 405, 563

Primordial

primordial cosmic clay 588

primordial cosmic inflation 462, 489

primordial density waves 467

primordial gravitational waves 467, 468, 473, 494

primordial nucleosynthesis 473

Principle

Anthropic cosmological principle 1, 8

bedrock principle, use of cumulative evidence 311, 458

Causal Principle 310

first principle, Richard Feynman (epigraph) 409

Heisenberg uncertainty principle. *See* Quantum mechanics, uncertainty principle

list of hermeneutical principles 147

Literary Primacy 185

holographic principle. *See* Holographic principle

PAP and TAP, agnostic principles. *See* Agnosticism

principles of Firstness, Secondness, and Thirdness 399

principles of life, liberty, and self-determination 56, 67, 363, 582, 584

principles, Truth Criteria. *See* Truth Criteria

Principle of Credulity. *See* Swinburne, Richard, Principle of Credulity

Principle of Reciprocity 84

Principle of Testimony. *See* Swinburne, Richard, Principle of Testimony

Prior, the. *See* Bayes' theorem, prior probability

Prior odds. *See* Bayes' theorem, prior probability

Priority

causal priority, the zetetic process 43

Marcan. *See* Gosepl of Mark, Marcan priority

Matthaean. *See* Gospel of Matthew, Matthaean Priority

Priscilliam, Bishop of A'vila 176

Probability

Bayesian inferential probability. *See* Bayes' theorem, Bayesian inference

epistemic probability. *See* Bayes' theorem, epistemic probability

frequentist probability. *See* Frequentist probability

mathematical probability 39, 250, 251, 309, 503, 521, 522, 524, 527, 561

non-zero probability for God's existence 15

odds. *See* Bayes' theorem, Odds form

posterior probability. *See* Bayes' theorem, posterior probability

prior probability. *See* Bayes' theorem, prior probability

Six Towers of God paradigm, not all towers

equiprobable 567

statistical probability (prediction) 2, 132, 136, 471, 472, 514, 569

Timeless existence of mathematical probability 521

Problems in cosmology

Matter-Antimatter Asymmetry Problem 464, 466

Boltzmann Brain Problem 464, 471-473, 481, 496, 502, 527

Cosmological Constant Problem 464, 486

Flatness Problem 464, 465

Fine-Tuning Problem 464

Horizon Problem 464, 465, 473, 474, 481

Large-Scale Structure Problem 464, 474, 496

Lithium Problem 464, 473, 474

Measure Problem 464, 471

Metallicity Problem 464, 466, 480

Monopole Problem 464

Singularity Problem. *See* Singularity, cosmological

Smallness Problem 486

Structure Problem 464, 466, 474, 496

Problem of Evil. *See* Evil, Problem of Evil and Evil, theodicy

Problem of the Priors. *See* Bayes' theorem, Problem of the Priors

Problem of Time. *See* Quantum mechanics, Problem of Time...

Process Theology (Process Metaphysics, Process Philosophy)

definition of 386

Process Metaphysics 386, 389

Process Philosophy 386-388, 405, 444, 542

Process Theology 3, 88, 384, 386, 387, 389, 392, 405, 531, 537, 542

Process Theology, doesn't address concept of eternity 390

Process Philosophy. *See* Process Theology

Prophet. *See* specific name of prophet (Abraham, Elijah, Ezekiel, Isaiah, Jeremiah, Jesus of Nazareth, John the Baptist, Malachi, Moses, Muhammad)

Protestantism (Protestant) 25, 29, 30, 40, 72, 120, 143, 144, 155, 158, 176, 235, 292, 294, 300, 335, 336, 350, 352, 355, 366, 587

Protestant Reformation 158, 176, 292

Proto-Christianity (compare with quasi-Christianity)

definition of 162

proto-Christianity 158, 178, 179, 203, 206, 209, 222, 233, 284, 285, 290, 299, 302, 305, 435, 539, 540

Proto-consciousness 443-445, 449

Proto-orthodox (*See Also* Proto-Christian) 162, 163, 165, 174, 175

Protocell 375

Protolife 379, 380, 405

Proton particle 10, 312, 373, 414, 454, 458, 493

Pseudepigrapha 166, 167

Pseudo-rationality 585

Pseudo-religion 85, 363

Pseudo-static 490, 495, 501

Pseudorealism. *See* Six Towers of God worldview

Pseudoscience 312, 409, 495

Psychical visions 173, 212, 273

Psychogenesis 385

Ptah-Seker-Osiris, deity 100

Ptolemaic (era or dynasty) 100, 101

Ptolemy, Claudius 372

Pulitzer Prize 269

Purgatory 301, 302

Pyrimidine (nucleotide molecule) 377

Q-source (Gospels) 202, 223

Quaker 358, 387

Quantal Bohmian trajectories 498

Quantized 324, 486

Quantum
    clock. *See* Time, quantum clock
    coherence 440, 442-444
    decoherence. *See Also* Wave function, collapse 440
    foam 324
    gravity. *See* Gravity, quantum gravity
    indeterminism (*See Also* Quantum mechanics, uncertainty principle) 438, 465
    nonlocality and entanglement 8, 444, 445, 478, 526
    superposition 318, 441
    states 318, 324, 439-441, 444, 449, 469, 472
    tensor network 526
    virtual particles 509
    wave function collapse (reduction). *See* Wave function, collapse

Quantum mechanics
    Bohm's Interpretation of 498
    Everett Interpretation 472, 498
    Many-Worlds Interpretation 11, 462, 472
    observer Effect of quantum 440
    Problem of Time, quantum gravity 469
    Problem of Time, quantum mechanics / field theory 494, 519
    uncertainty principle (*See Also* Quantum, indeterminism) 354, 439

Quark particle 10, 19, 312, 373, 380, 414, 458, 520

Quasar 9, 474, 553, 580

Quasi-Christianity (compare with proto-Christianity)
    abundance of cults 539
    Christian-like sects (early Christians) 153, 160, 161, 302
    compared to orthodox and proto-Christians 162
    Constantine I (Constantine the Great) 161
    definition of 153
    lack of extant literary works 236
    literary reference to Jesus and the resurrection 209
    list of sects 162
    on Jesus' humanity and divinity 270
    orthodox Christianity evolved from and in the midst of 278, 302
    quasi-Christian / quasi-Jewish 162

Quasi-time. *See* Time, quasi-time

Quine, Willard Van Orman (*See Also* Duhem-Quine thesis) 524

Quintessence 372, 486, 490

Qumranites 152, 203

Qur'an
    Qur'an 72, 84, 93, 107, 109, 148, 343, 537
    Sura 11 and 71 115

Radicalism, religious. *See* Fanaticism, violent religious

Radiocarbon. *See* C-14 (carbon-14) dating

Raglan, Lord. *See* Somerset, Baron FitzRoy Richard

Raman Spectroscopy. *See* Spectroscopy

Ramified Natural Theology 44, 59, 264, 265, 308, 309, 541

Rationalism 25, 44

Ratzinger, Joseph, Cardinal (*See Also* Pope, Benedict XVI) 355

Reactants 377, 378

Real, the (pluralistic concept by John Hick). *See* Hick, John, Ultimate Reality

Reality-consciousness (Vedic concept) 444

Reality (*See Also* Truth Criteria)
    defintion of 513
    distortions of reality. *See* Bias and Bias, types of
    dualism / monism. *See* Dualism and Monism
    dyadic mental-ordering of reality 428
    external reality (larger reality) apart from the self 45, 146, 407, 424, 544, 584
    external reality (outside of the universe) 548
    extra dimensions of reality. *See* Dimensions, extra-dimensional
    false reality 53, 427

Reality (*continued*)

fundamental truths. *See* Truth Criteria

greater universe. *See* Greater universe

imaginary reality vs. real reality 543

reality as a simulation. *See* Cosmic simulation and Simulation

two-worlds' interpretation of reality 45

the Ultimate / the Real. *See* Hick, John, Ultimate Reality

Reasoning

abductive 19, 42, 54, 185-187, 251, 278, 309, 409

circular 49, 357, 400, 542

deductive 54, 329, 409

inductive 19, 42, 54, 251, 254, 309, 310, 313, 333, 334, 380, 409, 416

reductive 12, 54, 251, 309, 373, 409

Redshift

cosmological 456, 492, 493

gravitational 456

Reductionism (*See Also* Reasoning, reductive) 373

Reformation. *See* Protestant Reformation

Reheating (cosmic inflation) 473

Reincarnation 67, 270

Relativity. *See* General relativity theory and Special relativity theory

Reliability (unreliability)

concerning reliability of Shroud testing 128

credibility of Christian artifacts 201

establishing credibility of fundamental claims of Christianity 161

poor record-keeping introduces reliability concerns with Bible 202

reliability of literary Jesus appearance accounts 217

reliability of our logic 3

Richard Swinburne's "princple of testimony" 265

unreliability of human cognition / mind 43, 434

unreliability of the Gospels (Matthew, Luke, John) 230

using Literary Primacy to adjudicate reliability of historical document 148

Religion-by-whatever-name 34

Religion-science 24, 66, 140, 307, 358, 366, 586

Religion

affiliation, United States adults 351

affiliation worldwide vs. population(chart) 350, 351

beginning (start) to religion 46, 85

defenders of religion 151

definition of, contrasted with spirituality 66

exclusivism. *See* Exclusivism

Great religions 57, 74, 108, 110

major religions (major religious) groups 29, 68, 76, 406

most dominant religion over history 86, 233

Research

investment dollars 411

perils of research 410, 412

Resurrection Hypothesis (RH)

Bayesian 258

Bayesian estimate, Richard Swinburne's 260, 266

Bayesian method as a rival hypothesis (HHTE) 274, 278

HHTE verdict, RH vs. Mortal Jesus Hypothesis 277, 278

summary, faults of Swinburne's Bayesian approach 281

Resurrection

bodily resurrected (Jesus), commentary for and against 194, 213, 214, 217, 229, 230, 239, 270, 273, 275, 283, 288, 541, 553

Claims to uphold Jesus' resurrection actually occurred 195

Claim 1 – Jesus' honorable burial 196, 197

Claim 2 – empty tomb 198, 199

Claim 3 – Paul and James' conversions 199

Claim 4 – Christian martyrs 200

Claim 5 (Part II) – Christian / Non-Christian writers 201, 203, 205, 207, 208

Claim 5 (Part I), 6, and 7 – The Jesus Appearance Accounts 211-217, 219-225, 227, 228, 230, 232, 233

Claim 8 – Alternate Naturalistic Hypotheses 234, 266

evidence for resurrection does not meet historical criteria 193

first authenticated extra-biblical literary references to the Empty Tomb 203

first authenticated extra-biblical literary reference to Jesus' "resurrection" 210

first authenticated non-Christian literary references to the Empty Tomb 204

first authenticated non-Christian literary reference to Jesus (Tacitus refers to "Christus") 208

first authenticated non-Christian literary reference to the Jesus' "resurrection" 210

first authenticated quasi-Christian remarks on "Jesus', "Christ", "resurrection" 209

See Foundational Truth Claims of Christianity

Gnostic gospels that do and do not mention resurrection 170

Gnostics held different interpretation 172

Resurrection (*continued*)

James Ossuary, may refute bodily resurrection of Jesus 134, 135, 137, 139

Jesus survived the resurrection, Michael Baigent 173

most resurrection literature by Bible scholars and philosophers, not historians 187

no resurrection, no Christian God 194, 199, 338

no prior concept of bodily resurrection prior to Jesus 270

testimony in all four NT Gospels 132

Revelation (deific)

divine (supernatural) revelation 44, 69, 148, 265, 308, 396, 552, 570

scriptural revelation 1, 543, 587

Revelation to John (literary work). *See* Johannine

Revelatory experience. *See* Personal Religious (Revelatory) Experience

Revolt. *See* Great Revolt

Rgveda, Hindu 12

RH. *See* Resurrection Hypothesis

Riess, Adam 453

Righteousness 75, 176

Rival theories / hypotheses

Bayes' theorem, rival hypotheses to God's existence 344

Bayes' theorem, rival hypotheses to resurrection hypothesis 255-257

HHTE, rival theories to resurrection hypothesis 186, 234, 274, 277

RNA (ribonucleic acid) 375, 377, 405

RNT. *See* Ramified Natural Theology

Robinson, Andrew 380, 394, 395, 399, 400, 402, 406, 543

Roman Emperor 121, 122, 158, 161, 162, 203, 206, 208, 210, 274, 292, 293, 540

Rubáiyát of Omar Khayyám (literary work) 589, 590

Rubenstein, Mary-Jane 338

Rule

Golden Rule. *See* Hick, John

Simple Rule. *See* Simple Rule

two-generation rule. *See* Two-generation rule

Rushdie, Salman 110

Russell, Bertrand (epigraph) 83, 505, 524

Rylands Papyrus P52 134, 149, 202

S-R-P. *See* Southgate-Robinson-Peirce

Sabellianism. *See Also* Modalism 299, 396

Sabellius 299

Sacks, Jonathan, Chief Rabbi 585

Sacred text 110, 113, 144, 352, 363

Sadducees 203

Sagan, Carl (epigraph) 8, 451

Saint 107, 120, 122, 166, 168-170, 175, 235, 271, 292, 336, 352

Sainthood (sainted) 121, 169, 175

Salvation (soteriology)

personal (eternal, universal) salvation 26, 76, 164, 167, 168, 218, 232, 242, 248, 277, 301, 343, 355, 445

Pope Francis (epigraph) 40

Sanhedrin

Jewish Sanhedrin Council 26, 157, 196, 197, 205, 234, 245, 247, 276

Mishnah Sanhedrin (literary work) 231

Satan (Satanists) 77, 159, 249, 301

The Satanic Verses (literary work) 110

Saul, King 90

Savior, divine 123, 168, 205, 209, 271, 326, 336, 343, 575

Scalar field 473, 475, 486, 489, 527, 553

Schayer, Milton M (letter to, by Einstein) 307

Schelling, Friedrich Wilhelm Joseph von 381, 388, 395, 542

Schism

East-West Schism 158, 335

Great Schism 292, 300

schisms (schismatic) 180, 299, 301, 304, 338, 352

Scholars ("the Dragons") 8, 24-26, 40, 60, 74, 85, 153, 190, 343, 358

Schrödinger, Erwin

Erwin Schrödinger 441

Schrödinger's cat experiment

Schrödinger's equation. *See* Equation, Schrödinger's equation

Science-religion 2, 361, 451

Science-theology 66

Scientism (Argument for God's existence) 307

Scientist, First 372

Scientology 172

SDE. *See* Shared-death experience

Sea of Galilee 190

Sea of Irrationality. *See* Irrational (irrationality) of belief / faith, Sea of Irrationality

Second Coming (of Jesus) 237, 271, 285, 385

Second Law of Motion. *See* Newton, Isaac

Second Law of Thermodynamics. *See* Thermodynamics

Secondness. *See* Principle, principle of Firstness...

Secret Gospel. *See* Gnostic, Secret Gospel of Mark

Secular (secularism, secularist, secularization)

secular 24, 25, 32, 59, 67, 572

Secular Humanist 340, 587

Self-caused 522, 526, 527

Self-Consistent 52

Self-determination. *See* Principle, principles of life...

Self-generated (attribute of God) 70, 106

Self-order 325

Self-organize (self-organizing)

ants 360, 442

autocells (self-organize, self-order) 325, 379

Self-transcendence 32, 431, 583

Semi-consciousness, state of 437

Semi-divine

angels and demons 159

Jesus 162, 180, 222

Semiotics (*See Also* Biosemiotics) 394, 395, 399-401, 405

Septuagint. *See* Bible (Greek), Septuagint

Series, completed / incomplete 511

Settlements (ancient) 89, 91, 92, 105, 538

Seven Sages of Ancient Greece 444

Seven Sins of academic behavior 412

Seventy disciples 199, 225, 226

Sextus Empiricus (wrote manual of skepticism) 77

Shamans 86

Shared-death experience (SDE) 437, 449

Sharia. *See* Law, Islamic law

Sharot, Tali 573

Sheet. *See* Shroud, Sheet

Sherman, Jeremy 377-380, 400, 543

Shermer

Shermer adapts Spinoza's hypothesis. *See Also* Spinoza's conjecture 431

Michael Shermer 428

Sherwin-White, A.N. 243-245

Shiite Muslims (*See Also* Islam) 587

Shimron, Aryeh 135

Shintoism 67

Shroud

age (dating) of the Shroud 126-128

burial shrouds of Jesus, general discussion 125-129

epigraph, dating of the shroud 113

serological testing of the Shroud 127, 138

Sheet 129

Shroud of Oviedo 129, 130, 140

Shroud of Turin 125, 126, 129, 137, 138, 140

Sindonology 125, 126, 129

Vatican curator of the Shroud of Turin 127

Shu, deity 100

Sicarii 203

Sikhism 67, 87

Simmonds, Douglas 115

Simon Peter the Apostle (Cephas) 161, 192, 198, 211, 212, 224, 225, 248

Simple Rule (statistics) 251, 256

Simplism 417, 434, 447

Simpson, Zachary 392

Simulation (*See Also* Cosmic simulation) 564

Simulator Creators / Operators 564

Sin, doctrine of Original 436

Sinaiticus. *See* Codex, Sinaiticus

Sindonology. *See* Shroud, Sindonology

Singularity, Cosmological (the Singularity Problem)

black hole singularity (See footnote) 457

different names for physical singularities 458

conical singularity 458, 459

curvature / over-curvature 458, 470, 483, 492, 498, 502, 523

Great Cosmological Singularity 460, 468, 469, 479, 480, 483, 484, 489, 498, 499

Singularity-free cosmogonic models

Cosmon Field Model 483

Emergent Universe 481

Hartle-Hawking No-Boundary proposal 480

Steady State Eternal Inflation / Aguirre-Gratton proposal 480

Sisyphus' tragedy 11

Six Towers of God worldview (paradigm)

adoption of the paradigm, challenges to 573, 575, 584

agnosticism (PAP and TAP) contrasted with Six Towers 571

category definitions ([U], [T], [O], [E], [K], [M], [C], [S]) 557

Buddhism contrasted with Six Towers of God 583

Deism and Tower 1 contrasted 570, 571

future alteration of the Six Towers of God paradigm 572

grand solution to religious discord 587

Inanimate Substantialism 567, 568

Ignosticism contrasted with Six Towers of God worldview 572

most defensible view on God's existence 576

personal and / or interactive God, least plausible scenario 573, 575

Six Towers of God worldview (*continued*)

plausibility of Six Towers of God worldview 566, 569, 570

"plausibility estimate" of Six Towers of God worldview (illustration) 569

Pseudorealism 567

Religious and Scientific Institutional Change needed (list) 585, 587

Six Towers of God worldview (illustration) 565

Theistic Transcendency 567

Tower 1 – The Purely Transcendent God 559

Tower 2 – The Meta-Transignification Creator 560

Tower 3 – The Adamite-Eveitite Universe 561

Tower 4 – The Branching Multiverse 562

Tower 5 – The Uncaused Temporally Eternal Universe 563

Tower 6 – Tower 6 – Reality as a Simulation / Ultra-Advanced "Aliens" 564

wisdom, a simple philosophy for the Common Man 588

zetetic journey does not end 582

Skepticism

contrasted with zeteticism 43

number of religiously-affiliated NT scholars outnumber skeptic scholars 154

Outlines of Sceptisim (literary work) 77

religion and science, both skeptically examined 56

Slices of time. *See* Time, time slices

Slipher, Vesto 453

Smallness Problem. *See* Problems in cosmology, Smallness Problem

Smith

Joseph Smith, Latter-day Saints founder 271

Mark S. Smith 91-93

Morton Smith 170-172

Socinianism (Socinian) 295, 297

Socrates 54, 232, 386, 435, 447

Socratic method 42

Sol Invictus, deity

colossal bronze statue of 161

worshiped by Roman Emperor Constantine I 161

Solomon, King 90

Solomon's Temple 90, 117, 119

Solomonoff, Ray 313

Soma (neuronal structure) 438, 442

Somerset, Baron FitzRoy Richard (Lord Raglan) 240

Something-ness 318, 470

Sorcerers 32

Sosthenes 224, 230, 236, 275

Sotloff, Steven 422

Soul (*See Also* Near-death experiences)

Anthropo-Cosmogenesis (Teilhard de Chardin) 385

Aristotle's views on the soul 435

attempt to weigh the mass of the soul 437

Augustine's views on the soul 436

Bible does not edify important aspects of the human soul 179, 449

Catholic position 394

Christian versus Islam beliefs 343

divine soul, Cosmic Christ (Teilhard de Chardin) 385

extra-dimensional location of the soul 548

Gnostic beliefs 165, 179, 540

human soul 70, 76, 179, 209, 394, 407, 435, 436, 445, 446, 448, 449

Jainism and Hinduism view on soul 394, 445

Origen's views on the Soul 436

Phaedo (On The Human Soul)—literary work 232, 435

Plato's views on the soul 435, 447

René Descartes, views on the soul 438

Second coming of Jesus introduces urgency for personal salvation 277

scientific overall view on the soul 449

Socrates' views on the soul 435, 447

Stuart Hameroff, views on the soul 444

Thomas Aquinas, unification of Jesus' human and divine soul 287

Thomas Aquinas, views on the soul 436

twelve centuries to develop a Christian doctrine on soul 436

Voltaire, views on the soul 447

World-Soul (Plato and Plotinus) 384

zetetic view on the soul 446

Source, the (God as a hyperessence) 341, 358, 404, 406

Southgate-Robinson-Peirce (S-R-P) 399

Southgate, Christopher 380, 394, 395, 399, 400, 402, 406, 543

Sozinni, Fausto and Lelio 295

Space, three-dimensional (*See Also* Spacetime, four-dimensional)

physical size of. *See* Universe, size

shape of. *See* Universe, shape

spaceless. *See* Spaceless

three-dimensional space 399, 496, 524, 525

vacuum condition during cosmic inflation 472

vacuum energy. *See* Vacuum, vacuum energy

vacuum of space 377, 457, 465, 509

Spacecraft (spaceship) 20, 38, 39, 45, 48, 51, 188, 325, 417

Spaceless (spacelessness) 71, 507, 520, 522

Spacetime, four-dimensional (*See Also* Space, three dimensional and Extra-dimensional)
  definition of 8
  edges of spacetime 9, 462, 479
  expansion of spacetime. *See* Expansion
  frozen block of spacetime 496
  God's existence inside or outside of universe (illustrations) 550, 551
  quantum-connected spacetime. *See* Quantum, tensor network
  quantum theory, spacetime should be significantly curved 465
  ripples in spacetime. *See* Gravitational waves
  singularities. *See* Singularity, Cosmological
  spacetime as a constituent of Reality. *See* Truth Criteria

Sparks
  Gnostic sparks 164, 165, 168, 222, 384, 540, 577
  sparks, Helena Blavatsky, Cosmogenesis (literary work) 384

Special relativity theory 452, 526

Spectroscopy
  Fourier Transform Infrared spectroscopy (FTIR) 127
  Raman spectroscopy 127

Spelke, Elizabeth 426

Sperry, Roger 373

Spilka, Bernard 65

Spinoza, Baruch 430

Spinoza's conjecture 431

Spirituality
  definition of 66
  New Age spiritualism 67
  three modes of 431

Stars
  Cepheid variable 456
  first stars in the universe 473
  number of stars in the observable universe 9
  pulsar 467
  supernova. *See* Supernovae
  white dwarf star 456, 520

Statistics, Bayesian. *See* Bayes' theorem

Stavrakopoulou, Francesca 97

Steinbeck, John (epigraph) 113

Stephen (disciple of Jesus, first martyr) 200, 212, 229, 235, 248, 318, 479

Sterile neutrinos 491, 492, 572

Stimoceiver 432

Stone Age. *See* Age, Stone Age

Stone of history 8, 60, 588

Straus, Ernst G. (discussion with Einstein) 505

String Theory / M-Theory. *See* Cosmogonic models, M-Theory and String Theory

Strobel, Lee 244

Stromata (literary work). *See* Clement of Alexandria

Stromatolites 581

Structures, large cosmic. *See* Walls (large cosmic structures)

Structural Spacetime Realism 524

Subatomic particles 273, 418, 439, 468, 526

Subjective experience 44, 45, 364, 525

Subjective truth. *See* Truth, subjective truth

Subjunctive possibility 511, 512

Subluminal 461, 501, 503

Substance (*See Also* Dualism, Monism)
  same substance. *See* Consubstantiality
  dispersed substance, property of God 337
  divine substance 298, 335, 397, 398
  God and universe as one substance. *See* Pantheism
  God-World substance 400, 401
  indivisible. *See* Indivisible, property of God
  nondivine substance 446
  quantized substance 324
  reactive substance (Adamite, Eveitite) 561

Substantialism. *See* Six Towers of God worldview, Inanimate Substantialism

Substantivalism (-ist) 524, 525

Suetonius (also called Gaius Suetonius Tranquillus) 208, 211

Sufism (*See Also* Islam) 335

Summa Theologica (literary work). *See* Aquinas, Thomas

Sunni Muslim (*See Also* Islam) 310, 422, 505

Superforce (combined elementary forces) 10

Supernatural Beings 25, 32, 116, 278, 283, 430

Supernovae
  planet-killers 580
  Type Ia 456, 496, 497
  SN 1987a (faster than lightspeed) 457
  supernova (general) 9, 36, 325, 456, 457, 466, 474, 580
  use for distance measurement 456

Superposition. *See* Quantum, superposition

Superstition

  learning 430, 448

  faith without reason leads to superstition 23

  survey, religion is based on superstition 30

Superstring theory. *See* **Cosmogonic models,
  Superstring Theories**

Supraluminal 316, 453, 455, 461, 466, 501

Swift satellite 497, 579

Swinburne, Richard

  a priori / a posteriori arguments. *See* Arguments, a
  priori / a posteriori

  biography of 250

  coherency requirements for Holy Trinity. *See* Holy
  Trinity, Richard Swinburne, for Trinity to be...

  coins term "Ramified Natural Theology" 44

  cosmological argument. *See* Induction, Richard
  Swinburne, inductive cosmological argument

  defense of God as three Persons. *See* Holy Trinity,
  Richard Swinburne, defense of exactly...

  defense, Christian God. *See* Arguments, Richard
  Swinburne's defense of the Christian God

  defense, generic God. *See* Arguments, Richard
  Swinburne's defense of a generic god

  faults in Bayesian analysis. *See* Resurrection
  Hypothesis, summary, faults...

  God is simple. *See* Intuition, God is simple

  God is subject to time. *See* Arguments, R. Swinburne
  & W. L. Craig...

  incoherent defense of God as three Persons 322

  necessary properties of God. *See* Arguments, Richard
  Swinburne's necessary features of God

  necessary properties of God. *See* Incoherent, Richard
  Swinburne, God's properties

  Principle of Credulity 250

  Principle of Testimony (*See Also* Reliability, Richard
  Swinburne's...) 250, 265

  Principle of Reciprocity. 84

  probability estimate, God's existence. *See* Bayes'
  theorem, Richard Swinburne's probability...

  probability estimate, God's existence. *See* Intuition,
  Richard Swinburne's probability estimate for existence
  of God

  probability estimate, resurrection. *See* Intuition,
  Richard Swinburne's probability estimate for
  resurrection

  probability estimate, resurrection. *See* Resurrection
  Hypothesis, Bayesian estimate...

  Swinburne's philosophy is unscientific

  The Christian God (literary work) 309, 322

  The Existence of God (literary work) 250, 309

The Resurrection of God Incarnate (literary work)
  250, 322

  understanding God requires inductive reasoning. *See*
  Induction, Richard Swinburne, defining God's nature /
  existence...

  view of Godhead. *See* Godhead, Richard Swinburne,
  view of...

Swingrover, Louis J. 522

Syllogism 506, 508, 517, 518, 528, 530

Symmetry, time-reversal. *See* Time, time-reversal
  symmetry

Synapse (neuronal structure) 438

**Syncretism (syncretistic, syncretic). Compare with
  Polyfaith** 32, 67, 92, 161, 163, 170, 205, 297, 350,
  352, 539

Systematic theology 14, 390, 435, 553

T-shaped cross. *See* **Crucifixion**

Tablet

  Ark Tablet 115, 116

  Jehoash Tablet 117, 135

  stone tablet of God's Ten Commandments 117

Tabor, James 132, 135

Tacitus (Publius Cornelius Tacitus) 208, 211

Talbott, William 333

Talpiot Tomb A (Garden Tomb) 130-136, 139, 197

Talpiot Tomb B (Patio Tomb) 130

Tammuz, deity 90, 239

Tanakh (Jewish Bible). *See* **Bible (Hebrew Tanakh)**

Tangential energy 385

Taoism 67, 88

TAP. *See* **Agnosticism, TAP**

Tatian the Assyrian 221

Taweret, deity 100

Taylor, Joseph H. 467

Teilhard de Chardin. *See* **de Chardin, Teilhard**

Teleodynamics 392

**Teleology / Teleological Argument (*See Also* Telos,
  Emergence, Autocells, Autocellularity)**

  Aristotle, Father of Teleology 372, 405

  autocell concept defeats and inspires teleogical
  arguments 381

  bundling of Teleological and other Arguments 536

  Christian Panentheism, a teleological philosophy 367,
  542

  Cosmon Field Model defeats all Teleological
  Arguments 488, 529

  defintion of 372

  Deism, a teleogical theology 570

  does biological emergence infer God must exist? 400

Teleology / Teleological Argument (*continued*)
emergence theory and teleology. *See* Emergence
New Sciences of Religion, a teleogical philosophy 361, 365
unsuccessful in affirming God's existence 407

Televangelist 302

Telos
author's goals for writing this book 56
natural (naturalistic) telos 374, 379, 380, 400, 405, 543
New Sciences of Religion, five concepts to discover God's existence 358
transcendental (divine) telos 374, 380, 381, 389, 390, 400, 401, 405, 406, 543

Temple
Asherah temples 96
Jewish temples 91, 93
Mormon temples 172
Solomon's Temple 117, 119
Temple of Venus 122

Temple Scroll (literary work) 197, 231

Templeton Prize 355, 388, 402, 583, 585

Templeton, Sir John Marks (epigraph) 371, 579

Tennyson, Alfred (Lord) 64, 65

Tensor. *See* Einstein, Einstein tensor

Tensor network. *See* Quantum, tensor network

Terrorism. *See* Fanaticism, violent religious

Tertullian of Carthage 164, 174, 176, 203, 204, 221, 271, 290

Testimonium Flavianum 206

Tetragrammaton (YHWH). *See* Yahweh, YHWH

Thales of Miletus 444

Theism
incoherencies of. *See* Incoherent, theism (many forms of), lack of coherency
Types of Theism (table) 87, 88

Theism-versus-nontheism 323

Theistic Creationsim. *See* Six Towers of God worldview, Theisitic Creationism

Theocracy 84, 232, 247, 422

Theodicy. *See* Evil, theodicy and Evil, Problem of Evil

Theological noncognitivism. *See* Noncognitivism, theological

Theology
Abrahamic theology 3
Apophatic theology. *See* Apophaticism
Bare Natural Theology (BNT). *See* Bare Natural Theology
Cataphatic theology. *See* Cataphaticism
Natural theology. *See* Natural theology
Negative theology. *See* Apophaticism
Perfect Being Theology. *See* Perfect Being Theology
Postive theology. *See* Cataphaticism
Process Theology. *See* Process Theology
Ramified Natural Theology (RNT). *See* Ramified Natural Theology
Systematic theology. *See* Systematic theology

Theophilus of Antioch 290

Therapeutae 163

Theriomorphism 85

Thermodynamics
closed system 477, 478
First Law of (Law of Conservation of Energy) 444
isolated system 326, 476-478, 520
open system 477
Second law of 477, 478
type of systems (open, closed, isolated) 477

Thich Nhat Hanh. *See* Hanh, Thich Nhat

Thirdness. *See* Principle, principle of Firstness...

Thomas
Gospel of Thomas. *See* Apocrypha, Gospel of Thomas
Thomas Aquinas. *See* Aquinas, Thomas
Thomas the Apostle (also Didymus Thomas) 72, 120, 167, 212
Thomas, Ryan 102

Thoreau, Henry David 583

Tiberius, Roman Emperor 208

Tillich, Paul 383

Time-bearing 515

Time (the property of)
A-series time. *See* A-theory (A-series) time
amorphous time 515, 516, 524
arrow of time, cosmological 478, 480
arrow of time, thermodynamic 477
atemporal 71, 79, 87, 298, 382, 397, 507, 514, 516, 549
B-series time. *See* B-theory / B-series time
Block time (static or growing block time). *See* Block Universe
changeless (eventless, empty) time 502, 514, 523-525
compare—atemporal, timeless, everlasting, eternal, omintemporal 71
Eternalism. *See* Block Universe, Static Block Universe
eventless (empty) time. *See* changeless time (above)
Growing Block Universe. *See* Block Universe, Growing time
imaginary time 480, 481, 494
irregular time 515, 516, 524
metric (differentiated) time 515

Time (*continued*)

Planck time (smallest unit of time). *See* Planck, time

Possibilism. *See* Block Universe, Growing Block Universe

Presentism / Nowism. *See* Presentism

Problem of Time. *See* Quantum mechanics, Problem of Time...

quantum clock 487

quasi-time 519

quasi-time, Grand Observer 8

reverse-time 470

time dilation (in special and general relativity) 502

time slices 525

Time Zero 514, 515, 517, 519

time-reversal symmetry 477

undifferentiated time 11, 516

Timeless (timelessness, timelessly)

Adamite and Eveitite reactive materials contrasted with a timeless God 528

Block Universe 528

compare—atemporal, timeless, everlasting, eternal, omintemporal 71

definition of (timelessness)—See footnote 11

dilemma of timeless knowledge, Free Will 338

Grand Observer's temporal state, quasi-temporal/timeless 8

ontological necessity of God and his status prior to Creation 319

Plotinus, world-universe emanated from timeless God 384

property of God 71, 79

property of God, Classical Theism 87, 382

Meta-Transignification hypothesis, no presumption of a timeless state 323

mathematical probability, timeless existence of (refer to truism T6) 521

multiverse, some universes may exist in a timeless state 514, 519

pre-universe, cannot determine if a timeless state existed 517

pre-universe, if timeless then changeless 517

pre-universe, temporal state prior to Big Bang 11

Six Towers of God (Tower 5), a state of timeless for universe 563

time as an illusion, reality as timeless 555

truisms of time and change (refer to truisms T5 and T6) 514

ultra-ancient universe in a timeless state, Cosmon Field Model 496, 503, 523

W. L. Craig KCA, First Cause must have been in timeless state 507, 513, 516

W. L. Craig, God changed from a timeless state to a temporal state (two phases) 383, 507, 516

W. L. Craig, God's necessary properties (timeless,...) 522

W. L. Craig, illustration of timeless–temporal existence of God 508

Timothy, First (book, Christian Bible) 294, 295

Tingley, Katherine 61, 353

Tischendorf, Canons of. *See* Canons

Titulus Crucis 122

Titus Flavius Clemens. *See* Clement of Alexandria

Titus Flavius Josephus 203, 206, 289

Tombs (*See Also* Graveyards)

Calvary (Golgatha) 122, 131

empty tomb. *See* Empty tomb

carved rock tomb 122, 131, 153, 157, 194-198, 202, 249

Garden Tomb (Jesus' family tomb?). *See* Talpiot Tomb A

Patio Tomb. *See* Talpiot Tomb B

Royal cemetery at Ur (Mesopotamia) 85

seconary burial (ossilegium). *See* Burial, secondary

Talpiot tombs. *See* Talpiot Tomb A and Talpiot Tomb B

Top-down (paradigm). *See* Approach (es)

Top-level 36

Toppino, T. 420

Torah (also called the Pentateuch). *See* Bible (Hebrew Tanakh)

Totemism (Animism) 86

Trajan, Roman Emperor 208

Trans-spatial 508, 529

Transcategorical 71, 79, 354, 356, 358

Transcendence

definition of 12

dimensional transcendence 381, 398, 449, 547, 548, 559, 570, 577

domain-piercing transcendence 548, 549

insuperable (transcendent) barrier 546, 559, 570

one-way transcendent barrier 546

ontological properties of a transcendent god (illustration) 550

pure transcendence (purely transcendent) 358, 381, 384, 398, 404-406, 449, 528, 537, 548, 552, 554, 559, 570, 572, 577, 587

Tower 1 – The Purely Transcendent God 559

Transcendental apophaticism (Buddhism) 339

Transcendental telos. *See* Telos, transcendental (divine) telos

Transcendentalism (transcendentalist) 583

Transmission of religion 29, 352

Transtheism 88

Transubstantiation 301, 335, 383

Triangulum Galaxy (M33) 78, 579

Trichotomics 395

Trinitarian, Niceno-Constantinopolitan 291, 300, 321, 540

Trinitarianism. *See* Holy Trinity, trinitarianism

Trinity. *See* Holy Trinity

Tritheism 321, 396, 541

Triune 70, 262, 290, 309, 320, 334, 335, 543

Truc Cross. *See* Cross, Truc Cross

Truth

    Christianity, truth claims. *See* Foundational Truth Claims of Christianity

    incoherency. *See* Incoherent

    objective truth 51

    subjective truth 51

Truth Criteria

    [TC-1] Accessibility Limits of Reality 50

    [TC-2] Dimensionality of Reality 50

    [TC-3] Temporality of Reality 50

    [TC-4] Jurisprudence of Reality 50

    [TC-5] Complexity of Reality 51

    [TC-6] Objectivity of Reality 51

    [TC-7] Temporal Relativity of Reality 51

    [TC-8] Coherency of Reality 52

Tubulins. *See* Microtubules

Twain, Mark. *See* Clemens, Samuel Langhorne

Twelve Basic Rules of Aland & Aland 147

Two-generation rule 244, 245, 276

Type I cognitive error 429, 430

Type Ia supernovae. *See* Supernovae

Type II cognitive error 429, 430

UFO 409, 433

Ufology 20

Ugarit 89-93, 95, 102, 103

Ultimate (the Real). *See* Hick, John, Ultimate Reality

Unconsciousness 234, 449

Unicity 355

Uniformitarian Panentheist 402

Uniformitarianism, modified 402

Unitarian Universalist 245

Unitarianism 107, 292

Universal truths 333, 362, 366

Universe (cosmos) (*See Also* Space... and Spacetime...)

    age of the universe according to Big Bang model) 9, 453, 455, 466, 474, 480, 493, 530

    age of the universe according to Cosmon Field Model 484, 486, 496, 503, 523

    barrenness of the universe 458

    Earth, center of the universe. *See* Geocentrism

    finely-tuned parameters of the universe 317, 318, 402, 403, 406, 458, 488, 514

    greater universe. *See* Greater universe

    heat death 471, 478, 514

    isotropy, anisotropy, homogeneity 466, 475

    laws (physical, natural) of the universe. *See* Law, laws of nature

    metallicity of the universe 464, 466, 480

    net energy of the universe, zero 464

    observable universe 9, 34, 35, 316, 454, 455, 458, 462, 464, 474, 475, 478, 484, 496, 497

    isolated, closed, or open system. *See* Thermodynamics

    isolated system, presumption 478

    shape, flat universe 458, 461, 464, 495, 497, 568

    shape, open (curved / hyperbolic) universe 464

    shape, spherically-shaped (closed) 464

    size, finite physical size 479, 481

    size, infinite physical size 479, 497, 499

    size of observable universe 455, 580

    scientific models of. *See* Cosmogonic models

    unobservable universe 45, 548

Upanishads

    Brihadaranyaka 12, 444

    Mukhya (Principal Upanishads) 12

Uracil (nucleobase molecule) 377

Vacuum

    vacuum energy 464, 465, 484

    Vacuum Fluctuation model. *See* Cosmogonic models

Valens, Roman Emperor 203

Values (more influential than rational thinking) 581

Vaticanus. *See* Codex, Vaticanus

Vedic (East Indian) 12, 444, 556

Verisimilitude 151, 157, 270

Vermes, Geza 238, 289

Vespasian, Roman Emperor 206

Vincentius of Thibaris 221

Virgin Mary (virgin birth). *See* Mary, virginity of Mary / virginal birth of Jesus

VMAT2 "God gene" 431

Voltaire (a pseudonym for François-Marie Arouet) 155

von Schelling. *See* Schelling

von Sicard, Harald 118

W. L. Craig. *See* Craig, William Lane

Wahhabism 422

Walls (large cosmic structures)

    Hercules-Corona Borealis Great Wall 474

    Great Coma Wall 474, 496

    Great Sloan Wall 474

Warp bubble 38

Wars

    Jewish-Roman Wars 178, 284

    holy war 27, 422

    Persian Gulf War 3

Wave function

    collapse (reduction) 440, 441, 443, 498

    definition of 439-441, 472, 487, 498, 519

    eigenstate (eigenvalue) 440

Wave-particle duality 354

Wave-particle duality problem solved (See footnote) 354

Weber, Bruce 380

Wetterich, Christof (*See Also* Cosmon Field Model) 482

Weyl

    field transformation 483

    scaling 483

White dwarf star. *See* Stars, white dwarf star

Whitehead, Alfred North (epigraph) 307, 383, 387, 388, 443, 542

Whitten, Ed 463

Wilde, Oscar (epigraph) 535

Wisdom, simple. *See* Philosophy, simple philosophy (wisdom)...

Wittgenstein, Ludwig 355

Wohlgemuth, Andrew 264

Wonderland story. *See* Alice's Adventures in Wonderland

Woolley, C. Leonard 85

World religion 2, 29, 57, 68, 189, 349, 354, 359, 361, 362, 434, 542

World Union of Deists. *See* Deism

World-Soul 384

World-universe 1, 13, 20, 88, 382, 384, 436, 526, 566

Wright, N.T. 199, 234, 271

Wright, Robert 91-93

X-shaped cross. *See* Crucifixion

Yahweh (deity)

    Allah, God, and Yahweh 184

    Asherah (deity), Bes (deity), and Yahweh 95-100, 102-105

    El (deity) and Yahweh 91, 93, 276, 538

    many ancient gods competed with Yahweh 159

    Marcion's belief about Yahweh 299

    Mortal Jesus Hypothesis—Yahweh and Asherah 247

    theonyms (epithets) for Yahweh 93

    Yahweh symbolism, as a young bull 102

    YAHWEH! Insta-Prayer (movie Bruce Almighty) 189

    YHWH (Tetragrammaton) 93, 97, 102, 180, 335

Yahwism (Yahwist), pagan 92, 93, 96, 305

Yam (Yamm), deity 95

YHWH. *See* Yahweh, YHWH

Yohanan Ben Ha'galgol 123

Zealots

    religious fanatic (*See Also* Fanaticism, violent religious) 3, 16, 26-28

    sub-group of the Sicarii (political-religious movement) 203

Zeteo Alétheia (*See Also* Zeteticism)

    continual seeking of the truth of reality 571, 582

    definition of 43, 146, 183, 535

    use of caution in applying principles 43, 434

Zeteticism (*See Also* Six Towers of God worldview and Zeteo Alétheia)

    author's primary goals, using zeteticism 56

    benefit to society and the indiviudal 583, 584

    initial / fundamental assumptions of 43, 146, 183, 308, 311, 380, 404

    initial assumptions on truth of reality. *See* Truth Criteria

    contrasted with skepticism 43

    definition of 42, 43

    dismantled traditional religion / reduced perimeter of God 341, 342

    dismantled most formalized theisms, showing them to be incoherent 404, 406, 573

    exposing postive / negative theology as incoherent 335

    parallels and differences with Hick's religious pluralism 356-358

    parallels and differences with New Sciences of Religion (NSoR) 361-364

    parallels with Kantian philosophy 44, 45

    parallels with Ramified Natural Theology 44, 308

    simple philosophy (wisdom) 2, 4, 56, 367, 582, 588

    six options to understand God's perimeter (*See Also* Six Towers of God worldview) 571, 572

Zeus, deity 160, 241

ACKNOWLEDGMENTS

The unbroken immersion of seemingly never-ending research, perpetual editing, and soul searching required a great wage to be paid. The specter of never finishing this book was persistently lurking in the shadows. My endeavor would have been made immeasurably more difficult if it weren't for the love and understanding from my wife Jennifer. Another inspiration is my mother Edith who instilled in me the values of devoting oneself to the task at hand, a tireless commitment to excellence, a deep compassion toward living creatures, and allowing me to be me. I also have to express an appreciation for her actions to indoctrinate me into the Catholic Christian faith. If I hadn't been exposed to Christianity, I may never have been motivated to fervently question the existence of God. And likewise, the simple philosophy that eliminates the tensions between theists (religionists) and atheists/agnostics (nonreligionists) would not have been discovered.

I also want to give tribute to my four-legged companions, all rescues from animal shelters, who accompanied me on an otherwise lonely journey. To Mocha, the Tonkinese cat, who cozied herself on my writing-room window sill to overlook my progress. To Devon, the doe-eyed and charmingly affectionate merle-coated cocker spaniel. To Piper, the effervescent and mightily agile miniature Schnauzer. And to Muppet (RIP), my treasured cocker who, though blind in sight, saw to buoying my spirits on countless occasions. I also express my gratitude to the following people— Burk U. Kladde, Leon G. Doris, Marvin P. and Donna L. Rezabek, Jessenia Avila, Bill Knutson, and Dennis J. Anderson—for listening to my views and sharing their own as these discussions have helped to shape aspects of this book (principally Chapter 1). Additionally, I thank Burk for his artful photography aptitudes which produced my author photo (refer to p. 743) and for providing me with many books which proved vital for my research. I was also provided with valuable critiques on the design of the book's cover from my youngest brother Dean.

I must also acknowledge the tremendous contribution of the Pew Research Center's forum on Religious & Public Life. If it weren't for their dedicated efforts to collect and interpret data to record the trends of religion in society, it would have been inordinately more difficult to capture the moving portrait of religion here in America and abroad.

Finally, I need to thank the multitude of scholars—the Dragons as I have called them—whose vital work was consulted to formulate this book. Their mastery over their subject matter and intellectual capacity is something I am in awe of. The scholar's job is largely a thankless one unless one is so lucky as to become elevated to high ground by their peers. Most toil long and hard with limited recognition for the immense contributions as they gather-up the nuggets of knowledge to be communally disseminated. My only wish is that scholars and the institutions they serve would be universally required to study and master forms of cognitive bias so that they may be better armed to conduct and report unbiased research outcomes.

Finally, I thank my alma maters, Iowa State University, Wichita State University, and Arizona State University and my many professors who contributed to the development of my critical thinking skills without which this book would not have been possible.

ABOUT THE AUTHOR

Brian Goedken is a research engineer, entrepreneur, and inventor whose contributions span multiple technological sectors within the domains of aeronautical, automotive, medical, and space systems engineering. He has engineered power modules for the *International Space Station Freedom*, communication arrays for orbital satellites, and before graduating college in 1991 had conceived an algorithm to compute the optimal trajectory to the planet Mars by use of a Solar Sail. At the time, solar sails were notional concepts for spacecraft that depend solely on sunlight for its propellant. Nearly two decades later, in 2010, NASA successfully launched and deployed its first solar sail technology demonstrator into low-Earth orbit.

Brian has also developed advanced analytical techniques for use in automotive power train design, invented a novel transparent armor for military personnel protection, and a range of crash protection technologies. He was a Principal and early founder of a startup technology firm located in Arizona. The company vectored to quickly become among one of the top five grossing small business firms in the state in terms of awarded-funding by the national *Small Business Innovation Research* program.

As an intellectual separated from the traditional realm of academia, Brian's ultimate concern is the substantive progression of human advancement through the discovery and application of new knowledge—technical and otherwise. As a formerly devout Catholic Christian for some 40 years, he recognized that hope for human advancement was being savaged by warped interpretations of God, too often at the hands of so-called violent religious radicalists. In the broadest context, something epic is playing-out on the world stage. The hegemony of scientific inquiry and religion-at-large, both longtime societal pincers, are being forced together tighter than ever to declare which of them are the truth bearers to ultimate reality. In response, some religionists foment violence to defend and fortify their conception of God against external influences. It is the general ignorance and lack of education, *specifically poorly-developed critical thinking skills*, that are underlying culprits for our retarded global progression as a species.

All the while, the contemporary Religion-Science Dialogue has continued on its wayward journey which most closely resembles a digressive closed loop. Sadly, so much of the exchange is laced with a heady froth of bias which in part explains why compelling discernments are lacking that, if it were otherwise, could heal a troubled society. While traditional religion has developed systematic theology to answer the full complement of questions concerning an existential Creator, many religious adherents have, perhaps unknowingly, artificed an unorthodox prescription for God leading to a personally pragmatic God that is no longer congruent with institutionalized religious precepts.

To make progress toward his audacious goal, the Big Questions became a central focus in Brian's mission—*How can we 'know' whether or not God is real? What is Reality and under what rules does it operate? What caused the universe to come about?* Brian, no stranger to dealing with complex problems and inconvenient truths, brings his full spectrum of research investigatory expertise and disciplinary rigor to deftly query high-brow scholastic mentation on these fundamental dilemmas. He applies the avant-garde approach that has served him so well by starting from first principles—eliminating all prior assumptions and conjectures—to architect a new paradigm using modern methods of inquiry. **To prevent religious terrorism from crippling the world, Brian has discovered a God–Science compatible paradigm that could, if embraced, offer an amicable peace between religionists and nonreligionists the world over.**

Brian Goedken and his wife Jennifer live in the Phoenix-Metro area where they devote energy to aid animal rights advocacies and animal rescue organizations.

INTERACT WITH THE AUTHOR

HTTP://WWW.ZETETICPATH.COM

89437149R00415

Made in the USA
Columbia, SC
21 February 2018